MEDIA LAW AND ETHICS

Fourth Edition

This is the first textbook to explicitly integrate both media law and ethics within one volume. A truly comprehensive overview, it is a thoughtful introduction to media law principles and cases and the related ethical concerns relevant to the practice of professional communication. With special attention made to key cases and practices, authors Roy L. Moore and Michael D. Murray revisit the most timely and incendiary issues in modern American media.

Exploring where the law ends and ethics begin, each chapter includes a discussion of the ethical dimensions of a specific legal topic. The Fourth Edition includes new legal cases and emerging issues in media law and ethics as well as revised subject and case indices. In addition to a separate chapter devoted exclusively to media ethics by Michael Farrell, a new chapter on international and foreign law by Dr. Kyu Ho Youm has also been added. Resources on the companion website include updated PowerPoint presentations and a sample syllabus for instructors, and a glossary, chapter review questions, chapter quizzes, and all seven of the book's original appendices for students.

An excellent integration of both law and ethics, this is the ideal text for undergraduate and graduate courses in media law and ethics.

Roy L. Moore is Professor of Journalism and Dean of the College of Mass Communication at Middle Tennessee State University. He holds a Ph.D. in Mass Communication from the University of Wisconsin-Madison and a J.D. from the Georgia State University College of Law.

Michael D. Murray is University of Missouri Board of Curators' Professor and Chair of the Faculty Senate and University Assembly at University of Missouri-St. Louis. He received his undergraduate degree from St. Louis University, and his Ph.D. from the University of Missouri-Columbia.

MEDIA LAW AND ETHICS

FOURTH EDITION

ROY L. MOORE
MICHAEL D. MURRAY

Routledge
Taylor & Francis Group

NEW YORK AND LONDON

Please visit the companion website at

www.routledge.com/cw/moore

Fourth edition published 2012
by Routledge
711 Third Avenue, New York, NY 10017

Simultaneously published in the UK
by Routledge
2 Park Square, Milton Park, Abingdon, Oxon OX14 4RN

Routledge is an imprint of the Taylor & Francis Group, an informa business

First edition published by Lawrence Erlbaum Associates, Inc. 1994
Third edition published by Routledge 2008

Library of Congress Cataloging in Publication Data
Moore, Roy L.
    Media law and ethics / Roy L. Moore, Michael D. Murray. — 4th ed.
    p. cm. — (Routledge communication series)
    Includes bibliographical references and index.
    1. Mass media—Law and legislation—United States—Cases. 2. Mass media—
    Moral and ethical aspects—Case studies. I. Murray, Michael D. II. Title.
    KF2750.M662 2011
    343.7309'9—dc23
    2011027522

ISBN: 978-0-415-89462-3 (hbk)
ISBN: 978-0-415-89463-0 (pbk)
ISBN: 978-0-203-14458-9 (ebk)

Typeset in Adobe Garamond, Optima, and Fritz Quadrata
by EvS Communication Networx, Inc.

Dedication

To the memory of our parents and parents-in-law –
Chester and Essie Moore,
Sam and Lila Vickers,
Marcella and Austin Murray,
and
Genevieve and Aloysius Ratermann.

Brief Contents

Contents

Preface
to the Fourth Edition

Thank you for your interest in the new fourth and thoroughly revised edition of the first college textbook to explicitly address both mass media law and media ethics under one cover. The intersection of these two vital areas often leads to more questions, creates more potential problems, attracts the most interest and provides the best promise for examining important decision-making by the mass media.

In the preface of the first edition of this textbook, growing interest was noted in having both law and ethics addressed together in a single course at many departments and schools of mass communication and journalism. This awareness has evolved as a well-accepted pattern and a concept endorsed not only by major media programs but also by professional organizations. We have come to even better understand the symbiotic relationship and importance of having these two areas simultaneously addressed.

Public confidence in the mass media continues to erode as more journalists and media outlets have been exposed for unethical conduct. The emergence of non-traditional "new media" creates another level of interest in related ethical issues. As a small step in addressing these challenges, the new edition continues with the dominant theme—an interspersing of legal and ethical concepts and concerns at every step along the way and, whenever possible, includes discussion of current views regarding the disposition of key legal cases in an ethical context. With changes taking place quickly in the current mass media environment, we offer the reader a look at the regulation of new and emerging technologies, including vast expansion via the Internet. The change in title that we made in the last edition—from "Mass Communication" to "Media"—continues to reflect an emphasis on and awareness of an ever-broadening field.

We have enlisted two colleagues, Dr. Michael Farrell and Dr. Kyu Ho Youm, to write highly specialized chapters devoted specifically to media ethics and international media law, respectively. Dr. Farrell has revised and expanded his chapter from the previous edition on media ethics, and Dr. Youm has contributed a new chapter on mass media international law.

Dr. Farrell, former managing editor of the *Kentucky Post,* is Associate Professor and Director of the First Amendment Center at the University of Kentucky. Dr. Youm is Professor and Jonathan Marshall First Amendment Chair in the School of Journalism at the University of

Oregon. He is current president of the Association for Education in Journalism and Mass Communication (AEJMC).

When the first edition of this book was published, the international influences and the impact of the Internet on such areas as intellectual property rights and privacy as well as public and governmental concerns over broadcast indecency were not major topics of discussion. We now function in a media regulation environment in which these issues often dominate. Now, even newer technologies have emerged, including high-definition television and HD and satellite radio. These technologies, along with handheld devices such as GPS, iPods, PDAs, and cell phones have created regulatory challenges and expanded the outlets for information, talent and even controversy. Some of the programming of the so-called new media has been forced to switch or has voluntarily crossed over from the traditional media outlets. Telecommunications issues remain the most controversial and this new fourth edition of Media Law and Ethics examines the most contentious issues and avenues for legal experts and mass media practitioners to explore in this evolving landscape.

Not only have we have continued with a separate chapter devoted exclusively to media ethics written by Dr. Farrell, but each of the other chapters still includes a discussion of the ethical dimensions of that specific legal topic. We do this to explore where the law ends and ethics begin. For example, although the First Amendment protects a reporter who publishes a rape victim's name from the public record, such disclosure is unethical in the eyes of many journalists. Appropriating another writer's ideas in a story is not copyright infringement so long as only ideas but not expressions are used, but is such conduct ethical? Snapping photos of a severely injured child being pulled from an automobile accident is generally not an invasion of privacy, nor is photographing parents at the moment of being informed of the loss of their child. However, most media outlets would refrain from publishing or broadcasting blood and gore from such an event out of respect for the child and the family.

Comprehension of the law is only the first step. Every journalist must establish a personal code of ethics. There is no shortage of ethical guidelines, but the standards are best understood within the context of mass media law. The question should not be "How do I avoid a lawsuit?" but rather "How do I do what is right?" Answering the latter question is often more difficult than ascertaining the appropriate legal principle, but, as professional communicators, we must be able to respond affirmatively to both queries. Mass media law and media ethics are inseparable and complement one another in a way that makes the bond between them stronger than the base on which they stand individually. We believe our enthusiasm and attention to the relationship of media law and media ethics are reflected in this text. Similarly, in addition to Dr. Youm's new chapter, we discuss relevant international cases and issues as they arise throughout the book.

We continue to welcome and benefit from comments from readers and adopters of this book, and we thank those who have helped us in improving this practical resource for both budding and seasoned journalists. We especially hope our student readers will adopt and practice high ethical principles and develop a keen understanding of media law so they can eventually enter one of the most exciting and noble professions in the world and do so well prepared.

Our special thanks go to our very devoted wives, Pam and Carol. When the authors met 35 years ago and shared office space as assistant professors in a converted dormitory at Virginia Tech, our wives set the tone and kept us "on track." They have supported us on assignments and chipped in on occasions when the burdens became too great. Now grown up, our children—

Derek, Ellen, and Kate—are always supportive and have always been there for us with patience, love, and understanding. Finally, thanks to our former students, our colleagues and our friends around the country for their comments and encouragement. We have been blessed with great teachers and exceptional students. We particularly thank Graduate Assistant Sarah E. Tollie, who provided editorial assistance with this new edition.

Roy L. Moore
Michael D. Murray

About the Authors

Roy. L. Moore is Professor and Dean of the College of Mass Communication at Middle Tennessee State University and Professor Emeritus of Journalism at the University of Kentucky. He served previously as Associate Vice President for Academic Affairs and Professor of Mass Communication at Georgia College & State University. At the University of Kentucky he was the Associate Dean of the College of Communications and Information Studies and Professor in the School of Journalism and Telecommunications. He also served as a Faculty Trustee on the Board of Trustees and Executive Director of the First Amendment Center. He earned his Ph.D. in Mass Communication from the University of Wisconsin-Madison and his J.D. from Georgia State University. He is a practicing attorney and a national authority on libel law and First Amendment issues. He has served as an expert witness in several media law cases. During 2001–2002 he was an American Council on Education (ACE) Fellow at the University of Georgia. In addition to the previous three editions of this textbook, he is also author of *Advertising and Public Relations Law* (second edition, 2011), co-authored with Carmen Maye and Erik L. Collins. He chaired the Law Division of the Association for Education in Journalism and Mass Communication (AEJMC) and was honored for life-long service by the Mass Communication and Society Division. He was named a "Great Teacher" by the University of Kentucky Alumni Association.

Michael D. Murray is University of Missouri Board of Curators' Distinguished Professor in Media Studies and Chair of the Faculty Senate and University Assembly on the UM-St. Louis campus. He earned his undergraduate degree at St. Louis University and Ph.D. from the University of Missouri-Columbia, where he was honored with a distinguished alumnus award. He wrote his dissertation on the controversial CBS *See It Now* programs on Senator Joseph McCarthy. He taught at Virginia Tech and the University of Louisville, where he founded the Communication program and also held post-doctoral fellowships at Stanford University, University of London and Cambridge University. He is an authority on the history of broadcast news and regulatory issues and has been honored by most of the major academic organizations with a mass media or regulatory component, including Association for Education in Journalism and Mass Communication (AEJMC), American Journalism Historians Association (AJHA),

Broadcast Education Association (BEA), International Radio & Television Society (IRTS) and the National Communication Association (NCA). He served as founding director of the Greenspun School of Journalism and Media Studies at the University of Nevada-Las Vegas and is author or editor of seven books including *Mass Communication Education*, co-edited with Roy L. Moore. He served as review and criticism editor for *Journal of Broadcasting and Electronic Media* and serves on the Publication Boards of the Broadcast Education Association and *Journal of Media Education*.

1

Sources and Types of American Law

Most high courts in other nations do not have discretion, such as we enjoy, in selecting the cases that the high court reviews. Our court is virtually alone in the amount of discretion it has.

—Sandra Day O'Conner (first female U.S. Supreme Court Justice—served 1981–2006)

When most of us conceptualize law, we focus on statutory or constitutional law, ignoring the source of law that has had the greatest impact on our legal history—common law. The concept of administrative law is rarely discussed and equity law is virtually unknown, except among legal experts. Yet these sources of law constitute *the law* as much as statutes do.

This chapter examines the sources and categories of American law from the U.S. Constitution's Bill of Rights to equity. Traditional categories of law, such as civil versus criminal and tort versus contract, are also distinguished as a background for later chapters that analyze specific court cases. But law is only part of the equation.

Chapter 4 is devoted specifically to *ethical dilemmas, issues and concerns in mass communication*, but all of the chapters go beyond the law to include discussions on ethics, which has become as important today as the law in news gathering and reporting. The public no longer expects the mass media to simply stay within the boundaries of the law but also to be objective and unbiased in their presentation of the news and to adhere to standards of professional conduct that ensure fairness. Polls from the past decade show a steady decline in public regard for journalists, their methods and the ethical considerations they make. Chapter 4 discusses in detail how and why public perceptions about the news media continue to grow negative.

A poll in 2002 during the 215th anniversary of the U.S. Constitution found that almost 90 percent of respondents agreed with the underlying principles of the Constitution, but more than 40 percent believed the Founding Fathers made freedom of the press too strong.[1] According to a Knight Foundation-sponsored poll three years later of 112,000 American high school students,[2] nearly 75 percent of them either did not know how they felt about the First Amendment or took it for granted. About the same percentage erroneously thought that flag burning was illegal and almost half erroneously believed the government had the right to restrict indecent materials on the Internet. An updated 2006 survey of almost 15,000 students and more than 800 teachers found a rise in support for First Amendment protection for the media and the right to report in school newspapers without approval from school officials. However, there was a slight increase in the number of students who thought the First Amendment, as a whole, went too far in its rights.[3]

In a 2009 national survey of American attitudes about the First Amendment, commissioned by the First Amendment Center at Vanderbilt University,[4] only 55 percent of the sample of 1,003 American adults identified free speech as one of the specific freedoms enunciated in the First Amendment, followed by 18 percent who cited freedom of religion and 16 percent who mentioned freedom of the press. Almost four in ten of those surveyed could not name a single freedom in the First Amendment. About 75 percent of the respondents said the First Amendment is not too broad in the rights it grants. However, less than half (48%) agree that the press has about the right amount of freedom, with 39 percent of those surveyed saying the press has too much freedom under the First Amendment. When asked whether there should be a constitutional amendment prohibiting flag-burning as a form of political protest, about 60 percent opposed such an amendment.

Against that backdrop, let's begin our look at the law with the supreme law of the land—the United States Constitution.

Constitutional Law

The Federal Constitution

More than 220 years ago, the authors of the U.S. Constitution debated numerous proposed provisions, few of which actually survived to become incorporated into the final draft. The general consensus among the delegates indicated that only a strong central government could overcome the serious problems that quickly doomed the Articles of Confederation. Although there was some strong disagreement, the representatives as a whole felt that such a strong central government had the best chance of maintaining unity and coordination among the individual states and commonwealths.

However, the conveners felt even more strongly that no one interest or person, including the head of state, should be accorded supreme authority over the federal government. Thus, a separation of powers, similar to the structure already established in a majority of the constitutions of the 13 original states, was created.

The idea of branches of government acting as checks and balances on one another had wide support at the constitutional convention in 1787. It still can claim strong backing today, but the implementation of that concept is as controversial now as it was then. Those concerns today are expressed in the form of complaints about gross inefficiency and erosion of states' rights and individual liberties.

The seriousness with which the U.S. Supreme Court[5] approaches the balance of powers was brought into sharp focus in June 1998 when the Court struck down the Line Item Veto Act of 1996 as unconstitutional. In *Clinton v. City of New York* (1998),[6] the justices ruled 6 to 3 that the Act violated Article I, §7 (the Presentment Clause) of the United States Constitution. Under the Presentment Clause, "Every Bill which shall have passed the House of Representatives and the Senate, shall, before it becomes a Law, be presented to the President of the United States" for approval or disapproval. If the President disapproves a bill, he has to veto it so it can be "returned" to the two houses so they can have the opportunity to override the veto by a two-thirds vote. The Court said the Constitution requires the return of the entire bill, not individual items of "new direct spending" that the Line Item Veto Act allowed. Thus, line item veto authority could be delegated to the President, according to the Court, only through an amendment to the Constitution.

The Constitution both limits and defines the powers of federal government, but it is principally an outline of the structure, powers, limitations, and obligations of government. Most of the details are left to statutory, common, and sometimes equity law. The first 10 amendments to the Constitution, commonly known as the Bill of Rights, clearly have had the most significant impact on individual privileges such as freedom of speech, freedom of the press guaranteed by the First Amendment, and freedom of religion.

The academic and professional debate over any significance of the position of the First Amendment in the Bill of Rights (i.e., whether first in line means that freedom of speech, press, and religion take priority over other rights in the Constitution when there is real conflict) has been intense in the last several decades. According to the general view of the U.S. Supreme Court during the so-called Burger era (when Warren Burger was chief justice of the United States, 1969–1986) and later during William H. Rehnquist's tenure (1986–2005), First Amendment rights are not to be favored over other individual rights granted in the Constitution. That view has generally continued under current U.S. Chief Justice John Roberts who assumed office in 2005, even though three new justices have joined the Chief Justice on the Court—Samuel Alito (appointed by president G.W. Bush in 2006); Sonia Sotomayor, the first Hispanic member of the court (appointed by President Obama in 2009); and Elena Kagan (appointed by President Obama in 2010).

The Bill of Rights did not even become an official part of the Constitution until December 15, 1791, more than three years after the Constitution became official and more than two years after the first U.S. Congress had convened, the first president had been inaugurated, and a federal court system with a Supreme Court had been created by Congress.

Under Article V of the U.S. Constitution, amendments are added through a two-stage process: the proposing of amendments and their ratification. They may be proposed in one of two ways: (a) by a two-thirds vote in each house of Congress or (b) if two-thirds of state legislatures (today that would be 34 states) petition Congress to call a convention for the purpose of proposing amendments, Congress would be required to hold such a convention. All 27 amendments to the Constitution have been proposed by Congress. This nation has held only one constitutional convention.

Moving to the next phase, amendments can be ratified by two methods: (a) by approval of three-fourths (38) of state legislatures or (b) by approval of three-fourths of state conventions. Congress selects which method of ratification will be used and has chosen state conventions on only one occasion, to approve the 21st Amendment to repeal prohibition which was ratified in 1933. Congress was concerned that state legislatures that were often dominated by rural interests would not agree to repeal prohibition. It is important not to confuse a single, national convention to propose amendments that would be called if 34 states petitioned Congress with conventions in each state to ratify amendments that Congress has the option of requiring regardless of how amendments are proposed.

The last amendment to the Constitution to be ratified was the 27th Amendment in 1992: "No law, varying the compensation for the services of the Senators and Representatives, shall take effect, until an election of Representatives shall have intervened." This amendment was one of the 12 articles proposed by Congress in 1789, 10 of which were ratified by the states and became the Bill of Rights.[7] It forbids Congress from passing any pay raise or decrease that would take effect before the next election of the House of Representatives. Michigan signed on as the necessary 38th state for ratification on May 7, 1992, more than 200 years after the amendment was originally proposed. Four other amendments without specific deadlines are awaiting ratification, including one calling for a new constitutional convention that has now been approved by 32 of the required 34 states although 3 of the 34 have rescinded their approvals. Prior to 1992, the 26th Amendment was the last to get the nod. It forbids states and the federal government from denying any citizen 18 years of age or older the right to vote in state and federal elections. All attempts to amend the Constitution since 1971 have been unsuccessful, including the so-called Equal Rights Amendment ("Equality of rights under the law shall not be denied or abridged by the United States or by any state on account of sex"), which died in 1982 when it fell 3 states short of the 38 required for ratification within the time frame (including one extension) specified by Congress.

State Constitutions

State constitutions are also important sources of U.S. law because they serve as the supreme laws in their respective states except when they are in direct conflict with the U.S. Constitution or valid federal statutes (i.e., federal statutes that do not conflict with the U.S. Constitution and fall within a power enumerated under the Constitution or permitted under the preemption doctrine that allows the federal government to preclude state and local governments from directly regulating certain activities, such as interstate commerce, considered to be national in nature).[8]

What happens if a federal regulation and state common law clash? The U.S. Supreme Court has generally been divided when this question has come before the Court. For example, in 2000, the Court held in a 5-to-4 decision that auto manufacturers could not be sued in state courts for not installing air bags in cars and trucks before the Highway Traffic Safety Administration required them to do so even though there was substantial evidence that air bags saved lives.[9] Three years later, however, the Court ruled unanimously that a state tort liability lawsuit against a boat engine manufacturer for not installing a propeller guard could proceed even though the company was not required to do so under the Federal Boat Safety Act nor by Coast Guard regulations.[10] The key difference between the two cases appears to be that the federal government specifically decided in the vehicle case *not* to impose a requirement but in the boat engine case had simply chosen not to make a decision. All of this illustrates how subtle and complicated interpretations of the preemption doctrine can be.

Most state constitutions require that a specified percentage (usually two-thirds or three-fourths) of those voting in that election approve any proposed amendments to the state constitution that are placed on the ballot after approval by the state legislature. Most state constitutions also provide for a state constitutional convention to consider amendments. Although the U.S. Constitution has never been rewritten, several states have approved new state constitutions.

How does one find state and federal constitutional law? Tracking down the specific constitutions is as easy as a trip to a local library; knowing their meaning is another matter. Constitutions focus on the basic issues of government authority, functions, and organization, as well as fundamental rights and limitations. Their interpretation is often a burdensome task that state and federal courts must constantly tackle. Anyone attempting to ascertain the meaning of a state or federal constitutional provision must consult appropriate statutes because they often pick up where the constitutions stop and yet cannot conflict with the constitutions and case law, where the courts have exercised the authority granted them to interpret constitutional law.

In *Marbury v. Madison* (1803),[11] the U.S. Supreme Court, in a landmark decision written by Chief Justice John Marshall, established the authority of the federal judiciary to determine the constitutionality of congressional actions, thereby effectively establishing the U.S. Supreme Court as the final arbiter or interpreter of the U.S. Constitution. The highest appellate court in each state (usually called the Supreme Court, although in some states such as New York the highest court may be called by another name) is generally the final arbiter of the meaning of that state's constitution.

Statutory Law

Laws in this country fall within a hierarchy of authority, with constitutional law at the top just above statutory law. Statutes take priority over all other types of law, except constitutional law. For example, unless a federal statute is determined to conflict with the U.S. Constitution by a court of competent jurisdiction (ultimately, the U.S. Supreme Court if it exercises its discretion to decide the case), that statute is presumed valid and preempts any conflicting administrative, common, or equity law—local, state, or federal.

Although the process of altering state constitutions and the federal constitution can be long and cumbersome, enacting statutes can be a relatively simple process despite the fact that committees and subcommittees often slow down the procedures. Today, most law is statutory; statutes can deal with problems never anticipated by the framers of the Constitution. They can also be considerably more flexible because they have the ability to deal with future problems and very complex issues.

Legislative bodies—the sources of all statutes and ordinances—number in the thousands and include city councils, county commissions, state legislatures, and Congress. All possess, with constitutional and other limitations, the authority to regulate social actions that range from setting the maximum fine for a particular type of parking violation (although not for a specific offender) to ratifying an international nuclear arms agreement.

All statutes, whether civil or criminal, are compiled in some official form so that affected individuals and organizations can have access to them. The typical university law library or courthouse contains myriad volumes of these written laws. The most convenient way to locate a particular statute is to consult the specific code in which that type of statute is collected. For example, federal statutes can be found in the official *United States Code* (U.S.C.) and in two commercially published codes: *United States Code Annotated* (U.S.C.A.) and *United States Code Service* (U.S.C.S.).

These codified texts conveniently arrange statutes by subject matter (such as copyright, obscenity, criminal acts, etc.) rather than chronologically. State laws are also codified under various names such as [State] *Revised Statutes* or [State] *Code Annotated*. Statutes can also be found chronologically by date of enactment in session laws. For example, federal session laws are compiled in *Statutes at Large*.

The role of the courts in statutory law is actually quite similar to that played in constitutional law. Contrary to popular belief, most statutes (state, federal, and local) are never challenged as unconstitutional. However, most courts have the authority to determine the constitutionality of statutes and, perhaps more significant, to interpret statutes. The federal courts, including the U.S. Supreme Court and most state courts, are prohibited from considering political questions because they can involve a usurpation of executive or legislative authority. Such disputes are characterized as "nonjusticiable" because they do not concern real and substantial controversies, but are merely hypothetical or abstract.

For instance, a U.S. District Court (the primary trial court in the federal system) could not determine in advance whether a proposed federal statute would be constitutional or unconstitutional even if Congress requested the court to do so.

Even the U.S. Supreme Court, the highest appellate court in the country, could not entertain the case because there are no real parties in interest already directly affected by the proposed law.

Administrative Law

Although constitutional and statutory law prevail when they are in conflict with administrative law, administrative law is playing an increasingly important role as society grows more complex. Administrative law is quite simply that "body of law created by administrative agencies in the form of rules, regulations, orders and decisions."[12]

Examples of such administrative agencies at the federal level are the Federal Communications Commission (which has primary authority over nearly all forms of broadcasting and telecommunications, including the Internet, commercial broadcasting, cable television, satellites, and interstate telephone communications), the Federal Trade Commission, the Interstate Commerce Commission, the Social Security Administration, the Veterans Administration, and the Homeland Security Department. Every state has similar agencies such as a department of transportation, an office of consumer protection, and an insurance commission. Each administrative agency (whether state, federal, or local) was created by a legislative act or acts and is responsible for (a) implementing the so-called *enabling legislation* that created the agency, (b) creating rules and regulations, and (c) issuing orders and decisions to carry out the legislative intent of the statutes. Thus, these agencies typically perform both quasi-legislative and quasi-judicial functions (i.e., creating laws in the form of rules and regulations and applying the law through case decisions).

Finding a specific administrative law, especially at the federal level, is a fairly simple task. If you know the approximate date a rule was promulgated, consult the *Federal Register* (Fed. Reg.), where federal administrative rules and regulations are published chronologically. Otherwise, check the *Code of Federal Regulations* (C.F.R.) under the specific topic.

Although most states publish their administrative rules and regulations in some official format, some do not. In the latter case, it may be necessary to contact the agency. Every state or local administrative agency is required, at a minimum, to make its rules and regulations available in some form so those individuals and entities it regulates will have constructive notice.

In some cases, there may be a charge for the complete set of rules and regulations, although a few states provide a free set to anyone on request and many provide free copies to news organizations.

All federal administrative decisions (both interpretative and enforcement) are available from the agencies. Several agencies such as the Federal Trade Commission, the Federal Communications Commission, and the Interstate Commerce Commission publish their own rules; these are also available through commercial publishers. An excellent general source for federal administrative agency and major federal and state trial and appellate court decisions affecting mass communication is the unofficial loose-leaf service, *Media Law Reporter*, published by the Bureau of National Affairs (BNA). The BNA, Commerce Clearinghouse (CCH), and Prentice-Hall (P-H) publish a variety of loose-leaf reporters on a broad range of topics, including mass communications, copyrights, trademarks, and antitrust and trade regulations. These services are especially useful in updating the law because they are published on a regular schedule, usually weekly or monthly.

Common Law

When the United States declared independence in 1776, all of the statutory and case law of England and the colonies prior to that time became the common law. This type of law still exists today, although its significance has declined considerably over the decades.

Whereas written laws in 13th and 14th century England could handle most problems, such statutes could not deal adequately and effectively with all disputes. Gradually, with the support of the monarchy, English courts began basing some decisions solely on prevailing customs and traditions. These decisions blossomed into an expanding body of law that eventually became known as common law. Inconsistencies naturally arose in this corpus of law because it was grounded in specific court decisions, rather than legislation.

However, these conflicts were gradually ironed out as decisions by more influential courts became precedents that effectively bound other courts to follow certain recognized legal principles. As the British colonists came to America, these precedents were generally accepted as American law as well. Thus, common law adhered to the doctrine of *stare decisis*.

Common law is often called "judge-made law" and "case law," although these terms do not represent the total picture. At least in theory, judges do not make law; they merely decide or ascertain the appropriate law and apply it to the given situation. In other words, the role of the judge is to determine the specific legal principle or principles appropriate to the particular case at hand, whether based on constitutional, statutory, or common law. Critics sometimes characterize this responsibility as "discovering the law." Common law is based on previous cases, if they exist, but statutory law and constitutional law are occasionally not based on prior decisions.

One way to understand the nature of the common law is to realize that this body of law fills in the gaps left by statutory and constitutional law but is *always* inferior to statutes and the Constitution. If a conflict occurs between common law and constitutional law or between common law and statutory law, common law gives way.

Tracking down common law is sometimes difficult. The only official source is court decisions, which are generally collected in two forms: case reporters, which are organized chronologically, and case digests, which are organized by topics. Every major federal court has at least one official or unofficial case reporter for its decisions. U.S. Supreme Court cases are officially published by volumes in *United States Reports* (U.S.) and unofficially in *Supreme Court Reporter* (S.Ct.) by West Publishing and in *United States Supreme Court Reports Lawyers' Edition* (L.Ed. and L.Ed.2d) by Lawyers Cooperative Publishing Company.

Official means the reporter was published with government approval. *Unofficial* reporters are usually more comprehensive and informative than the official reporters because they typically include the complete text of a decision plus useful annotations not found in the official report-ers. When attorneys argue their cases in court, they use official reporters.

U.S. Court of Appeals decisions from all 12 circuits are published in the *Federal Reporter* (F.2d) by West. Prior to 1932, U.S. District Court decisions were also reported in the *Federal Reporter.* Since 1932, these decisions have appeared in West's *Federal Supplement* (F.Supp.). Most court decisions, whether state or federal, are not based on common law, and thus these reporters serve primarily as sources for cases dealing with statutory and constitutional law. Unfortunately, the only accurate and effective way to find the common law is by sorting through the cases in the reporters or digests when they are available or by searching through an electronic legal database service such as WestLaw or Lexis.

The highest appellate court in every state has at least one official reporter and most have at least one unofficial reporter. All but a few states also report cases for their intermediate appel-late courts. Reporters generally are not available for trial level courts, although more populous states such as New York and California publish at least some trial court decisions.

Most state appellate court decisions can be found in regional reporters published by West. For example, Georgia cases are in the *South Eastern Reporter* and Kentucky cases can be found in the *South Western Reporter.* As noted earlier, reporters organize cases chronologically. Cases are also compiled by topics in digests, which are convenient to consult because they are divided into hundreds of legal subjects. For example, West uses a Key Word scheme that makes cases very accessible.

A typical court decision, whether trial or appellate, usually touches on several topics and thus, if cited, can be readily tracked in a digest. Several digests are published for the federal courts, including *United States Supreme Court Digest* by West and *United States Supreme Court Digest, Lawyers Edition* by Lawyers Cooperative. Although these two digests contain only U.S. Supreme Court cases, summaries of decisions of all federal courts can be found in a series of digests published by West.[13]

Equity Law

Although equity law falls at the bottom in the hierarchy of laws, it plays an important role in our judicial system, especially in communication law. In this country, equity law can be traced to British courts of chancery that developed primarily during the 14th and 15th centuries. Over the decades, aggrieved individuals found that courts of law (i.e., common law) were often too rigid in the kinds of actions they could consider and remedies they could provide. For example, courts of common law adhered to the maxim that damages (money) could right any wrong. In many instances, such as disputes over land ownership, damages simply were not adequate. Par-ties would then appeal to the king for justice because the sovereign was above the law. Eventu-ally, the king created special courts of chancery that could be used when a remedy at law was not available or was inadequate or unfair. One of the great strengths of equity law was that it could provide prevention.

Courts of law and courts of equity were separate in England for many centuries, whereas today they are merged procedurally in the British courts and in all federal and nearly all state courts in the United States. Thus, plaintiffs seeking equitable relief generally will file suit in the same court as they would in seeking a remedy at law. In fact, the suit could include a request for relief at law and equity or for either (e.g., for equity or, in the alternative, for damages). However, in some states lower level or inferior courts have either limited or no power of equity (i.e., authority to grant equitable relief).

There are several major differences between equity law and common law that can be confusing to the uninitiated. Reporters, editors, and other journalists who cover the courts are often unfamiliar with these crucial distinctions, leading to inaccurate and sometimes downright misleading information in stories.

First, equity decisions are strictly discretionary. In many *civil actions* (this term is defined shortly), a court of law is required (usually by statute) to hear and render a decision in a particular case. However, courts of equity are generally not bound to hear any specific case.

This discretionary power sometimes frustrates parties who feel they have strong justification for equitable relief, but are nevertheless unsuccessful in convincing a court of equity to entertain the case. For example, the equity court may simply dismiss the case as more appropriate for a court of law or even grant damages at law while denying any equitable relief when both damages and an equitable remedy have been sought.

Second, there are certain recognized principles or maxims that equity follows but that are not applicable to actions at law: (a) "equity acts in personam," (b) "equity follows the law," (c) "equity looks upon that as done which ought to have been done," and (d) "equity suffers not a right without a remedy."[14]

"Equity acts in personam" simply means that equity courts grant relief in the form of judicial decrees rather than the traditional damages granted in courts of law. For example, a court of equity could issue an injunction (the different types of injunctions are examined in Chapter 3) prohibiting a credit bureau from disseminating further information about a particular consumer or, conversely, ordering the bureau to disclose its records to the consumer whom it had investigated. That same court could order an employer to rehire a fired employee or command an individual or company to comply with the terms of a contract (i.e., granting specific performance). An example of the use of equity in communication law is a U.S. District Court ordering the Federal Trade Commission to reveal records requested by a media organization under the federal Freedom of Information Act.

"Equity follows the law" is the idea that equity courts will follow substantive rules already established under common law, where those rules are applicable. However, this does not mean that equitable relief must be analogous to relief at law. Equity simply takes over where the common law ends.

One of the real limitations (although some litigants may justifiably perceive it as an advantage) of equity is that it will render relief, especially in contractual disputes, based on that which would be available if the final actions anticipated by the parties occurred exactly as the parties would have expected them to be executed, not as the parties would actually have performed. This principle is congruent with the notion that equity decisions are based on fairness or justice, not according to strict rules of law. Thus, "equity looks upon that as done which ought to have been done."

Even today, remedies at law can be harsh, unjust, inappropriate, or totally lacking, but "equity suffers not a right without a remedy." Although generally only money damages per se are available at law, equity can be broad and flexible. For example, a client who contracted with an owner to purchase a unique or rare manuscript could seek an order for specific performance, which, if granted, would compel the owner to transfer possession and title (ownership) to the client. A court of law would be confined to awarding monetary damages even though money would clearly be inadequate.

Third, equity cases are usually not tried before juries. There are rare exceptions such as divorce cases in Georgia (remember divorces are granted in the form of decrees) and cases in which advisory juries are impaneled. For instance, in *Penthouse v. McAuliffe* (1981),[15] a U.S. District Court judge in Atlanta, Georgia, ruled that the X-rated version of the movie *Caligula* was not obscene because it had serious political and artistic value and did not appeal to prurient interests. Bob Guccione, owner and publisher of *Penthouse* magazine, had purchased the rights to distribute the film in the United States. Prior to showing the film in Georgia, he sought in equity court a declaration that the film was not obscene and a permanent injunction prohibiting the county solicitor general (prosecuting attorney) from bringing criminal suit against him or anyone else involved with distributing or showing the film.

On the advice of the jury that viewed the movie and heard the evidence presented by attorneys for both sides, the judge declared the film not obscene. (The judge did not grant the request for the injunction because he felt declaring the movie not obscene was tantamount to preventing any criminal actions against it.) Obviously, Judge Richard C. Freeman was not bound by the advice of the jury (which can be impaneled in such cases under the Federal Rules of Civil Procedure). However, he apparently felt this body of citizens was in the best position of evaluating whether the work violated contemporary community standards (a finding of fact under obscenity laws). Juries may also be used in those cases in which the primary issue to be decided is one of law, although collateral issues and/or relief sought may be in equity.[16]

Finally, court procedures in equity courts differ somewhat from those in courts of law, although equity and common law courts have been merged. Journalists must understand these distinctions when covering equity cases.

Civil versus Criminal Law

One of the most confusing concepts in our judicial system is civil law. The U.S. judicial system is based on common law, whereas many other Western countries such as Germany and France as well as the state of Louisiana have judicial systems based on a civil code. Most of the civil code systems can trace their origins to the Roman Empire—in particular, the Justinian Code (A.D. 529) and its successors (compiled into the *Corpus Juris Civilis*).

The civil law of France was known as the *Code Civil*, which later became the *Code Napoleon*, from which most of the Louisiana Civil Code is derived. There are other types of judicial systems, such as that of Vatican City, which is based on so-called ecclesiastical law or *religious* or *church law*. Iran's law is also primarily ecclesiastical.

The confusion over civil law arises from the fact that legal actions in our common law system can be either civil or criminal. *Civil law* or action in this sense refers to that body of law dealing with those cases in which an individual or legal entity (such as a corporation, partnership, or even governmental agency) is requesting damages or other relief from another individual or entity. Examples of civil actions are divorce, child custody, libel (except criminal libel), invasion of privacy (in most instances), and copyright infringement.

The vast majority of court cases are civil, although criminal cases tend to attract the most attention in the mass media. A local, state, or federal government can bring action against an individual or organization for the commission of a crime or crimes such as murder, burglary, rape, and assault. (Assault can sometimes be a civil action as well.) The judicial processes involved in criminal and civil cases differ substantially. Both state and federal courts have separate rules of procedure and separate rules of evidence in civil and criminal cases.

Whether a case is civil or criminal is not always readily apparent from the line-up of the litigants. Whereas the government (local, state, or federal) is always the plaintiff (the party bringing the suit) in criminal cases, the government can be a plaintiff or defendant (the party against whom the action is brought) in a civil case.

One easy way to distinguish the two is to look at the possible result if the defendant loses. An individual can rarely be incarcerated in a civil action, except for civil contempt of court. In contrast, the major objectives in a criminal case are to determine guilt or innocence and then punish the guilty. Punishment can include fines, incarceration (jail and/or prison), and even execution for the commission of certain felonies. The primary purposes in civil actions are to determine the liability of the defendant and provide relief, when warranted, for the aggrieved plaintiff(s). Of course, relief in a civil case can also include equity. Punishment can be meted out in civil cases in the form of punitive damages (usually for intentional torts), but the punishment would not include incarceration (except for civil contempt).

The O. J. Simpson cases are prime illustrations of how criminal and civil law intersect and yet have major differences. In 1995, Simpson was acquitted of the murders of Nicole Brown Simpson and Ronald Goldman. The prosecution in the case had to prove that Simpson, the defendant, was guilty *beyond a reasonable doubt*. Under California law, the jury had to render a unanimous verdict. Simpson could not be forced to testify in the criminal case because of his 5th Amendment right ("nor shall [any person] be compelled in any criminal case to be a witness against himself"), and he chose not to take the witness stand. The trial was held in Los Angeles where the crimes occurred. By contrast, in the civil case in which Simpson was tried and found liable less than two years later for the wrongful deaths of the same two victims, the plaintiffs had to prove the defendant liable only by *preponderance of the evidence*. Although the verdict of $8.5 million in compensatory damages for the Goldmans was unanimous, only 9 of the 12 jurors had to agree on the verdict. In fact, the award of $25 million in punitive damages for the Goldmans and the Browns was not unanimous. Ten of the 12 jurors agreed to award the two families $12.5 million each.

During the civil trial, Simpson had to testify because he could no longer assert his 5th Amendment rights. (These rights apply only in criminal cases.) Also, in the civil case, Simpson faced no criminal punishment *per se*; he merely had to pay damages for the wrongful deaths.

Because of his 5th Amendment right not to have to face double jeopardy ("nor shall any person be subject for the same offense to be twice put in jeopardy of life or limb"), Simpson's acquittal in the criminal trial meant that he could not be imprisoned even when found liable for the wrongful deaths in the civil case, but the double jeopardy rule does not prevent a defendant from being tried in a civil case that involves the same set of facts for which the person has been

Weather: Cloudy, snow tonight, 38/32   SPORTS ★ FINAL   Saturday, December 6, 2008

DAILY◉NEWS

75¢   *2.5 MILLION READERS EVERY*   NYDailyNews.com

He dodged the country's most infamous murder rap. Now he faces spending the rest of his life behind bars

IT'S O.JAIL!

SEE STORY ON PAGES 4-5

GIRL MISSING IN CLUBLAND HORROR PAGE 7

Figure 1.1 *Daily News* front page dated December 6, 2008 (NY Daily News Archive/New York Daily News/Getty Images).

found not guilty of criminal liability. Furthermore, acquittal in the first case did not mean that new evidence could not be introduced in the second trial, as witnessed by the 30 photos presented in the wrongful death trial that showed Simpson wearing Bruno Magli shoes.

There were other differences between the two trials, including the sites for the trial (Los

Angeles versus Santa Monica) and the status of cameras in the courtroom (present in the criminal case but banned in the civil trial), but these were not due to the fact that one action was criminal and one was civil. The Simpson criminal trial apparently had a particularly negative impact on public perceptions of the criminal judicial system. An estimated 5 to 15 million people watched at least some of the trial each day on one of the three cable networks carrying the trial live—Cable News Network, E! Entertainment, and Court TV (now known as truTV). A 1995 *American Bar Association Journal* poll revealed that the percentage of individuals who had no confidence in the criminal judicial system increased from 28 in 1994 to 45 percent in 1995.[17] Almost three-fourths of the respondents predicted the trial would result in a hung jury, and only 5 percent said Simpson would be found guilty.[18]

Simpson wrote a book in 2006 entitled *If I Did It* in which he discussed hypothetically how he would have committed the murders if he had been the murderer. After an intense uproar over the announcement that the book would be published and an interview with Simpson would be broadcast on Fox television, Fox and the publisher cancelled the book's publication and the interview. In 2007 the Goldman family purchased the rights to the book from a court-approved trustee handling Simpson's bankruptcy proceedings. The Goldmans purchased all rights to the book, including the copyright and media and movie rights.[19]

Under a bankruptcy settlement reached in 2007, a federal judge awarded Nicole Brown Simpson's family, the Browns, a portion of the first 10 percent of gross proceeds from the book, and the Goldmans the rest.[20]

The O. J. Simpson story took another dramatic turn in 2007 when the former pro-football star was charged and then later tried and convicted of armed robbery and kidnapping—criminal offenses—after a violent confrontation at a Las Vegas hotel.[21] The 61-year-old Hall of Famer claimed at the 2008 trial that he and five companions had stormed the hotel room simply in an attempt to recover sports memorabilia and other items, including his first wife's wedding ring, he said had been stolen from him. His defense was unsuccessful, and he was sentenced to a minimum of nine years in a Nevada state prison. During the sentencing, Judge Jackie Glass noted several times that there was no connection between Simpson's 1995 acquittal and the second criminal trial.[22]

In 2010, the tan Armani suit, white dress shirt and gold tie that Simpson wore in court on the day he was acquitted of murder in 1995 were donated by Simpson's former manager to the Newseum in Washington, D.C., where it is now on display as part of an exhibit on the "trial of the century."[23] The clothing had been offered first to the Smithsonian Institution, which declined the donation as not appropriate.[24]

The first Simpson criminal trial had an impact on subsequent, highly publicized trials such as the Scott Peterson trial in 2004 in which Peterson was found guilty of first-degree murder in the death of his pregnant wife and of second-degree murder in the death of their unborn son. Peterson was sentenced by the judge to death after a jury recommended the punishment. The judge barred cameras in the case, but he did allow a live audio feed of the jury's verdict. In a case with many parallels to the Simpson trials, 72-year-old Robert Blake (a child actor in the *Our Gang* TV series and later an adult actor in *Baretta* on network television) was acquitted in 2005 of the murder of his wife four years earlier. Later in the same year, Blake was found liable to the tune of $30 million by a jury in a civil lawsuit filed on behalf of his wife's four children.[25]

Torts versus Contracts

Civil actions (as defined earlier) are generally classified as arising either *ex contractu* (breach of contract) or *ex delicto* (tort). For example, a publisher who failed to properly (i.e., in good faith) market an author's work after making a binding promise to do so could be held liable for damages at law to the author or, if warranted, ordered to perform the terms of the contract (specific performance). Such actions would be classified as *ex contractu* (breach of contract). A newspaper that published false and defamatory information about an individual could be held liable for harm to the person's reputation. Such an action would be *ex delicto* (tort).

A *tort* is simply "a private or civil wrong or injury, other than breach of contract, for which the court will provide a remedy in the form of an action for damages."[26] The three basic elements of any tort action are (a) a legal duty owed a plaintiff by the defendant, (b) infringement on a legal right of the plaintiff by the defendant, and (c) harm resulting from that infringement.

Summary

There are five major categories of law under our common law judicial system that form a hierarchy of authority: *constitutional law* is at the top, followed by *statutory law, administrative rules and regulations, common law,* and, finally, *equity*. The courts play a major role in the development of each type of law. Two of the most important roles are interpreting constitutional and statutory law and determining the constitutionality of statutes and administrative law.

The task of tracking down a particular law can range from simply reading the U.S. Constitution or a state constitution to getting a copy of a local ordinance. It is also important to check an official or unofficial reporter or digest and read the case law, especially that of higher appellate courts such as the U.S. Supreme Court and the highest appellate court in a particular state.[27]

Civil cases are generally those in which a *plaintiff* (an individual, organization, or government agency) requests damages and/or equitable relief from a *defendant*. Such cases can be either *ex contractu* (breach of contract) or *ex delicto* (tort). When the state (government) brings action against an individual or organization for the commission of a crime or crimes, the case is known as a *criminal suit*; penalties can range from a small fine to incarceration or even death for certain felonies.

Endnotes

1. The poll was conducted in July 2002 for the National Constitution Center. *See* Steven Thomma, *Most People Vague on Constitution's Content*, Lexington (Ky.) Herald-Leader (Knight Ridder), Sept. 17, 2002.
2. *Future of the First Amendment: What America's High School Students Think About Their Freedoms*, The John S. and James L. Knight Foundation, Jan. 2005 (study conducted by David Yalof and Kenneth Dautrich).
3. *Id.* September 2006 survey update.
4. Available online at http://www.firstamendmentcenter.org/pdf/SOFA2009.analysis.tables.pdf
5. The official name of the Supreme Court is "Supreme Court of the United States." To save space and make for easier reading, the generic name, "U.S. Supreme Court," is used throughout this textbook, but be aware that this is *not* the official name.

6. *Clinton v. City of New York,* 524 U.S. 417, 114 S.Ct. 2091, 141 L.Ed.2d 393 (1998).

7. DeBenedictis, *27th Amendment Ratified,* 78 A.B.A. J. 26 (Aug. 1992).

8. Preemption is a U.S. Supreme Court doctrine derived from the supremacy clause of Article VI of the U.S. Constitution, which reads: "This Constitution and the Laws of the United States which shall be made in Pursuance thereof; and all Treaties made, or which shall be made, under the authority of the United States, shall be the supreme Law of the Land; and the Judges in every State shall be bound thereby, any Thing in the Constitution or Laws of any State to the Contrary notwithstanding."

9. *Geier v. American Honda Motor Co.,* 529 U.S. 861, 120 S.Ct. 1913, 146 L.Ed.2d 914 (2000). *See* also David G. Savage, *Tort Lawsuit Cruises Along,* 89 A.B.A. J. 28 (Feb. 2003).

10. *See Sprietsma v. Mercury Marine,* 122 S.Ct. 2585, 153 L.Ed.2d 776 (2002). See also Savage, *supra,* note 9.

11. *Marbury v. Madison,* 5 U.S. 137, 2 L.Ed. 60, 5 Cranch 137 (1803).

12. Henry Campbell Black and Brian A. Garner (eds.), *Black's Law Dictionary* 43 (7th ed. 2000).

13. An excellent resource on how to conduct legal research in media law is Carol Lomicky and Geertruida's *A Handbook for Legal Research in Media Law* (Blackwell Publishing, 2005). This comprehensive text covers in clear detail how to gather and analyze facts, identify and organize legal issues, find the law, update the law, and conduct computerized legal research.

14. *Black's Law Dictionary,* 484–485.

15. 610 F.2d 1353.

16. In *Ross v. Bernhard,* 396 U.S. 531, 90 S.Ct. 733, 24 L.Ed.2d 729 (1970), the U.S. Supreme Court held that a jury trial is required under the Seventh Amendment when the underlying nature of the issue at hand is one of law. Earlier (1959) the court ruled, in *Beacon Theatres, Inc. v. Westover,* 359 U.S. 500, 79 S.Ct. 948, 3 L.Ed.2d 988, that when there is a legal issue that involves both relief at law and in equity, the legal issue must be tried first with a jury before the judge can decide the equitable issue.

17. *See* Steven Keeva, *Storm Warnings,* 81 A.B.A. J. 32 (June 1995).

18. *Id.*

19. *See* Kelli Kennedy, *Goldman Family Buys Rights to O.J. Book,* Associated Press, July 3, 2007.

20. *See* Curt Anderson, *Goldmans Awarded Rights to Simpson Book,* Associated Press, July 31, 2007.

21. *See O.J. Simpson to Serve Up to 33 Years,* Murfreesboro (TN) Daily News Journal (Associated Press), Dec. 6, 2008.

22. *Id.*

23. *See* Linda Deutsch, *O.J. Simpson Acquittal Suit Goes to Newseum in DC,* Associated Press, April 6, 2010.

24. *Id.*

25. *See* Andrew Blankstein, *Civil Trial Jury Finds Robert Blake Liable for Wife's Murder,* Lexington (Ky.) Herald-Leader (Los Angeles Times), Nov. 19, 2005.

26. *Black's Law Dictionary.*

27. 28 U.S.C.A. §§1251 *et seq.* specifies the scope and extent of federal court jurisdiction. Under the U.S. Constitution, Congress possesses the authority to define and limit the jurisdiction of the federal courts, except those matters specifically mentioned in the Constitution as within either the original or appellate jurisdiction of the U.S. Supreme Court. *See* Article III, §2.

2

The U.S. Legal System

A court which is final and un-reviewable needs more careful scrutiny than any other. Un-reviewable power is the most likely to self-indulge itself and the least likely to engage in dispassionate self-analysis … In a country like ours, no public institution, or the people who operate it, can be above public debate.

—Warren E. Burger, Circuit Court of Appeals Judge, to Ohio Judicial Conference on September 4, 1968—nine months before being named Chief Justice of the United States

Our Republic and its press will rise or fall together. An able, disinterested, public-spirited press, with trained intelligence to know right and courage to do it, can preserve that public virtue without which popular government is a sham and a mockery.

—Joseph Pulitzer

The structures, functions, and procedures of our federal and state judicial systems can be confusing, complex, and even intimidating to the layperson, but journalists must be familiar with the basics as well as some of the intricacies. Today, most major news media outlets devote a substantial amount of coverage to judicial decisions and proceedings. These include civil and criminal trials, criminal pretrial proceedings, and, frequently, appellate court rulings. Some of this increased coverage can be traced to a series of U.S. Supreme Court decisions favoring greater access of the public and the press to the judicial process.

Most states now provide for routine access of video, film, and still cameras to criminal and, in some cases, civil trials, although such access has become more difficult since 9/11. In 2010, the Judicial Conference, the policy-making body of the federal courts, announced a three-year pilot project that would allow the televising of some civil trials but under some fairly strict conditions.[1] The conditions include consent from both sides in the case, a ban on recording the faces of witnesses or jurors, and all cameras must be set up and operated by court personnel.

Earlier in the same year, the U.S. Supreme Court initiated a new policy of releasing audio recordings on its website on Friday of the week in which oral arguments are made. Unfortunately,

Figure 2.1   U.S. President George W. Bush poses with 2007 Nobel peace prize laureate Al Gore, in the Oval Office of the White House in Washington, DC, November 26, 2007 (Mandel Ngan/AFP/ Getty Images).

at the same time the Court ended its previous policy of audio recordings of oral arguments on the same day they occurred in selected major cases such as in the *Bush v. Gore* case, which decided the outcome of the 2000 presidential election.[2] These recordings often generated strong media attention. Since 1996 federal appellate courts have been able to decide whether to allow cameras for oral arguments, and two circuits have participated so far. Cameras continue to be prohibited in most other federal courts.

Major U.S. Supreme Court cases are usually handed down each week the court is in session from the first Monday in October until late June or early July. These decisions frequently lead radio and television newscasts, including those of the major networks, and receive front-page attention in major dailies. Occasionally, even lower federal and state appellate court decisions attract headlines.

The trend toward more specialized beats such as consumer reporting and legal affairs has accelerated the need for journalists to have broad bases of legal knowledge. For example, professional athletes and team owners and managers frequently battle in the courts over contracts, antitrust issues, and even liability for personal injuries of spectators. The sports writer who cannot distinguish a judgment non obstante veredicto from a directed verdict or a summary judgment from a summary jury may not be able to write a complete story about a major league baseball player's suit against a team mascot for injuries suffered in a home plate collision. Not only should the writer understand and know how to explain to the readers the issues being litigated, but he or she should also comprehend the basis or bases on which the case was decided at trial and later on appeal.

Significantly more mass communication law now involves court decisions than in the past. Much of our knowledge of communication law is derived from cases decided in the last two decades in which trial and appellate courts either established constitutional boundaries and limitations; interpreted federal or state statutes; or set, affirmed, or rejected precedents at common law. Law (whether constitutional, statutory, administrative, common, or equity) usually has little meaning until an appropriate court or courts interpret it and thus ultimately determine its impact.

Attorneys, judges, and other legal experts sometimes hurl criticism and scorching comments at the press for what they perceive as weak, inaccurate, and even distorted coverage of court cases. Law degrees are not necessary to enable journalists to understand the judicial system, but they must possess thorough and comprehensive knowledge of the system and its processes.

The Federal Court System

Although we usually refer to the U.S. judicial system, there are actually 51 separate and distinct judicial systems. Each state has its own, and there is an independent federal judicial system.

As Figure 2.2 illustrates, there are three basic levels of courts in the federal system—U.S. District Courts, U.S. Courts of Appeals, and the Supreme Court of the United States. Other specialized courts such as U.S. Tax Court, U.S. Claims Court, and U.S. Court of International Trade are also part of the federal system, but these courts are rarely connected with communication law.

The "work horse" or primary trial court in the federal system is the U.S. District Court. Every state has at least one such court and most states have two or more; highly populated states such as California, Texas, and New York have as many as four. Each district court serves a specific geographic area in that state (or can include an entire state as in the case of 26 states that have only one federal district court). Altogether, there are 94 federal judicial districts—counting those in the District of Columbia, Guam, Northern Mariana Islands, Puerto Rico, and the Virgin Islands—and the number of judges in each ranges from 1 to 28. In 2010, U.S. District Court judges earned $174,000 a year (the same as members of Congress), and Circuit Court judges made $184,500.[3] The Chief Justice's salary was $223,500, and the Associate Justices earned $213,900.[4] Salaries have been periodically increased under a 1989 statute that banned nearly all sources of outside income for federal judges but at the same time provided regular raises tied to the cost of living.[5] The total budget in 2009 for the whole federal court system, including the U.S. Supreme Court, was slightly more than $6.9 billion, with about $74 million of that going to the Supreme Court.[6]

A specific U.S. District Court is designated by the region it serves: for example, U.S. District Court for the Northern District of Georgia, U.S. District Court for the Eastern District of Kentucky, U.S. District Court for the Central District of California, or U.S. District Court for the District of Massachusetts. U.S. District Courts are primarily trial courts. A trial court, also known as a court of original jurisdiction, is the court in which litigation in a case is likely to be initiated, and if there is a trial, the court in which the trial will occur. Jury trials take place only in trial courts. The primary purposes of any civil or criminal trial, whether a bench trial (judge only, no jury) or a jury trial, are (a) to seek to determine the facts in the case (similar to the traditional who, what, when, where, why, and how used to organize a news story), (b) to

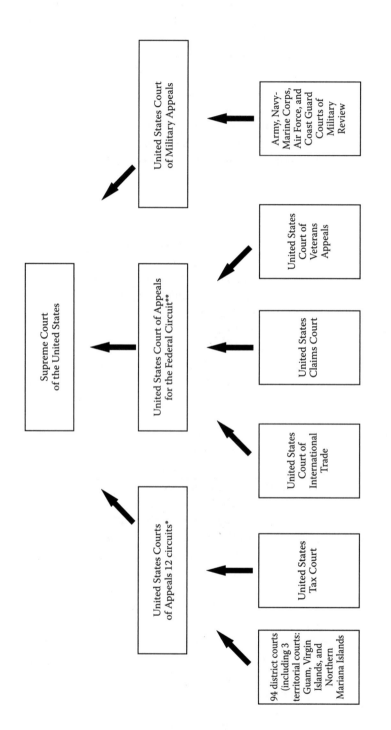

Figure 2.2 The United States Court System.

* The 12 regional courts of appeals also review cases from a number of federal agencies.

** The Court of Appeals for the Federal Circuit also receives cases from the International Trade Commission, the Merit Systems Protection Board, the Patent and Trademark Office, and the Board of Contract Appeals.

ascertain the appropriate law or legal principles (whether constitutional, statutory, common, or administrative law) in the case, and (c) to apply those principles to the facts as determined at trial. In a jury trial, the jury decides the facts in the case and then applies the law, as determined by the judge, to those facts.

Numerous studies have shown that most of the federal courts and many state courts are under-staffed and overloaded with cases. However, the vast majority of both civil and criminal cases never go to trial. In fact, the trend in both state and federal courts is that fewer civil and criminal cases are tried by a judge or jury even though the workloads have risen dramatically. Part of this trend can likely be explained by the push on the part of the courts to encourage parties to settle through alternative forms of dispute resolution such as mediation, arbitration, and facilitation.

Settlement not only saves the expenses of having a much larger court system with more judges, clerks and buildings but, ironically, may result in a better financial outcome for plaintiffs in civil lawsuits, than would have occurred from a trial. That's the conclusion of one study reported in the *New York Times*. According to the report, which was based on a review of state court trials over four decades, "most of the plaintiffs who decided to pass up a settlement offer and went to trial ended up getting less money than if they had taken that offer." [7] The researchers calculated that plaintiffs lost an average of $43,000 by continuing to trial rather than settle out of court.

A relatively small percentage of civil and criminal cases are appealed. Criminal defendants generally have statutory or constitutional rights to at least one appeal when they lose at trial, and both defendants and plaintiffs in civil cases have such rights. Typically, a higher percentage of criminal convictions than civil decisions are appealed. In a civil case, usually only the losing side will appeal the decision. In rare cases, a plaintiff who is dissatisfied with the amount of damages awarded may appeal to a higher court for a new trial on the basis that the damages awarded were inadequate. For instance, a libel plaintiff granted only nominal damages may appeal the jury or judge's decision even though that party technically won the case. In that same situation, the defendant may appeal the decision in hopes of having the verdict overturned.

Most appeals are made on grounds of either (a) errors in court procedures such as presentation of evidence or jury instructions or (b) errors in substantive law by the court such as the judge's application of the wrong criteria for determining whether a plaintiff is a public figure in a libel suit.

Appeal rights are considerably different in criminal cases than in civil cases. If an accused criminal is acquitted, the prosecution is prohibited from appealing the court's decision, whether by a judge or a jury, even if new evidence against the defendant for the same crime(s) emerges later. The 5th Amendment to the U.S. Constitution specifically prohibits double jeopardy ("nor shall any person be subject for the same offence to be twice put in jeopardy of life or limb"). Even if defendants later admit to crimes, they cannot be tried again.

This can lead to what can be described as an "injustice," as illustrated in the classic case of the 1955 murder of Emmett Till, a 14-year-old African American boy, in Money, Mississippi. The case has been the subject of several documentaries and books. Till was found in the Tallahatchie River—shot through the head. A 70-pound fan was wrapped around his neck with barbed wire. The murder attracted widespread international and national media attention. Till's mother insisted that his casket be open for public viewing, and *Jet* magazine and other publications showed graphic photos of the horribly disfigured body in the open casket. Two white men were arrested for the murder and admitted to kidnapping Till. An all-white, all-male jury acquitted them at trial. In a *Look* magazine article only four months later, the pair bragged about the murder and provided extensive details about how they committed the crime.[8] In spite of this obvious injustice, the two could not be retried because of the prohibition against double jeopardy.

Double jeopardy applies only to criminal charges. A person acquitted of a particular crime can still be successfully sued for a similar civil offense using the same or similar evidence presented in the criminal suit because the common standard of proof in civil cases is preponderance of the evidence rather than beyond a reasonable doubt.

The U.S. Supreme Court has added interesting twists to the double jeopardy clause over the years. In 1996, the Court ruled in *United States v. Ursery*[9] that the clause prohibits successive prosecutions but not successive punishments. In an 8 to 1 decision, the Court held that Guy Jerome Ursery was not placed in double jeopardy when he was prosecuted and convicted for growing marijuana after he had earlier paid the federal government $13,250 to settle a civil forfeiture claim against his house where authorities found the plants. The Court invoked an old legal principle that holds that forfeiture is not double jeopardy because it is against property, not against an individual. (Forfeiture involves under the law what is known as an in rem proceeding.) The Court held that such "in rem civil forfeitures are neither punishment nor criminal for purposes of the Double Jeopardy Clause."

In *Sattazahn v. Pennsylvania* (2003)[10] the Court held in a 5 to 4 decision that the double jeopardy ban does not prevent a state from seeking the death penalty against a defendant in a new trial even though he automatically received a life sentence in the original trial because of a hung jury during the penalty phase of the trial. The majority reasoned that a life sentence is not an acquittal and thus does not invoke the prohibition against double jeopardy.

There are no constitutional or statutory limits on how many times a defendant can be tried for the same crime unless the defendant has actually been acquitted. A hung jury is not the same as an acquittal, as illustrated in the case of Curtis Kyles, who was tried five times over a period of nearly 14 years in a 1984 murder in New Orleans.[11] Trial one led to a hung jury, but a second trial resulted in a guilty verdict and a death sentence. On appeal, Kyles' conviction was overturned by the U.S. Supreme Court, leading to three subsequent trials with all resulting in hung juries. Fourteen years after the murder, the local prosecutor dropped the charge, and Kyles was freed from prison.

If convicted, a criminal defendant can appeal the trial court's decision on various grounds. These include violation of the 6th Amendment right "to a speedy and public trial, by an impartial jury of the State and district wherein the crime shall have been committed" to failure of the state (i.e., the prosecutor) to prove its case beyond a reasonable doubt. Although the U.S. Supreme Court has not mandated a specific time frame during which a trial must be conducted in order to meet the 6th Amendment requirement for a speedy trial, most states have established their own standards. For example, California requires that the trial be held within 60 days from the time the defendant is formally charged unless the defendant waives this right.

Defendants often do waive the right so they will have more time to prepare their defense, but asserting this right can sometimes work to a defendant's advantage, as witnessed by the 1995 O. J. Simpson murder trial discussed in Chapter 1. Simpson's attorneys refused to waive the 60-day requirement, forcing the prosecution to prepare its case against the former pro-football star within a very short time frame. Simpson was acquitted, and the prosecutors were criticized in the press for the many strategic mistakes they committed during the trial. Prejudicial pretrial or during-trial publicity may also be shown to have violated a defendant's 6th Amendment right to an impartial jury. If Simpson had been convicted, it is likely that he would have cited the massive publicity surrounding the criminal trial.

Once the defendant (now the appellant or petitioner) files an appeal, that individual effectively waives a claim of double jeopardy. Appellate courts lack authority to ascertain guilt or innocence because this determination is a question of fact for the trial court, not a question of law. Thus the appellate court could order a new trial, pending further appeals, but it cannot declare the appellant guilty or not guilty. Therefore, the criminal defendant granted a new trial by the appellate court could be retried for the same offense(s), but any new trial would have to follow closely the guidelines or standards established by the appellate court.

For instance, three men sentenced to die by a Georgia trial court in the murder of six members of the same family were granted new trials by an 11th Circuit U.S. Court of Appeals more than 14 years after their convictions because of "prejudicial pretrial publicity." One of the men was reconvicted three years after the original convictions were overturned by the federal appellate court and again given the death sentence after a jury trial. A second defendant received a life sentence after a jury deadlocked on the death penalty. The third man also faced only a life sentence because the county prosecutor did not seek the electric chair for him, thanks to a new state statute that prohibited the execution of mentally retarded defendants.

A filtering process further assures that higher appellate courts such as state supreme courts and the U.S. Supreme Court consider a very small percentage of cases from lower appellate and trial courts. The U.S. Supreme Court can exercise its discretion and refuse to hear most appeals. During the 1980s the Court typically granted full-scale review to 150 to 200 of the approximately 5,000 cases appealed to it each year, but by the mid-2000s the Court heard about 80 cases each term or only about one percent of the approximately 8,000 cases filed for discretionary appeal known as a writ of certiorari.[12]

The "Alday family murders" case illustrates another major appellate right of convicted criminals. A defendant convicted in any state court may appeal to the federal courts through a writ of habeas corpus[13] on grounds that the person's constitutional rights (typically 5th or 6th Amendment rights) were violated during the judicial process that led to conviction. Such appeals normally begin in a U.S. District Court and then wend their way eventually to the U.S. Supreme Court. If it believes such grounds may exist, the federal court has the discretion to hear the appeal and to order a new trial in state court, if warranted. All the federal court needs to do to hear the appeal is to simply issue the writ of habeas corpus, which then requires police to release the prisoner until the legality of the detention can be established. The purpose of the writ is to enable the court to ascertain the validity of the petitioner's detention or imprisonment, not to determine the person's innocence or guilt.

In 1996, President Bill Clinton signed into law the "Antiterrorism and Effective Death Penalty Act," which set up a gatekeeping function for the federal courts, requiring them to dismiss any habeas corpus petition filed by a state prisoner who had already had a previous claim considered. Under the statute, (a) federal courts must defer to state court decisions regarding habeas corpus petitions except when they conflict with federal law or are applied in an unreasonable manner, (b) inmates must file any federal habeas corpus petitions within one year of conviction, and (c) prisoners have to file all such petitions after the first one for consideration by a three-judge panel of the U.S. Court of Appeals. The panel then determines whether the petition falls within one of the few exceptions such as when "the applicant shows that the claim relies on a new rule of constitutional law."[14] If an exception did not apply, the claim is automatically dismissed. The law was immediately challenged on the ground that it violated the U.S. Constitution's Suspension Clause, which says that the "Privilege of the Writ of Habeas Corpus shall not be suspended, unless when in Cases of Rebellion or Invasion the public safety may require it."[15]

In *Felker v. Turpin, Warden* (1996),[16] the U.S. Supreme Court held "that although the Act does impose new conditions on our authority to grant relief, it does not deprive this Court of jurisdiction to entertain original habeas corpus petitions."[17] Thus the Court was acknowledging that the new law made it more difficult for prisoners to have more than one application for habeas corpus relief considered, but upheld it as constitutional because it did not specifically prohibit the Court itself from considering such petitions. The purpose and effect of the law are to keep prisoners, especially those on death row, from clogging the courts with petitions.

The Sam Sheppard case[18] of the 1960s is one of the best examples of how a writ of habeas corpus works. In this case, the U.S. Supreme Court granted a writ and agreed to hear Sheppard's appeal of a murder conviction on grounds of prejudicial publicity. The defendant, a prominent osteopath from Cleveland, had been serving 12 years of a life sentence in an Ohio state prison but was freed, pending the outcome of a new trial, when the Court issued the writ and overturned his conviction. Even the highest court in the land, like all appellate courts, lacks the authority to decide a defendant's guilt or innocence. Thus the Supreme Court could merely order Sheppard freed until a new trial could be conducted. Previous appeals by Sheppard and his lawyers had failed, including one made earlier to the Supreme Court. Sheppard was ultimately acquitted at trial by a state jury, but his fate is unusual because most individuals who win new trials in criminal cases are subsequently found guilty again.

Code of Conduct for United States Judges

All federal judges must adhere to the Code of Conduct for United States Judges, which includes seven canons as well as other guidelines and principles for ethical conduct. For example, judges are required to disqualify themselves from cases in which they have personal knowledge of the facts in controversy, any personal bias concerning any of the parties, previous involvement earlier in the case as an attorney, or any financial interest in any party or subject matter involved. This Code of Conduct has been adopted by the Judicial Conference of the United States, the national policy-making body for the federal courts. The conference is chaired by the Chief Justice of the United States and includes 26 other members—the chief judge of each court of appeals, one district court judge from each regional judicial circuit, and the chief judge of the Court of International Trade.[19]

The seven canons state that:

1. A judge should uphold the integrity and independence of the judiciary.
2. A judge should avoid impropriety and the appearance of impropriety in all activities.
3. A judge should perform the duties of the office impartially and diligently.
4. A judge may engage in extra-judicial activities to improve the law, the legal system, and the administration of justice.
5. A judge should regulate extra-judicial activities to minimize the risk of conflict with judicial duties.
6. A judge should regularly file reports of compensation received for law-related and extra-judicial activities.
7. A judge should refrain from political activity.[20]

Venue versus Jurisdiction

No state or federal court has the authority to render a judgment unless it has both jurisdiction and venue in the case. Jurisdiction, the legal right of a court to exercise authority in a particular case, is an enormously complex concept that has been the subject of many scholarly books, treatises, and law review articles. Attorneys must be familiar with such terms as *pendent, ancillary, concurrent,* and *primary jurisdictions,* but for our purposes, only personal jurisdiction and subject matter jurisdiction are relevant.

Personal jurisdiction (also called in *personam jurisdiction*) is the authority of the court over a defendant in a given case. Unless the court possesses personal jurisdiction over the defendant, the court cannot effect a binding judgment against that individual or other entity. The federal and state rules regarding personal jurisdiction can be highly complex, especially in their application, but one of the viable grounds for appeal by a defendant in a civil case can be that the trial court lacked in personam jurisdiction.

In the case of property, whether personalty (such as an automobile or a book) or realty (land and that which is attached to it such as a building), the court must also have jurisdiction *in rem* before it can establish the rightful ownership of that property when there is a dispute.

Jurisdiction of the subject matter is simply the power of the court to hear a particular type of case. Most state court systems include a two-tiered trial court structure. Usually the system includes a lower trial court with limited jurisdiction that can adjudicate only those civil cases in which the amount in dispute is less than a specified monetary sum and/or only certain criminal cases such as misdemeanors (but no felonies). A higher trial court typically has general jurisdiction or the authority to hear all civil and criminal cases that can be tried in that court system, including those that could have been heard in the lower trial court (but which the higher trial court permitted to bypass the lower court).

Examples of subject matter are divorce, equity, felonies, misdemeanors, child custody, and contracts. Even if a particular court may have personal jurisdiction over the parties to the suit, the court cannot hear that case unless it also has subject matter jurisdiction. On rare occasions, an appellate court will reverse a trial court decision on grounds that the lower court lacked jurisdiction (either personal or subject matter). Usually, it is clear which specific court (or courts) has jurisdiction, but the U.S. Supreme Court and other appellate courts have struggled for decades with the issue of jurisdiction, especially *jurisdiction in personam.*

Venue, a relatively simple concept compared to jurisdiction, is the county or other geographical area where a case is to be litigated. Journalists often confuse jurisdiction with venue, but the concepts are not synonymous. An easy way to remember the difference is to keep in mind that venue bears only on the specific geographic location where the case is to be tried and is derived from the Latin, *venire* ("to come").

Ascertaining proper venue involves two major steps. First, it must be determined which particular type of court has both personal and subject matter jurisdiction to hear the case. (In diversity cases and in a limited number of other types of cases as discussed in the next section, both a state court and a U.S. District Court may have jurisdiction. Thus a case could be heard in either court but not both.)

For instance, in a libel suit in which a citizen in Tennessee is suing a newspaper whose primary place of business is in Alabama, a U.S. District Court in Tennessee would likely have both personal and subject matter jurisdiction. Once a judicial determination has been made that a U.S. District Court has such jurisdiction, the question of venue faces the court and the parties. In the vast majority of cases, this question is easily resolved. In the libel case at hand, the U.S. District Court in Alabama— whose geographic authority includes the city or town in which the newspaper is published—would have venue authority. Venue in such a libel suit could (but not necessarily would) lie in another U.S. District Court, such as the plaintiff's state of residence or domicile (Tennessee in this case) if a substantial number of copies of the newspaper were distributed there. Venue could also lie in an Alabama or Tennessee state trial court (assuming that court had jurisdiction).

In summary, think of jurisdiction as the authority of a specific type of court such as a state circuit court as opposed to a state district court, for example, to hear the particular subject matter(s) in the case (e.g., worker's compensation or divorce) and the authority over the parties in the suit (especially the defendant). Venue is simply the specific court, from a geographic perspective, of that type or level of court (U.S. District Court, state superior court, etc.) in which the case can be litigated.

These distinctions are not trivial. A reporter writing a news story about an invasion of privacy suit should be specific in citing the court on first reference (e.g., the "U.S. District Court for the Eastern District of Kentucky" or the "Fulton County [Georgia] Superior Court," not simply "in federal court" or "in superior court").

Federal prosecutors in criminal cases generally must try a defendant in the district where the crime occurred, as required under the 6th Amendment. However, this constitutional restriction on venue does not prevent a defendant from being granted, on request, a change to the same type or level of court in another location within that state. By requesting this voluntary change of venue, the defendant effectively waives a 6th Amendment right to be tried in the state or district where the alleged crime was committed. A change of venue is usually granted by the judge when adverse pretrial and/or during-trial publicity is likely to interfere with the defendant's 6th Amendment "right to a speedy and public trial, by an impartial jury"—often characterized as the right to a fair trial.

For example, U.S. District Court Judge Richard Matsch moved the federal trial in 1997 of Timothy McVeigh from Oklahoma City, Oklahoma, to Denver, Colorado. McVeigh was on trial for the April 1996 bombing of the Alfred P. Murrah Federal Building that killed more than 169 people and injured more than 500 in the deadliest bombing in the United States. A closed-circuit telecast was arranged in Oklahoma City, where the blast occurred, for survivors of the attack and relatives of those killed. McVeigh was found guilty of all charges and given the death penalty by a unanimous jury (as required). He was executed by lethal injection on June 11, 2001. On rare occasions, a change of venue would be made when important witnesses in a civil or criminal case would have difficulty appearing.

Most state constitutions or statutes have venue requirements similar to those under federal law. Although subject matter and personal jurisdiction can usually be challenged during an appeal even if they were not challenged earlier, any objections to a court's venue must be established by the defendant early in the suit (usually no later than in a pretrial motion to dismiss or in the answer) or be deemed waived.

Can a trial court choose not to hear a civil suit even though the court meets all of the statutory and constitutional requirements for venue? In relatively rare situations in which another trial court satisfies all of the venue requirements and in which a clearly more convenient forum than that selected by the plaintiff can be found, a court may invoke a judicial doctrine known as *forum non conveniens*—a discretionary power of the court to decline jurisdiction. This power can be invoked only when (a) a defendant files a motion to dismiss based on forum non conveniens, (b) the plaintiff's forum is clearly inconvenient for the litigants and/or witnesses, and (c) there is another forum in which the suit can be brought.

Forum non conveniens is always discretionary on the part of the court, and thus the judge could still permit the case to be heard even if all of the aforementioned conditions were met. In fact, many states have statutes that prohibit a court from granting a motion to dismiss on grounds of forum non conveniens if the plaintiff is a legal resident of the state in which the suit has been brought.

Forum non conveniens per se is no longer a real issue in the federal courts because Congress codified the doctrine in what is known as a *transfer statute*. Under 28 U.S.C. §1404, a federal trial court can transfer a case to another court within the same court system in which the suit could have been filed originally. Obviously, the other court would also have to have both proper jurisdiction and venue in the case. There are two major differences, however, between the traditional forum non conveniens and transfer: either side may request a transfer and the cause of action is not dismissed and then brought again in the new court when there is a transfer as is done for forum non conveniens. However, transfers can only occur when the two courts involved are in the same system. Thus forum non conveniens would have to be used for changing from a federal court to a state court or vice versa and for changing from a court in one state to one in another state.

Transitory versus Local Causes of Action

In civil cases in state courts, lawsuits can be distinguished as either transitory or local. If a cause of action is deemed local, the plaintiff can file suit only in the specific court designated by statute or by a provision in the state constitution. Local actions nearly always involve real property, whether the dispute concerns ownership, alleged trespassing, or damage to real property. Thus the suit must be brought in the county in which the property is located.

Transitory causes of action, on the other hand, can be brought in "any court of general jurisdiction in any district wherein the defendant can be found and served with process" (i.e., with the complaint or petition).[21] Transitory actions do require what are commonly called *minimum contacts* in the case of a foreign corporation or a nonresident defendant. (*Foreign* means out of state, not just out of the country.) The U.S. Supreme Court first adopted the minimum contacts test for assuring due process for in personam jurisdiction in 1945 in *International Shoe Company v. Washington*.[22] In a series of cases since *International Shoe*,[23] the Court has established minimum contacts, fair play, and substantial justice as the constitutional standard for personal jurisdiction.

The U.S. Courts of Appeals

As discussed earlier, appellate courts such as the U.S. Courts of Appeals are not trial courts but merely serve to consider appeals from trial courts and from federal agencies. Such appeals are usually based on alleged violations of procedural and/or substantive law. State and federal appeals courts generally have three basic options with any appeal they hear: (a) affirm or reverse the criminal or civil verdict or judgment of the lower trial court, (b) dismiss the appeal, or (c) remand (send back) the case to the trial court for further consideration (usually for proceedings consistent with the appellate court's decision). The court also has the option of reversing the trial court decision and sending the case back with an order to dismiss.

The 94 judicial districts of the federal court system are organized into 12 regional circuits, each of which has limited jurisdiction over a specific geographical area or circuit, as shown in Figure 2.3.

These regional courts also hear appeals from cases decided by federal administrative agencies. Eleven of these circuits are numbered, but one is designated the U.S. Court of Appeals for the District of Columbia Circuit (no number). There is also a 13th circuit court, the Court of Appeals for the Federal Circuit—the only federal appellate court that has national jurisdiction other than the U.S. Supreme Court. This court hears specialized appeals such as those involving international trade, patent litigation, and claims for damages against the federal government. The geographic areas covered by the 11 numbered circuits vary from three to nine states. The judicial caseloads for most of the federal courts continue to climb each year. For the 12-month period ending March 31, 2010, 60,358 cases were filed in the U.S. Courts of Appeals, excluding the Federal Circuit,[24] the vast bulk of which were from the lower district courts, U.S. Tax Court, and federal administrative agencies. By comparison, 282,307 civil and 77,287 criminal cases were filed in the U.S. District Courts during that same period.[25]

The Court of Appeals for the Federal Circuit has *exclusive appellate jurisdiction* over some 15 specific types of cases such as final decisions of the U.S. Claims Court and the Court of International Trade and most patent appeals. *Exclusive jurisdiction* (whether original or appellate) is, as the term implies, the power of that specific court to hear and decide that particular matter to the exclusion of any other court.

Nonexclusive jurisdiction means, of course, that one or more other courts could hear the case, although not at the same time. All of the federal courts have original and exclusive jurisdiction over certain types of cases, such as violations of federal laws, but this jurisdiction varies from court to court. For example, the federal courts have original and exclusive jurisdiction over all controversies between two or more states. Federal courts also have *concurrent jurisdiction* with state courts in certain types of cases such as those involving *diversity* or actions between citizens of different states, as discussed in the next section.

Diversity

Article III, §2 of the United States Constitution specifies the judicial power of the federal courts, noting that this power "shall extend to all Cases, in Law and Equity, arising under this Constitution, the Laws of the United States, and Treaties made, or which shall be made, under their authority." This section then lists the other types of cases over which the federal courts have jurisdiction, including those involving the United States as a party, controversies between two or more states, and admiralty and maritime cases. Such cases qualify for federal jurisdiction because they involve what are known as federal questions or matters that directly involve the federal issues or the federal government and its interests. There is one other way in which a case can be heard in federal court—diversity of citizenship.

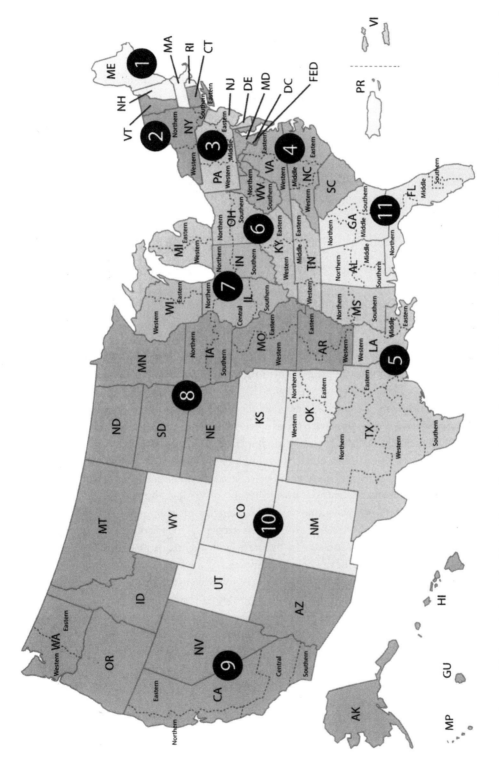

Figure 2.3 Geographic boundaries of the United States Court of Appeals and the United States District Court (www.uscourts.gov/court_locator.aspx).

Diversity of citizenship, or *diversity* as it is usually known, under §2 involves controversies "between Citizens of different States." When the conditions for diversity are met, a plaintiff can choose to have a case tried in either state or federal court. The requirements include (a) meeting a jurisdictional or threshold amount in dispute, which has been $75,000 since 1997, and (b) having complete diversity. The jurisdictional amount is set by Congress and has increased over the years from $10,000 in 1958 to $75,000 today.[26] The requirement of complete diversity, which means that in multi-party suits no plaintiff can be a citizen of the same state as any defendant, was established by the U.S. Supreme Court in 1806 in *Strawbridge v. Curtiss*.[27]

To avoid the problem of plaintiffs engaging in forum shopping or deciding whether to take a case to federal or state court based upon which court would be most likely to render a favorable verdict, the Supreme Court established the principle that the same substantive law—usually state law—will apply in diversity cases as would apply if the case were tried in state court. Beginning with *Erie Railroad Co. v. Tompkins* (1938) through *Hanna v. Plumer* (1965),[28] the Court created an outcome test under which an analysis is conducted to ensure that a final decision in a diversity case is the same as what would have occurred if the case had been tried in state court. However, the rules of civil procedure may be different because federal rules will apply in federal court and state rules in state court.

In 2001, the U.S. Supreme Court held in *Semtek International v. Lockheed Martin*[29] that a Maryland Court of Special Appeals was wrong when it dismissed a case filed in that state's court system after the same case had earlier been dismissed in U.S. District Court in California. The federal court in California dismissed the case because the lawsuit had been filed past the statute of limitations deadline. The plaintiff then filed the suit in a trial court in Maryland where the statute of limitations had not expired. However, the Maryland court dismissed the case on the ground of res judicata—Latin for "the thing that has been decided." This is the judicial doctrine that, once a court with proper jurisdiction has made a decision based upon the merits of the case, the decision is final and further lawsuits are barred.

The U.S. Supreme Court said the lawsuit could go forward in Maryland because federal courts apply state substantive law in diversity cases, not federal law. The Court cited *Erie Railroad Co. v. Tompkins* in its reasoning, noting that nation-wide uniformity under which state law applies in diversity cases was necessary to prevent forum shopping. The concern of the Court is that the outcome be the same, whether a diversity case is tried in federal court or state court, not that the result be the same regardless of which state court hears the case.

In *Hertz Corp. v. Friend* (2010),[30] the U.S. Supreme Court unanimously ruled the phrase "principal place of business" under federal diversity-of-citizenship statutes refers to the place where a corporation's high level officers direct, control, and coordinate the corporation's activities. The Court applied a test known as the "nerve center" test rather than a "business activity" test. The former test makes it easier, according to the Court, for lower courts to determine where a corporation predominantly has its business activities. Hertz successfully argued that its principal place of business was New Jersey, its headquarters, and not California where the plaintiffs resided and where Hertz conducted business.

The U.S. Supreme Court

No court in this country has attracted more media and public attention than the U.S. Supreme Court. There is no better example of this than the intense coverage of *Bush v. Gore* (2000), in which the Court effectively decided who won the presidential election that year. The per *curiam* opinion (an unsigned opinion representing the whole court) technically dealt with only whether the Florida Supreme Court in ordering a state-wide recount of disputed presidential ballots had violated Article II, §1, clause 1 and the Equal Protection and Due Process provisions of the U.S. Constitution. Clause 1 deals with the appointment of electors. Equal Protection and Due Process are guarantees contained in the 14th Amendment: The Equal Protection clause prohibits states from unlawfully discriminating against citizens, and the Due Process clause assures that states may not deprive citizens of life, liberty, or property without proper administration of justice.

In *Bush v. Gore*,[31] the Court abruptly and decisively ended the protracted uncertainty over whether Al Gore or George W. Bush won the election in which Gore officially won the popular vote but Bush won the electoral vote, thanks to a razor-thin margin of 1,784 votes out of more than 5.8 million cast in Florida. Everyone— the presidential candidates, the American public, and Congress—deferred to the Supreme Court for the final decision, an indication of just how powerful the Court can be. For more than a month, chads (small bits of cards left after ballots are punched with a Votomatic machine) of all sorts—dimpled, pregnant, scratched, and punched—were subjects of intense discussion in a national debate over who won the election.

The answer ultimately boiled down to the decision of five justices that the recount process ordered by the Florida Supreme Court could not be done prior to December 12, the deadline under the U.S. Constitution for electors to select a president. According to the Court, "having once granted the right to vote on equal terms, the State may not, by later arbitrary and disparate treatment, value one person's vote over another." Only three days earlier, the Court had granted an injunction to halt a recount ordered by the Florida Supreme Court pending a hearing and a decision in the case by the U.S. Supreme Court. The Court's final decision did not escape criticism that included the opinions of the four dissenting justices. In his book, *Supreme Injustice: How the High Court Hijacked Election 2000*, Harvard law professor and legal expert Alan M. Dershowitz said, the decision "has left a permanent scar on the credibility of the Supreme Court."[32] In his national bestseller, *The Nine: Inside the Secret World of the Supreme Court*, CNN legal analyst Jeffrey Toobin offers a rare inside look at the decision-making process in the case and its impact on the justices themselves, including the fact that Justice Souter "seriously considered resigning" and "his attitude toward the Court was never the same. There were times when David Souter thought of *Bush v. Gore* and wept."[33] Souter did resign nine years later and was replaced by Second Circuit U.S. Court of Appeals Judge Sonia Sotomayor.

Bush v. Gore made history in another way. For the first time, audiotapes were made available to the press immediately following the conclusion of the one-hour oral arguments. In the past, audio recordings were not released until the beginning of the next term of the Court, although transcripts of the Court's decisions are publicly available on the Court's website: (www.supremecourtus.gov) within minutes after opinions are issued. Three years later the Court allowed the press to have immediate access to the recordings in the combined cases of *Grutter v. Bollinger* and *Gratz v. Bollinger*,[34] challenging the University of Michigan's affirmative action policies for undergraduate and law school admissions. In both instances it was clear that the Court provided such quick access to the recordings because of the intense public interest in the cases. As noted earlier in this chapter, in 2010 the Court discontinued its policy of providing same-day release of audio recordings in select cases. The Court now posts each week's oral arguments on Fridays on its website.

Distinguishing Characteristics of the U.S. Supreme Court

The U.S. Supreme Court is unique in several significant ways. First, it is the only court specifically established by the U.S. Constitution. Article 3, §1 of the Constitution creates "one supreme Court," while granting Congress the authority to ordain and establish "inferior courts," if it so chooses. Thus Congress could constitutionally abolish all of the federal courts except the Supreme Court. As noted previously, the Supreme Court does have original jurisdiction over specific types of cases enumerated in Article 3, §2(2), but the Court functions primarily as an appellate court. Typically, the Court decides one or two original jurisdiction cases each nine-month term.

In 2004, for example, the Court decided an original jurisdiction case involving a dispute between the states of Kansas and Colorado over a 1949 compact involving the Arkansas River.[35] The case could be traced all the way back to 1985 when Kansas claimed that Colorado had violated the agreement by drilling new irrigation wells that depleted the water from the river. Per tradition, the Court first appointed a Special Master to hear evidence and arguments on both sides and then make recommendations in the form of a "Special Master's Report." Because the two sides could not agree on the recommendations, the Supreme Court faced the task of deciding the case under its original jurisdiction authority. Over the years, there were four Special Master's Reports, with the Court essentially agreeing with the recommendations each time, including the most recent one.[36] Kansas was unhappy with some of the recommendations in the last report and asked the Court to overrule those recommendations. The Supreme Court sided with the Special Master once again.

In contrast, until the last decade or so, under its appellate jurisdiction, the Court traditionally heard oral arguments and issued decisions for about 160 cases each term from the approximately 7,500 it was formally requested to consider. Since the early 1990s, though, the Court has substantially reduced its load, typically hearing only 75 to 80 cases each term.

A second unique feature is that the U.S. Supreme Court, as one of the three branches of government (along with the President and Congress), both interprets and applies the U.S. Constitution in cases in which the other branches play a role. In other words, the Court is the final arbiter of the Constitution. This authority is quite wide ranging and has invoked considerable controversy over the years, but especially in the last two decades. The debate is usually framed in terms of a liberal versus conservative court but really revolves around the issue of whether the Court merely interprets the law or both interprets and makes the law. Former President Ronald Reagan was particularly proud of the fact that he had been able to select (with approval of the U.S. Senate) Chief Justice William H. Rehnquist (who had been nominated as Associate Justice by President Richard M. Nixon) and Associate Justices Sandra Day O'Connor, Antonin Scalia, and Anthony M. Kennedy. The senior President George Bush got to appoint two Associate Justices—Souter in 1990 and Thomas the next year. President Bill Clinton also appointed two justices—Ruth Bader Ginsburg in 1993 and Stephen G. Breyer in 1994. President George W. Bush appointed Chief Justice John G. Roberts in 2005 and Associate Justice Samuel Alito in 2006. President Barack Obama made history twice with two appointments to the Supreme Court—Justices Sonia Sotomayor (2009) and Elena Kagan (2010). He was the first President to appoint two women to the Court and to appoint the first Hispanic member to the Court.

A third feature is the intricate but fascinating process by which the Supreme Court reviews cases. Other federal courts and some state courts may follow some of the steps followed by the

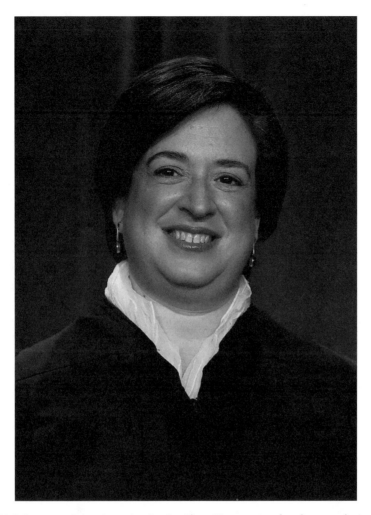

Figure 2.4   U.S. Supreme Court Associate Justice Elena Kagan poses for photographs in the East Conference Room at the Supreme Court building in Washington, DC, October 8, 2010 (Chip Somodevilla/Getty Images News/Getty Images).

Supreme Court in its decision making, but the process as a whole is rather unique. There are three ways in which a case can be heard on appeal by the Court: direct appeal, writ of certiorari, and certification. The grounds on which each of these types of appeals can be heard are enumerated in Title 28 of the U.S. Code.

Mandatory versus Discretionary Jurisdiction

Until 1988, under Title 28 and other federal statutes, some litigants had a right, theoretically, to have an appeal heard by the Supreme Court. For example, if a U.S. Court of Appeals held that a state statute or treaty was invalid because it violated the Constitution, laws, or treaties of the United States, the state had a statutory right to have the case ultimately decided by the Supreme Court. A similar right existed if the state's highest appellate court held the statute or treaty unconstitutional. However, for at least 50 years the Supreme Court rejected the vast majority of such appeals "for want of a properly presented federal question" or "because of the inadequacy of the record"[37] or other basis. Thus a seemingly obligatory appeal was in practice discretionary.

In 1988, the picture changed dramatically for mandatory jurisdiction. For almost a decade Congress tried unsuccessfully to grant the unanimous request of the U.S. Supreme Court that it be given greater choice in selecting cases for review. More specifically, the justices called for Congress to essentially kill the body's mandatory jurisdiction. With the support of the Reagan administration, then-Chief Justice Rehnquist and various legal organizations such as the American Bar Association, a bill passed Congress that granted the Court's wish. Congressman Robert Kastenmeier (D-Wis.), chairman of the House subcommittee on courts, characterized the new statute as the "most significant jurisdictional reform affecting the high court in over 60 years."[38]

Over the years Congress narrowed or eliminated various mandatory appeals that ranged from antitrust cases to suits contesting the constitutionality of state and federal statutes, but it took the 1988 legislation to kill nearly all appeals based on mandatory jurisdiction. To understand the real impact of this statute, one must realize that during its 1987–1988 term, the Court handled 248 mandatory appeals, with 206 decided summarily (i.e., without full briefing or oral argument), including 120 dismissed for lack of jurisdiction and 83 for lack of a federal question.[39] Thirty-two of the appeals were actually accepted for review, none of which the Court would have had to have decided if the 1988 legislation had been in effect at that time. Until the 1988 statute, the Court typically decided only about 200 cases on the merits each term, with about one-fifth of the load involving mandatory jurisdiction. These summary decisions were nevertheless binding on state and other federal courts because they had been decided on the merits, leaving the lower courts with little or no guidance beyond the vote of the Court.

The law that amended or repealed several sections of Title 28 did not eliminate all mandatory jurisdiction. Specific appeals under the Civil Rights and Voting Rights Acts and the Presidential Election Campaign Act retain their mandatory status.[40]

The statute law left intact another way in which the court could hear an appeal: certification. Under §254(3) of Title 28, questions of law in any civil or criminal case can be certified by a court of appeals to the Supreme Court. For example, if a U.S. Court of Appeals is uncertain about the constitutionality of a new federal criminal statute, it can certify this question of law to the Supreme Court for a determination. As with all other judicial cases, there must be a real case in controversy. The federal courts, including the Supreme Court, are prohibited from deciding purely political questions because they are not "justiciable" matters for the courts.

Writ of Certiorari

By far the most common way and now virtually the only way cases are heard by the Supreme Court is *writ of certiorari*. There are three major situations in which the Court will hear an appeal under this writ: (a) before or after judgment or decree in a civil or criminal case in a court of appeals; (b) final judgments or decrees of the highest appellate court of a state, Puerto Rico, or the District of Columbia involving the constitutionality of a state or federal treaty or statute or any title, right or privilege claimed under the U.S. Constitution; and (c) certain types of decisions by the U.S. Court of Military Appeals. Most states have abandoned this discretionary writ in their courts, but Congress and the Supreme Court continue to cling to what many legal critics contend is an outmoded process.

"Granting cert" (press and legal shorthand for granting a writ of certiorari) is a relatively simple process by which the Supreme Court (after agreeing to hear a case) formally orders the lower appellate court to certify the record and then turn it over to the Supreme Court. Denial by the Supreme Court of the request to issue the discretionary writ is tantamount to a denial of the party's appeal.

Certiorari begins when an attorney for one side in a case (nearly always the losing side) files a written petition with the U.S. Supreme Court. Such petitions can be filed in other courts, but they are much less common now than in the past. Under a working rule adopted by the court (known as the "rule of four"), four justices must agree to hear the appeal before the Court will review the lower court decision. This rule is based on the belief that a legal question is substantial enough to be considered when at least four members are willing to grant a writ of certiorari. When four votes are not available, which occurs about 90 percent of the time, the petition is thereby denied and the lower court (i.e., the last court in which the appeal was decided) ruling stands. Although news stories occasionally unintentionally mislead the public into believing otherwise, denial does not necessarily mean that the Court agrees with the lower court decision but merely that the justices did not feel the appeal warranted their attention because of the lack of a major legal issue. When the Court declines to hear an appeal, it is inaccurate to publish or broadcast that the Court "upheld" the lower court decision. However, it is accurate to say the Court allowed the lower court decision to stand, although it is more accurate to indicate the Court did so by rejecting the appeal from the lower court.

Appellate Briefs and Oral Arguments

If the Court votes to hear the case, the writ is then issued and a tentative date is set for oral arguments. Prior to the oral hearing, the attorneys for the two sides are required by a specified deadline to submit written briefs detailing their positions and arguments. A well-written appellate brief will normally contain an extended statement of the issues involved, a summary of the facts in the trial court case, relevant laws, arguments based on the law and trial and appellate court decisions that support that position, and a summary of and justification for the particular relief sought.

The form and the content of appellate briefs are usually dictated by the particular court hearing the appeal, and the U.S. Supreme Court is no exception. There are other types of briefs, such as a trial brief, but these are not the same as appellate briefs. Although they presumably summarize, appellate briefs are rarely "brief" and are typically lengthy and detailed. The briefs are presumably read by all of the justices before the oral arguments that typically last 30 minutes for each side. The Court is quite strict about the time frame, and the justices, including the Chief Justice, will often interrupt the presenting attorneys' arguments with pointed questions while the clock is running. In a major case, it is not unusual for attorneys to fail to complete oral arguments because of these interruptions. Except in rare cases such as those involving sensitive national security matters, the oral arguments are open to the press and to the public, unlike Supreme Court deliberations that are always secret.

The court has lost a bit of its mystique, in the eyes of some folks, over the years. In 1993, Librarian of Congress James H. Billington opened the late Justice Thurgood Marshall's files to the public. Marshall donated 173,700 items from his career that cover more than 3,000 Supreme Court cases.[41] The materials provide considerable insight into the decision-making process of the Court and included Marshall's handwritten tallies of justices' votes, hundreds of internal memos, and Marshall's personal comments. The justice's widow criticized the Library of Congress for releasing the documents so soon after Marshall's death, but Library of Congress officials said the justice had agreed there should be no restrictions on access after he died.

Later in the same year Peter Irons, a University of California-San Diego political science professor, published a package entitled "May It Please the Court." It included 23 edited recordings and transcripts of selected oral arguments of major Supreme Court decisions. Most of the justices criticized the release of the tape recordings and transcripts, just as they had the release of Justice Marshall's papers. Professor Irons gained access to the tapes in 1990 as part of a research project in which he agreed to limit their use to private research and teaching purposes and not to reproduce them. Excerpts were broadcast on National Public Radio and C-SPAN. The Court issued a warning before the package was actually published threatening legal steps because Irons violated contractual commitments but then announced three months later that it had decided not to pursue legal remedies against the author but instead to make the tape recordings in the National Archives publicly available on a "generally unrestricted basis."[42]

Deliberations

Later, after oral arguments have been presented in a case, the U.S. Supreme Court justices deliberate in chambers to hammer out a decision. The sessions are so secret that even the law clerks and assistants are excluded. The discussion begins with the Chief Justice enunciating his views (although usually not his vote), followed by the Associate Justices in order of seniority (highest to lowest) on the Court. According to books purporting to offer insights into the Court such as Bob Woodward's *The Brethren*, the views and subsequent votes sometimes change as the justices attempt to forge a majority opinion.

Tentative votes are usually taken first. However, when the final vote is made, the justices state their decisions beginning with the justice with the shortest tenure on the court on up to the most senior justice, with the Chief Justice voting last in the case of a tie. If the Chief Justice is a member of the majority in the decision, he or she has the option of writing the majority opinion or designating the justice who will write the opinion. If the Chief Justice is in the minority, the most senior justice in the majority can write the opinion or select the justice to do so.

Types of Opinions

Initially, the draft of a majority opinion is written, usually with the assistance of law clerks, and then circulated to the other members, including those in the minority. Each justice has the option of (a) agreeing with the majority opinion, (b) writing a separate concurring opinion agreeing with the conclusions, outcome, or result of the majority opinion but disagreeing with the majority's reasons or rationale, (c) writing a dissenting opinion disagreeing with the majority opinion's conclusions, outcome, reasons, and rationale, or (d) concurring with the majority in part and dissenting in part. For the latter, the justice agrees with a portion or portions of the majority opinion but disagrees with another portion or portions.

Majority opinions are ideal because they can establish a *precedent* to guide future cases, but sometimes justices cannot reach a majority opinion or they may wish to merely issue a brief majority opinion. A *plurality opinion* results when fewer than a majority and more than required for a *concurring opinion* join in an opinion. Plurality opinions never establish precedents but they sometimes influence lower court decisions, as witnessed by the Supreme Court's three-justice plurality decision in *Rosenbloom v. Metromedia*,[43] a 1971 libel case. Although the Court explicitly rejected the plurality decision three years later, many lower courts, especially trial courts, adopted the rule cited in the plurality opinion that the actual malice rule of *New York Times v. Sullivan*[44] included involuntary public figures.

Another type of opinion worthy of attention is the *per curiam opinion*, as noted earlier in the discussion of *Bush v. Gore* (2000). These unsigned opinions written by one or more justices but representing the views of the whole Court are usually brief because they require the agreement of each justice. There are many theories about why the Court issues per *curiam* opinions, including the desire by each justice not to have his or her name specifically attached to the opinion. *Per curiam* decisions, even in First Amendment cases, are fairly uncommon.

A final option of the Court is a *memorandum decision* in which the Court gives its ruling in the case but offers no opinion. A memorandum decision is technically not a judgment but merely an announcement of the Court's vote. Such decisions, which can be rather frustrating for litigants who are looking for precise answers, are becoming more common as the workload of the Court continues to increase each year.

Terms of Service on the Court

Much of the aura surrounding the Supreme Court can be attributed to the fact that justices are appointed for life[45] and can be removed from office only upon impeachment. Judges of the U.S. courts of appeals, the district courts, and the Court of International Trade also serve for life, but other federal judges, including bankruptcy and magistrate judges and those serving on the Court of Federal Claims serve for specific periods. Many U.S. Supreme Court justices have served on the Court until their deaths, with some staying on the Court even in their 80s. Although there have been instances in which suggestions have been made that particular justices be impeached, such as Michigan Congressman Gerald Ford's[46] campaign to have Associate Justice William O. Douglas impeached in the late 1960s, only one U.S. Supreme Court Justice has ever been impeached. The U.S. House of Representatives impeached Associate Justice Samuel Chase (not to be confused with Samuel P. Chase, who joined the Court later and served as Chief Justice) in 1804 for his political activities outside the courtroom while he was still serving on the Court. However, the U.S. Senate could not muster enough votes to convict him.[47]

In recent years, the trend has been for the President to nominate relatively young justices to serve on the Court to ensure that a conservative majority sits on the Court for many years to come, regardless of who may become President later. Associate Justice Clarence Thomas, the only African American serving on the Court, was 43 when he was approved 52 to 48 to succeed Associate Justice Thurgood Marshall in October 1991 by the Senate in one of the closest votes in Supreme Court history. His nomination by the senior President George Bush was extremely controversial because of his staunchly conservative views.

The Senate approved the chief executive's choice in spite of an unprecedented Senate Judicial Committee extended hearing over University of Oklahoma Law Professor Anita Hill's sexual harassment allegations. When he assumed the role of Chief Justice in October 2005, Justice Roberts, at age 50, became the second youngest Chief Justice in history, with Justice John Marshall, who served from 1801 to 1835, having been the youngest at 46. Sonia Sotomayor was 55 when she became Associate Justice in 2009, and Elena Kagan was 50 when she took the oath of office in 2010. Both Sotomayor and Kagan were nominated by President Obama. The current court is not only the most diverse court in history but also one of the youngest, with the average age of the justices at 64 in 2011, compared with an average of 76 in 2005.[48]

Size of the Court

One common myth about the Supreme Court is that the U.S. Constitution requires the court to have nine justices. In fact, the Constitution does not provide for any specific number; instead Congress was left with the task of setting the number. Before Congress set the number in 1867 at nine (which has continued to today), the number of justices on the Court changed six times and ranged from 6 to 10. As of 2011, 112 justices have served on the Court, with 17 of them serving as chief justices. Only five associate justices later became chief justices, including the late Chief Justice William H. Rehnquist.

According to another myth, President Franklin Delano Roosevelt appointed the most members to the Court. Actually, President George Washington holds the record because he appointed the six original justices plus another four during his second term. However, President Roosevelt is second because he appointed eight justices and selected Associate Justice Harlan Fiske Stone as Chief Justice. President Ronald Reagan appointed three justices and picked Associate Justice Rehnquist as Chief Justice. The senior President George Bush had the chance to appoint two Associate Justices, and President Bill Clinton appointed two. President George W. Bush appointed the current Chief Justice Roberts and Associate Justice Alito, and President Barack Obama has appointed two Associate Justices.

The Court's Schedule

The Supreme Court adheres to a rather strict schedule. Each annual session begins on the first Monday in October and typically ends by the July 4 holiday. Court sessions alternate among hearings, delivering opinions, and recesses. Hearings and opinions are known as sittings. The usual rotation between sittings and recess is every two weeks. Opinions are written during the recesses. The sittings begin at 10:00 a.m. each day and typically end by 3:00 p.m.

Each sitting begins promptly at 10:00 a.m. when, at the sound of the gavel, everyone stands and the Court Marshal announces: "The Honorable, the Chief Justice and the Associate Justices of the U.S. Supreme Court. Oyez! Oyez! Oyez! All persons having business before the Honorable, the U.S. Supreme Court, are admonished to draw near and give their attention, for the Court is now sitting. God save the United States and this Honorable Court!" The audience then sits after the justices have been seated.

About two dozen cases are heard during each sitting, but the Court conducts other business during this time; it may release a list of orders, admit new attorneys to the Court bar, and release opinions. Opinions are not announced in advance, and thus reporters and others covering the Court do not know which opinions will be released on any given day, lending an element of surprise to the proceedings. Oral arguments and some of the other business are announced in advance. Public sessions are conducted only on Mondays, Tuesdays and Wednesdays.

During May and June, the last two months of its sessions, the Court conducts no other public business except to announce opinions. When the last opinion has been announced, usually in late June, the Court recesses until the following October. However, during the summer hiatus numerous petitions for review and motions are processed.

Until 1935 the U.S. Supreme Court had no building of its own in which to meet but instead convened at various locations in the District of Columbia, including the U.S. Capitol. In 1929 Chief Justice William Howard Taft, the only member of the Court to have previously served as a U.S. President, convinced Congress to build the Court a permanent home. Construction began that year and was completed in 1935. The building was designed by architect Cass Gilbert, who died before the building was completed, as did Chief Justice Taft.

Mootness, Ripeness, and Standing

Before this discussion of the Supreme Court ends, three more terms need to be explained: *mootness*, *ripeness*, and *standing*. Legal scholars sometimes refer to these concepts as the three horsemen. Mootness refers to the refusal of a court to hear a case when the outcome has already been determined, and thus any decision by the Court would have no impact on the case. In other words, the Court will not decide "dead" or merely academic issues. From time to time, the Supreme Court will deny certiorari in a case on the grounds that the issue in the case is non-justiciable. The basis for this refusal is, once again, that Article III, §2 of the U.S. Constitution restricts all federal courts including the U.S. Supreme Court to real "cases" and "controversies."

For example, a fired government "whistle blower" who sues his federal employer for violating his First Amendment rights but subsequently settles out of court will not be permitted to continue his suit simply to have the Court determine whether his rights were violated, even if any claim for damages is sought. In most cases, the death of a plaintiff does not render a suit moot. For instance, if a plaintiff in a libel suit dies before the case comes to trial or dies while a case is being appealed, the legal representative(s) can continue the case on the victim's behalf.

A good example of how the death of a plaintiff does not automatically render a case moot is *Tory v. Cochran* (2005),[49] a U.S. Supreme Court decision discussed in more detail in Chapter 8. Johnnie Cochran, who served as the lead attorney in O. J. Simpson's murder trial, died one week after the U.S. Supreme Court heard oral arguments in an appeal of a gag order. The Court granted a motion by Cochran's attorney that Cochran's widow be substituted for her husband. The permanent order had been issued by a California trial court five years earlier and upheld by two state appellate courts. It prohibited a former client of Cochran and an associate from uttering any statements about the lawyer or his law firm in any public forum and was issued after the trial court ruled that Cochran had been defamed by picketing outside his office.

In a 7 to 2 decision, the Supreme Court said the case was not moot because the restrictive order remained in effect even though Cochran had died. The Court held that the order was unconstitutional prior restraint, ruling that "the injunction, as written, now amounts to an overly broad prior restraint on speech, lacking plausible justification." However, the Court refused to rule on whether the First Amendment prohibits such an injunction in a libel case, arguing that Cochran's death made it unnecessary to make such a determination.

The 2001 U.S. Supreme Court decision in *City News & Novelty v. Waukesha*[50] illustrates the concept of mootness. The case involved an adult-oriented store whose business license was not renewed by the city because of alleged violations of a city ordinance. The denial was upheld in administrative proceedings and by the state courts on appeal. In its appeal, City News raised three questions, but the U.S. Supreme Court agreed to hear only one—whether the constitutional right to a prompt judicial review in such a case meant a determination on the merits of the denial of the license or simply prompt access to judicial review.

In a 1965 decision, *Freedman v. Maryland*,[51] the U.S. Supreme Court ruled that before the government can restrict adult-oriented materials or businesses, certain procedural safeguards must be followed to assure that the First Amendment is not violated. One of those safeguards is that there must be a prompt final judicial decision. At the time of the appeal, some of the federal circuit courts had held that the requirement meant a prompt judicial determination on the merits of a permit denial, but other courts, including the Wisconsin Court of Appeals, determined that the requirement simply meant prompt access to judicial review. With a conflict among the courts, this issue was clearly one that needed to be resolved, not only for the parties in the case but for the country as a whole. Unfortunately, the question ultimately remained unresolved.

After petitioning the U.S. Supreme Court for certiorari, City News withdrew its renewal application and shut down. In a unanimous opinion by Justice Ginsburg, the U.S. Supreme Court dismissed the petition on the ground that the case was moot because "City News is not properly situated to raise the question on which this Court granted review."[52]

Vacatur, a process in which the parties to a case seek to set aside a judgment, is often used by the U.S. Supreme Court to render a case moot, especially when there has been a settlement. A 1994 U.S. Supreme Court decision, however, significantly limits the use of vacatur, at least in the federal courts. In *U.S. Bancorp Mortgage Co. v. Bonner Mall Partnership*,[53] the Court in a unanimous opinion written by Justice Scalia held that "mootness by reason of settlement does not justify vacatur of a judgment under review."

An equitable remedy, vacatur is frequently used by business and government to have adverse rulings set aside to avoid having a judgment against them on the record as well as to avoid an unfavorable precedent.[54] After U.S. Bancorp reached a settlement with Bonner Mall in a bankruptcy suit, the mortgage company asked the U.S. Supreme Court to vacate the decision of the 9th Circuit Court of Appeals on the ground that the settlement had made the ruling moot. U.S. Bancorp made a rather interesting argument to support the idea of "routine vacatur," as it is known—by leaving an issue unsettled, vacatur encourages "continued examination and debate."

U.S. Bancorp also told the Court the process facilitates settlements, thus reducing the workload on the federal courts. The Supreme Court found neither argument compelling, noting: (a) "The value of intra-circuit debate seems to us far outweighed by the benefits that flow to litigants and the public from the resolution of legal questions" and (b) "We find it quite impossible to assess the effect of our holding, either way, upon the frequency or systemic value of settlement."[55]

A second obstacle that may confront litigants or appellants in a case is lack of *ripeness*. Citing Article III, §2, the Court will sometimes refuse to hear a case because it believes the controversy is not ready (ripe) for review. The rationale for this ripeness doctrine is to prevent courts from engaging in premature, abstract, or political decisions. For example, a newspaper that wanted to challenge the constitutionality of a proposed federal law restricting access to government records could not have its case decided because this issue would not have been ripe for consideration. Instead of hearing the suit, the Court would dismiss it and probably note that the newspaper must wait until the law is enacted and the paper was actually denied access—and thus suffered some harm or abridgement of its First Amendment rights.

A good illustration of the concept of ripeness is the U.S. Supreme Court's decision in *Palazzolo v. Rhode Island*[56] in which a landowner sued the state after a state regulatory agency designated salt marshes, such as the one on the owner's land, as protected coastal wetlands on which development was severely restricted. The owner claimed the regulations constituted a taking of his property without compensation under the Takings Clause of the 5th Amendment.[57] The owner had originally been one of several partners in the company that owned the property but eventually bought out his associates and became sole owner. When the owner sought permission from the state agency to construct a wooden bulkhead and fill the entire marsh area, his application was denied, as was his later request to fill 11 of the property's 18 wetland acres to build a private beach club. He then sued the state, arguing that the regulations violated the 5th and 14th Amendments as a taking. A trial court ruled against him, and the State Supreme Court affirmed, ruling, among other things, that the owner's suit was not ripe because the owner had not sought permission to make other uses of the land.

The U.S. Supreme Court disagreed, holding that the two application denials by the agency had been a final determination on the permitted use for the land. According to the Court, there was no "genuine ambiguity in the record as to the extent of permitted development on petitioner's property, either on the wetlands or the uplands."[58] The regulations were unequivocal in their restrictions, the Court said.

Finally, litigants in federal court must have *standing* to avail themselves of justice in the federal courts. Standing has been interpreted to mean a plaintiff must have suffered actual injury or must be threatened with injury in the case of governmental action. In other words, this standing to sue doctrine requires that a party be "sufficiently affected so as to insure that a justiciable controversy is presented to the court."[59]

In a 1997 case, *Raines et al. v. Byrd et al.*,[60] the Court held that six members of the U.S. Congress—two Representatives and four Senators—had no standing to file a complaint against the Secretary of the Treasury and the Director of the Office of Management and Budget to determine the constitutionality of the Line Item Veto Act. The Act, passed by the both the Senate and the House of Representatives in March 1996, granted the President the authority to "cancel" specific spending and tax items after the President had already signed them into law, simply by notifying Congress within five days after the particular Act takes effect.

The U.S. District Court of the District of Columbia had earlier sided with the plaintiffs in holding that the Act was unconstitutional. President Bill Clinton had made no line item vetoes when the complaint was filed. The Act included a provision requiring the Court to grant expedited review, and thus the trial court decision was directly appealed to the Supreme Court. Stressing that a plaintiff bears the burden of proof in establishing standing and that "the alleged injury must be legally and judicially cognizable," the Court held "that these individual members of Congress do not have a sufficient 'personal stake' in this dispute and have not alleged a sufficiently concrete injury to have established Article III standing."[61] The Court characterized any injury to the appellees as "wholly abstract and widely dispersed" and their claim as "contrary to historical experience."[62]

State Court Systems

If you intend to become a practicing journalist, you should thoroughly review your state court system. State and federal courts play an increasingly important role in news and news gathering, and thus it is not unusual now for most reporters, editors, and writers to occasionally cover a state court decision or a trial, regardless of the specific beat assigned.

A state court is a hierarchy, organized by levels from limited or general jurisdiction trial courts to intermediate appellate courts to the highest appellate court (usually, but not always, called the supreme court). The review process is quite similar to that of the federal courts, discussed earlier, with the higher courts having the power to review and, of course, reverse lower court decisions.

Figures 2.5 and 2.6 illustrate the court system and the appeals process of one state—Kentucky. Both the system and the appeals process in Kentucky are similar to those of many other states, but you should consult appropriate references to learn more about your own jurisdiction.

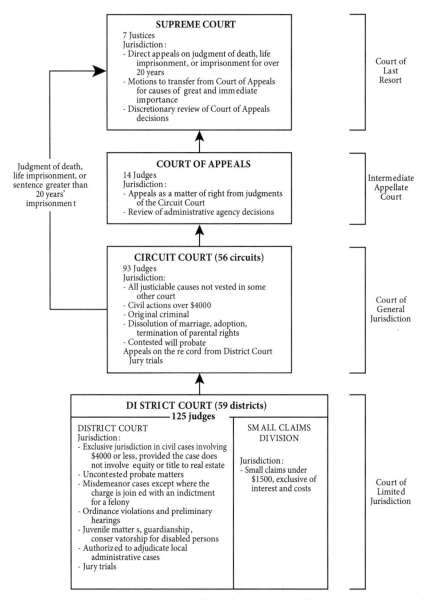

Figure 2.5   Kentucky Court System (Compiled by Administrative Office of the Courts, Frankfort, KY. Reprinted with permission).

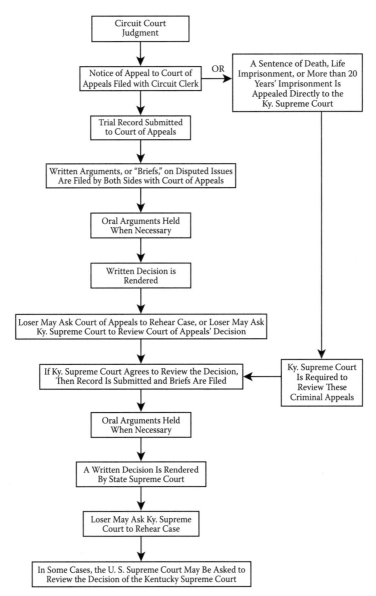

Figure 2.5 Kentucky Appellate Process (Compiled by Administrative Office of the Courts, Frankfort, KY. Reprinted with permission).

Although the federal court system and the 50 individual state court systems are independent, links allow cases to flow from one to the other, especially between the federal and state courts. Although most cases that move from one court system to another are cases appealed from a state court to a federal court (nearly always to the U.S. Supreme Court), on rare occasions a court in one state may refuse to hear a case on grounds that a court in another state is the more appropriate or convenient forum. In other relatively rare cases, a court in one state may invoke the law of another state under a doctrine known as choice of law, which arises when a determination must be made as to which state's laws apply when a conflict exists between the two states' laws.

For example, suppose a sports celebrity sues a food conglomerate for using her picture and name to sell one of its popular cereals. The company has headquarters in Atlanta, the ads appear primarily in New York, and the celebrity resides in Oklahoma. If the case is tried in Oklahoma, whose appropriation (the alleged tort committed here) laws will prevail if the laws of the three states involved conflict with each other? As any other state court would do under the circumstances, the Oklahoma court would apply its own conflict of law rules to make that determination.[63]

The final matter to consider about state courts is their relationship to the federal courts, including interpreting federal laws such as the U.S. Constitution. As pointed out in the next chapter, state courts in some circumstances have the authority to interpret and apply federal laws, including the U.S. Constitution. Although the Supreme Court, as mentioned earlier, has declared that it will be the final arbiter of the meaning of the U.S. Constitution, state courts can indeed decide cases involving the Constitution and even federal statutes when Congress has specifically permitted state courts to interpret and apply federal laws. On the other hand, federal courts will apply state laws in certain types of cases, such as those involving diversity (in which the parties are residents of different states).

Summary

The federal court and most state courts have three basic levels—a general trial court, an intermediate appellate court, and a supreme court. The primary trial court in the federal system is the U.S. District Court. Trial courts determine the facts in a case, ascertain the appropriate law or legal principles, and then apply the law to the facts. Appellate courts such as the U.S. Court of Appeals and the U.S. Supreme Court merely hear appeals from cases tried in the trial courts and from federal agencies and thus do not conduct trials except in those rare instances in which a court has original jurisdiction. Appellate courts do not determine guilt or innocence.

Before a federal or state court can hear a case, it must have both jurisdiction and venue. Jurisdiction includes both personal and subject matter jurisdiction. In civil cases in state courts, suits are classified as either transitory or local. The U.S. Supreme Court is the only federal court created by the U.S. Constitution. This court is the final arbiter of the Constitution and hears cases by direct appeal, writ of certiorari, and certification.

Virtually all appeals heard by the court are now by writ of certiorari since a 1988 federal statute eliminated nearly all mandatory jurisdiction by the U.S. Supreme Court. But before a case can be heard by the court by writ of certiorari, at least four justices must agree to consider the appeal. If at least five justices agree, a majority opinion is reached and a precedent can be established. A plurality opinion (one written by less than a majority) never sets a precedent. Other types of decisions are per *curiam* opinions and memorandum decisions. If a case is moot or not ripe, or if the parties have no standing, the Court will refuse to hear the case per Article III, §2 of the U.S. Constitution.

It is imperative that journalists and aspiring journalists be familiar with legal concepts, judicial principles, and the structures of the state and federal court systems to ensure that their stories are accurate and complete. Media consumers have already been confused and even misled in television shows and novels about lawyers and the courts, with a few notable exceptions.

Endnotes

1. Rosemary Lane, *Flights, Camera and Some Action*, 34 News Media & Law 33 (Fall 2010).
2. *Id.*
3. *See* "Judicial Salaries Since 1968" at http://www.uscourts.gov.
4. *Id.*
5. *See* Hope Viner Samborn, *The Vanishing Trial*, 88 A.B.A. J. 24 (Oct. 2002).
6. *See* "Frequently Asked Questions" at http://www.uscourts.gov.
7. *See* Jonathan D. Glater, *The Cost of Not Settling a Lawsuit*, New York Times, Aug. 8, 2008. The study itself was published in the Journal of Empirical Legal Studies.
8. *See* Thomas Doherty, *The Ghosts of Emmett Till*, Chron. Higher Educ., Jan. 17, 2003, for a review of various documentary films and publications about the case.
9. *United States v. Ursery*, 518 U.S. 267, 116 S.Ct. 2135, 135 L.Ed.2d 549 (1996).
10. *Sattazahn v. Pennsylvania*, 537 U.S. 101, 123 S.Ct. 772, 154 L.Ed.2d 588 (2003).
11. *See* Pamela Coyle, *Tried and Tried Again*, 84 A.B.A. J. 38 (Apr. 1998).
12. *See* Anne Gearan, *Justices Reject Almost 2,000 Appeals*, Lexington (Ky.) Herald-Leader (Associated Press), Oct. 8, 2002.
13. The official name is *writ of habeas corpus ad subjiciendum.* There are other writs of habeas corpus but the use of the term, *writ of habeas corpus*, is nearly always in reference to a *writ of habeas corpus ad subjiciendum.*
14. Pub. L. 104-132, 110 Stat. 1217, 18 U.S.C. 153 (1996).
15. U.S. Const., Art. I, §9, cl. 2.
16. *Felker v. Turpin, Warden,* 518 U.S. 651, 116 S.Ct. 2333, 135 L.Ed.2d 827 (1996).
17. *Id.*
18. *Sheppard v. Maxwell,* 384 U.S. 333, 86 S.Ct. 1507, 16 L.Ed.2d 600 (1966).
19. *See* Understanding the Federal Courts, downloadable free at the website for the Administrative Office of the U.S. Courts: http://www.uscourts.gov.
20. *Id.*
21. *Black's Law Dictionary,* 1343.
22. *International Shoe Company v. State of Washington*, 326 U.S. 310, 66 S.Ct. 154, 90 L.Ed. 95 (1945).
23. See especially *Shaffer v. Heitner*, 433 U.S. 186, 97 S.Ct. 2569, 53 L.Ed.2d 683 (1977) and *Kulko v. Superior Court of California,* 436 U.S. 84, 98 S.Ct. 1690, 56 L.Ed.2d 132 (1978).
24. These statistics were gathered from the website of the Administrative Office of the Courts: http://www.uscourts.gov.
25. *Id.*
26. 28 U.S.C.A. §1332 (2011).
27. *Strawbridge v. Curtiss,* 7 U.S. 267, 2 L.Ed. 435, 3 Cranch 267 (1806).
28. *Erie Railroad Co. v. Tompkins*, 304 U.S. 64, 58 S.Ct. 817, 82 L.Ed. 1188 (1938) and *Hanna v. Plumer*, 380 U.S. 460, 85 S.Ct. 1136, 14 L.Ed.2d 8 (1965).
29. *Semtek International v. Lockheed Martin,* 531 U.S. 497, 121 S.Ct. 1021, 149 L.Ed.2d 32 (2001).
30. *Hertz Corporation v. Friend,* ___ U.S. ___, 130 S.Ct. 1181, 175 L.Ed.2d 1029 (2010). The statutory provisions are in 28 U.S.C. §§1332(d)(2) and (c)(1).
31. *Bush v. Gore*, 531 U.S. 98, 121 S.Ct. 525, 148 L.Ed.2d 388.
32. *Id.*
33. Alan M. Dershowitz, *Supreme Injustice: How the High Court Hijacked Election 2000*, 206 (2001).
34. Jeffrey Toobin, *The Nine: Inside the Secret World of the Supreme Court*, 208 (2008).
35. *Grutter v. Bollinger*, 539 U.S. 982, 124 S.Ct. 35, 156 L.Ed.2d 694 (2003) and *Gratz v. Bollinger*, 539 U.S. 244, 123 S.Ct. 2411, 156 L.Ed.2d 257 (2003).
36. *Kansas v. Colorado*, No. 105 Orig. (2004).
37. *Kansas v. Colorado*, 533 U.S. 1, 121 S.Ct. 2023, 150 L.Ed.2d 72 (Kansas III) (2004).
38. *See* Gunther, Gerald, *Constitutional Law: Cases and Materials*, 10th ed., 1670 (Mineola, NY: Foundation Press, 1980).
39. *See* Marcotte, *Some Relief for Supreme Court*, 74 A.B.A. J. 33 (Sept. 1988).

40. *See* Stern, Gressman, and Shapiro, *Epitaph for Mandatory Jurisdiction*, 74 A.B.A. J. 68 (December 1988).

41. *Id.*

42. *See* B. Weiser and J. Biskupic, *Justice's Papers Offer Rare Look Inside Supreme Court*, Lexington (Ky.) Herald-Leader (Washington Post), May 23, 1993; *Librarian of Congress Defends Release of Papers from Justice Marshall*, Lexington (Ky.) Herald-Leader (Washington Post), June 12, 1993.

43. *See* H. J. Reske, *Publicity-Shy Justices Criticize Prof*, 79 A.B.A. J. 36 (Nov. 1993); H. J. Reske, *Justices' Reversal*, 80 A.B.A. J. 31 (January 1994); D. O. Stewart, *May It Please the Court …*, 80 A.B.A. J. 50 (March 1994).

44. *Rosenbloom v. Metromedia*, 403 U.S. 29, 91 S.Ct. 1811, 29 L.Ed.2d 296, 1 Med.L.Rptr. 1597 (1971).

45. *New York Times v. Sullivan*, 376 U.S. 254, 84 S.Ct. 710, 11 L.Ed.2d 686, 1 Med.L.Rptr. 1527 (1964).

46. Technically, all federal judges serve during "good behavior," which has been interpreted to mean for life unless impeached.

47. Ford became President in 1974 when President Richard Nixon was forced to resign after revelations of a conspiracy to cover up the Watergate break-in.

48. These and other interesting facts about the Court can be found in a booklet, *The Supreme Court of the United States*, updated each term and available from the main office of the court. Also see *Understanding the Federal Courts, supra*, note 19.

49. *See* Joan Biskupic, *With 3 Women on Bench, Court Ready to Open New Era*, Murfreesboro (TN) Daily News Journal (USA Today), Oct. 3, 2010.

50. *Tory v. Cochran*, 544 U.S. 734, 125 S.Ct. 2108, 161 L.Ed.2d 1042, 33 Med.L.Rptr. 1737 (2005).

51. *City News & Novelty v. Waukesha*, 531 U.S. 278, 121 S.Ct. 743, 148 L.Ed.2d 757 (2001).

52. *Freedman v. Maryland*, 380 U.S. 51, 85 S.Ct. 734, 13 L.Ed.2d 649 (1965).

53. *Id.*

54. *U.S. Bancorp Mortgage Co. v. Bonner Mall Partnership*, 513 U.S.18, 115 S.Ct. 386, 130 L.Ed.2d 233 (1994).

55. *See* H. J. Reske, *Supreme Court Bans Routine Vacatur*, 81 A.B.A. J. 18 (Feb. 1995).

56. *U.S. Bancorp Mortgage Co.*

57. *Palazzolo v. Rhode Island*, 533 U.S. 606, 121 S.Ct. 2448, 150 L.Ed.2d 592 (2001).

58. See Amendment Five of U.S. Constitution of the United States, which states, in part, that no person shall "be deprived of life, liberty, or property, without due process of law; nor shall private property be taken for public use, without just compensation."

59. *Palazzolo v. Rhode Island*.

60. *Black's Law Dictionary*, 1260.

61. *Raines et al. v. Byrd et al.*, 521 U.S. 811, 117 S.Ct. 1489, 137 L.Ed.2d 699 (1997).

62. *Id.*

63. *Id.*

64. Choice-of-law principles go by such colorful names as *lex fori, center of gravity, renvoi*, and *grouping of contracts*. This topic has been the subject of numerous books, articles, and treatises and, in fact, is regularly taught as an elective course at most law schools.

3

The Judicial Process

This chapter introduces you to the basics of the judicial process, including descriptions of a typical civil lawsuit and trial and a typical criminal lawsuit and trial. Put aside any images you may have from television shows and movies—you are now in the real world of law. You will encounter some strange new terms, but take them to heart because you will find them indispensable later, especially if you become a practicing journalist.

The Civil Lawsuit

The vast majority of lawsuits never reach trial but are either dropped by the plaintiff or settled out of court by the parties. The courts could never handle the load if all or even half of all cases went to trial because they are extremely busy processing and ruling on motions and other pretrial proceedings. Most court cases are civil, although criminal cases often attract the most intense media attention. For example, during the 2010 fiscal year, 282,307 new civil cases and 77,287 new criminal cases were filed in the federal district courts.[1]

In the federal courts, the *Federal Rules of Civil Procedure* and the *Federal Rules of Evidence* (that also apply to criminal cases) generally dictate the procedures and rules governing civil litigation, both for actions within the courtroom and for those outside the courtroom. Most states have either adopted the federal rules for their state courts or use similar rules with modifications. This chapter relies primarily on the federal rules, but you should consult your own state's rules if you plan to cover state courts.

The Complaint

Figure 3.1 illustrates the civil case process for Kentucky, which is similar to the processes in most other states. As the diagram indicates, a civil suit typically is formally initiated with the filing of a legal document known as a *complaint*. The primary purposes of the complaint are to give the defendant notice and to inform the person or organization of the nature and basic facts of the case. A complaint states the specific claim(s) against the defendant, the basis on which the court can exercise jurisdiction over the case, the basic facts, and the particular relief sought (which need not be stated in specific dollar amounts but instead can indicate the type of damages requested, such as punitive and actual).

All of the claims are mere allegations and should never be cited in a news story without attribution and qualification. For example, if a plaintiff says in a complaint that her telephone was wiretapped by the defendant without her permission, do not assume that her statement is a proven fact. Instead, you should note in the story: "According to a complaint filed today in state circuit court, Jane Smith's home telephone was bugged by her ex-husband. Mrs. Smith is seeking $125,000 for alleged invasion of privacy."

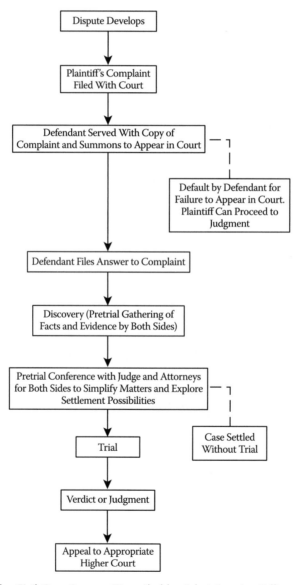

Figure 3.1 Kentucky Civil Case Process (Compiled by Administrative Office of the Courts, Frankfort, KY. Reprinted with permission.)

A complaint in a civil suit is nearly always a public document and thus available under state and federal open records laws. In most states, you can simply go online for access. You can also go to the clerk of the appropriate court and ask to see the case files. If you have a case number, you will save some search time, but court clerks are usually helpful in tracking down particular documents if you have a name of one of the parties. Local attorneys, who can often be found perusing documents in the courthouse, can also be helpful, but the best way to learn the system is to practice a few trial runs, whether you are seeking access online or in-person, before you have to find a document under deadline pressures.

Once the complaint has been filed, the court clerk will issue a signed *summons* with the seal and name of the court. Under the federal rules, called the *Federal Rules of Civil Procedure*, the summons must also contain the name and address of the plaintiff's attorney, the time frame within which the defendant must respond under the federal rules, and a statement that if the defendant fails to answer ("failed to plead or otherwise defend"), judgment by default can be entered against the defendant.[2]

Under the federal rules, the complaint and the summons must be served together[3] in person by an individual who is not a party to the suit and who is at least 18 years of age. Service can also be made under certain conditions by a U.S. marshal, deputy marshal, or other person specially appointed by the court for that purpose. Personal (i.e., in hand) service to the named defendant is known as *actual service*. It is usually not necessary that the defendant be served so long as a "person of suitable age and discretion" within the dwelling is handed the copy. Appointed agents and individuals specified under the law can be served in lieu of the actual defendant in some cases, and federal and state agencies can sometimes be served via certified mail.

Service methods such as mail and delivery to an agent or other representative are called *substituted service*. The rules are quite complex because they are designed to assure compliance with the due process clause of the 14th Amendment to the U.S. Constitution. The rules are also complicated by the fact that each local federal district court can set its own rules and because state statutes frequently come into play in federal courts because the federal rules permit federal courts to adopt local (i.e., state) rules for service. In some limited circumstances, *constructive service*—service via publication in an official organ—is permitted, such as when a defendant cannot be found or actual or substituted service is not possible.

Service via e-mail is permissible under some circumstances, at least according to one U.S. Circuit Court of Appeals. In the first federal court appellate ruling on this new substitute service, the 9th Circuit U.S. Court of Appeals allowed a plaintiff in a case to serve the defendant, a foreign-based Internet gambling firm with no physical location, with the complaint by e-mail. The court allowed such service under Rule 4(f)(3)[4] but only after the plaintiff had tried to serve the complaint via several other means including snail mail and personal service.[5]

Filing a complaint is obviously a serious matter because the allegations become public record and therefore subject to public scrutiny. Thus sanctions are in place for individuals and their attorneys who file frivolous or unsubstantiated claims. Rule 11 of the Federal Rules of Civil Procedure requires that every "pleading, written motion, and other paper shall be signed by at least one attorney of record."[6] With their signatures, attorneys certify that they have read the document and have made a reasonable inquiry into the merits of the case to assure that the pleading or motion "is warranted by existing law or by a non-frivolous argument for the extension, modification, or reversal of existing law or the establishment of new law."[7] The court can exercise various sanctions, including fines, when the judge believes the rule has been violated.

Congress added more teeth to the rule, including revisions in the 1980s, and federal judges have been enforcing the rule more rigorously. The result has been a noticeable increase in the number of attorneys sanctioned and considerable controversy among legal authorities over how and when the rule should be enforced. Because attorneys are certifying that their purpose in filing the suit or motion is not "for any improper purpose, such as to harass or to cause unnecessary delay or needless increase in the cost of litigation,"[8] it is not unusual for federal judges to cite delaying tactics and harassment in imposing fines. Many states have adopted the federal rules, complete with Rule 11, for their courts, and most of the other states have at least a parallel rule.

Another remedy for the problem of frivolous lawsuits that can be more effective than Rule 11 sanctions, when available, is *malicious prosecution of a civil suit*, which requires that the defendant win the original suit and prove that the plaintiff had no probable cause in initiating legal action.

The Answer

The next typical step in a civil suit is the filing of an *answer* by the defendant. Under the federal rules, a defendant generally has 20 days from time of service to file an answer or other appropriate *pleading*. If the defendant is the United States or a federal officer or agency, the maximum time for an answer is 60 days. Similar time constraints apply in most state courts, although the periods do vary among states.

The defendant has a host of options in answering the plaintiff's complaint. These options are generally not mutually exclusive and thus can be used alternatively or in combination. The primary purpose of the answer, also called the defendant's *responsive pleading*, is to counteract the plaintiff's allegations. In other words, the defendant should demonstrate why the plaintiff should not prevail. The defendant can also enter various denials, as discussed shortly, plead an affirmative defense and even file a *counterclaim*, asking for damages from the plaintiff or other individuals or entities.

Denials

Denials fall into five general categories: general, specific, qualified, insufficient knowledge, and denial on information and belief. A *general denial*, asserting that all of the averments in the complaint are false, was once rather commonly used. But, because Rule 8(b) now requires that "denials shall fairly meet the substance of the averments denied,"[9] general denials are rare in the federal courts today. Typically, the defendant will file a *specific denial*, which designates the specific statements and/or paragraphs being denied and usually the specific statements and paragraphs admitted.[10] Under Rule 8(d), if the defendant does not deny those averments "to which a responsive pleading is required" (except the amount of damage), the averments are deemed to have been admitted. In other words, those allegations and other statements made by the plaintiff in the complaint that are not denied by the defendant are generally considered to have been admitted by the defendant. There are certain exceptions to this rule, but these are beyond the scope of this book.

An example of a specific denial would be a media defendant in an invasion of privacy suit denying that it had subjected the plaintiff to public ridicule when it published a story about his financial dealings. On the other hand, the paper would probably admit that the story was actually published on January 25, 2012, and that it contained the statements cited in the complaint.

Another fairly common type of denial is a *qualified denial* in which the defendant denies some but not all of the statements in particular paragraphs or denies a portion of a specific sentence but admits other portions.

The federal courts and most state courts also allow a defendant to make a denial on the basis that the person or company "is without knowledge or information sufficient to form a belief as to the truth of an averment."[11] Attorneys are justifiably cautious about asserting this type of denial because of the requirements of Rule 11.

Finally a defendant may make a *denial on information and belief,* on grounds that only second-hand information about the truth or falsity of the allegations is available at the time the answer is filed. It is unusual to see this type of denial in media law cases. It is fairly common for defendants, including those in media law cases such as libel and invasion of privacy suits, to include affirmative defenses in lieu of or in addition to denials in the answer. An *affirmative defense* is, in effect, saying that defendant admits that the plaintiff's allegations are true (for purposes of the defense only), but that there are additional facts that, when proven, will mean dismissal of the suit.

The wide range of affirmative defenses have technical names such as assumption of risk, accord and satisfaction, and estoppel, but the most common asserted in media law cases is the *statute of limitations*, which is the specified time period during which that particular cause of action must be filed after the right to sue occurs. In other words, if the suit is not filed within that time frame, the court will automatically dismiss the case when it is filed later. For example, the typical statute of limitations for a libel or invasion of privacy suit is one year, although some states have longer periods. Under Rule 12(b), if affirmative defenses are to be asserted by the defendant, they must be included in the answer or be effectively waived. In some cases such as "failure to state a claim upon which relief can be granted," the defense can be made by motion (in this case a motion to dismiss, as discussed below). Affirmative defenses usually do not play a major role in media law cases, but, when they are available, they can have a significant impact on a case—for example, permitting the judge to dismiss the suit before trial. Affirmative defenses can be particularly determinative in criminal cases, where many such defenses can be invoked.

Counterclaims

One more item sometimes included in an answer is a *counterclaim.* A counterclaim is simply a claim made by a defendant against a plaintiff, which, if proven, may cancel or decrease the amount of damages to which the plaintiff would be entitled. For example, if a defendant in an auto accident (personal injury) case also suffered personal injuries and property damage, he or she could file a counterclaim against the plaintiff, alleging that the plaintiff was at fault and, therefore, should be required to pay damages to the defendant. Counterclaims are relatively rare in media law cases, especially in libel and invasion of privacy suits. Counterclaims represent a fairly complex topic. Counterclaims can be filed with an answer or as a separate document. If a counterclaim is filed, the plaintiff is generally required to respond in the same manner as any defendant would to a claim and thus must follow the usual procedural rules.

Motions in General

The next step for both sides is usually filing motions, which is known as *challenging the pleadings*. Although journalists sometimes confuse pleadings with motions, the two processes are not the same. Pleadings are always written statements of fact and/or law filed by the parties, whereas motions are requests ("applications") made to a judge or a court. Under Rule 7 of the Federal Rules of Civil Procedure, pleadings are limited to a complaint; answer; and if appropriate, a reply to a counterclaim; an answer to a cross-claim (a claim by co-defendants or co-plaintiffs against one another rather than someone on the other side); and a third party answer (if a third party complaint has been filed).[12]

Although the federal rules and most state rules are rather strict about the types of pleadings that can be made, those same rules are quite flexible in allowing rather liberal supplementation or amendment of pleadings, in contrast to the old days of common law pleadings when the requirements were rather rigid. The idea of modern pleadings is to allow cases to be tried on their merits, not on technicalities.

Motions are typically filed throughout the judicial process, including during and after the trial, but certain specific motions are commonly filed pretrial. Space limitations do not permit a discussion of all of these motions, but it is important that you be familiar with the most common ones.

Pretrial Motions

The two most common pretrial motions in mass communication law suits, especially libel and invasion of privacy cases, are the *motion to dismiss* and the *motion for summary judgment*. A *motion to dismiss* simply requests that the court dismiss the case because the plaintiff has failed in the pleadings "to state a claim upon which relief can be granted."[13] In other words, the defendant is contending that the plaintiff's suit has no legally sound basis even if all of the allegations made by the plaintiff are true. The defendant is, of course, not admitting that the allegations are true, but is, in effect, saying, "Even if the plaintiff were to prove all of the facts, so what?" This motion is commonly referred to as a 12(b)(6) motion (the number designated under the federal rules) by lawyers in the federal courts. A similar one is available in the state courts.

Here's an extreme but useful hypothetical case in which a motion to dismiss would almost certainly be granted. Suppose a television viewer is highly offended by some grisly videos she sees on a cable news network that show mangled bodies of American soldiers fighting in Afghanistan. The viewer becomes so upset with the videos that she instantly experiences a psychological breakdown. She recovers long enough to see an attorney, who files suit on her behalf, claiming intentional infliction of emotional distress. Let's assume, for purposes of argument, that this individual suffered emotional damages as a direct result of exposure to the news reports, and yet we know her suit will be immediately dismissed. Why? There is simply no legal basis for her suit. No court has ever recognized a cause of action under such circumstances, and there is no law—common, statutory, administrative, or constitutional—establishing a cause of action. Therefore, the judge will grant the news network's motion to dismiss.

There are other bases on which a case can be dismissed at this stage or later under certain conditions including lack of subject matter jurisdiction, improper venue, lack of personal jurisdiction, and insufficiency of service of process.

A second common motion filed by a defendant in a media law case is a *motion for summary judgment*. This motion is a much-debated topic in libel and was the focus of a 1986 U.S. Supreme Court libel decision.[14] Briefly, this motion is frequently filed in libel suits when no dispute exists between the parties about the substantive facts in the case, but the two sides differ on the applicable law. A summary judgment has the major advantage that it is made prior to the trial. Thus a potentially expensive trial is avoided, saving both sides considerable time and money. Why then does so much controversy surround this type of judgment? Summary judgments are far more likely to be decided in favor of defendants, whereas full-blown trials in libel and invasion of privacy suits are much more likely to result in an award of damages to a plaintiff, especially if the trial were before a jury.

A summary judgment can be granted only when the judge or court is convinced that there is no dispute of facts, only a difference regarding the law. Even though a summary judgment is made without a trial, it is a binding decision and thus can be appealed to a higher (i.e., appellate) court. A motion for summary judgment can usually be made any time after the pleadings have been closed, including up to the time of the trial, so long as the motion is made "within such time as not to delay the trial."[15]

Although the motion to dismiss and most other pretrial motions are granted based on the pleadings alone, the court is not limited to the pleadings when deciding a summary judgment and can certainly consider other evidence. In fact, under the federal rules, if matters outside the pleadings are presented to the court in making a decision on whether to grant a motion for judgment on the pleadings, the motion is automatically converted into a motion for summary judgment.[16]

Two other less common motions need to be briefly considered. A *motion for more definite statement* would be filed when a pleading such as a complaint or answer is "so vague or ambiguous that a party cannot reasonably be required to frame a responsive pleading."[17] The idea is that the party filing the motion cannot make sense of the particular contentions of the other side, whether factual or legal, and thus those statements must be made clear before the party can be expected to respond to them.

Finally, a *motion to strike* is sometimes used. This is a request that the court strike (i.e., delete) certain statements from the pleadings, including "any insufficient defense or any redundant, immaterial, impertinent, or scandalous matter."[18] If the court rules in favor of the party filing the motion, the statements will be officially struck from the records.

Discovery in General

The next step in the judicial process, which has no exact parallel in a criminal case even though it is permitted on a limited basis, is *discovery*. This is the much-publicized, formal process by which each side discovers the information and evidence to be presented at trial by the other side. The primary purpose of this often lengthy and expensive process is to avoid surprises at the trial. In a nutshell, when both sides do their homework, there are likely to be few, if any, surprises at trial. Although surprise witnesses and last-minute revelations pervade television shows and movies with law themes, the real world is much different. You have probably heard the axiom for lawyers: do not ask a question of a witness at trial to which you don't already know the answer. Those answers are already known, thanks to discovery. A check of recent issues of law journals, such as *Trial* and the *American Bar Association Journal*, will usually reveal several articles on discovery—a clear indication of the importance of this process. Literally dozens of how-to books on discovery and numerous workshops focus on the topic every year.

Ideally, most of the discovery process takes place extrajudicially (i.e., outside the courtroom). This is made possible by the very liberal discovery rules adopted by the federal courts and most state courts. Twelve of the 86 *Federal Rules of Civil Procedure* deal directly with depositions and discovery. Although sometimes complex, they are designed to facilitate the process, not to make it more difficult. The rules are also geared toward keeping discovery from becoming unreasonably long or unduly burdensome.

For example, Rule 16(b) requires a scheduling conference, followed by a scheduling order from the judge that, among other matters, limits the time for filing motions and completing discovery. The order must be made within 90 days after the defendant appears in court or 120 days after the complaint has been served on the defendant. Federal Rule 26(b)(2) specifically permits a court to limit the number of depositions and interrogatories, the length of depositions and the frequency or use of discovery methods under certain conditions. Rule 26(f) mandates, except in rare cases, a discovery planning conference at least 21 days before the scheduling conference or order under Rule 16(b) at which the attorneys must try in good faith to agree on a proposed discovery plan. Most state courts have adopted similar rules limiting time for discovery. In the past, discovery occupied so much time that what was supposed to be a battle of the facts and the wits became an endurance contest instead. The picture has dramatically changed over the decades, but discovery still remains the most time-consuming and expensive part of the civil judicial process, with the trial often being an anticlimax.

Federal Rule 37 permits the court to impose various sanctions from paying the other side's attorney's fees and other expenses to charges of contempt of court for parties, witnesses, and attorneys who fail to appear at or to cooperate in discovery.

Depositions

The two most common methods of discovery are depositions and interrogatories, with depositions clearly leading the pack. A *deposition* is technically any out-of-court statement made under oath by a witness for use at trial or for preparing for trial. This device is by far the most expensive of the two but is the most useful and effective. Generally, either side may depose the other side and any witnesses. For example, a plaintiff in a copyright infringement suit would almost certainly orally depose the defendant and vice versa. Depositions can be taken orally or in writing, but are usually oral.

The procedure is for the plaintiff's attorney to file a formal notice of deposition with the defendant's attorney, specifying the exact day, time, and location. Because both sides have the right to be present during the deposition, attorneys for both usually appear. The plaintiff's attorney then questions the defendant under oath. The party or witness being deposed is administered the oath, usually by an independent court reporter at the beginning of the deposition. No judge is present, but a court reporter hired by the deposing attorney records the proceedings. A common procedure today is to record depositions on videotape, which can save the considerable cost of transcription. Depositions can be taken via phone as well, and many state and all federal courts now permit them to be taken with new technologies such as satellite television.

The primary purpose of depositions is to enable the attorney to learn before trial the content of the testimony that witness will offer at trial. For example, if a defense attorney in a libel suit wants to know what the plaintiff's expert witness is going to testify at trial about the defendant's alleged negligence, the lawyer would depose that witness. This information would be particularly useful in deciding how to use one's own expert witnesses, who would likely be deposed by the plaintiff's attorney.

The procedure in an oral deposition is relatively simple. The witness and that person's attorney or the attorney representing the side using the witness at trial appear at the designated time and place. The deposition is often taken in a law office, usually that of the attorney who is deposing the witness, although this can certainly vary. After the usual courtesy introductions, the court reporter then swears in the witness. The witness is questioned by the deposing attorney (a process known as *direct examination*), with the attorney for the other side present only to object if the questioning becomes improper, such as when the deposing attorney poses a question that would require a lay witness to assert a legal opinion or when the deposing attorney badgers the witness.

It is not unusual for even expert witnesses to find depositions stressful because the questioning can be intense and long. Once the deposing attorney has completed questioning, the opposing attorney has the option of conducting a *cross examination* of the witness. Unlike in a trial in which cross examination is conducted by the attorney representing the side opposite the one that called the witness, cross examination in a deposition is typically conducted by the attorney who has selected that witness to testify at trial. Cross examination is particularly important when the direct examination has severely damaged the credibility of a witness and thus some "restoration" is in order, or when a deposing attorney has failed to elicit information that could be favorable to the other side.

Interrogatories

Interrogatories are written questions submitted to an adverse party to be answered under oath. The procedure is for the attorney interrogating the witness to submit a series of questions in writing to the opposing party or a witness for the opposing party through the opposing party's attorney. Federal Rule 33 permits parties only (not other witnesses) to be deposed, and requires that the interrogatories be written under oath. Only 25 items, including discrete subparts, may be served under Rule 33(a). The attorney for the party being questioned is permitted to work with the party in composing the answers, although all answers must represent the views and direct knowledge of the party. A few state jurisdictions permit interrogatories directed to all witnesses—not only parties—but most follow the federal model.

The major advantage of interrogatories is cost. They are much less expensive to administer than depositions. However, you get what you pay for, as the old saying goes. It is easy for a party to manipulate answers or be evasive, and because the questions are prepared in advance without benefit of previous answers, it is difficult to anticipate a party's answers. Thus interrogatories are used principally as a means of getting the discovery process started. Because of the burdensome nature of interrogatories, attorneys can make objections in lieu of answers if reasons are also provided. Conversely, an attorney submitting an interrogatory can request that the judge order that an answer be given or that a party who refuses to cooperate in an interrogatory be forced to respond.[19]

Written Depositions

Written depositions (depositions upon written questions) are sometimes confused by journalists with interrogatories, but they are not the same. Unlike interrogatories that are limited to parties, written depositions can be submitted to any witness including a party to a suit. They are much less expensive than oral depositions because no attorneys need to be present, and they can be answered over a longer period.

In the case of a written deposition, the deposing attorney submits a list of proposed questions to the attorney for the other side who then makes any objections known and submits proposed questions for cross examination. The witness then appears before a court reporter, usually in the home or office of the witness rather than in an attorney's office, and answers the questions under oath. The answers are recorded by the reporter and the word-for-word transcript or videotape is then made available to the attorneys for both sides. The process takes some time, but a witness has an opportunity to prepare responses. Written depositions are rarely taken of parties or of major witnesses.

Except for accepting motions or considering objections to the scope or conduct of the process, the court is rarely involved in discovery, especially in the federal system. The idea is for the attorneys to cooperate in seeing that each side is fully informed before trial. In most cases, an attorney has no obligation to make information available to the other side unless the opponent has made a formal request, but does have a duty to provide such information if requested. There are exceptions to this requirement, but most attorneys cooperate with one another, even though they represent clients on different sides.

Witnesses are important in any case, but witnesses alone are usually not sufficient to build a case. Discovery also permits access to and copying of documents and other evidence. The usual procedure for obtaining documents and other items from a party is for the attorney to file a formal request through the attorney for the other side that specifies the documents or other materials sought. The federal rules and all state court rules also permit an attorney for one side to have the party on the other side submit to a physical examination under certain circumstances, such as when the party's physical or mental condition is an issue in the case.

Subpoenas

For nonparties, a subpoena is traditionally used to compel them to testify or produce documents or other materials. If a witness is to appear to simply testify and not to bring documents or other physical evidence, an ordinary *subpoena* would be issued, notifying the witness of the specific time, place, and type of information sought. If the witness is to produce "books, papers, documents, or tangible things," a *subpoena duces tecum* would be served on that individual. The process of serving a subpoena or a subpoena duces tecum is fairly similar to that of serving a complaint and summons. In the federal courts, a federal marshal, deputy marshal, or anyone who is not a party to the suit and is at least 18 years old simply delivers the subpoena to the witness. In the federal courts, all subpoenas must be issued by the district court clerk.[20] The power of the federal district courts to subpoena nonparty witnesses extends within a 100-mile radius of the court. There is no 100-mile limit for parties. The subpoena power of state courts traditionally resides within the state boundaries, although all states have some form of a *long-arm statute*, which permits personal jurisdiction, including subpoena powers, beyond the borders under certain conditions.

The rules for subpoenaing witnesses and documents for a hearing or trial are similar to the authority covering subpoenas for depositions. Both federal and state rules allow courts to cite an individual for contempt for failing to comply with a valid subpoena. However, those same rules permit a subpoenaed witness to make objections, usually in writing, within a specified period—typically 14 days—which the court will ultimately decide whether to sustain or overrule.[21]

Journalists have been plagued in recent decades by a considerable increase in the number and scope of subpoenas in both civil and criminal cases. All journalists, whether or not they cover the courts, must have a strong, basic knowledge of subpoenas because they are routinely called and forced to testify and produce documents, despite the vehement and vociferous protests of their employers and news organizations. There is no federal shield law to protect journalists and state shield laws, where they exist, are often ineffective in offering protection. One type of protection that journalists sometimes successfully seek is a protective order. Federal Rule 26(c) allows a court to issue a *protective order* "to protect a party or person from annoyance, embarrassment, oppression, or undue burden or expense."[22] The court has several options affecting the impact of such an order including prohibiting the discovery entirely, allowing the discovery only under certain terms and conditions, and limiting the scope of the discovery matters.[23]

Although various constitutional, statutory, and common law rights cover public and press access to court documents, no such rights have been established thus far for access to discovery materials including depositions. On rare occasions, a court will order that a transcript or videotape of a deposition be made public, but usually only when a strong public interest—for example, when the government is a party in a suit—is involved. Thus depositions are almost always conducted in private, with journalists and the public having no access to the proceedings or to the transcripts or videotapes.

Privileged Discovery

In general, any relevant evidence can be discovered. However, there are certain exceptions. The federal rule notes, "Relevant information need not be admissible at the trial if the discovery appears reasonably calculated to lead to the discovery of admissible evidence."[24] The two major exceptions are privilege, including attorney–client privilege and attorney work product. *Privileged communications* are statements made within a particular context or relationship and protected from disclosure because the nature of that relationship is so sacred that the benefits of disclosure (viz., revelation of the truth) are outweighed by the need to preserve that type of relationship. Typical protected relationships are attorney–client, husband–wife, physician–patient, and clergy–penitent.

Federal and state rules of evidence, rather than rules of civil procedure, govern when privileged communications are permitted (i.e., when the content of such communication does not have to be disclosed). For example, the federal courts and all state courts protect attorney–client communications, although the protection is not absolute, whereas some state courts do not allow physician–patient privilege, which is available in the federal courts. Reporter–source privileges exist in some form in more than half of the states, but the federal courts do not recognize this privilege, although the federal Privacy Protection Act of 1980 does offer some procedural protection for federal and state searches for evidence held by journalists.

Finally, the *attorney work product doctrine* recognized in most states and now incorporated in the federal rules places strict limits on the discovery of information specifically prepared for litigation or for trial by a party or a party's attorney. Under the Federal Rules of Civil Procedure, such information can be discovered "only upon a showing that the party seeking discovery has substantial need of the materials in the preparation of the party's case and that the party is unable without due hardship to obtain the substantial equivalent of the materials by other means."[25] The federal rule offers absolute protection "against disclosure of the mental impressions, conclusions, opinions, or legal theories of an attorney or other representative of a party concerning the litigation."[26]

In *Swidler & Berlin et al. v. United States* (1998),[27] the U.S. Supreme Court ruled in a 6 to 3 decision written by Chief Justice Rehnquist that attorney–client privilege survives a client's death even in the criminal context. The Court noted that this privilege is "one of the oldest recognized privileges for confidential communications." The case arose after independent counsel Kenneth Starr tried to force Washington attorney James Hamilton to turn over three pages of notes he had taken during a meeting with Deputy White House Counsel Vincent Foster nine days before Foster committed suicide. Starr wanted the notes as possible evidence in his criminal investigation of First Lady Hillary Rodham Clinton.

In overturning the decision of the U.S. Court of Appeals for the D.C. Circuit, the U.S. Supreme Court said that case law overwhelmingly supported the principle that this common law privilege did not end when a client died. While acknowledging that a client might consult an attorney regarding possible criminal liability, the Court said that was only one of many reasons for consultation such as seeking advice on personal and financial problems.

Pretrial Conferences

The debate among legal scholars and jurists over the appropriate point at which a case should come into focus—so the issues and facts are jelled or at least clear to both sides and the court—has been going on for many decades. Some courts have opted for rigid pleadings, an approach designed to hone the issues and facts early in the case. The federal courts and many state courts have chosen more liberal pleadings, but obviously at some point the issues and facts must congeal. The pretrial conference is typically the point at which the judge begins to establish firm control over the case by requiring the attorneys to establish time parameters for pretrial proceedings and/or agree on undisputed facts or issues. Most judges hold several pretrial conferences with the attorneys in a case, but two types of pretrial conferences are frequently employed in the federal courts. After all the initial pleadings have been filed, a *scheduling and planning conference* is held among the judge or magistrate and attorneys for both sides to establish time limits for various proceedings including discovery and schedule dates for further pretrial conferences.[28]

The second type of pretrial conference is the *issue conference*. The attorneys and the judge hammer out the issues and facts in the case so an agreement can be reached on undisputed facts and law, also known as *stipulations*. The primary purpose is to narrow the case to the point at which either an out-of-court settlement can be reached or, at the very least, the issues and the facts in the case are crystallized so that the trial itself can focus on important matters and not be bogged down with trivial and undisputed points. Some judges apply more pressure than others, but all of them are certainly interested in having cases settled before trial, if possible. Most courts are overloaded with cases, and trials can be quite expensive. Thus it is not unusual for a case to be settled before trial.

One type of pretrial conference is nearly always required by federal district court judges—the *final pretrial conference*. Federal Rule 16(d) provides that this conference be held close to the time of the trial and that a plan for the trial be established by this point. Cases are sometimes settled at this conference, but the chances of a settlement have usually decreased by this point; both sides have probably expended considerable time and expense and virtually all that remains is the trial itself. After the final pretrial conference, the judge will issue pretrial orders including a list of trial witnesses, stipulations, and other agreements reached at the conference.[29] Under the federal rules, the pretrial orders can be changed only "to prevent manifest injustice."[30]

The Civil Trial

The vast majority of cases, for one reason or another, do not make it to the trial stage. Once a case is placed on a court's trial docket with a specific date set, the wheels of justice begin moving again. It is not unusual for at least one *continuance* or postponement to occur before a trial begins.

Both civil and criminal cases can be tried before a jury and a judge or before a judge alone. The latter is known as a *bench trial*. Obviously, jury trials are substantially more time consuming and expensive, both for the parties and for the court, but many litigants and their attorneys prefer jury trials. Although the reasons for this preference vary, there seems to be a widespread belief among trial lawyers and their clients that juries render better or fairer verdicts. The general rules of order are virtually the same for jury and bench trials regardless of jurisdiction. Rather than separate the two types of trials, this chapter analyzes them together and notes differences where applicable.

According to the 7th Amendment to the U.S. Constitution, "In suits at common law, where the value in controversy shall exceed twenty dollars, the right of trial by jury shall be preserved." Although this right to a trial by jury is binding only on the federal government, not on the states, every state recognizes such a right in its own constitution or by statute. The difficulty lies in knowing what suits existed at common law in determining when the right can be invoked. In 1970, the U.S. Supreme Court, for the first time, enunciated a constitutional test for deciding when the right exists.[31] The test focuses on whether the issue in a case is primarily equitable or legal. As discussed in Chapter 1, no jury trials are held in equity cases, but cases can become complicated when they appear to involve issues of both law and equity. The Supreme Court has adopted the rule that when legal and equitable claims are intertwined, the legal issue will be tried first by the jury (if a jury trial is chosen) and then the equitable claim will be tried by the judge alone.[32]

When most people hear the term *officers of the court*, they immediately think of judges, clerks, and bailiffs. The judge presides over the trial, and the court clerk helps the judge administer and keep track of the trial, including the various exhibits. The bailiff has the responsibilities of maintaining order in the courtroom, calling witnesses, escorting the jury and, in some jurisdictions, administering oaths to witnesses and jurors. Lawyers are also officers of the court and are thereby bound by its rules and procedures.

Jury Selection

One of the most critical stages in a jury trial is the jury selection process. In the past, courts and legislators paid relatively little attention to the process as a whole, although everyone knew that successful jury selection was extremely important in a trial. Over the decades, the topic of jury selection attracted extensive Supreme Court attention, with the Court handing down several decisions related to the process. Two of the most important decisions were issued in the early 1970s. In 1970, the Supreme Court held that nonunanimous verdicts in criminal cases did not violate the 6th Amendment.[33] Three years later, the Court ruled that juries with fewer than 12 members (in this case, 6 members) were permissible in civil cases.[34]

As a result of these decisions, many jurisdictions including the federal courts now routinely opt for 6-member juries because of the savings in time and expense. More states also allow, either by experiment or by statute, jury verdicts based on agreements of three-fourths or five-sixths of the members, especially in civil and misdemeanor cases.

In 1991 the United States Judicial Conference, the governing body of the federal courts, revised Rule 48 of the *Federal Rules of Civil Procedure* to explicitly allow juries of fewer than 12 members. The rule still requires that the verdict be unanimous, unless the parties agree otherwise, and sets a minimum of 6 members.[35] Five years later, after extensive debate, the Conference decided to stick with the current rule rather than return to mandated 12-person juries.[36]

In both civil and criminal cases, jurors are selected at random from a pool or list (also called *venire facias*), usually compiled from property tax rolls, automobile registration lists, and voter registration printouts. In the federal district courts, potential jurors are chosen at random solely from voter lists or combined lists of voters and drivers licensed in that particular judicial district. A court official, usually a jury commissioner appointed by a judge, initially screens the prospective jurors to narrow the list to only qualified and eligible individuals based upon their answers on questionnaires they complete. At one time, a fairly long list of occupational exemptions allowed many people to escape serving as jurors. People in these occupations (e.g., physicians, teachers, students, and lawyers) were never prevented from serving, but they were allowed to exempt themselves. Many of them exercised the exemption because serving usually meant taking time from work with little or no pay. In the 1970s, however, many states began revising their statutes to eliminate or severely limit exemptions.

Once the *array*, as it is sometimes known, of qualified *veniremen* (prospective jurors) is in order, the process of selecting the actual jurors for trial begins. On rare occasions, an attorney will move that the court disqualify the entire array because the list was compiled in violation of some constitutional or statutory right. For example, the list may have somehow excluded all minority group members. Any systematic exclusion of a particular community group may be grounds for violation of that defendant's 6th Amendment right in a criminal case to a trial by an impartial jury of the state or district where the alleged crime was committed or, in the case of a civil suit, the 7th Amendment right of trial by jury. The motion in such a case is known as *challenge to the array*, and is more likely to occur in a criminal suit.

The jury selection process begins when panels (usually 12 people at a time) of individuals selected from the array are called. With each panel, the court clerk calls the set of names or numbers and then has the individuals sit in the jury box. To preserve anonymity, more courts are now assigning potential jurors numbers for identification. After offering the panel a brief overview of the case, the judge then asks that any juror who feels unable to serve for any reason to make it known. Occasionally, potential jurors will be excluded at this point for poor health, personal acquaintance with one of the parties, or on another basis.

The next step in the process varies depending on the particular jurisdiction. In *voir dire,* potential jurors are questioned about a variety of matters from their names and occupations to their views on the particular type of case. In the past, most federal judges conducted voir dire themselves, preventing the attorneys from playing an active role, except for giving them opportunities to provide the court with potential questions in advance. Now federal judges generally follow the state court model that allows the attorneys to do most of the questioning.

The types of questions that can be asked, whether by the attorneys or the judge, can be highly personal and intimate. Depending upon the subject matter of the case, potential jurors may be asked during voir dire about their religious beliefs, their views on capital punishment, whether they have ever been victims of a crime, the political parties to which they belong, and whether they are married or single.

Dozens of legal treatises and hundreds of articles have been published about voir dire, and several companies offer advice on jury selection, some of which will, for a fee, sit with counsel during voir dire to observe the verbal and nonverbal communications of prospective jurors and make recommendations regarding which jurors should be struck during the peremptory challenges, discussed shortly.

Most attorneys no doubt still rely on experience and instinct or "gut feelings" in their juror challenges, but scientific techniques are making headway in the process, as indicated by the growing use by attorneys of psychological and sociological experts (and occasionally even communication specialists) for consultation during voir dire. One of the criticisms leveled at the prosecutors in the 1995 murder trial in which O. J. Simpson was acquitted was that they had turned down an offer from a pro bono jury consultant to help in voir dire. The defendant's legal team, on the other hand, hired trial consultant Jo-Ellen Dimitrius, a former college professor, who became widely known as a result of her work in the Simpson case.[37]

Jury consultants are no longer unusual, particularly in high profile cases. For example, defense attorneys hired them in both the 1991 William Kennedy Smith rape trial in which Kennedy was acquitted and in 1994 in the separate trials of Lyle and Erik Menendez for the murders of their parents. The first Menendez trials led to hung juries, but the brothers were later convicted at retrial.

The major goal of voir dire is to weed out those prospective jurors who may have biases or prejudices that would prevent them from making a fair and independent decision in the case. After a panel has been questioned, the attorney for either side can request the judge to dismiss individuals *for cause.* Suppose in a libel case against a newspaper a prospective juror indicates during voir dire that she believes newspapers never tell the truth and are always out to get prominent people. The defense attorney would clearly have grounds for asking the court to dismiss the individual for cause, and this request would very likely be granted.

Judges and attorneys are not necessarily looking for uninformed jurors but for fair and impartial jurors. Only the judge can dismiss jurors for cause, but this can be done either at the request of an attorney or on the judge's own initiative. There is no limit on the number of individuals an attorney can challenge for cause, nor on the number of dismissals a judge can make.

The judge will continue calling prospective jurors until a panel of qualified jurors twice the size of the jury (including alternate jurors) actually needed for trial survives voir dire without dismissal for cause. If there are to be 12 jurors at trial plus an alternate, the final panel would have 26 members. In highly publicized cases involving concern about pretrial exposure of jurors to potentially highly prejudicial information in the mass media, voir dire can take days or even months. Typically, the process occupies only a few hours.

Art, science, and gut instinct tend to play major roles in the next step of the jury selection process—*peremptory challenges*. In civil cases, each side usually gets to "strike" (i.e., make a peremptory challenge of) an equal number of jurors. An attorney can excuse a juror for any or no reason. In fact, the attorney need not state a reason. However, there are two exceptions to the general rule that peremptory challenges can be made for any reason. In 1986 in the landmark case of *Batson v. Kentucky*,[38] the U.S. Supreme Court held that the equal protection clause of the 14th Amendment to the U.S. Constitution[39] prohibits a prosecutor in a criminal trial from exercising peremptory challenges against jurors solely because of race or because the attorney believed that members of that racial group would not be able to render a fair and impartial decision.

The Court established a three-prong test for determining whether a peremptory jury strike violated the 6th Amendment. First, the challenger of the strike (typically the criminal defendant) must make a prima facie case for discrimination. Second, the proponent of the strike (typically the prosecution) must then offer an acceptable race-neutral explanation for the strike. Finally, the challenger of the strike must prove that the discrimination was intentional.[40]

In 1994, the U.S. Supreme Court took another significant step toward what some critics predict will eventually lead to the elimination of peremptory challenges altogether. In *J.E.B. v. Alabama ex rel. T.B.*,[41] the justices ruled 6 to 3 that litigants may not strike potential jurors solely based on gender. In the majority opinion written by Justice Blackmun (joined by Justices Stevens, O'Connor, Souter, and Ginsburg with Justice Kennedy concurring in the judgment), the Court held that the Equal Protection clause of the 14th Amendment bars discrimination in jury selection based on gender or on the assumption that a potential juror will be biased in a case because of his or her sex. The Court applied the logic and reasoning of *Batson*, noting that it had already extended the *Batson* rule to include civil cases.[42] However, the justices were careful to note:

> Our conclusion that litigants may not strike potential jurors solely on the basis of gender does not imply the elimination of all peremptory challenges. Neither does it conflict with a State's legitimate interest in using such challenges in its effort to secure a fair and impartial jury. Parties may still remove jurors whom they feel might be less acceptable than others on the panel; gender simply may not serve as a proxy for bias. Parties may also exercise their peremptory challenges to remove from the venire any group or class of individuals normally subject to *rational basis* review.[43]

The gist of this decision is that if it is apparent that a potential juror may have been struck by a party in either a civil or a criminal suit because of that person's race or sex or because the party believed the person would be biased because of his or her race or sex, the selection process will be subject to the heightened scrutiny test of the 14th Amendment rather than the traditional rational review. Both potential jurors and litigants enjoy this right under the Equal Protection clause "to jury selection procedures that are free from state-sponsored group stereotypes rooted in, and reflective of, historical prejudice." Thus, just as a litigant has a right to keep the other side from excluding a potential juror from a case based on sex or race, a potential juror also has the right not to be excluded.

J.E.B. v. Alabama arose from a paternity and child support trial in which the state of Alabama, at the request of the mother of a minor child, filed a complaint against J.E.B. for paternity and child support. Voir dire began with 36 potential jurors but 3 were struck for cause. Only 10 of the remaining individuals were men, and the state used 9 of its 10 strikes to eliminate males. Consequently, the trial jury was all women. The trial court judge overruled the defendant's objection to the state's use of the peremptory challenges to eliminate men. The jury found that the defendant was the child's father and had to pay support.

In a highly critical dissent, Justice Scalia, joined by Justice Thomas and Chief Justice Rehnquist, concluded:

> In order, it seems to me, not to eliminate any real denial of equal protection, but simply to pay conspicuous obeisance to the equality of the sexes, the Court imperils a practice that has been considered an essential part of fair jury trial since the dawn of the common law. The Constitution of the United States neither requires nor permits this vandalizing of our people's traditions.[44]

In a separate dissent, the Chief Justice distinguished sex discrimination from race discrimination in peremptory challenges:

> The two sexes differ, both biologically and, to a diminishing extent, in experience. It is not merely *stereotyping* to say that these differences may produce a difference in outlook which is brought to the jury room. Accordingly, use of peremptory challenges on the basis of sex is generally not the sort of derogatory and invidious act which peremptory challenges directed at black jurors may be.[45]

In 1995, the Court appeared to be backing away from *Batson* in a 7 to 2 *per curiam* opinion. In *Purkett v. Elem*,[46] the Court overturned an 8th Circuit U.S. Court of Appeals reversal of a robbery conviction in a case in which a prosecutor had said he dismissed an African American potential juror because he had "long, curly … unkempt hair" and a "mustache and a goatee." According to the Court, a facially neutral reason is a proper basis for a peremptory challenge even if it is "implausible or fantastic." The general consensus among legal experts is that, at the very least, *Purkett* made it more difficult for an attorney to challenge a peremptory strike based on race.[47]

In 2000, in *United States v. Martinez-Salazar*,[48] the U.S. Supreme Court held that a criminal defendant's 5th Amendment due process rights were not violated when he was forced to exercise one of his peremptory challenges after the trial court judge denied his request to strike a prospective juror for cause. The defendant, who was on trial in federal court for a variety of federal offenses, had asked the judge twice to dismiss a prospective alternate juror who had indicated several times during voir dire that he favored the prosecution. When the judge refused to grant the request, the defendant exercised one of his ten allotted peremptory challenges to eliminate the prospective juror. First, the Court said no constitutional right was involved because peremptory challenges are products of Rule 24 of the Federal Rules of Criminal Procedure, not creations of the 6th Amendment. The Court then went on to say that the defendant's rights under Rule 24 also were not violated so long as the end result was an impartial jury. If exercising the peremptory challenge had somehow led to an unfair trial, the defendant then had the option of challenging the verdict on appeal on the ground that his 6th Amendment rights had been violated. According to the Court in its unanimous decision, "A hard choice is not the same as no choice. Martinez-Salazar received and exercised 11 peremptory challenges. That is all he is entitled to under the Rule."[49]

Three years later, the Court in an 8 to 1 opinion in *Miller-El v. Cockrell*[50] ruled that a Texas death row inmate had been wrongfully denied a hearing to determine whether his 6th Amendment rights had been violated after state prosecutors had used 10 of their 14 peremptory strikes to exclude all but one of the eligible African American members of the jury pool. The convicted murderer had unsuccessfully appealed the jury's verdict to the federal courts, including the U.S. Court of Appeals, on a petition for a writ of habeas corpus.

The U.S. Supreme Court made it clear that federal courts should not blindly defer to the state courts in such situations, particularly when such strong evidence of potential discrimination is present. The evidence in the case, as pointed out by the Court, included the fact that African American jurors, unlike white jurors, were offered descriptions of the execution process before they were asked about their attitudes toward capital punishment. Other evidence included an historical pattern of racial discrimination, confirmed by testimony from former prosecutors, including a 1963 circular from the district attorney's office instructing prosecutors to specifically exercise peremptory strikes against "Jews, Negroes, Dagos, Mexicans or a member of any minority race on a jury, no matter how rich or how well educated."[51] In its decision, the U.S. Supreme Court directed the 5th Circuit U.S. Court of Appeals to issue Miller-El a *certificate of appealability*, an order that would have given him the opportunity to make a full-blown case in the federal court.

Different jurisdictions have different rules regarding the number of peremptory challenges permitted by each, with some states, for example, permitting a criminal defendant to strike more jurors than the prosecutor, but the number of challenges in civil cases tends to be the same for both sides. All jurisdictions do limit the total number of peremptory challenges, however, unlike challenges for cause. In Kentucky, for example, each side in a civil case is entitled to three peremptory challenges, and in criminal cases involving a felony, each side has eight challenges. Once the two sides have exercised their strikes, the jurors, including any alternates, are sworn in by the court clerk. Those who were not selected are then permitted to leave.

One of the difficulties in getting jurors to serve is the perception that trials often go on too long. That perception may have some validity, as witnessed by a trial in 1994 in New York City in which the jurors told the judge that if the trial had not ended by January 1, 1995, they were quitting. The jury sat through four months of testimony in the libel case and the plaintiff's side had yet to rest its case. The judge ordered a mistrial after he realized the case could not end by the deadline. Some of the jurors later said they were merely bluffing.[52] Rule 16 of the Federal Rules of Civil Procedure allows judges to set reasonable time limits on trials.

Juries receive little compensation for their service—typically $25 to $50 per day. Jurors in federal court currently receive $40 daily plus meal and travel allowances under certain conditions.[53] Under federal law and the law in most states, employers are required to allow employees to take time off to serve as jurors, and they cannot fire an employee because of jury service.

Ethical Concerns in Covering Juries

Careful thought should always be given to the ethical dimensions of covering a trial. The U.S. Supreme Court in 1984 unanimously held that there was a "presumptive openness" in voir dire so that the press and the public had a constitutional right to attend, except in rare circumstances.[54] Thus journalists frequently cover jury selection, especially in cases with strong public interest. One of the ethical concerns facing journalists is whether to publish names and other personal information about jurors including potentially embarrassing facts that may have been disclosed during voir dire. Some jurisdictions now allow judges, under certain circumstances, to impose prior restraint on reporters by issuing gag orders that forbid publication of names and other information about jurors. Although such orders could, in most situations, be overturned as a violation of the First Amendment, media outlets usually choose not to contest them, particularly when individual jurors might be adversely affected by disclosure.

In rare cases such as when a trial is likely to attract a lot of media attention or when a notorious or well known figure is on trial, judges will order that jurors' identities be kept secret. That was the case in the both the O. J. Simpson and Susan Smith murder trials in 1995. Simpson was acquitted of the murders of his ex-wife and her friend, although he was found liable in a jury trial two years later for their wrongful deaths and other civil offenses to the tune of $33.5 million in compensatory and punitive damages. Smith was tried, convicted, and given a life sentence for murdering her two young sons. When several jurors were dismissed in the Simpson case, each one held press conferences and one even wrote a book about his experience on the jury. Several jurors in the Smith case also spoke out after the trial ended.

Sequestration

Both witnesses and the jury can be sequestered during a trial, whether civil or criminal. Witnesses are sequestered by keeping them separated and out of the courtroom except when giving their testimony. The idea is to prevent one witness from being influenced by the testimony of a previous witness. In reality, sequestration of witnesses probably does not work so well because witnesses have often seen the depositions of the witness on the stand, especially in the cases of expert witnesses. But some judges apparently feel more comfortable separating witnesses than allowing them to interact. Parties (who can also be witnesses) have a constitutional right to be present during trial and thus cannot be involuntarily sequestered.

Sequestration of a jury is a somewhat different process. The jurors are allowed to interact with one another, but are not allowed to talk with other people, except under highly supervised circumstances. Sequestered jurors are kept together, usually in a local hotel, where they eat together, watch television programs, and read newspapers. All of their media content is edited so any prejudicial news is not disseminated to them. Jury sequestration is aimed at ensuring a fair trial by keeping the members from being exposed to outside prejudicial information. Obviously, jurors will hear and see biased, or at least one-sided, information in the courtroom as both sides try to sway them, but this material is presented as evidence following strict rules to ensure fairness and relevance.

Opening Statements and Burden of Proof

A trial begins with opening statements by each side. In a civil suit, the plaintiff's attorney is first, whereas in a criminal suit the prosecutor goes first. According to the rule, the party with the burden of proof begins the trial. *Burden of proof* is a term frequently confused with *standard of proof.* Both are evidentiary terms whose impact is dictated by the appropriate rules of evidence (civil versus criminal). State and federal rules of evidence place an affirmative duty on the party initiating the suit (the plaintiff in a civil case or the prosecuting attorney in a criminal case) to prove the facts on a particular issue.

For example, in a libel suit, the plaintiff has the burden of proving that the necessary elements of the tort occurred—defamation, identification, publication and, sometimes, special damages. The plaintiff also has the burden of showing the defendant was at fault by acting with negligence or with actual malice, depending on the status of the plaintiff and the jurisdiction, and that harm occurred as a result. In a criminal suit, a prosecutor must prove that the necessary elements of the particular crime or crimes with which the defendant is charged were present.

Standard of proof, a related but much different concept from burden of proof, is the extent or degree to which the evidence must be demonstrated by the party having the burden of proof. For most torts, the standard of proof is "a preponderance of the evidence," although occasionally other standards such as "clear and convincing evidence" apply. In criminal prosecutions, the standard is always "beyond a reasonable doubt." Figure 3.2 illustrates the concept.

The phrase *beyond a reasonable doubt* holds considerable mystique in the criminal justice system, but there has never been strong agreement, even among U.S. Supreme Court justices, on the precise meaning of the concept. This confusion was illustrated in two consolidated decisions in March 1994. In *Victor v. Nebraska* and *Sandoval v. California* (1994),[55] the Court upheld jury instructions in both cases that included archaic references with which the justices were clearly uncomfortable but nevertheless considered them *taken as a whole* to be constitutional. Justice O'Connor wrote the majority opinions in both cases. In *Sandoval,* the jury instructions defined *reasonable doubt* as including "not a mere possible doubt" but "depending upon moral evidence" so that the jurors could not say that they felt an abiding conviction "to a moral certainty" of the truth of the charge. Writing for a unanimous court in *Sandoval,* O'Connor noted that while the phrase *moral evidence* "is not a mainstay of the modern lexicon … we do not think it means anything different today than it did in the 19th century."

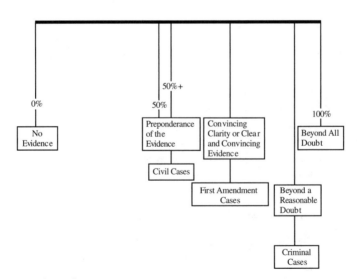

Figure 3.2   Burden of Proof.

The jury instructions in both *Sandoval* and *Victor* were based on those enunciated by Massachusetts Supreme Judicial Court's Chief Justice Lemuel Shaw in 1850. The instructions in *Victor,* which the Court upheld in a 7 to 2 decision (Justices Blackmun and Souter dissenting), also included reference to *moral certainty* and equated *reasonable doubt* with *substantial doubt:* "A reasonable doubt is an actual and substantial doubt arising from the evidence, or from the lack of evidence on the part of the state, as distinguished from a doubt arising from mere possibility, from bare imagination, or from fanciful conjecture." Justice O'Connor agreed that this construction was "somewhat problematic" but felt that "[a]ny ambiguity, however, is removed by reading the phrase in the context of the sentence in which it appears."

The impact of the Court's decision in the two cases has been rather minimal. The message appears to be, as lawyer David O. Stewart contends, "After *Victor* and *Sandoval*, it is apparent that the Supreme Court will not lead an effort to rewrite reasonable doubt instructions, nor will the due process clause serve as a tool for prodding such an effort."[56]

No case would ever require proof beyond all doubt nor would any suit be permitted to go forward with absolutely no evidence. However, it is clear, as the chart illustrates, that preponderance of the evidence is a lower evidentiary standard than clear and convincing evidence, which is a lower standard than beyond a reasonable doubt. Preponderance of the evidence is definitely a burden on the plaintiff because the standard requires that the greater weight of the evidence be in favor of the plaintiff. If a judge (in a bench trial) or jury is convinced that the evidence is a dead heat for the two sides, the judge or jury ("trier of fact") must find in favor of the defendant. In other words, 50/50 is not enough for the plaintiff; the plaintiff must be at least slightly ahead.

Under the civil and criminal rules of evidence, opening statements cannot be argumentative and must be confined to the facts to be proven at trial. News stories sometimes call opening statements "opening arguments" but such a reference is inaccurate. Opening statements are usually relatively brief (typically 30 to 45 minutes for each side) although some courts impose time limits to avoid lengthy statements. The tendency of some lawyers to be long in their opening statements is probably linked to the widespread belief, bolstered by a few scientific studies and pronouncements by some experienced attorneys, that most jurors have made up their minds by the end of the opening statements.

Opening statements are always optional, but it is rare for an attorney not to make an opening statement except in those jurisdictions that allow the defense attorney to postpone opening statements until the plaintiff's attorney or prosecutor has presented that side. Litigation expert James W. McElhaney says that "the first job in an opening statement is to tell the story, to make sense out of the facts. How you do that makes all the difference."[57]

Evidence is the core of any trial, and thus the rules of evidence, both criminal and civil, are enormously complex. Many lawyers will tell you the most difficult topic in law school was Evidence, especially Hearsay. (Not surprisingly, this topic is probably the most dreaded on the state bar exams.) An indication of this complexity is the fact that there are not only strict, complicated rules about what kinds of evidence can be presented, but even stricter rules about how evidence can be presented. In addition, there are so many exceptions to the general rule of hearsay evidence (second-hand information, i.e., information based on communication from a third party, not on personal knowledge) that some law professors are fond of saying the exceptions actually swallow the rule.

Presentation of Evidence

After each side has presented an opening statement, the heart and soul of the trial— the presentation of evidence—begins. Opening statements may have an impact on the trial, but the evidence is what the jury or judge weighs in reaching a verdict. Evidence comes in two types and two forms. When most people think of evidence as presented at trial, they probably think of what is known as *direct evidence*, which *Black's Law Dictionary* defines as "that means of proof which tends to show the existence of a fact in question, without the intervention of the proof of any other fact."[58] In other words, direct evidence directly proves a fact without having to be tied to other facts or presumptions. The best examples of direct evidence are oral testimony from an eyewitness, a confession (in a criminal case), an admission (in a civil or criminal case), and a murder weapon.

The other type is *indirect evidence*, also known as *circumstantial evidence*. *Black's Law Dictionary* defines circumstantial evidence as "testimony not based on actual personal knowledge or observation of the facts in controversy, but other facts from which deductions are drawn, showing indirectly the facts sought to be proved."[59] In other words, indirect evidence consists of facts that must be proven by inference or by implication. Examples in an invasion of privacy suit in which a defendant is accused of taping a private phone conversation (a tort known as "intrusion") would be the receipts showing the defendant had purchased such equipment and the fact that the person had been fired from a previous job for listening in on other employees' phone conversations. An example in a criminal case would be the physical appearance of the scene of a crime.

The two forms of evidence are *oral testimony of witnesses* and *exhibits*, including documents. Both direct and indirect evidence can be presented in either form.

Direct Examination versus Indirect Examination

Under the federal and state rules of civil procedure and criminal procedure, the side with the evidentiary burden of proof—the plaintiff in a civil case and the state in a criminal case—begins the presentation of evidence. This is accomplished by calling witnesses for *direct examination* or questioning by the attorney for the side that called the witness. Beginning journalists sometimes confuse direct examination with direct evidence. They are not the same. Direct examination deals with the interrogation process, whereas direct evidence relates to a type of evidence. The confusion arises from the fact that in a direct examination, the attorney can have the witness offer both direct and indirect evidence.

Direct examinations are usually fairly straightforward, with the attorney asking questions designed to induce the witness to make factual statements and identify documents, photos, and other physical items to be introduced into evidence. The particular rules of evidence (state or federal) dictate what evidence can be introduced and how and even the forms and types of questions that can be asked. For example, *leading questions*, which suggest specific answers, are not permitted under most circumstances in direct examination. In fact, Rule 611(c) of the Federal Rules of Evidence says that leading questions "should not be used on the direct examination of a witness except as may be necessary to develop the witness' testimony." Exceptions include hostile witnesses[60] and questions designed to elicit basic information such as a witness' name, age and address.

The plaintiff or state (in a criminal case) presents its witnesses first. After each witness is sworn in and questioned by the attorney, the defense attorney has the opportunity to conduct a *cross examination* of that witness. Unlike in direct examination, during cross examination leading questions are not only permitted but expected. "Ordinarily leading questions should be permitted on cross examination," according to Rule 611(c) of the Federal Rules of Evidence. All states have similar rules permitting this type of interrogation. Cross examinations are generally "limited to the subject matter of the direct examination and matters affecting the credibility of the witness,"[61] so attorneys conducting them feel they must use leading questions if they are to accomplish the primary goal of destroying the witness' previous testimony during direct examination and if possible, making the witness give testimony favorable to their side. Another goal of cross examination, especially with expert witnesses, is to *impeach* or destroy the credibility (not just the content) of the witness' testimony.

Cross examination has become an art that few attorneys probably feel they have ever fully mastered, but nevertheless is often critical to a case, especially in media law suits such as those for libel and invasion of privacy. One litigation expert, Professor James W. McElhaney of the Case Western University School of Law, advises attorneys not only to ask leading questions in cross examination but also to ask very short questions, use simple words, use headlines and to get one fact straight at a time.[62] According to McElhaney, "Cross examination is not for the witness. It is for you. It is your opportunity to present your side of the witness' story, punctuated by the witness' reluctant agreement that what you say is true."[63]

To help you understand the difference between leading versus nonleading questions, Table 3.1 provides some examples of how the same information may be sought using both types of questions.

Nonleading	Leading
How many years have you been a reporter?	You've been a reporter only two years, haven't you?
How reliable was John Jones as a confidential source?	You had reason to believe John Jones lied, didn't you?
When, if ever, do you recored your phone conversations?	Don't ou routinely record your phone conversations?

As mentioned earlier, hearsay testimony is generally not admissible, although there are many exceptions. In fact, the federal rules of evidence specifically cite 23 exceptions, even when a declarant is available to testify, including a catch-all "other" category.[64] Five categories of exceptions are available if a declarant is unavailable as a witness.[65] Even hearsay within hearsay is permitted under certain circumstances.[66] Journalists sometimes get trapped by making statements under the pressure or heat of the moment that come back to haunt them.

For example, a reporter writing a story about a politician who is allegedly a drug trafficker may accidentally blurt out that he knows the person is a crook and all that's left is to prove it. That statement could be admitted as either an "excited utterance" (an exception to the general hearsay rule) or possibly as an "admission by a party-opponent" (which the federal rules do not even consider as hearsay anyway). *The moral of the story is to be very careful at all times about what you say because your statements may come back to haunt you later in a libel or invasion of privacy suit.*

The opposing counsel can always object to the court during direct examination and cross examination when impermissible questions are asked or irrelevant evidence is sought. If the judge overrules the objection, the witness is allowed to answer the question, but the judge's ruling may be the basis for an appeal if an unfavorable verdict is rendered. If the judge sustains the objection, the attorney may either rephrase the question or start another line of questioning.

Following Cross Examination

After a witness has been directly examined by the attorney who called him or her and then cross examined by the attorney for the other side, the attorney who called can then conduct a redirect examination, followed by a recross examination by the other side. Both steps are optional, although a recross can be conducted only after a prior direct examination. It should be noted that the recross can be followed by another redirect and so on, but such exchanges are rare, and the judge has the authority to end the process when deemed appropriate. Redirect and recross examinations are usually short because they can deal only with matters handled in the preceding step.

Motion for Directed Verdict versus Judgment Notwithstanding the Verdict

Once the plaintiff or state (in a criminal suit) has rested its case after calling all of its witnesses, which have also been cross examined, and so on, the defendant can (and usually does) make an oral motion for a directed verdict. This motion is made outside the hearing of the jurors in a jury trial and can be made in both civil and criminal cases. In a criminal case, however, it is usually a motion to dismiss because acquittal in a criminal case either by a judge or a jury is final and the 5th Amendment bars double jeopardy ("nor shall any person be subject for the same offence to be twice put in jeopardy of life or limb").

The concept of directed verdict is sometimes difficult for beginning journalists to understand, especially when coupled with the concept of *judgment notwithstanding the verdict* (also called *non obstante veredicto* or *jnov).* The two concepts— directed verdict and jnov—are the same, except for the timing. If the judge in a civil case determines *before* the jury renders a verdict that there is either (a) insufficient evidence for a case to go to the jury or (b) the evidence is so compelling that any reasonable person would clearly find for the plaintiff, the judge will issue a directed verdict. If the judge makes this determination after the jury has rendered a verdict, a jnov is issued. Obviously, a directed verdict or a jnov in a civil case can be in favor of either the defendant or the plaintiff. If the evidence is sufficiently weak so there is no question of fact for the jury to decide, the directed verdict will be for the defendant. If the evidence is so compelling that there is also no question of fact for the jury, the directed verdict or jnov will be in favor of the plaintiff.

Within the same jurisdiction, the test the judge applies is the same for both the directed verdict and the jnov, but, to add to the confusion, there are two different tests. Most jurisdictions, including the federal courts, now apply the *substantial* evidence test. When a motion for a directed verdict or a jnov is made, the judge is required to look at all of the evidence but view it in the light most favorable to the side *not* requesting the directed verdict or jnov—also called the *nonmovant*. If the evidence that would allow a jury to find in favor of the side not making the motion is insufficient, the judge will then deny the motion for the directed verdict or jnov. The second test, which is used in a minority of jurisdictions, is the *scintilla test* that allows the judge to deny the motion if there is *any* evidence whatsoever to warrant jury consideration.

One of the confusing aspects of the motion for a directed verdict and the jnov is the timing. The directed verdict may first be made by the defendant right after the plaintiff or state has rested its case. In a civil case, as mentioned earlier, the plaintiff must prove the case by a preponderance of the evidence, not beyond a reasonable doubt, as in a criminal case. How then would a judge be able to grant a directed verdict before the defendant has ever presented that side? Recall that the plaintiff or state has the burden of proof. If the proof is so weak that reasonable minds would not differ, the judge can obviously rule in favor of the defendant even though the defendant has not presented that side because there is so little evidence for the defendant to counter anyway. The defendant, of course, has no reason to contest the judgment because it favors that party.

For example, in a 2009 lawsuit filed against health insurer Blue Shield of California, an Orange County Superior Court Judge issued a directed verdict in favor of the company after he determined that Blue Shield had acted in good faith when it cancelled a client's medical insurance. The judge issued the ruling in mid-trial on the grounds that the plaintiff in the case had intentionally misrepresented his medical record on his insurance application.[67]

Why can't a directed verdict be issued in favor of the plaintiff after the plaintiff has rested that side of the case? Even if the evidence is overwhelming, the defendant must be allowed to counter this evidence with other evidence that may substantially negate the plaintiff's case.

If a directed verdict and a jnov are granted on the same basis, then why would a judge wait until a jury had rendered its verdict before issuing a jnov? At first analysis, there would appear to be no real reason; one major purpose of issuing the directed verdict when it is warranted is to save the expense and time of continuing the trial. By waiting until the jury has made its decision, the judge would certainly defeat this purpose. However, many judges prefer to allow the jury to deliberate even though they know they would overturn a verdict if the jury did not decide in favor of the *correct* party for whom the judge would issue the directed verdict.

There are two major reasons for this preference. First, the jury may very well decide in favor of the correct side, thus negating the need for a jnov. The typical juror feels frustration and, perhaps, anger when he or she returns from a recess—after hearing the plaintiff (or state) present its side or hearing both sides in a civil suit when the directed verdict is in favor of the plaintiff—and is dismissed because the jury has no need to deliberate. Second, the odds of a directed verdict being overturned by an appellate court are typically much higher than for a jnov. In fact, even if a jnov is overturned on appeal, all the appellate court must do is reinstate the jury's decision. If a directed verdict is overturned on appeal, there is no jury verdict to reinstate and thus a new trial will be necessary.

A jury may never know that a jnov overturning its verdict has been issued because there is a period—usually 10 to 20 days after the jury's verdict—during which the motion can be filed, and the judge has some time to consider whether to grant the motion. Unless the judge's decision is reported in the media, the jurors will likely never learn their decision was overruled. The federal courts and most state courts do not allow a jnov unless the side requesting it has previously made a motion for a directed verdict at the appropriate time.

Assuming no directed verdict is granted in favor of the defendant after the plaintiff or state (in a criminal case) has presented all of its witnesses and the defendant has had the opportunity to cross examine each of those witnesses, the defense then calls its witnesses. The process is exactly the same as for the plaintiff except that the defendant conducts a direct examination of each witness, followed by the plaintiff's cross examination, the defendant's redirect (if exercised), and so on. It is quite possible that the plaintiff or state may have already called some of the witnesses testifying on behalf of the defense. If so, the plaintiff is permitted to ask leading questions, even though conducting a direct examination. For example, in a libel or invasion of privacy case, the plaintiff's attorney may wish to build the case with testimony from the reporters who wrote the story, the managing editor, the copy desk chief, and other journalists in an attempt to establish negligence or even actual malice from the beginning and thus form a strong impression on the jury.

Expert Witnesses

According to litigation expert James W. McElhaney, "The point of calling an expert is to put a teacher on the stand—an explainer who brings another set of eyes into the room through which the judge and jury can see the facts and understand your case."[68] Both sides may call expert witnesses, hired to offer their opinions on a particular aspect of the case. By definition, expert witnesses must possess special skills and/or knowledge not held by the average person but gained through specialized experience or education or a combination of both. In other words, the expert witness must be qualified to testify on a particular issue. For example, a professor of journalism may be hired in a libel case by the defendant to testify that the reporter was not negligent and that the story was not published with actual malice, just as the plaintiff could hire a similar expert to offer evidence of negligence or actual malice. An example in a criminal case would be a forensic psychiatrist hired by a prosecutor to testify that the defendant was mentally competent to stand trial.

Expert witnesses are usually paid for their services, and their fees generally range from fifty to several hundred dollars an hour plus expenses. Although the importance of expert witnesses varies from case to case (in both civil and criminal cases), sometimes the expert with the strongest testimony makes such a positive impression on the jury or judge (in a bench trial) that the decision sways in favor of the party for whom the expert testimony is offered. In most cases, however, the experts cancel out one another in the eyes of the jury. Thus it is not all that unusual for the attorneys for both sides to forego the experts.

The judge plays a major role in the conduct of any trial, including ruling on whether a particular piece of evidence is admissible under the federal or state rules of evidence. The difficulty is assuring that jurors do not hear inadmissible evidence. However, all too often, the inadmissible evidence is heard by the jury anyway because the other side is unable to object until after the fact. The judge must then admonish the jury to disregard the inadmissible evidence. Is such an admonition effective? If one study is any indication, the answer is "probably not." An American Bar Foundation researcher[69] found in an experiment with more than 500 adults called to jury duty in Cook County, Illinois, that jurors' decisions in a hypothetical civil case involving clear police misconduct in a raid were affected by the evidence police did or did not find. Even though the jurors were instructed by the judge to disregard the inadmissible evidence, their decision was affected by that evidence. Even the amount of damages was affected by the illegally obtained evidence, apparently because the information remembered by the jurors during their deliberations was influenced by what the police found. For example, the study's participants who heard that the fruits of the illegal search included evidence that the plaintiff was guilty of selling heroin awarded the plaintiff an average of $7,359 in punitive damages versus an average of $23,585 if the evidence indicated the plaintiff was *innocent* of possession of marijuana.

Closing Arguments

In both civil and criminal cases, the trial ends with closing arguments by both sides. The opening statements, as mentioned earlier, are summaries of the facts to be presented, *not* arguments. The closing comments can, and indeed nearly always are, arguments designed to sway the jury to a particular side. Even though some studies indicate that jurors often make up their minds during the opening statements, attorneys know that closing arguments can play a key role in influencing jurors—especially those who may still be undecided after hearing all of the evidence. Thus, it is not unusual, especially in civil cases, for attorneys to make strong, emotional appeals. Indeed, some of the most colorful and memorable statements from great lawyers such as Clarence S. Darrow, who unsuccessfully defended public school teacher John T. Scopes in the famous Tennessee "Monkey" trial over the teaching of evolution, have come from closing arguments.

In fact, unless the opposing side objects, judges in both civil and criminal cases are generally lax in what they permit attorneys to say in closing.

Rule 61 of the Federal Rules of Civil Procedure and a very similar Rule 61 of the Federal Rules of Criminal Procedure are usually cited as the bases for ignoring potential errors in closing arguments because "the court at every stage of the proceeding must disregard any error or defect in the proceeding which does not affect the substantial rights of the parties."[70] Consider the excerpts from the following closing arguments made by the plaintiff's attorney in a libel suit discussed in Chapter 8:

> Since he talked with you about the University of Georgia and when he was there, I think I likewise have a right to mention to you briefly that I probably have known Wally Butts longer than any man in this case. I was at Mercer University with Wally Butts when he played end on the football team there. He was in some respects a small man in stature, but he had more determination and more power to win than any man that I have ever seen in my life. I would not stand before you in this case today arguing in his behalf if I thought that Wally Butts would not tell you the truth when he raises his hand on this stand and swears to Almighty God that what he is going to tell you is the truth....
>
> Somebody has got to stop them. There is no law against it, and the only way that type of, as I call it, yellow journalism can be stopped is to let the *Saturday Evening Post* know that it is not going to get away with it today, tomorrow, or anymore hereafter and the only way that lesson can be brought home to them, Gentlemen, is to hit them where it hurts them, and the only thing they know is money. They write about human beings; they kill him, his wife, his three lovely daughters. What do they care?
>
> I say, Gentlemen, this is the time we have got to get them. A hundred million dollars in advertising, would ten per cent of that be fair to Wally Butts for what they have done to him?

> You know, one of these days, like everyone else must come to, Wallace Butts is going to pass on. No one can bother him then. The *Saturday Evening Post* can't get at him then. And unless I miss my guess, they will put Wallace Butts in a red coffin with a black lid, and he will have a football in his hands, and his epitaph will read something like this: "Glory, Glory to old Georgia."[71]

The jury of 12 men awarded plaintiff Butts $60,000 in compensatory damages and $3 million in punitive damages. The trial court judge reduced the award to $460,000, the equivalent of two cents for each of the 23 million issues in which the story appeared. Both a U.S. Circuit Court of Appeals and the U.S. Supreme Court upheld the trial court's decision.

Judge's Instructions to the Jury

After the closing arguments have been delivered, the judge instructs the jury on the appropriate law to be applied in deciding the case. In most jurisdictions including the federal system, the attorneys for both sides have the opportunity to submit to the judge specific instructions for the jury. Such requests must be filed and the judge must rule on them before the closing arguments are made, but the instructions are not usually given to the jury by the judge until *after* the closing arguments. Under Rule 51 of the Federal Rules of Civil Procedure and most state rules, the judge can instruct the jury before or after the closing arguments or both, although judges rarely depart from the tradition of waiting until the arguments conclude. In complex cases, these instructions can be long, complicated, and intensely boring for the jury, but they are important in the judicial process.

A study by the Capital Jury Project (CJP), which included interviews with more than 500 jurors who served in trials for capital offenses, found that jurors often misunderstand or ignore instructions by the judge.[72] According to the research, more than half had already formed opinions before the sentencing hearing, and almost 40% of them had improperly discussed punishment while they were deliberating on guilt. (Under federal and state rules, guilt or innocence is to be determined before punishment is set.)

Jury Deliberations

Once the jury instructions have concluded, the members deliberate behind closed doors. After a foreperson is elected by the body, a tentative vote is first taken, usually by secret ballot. If a unanimous verdict is required (often it is not) and the vote is unanimous with no undecideds on the first ballot, the jury returns to the courtroom to announce its verdict. Generally, however, the first vote will not be unanimous and deliberations will last from a few hours to days and even weeks. In criminal cases in both federal and state courts, a unanimous verdict is required. In the federal courts and most state courts, civil cases require a unanimous verdict unless the two sides have agreed otherwise before the trial.

In most cases the same jurors serve throughout a trial but in rare instances substitutions may have to be made. In the highly publicized 1993 Los Angeles trial in which two defendants were charged with beating Reginald Denny during the 1992 L.A. riots, five of the original twelve jurors were replaced. Two became ill during testimony and were dismissed, one was removed for discussing the case with neighbors, and two were taken off the jury during deliberations.

One of the latter was a woman about whom the other jurors sent a note to the judge indicating they could not work with her.[73] In the 1997 civil trial of O. J. Simpson for the wrongful deaths of Ronald Goldman and Nicole Brown Simpson, one juror was removed and replaced by an alternate after the jury had already begun deliberations. Only a handful of states give judges the discretion to replace a juror with an alternate any time during the trial and then only for "good cause."

The Verdict

In a civil case, there are three major types of verdicts. The judge always determines which type of verdict is needed. The most frequent type is the *general verdict*; the judge instructs the jury on the applicable law and requests that the members apply that law to the facts in the case and determine which side wins and the amount of damages or other relief if the plaintiff wins. Thus the jury is granted considerable flexibility in reaching its decision. With a *special verdict*, the court requires the jury to render a verdict "in the form of a special written finding upon each issue of fact."[74] In other words, the jury is confined to making specific findings of fact, and the judge actually applies the appropriate law to the facts and renders the final verdict. The procedure is for the judge to submit to the jury a series of written questions, along with explanations and instructions, which the members answer in writing based on their findings during deliberations. Any party in a civil suit can request a special verdict, but the judge makes the final decision regarding the form of the verdict.

In the Simpson civil trial, the jury was asked to answer eight questions in its special verdict, including:

1. Do you find by a preponderance of the evidence that defendant Simpson willfully and wrongfully caused the death of Ronald Goldman?
2. Do you find by a preponderance of the evidence that defendant Simpson committed battery against Ronald Goldman?
3. Do you find by clear and convincing evidence that defendant Simpson committed oppression in the conduct upon which you base your finding of liability for battery against Ronald Goldman?
4. Do you find by clear and convincing evidence that defendant Simpson committed malice in the conduct upon which you base your finding of liability for battery against Ronald Goldman?

The next three questions were the same as questions 2, 3, and 4, except that they related to Nicole Brown Simpson instead of Ronald Goldman. The jury was not presented with the question of whether Simpson had willfully and wrongfully caused the death of Nicole Brown Simpson because her parents chose to file the suit on behalf of their daughter's estate to avoid putting the two grandchildren in the position of suing their father for their mother's death. The last question focused on the compensation of Goldman's parents for the loss of companionship of their son. (Nicole Simpson's estate sought no such damages.) A unanimous jury answered "yes" to all eight questions. In order to award punitive damages, the jury had to find that the defendant committed oppression and malice by clear and convincing evidence, not merely by a preponderance of the evidence.

Noting that it is an old procedure, one legal expert calls the special verdict "a valuable tool for lawyers involved in civil litigation" that, when used with care, "is helpful in defining issues, focusing the jury's attention on those issues, sorting out the liabilities of the parties, and producing a record of the jury's fact findings."[75]

A third type of verdict, a sort of compromise between general and special verdicts, is the *general verdict accompanied by answers to interrogatories.*[76] This form of verdict, in which the judge requests a general verdict accompanied by written answers to one or more factual issues, has the advantage that the judge can compare the answers to the interrogatories to see whether they are in line with the verdict. If they are consistent, all's right with the world, and the judgment is entered into the record. If the verdict and answers are at odds, the judge can either send the case back to the jury for further consideration or grant a new trial. This verdict form has the advantage that it allows the judge to head off the possibility of a successful appeal. Unfortunately, such a verdict can be very time consuming and potentially confusing to the jury.

Although its deliberations are secret, the jury verdict in both civil and criminal cases is announced in open court either by the jury foreperson or by the court clerk, depending on the tradition in that particular jurisdiction. If the jury has been unable to reach a verdict (for example, if it is unable to reach a unanimous verdict when required), the result is a *hung* jury. If the judge is convinced that the jury could reach a verdict if given more time, the judge may order the jury to reconvene to try to reach a decision. Otherwise, the judge may declare a *mistrial*. Mistrials are relatively rare in civil cases, but they do occasionally occur in criminal cases.

6th Amendment Ban on Double Jeopardy

Can a defendant be tried again if there is a mistrial? The answer is "yes" in both civil and criminal cases. The 6th Amendment ban on double jeopardy does not apply to civil cases, and there is no double jeopardy in a mistrial in a criminal case because no verdict has been rendered. However, if a defendant in a criminal suit is acquitted, the decision is final, and the defendant cannot be tried again for that same crime. If an individual has been acquitted of a federal crime but the same facts and circumstances support a trial on state charges, the person could face trial in state court. No double jeopardy arises because the two alleged crimes are not the same even though the facts surrounding them are similar or even identical. The same would hold true if the acquittal were on state charges but the facts supported federal charges.

The judge always has the option in a criminal case of either granting an acquittal or a directed verdict, of course, before the case goes to the jury. In this case, the judge must be convinced that a guilty verdict cannot be reasonably supported by the facts. The court can also order a new trial because of substantive procedural errors, but such decisions are unusual in both civil and criminal cases.

In *Renico v. Lett* (2010),[77] the U.S. Supreme Court reversed a Sixth Circuit U.S. Court of Appeals decision in favor of a criminal defendant in a first degree murder case who claimed double jeopardy after being tried twice. The judge in the first trial had declared a mistrial. Based on statements from the jury foreperson after the jury was called back into the courtroom, the judge was convinced that the jury was unable to reach a unanimous verdict. Before the judge had called the jurors back, she had received seven notes from the body. The jury had been deliberating about four hours, and the entire trial took about nine hours. At the second trial, a different jury deliberated for 3 hours and 15 minutes before finding him guilty of second degree murder. The Supreme Court noted in its decision that "the trial judge could have been more thorough before declaring a mistrial'" but that she did not violate "clearly established Federal law" that judges can discharge juries on the grounds that a jury cannot reach a verdict without violating the Double Jeopardy Clause. [78]

Impeachment of the Verdict

In rare situations, a jury verdict may be *impeached* based on juror testimony. The rule in most states, but not in the federal courts, is that juror testimony *cannot* be used to impeach a verdict. This rule, popularly known as the "Mansfield rule," does not prohibit the use of other evidence such as someone else's observations of jury misconduct for impeachment. A few states adhere to the "Iowa rule," under which jurors can testify regarding overt acts, but not opinions, of other members. For example, a juror could testify that another juror read newspaper stories about the trial even though the jurors had been instructed not to read such stories. Federal Rule of Evidence 606 allows inquiry into testimony by a juror only "on the question whether extraneous prejudicial information was improperly brought to the jury's attention or whether any outside influence was improperly brought to bear upon any juror."

Debriefing Jurors

While jurors may be prohibited from discussing a case while a trial is in progress, they are certainly free to talk once they have rendered a verdict and the trial is over or otherwise concluded. Thus a journalist or anyone else can debrief a juror with that person's consent. Many news media outlets now routinely interview jurors when a trial is concluded to ascertain how the decision was reached and what factors influenced the jurors. Jurors are sometimes reluctant to discuss cases, especially because they were ordered not to do so while the trial was in session. However, a thoughtful and enterprising reporter can usually make such former jurors feel at ease and thus get an important "inside" story that helps readers better understand the verdict. Judges sometimes issue bans prohibiting post-verdict contacts with jurors by journalists. Whether such bans can pass constitutional muster is an open question, but the news media usually threaten to fight such bans in court, which usually discourages judges from imposing such orders. Although the jury may have come and gone, its decision is not final until the judge enters a judgment on the decision, which may come a few or even several days later. Any specified deadlines for filing appeals and other motions do not begin to run until the judgment is entered.

Determining Damages

Unless there are applicable statutory limits, the jury has considerable discretion and leeway in setting damages in civil cases. However, in nearly all cases the judge has the authority to increase or decrease the amount of damages awarded by the jury and even to modify the judgment in other ways before the final judgment is actually entered. For example, when actress and comedienne Carol Burnett was awarded $1.6 million in 1981 by a California jury for libel against the *National Enquirer*, the judge cut the total to $800,000. [79] In the same year when a former "Miss Wyoming" won a total of $26.5 million in damages in a jury trial for libel against *Penthouse* magazine, the federal court judge immediately halved the damages,[80] which the plaintiff never collected because she ultimately lost before a U.S. Court of Appeals.

An exception to the general rule that judges have wide discretion to revise damages awarded by juries can be found in a 1910 amendment to the Oregon constitution providing that a judge cannot review the amount of *punitive damages* awarded by a jury "unless the court can affirmatively say there is no evidence to support the verdict." In 1994, the U.S. Supreme Court struck down this standard, which made it extremely difficult to alter punitive damage awards, as a violation of the 14th Amendment's Due Process clause. In *Honda Motor Co., Ltd. et al. v. Oberg*,[81] the Court held 7 to 2 in an opinion written by Justice Stevens that the amendment was unconstitutional because:

> Punitive damages pose an acute danger of arbitrary deprivation of property. Jury instructions typically leave the jury with wide discretion in choosing amounts, and the presentation of evidence of a defendant's net worth creates the potential that juries will use their verdicts to express biases against big businesses, particularly those without strong local presences. Judicial review of the amount awarded was one of the few procedural safeguards which the common law provided against that danger. Oregon has removed that safeguard without providing any substitute procedure and without any indication that the danger of arbitrary awards has in any way subsided over time.[82]

The majority opinion pointed out, "Judicial review of the size of punitive damage awards has been a safeguard against excessive verdicts for as long as punitive damages have been awarded." The Court further noted, "No Oregon court for more than half a century has inferred passion and prejudice from the size of a damages award, and no court in more than a decade has even hinted that courts might possess the power to do so." The Court was effectively saying that the standard for judicial review under the state constitution was so high that it essentially prevented any review of punitive damages by a judge.

The case arose when Honda Motor Co. appealed a jury's awards of $5 million in punitive damages and $919,390.39 (reduced to $735,512.31 by the judge because of the plaintiff's own negligence) in compensatory damages. The damages were awarded as a result of an accident in which a three-wheeled all-terrain vehicle overturned, resulting in severe and permanent injuries to the male driver. The U.S. Supreme Court remanded the case back to the Oregon Supreme Court for reconsideration of the $5 million punitive award in light of the $735,512 compensatory damages.

Most jury trials, whether civil or criminal, last no more than three or four days. However, some may go no longer than a few hours and others may continue for years. The record for the longest trial is the three-and one-half-year *Kemner v. Monsanto* dioxin trial. The trial over whether 65 plaintiffs were injured when a half teaspoon of extremely toxic dioxin leaked from a railroad tank car during an accident began on February 22, 1984, and ended on October 22, 1987, with a jury verdict that ordered the defendant to pay $16.25 million in punitive damages.[83]

The transcript in the trial was more than 100,000 pages, including testimony from 182 witnesses and some 6,000 exhibits. One report about the trial noted that one 27-year-old lawyer had worked on this single case since he graduated from law school,[84] and another article described how one juror was dismissed less than an hour before jury deliberations began after she had sat through all of the previous three years of trial proceedings.[85] The jurors awarded the 65 plaintiffs $1 each in compensatory damages.[86]

Final Judgment

As attorney James R. Laramore points out, "To the uninitiated, a final judgment marks the end of lengthy and expensive litigation. It is, however, only the beginning of the end."[87] These procedures include various post-judgment motions such as motions for a *judgment notwithstanding the verdict* and a *directed verdict* (discussed earlier in this chapter) as well as the appeals process (see Chapter 2) and also include enforcement of the judgment via garnishments and property liens.[88]

The Criminal Trial

The procedures and proceedings in a civil trial and a criminal trial are quite similar, but there are a few differences. First, the pretrial procedures in criminal cases are substantially different, primarily because various constitutional rights come into play, as discussed earlier, such as the 6th Amendment right to a speedy and public trial and the 5th Amendment right of due process. There are three major ways in which criminal charges are brought against an individual or legal entity such as a corporation. First, a grand jury can issue an *indictment*, which is not a finding of guilt. It is merely a finding that there is sufficient evidence—defined as *probable cause*—to warrant a trial. Figure 3.3 illustrates the felony process for Kentucky, which is similar to that in most other states.

Grand Jury Indictments

The grand jury system has a long bloodline that goes back nine centuries ago to England and continues through colonial times in this country as a means of formally accusing the guilty. However, in the American colonies, grand juries also assumed the role of protecting innocent citizens from prosecutorial zeal.[89] The process has the advantage that it serves as a mechanism for filtering out criminal cases that have little merit. At the same time it can be argued that all too often grand juries have become mouthpieces for prosecutors. Only the federal court system, 12 states, and the District of Columbia require grand jury indictments in all cases. Four states require indictments only in capital cases or cases that carry potential life sentences.[90] The federal requirement comes from the 5th Amendment: "No person shall be held to answer for a capital, or otherwise infamous crime, unless on a presentment or indictment of a Grand Jury, except … [followed by exception]." The U.S. Supreme Court has yet to rule whether this clause applies to the states through the 14th Amendment.[91]

Unlike trial juries (technically known as *petit juries*), grand juries sit for more than one case. In the federal system, grand jurors may serve up to 18 months and can hear hundreds of potential cases during that time. The grand jury is also much larger than a trial jury—typically with 16 to 23 members in federal cases and a similar number in state cases.

Two characteristics of the grand jury system that could be criticized as inherent weaknesses are (a) deliberations are always conducted in secret, away from the scrutiny of the press and

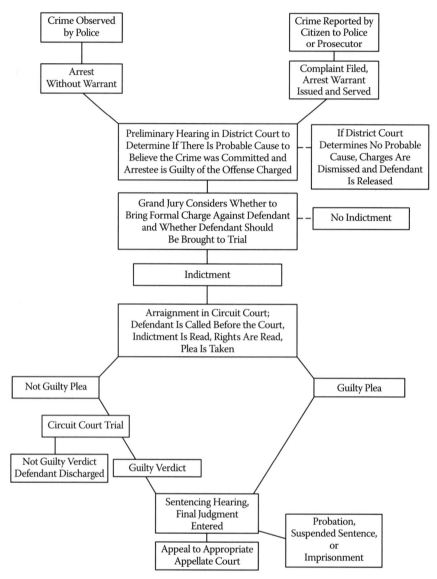

Figure 3.3   Kentucky Felony Case Process (Compiled by Administrative Office of the Courts, Frankfort, KY. Reprinted with permission.)

the public and (b) the prosecutor or, in the federal system, the U.S. Attorney for that district, presents the evidence to the grand jury, without the opportunity for any potential defendant or actual defendant to present the opposing side. Even the federal government acknowledges that it is rare for a grand jury not to issue an indictment requested by a prosecutor.[92]

According to the rationale for secrecy, witnesses will feel free to give their testimony without fear of revenge. By the same token, it could be argued that such a witness is more likely to exaggerate or even lie if that person knows the testimony will not be subject to public scrutiny. Not only are the grand jurors restricted from publicly disclosing any information about the proceedings while the grand jury is in session but even the U.S. Attorney or prosecutor is gagged.

In the federal system and in the few states that use the grand jury system, the press is usually allowed to watch witnesses as they enter and leave the grand jury room, but witnesses are not permitted to talk with anyone except authorized officials until after they have given their testimony. Once the witness has testified in secret, he or she can, if willing to do so, talk freely about the testimony. The enterprising journalist is always on the lookout for witnesses who volunteer to talk. Be careful! Witnesses can talk, if they wish, only *after* the testimony; the journalist who publishes information leaked by a grand juror or a prosecutor faces the real possibility of a subpoena to identify the source in court or may face contempt of court charges including a fine and/or a jail sentence.

After hearing the evidence in the forms of testimony and materials and/or documents, the grand jury votes to determine whether there is *probable cause* to believe that a person has committed a crime and thus should be tried. *Probable cause* is a relatively low standard. It simply means that there is more evidence as a whole for the grand jurors, acting as reasonably prudent individuals, to believe that the accused committed the crime than that the person did not. This is sometimes known as *reasonable cause* or *reasonable belief.* If the specified number of members (12 in the federal system) finds probable cause, the grand jury will issue a *bill of indictment*, also known as a *true bill*, charging that individual with a particular crime or crimes. Unless the indictments have been ordered sealed, which occurs in rare circumstances, they are read and made available in open court and then filed as open records, usually in the court clerk's office.

Seasoned journalists know that all defendants' names appear on an indictment in all capital letters and that all charges are individually listed. Read names carefully because witnesses and other individuals may also be listed, but they are not defendants. (These names are not in all capital letters in the indictment.) For example, characterizing someone as a defendant who was merely a witness simply because you did not carefully read the indictment could bring you an unwanted suit for libel or false light.

Filing of an Information

The second method by which criminal charges can be brought is *filing of an information* by a prosecutor such as a district or county attorney. This is simply a process by which the individual is formally accused without the use of a grand jury. Constitutional standards including the 6th and 14th Amendments, require, just as in an indictment, that the exact (or approximate if exact cannot be determined) date, time, and place of the alleged criminal act be specified. The information must also include the role the defendant played in the alleged crime and other known details. The idea is that defendants should be sufficiently informed so they can adequately defend themselves.

The filing of an information is often based on evidence obtained through a search warrant, which must conform to 4th Amendment standards enunciated by the U.S. Supreme Court in a series of complicated decisions over the years. Basically, the Court has said that a warrant must be specific and narrowly drawn to ensure that a constitutionally valid search is conducted. If a search warrant is improper, then the evidence garnered from the search generally cannot be used at trial, although the Supreme Court has carved out a series of "good faith exceptions" that some legal experts, especially criminal defense attorneys, find troubling.

One variation of the filing of an information occurs when charges are initiated by one individual filing a criminal complaint against another, such as a wife filing charges against her husband for assault. However, the prosecutor has the discretion on whether to act on the charges by a filing of an information. In other words, the original criminal complaint basically serves as a request to the prosecutor to take further steps. The prosecutor can always choose *not* to proceed further, especially if there appears to be no probable cause to do so.

Citations

Finally, for certain misdemeanors and other relatively minor crimes such as traffic violations, but *not* felonies, charges can be brought via a *citation* from a law enforcement or other designated officer. No grand jury or filing of an information is required under these circumstances.

Arrest Warrant

Once a grand jury has returned an indictment or a prosecutor has filed an information, the court clerk issues an *arrest warrant* if the person is not already in custody. For example, the individual may already have been charged with another crime and thereby arrested or may have been detained at the time the alleged criminal act took place. Since a 1966 U.S. Supreme Court decision in the case of *Miranda v. Arizona*,[93] police have been required, primarily under the 5th Amendment ban on forced self-incrimination, to inform suspects in police custody of their constitutional rights *before* any questioning can begin.

Television shows and movies are fond of including the Miranda warnings, probably as a way of lending authenticity to their products. Almost any first grader can utter, "Read me my rights." Television shows such as *Law and Order, Cold Case*, and *Crime Scene Investigation* have made the line "You have the right to remain silent …"[94] as familiar as some of the theme songs that accompany the shows. One stipulation to the requirement that the Miranda Rule be followed is that the suspect must be in custody or be in a situation in which the ability to voluntarily leave is significantly restricted by police. If police fail to give the warnings when the rule is in effect, any confession or other incriminating evidence disclosed by that person generally may not be used to convict the person.

Preliminary Hearing

Unless a defendant has been indicted by a grand jury, the next major step in a criminal procedure is an *initial* or *first appearance*, which is known in some jurisdictions as a *preliminary hearing* or *arraignment*. (Journalists should learn the proper terminology in their jurisdictions.) First, the judge will inform defendants of the specific charges brought against them and then inform them of their legal rights. At this stage, a judge must also decide if there is *probable cause* (i.e., sufficient evidence) to warrant bringing defendants to trial. If the judge believes the evidence is insufficient, the judge will dismiss the charge(s) and order that the defendant be released.

If the judge finds probable cause to charge defendants, the judge will first determine whether they need legal representation. If the defendants cannot afford an attorney, the judge will make arrangements for a public defender to serve. Finally, the judge determines whether defendants will be allowed to post bail and, if so, how much must be posted prior to their release from custody.

The judge has several options, including allowing defendants to post a specified amount for *bail*, releasing defendants on their *own recognizance* (without having to post bond), and even denying bail in extreme circumstances such as when a defendant has a history of "jumping" bail.

The fact that dangerous individuals are frequently released on bail has drawn much criticism from the public over the years, but judges are bound by the 8th Amendment prohibition against excessive bail.

The rationale in granting bail is to allow the defendant to prepare adequately for defense while a stick is held over the accused's head in the form of a posted bail bond that is forfeited if the defendant fails to appear at trial. A judge does have the option of imposing certain conditions on the bail such as restricting the defendant's travel and personal contacts, so long as the restrictions are reasonable. A judge can always set the amount of the bond sufficiently high to ensure that the defendant does appear at trial.

Arraignment

If defendants have already been indicted, the first major step after indictment and arrest is *arraignment*. At this stage, the individuals are read the indictment, the judge explains the legal rights, and the individuals enter a plea. If an initial appearance, as explained earlier, has already been made, the judge simply hears the plea. If the defendants plead guilty, they will either be immediately sentenced, especially in the case of misdemeanors and minor offenses, or a date will be set for sentencing. If they plead not guilty, a tentative trial date is announced. It is not unusual for a trial date to be postponed one or more times before the actual trial.

In the case of federal crimes and in some states, a judge can also entertain a plea of *nolo contendere* (from the Latin meaning "I will not contest it"). Federal Rule of Criminal Procedure 11(b) permits this plea only with the consent of a judge who must consider the rights of the parties and the public interest in effective administration of justice. Basically, the defendant is saying "I am neither admitting nor denying the charges but simply not fighting." Obviously, the judge in such a case can reject the plea or, if the judge accepts the plea, he or she can still fine and/or sentence the person. The major advantage for the defendant is that, unlike with a guilty plea, a plaintiff cannot use the plea as evidence against the defendant in a civil suit arising from the same actions as those associated with the criminal charges. In other words, a nolo contendere plea cannot be used as evidence in a civil suit.

A defendant may also enter an *Alford plea* in which the defendant claims innocence but agrees to plead guilty in exchange for a reduction in the charges. The plea owes its origins to the 1970 U.S. Supreme Court decision, *North Carolina v. Alford*.[95] The case involved a defendant who pled guilty after the prosecutor agreed to reduce the charge against him from first degree to second degree murder. After being sentenced to 30 years imprisonment, he appealed his conviction on the ground that he had pled guilty only to avoid the death penalty and thus his plea had been involuntary. According to the U.S. Supreme Court, "An individual accused of a crime may voluntarily, knowingly, and understandingly consent to the imposition of a prison sentence even if he is unwilling or unable to admit his participation in the acts constituting the crime."[96]

Settlement Prior to Trial

The overwhelming majority of criminal and civil cases never go to trial because an agreement is reached between the two sides beforehand. For example, in 2001, only 2% of civil cases filed in federal court were tried, and only 15% of defendants in criminal cases chose to go to trial.[97] For civil cases, this means out-of-court settlements. In criminal cases, the filtering process is called *plea bargaining*. Plea bargaining can occur at any stage, but most agreements are made after the arraignment but before trial. The courts could not begin to handle the caseload if even only twice as many defendants insisted on having trials to which they are constitutionally entitled. Plea bargaining has become *the* way of settling criminal cases.

The public is often appalled when an incorrigible has a prosecutor agree to ask a judge to charge the incorrigible with a lesser offense than in the original complaint and/or grant leniency in sentencing in exchange for a guilty plea. Some people are particularly concerned because the plea bargaining process takes place out of the public view. The agreement usually becomes public only when the defendant appears in court. It is not well known that a judge is not bound by any agreement between a prosecutor and a defendant. In other words, a judge can refuse to honor an agreement, although judges rarely override the recommendations of a prosecutor.

If a defendant does plead guilty, a judge can immediately impose a sentence, but will usually schedule a hearing instead for later. If a defendant pleads not guilty, the judge will then schedule a trial.

Discovery

If a criminal case has not already been settled by a guilty plea or dismissal, the last major step before trial is *discovery*. The discovery process is somewhat different in criminal and civil suits. One of the most important differences is that depositions and interrogatories, which are almost essential in any civil case that goes to trial, are almost never conducted in criminal cases. They are usually unnecessary because (a) the 5th Amendment prevents a criminal defendant (but generally not a civil defendant) from being forced to give testimony and (b) the federal system and most states have fairly strong disclosure provisions that require each side to keep the other side informed, including exchanging lists of witnesses each side expects to use at trial. The prosecutor is also required to reveal to the defense any evidence found during the investigation or discovery that would reflect on the defendant's guilt or innocence. This requirement is usually enforced in the form of a judge's order and can encompass the defendant's criminal records; documents, photos, and other materials to be used at trial; medical reports and results of other tests such as a polygraph examination; and any recorded statements made by the defendant to police or other officials. There are often restrictions that allow prosecutors to keep the identities of government informants and other witnesses who might face intimidation or harm confidential.

In the federal system and in most states, the prosecution also has the right of access to evidence to be used by the defense at trial, although, of course, the prosecution cannot get information that would be covered by attorney–client privilege or by some other exemption to the general rule of disclosure.

Much of the information exchanged by the two sides is public record, including discovery orders and responses. The astute journalist will frequently check with the court clerk to see if new documents have been added to the case file. It is particularly a good idea to establish rapport with the clerk because processing a document that has been filed may take a while, especially if the clerk's office is overloaded at the time. Most court clerks are usually willing to allow a journalist to make a copy of a document as soon as it has been filed (i.e., officially received and stamped), but you should set up a cooperative arrangement with the clerk for doing this.

Sentencing

If a judge or jury determines that a defendant is guilty beyond a reasonable doubt, a judge in the federal system determines the defendant's sentence, applying special guidelines established by the United States Sentencing Commission.[98] Until 2002, in five states, including Arizona, the judge, rather than the jury, decided whether to sentence a defendant convicted of a capital offense to death. In four other states, juries made sentence recommendations but the final decision was in the hands of the judge. In the other 29 states with the death penalty and in the federal system, juries decided whether there were aggravating circumstances and then balanced those against any mitigating circumstances before imposing a death sentence on a capital defendant.

In *Ring v. Arizona* (2002),[99] the U.S. Supreme Court held in a 7 to 2 decision that it was a violation of the 6th Amendment for a judge to have sole responsibility for deciding whether to sentence an individual to death in a jury trial. In issuing its ruling, the Court overturned *Walton v. Arizona*—1990 precedent[100] in which the Court upheld the same sentencing scheme as constitutional. As a result, in all 38 states with the death penalty and in the federal system, the decision is now in the hands of the jury. In 2000 in *Apprendi v. New Jersey*,[101] the Court had ruled that a defendant's 14th Amendment due process rights were violated in a hate crimes case by a New Jersey statute that removed the jury from determining whether a defendant could face an increase in the maximum sentence. According to the majority opinion, *Walton* and *Apprendi* were irreconcilable. "Capital defendants, no less than non-capital defendants, we conclude, are entitled to a jury determination of any fact on which the legislature conditions an increase in their maximum punishment."[102]

Alternative Dispute Resolution

As the workloads of most courts continue to increase, alternatives will get more attention and thereby begin to look more attractive. Clearly, the courts remain the best forums for many types of cases, but there are indeed some viable alternatives, many of which have long, distinguished histories. These options go by colorful names such as summary jury trials, minitrials, facilitation, arbitration, and mediation. They all provide ways of resolving disputes outside the traditional trial. Some—such as summary jury trials—are more shortcuts than real alternatives, but they are becoming more popular as attorneys, judges, and other legal experts discover their advantages and begin to feel comfortable in recommending them to clients and parties.

Alternative dispute resolution (ADR) is not without critics. One of the most common criticisms is that in providing privacy for the parties, ADR, particularly arbitration and mediation, undermines the whole doctrine of *stare decisis*. Both the proceedings and the outcomes are shrouded in secrecy, preventing both trial courts and appellate courts from interpreting and applying law so that future litigants will have some guidance on how a case is likely to be decided. Journalists are often among the most vocal critics because they are prevented from gaining access to decisions in lawsuits that clearly have a strong public interest. As one U.S. District Court judge noted, "Everybody knows what is happening in a jury trial. It creates an open forum to understand how the law works. If we lose that, we lose something very important."[103] We will briefly explore the more popular alternatives so you will recognize their features and can learn, on your own if necessary, their inner workings.

Summary Jury Trial

In 1980, a U.S. District Judge in Cleveland, Thomas Lambros, proposed a new process for encouraging negotiated settlements in civil cases. Several federal trial court judges have used the technique, known as a *summary jury trial,* usually with the consent of litigants on both sides. The idea of a summary jury trial is, at least intuitively, rather appealing. Instead of the usual drawn-out trial involving opening statements, direct examinations, cross examinations, closing arguments, objections, motions, and so on, the attorney for each side is granted a specific amount of time to summarize the case before a six-person jury, which then deliberates and renders a *nonbinding* verdict. Most summary jury trials take no more than a few hours to a day and they, theoretically at least, afford the parties an opportunity to see how a full jury would weigh the evidence and decide.

In 1987, however, this procedure received a serious, although certainly not fatal, blow when the U.S. Court of Appeals for the 7th Circuit held that federal judges lacked the authority to require parties and attorneys to use summary jury trials.[104] Because the issue in the case was whether litigants could be forced to use the technique, the court did not rule on the legality of such trials to which both sides consented.[105]

The case arose when an attorney was cited for contempt and fined $500 by the trial court judge after he refused to participate in a summary jury trial even though ordered to do so. The trial court judge did not order that the case be settled with this process but merely that this alternative be used to attempt to induce a settlement. He used Rule 16 of the Federal Rules of Civil Procedure, which grants federal judges discretion in directing attorneys and parties to participate in pretrial conferences. The judge also cited a 1984 resolution by the Judicial Conference of the United States endorsing summary jury trials.[106] Nevertheless, the court of appeals noted that although the rule "was intended to foster settlement through the use of extrajudicial procedures, it was not intended to require that an unwilling litigant be sidetracked from the normal course of litigation."[107] In 1990, Congress approved the use of summary jury trials through the Judicial Reform Act.[108]

Decades after Judge Lambros came up with the idea of summary jury trials, the process is still struggling to capture acceptance, with still relatively few judges using this alternative dispute resolution.[109] One of the most prominent critics of compulsory use of this technique is 7th Circuit U.S. Court of Appeals Judge Richard Posner, who argues that it can actually increase cost and that it bypasses the opportunity for jurors to judge the credibility of witnesses.[110]

Arbitration

Certainly the oldest ADR mechanisms still in use today are arbitration and mediation. These processes are often confused with one another, but they are quite different. The Council of Better Business Bureaus (BBB) defines *arbitration* as "a process in which two or more persons agree to let an impartial person or panel make a decision to resolve their dispute."[111] Except in very unusual circumstances, such as when an arbitrator or panel violates established rules or when the arbitrators clearly exceed their legal authority, a court will not even hear an appeal of an arbitration decision, let alone reverse it. Thus arbitration decisions are legally binding on all the parties involved, unlike court decisions that can generally be appealed at least once. This is one of the major advantages of arbitration. The parties must agree to abide by the decision, regardless of whether it is favorable or unfavorable to a particular party, so both sides know from the beginning that the arbitrator's decision will settle the dispute once and for all. The savings in cost, time, and attorneys' fees can be considerable. In fact, for most arbitration hearings, parties are not required to be represented by attorneys although each side has the option of using legal counsel.

The Better Business Bureau is one of several private organizations that conduct arbitration hearings. The BBB provides both binding and conditionally binding arbitration as well as mediation and informal dispute settlement. In conditionally binding arbitration, the consumer does not have to accept the arbitrator's decision, although the business involved does. In informal dispute settlement the two parties present their sides to an impartial third party (hearing officer) who issues a nonbinding decision.[112] Even governmental agencies are involved in alternate methods, for example, the Federal Mediation and Conciliation Service (FMCS)[113] whose work includes resolving labor–management conflicts, and the Community Relations Service (CRS) whose primary concern is improving law enforcement–community interactions.[114] Both are little known among the general public, but they provide services such as arbitration, mediation, and conciliation that are becoming more common each day. The FMCS was established in 1947 to mediate labor–management disputes, whereas the CRS was created via the Civil Rights Act of 1964 to provide help in resolving racial conflicts.[115] Many states now have public agencies for arbitrating and mediating disputes, usually connected with a state consumer protection agency.

Mediation

Mediation is a process by which a neutral party or parties intermediate between two or more parties in conflict, with their consent, in an attempt to have the opposing sides settle a dispute on mutually satisfying terms. A mediator uses the power of persuasion, *not* coercion, to convince the two sides to reach an agreement. The mediator hears both sides, asks questions, and works hard to convince the parties to settle but does *not* issue a decision. If the parties, with the aid of the mediator, reach a final agreement, it is usually legally binding. With arbitration, on the other hand, the arbitrator, after hearing both sides, will actually render a legally binding decision, usually in favor of one side.

ADR has become so popular that many major law firms and attorneys in private practice now offer arbitration, mediation, and other forms of ADR as part of their service. Many prominent law schools such as Harvard University hold seminars in mediation and negotiation. Mediation has been particularly successful in family courts in some parts of the country. More states are now routinely referring cases involving divorce, child custody, and other domestic matters to mediation. In Kentucky, for example, all 22 jurisdictions that have family courts now use mediation and use of the process is growing as more mediators and judges are trained.[116] As mediation expert Carol B. Paisley notes in discussing family court mediation in Kentucky, "Mediation is here to stay. In family cases, the parties are empowered in the mediation process, and, therefore, generally satisfied with the results they reach."[117]

American Arbitration Association

By far the most widely known, prestigious, and largest full-service ADR provider is the American Arbitration Association (AAA), founded in 1926. The AAA describes itself as "a not-for-profit, public-service organization committed to the resolution of disputes through the use of arbitration, mediation and other voluntary procedures."[118] Its corporate headquarters are in New York, and with 37 offices in the United States and Europe, it can provide service around the world. In 2002, more than 230,000 cases were handled by AAA, including disputes regarding construction, health care, energy, employment, insurance, and consumer finance.

Each type of arbitration—commercial, construction industry, securities, sports, and so on—has its own set of rules, copies of which are always available from the organization under whose auspices the process is conducted. If, as a journalist, you are assigned to cover the business, labor, or even the sports beat, it is likely that you will be assigned a story involving arbitration or mediation. Thus it would be well worth the effort to read and know the ADR rules governing a particular type of dispute.

Two services offered by the same ADR organizations, of which many individuals including lawyers are not aware, are divorce mediation and divorce arbitration. Divorce arbitration has been growing over the years, with two states—North Carolina and Michigan—leading the way by passing statutes that specifically permit arbitration in family law cases.[119] The typical arbitrator, who must undergo training, is a divorce lawyer or retired judge, and the going rate for the arbitrator's services is $250 to $450 an hour. Divorce arbitration provides many benefits including reduced expenses, assurance of privacy, and quicker, more satisfying resolutions. However, arbitration is still relatively uncommon in divorce cases.[120]

Arbitration and mediation procedures are traditionally conducted in private, although parties will sometimes consent to opening them to the press and to the public, and a few states have statutes requiring that arbitration proceedings be public under specific conditions (such as when a governmental entity is an interested party). If you are a journalist doing a story about a dispute, do not hesitate to ask a party whether he or she is willing to talk about the conflict on the record. You can also ask the parties to consent to making the decision public. It is usually fruitless, on the other hand, to question arbitrators because they are bound to neutrality and fairness, and thus it is usually not appropriate for them to make any comments, no matter how objective such statements might be.

Some of the options offered by AAA are *mini-trials* ("a confidential, nonbinding exchange of information, intended to facilitate settlement"), *fact-finding* ("a process by which parties present the arguments and evidence to a neutral person who then issues a nonbinding report on the findings"), and mediation–arbitration (a neutral party serves as both a mediator and an arbitrator).[121]

The U.S. Supreme Court handed ADR proponents two major victories in 1995. The Court ruled 7 to 2 in a decision written by Justice Breyer that Section 2 of the Federal Arbitration Act should be read broadly to include the maximum authority granted Congress to regulate commerce under the Commerce Clause of the U.S. Constitution. *Allied-Bruce Terminix Companies, Inc. and Terminix International v. G. Michael Dobson* (1995)[122] began when Steven Gwin bought a lifetime termite protection policy from a local Allied-Bruce Terminix office. The plan's contract included a typical arbitration clause that said, in part, "any controversy or claim … arising out of or relating to the interpretation, performance or breach of any provision of this agreement shall be settled exclusively by arbitration." Gwin and his wife sold their house to the Dobsons after an inspector from the termite company said there were no termites in the house. The lifetime contract was transferred to the Dobsons upon the sale of the house. The new owners immediately discovered termites and had the termite company treat and repair the house.

Because they were not satisfied with the repairs and treatment, the Dobsons sued the company and the Gwins. The termite company asked the court for a stay to permit arbitration as specified in the contract, but the court denied the request. On appeal, the Alabama Supreme Court upheld the denial on the ground that a state statute made such written, predispute arbitration agreements invalid and also held that the Federal Arbitration Act did not apply even though it contains a provision preempting state law because there was only a minimal connection between the contract and interstate commerce. As the state court saw it, the federal statute applied only if the parties to the contract "contemplated substantial interstate activity" at the time they formed the contract.

The U.S. Supreme Court reversed the Alabama Supreme Court, noting that "the basic purpose of the Federal Arbitration Act is to overcome courts' refusals to enforce agreements to arbitrate." The Court also said that the phrase "involving commerce" in the Act is functionally equivalent to the phrase "affecting commerce" from the Constitution's Commerce Clause. The Court also said that such a broad interpretation is in line with the basic intent of the Act of putting arbitration terms on the "same footing" as the other terms in the contract. The Court concluded:

> States may regulate contracts, including arbitration clauses, under general contract law principles and they may invalidate an arbitration clause *upon such grounds as exist* at law or in equity for the revocation of any contract. 9 U.S.C. §9 (emphasis added). What states may not do is decide that a contract is fair enough to enforce all its terms (price, service, credit), but not fair enough to enforce its arbitration clause. The Act makes any such state policy unlawful, for that kind of policy would place arbitration clauses on an unequal *footing,* directly contrary to the Act's language and Congress's intent. [cite omitted][123]

The Supreme Court continued its support of arbitration less than two months following *Allied-Bruce Terminix* when it voted 8 to 1 (with only Justice Thomas dissenting) to reverse a U.S. Court of Appeals for the Federal Circuit decision upholding a district court ruling that disallowed punitive damages in an arbitration. In *Mastrobuono v. Shearson Lehman Hutton, Inc.,*[124] both lower courts killed the punitive damages because a choice-of-law provision in the contract said that New York law would apply, and New York law allows courts only, not arbitrators, to grant punitive damages. (An arbitration panel had awarded damages to the plaintiffs.)

Citing *Allied-Bruce Terminix,* the Court once again emphasized that its previous decisions make it clear that contract terms involving arbitration, including the award of punitive damages, will be enforced even if they conflict with a state law, thanks to the Federal Arbitration Act. The Court noted that while the agreement did not specifically mention punitive damages, the agreement strongly implied punitive damages were appropriate. Thus the Court resolved the perceived conflict between the choice-of-law provision and the arbitration provision in the contract by interpreting the "laws of New York" phrase to include the substantive principles of state law but not any special rules affecting the authority of arbitrators. If state courts did not get the message from previous decisions, surely they heard the Court this time. This decision loudly and clearly says that when state laws conflict or are interpreted or misinterpreted to conflict with the Arbitration Act, the Act prevails.

In more recent years, the U.S. Supreme Court under Chief Justice John Roberts has backed away somewhat from its favorable rulings toward arbitration in general toward a more pro-business stance. In 2010, for example, the Court handed down three decisions centering on the interpretation of arbitration agreements—*Stolt-Nielsen v. AnimalFeeds,*[125] *Rent-A-Center v. Jackson*[126] and *Granite Rock Co. v. Teamsters.*[127] In *Stolt Nielsen,* the Court decided 5–4 that requiring class arbitration for parties who had not specifically agreed to such arbitration violated the Federal Arbitration Act. Before the lawsuit commenced, the parties in the case had signed an arbitration agreement for settling disputes, but the agreement was silent on class arbitration. The case arose when AnimalFeeds and other customers demanded class arbitration against Stolt-Nielsen, and the arbitrators ruled in favor of such arbitration. Stolt-Nielsen challenged the ruling and the Supreme Court sided with the company.

In *Rent-A-Center,* the Court, in another 5–4 opinion, held that when an arbitration agreement has a provision allowing the arbitrator to determine the enforceability of the agreement, the enforceability of the contract as a whole would be a matter for the arbitrator to determine. However, if a party is challenging the validity of the agreement, the district court would determine the enforceability. The impact of the decision is to better delineate what aspects of an arbitration agreement fall under the jurisdiction of the court and which fall within the purview of the arbitrator(s).

Finally, in *Granite Rock Company,* the Court held that the District Court, not the arbitrator, has the authority to settle a dispute over the actual ratification date in an arbitration agreement.

Summary and Conclusions

Each jurisdiction, whether state or federal, has its own rules of civil procedure, criminal procedure, and evidence that determine the specific steps involved in a civil or criminal case. Most states, however, conform fairly closely to the federal rules, with which any journalist who covers legal matters should become quite familiar. The trial process for a civil matter is similar to that of a criminal case, whereas the pretrial procedures and evidentiary standards are rather different. For example, the typical civil case begins with the filing of a complaint; a criminal case can begin with an arrest, with the prosecutor's filing of an information, or with a grand jury indictment. Both types usually involve discovery whereby the two sides disclose to one another the witnesses, documents, and other evidence expected to be used at trial. In many jurisdictions, the prosecution has an affirmative duty to disclose to the defense any evidence uncovered during the investigation or otherwise found that would aid the defendant at trial. There is obviously no such duty imposed on attorneys in civil cases although a motion to discover is sometimes used to compel the other side to disclose books, records, and other documents relevant to the case.

The three most common evidentiary standards are *preponderance of the evidence* and *clear and convincing evidence* in civil cases and *beyond a reasonable doubt* in criminal cases. For example, in a libel suit by a public figure against a media defendant, the plaintiff must show by clear and convincing evidence that the false information was published with actual malice. In any criminal case, the jury must be convinced beyond a reasonable doubt that defendants committed the alleged crime before it can find them guilty.

Because both civil and criminal trials absorb considerable time and resources including great strain on the courts, more judges and attorneys are using alternative ways of resolving disputes, popularly known as *alternative dispute resolution* (ADR). For criminal cases, the answer to the ever-growing backlog still remains plea bargaining by which a defendant pleads guilty in return for the prosecutor's agreement to ask the judge to reduce the alleged crime to a lesser offense, that the judge be lenient in sentencing, and so on. Viable alternatives in civil cases include minitrials, arbitration, mediation, summary jury trials, and other forms of dispute resolution that are much faster, considerably less expensive, and less burdensome on the participants and the court systems. One downside to ADR is that such proceedings are nearly always closed to the press and to the public even when there is strong public interest in a case. The second concern is that by bypassing the trial process, decisions and settlements in ADR cases set no precedents and thus make no contribution to our understanding and interpretation of law.

Endnotes

1. *See* "U.S. District Courts—Civil Cases Commenced, Terminated, and Pending During the 12-Month Periods Ending March 31, 2009 and 2010," and "U.S. District Courts—Criminal Cases Commenced, Terminated, and Pending (Including Transfers) During the 12-Month Periods Ending March 31, 2009 and 2010," downloadable free at the website for the Administrative Office of the U.S. Courts: http://www.uscourts.gov.
2. *See* Fed. R. Civ. P. 55(b) (2010).
3. *Id.* 4(c).
4. Rule 4(f)(3) allows service at locations outside U.S. jurisdiction such as in a foreign country via any manner "not prohibited by international agreement as may be directed by the court."
5. See Terry Carter, *Cyber-Served: E-Mail Delivery of Lawsuit is OK, 9th Circuit Says*, A.B.A. J. e-Report (Mar. 29, 2002).
6. Fed. R. Civ. P. 11(a) (2010).
7. *Id.* (b)(2).
8. *Id.* (b)(1).
9. *Id.* 8(d).
10. *Id.*
11. *Id.* 8(b).
12. *Id.* 7(a).
13. *Id.* 12(b)(6).
14. *See Anderson v. Liberty Lobby, Inc.*, 477 U.S. 242, 106 S.Ct. 2505, 91 L.Ed.2d. 202 (1986).

15. Fed. R. Civ. P. 12(b)(6) and 12(c) (2010).
16. *Id.* 12(c).
17. *Id.* 12(e).
18. *Id.* 12(f).
19. *Id.* 33(b).
20. *Id.* (c)(2).
21. *Id.* 45(c).
22. *Id.* 26(c).
23. *Id.* 26(c).
24. *Id.* (b)(1)
25. *Id.* 26(b)(3).
26. *Id.*
27. *Swindler & Berlin et al. v. United States,* 524 U.S. 399, 118 S.Ct. 2081, 141 L.Ed.2d 379 (1998).
28. *See* Fed. R. Civ. P. 16(b).
29. *Id.* 16(c).
30. *Id.* 16(e).
31. *See Ross v. Bernhard,* 396 U.S. 531, 90 S.Ct. 733, 24 L.Ed.2d 729 (1970).
32. *Beacon Theatres, Inc. v. Westover,* 359 U.S. 500, 79 S.Ct. 948, 3 L.Ed.2d 988 (1959).
33. *Apodaca v. Oregon,* 400 U.S. 901, 91 S.Ct. 145, 27 L.Ed.2d 138 (1970).
34. *Colgrove v. Battin,* 413 U.S. 149, 93 S.Ct. 2448, 37 L.Ed.2d 522 (1973).
35. Fed. R. Civ. P. 48.
36. *See* Henry J. Reske, *Downward Trends,* 82 A.B.A. J. 24 (Dec. 1996).
37. Marc Davis and Kevin Davis, *Star Rising for Simpson Jury Consultant,* 81 A.B.A. J. 14 (Dec. 1995).
38. *Batson v. Kentucky,* 476 U.S. 79, 106 S.Ct. 1712, 90 L.Ed.2d 69 (1986).
39. §1 states, "nor shall any State deprive any person of life, liberty, or property without due process of law; nor deny to any person within its jurisdiction the equal protection of the laws."
40. *See* Edward D. Tolley and Jason J. *Carter, Striking Out in the Batson Box: A Guide to Non-Discriminatory Jury Selection in Georgia,* 8 Ga. B. J. 13 (Dec. 2002).
41. *J.E.B. v. Alabama ex rel. T.B.,* 511 U.S. 127, 114 S.Ct. 1419 128 L.Ed.2d 89 (1994).
42. The majority cited *Powers v. Ohio,* 499 U.S. 400, 111 S.Ct. 1364, 113 L.Ed.2d 411 (1991); *Edmonson v. Leesville Concrete Corp.,* 500 U.S. 614, 111 S.Ct. 2077, 114 L.Ed.2d 660 (1991); and *Georgia v. McCollum,* 505 U.S. 42, 112 S.Ct. 2348, 120 L.Ed.2d 33 (1992).
43. *J.E.B. v. Alabama ex rel.* T.B.
44. *Id.* (Scalia dissent).
45. *Id.* (Rehnquist dissent).
46. *Purkett v. Elam,* 514 U.S. 765, 115 S.Ct. 1769, 131 L.Ed.2d 834 (1965).
47. *See* Richard C. Reuben, *Excuses, Excuses,* 82 A.B.A.J. 20 (Feb. 1996).
48. *United States v. Martinez-Salazar,* 528 U.S. 304, 120 S.Ct. 774, 145 L.Ed.2d 792 (2000).
49. *Id.*
50. *Miller-El v. Cockrell,* 123 S.Ct. 1029, 154 L.Ed.2d 931 (2003).
51. *Id.,* citing manual titled "Jury Selection in a Criminal Case."
52. *See* Mark Hansen, *Jurors Demand a Speedy Trial,* 81 A.B.A. J. 26 (Mar. 1995).
53. *See Understanding the Federal Courts* downloadable free at the website for the Administrative Office of the U.S. Courts: http://www.uscourts.gov.
54. *Press-Enterprise v. Superior Court,* 464 U.S. 501, 104 S.Ct. 819, 78 L.Ed.2d 629, 10 Med. L.Rptr. 1161 (1984).
55. *Victor v. Nebraska* and *Sandoval v. California,* 511 U.S. 1, 114 S.Ct. 1239, 127 L.Ed.2d 583 (1994).
56. David O. Stewart, *Uncertainty about Reasonable Doubt,* 80 A.B.A. J. 38 (June 1994).
57. James W. McElhaney, *Opening Statements: To Be Effective with the Jury, Tell a Good Story,* 81 A.B.A. J. 73 (Jan. 1995).
58. *Black's Law Dictionary.*
59. *Id.*
60. Fed. R. Evid. 611(c).

61. *Id.* 611(b).

62. James W. McElhaney, *Cross-Examination*, 74 A.B.A. J. 117 (Mar. 1988).

63. *Id.*

64. Fed. R. Evid. 803(1)–(23).

65. *Id.* 804(b)(1)–(5).

66. *See* Fed. R. Civ. P. 50(b).

67. *See Judge Orders Verdict in favor of Blue Shield*, Atlanta Journal-Constitution (Associated Press), May 29, 2009.

68. James W. McElhaney, *Terms of Enlightenment,* 83 A.B.A.J. 82 (May 1997).

69. Marcotte, *The Jury Will Disregard* …, 73 A.B.A. J. 34 (Nov. 1987).

70. Fed. R. Civ. P. 61 and Fed R. Crim. P. 61.

71. *Curtis Publishing Company v. Butts*, 351 F.2d. 702, 388 U.S. 130, 1 Med.L.Rptr. 1568 (5th Cir. 1965).

72. *See* Scott Burgins, *Jurors Ignore, Misunderstand Instructions,* 81 A.B.A. J. 30 (May 1995).

73. *See* M. Hansen, *Juror's Dismissal Debated*, A.B.A. J. 26 (Jan. 1994). The other jurors claimed the woman "doesn't use common sense" and "cannot comprehend anything that we've been trying to accomplish."

74. Fed. R. Civ. P. 49(a).

75. George H. Chamblee, *The Special Verdict: Old Procedure with New Applications*, 1 Ga. B. J. 18 (Oct. 1995).

76. Fed. R. Civ. P. 49(b).

77. *Renico v. Lett*, ___ U.S. ___, 130 S.Ct. 1855, 176 L.Ed.2d 678 (2010).

78. *Id.*

79. *Burnett v. National Enquirer*, 144 Cal.App.3d 991, 193 Cal.Rptr. 206, 9 Med.L.Rptr. 1921 (Cal. App. 1983).

80. *Pring v. Penthouse*, 695 F.2d. 438, 8 Med.L.Rptr. 2409 (10th Cir. 1983).

81. *Honda Motor Co., Ltd., et al. v. Oberg*, 512 U.S. 415, 114 S.Ct. 2331, 129 L.Ed.2d 336 (1994).

82. *Id.*

83. *See* Blodgett, *Longest Trial is Over*, 73 A.B.A. J. 22 (Nov. 1987) and Blodgett, *Longest Trial Verdict In*, 73 A.B.A. J. 34 (Dec. 1987).

84. Dadisman, *What Did You Do in Trial Today, Daddy?*, 14 Barrister 23 (Fall 1987).

85. Blodgett, *Juror Dismissed after 3 Years*, 73 A.B.A. J. 23 (Nov. 1987).

86. Marcotte, *The Longest Trial, Cont.*, 74 A.B.A. J. 30 (Sept. 1988).

87. James R. Laramore, *Final Judgment: The Beginning of the End,* Ky. Bench & Bar (Summer 1994), at 8.

88. *See id.* for a discussion of these procedures. Although the article is written from the perspective of Kentucky law, much of it is relevant to practice in other states.

89. *See* John Gibeaut, *Indictment of a System*, 87 A.B.A. J. 35 (Jan. 2001).

90. *Id.*

91. *Id.*

92. *Id.* at 36.

93. *Miranda v. Arizona,* 384 U.S. 436, 86 S.Ct. 1602, 16 L.Ed.2d 694 (1966).

94. The Miranda warning states: "Before we ask you any questions, you must understand your rights. You have the right to remain silent. Anything you say can and will be used against you in a court of law. You have the right to talk to a lawyer for advice before we ask you any questions and to have him with you during questioning. If you cannot afford a lawyer, one will be appointed for you before any questioning if you wish. If you decide to answer questions now without a lawyer present, you will still have the right to stop answering at any time. You also have the right to stop answering at any time until you talk to a lawyer. Do you understand these rights?"

95. *North Carolina v. Alford*, 400 U.S. 25, 91 S.Ct. 160, 27 L.Ed.2d 162 (1970).

96. *Id.*

97. Hope Viner Samborn, *The Vanishing Trial*, 88 A.B.A. J. 24 (Oct. 2002).

98. *See Understanding the Federal Courts, supra,* note 53.

99. *Ring v. Arizona*, 536 U.S. 584, 122 S.Ct. 2428, 153 L.Ed.2d 556 (2002).

100. *Walton v. Arizona,* 497 U.S. 639, 110 S.Ct. 3047, 111 L.Ed.2d 511 (1990).

101. *Apprendi v. New Jersey*, 530 U.S. 466, 120 S.Ct. 2348, 147 L.Ed.2d 435 (2000).

102. *Id.*

103. U.S. District Judge W. Royal Furgeson of the Western District of Texas, quoted in Hope Viner Samborn, *supra,* note 98.

104. *In Re Strandell v. Jackson County*, 838 F.2d 884 (1987).

105. Marcotte, *No Forced Summary Jury Trials*, 74 A.B.A. J. 32 (Apr. 1988).

106. Postell, *Summary Jury Trials: How Far Can Federal Judges Go?* 24 Trial 91 (May 1988).

107. *In Re Strandell, supra,* note 105.

108. Molly McDonough, *Summary Time Blues*, 90 A.B.A. J. 18 (Oct. 2004).

109. *Id.*

110. *Id.* (summarizing a 1986 University of Chicago Law Review article by Judge Posner).

111. *See The Commonsense Alternative* at the BBB website: http://www.dr.bbb.org.

112. *Id.*

113. *See* Schweber, *You're in Good Company: An Overview of Dispute Resolution Providers*, Cons. Arbitration 6 (Fall 1988) for a description of major ADR providers.

114. *See* 29 U.S.C.A. §172 *et seq.*

115. Schweber, *supra,* note 114 at 6.

116. Carol B. Paisley, *Family Court Mediation*, Ky. Bench & Bar (Nov. 2004), at 26.

117. *Id.*

118. *See* Rules and Procedures: Supplementary Procedures for Consumer-Related Disputes Questions and Answers, at the AAA website: http://www.adr.org.

119. Rachel Emma Silverman, *Making Divorce Quicker, Less Costly*, Wall Street Journal, Oct. 28, 2004, at D-2.

120. *Id.*

121. *See* AAA Glossary of Dispute Resolution Terms at the AAA website: http://www.adr.org.

122. *Allied-Bruce Terminix Companies, Inc. and Terminix International v. G. Michael Dobson,* 513 U.S. 265, 115 S.Ct. 834, 130 L.Ed.2d 753 (1995).

123. *Id.*

124. *Mastrobuono v. Shearson Lehman Hutton, Inc.,* 514 U.S.52, 115 S.Ct. 1212, 131 L.Ed.2d 76 (1995).

125. *Stolte-Nielsen v. AnimalFeeds,* ___ U.S. ___, 130 S. Ct. 1758; 176 L. Ed. 2d 605 (2010).

126. *Rent-A-Center v. Jackson,* ___ U.S. ___, 130 S.Ct. 2772, 177 L.Ed.2d 403 (2010).

127. *Granite Rock Co. v. Teamsters,* ___ U.S. ___, 130 S.Ct. 2847, 177 L.Ed.2d 567 (2010).

4

Ethical Dilemmas, Issues, and Concerns in Mass Communication

*Mike Farrell**

The First Amendment guarantees broad rights to journalists—the government can prevent publication of news only in the most extraordinary circumstances, usually related to national security, and journalists are virtually immune from criminal penalties for criticizing public officials. The First Amendment does not allow the government to license journalists. Doctors, lawyers, teachers, engineers, and other professionals generally face licensing requirements— they must meet certain education standards, agree to follow accepted procedures, and usually attend continuing education classes. If they fail to meet these standards, the government can yank their licenses and forbid them from practicing.

No such requirements exist for journalists. To the dismay of the media's many critics, the First Amendment does not balance those rights and protections by requiring journalists to be responsible. The First Amendment does not force journalists to be fair or balanced, to thoroughly research every story, to report a story within its context, or even to acknowledge and apologize for errors. Many journalism associations, including the Society of Professional Journalists and the Radio–Television Digital News Association (formerly the Radio-Television News Directors Association), have ethics codes, but journalists do not have to belong to such organizations. Following a code of ethics is not a requirement to be a journalist.

The absence of these responsibilities and the performance of the media have undermined public support for the First Amendment and for journalists. A seemingly unending list of public opinion surveys has found that the public holds journalists and the news media in low regard. An analysis of more than 1,000 studies of public opinion about the media conducted between 1986 and 2006 found "there is ample evidence to suggest that Americans at large no longer trust, if they ever did, the American media."[1] In a 2007 Gallup survey, 9% of Americans

---

* Mike Farrell teaches reporting, editing, media law, journalism history and media ethics as an associate professor in the School of Journalism and Telecommunications at the University of Kentucky. He also serves as director of the Scripps Howard First Amendment Center and serves as a member of the Ethics Committee of the Society of Professional Journalists. He worked as a journalist for almost 20 years, the last 11 as managing editor of *The Kentucky Post*. He earned his master's and doctoral degrees in communication from the University of Kentucky.

said they had a great deal of trust and confidence in the mass media to report the news "fully, accurately, and fairly," while 38% said they had a "fair amount" of trust. In 1976, 72% of Americans said they had a great deal or fair amount of trust in the media. The 2007 result, 53%, was nearly identical to the 2004 and 2005 results.[2]

A 2007 survey found that 35% of Americans think the news media care about people, down from 41% in 1985. Fifty-five percent think the news is biased, and 53% think the news is often inaccurate. Only 44% think the press protects democracy, down from 54% in 1985.[3] Study after study has produced similar results: Americans largely do not trust the news media.[4] When the First Amendment Center at Vanderbilt University conducted surveys for its annual "American Attitudes about The First Amendment" report in 2009, it found 39% of those surveyed said the press has too much freedom while only 7% said it has too little. And only 16% could name freedom of the press as one of the five freedoms guaranteed in the First Amendment, while 39% could not name one of the five freedoms—assembly, petition, press, religion, and speech.[5]

An earlier study by the American Society of Newspaper Editors found some lessons about the credibility of journalists:[6]

- The public and the press agree journalists make too many factual errors and spelling or grammar mistakes. Those errors undermine public confidence in newspapers.
- The public believes that newspapers do not consistently demonstrate respect for and knowledge of their readers and communities. Readers believe that journalists are willing to hurt people just to publish a story.
- The public believes that journalists' points of view and biases influence what stories are covered and how they are covered. The public feels that advertisers and people in positions of power maneuver the press to ensure that their viewpoints are presented. At the same time, the less powerful and the underprivileged have little voice. Commenting on the finding, *Editor & Publisher* said, "Americans are coming to the nearly unanimous conclusion that the press is biased, that powerful people and organizations can kill or steer news stories."[7]

Readers believe newspapers over-cover sensational stories because they are exciting and because they sell newspapers. Journalists have responded for years that they are simply giving readers what they want (which, they believe, is why sensational stories sell newspapers.) In broadcast news, a similar theme, emphasizing sensational content—"If it bleeds, it leads"—is heard often. These kinds of assumptions create circular arguments and negative feedback that fail to address the issues or settle the debate.

The public believes journalists are too quick to invade the privacy of individuals. The public says journalists should hold a story until facts can be double-checked for accuracy, the names of suspects should not be published until charges are filed, and long-ago transgressions of public officials should be overlooked.

These surveys illustrate what journalists have long known: The public does not like the way a lot of journalists practice their profession. In an earlier study, University of Oklahoma Professor Charles Self examined reasons behind public distrust of the media.[8] He listed four:

- insensitivity, arrogance, and generally bad behavior of journalists
- stories that are inaccurate, incomplete, or reflect poor reporting practices

- disapproval of the type of news that reporters write about and their overall news judgment
- disagreements over the task of news in the life of the reader: whether the most important task of a news report is to give facts objectively, explain the facts, or report all sides of a story fairly

Media critics recognize that good journalism is difficult and journalists fall short of ethical ideals for a number of reasons that do not add up to deliberate lapses:

> We do not mean to imply that journalists are a morally defective lot. American journalists, both print and electronic, are often fair, competent, even altogether virtuous. They are sometimes criticized indiscriminately, perhaps as a result of inflated expectations, and many of their failures are understandable in context. Given the catch-it-on-the-fly nature of daily journalism, it would be unreasonable to expect the total output of even a generally competent and fair-minded group of professionals to be uniformly satisfactory. Journalism being what it is, even the most virtuous journalists, operating from what they view as the best of motives, inevitably will produce some morally unsatisfactory results.[9]

In his book on media ethics, French professor Claude-Jean Bertrand wrote, "Paradoxically, the media are accused of every sin at a time when they have never been better." Still, Bertrand labeled the media's performance "mediocre."[10]

The Bad Old Days

An ethical profile of journalists from 1850 to 1950 found instances of reporters who accepted—and sometimes demanded—free theater tickets, liquor, and meals.[11] Another reporter who needed a raise to support his family was offered the opportunity to write the book review column and told he could sell the books he did not want.

Fred Fedler's research also found that reporters often resorted to deception to obtain information for stories: some posed as police officers. A New York City reporter obtained a firefighter's uniform so he could inspect theaters and write a story about the poorly constructed dressing rooms and firetraps backstage. Some reporters were quick to eavesdrop, even showing up unannounced outside a hotel room to listen before seeking an interview. During the early part of the 20th century, some reporters accepted second jobs as press agents, while ambulance-chasing lawyers looking for clients constantly approached others. Fedler found one reporter who said he was promised $50 for each accident case he found and another $50 if the attorney won the case. According to Fedler, the reasons reporters gave for behavior that was often illegal and certainly unethical included:

- beating the competition
- belief that obtaining information was so important it justified any means
- fear for their jobs
- belief that other professions included people who followed the same practices
- low salaries
- loyalty to their editors and newspapers

- a culture that failed to condemn such practices as unethical
- bad examples set by many of the people they covered[12]

Even though reporters today work in a world with totally different ethical expectations, some journalists are far from satisfied with the way their craft is practiced. Magazine editor James Fallows warned that journalism must change or it will destroy itself and democracy. He reported, "Americans believe that the news media have become too arrogant, cynical, scandal-minded, and destructive."[13]

Howard Kurtz, then a media critic for CNN and the *Washington Post*, accused the media of arrogance and hypocrisy: "While news organizations make their living pointing fingers and hurling accusations, they are notoriously slow to 'fess up to their own mistakes. With varying degrees of stubbornness, stupidity and arrogance, media executives often circle the wagons when their own actions come under scrutiny."[14]

The Credibility Factor

Stupidity and arrogance, however, are not the most troubling issues for journalists. The too-frequent lapses of ethical practice by those who call themselves journalists undermine public confidence in the news media. Obviously, when the public has little trust in the media, the effort to publish news the public finds credible becomes much more difficult. One ethicist wrote, "This problem of credibility is extremely important, especially to journalists. If their stories cannot be believed, then the whole of journalism is on a shaky foundation."[15] Dave Aeikins, president of the Society of Professional Journalists in 2009, addressed the issue in *Quill*. "The public needs professionally reported and written information so it can make important decisions in their lives. If the public does not trust or believe what it reads or hears on the news, then we as journalists are finished."[16]

At a time when the newspaper industry is under increasing economic pressure as readers and advertisers migrate to the Internet, recovering the public trust becomes an even more daunting undertaking.[17]

Journalism credibility is tied directly to the perception that journalists are ethical. Ethics is the study of journalistic behavior, specifically the right and wrong of how journalists do their jobs. It involves defining the values of the individual, organization, profession, and society and using those values as a basis of human behavior.[18] It is not the same as morality.

Ethics is related to duty—duty to self, duty to community, duty to profession, and duty in this case to the First Amendment. Ethical behavior involves a choice, sometimes choosing one good over another, sometimes choosing to do wrong in order to accomplish some good. For example, would it be ethical to get a job as a janitor in a courthouse so you could search for a report that might prove a prosecutor is accepting money to dismiss drunken driving charges? Taking bribes is certainly illegal and a violation of the public trust. But are there ethical limits on how a reporter should gather the information needed to expose such behavior? Many times, the more important a story becomes, the more obstacles reporters encounter trying to gather the information for the story. At some point, a reporter who suspects something illegal or unethical is going on inside the government but cannot prove it may consider whether some surreptitious tactic is justified in catching someone who has been betraying the public trust.

Journalism has been beset by ethical problems that have over the years eroded the credibility of journalists. Some examples of ethical issues arising in recent years follow.

At a meeting of then-Secretary of Defense Donald Rumsfeld and troops in Kuwait in December 2004, a soldier asked Rumsfeld why some of the vehicles used by troops in Iraq lacked armor. A reporter for the *Chattanooga* (Tenn.) *Times Free Press* embedded with a Tennessee National Guard unit played a role in formulating the question. He also tried to make sure that the soldier was called upon during the question-and-answer session in which only soldiers were allowed to question the defense secretary. In his story about the soldier's question that made national headlines, the reporter failed to disclose his role in the incident.[19]

CBS News acknowledged in September 2004 that it could not vouch for the authenticity of documents it used to support a *60 Minutes II* segment—repeated on the *CBS Evening News*—alleging that former military superiors of President George W. Bush had been asked to "sugarcoat" his performance evaluations during the Vietnam era. The documents also purported to show that as a young officer, Bush ignored direct orders to complete a physical exam. Almost immediately, document experts questioned the veracity of the documents used to support the allegations, supposedly written by his late squadron leader. It was pointed out, for example, that the memos appeared to have been created by a computer, not a manual typewriter from the 1970s. While Dan Rather, anchor of *CBS Evening News*, later apologized for the use of bogus memos as support, CBS President Andrew Heyward appointed an investigative committee to uncover how the hoax had taken place.[20] Before the committee returned its 224-page report, Rather announced he was stepping down from the anchor's desk, a position he had held for 24 years.[21] CBS subsequently fired three top executives and a producer.[22]

The top editors of the *New York Times*—Executive Editor Howell Raines and Managing Editor Gerald Boyd—resigned in June 2003 amid a scandal that developed the previous month when 27-year-old reporter Jayson Blair was exposed for journalistic fraud at the paper. In the same month, 43-year-old Pulitzer Prize-winning reporter Rick Bragg had resigned after being suspended for publishing a story under his byline that had been mainly reported by a freelance writer who was not credited. In a four-page investigative report, the *Times* revealed that Blair included fabrications, inaccuracies, plagiarism, and other serious errors in at least 36 of the 73 articles he had written for the newspaper during a six-month period. Fourteen months before Raines and Boyd stepped down, the *Times* under their leadership had won a record seven Pulitzers, all but one for its coverage of the terrorist attacks on September 11, 2001.[23]

Three of the nation's most respected newspapers—the *New York Times*, the *Washington Post,* and the *Wall Street Journal*—agreed in 2000 to accept details about a proposed $5 billion merger between two of the nation's major airlines provided they broke the story without calling outside sources for details. The deal fell apart when another media outlet broke the story using its own independent reporting.[24]

The *Cincinnati Enquirer* published a comprehensive expose on Chiquita, the banana company, accusing it of unethical business practices in Central America—bribing foreign officials, mistreating workers and evading foreign laws—only to retract its story days later. The newspaper paid Chiquita $14 million because the story had been based, in part, on information stolen from the company voice mail system.[25] What makes the incident more complicated ethically is that the lead reporter on the Chiquita story not only revealed the identity of his confidential source, but he also pleaded guilty in exchange for his testimony against his source, a former Chiquita lawyer who was accused of telling the reporter how to access the Chiquita voice mail.[26]

The top news executive of CNN acknowledged in an opinion piece in the *New York Times* that the television network had for years failed to report some of the atrocities its correspondents witnessed in Iraq under the regime of Saddam Hussein because he feared Saddam Hussein would close the Baghdad office. Eason Jordan wrote, for example, that he never reported that Saddam Hussein's eldest son had told him in 1995 that he planned to kill two of his brothers-in-law who had defected because he was sure the Iraqis would have responded by killing the Iraqi translator.[27] (A few months later, Uday Hussein "lured the brothers-in-law back to Baghdad; they were soon killed.")

The editor of the *Salt Lake Tribune* fired two reporters after he learned they had received $20,000 from the *National Enquirer* for selling the tabloid "salacious rumors" related to the kidnapping of Elizabeth Smart, rumors the *Tribune* never printed. After the firings, the editor also resigned in 2003 because he said the newsroom had lost faith in him.[28]

NBC's *Dateline* reported that the gasoline tanks of GMC pick-up trucks built between 1973 and 1987 were prone to fire and explosion during accidents. As part of the 15-minute segment that aired November 17, 1992, *Dateline* showed an empty pick-up truck bursting into flames after a collision. NBC later acknowledged that the explosion viewers witnessed was staged. The gas tank was filled to the brim, the gas cap was defective, and a toy rocket had been rigged to ensure the tank exploded and was activated by a remote device just before the staged crash.[29]

In the aftermath of Hurricane Katrina in 2005, one of the worst natural disasters to hit the United States, the media were widely criticized for publishing and broadcasting incorrect information and uncorroborated rumors that officials later said delayed the relief efforts. Lt. Gen. Russel L. Honore, commander of Joint Task Force Katrina, told the *Washington Post* that reporters got bogged down trying to tell people how bad the situation was rather than "gathering facts and corroborating that information." The *Post* also reported that officials told reporters that accounts of widespread looting, gunfire directed at helicopters, homicides, rapes, and life-or-death struggles at the Louisiana Superdome frequently turned out to be overblown and even untrue.[30]

But the presidential election in November 2000 proved to be one of the media's worst moments. The television networks prematurely projected that then-Vice President Al Gore had won the electoral votes of Florida that would have ensured his election, only to withdraw that prediction two hours later after then-Texas Gov. George W. Bush on television told the networks and the nation that the projection was wrong. Several hours later, the networks went the other way, announcing Gov. Bush had won Florida and the presidency, only to withdraw that announcement a short time later. The debacle brought a reprimand from the Society of Professional Journalists. The co-chairman of SPJ's Ethics Committee, Gary Hill, a broadcast journalist, said journalists failed to follow a central tenet of SPJ's Code of Ethics: act independently. "Election night 2000 was another chance for the national media to reaffirm its central role in our democracy, and it was a chance for journalists to wrap themselves in glory, to regain some of their lost credibility, but it didn't work out that way," Hill said in an SPJ release.[31]

It probably did not surprise a survey team for the Freedom Forum a few months later that 80% of those they questioned opposed the right of television networks to project winners of an election while people are still voting.[32]

Public confidence in the media—which seems to rely in great part on a perception that the media are ethical—is critical today, critical to the health of a democracy. Most information that citizens glean about public issues comes through the media either directly—they read newspapers or Internet websites, watch TV news shows, listen to radio—or indirectly by talking with someone who read a story, saw a show, or listened to a program. The practice of a town turning out to hear a prominent citizen extol the virtues of his party's candidate for president or member of Congress is as much a part of history as the Model T Ford.

The Foundation of Ethics

Any discussion of journalism ethics should begin with the First Amendment. While the courts have found that freedom of the press does not carry with it all the ethical responsibilities that its critics would like it to require, democracy requires a free press. As President Lincoln framed it in his Gettysburg Address in 1863, the theory of democracy is that government is "of the people, by the people, for the people." Citizens established the government by ceding to it the authority to rule over them. Citizens participate in their government by electing those who will represent their convictions in the debates of important issues that require government actions. Finally, the government exists solely for the benefit of citizens, the governed, and not the governors.

The role journalists play in this citizen-based democracy is as essential as the role the courts play. The preamble to the Code of Ethics of the Society of Professional Journalists (see www.spj.org/ethicscode.asp) explains that the duty of journalists is to further justice and democracy "by seeking truth and providing a fair and comprehensive account of events and issues."

The media play major roles in a democracy. The first is the informative role. Journalists inform citizens of what is happening in the world, in the community, in their government. Citizens must understand the issues and the problems confronting society. They need to know what their elected representatives are doing about those problems. Another role is deliberation. The press publishes stories about issues and points of view so that they can be debated. A third is the agenda-setting role. The press calls attention to pressing public issues that editors and reporters believe should be addressed. A fourth is the watchdog role. The press examines critically what the governors are doing so that they do not abuse the trust of those who elected them.

Inform and Entertain

The news media function as a political institution to inform and to entertain citizens. This is essential for democracy; citizens who participate in their government need information on the issues, the actions of their governors, and the outcomes of government's decisions. The media also allow the government to speak to citizens. The president can address a community luncheon and speak to not only the 500 people in the hall but also to the entire nation via the media. The governor addresses the state legislature, and the next day newspaper readers all across the state who didn't watch it live can learn what he said.

The informative role is essential in a democracy for citizens to play their proper role in their government and for their individual well-being. How would citizens know a city government was going to raise the payroll tax if the news media didn't report it? Surely no one thinks that city officials would send a letter to taxpayers inviting them to city hall to express their opinions about raising taxes. Most city councils would shudder at the thought of even 50 people coming to a council meeting to debate an issue.

The idea that New York City could host a town meeting to debate a tax increase is as fictional as any novel on the best-seller list. The city does not have a stadium or meeting hall large enough to house even a small share of eight million people. How would citizens know that a deadly disease had broken out in the United States if the media did not report it? It is difficult to protect yourself against a danger if no one has informed you about that danger. Providing information is the most basic function of the press.

The Marketplace of Ideas

In a democratic system of government like the United States, the free expression of ideas is essential. Hidden behind the political infighting of the Republican and Democratic parties are basic differences in the philosophies of those parties. For example, Democrats generally believe that government can help solve societal problems. Republicans generally believe that individuals singly and collectively can do a better job of that. Debating those philosophies is the essence of American politics.

The media function as a forum in which political parties and others can debate important issues and how they should be addressed. Essential to this role is the independence of the media from government. Freedom of the press, as embodied in the First Amendment and interpreted by the courts, is essential because government officials usually have some stake in the outcome of a public debate and because giving government exclusive access to the channels of communication—as happens in authoritarian governments—necessarily forces other voices and ideas to seek underground media.

First Amendment scholar Richard Labunski argues that the protection given freedom of expression by American courts is essential to democratic government. According to Labunski, "The special position that the First Amendment is granted in our system is recognition of the paramount importance of the free exchange of ideas to self-government. Freedom of speech and press provisions of the First Amendment are designed to prevent interference with the exchange of information if citizens are to make intelligent decisions when choosing public officials and shaping policy."[33]

The forum for political debate—the so-called marketplace of ideas—represents the democratic ideal that in political debate, many voices will be heard and no voice will be silenced in the search for truth. The assumption is that in the end, the best idea will prevail in the debate. The marketplace of ideas, while not an American creation, has been elevated to the capstone of democracy and individual liberty by a long string of judicial decisions. This metaphor is based on the assumption that if citizens are to be seen as governing through those whom they elect, citizens must be informed. According to James Madison, who played a central role in the constitutional convention and the drafting of the Bill of Rights, political speech is a means to further the ideal of deliberative democracy.[34]

The marketplace of ideas is rooted in the work of John Milton in his 1644 work *Areopagitica*. This passage underscores Milton's objection to a 1643 act of Parliament that required government licensing before something could be published, a process of overt censorship:

> And though all the winds of doctrine were let loose to play upon the earth, so Truth be
> in the field, we do injuriously by licensing and prohibiting, to misdoubt her strength.
> Let her and Falsehood grapple, who ever knew Truth put to the worse, in a free and
> open encounter.

Milton's theory, labeled the self-righting principle, was simple: expose people to the truth and to false arguments and the truth will win out every time. So strong is truth, Milton wrote in *Areopagitica,* that truth needs no authoritative champion in the marketplace of ideas. No reason existed for government censorship because lies would always be exposed and ultimately discounted. It must be noted, however, that Milton felt free speech had its limits. He did not want it extended to those who disagreed with his religious beliefs.

British philosophers John Locke and John Stuart Mill advanced Milton's theory of censorship. Mill insisted that freedom of thought, discussion, and investigation were goods in their own right, and that in the end, the open exchange of ideas benefits society above all else. Mill, considered by some the father of liberalism, argued that repression may interfere with society's ability to seek truth. First, if the censored opinion contains truth, its silencing will lessen the chance of discovering that truth. Second, if each conflicting opinion contains part of the truth, the clash between them is the only method of discovering the contribution of each toward the whole of the truth. Third, even if the accepted opinion contains the whole truth, the public tends to hold it as a prejudice unless forced to defend it. In Mill's view, expressed in *On Liberty,* every idea has some societal value and therefore deserves protection from the government. According to Mill:

> If all mankind minus one were of one opinion, mankind would be no more justified in silencing that one person than he, if he had the power, would be justified in silencing mankind. Were an opinion a personal possession of no value except to the owner; if to be obstructed in the enjoyment of it were simply a private injury, it would make some difference whether the injury was inflicted only on a few persons or on many. But the peculiar evil of silencing the expression of an opinion is, that it is robbing the human race; posterity as well as the existing generation; those who dissent from the opinion, still more than those who hold it.

Nearly 300 years later, Milton's self-righting principle was recast into a 20th-century metaphor and introduced into American jurisprudence. The marketplace of ideas, despite numerous criticisms, today guides American thought and Supreme Court decisions about the First Amendment freedoms of expression.[35]

U.S. Supreme Court Justice Oliver Wendell Holmes introduced the concept of the marketplace of ideas in a decision, albeit a dissenting one, in a World War I free speech case. Holmes, in one of the most famous high court reversals of philosophy, changed his position in just a few months. He moved from writing a majority decision upholding the repression of free expression to writing a dissenting opinion that advocated for greater meaning for the First Amendment.[36]

But the marketplace analogy is often criticized.[37] One of the major objections has been that the analogy is utopian and impractical because of the barriers to having everyone's voice heard in the market. Other commentators question whether Holmes' analogy is a fitting one and whether a free trade in ideas is likely to identify the best course of action. Critics ask whether the marketplace is truly representative when the voice of the poor is hard to hear because of monopolistic practices, unequal distribution of resources, and limitations of communication technology. But other weaknesses are also apparent. If people cannot hear the debate or understand the arguments, or if people cannot articulate ideas in order that they can be understood, the marketplace does not function well.

As many critics have observed, while the First Amendment protects the media from government control, the media have become almost partners with government, so closely are journalists tied to reporting the actions of government through the eyes of the officials who make those decisions. Despite these weaknesses, the role of the press in maintaining a forum for public debate is a key element of the freedoms enjoyed by Americans. That role also makes the First Amendment essential.

Agenda Setting

A third important role is agenda setting, the power of the media to broadcast and publish stories about issues, resulting in widespread public attention to those issues. Stated another way, it is not the power of the media to tell citizens what to think but to tell citizens what to think about.

Journalist Walter Lippmann, a scholar of public opinion and propaganda, noted in the 1920s that ordinary people had limited opportunities to see important events first-hand and they were thus dependent on the media to provide them accounts of these events. In *Public Opinion*, Lippmann wrote about "The World Outside and the Pictures in our Heads." His thesis was that the media serve as the principal connections between what transpires in the world and the pictures of those events drawn in our heads.

Professors Maxwell McCombs and Donald Shaw, then at the University of North Carolina, coined the term "agenda setting."[38] They studied voter information sources during the 1968 presidential election featuring Richard Nixon, the Republican; Hubert Humphrey, the Democrat; and George Wallace, the independent. McCombs and Shaw selected 100 undecided voters in Chapel Hill, North Carolina, and personally interviewed each of them during a three-week period before the election. They were asked, "What are you most concerned about these days? That is, regardless of what politicians say, what are the two or three main things that you think the government should concentrate on doing something about?" Five main themes—foreign policy, law and order, fiscal policy, public welfare, and civil rights—emerged as the major concerns.

The researchers then analyzed the subjects of the election campaign news stories in the nine media outlets—five newspapers, two network TV news broadcasts, and two weekly news magazines—that served Chapel Hill. What they found when they compared the two lists was that the concerns of the voters almost identically matched the subjects of the media reports.[39]

The study, of course, had its weaknesses, but it was ground-breaking. Some 350 studies on agenda-setting effects of the media were published in the 25 years after the North Carolina study, and many more in the past decade and a half. Those studies support the theory that a strong correlation exists between what issues the media tell their audiences are important and what eventually becomes an issue the public recognizes as important.[40] Agenda-setting theory was a major turning point in communications research because it focused the attention of researchers on the process by which the media play a significant part in generating a common culture.

Agenda setting allows the media to call attention to issues needing public attention that otherwise might go unaddressed. Nursing home abuses and deteriorating education systems are only two of the many issues that have been spotlighted over the years by the media.

The gate-keeping function of the media is a corollary; i.e., from the many happenings of a day, the media choose events, issues, and people and present them as the most important information for the news consumer on that particular day. Reporters and editors choose what events they will report and what events they will ignore. They are faced daily with more stories to cover than time in which to cover them. Most reporters have "to-do" lists of stories already assigned to them by editors or lists of ideas of their own. Assignment editors daily receive press releases or news alerts by mail, by fax, and by electronic messaging urging coverage of some announcement or event. Government hearings, commission meetings, and legislative sessions abound. And the judiciary offers an endless stream of human stories that are told through court filings, indictments, arraignments, and trials. The dilemma is not one of finding enough to fill a news hole or telecast; the dilemma is having enough reporting and editing time to prepare stories.

It is an oversimplification to say, however, that the media decide alone or in isolation what the news is. Politicians use the media as well to help set the public agenda by serving as sources for news stories and by convincing reporters of the importance of certain issues. Indeed, political actors anticipate what actions and words will increase the chance that journalists will cover a story and tailor their actions accordingly. The three separate branches of government and the actors in both political parties use the media to send signals to each other and to fight their ideological and political battles. There is a significant reason that Washington overflows with men and women whose jobs are to serve as media representatives for elected officials and government agencies.

Today's media environment, with blogs, Twitter and Facebook accounts, offers countless avenues for those who don't work for media outlets the opportunity to draw attention to their own "news items."

Watchdog Function

The media report on the government. It is as simple as that. A basic rule of human behavior is that when people believe they are accountable, they do a better job. Or, put another way, power corrupts. When public officials think no one is looking, they are capable of abusing their power. When a city government passes a budget, a good reporter will examine that budget to see how the money is going to be spent. By reporting what she finds, she helps ensure that the city government is accountable to the taxpayers. When police arrest a suspect and he appears in court with a couple of black eyes, reporters will ask how it happened. Police abuse is not unheard of, although force is sometimes necessary in subduing people. And prisoners do fight with other prisoners.

Another watchdog role involves uncovering conflicts of interest. The Washington media today pay a great deal of attention to the connections of people and special interest groups who help fund election campaigns and the types of legislation elected candidates support. Congressional budget bills are examined so that reporters can find deep in the fine print special interest legislation that benefits someone who made sure the budget chairman received thousands of dollars in campaign contributions.

One of the most-cited examples of the watchdog function is the scandal known as Watergate. Reporters traced what appeared to be nothing more than a minor burglary in the Democratic offices in the Watergate Hotel all the way to the office of the president, and Richard Nixon stepped down as the nation's chief executive.[41]

These roles of the media in a democracy—informing and entertaining, creating a marketplace of ideas, agenda-setting and watchdog—were pointed out by the Supreme Court of the United States in 1966:

> Whatever differences may exist about interpretations of the First Amendment, there is practically universal agreement that a major purpose of that Amendment was to protect the free discussion of governmental affairs.... Thus the press serves and was designed to serve as a powerful antidote to any abuses of power by governmental officials and as a constitutionally chosen means for keeping officials elected by the people responsible to all the people whom they were selected to serve. Suppression of the right of the press to praise or criticize governmental agents and to clamor and contend for or against change ... muzzles one of the very agencies the Framers of our Constitution thoughtfully and deliberately selected to improve our society and keep it free.[42]

If the First Amendment does not demand that journalists carry out their responsibilities in an ethical manner, the relationship of journalism and democracy certainly does. The essential roles journalists play require them to be ethical. Citizens must be informed in a democracy; if those citizens do not find the media credible or if the media do not report in an ethical manner, democracy as it exists in the United States will be in trouble.

What also should not be overlooked here is that journalists play a significant role in American political life and that they wield a powerful tool. After almost 100 years of research on the effects media have on its readers or viewers, scholars are divided over the extent of that impact. Lippmann's "pictures in our heads" statement is worth enlarging. The media help people construct their view of the world through the images portrayed in newspapers and on the television news. In fact, the media are responsible for the perceptions most people have of the world beyond their own experiences.

If the media focus disproportionately on crime, if they splash murder after murder on the front page or at the top of each newscast and fail to point out that the number of murders is actually 25% lower than at the same time last year, news consumers grow more concerned about safety and critical of their city leaders who are failing to deliver on their pledges of safe communities. If the media focus their coverage on white leaders, white business officials, white schools, and the white community, readers and viewers will fail to understand they live in a diverse community. Even those who refuse to read newspapers or show no interest in television news will learn of these perceptions through their families, friends, and coworkers who do pay attention to the media.

Why Journalism's Ethical Problems Are Different

Ethical problems are not exclusive to journalists. Public officials, lawyers, doctors, the clergy, law enforcement professionals, scientists, and educators all encounter ethical dilemmas. Two factors, however, make journalism ethics different.

First, journalists are able to shape public values and mold public opinion about the values to which they should be held on a broader scale. Journalists cover and comment on the ethical dilemmas and lapses of others daily as part of their job. This is critical because certain elements of the media have tended to have undue influence. And lapses by the *New York Times* and *60 Minutes*, for example, two of the most respected elements of the American mass media, have led to widespread dissent and second-guessing. For the media, however, no "other" voice critiques its work in a way that can influence public opinion to the same extent. Politicians who take on the media do not often succeed. Media purists argue that the media should critique themselves and report on their own lapses. But the media's poor performance on Election Day 2000 received little public airing as the media rushed to cover the unsettled election between George W. Bush and Al Gore.

Second and conversely, the choices lawyers, doctors, police, prosecutors, and the others make as results of the dilemmas they face come under public scrutiny only occasionally. While politicians and business people may commit their ethical lapses behind closed doors, the media's lapses are often plastered across the front page or recounted on the evening news. As a result of the pervasive reach of media today, the public has become increasingly suspicious of the way reporters and editors do their jobs. As one media ethics text points out:

> How well journalists have met their responsibilities is a judgment call open to scrutiny with the production of every story. The primary news critics—the subjects and consumers of the resulting news story—do not hesitate to voice judgments about the rights and wrongs of journalistic action. Thus, the practice of journalism ethics begins. No other professional behavior is as open to scrutiny by those working in the profession, those who are used by the profession, and those who consume the final products.[43]

The Internet has brought increased accountability to journalism as well. Much of the questioning of journalism ethics was once left to politicians, ethics textbooks and academic reviews, the *Columbia Journalism Review* and *American Journalism Review*. Some newspapers have hired an ombudsman or a public editor, Howard Kurtz covered the media as a beat for *The Washington Post* for 20 years, and PBS, NPR, CNN, and Fox News all have focused on the industry and its problems.

Since 1999, Jim Romenesko, a senior online reporter at the Poynter Institute, has brought media controversies to public attention almost instantly.[44] "What's new," one commentator wrote in 2005, "is the way the Romenesko megaphone distributes the news of these offenses, allowing journalists to box their peers' ears while the subject is still green in memory." That instant criticism is widely known as "The Romenesko Effect."[45]

The column, subtitled "Your daily fix of media industry news, commentary, and memos," serves as "an ad hoc, post-publication, peer review mechanism for the journalism profession. It also contributes to journalistic transparency. No newsroom memo or in-house letter of any consequence circulates inside a newspaper for very long before being posted on 'Romenesko Memos' or 'Romenesko Misc.'"[46] Its widespread distribution means news of the latest plagiarism accusation zips from coast to coast at the speed of light.

Other online sites also serve as clearinghouses for news emanating from the profession: The Daily Briefing by the Project for Excellence in Journalism,[47] Mediabistro.com[48] with its "Morning Newsfeed" and blogs, I Want Media[49] with its emphasis on the business of news, and CJRDaily,[50] a site born from *Columbia Journalism Review*.[51] "Regret The Error: Mistakes Happen" is a website that reports on media mistakes, including a yearly round-up on mistakes and corrections.[52]

But the cry for journalistic responsibility is much older than the Internet. It dates back decades. In response to concerns about the printed press, the Hutchins Commission, comprised of an impressive array of scholars and experts, issued a report in 1947 that listed five requirements for a responsible press. "The five requirements (listed below) suggest what our society is entitled to demand of its press," the report said.[53]

- "A truthful, comprehensive and intelligent account of the day's events in context which gives them meaning." In other words, the media's reporting must be accurate. Reporters and editors must also be trained and competent, able to choose the most authoritative sources for a story and to separate fact from opinion.
- "A forum for the exchange of comment and criticism." The media must view themselves as carriers of public discussion, willing to publish viewpoints contrary to their own.
- "The projection of a representative picture of the constituent groups in the society." The media should portray society as the pluralistic mix that it is, not ignoring members of any race, gender or religion. At the same time, reporting should not fall into stereotypical roles.
- "The presentation and clarification of the goals and values of the society." The media, recognized for reporting heavily on the failings of people and government, should assume an educational role in clarifying the ideas toward which a democratic community should strive.
- "Full access to the day's intelligence." Citizens in a modern society require vast amounts of information. That information should not be available only to a few but the media should widely disseminate it.

The report of the Hutchins Commission was not welcomed by all members of the media. The report concluded that the press must be accountable if it was to remain free. Publishers and editors, who were not part of the commission, argued that any involvement of the government in an effort to achieve responsibility would involve government authority.[54] Journalists, of course, believe that the First Amendment guarantees the press would remain free of government controls. But one result of that report was the creation of the position of newspaper ombudsman, an employee who critiqued the newspapers' performance and listened to and evaluated complaints from readers and those who were subjects of stories.

Another factor in the public's perception of unethical media is related to the growing breadth of media outlets. As the 20th century dawned, the public depended solely on the newspapers for news. Twenty years later, along came radio and before long stations began reporting the news. Thirty years after that, television was born and owners soon found they could make money producing news. Cable television came next, and around-the-clock news resulted, along with competition with and among the three major television networks.

Soon entertainment news filled the network line-ups. The century ended with the birth of the Internet and the capacity for almost anyone to set up a Web page filled with "news," even if some of that news is, as critics maintain, biased opinion masquerading as news. Today, the "word" is social networking, with websites like MySpace and Facebook and instantaneous news feeds to your iphone.

Online journalists often work far outside the code of ethics that more traditional journalists and media outlets endorse. Still, they claim to be "media" and the public does not always draw or perceive a line when expressing disgust with the ethics of those who provide information. People with conservative philosophies rail against what they perceive as the liberal bent of some media outlets while people with liberal philosophies rail against what they perceive as the conservative bent of others.

Approaches to Ethics

A number of approaches exist for ethical decision-making. One system classifies the approaches as teleological and deontological. Teleological principles measure the ethical nature of a decision by weighing the alternatives, considering the consequences and speculating about the outcomes. The ethical decision is the one that produces the greater good, presumably for the most people, or alternatively, the greater good for the decision-maker. Stealing is not wrong when it means a starving child gets food. Lying is not wrong if it means a would-be killer is misled about the whereabouts of an intended victim.

Journalists go about their work reporting and editing with the intent of serving society, providing information they believe is essential for citizens. One of the attractions of this form of ethics is its process. It assumes journalists are thinking people who carefully weigh alternatives and choose courses that are most beneficial to society or the community. It exalts the role of a journalist.

But critics argue that a teleological approach requires some form of omniscience. The decision-maker must be able to accurately predict the outcomes of the choices in order to make the right decision. For example, reporter Smith learns that police have figured out that a serial killer lures victims from a particular park and strikes only on the third Friday of the month just after sundown. Police beg the reporter not to print this information because it will warn the killer that police have figured out his modus operandi.

But not printing the story also means that unsuspecting park-goers are at risk. If the reporter cooperates with police and the serial killer is caught before another victim dies, then not running the story appears to have been the right decision. But if the killer strikes the next time on the second Friday and lures a victim from the same park, or strikes a victim on the third Friday in a different section of the park, the reporter's decision had a horrifying outcome. Even if withholding the information ultimately led to the serial killer's capture, the death of an additional victim makes the reporter's decision not to warn the public at best highly problematic and at worst a blatant betrayal of the reporter's public trust.

On the other hand, if the reporter prints the information and the serial killer begins luring victims from another park because he knows the police are onto him, the reporter has again acted in a way that appears to have contributed to the deaths of others.

Another teleological dilemma occurs if the reporter learns the modus operandi from a regular source, a police investigator who discloses the information during a conversation he believes is confidential as similar ones have been in the past. Now the reporter must decide whether the greater good is served by betraying the confidence of a source with the intention of warning the public and scooping the competition or by protecting the source and relying on the police to prevent another murder.

But what if the reporter recognizes that this scoop would likely bring a pay raise as newsroom evaluations are just around the corner? The reporter must decide whether the greater good outweighs his possible advantage, regardless of the consequences to the investigator or the seemingly unlikely result that someone's life could be in danger.

By its nature, journalism (and the journalist, by extension) is supposed to serve the public, so any ethical dilemma in which a reporter or editor chooses personal gain ahead of societal good is unethical journalism.

By contrast, the deontological approach looks not at the results but at the nature of the act itself. It holds that some activities are inherently wrong. To lie, to deceive, to kill, to steal, for example, are all wrong. The deontological approach is generally grounded in faith or religion, in the belief that God has fixed some behavior as wrong and transmitted that decree to human beings through sacred writings such as the Bible, the Torah, or the Koran, or a religion's prophets.

In turn, a journalist sees his duty as doing that which is right in the pursuit of the story. For a deontologist, the end never justifies the means. It is wrong to lie, so a reporter should never give someone his word that he will keep information confidential and then print it. At the same time, journalists believe they have an obligation to present the news, not to withhold it. If publishing or broadcasting a story has unpleasant consequences, the outcome is outside the journalist's responsibility. The public depends upon the media to report information and report it accurately. Journalists are not in the business of keeping secrets from the public.

A journalist who follows the deontological approach would present the information to the public that the police had figured out how the serial killer operates *unless* he had received the information in a confidential manner. Even then, he would struggle to convince the source to allow him to write the story so that the public could be warned of the danger.

Journalism is not a profession practiced by bodies lacking consciences, souls, or values. A reporter's own values are tested repeatedly in ethical dilemmas.

Many reporters studied to be journalists because of deep personal commitments to truth, justice, freedom, and humanitarianism. Some of the nation's most revered journalists are associated with these traits and values. Those personal values form the basis of a reporter's ethical behavior. In many ways, journalism could be more ethical if it could be limited to people who shared deep commitments to ethical values.

In any event, deontology and teleology are simply approaches. They are not sure-fire methods of resolving ethical dilemmas. Sometimes, as Edmund Lambeth points out in his book on journalism ethics, the approaches can lead journalists to the same result but for different reasons.[55] For the most part, these approaches provide only a way to reason through a dilemma. Many ethical situations call for journalists to evaluate outcomes, set priorities, and strive to be fair. It is seldom an easy call.

Ethics Codes

One result of the ethical dilemmas journalists often faced was the development of codes of ethics. The first American code was developed in 1910 by the state press association of Kansas, a code that applied to both editors and publishers.[56] The Canons of Journalism were adopted in 1923 by the American Society of Newspaper Editors, at its first meeting, just after embarrassing revelations about the role of some journalists in the Teapot Dome Scandal under the administration of President Warren G. Harding. Three years later ASNE censured and suspended from its membership the editor of the *Denver Post* for his role in the scandal.[57]

Since that time, a number of professional organizations have developed codes, as have many newspaper publishing and broadcasting groups. The codes of the professional organizations establish a standard to guide ethical decision-making while serving as a crucial accountability tool for members even though the codes are advisory. No journalist is likely to be kicked out of the Society of Professional Journalists or the Radio Television Digital News Association for an ethical violation. These codes lack muscle to hold anyone accountable for ethical violations.[58]

The Society of Professional Journalists explains that it has debated the issue of holding its members accountable. "The majority has felt that establishing a quasi-judicial system, such as those found in some other professions, would inevitably lead to actions by governments, courts or their proxies that would restrict the rights to free speech and free press guaranteed by the First Amendment to the U.S. Constitution."[59] Instead, the SPJ has decided "the best enforcement is in publicizing, explaining and applying those principles and weighing alternatives, as individuals, as journalists and as an organization, in the form of comment and opinion, without issuing definitive, quasi-legal judgments that might be put to improper use."[60] The society does, however, periodically issue statements criticizing journalists and news organizations whose conduct it deems problematic or unethical. Those statements usually refer to the society's code as the basis for the criticism.

The ethics codes of individual news organizations have muscle. Employees can be reprimanded or fired for violating the established practices of their employee. Organizations use their codes to clarify ethical expectations for employees as well as the public. In 2003, the *New York Times* published its ethics code online, a significant step in journalistic transparency that allowed readers to compare the practice demonstrated in a story with the principles the newspaper established.[61]

Today, repercussion can come in the form of criticism from a professional society or a journalism review, although both are rare. However, with the growing presence of media critics on the Internet, journalists can be stung by the publicity and the reaction from their colleagues. On the other hand, media owners and organizations can be aggressive in enforcing their own ethical and professional codes. For example, running for political office will almost certainly mean that a journalist loses his or her reporting or editing job. Donating money to political campaigns is also usually prohibited. MSNBC suspended hosts Keith Olbermann and Joe Scarborough for donating to political candidates during the 2010 election cycle. Dating a news source such as the mayor can cost a reporter a job. An editor who learns a reporter committed plagiarism may suspend or fire the reporter.

Ethics codes are not universally viewed positively. Critics argue codes are too vague to be applied when decisions have to be made, especially when those decisions must be made on a deadline with little time for discussion and clarification.

A Reporter's Duty

The codes usually begin by talking about the role of journalism and the duties of a journalist. "(P)ublic enlightenment is the forerunner of justice and the foundation of democracy. The duty of the journalist is to further those ends by seeking truth and providing a fair and comprehensive account of events and issues. Conscientious journalists from all media and specialties strive to serve the public with thoroughness and honesty" (Society of Professional Journalists).

"Our primary role is to report visually on the significant events and on the varied viewpoints in our common world. Our primary goal is the faithful and comprehensive depiction of the subject at hand. As photojournalists, we have the responsibility to document society and to preserve its history through images" (National Press Photographers Association Code of Ethics).

"The primary purpose of gathering and distributing news and opinion is to serve the general welfare by informing the people and enabling them to make judgments on the issues of the time…. The American press was made free not just to inform or just to serve as a forum for debate but also to bring an independent scrutiny to bear on the forces of power in the society, including the conduct of official power at all levels of government" (American Society of News Editors Statement of Principles).

"Professional electronic journalists should operate as trustees of the public, seek the truth, report it fairly and with integrity and independence, and stand accountable for their actions" (Radio Television Digital News Association).

The Journalist's Code

Each code addresses the most important issues in a different way. The SPJ code addresses the responsibility of a journalist *to seek truth and report it,* stressing the obligation to report accurately, test the accuracy of sources, seek out all sides diligently, identify sources "whenever feasible," not use undercover or surreptitious means except if it is the only alternative to obtain information deemed vital to the public.

The second paragraph urges journalists *to minimize harm,* showing compassion and sensitivity toward those affected by grief and tragedy, urging the use of good taste, exercising caution before identifying juveniles who are accused of sex crimes or are victims of sex crimes or before identifying those who are suspected of crimes before formal charges are filed, and balancing the right of a criminal to a fair trial with the right of the public to be informed.

The third paragraph advises journalists *to act independently,* avoiding conflicts of interest or disclosing any that are unavoidable, refusing gifts or favors, and being diligent to hold those in power accountable for their actions. The final paragraph suggests that journalists should *be accountable* to their readers and to each other, encouraging journalists to acknowledge mistakes promptly and correct them, expose unethical practices of other journalists and media, and live by the same high standards to which they hold others.[62]

The American Society of News Editors' statement of principles parallels the SPJ code on many issues. It addresses the independence of journalists and the requirements for truth and accuracy, balanced reporting, and fair play. It also includes a paragraph addressing freedom of the press.[63]

The electronic journalist's code also addresses many of the same issues, stressing the need to be "balanced, accurate and fair," as well as free from conflicts of interest. Broadcasters are warned to clearly label opinion and commentary, an effort to ensure that viewers and listeners understand where news begins and ends. They are also urged to air the materials of other broadcasters only with permission.[64]

The ethics code of the National Press Photographers emphasizes the responsibility of photographers "at all times to strive for pictures that report truthfully, honestly and objectively." It also includes a statement about manipulation of photographs: "[W]e believe it is wrong to alter the content of a photograph in any way that deceives the public."[65]

Being Ethical

Ed Lambeth, who originated a national workshop on the teaching of ethics in journalism, outlined five ethical principles for journalists:

- Be truthful, which covers being unbiased, accurate, and competent.
- Be just, which means being fair, treating with caution highly emotional issues, and examining government decisions to see that they are just to others.
- Be free, which covers a reporter's autonomy from government and other social sources such as advertising and business and "use" by any source.
- Be humane, which involves assisting others and is defined as "the very minimum that one human owes another."
- Be a good steward, which Lambeth defined as "the responsibility to manage his life and property with proper regard to the rights of others.…." To this end, journalists must guard the rights of free press and speech for, as Lambeth points out, "These rights belong to all, though they are exercised more frequently by the press than others."[66]

Ethical Issues

The list of issues that have created ethical problems for the media is endless.

September 11, 2001: The Falling Man Picture

On September 11, 2001, four jets were hijacked in the United States almost simultaneously. One crashed into the Pentagon in Washington, D.C., and a second crashed in Pennsylvania after passengers overwhelmed the hijackers. The other two jets were flown into the twin towers of the World Trade Center in New York City. Filled with jet fuel for transcontinental flights, the planes brought an inferno to the buildings, killing more than 2,800 people.

Some of those trapped on the upper stories chose to jump 100 stories to their death rather than be burned to death. *USA Today* later estimated that at least 200 people jumped from both buildings, but mostly from the North Tower, which was hit first. Some jumped alone, some jumped in pairs, some jumped in groups.[67] A picture of a man jumping appeared in newspapers the next day, including the *New York Times* and the *Washington Post* but not *USA Today,* and video of the action was shown several times on television. The pictures brought cries of sensationalism from readers and viewers, but their use was defended on the grounds that the faces of the jumpers were indistinguishable. The media also argued the pictures conveyed the horror experienced by those trapped in a way that words could not.[68]

The Associated Press photograph of one man falling from the North Tower ran once and never again. *Esquire* reported that "papers all over the country, from the *Fort Worth Star-Telegram* to the *Memphis Commercial Appeal* to *The Denver Post,* were forced to defend themselves against charges that they exploited a man's death, stripped him of his dignity, invaded his privacy, turned tragedy into leering pornography. Most letters of complaint stated the obvious: that someone seeing the picture had to know who it was."[69]

Tragic events—and this was one of the worst in the history of the United States compounded by the fact that it was not a natural disaster—produce emotional responses that ebb with time. Editors and broadcasters have, of course, few precious moments in today's instant media age to ponder the ramifications short- and long-term of stories and pictures.

This raised ethical questions: In a day filled with images that were seared into the mind of a nation, was it essential to include at least one picture of someone who chose to die that way rather than to perish in an inferno that eventually collapsed? Was it an invasion of a family's privacy, even though no one is absolutely sure of the victim's identity? Was this an appeal to lurid curiosity or an effort to paint a fuller picture of the truth? Was this the only way to capture the horror that morning brought to innocent civilians who were simply going about their daily routine?

Are Journalists Allowed To Be Patriots, Too?

The events of September 11, 2001, led to invasions of Afghanistan and Iraq. Flags flew everywhere and patriotism surged throughout the country. A debate began over how patriotic the media should be. At the University of Missouri in Columbia, the university-owned NBC affiliate station debated whether anchors should be permitted to wear American flags on their lapels during delivery of the news. Some newspapers published flags on their mastheads or even a full-page flag that could be displayed in a window. Reuters would not allow reporters to refer to the September 11 hijackers as terrorists. In the face of criticism, CNN decided to balance reports of civilian casualties in Afghanistan with reminders of the death toll in the United States on September 11.[70]

But questions deeper than lapel flags arose. Congress almost unanimously empowered President Bush "to use all necessary and appropriate force" to seek out and destroy the terrorists. No one, including reporters, was asking senators and representatives or the administration what the cost was going to be, either in war supplies or in American lives.[71] In the name of patriotism, the marketplace of ideas was confined to a small corner and a few debaters, and the watchdogs turned their eyes on the terrorists and stopped watching their own government.

This raised ethical questions: At what point does life become so dangerous that journalists shed their roles as watchdogs and instigators of debate to further the interests of patriotism? When, if ever, is it no longer practical to strive to be an objective observer, presenting a balanced and fair reporter that takes all sides into account?

Reporting the Truth

One of the great outrages inflicted by the American system of justice also brought shame on the media in March 2006. Michael Nifong, a prosecutor in North Carolina armed with little evidence, publicly tarred the reputations of three Duke University lacrosse players and boldly proclaimed that a young black woman, a stripper paid to attend a team party, had been raped. He called the lacrosse players "hooligans."[72]

Kelly McBride, who writes about media ethics for the Poynter Institute, described what happened as the media learned about the story: "Commentators and pundits on television, in print, on the radio and, of course, on the Internet then magnified an already distorted reality by shouting over each other. In their attempt to shed light, they lit a fire of public scorn."[73]

The Duke students were indicted even as Nifong's case was imploding because of contradictory evidence and victim and witness statements. Justice was served a year later when he resigned his office and was disbarred the next day. If Nifong was the perpetrator, he had plenty of accomplices. "Fueled by Nifong, the media quickly latched onto a narrative too seductive to check: rich, wild, white jocks had brutalized a working-class, black mother of two," according to "Justice Delayed," written by Rachel Smolkin, managing editor of the *American Journalism Review*. Broadcasters and newspaper columnists talked and wrote as if the players had already been convicted. Because the accused would not grant interviews, most of the coverage was totally unbalanced.[74]

CNN's Nancy Grace was one of those responsible for especially unfair coverage. "I'm so glad they didn't miss a lacrosse game over a little thing like gang rape!" she exclaimed during a March 31 broadcast in which she portrayed the athletes as rich, privileged jocks.[75]

The senior who served as editor of the independent student newspaper at Duke, *The Chronicle*, also found lessons for the media. Ryan McCartney said he hoped that "this case will kind of go down in the books as a lesson to media organizations on all levels to … second-guess themselves any time they think a story is clear-cut."[76] *The Chronicle* was credited with coverage that consistently outclassed most of the national media.[77]

While many journalists on television and in print were trying and convicting the three young men, believing the lies told them by a prosecutor running for re-election, bloggers were pointing out the inconsistencies of his statements and some were far more accurate than professional media.[78]

Smolkin summed up the ethical issues: "The lessons of the media's rush to judgment and their affair with a sensational, simplistic storyline rank among journalism's most basic tenets: Be fair; stick to the facts; question authorities; don't assume; pay attention to alternative explanations."[79]

Naming Those Who Say They Have Been Raped

The Duke case raised another ethical question: Should the media disclose the name of a rape victim? Many news outlets, newspapers, and television stations, have a policy not to identify victim to protect them from the stigma associated with rape and other sex-related crimes.

While newspapers and television broadcasters routinely identified the three Duke students indicted on the rape charges, most media outlets refrained from identifying their accuser. The name of the woman at the center of this case did appear in some of the blogs, however. She was named by some outlets after the charges against the former lacrosse players were dropped. According to *American Journalism Review*, her name was published by *The Chicago Sun-Times*, the *Charlotte Observer* and the *New York Post* after the charges were dropped. CBS' *60 Minutes* also used her name. Many major news organizations, including the *New York Times, the Washington Post, Newsday,* and the Associated Press, never identified her.[80]

Kelly McBride, the Poynter ethics specialist, cited three guiding principles from the SPJ Code of Ethics on whether to name an accuser several months before the prosecution's case against the players collapsed. Journalists should (1) report the truth as fully as possible, (2) remain independent and (3) minimize harm.[81]

The *Raleigh News & Observer* did publish the accuser's name after the charges were dropped even though the newspaper has a policy to protect the identity of victims of sex-related crimes. Executive Editor Melanie Sill told the *American Journalism Review* that before editors decided, they sought advice from advocates for sexual assault victims, defense lawyers and ethicists, among others. "They almost uniformly did not want to see the newspaper identify sexual assault victims," Sill said. But no one criticized the newspaper's decision.[82]

Not everyone agrees with the standard practice. Geneva Overholser, director of the School of Journalism at the University of Southern California Annenberg School for Communication, believes printing an accuser's name is the only acceptable decision in nearly all instances. Overholser was editor of the *Des Moines Register* when it won a Pulitzer Prize in 1991 for a story on a rape victim who agreed to let the newspaper publish her name. "In the long run, we'll never get rid of the stigma if we don't treat these like regular crimes." She also told the *American Journalism Review* that naming the accused and not the accuser is unfair. "It's just not ethical to make a choice about guilt or innocence, which is effectively what we do. It makes us look like we are assuming innocence on one part, guilt on another," she said.[83]

Working With the Police to Catch a Predator

A television investigation that raised ethical questions was NBC's "To Catch a Predator." *Dateline*, the network's news magazine, collaborated with Perverted Justice, whose members pose as children on the Internet to identify adult predators. The news team essentially created a sting. Perverted Justice members entered Internet chat rooms, engaged men looking to have sex with young teens and set up an encounter. Waiting at the house where the men were lured was *Dateline*. After the encounter was filmed and the suspect interviewed, he walked outside where he was arrested.

Several ethical questions have been raised. First, is it proper for journalists to work essentially as an arm of law enforcement? For one episode in Greenville, Ohio, police deputized members of Perverted Justice so that the evidence they gathered could be used in court. McBride, an ethics specialist at the Poynter Institute, told the *Los Angeles Times*, "By working with a group that has been deputized, *Dateline* is essentially partnering with local law enforcement. Even if the outcome is a desirable outcome, in the long run it undermines their ability to serve as a watchdog."[84]

Another ethical issue is the money, more than $100,000 that *Dateline* has paid Perverted Justice to assist in the sting. NBC's senior producer of the segments, Allan Maraynes, said that the network had no qualms about the expenditure, although, as the *Washington Post* reported, news organizations typically avoid paying sources to prevent an undue influence on the source's actions or information. "We've raised the public's consciousness of a very serious issue," Maraynes told the *Post*. "We think we've created a model [for reporting on Internet pedophilia] that accurately reflects what happens in real life."[85]

Also at issue is whether *Dateline* was essentially assisting in entrapment because at least some of the time the decoy introduced the idea of sex into the conversation.[86]

The questions Brian Montopoli, editor of Public Eye, the CBS News blog that covers the media, outlined are difficult because those who are caught in the camera's eye are far from sympathetic:[87]

> It can be extremely difficult to discuss journalistic ethics when dealing with a topic such as this. *Dateline*, many would argue, is exposing predators and getting them off the streets, and so high-minded debates about the ethics of the program's methods do not come into the equation. I am sympathetic to that argument, and, indeed, I find the actions of the men featured in the program disturbing. But I don't think we can abandon questions of journalistic conduct just because our first instinct is that the ends justify the means.

Journalists and Politicians

In its 2004 post-election survey, the Pew Research Center for the People and the Press found increasing voter anger over what voters see as the media's unfair treatment of political candidates. Almost four in ten of those surveyed believed the media were unfair to Republican candidate George W. Bush, while three in ten felt the media were unfair to Democratic candidate John Kerry. Both unfair measures were 10 percentage points higher than those cited for Bush and former Vice President Al Gore in 2000.[88] After the 2008 election, 30% of those surveyed believed the press unfairly covered Sen. Barack Obama's campaign compared to 44% who said Sen. John McCain's campaign was covered unfairly.[89]

Those perceptions were probably buoyed by a report issued in June 2007 by MSNBC that it had found 143 journalists who had given money to political candidates since 2004.[90] Some news organizations have ethics codes that prohibit contributions to candidates or working on behalf of the candidates. Some news organizations do not.

In response to the story, the Kentucky Republican Party issued a call for the dismissal of the copy desk chief for the *Lexington Herald-Leader,* who donated $250 to the campaign of 2004 Democratic presidential nominee John Kerry. The editor of the newspaper said the employee had not violated the newspaper's policy and would not be fired. She also said the newspaper would review its policy on political contributions.[91]

The Society of Professional Journalists, one of the nation's oldest and largest journalism-advocacy organizations, said journalists who give money to candidates violate the society's ethics code, which says the news media should "abide by the same high standards to which they hold others."

Andrew Schotz, chairman of SPJ's ethics committee and a reporter in Hagerstown, Maryland, said, "Contributing to a political cause clearly damages the credibility of anyone who professes to be a detached reporter of events … (I)t's disturbing to see that so many journalists don't see the problem here. It's also unfortunate that so few media organizations have communicated a clear policy to their employees, if they even have a policy at all.

"Ethical journalists sacrifice rights of activism and affiliation that the public at-large has. The degree to which we excuse ourselves from community involvement remains a personal choice and a workplace policy. But we encourage journalists to think through their commitments before they make them and to err on the side of neutrality," Schotz said in SPJ's statement.[92]

Another ethical problem arises out of the relationship between journalists and politicians. A political reporter had an affair with Los Angeles Mayor Antonio Villaraigosa, who subsequently took responsibility for the end of his 20-year marriage in 2008. The station suspended the reporter, who had covered a number of the mayor's initiatives and had announced on the air the break-up of the mayor's marriage without reporting that she had been secretly dating the mayor. The station reassigned her, and when she failed to show up for the assignment, the station announced that she had quit her job.[93]

The next year, another reporter found herself in a similar situation. Villaraigosa began dating another Los Angeles television reporter, a former beauty queen. The station learned of the relationship after the journalist, working as a weekend anchor, reported that the mayor had chosen not to run for governor, but the station manager said the relationship was not a problem and she would no longer report news about the mayor.[94]

The issue played out a different way when Arnold Schwarzenegger was elected governor of California in 2004. His wife, NBC journalist Maria Shriver, quit her television job to devote time to her role as the state's first lady. The decision clearly removed the possibility of conflict between her duties as a journalist and wife of a high-profile politician.[95]

The SPJ Code of Ethics, while encouraging journalists to act independently, advises them to remain "free of any obligation to any interest other than the public's right to know." That includes, the code says, remaining free of associations that "could compromise integrity or damage credibility."

Plagiarism

Plagiarism is using the work of another without consent or attribution and representing it as your own. The ethics committee of the American Society of Newspaper Editors reported in 1986 that one of every six editors had encountered plagiarism in the newsroom.

Plagiarism can consist of copying a statement a news source made to a reporter and publishing it as though the statement were made to another reporter. Sometimes it involves taking and publishing material already published by one media outlet when a reporter does not have time to research and write the information on deadline. In any case and for whatever reason, stealing material from another reporter or publication is always unethical. The solution is simple: attribute, give credit to the original author.

Plagiarism is the subject of the briefest entry in SPJ's Code of Ethics: "Never plagiarize." Sadly, the list of violations is not brief:

- Maureen Dowd, Pulitzer-Prize winning columnist for the *New York Times,* acknowledged in 2009 plagiarizing a statement in her column that she failed to attribute. The declaration had originated in a column on a political website.[96]

The *American Journalism Review* in March 2001 reported on these plagiarism revelations of the media:[97]

- *The Sacramento Bee* fired political reporter Dennis Love a few weeks after the 2000 election for plagiarizing and fabricating material in his stories on the presidential campaign. He acknowledged "borrowing" material from *U.S. News & World Report, USA Today,* the *Boston Globe,* and the *Dallas Morning News.*
- Medill News Service reported it could not verify information in two stories reported by a student journalist. *American Journalism Review* reported that newspapers where the student interned—the *San Jose Mercury News,* the *Philadelphia Daily News,* and the *San Francisco Examiner*—could not locate sources from stories the intern wrote.
- The *Detroit News* admitted it lifted a paragraph from the pages of a suburban newspaper.
- *The San Jose Mercury News* fired an intern for plagiarizing material from the *Washington Post* and the *San Francisco Chronicle.*
- Tom Squitieri, a staff writer for *USA Today,* apologized in May 2005 for not attributing quotes in his story that were originally published in a 2004 story by the *Indianapolis Star.* Then he resigned.[98]
- *The New Republic* fired reporter Stephen Glass in May 1998 and later reported it found evidence that he had fabricated material in 27 of the 41 articles he had written wrote for the magazine.

Plagiarism obviously is more widespread than these examples. In newsrooms already strapped by financial constraints that have reduced their reporting and editing staffs, it is almost unthinkable that a staff member might be assigned to check stories for material lifted from other publications or to call sources in stories to confirm that a reporter had interviewed them.

What has made plagiarism a more widespread offense today is the Internet. Newspaper stories are available nationwide. Now a reporter in Los Angeles writing a story about anthrax found in a Senate office building can read what a reporter wrote about the story in Washington.

But the availability also makes it more likely that plagiarists will be caught. The *American Journalism Review* reported that the *Sacramento Bee* searched the Internet for a review it published about a Shania Twain concert. The newspaper reported it popped up on about 100 websites, most of them fan sites and music pages.[99]

The practice of "borrowing" from other reporters is as wrong as cheating on an exam in a college class. However, differentiating between plagiarism and research is sometimes difficult. Events in a news story can't be copyrighted like a novel. And it is fairly easy to rewrite information in your own words. The solution is rather easy. When in doubt, attribute. Give credit to the originator.

Here are situations reporters sometimes face:

- Using material from a newspaper's own library of previously published stories. Reporters should paraphrase the material rather than quote it verbatim. It is also appropriate, if the material was original and not reported repeatedly, to introduce the material by writing that the newspaper reported the material on the date it was published. This avoids any implication that the reporter whose byline appears on the new story originated this information.
- Using material from a wire service. Newspapers routinely localize national and state stories from wire services. This involves finding local aspects or local examples of the story. Even if the newspaper originates more than half of the story it publishes, the wire service should be credited in the body of the story or with a trailer at the end that makes it clear information in the story was produced by the wire service.
- Using the work of a fellow reporter without giving the reporter credit. News outlets have different standards for how this is handled, but if plagiarism means taking someone else's work and claiming it as your own, then reporters who contribute to any degree deserve credit—either a joint byline or a credit at the bottom of the story.
- Using material from other publications. Reporters should first try to confirm this information independently. However, if the source is not available or deadlines make confirmation impossible, then reporters and editors should choose either not to use the information or to give credit to the media outlet that reported the information.
- Using unedited news releases or news videos. The companies and individuals who send them out are delighted to see them on the air or in print and are unlikely to complain. But reporting requires independent work, and accepting at face value material from a source without checking it is a violation of the trust between a newspaper and its readers or a broadcaster and the audience. Running such items without checking them also puts the media at risk of becoming victims of a hoax. It is not hard today with faxes and computer graphics to mimic a company letterhead and invent a press release.
- Using old stories or columns a second time. Recycling material is certainly not a new problem. Newspapers republish the classic "Yes, Virginia, There is a Santa Claus" column. Ethically, the only problem is passing old material off as new. Readers have a right to know they are reading recycled material, and they probably are not going to object to reading old columns when a columnist goes on vacation or sick leave if they are told that is what they are reading.

And what is the answer to plagiarism? Certainly, a strong link exists between repeated discoveries of plagiarism and the falling credibility of the media. Reporters would be quick to point fingers at public officials who stole money from the taxpayers, but they are not as quick to recognize that deceiving the audience by claiming something that is not their own is just as harmful.

Making It Up And Calling It Journalism

The second plagiarism issue is fabrication, inventing a person or a story. One journalism ethics scholar identified "the most famous hoax of the modern era of American journalism" as "Jimmy's World," the story for which Janet Cooke, a 26-year-old reporter for the *Washington Post*, won the 1981 Pulitzer Prize. The story described the life of an eight-year-old inner-city heroin addict. Police could not locate the boy after an extensive search, and Cooke refused to tell police where they could find him because of her pledge of confidentiality. When the prize was announced, reporters found holes in Cooke's resume, which led to questions about her story. There was no Jimmy; she claimed he was a composite of inner-city drug addicts she had found in her reporting. The newspaper returned the Pulitzer, and Cooke was out of work.[100]

Unfortunately, other notable instances of fabrication exist in the annals of American journalism. Patricia Smith, an award-winning columnist for the *Boston Daily Globe*, resigned in 1998. Questions were raised about 52 columns she wrote. She admitted to an editor that she invented four of the characters that appeared in her columns.[101]

Smith, of course, was not the first columnist who has written about people who did not exist. The late Mike Royko, a legendary Chicago columnist, used the device regularly; the difference is that readers knew Royko's foils were fictional. Smith passed off her characters—just as Janet Cooke passed off her character—as living, breathing people.

Sacramento Bee columnist Diana Griego Erwin resigned in 2005 during an investigation. The newspaper said it found 43 sources it could not verify in her work. The 12-year columnist denied any wrongdoing and said she had quit because of personal problems.[102]

Celebrities In The Public Eye

Often the public criticizes the media for focusing too much attention (or more accurately, an around-the-clock siege) on politicians and celebrities when they end up in the news for the wrong reasons. But journalists aren't always sure what to make of such criticism. A 2000 survey uncovered two factors that undermine the public's reaction. First, the public tends to confuse news with non-news programming, especially entertainment, on television. Second, the survey found that while the public may decry the media attention on a fallen star, the survey's respondents acknowledged they drink in the very kind of news the media are providing. "What Americans said they want in news and how they will actually behave are entirely different," the pollster concluded.[103]

Tiger Woods provides a glaring example. Perhaps the world's most recognizable athlete, the man named athlete of the first decade of the 21st century was on his way to shattering records in professional golf when he stumbled. He became a household name because of his amazing ability on the course, his rise from child star to adult superstar and because his Mr. Clean reputation had been honed by his managers. Apart from his winnings on the golf courses of the world, his product endorsements brought in an estimated $900 million.

In a statement issued several days after he wrecked his car by hitting a fireplug and several women publicly announced they had had affairs with the married Woods, he acknowledged the public had an interest in his life because he's a public figure. But he also asserted "an important and deep principle (was) at stake, which is the right to some simple, human measure of privacy."

He also declared "Personal sins should not require press releases and problems within a family shouldn't have to mean public confessions."[104]

ESPN.com senior writer Howard Bryant summarized the arguments:

> In defense of Tiger, supporters argue that the details of whatever occurred in his driveway on Nov. 27 and its fallout did not belong to the public, certainly didn't belong as front-page news for two-thirds of a month, as they were in the *New York Post*, which ran a Tiger headline on its front page for 20 consecutive days. He is, for goodness sake, a golfer, not the head of the U.N. Security Council. And he is a young male who has earned $1 billion, and he isn't yet 34 years old. Opportunities for female company, naturally, would be virtually unlimited.
>
> That argument is porous for many reasons, the most important one being this: He took the money. Tiger—like Michael Jordan before him, LeBron James after him, and virtually every contemporary big-time athlete in between (Tim Duncan is a noteworthy exception)—allowed his name to be used and manipulated for financial gain. For money, he allowed himself to be marketed and characterized with a virtuousness the world is now finding he did not possess. He allowed himself to be a pitchman to the lucrative family and children's demographic ("I'm Tiger Woods!") for dollar sums, and he is now left exposed. He sold his right to privacy—the right to be unapologetically authentic—as just another commodity.[105]

Reporters are taught to "seek the truth and report it," in the words of the ethics code of the Society of Professional Journalists. When they learn someone has become rich or famous or powerful perpetrating a lie upon the public, the race is on to tell the story and expose the hypocrisy with many, if not all, of the sordid details. Tiger Woods had made a fortune passing himself off as someone he was not. If he had only played golf and not created a phony persona, perhaps his plea for privacy would have been received with some sympathy. If the world's most public athlete truly believed he was entitled to an exemption for the salacious details of his marital infidelity, it only demonstrates he believed his own propaganda machine. When he signed all those endorsement contracts based on the public image he created, he pretty much forfeited any privacy.

But athletes aren't the only ones who declare they are entitled to privacy when they find themselves in the middle of a media frenzy over their private indiscretions. Public officials—governors, senators, and others—have tried to declare their private lives off-limits in the middle of crises resulting from the exposure of private failings. It seldom works. People have differing ideas about how much privacy public sinners are entitled to in the middle of these storms.

Non-celebrities Caught in the Media Eye

The all-seeing eye of the media captures more than just the famous who prove to be unfaithful to their spouses or who end up in jail for using illegal drugs, drinking too much alcohol, or getting involved in some kind of fight. The non-famous also can become the infamous through the media, particularly because the media have an enlarged capacity on the Internet.

Time magazine documented a new trend online: mug-shot galleries. The news magazine said the Orlando *Sentinel* garnered 2.5 million page views a month for its mug-shot gallery of those arrested, quoting the digital-news manager.[106] But the *Sentinel* was not the only news site where the arrested could be viewed. The *Daily News* in Newport News, Virginia, CBS-13.com in Sacramento, California, and the *Chicago Tribune* are among the websites that have displayed those with recent brushes with the law.

"Mug shot mania" has even given birth to new publications. Pick up a copy of *The Slammer* in Raleigh, N.C., *Cellmates* in Tampa Bay, Florida, and *Jail* in Orlando, Florida, for an update on who has been to the pokey. According to the *Christian Science Monitor,* the circulation for *The Slammer* had grown to 29,000 by January 2009, selling at 500 convenience stores for $1. Bob Steele, one of ethical journalism's leading voices, told the *Monitor* it was a sad commentary on the state of journalism. "It's really painful to know that so many publications are struggling terribly and something as schlocky as this is succeeding."[107]

This practice obviously multiplies the embarrassment for those who are arrested, some of whom will not be convicted. But does it offend ethical standards of journalism? Steele, whose credentials include his association with the non-profit Poynter Institute and Pulliam Distinguished Professor at DePauw University in Greencastle, Indiana, believes it does.

Police mug shots are anything but flattering to the one who poses. The lighting and background suggest anything but innocent until proven guilty. Publishing the names and mug shots of those who have been arrested for serious crimes—armed robbery, rape, murder, defrauding people of their life savings—is a standard practice across all media platforms. The practice serves not only to inform the public that a crime has been committed but also to inform them that the judicial system is working.

The better question is whether anything is achieved by publishing the mug shots of those arrested on misdemeanor charges, lesser offenses that otherwise would not be fodder for local news reports. The SPJ ethics code exhorts journalists to "minimize harm." That imperative includes not pandering to lurid curiosity and balancing a suspect's right to a fair trial with the public's right to be informed.

Accepting Gifts and Trips

The issue here is receiving anything as a gift that would tend to make a reporter or editor feel he or she owes the source something. Even something that creates good will for the source should be suspect. Reporters should never allow sources to buy them food or drinks or "sponsor" coverage. It sends the wrong message. Media outlets should give reporters expense money if they expect reporters to have lunch regularly with sources or attend all-expenses-paid meetings in exotic locales.

Reporters and editors should never accept gifts from sources for Christmas, other holidays, or birthdays. Yes, Christmas may be the season for giving and good will, but the reporter will then find it uncomfortable after he accepts a tie from the mayor to write about the mayor's inflated expense account, particularly if the tie is one of the items on the tab. It once was not uncommon for a reporter to come back from city hall the week before Christmas with bottles of liquor from the mayor, city manager, or county judge. Today, conduct like that is considered highly unethical.

These gifts may or may not be given in expectation of favorable coverage. Even if that is not the case, it will be hard to explain to a media audience that a reporter was not influenced favorably by a gift. And if the mayor has an opponent in the next election, the opponent would certainly be suspicious if she learned about the gift and would interpret it as evidence the reporter is too cozy with the incumbent to cover the race fairly.

The appearance of impropriety is just as dangerous to the credibility of a journalist as impropriety. Journalists must not only act ethically; they must also be perceived as ethical.

The scale may be dramatically different, but the principle is akin to an issue journalists raise all the time about the relationships of candidates, campaign contributions, and the influence those contributions have on officials' positions and votes on issues. As is always the case with ethical issues, it is not enough to be accurate, fair, and balanced. A reporter must also appear accurate, fair, and balanced. That makes ethical conduct even more critical. Ralph Otwell, former managing editor of the *Chicago Sun-Times,* summed up the issue for *Editor & Publisher* in an article in 1974:

> But in the performance of our journalistic jobs there is more than a conscience to be served; it is not enough to know down deep inside that you are not being bought or influenced, that the "freebie" has not dulled your critical senses or lulled your watchful vigilance. The conflict of interest might not be felt on the inside … but it may be imagined or perceived on the outside. And there is the rub … the point where self-image and self-confidence end and public confidence begins.[108]

The problem involves more than beat reporters eating lunches paid for by city council members. What is the effect if the sponsors of major sporting events throw a media party complete with food and drink the night before an extravaganza? Or if the television networks make television stars available for interviews weeks before the fall program season begins? Or if airlines initiate international flights by offering local reporters free rides on maiden voyages? Or if food companies supply food editors with new lines of frozen entrees for tasting? This is not a new problem. Consider this statement almost 30 years ago by Charles Long, then editor of the *Quill*, the SPJ magazine:

> There's nothing new about the "freebie game." It is being played all the time and shows up in hundreds of different places and with varying sets of rules. Freebies—meaning token as well as expensive gifts, tickets to events large and small, junkets to simple and exotic places—have been floating in and about newsroom operations for as long as there has been a way of saying thanks for good publicity.[109]

One of the biggest examples of the freebie game was Disney World's invitation in 1986 to thousands of journalists to go to Florida to celebrate the park's 15th anniversary and the Constitution's 200th birthday. Some 5,000 journalists (each could bring one guest) generated lots of free publicity for Disney. The junket cost about $7.5 million, and a financial arm of the Walt Disney Co. paid $1.5 million of that. All areas of the tourist industry—Orlando-area hotels, airlines, convention bureaus, even state and local governments—kicked in most of the rest. Journalists who insisted on paying for part of it were billed $150, and some paid their own way.

Disney estimated that television and radio crews broadcast more than 1,000 hours of coverage while they attended the park's anniversary. Disney's media relations division also supplied plenty of press releases to the reporters, talk show hosts, travel writers, radio disc jockeys, and magazine writers to read on the plane rides home. As one ethics text explains, the trip—and similar trips Disney staged for its 20th and 25th anniversary—raised serious news-gathering questions:

> The problem for news on the national and local levels is recording faithfully both the good and bad associated with the trip. However, to expect reporters on free trips to

report carefully on both sides is to assume that reporters are willing to "bite the hand that feels them. That is more than one should normally expect of mere mortals. Thus, agreeing to free trips is tantamount to accepting the proposition that it is morally permissible to write puffery.[110]

Checkbook Journalism

Another practice that American journalists frown upon is purchasing information. The concern is that paying for information will create a market for stories that sound true but are not. "Money-hungry sources will be likely to embellish and fabricate to drive their prices higher."[111] More importantly, according to John Michael Kittross, editor of *Media Ethics,* checkbook journalism destroys the credibility of all journalists. "If we believe that information is only a commodity to be bought and sold, how long will it be before we, ourselves, also are on the block? What will be our price?"[112]

The Ethics Committee of the Society of Professional Journalists issued a statement in March 2010 criticizing ABC News for a $200,000 payment to the family of a woman accused of murdering her two-year-old daughter, Caylee Anthony. The payment was revealed during a court hearing. The network said it had given the money for exclusive access to the family's photos and home movies.[113]

SPJ also criticized NBC News, which provided a New Jersey man, David Goldman, transportation on a private plane from Brazil to the United States after he was granted custody of his son, who had been living with his mother and step-father until his mother died. SPJ pointed out that the network conducted an exclusive interview with Goldman during the flight and another one after father and son returned.

"The public could rightly assume that NBC News bought exclusive interviews and images, as well as the family's loyalty, with an extravagant gift," Ethics Committee Chairman Andrew Schotz said in a statement the organization issued.[114] "Mixing financial and promotional motives with an impartial search for truth stains honest, ethical reporting," Schotz said. "Checkbook journalism has no place in the news business."[115]

The list of payouts grew in 2010 and 2011. ABC paid a so-called licensing fee for a picture of an alligator to the workman who found the body of Caylee Anthony. He was interviewed by ABC. The network paid between $10,000 and $15,000 for pictures a woman sent to then-Rep. Anthony Weiner, D-NY, a congressman who resigned after he emailed lewd pictures of himself. She was interviewed by ABC. Jaycee Lee Dugard, kidnapped and held hostage by a couple for 18 years, received a six-figure licensing fee for home movies, according to the *New York Times.* She was interviewed by Diane Sawyer in a highly promoted ABC exclusive.

NBC received an exclusive interview with a Washington high school student who faked a pregnancy for her senior project after the network put money in a trust fund for her education.

Responding to questions about the practice of paycheck journalism and SPJ's stand against it, SPJ's 2010-11 President Hagit Limor, a broadcast journalist, told the *Washington Post,* "When you pay for a story, you're making a contract with the person who supplies it and that means you're no longer acting independently.

"People will say anything in pursuit of money. The public should assume you're reporting something because it's true, not because someone received money to say it," Limor said.

In August 2011, ABC announced it would stop paying "license fees" for photos and videos, a cover to avoid directly paying for exclusive interviews, except in "extraordinary circumstances," which it did not define. That left NBC as the top network in the pay-for-information field.

One event that attracted money offers of all kinds was the trial of former football star O. J. Simpson, who was arrested in 1994 for the murder of his former wife and a friend but subsequently found not guilty. *Hard Copy* paid one witness $5,000 for her recollections of Simpson driving wildly near his home on the night of the murders. Two prosecution witnesses, the owner and a salesman at a cutlery store where Simpson bought a knife shortly before the murders, received part of a $12,500 check from the *National Enquirer* for their stories. Kato Kaelin, a key witness who was staying at Simpson's guest house on the night of the murders, received an offer of $250,000 from *The Enquirer,* according to his attorney.[116]

In the spring of 2001, ABC News tested a claim of a former New York City police commissioner that many rapists go unidentified because law enforcement departments lack the money to pay for DNA tests. The network paid for Baltimore's police department to have evidence scientifically analyzed in 50 rape cases. As a result, four men were charged in unsolved cases involving rape and murder. A man who had been imprisoned for three months was released, exonerated by the DNA analysis.

Another outcome was the result of information purchased by Larry Flynt, publisher of *Hustler Magazine.* In October 1998 while Congress was debating whether to impeach President Bill Clinton, Flynt paid $85,000 to place an ad in the *Washington Post* offering up to $1 million to the person who could provide evidence that a member of Congress had carried on an adulterous affair. Before the year ended, Rep. Bob Livingston, R-La., who had been chosen to serve as speaker of the House of Representatives when the new Congress was sworn in during January 1999, abruptly resigned.[117] Flynt took credit for the resignation,[118] issuing a statement that *Hustler* was preparing a story that Livingston had had several affairs.

The Internet has caused dramatic changes in the way people access—and the ways journalists report—the news. Those dramatic changes are raising more ethical issues. A national survey conducted by researchers at George Washington University found that 89% of journalists said they use blogs for research, 65% visit social media pages such as Facebook and LinkedIn, and 52% to services such as Twitter.[119]

One of the ethical issues raised is the use of information from personal pages such as Facebook. Journalists who find information on social media sites must decide whether the information there is private even though in most cases the person disclosed it himself. In December 2009, an 11-year-old accidentally shot and killed his 20-year-old brother, who was scheduled to report for Air Force training a week later. In the story the *Knoxville News Sentinel* posted on its website, the reporter quoted from the Facebook page of the victim: "My ultimate goal is to go to the 2012 Olympics in London."[120]

Twitter allows journalists to cover and report on events as they happen without delay. In one respect, it allows traditional print reporters access to an audience instantly, a privilege that formerly belonged to broadcasters. A reporter for the now-defunct *Rocky Mountain News* attended the funeral of a three-year-old killed when a car crashed through the front of an ice cream store and using Twitter, sent updates on what family and the rabbi said. The newspaper was criticized, although the editor made clear that the family had given the reporter permission to cover the service.[121]

As the technology continues to evolve and journalists master new ways to use it to research and to communicate with the audience, more ethical issues will develop. Some commentators believe that the issues can be addressed by applying principles from the existing ethics codes, while others suggest the new media environment will require new ethical standards.[122]

The Reporter's Privilege

Few issues straddle the worlds of journalism ethics and media law more than reporter's privilege. Journalists believe they have an ethical duty to protect the identities of sources to whom they pledge confidentiality—they have given their word and they must keep it. The SPJ Code of Ethics speaks to that obligation:

> Always question sources' motives before promising anonymity. Clarify conditions attached to any promise made in exchange for information. Keep promises.

Journalists argue that they should be allowed to protect the identities of confidential sources because often a pledge of confidentiality is the only way the media are able to tell stories. Even though the Supreme Court ruled that all citizens have a duty to tell whatever they know to a grand jury, journalists argue that doing so will hurt the public by diminishing the ability of journalists to fulfill the watchdog role of the media. The First Amendment is not a private right of journalists to be above the law; it is a right given to ensure the continued function of the media on behalf of the public, intending that the public will be exposed to more information about the conduct of government at all levels as a result.

Many journalists have refused to reveal the identities of their sources even when ordered to do so by judges who believe the law requires the journalists to testify about what they know before a grand jury or in a libel trial. Using a confidential source can prove problematic for a journalist if a lawyer comes knocking on the door with a subpoena in hand, demanding to know the identity of an informant. Here are some examples.

Marie Torre, the entertainment columnist for the *New York Herald-Tribune,* reported comments in 1957 of an anonymous CBS executive that singer-actress Judy Garland said libeled her.[123] Garland sued CBS, and when her lawyer deposed the reporter, Torre refused to reveal her source and was found in contempt of court. Torre, who had two small children, spent 10 days in jail, but Garland never learned the identity of her critic from the reporter.[124] Torre was one of the first journalists to win national attention for refusing to identify a source, and the court's decision that sent her to jail set the stage for a Supreme Court decision a decade later.[125]

National Public Radio legal affairs correspondent Nina Totenberg and *Newsday* reporter Tim Phelps were asked in 1992 by a special independent counsel how they had received a copy of a confidential affidavit sent to the Senate Judiciary Committee. The document outlined law professor Anita Hill's claims of sexual harassment against then-U.S. Appeals Court Judge Clarence Thomas. The memo surfaced during hearings for Thomas, who had been nominated for the Supreme Court of the United States.[126] The reporters refused to answer; the independent counsel threatened contempt, but the reporters sat silent. U.S. Senators Wendell Ford, D-KY, and Ted Stevens, R-AK, the chairman and ranking member of the Senate Rules Committee, rebuffed efforts of the independent counsel to hold the reporters in contempt of Congress.[127]

Wally Wakefield, a 74-year-old retired elementary school teacher who covered high school sports for a Minnesota weekly newspaper, was fined $200 per day for refusing to identify his source in a story that reported the firing of a high school football coach. The coach's contract was not renewed after accusations of misconduct and maltreatment of players surfaced, according to court records. The state Supreme Court ordered Wakefield to identify his source after the coach sued the school district for libel, but Wakefield refused. Reporters in Minnesota raised about $24,000 to pay the fine.[128] The former coach and the school board settled their lawsuit out of court in 1994, stopping the fine for Wakefield at $18,200.[129]

The battle over confidential sources escalated after the turn of the century. The most publicized event was intertwined with politics and the U.S. invasion of Iraq. The CIA dispatched Joseph C. Wilson IV, a former ambassador, to Niger in February 2002 to investigate whether Iraq had tried to buy uranium in that country. The uranium issue was part of the Bush administration's justification for the invasion of Iraq. After U.S. troops toppled Saddam Hussein, Wilson wrote an opinion piece published by the *New York Times* on July 6, 2003, arguing that President Bush misled the country because Wilson had found no evidence that Iraqi agents had gone to Niger.[130] A week later, *Chicago Sun-Times* columnist Robert Novak wrote that administration sources had told him Wilson was chosen for the trip because of the influence of his wife, Valerie Plame, a CIA agent.[131]

It can be a federal crime for a government employee to reveal the identity of a secret government agent. A special prosecutor was appointed and a grand jury impaneled to identify the source of that leak. A number of reporters were subpoenaed, among them Tim Russert of NBC's *Meet the Press* and Matthew Cooper of *Time* magazine.[132] Four months later, a federal judge held Cooper in contempt and ordered that he be jailed and fined $1,000 per day until he testified. The judge suspended the penalties while Cooper appealed. NBC said that Russert had testified, but he had not been told about Plame's work for the CIA.[133]

Washington Post reporter Walter Pincus, who had covered national security and intelligence for the paper for 30 years, gave a deposition about his conversation with his source; he refused to identify his source even though the source had identified himself to the special prosecutor.[134]

New York Times reporter Judith Miller, who never wrote about what sources told her about Wilson and Plame, also was subpoenaed, found in contempt when she refused to testify, and, with Cooper, appealed the judge's decision to the U.S. Court of Appeals.[135] After the Court of Appeals upheld the contempt decision and the Supreme Court refused to review it,[136] *Time* announced the magazine would turn over Cooper's notes to the prosecutor, a decision that brought howls of protest from journalists.[137]

Before he went to jail, however, his source, presidential adviser Karl Rove, waived the confidentiality agreement.[138] Judith Miller, however, was sent to jail for 85 days before finally agreeing to testify after she had tangible evidence her source waived his right to anonymity. "If journalists cannot be trusted to guarantee confidentiality," she told Judge Thomas F. Hogan before she was taken into custody, "then journalists cannot function and there cannot be a free press."[139]

In the end, no one was indicted for revealing the name of a covert agent. However, Lewis "Scooter" Libby, chief of staff for Vice President Dick Cheney who had been Miller's source, was convicted of perjury before the grand jury investigating the leak.

A different outcome resulted from subpoenas issued reporters who published stories about Wen Ho Lee, a scientist at the Los Alamos National Laboratory in New Mexico. Lee, indicted on 59 counts of mishandling classified information and accused of transferring nuclear weapons technology to China, eventually pleaded guilty to one count and the other 58 were dismissed. A federal judge apologized for the way the government had treated him.

Figure 4.1   Former CIA covert agent Valerie Plame Wilson is sworn in before testifying before the U.S. House of Representatives Committee on Oversight and Government Reform on Capital Hill in Washington, D.C., March 16, 2007 (Mannie Garcia/AFP/Getty Images).

Lee sued the U.S. Department of Justice in 1999 contending the government had violated his privacy by telling reporters about his employment history, finances, travels, and polygraph tests.[140] He subpoenaed reporters for the *Los Angeles Times*, the *New York Times*, the *Washington Post*, the Associated Press, and CNN. (The CNN reporter later went to work for ABC News.) Lee's attorney sought to learn the sources of the information they had published or broadcast, but the reporters refused and were found in contempt. The U.S. Court of Appeals in Washington, D.C., upheld that ruling in June 2005.[141]

In a dramatic conclusion to the lawsuit, the government and five news organizations agreed to pay Lee more than $1.6 million. Henry Hoberman, a senior vice president of ABC, explained this startling development. "The journalists found themselves between a rock and a hard place. Given the absence of a federal shield law and the consistently adverse rulings from the federal courts in this case, the only way the journalists could keep their bond with their sources and avoid further sanctions, which might include jail time, was to contribute to a settlement between the government and Wen Ho Lee that would end the case."[142]

A television reporter was sentenced to six months of home incarceration for his refusal to identify the person who gave him videotape that his station then broadcast. The federal judge who sentenced him said the only reason the reporter was not going to jail was concern about his health.

WJAR, a Providence, Rhode Island, affiliate of NBC, aired the tape on February 1, 2001. It showed a top aide to the city's mayor accepting a $1,000 bribe. At the time, the senior U.S. district judge had issued an order banning dissemination of the FBI tape by members of the prosecution and defense teams. The protective order was issued to ensure fair trials for the mayor and his codefendants, who were later tried and convicted.

Jim Taricani, a veteran investigative reporter who has won four Emmys, received the videotape from a defense attorney whose client pleaded guilty before the trial. His station then broadcast the tape. The judge ordered a special prosecutor to investigate the source of the tape, but interviews with 14 people failed to uncover the source. The judge then found Taricani in civil contempt and fined him $1,000 for each day he continued to refuse to name his source. Taricani paid a fine of $85,000, for which his employer reimbursed him. When Taricani still refused to turn over the information, the judge held Taricani in criminal contempt.

Before the reporter was sentenced, the attorney who handed over the videotape came forward and admitted his role. He also admitted he lied under oath to the special prosecutor. The judge still sentenced Taricani to home incarceration.

Before his sentencing, Taricani said, "'I wish all my sources could be on the record, but when people are afraid, a promise of confidentiality may be the only way to get the information to the public, and in some cases, to protect the well-being of the source. I made a promise to my source, which I intend to keep."[143]

New York Times reporter James Risen was subpoenaed by the Justice Department under President Bush and again under President Obama, seeking to compel him to testify before a grand jury about his confidential sources for his 2006 book on the Central Intelligence Agency. The subpoena required Risen to provide documents about sources for a chapter that focuses on covert CIA efforts to disrupt alleged Iranian nuclear weapons research. The first subpoena expired when the grand jury adjourned; a federal judge quashed the second one. In July 2011, a federal judge greatly limited his testimony in the trial of a former CIA agent accused of leaking information to Risen.[144]

The most famous anonymous source remains Deep Throat, a confidential source relied upon by *Washington Post* reporters Bob Woodward and Carl Bernstein in their investigation of the burglary of the Democratic National Headquarters in the Watergate Hotel and the subsequent cover-up that eventually resulted in the resignation of President Richard Nixon in 1974. In the *All the President's Men* movie, Deep Throat was portrayed as a shadowy image standing in a parking garage, smoking a cigarette, and listening as Woodward begs for help. All Woodward's leads had gone dead. Finally, Deep Throat said, "Just follow the money."

Three decades later, the shadowy figure in the parking garage who helped Woodward and Bernstein unravel the Watergate cover-up unmasked himself.[145] Despite White House pressure on the *Washington Post,* the impeachment proceedings and related hearings in Congress, and years of inquiries and speculations, Woodward and Bernstein consistently refused to reveal Deep Throat's identity. Mark Felt, former deputy director of the FBI, was identified in June 2005 as Deep Throat by his family in an article in *Vanity Fair.* Felt, then 91, was identified in part because his family believed he deserved to be honored for his actions while he was still alive.[146] Felt died in 2008 at age 95.

When journalists debate the unnamed source issue, Deep Throat is a trump card against those who want to ban confidential sources from all publications and television broadcasts. It is safe to say that no anonymous source played a more pivotal role on the national stage by unveiling government secrets than Deep Throat.

The Case for Protecting Sources

Reporters refuse to disclose their sources, often even when a court orders them to do so, on two grounds: ethical, because they gave their word that they would not, and legal, because they believe the law gives them a special privilege to protect their sources' identities. A privilege, according to *Black's Law Dictionary,* is a "particular and peculiar benefit or advantage enjoyed by a person, company or class, beyond the common advantages of other citizens." In tort law, according to *Black's,* it is "the ability to act contrary to another individual's legal right without that individual having legal redress for the consequences of that defense."[147]

The law has long recognized that certain relationships are so personal that they deserve protection against disclosure of confidential communication. The law recognizes that discussion between a husband and wife, a lawyer and a client, a clergyman and a layman, or a doctor and a patient are so personal that they warrant unbroken confidentiality. A husband cannot be forced to testify against his wife, a lawyer cannot be forced to testify as to what a client confided, and a priest cannot be forced to testify what a penitent confessed. The law recognizes only a few exceptions to these privileges.

Journalists argued as early as the colonial period that the law should recognize another privilege: the journalist's privilege to protect the confidentiality of sources. Printers in that era provided confidentiality to many contributors. Some of them even resisted demands of the legislative branch to reveal sources' names. They argued that journalistic ethics and their own livelihoods required them to avoid revealing the identities of confidential sources.

The public interest in good government also required journalists to protect those sources because some stories could be told only if reporters promised confidentiality to those who had information about government corruption. By the end of the 19th century, Maryland's legislature enacted the first journalist's privilege by statute. Today, 40 states and the District of Columbia have enacted reporter shield laws. The most recent was West Virginia, which enacted legislation, the Whistleblower Protection Act, in April 2011.[148] Courts in other states have recognized reporter's privilege under their state constitutions so that only Wyoming offers no shield law protection.

The terms of the protection offered journalists vary. For example, the Minnesota Supreme Court ruled the state shield law did not prevent the court from fining Wally Wakefield when he refused to disclose his source to a former coach who sued for libel.[149] On the other hand, a reporter for the *Phoenix New Times* invoked the Arizona shield law when he received a subpoena from a grand jury investigating the arson of a number of homes. The reporter had met one of the arsonists for an hour-long interview after promising not to reveal the arsonist's identity. The article was published,[150] and the grand jury subpoena followed. The state judge quashed the subpoena, ruling the state's shield law protected the reporter.[151] The arsonist was arrested some time later.

The case for a privilege to protect confidential sources is best made by Bruce Sanford, one of the nation's leading media lawyers and a staunch defender of the First Amendment:[152]

> It is termed a "reporter's" privilege, but the authority under which reporters refuse to divulge sources and information, more than any other privilege recognized by United States courts, is "the people's" privilege. Unlike privileges for private communications between husband and wife, attorney and client, or doctor and patient, the reporter's privilege protects actions and communications that are undertaken for the express purpose of improving the public's access to information.
>
> The main purpose of any evidentiary privilege is to encourage openness in certain relationships where such openness is deemed beneficial to society. We as a society want people to be able to speak frankly with their doctors and spouses without fear that their words will be subject to scrutiny in a court of law. In no case is the benefit to society so direct as when sources feel free to share important information with the press, and through it, with the public.
>
> In a country where we have many freedoms, this particular freedom is essential because the success of our democratic government rests on the ability of citizens to make informed decisions about matters of public concern. Without reporters being able to have confidential communications with leaders in politics, business and other fields, the public will be deprived of information about what is *really* going on in their government and their world.
>
> The reporter's privilege is repeatedly challenged. In particular, many chafe at the idea that reporters should receive "special treatment" by being exempt from civic duties. In my view, these people miss the point. The reporter's privilege is about elevating the public discourse, not the press' stature. And when this privilege is not recognized, the public—not the press—are the real losers.

The Seminal Case

The 1960s and 1970s were turbulent decades in the United States. Turmoil boiled over amid the civil rights struggles, the assassinations of a president and a presidential candidate, the protracted conflict in Vietnam, and the Watergate scandal. In that environment, many reporters relied on confidential sources to report stories that otherwise would have gone unreported. Chief among them was the Watergate investigation of reporters Woodward and Bernstein.

From this era came the seminal Supreme Court decision on the right of reporters to protect the confidentiality of sources. The decision came in the context of four merged cases—*In re Pappas*,[153] *Caldwell v. United States*,[154] *Branzburg v. Meigs*,[155] and *Branzburg v. Hayes*[156] recorded under the latter title.[157]

Paul Pappas was an investigative reporter-photographer for WTEV-TV in New Bedford, Massachusetts. He was covering civil unrest, including fires and "other turmoil" in progress in New Bedford in July 1970. The Black Panthers, a radical black group, allowed Pappas to enter group headquarters on the condition he would not report anything he saw or heard inside. Two months later, a grand jury investigating the violence subpoenaed Pappas to testify about what he had seen and heard at the Black Panthers' headquarters. Pappas refused. He was found in contempt in state court, and the state supreme court upheld the decision. He appealed to the U.S. Supreme Court.

Earl Caldwell was one of the black reporters who made his mark covering the civil rights era. A member of the *New York Times* national staff, he was assigned to cover the activities of the Black Panthers in Oakland, California. In a 1968 article, one 27-year-old Panther told Caldwell, "We're young revolutionaries. We're revolutionaries and we're fighting a war.... We are ready to die for what we believe."[158]

J. Edgar Hoover, the long-time director of the FBI, labeled the Panthers the greatest threat to the internal security of the United States. A federal grand jury began investigating the group and subpoenaed Caldwell, ordering him to testify about his reporting and to bring with him his notes and any tape recordings of interviews with the Panthers. Caldwell refused, arguing that if he testified, his effectiveness as a reporter on the activities of the Black Panthers would be fatally compromised.[159] A federal district judge recognized a limited newsman's privilege to protect his sources but said the grand jury could compel his testimony.[160] Caldwell appealed to the Ninth U.S. Circuit Court of Appeals. This time Caldwell won, but the government appealed to the Supreme Court.

The other two cases involved Paul Branzburg, a reporter for the Louisville *Courier-Journal.* In 1969, he wrote an eyewitness account of two men engaged in the manufacture of hashish from marijuana in a makeshift laboratory in south central Louisville. Branzburg reported that the pair hoped to produce enough of the illegal drug to net them up to $5,000 for three weeks of work. The story concluded that the reporter promised the hashish makers that he would not identify them if they allowed him to observe what they were doing. He said to persuade the men to talk to him he even showed one a copy of the Kentucky reporter's privilege statute, or shield law, to prove he could not be forced to reveal their identities.[161] Fourteen months later, the newspaper published a story under Branzburg's byline detailing his observation of the use of marijuana in Frankfort as part of his effort to describe the drug scene in the state capital.

Local and federal narcotics agents read Branzburg's stories and decided to break up the drug trade. When Branzburg was subpoenaed, he refused to reveal the identities of those who had talked to him, arguing that the Kentucky reporter's privilege statute,[162] the state Constitution, and the First Amendment to the U.S. Constitution protected his right not to identify his informants. He was ordered to testify by state judges, and he appealed to the U.S. Supreme Court.

In 1972, the Supreme Court took up the issue.[163] The sole question before the Court, according to the majority opinion written by Justice Byron White, was "the obligation of reporters to respond to grand jury subpoenas as other citizens do and to answer questions relevant to an investigation into the commission of crime."[164] In a 5-to-4 decision, the Court ruled that the First Amendment freedom of the press did not include the right of reporters to refuse to appear before a grand jury and answer its questions about criminal activity they had witnessed. The majority held that the public's interest in law enforcement outweighed the concerns of the press. While journalists had been arguing that protecting sources was vital to their ability to inform the public, the courts had a long tradition of enforcing grand jury subpoenas.

The Supreme Court said as early as 1919 that testifying before a grand jury was recognized as a public duty except for the possibility that those subpoenaed could incriminate themselves in their testimony. "[I]t is clearly recognized that the giving of testimony and the attendance upon court or grand jury in order to testify are public duties which every person within the jurisdiction of the government is bound to perform upon being properly summoned."[165]

The *Branzburg* majority opinion was limited by the fifth vote. Justice Lewis Powell, while subscribing to the majority opinion, wrote his concurring opinion to emphasize what he believed was "the limited nature of the ruling." He suggested judges who review reporters' motions to quash grand jury subpoenas should balance freedom of the press against the obligation of all citizens to testify before a grand jury.[166] Justice Potter Stewart in a speech in 1974 characterized the decision as "considering Mr. Justice Powell's concurring opinion, perhaps by a vote of four and a half to four and a half."[167] And Justice Powell, dissenting in another case, commented that the *Branzburg* ruling did not leave reporters without First Amendment rights to protect the identities of their sources.[168]

The dissenters broke into two sides. Justice William O. Douglas insisted that the First Amendment provided reporters with an absolute and unqualified privilege to protect sources.[169] The others—Justices Stewart, William Brennan, and Thurgood Marshall—argued in an opinion written by Stewart that the Court was going to impose a governmental function on the media, an argument at which Justice Powell scoffed.[170] In his dissent, Stewart proposed a three-part test. The government would have to prove all three of these conditions or reporters would be allowed to protect the confidentialities of their sources:

- A probable cause exists that the reporter has information that is clearly relevant to a specific crime.
- The information sought cannot be obtained by alternative means less destructive of First Amendment rights.
- The state has a compelling and overriding interest in the information.[171]

Powell's concurring opinion raised another question. What if the Court framed the decision in terms of this question: "Do journalists have a right to protect their sources by refusing to disclose their identity?" The answer to that question, it appears from the opinions, would have been "yes, under certain circumstances." Five of the justices—Powell, who concurred with the majority; Stewart, whose dissent was joined by Brennan and Marshall; and Douglas, who wrote a separate dissent—recognized some privilege for journalists in protecting confidential sources.[172] As a result, many courts have recognized some privilege for reporters in protecting their sources.

In the aftermath of the Court's decision, the American Society of Newspaper Editors and Sigma Delta Chi, now known as the Society of Professional Journalists, called for Congress to pass legislation that would protect the confidentiality of journalists' news sources.[173] While the issue has been taken up several times, Congress has never passed such legislation.[174] One of the obstacles has been agreement on its terms, including who could be considered a journalist and under what circumstances a journalist could refuse to testify. After the rash of subpoenas between 2001 and 2004, U.S. Senator Christopher Dodd, D-Conn., announced he would introduce legislation to create a federal shield law to protect reporters from federal subpoenas.[175] Dodd's bill went nowhere, but new proposals were introduced in both the House of Representatives and the Senate in 2005, by two Democrats and two Indiana Republicans, who asserted in an opinion piece published by the *Washington Post* that freedom of the press was under attack and that a shield law was essential.[176] The House passed the proposal in 2007,[177] but the bill never made it to the floor of the Senate and Bush administration officials vigorously opposed it.[178] The House passed the bill on voice vote in April 2009. After several committee meetings and compromises with the Obama administration, the Senate Judiciary Committee in December 2009 approved a different version by a vote of 14–5.[179] But after more than 75,000 classified documents related to the war in Afghanistan were posted online by WikiLeaks, support for the proposal eroded and the law died without a vote of the full Senate.[180]

As is often the case, the court's decision in the *Branzburg* case left many unanswered questions with which lower courts have grappled. More than three decades after *Branzburg*, the Supreme Court has refused opportunities to take up the issue again, but the lesson of *Branzburg* and more recent cases is clear: Reporters should consider carefully any request from a source who wants to provide information confidentially. Information that could be construed as damaging someone's reputation or related to criminal activity can lead a reporter to an unpleasant choice: go to jail or break a promise and reveal a source.

The Real Impact

No chapter about journalism ethics could begin to detail all the ethical dilemmas that journalists encounter in their day-to-day work. The reporter or photographer decides many of those dilemmas quickly and easily. Reporters and editors vigorously debate other issues. To most journalists, their ethical decisions are critical; they do not want to be viewed as unethical or do anything that would undermine the credibility of their newspapers, broadcast stations, or Internet sites.

For every bad decision that is made and written about, hundreds of right decisions are made; most of them are never acknowledged publicly. But every bad decision serves to further undermine the public trust in journalism, and that is harmful to all journalists and also to democracy. Rising discontent with the media turns into weakened support for the First Amendment, and that means trouble for the American form of government. That is precisely why journalists must be ethical. The First Amendment may not require it; democracy does.

The British Media Scandal of 2011

In what must have been one of the largest news media scandals in a decade, Rupert Murdoch's News Corporation was scalded in 2011 by politicians, investigators, and other media for its phone-hacking practices.

The *News of the World,* Britain's largest circulation Sunday tabloid, was closed in July 2011 and 200 employees dismissed after revelations that reporters had hacked the phone of a missing 13-year-old schoolgirl in 2002. Journalists deleted voicemails, giving her parents hope she was still alive when she had been murdered. *The Guardian* reported police feared evidence had been destroyed. Murdoch, owner of *News of the World,* personally visited the family of the deceased teen and apologized to them.

The scandal widened, with reports that journalists had hacked phones belonging to the families of people killed in the July 7, 2005, bombings in the London transit system. Scotland Yard was asked to investigate reports that the tabloid's executives had paid police officers for information and lied to Parliament. In the United States, Attorney General Eric Holder announced that the FBI would investigate rumors that *News of the World* reporters had hacked the phones of the families of victims of the September 11, 2001, terrorist attacks.

Figure 4.2   Media mogul Rupert Murdoch, his son James, and Rebekah Brooks found themselves at the center of a phone-hacking scandal in Great Britain in July 2011. As News International officers, Murdoch and his son became subject of government and police investigations. Brooks, who served earlier as the chief executive of "News of the World," the highly successful Sunday tabloid Murdoch closed because of the hacking scandal, was arrested but was not charged with anything at that time.

There had been previous hacking incidents. A private investigator and the royal editor of the *News of the World* were jailed in 2007 after the phones of Princes William and Harry and their aides were hacked.

As the British investigation of the scandal moved forward, 11 people, most of them former Murdoch employees, were arrested and two British police officials resigned. The arrests include Rebekah Brooks and Andrew Coulson, both former editors of *News of the World*. Murdoch also withdrew his bid for the $12 billion pay-TV British Sky Broadcasting.

Murdoch, 80, and his son James, 38, were questioned by British lawmakers for three hours about allegations the tabloid had hacked the phones of murder victims and paid police for stories. During his testimony, an attempt was made to hit Murdoch in the face with a pie, but his wife slugged the intruder.

Murdoch's holdings in the United States include Fox Broadcasting Company, the *Wall Street Journal, the New York Post,* and the movie studio 20th Century Fox. His conglomerate in one of the largest media companies in the world.

The scandal involved both legal and ethical violations. Breaking into someone's voicemail and interfering with a police investigation into a murder are illegal in both the United States and Great Britain. The ethics code of the Society of Professional Journalists warns reporters to "(a)void undercover or other surreptitious methods of gathering information except when traditional open methods will not yield information vital to the public." Certainly, the information to be gathered from the teenager's phone could not be considered vital to the public and what information there was could have been gathered from the police. In addition, the SPJ code makes it clear journalists should show compassion toward those affected adversely by the news.

Endnotes

1. Tom Cooper, *Between the Summits: What Americans Think About Media Ethics*, Journal of Mass Media Ethics, 2008(1), 25.
2. Frank Newport, *Republicans Deeply Distrustful of News Media, Democrats much more positive*, Gallup News Service, Oct. 8, 2007, http://www.gallup.com/poll/101677/Republicans-Remain-Deeply-Distrustful-News-Media.aspx.
3. *Internet News Audience Highly Critical of News Organization*, Pew Research Center for the People and the Press, Aug. 9, 2007, http://people-press.org/report/348/internet-news-audience-highly-critical-of-news-organizations.
4. Cooper, *supra* note 1, 20–22.
5. Results are available at http://www.firstamendmentcenter.org/sofa_reports/index.aspx.
6. *Examining Our Credibility, 1999*, American Society of Newspaper Editors. Summary available at http://204.8.120.192/index.cfm?ID=2632.
7. Editor & Publisher, Dec. 28, 1998, 12.
8. Charles Self, *A Study of News Credibility*, International Communication Bulletin (Spring 1988), 23. See also Self, *Perceived Task of News Reports as a Predictor of Media Choice,* Journalism Quarterly, Spring 1988, 119–125.
9. Stephen Klaidman and Tom L. Beauchamp, *The Virtuous Journalist* (Oxford University Press, 1987), 4–5.
10. Claude-Jean Bertrand, *Media Ethics and Accountability Systems* (Transaction Publishers, 2000), 2.
11. Fred Fedler, *Actions of Early Journalists Often Unethical, Even Illegal,* Journal of Mass Media Ethics, 1997(3), 160–170.
12. *Id.*
13. James Fallows, *Breaking the News: How the Media Undermine American Democracy* (Vintage Books, 1997), 3.
14. Howard Kurtz, *Why the Media is Always Right,* Columbia Journalism Review, May-June 1993.
15. John C. Merrill, *Journalism Ethics: Philosophical Foundations for News Media* (St. Martin's Press, 1997), 6–7.
16. Dave Aeikins, *Restoring the Public's faith in News media Credibility*, Quill, http://www.spj.org/quill_issue.asp?ref=1498.
17. Bastian Vanacker and Genelle Belmas, *Trust and the Economics of News,* Journal of Mass Media Ethics, 2009 (2-3), 110–126.
18. Philip Seib and Kathy Fitzpatrick, *Journalism Ethics* (Harcourt and Brace, 1997), 1–3.
19. Mark Memmott, *Soldier, Reporter Teamed Up for Question Asked Rumsfeld,* USA Today, Dec. 10, 2004, 9A.
20. David Bauder, *CBS Says It Cannot Vouch for Authenticity of Bush Documents*, Las Vegas (Nevada) Sun, Sept. 20, 2004, A8. *See also* K. C. Howard, *Filmmaker Tells 'Slacker Friends' to Get Out, Vote*, Las Vegas (Nevada) Review-Journal, Oct. 16, 2004, A9.
21. Howard Kurtz, *Dan Rather to Step Down at CBS: Anchor's Decision Comes Amid Probe of Flawed Bush Report*, Washington Post, Nov. 24, 2004, Page A01.
22. Howard Kurtz, *CBS Fires 4 Staffers In Wake Of Probe; Panel Faults Rather For His Defense of Bush Guard Story,* Washington Post, Jan. 11, 2005, Page A01.
23. Jacques Steinberg, *Times' 2 Top Editors Resign After Furor on Writer's Fraud*, New York Times, June 6, 2003, Page A1.
24. Fred Brown, *Just What Would You Give (or Give Up) for that Story?* Society of Professional Journalists, June 6, 2000, http://www.spj.org/news.asp?ref=505.
25. Dan Horn, *Enquirer Paid Chiquita $14 Million in Settlement, Magazine Reports*, The Cincinnati Enquirer, Jan. 24, 2001.
26. Alicia C. Shepard, *The Chiquita Aftermath*, American Journalism Review, May 1999, 445.
27. Eason Jordan, *The News We Kept to Ourselves,* New York Times, April 11, 2003, A25.
28. Glen Warchol, *Trib Editor Resigns Amid Controversy*, Salt Lake Tribune, May 2, 2003, A1.
29. Clifford G. Christians et al., *Media Ethics: Cases and Moral Reasoning*, 6th ed. (Longman, 2001), 41.

30. Robert E. Pierre and Ann Gerhart, *News of Pandemonium May Have Slowed Aid,* Washington Post, Oct. 5, 2005, A08.

31. *SPJ Says Hasty Coverage of Election Violated Ethics Code,* http://www.spj.org/news.asp?ref=71.

32. *American Attitudes about the First Amendment 2001,* available at http://www.freedomforum.org.

33. Richard Labunski, *The First Amendment under Siege* (Greenwood Press, 1981), 3.

34. Alexander Hamilton, James Madison, John Jay, *The Federalist Papers,* The Federalist No. 10. ("The effect … is … to refine and enlarge the public views, by passing them through the medium of a chosen body of citizens, whose wisdom may best discern the true interest of their country, and whose patriotism and love of justice will be least likely to sacrifice it to temporary or partial considerations. Under such a regulation, it may well happen that the public voice, pronounced by the representatives of the people, will be more consonant to the public good than if pronounced by the people themselves, convened for the purpose.")

35. W. Wat Hopkins, *The Supreme Court Defines the Marketplace of Ideas,* 73 Journalism and Mass Communication Quarterly, 1996 (1), 40.

36. *Abrams v. United States,* 250 U.S. 616, 40 S.Ct. 17, 63 L.Ed. 1173 (Holmes, J., dissenting) (1919).

37. See, *e.g.,* Stanley Ingber, *The Marketplace of Ideas: A Legitimizing Myth,* Duke Law Journal, 1984 (1) 3–4; Robert Post, *Reconciling Theory and Doctrine in First Amendment Jurisprudence,* 88 California Law Review, 2000, 2353, 2356; Ken Greenawalt, *Free Speech Justifications,* 89 Columbia Law Review, 1990, 119.

38. Denis McQuail, *Mass Communication Theory: An Introduction,* 3rd ed. (Sage Publications, 1994), 356.

39. Maxwell McCombs and Donald L. Shaw, *The Agenda Setting Function of Mass Media,* 36 Public Opinion Quarterly, 1972, 176.

40. J. W. Dearing and E. M. Rogers, *Agenda Setting* (Sage Publications, 1996), 89.

41. See Carl Bernstein and Bob Woodward, *All The President's Men* (1974).

42. *Mills v. Alabama,* 384 U.S. 214, 218; 86 S.Ct. 1434; 16 L.Ed.2d 484; 1 Media L. Rep. 1334 (1966).

43. Elliott D. Cohen and Deni Elliott, *Journalism Ethics* (ABC-CLIO, 1997), 1.

44. http://www.poynter.org/column.asp?id=45

45. Jack Shafer, *The Romenesko Effect: How a One-man Web site Is Improving Journalism,* Slate, posted Monday, April 18, 2005, http://www.slate.com/id/2116903.

46. *Id.*

47. http://www.journalism.org/dailybriefings

48. http://www.mediabistro.com

49. http://iwantmedia.com

50. http://www.cjr.org

51. Mark Jurkowitz, *The Romenesko Effect: How a Media Web Site Is Changing the Face—and Pace—of Media Culture,* The Boston Phoenix, Aug. 26, 2005, http://www.bostonphoenix.com/boston/news_features/dont_quote_me/multi-page/documents/04927098.asp

52. http://www.regrettheerror.com

53. Commission on Freedom of the Press, *A Free and Responsible Press* (University of Chicago Press, 1947), 20.

54. Edmund B. Lambeth, *Committed Journalism: An Ethic for the Profession* (Indiana University Press, 1986), 6–7.

55. *Id.*

56. Bertrand, *supra,* note 10, 44.

57. Philip Meyer, *Ethical Journalism,* (Longman Press, 1987), 18.

58. *Id.*

59. *Why Doesn't SPJ Enforce its Code of Ethics?,* http://www.spj.org/ethicsfaq.asp

60. *Id.*

61. Bonnie Brennen, *Conflicted interests, contested terrain: The code of ethics.* In Philip Patterson and Lee Wilkins (eds.) *Media Ethics: Issues and Cases,* (McGraw-Hill, 2008), pp. 111–113.

62. The SPJ Code of Ethics, last revised in 1996, is available online at http://www.spj.org/ethicscode.asp The society, originally known as Sigma Delta Chi, borrowed its first code from the American Society of Newspaper Editors in 1926 before creating its own in 1973. The code was modified in 1984 and 1987.

63. The ethics code of the American Society of News Editors is available online at http://www.asne.org/kiosk/archive/principl.htm The code, first adopted in 1922 as the "Canons of Journalism" was revised and renamed "Statement of Principles" in 1975. Its most recent update was in 2006.

64. The ethics code of the Radio Television Digital News Association is available online at http://www.rtdna.org/pages/media_items/code-of-ethics-and-professional-conduct48.php It was adopted in 2000.

65. The ethics code of the National Press Photographers Association is available at http://www.nppa.org/professional_development/business_practices/ethics.html. The code, devised in 1946, was most recently revised in 2004.

66. Lambeth, *supra*, note 54, 5.

67. Dennis Cauchon and Martha Moore, *Desperation forced a horrific decision*, USA Today, Sept. 3, 2002, 5A.

68. See Phil Nesbitt, *Tragedy in Photos, a New Standard?* American Press Institute, Sept. 14, 2001, available at http://www.americanpressinstitute.org/content/364.cfm?sects=Managing%20And%20Reporting%20a%20News%20Crisis&template=details_cov&id=364&CFID=2180891&CFTOKEN=52956925.

69. Tom Junod, *The Falling Man*, Esquire, Sept. 11, 2008, http://www.esquire.com/features/ESQ0903-SEP_FALLINGMAN.

70. Jim Rutenberg and Bill Carter, *A Nation Challenged: Network Coverage a Target of Fire from Conservatives*, New York Times, Nov. 7, 2001, at B2.

71. Ted Gup, *A Question of Dependence: The journalistic covenant post 9/11*, Columbia Journalism Review, March/April 2004, 59–60.

72. Stuart Taylor Jr. and KC Johnson, *Until Proven Innocent: Political Correctness and the Shameful Injustices of the Duke Lacrosse Rape Case*, (St. Martin's Press, 2007).

73. Kelly McBride, *Winners and Losers in the Duke Lacrosse Story*, Poynter Online, April 11, 2007, available at http://www.poynter.org/column.asp?id=67&aid=121262

74. Rachel Smolkin, *Justice Delayed*, American Journalism Review, August/September 2007, 18.

75. *Id.* at 21

76. *Id.*

77. Taylor and Johnson, *supra* note 72, at 124–125.

78. *Id.* at 269.

79. Smolkin, *supra* note 74, at 20.

80. Sally Dadisman, *Naming Names: Should News Organizations Identify the Accuser in the Duke Lacrosse Case?*, American Journalism Review, August/September 2007, 22–23.

81. Kelly McBride, *Duke Lacrosse Case: Should We Name the Accuser?*, Poynter Online, Jan. 29, 2007, available at http://www.poynter.org/uncategorized/80052/duke-lacrosse-case-should-we-name-the-accuser/

82. Dadisman, *supra* note 80.

83. *Id.*

84. Matea Gold, *'Dateline' Too Close to Cops?*, Los Angeles Times, April 26, 2006, E9.

85. Paul Farhi, *'Dateline' online string: One more point; NBC Collaboration Raises Eyebrows as Well as Awareness*, Washington Post, April 9, 2006, D1.

86. Brian Montopoli, *Does "Dateline" Go Too Far "To Catch A Predator?*,*" CBS News Public Eye, February 7, 2006, available at http://www.cbsnews.com/blogs/2006/02/07/publiceye/entry1290135.shtml?tag=contentMain;contentBody.

87. *Id.*

88. Pew Research Center for the People & the Press, *Voters Likes Campaign 2004, But Too Much Mud Slinging*, Nov. 11, 2004, available at http://www.people-press.org/report/233.

89. Pew Research Center for the People & the Press, *High Marks for the Campaign, a High Bar for Obama*, Nov. 13, 2008, available at http://www.people-press.org/report/?pageid=1429.

90. Bill Dedman, *Journalists Dole Out Cash to Politicians (quietly)*, MSNBC.com, June 25, 2007, available at http://www.msnbc.msn.com/id/19113485.

91. John Stamper, *State GOP Calls for Dismissal of Newspaper Employee*, Lexington Herald-Leader, June 26, 2007, B2.

92. SPJ News, *SPJ Leaders Respond to MSNBC.com's Investigative Report Concerning Journalists' Political*

Contributions, Offers Journalism Ethics Resources, June 26, 2007, available at http://www.spj.org/news. asp?REF=682#682.

93. Shawn Hubler, *The Mayor and His Mistress,* Los Angeles Magazine, May 2008, http://www.lamag.com/ article.aspx?id=1112. David Zahniser, *'I regret hurting people,'* Los Angeles Times, April 10, 2008, available at http://www.articles.latimes.com/2008/apr/10/local/me-salinas10.

94. Phil Wilson, *L.A. mayor is dating local newscaster,* Los Angeles Times, June 2, 2009, http://www.articles.latimes.com/2009/jun/02/local/me-villaraigosa2.

95. Elizabeth Jensen, Carla Hall, and Jeffrey L. Rabin, *Shriver to Quit Job at NBC News,* Los Angeles Times, Feb. 4, 2004, available at http://www.articles.latimes.com/2004/feb/04/local/me-maria4.

96. Maureen Dowd, *Cheney, Master of Pain,* New York Times, May 16, 2009, http://www.nytimes.com/2009/05/17/opinion/17dowd.html?_r=1&scp=10&sq=Maureen%20Dowd&st=cse. See also Belinda Luscombe, *Is Maureen Dowd Guilty of Plagiarism?,* Time Magazine, May 18, 2009, http://www.time.com/time/arts/article/0,8599,1899530,00.html.

97. Lori Robertson, *Ethically Challenged,* American Journalism Review, March 2001, 21.

98. Lori Robertson, *Confronting the Culture,* American Journalism Review, August/September 2005, 37.

99. Robertson, *supra* note 97.

100. Ron F. Smith, *Ethics in Journalism*, 6th ed. (Blackwell Publishing, 2008) 99–100.

101. Sinead O'Brien, *Secrets and Lies,* American Journalism Review, Sept. 1998, 41.

102. Robertson, *supra* note 97.

103. The survey was conducted for publication in the magazine *Brill's Content*, a media watchdog journal. The results were reported by Herbert N. Foerstel, *From Watergate to Monicagate: Ten Controversies in Modern Journalism and Media* (Greenwood Press, 2001), 7–8.

104. *Tiger Woods Issues Statement: "Personal Sins Should Not Require Press Releases,"* Wall Street Journal, Dec. 2, 2009, available at http://blogs.wsj.com/speakeasy/2009/12/02/tiger-woods-makes-statement-personal-sins-should-not-require-press-releases/

105. Howard Bryant, *Why Tiger Matters,* ESPN.com, Dec. 23, 2009, available at http://sports.espn.go.com/espn/commentary/news/story?page=bryant/091223

106. Tim Padgett, *Mug-Shot Mania,* Time magazine, Sept. 21, 2009, 82.

107. Patrik Jonsson, *A Crime Paper Flourishes by Printing Mug Shots,* The Christian Science Monitor, Jan. 6, 2009.

108. Quoted in John L. Hulteng, *The Messenger's Motives: Ethical Problems* of *the News Media,* 2d ed. (Prentice Hall, 1985), 34.

109. *Id.*

110. Christians et al., *supra* note 29, at 47–49.

111. Seib, *supra* note 18, at 110.

112. A. David Gordon and John Michael Kittross, *Controversies in Media Studies,* 2d ed. (Longman, 1999), 270–273.

113. *Society of Professional Journalists, SPJ Ethics Committee Condemns Major Broadcast Networks' Practice of "Checkbook Journalism,"* March 23, 2010, http://www.spj.org/news.asp?ref=954.

114. Society of Professional Journalists, *NBC News' 'C'heckbook Journalism' Crossed Ethical Line,* Dec. 28, 2009, http://www.spj.org/news.asp?REF=944#944.

115. The author of this chapter was a member of the Ethics Committee of the Society of Professional Journalists and participated in email discussions of both statements before they were issued.

116. Jeffrey Toobin, *Buying Headlines,* Quill, November/December 1994, 20.

117. Katharine Q. Seelye, *Impeachment: The Speaker-Elect; After Spotlight, Livingston Exits Center Stage,* New York Times, Dec. 19, 1998, 3B.

118. Bernard Weintraub, *Hustler Behind Sex Story,* New York Times, Dec. 19, 1998, B3.

119. *National Survey Finds Majority of Journalists Now Depend on Social Media for Story Research,* http://www.gwu.edu/explore/mediaroom/newsreleases/nationalsurveyfindsmajorityofjournalists nowdependonsocialmediaforstoryresearch.

120. Matt Lakin, *Sheriff: Lockett's Younger Son Accidentally Shot Brother*, Dec. 22, 2009, http://www.knoxnews.com/news/2009/dec/22/sheriff-locketts-younger-son-accidentally-shot-bro/

121. Cara Degette, *RMN 'Tweets' the Funeral of 3-Year Old Boy Killed in Ice Cream Shop*, The Colorado Independent, Sept. 8, 2008, http://coloradoindependent.com/7717/rmn-tweets-the-funeral-of-3-year-old-boy/ John Temple, *Temple: New Tech Raises Taste Questions*, Sept. 12, 2008, http://www.rocky-mountainnews.com/news/2008/sep/12/temple-new-tech-raises-taste-questions/

122. Ginny Whitehouse, *Newsgathering and Privacy: Expanding Ethics Codes to Reflect Change in the Digital Media Age*, Journal of Mass Media Ethics, 25:4, October 2010 , pp. 310–32.

123. *Garland v. Torre*, 259 F.2d 545, 547 (2d Cir.), cert. denied, 358 U.S. 910 (1958).

124. Torre's story reported that one executive told her Garland balked at plans for a CBS special because of her inferiority problems and "because she thinks she is terribly fat." Garland sued the network for $1.39 million and subpoenaed the journalist. Torre died in 1997. Her obituary quoted her family as maintaining she never told anyone, even them, who the source was. Nick Ravo, *Marie Torre, 72, TV Columnist Jailed for Protecting News Source,* New York Times, Jan. 5, 1997, A24. Dorothy Kilgallen, the gossip columnist, said she never expected anyone would go to jail for reporting that Garland had personal problems. Gerald Clarke, *Get Happy: The Life of Judy Garland* (Dell Publishing, 2001), 329.

125. See Stephen Bates, *Garland v. Torre and the Birth of Reporter's Privilege*, 15:2 Communication Law and Policy, 2010, 91–128.

126. Felicity Barringer, *Newsday Refuses to Reveal Source of Thomas Report*, New York Times, Feb. 14, 1992, A20. Neil A. Lewis, *Second Reporter Silent in Senate Leak Inquiry*, New York Times, Feb. 25, 1992, A13.

127. Helen DeWar, *Senate Counsel Loses Bid For Reporters' Testimony; Probe Continues on Sources of Thomas Leaks*, Washington Post, Mar. 26, 1992, A1.

128. Doug Grow, *Scribe Takes a Stand—an Expensive One: Refusing to Reveal Sources Has Made Wally Wakefield a Journalistic Hero*, Star Tribune (Minneapolis), April 13, 2004, 2B.

129. Associated Press, *Fines End for Reporter after Coach, School District Settle Lawsuit*, July 12, 2004, available at http://www.firstamendmentcenter.org/news.aspx?id=13686.

130. Joseph C. Wilson IV, *What I Didn't Find in Africa*, New York Times, July 6, 2003, D9.

131. Robert Novak, *The Mission to Niger*, Chicago Sun-Times, July 14, 2003, 31.

132. Adam Liptak and Peter T. Kilborn, *Two Journalists Subpoenaed over Source of Disclosure*, New York Times, May 23, 2004, A22.

133. Adam Liptak, *Reporter from Time is Held in Contempt in CIA Leak Probe*, New York Times, Aug. 10, 2004, A1.

134. Susan Schmidt, *Post Source Reveals Identity to Leak Probers*, Sept. 16, 2004, A2.

135. Adam Liptak, *Reporters Face Scrutiny in CIA Leak Inquiry*, New York Times, Sept. 28, 2004, A18.

136. Carol Leonnig, *Reporters Lose Appeal, Face Jail Time; Supreme Court Refuses to Review Contempt Charge in Probe of Leak about CIA Agent*, Washington Post, June 28, 2005, A7.

137. Lorne Manly, *Editors at Time, Inc., Offer Reassurances to Reporters*, New York Times, July 13, 2005, A18.

138. Howard Kurtz, *Lawyers Secured Rove's Waiver; Executives Hear Reporters' Anger*, Washington Post, July 16, 2005, A6.

139. Adam Liptak, *Reporter Jailed After Refusing to Name Source*, New York Times, July 6, 2005, A1.

140. Christopher Lee, *Five Journalists Won't Name Sources; Wen Ho Lee Is Suing U.S. over Leaks from Spy Probe*, Washington Post, Jan. 11, 2004, A9.

141. Adam Liptak, *Judges Affirm Decision That Found 4 Reporters in Contempt*, New York Times, June 29, 2005, A16.

142. Adam Liptak, *News Media Pay in Scientist Suit*, New York Times, June 3, 2006, A1.

143. Pam Belluck, *Reporter Is Found Guilty for Refusal to Name Source*, New York Times, Nov. 19, 2004, A24.

144. Charlie Savage, *U.S. Subpoenas Times Reporter Over Book on C.I.A.*, New York Times, April 29, 2010, 21A; *U.S. Gathered Personal Data on Times Reporter in Case Against Ex-C.I.A. Agent*, Feb. 26, 2011, 14A; *Judge Agrees to Limit Writer's Testimony*, July 30, 2011, A15.

145. According to Bernstein, they would not have revealed the identity of Deep Throat until he died. Brady Dennis, *Ex-Watergate Writer Laments 'Idiot Culture,'* St. Petersburg Times, Mar. 19, 2004, 3B.

146. *Deep Throat Speaks*, Washington Post, June 1, 2005, A18.

147. *Black's Law Dictionary*, 6th ed., (1990), 1197.

148. Kristen Rasmussen, *West Virginia Acting Governor Signs Reporter Shield Law*, Reporters Committee for Freedom of the Press, April 6, 2011, available at http://www.rcfp.org/newsitems/index.php?i=11810.

149. *Weinberger v. Maplewood Review,* 668 N.W.2d 667: 2003 Minn. LEXIS 559; 31 Media L. Rep. 2281 (2003).

150. James Hibbert, *An Exclusive Interview with the Preserves Arsonist: He is Smart. He is Professional. He is Everything You Don't Expect,* Phoenix New Times (Arizona), Jan. 25, 2001.

151. John T. White, *Smoke Screen: Are State Shield Laws Really Protecting Speech or Simply Providing Cover for Criminals Like the Serial Arsonist?* 33 Ariz. St. L.J. 909 (2001).

152. Interview with the author.

153. 358 Mass. 604, *aff'd.* 266 N.E. 2d 297 (1970).

154. 311 F. Supp. 358, 1434 (N.D. Cal.), *rev'd.* F.2d 1081 (9th Cir. 1970).

155. 503 S.W.2d 748 (Ky. Ct. App. 1971), *aff'd. sub nom., Branzburg v. Hayes.*

156. 461 S.W.2d 345 (1971).

157. *Branzburg v. Hayes,* 408 U.S. 665 (1972); 92 S.Ct. 2646; 33 L.Ed.2d 626; 1 Media L. Rep. 2617 (1972).

158. Earl Caldwell, *Black Panthers, 'Young Revolutionaries at War,'* New York Times, Sept. 6, 1968, 49.

159. A. David Gordon, *Protection of News Sources: The History and Legal Status of the Newsman's Privilege* (1971), 93 (unpublished Ph.D. dissertation on file with University of Wisconsin Library).

160. *United States v. Caldwell,* 311 F.Supp. 358, 360 (1970).

161. Andrew Wolfson, *Paul Branzburg's Secret,* Courier-Journal (Louisville), Sept. 17, 1987.

162. "No person shall be compelled to disclose in any legal proceeding or trial before any court, or before any grand or petit jury, or before the presiding officer of any tribunal, or his agent or agents, or before the General Assembly, or any committee thereof, or before any city or county legislative body, or any committee thereof, or elsewhere, the source of any information procured or obtained by him, and published in a newspaper or by a radio or television broadcasting station by which he is engaged or employed, or with which he is connected." Ky. Rev. Stat. 421.100 (1962).

163. *Branzburg v. Hayes,* 408 U.S. 665; 92 S.Ct. 2646; 33 L.Ed.2d 626; 1 Media L. Rep. 2617 (1972).

164. *Id.* at 682.

165. *Blair v. United States,* 250 U.S. 273, 281; 39 S.Ct. 468; 63 L.Ed. 979 (1919). In *Wilson v. United States,* 221 U.S. 361, 372; 31 S.Ct. 538; 55 L.Ed. 771 (1911), the Court upheld a lower court decision to hold in contempt a U.S. citizen who had been subpoenaed to appear before a grand jury and had fled to France to avoid the subpoena. That decision quoted Lord Ellenborough: "The right to resort to means competent to compel the production of written, as well as oral, testimony, seems essential to the very existence and constitution of a court of common law, which receives and acts upon both descriptions of evidence, and could not possibly proceed with due effect without them." *Amey v. Long,* 9 East 484.

166. "The asserted claim to privilege should be judged on its facts by the striking of a proper balance between freedom of the press and the obligation of all citizens to give relevant testimony with respect to criminal conduct. The balance of these vital constitutional and societal interests on a case-by-case basis accords with the tried and traditional way of adjudicating such questions." *Branzburg,* at 709 (Powell, J., concurring).

167. Potter Stewart, *Or of the Press,* 26 Hastings L.J. (1974), 631. Reprinted in *Freedom of Expression: A Collection of Best Writings* (Kent Middleton & Roy M. Mersky, eds., 1981), 427.

168. *Saxbe v. Washington Post Co.,* 417 U.S. 843, 859–860; 94 S.Ct. 2811; 41 L.Ed.2d 514; 1 Media L. Rep. 2314. (Stewart, J., dissenting) (1974).

169. *Branzburg,* at 712, (Douglas, J., dissenting).

170. *Id.* at 725. "The Court thus invites state and federal authorities to undermine the historic independence of the press by attempting to annex the journalistic profession as an investigative arm of government."

171. *Id.* at 743 (Stewart, J., dissenting.)

172. Douglas said the First Amendment provided an unqualified privilege for journalists to protect their sources. "It is my view that there is no 'compelling need' that can be shown which qualifies the reporter's immunity from appearing or testifying before a grand jury." *Id.* at 712.

173. Richard Phalon, *Congress Urged to Act on Issue: Law Is Sought to Protect Confidentiality of News Sources,* New York Times, June 30, 1972, 15.

174. Jennifer Elrod, *Protecting Journalists from Compelled Disclosure: A Proposal for a Federal Statute,* 7 NYU Journal of Legislative and Public Policy 124, note 58 (2003).

175. Associated Press, *Federal Bill Would Protect Reporters,* New York Times, Nov. 20, 2004, A15

176. Mike Pence and Richard G. Lugar, *Protecting the Press ... and the Public,* Washington Post, Apr. 15, 2005, A25.
177. Elizabeth Williamson, *House Passes Bill to Protect Confidentiality of Reporters' Sources,* Washington Post, Oct. 17, 2007, A2.
178. Walter Pincus, *Cabinet Officials Cite Concerns About Senate Version of Reporter's Shield Law,* Washington Post, April 21, 2008, A13.
179. Associated Press, *Senate Committee Passes Shield Law,* New York Times, Dec. 11, 2009, 28A.
180. Charlie Savage, *After Afghan War Leaks, Revisions in a Shield Bill,* New York Times, Aug. 4, 2009, 12A.

5

Prior Restraint

Every freeman has an undoubted right to lay what sentiments he pleases before the public; to forbid this is to destroy the freedom of the press; but if he publishes what is improper, mischievous, or illegal, he must take the consequences of his own temerity.[1]

—British jurist Sir William Blackstone (1723–1780)

Our [WikiLeaks] founding values are those of the U.S. revolution. They are those of people like Jefferson and Madison. If you are a whistle-blower and you have material that is impartial, we will accept it, we will defend you, and we will publish it. You cannot turn away material simply because it comes from the United States.[2]

—Julian Assange, *The Man Behind WikiLeaks*, CBS News' *60 Minutes* (January 30, 2011)

The website WikiLeaks used on-line technology to establish electronic drop-boxes in order to aggregate government and corporate secrets and then shared information with news sources around the world, including the *New York Times*. In an interview with CBS *60 Minutes'* correspondent Steve Kroft identified the site's founder, Julian Assange, an "Internet muckraker" and said that he must have known that he was "screwing with the forces of nature," adding: "You had made some of the most powerful people in the world your enemies … You took, you gathered, you stored, all sorts of classified cables and documents then released them to the world on the Internet. They see that as a threat."[3] As the *60 Minutes* report on Assange and his organization pointed out, public awareness of WikiLeaks began for many people in April 2010 when it released a video showing U.S. forces attacking and killing people from an Apache helicopter in Baghdad including journalists from the international news agency Reuters. Then in July 2010, 76,000 field reports from U.S. military operations in Afghanistan were also released by WikiLeaks, as were additional documents published against the claim that it had failed to redact the names of Afghans who helped the United States and had therefore become vulnerable to identification and retaliation.

In October 2010 WikiLeaks released 400,000 additional documents from Iraq showing civilian casualties there were greater than the U.S. State Department had earlier claimed. Thousands of additional documents were released by the WikiLeaks organization showing the U.S. State Department had been collecting intelligence on international leaders from the United Nations. Much of this material had been provided by a U.S. Army Private First-Class, Bradley Manning, placed under military arrest at that time. U.S. Attorney General Eric Holder condemned WikliLeaks for putting national security at risk noting that criminal investigations for possible prosecution on espionage charges were also under way.

The serious claims that the unedited Internet postings by WikiLeaks placed the lives of cooperating individuals at risk became part of government arguments against WikiLeaks, complicated by the sharing and publishing of some of the same material by the *New York Times*, and other major news outlets. This occurred while Assange—without actually saying it—was in effect claiming that his organization had acted responsibly and indeed engaged in a form of prior restraint—by maintaining that he had held back one-in-five documents received. The widespread debate concerning the actions of WikiLeaks and its methods placed prior restraint considerations at the apex of responsible journalism practice while also questioning whether Assange could even be appropriately dubbed "a journalist." This case developed against the backdrop of what we may view as more typical prior restraint cases:

- At about the same time, in a case involving the *Los Angeles Times*, a panel of California's 2nd District Court ordered L.A. County Supreme Court Judge, Hilleri G. Merritt, to end prior restraint on publishing a photo of a criminal defendant taken earlier with the Judge's permission by one of that newspapers' photojournalists. The Judge maintained that the defendant's due process rights could be placed at risk, while the newspaper noted the photos had already been published. An Appellate court vacated as unconstitutional the prohibition on publishing the "lawfully obtained photographs."[4]
- Lawyers for an author who wrote a novel offered as a sequel to J.D. Salinger's *Catcher in the Rye*, described as unconstitutional prior restraint, efforts to prevent its publication at a time when the late author was said to have created yet other undiscovered works.[5]
- Debate over any relationship between violent acts and media use has continued unabated. After the 2010 attempt on the life of a U.S. Representative, Gabrielle Giffords (D-AZ), media pundits used public statements by a Tucson, Arizona, police official to question whether the murder attempt was somehow provoked by media coverage. No relationship was found.
- Over a decade earlier, in December 1, 1997, 14-year-old Michael Carneal walked into the lobby of Heath High School in Paducah, Kentucky, and shot at a crowd of his fellow students, killing three and wounding five. Carneal was later convicted of murder. During the investigation process, officials discovered Carneal frequently played violent computer games such as "Doom," "Quake," "Redneck Rampage," "Resident Evil," and similar games. He had also apparently watched a video of "The Basketball Diaries" whose plot includes a character who dreams about shooting a teacher and several fellow students to death. When the investigators examined Carneal's computer, they found that he had visited various pornographic websites on the Internet. The families of the murder victims of the school shootings filed a civil suit for wrongful deaths against the manufacturers of the video games, the production company of the movie, and several Internet service

providers, claiming their products desensitized Carneal to violence and caused him to commit the crimes for which he was convicted. The plaintiffs also claimed that the companies marketed defective products and thus should be held strictly liable under state law for the harm that occurred to the murder victims.[6] The U.S. District Court judge in the case granted the defendants' motion to dismiss the case on the grounds that the plaintiffs had failed to state a claim on which relief could be granted. On appeal, the 6th Circuit U.S. Court of Appeals upheld the trial court's dismissal.[7] Upon appeal of the appellate court's decision, the U.S. Supreme Court denied certiorari in January 2003.[8]

- Following the terrorist attacks of September 11, 2001, the major U.S. television networks agreed not to broadcast any video messages from Osama bin Laden without screening them first—after National Security Adviser Condoleezza Rice (who later succeeded Colin Powell as Secretary of State) asked them to consider such a policy. The purpose of the screening at the time was to make sure that the video contained no coded messages to bin Laden supporters about conducting terrorist attacks. Subsequent reviews of such videos centered on tape authenticity.[9]

- On May 2, 2011, almost a decade after the 9/11 attacks, U.S. Navy SEALS, in an operation officially approved by President Barack Obama, covertly entered a private residential compound in Abbottabad, Pakistan, where bin Laden was living. He was shot to death during the attack, and his body was buried at sea. Although photos and video recordings of the operation were released to the public, President Obama ultimately decided that no photos or recordings would be released showing bin Laden's body. The President said he was concerned about potential violence against Americans from bin Laden supporters. Four days after his death, Al-Qaeda confirmed that bin Laden had been killed.

- During the first Iraq war, country music trio, the Dixie Chicks had their songs banned from some music radio stations and denounced by commentators and others as traitors. They received hate mail—electronically and in hard copy—after one member, Natalie Maines, told a London audience on the eve of military conflict that she was "ashamed" that President Bush was from her home state. As a result of the blacklisting, sales of the group's albums dropped, and their concerts were picketed at that time as part of an anti-Dixie Chicks campaign.[10]

- According to an article published in the *Journal of Epidemiology and Community Health* that reviewed 42 studies, when news stories are published about the suicides of popular entertainment and political figures, it is 14.3 times more likely that copycat suicides will follow than when such stories appear about non-celebrities.[11]

- In a 6 to 5 *en banc* decision in 2002, the 9th Circuit U.S. Court of Appeals held that the First Amendment does not protect "wanted" posters placed on the Internet by anti-abortion groups to indicate doctors who perform abortions. The Web pages for the groups included the names of and personal information about the doctors with lines drawn through the photos of those murdered.[12]

- In 2004 military contractor Maytag Aircraft fired a Kuwait-based employee who had photographed flag-draped coffins of American soldiers killed in Iraq as they were loaded onto a cargo plane. The cargo worker's photos were published in the *Seattle Times* and later in other publications. Under a U.S. government policy then in effect journalists have been prohibited from taking such photos. The ban was lifted under President Obama.

- On April 16, 2007, a Virginia Tech University student, Seung-Hui Cho, murdered 32 people and wounded 25 before killing himself. On the same day as the massacre, Cho sent a multimedia manifest of photos, videos, and writings to NBC News. While the network prepared for saturation coverage by sending their news anchors to the Blacksburg, Virginia, campus, the material sent to NBC News set off an internal debate about whether to air any of the material sent by the killer. NBC decided to take a cautious approach with limited exposure. An analysis of the top 10 mass shootings covered by the U.S. network news (August 1987–April 2007) showed that nine, including Virginia Tech and Columbine, had occurred in just the past 10 years. While the Virginia Tech massacre was still fresh in the minds of viewers, an on-campus poster read: "VT STAY STRONG — MEDIA STAY AWAY."

As each of the above examples illustrates, prior restraint takes many forms. Some situations do not directly involve prior restraint. In one example, TV news networks volunteered to screen bin Laden videos. One of the requirements of impermissible prior restraint is that it must be compulsive, not voluntary. Granted, the networks agreed on a policy only after being pressured by government officials, but that pressure was not sufficiently coercive to make the networks' actions become involuntary. In the case of the Dixie Chicks, the government was not directly involved. One requirement of unconstitutional prior restraint is that it must originate with the

Figure 5.1   Although a permit may be required to distribute materials in a "First Amendment Expression Area" on public property such as at this welcome center in Gatlinburg, Tennessee, the U.S. Supreme Court ruled that a governmental entity may not discriminate based on content. The Court, however, said that reasonable time, place, and manner restrictions may be imposed so long as they are "content-neutral" (Photo by Roy L. Moore).

government. However, as discussed later in this chapter, government action can be broadly interpreted within the context of prior restraint as an abridgement of freedom of expression.

Copycat suicides and murders represent a very serious problem, but dealing with them is usually an ethical issue, not a legal one. The First Amendment would never allow a newspaper or other media outlet to be barred from publishing accurate details about suicides, but that does not prevent news or entertainment media from voluntarily adopting ethical standards that discourage reporting the details of celebrity suicides.

Only the remaining three examples—the Heath High School case, the Web page "wanted" posters case, and the coffin photos—involved direct prior restraint. In the case of the coffin photos, it is highly unlikely that a court challenge of the policy would have been successful because the courts have generally deferred to the government when access is denied to military property, whether the ban applies to the public or to the news media or to both.

Not surprisingly, two court cases led to two different results, illustrating the difficulty courts typically have in determining permissible and impermissible prior restraint. What is the difference between a Web page that appears to glorify the murders of physicians who perform abortions and a video game or movie that glorifies violence and murder of fictional individuals or cartoon characters? In the majority opinions in both cases, the appellate courts referred to the legal doctrine of *foreseeability*— whether a reasonable person would foresee that a particular statement or act could be perceived as a serious intent to harm someone or that it could result in serious harm. Note that each court came to a different conclusion.

As an illustration of how inconsistent prior restraint decisions can be, consider how, in 1988, a federal jury in Texas returned a $9.4 million verdict against *Soldier of Fortune* magazine for running a classified ad that prompted a husband to hire an assassin to murder his wife. The 5th Circuit U.S. Court of Appeals overturned the verdict, holding that the magazine had no duty to withhold publication of a "facially innocuous ad."[13] One year later, the U.S. Supreme Court denied certiorari. The classified ad read: "Ex-Marines—67–69 'Nam Vets, Ex-DI, weapons specialist—jungle warfare, pilot, M.E., high risk assignments, U.S. or overseas." The appellate court did say that the magazine owed a duty of reasonable care to the public and that the ad posed "a risk of serious harm," but it noted that such daily activities as interstate driving involved risks as well. "Given the pervasiveness of advertising in our society and the important role it plays, we decline to impose on publishers the obligation to reject all ambiguous advertisements for products or services that might pose a threat of harm," the court said.[14]

Two years after the federal circuit court ruled in its favor, *Soldier of Fortune* lost a round in a trial court when a U.S. District Court jury in Alabama awarded two brothers $2.375 million in compensatory damages and $10 million in punitive damages for the death of their father.[15] The judge in the case reduced the punitive damages to $2 million. Michael and Ian Braun's father was gunned down by a man hired by Braun's business partner after the following ad appeared in the magazine: "GUN FOR HIRE. 37-year-old professional mercenary desires jobs. Vietnam Veteran. Discreet and very private. Body guard, courier, and other special skills. All jobs considered." The classified ad also included an address and phone number. Citing the earlier 5th Circuit decision, the Alabama federal judge ruled, in denying a motion for summary judgment, that this ad, unlike the earlier one, was not facially innocuous and that the magazine had breached its duty of reasonable care. The 11th Circuit U.S. Court of Appeals affirmed the district court decision in 1992, and the U.S. Supreme Court denied certiorari the next year.[16]

Contempt of Court

Contempt of court is, without doubt, one of the most serious prior restraint problems facing journalists in the 21st century. Most other types of prior restraint have become less of a threat than in the past, thanks to generally favorable rulings from the U.S. Supreme Court and other courts.

At first glance, contempt of court may appear to be unrelated to prior restraint. After all, contempt is generally either used to attempt to coerce an individual into complying with a court order, such as to provide the identity of a confidential source, or as a means of punishing someone for demonstrating disrespect for the court or the judicial process. However, a fairly frequent use of what is known as *criminal contempt* is to punish individuals for disobeying a court order—such as a gag order prohibiting attorneys and witnesses from discussing a case with reporters. Thus, news sources are effectively restrained from speaking out.

Contempt of court is generally defined as "any act which is calculated to embarrass, hinder, or obstruct court in administration of justice, or which is calculated to lessen its authority or its dignity."[17] There are two different ways of classifying contempt. First, contempt can be either *civil* or *criminal*. Unfortunately, this classification can be quite confusing because the distinction of civil versus criminal for purposes of contempt does not precisely parallel the traditional criminal versus civil division in law. Instead, the categorization is a rather artificial one that has been known to confuse journalists. *Civil contempt* involves the failure or refusal to obey a court order granted for the benefit of one of the litigants in a case. The offense, in other words, is not against the dignity of the court but against the party for whom the order was issued. The confusion is compounded by the fact that civil contempt can occur in both civil and criminal cases. *Criminal contempt*, on the other hand, is indeed an affront to the court and the purpose of any fine and/or jail term imposed is to punish the offender.

Civil Contempt

The purpose of a fine or sentence for civil contempt is to coerce an individual into complying with a court order. The penalty imposed must be lifted once the person obeys or once judicial deliberations have ended. However, civil contempt orders can remain in effect indefinitely in some cases, as dramatically demonstrated in the case of Dr. Elizabeth Morgan, who served longer (25 months) than any other U.S. woman not convicted of a crime.

What was the former affluent plastic surgeon and medical writer's offense? She refused to obey District of Columbia Superior Court Judge Herbert Dixon's order to disclose the whereabouts of her young daughter in a contentious custody battle with the girl's father, whom Morgan accused of sexually abusing the child. He strongly denied the claims. A three-judge panel of the U.S. Court of Appeals for the District of Columbia Circuit ruled 2 to 1 that Morgan should have been released because it appeared highly unlikely that she would disclose the location of her daughter and thus the efforts to force Morgan to comply with the trial court judge's order served no further purpose. However, the Circuit Court, meeting *en banc* (i.e., as the full court) soon overturned the appeal panel's decision so that Morgan was never released from jail. The full court did rule that she was entitled to a new hearing on her appeal of the civil contempt citation.

Morgan was freed on September 25, 1989, after the U.S. Congress passed a bill, specifically aimed to free her, limiting imprisonment for civil contempt in the District of Columbia to 12 months. The senior President George Bush signed the bill on September 23, 1989, and the D.C. Court of Appeals ordered her released two days later. She still faced possible civil contempt charges again because the bill limited the maximum term on a *single citation*, and the judge could have issued a new contempt citation so long as she refused to obey the order. However, the judge chose not to do so. The bill affected only *civil contempt citations* and only those in the District of Columbia. No court ever determined whether Morgan's spouse had abused the daughter.

ABC-TV broadcast a made-for-TV movie in 1992 entitled *A Mother's Right: The Elizabeth Morgan Story* about the case. Although the mother was permitted to return to the United States, it took another act of Congress to permit her to return with her daughter without facing contempt for not allowing the daughter to see her father. In 1996, both houses of Congress approved legislation—tacked onto a transportation bill—that forbids the father from visiting his daughter unless the child gives her consent, which she refused to do.[18] After she was freed, Morgan flew to New Zealand to be with her daughter, staying with grandparents.

The person jailed the longest for civil contempt is Odell Sheppard, whose contempt citation was upheld by the Illinois Supreme Court in November 1994.[19] Sheppard served more than 10 years in jail from October 1987 to January 1998 because he refused to comply with a judge's order that he inform authorities of the whereabouts of his then-five-year-old daughter. He had served a three-year prison sentence for kidnapping the girl. He was released after the death of the child's mother, who had been granted the protective order that led to the contempt citation. Norelle Sanders died without ever learning the whereabouts of her daughter.[20]

Journalists are most often faced with civil contempt when they refuse to reveal confidential information or sources. Although most civil contempt citations against journalists usually result in incarceration for a few days, freelance Texan journalist Vanessa Leggett served 168 days in jail—the record at that time for a journalist for civil contempt. Leggett was cited for contempt after she refused to turn over her notes to a federal grand jury investigating the murder of a Houston socialite. She was doing research for a possible magazine article about the case at the time. The article was never published, but Leggett conducted confidential interviews with various individuals connected with the case, including police and the brother of the victim's husband, who confessed to the murder. In one interview, the brother said he had acted alone, but in another interview his account varied. Leggett gave prosecutors tapes of the interviews containing inconsistent confessions, but they were not used at trial. After the brother was acquitted on state charges, federal prosecutors filed federal charges and subpoenaed Leggett's notes and tapes from other interviews. She refused and was cited for contempt.[21] Leggett appealed her citation, but the U.S. Supreme Court denied certiorari in 2002. Leggett later published a book about the case. She was released after the grand jury's term ended. Freelance videographer Josh Wolf holds the current record for a journalist jailed for civil contempt. He was released in April 2007 after serving 224 days for refusing to turn a videotape over to federal authorities he had made of a violent protest in California. He also refused to appear before a grand jury investigating the event. He was freed after he turned over the tape, which he had posted in his website. He did not have to testify before a grand jury, as originally ordered.[22]

As discussed in the previous chapter, *New York Times* reporter Judith Miller was released from jail after 85 days for refusing to reveal a confidential source to a federal grand jury in 2005 investigating the leak concerning undercover CIA officer Valerie Plame. Plame's husband, Joe Wilson, had been asked by the CIA to go to Africa to try to determine the veracity of a report that Niger had sold uranium to Iraq, whose president then was Saddam Hussein. When Wilson returned, he wrote a *New York Times* piece in which he claimed the report was false. Almost a week later, Robert Novak revealed in his syndicated column that two "senior administration officials" informed him that Plame was a CIA agent. Miller was released after she obtained a voluntary waiver from her source, who turned out to be Vice President Dick Cheney's chief of staff, I. Lewis "Scooter" Libby. Miller later resigned from the *Times* amid criticism from the newspaper's publisher and other journalists for the manner in which she handled her sourcing. Libby was indicted by a grand jury for perjury for allegedly lying about what he knew in the case. Libby was later convicted of perjury and obstructing justice by a jury and sentenced to 30 months in prison. President George W. Bush commuted Libby's sentence, calling it "excessive." A $250,000 fine remained, which Libby paid. He never served a day in jail or prison for his offenses.

In 1970 William Farr,[23] a *Los Angeles Herald-Examiner* reporter, was assigned to cover the trial of the notorious mass murderer, Charles Manson. To ensure that Manson received a fair trial, the judge issued a *restrictive* or *gag order* prohibiting out-of-court statements by attorneys and witnesses. *Gag order* is a pejorative term used by the press to label what courts usually call *restrictive orders*. The judge also ordered the jury sequestered. Although the gag order was not aimed specifically at journalists, Farr was ordered by the judge to identify his sources for a story based on pretrial statements of a witness to whom Farr had promised confidentiality. The story attracted considerable attention because it contained grisly details allegedly revealed by one defendant, Susan Atkins, about the so-called Tate–Labianca murders and others planned by the Manson "family" against movie stars such as Elizabeth Taylor and Frank Sinatra. It was clear that some of the information reported by Farr in his stories could have been obtained only from sources the judge had ordered not to discuss the case publicly or with the media.

California Superior Court Judge Charles Older queried Farr about the source of his information, but Farr, claiming protection under a California shield law, steadfastly refused to disclose the name. Judge Older took no further action until the trial was over when he ordered Farr again to reveal the name. By this time, Farr had obtained a new position as an assistant to a county district attorney. Farr still refused to provide the information, although he did indicate that he had received the information from two of the six attorneys involved. However, he would not identify the specific two, and thus the judge cited him for civil contempt with an indefinite jail sentence. The judge noted that the former reporter could no longer claim protection under the state's shield law because he now did not meet the definition of journalist under the statute. Some 46 days later, Farr was released when a state appellate court vacated the district court judge's contempt order, but only pending appeal. A cloud of doubt loomed over his fate, however, because if the judge's ruling were ultimately upheld by the appellate courts, Farr could have faced an indefinite jail term as long as he continued to refuse to obey the order to disclose. In late 1976, the California Court of Appeals permanently lifted the contempt order, five years after the case had begun and after the California Supreme Court[24] and the U.S. Supreme Court[25] refused to hear Farr's appeals. In 1980, California residents, apparently largely in reaction to the Farr case, approved Proposition 5, which for the first time gave state constitutional protection for journalists in protecting confidential sources.[26]

The Farr case illustrates a "Catch 22" for states that have chosen to grant protection for journalists against prior restraints imposed by restrictive orders and contempt citations. No matter how strong the protection the legislation or constitutional provision may be designed to offer, the courts always have the authority to limit the protection or even strike the law down on the grounds that it violates the separation of powers of the U.S. Constitution. Although, as one U.S. constitutional scholar has noted, "As an examination … readily reveals, separation was not intended to be total and airtight,"[27] both state and federal courts have been very reluctant to allow legislators to restrict their authority to regulate judicial proceedings, including the ability to cite individuals for contempt. The California Court of Appeals in the Farr case no doubt reflected the reasoning of the vast majority of state and federal courts when it clung to the long-standing constitutional premise that courts have an inherent power to control judicial proceedings free from any interference. In sum, even when its use may mean serious prior restraint, contempt power is near and dear to the hearts of judges and justices, and thus courts will almost inevitably uphold its constitutionality except in extreme cases such as *Nebraska Press Association v. Judge Stuart.*[28]

Efforts to enact a national shield law continue to fail despite fairly broad bipartisan support in Congress and apparently strong public approval, as reflected in a 2005 poll commissioned by the First Amendment Center in collaboration with *American Journalism Review.*[29] The poll found that 69% of Americans either strongly agree or mildly agree "journalists should be allowed to keep a news source confidential."[30]

Dickinson Rule

Probably the most serious "Catch 22" situation facing journalists in the area of prior restraint is the so-called Dickinson rule formulated by the U.S. Court of Appeals for the 5th Circuit in 1972.[31] The case began when two Louisiana newspaper reporters were covering a hearing in a U.S. District Court in which a black civil rights VISTA (Volunteers in Service to America) volunteer challenged his indictment by a state grand jury for conspiracy to murder the local mayor. During the hearing, the judge issued a verbal order prohibiting publication of any information about the testimony given at the hearing even though the information had been disclosed in open court. The judge's order permitted the reporters to publish that the hearing had been held, but essentially nothing more.

In spite of the order, both reporters wrote news stories giving details of the hearing. For their defiance of his order, the judge in a summary hearing found them guilty of criminal contempt and fined both $300. Although the reporters were never jailed and the fines were relatively minimal, the *Baton Rouge Morning Advocate and State Times* newspaper chose to appeal the convictions. Most First Amendment experts would probably have concluded that the order was indeed unconstitutional, and, in fact, the U.S. Court of Appeals for the 5th Circuit agreed and sent the case back to the District Court judge for further consideration. Not surprisingly, the judge reinstated the fines, and the newspaper filed another appeal. The Circuit Court then upheld the citations by reasoning that even constitutionally invalid restrictive orders require compliance because (citing an earlier decision), "people simply cannot have the luxury of knowing that they have a right to contest the correctness of the judge's order in deciding whether to willfully disobey it."[32]

The court also reasoned that if individuals including journalists are permitted to disobey court orders, the judicial process would be seriously affected. After all, the court noted, such orders are to be used only "sparingly."[33] A journalist can request expedited review by the appeals court, but reviews are rare and unlikely to be granted in a case such as this one. The upshot is that journalists face the dilemma of disobeying an order, risking fines and even jail sentences and getting the story published, or complying with the order by withholding the information from the public while waiting months or longer for the appeal to be heard. The Dickinson decision was appealed to the U.S. Supreme Court, but the court denied certiorari in 1973.[34]

Direct versus Indirect Contempt

Contempt can also be categorized into direct and constructive or indirect. *Direct contempt* is committed in or near the presence of the court ("so near thereto as to obstruct the administration of justice").[35] *Indirect* or *constructive contempt*, on the other hand, occurs or relates to matters outside court. Although such a distinction may seem artificial or contrived at first glance, there are major differences in the procedures followed in the two types of contempt and in the constitutional and statutory rights involved.

Suppose a judge issues a restrictive order forbidding all news media in the area from publishing or broadcasting the details of testimony given at the trial of a grandfather accused of sexually abusing his grandchildren. The judge exercises discretion under state statutes and the rules of criminal procedure by closing the testimony of the young victims to the public and the press. The judge had earlier issued an order barring all trial participants including witnesses, jurors, and attorneys from discussing the case with anyone including journalists.

In this hypothetical case, a reporter for the local television station convinces one of the social workers who accompanied the children to the trial and sat in the courtroom while the children testified to disclose the details of the testimony. The reporter broadcasts a summary of the testimony on the six o'clock news. What is the judge likely to do?

First, there are two potential violations leading to contempt—the broadcast and the disclosure of information by the social worker. Assuming the reporter refuses to disclose the confidential source of her information, there is even a third possible contempt. Let's begin with the first. When the reporter is called before the judge to explain why she violated the judge's order and is ordered to name her source but refuses, her refusal constitutes direct criminal contempt. That is because (a) the contempt has occurred within the presence of the court and (b) her refusal can be considered an affront to the dignity of the court (i.e., an interference with the orderly administration of justice). What can the judge do? The judge has the clear authority in this case to exercise summary jurisdiction in a summary proceeding. The judge can immediately cite the reporter for contempt and immediately punish her within certain constitutional parameters. Within a matter of minutes or even seconds after she refuses to disclose her source, the judge can accuse her of contempt, determine that contempt has occurred and sentence her to jail. Journalists are often shocked by the swiftness of the summary proceeding, but state and federal rules of criminal and civil procedure grant this authority to judges and the courts have consistently upheld its constitutionality.

What are the reporter's options? She can plead with the judge not to find her in contempt, but, assuming the judge does not accept the reporter's plea, she can appeal her conviction to a higher court or serve her time in jail. Can the judge also punish her for broadcasting the report in defiance of the order? Yes, but the punishment would be for indirect criminal contempt because the broadcast interferes with the administration of justice (criminal contempt), and the action occurred outside court. With indirect contempt, unlike direct contempt, the accused is entitled to notice of the alleged offense and to a formal, separate hearing on the matter. The reporter thus would have the opportunity to mount some type of defense, although the judge is still likely to ultimately punish her and probably even fine the station for defying the restrictive order.

Ironically, the reporter could also face civil contempt charges for failing to identify her source and thus be confined for an indefinite time in jail and forced to pay fines as a means of coercing her to testify. Her confinement, as already indicated, could continue until the judge decided it fruitless to keep her in jail, the name disclosed by someone else, the trial ended or, if she relented and testified.

If the reporter does disclose her source's identity or the judge somehow determines the social worker violated the earlier order, what are the consequences? Although the social worker may have actually communicated the information to the reporter outside the courtroom, the worker would in all likelihood be cited for direct criminal contempt because "so near thereto" can be broadly interpreted to include such defiance. Because the purpose of citing the worker would be as punishment, criminal contempt has occurred. (There is nothing to coerce the worker to do.)

In some cases, civil contempt can ultimately turn into criminal contempt, as illustrated in the case of a Providence, Rhode Island television reporter. In 2001, WJAR-TV reporter Jim Taricani broadcast part of a videotape that had been sealed as evidence in an FBI investigation. The tape showed a city official taking a bribe from an FBI undercover informant. More than three years later, after Taricani refused to name his source for the tape in court, the judge held him in civil contempt. The station owner, NBC, paid $85,000 in fines, but the judge still held the reporter in criminal contempt and sentenced him to jail for six months, of which he served four.[36]

Constitutional Limits on Contempt Power

Bridges v. California and Times-Mirror Co. v. Superior Court (1941)

Although judges have considerable power to cite and punish individuals, including journalists, for contempt, some First Amendment limits have been recognized by the courts. The greatest protection is for information disseminated outside the courtroom. In 1941, the U.S. Supreme Court held in *Bridges v. California* and *Times-Mirror Co. v. Superior Court* (the two appeals were decided together by the Court)[37] that a judge may not cite journalists for contempt for publishing information about pending court cases unless there was a "clear and present danger" to the administration of justice. The Court noted that this clear and present danger standard was "a working principle that the substantive evil must be extremely serious and the degree of imminence extremely high before utterances can be punished."[38]

In *Bridges*, a union official sent a telegram to the U.S. Secretary of Labor that was published in local newspapers in California. In the telegram, sent while the ruling on a motion for a new trial in a labor dispute was pending, Harry Bridges threatened to have his union strike if the judge's "outrageous" decision were enforced. The lower appellate courts upheld the leader's conviction for contempt as an interference with the "orderly administration of justice."

In *Times-Mirror*, while a decision was pending in the sentencing of two union members convicted of assaulting nonunion employees, the *Los Angeles Times* published a series of editorials in which it called the two "sluggers for pay" and "men who commit mayhem for wages"

and contended that the judge would be committing a "serious mistake" if he granted probation. The paper was convicted of contempt and fined. The lower appellate courts, including the
California Supreme Court, upheld the conviction. But the U.S. Supreme Court reversed the
convictions of Bridges and the *Times* on the grounds that no clear and present danger had been
shown.

Post-Bridges Decisions

In three more major cases since *Bridges*, the Court elaborated on the clear and present danger
standard. First, in 1946, in *Pennekamp v. Florida*,[39] the Court reversed the contempt convictions of the *Miami Herald* and its associate editor for a series of editorials and an editorial
cartoon accusing local judges of being more interested in assisting criminals than serving the
public. The Court noted that the editorials had been based on false information, but it characterized the errors as relatively minor in light of the need for permissible commentary on the
judiciary. No clear and present danger could be demonstrated, according to the majority.

In the second case, *Craig v. Harney*,[40] the Court also acknowledged that newspaper criticism
aimed at a judge had been based on inaccuracies. "The fact that the discussion at this particular point in time was not in good taste falls far short of meeting the clear and present danger
test," the majority asserted. The newspaper severely criticized in an editorial and articles the
judge's handling of a civil case in which he directed a jury three times to find for a plaintiff in a
landlord–tenant dispute. The first two times the jury found for the defendant; he was stationed
overseas in the military and had failed to pay rent to the landlord, who was now seeking repos-
session of the building. Each time the Texas judge sent the jurors back to decide in favor of the
plaintiff. Finally, they found for the plaintiff but made their objections known to the judge. The
defendant's attorney filed a motion for a new trial. While the Court was deciding on whether to
grant it, the newspaper published the articles and an accompanying editorial that Justice William O. Douglas, writing for the majority, characterized as "unfair" because of the inaccuracies.
But Justice Douglas said the articles and editorial did not warrant the contempt citation and
consequent three-day jail sentence imposed on the editor.

According to the Court, "the vehemence of the language used is not alone the measure of the
power to punish for contempt. The fires which it kindles must constitute an imminent, not just
likely, threat to the administration of justice. The danger must not be remote or even probable;
it must immediately imperil."[41] The majority said, "Judges are supposed to be made of fortitude,
able to thrive in a hardy climate." The Court is saying judges must be able to withstand criticism, no matter how harsh or unfair. Justice Robert H. Jackson, in a strongly worded dissent,
contended that the majority "appears to sponsor the myth that judges are not as other men are."

In the last case in which the Court directly applied the clear and present danger test in a
contempt case within a First Amendment context, Chief Justice Earl Warren, writing for the
majority in *Wood v. Georgia*,[42] reversed the conviction for contempt of a Bibb County, Georgia,
sheriff. The sheriff issued a news release criticizing a judge's actions in a grand jury investigation of a voting scandal. Upset because the judge ordered the grand jury to investigate rumors
and accusations of "Negro bloc voting," Sheriff James I. Wood launched a news release calling the investigation "one of the most deplorable examples of race agitation to come out of
Middle Georgia in recent years.... Negro people will find little difference in principle between

attempted intimidation of their people by judicial summons and inquiry and attempted intimidation by physical demonstration such as used by the KKK."[43]

A month later, Wood was cited for contempt for creating a "clear, present and imminent
danger" to the investigation and "to the proper administration of justice in Bibb Superior
Court."[44] The defendant issued another press release the next day, essentially repeating his previous claims, and his contempt citation was amended to include this release as well. The U.S.
Supreme Court noted that there were no witnesses at the contempt hearing and no evidence
was presented to demonstrate a clear and present danger to the administration of justice. The
Court reversed the convictions that had been affirmed by the Georgia Court of Appeals except
for a contempt charge based on an open letter the sheriff sent to the grand jury, set aside by the
state appellate court. According to the U.S. Supreme Court:

> Men are entitled to speak as they please on matters vital to them; errors in judgment
> or unsubstantiated opinions may be exposed, of course, but not through punishment
> for contempt for the expression. [In] the absence of some other showing of substantive
> evil actually designed to impede the course of justice in justification of the exercise of
> the contempt power to silence the petitioner [Wood], his utterances are entitled to be
> protected.[45]

The *Bridges–Pennekamp–Craig–Wood* line-up offers strong but not absolute constitutional
insulation for journalists from contempt citations when they publish information about the
judicial process, especially criticism of judges and information obtained in open court, even
when such information is based on inaccurate data. Nevertheless, the contempt power of judges
remains strong, including coercion and punishment for refusing to reveal confidential information. The greatest protection appears to be for overt prior restraint, such as prohibiting someone
from speaking out rather than when information is actually being sought for disclosure.

The Classic Case: Near v. Minnesota (1931)

The most significant prior restraint case decided by the U.S. Supreme Court is *J.M. Near v.
Minnesota ex rel. Floyd B. Olson, County Attorney of Hennepin County, Minnesota*,[46] otherwise
known as *Near v. Minnesota*. No other prior restraint case has been cited as often, and the
Supreme Court consistently cites the holding in this case as controlling whenever it issues an
opinion in any prior restraint case even though *Near* was decided six decades ago by a very
slim 5 to 4 majority. Even the rather conservative court headed by Chief Justice William H.
Rehnquist generally upheld the principles first enunciated in *Near*.

This demonstrates how extreme actions are sometimes necessary to ascertain outer limits of
the First Amendment—the Larry Flynts, J. M. Nears, flag burners, and cross burners of the
world give courts an opportunity to enunciate how far our constitutional rights extend.

As the late CBS News President and Columbia University Professor Fred Friendly pointed
out in his superb account of the *Minnesota Rag* case,[47] Minneapolis was a politically corrupt
city in the 1920s and politicians had little tolerance for outspoken publications like J. M. Near's
The Saturday Press. Near and his co-publisher, Howard Guilford, accused various local politicians and officials, including the police, of ignoring widespread racketeering, bootlegging, and
illegal gambling. According to the newspaper in a series of blatantly sensational, anti-Semitic

articles, a "Jewish gangster" controlled these activities. The Minnesota legislature passed a statute in 1925 that allowed authorities to halt publication of "obscene, lewd and lascivious ... or malicious, scandalous, and defamatory newspaper, magazine, or other periodical" as a public nuisance. Anyone guilty of such a nuisance could be enjoined from further publication (except presumably with approval of a judge).

A quick look at old issues would probably convince most people even today that indeed the paper met all the criteria of a scandalous and defamatory newspaper. One of the editorials introduced into evidence referred to "Jew gangsters, practically ruling Minneapolis" and contended "practically every vendor of vile hooch, every owner of moonshine still, every snake-faced gangster and embryonic yegg in the twin cities is a JEW" (capital letters in the original).[48]

Hennepin County Attorney Floyd Olson, who years later was elected state governor as a Populist, filed a criminal complaint against the paper and its publishers. It charged that nine issues of the paper from September to November 1927 contained "malicious, scandalous and defamatory articles" making false accusations against police and various public officials. After the prosecution presented its side and the defense immediately rested its case without presenting any evidence, the Minnesota trial court determined that Near and Guilford had violated the statute by creating a public nuisance. The judge then ordered that the paper be abated and that the defendants be "perpetually enjoined" from publishing "under the title of *The Saturday Evening Press* or any other name or title ... any publication whatsoever which is a malicious, scandalous or defamatory newspaper." In other words, Near and Guilford were prevented not only from publishing more issues of the *Press* but essentially any other newspapers of that type.

On appeal one year later, the Minnesota Supreme Court held the statute was constitutional under both state and federal constitutions as a valid exercise of the police power of the state and that the order did not prevent Near and Guilford from "operating a newspaper in harmony with the public welfare." In a 5 to 4 decision that could have gone the other way had it not been for a few twists of fate such as the death of an associate justice,[49] the U.S. Supreme Court reversed the order and struck down the statute as unconstitutional.

In delivering the majority opinion of the Court, Chief Justice Charles Evans Hughes characterized the statute as "unusual, if not unique." The decision, as fate would have it, was read as the last one on the last day of the Court's 1930–1931 term.[50] Drawing heavily on the ideas of British legal scholar Sir William Blackstone (1723–1780), the court quoted him saying, "The liberty of the press is indeed essential to the nature of a free state; but this consists in laying no *previous* restraints upon publications, and not in freedom from censure for criminal matter when published."[51] Justice Hughes' opinion reasoned the First Amendment ban on prior restraint is "not absolutely unlimited" but constitutionally "exceptional cases":

> When a nation is at war, many things that may be said in time of peace are such a hindrance to its effort that their utterance will not be endured.... No one would question but that a government might prevent actual obstruction to its recruiting service or the publication of sailing dates of transports or the number and location of troops. On similar grounds, the primary requirements of decency might be enforced against obscene publications. The security of the community life may be protected against incitements to acts of violence and the overthrow by force of orderly government.[52] [cites omitted]

This decision offers the first hint of later versions of reasonable time, place, and manner restrictions permitted on speech. These exceptions also point to more modern limitations usually grouped under the rubrics of obscenity, national security, and military secrets. Did any of the exceptions apply? According to the Court, "These limitations are not applicable here.… We hold the statute, so far as it authorized the proceedings in this action … to be an infringement of the liberty of the press guaranteed by the 14th Amendment."[53] Why did the Court invoke the 14th Amendment?

The U.S. Supreme Court has over the decades selectively incorporated various rights under the Constitution's Bill of Rights, including those granted under the First Amendment. Until the *Near* decision, the Court had not specifically ruled whether First Amendment rights applied to the states. If this fact seems strange, closely examine the wording of the First Amendment, especially the reference that "Congress shall make no law." State and local governments are not mentioned. Theoretically, one's First Amendment rights could not be trampled upon by the federal government, but a state agency could infringe on those rights so long as it did not violate the state constitution or state or federal statutes.

However, the Supreme Court went beyond its traditional turf by asserting, "It is no longer open to doubt that the liberty of the press and of speech is within the liberty safeguarded by the due process clause of the 14th Amendment from invasion by state action."[54] In other words, according to the Court, section 1 of the 14th Amendment ("nor shall any State deprive any person of life, liberty, or property without due process of law") includes freedom of speech and of the press.[55]

A close reading of the majority opinion, especially the reasoning, provides a portentous glimpse at troubling decisions such as the Pentagon Papers case[56] emerging decades later from the Court. *Near* was a strong affirmation of First Amendment rights. The Court reasoned (a) "Remedies for libel remain available and unaffected" (officials had the option of suing for libel, perhaps criminal as well as civil, after the publication appeared); (b) the statute is too broad because it bans not only "scandalous and defamatory statements" aimed at private citizens but also charges against public officials of "corruption, malfeasance in office, or serious neglect of duty" (a preview of the *New York Times v. Sullivan* "actual malice" rule?)[57]; (c) "the object of the statute is not punishment, in the ordinary sense, but suppression of the offending newspaper or periodical" (that is, prior restraint is the real evil); and (d) "the statute not only operates to suppress the offending newspaper or periodical, but to put the publisher under an effective censorship." The kiss of death for the statute is that the prior restraint can be indefinite.[58]

The Court made two more major points that have stood the test of time. First, the Court indicated, "In determining the extent of the constitutional protection [of the First Amendment], it has generally, if not universally, considered that it is the chief purpose of the guaranty to prevent previous restraints upon publication."[59] The majority opinion then traced the historical background of freedom of the press, liberally quoting Blackstone and his progeny as well as his critics. The obvious purpose of the analysis was to attempt to delineate the primary meaning of the First Amendment. *Near* was a major step toward accomplishing this task. The Supreme Court continues to struggle with the boundaries of the freedom that undergirds all other constitutional rights.

Second, the Court effectively killed the idea that a prior restraint statute can be justified if it includes, as the Minnesota law did, a provision that permits the accused to use the defense that the information published was true and that it was "published with good motives and for justifiable ends." According to the Court, if this exception to the unconstitutionality of prior restraint were allowed, "it would be but a step to a complete system of censorship" because legislatures could thus arbitrarily determine what constituted justifiable ends. Clearly, if *Near* has any meaning, it is that legislatures cannot have unbridled discretion in determining permissible versus impermissible speech and publication. In actions involving prior restraint, the burden, as discussed shortly, always rests on the government to show that the communication falls into one of the exceptions, *not* on the speaker or publisher to show that the communication is justified.

In analyzing the *Near* case, legal scholars usually include some discussion of the dissenting opinion of Associate Justice Pierce Butler, with which three of the other justices concurred. Although Justice Butler's view has yet to be shared by a majority of justices, it does represent a perspective that has some following among jurists and other legal scholars. Justice Butler contended that because the state clearly had the right to punish the "transgressions" that occurred as a result of the publication of the newspaper, there is no reason the state should not be permitted to prevent continuance of the harm. According to Justice Butler, "The Minnesota statute does not operate as a previous restraint on publication ... [because] ... [i]t does not authorize administrative control in advance ... but prescribes a remedy to be enforced by a suit in equity."[60] He was concerned that the doctrine espoused in the majority opinion in *Near* "exposes the peace and good order of every community and the business and private affairs of every individual to the constant and protracted false and malicious assaults" of ill-motivated publishers.[61]

Whereas Butler's reasoning may appear, at first reading, to expose a major weakness of the *Near* rationale, his reasoning begins to crumble under scrutiny when one realizes, as Chief Justice Hughes pointed out, that legislators and officials would have enormous power in silencing unpopular views. These might include religious, political, or social views. All of this censorship would be accomplished with the blessing of courts beholden to the public that elected them or to the officials who appointed or hired them. The real evil of prior restraint arises when unpopular views or views simply perceived by officials as unpopular or threats to their authority are arbitrarily silenced with no opportunity for society to accept or reject them. In a democracy such as ours, we must take the risk that some individual or other entity may suffer harm from the publication of false information in order to ensure that all views have opportunities to be heard. As Sir Blackstone believed, it is better to allow the potentially harmful information to be disseminated and then punish the offender, if justified, than to prohibit the publication.

There is an interesting footnote to the story of the *Saturday Press*. J. M. Near went virtually unmentioned in news accounts of the Supreme Court's decision, but more than a year later, the newspaper reappeared under Near's editorship with a front-page proclamation that said, "The only paper in the United States with a United States Supreme Court record of being right; the only paper that dared fight for freedom of the press and won."[62]

New York Times Co. v. United States *(1971)*

Some 40 years after the U.S. Supreme Court's decision in *Near*, the Court agreed to hear an appeal in a case that had the potential of answering many of the questions surrounding prior restraint that had not been answered in *Near*. From the beginning, the case had the makings of a landmark decision, although the pinnacle was never reached.

In 1967, U.S. Secretary of Defense Robert S. McNamara commissioned what ultimately became a 47-volume, 7,000 page study of America's Vietnam policy. In his book, *In Retrospect: The Tragedy and Lessons of Vietnam*, McNamara noted:

> … It [the study] had shortcomings, in part reflecting the natural limitations of history written so close to the event and in part because Les [Leslie H. Gelb, who directed the study] and his team in fact lacked access to the White House files and some top-level State Department materials. But overall the work was superb, and it accomplished my objective: almost every scholarly work on Vietnam since then has drawn, to varying degrees, on it.[63]

Daniel Ellsberg, a political scientist and military defense expert, was among those working on the study. Ellsberg gained access to the classified study titled *History of U.S. Decision-Making Process on Viet Nam Policy* that was completed in 1969 and that later became popularly known as the "Pentagon Papers." Ellsberg spent several months reading the volumes and other documents he carried from the Washington, D.C. field office of the Rand Corporation where he worked to company headquarters in Santa Monica. According to one account, Ellsberg had access to all 47 volumes and the sole but temporary custody of 27 of the volumes.[64]

After Ellsberg read the papers, he was convinced "beyond any doubt that the information in the Pentagon Papers, if widely available, would be explosive."[65] After several unsuccessful attempts to have members of Congress including U.S. Senator and Democratic presidential candidate George McGovern accept the papers and presumably make them public, Ellsberg, in March 1971, delivered photocopies of all but the last four volumes to Neil Sheehan, a Washington correspondent for the *New York Times*. He apparently considered those too sensitive to disclose.[66]

For the next three months, Sheehan and other *Times* staffers spent hundreds of hours reading and digesting the documents into article form—usually while in a hotel suite away from the hubbub of the news office. The ultimate decision was to publish the report in a comprehensive series of articles. Much of the writing for "Project X" (as the secret effort became known at the *Times*) was done at group headquarters at the New York Hilton, with security guards to watch the three-room suite when no one was there.[67]

On Monday, June 13, 1971, the *Times* published the first installment of what was intended to be a series of 10 articles summarizing and analyzing the Pentagon Papers. The next day, the second article appeared, and U.S. Attorney General John Mitchell asked the newspaper to voluntarily stop publication of the top secret documents. (Mitchell would serve 19 months in a federal minimum security prison for involvement in criminal activities in the Watergate affair.) When the *Times* rebuffed him, Mitchell began a series of legal maneuvers to halt further publication. He claimed prior restraint was justified under the Espionage Act of 1918 because publication would create infringement on national security.

On Tuesday, the third article appeared, but the government was able to convince Judge Murray Gurfein of the U.S. District Court for the Southern District of New York to issue a temporary restraining order (TRO) to prevent further publication in the *Times* until a hearing could be set on a permanent injunction. A TRO can be granted without hearing from the opposing side if it can be shown that irreparable harm will occur if such an order is not granted and that a reasonable effort was made to notify the other side. The TRO would be issued, pending a hearing at which both sides appear—before either a temporary or permanent injunction could be issued. Both appeared and the judge ruled in favor of the government. So for the first time in U.S. history, a judge imposed prior restraint on a media outlet to prevent it from publishing content. In *Near*, the judge prevented the editor from publishing any further issues of that or similar papers that constituted a public nuisance. Thus the injunction was not against a specific article.

In the meantime, the *Washington Post* obtained photocopies of most of the Pentagon Papers and, after protracted debate among editors and lawyers, on Friday, June 17, published the first of a planned series, along the lines of those in the *Times*. As expected, Attorney General Mitchell immediately requested the *Post* to voluntarily cease publication. The *Post* refused, and he immediately sought a TRO in the U.S. District Court for the District of Columbia. The Judge rejected Mitchell's request, and the government immediately appealed to the U.S. Court of Appeals for the District of Columbia Circuit. After a hearing in which both sides participated, that appeals court upheld the lower court refusal.

During this same period, the federal trial court judge in New York, Judge Gurfein, denied the federal government's request for a permanent injunction. The government immediately appealed to the U.S. Court of Appeals for the Second Circuit. In a controversial 2 to 1 decision, that court reversed Judge Gurfein and reinstated the injunction. The court ruled that the ban should remain until a hearing could be conducted at which the government would have the opportunity to demonstrate why further publication would pose a serious threat to national security.

As a result of these decisions in two different appeals court circuits, the *Times* was legally prevented from any further publication of the Pentagon Papers and the *Post* effectively had the court's blessing to continue. Other newspapers, including the *Boston Globe, St. Louis Post Dispatch, Chicago Sun-Times,* and *Los Angeles Times*, entered the fray. In another illustration of how inconsistent federal courts and the government can be in prior restraint cases, the *Globe* and the *Post Dispatch* were enjoined by the courts, but the government chose not to seek injunctions against the other two.

On June 24, one day after the federal appeals court in New York ruled against the newspaper, the *Times* filed a motion for expedited review and petition for a writ of certiorari with U.S. Supreme Court. The next morning (Saturday), at government urging, in an unprecedented 5 to 4 decision, the Court temporarily banned *all* further publication of Pentagon Papers, not only in the *Times* and *Post*, pending an expedited review. The Court rarely deliberates on weekends, indicating this was no ordinary case. The Court's action was without precedent: The U.S. Supreme Court had never granted an injunction, even a temporary one, against a news medium.

In another unusual move, the Supreme Court heard oral arguments on Sunday. They were predictable. The U.S. Solicitor General, representing the government, contended that further publication of the documents would have a potentially serious adverse impact on the course of the Vietnam War and cause irreparable harm to national security. The newspaper lawyers asserted that the government failed to show that such harm would occur and that such prior restraint violated the First Amendment. With surprising swiftness, the Supreme Court rendered its decision five days later, on Thursday, June 30, 1971.[68] For those who awaited a strong reaffirmation of *Near* and a ringing victory for First Amendment rights, the Court's decision was a hollow win and, to many, a major disappointment.

In a brief *per curiam* opinion, the Court merely held that the government failed to meet the heavy burden required in justifying prior restraint. The 6 to 3 decision in favor of the *Times* and the *Post* included separate opinions from each of the nine justices. In the unsigned opinion, the Court quoted a 1963 decision involving prior restraint—*Bantam Books, Inc. v. Sullivan*:[69] "Any system of prior restraints of expression comes to this Court bearing a heavy presumption against its constitutional validity." The opinion then went on to note that "the government thus carries a heavy burden of showing justification for the enforcement of such restraint" (citing a decision earlier in the year, *Organization for a Better Austin v. Keefe*).[70] The citations also included *Near*, but none of the opinions, including the *per curiam* opinion, shed light on the limits for prior restraint. No consensus was reached regarding whether the injunctions had been constitutional, only that a heavy evidentiary burden had not been met.

Both the concurring justices and the dissenters looked to *Near*, but none of them went to great lengths to reaffirm the principles in *Near*. Instead they used the reasoning in *Near* to bolster their opinions. Justice William O. Douglas, who had a long and distinguished record of defending First Amendment rights, was joined by Justice Hugo Black (serving his last term on the Court; he died three months later) in one concurring opinion, and Black wrote another separate opinion joined by Douglas.

Black, joined by Douglas, argued that "in seeking injunctions against these newspapers and its presentation to the Court, the executive branch seems to have forgotten the essential purpose and history of the First Amendment." According to Black, "In revealing the workings of government that led to the Vietnam War, the newspapers nobly did precisely that which the Founders hoped and trusted they would do." He claimed that ruling that prior restraint may be imposed on news, as several of the justices advocated, "would make a shambles of the First Amendment."[71]

Douglas, joined by Black, took an absolutist view that "no law" means "no law." The First Amendment means there is "no room for governmental restraint on the press," according to Douglas. Even though disclosures such as those made by the newspaper in this case "may have a serious impact … that is no basis for sanctioning a previous restraint on the press," he argued. "Secrecy in government is fundamentally anti-democratic, perpetuating bureaucratic errors. Open debate and discussion on public issues are vital to our national health."[72]

In a third concurring opinion, Justice William J. Brennan, Jr., also known for his unwavering support of a strong First Amendment, vociferously argued, "The error that has pervaded these cases from the outset was the granting of any injunctive relief whatsoever, interim or otherwise." He noted that "never before has the United States sought to enjoin a newspaper from publishing information in its possession." Brennan freely cited *Near* as affirming that prior restraint should be imposed in only the rarest of cases.[73]

Justices Potter Stewart and Byron R. White each wrote separate concurring opinions with which the other joined. Stewart, joined by White, made it clear that he did not share an absolutist view of the First Amendment on prior restraint. His opinion included a now famous quote, "For when everything is classified, then nothing is classified," arguing that governmental secrecy must not be secrecy for secrecy's sake. "I am convinced that the executive is correct with respect to some of the documents involved," Justice Stewart concluded. "But I cannot say that disclosure of any of them will surely result in direct, immediate, and irreparable damage to our Nation or its people." In his view, the government failed to overcome the heavy burden imposed by the Constitution to demonstrate that the prior restraint was justified under the circumstances.[74]

In his concurring opinion, White, joined by Stewart, went beyond the previous concurring opinion with Stewart to note that whereas the government had not been able to show the constitutionally mandated "unusually heavy justification" for prior restraint, the "failure by the Government to justify prior restraints does not measure its constitutional entitlement to a conviction for criminal publication."[75] White did not rule out the possibility that the government may have been able to seek criminal sanctions provided in the statutes *after* the publication even though it could not prevent publication.

In the final concurring opinion, Justice Thurgood Marshall focused on the doctrine of separation of powers, concluding that "this Court does not have authority to grant the requested relief [sought by the executive branch]. It is not for this Court to fling itself into every breach perceived by some government official."

If read carefully, the dissenting opinions present a narrow view of First Amendment rights. In his dissent, Chief Justice Warren Burger noted, "The prompt setting of these cases reflects our universal abhorrence of prior restraint. But prompt judicial action does not mean unjudicial haste." The Chief Justice characterized the Pentagon Papers as "purloined documents," pointing out "it is not disputed that the *Times* has had unauthorized possession of the documents for three to four months." Burger criticized the newspaper for not submitting the materials to government officials so the parties could negotiate declassification. "The consequence of all this melancholy series of events is that we literally do not know what we are acting on," according to the Chief Justice.

On the surface, Burger's arguments may seem reasonable. However, a closer look reveals that he is advocating that the newspaper impose self-censorship and submit the "stolen property" to governmental authorities so they could determine what, if anything, could be declassified. Barring such voluntary action by the *Times*, the Chief Justice would permit the trial court to continue the injunction until all of the facts were in and the case could be resolved at trial. Further, although he would have directed that "the district court on remand give priority to the *Times* case to the exclusion of all other business of that court ... [he] would not set arbitrary deadlines." Throughout his opinion, Burger expresses his distaste for the speedy manner in which the case was granted certiorari and ultimately decided by the Court.[76]

Justice John M. Harlan, joined by Burger and Justice Harry A. Blackmun, also chided the majority for the swiftness with which the case was decided. He felt that the Court had been "almost irresponsibly feverish" in hearing and deciding this case. "This frenzied train of events took place in the name of the presumption against prior restraints created by the First Amendment," he complained. "Due regard for the extraordinarily important and difficult questions involved in these litigations should have led the Court to shun such a precipitate timetable." Harlan raised seven major questions to be considered before deciding the case on its merits, including whether the newspapers were entitled to retain and use the "purloined" documents and "whether the unauthorized disclosure of any of these particular documents would seriously impair the national security."[77] These three dissenters would have continued the injunctions at least until the lower courts could decide the cases on their merits. They make no mention of the fact that such deliberations, even if expedited, could take months or years while the documents continued to be suppressed.

Finally, in a separate dissent not joined by any of the other justices, Blackmun carefully avoided criticizing any judges or lawyers in the case. He indicated he "would remand these cases to be developed expeditiously, of course, but on a schedule permitting the orderly presentation of evidence from both sides, with the use of discovery, if necessary." Blackmun studied affidavits and portions of the Pentagon Papers. He believed if the newspapers published the documents because of the majority opinion in the case, soldiers would be killed, alliances destroyed, negotiations with the enemy would be more difficult, and the war would be prolonged, resulting in "further delay in the freeing of United States prisoners."[78]

Minus the four missing volumes that Daniel Ellsberg initially considered too sensitive to disclose and that were never officially declassified, the Pentagon Papers were eventually published by newspapers throughout the United States, including the *Times* and the *Post*. At least three versions of the 43 volumes were published in book form—the official version for the media and interested parties by the Government Printing Office, a Bantam Books paperback edition based on the *New York Times* stories, and a Beacon Press "Gravel" edition; named after Senator Mike Gravel (D-Alaska), who managed, over the opposition of many of his colleagues, to have the documents officially entered into the record of a Senate Subcommittee hearing. Gravel was one of several members of Congress who had the opportunity to gain access to copies of the Pentagon Papers before they were eventually published, but he was the only one willing to publicly disclose them.[79]

By most, if not all, accounts, publication of the Pentagon Papers had virtually no impact on the Vietnam War. The Nixon administration chose to prosecute Ellsberg and Anthony J. Russo, Jr., who had helped Ellsberg photocopy the documents, charging them primarily with violating the U.S. Espionage Act[80] and for stealing government property. Both were indicted based on evidence presented by the U.S. Justice Department to a federal grand jury. The first trial court jury impaneled in the case in July 1972 was dismissed after some complicated legal maneuvering. Charges were dismissed on May 11, 1973, after it became known that President Nixon's Watergate "plumbers" burglarized the offices of Ellsberg's psychiatrist and also conducted illegal wiretaps against individuals from 1969 through 1971 in an effort to plug government "leaks."

The fates of the two major players in the Pentagon papers case could not have been more different. In 1975, Attorney General Mitchell was convicted of conspiracy, perjury, and obstruction of justice for participating in planning the Watergate break-in and cover-up. He became the first and, so far, only U.S. Attorney General to be convicted of criminal acts and sent to prison. Three decades after the Pentagon Papers, Ellsberg switched criticism from Vietnam to Iraq, pointing out the parallels he saw between wars.[81]

Although most media hailed the Court's decision as a triumph for the press, at least some First Amendment scholars saw the decision as a hollow victory at best. Prior restraint had been imposed on major news media for two weeks with the consent of the federal courts, including the U.S. Supreme Court. The ultimate decision was merely that the U.S. government had failed to meet the heavy evidentiary burden in demonstrating that the prior restraint was constitutionally permissible. There is also little solace in the fact that each of the nine justices took somewhat different views of the meaning of the principles established in *Near v. Minnesota*.

Impact on the Vietnam War was minimal. There was no public clamor over the Court's ruling or over the ultimate publication of the Pentagon Papers. Apparently few people other than journalists read the Papers in detail, although the *Times* book version sold more than a million copies.[82] Thousands of U.S. soldiers died in the Vietnam War. The war continued until a cease-fire agreement was signed in 1973. U.S. troops made a relatively quick withdrawal. The war ended in 1975 when the North Vietnamese gained military control over the south with its final offensive against the South Vietnamese forces. Officially, 47,393 U.S. soldiers died in combat,

10,800 died from other causes, and 153,363 were wounded.[82] Thousands of others were missing in action and presumed dead.

Ethical Concerns in the Pentagon Papers Case

The legal battle over the Pentagon Papers was certainly complex and even convoluted. It also raised serious ethical questions that make the case even more complicated. Putting the legalities aside (they were never resolved), was it ethical for the newspapers to agree to accept stolen government property? It can be argued that Daniel Ellsberg had legal access to the classified materials. There is no doubt that he did not have authority to disclose the documents to the *Times* or to others (such as members of Congress). Should a journalist agree to accept documents knowing they are classified, illegally obtained or copied? When do the ends justify the means? The *Code of Ethics of the Society of Professional Journalists* and all of the other major media codes of conduct are silent on this issue.

Twenty years after the Pentagon Papers case, the U.S. Supreme Court held that a journalist who innocently obtained and then broadcast an illegally recorded cellular phone conversation could not be held liable for civil damages. In *Bartnicki v. Vopper* (2001),[84] a radio commentator played a tape on his talk show of a cell phone discussion between a local teacher's union president and the chief union negotiator concerning ongoing collective bargaining negotiations. The person who secretly recorded the call and the broadcaster clearly violated a provision of the federal Omnibus Crime Control and Safe Streets Act of 1968[85] as well as state statutes. No one was able to determine who had surreptitiously recorded the conversation because the tape was anonymously delivered. The *Bartnicki* Court held that the First Amendment protected such disclosures even if the journalist knew or had reason to know the interception was unlawful—so long as the topic of the conversations was a matter of public concern. Bartnicki was handed down two decades after the Pentagon Papers decision but presumably could justify the publication of documents like the Pentagon Papers—if the journalist played no direct role in illegally obtaining them and publication posed no serious threat to national security.

Most newspapers would probably not have been able to endure the agony and expense of the Pentagon Papers case. The *Times* spent $150,000 in legal fees in the two weeks between the time the injunction was sought and the U.S. Supreme Court issued its decision, and the *Post* faced a $70,000 bill.[86] Obviously, the expenses involved for the *Times* in researching the Papers and writing the articles were also high. Smaller newspapers and newspapers with weaker finances could ill afford to fight such a battle, and even the *Times* and the *Post* could not tackle many such matches. Every media outlet should adopt a consistent policy for dealing with such ethical issues, including who has authority to review such materials and who will oversee publication. The Pentagon Papers were historical documents whose ultimate disclosure caused apparently no harm to U.S. security and diplomatic matters. What if there were a chance that such harm would occur but there was no way of determining precisely what would happen? Should a newspaper or magazine go ahead and publish the materials?

These are thorny questions that were raised again, but never answered, in the strange and almost unbelievable *Progressive* magazine story in the next section. It was inevitable that, at some point, a case would arise to test the constitutionality of prior restraint involving national security matters outside the historical context of the Pentagon Papers.

United States v. The Progressive, Inc. (1979)

Under the U.S. Atomic Energy Act of 1954:

> Whoever, lawfully or unlawfully, having possession of, access to, control over, or being entrusted with any document, writing, sketch, photograph, plan, model instrument, appliance, note, or information involving or incorporating Restricted Data.…
>
> (b) communicates, transmits, or discloses the same to any individual or person, or attempts or conspires to do any of the foregoing, with reason to believe such data will be used to injure the United States or to secure an advantage to any foreign nation, shall, upon conviction, be punished by a fine of not more than $10,000 or imprisonment for not more than ten years, or both.[87]

Every aspiring journalist planning to write about nuclear weapons and nuclear energy should read the Act, still in effect. The basic provisions of the act are quite broad. Its definition of restricted data is: "all data concerning (1) design, manufacture or utilization of atomic weapons; (2) the production of special nuclear material; or the use of special nuclear fuels in the production of nuclear energy."[88] The Act grants the U.S. Attorney General the authority to seek "a permanent or temporary injunction, restraining order, or other order" in court to prohibit "any acts or practices" that violate or would violate any provision of the act.[89]

In early 1979, *The Progressive*—a relatively small circulation monthly magazine founded in 1909 by Robert M. LaFollette as the official organ of the Progressive political party—hired a freelancer, Howard Morland, to write an article about the ease with which an H-bomb could be made. Morland and magazine editor Erwin Knoll claimed that all the material for the article, "The H-Bomb Secret: How We Got It, Why We're Telling It," came from public documents and sources. The U.S. government, on the other hand, claimed the article revealed secret technical concepts whose dissemination would violate the Atomic Energy Act, although the government conceded during the trial that much of the information appeared in documents available to the public at the Los Alamos (New Mexico) Scientific Laboratory Library. When this fact became known, the government removed the documents from public circulation and had them classified as secret.

How did the government learn about the article in advance? Morland circulated a rough draft among several scientists for criticism on the technical accuracy of the article, and eventually the government learned of the article's existence. The U.S. Attorney General, citing the provisions of the Atomic Energy Act discussed earlier, moved immediately to stop publication of the article by seeking an injunction in federal court in Madison, Wisconsin, where the magazine, which specializes in social and political commentary, is published. The federal government took this legal action after editor Knoll refused to delete approximately one-tenth of the article the government contended endangered national security.

In March 1979, after hearing evidence presented by U.S. attorneys in a closed hearing in Milwaukee, U.S. District Court Judge Robert W. Warren granted the government's request for a temporary restraining order. The TRO was soon replaced by a preliminary injunction on March 26 after Judge Warren heard arguments on both sides. He based his decision on grounds that the information, if published, would violate the Atomic Energy Act and that even though the article was not a "'do-it-yourself' guide for the hydrogen bomb … [it] could possibly provide sufficient information to allow a medium size nation to move faster in developing a hydrogen weapon."[90]

Warren seemed concerned that the article could start a nuclear war. While noting serious First Amendment ramifications (he cited the case as "the first instance of prior restraint against a publication in this fashion in the history of this country"), he believed that a "mistake in ruling against the United States could pave the way for thermonuclear annihilation for us all. In that event, our right to life is extinguished and the right to publish becomes moot."[91]

What precedents did Warren cite in his decision? As expected, *Near* set the standard, although the judge also reverted to the test proposed by Justice Stewart in the Pentagon Papers decision. This test holds value as precedent because only Justice White joined the concurring opinion. Ironically, Justice Stewart found that in applying the test ("direct, immediate, and irreparable damage to our Nation or its people"), the *Times* and the *Post* should not have been enjoined because he was not convinced that publication would cause such harm. *The Progressive*'s attorneys contended that the purpose of the article was not to enable someone to build an H-bomb, but to make the public aware of the dangers of nuclear war by demonstrating how easy it was to construct such weapons. Judge Warren called this goal a "laudable crusade" but held the portions of the article found objectionable by the government "fall within the narrow area recognized by the Court in *Near v. Minnesota* in which a prior restraint on publication is appropriate." *Near*, of course, makes no mention of hydrogen bombs, but Warren drew a parallel between troop movement exception ("publication of the sailing dates of transports or number and location of troops") and H-bombs:

> Times have changed significantly since 1931 when *Near* was decided. Now war by foot soldiers has been replaced in large part by war by machines and bombs. No longer need there be any advanced warning or any preparation time before a nuclear war could be commenced. In light of these factors, this court concludes that publication of the technical information of the hydrogen bomb contained in the article is analogous to publication of troop movements or locations in time of war and falls within the extremely narrow exception to the rule against prior restraint.[92]

How was this case different from the Pentagon Papers? Judge Warren contended that the Pentagon Papers were "historical data," whereas *The Progressive* article involved "the most destructive weapon in the history of mankind, information of sufficient destructive potential to nullify the right to free speech and to endanger the right to life itself."[93] He noted the U.S. government had simply failed to meet its heavy evidentiary burden in the earlier case. Although no federal statute applied in the Pentagon Papers, a specific federal statute (the Atomic Energy Act) granted the government authority to seek the injunction.

The preliminary injunction kept the article from being published. The magazine appealed the judge's decision to the 7th Circuit U.S. Court of Appeals in Chicago, seeking a writ of mandamus from the U.S. Supreme Court to order the trial court to conduct an expedited review. On July 2, the Supreme Court, in a 7 to 2 *per curiam* opinion that was a decision only on the request for expedited review, not a decision on the merits of the prior restraint, denied the motion (only Justices White and Brennan dissented.) The Court denied the motion primarily on the grounds that *The Progressive* spent almost three months preparing the required briefs arguing the merits of the case and, in the eyes of the Court, negated need for expedited review. On September 13, six months after the initial prior restraint had been imposed on the magazine, the U.S. Court of Appeals finally heard oral arguments on both sides, which essentially were the same as those made prior to the earlier decision.

Three days later on September 16, the case took a bizarre turn. A small circulation newspaper, the *Madison* (Wisconsin) *Press Connection*—published by a group of employees then on strike against the two daily newspapers[94]—published a letter from a 32-year-old computer programmer and freelance writer who had developed a keen interest in the hydrogen bomb. The letter from Charles Hansen was addressed to liberal U.S. Republican Senator Charles Percy of Illinois. Copies were sent to various newspapers. Hansen was miffed at what had happened to *The Progressive* and included essentially the same information—including a diagram of how the bomb works and a description of the process of manufacturing the device in his letter repressed from the magazine.

The U.S. government's reaction was immediate. Instead of hopping to court to seek another injunction or to criminally prosecute the magazine, the government dropped all efforts to seek a permanent injunction. Why? Officially, the U.S. Justice Department indicated that because the letter exposed most of the information the United States was seeking to prevent *The Progressive* from publishing, there was no longer any need for the injunction. The secrets were out and the damage was done.

Would the government have ultimately prevailed had this case gone to the U.S. Supreme Court on its merits? No one knows. If the Court chose, it could certainly have distinguished this case from the Pentagon Papers case, just as U.S. District Court Judge Warren had done. Once again, many questions were left unanswered; the Republic apparently was not harmed and life went on. Several newspapers published the letter later, and in its November 1979 issue, *The Progressive* finally published the original article under the title, "The H-Bomb Secret: To Know How Is To Ask Why." Judge Warren did not formally dismiss the case against the magazine until September 4, 1980, but the government's request the case be dismissed effectively blocked any obstacles to publication.

Was this a media victory? No. But it was not a defeat. Press reaction was mixed. The *New York Times* editorially supported the magazine. The *Washington Post* (the same that fought to publish the Pentagon Papers) criticized the publication. Journalists feared that if the U.S. Supreme Court heard the case on its merits, an adverse ruling would have emerged with dire consequences for First Amendment rights. Ignorance may be bliss, they reasoned.

When *The Progressive* Editor Erwin Knoll died in 1994, most of the obituaries recalled his First Amendment battle with the government over the article. He had been editor of the magazine since 1973.

Judicial Prior Restraints

Most prior restraints occur when an agency of the executive branch such as the U.S. Justice Department or a local prosecutor seeks a court order to prohibit publication, but prior restraint can originate from any branch of government including the judiciary. In 1976, for the first and thus far only time, the U.S. Supreme Court confronted the constitutionality of restrictive orders imposed on the press in attempting to preserve the constitutional rights of criminal defendants.

Nebraska Press Association v. Stuart (1976)

On October 18, 1975, six members of the Henry Kellie family were viciously murdered in their home in Sutherland, a small Nebraska hamlet. The state later charged that the murders occurred in the course of a sexual assault, including that of a 10-year-old girl. This attracted widespread attention from local, regional, and national news media. Police released a description of a suspect who was quickly arrested and arraigned in Lincoln County Court. The suspect, Ervin Charles Simants, through his attorney and joined by the county attorney, moved to close the proceedings to the press and the public. The county court judge heard oral arguments (probably a misnomer because both attorneys supported a restrictive order and no attorney for the media was there to protest) and granted the motion for the restrictive order.

As requested, the order strictly prohibited anyone at the hearing from releasing or authorizing for public dissemination in any form or matter whatsoever any testimony given or evidence and required the press to adhere to the Nebraska bar–press guidelines. These are sometimes called bench–bar–press guidelines, drawn up in many states to provide guidance to the media on how criminal trials and other judicial proceedings should be covered. Guidelines are *voluntary* and bear no sanctions or penalties for violation. However, the county court judge ordered the press to abide by the guidelines.

Surprisingly, the judge did not close the preliminary hearing for the defendant but made the hearing subject to restrictive order. In other words, the media were permitted to attend the hearing but prohibited from reporting anything that took place. The judge's justification for that order was to preserve the 6th Amendment right of the defendant to "a speedy and public trial, by an impartial jury."

The county court bound Simants over to the district court for further proceedings. On October 23, members of the news media including the Nebraska Press Association, publishers, and reporters filed a motion for leave to intervene in the district court, requesting that the restrictive order be lifted. After a hearing that included testimony from the county court judge and admission into evidence of news articles about the case, District Court Judge Hugh Stuart granted the motion to intervene. On October 27, however, he issued his own restrictive order to be tentatively applied until the trial court jury was selected and could have been extended longer at the judge's discretion. The order was broad, prohibiting the news media from reporting:

> (1) the existence or contents of a confession Simants had made to law enforcement officers, which had been introduced in open court arraignment; (2) the fact or nature of statements Simants had made to other persons; (3) the contents of a note he had written the night of the crime; (4) certain aspects of the medical testimony at the preliminary hearing; and (5) the identity of the victims of the alleged sexual assault and the nature of the assault.[95]

As with the prior one, this order required the press to follow the Nebraska bar–press guidelines and even prohibited publication of the exact nature of the order. The order prohibited public dissemination of virtually any information that could possibly prejudice potential jurors.

On October 31, the Nebraska Press Association and its supporters simultaneously asked the district court to vacate its order and filed a writ of mandamus, a stay, and an expedited appeal with the Nebraska Supreme Court. The prosecuting attorney and Simants' attorney intervened and the state supreme court heard oral arguments on November 25. One week later, the state supreme court issued a *per curiam* opinion that modified the district court order but still prohibited dissemination of: "(a) the existence and nature of any confessions or admissions made by the defendant to law enforcement officers, (b) any confessions or admissions made to any third parties, except members of the press, and (c) other facts 'strongly implicative' of the accused."[96]

Although this version of the order was not quite as restrictive as the original, the restraint on the press was still very broad. The Nebraska Supreme Court applied a balancing test pitting the standard enunciated in the Pentagon Papers ("heavy presumption against … constitutional validity" of governmental prior restraint) against the 6th Amendment rights of the defendant. The court found that Simants' right to trial by an impartial jury outweighed the First Amendment considerations. The state supreme court did not use the state bar–press guidelines as justification, but instead referred to state statutory law permitting closure in certain circumstances. The Nebraska Supreme Court specifically rejected the "absolutist position" that prior restraint by the government against the press is never constitutionally permissible.

The Nebraska Press Association and the other petitioners quickly appealed the state supreme court decision to the U.S. Supreme Court, and in late 1975 the Court granted a writ of certiorari to hear the case. In the meantime, Simants was tried and convicted of first degree murder and sentenced to death in January 1976. On April 19, 1976, the U.S. Supreme Court heard oral arguments in the appeal of the restrictive order and issued its decision on June 30. The Court had jurisdiction to hear the case despite the fact Simants was already convicted because the particular controversy was "capable of repetition." In other words, the Court felt this case was important enough to decide because of its implications for future cases even though the decision would have no impact on the case from which it originally arose.

The U.S. Supreme Court held that the restrictive order was unconstitutional. In the unanimous opinion written by Chief Justice Warren E. Burger, the Court contrasted the impact of prior restraint versus the after-the-fact impact of punishment on press freedom. "A prior restraint, by contrast and by definition, has an immediate and irreversible sanction," according to the Court. "If it can be said that a threat of criminal or civil sanctions after publication 'chills' speech, prior restraint 'freezes' it at least for the time."[97]

The Court saw three major issues that had to be addressed before the constitutionality of the order could be determined: "(a) the nature and extent of pretrial coverage; (b) whether other measures would be likely to mitigate the effects of unrestrained pretrial publicity; and (c) how effectively a restraining order would operate to prevent the threatened danger."[98] Although the Court felt "that the trial judge was justified in concluding that there would be intense and pervasive pretrial publicity … [and] … that publicity might impair the defendant's right to a fair trial …," it characterized the judge's conclusions regarding the effect on potential jurors as "speculative, dealing as he was with factors unknown and unknowable."[99] A major problem resulted because the judge did not demonstrate that measures short of the restrictive order would not have prevented or mitigated any potential violations of the defendant's 6th Amendment rights. The Court listed several examples of measures that should have been attempted first by the judge before issuing the restrictive order. These included:

> (a) change of trial venue to a place less exposed to the intense publicity that seemed imminent in Lincoln County [footnote omitted]; (b) postponement of the trial to allow public attention to subside; (c) use of searching questions of prospective jurors … to screen out those with fixed opinions as to guilt or innocence; (d) the use of emphatic and clear instructions on the sworn duty of each juror to decide the issues only on evidence presented in open court.[100]

Other measures mentioned by the Court were sequestration of jurors and restricting what the lawyers, police, and witnesses could say outside the courtroom. Most of these measures were first enunciated in a 1966 case, *Sheppard v. Maxwell*.[101]

As in *Near* and the Pentagon Papers case, the Court made it clear that whereas the burden of overcoming the strong presumption against the constitutionality of prior restraint had not been met in the case at bar, "this Court has frequently denied that First Amendment rights are absolute and has consistently rejected the proposition that prior restraint can never be employed."[102]

Because the composition of the Court has changed almost entirely since this case was decided in 1976, it is difficult to predict how the Court would decide other prior restraint cases involving restrictive orders, especially if such an order were narrowly tailored to protect rights of a defendant when those rights were in jeopardy and other measures would be highly unlikely to be effective.

United States v. Noriega (In re Cable News Network, Inc.) (1990)

The Cable News Network (CNN) aired an audiotape it obtained through an anonymous source that included a conversation between former Panamanian dictator Manuel Noriega and one of his attorneys on November 7, 1990. At the time, General Noriega was in federal jail in Florida awaiting trial on various federal charges, including drug trafficking. He had been captured a year earlier in a U.S.-led invasion of Panama. The tape was one of several recorded by prison officials who argued that the monitoring and recording of outgoing phone calls were in line with established policies and procedures. Noriega's lawyers denied the federal government's claim that the former dictator had been aware of the taping. In the story about the tape, CNN included an interview with one of the defendant's attorneys who indicated the tape was authentic.

Noriega's defense team immediately requested a temporary restraining order in U.S. District Court before the judge presiding over the criminal case, but CNN aired additional tapes before a hearing could be conducted the next day. At the hearing, the attorneys argued that further broadcasts of the tapes could jeopardize the deposed leader's 6th Amendment right to a fair trial and violate attorney–client privilege. At the hearing the Judge granted the request and then ordered the network to turn over all tapes in its possession so he could determine through an *in camera* inspection whether broadcast constituted "a clear, immediate and irreparable danger" to Noriega's 6th Amendment rights.[103]

After conferring with its attorneys, CNN defied both the restraining order and the order to relinquish the tapes, claiming First Amendment protection. The network sought relief from the 11th Circuit Court of Appeals, but two days later, the appellate court upheld the trial court's orders and, in a decision that severely criticized CNN, held that it must immediately produce the tapes.[104]

In an expedited review, the U.S. Supreme Court in a 7 to 2 vote on November 18, with Justices Marshall and O'Connor dissenting, denied certiorari,[105] thus allowing the 11th Circuit decision to stand. Two days later, CNN complied by delivering the tapes to the district court. A week later, after hearing arguments on both sides regarding Noriega's request for a permanent injunction and listening to the tapes, the Judge ruled further airing of the recorded conversations would not interfere with Noriega's right to a fair trial.[106] The tapes were then returned to CNN. Noriega was tried and convicted.

During a four-day trial in September 1994, CNN claimed it had the right to broadcast the

Noriega tapes under the First Amendment, and the government argued simply that CNN had a responsibility to abide by a gag order until it was overturned. The next month, the Judge convicted the network of criminal contempt. In December he told CNN it had two options in accepting punishment—it could pay a fine of up to $100,000 plus the $85,000 cost of prosecuting the case, or it could apologize on the air and pay only the prosecution cost. CNN chose the latter and aired the following apology each hour for 22 hours beginning on December 19, 1994: "CNN realizes that it was in error in defying the order of the court and publishing the Noriega tape while appealing the court's order."

Ten years after the CNN case, the U.S. Supreme Court again allowed prior restraint to be imposed on the news media covering a criminal trial. This time it involved the rape trial of NBA star Kobe Bryant. After a court reporter mistakenly emailed the transcript of an *in camera* hearing concerning details of the alleged victim's sexual past, the Colorado trial court judge imposed a ban on publication of the transcript and ordered the press to destroy electronic and hard copies.[107] On appeal, the Colorado Supreme Court in a 4 to 3 decision upheld the trial court's ban on publication but reversed the order that copies be destroyed.[108] The charges were eventually dropped after the alleged victim refused to testify at trial.

Strategic Lawsuits against Public Participation (SLAPPs)

The last provision of the First Amendment grants citizens the right "to petition the Government for a redress of grievances." This right received renewed attention in 1996 with the publication of the results of a national project initiated in the mid-1980s by University of Denver Professors George W. Pring and Penelope Canan. In a landmark book entitled *SLAPPs: Getting Sued for Speaking Out*,[109] the authors describe how individuals and organizations "are now being routinely sued in multimillion-dollar damage actions for … circulating a petition, writing a letter to the editor, testifying at a public hearing, reporting violations of law, lobbying for legislation, peaceably demonstrating, or otherwise attempting to influence government action."[110] They call such legal actions "strategic lawsuits against public participation" (SLAPPs) and characterize them as "a new breed of lawsuits stalking America."

The California Anti-SLAPP Project that was formed to help both attorneys and members of the public fight SLAPPs notes on its Web site, "While most SLAPPs are legally meritless, they effectively achieve their principal purpose: to chill public debate on specific issues."[111] Many states now have anti-SLAPP statutes, but they vary considerably in scope from broad protection to very limited protection.[112] The Society of Professional Journalists is promoting a model anti-SLAPP statute that it hopes will be adopted by the states.[113] Two media law attorneys have characterized Georgia's statute enacted in 1996 as "a powerful weapon to protect Georgia citizens and organizations from lawsuits designed to silence the exercise of First Amendment freedoms."[114]

According to Pring and Canan, the largest categories of SLAPPs involve real estate development, zoning, land use, and criticism of public officials and employees.[115] They point out that most SLAPP suits are eventually dismissed but only after an average of 40 months of litigation.[116] To avoid a chilling effect on citizens and groups who speak out, anti-SLAPP statutes usually permit defendants who win to recover attorney fees.

SLAPP suits will undoubtedly continue to increase, posing serious risks to First Amendment rights unless more states pass effective anti-SLAPP legislation. Although freedom of speech and freedom of press have attracted far more attention than the allied right to petition the government for a redress of grievances, the latter right is just as important in protecting not only individuals and organizations but the news media as well. The mass media are by no means immune from such suits but have simply been able to generally avoid facing SLAPPs because they usually have substantial resources to fend off the litigation.

Prior Restraint on Freedom of Speech

The First Amendment grants not only freedom of the press but freedom of speech and the right to peaceably assemble as well. Some of the most controversial cases to be decided by the U.S. Supreme Court evolved from free speech and free assembly conflicts. Troublesome speech cases often produce inconsistent and confusing opinions. This section deals only with noncommercial speech because commercial speech is the focus of the next chapter.

One of the earliest U.S. Supreme Court decisions on free speech was *Jay Fox v. State of Washington* in 1915 in which a unanimous court ruled that a Washington State statute banning speech "having a tendency to encourage or incite the commission of any crime, breach of the peace, or act of violence" did not violate the First or 14th Amendments. According to the decision written by the famous Justice Oliver Wendell Holmes, "In this present case the disrespect for law that was encouraged was disregard of it, an overt breach and technically criminal act."[117] The defendant published an article encouraging a boycott of officials and others who were arresting members of a local nudist colony for indecent exposure. He was charged with inciting indecent exposure under a statute that made such an act a misdemeanor. This was an early indication of a distinction made many years later between speech versus action or symbolic speech versus action speech.

Schenck v. United States (1919)
One of the most famous of the early free speech cases was *Schenck v. United States* (combined with *Baer v. United States*)[118] in 1919 in which the U.S. Supreme Court for the first time applied the "clear and present danger" test in determining impermissible speech. Charles T. Schenck and Elizabeth Baer, members of the U.S. Socialist Party, were indicted and ultimately convicted by a federal jury of three counts of violating the federal Espionage Act of 1917. This act provided criminal penalties of up to a $10,000 fine and/or imprisonment for up to 20 years for conviction of various offenses during wartime including "willfully obstruct[ing] the recruiting or enlistment service of the United States, to the injury of the service or of the United States." Both defendants were involved in sending brochures to potential draftees during World War I characterizing a conscript as little better than a convict and "in impassioned language … intimated that conscription was despotism in its worst form and a monstrous wrong against humanity in the interest of Wall Street's chosen few."[119] According to Justice Holmes:

> We admit that in many places and in ordinary times the defendants in saying all that was said in the circular would have been within their constitutional rights. But the character of every act depends upon the circumstances in which it is done. The most stringent protection of free speech would not protect a man in falsely shouting fire in a theatre and causing a panic. The question in every case is whether the words are used in such circumstances and are such a nature as to create a clear and present danger that they will bring about the substantive evils that Congress has a right to prevent. It is a question of proximity and degree.[120]

The Court upheld the convictions on the grounds that the state was within its rights to punish Schenck and Baer because of the possibility that the circulars could have obstructed recruiting even though no such obstruction was demonstrated by the state. According to the unanimous opinion, "If the act (speaking, or circulating a paper), its tendency and the intent with which it is done are the same, we perceive no ground for saying that success alone warrants making the act a crime."[121]

The clear and present danger test has had many advocates among the U.S. Supreme Court justices over the years, and the example of falsely shouting fire in a crowded theater has been frequently cited by the public and jurists alike in supporting restrictions on certain kinds of speech. But is it an appropriate test? Can it be fairly and consistently applied or does it become merely arbitrary? In *Schenck*, the Court emphasized that the country was at war and that Congress had specific authority under the federal statute to prohibit such actions. What if there had been no war at the time? What if no federal statute covered the speech?

Abrams v. United States (1919)

On May 16, 1918, Congress amended the 1917 Espionage Act to include a series of additional offenses such as promoting curtailment of the production of war materials. That same year Jacob Abrams and four other defendants, all Russian emigrants, were convicted in a federal court in New York of violating the act, including the 1918 amendments, for publishing information "intended to incite, provoke and encourage resistance to the United States" during the war and for conspiring "to urge, incite and advocate curtailment of production [of] ordnance and ammunition, necessary [to] the prosecution of the war."[122] What were their specific acts? They printed and distributed two different leaflets printed in English and Yiddish and threw copies out of the window of a building to passers-by. One of the leaflets, as described in Justice Holmes' dissent (joined by Justice Louis D. Brandeis), said:

> The President's [Woodrow Wilson] cowardly silence about the intervention in Russia reveals the hypocrisy of the plutocratic gang in Washington.… The other leaflet, headed 'Workers—Wake Up,' with abusive language says that America together with the Allies will march for Russia to help the Czecko-Slovaks in their struggle against the Bolsheviki, and that this time the hypocrites shall not fool the Russian emigrants and friends of Russia in America.[123]

In a 7 to 2 decision, with Justices Holmes and Brandeis dissenting, the Court upheld the trial court convictions, noting, "All five of the defendants were born in Russia. They were intelligent, had considerable schooling, and at the time they were arrested they had lived in the United States for terms varying from five to ten years, but none of them had applied for naturalization."[124]

In his dissent, Justice Holmes applied the clear and present test that he had formulated in the majority opinion in *Schenck* to the acts committed by Abrams and his co-defendants, but found a lack of proof of intent on the part of the defendants "to cripple or hinder the United States in the prosecution of the war." According to Justice Holmes: "I think that we should be eternally vigilant against attempts to check the expression of opinions that we loathe and believe to be fraught with death, unless they so imminently threaten immediate interference with the lawful and pressing purposes of the law that an immediate check is required to save the country."[125]

Does this case indicate the arbitrariness with which the clear and present danger test can be applied? The majority essentially applied the clear and present danger test but upheld the convictions, whereas the architect of the test, Justice Holmes, applied the test but found no imminent danger. In other cases decided by the Court in 1919 and 1920, a majority of the justices consistently upheld convictions for speech, usually involving the distribution of pamphlets or attempts to obstruct recruiting under the Espionage Act of 1917.[126]

Applying the First Amendment Through the 14th Amendment: *Gitlow v. New York* (1925)

In 1925, the U.S. Supreme Court tackled the first of a long series of cases that eventually broadened free speech rights and established much clearer guidelines on permissible versus impermissible speech. In *Gitlow v. New York*,[127] the Court upheld the conviction of Benjamin Gitlow for the distribution of 16,000 copies of *The Revolutionary Age*, an organ of the radical left wing section of the Socialist Party. Gitlow, an active member of the left wing who made speeches throughout New York, served on the paper's board of managers and as business manager, was indicted and convicted under the state criminal anarchy statute. The law, enacted in 1902 after the assassination of President William McKinley by an anarchist a year earlier, made it a felony for anyone to advocate criminal anarchy. Anarchy was defined as advocating, advising, or teaching "the duty, necessity or propriety of overthrowing or overturning organized government by force or violence."[128]

There was no question regarding Gitlow's guilt. He freely admitted violating the statute, but he contended that (a) his conviction was a violation of the due process clause of the 14th Amendment[129] and (b) "as there was no evidence of any concrete result flowing from the publication of the Manifesto or of the circumstances showing the likelihood of such a result, the statute ... penalizes the mere utterance ... of 'doctrine' having no quality of incitement, without regard either to the circumstances of its utterance or to the likelihood of unlawful consequences."[130] In a 7 to 2 decision with Justices Holmes and Brandeis dissenting, the Court held that even though there "was no evidence of any effect resulting from the publication and circulation of the Manifesto," the jury was "warranted in finding that the Manifesto advocated not merely the abstract doctrine of overthrowing organized government by force, violence and unlawful means, but action to that end."

Gitlow's First Amendment rights were not violated because the statute did not penalize communication of abstract doctrine or academic discussion but instead prohibited language that implied an urging to action, of which Gitlow was judged guilty. This was the Court's first hint of a distinction that was to come many years later between advocacy to action versus mere abstract doctrine.

What about 14th Amendment? The Court said it applied: "For present purposes, we may and do assume that freedom of speech and of the press—which are protected by the First Amendment from abridgement by Congress—are among the fundamental personal rights and 'liberties' protected by the due process clause of the 14th Amendment from impairment by the States."[131]

For the first time, the Court incorporated First Amendment rights into the 14th Amendment so that citizens of all states would have the same freedom of speech and of the press because the 14th Amendment prohibits both federal and state abridgement of these rights as originally granted in the Constitution.

Gitlow won his argument that the First Amendment applied to the states (the statute was a New York law) through the 14th, but he lost the argument that his First Amendment rights had been violated. Thus, his convictions stood. The majority applied a *bad tendency test* (implying an urging to action, as just mentioned), whereas Justices Holmes and Brandeis applied the clear and present danger test, noting in their dissent that "there was no present danger of an attempt to overthrow the government by force.... The only difference between an expression of an opinion and an incitement in the narrower sense is the speaker's enthusiasm for the result."[132]

Gitlow served three years of his five- to ten-year sentence. New York Governor Alfred E. Smith, who later ran unsuccessfully for the U.S. presidency, pardoned him. Gitlow became an anti-Communist informer during the 1940s and died in 1965.[133]

Two years after *Gitlow*, the U.S. Supreme Court had another opportunity to expand freedom of speech but chose once again not to do so. In *Whitney v. California* (1927),[134] the Court upheld the conviction of a Communist Labor Party (CLP) member for violating California's 1919 Criminal Syndicalism Act. What was Anita Whitney's crime? She attended a 1919 Chicago convention of the Socialist Party at which a radical right wing of the party—the Communist Labor Party—was formed. The state statute provided that any individual who "organizes or assists in organizing, or is or knowingly becomes a member of any organization, society, group or assemblage of persons organized or assembled to advocate, teach or aid and abet criminal syndicalism ... [i]s guilty of a felony and punishable by imprisonment." Criminal syndicalism was defined "as any doctrine or precept advocating, teaching or aiding and abetting the commission of a crime, sabotage ... or unlawful acts of force and violence or unlawful methods of terrorism."

Whitney admitted that she had joined and helped organize the CLP of California but argued that "the character of the state organization could not be forecast when she attended the convention" and that she did not intend to create "an instrument of terrorism and violence." Furthermore, she contended that the CLP's endorsement of acts of criminal syndicalism took place over her protests. The majority opinion rejected Whitney's argument that her First and 14th Amendment rights had been violated because "her mere presence in the convention, however violent the opinions expressed therein, could not truly become a crime."[135]

With Justice Louis D. Brandeis (joined by Justice Holmes) concurring in a separate opinion, the Court ruled that the jury had the authority to convict Whitney because the state statute as applied was not "repugnant to the due process clause." Citing *Gitlow*, the majority held that a state may punish those who abuse freedom of speech "by utterances inimical to the public welfare, tending to incite to crime, disturb the public peace, or endanger the foundations of organized government and threaten its overthrow by unlawful means."[136] What about the clear and present danger test? The majority refused to apply the test, but Justice Brandeis strongly argued that the test should apply in such cases, and he greatly clarified the conditions necessary to meet the test. Why did Justices Brandeis and Holmes then concur with the majority? According to Justice Brandeis, Whitney had not adequately argued her case on constitutional grounds at the time of her trial:

> Whenever the fundamental rights of free speech and assembly are alleged to have been invaded, it must remain open to a defendant to present the issue whether there actually did exist at the time a clear danger; whether the danger, if any, was imminent, and whether the evil apprehended was one so substantial as to justify the stringent restriction interposed by the legislature … [Whitney] claimed below that the statute as applied to her violated the Federal Constitution; but she did not claim that it was void because there was no clear and present danger of serious evil.[137]

This concurring opinion illustrates a fatal flaw that even modern appeals of trial court decisions involving First Amendment issues sometimes suffer—the failure to attack a statute or state action on sufficient constitutional grounds. Although it is unlikely that Whitney's conviction would have been reversed if the arguments at trial had met the criteria enunciated in Justice Brandeis' opinion, in other cases it could have made a difference. How should the clear and present danger test be applied? Justice Brandeis refined the test considerably:

> Fear of serious injury cannot alone justify suppression of free speech and assembly.… To justify suppression of free speech there must be reasonable ground to fear that serious evil will result if free speech is practiced. There must be reasonable ground to believe that the danger apprehended is imminent. There must be reasonable ground to believe that the evil to be prevented is a serious one. Every denunciation of existing law tends in some measure to increase the probability that there will be violation of it. Condonation of a breach enhances the probability. Expressions of approval add to the probability. Propagation of the criminal state of mind by teaching syndicalism increases it. Advocacy of lawbreaking heightens it further. But even advocacy of violation, however reprehensible morally, is not a justification for denying free speech where the advocacy falls short of incitement and there is nothing to indicate that the advocacy would be immediately acted on.
>
> The wide difference between advocacy and incitement, between preparation and attempt, between assembly and conspiracy, must be borne in mind. In order to support a finding of clear and present danger it must be shown either that immediate serious violence was to be expected or was advocated, or that the past conduct furnished reason to believe that such advocacy was then contemplated.[138]

Justice Brandeis' formulation was part of a concurring opinion rather than the majority opinion that rejected the test. His opinion was apparently a major influence on a decision 42 years later in which the Court, in a *per curiam* decision, unanimously overruled *Whitney*. In *Brandenburg v. Ohio*,[139] the Court overturned the conviction of a Ku Klux Klan (KKK) leader who had been fined $1,000 and sentenced to one to ten years in prison for violating Ohio's criminal syndicalism statute, quite similar to the statute in *Whitney*. Brandenburg telephoned an announcer–reporter for a Cincinnati television station and invited him to attend a KKK rally at a nearby farm. With the cooperation of the KKK, the reporter and a cameraperson attended and filmed the events that included a cross burning and speeches denouncing Jews and Blacks including phrases: "Send Jews back to Israel" and "Bury the Niggers." Portions were broadcast by the station and over network TV. The Court held the statute under which the defendant was prosecuted was unconstitutional because it "by its own words and as applied, purports to punish mere advocacy and to forbid … assembly with others merely to advocate the described type of action."[140]

The concept of "fighting words" first emerged in 1942 in *Chaplinsky v. New Hampshire*[141] in which the Court unanimously held such words have no First Amendment protection if, as the New Hampshire Supreme Court ruled earlier, they are "likely to cause an average addressee to fight." The Court upheld the conviction of a Jehovah's Witness who provoked a city marshal to fight on a sidewalk after he called the official "a God damned racketeer" and "a damned Fascist" and the government of Rochester, New Hampshire, "Fascists or agents of Fascists."[142] Fighting words, according to the majority, are "those which by their very utterance inflict injury or tend to incite an immediate breach of the peace."[143]

The U.S. Supreme Court tackled another free speech case involving Jehovah's Witnesses in 1951. Several members of the religious sect held a meeting in a city park in Havre de Grace, Maryland, after they had been denied a permit by the park commissioner. Two speakers were arrested, convicted, and fined $25 each for violating a state "practice" (no statute was involved) or tradition for anyone to seek a permit before holding a meeting in a public park. In a unanimous opinion, the Court held that such an arbitrary and discriminatory refusal to issue a permit was a clear violation of equal protection under the 14th Amendment.[144]

In another case[145] decided the same day, the U.S. Supreme Court upheld the disorderly conduct conviction of a college student, Irving Feiner, who told a group of approximately 75 African Americans and whites that President Harry S. Truman and the mayor of Syracuse, New York, were "bums" and the American Legion was a "Nazi Gestapo." He also said, "The negroes don't have equal rights; they should rise up in arms and fight them." Why was Feiner arrested? A man in the crowd told police, "If you don't get that son of a bitch off, I will go over and get him off there myself." At trial, a policeman testified he "stepped in to prevent it resulting in a fight." That was enough for the trial court to find that police "were motivated solely by a proper concern for the preservation of order and protection of the general welfare." The Court concluded Feiner "was thus neither arrested nor convicted for the making or the content of his speech. It was the reaction it actually engendered."[146]

It is unlikely today that Feiner's conviction would be upheld, especially based on evidence that one person's reaction might cause an adverse impact on the public welfare. The decision does illustrate how easily states can legally suppress freedom of speech. Indeed, 14 years after *Feiner*, the U.S. Supreme Court faced a similar set of circumstances. In two cases commonly known as *Cox I*[147] and *Cox II*,[148] the Court appeared to back substantially away from *Feiner*, although the majority opinion called the circumstances a "far cry" from those of *Feiner*. In *Cox I*, the Court held that a civil rights minister's conviction under a Louisiana disturbing-the-peace statute was an unconstitutional restraint on his freedom of speech and assembly. The minister, a field secretary for the Congress of Racial Equality (CORE), was arrested and convicted for breach of the peace and for obstructing a sidewalk after he gave a speech protesting the arrests of 23 African American college students after they picketed stores with segregated lunch counters. Cox encouraged a group of about 2,000 students to sit in at lunch counters, while a group of 100 to 300 whites gathered on the opposite sidewalk. When some members of the crowd reacted with muttering, Reverend Cox was arrested and convicted. The defendant was also convicted of violating a state statute banning courthouse demonstrations, and this conviction was reversed in *Cox II* by the Supreme Court on the same grounds as *Cox I*.

One more case decided prior to *Brandenburg* that deserves attention is *Dennis v. United States*[149] in which the Court applied a variation of the clear and present danger test, *ad hoc* balancing, to uphold the convictions of 11 members of the U.S. Communist Party for violating the conspiracy provisions of the Smith Act of 1940— a peacetime sedition act enacted by Congress. The Court voted 6 to 2 to uphold the convictions, but only four justices could agree on the specific test to be applied. Party members were convicted for "willfully and knowingly conspiring (1) to organize as the Communist Party ... a society, group and assembly of persons who teach and advocate the overthrow and destruction of the Government ... by force and violence and (2) knowingly and willfully to advocate and teach the duty and necessity of overthrowing and destroying the Government ... by force and violence."[150] The plurality opinion written by Chief Justice Fred M. Vinson applied the test articulated by Chief Judge Learned Hand in the 2nd Circuit U.S. Court of Appeals decision in the case: "In each case [courts] must ask whether the gravity of the 'evil,' discounted by its improbability, justifies such invasion of free speech as is necessary to avoid the danger."[151]

In *Dennis*, the trial court judge reserved the question of whether there was a clear and present danger for his own determination rather than submitting the issue to the jury. The defendants argued that the question should have been a jury issue because it was a question of fact. The U.S. Supreme Court agreed with the trial judge that the presence or absence of such a danger is a question of law, so for the judge to determine. The distinction is extremely important because juries are often more lenient with defendants in free speech cases than judges are. In a criminal case such as *Dennis*, a jury verdict in favor of the defendant cannot be overruled by the judge, and a judge's decision can only be reversed by an appellate court.

The thesis mentioned earlier—that extreme examples often provide the courts with the opportunity to delineate the outer boundaries of our First Amendment rights was well illustrated in a 1977 U.S. Supreme Court decision involving the National Socialist Party, otherwise known as the American Nazis. The Village of Skokie, Illinois, would seem on a map to be a fairly typical, small midwestern town, but appearances can be deceiving. During the Holocaust of 1933 through 1945, more than 6 million European Jews were systematically murdered in Nazi Germany while held in concentration camps. During the 1970s, more than 100,000 survivors were scattered around the world, with about 600 living in Skokie.[152] Frank Collins, a leader of the National Socialist Party, chose to march with his band of Nazi followers in Skokie after his request was strongly rebuffed by Skokie officials who told him he would have to purchase a $350,000 insurance bond to cover any damages. Shortly after the Nazis announced their plans to demonstrate in protest of the insurance requirement, the village council authorized its attorney to sue to obtain an injunction to prevent the march. An Illinois trial court judge granted the request and banned the party from conducting a number of actions from parading in uniform to distributing leaflets. The Nazis appealed the decision to the Illinois Appellate Court, which refused to stay the injunction, and then to the state Supreme Court, which denied their petition for expedited review. The party wanted a quick review so it could seek approval to demonstrate while the media attention was focused on its planned actions.

When the Illinois Supreme Court rendered its decision, the party filed a petition to stay pending expedited review in the U.S. Supreme Court. In a 5 to 4 *per curiam* decision, the U.S. Supreme Court treated the stay petition as a petition for a writ of certiorari and summarily reversed the Illinois Supreme Court. The Court said the injunction would deprive the Nazis of First Amendment rights during the appellate review process, which the Court noted could take at least a year to complete. The Court went on to hold, "If a State seeks to impose a restraint of this kind, it must provide strict procedural safeguards … including immediate appellate review. Absent such review, the State must instead allow a stay."[153]

The Court did *not* hold that the village could not ultimately have halted the march, but instead that the Nazis should have been granted an expedited decision rather than having to wait the usual long period involved in appealing trial court decisions. By refusing to grant expedited review on a First Amendment matter as serious as this one, the Illinois appellate courts infringed on the party's freedom of speech and freedom of assembly.

Following the dictates of the U.S. Supreme Court, the Illinois Appellate Court set aside the original injunction except for a provision banning the marchers from displaying the swastika.[154] On appeal, the state Supreme Court lifted the complete injunction on grounds that the ban was unconstitutional prior restraint.[155]

The battle was not over, however. While the case was on appeal, the Village of Skokie enacted several ordinances effectively banning demonstrations such as that proposed by the National Socialist Party. After fighting the ordinances in the federal courts—including the 7th Circuit U.S. Court of Appeals that ruled against the village and the U.S. Supreme Court that refused to stay the Court of Appeals decision—the march was presumably ready to begin. However, three days before the march was scheduled, Nazi leader Collins canceled plans for the rally. Instead two demonstrations were held in downtown Chicago, one at the Federal Plaza and the other in a public park two weeks later. Both marches involved a relatively small band of uniformed Nazis surrounded by thousands of police and counterdemonstrators. After short speeches, each was over almost as quickly as it had begun and the front page and lead stories in television newscasts about the marches faded away.

The ability of the government to impose prior restraint on private citizens appears rather limited, but such censorship is routinely permitted against the government's own employees. A long line of cases in the Supreme Court has established the principle that the government can impose criminal penalties and recover civil damages when employees disclose classified information, but the Court had never determined until 1980 whether the government can punish or recover damages from ex-employees who disclose nonclassified information after signing prepublication review agreements as conditions for employment.

Frank Snepp, a former CIA intelligence expert during the Vietnam War, wrote a book titled *Decent Interval*, sharply critical of U.S. involvement in Vietnam, especially during the interval in which U.S. troops were withdrawn. Snepp's book was published in 1977, four years after U.S. troops began withdrawing and two years after the Communists defeated the South Vietnamese Army. When hired by the agency in 1968, Snepp signed a prepublication review agreement, typically signed by CIA workers, specifying he would submit any materials to be published based on information he acquired as an employee. Such agreements, commonplace for federal employees with access to sensitive information, require prepublication review for the rest of the employee's life, even if the person is no longer employed by the government. This type of contract is obviously prior restraint because it involves governmental censorship of individuals, but is it unconstitutional?

It was undisputed in the case that Snepp did not seek CIA preclearance of his manuscript and he knowingly signed the contract. No classified information was published because the agency never made any claim that secrets were disclosed. Instead, the government argued that Snepp intentionally breached his contract with the CIA and was therefore obligated to pay all royalties to the agency. The CIA asserted that he should also be subject to punitive damages. The U.S. government successfully sought an injunction in U.S. District Court[156] to prohibit Snepp from committing further violations of his agreement with the CIA. The injunction imposed a *constructive trust* on previous and future royalties. A *constructive trust* is a legal mechanism created to force an individual or organization to convey property to another party on the ground that the property was wrongfully or improperly obtained.

The 4th Circuit U.S. Court of Appeals[157] upheld the trial court's injunction but ruled there was no basis for a constructive trust, although the court did hold that punitive damages could be imposed. In a 6 to 3 *per curiam* opinion,[158] the U.S. Supreme Court held that Snepp could not be forced to pay punitive damages but that a constructive trust was permissible because he had breached a fiduciary duty he owed to the government. *Fiduciary duty* simply means the duty of an individual or organization acting as a trustee for another after having agreed to undertake such a duty. By signing the agreement, Snepp created a duty to act on behalf of the CIA in protecting and withholding information from public disclosure that he acquired during the course of his work for the agency. By publishing the book, he breached that duty and could therefore be held accountable for the profits or gains from the book because he was not legally entitled to the proceeds.

Although Snepp argued First Amendment rights were violated by prior restraint, the Court mentioned First Amendment rights only once—a footnote said: "The Government has a compelling interest in protecting both the secrecy of information important to our national security and the appearance of confidentiality so essential to the effective operation of our foreign intelligence service. The agreement that Snepp signed is a reasonable means of protecting this vital interest."[159] Although oral arguments are traditional in most Supreme Court cases heard under the grant of a writ of certiorari, the Court declined to hear oral arguments in this case.

Symbolic Speech

Burning Cards, Flags, and Crosses

Most of the cases discussed previously involved the communication of verbal information such as publishing classified materials or some direct action such as making an inflammatory speech or mounting a demonstration, but some of the most troublesome and controversial free speech decisions have involved so-called symbolic speech. Symbolic speech can range from wearing a black arm band to desecration of the American flag.

United States v. O'Brien (1968): Burning Cards

During the turbulent 1960s, the free speech case that evoked the most public controversy was *United States v. O'Brien* (1968).[160] The decision came in the same year as the Tet offensive in which North Vietnamese Communists scored a major psychological victory over U.S. and South Vietnamese troops in the Vietnam War by demonstrating how easily they could invade urban areas of the south. Two years before the Tet offensive, at a time when the United States was becoming politically polarized by the war, David Paul O'Brien and three other war protesters burned Selective Service registration certificates (draft cards) on the steps of the South

Boston Courthouse in defiance of the Universal Military Training and Service Act of 1948 requiring Selective Service registrants to have certificates in possession at all times with criminal penalties for one "who forges, alters, knowingly destroys, knowingly mutilates, or in any manner changes any such certificate."[161]

O'Brien was indicted, tried, convicted, and sentenced in the U.S. District Court for the District of Massachusetts. He did not deny burning the card, but said he attempted to influence other people to agree with his beliefs and his act was protected symbolic speech under the First Amendment. The U.S. Court of Appeals essentially agreed by ruling the 1965 amendment was unconstitutional because it singled out for special treatment individuals charged with protesting. In a majority opinion written by Chief Justice Earl Warren, the U.S. Supreme Court disagreed. The Court held:

> We cannot accept the view that an apparently limitless variety of conduct can be labeled 'speech' whenever the person engaging in the conduct intends thereby to express an idea.… This Court has held that when 'speech' and 'nonspeech' elements are combined in the same course of conduct, a sufficiently important governmental interest in regulating the nonspeech element can justify incidental limitations on First Amendment freedoms. To characterize the quality of the governmental interest which must appear, the Court has employed a variety of descriptive terms: compelling; substantial; subordinating; paramount; cogent; strong. Whatever imprecision inheres in these terms, we think it clear that a government regulation is sufficiently justified if it is within the constitutional power of the Government; if it furthers an important or substantial governmental interest; if the governmental interest is unrelated to the suppression of free expression, and if the incidental restriction on alleged First Amendment freedoms is no greater than is essential to the furtherance of that interest. We find that the 1965 Amendment to §12(b)(3) of the Universal Military Training and Service Act meets all of these requirements, and consequently that O'Brien can be constitutionally convicted for violating it.[162]

A Matter of Scrutiny

Considerable criticism of the Court's reasoning arose in this case, although the particular test enunciated has stood the test of time. In the decades following the decision, the Court frequently applied the "O'Brien test" in those First Amendment cases in which the justices felt an *intermediate* level of judicial scrutiny was appropriate. This level of scrutiny falls somewhere on the scale between *strict* scrutiny in which the Court requires that the government demonstrate a compelling interest and simply *heightened* scrutiny in which only a strong governmental interest must be shown. Seasoned observers know that when the Court applies a strict scrutiny test, the odds are high that the government will be on the losing side in the decision, but when the Court adopts heightened scrutiny, the government will often come out a winner. When the justices choose intermediate scrutiny, all bets are off, with one side just as likely as the other to win.

What was the "substantial government interest" in *O'Brien*? According to the Court, the country "has a vital interest in having a system for raising armies that functions with maximum efficiency and is capable of easily and quickly responding to continually changing circumstances."[163] The continuing availability of the draft certificates, the Court asserted, is essential to preserving this substantial interest, and destroying them frustrates this interest. Would burning a registration card today be punishable under the Constitution? O'Brien burned his card during the Vietnam War era when men were drafted into the armed forces. The draft has now been eliminated, although all men are required to immediately register when they reach 18 years of age. Is there still a substantial government interest to be protected in preserving nondraft registration cards?

Street v. New York *(1969): Flag Burning Protected*

One year after *O'Brien*, the U. S. Supreme Court tackled another thorny case involving prior restraint of symbolic speech. In *Street v. New York* (1969),[164] the Court split 5 to 4 in reversing the conviction of an African American man for protesting the sniper shooting in Mississippi of civil rights leader James Meredith by burning an American flag at a public intersection in Brooklyn, New York. After the defendant burned the flag he owned, a police officer arrested him. The Court held that the provision in the state statute under which Street was punished was unconstitutionally applied in his case because it allowed the defendant to be punished simply for uttering defiant or contemptuous words about the American flag.

The majority opinion contended that none of four potential governmental interests were furthered by the statute in this case, including (a) deterring the defendant from vocally inciting other individuals to do unlawful acts, (b) preventing him from uttering words so inflammatory as to provoke others into retaliating against him and thus causing a breach of the peace, (c) protecting the sensibilities of passers-by, and (d) assuring that the defendant displayed proper respect for the flag. The four dissenting justices, including Chief Justice Earl Warren, characterized Street's burning of the flag as action, not mere words.

Flag Desecration Protection Continues

The U.S. Supreme Court decided yet another flag desecration case in 1974. A college student was arrested in 1970 for violating a Washington State statute that banned the display of any American flag to which any word, figure, mark, picture, design, drawing, or advertisement had been attached. The student attached large peace symbols made of removable tape to both sides of a flag he owned and displayed the altered flag from a window of his apartment.

At trial, he testified that he had done so to protest the invasion of Cambodia on April 30, 1970, by U.S. and South Vietnamese soldiers and the killing of four students by national guardsmen at Kent State University in Ohio during a war protest on May 4. "I felt there had been so much killing and that this was not what America stood for," he testified. "I felt that the flag stood for America and I wanted people to know that I thought America stood for peace." He also testified that he used removable tape to make the peace symbols so the flag would not be damaged.[165] The defendant was convicted under a so-called *improper use statute* rather than the state's flag desecration statute because the desecration statute required a public mutilation, defacing, defiling, burning, or trampling of the flag, and the other statute merely required placing a word, figure, and so forth, on a flag that was publicly displayed.

In a 6 to 3 *per curiam* decision, the Court reversed the conviction on grounds that "there was no risk that appellant's acts would mislead viewers into assuming that the Government endorsed his viewpoint. To the contrary, he was plainly and peacefully [footnote omitted] protesting the fact that it did not.… Moreover, his message was direct, likely to be understood, and within the contours of the First Amendment."[166] The Court noted the flag was privately owned and displayed on private property. Dissenters, led by then-Associate Justice (later Chief Justice) William H. Rehnquist, said Washington State "has chosen to set the flag apart for a special purpose, and has directed that it not be turned into a common background for an endless variety of superimposed messages."[167]

Texas v. Johnson *(1989) and* United States v. Eichman *(1990): More Flag Burning*

Twenty years after *Street v. New York*, the U.S. Supreme Court returned to flag burning. In *Texas v. Johnson*,[168] the Court reversed the conviction of a Revolutionary Communist Youth Brigade member in Texas for burning the American flag at the 1984 Republican National Convention in Dallas. In a split 5 to 4 decision in 1989 that surprised many politicians and legal scholars, the Court held that when Gregory Lee "Joey" Johnson burned an American flag in a nonviolent demonstration against President Ronald Reagan's administration, he was engaging in symbolic speech protected by the First Amendment. During the demonstration of approximately 100 protestors, the participants chanted, "America, the red, white and blue, we spit on you." Johnson was the only individual charged with a criminal offense. He was arrested and sentenced to a year in jail and fined $2,000 for violating a Texas flag desecration statute, similar to a federal statute and laws then existing in most states.[169] Such laws typically prohibit desecration of a venerated object such as a state or national flag, a public monument, or a place of worship or burial. The Texas Court of Criminal Appeals overturned the trial court decision, holding that the First Amendment protected Johnson's flag burning as expressive conduct and the statute was not narrowly drawn enough to preserve the state's interest in preventing a breach of the peace.

The U.S. Supreme Court affirmed the Texas appeals court decision to overturn the conviction. The Court did not invalidate the Texas statute nor any of the federal and state statutes. It merely ruled that the Texas law as applied in this case was unconstitutional. The majority opinion written by Associate Justice William J. Brennan, Jr. specifically pointed out that statutes banning flag desecration and similar acts when such acts provoke a breach of the peace and incitement to riot were not affected by the decision.

The line-up of the justices and the way in which the decision was delivered were somewhat surprising as well. Justice Brennan, the most senior member of the Court at 83 and the most liberal, wrote the majority opinion, but he was joined by two justices considered among the more conservative on the Court—Justices Anthony M. Kennedy and Antonin Scalia, both appointed by President Ronald Reagan. According to the majority:

> If there is a bedrock principle underlying the First Amendment, it is that the Government may not prohibit the expression of an idea simply because society finds the idea itself offensive or disagreeable.… We have not recognized an exception to this principle even where our flag has been involved.… The way to preserve the flag's special role is not to punish those who feel differently about these matters. It is to persuade them that they are wrong.…[170]

The majority reasoned because no violence or disturbance of the peace erupted at the demonstration, the state was banning "the expression of certain disagreeable ideas on the unsupported presumption that their very disagreeableness will provoke violence." The Court also contended a government cannot legislate that the flag may be used only as a symbol of national unity so that other messages cannot be expressed using that symbol.

Justice Kennedy wrote a brief concurrence with the majority, noting, "The hard fact is that sometimes we must make decisions we do not like. We must make them because they are right, right in the sense that the law and the Constitution, as we see them, compel the result."[171] This contention prompted one expert to quip, Justice Kennedy saying, "You hold your nose and follow the Constitution."[172] Kennedy went on to assert, "It is poignant but fundamental that the flag protects those who hold it in contempt."

Certainly the most elaborate, eloquent, and emotional plea came from Chief Justice Rehnquist in his dissent. The Chief Justice quoted extensively from Ralph Waldo Emerson's "Concord Hymn," Francis Scott Key's "The Star Spangled Banner," and John Greenleaf Whittier's "Barbara Frietchie" poem that describes how a 90-year-old woman flew the Union flag when Stonewall Jackson and his Confederate soldiers marched through Fredericktown during the Civil War. According to Chief Justice Rehnquist:

> The American flag, then, throughout more than 200 years of our history, has come to be the visible symbol embodying our Nation.... The flag is not simply another 'idea' or 'point of view' competing for recognition in the marketplace of ideas. Millions and millions of Americans regard it with an almost mystical reverence regardless of what sort of social, political or philosophical beliefs they have....[173]

The U.S. Supreme Court decision in *Texas v. Johnson* did not end the controversy over flag desecration. The senior President George Bush pushed strongly for a constitutional amendment to prohibit flag desecration in a variety of forms. President Bush had the strong support of most political conservatives and certainly the general public in his efforts to secure a constitutional amendment, but at least two traditionally conservative political writers, *Washington Post* syndicated columnist George F. Will and syndicated Washington columnist James J. Kilpatrick,[174] opposed such an amendment. Will believed the case was wrongly decided by the Supreme Court, whereas Kilpatrick said, "given the undisputed facts, the Texas law and the high court precedents, the case was properly decided."[175]

A proposed amendment quickly garnered 51 votes in the U.S. Senate, but that was 15 short of the two-thirds necessary to pass it on to the states. Before becoming part of the U.S. Constitution, the amendment required ratification by at least 38 of the state legislatures. Congress then enacted the Flag Protection Act of 1989 that became law without President Bush's signature. The President chose not to sign the bill because he believed it would eventually be struck down by the U.S. Supreme Court as unconstitutional, just as the Court had done the previous year in *Texas v. Johnson*. Thus, for the President, the remedy was a constitutional amendment.

In *United States v. Eichman* and *United States v. Haggerty*,[176] Justice Brennan, joined by Justices Marshall, Blackmun, Scalia, and Kennedy (the exact same line-up as *Texas v. Johnson*), struck down the federal statute on essentially the same grounds employed in the earlier decision. This time, though, Justice Stevens' dissent lacked much of his impassioned rhetoric of the *Johnson* decision, and he did not read it from the bench.

The case began when Shawn Eichman and two acquaintances deliberately set fire to several U.S. flags on the steps of the Capitol building as a protest of U.S. domestic and foreign policy. They were arrested and charged with violating the criminal statute that provided:

(a)(1) Whoever knowingly mutilates, defaces, physically defiles, burns, maintains on the floor or ground, or tramples upon any flag of the United States shall be fined under this title or imprisoned for not more than one year, or both. (2) This subsection does not prohibit any conduct consisting of the disposal of a flag when it has become worn or soiled. (b) As used in this section, the term 'flag of the United States' means any flag of the United States, or any part thereof, made of any substance, of any size, in a form that is commonly displayed.[177]

Mark John Haggerty and three other individuals were also prosecuted by the federal government for setting fire to a U.S. flag to protest the passage of the federal Flag Protection Act. The convictions of both Eichman and Haggerty were dismissed by separate federal trial courts as unconstitutional. The U.S. District Court for the Western District of Washington and the U.S. District Court for the District of Columbia Circuit, respectively, cited *Johnson* as precedent. On appeal by the United States, the Supreme Court consolidated the two cases. The government bypassed the U.S. Court of Appeals by invoking a clause in the 1989 Federal Flag Protection Act that provided for a direct appeal to the Supreme Court and expedited review under certain conditions.

The Court expressly rejected the government's argument that the U.S. statute, unlike the Texas law in *Johnson*, did not "target expressive conduct on the basis of the content of its message." According to the majority opinion, "The Act still suffers from the same fundamental flaw: it suppresses expression out of concern for its likely communicative impact."[178] The government also asserted that the statute should have been viewed as an expression of a "national consensus" supporting a ban on flag desecration. "Even assuming such a consensus exists, any suggestion that the government's interest in suppressing speech becomes more weighty as popular opposition to that speech grows is foreign to the First Amendment,"[179] according to the Court.

President Bush and a number of prominent politicians, principally Republicans, immediately called for a constitutional amendment to overturn *Texas v. Johnson* and *U.S. v. Eichman*, but the clamor gradually subsided after the measure appeared doomed.

Cross Burning and the First Amendment: R.A.V. v. City of St. Paul, Minnesota *(1992)* and Virginia v. Black *(2003)*

The U.S. Supreme Court handed down one of its most controversial free speech decisions in 1992. In *R.A.V. v. City of St. Paul, Minnesota*,[180] the justices unanimously ruled a city ordinance unconstitutional that provided criminal penalties for placing "on public or private property a symbol, object appellation, characterization or graffiti, including, but not limited to, a burning cross or Nazi swastika, which one knows or has reasonable grounds to know arouses anger, alarm or resentment in others on the basis of race, color, creed, religion or gender."[181]

The case began when several teenagers allegedly burned a cross made by taping together broken chair legs inside the fenced yard of an African American family in St. Paul, Minnesota. When charged with violating the ordinance as a result of the incident, one of the juveniles filed a motion to dismiss, claiming the law was too broad and impermissibly based on content, thus invalid under the First Amendment. A trial court judge granted the motion, but the Minnesota Supreme Court reversed on the ground that the provision simply regulated *fighting words* can be punished as affirmed by the U.S. Supreme Court. The Minnesota Supreme Court particularly cited *Chaplinsky v. New Hampshire* (1942),[182] in which the U.S. Supreme Court held words "likely to provoke the average person to retaliation, and thereby cause a breach of the peace" (known as *fighting words*) were not protected by the First Amendment.[183]

Justice Scalia wrote the majority opinion for the U.S. Supreme Court. He was joined by Chief Justice Rehnquist and Associate Justices Kennedy, Souter, and Thomas. The majority indicated it was bound by the construction given the ordinance by the Minnesota Supreme Court, including the interpretation that the law restricted only expressions that would be considered fighting words. However, the opinion skirted the issue of whether the ordinance was substantially too broad, as the petitioner (R.A.V.) contended. Instead, the Court said: "We find it unnecessary to consider this issue. Assuming, *arguendo*, that all of the expression reached by the ordinance is proscribable under the 'fighting words' doctrine, we nonetheless conclude that the ordinance is facially unconstitutional in that it prohibits otherwise permitted speech solely on the basis of the subjects the speech addresses."[184] According to the Court:

> Although the phrase in the ordinance, 'arouses anger, alarm or resentment in others,' has been limited by the Minnesota Supreme Court's construction to reach only those words or displays that amount to 'fighting words,' the remaining unmodified terms make clear that the ordinance applies only to 'fighting words' that insult or provoke violence, 'on the basis of race, color, creed, religion or gender.' Displays containing abusive invective, no matter how vicious or severe, are permissible unless they are addressed to one of the specified disfavored topics.[185]

The Court made it clear that "burning a cross on someone's front yard is reprehensible. But St. Paul has sufficient means at its disposal to prevent such behavior without adding the First Amendment to the fire." In a footnote in the decision, the majority indicated the conduct at issue might have been punished under statutes banning terrorist threats, arson or criminal property damage.

In a concurring opinion joined by Justices Blackmun, O'Connor, and Justice Stevens in part, Justice White strongly disagreed with the majority's standard for evaluating the ordinance. According to Justice White, the ordinance should have been struck down on overbreadth grounds. He characterized the decision as "an arid, doctrinaire interpretation, driven by the frequently irresistible impulse of judges to tinker with the First Amendment. The decision is mischievous at best and will surely confuse the lower courts."

The St. Paul ordinance was enacted at a time of considerable concern about so-called hate speech and what has become known as "politically correct" (PC) speech. In a proliferation of incidents including many on college and university campuses, members of racial, ethnic, and sexual preference minority groups were targeted with epithets, anonymous hate letters, slogans painted on doors and walls, and other forms of hate speech. To counter this behavior, a number of cities and private and public universities instituted codes of conduct that specifically banned this type of behavior.

At the same time, political correctness (PC) became a buzzword for the idea that both oral and written communications including those of the media should demonstrate greater sensitivity to race and gender bias, leading to guides such as *The Dictionary of Bias-Free Usage: A Guide to Nondiscriminatory Language* and *The Elements of Non-Sexist Usage: A Guide to Inclusive Spoken and Written English*. Critics view the PC speech campaign with disdain. They believe it inhibits freedom of speech and a free press, whereas PC supporters saw this movement as a legitimate means of persuading writers and speakers to abhor sexist, racist, and other biased speech.

Prior Restraint in the 21st Century: Cross Burning II

Hate speech and PC speech are two sides of the coin, and the controversies they stir revolve around prior restraint. Can political and social hate groups be muzzled without denying their members their First Amendment rights? On the other hand, can policies and codes that either punish or strongly discourage sexist, racist, or other biased language pass constitutional muster? What about a policy that simply strongly encourages bias-free speech as a means of consciousness raising? Journalists appear to be splintered on these issues, as are civil rights and civil liberties groups. Some view the PC movement and the anti-hate speech campaign as unjustified attempts to restrict freedom of speech and freedom of the press, and others contend that the rights of minorities to be free of hatred and bias directed toward them should take precedence over any First Amendment right that may exist in such contexts. It was inevitable that the U.S. Supreme Court would have the opportunity to wrestle with some of these issues.

Virginia v. Black (2003)

In Virginia v. Black,[186] the U.S. Supreme Court held that states may outlaw cross burnings that are clearly intended to intimidate. In affirming conviction of two men who burned a cross in a family's yard without permission, the Court ruled that state statutes banning such cross burning do not violate the First Amendment. At the same time, the Court overturned the conviction under the same Virginia statute as a Ku Klux Klan leader who burned a cross at a rally on a willing owner's property because the statute, as written at the time, said cross burning on its face was evidence of intent to intimidate. The statute was subsequently revised. The majority opinion written by Associate Justice O'Connor said such a presumption would violate the First Amendment: "It may be true that a cross burning, even at a political rally, arouses a sense of anger or hatred among the vast majority of citizens who see a burning cross. But this sense of anger or hatred is not sufficient to ban all cross burnings."[187]

The ruling produced five different opinions, reflecting the complexity of the struggle the justices had with this controversial issue. In upholding the state statute, the Court split the difference, handing both sides limited, symbolic victories. The advocates for strong First Amendment protection for speech could claim victory because the Court made it clear that an intent to intimidate must have been demonstrated, not simply presumed, to warrant punishment of cross burning. On the other hand, those who opposed hate speech now had a tool in their arsenals.

Citing *Chaplinsky*, the majority emphasized that the "protections the First Amendment affords speech and expressive conduct are not absolute. This Court has long recognized that the government may regulate certain categories of expression consistent with the Constitution."[188] Noting that a state is permitted under the First Amendment to ban real threats, the Court said it is not necessary for a speaker to actually carry out a threat in order for such speech to be prohibited. The problem is the intimidation: "Intimidation in the constitutionally proscribable sense of the word is a type of true threat, where a speaker directs a threat to a person or group of persons with the intent of placing the victim in fear of bodily harm or death."[189] The Court went on to note that Virginia was allowed under the First Amendment to ban "cross burnings done with the intent to intimidate because cross burning is a particularly virulent form of intimidation," pointing to "cross burning's long and pernicious history as a signal of impending violence."[190]

During oral arguments, Justice Clarence Thomas, the only African American on the Court, was outspoken. Thomas, with a reputation for rarely speaking in that context, condemned cross burning. Pointing to a decade of lynchings of African Americans in the South, Thomas said cross burning "is unlike any symbol in our society. It was intended to cause fear and terrorize a population." Interrupting one of the attorneys for the state of Virginia, who was arguing in favor of the statute, Thomas said, "My fear is that you're actually understating the symbolism and effect of the burning cross." His dissent in the case reflected the same concerns. Thomas noted at the outset of his dissenting opinion that although he agreed with the majority that cross burning can be constitutionally banned when carried out with the intent to intimidate, he believed the majority erred "in imputing an expressive component" to cross burning. After detailing the history of the Ku Klux Klan's use of cross burning to intimidate and harass minorities and other groups, Justice Thomas concluded:

> It is simply beyond belief that, in passing the statute now under review, the Virginia legislature was concerned with anything but penalizing conduct it must have viewed as particularly vicious. Accordingly, this statute prohibits only conduct, not expression. And, just as one cannot burn down someone's house to make a political point and then seek refuge in the First Amendment, those who hate cannot terrorize and intimidate to make their point. In light of my conclusion that the statute here addresses only conduct, there is no need to analyze it under any of our First Amendment tests.[191]

In a note, the majority opinion acknowledged Justice Thomas' point that cross burning is conduct rather than expression but contended that "it is equally true that the First Amendment protects symbolic conduct as well as pure speech."[192]

Prior Restraint in the Classroom

Tinker v. Des Moines Independent Community School District (1969)
In *Tinker v. Des Moines Independent Community School District* (1969),[193] the U.S. Supreme Court held that the wearing by students of black armbands in a public school was a symbolic act protected by the First Amendment. With the support of their parents, two high school students and one junior high school student wore black armbands to class in December 1965 to protest the Vietnam War. Two days earlier, local school principals met to issue a regulation specifically prohibiting the armbands after a high school student in a journalism class asked his teacher for permission to write an article on Vietnam for the school newspaper. As the Court noted in its 7 to 2 opinion, students in some of the schools in the district had been allowed to wear political campaign buttons and even the Iron Cross, the traditional Nazi symbol.

A federal district court upheld the regulation as constitutional because school authorities reasonably believed that disturbances could result from the wearing of armbands. Indeed, a few students were hostile toward the students outside the classroom. However, according to the U.S. Supreme Court, "There is no indication that the work of the schools or any class was disrupted."[194] The official memorandum prepared by school officials after students were suspended was introduced at trial; it did not mention disturbances.

The test, the Court said, for justifying prior restraint would be whether "the students' activities would materially and substantially disrupt the work and discipline of the school." The Court held:

> These petitioners [students] merely went about their ordained rounds in school. Their deviation consisted only in wearing on their sleeve, a band of black cloth, not more than two inches wide. They wore it to exhibit their disapproval of the Vietnam hostilities and their advocacy of a truce, to make their views known, and, by their example, to influence others to adopt them. They neither interrupted school activities nor sought to intrude in the school affairs or the lives of others.[195]

In an attack on the majority, Justice Hugo L. Black appeared to compare the classroom to a church or synagogue and settings such as the Congress and the Supreme Court: "It is a myth to say that any person has a constitutional right to say what he pleases, where he pleases, and when he pleases. Uncontrolled and uncontrollable liberty is an enemy of domestic peace. We cannot close our eyes to the fact that some of the country's greatest problems are crimes committed by youth, too many of school age."[196]

Hazelwood School District v. Kuhlmeier *(1988): A Retreat from Tinker?*

The Court issued a decision in *Hazelwood School District v. Kuhlmeier*[197] (1988) that generated concern and comment among First Amendment scholars and journalists. The case began innocently when the May 13, 1983, edition of the Hazelwood East (St. Louis, Missouri) High School student newspaper, *Spectrum*, was ready to go to press. The paper was produced by a Journalism II class under the supervision of a faculty adviser. This edition featured a special, two-page report, "Pressure Describes It All for Today's Teenagers." The articles touched on: teenage pregnancy, birth control, marriage, divorce, and juvenile delinquency.

On the day before the paper was ready to be printed, the new faculty adviser, Howard Emerson, took the page proofs to the school principal, Robert E. Reynolds who deleted the special report. Reynolds did not consult with the students and later said the article focusing on the pregnancies of three students was too sensitive for younger students. He was concerned that the students quoted in the article would suffer from invasion of privacy although pseudonyms were used. He killed the second article analyzing the effects of divorce on teenagers because he said the father of one student quoted as criticizing him as abusive and inattentive was not given an opportunity to respond to the allegations.[198] Reynolds ordered the adviser, who had been appointed only 10 days earlier, to publish the paper without the special section. None of the articles contained sexually explicit language, but included discussions of sex and contraception. Most information in the articles was garnered from questionnaires completed by students at the school and personal interviews conducted by newspaper staff. All the respondents had given permission for their answers and comments to be published.

With assistance from the American Civil Liberties Union (ACLU), three of the students on the *Spectrum* staff—a layout editor and two reporters—filed suit against the school district and school officials in the U.S. District Court (E.D. Mo.) three months after the incident. The students unsuccessfully tried to convince the principal to allow the articles to be published. The complaint alleged that the students' First Amendment rights had been violated and requested declaratory and injunctive relief and monetary damages. ACLU attorneys argued in the federal trial court that the newspaper constituted a public forum and thus deserved full First Amendment protection and, as government officials, school authorities could impose prior restraint on the paper only if it were obscene or libelous or could cause a serious disruption of normal school operations as the Court held in *Tinker* in 1969.[199] Attorneys for the school district argued that, because the newspaper staff was taking the journalism class for credit, just as any other course would be taken for credit, the newspaper was, therefore, not a public forum but merely part of the school curriculum.

In May 1985, the U.S. District Court decided in favor of the school and denied all relief requested. On appeal by the students, the 8th Circuit U.S. Court of Appeals reversed the U.S. District Court ruling. The appeals court held in a 2 to 1 decision that the newspaper was a public forum even though the faculty adviser maintained considerable editorial control over the paper. According to the majority opinion, prior restraint was permitted, in line with *Tinker*, only if the school officials could demonstrate that such censorship was "necessary to avoid material and substantial interference with school work or discipline" (citing *Tinker*).[200]

In a move that surprised many First Amendment scholars, the U.S. Supreme Court granted certiorari on appeal of the decision by the school board. Oral arguments were heard in October 1987 and exactly three months later, the Court handed down its decision that provoked a torrent of criticism from professional journalism organizations such as the Society of Professional Journalists, the Reporters Committee for Freedom of the Press, the Student Press Law Center, and the Association for Education in Journalism and Mass Communication, all of which either filed or joined *amicus curiae* ("friend of the court") briefs with the Supreme Court to support the students and the federal appeals court decision.

Fate was not on the side of the students, however. In a 5 to 3 decision written by Justice Byron R. White, the Court reversed the U.S. Court of Appeals and held that the First Amendment rights of the students had not been violated.[201] The Court began by reaffirming its principle in *Tinker* that it "can hardly be argued that either students or teachers shed their constitutional rights to freedom of speech or expression at the schoolhouse gate."[202] The Court went on to say that *Tinker* applies only to "educators' ability to silence a student's personal expression that happens to occur on the school premises" so that prior restraint is permitted when it is "reasonably related to pedagogical concerns." In other words, expression that occurs within the context of curriculum can be censored unless restrictions have "no valid educational purpose."

The Court reasoned the school was publisher and had no manifest intention to make *Spectrum* a public forum. As publisher, the school could impose greater restrictions so that students "learn whatever lessons the activity is designed to teach, that readers or listeners are not exposed to material that may be inappropriate for their level of maturity, and that the views of the school are not erroneously attributed to the school."[203] The majority noted:

> A school must be able to set high standards for the student speech that is disseminated under its auspices—standards that may be higher than those demanded by some newspaper publishers or theatrical producers in the "real" world—and may refuse to disseminate student speech that does not meet those standards.[204]

As expected, Justice William J. Brennan, Jr., wrote a very strong dissent to the majority decision. He was joined in his dissent by Justices Thurgood Marshall and Harry A. Blackmun. "In my view, the principal … violated the First Amendment's prohibition against censorship of any student expression that neither disrupts class work nor invades the rights of others, and against any censorship that is not narrowly tailored to serve its purpose," Justice Brennan wrote. He reasoned, unlike the majority, that *Tinker* did apply to this case and thus the paper could be censored only if its content materially and substantially disrupted the educational process or interfered with the rights of others (such as the right of privacy). According to Justice Brennan, *Tinker* should have applied to all student expression, not only to personal expression, as the majority ruled.

One of the most surprising aspects of the majority opinion was the extension of its holding to include virtually all school-sponsored activities, not only laboratory newspapers. The U.S. Supreme Court, especially the Rehnquist Court, usually limited its rulings on the First Amendment to the particular issue at hand, but in *Hazelwood* the Court chose to substantially broaden the scope of the activities affected by the decision. The Court provided no direct indication as to why it had taken this unusual step in *Hazelwood*, but it is likely the Court wanted to avoid having to tackle prior restraint on student expression on a situational basis. The Court may have been attempting to forestall a flood of litigation likely to arise if the Court narrowed the scope of the decision to include lab newspapers.

What was covered by *Hazelwood*? According to the Court, any public school has a constitutional right to disassociate itself from all speech that others, including students, parents, and the general public "might reasonably perceive to bear the imprimatur of the school."[205] The Court cited examples such as theatrical productions, but it is apparent that other activities such as art shows, science fairs, debates, and research projects come under the aegis of *Hazelwood*. As the Student Press Law Center indicated in its legal analysis of the case, "Any school-sponsored, non-forum student activity that involves student expression could be affected."[206]

The impact of *Hazelwood* was both immediate and long term. Literally within hours, high school and even college newspapers felt the heavy hand of censorship. According to one report, a high school principal in California ordered a school newspaper not to publish a story based on an interview with an anonymous student who tested positive for AIDS. Less than two hours after the Court's decision, the principal told the newspaper staff, "You won't run that story now."[207] In the years that followed, headlines such as "Concern Rises over High School Journalism"[208] and "Censorship on Campus: Press Watchers Fear Rise"[209] are not very unusual.

A survey of high school principals in Missouri—the home of the *Hazelwood* case, found that while 61.5% of them considered their student newspapers to be open forums and only 35.6% kept material from being printed in student publications, almost 90% of them said they might suppress "dirty language" in a student publication if they found it objectionable. More than 60% said they might suppress content dealing with sex. Articles on drugs might have been censored by 56.8% of the principals, and almost 42% might have restrained content dealing with student pregnancy.[210] A 1988 report jointly sponsored by the American Library Association and the American Association of School Administrators listed four major categories of motivation for school censorship—family values, political views, religion, and minority rights,[211] all common topics in high school newspapers.

One analysis of the case concluded, "The [Supreme] Court's view of the state's permissible role in restricting student expression has gone from expansive to narrow and back, culminating in its broad discretion to school authorities in *Hazelwood*."[212] The law review note suggests that school officials be required to conform to written regulations that would permit discretion while offering students the opportunity "to learn the full responsibilities of the first amendment through using it responsibly."[213]

As discussed in Chapter 1, states can always expand rights recognized by the Court under the First Amendment. Although the states made no mad dash to enact legislation to expand high school student rights after *Hazelwood*, a few states offer broader protection. Section 48907 of the California Education Code provided extensive protection 10 years before *Hazelwood*. Under the code, public school students have the right to exercise an extensive array of speech and press activities regardless of whether such activities are financially supported by the school, except "obscene, libelous, or slanderous" expression or "material which so incites students as to create a clear and present danger of the commission of unlawful acts on school premises or the violation of lawful school regulations, or the substantial disruption of the orderly operation of the school."[214]

Massachusetts had a statute even earlier than the California law, but the provision affecting school publications was optional until it became mandatory in July 1988.[215] In May 1989, Iowa became the first state to enact legislation specifically geared to respond to the concerns of *Hazelwood*.[216] The statute is very similar to that of California, especially in its exceptions.[217]

The *Hazelwood* Court specifically avoided the question of whether its ruling would apply to college newspapers. In a footnote, the majority opinion stated, "We need not now decide whether the same degree of deference is appropriate with respect to school-sponsored activities at the college or university level."[218]

The ripples from *Hazelwood* continue to be felt. The 7th Circuit U.S. Court of Appeals ruled that the policy of a public elementary school in Racine, Wisconsin on non-school-sponsored publications did not violate the First Amendment in 1996. In *Muller v. Jefferson Lighthouse School*,[219] the appellate court held the school had the right to prohibit a student from giving his classmates fliers inviting them to his church. The 6th Circuit U.S. Court of Appeals held in an *en banc* (full panel) decision in *Kinkaid v. Gibson*[220] that First Amendment rights of students at Kentucky State University were violated when university officials banned the distribution of a yearbook. The court said the yearbook was a limited public forum and noted that *Hazelwood* did not apply to college students.

A much different result occurred when the 7th Circuit U.S. Court of Appeals in an *en banc* 7 to 4 decision in *Hosty v. Carter (2005)* held "that *Hazelwood*'s framework applies to subsidized student newspapers at colleges as well as elementary and secondary schools."[221] Two years earlier, a three-judge panel of the same court unanimously ruled[222] that college students, unlike high school students, enjoy First Amendment protection. The panel said the editors of *The Innovator*, a student newspaper at Governors State University, a public institution in University Park, Illinois, could sue the dean of students for requiring the newspaper's printer to get the dean's approval before publishing. The court held that the dean did not enjoy qualified immunity that would protect her from such suits. The court also said *Hazelwood* did not apply to college students.

The *en banc* court, on the other hand, decided the dean did enjoy qualified immunity. The court said the evidence presented to the trial court, when considered in the light most favorable to the plaintiff (the standard when attempting to establish a constitutional claim), "would permit a reasonable trier of fact [i.e., a judge or jury] to conclude *The Innovator* operated in a public forum beyond control of the University's administration." The court concluded, "Qualified immunity nonetheless protects Dean Carter from personal liability unless it should have been 'clear to a reasonable [public official] that his conduct was unlawful in the situation he confronted'" (citing an earlier U.S. Supreme Court decision).

The student journalists appealed the 7th Circuit's opinion, but in 2006 the U.S. Supreme Court denied certiorari, allowing the lower court decision to stand.[223] Critics of the decision such as Mark Goodman and John K. Wilson, expressed concern that the 7th Circuit's decision, while technically applicable only to public institutions of higher education in Wisconsin, Indiana, and Illinois, might be used to censor colleges and universities nationally. Goodman contended the Supreme Court's refusal to hear the appeal "may be interpreted as a green light by some college administrators."[224] Wilson said the dismissal, coupled with controversy concerning anti-Muslim cartoons in college newspapers and other publications, "should make us worry about how the new power to censor granted to administrators will be used."[225]

Hosty concerned activities within the classroom. What about outside? The U.S. Supreme Court held in *Morse v. Frederick (2007)* [226] that a high school principal did not violate student First Amendment rights when she confiscated a banner held up during an Olympic torch run that read "Bong Hits 4 Jesus." The Court ruled 5–4 that the principal could conclude the banner promoted drug use, a violation of school policy.

Prior Restraint and National Security

When President George W. Bush initiated the attack on Iraq that led to what appeared to be a rather quick military victory with the removal of Saddam Hussein as president, the Pentagon approved the embedding of about 600 U.S. and international reporters within American armed forces fighting in Iraq. The result was extensive, direct media coverage of the war that was in sharp contrast to the coverage of the Persian Gulf Conflict in early 1991 under the senior President George Bush. Only one embedded reporter was formally pressured by the military to leave during the 2003 Iraq War—Fox's Geraldo Rivera drew a map in the sand pointing to troop locations.

During the 1991 war, a ban was imposed on press access to the war zone. A few journalists were killed during the Iraq war, either in accidents or during hostile fire, but the press made little criticism regarding access. However, from the 1980s through the 2000s, national security issues provided the federal government with opportunities to impose prior restraint on the media.

Until 1985 no one in this country had ever been convicted of a crime for leaking national security information to the press; in October of that year, Samuel Loring Morison was convicted in U.S. District Court in Baltimore[227] for providing three classified photographs to the British magazine *Jane's Defence Weekly* in 1984. The magazine published the photos and then made them available to various news agencies. One of the photos also appeared in the *Washington Post*.[228] Morison was not employed by the magazine at the time, although he worked for *Jane's Fighting Ships*, another magazine owned by the same company. He gained access to the classified photos when he previously worked for the U.S. Navy as an intelligence analyst. His prosecution came during a campaign under President Ronald Reagan to halt unauthorized leaks of sensitive government information.

Morison freely admitted to furnishing the pictures to the magazine, but he contended that he was not paid for the materials even though he had been paid by the magazine for his writing.

His confession was ruled inadmissible at trial. The government did not argue that he had been compensated for providing the materials. In his defense, Morison claimed that the statute under which he was prosecuted did not apply in his case but instead was intended to apply to the disclosure of classified information to foreign governments and thus not the press. Morison was sentenced to two years at a federal medium security prison in Danbury, Connecticut, for violating two sections of the U.S. Espionage Act of 1917.[229] He appealed the decision to the 4th Circuit U.S. Court of Appeals, but on April 1, 1988, a three-judge panel upheld the trial court decision, rejecting all Morison's major contentions: he had not used the documents for personal gain, he did not know the documents were classified, and Congress intended to restrict application of the law to traditional spying rather than disclosures to the press.[230]

In October 1988, the U.S. Supreme Court denied certiorari,[231] effectively closing the case, while Morison continued to serve his prison term. Denial of certiorari does not necessarily mean the Supreme Court agrees with a lower court's decision. It does indicate that at least six justices did not feel a case deserves consideration because at least four justices must agree to hear a case before a writ of certiorari can be granted.

Prior Restraint on Crime Stories

"Son of Sam" Laws: Simon & Schuster v. New York State Crime Victims Board *(1991)*
In 1977, the New York legislature enacted a statute that, as later amended, required that any income received by convicted or accused criminals for sales of their stories be placed in an escrow account for five years during which their victims would have the right to sue in civil actions for damages. The statute also mandated that any publisher contracting with an accused or convicted criminal must submit a copy of the contract to the Crime Victims Board. If a victim won a civil judgment against the criminal, the person would then be entitled to a share of the proceeds from the sale of the story. The law also permitted the use of proceeds from such sales under certain circumstances for other uses such as legal fees and for payments to creditors of the accused or convicted person. The statute was popularly know as the "Son of Sam" law because it was initiated in reaction to stories that David Berkowitz, convicted of killing six people in New York City after a highly publicized and sensationalized arrest and trial, planned to sell a "Son of Sam" story.

The statute was challenged in the courts as unconstitutional prior restraint. In 1991 in *Simon & Schuster, Inc. v. Members of the New York State Crime Victims Board,*[232] the U.S. Supreme Court ruled 8–0 that through the "Son of Sam law, New York singled out speech on a particular subject for financial burden that it places on no other speech and no other income. The State's interest in compensating victims from the fruits of crime is a compelling one, but the Son of Sam law is not narrowly tailored to advance that objective."[233]

The justices noted that any statute that imposes a financial burden on a speaker because of the content of the speech "is presumptively inconsistent with the First Amendment." The law in this case was so broad, the Court said, that a person who had never been accused or convicted of a crime but who admitted in a book or other publication that she or he had committed a crime would be included. The case arose after the board ordered publisher Simon & Schuster to turn over all monies payable to admitted organized crime figure Henry Hill for his book

Wiseguy (which later inspired the classic crime film *Goodfellas*, which won the 1990 Academy Award for Best Picture). Hill was also ordered to turn over monies he had already received.

Simon & Schuster sued the board, seeking a declaratory judgment that the law was unconstitutional. A U.S. District Court judge ruled against the publisher and the 2nd Circuit U.S. Court of Appeals affirmed. The Court reversed, pointing out that works such as the *Autobiography of Malcolm X* and even the *Confessions of St. Augustine* would have fallen under the shadow of the law if the law had been on the books when they were written. The Court cited other constitutional means of obtaining such proceeds such as securing a judgment against the criminal's assets in a civil suit.

All but about 10 states[234] have "Son of Sam" laws designed to overcome the constitutional problems of the original New York Statute. California is among the states that have such statutes, but the California Supreme Court later unanimously struck down that state's statute. The law was challenged by a felon convicted in the 1963 kidnapping of 19-year-old Frank Sinatra, Jr., who was released unharmed after his family paid a ransom of nearly a quarter of a million dollars. The convict, Barry Keenan, would have received $485,000 of the $1.5 million offered for film rights to a magazine story about the crime, but the statute prevented him from doing so.[235] The law specifically barred convicted felons from receiving funds from media dealing with their crimes. Any proceeds would instead go to the victims or to the state. The California Supreme Court said the state had a compelling interest in compensating crime victims but the law violated the First Amendment because it restricted speech more than necessary to serve that interest.[236]

The Nevada Supreme Court struck down that state's "Son of Sam" law in 2004[237] as a violation of the First Amendment on grounds similar to those on which other courts struck down such statutes.[238] The Court conducted a strict scrutiny analysis because the restrictions were content-based and the statute was later revised to attempt to conform with the ruling by the U.S. Supreme Court.

Free Speech Rights in a Political Context: Public and Private Protests

Offensive Language on Clothing: Cohen v. California *(1971)*

The distinction between "action speech" and "pure speech" has proven troublesome for courts, despite the Supreme Court's attempts to clarify the difference. How far does an individual have to proceed to transform words into deeds? Suppose an individual were to wear in public a jacket with an expression deemed obscene by some and at least indecent by most. Suppose women and children are present and can clearly read the expression. Can the individual be banned from wearing the jacket? Can he be convicted for maliciously and willfully disturbing the peace by offensive conduct?

In *Cohen v. California* (1971),[239] the U.S. Supreme Court reversed the conviction of a man for wearing a jacket with the clearly visible words, "Fuck the Draft," in a corridor outside a courtroom of the Los Angeles County Courthouse. The defendant testified at trial that he wore the jacket to protest the draft and the Vietnam War. He was convicted of violating Section 415 of the state penal code that bans maliciously and willfully disturbing the peace by offensive conduct and was sentenced to 30 days in jail. According to the Court, "There were women and children present in the corridor.… The defendant did not engage in, nor threaten to engage in, nor did anyone as the result of his conduct in fact commit or threaten to commit any act of violence."[240]

The majority opinion characterized the situation as involving speech. Dissenters saw it differently. Writing for the majority, Justice John M. Harlan, said:

> The conviction quite clearly rests upon the asserted offensiveness of the words Cohen used to convey his message to the public. The only 'conduct' which the State sought to punish is the fact of communication. Thus we deal here with a conviction resting solely upon 'speech' ….not upon any separately identifiable conduct which allegedly was intended by Cohen to be perceived by others as expressive of particular views.…[241]

Citing *Chaplinsky*, the Court noted that states "are free to ban the simple use, without a demonstration of additional justifying circumstances, of so-called 'fighting words,' those personally abusive epithets which, when addressed to the ordinary citizen, are, as a matter of common knowledge, inherently likely to provoke violent reaction."[242] The Court also concluded that (a) the words were not obscene because they were in no way erotic, (b) no person would reasonably regard the words as a direct personal insult and thereby be provoked to violence, and (c) the jacket was not akin "to the raucous emissions of sound trucks blaring outside … residences" because the people in the courthouse could simply turn their eyes to "effectively avoid bombardment of their sensibilities."[243] Justice Harry A. Blackmun, joined by Chief Justice Warren Burger and Justice Hugo Black, called Cohen's effort an "absurd and immature antic" that "was mainly conduct and little speech."[244]

Abortion Protests

At least one abortion protest case seems to crop up every year in the Supreme Court. One of the most important of these cases was handed down in 1994. *National Organization for Women v. Scheidler* (*Scheidler I*) (1994)[245] involved an interpretation of the Racketeer Influenced and Corrupt Organizations (RICO) chapter of the Organized Crime Act of 1970. Under Section 1962(a) of the Act, any individual associated with an enterprise is prohibited from operating through a pattern of racketeering activity. NOW, a nonprofit organization promoting the legal availability of abortion, and two health care centers that perform abortions sued Pro-Life Action Network (PLAN), a coalition of anti-abortion groups, Joseph Scheidler, and other anti-abortion activists in U.S. District Court. NOW claimed members of PLAN and other protesters violated RICO and other federal statutes in their admitted attempts to shut down abortion clinics and convince women not to have abortions. NOW further asserted defendants were part of a national conspiracy to close clinics through a pattern of racketeering activity.

The federal trial court dismissed NOW's suit, primarily because the court said that RICO required proof that pre-racketeering and racketeering activities were motivated by an economic (profit generating) motive, which the court said NOW had failed to show. The 7th Circuit Court of Appeals affirmed, but in a unanimous opinion by Chief Justice Rehnquist, the U.S. Supreme Court held that the statutory language of RICO and the legislative history of the Act make it clear that no economic motive is required:

We therefore hold that petitioners may maintain this action if respondents conducted the enterprise through a pattern of racketeering activity. The questions of whether the respondents committed the requisite predicate acts, and whether the commission of these acts fell into a pattern, are not before us. We hold only that RICO contains no economic motive requirement.[246]

Nine years later, NOW and Joseph Scheidler and his supporters were again lined up on opposite sides in a U.S. Supreme Court decision regarding the RICO act. However, this time the protesters were on the winning side. In *Scheidler v. NOW* (*Scheidler II*, 2003),[247] the U.S. Supreme Court in an 8 to 1 decision reversed a jury award of more than $85,000 in civil damages against the anti-abortion protesters. The Court also lifted a permanent nationwide injunction[248] imposed by the federal trial court that banned the group from blocking access to abortion clinics, trespassing on and damaging clinic property, and using violence or threats of violence. The Court also held that Scheidler and his Pro-Life Action Network (PLAN) did not commit extortion as NOW had claimed, within the meaning of the Hobbs Act. That federal statute defines extortion as "the obtaining of property from another, with his consent, induced by wrongful use of actual or threatened force, violence, or fear, or under color of official right."[249]

The Court agreed that the protesters "interfered with, disrupted, and in some instances completely deprived respondents of their ability to exercise their property rights."[250] The Court also recognized that some of the conduct was criminal (as acknowledged by the protesters themselves) and that such interference and disruptions may have accomplished their goal of shutting down the clinics. However, the Court said, these acts did not constitute extortion because the protesters did not "obtain" the property. The Court declined to rule whether civil injunctions were available under RICO to private litigants such as NOW because the jury's decision that extortion had been committed had not been supported.

The battle did not end, however. The end did not occur until three years later. In 2006, the U.S. Supreme Court appeared to finally end the 20-year dispute between NOW and Scheidler and his supporters by ruling 8 to 0 (newly appointed Justice Alito did not participate) that the Hobbs Act and the RICO Act could not be used to prosecute protesters who block abortion clinics even when they commit violence. In *Scheidler v. NOW* (*Scheidler III*),[251] Justice Breyer wrote in the majority opinion, "Physical violence unrelated to robbery or extortion falls outside the Hobbs Act scope. Congress did not intend to create a freestanding physical violence offense. It did not intend to forbid acts or threats of physical violence in furtherance of a plan or purpose to engage in what the Act refers to as robbery or extortion (and related attempts or conspiracies)." This final case arose after *Scheidler II* was remanded to the U.S. Court of Appeals. That court then remanded the case to the federal district court on the grounds that an alternative argument made by NOW had not been considered. That argument basically was that the original jury's verdict finding the protesters guilty under the Hobbs Act could have been based on threats of physical violence not connected to extortion, not only on extortion-related conduct. The U.S. Supreme Court then jumped into the fray, agreeing to hear the case one more time. These rulings, especially the 2006 holding, make it clear that Congress intended for the RICO and Hobbs statutes to be used to ban such acts or threats of violence only "in furtherance of a plan or purpose to engage in robbery or extortion."

Anti-abortion activists have experienced both victories and defeats in their attempts to obtain First Amendment protection for their acts of protest. One mild blow came in 1994 when the U.S. Supreme Court handed down its 6 to 3 decision in *Madsen v. Women's Health Center*.[252] The case began in September 1992 when a Florida state trial court judge issued an injunction barring anti-abortion groups from blocking or interfering with public access to a clinic in Melbourne. Six months later, the judge broadened the injunction at the request of Women's Health Center, which operates abortion clinics throughout central Florida. The judge believed the protesters were continuing to block access by congregating on the road leading to the clinic and created stress for patients and medical personnel, especially with their noise that included singing, chanting, and speaking with loudspeakers and bullhorns. The protesters also picketed the fronts of private residences of physicians and other clinic workers.

The broader injunction that anti-abortion activist Judy Madsen and others filed suit to over-turn prohibited anti-abortion organizations "and all persons acting in concert" at all times and all days from entering clinic premises, from interfering with access to the building or parking lot, from "congregating, picketing, patrolling, demonstrating or entering" the public right-of-way or private property within 36 feet of the clinic's property line, and from physically approaching anyone visiting the clinic to communicate (unless the person indicated a desire to communicate) within 300 feet of the clinic, and protesting, demonstrating, and using bull-horns and other devices within 300 feet of the private residence of a clinic employee. The order also banned singing, whistling, and similar noises during certain hours and "sounds or images observable to or within earshot of the patients inside the clinic."

On appeal, the Florida Supreme Court upheld the injunction as content-neutral, "narrowly tailored to serve a significant government interest," and leaving "open ample alternative channels of communication."[253] Around the same time, the 11th Circuit U.S. Court of Appeals struck down the injunction as "content-based and neither necessary to serve a compelling state interest nor narrowly drawn to achieve that end."[254]

The U.S. Supreme Court assumed the task of resolving the conflict. First, the majority opinion written by Chief Justice Rehnquist held that the injunction was not content-based because, although it was written to regulate the activities of a specific group, it was based on the past activities of the group. (In a long dissent, Justice Scalia, joined by Justices Kennedy and Thomas, strongly disagreed with this analysis, saying that while the press would characterize the decision as an abortion case, the law books will cite it "as a free speech injunction case—and the damage its novel principles produce will be considerable.") The Chief Justice went on to say that the injunction protected significant government interests including a woman's right to seek lawful services. However, because the case involved an injunction, he said its constitutionality must be analyzed against a stronger standard than a content-neutral standard. The latter test would be whether it was narrowly tailored to serve a significant government interest as a reasonable time, place, and manner restriction. On the other hand, the test here is the more rigorous First Amendment standard: "whether the challenged provisions of the injunction burden no more speech than necessary to serve a significant government interest."

In applying this test, the Court held the 36-foot buffer zone in general was constitutional because the court had few other options to protect access. The portion of the zone at the back and side was not constitutional because there was no evidence access was obstructed by allowing the protesters in those areas. The Court also ruled that the noise restrictions were constitutional because noise control is particularly important for medical facilities during surgery and recovery of patients. The 300-foot no-approach zone and the prohibition on images observable did not survive the test's scrutiny.

According to the Court, "It is much easier for the clinic to pull its curtains than for a patient to stop up her ears, and no more is required to avoid seeing placards through the windows of the clinic."[255] Both the 300-foot zone around private residences and the 300-foot zone around the clinic violated the First Amendment because they were broader restrictions than necessary. The Court said "a limitation on the time, duration of picketing, and number of pickets outside a smaller zone could have accomplished the desired result."[256] Finally, the justices rejected the protesters' argument that the "in concert" provision of the injunction violated their First Amendment right of association: "The freedom of association protected by the First Amendment does not extend to joining with others for the purpose of depriving third parties of their lawful rights."[257]

Three years after *Madsen*, protesters won a major victory when the U.S. Supreme Court handed down its decision in *Schenck et al. v. Pro Choice Network of Western New York et al.*[258] In 1990, three physicians and four medical clinics, all of which provided abortion services, and the Pro Choice Network of Western New York, a nonprofit corporation founded to maintain access to family planning and abortion services, filed suit against 50 individuals and three organizations involved in anti-abortion protests. The plaintiffs sought a temporary restraining order (TRO), a permanent injunction, and damages against the defendants who engaged in numerous large-scale blockades of the clinics that included protesters marching, standing, kneeling, sitting, and lying in driveways and doorways. These actions were intended to prevent or discourage patients, physicians, nurses, and other employees from entering the facilities. Other activities outlined in the Supreme Court's discussion of the case included protesters crowding around parked cars, milling around doorways, handing out literature, and shouting at, shoving, grabbing, and pushing women entering the clinics. Some of the protesters followed the women as they walked toward the clinic, handing them literature and talking with them in attempts to persuade them not to have abortions. The tactics were so aggressive and continuous that local police were unable to control the protesters who usually dispersed as soon as police arrived and then returned later. They harassed the police, verbally and by mail.

The U.S. District Court judge in the case granted the plaintiffs' request for a TRO three days after the complaint was filed. The TRO enjoined the defendants from physically blocking the clinics, physically abusing or harassing anyone entering or leaving a clinic, and demonstrating within 15 feet of any person entering or leaving the premises. The defendants were allowed to place two "counselors" within the 15-foot "buffer zone" to have "a conversation of a nonthreatening nature" with people entering or leaving the clinic unless the persons indicated they did not want such "counseling." As a result, the protesters cut back on some of their activities but continued to set up blockades and to harass patients and staff entering and leaving the clinics. The District Court changed the TRO to a preliminary injunction after 17 months and eventually cited five protesters for civil contempt for allegedly violating the terms of the order. The injunction was broader than the TRO, banning demonstrations "within fifteen feet from either side or edge of, or in front of, doorways or doorway entrances, parking lot entrances, driveways and driveway entrances" of the clinics.[259]

The Supreme Court called these "fixed buffer zones." The injunction also banned protesters from coming "within 15 feet of any person or vehicle seeking access to or leaving such facilities." The order also said that once the two sidewalk "counselors" had entered the buffer zones, they had to "cease and desist" their "counseling" if the person asked them to stop and then retreat 15 feet from the person and remain outside the buffer zones (characterized by the Court as "floating buffer zones"). When the defendants asserted that these restrictions constituted a violation of the First Amendment, the district court judge applied the traditional time, place, and manner analysis and found that the injunction did not infringe on the defendants' First Amendment rights.

The court held that the injunction was content-neutral, was narrowly tailored to serve a government interest, and left open alternative means of communication. In a split vote, a three-judge panel of the 2nd Circuit U.S. Court of Appeals, applying the *Madsen* test discussed *supra*, reversed the trial court decision. Meeting *en banc,* the Court of Appeals affirmed the District Court decision in a divided vote. The U.S. Supreme Court held by 6–3 the fixed buffer zone around clinic driveways and entrances was permissible under the First Amendment but ruled 8 to 1 the floating buffer zones around patients and vehicles were not permissible.

In a majority opinion written by Chief Justice Rehnquist, the Court, applying the *Madsen* test, reasoned that the same significant government interests applied in this case as in *Madsen*—"ensuring public safety and order, promoting the free flow of traffic on streets and sidewalks, protecting property rights, and protecting a woman's freedom to seek pregnancy related services." Fixed buffer zones did not burden any more speech than was necessary to serve those interests. Rehnquist was joined by Justices Stevens, O'Connor, Souter, Ginsburg, and Breyer in this part of the decision. Justices Scalia, Kennedy, and Thomas dissented, as earlier in *Madsen.*

On the issue of floating buffer zones for people and vehicles, however, all justices except Breyer voted to strike down that portion of the injunction. The Court indicated that such prohibitions are too broad and hard to enforce and thus burden more speech than is necessary to serve relevant governmental interests. The Court noted, for example, that protesters might have to go to great lengths to maintain the 15-foot distance from a person entering or leaving the clinic while still communicating with the person. According to the Court, "Leafleting and commenting on matters of public concern are classic forms of speech that lie at the heart of the *First Amendment,* and speech in public areas is at its most protected on public sidewalks, a prototypical example of a traditional public forum."[260]

The justices had given a hint of how they were likely to rule on the floating buffer zones during oral arguments the previous October. Noting that the sidewalks near the clinic were only 15 feet wide, the justices questioned whether a 15-foot barrier could be fairly enforced. The Court did not rule out the possibility that a "zone of separation between individuals entering the clinics and protesters, measured by the distance between the two" could be imposed. Instead, the Court said there had been no justification made for a zone of privacy. The majority opinion acknowledged the "physically abusive conduct, harassment of the police that hampered law enforcement, and the tendency of even peaceful conversations to devolve into aggressive and sometimes violent conduct." Thus the justices appeared to open the door for further litigation on this issue, which is likely to arrive at the Court's doorsteps someday. More recently, cases involving protests at the funerals of military veterans have resurrected concerns over safe distance buffers.

In *Lelia Hill v. Colorado* (2000),[261] the U.S. Supreme Court upheld as constitutional a state statute that made it unlawful for any person who was within 100 feet of a health care facility's entrance to "knowingly approach" within 8 feet of another person without that individuals' consent to hand a leaflet or handbill, display a sign or engage in oral protest, education, or counseling. The Court ruled in a 6 to 3 decision that the statutory provision was a reasonable time, place, and manner regulation that was narrowly tailored to serve a legitimate public interest while also leaving open alternative channels of communication. Citing both *Schenck* and *Madsen*, the Court said the regulation was not unconstitutionally vague.

In 2011 the U.S. Supreme Court handed down decisions in three major prior restraint cases that, taken together, send a clear signal that the current Roberts Court, although conservative on most issues, is generally highly protective of First Amendment rights. In all three cases the U.S. Supreme Court applied strict scrutiny in its analysis, and each time the particular prior restraint involved failed to pass Constitutional muster.

Funeral Protests

The first case, *Snyder v. Phelps et al.* (2011),[262] involved a highly emotional and complex situation that shares many similarities with the abortion protest cases. Seven members of the Westboro Baptist Church (WBC) of Topeka, Kansas—founder Fred Phelps, two of his daughters and four of his grandchildren—picketed the 2006 funeral of Marine Lance Cpl. Matthew Snyder in his hometown of Westminster, Maryland. Snyder died in military action in Iraq. For more than two decades, members of the church, which Phelps founded in 1955, have picketed funerals of soldiers and other individuals across the country. The church members typically hold signs, as they did in this case, that say "Thank God for Dead Soldiers," "Fags Doom Nations," "America is Doomed," "Priests Rape Boys," "You're Going to Hell," "Thank God for IEDs," "God Hates Fags," "God Hates the USA/Thank God for 9/11," and other highly offensive messages. WBC, which had picketed more than 600 funerals when the case came before the Court, believes that God hates this country because it tolerates homosexuality, including in the military. According to press accounts, Matthew Snyder was not gay and apparently most of the soldiers whose funerals WBC has picketed were not gay either.

The protests in this case were on public land about 1,000 feet from the local Catholic Church, the site of the funeral. (WBC also condemns the Catholic Church for its sexual scandals involving priests raping young boys and girls.) The church also posted Internet messages attacking Albert Snyder and his spouse, Julie Snyder, as parents and as Catholics. Albert Snyder saw only the tops of the signs when he drove to his son's funeral and did not learn of their actual messages until he watched the news later that evening.

Albert Snyder sued Phelps and the other members of the church in federal court in a diversity action, claiming defamation, intentional infliction of emotional distress, intrusion upon seclusion, publicizing private life, and civil conspiracy. The U.S. District Court judge in the trial court case granted summary judgment to the church on the defamation and invasion of privacy claims. He allowed the other three claims to go to the jury, which awarded the plaintiff $10.9 million in damages, which the District Court later reduced to $5 million. The Fourth U.S. Circuit Court of Appeals reversed the District Court decision, holding the church's protests were protected by the First Amendment because they focused on issues of public concern, were not provably false and were communicated solely as rhetorical hyperbole.

In an 8–1 decision, with Justice Alito dissenting, the U.S. Supreme Court upheld the appeals court decision. The Court said the First Amendment protected such protests at military funerals and thus shielded WBC from tort liability. In his dissent, Justice Alito likened these protests instead to unprotected "fighting words," which do not enjoy First Amendment protection. While noting the need to have vigorous public debate, Alito added, it is "not necessary to allow the brutalization of innocent victims."[263] The Supreme Court decided that even the most offensive and outrageous forms of speech, including public picketing at a soldier's funeral, are protected by the U.S. Constitution if that speech addresses important public issues and occurs peaceably in a public place.

Maryland had no law at the time of the protests in the case that specifically targeted funerals, but it did pass such legislation four months after Snyder sued the church. In its decision, the Supreme Court noted that it was thus making no judgment whether the state statute was a "reasonable time, place and manner" restriction under standards enunciated in earlier decisions by the Court. Several states have passed statutes similar to that of Maryland. Some have been struck down by state appellate courts. Typically, the laws classify specific types of funeral protests as misdemeanors and ban picketing except outside a "buffer zone" (similar to that in abortion protest cases). There is a federal statute, known as the "Respect for America's Fallen Heroes Act," that applies only to national cemeteries.

There is a long tradition in the U.S. Supreme Court of defending otherwise offensive speech such as the rants of white supremacists that effectively provide a "bully pulpit" for what many citizens consider a form of bullying behavior. According to Justice Alito, a funeral should be a private event, which was consistent with the claim by the soldier's father that the protests caused him emotional distress. He also noted in his dissent that "our profound national commitment to free and open debate is not a license for the vicious verbal assault that occurred in this case."[264]

Violent Video Games

In the second of its three major prior restraint decisions in 2011, the U.S. Supreme Court in a 7–2 decision written by Justice Scalia struck down as unconstitutional a California statute banning the sale or rental of violent video games to minors and requiring their packaging to be labeled "18." In *Brown, Governor of California, et al. v. Entertainment Merchants Association et al.* (2011),[265] the Court agreed with both the Federal District Court and the Ninth Circuit U.S. Court of Appeals that video games, including those that depict extreme violence, enjoy the same protection under the First Amendment as books, plays, movies, and other traditional forms of communication.

The California statute covered "games in which the range of options available to a player includes killing, maiming, dismembering, or sexually assaulting an image of a human being, if those acts are depicted" such that a "reasonable person, considering the game as a whole, would find appeals to a deviant or morbid interest of minors" that is "patently offensive to prevailing standards in the community as to what is suitable for minors" and that "causes the game as a whole, to lack serious literary, artistic, political, or scientific value for minors."[266] The penalty for violating the statute was a fine of up to $1,000. After the Act was passed, the video software industry successfully sought a permanent injunction in the courts prohibiting enforcement.

Both Justices Thomas and Breyer dissented in the case but for separate reasons, and Justice Alito wrote a concurring opinion, which Chief Justice Roberts joined. In the concurring opinion, Justice Alito pointed to the fact that today's advanced video games can produce high definition images that may soon be experienced in 3-D. He called the violence in some of the games "astounding," with victims "dismembered, decapitated, disemboweled, set on fire, and chopped into little pieces. They cry out in agony and beg for mercy. Blood gushes, splatters and pools. Severed body parts and gobs of human remains are graphically shown."[267] He cites other examples of violence, including a game whose objective is to rape a mother and her daughters and others that involve raping Native American women and gunning down African Americans, Latinos and Jews.

In his majority opinion, Justice Scalia was not persuaded by Alito's examples, noting that "Justice Alito recounts all these disgusting video games in order to disgust us—but disgust is not a valid basis for restricting expression." Justice Scalia also pointed to the tradition of violence even in fairy tales such as doves pecking out the eyes of Cinderella's evil stepsisters, *Grimms' Fairy Tales* ("grim indeed," according to Justice Scalia), and the savage murder of a schoolboy by other children in the classic novel *Lord of the Flies* often read in high school.[268] In his dissenting opinion, Justice Breyer, a member of the liberal wing of the Court, cited 15 pages of research on the effects of violent video games on children. According to the majority opinion, "No doubt a state possesses legitimate power to protect children from harm, but that does not include a free-floating power to restrict the ideas to which children may be exposed."

The decision makes it clear that violent video games marketed to minors do not fall within the exceptions the Court has enunciated for imposing prior restraint on content, as *Near v. Minnesota* established—obscenity, incitement to violence, and imminent harm to national security.

The Court had echoed similar sentiments the previous year in a case that concerned a federal statute providing imprisonment of up to five years creating, selling or possessing depictions of animal cruelty "in which a living animal is intentionally maimed, mutilated, tortured, wounded or killed" if such harm was illegal where it occurred. The statute was aimed at so-called "crush videos" in which helpless animals are tortured and killed. The law exempted from prohibition any depiction that had serious religious, political, scientific, educational, journalistic, historical, or artistic value. The case arose after a defendant appeal his conviction of five years imprisonment for selling videos of dog fighting.

In *United States v. Stevens* (2010),[269] the Court in an 8–1 decision, written by Chief Justice Roberts with only Justice Alito dissenting, struck down the statute as overbroad under the First Amendment. The Court found the statute was "an impermissible content-based restriction on speech. There was no American tradition of forbidding the *depiction of* animal cruelty—though States have long had laws against *committing* it"[270] (emphasis in the original).

Data Mining and the First Amendment

In the final prior restraint case in 2011, the Court in a 6–3 decision in *Sorrell v. IMS Health* (2011)[271] held that Vermont's Prescription Confidentiality Law violated the First Amendment. The Court ruled the statute was subject to heightened judicial scrutiny because it imposed content- and speaker-based burdens on protected expression. The law restricts the sale, disclosure, and use of pharmacy records that reveal the prescribing practices of individual physicians. In general, such data cannot be sold, disclosed by pharmacies for marketing, or used in marketing by pharmaceutical companies. These companies employ a process known as "detailing," which typically involves visiting the physician to attempt to convince him or her to prescribe particular drugs by explaining the benefits for patients. When they process prescriptions, pharmacies gain access to the prescribing patterns of specific physicians through what is known as "prescriber identifying information." Pharmacies often sell this information to "data miners," companies that analyze the data and then lease their reports to pharmaceutical manufacturers who use the information to improve their marketing and sales.

Data miners, joined by an association of brand-name pharmaceutical manufacturers successfully sought a ruling in the Second U.S. Circuit Court of Appeals that the law was unconstitutional. (A U.S. District Court ruled in favor of the State.) The Supreme Court agreed with the federal appellate court. Vermont argued in its appeal that the statute advanced important public policy goals by lowering he costs of medical care and promoting public health by preventing drug companies from promoting brand-name prescriptions that are more expensive and may be less safe than generic drugs. The Court rejected this argument, noting that just because "the State finds expression too persuasive does not permit it to quiet the speech or to burden its messengers."[272] The Court also addressed the State's personal privacy concerns:

> The capacity of technology to find and publish personal information, including records required by the government, presents serious and unresolved issues with respect to personal privacy and the dignity it seeks to secure. In considering how to protect those interests, however, the State cannot engage in content-based discrimination to advance its own side of a debate.[273]

Signs: City of Ladue v. Gilleo *(1994)*

In *City of Ladue v. Gilleo* (1994),[274] a unanimous U.S. Supreme Court recognized a clear violation of the First Amendment with which few people would disagree. The case arose when Margaret P. Gilleo, a resident of Ladue, an affluent suburb of St. Louis, placed a 24- × 36-inch sign on her front lawn during the 1990 Persian Gulf Conflict that read "Say No to War in the Persian Gulf, Call Congress Now." The sign quickly disappeared and a replacement was knocked down. When Gilleo complained to police, she was informed the city had an ordinance barring homeowners from displaying signs on their property except "For Sale" or similar signs.

However, under the Ladue ordinance, businesses, churches, and so on were allowed to have certain signs not allowed by private residents. Gilleo sued the city council after it denied her request for a variance. She then successfully sought a preliminary injunction against enforcement of the ordinance in U.S. District Court and placed an 8.5- × 11-inch sign in the second story window of her home that read "For Peace in the Gulf." The Ladue City Council enacted a replacement ordinance that more broadly defined *signs* and listed 10 exemptions. One of the stated reasons for the enactment of the ordinance was:

> … proliferation of an unlimited number of signs … would create ugliness, visual blight and clutter, tarnish the natural beauty of the landscape as well as the residential and commercial architecture, impair property values, substantially impinge upon the privacy and special ambience of the community, and may cause safety and traffic hazards to motorists, pedestrians, and children.[275]

Gilleo challenged the new ordinance as well, and both the U.S. District Court and the 8th Circuit U.S. Court of Appeals ruled in her favor. The unanimous opinion of the U.S. Supreme Court noted that with this ordinance:

> … Ladue has almost completely foreclosed a venerable means of communication that is both unique and important. It has totally foreclosed that medium to political, religious or personal messages.… Displaying a sign from one's own residence often carries

Figure 5.2   The city limits sign for Ladue, Missouri, the origin of *Ladue v. Gilleo*, a 1994 U.S. Supre-meme Court case (Photo by Roy L. Moore).

a message quite distinct from placing the same sign someplace else, or conveying the same text or picture by other means. Precisely because of their location, such signs provide information about the identity of the "speaker".... Residential signs are an unusually cheap and convenient form of communication. Especially for persons of modest means or limited mobility, a yard or window sign may have no practical substitute.[276]

The justices made it clear this right is not absolute:

Our decision that Ladue's ban on almost all residential signs violates the First Amendment by no means leaves the City powerless to address the ills that may be associated with residential signs. It bears mentioning that individual residents themselves have strong incentives to keep their own property values up and to prevent 'visual clutter' in their own yards and neighborhoods—incentives markedly different from those of persons who erect signs on others' land, in others' neighborhoods, or on public property....[277]

Those remarks appear to open the door to private communities imposing their own rules on signs. For example, many new subdivisions now routinely include covenants in the so-called master plans that bar displays of political signs, flags, religious symbols, and even prohibit erection of outside satellite dishes. Would such restrictions pass constitutional muster under *Ladue*?

The key question would be whether community associations that are responsible for enforcing these rules are acting as governmental or quasi-governmental bodies for purposes of the First Amendment. Because they usually have the authority to enforce their decisions and interpretations in court, it could be argued that they are tantamount to governmental authorities. On the other hand, their authority is limited and can ultimately be enforced only indirectly (i.e., through the judicial system). According to a *New York Times* article, about 50 million Americans live in communities governed by such associations.[278] Most of the lawsuits filed by homeowners associations against residents concern violations such as failures to pay dues and improper parking, but these groups are quite capable of imposing prior restraint on speech, as *Ladue* illustrated very well.

Workplaces and Restricted Zones

Occasionally, prior restraint in the workplace attracts the attention of the U.S. Supreme Court, sometimes with confusing results. For example, in *Waters v. Churchill* (1994),[279] a nurse was fired from a public hospital for statements she made during a work break that were critical of her employer. Her precise statements are in dispute. The hospital claimed they were disruptive comments critical of her department and the hospital, but she testified that her conversations were nondisruptive and focused primarily on a specific hospital policy she believed threatened patient care.

The plurality opinion said that under an earlier Court decision, *Connick v. Myers*,[280] the First Amendment protects a government employee's speech if it is on a matter of public concern and the employee's interest is not outweighed by any injury the speech could cause to the government's interest. The *Connick* test, the justices said, should be applied to what the employer reasonably thought was said, not what the judge or jury ultimately determines to have been said. The opinion went on to say that circumstances such as those in this case require the supervisor to conduct an investigation to determine whether there is a substantial likelihood that the type of speech uttered was protected under the First Amendment. *Waters* symbolizes the ongoing struggle within the Supreme Court over the limits of the First Amendment, especially in the area of freedom of speech.

In *Legal Services Corporation v. Velazquez* (2001),[281] the U.S. Supreme Court declared unconstitutional a restriction imposed by Congress banning funding of any organization that represented individuals in an attempt to change or challenge current welfare law. In a 5 to 4 decision the Court distinguished this case from *Rust v. Sullivan*, handed down 10years earlier. In *Rust*, the Court upheld in another 5 to 4 decision certain regulations imposed by the U.S. Department of Health and Human Services. The regulations banned programs that received federal funding from providing abortion counseling, referral, or advocacy and requiring health care workers on those projects to refer pregnant women to agencies that provided prenatal care but not abortions. The Court said the two cases were different because *Rust* involved governmental speech but *Legal Services Corporation* involved a project "designed to facilitate private speech, not to promote a governmental message. An LSC attorney speaks on behalf of a private, indigent client in a welfare benefits claim, while the Government's message is delivered by the attorney defending the benefits decision."[282]

In a case somewhat parallel to *Rust*, the U.S. Supreme Court held in *Rumsfeld v. Forum for Academic and Institutional Rights* (2006)[283] that no First Amendment violation occurs when the federal government requires universities and presumably other institutions that receive federal funding to provide equal access to military recruiters even if violating a school's antidiscrimination policies.

Such a case arose when FAIR, a group of law schools and law faculties, requested a preliminary injunction to stop enforcement of a federal statute known as the Solomon Amendment that allows the federal government to withhold federal funds from educational institutions if they denied military recruiters the same access provided to other recruiters on campus. FAIR opposed the military's "Don't ask, don't tell" policy against homosexuals. The U.S. District Court denied the request, characterizing recruitment as conduct rather than speech, but also questioned the Department of Defense's interpretation. Congress revised the statute to meet the court's concerns.

On appeal, the Third Circuit U.S. Court of Appeals ruled in favor of FAIR, holding that the revised amendment violated the unconstitutional conditions doctrine by forcing law schools to decide whether to assert their First Amendment rights or receive certain federal funding. The U.S. Supreme Court disagreed, holding that the amendment did not violate the schools' freedom of speech and freedom of association rights under the First Amendment. The Court reasoned that, although the right is not absolute, Congress does have the authority to set conditions for federal funding, and such a requirement is not unconstitutional if it could be constitutionally imposed directly, as it was in this case.

The debating points about military recruiting narrowed considerably when the U.S. Senate voted in 2010 to repeal the "don't ask, don't tell" policy against gays and lesbians serving openly in the armed services.[284] The subject had been brought up earlier during the Supreme Court confirmation hearings for the then-Solicitor General, Drew Faust, the former Harvard Law School President who supported the policy prohibiting military from officially recruiting on campus because of the earlier ban. U.S. Senator Scott Brown earlier blasted Harvard's ban on ROTC saying the school had its priorities mixed-up, "favoring illegal immigrant students over military-affiliated students." [285]

One way in which city governments have attempted to reduce crime in certain areas of cities is to turn those areas into restricted zones in which all visitors must obtain permission to enter from appropriate authorities such as the police. The Richmond, Virginia City Council turned over the streets of one low-income housing development to the Richmond Redevelopment and Housing Authority, a political subdivision of the state in 1997. Under RRHA rules, anyone who wanted to engage in free speech such as distributing leaflets, speaking, or simply visiting family members had to obtain permission from police or a housing authority official. In a unanimous opinion written by Justice Scalia, the U.S. Supreme Court held in *Virginia v. Hicks*[286] that this trespass policy was not overly broad and thus did not violate the First Amendment.

In *Thomas v. Chicago Park District* (2002),[287] the U.S. Supreme Court held in a unanimous decision written by Justice Souter that a city ordinance requiring individuals to obtain permits before conducting large-scale events in public parks did not violate the First Amendment. According to the Court, the restriction was not prior restraint based on subject matter but a content-neutral time, place, and manner regulation of the use of a public forum.

Public Accommodation

Public parades are very effective ways in which groups can express their political, social, and religious views, usually to large audiences, with little likelihood of confrontation. But what if individuals with views opposed by the parade organizers want to be part of the parade? Can the organizers be forced to provide accommodation? In a unanimous opinion delivered by Justice Souter, the U.S. Supreme Court held in *Hurley v. Irish-American Gay, Lesbian and Bisexual Group of Boston* (1995)[288] that a Massachusetts court's application of a public accommodations statute to require a parade organizer to include marchers for a cause it opposed violated the First Amendment. The ruling is, essentially, a strike against at least some forms of political correctness, but it is clearly a major boost for First Amendment rights. Much of the media coverage focused on the fact that the excluded marchers belonged to an organization of gays, lesbians, and bisexuals. Unfortunately, most of the stories and headlines missed the real significance of the case—its recognition that under the First Amendment speakers cannot be forced to accommodate views with which they disagree. The fact that the group excluded in this case consisted of gays, lesbians, and bisexuals may have been interesting, but it was merely coincidental (i.e., any group could have been excluded including pro-choicers, pro-lifers, Christians, Jews, Muslims, etc.). Also missed in much of the analysis surrounding the decision was the fact that the Court did not declare the state statute unconstitutional; only the manner in which it was applied was a problem.

The case originated when a group known as the Irish-American Gay, Lesbian and Bisexual Group of Boston (GLIB) was excluded from the annual St. Patrick's Day Parade in South Boston by the sponsor, the South Boston Allied War Veterans Council led by John Hurley. The parade that typically attracts as many as 20,000 marchers and 1,000,000 spectators is not officially sponsored by the city, although the city provides funding for the sponsor and allows it to use the official city seal. No group other than the veterans association has ever applied for the parade permit since the city gave up sponsorship in 1947. When GLIB asked the sponsor for permission to march in the parade, the veterans council denied the request. GLIB successfully sought a court injunction that required the council to allow it to march. The march, which included GLIB, created no problems, but GLIB was nevertheless denied permission the next year. The group and some of its members then sued the city, the council, and the council leader, claiming state and federal constitutional rights had been violated.

They also asserted that the denial of their permit violated Massachusetts' public accommodations law that bans "any distinction, discrimination or restriction on account of ... sexual orientation ... relative to the admission of any person to, or treatment in any place of public accommodation, resort or amusement."[289] The state trial court ruled in favor of the plaintiffs, holding that the parade met the definition of *public accommodation* as defined under Massachusetts law. Interestingly, the court chided the council for not recognizing that "a proper celebration of St. Patrick's Day and Evacuation Day requires diversity and inclusiveness."[290] The Supreme Judicial Court of Massachusetts affirmed the trial court decision.

Justice Souter's opinion notes that by the time the case reached the U.S. Supreme Court, only the veterans council was asserting a First Amendment claim. GLIB rested its case on the ground that its exclusion from the parade violated the state public accommodations law; it did not claim any violation of its free speech rights. The opinion also noted that the U.S. Supreme Court was required to conduct a *de novo review*, an independent appellate review in line with *Bose v. Consumers Union* (1984).[291]

The Court had no difficulty characterizing parades of this type as "a form of expression, not just motion, and the inherent expressiveness of marching to make a point explains our cases involving protest marches." The court agreed with the state courts that the council had been rather lenient in allowing others to march while excluding GLIB. "But," the Court said, "a private speaker does not forfeit constitutional protection simply by combining multifarious voices, or by failing to edit their themes to isolate an exact message as the exclusive subject matter of the speech." The Court had no problem with the public accommodations statute itself, noting that it had a "venerable history" and its provisions including a variety of types of discrimination were "well within the State's usual power to enact when a legislature has reason to believe that a given group is the target of discrimination, and they do not, as a general matter, violate the First or 14th Amendments." The opinion pointed to the peculiar manner in which the law was applied:

> … Although the state courts spoke of the parade as a place of public accommodation … once the expressive character of both the parade and the marching GLIB contingent is understood, it becomes apparent that the state courts' application of the statute had the effect of declaring the sponsors' speech itself to be the public accommodation.[292]

The Court rejected the state's argument that *Turner Broadcasting v. FCC* (1994)[293] supported the state's position. In *Turner Broadcasting,* which involved the FCC requirement that cable companies set aside channels for designated broadcast stations, the Court applied an intermediate level of scrutiny rather than the traditional strict scrutiny employed in First Amendment cases. "Parades and demonstrations," the *Hurley* Court said, "… are not understood to be so neutrally presented or selectively viewed [as channels are on a cable network]." The Court's criticism of the state courts' decisions grew particularly harsh toward the end:

> … The very idea that a noncommercial speech restriction be used to produce thoughts and statements acceptable to some groups or, indeed, all people, grates on the First Amendment, for it amounts to nothing less than a proposal to limit speech in the service of orthodox expression. The Speech Clause has no more certain antithesis. [cites omitted] While the law is free to promote all sorts of conduct in place of harmful behavior, it is not free to interfere with speech for no better reason than promoting an approved message or discouraging a disfavored one, however enlightened either purpose may strike the government.[294]

The crystal clear message of *Hurley* is that under the First Amendment a speaker engaging in protected speech cannot be forced to accommodate another speaker with whom he or she chooses not to associate, no matter how worthy the government's goal in forcing the accommodation. The *faux pas* of the Massachusetts courts was converting what was expression or expressive conduct into unprotected (discrimination) simply because the speaker chose not to accommodate views of a protected group.

Gay and lesbian rights and other groups were not universally critical of the decision. For example, the legal director for the Lambda Legal Defense Fund in New York was quoted as saying, "This was a First Amendment decision that didn't have much to say about gay rights. What it does say is actually positive for us."[295]

The U.S. Supreme Court tackled the issue of forced public accommodation again—back in 2000, this time within the context of a private, not-for-profit organization—and homosexual rights were at the center of the case. In *Boy Scouts of America v. Dale* (2000),[296] the Court held in a 5 to 4 decision written by Chief Justice Rehnquist that a New Jersey public accommodations statute requiring the Boy Scouts of America (BSA) to admit a gay Scout violated that organization's First Amendment right of expressive association. The BSA argued that homosexual behavior violated the system of values it tried to instill in young males. An adult assistant scoutmaster for a New Jersey troop filed the suit against the Scouts after he was removed from his position when the organization learned that he was a gay rights activist and avowed homosexual. The state statute prohibited discrimination based on sexual orientation in places of public accommodation.

The Court cited *Hurley* extensively in its decision, noting that the standard of review in such cases is the traditional First Amendment analysis or strict scrutiny of *Hurley*, not the intermediate standard of review discussed earlier in this chapter.[297] In its reasoning, the Court said that (1) it disagreed with the New Jersey Supreme Court's view that group's ability to communicate its values would not be significantly affected by the forced inclusion of the gay assistant scoutmaster, (2) even if the BSA discourages its leaders from expressing views on sex, its method of expression has First Amendment protection, and (3) "the First Amendment does not require that every member of a group agree on every issue in order for the group's policy to be 'expressive association.'"

Is it forced accommodation if members of a group are assessed a mandatory fee by a public agency that distributes some of the fee to support organizations whose views are contrary to those of some members of the group? That's the question facing the U.S. Supreme Court in *Board of Regents, University of Wisconsin System v. Southworth*.[298] The case involved a required fee paid by students at the University of Wisconsin-Madison that was used to support various campus services and extracurricular activities. Some of the funds were allocated to registered student organizations that engaged in political and ideological expression with which some students strongly disagreed. A group of students filed suit against the university's governing board, claiming that the fee violated their First Amendment rights because they were forced to fund political and ideological speech offensive to their personal views. In a unanimous opinion written by Justice Kennedy, the U.S. Supreme Court held, "The First Amendment permits a university to charge its students an activity fee used to fund a program to facilitate extracurricular student speech, provided that the program is viewpoint neutral."[299] The Court did say that a university could set up an optional or refund system under which students would not have to subsidize speech they found objectionable, but the Constitution did not impose a requirement. According to the Court, the key to avoid violating the First Amendment is that the university must maintain viewpoint neutrality in its allocation of funding.

Religious Speech

In *Board of Regents v. Southworth*, the Court cited its 5 to 4 decision five years earlier in *Rosenberger v. Rector and Visitors of the University of Virginia* (1995).[300] Justice Kennedy wrote the majority opinion in that case as well. In *Rosenberger*, the Court held that the University of Virginia, a state-supported institution, violated the First Amendment right to freedom of speech when it denied a student-run Christian newspaper funds for printing. University guidelines prohibited expending student activities fees to organizations that promoted or manifested beliefs in a deity or "an ultimate reality" (i.e., religious organizations). The case involved a publication called *Wide Awake: A Christian Perspective*. The university collects mandatory fees from each student that are then placed into a Student Activities Fund to support a wide range of student activities including printing costs associated with student newspapers. When the university refused a request for reimbursement for printing costs because the paper was sponsored by a religious organization, the publisher appealed on the grounds that the action abridged the First Amendment right to freedom of speech and freedom of religious expression. The U.S. District Court issued a summary judgment for the school, and the Fourth Circuit Court of Appeals affirmed, holding that even though the university's discrimination violated freedom of speech, the Establishment Clause forced the university to do so.

The U.S. Supreme Court cited its 1993 decision in *Lamb's Chapel v. Center Moriches Union Free School District*[301] in which it held that it was a violation of the First Amendment for a public school to allow its premises to be used for all forms of speech except those dealing with religion. The justices also cited *R.A.V. v. City of St. Paul,* discussed earlier, as well as a line of similar prior restraint cases, to support the principle that a public university does not violate the Establishment Clause when it provides access to its facilities and resources on a content-neutral basis to student groups, even if some of them espouse religious views.

In another case involving religious speech, *Good News Club v. Milford Central High School* (2001),[302] the Court held that a public high school violated the First Amendment when it refused to allow a Christian organization for 6- to 12-year-olds to hold after-school weekly meetings using the school's facilities. Under school policy, other nonreligious groups (but not religious organizations) were permitted to meet. The school argued that meetings of religious groups would violate the Establishment Clause of the U.S. Constitution, but the U.S. Supreme Court held that such exclusion discriminated against the club on the basis of its religious viewpoint and thus violated the Free Speech Clause.

Political Communication

The Supreme Court has also devoted considerable attention over the decades to prior restraint on communication within political contexts. This is not surprising in light of the Court's consistent recognition of the importance of political speech.

The First Amendment rights of taxpayers or, more accurately, "Concerned Parents and Taxpayers" were at stake in a 1995 case—*McIntyre v. Ohio Elections Commission*.[303] In a decision written by Justice Stevens (with only Chief Justice Rehnquist and Justice Scalia dissenting), the Court held that a provision of the Ohio Code[304] barring the dissemination of anonymous campaign literature violated the First Amendment. Margaret McIntyre (who died before her appeal reached the U.S. Supreme Court) handed out leaflets at a public meeting at an Ohio middle school in 1988. The leaflets, which expressed opposition to a proposed school tax levy, had been word processed and printed on McIntyre's home computer. There was one problem—some of the circulars omitted her name and instead were signed by "CONCERNED PARENTS AND TAXPAYERS." When a school official who supported the tax told McIntyre that her leaflets violated Ohio law because they were anonymous, she ignored him and handed out more at a meeting the next evening. When the levy passed after first failing in two elections, the official filed a complaint against McIntyre with the Ohio Elections Commission. The commission fined her $100, but a state trial court reversed on the grounds that the statutory provision violated the First Amendment and that McIntyre did not "mislead the public nor act in a surreptitious manner." The Ohio Court of Appeals reinstated the fine in a divided vote, and the Ohio Supreme Court affirmed in a divided vote.

The Ohio appellate courts viewed the mandatory disclosure as a minor inconvenience that provided voters a means of evaluating the validity of political messages and helped prevent fraud, libel, and false advertising. In his opinion, Justice Stevens pointed to the role anonymous publications had played in history, and he cited the principles established the previous year in *Ladue*, discussed above. His opinion stressed the strong protection afforded political communication by the First Amendment. The Court rejected both arguments, noting "the identity of the speaker is no different from other components of the document's content that the author is free to include or not include." The Court was not convinced that the identification requirement would prevent fraud and libel, noting "the prohibition encompasses documents that are not even arguably false or misleading." According to the *McIntyre* Court:

> Under our Constitution, anonymous pamphleteering is not a pernicious, fraudulent practice, but an honorable tradition of advocacy and of dissent. Anonymity is a shield from the tyranny of the majority. [cite omitted] It thus exemplifies the purpose behind the Bill of Rights, and of the First Amendment in particular: to protect unpopular individuals from retaliation *and their ideas from suppression* at the hand of an intolerant society. The right to remain anonymous may be abused when it shields fraudulent conduct. But political speech by its nature will sometimes have unpalatable consequences, and, in general, our society accords greater weight to the value of free speech than to the dangers of its misuse. [cites omitted] Ohio has not shown that its interest in preventing the misuse of anonymous election-related speech justifies a prohibition of all uses of that speech.[305]

McIntyre is a resolute affirmation of First Amendment rights—in this case, those connected with political speech, a category that has traditionally had strong protection against prior restraint. This decision illustrates how First Amendment rights often emerge in the courts in cases involving private individuals. Margaret McIntyre was fined only $100, but her appeal, which was ultimately heard by the U.S. Supreme Court, must have cost her and her estate many times the amount of the fine. She died before the appeal reached the high court, but her contribution to the cause of freedom of speech lives on. As the majority opinion noted, "Mrs. McIntyre passed away during the pendency of this litigation. Even though the amount in controversy is only $100, petitioner, as executor of her estate, has pursued her claim in this Court. Our grant of certiorari ... reflects our agreement with his appraisal of the importance of the question presented."[306] Unlike many other First Amendment cases, this case received little attention in the mass media.

In *Colorado Republican Federal Campaign Committee et al. v. Federal Election Commission* (1996),[307] the U.S. Supreme Court held that the provision of the Federal Election Campaign Act (FECA) of 1971 that restricts the amount of funds a political party can spend in the general election campaign of a congressional candidate was a violation of the First Amendment, at least as applied in the particular case at hand. The facts in the case were quite simple: the Federal Election Commission charged the Colorado Party with violating the "party expenditure" provision of FECA after the party exceeded the expenditure limits when it bought radio ads attacking the likely opponent of a candidate the party had endorsed. The opinion reflects the stance of the Court in limits on political campaign expenditures—reasonable limits on candidate expenditures are permissible but limits on spending by political parties and groups often fail constitutional muster.

A 1997 Supreme Court decision dealt with whether a state could prohibit multiple party or "fusion" candidates for elected office. In *Timmons et al. v. Twin Cities Area New Party*,[308] the Court in a 6 to 3 vote upheld Minnesota's laws preventing a person from appearing on a ballot as a candidate for more than one party. The laws did not violate either the First or the 14th Amendments, according to the majority opinion written by Chief Justice Rehnquist. The Court said states' interests in protecting the integrity, fairness, and efficiency of their ballots and the election processes are sufficiently strong to justify such restrictions. The fusion ban did not severely burden the party's associational rights...nor its ability to endorse, support, or vote for any candidate, according to the majority opinion.

In *Nixon v. Shrink Missouri Government PAC*,[309] the Court upheld as constitutional Missouri's limits on political campaign contributions for state candidates that ranged from $275 to $1075 in 2000. In the 6 to 3 decision written by Justice Souter the Court applied a strict scrutiny test, as it had done in an earlier decision, *Buckley v. Valeo* (1976),[310] which upheld provisions of the Federal Election Campaign Act limiting contributions to federal candidates to $1000 per election. In *Buckley*, the Court did strike down limits on how much candidates could spend.

In *Federal Election Committee v. Colorado Republican Federal Campaign Commission* (2001),[311] the Court answered a question about the Federal Election Campaign Act of 1971 that had been left open in previous Court decisions: does the First Amendment allow coordinated election expenditures by political parties to be treated as contributions, just as coordinated expenditures are treated for other groups? The Republican Party in this case argued such spending in which the party works closely with the candidate is essential because "a party's most important speech is aimed at electing candidates and is itself expressed through those candidates."[312] Thus political parties should have greater freedom to engage in coordinated spending with the candidates themselves. The Court held coordinated election expenditures were contributions for purposes of the law and could be limited; noting that the FEC presented sufficient evidence that such limits could help to prevent corruption of the political process.

In *Republican Party of Minnesota v. White* (2002)[313] the Court held in a 5 to 4 decision that a state statute prohibiting judicial candidates from announcing their views on disputed legal and political issues was unconstitutional. Minnesota and eight other states then had such statutes that were similar to a provision in the American Bar Association's Model Code of Judicial Conduct. The ABA Code was revised after the decision to state that judicial candidates could not make pledges or promises that commit or appear to commit them on issues that could come before the courts. In other words, candidates can express their views on issues but cannot promise to vote a particular way on an issue. In *Minnesota Republican Party*, the Court had not ruled on the provision that banned promises or pledges on issues.

A year later the Court ruled in *Federal Election Commission v. Beaumont* (2003)[314] the federal statutory provision that bans direct contributions to candidates in federal elections by corporations including nonprofit advocacy groups did not violate the First Amendment. The Court reasoned that such a ban was important in preventing political corruption and that corporations could still make contributions through PACs (political action committees).

Congress amended the Federal Election Campaign Act (FECA) of 1971 to impose strict limits on political donations, especially "soft money"—contributions not made directly to candidates and used instead to support activities such as get-out-the-vote drives, generic party ads, and ads supporting specific legislation in 2002.

The Bipartisan Campaign Reform Act (BCRA) also known as the McCain-Feingold Act, attempted to close a loophole in FECA. The loophole allowed parties and candidates to spend unlimited funds on issue ads that were designed to influence election outcomes but nevertheless could skirt restrictions by avoiding so-called "magic words" such as "Vote for Jack Smith" or "Vote Against Mary Jones." The BCRA strictly regulated without banning the expenditure of soft money by political parties, politicians, and political candidates. It barred corporations and unions from spending general funds for advertisements and other forms of communication intended to impact or affect elections.

In *McConnell v. Federal Election Commission* (2003),[315] the U.S. Supreme Court upheld all the main provisions of the BCRA. There were three majority opinions in the case as well as five others—concurring, dissenting or concurring in part and dissenting in part. When the dust settled, it was clear that the Act had withstood constitutional challenge.

Clingman v. Beaver,[316] handed down by the U.S. Supreme Court in 2005, was technically a freedom-of-assembly or right-to-associate case ("… the right of the people peaceably to assemble") rather than a traditional prior restraint case, but it has implications for political communication including prior restraint.

The case involved an Oklahoma statute that permits only registered members of a particular political party and registered Independents to vote in the party's primary. The Libertarian Party of Oklahoma and members of other political parties filed suit against the state election board, claiming this "semiclosed primary" violated their association rights under the First Amendment.

In a decision written by Justice Thomas, the Supreme Court ruled the statute did not violate the Constitution because any burden it imposed on associational rights was not severe and justified by legitimate state interests. The Court agreed with the state that such a primary "preserves the political parties as viable and identifiable interest groups, insuring that the results of a primary election, in a broad sense, accurately reflect the voting of the party members."[317] The Court said the system helped parties' electioneering and party-building efforts "by retaining the importance of party affiliation" and the state had an interest in preventing "party raiding, or 'the organized switching of blocs of voters from one party to another to manipulate the outcome of the other party's primary election.'"

In a plurality opinion written by Chief Justice John G. Roberts, the U.S. Supreme Court in 2007 appeared to strike down the section of the Bipartisan Campaign Reform Act of 2002 that banned corporations and unions from broadcasting ads that refer to a candidate for federal office within 30 days of a federal primary election or 60 days of a federal general election. In *Federal Election Commission v. Wisconsin Right to Life* (2007),[318] the Court said the decision was applicable only to the specific campaign involved, but noted that the section was subject to strict scrutiny. The Federal Election Commission had held that the ad at issue was a thinly veiled attack on Wisconsin Senator Russ Feingold (a co-sponsor of the BCRA), but the Court's plurality opinion said the ad was more like a "genuine issue ad." Viewed from a political context, as important as ever was the U.S. Supreme Court's overruling of two important precedents concerning First Amendment rights of corporations.

In a 5–4 decision three years later, the Court determined in *Citizens United v. Federal Election Commission* (2010) that the government had no business regulating political speech in the form of political spending by corporations in elections. While the decision was considered a boon to political advertising, President Barack Obama termed it "a major victory for big oil,

Wall Street banks, health insurance companies and the other powerful interests that marshal their power every day in Washington to drown out the voices of everyday Americans."[319]

Nontraditional Speech Contexts

The courts, including the U.S. Supreme Court, have also looked at speech in contexts outside the traditional protest and political arenas. For example, in *Lebron v. National Railroad Passenger Corporation* (1995),[320] the U.S. Supreme Court focused on a simple but significant question: Is Amtrak (the National Railroad Passenger Corporation) a government corporation for purposes of the First Amendment? In an 8 to 1 opinion written by Justice Scalia (with only Justice O'Connor dissenting), the Court said "yes." Michael Lebron, who creates controversial billboard displays, signed a contract to display a lighted billboard 103 feet long and 10 feet high in Amtrak's Pennsylvania Station in New York City, subject to content approval by Amtrak. When the corporation learned Lebron's display was a satirical takeoff of a Coors Beer ad, it backed out. Captioned "Is It the Right Beer Now?" (a play on Coors' "Right Beer" campaign), the display showed Coors drinkers juxtaposed with Nicaraguan villagers toward whom a can of Coors was aimed like a missile. The text criticized the Coors family for backing right-wing causes such as the Nicaraguan contras.

Lebron sued Amtrak, claiming it had violated his First and 5th Amendment rights. A U.S. District Court granted his request for an injunction and ordered Amtrak to display his billboard. The trial court held that Amtrak was a government corporation for purposes of the First Amendment. On appeal by the railroad company, the U.S. Court of Appeals for the 2nd Circuit reversed on the basis that Amtrak was not created as a government corporation and thus its actions could not be considered state actions.

Although Lebron did not specifically argue in his original suit in trial court that Amtrak was a government entity for purposes of the First Amendment, the Supreme Court said he could still make such an argument at the appellate level, which he had done. The Court traced the history of Amtrak and other agencies created by Congress and concluded:

> We hold that where, as here, the Government creates a corporation by special law, for the furtherance of governmental objectives, and retains for itself permanent authority to appoint a majority of the directors of that corporation, the corporation is part of the Government for purposes of the First Amendment.[321]

The Court did not determine whether Lebron's First Amendment rights had been violated, but left that judgment to the lower court.

Lebron is an important First Amendment victory because it clarifies that when government-created entities are established to fulfill governmental objectives and are effectively controlled by the government, it does not matter, for purposes of the First Amendment, what the enabling statute says about an agency's status. In colloquial terms, if it walks like a duck and quacks like a duck, it is a duck for purposes of the First Amendment. *For purposes of the First Amendment* is a crucial limitation of this precedent, which does not affect the status of such an agency for other purposes such as its independence in conducting certain business activities. Nevertheless, the Court's broad interpretation of *governmental agency* appears to encompass a wide range of entities.

In *United States v. National Treasury Employees Union* (1995),[322] the Court ruled that a provision of the Ethics Reform Act of 1989 was unconstitutional because the government failed to meet its heavy burden of proof that a ban on government employees accepting honoraria was justified. The majority opinion written by Justice Stevens (joined by Justices Kennedy, Souter, Ginsburg, and Breyer, with Justice O'Connor concurring in part and dissenting in part) struck down the provision that prohibited all members of Congress, government officers, and all other federal employees from accepting payments for any appearances, speeches, and articles even when such activities had no connection to their official duties.

The suit was brought by a union representing all executive branch workers below grade GS-16. The Court said that when a provision such as this one serves as "a wholesale deterrent to a broad category of expression by a massive number of potential speakers," the government must show that the interests of both the employees and their potential audiences is outweighed by the expression's "necessary impact on the actual operation" (quoting from an earlier decision by the Court) of the Government. The Court acknowledged that Congress' interest in curbing abuses of power of government employees who accept honoraria for their unofficial and non-political communication activities was "undeniably powerful." But, the Court said, the government had not demonstrated evidence of a problem with the group of employees represented by the union in its suit. The Court did reverse the portion of the lower court's decision that applied to senior federal employees. The Supreme Court said this interpretation was too inclusive—it confined the holding to the group of employees for whom the union filed suit.

National Treasury Employees Union is a fairly narrow holding, but it illustrates once again the Court's reluctance to approve governmental prior restraint, even if the purpose of the restriction may be noble, especially when the government fails to demonstrate substantial harm. Under the ruling, Congress is free to fashion a provision friendly to the First Amendment—for example, one that would more effectively define the connection or "nexus" between government employment and the restricted speech. Justice Stevens noted that at least two of our great American literary figures, Herman Melville and Nathaniel Hawthorne, were government employees who wrote when they were not at work. The defectors in this case were Justices Kennedy and O'Connor (with her partial concurrence in the judgment). The conservative at the time—Chief Justice Rehnquist and Justices Thomas and Scalia—dissented.

United States v. National Treasury Employees Union and *Waters v. Churchill,* discussed earlier, were both cited several times in a decision handed down by the Court in 1996 that decided the extent to which the First Amendment protects independent contractors from firing under termination-at-will contracts for exercising their free speech rights. In *Board of County Commissioners, Wabaunsee County, Kansas v. Umbehr* (1996),[323] the Court held that the First Amendment provides such protection and the appropriate test for determining the extent of the protection is a balancing test, known as the *Pickering* test, adjusted to consider the government's interests as contractor rather than employer.

The case involved Keen A. Umbehr, a man who had been hired as an independent contractor to haul trash for a county government. His contract was not renewed after six years of service during which he openly criticized the local board of county commissioners at board meetings and in letters and editorials in local newspapers. His targets of criticism included landfill user rates, alleged violations of the state's Open Meetings Act, and alleged mismanagement of taxpayers' funds. Umbehr sued the two members of the three-member board who voted against renewal of the contract, claiming that their action was in retaliation for his outspokenness.

In an opinion written by Justice O'Connor and joined at least in part by all the other justices except Justices Thomas and Scalia, the Court said the appropriate test is a modified version of one first enunciated by the Court in 1968 in *Pickering v. Board of Education, Township High School District 205, Will County*.[324] In order for the plaintiff to win in this case, according to the Court, he must first show that his contract was terminated because he spoke out on a matter of public concern, not simply that the criticism occurred before he was fired. In its defense, the board could prove, however, by preponderance of the evidence that the members would have terminated the contract regardless of his speech.

The majority opinion made it clear that the holding in this case was narrow but did acknowledge that, subject to limitations outlined in the decision, "we recognize the right of independent government contractors not to be terminated for exercising their First Amendment rights."[325] Thus the decision effectively expands the conditions under which First Amendment rights against governmental prior restraint apply.

In 1996, the Supreme Court dealt with a similar situation in *O'Hare Truck Service, Inc. et al. v. City of Northlake et al.*[326] A towing company owner sued the local government after his company was taken off the list of businesses approved to provide towing services for the city. The owner claimed the removal was in retaliation for his failure to contribute to the mayor's reelection campaign and support for the mayor's opponent. The 7 to 2 decision, written by Justice Kennedy, held that government officials may not fire public employees, including a contractor or someone who regularly provides services, for exercising their "rights of political association or the expression of political allegiance." The Court did indicate, however, that the person or company could still be terminated if the government "can demonstrate that party affiliation is an appropriate requirement for the effective performance of the public office involved" (citing an earlier Court decision).

Five years later in *Borough of Duryea, Pennsylvania, et al. v. Guarnieri* (2011)[327] the U.S. Supreme Court, in a 5–4 opinion written by Justice Kennedy, held that when a government agency (in this case a borough in Pennsylvania) allegedly retaliates against an employee, it cannot be held liable for violating the employee's First Amendment rights under the Petition Clause (" … and to petition the Government for a redress of grievances") unless the petition addresses a matter of public concern. In so ruling, the Court affirmed what every other federal circuit had decided that had weighed in on this issue, except the Third Circuit, from which this case had been appealed. The employee in this case was a police chief who had been issued directives on how to perform his duties after he had been fired, filed a union grievance and then been reinstated. The Court's stated rationale was that petitions concerning private matters can interfere with the efficient and effective operation of government. The Court noted that it had previously applied this "public concerns" test in earlier cases involving government employees under the Speech Clause and saw no reason to set a different standard for the Petition Clause.

Prior Restraint: Post 9/11

The terrorist attacks of September 11, 2001, and the wars that followed in Afghanistan and Iraq continue to have adverse impacts on freedom of the press and freedom of speech in the United States. Much of the impact has appeared in the form of self-censorship, often under pressure.[317] A month after the 9/11 attacks, the Bush administration—primarily the then-National Security Advisor Dr. Condoleezza Rice (who later became Secretary of State)—successfully pushed the major U.S. television networks to carefully review video messages from Osama bin Laden before airing them to make sure national security was not at risk.[328]

Seven TV stations were asked not to carry an April 30, 2004, ABC-TV Nightline program in which the host recited names of more 700 U.S. service men and women who died in initial conflict in Iraq.[329] Among critics of that action was Republican Senator John McCain of Arizona, who had been a prisoner of war in Vietnam.[320] One New Mexico teacher was suspended by his school after some of the students in his ninth grade made posters protesting that war. He refused to remove them.[330]

Public support for the First Amendment often appears to be in decline. National polls often find that about half of the American public feel some form of prior restraint should be imposed on media coverage of certain grizzly events such as the Abu Ghraib prisoner abuse scandal in Iraq that eventually led to conviction and punishment of U.S. soldiers.[331] According to Charles Lewis, a former CBS News producer and head of the Center for Public Integrity, "This ambivalence, in which at least half the country equates draconian security and secrecy measures with its own safety, is quite serious and very possibly insurmountable."[332]

Some of the censorship appears in private quarters, which does not meet the legal definition of prior restraint, so is permissible. For example, the world's largest retailer, Wal-Mart, banned content over the years including magazines such as Maxim, Stuff, and FHM[333]and an infamous anti-Semitic book (considered fake) that it sold online until it received complaints from Jewish groups.[334]

The Internet continues to add new wrinkles to the prior restraint picture as illustrated by the publication of false information attributed to political figures including a series of stories involving political commentator and former vice presidential candidate, Sarah Palin's comments, which were totally fabricated.

Conclusions

Even in the aftermath of WikiLeaks disclosures, with the 9/11 attacks still in the memory of many Americans, attempts to justify prior restraint remain substantial. With public support declining for the First Amendment, which is not unusual—particularly during wartime, freedom of the press and freedom of speech can be expected to continue to come under fire as local, state, and federal government agencies challenge the public dissemination of information, especially criticism and exposure of corruption and wrongdoing, on national security and safety grounds. Freedom of speech, especially political communication, continues to enjoy more protection under the First Amendment than freedom of the press.

The broad view is that some erosion of such rights has occurred in recent decades as illustrated in *Virginia v. Hicks*, *Thomas v. Chicago Park District*, and *McConnell v. Federal Election Commission*. In context, the U.S. Supreme Court and other courts have been broadening First Amendment rights, as demonstrated in the 7th Circuit's decision in *Hosty v. Carter* and the 6th Circuit's ruling in *Kinkaid v. Gibson*, expanding college press rights.

We still lack definitive answers to certain simple questions: What is symbolic speech? What is "government" for purposes of prior restraint? What is prior restraint? Why is wearing a black armband in a public school protected speech, when burning a draft card is not symbolic speech and therefore can be punished? Why is burning an American flag or protesting at a military funeral considered protected expression while the publication of information obtained from publicly available sources (as in the *Progressive* case) is apparently not covered?

Some trends are discernible. Student journalists, especially in elementary and secondary public schools, appear to have the least protection of all against prior restraint, although the emergence of blogs and bloggers has opened another area for consideration.

Hazelwood made it clear many years ago that the high school press is perceived by the U.S. Supreme Court as essentially a training ground for budding journalists, not an opportunity for them to exercise First Amendment rights. *Morison* and similar cases such as *Snepp* illustrate how easily the government can justify prior restraint including criminal prosecution in certain contexts such as national security matters even though disclosure of such information probably would have limited, if any, impact on national security. Finally, speech within a public forum and individual public speech generally have the strongest protection of all against governmental censorship as *City of Ladue v. Gilleo, Skokie, Lebron v. National Railroad Passenger Corporation, Texas v. Johnson, U.S. v. Eichman*, and *Tinker* demonstrate, but even this principle must be tempered by the Court's stand in *Rust v. Sullivan* that the government can selectively censor information about activities it does not wish to promote when it has subsidized another activity.

As *Rumsfeld v. Forum for Academic and Institutional Rights* indicates, there is no First Amendment violation when the federal government requires universities and presumably other institutions that receive federal funding to provide equal access to military recruiters even when such access violates the schools' antidiscrimination policies.

The Court also appears to be broadening the protection for public protesters, although still specifying limits under the First Amendment, as illustrated in *Madsen v. Women's Health Center, Schenck v. Pro Choice Network, Scheidler I, Scheidler II,* and *Scheidler III*. However, the U.S. Supreme Court has had no problem drawing some demarcations for First Amendment protection including "floating buffer zone" versus "fixed buffer zone" in abortion protests and "contributions" versus "expenditures" in political campaigns. More recent cases involving protests at military funerals have raised the specter of the need for lines of demarcation.

Even U.S. Supreme Court justices sometimes face personal encounters with the First Amendment, as Justice Antonin Scalia can attest. He once faced criticism in the media after an incident in which a federal marshal assigned to protect him ordered reporters to erase audio recordings of a speech he made to students about the importance of the U.S. Constitution. Scalia had a policy at that time, of which the journalists were unaware, prohibiting electronic recording of his public speeches. He later changed the policy.

Endnotes

1. W. Blackstone, *Commentaries on the Laws of England* (1820), 151.
2. *Julian Assange: The Man behind WikiLeaks*, CBS News' 60 Minutes, Steve Kroft, Correspondent, January 30, 2011.
3. *Id.*
4. *Los Angeles Times Communications, LLC v. Superior Court of Los Angeles County*, 2010 WL 3260056 (Cal Ct. App. Aug 19, 2010). See also Tim Rutten, *Judicial Myopia in L.A.,* Los Angeles Times, August 7, 2010, at A-23. Another recent case barred the *National Law Journal* from publishing content of court records released while intended "sealed." See *POM Wonderful, LLC v. ALM Media Properties, LLC*, No. 2010-CAB-005533 (D.C. Super Ct. 2010).

5. Dave Itzkoff, *Re-evaluation Ordered in 'Rye' Sequel Ruling*, New York Times, May 1, 2010, at C-2. And see also, Thomas Mitchell, *Upholding the State Prior Restraint*, Las Vegas Review-Journal, June 6, 2010, at D-2.

6. *James et al. v. Meow Media, Inc. et al.*, 300 F.3d 683, 30 Med.L.Rptr. 2185 (6th Cir. 2002).

7. *Id.*

8. *James et al. v. Meow Media, Inc. et al.*, cert. denied, 537 U.S. 1159, 123 S.Ct. 967, 154 L.Ed.2d 893, (2003).

9. *See* Sumana Chatterjee, *TV Networks Agree to Review bin Laden Tapes before Airing*, Lexington (Ky.) Herald-Leader, Oct. 11, 2001, at A5. For an update, including discussion of the prospect of fraudulent tapes, Richard Engel, *Bin Laden Issues New Threat*, MSNBC, March 25, 2010, available at http:// http:// www.msnbc.msn.com, Scott Shane, *Bin Laden Resurfaces in Recording*, New York Times, October 2, 2010, at A-6.

10. *See* Mark Washburn, *Audience Cheers Chicks on First Return Gig in U.S.*, Lexington (Ky.) Herald-Leader), May 2, 2003, at A2.

11. Simon Stack, 57 J. Epidemiol. Commun Health (April 2003), at 238.

12. *Planned Parenthood of Columbia/Willamette Inc. v. American Coalition of Life Activists*, 290 F.3d 1058 (9th Cir. 2002). *See* also Stephanie Francis Cahill, *Threatening Posters Banned*, ABA J. eReport (May 24, 2002). And regarding the shooting at Virginia Tech, see: Ben Grossman, *The Impact of Virginia Tech on the News*, Broadcasting & Cable, April 23, 2007, and *Tyndall Report: The History of Saturation Coverage*, Broadcasting & Cable, April 23, 2007, and also, Thomas Mitchell, *Upholding the State Prior Restraint*, Las Vegas Review-Journal, June 6, 2010, at D-2.

13. *Eimann v. Soldier of Fortune Magazine Inc.*, 880 F.2d 830 (5th Cir.), 16 Med.L.Rptr. 2148 (1989), cert. denied, 493 U.S. 1024, 110 S.Ct. 729, 107 L.Ed.2d 748 (1990).

14. *Id.*

15. *Braun v. Soldier of Fortune Magazine Inc.*, 757 F.Supp. 1325, 18 Med.L.Rptr. 1732 (M.D. Ala. 1991).

16. *Id.*, 968 F.2d 1110, 20 Med.L.Rptr. 1777 (11th Cir. 1992), cert. denied, 506 U.S. 1071, 113 S.Ct. 1028, 122 L.Ed.2d 173 (1993).

17. *Black's Law Dictionary*, 5th ed. (1979), 288.

18. *Congress Passes Bill To Allow Mother, Child Back into U.S.*, Lexington (Ky.) Herald-Leader, Sept. 19, 1996, at A4. For the Court's more recent view regarding impending issues of representation, see also, Adam Liptak, *Court to Weigh Legal Aid in Contempt Case*, New York Times, November 1, 2010, at A-22.

19. *Sanders v. Shepard*, 258 Ill.App.3d 626 (1994). *See* Sharon Cohen and Sarah Nordgren, *Seven Years for Keeping Mum*, 80 A.B.A. J. (Feb. 1995), at 16.

20. Cindy Richards, *A Mother's Long Nightmare Comes to an End in Tragedy* (editorial), Chicago Sun-Times, Jan. 30, 1998, at 33.

21. David D. Kirkpatrick, *Book Contract for Writer Jailed for Contempt*, New York Times, Apr. 30, 2002, at A26.

22. Jesse McKinley, *8-Month Jail Term Ends as Maker of Video Turns Over Copy*, New York Times, April 4, 2007, at A9.

23. *Farr v. Superior Court of Los Angeles County*, 22 Cal.App.3d 60, 99 Cal.Rptr. 342, 1 Med. L.Rptr. 2545 (1971).

24. 22 Cal.App.3d. 60 (1971).

25. Cert. denied, 409 U.S. 1011, 93 S.Ct. 430, 34 L.Ed.2d 305 (1972).

26. California Constitution, §2, subd. (b). Farr's troubles did not end with the California Court of Appeals decision. Two of the six lawyers Farr named when he refused to identify specific sources sued him for libel but were unsuccessful because they failed to file suit within California's five-year statute of limitations.

27. G. Gunther, *Constitutional Law*, 5th ed., Foundation Press, Stamford, CT (1980), 384.

28. *Nebraska Press Association v. Judge Stuart*, 427 U.S. 539, 96 S.Ct. 2791, 49 L.Ed.2d 683, 1 Med.L.Rptr. 1064 (1976).

29. Rachel Smolkin, *A Source of Encouragement*, Am. Journal. Rev., Aug.–Sept. 2005, at 30.

30. *Id.*

31. *United States v. Dickinson*, 465 F.2d 496 (5th Cir. 1972), cert. denied, 414 U.S. 979, 94 S.Ct. 270, 38 L.Ed.2d 223 (1973).
32. *Id.*
33. *Id.*
34. *United States v. Dickinson*, cert. denied, 414 U.S. 979, 94 S.Ct. 270, 38 L.Ed.2d 223 (1973).
35. 18 U.S.C.A. §401.
36. *Jail Birds*, Am. Journal. Rev. Aug.–Sept. 2005, at 18. The report is based on information from the Reporters Committee for Freedom of the Press.
37. *Bridges v. California*, 314 U.S. 252, 625 S.Ct. 190. 86 L.Ed. 192 (1941).
38. *Id.*
39. *Pennekamp v. Florida*, 328 U.S. 331, 66 S.Ct. 1029, 90 L.Ed.2d 1295 (1946).
40. *Craig v. Harney*, 331 U.S. 367, 67 S.Ct. 1249, 91 L.Ed. 1546 (1947).
41. *Id.*
42. *Wood v. Georgia*, 370 U.S. 375, 82 S.Ct. 1364, 8 L.Ed.2d 568 (1962).
43. *Id.*
44. *Id.*
45. *Id.*
46. *Near v. Minnesota*
47. F. Friendly, *Minnesota Rag,* Random House (1981).
48. *See* note 1 of Associate Justice Pierce Butler's dissent.
49. *See* Friendly and Elliott, *supra*, for a telling account of circumstances surrounding the decision.
50. *Id.* at 46.
51. *Near v. Minnesota*, 283 U.S. 697, 51 S.Ct. 625, 75 L.Ed.2d 1357, 1 Med.L.Rptr. 1001 (1931).
52. *Id.*
53. *Id.*
54. *Id.*
55. The Fourteenth Amendment also states, "No State shall make or enforce any law which shall abridge the privileges or immunities of citizens of the United States [known as the privileges and immunities clause]; nor shall any State deprive any person of life, liberty, or property, without due process of law [due process clause]; nor deny to any person within its jurisdiction the equal protection of the laws" [equal protection clause]; §5 grants Congress the authority to enforce the amendment.
56. *New York Times Co. v. U.S.* and *U.S. v. The Washington Post Co.*, 403 U.S. 713, 91 S.Ct. 2140, 29 L.Ed.2d 822, 1 Med.L.Rptr. 1031 (1971).
57. *New York Times v. Sullivan*, 376 U.S. 254, 84 S.Ct. 110, 11 L.Ed.2d 686, 1 Med.L.Rptr. 1527 (1964).
58. *Near v. Minnesota.*
59. *Id.*
60. *Id.*
61. *Id.*
62. *See* Friendly and Elliott, *supra*, at 49.
63. Robert S. McNamara, *In Retrospect: The Tragedy and Lessons of Vietnam,* New York: Random House (1995), at 281.
64. S. Ungar, *The Papers and the Papers*, (New York: E.P. Dutton, 1989), at 69. This is a highly informative account of the legal and political battles in the Pentagon Papers case.
65. *Id.* at 65.
66. *Id.* at 83.
67. *Id.* at 95
68. *New York Times Co. v. United States* and *United States v. The Washington Post.*
69. *Bantam Books, Inc. v. Sullivan*, 372 U.S. 58, 83 S.Ct. 631, 9 L.Ed.2d 584, 1 Med.L.Rptr. 1116 (1963).
70. *Organization for a Better Austin v. Keefe*, 402 U.S. 415, 91 S.Ct. 1575, 29 L.Ed.2d. 1, Med. L.Rptr. 1021 (1971).
71. *New York Times Co. v. United States* and *United States v. The Washington Post.*
72. *Id.*
73. *Id.*

74. *Id.*

75. *Id.*

76. *Id.*

77. *Id.*

78. *Id.*

79. *See* chapter 3 in S. Ungar, supra, for an insightful account of Gravel's efforts including a filibuster that was cut short after he began crying while he was trying to read "a section of the Papers describing the severing of arms and legs in battle" (p. 262).

80. 18 U.S.C. §641.

81. For example, he told an audience at Eastern Kentucky University in 2004, "Vietnam would have been avoided if the truth had been told. The biggest lie of this year is that the war against Iraq is connected to the war against terror." See Adam Baker, *Against the Grain: Whistle-Blower Sees Similarities in Iraq, Vietnam,* The Eastern Progress (Eastern Kentucky University), Apr. 1, 2004, at A10.

82. Ungar, *supra,* at 301.

83. *The World Almanac and Book of Facts* (1989), at 209.

84. *Bartnicki v. Vopper,* 532 U.S. 514, 121 S.Ct. 1753, 149 L.Ed.2d 787 (2001).

85. 18 U.S. C. §2511(1)(a).

86. Ungar, *supra,* at 306.

87. 42 U.S.C. §2011 et seq.

88. *Id.* at §2014 (y).

89. *Id.* at §2280.

90. *U.S. v. The Progressive, Inc.* 467 F.Supp. 990 (W.D. Wisc. 1979), appeal dismissed as moot, 610 F.2d 819 (7th Cir. 1979).

91. *Id.*

92. *Id.*

93. *Id.*

94. The *Wisconsin State Journal* and the *Capital-Times.*

95. *Nebraska Press Association v. Judge Hugh Stuart,* 427 U.S. 539, 96 S.Ct. 2791, 49 L.Ed.2d 683, 1 Med.L.Rptr. 1059 (1970).

96. *Id.*

97. *Id.*

98. *Id.*

99. *Id.*

100. *Id.*

101. *Sheppard v. Maxwell,* 384 U.S. 333, 86 S.Ct. 1507, 16 L.Ed.2d 600, 1 Med.L.Rptr. 1220 (1966).

102. *Nebraska Press Association v. Judge Stuart,* supra.

103. *United States v. Noriega,* 752 F.Supp. 1045 (S.D. Fl. 1990).

104. *In re Cable News Network, Inc.,* 917 F.2d 1543 (11th Cir. 1990).

105. *In re Cable News Network, Inc.,* cert. denied, 498 U.S. 976, 111 S.Ct. 451, 112 L.Ed.2d 432, 18 Med.L.Rptr. 1359 (1990).

106. *United States v. Noriega.*

107. Associated Press v. District Court for the Fifth Judicial District of Colorado, 542 U.S. 1301, 125 S.Ct. 159 L.Ed.2d 800 (2004) (stay denied).

108. *The People of the State of Colorado v. Kobe Bean Bryant,* 94 P.3d 624, 32 Med.L.Rptr. 1961 (Colo. 2004).

109. George W. Pring and Penelope Canan, *SLAPPs: Getting Sued for Speaking Out,* Philadelphia: Temple University Press (1996).

110. *Id.*

111. http://www.casp.net/into.html.

112. Margaret Graham Tebo, *Offended by a SLAPP,* 91 A.B.J. (Feb. 2005), at 16.

113. *Id.*

114. *Id.* at 32.

115. *See* Alexander D. Lowe, *The Price of Speaking Out,* 82 A.B.J. (Sept. 1996), at 48.

116. *Id.*

117. *Jay Fox v. State of Washington*, 236 U.S. 273, 35 S.Ct. 383, 59 L.Ed. 573 (1915).
118. *Schenck v. United States* and *Baer v. United States*, 249 U.S. 47, 39 S.Ct. 247, 63 L.Ed. 470 (1919).
119. *Id.*
120. *Id.*
121. *Id.*
122. *Jacob Abrams v. United States*, 250 U.S. 616, 40 S.Ct. 17, 63 L.Ed. 1173 (1919).
123. *Id.* (Holmes dissent).
124. *Id.* (majority opinion).
125. *Id.* (Holmes dissent).
126. *See*, for example, *Jacob Frohwerk v. United States*, 249 U.S. 204, 39 S.Ct. 249, 63 L.Ed. 561 (1919); *Eugene V. Debs v. United States*, 249 U.S. 211, 39 S.Ct. 252, 63 L.Ed. 566 (1919); *Peter* Schafer v. United States, 251 U.S. 466, 40 S.Ct. 259, 64 L.Ed. 360 (1920); and *Pearce v. United States*, 252 U.S. 239, 40 S.Ct. 205, 64 L.Ed.542 (1919).
127. *Benjamin Gitlow v. New York*, 268 U.S. 652, 45 S.Ct. 625, 69 L.Ed. 1138 (1925).
128. New York Penal Law §§160, 161 (as cited in *id.*).
129. Clause 1: "nor shall any State deprive any person of life, liberty or property, without due process of law. ..."
130. *Gitlow v. New York, supra.*
131. *Id.*
132. *Id.*
133. *See* F. Friendly and M. Elliott, *supra*, at 79.
133. *Whitney v. California*, 274 U.S. 357, 47 S.Ct. 641, 71 L.Ed. 1095 (1927).
135. *Id.*
136. *Id.*
137. *Id.*
138. *Id.*
139. *Clarence Brandenburg v. Ohio*, 395 U.S. 444, 89 S.Ct. 1827, 23 L.Ed.2d 430 (1969).
140. *Id.*
141. *Chaplinsky v. New Hampshire*, 315 U.S. 568, 62 S.Ct. 766, 86 L.Ed. 1031 (1942).
142. *Id.*
143. *Id.*
144. *Daniel Niemotko v. Maryland* and *Neil W. Kelly v. Maryland*, 340 U.S. 268, 71 S.Ct. 303, 95 L.Ed. 295 (1951).
145. *Irving Feiner v. New York*, 340 U.S. 315, 71 S.Ct. 303, 95 L.Ed. 295 (1951).
146. *Id.*
147. *Cox v. Louisiana* (Cox I), 379 U.S. 536, 85 S.Ct. 453, 13 L.Ed.2d 471 (1965).
148. *Cox v. Louisiana* (Cox II), 379 U.S. 559, 85 S.Ct. 476, 13 L.Ed.2d 487 (1965).
149. *Dennis v. United States*, 341 U.S. 494, 71 S.Ct. 857, 95 L.Ed. 1137 (1951).
150. *Id.*
151. *Id.*
152. *Nationalist Socialist Party v. Village of Skokie*, 432 U.S. 43, 97 S.Ct. 2205, 53 L.Ed.2d 96 (1977). *See* F. Friendly and M. Elliott, *supra*, at 81. Chapter 5 gives a detailed and colorful account of the Skokie case.
153. *Nationalist Socialist Party v. Village of Skokie.*
154. 366 N.E.2d 347 (1977).
155. 373 N.E.2d 21 (1978).
156. *United States v. Snepp*, 456 F.Supp. 176 (E.D. V. 1978).
157. *Snepp v. United States*, 595 F.2d 926 (4th Cir. 1979).
158. *Frank W. Snepp v. United States* and *United States v. Frank W. Snepp*, 444 U.S. 507, 100 S.Ct. 763, 62 L.Ed.2d 704 (1980).
159. *Id.*
160. *United States v. O'Brien*, 391 U.S. 367, 88 S.Ct. 1673, 20 L.Ed.2d 672 (1968).
161. 50 U.S.C. §462(b)(3) of the Universal Military Training and Service Act of 1948 and §12(b)(3) of the amendment.

162. *United States v. O'Brien.*

163. *Id.*

164. *Street v. New York*, 394 U.S. 576, 89 S.Ct. 1354, 22 L.Ed.2d 572 (1969).

165. *Spence v. Washington*, 418 U.S. 405, 94 S.Ct. 2727, 41 L.Ed.2d 842 (1974).

166. *Id.*

167. *Id.*

168. *Texas v. Johnson*, 491 U.S. 397, 109 S.Ct. 2533, 105 L.Ed.2d 342 (1989).

160. Epstein, *High Court Upholds Right to Burn Flag*, Lexington (Ky.) Herald-Leader, June 22, 1989, at A1.

170. *Texas v. Johnson.*

171. *Id.*

172. Media Access Project's Andy Schwartzman, quoted in *And the First Shall Be First*, Broadcasting (July 3, 1989), at 25.

173. *Texas v. Johnson.*

174. George F. Will, *The Justices Are Wrong—But Keep Off the Constitution*, syndicated column published in Lexington (Ky.) Herald-Leader, July 2, 1989, at F7.

175. James J. Kilpatrick, *First Amendment: It Ain't Broke, So Don't Fix It*, syndicated column published in Lexington (Ky.) Herald-Leader, June 29, 1989, at A19.

176. *United States v. Eichman et al.* and *United States v. Haggerty et al.*, 496 U.S. 310, 110 S.Ct. 2404, 110 L.Ed.2d 287 (1990).

177. 103 Stat. §777, 18 U.S.C. §700 (Suppl. 1990).

178. *Id.*

179. *Id.*

180. *R.A.V. v. City of St. Paul*, 505 U.S. 377, 112 S.Ct. 2538, 120 L.Ed.2d 305 (1992).

181. St. Paul, Minn. Legis. Code §292.02 (1990).

182. *Chaplinsky v. New Hampshire*, 315 U.S. 568, 62 S.Ct. 766, 86 L.Ed. 1031 (1942).

183. *In re Welfare of R.A.V.*, 464 N.W.2d 507 (Minn. 1991).

184. *R.A.V. v. City of St. Paul.*

185. *Id.*

186. *Virginia v. Black*, 538 U.S. 343, 123 S.Ct. 1536, 155 L.Ed.2d 535 (2003).

187. *Id.*

188. *Id.*

189. *Id.*

190. *Id.*

191. *Id.* (Thomas dissent).

192. *Id.* (note 2).

193. *Tinker v. Des Moines Independent Community School District*, 393 U.S. 503, 89 S.Ct. 733, 21 L.Ed.2d 731 (1969).

194. *Id.*

195. *Id.*

196. *Id.*

197. *Hazelwood School District v. Kuhlmeier*, 484 U.S. 260, 108 S.Ct. 562, 98 L.Ed.2d 592, 14 Med.L.Rptr. 2081 (1988).

198. *October 13: The Student Press's Turn*, 3 Student. Press L. Ctr. Rep. (Winter 1987–1988), at 3.

199. *Id.*

200. *Kuhlmeier v. Hazelwood School District*, 795 F.2d 1368 (8th Cir. 1986).

201. *Hazelwood School District v. Kuhlmeier.*

202. *Tinker v. Des Moines School District.*

203. *Hazelwood School District v. Kuhlmeier.*

204. *Id.*

205. *Id.*

206. *See* Hazelwood: *A Complete Guide to the Supreme Court Decision*, 9 Student Press L. Ctr. Rep. (Spring 1988), at 3 for a detailed analysis of the decision including Model Guidelines for Student Publications.

207. *P. Parsons, Student Press Censorship Reborn within Hours of Hazelwood Ruling*, 15 Media L. Notes (Winter 1988), at 12.
208. Anderson, 11 Presstime (Feb. 1989), at 6.
209. Johnson, Louisville (Ky.) Courier-Journal, Nov. 13, 1988.
210. *Dickson, Attitudes of High School Principals about Press Freedom after Hazelwood*, 66 Journal. Q. (1989), at 169.
211. *Censorship and Selection: Issues and Answers for Schools* [summary], 76 Quill (Oct. 1988), at 49.
212. *Only the News That's Fit to Print: Student Expressive Rights in Public School Communications Media after Hazelwood v. Kuhlmeier* [note], 11 Hastings Comm. Ent. L.J. 35 (1988).
213. *Id.* at 74.
214. Cal. Educ. code §48907 (West Suppl. 1987).
215. Mass. Gen. L., Chap. 71, §§82, 86 (Suppl. 1988).
216. *Iowa Expression Law Loosens Hazelwood's Grasp*, 10 Student Press L. Ctr. (Fall 1989), at 3.
217. *Id.* at 4.
218. *Hazelwood v. Kuhlmeier*, note 7.
219. *Muller v. Jefferson Lighthouse School*, 604 F. Supp. 655 (7th Cir. 1996); cert. denied, 117 S.Ct. 1335, 137 L.Ed.2d 495 (1997).
220. *Kinkaid v. Gibson*, 236 F.3d 342, 29 Med.L.Rptr. 1193 (6th Cir. 2001).
221. *Hosty v. Carter*, 412 F.3d 731, 33 Med.L.Rptr. 1897 (7th Cir. 2005).
222. *Hosty v. Carter*, 325 F.3d 945, 31 Med.L.Rptr. 1577 (7th Cir. 2003).
223. *See* Gina Holland, *Court Won't Hear Campus Newspaper Appeal*, Seattle Post-Intelligencer, Feb. 21, 2006, online edition.
224. *Hosty v. Carter*, cert. denied, 546 U.S. 169, 126 S.Ct. 1330, 164 L.Ed.2d 47 (2006). *Also see* Sara Lipka, *Stopping the Presses*, Chron. Higher Educ. Mar. 3, 2006, at A35.
225. *See* John K. Wilson, *A Threat to Freedom*, insidehighered.com., Feb. 23, 2006, online edition.
226. *Deborah Morse v. Joseph Frederick*, 127 S.Ct. 2618, 168 L.Ed. 2d 290 (2007).
227. *United States v. Morison*, 604 F. Supp. 655 (Md. 1985).
228. *See* C. Crystal, *Media Fight Man's Sentence in Navy 'Leaks' Case, 1987–1988*, Sigma Delta Chi Freedom of Info. Rep., at 24. D.M. Brenner, Sigma Delta Chi Freedom of Info. Rep. 1988–1989, at 20.
229. 8 U.S.C. §641, 793 (1953).
230. 844 F.2d 1057, 15 Med.L.Rptr. 1369 (4th Cir. 1988).
231. *Morison v. United States*, cert. denied, 488 U.S. 908, 109 S.Ct. 259, 102 L.Ed.2d 247 (1988).
232. *Simon & Schuster, Inc. v. Members of the New York State Crime Victims Board*, 502 U.S. 105, 112 S.Ct. 501, 116 L.Ed.2d 476, 19 Med.L.Rpt. 1609 (1991).
233. *Id.*
234. *See* David Kravets, *Cashing in on Crimes*, A.B.A. J. eReport (Mar. 1, 2002).
235. *Id.*
236. *Keenan v. Superior Court*, 27 Cal. 4th 413, 40 P.3d 718, 30 Med.L.Rptr. 1385 (Cal. 2002).
237. Nev. Rev. Stat. §217.007.
238. *Seres v. Lerner*, 102 P.3d 91, 33 Med.L.Rptr. 1139 (2004).
239. *Cohen v. California*, 403 U.S. 15, 91 S.Ct. 1780, 29 L.Ed.2d 284 (1971).
240. *Id.*
241. *Id.*
242. *Id.*
243. *Id.*
244. *Id.*
245. *National Organization for Women v. Scheidler (Scheidler I)*, 510 U.S. 249, 114 S.Ct.798, 127 L.Ed.2d 99 (1994).
246. *Id.*
247. *Scheidler v. National Organization for Women (Scheidler II)*, 537 U.S. 393, 123 S.Ct. 1057, 154 L.Ed.2d 991 (2003).
248. Such injunctions are permitted under 18 U.S.C. §1964 of the Racketeer Influenced and Corrupt Organizations Act.

249. *See* 18 U.S.C. §1951(b)(2).

250. *Scheidler II.*

251. *Scheidler v. NOW (Scheidler III)*, 547 U.S. 9, 126 S.Ct. 1264, 164 L.Ed.2d 10 (2006).

252. *Madsen v. Women's Health Center*, 512 U.S. 753, 114 S.Ct. 2516, 129 L.Ed.2d 593 (1994).

253. *Operation Rescue v. Women's Health Center*, 626 So.2d 664 (Fl. 1993).

254. *Cheffer v. McGregor*, 41 F.3d 1422 (11th Cir. 1994).

255. *Madsen v. Women's Health Center.*

256. *Id.*

257. *Id.*

258. *Schenck et al. v. Pro Choice Network of Western New York et al.*, 519 U.S. 357, 117 S.Ct. 855, 137 L.Ed.2d 1 (1997).

259. *Id.*

260. *Id.*

261. *Lelia Hill v. Colorado*, 530 U.S. 703, 120 S.Ct. 2480, 147 L.Ed.2d 597 (2000).

262. *Snyder v. Phelps et al.*, 562 U.S. ___, 131 S.Ct. 1207, 179 L.Ed.2d 172, 34 Med.L.Rptr. 1353 (2011).

263. *Id.*

264. *Id.* Alito dissenting.

265. *Brown, Governor of California, et al. v. Entertainment Merchants Association et al.*, 564 U.S. ___ (2011).

266. *Id.* (citing Calif. statute).

267. *Id.* Roberts concurring.

268. *Id.* (majority opinion).

269. *United States v. Stevens*, 563 U.S. ___, 130 S.Ct. 1577, 176 L.Ed.2d 435 (2010).

270. *Id.*

271. *Sorrell, Attorney general of Vermont, et al. v. IMS Health Inc. et al.*, 564 U.S. ___ (2011).

272. *Id.*

273. *Id.*

274. *City of Ladue v. Gilleo*, 510 U.S. 1037, 114 S.Ct. 677, 126 L.Ed.2d 645 (1994).

275. *Id.*

276. *Id.*

277. *Id.*

278. Motoko Rich, *Homeowner Boards Blur Line of Who Rules Roost*, New York Times, July 27, 2003 (electronic version).

279. *Waters v. Churchill*, 511 U.S. 661, 114 S.Ct. 1878, 128 L.Ed.2d 686 (1994).

280. *Connick v. Myers*, 461 U.S. 138, 103 S.Ct. 1684, 75 L.Ed.2d 708 (1983).

281. *Legal Services Corporation v. Velazquez*, 531 U.S. 533, 121 S.Ct. 1043, 149 L.Ed.2d 63 (2001).

282. *Id.*

283. *Rumsfeld v. Forum for Academic and Institutional Rights*, 547 U.S. 47, 126 S.Ct. 1297, 104 L.Ed.2d 156 (2006). See also: Tamar Lewin and Anemonia Hartocollis, *College Rethink ROTC After 'Don't Ask' Repeal*, New York Times, December 21, 2010, at A-10.

284. See Carl Hulse and Jeff Zeleny, *Court Nominee Figures in Midterm Campaigns*, New York Times, May 12, 2010, at A-10, and Jay Fitzgerald, *Sen. Brown Blasts Harvard's Faust for Continuing to Ban ROTC*, September 23, 2010, via Bostonherald.com.

285. *Id.*

286. *Virginia v. Hicks*, 539 U.S. 113, 123 S.Ct. 2191, 156 L.Ed.2d 148 (2003).

287. *Thomas v. Chicago Park District*, 534 U.S. 316, 122 S.Ct. 775, 151 L.Ed.2d 783 (2002).

288. *Hurley v. Irish-American Gay, Lesbian and Bisexual Group of Boston*, 515 U.S. 557, 115 S.Ct. 2388, 132 L.Ed.2d 487 (1995).

289. Mass. Gen. L. §272:98.

290. *Hurley*, citing trial court ruling.

291. *Bose Corp. v. Consumers Union of the U.S., Inc.*, 466 U.S. 485, 104 S.Ct. 1949, 80 L.Ed.2d 502, 10 Med.L.Rptr. 1625 (1984).

292. *Hurley.*

293. *Turner Broadcasting v. FCC*, 512 U.S. 622, 114 S.Ct. 2445, 129 L.Ed.2d 497 (1994).

294. *Hurley.*
295. *See* David G. Savage, *Court Says Parade Can Exclude Gays*, Lexington (Ky.) Herald-Leader, June 20, 1995, at A1.
296. *Boy Scouts of America v. Dale*, 530 U.S. 640, 120 S.Ct. 2446, 147 L.Ed.2d 554 (2000).
297. *United States v. O'Brien*, 391 U.S. 367, 88 S.Ct. 1673, 20 L.Ed.2d 672 (1968).
298. *Board of Regents, University of Wisconsin System v. Southworth*, 529 U.S. 217, 120 S.Ct. 1346, 146 L.Ed.2d 193 (2000).
299. *Id.*
300. *Rosenberger v. Rector and Visitors of the University of Virginia*, 515 U.S. 819, 115 S.Ct. 2510, 132 L.Ed.2d 700 1995).
301. *Lamb's Chapel v. Center Moriches Union Free School District*, 508 U.S. 384, 113 S.Ct. 2141, 124 L.Ed.2d 352 (1993).
302. *Good News Club v. Milford Central High School*, 533 U.S. 98, 121 S.Ct. 2093, 150 L.Ed.2d 151 (2001).
303. *McIntyre v. Ohio Elections Commission*, 514 U.S. 334, 115 S.Ct. 1511, 131 L.Ed.2d 426 (1995).
304. Ohio Code §3599.09 (A).
305. *McIntyre.*
306. *Id.*
307. *Colorado Republican Federal Campaign Committee et al. v. Federal Election Commission*, 518 U.S. 604,116 S.Ct. 2309, 135 L.Ed.2d 795 (1996), and more recently, Thomas Mitchell, *Upholding the State Prior Restraint*, Las Vegas Review-Journal, June 6, 2010, at D-2.
308. *Timmons et al. v. Twin Cities Area New Party*, 520 U.S. 351, 117 S.Ct. 1364, 137 L.Ed.2d 589 (1997).
309. *Nixon v. Shrink Missouri Government PAC*, 528 U.S. 377, 120 S.Ct. 897, 145 L.Ed.2d 886 (2000).
310. *Buckley v. Valeo*, 424 U.S. 1, 96 S.Ct. 612, 46 L.Ed.2d 659 (1976).
311. *Federal Election Commission v. Colorado Republican Federal Campaign Committee*, 533 U.S. 431, 121 S.Ct. 2351, 150 L.Ed.2d 461 (2001).
312. *Id.*
313. *Republican Party of Minnesota v. White*, 536 U.S. 765, 122 S.Ct. 2528, 153 L.Ed.2d 694 (2002). *See* also Terry Carter, *Limit on Judicial Speech Thrown Out*, A.B.A. J. eReport (June 28, 2002).
314. *Federal Election Commission v. Beaumont* (2003).
315. *McConnell v. Federal Election Commission*, 540 U.S. 93, 124 S.Ct. 619, 157 L.Ed.2d 491 (2003).
316. *Clingman v. Beaver*, 544 U.S. 581, 125 S.Ct. 2029, 161 L.Ed.2d 920 (2005).
317. Adam Liptak, *Justices, 5-4, Reject Corporate Spending Limit*, New York Times, January 22, 2010, at A-1.
318. *Federal Election Commission v. Wisconsin Right to Life*, 127 S.Ct. 2652, 168 L.Ed.2d 329 (2007).
319. *Id.*
320. *Lebron v. National Railroad Passenger Corporation*, 513 U.S. 374, 115 S.Ct. 961, 130 L.Ed.2d 902 (1995).
321. *Id.*
322. *United States v. National Treasury Employees Union*, 513 U.S. 454, 115 S.Ct. 1003, 130 L.Ed.2d 964 (1995).
323. *Board of County Commissioners, Wabaunsee County, Kansas v. Umbehr*, 518 U.S. 668, 116 S.Ct. 2342, 135 L.Ed.2d 843 (1996).
324. *Pickering v. Board of Education of Township High School District 205, Will County*, 391 U.S. 563, 88 S.Ct. 1731, 20 L.Ed.2d 811 (1968).
325. *Id.*
326. *O'Hare Truck Service, Inc. et al. v. City of Northlake et al.*, 518 U.S. 712, 116 S.Ct. 2353, 135 L.Ed.2d 874 (1996).
327. *Borough of Duryea, Pennsylvania, et al. v. Guarnieri*, 564 U.S. ___ (2011)
328. *Sonya Ross, Boycott of MCI Threatened Over Spokesman's War View*, Lexington (Ky.) Herald-Leader, May 19, 2003, at A7.
329. Sumana Chatterjee, *TV Networks Agree to Review bin Laden Tapes before Airing*, Lexington (Ky.) Herald-Leader, Oct. 11, 2001, at A5. For discussion of the prospect of fraudulent bin Laden tapes, see Richard Engel, *Bin Laden Issues New Threat*, MSNBC, March 25, 2010, available at http://www.msnbc.

msn.com, and also, Scott Shane, *Bin Laden Resurfaces in Recording*, New York Times, October 2, 2010, at A-6.

330. Lynn Elber, *TV Group Draws Criticism for Not Airing 'Nightline,'* Lexington (Ky.) Herald-Leader, May 1, 2004, at C7.

331. Pauline Arrillaga, *Freedom of Speech Can Have Different Meaning in Wartime*, Lexington (Ky.) Herald-Leader, April 13, 2003, at A3. Regarding more recent political speech and potential relationship to violent acts, see Carl Hulse and Kate Zernike, *Bloodshed Puts New Focus on Vitriol in Politics*, New York Times, January 8, 2011, at A1; *Sarah Palin Accuses Media of 'Blood Libel' After Tucson Shooting*, CBS News, January 12, 2011, available at http//www.cbsnews.com and Jeremy W. Peters and Brian Stelter, *After Tucson, Blanket Accusations Leave Much to Interpretation*, New York Times, January 16, 2011, at B-3,

332. Charles Lewis, *Press v. White House: Has the Post-9/11 Tug-of-War between the Media and the Bush Administration Tipped the Balance in Favor of the Power Structure*, IPI Global Journalism (3rd Q. 2004), at 12.

333. See *The Wal-Marting of America*, The Week (Aug. 15, 2003). More recent concerns focus on on-line alternatives, especially Facebook and the search-engine Google. See, for example, Ken Auletta, *Googled: The End of the World as we Know It* (2009), and Siva Vaidhyanaha, *The Googlization of Everything*, Berkeley: U of California Press, (2011). Professor of Media Studies at the University of Virginia, Vaidhyanaha examines effects of Google on information gathering.

334. See *Wal-Mart Ends Anti-Semitic Book Sale*, CNN Money, (Sept. 24, 2004) online edition. For an update on related issues see, Publisher's Weekly, *The Googlization of Books: Siva Vaidhyanaha Interview*, Vol. 258, Issue, 5, (Jan. 21, 2011).

6

Corporate and Commercial Speech

Unfortunately, the lawyers in this case elected to sue first and ask questions later—and got their "facts" absolutely wrong. We plan to take legal action for the false statements being made about our food.

—Greg Creed, President and Chief Concept Officer, Taco Bell Corp, Statement Regarding Class Action Law Suit, Jan. 25, 2011. In response to a lawsuit claiming that Taco Bell used false advertising when it called its food "beef."

A class action lawsuit was filed in California federal court in early 2011 claiming the highly successful fast food chain Taco Bell falsely advertised some of its products as "beef," allegedly using a meat mixture in its burritos and tacos that did not meet U.S. Department of Agriculture standards. When that beef content was called into question by way of the announcement of the lawsuit, the company immediately and publically labeled the lawsuit as "bogus," and "completely inaccurate," promising to fight back and "set the record straight." That is exactly what it did. Taco Bell launched full page ads in the *New York Times, Wall Street Journal,* and *USA Today*, as well as part of an aggressive online ad campaign using a very direct approach and reading: "Thank you for suing us. Here's the truth about our seasoned beef." The company then took the opportunity to aggressively explain how proud it was of products stating that its beef was 100% USDA inspected, like that purchased in supermarkets. An attorney specializing in fast-food litigation said this case was thin in potential legal liability because those making the allegations would have to prove that consumers were unaware that tacos contain products other than beef.[1]

Few such product oriented lawsuits make it to the highest court but once in a great while, the U.S. Supreme Court grants certiorari in a case that both sides anticipate will lead to a decision that will significantly alter the First Amendment landscape. *Nike v. Kasky* was such a case. It began in the mid-1990s when Nike came under fire from critics after news stories in several media outlets claimed that some of firm's athletic shoes and apparel were manufactured in sweat shops in China, Vietnam, and other Asian countries. The reports pointed to allegedly adverse work conditions in the factories, including low wages, poor safety, verbal and sexual abuse, and exposure to toxic chemicals.[2] The company, known worldwide for its "swoosh" and "Just Do It" trademarks, fought back with a massive publicity campaign that included press releases, a website, full-page newspaper ads, and letters to newspapers, university presidents, and athletic directors. None of the publicity attempted to directly sell any of Nike's products. Instead, Nike vigorously tried to counter the accusations by arguing that its products were made in safe and comfortable work environments and that employees were paid fair wages.

Mark Kasky, a consumer and labor activist, filed suit against Nike, using a California law, known as the "private attorney general" rule that allows a state resident to sue as a representative of all consumers in the state. Kasky claimed that some of Nike's statements in its press releases constituted false advertising and unfair trade practice even though all of Nike's statements were made outside of any direct product advertising. He argued that Nike should be held liable even though he acknowledged in his complaint that he had not purchased any Nike products as a result of the publicity and that he had not been harmed by any of Nike's statements. He also argued that the statements, although not part of a product advertising campaign, were aimed not only at countering criticism but also at influencing consumers who purchased or might purchase the company's products. The purpose of this argument was to convince the courts that Nike had engaged in commercial speech, which, as you will see later in this chapter, has substantially less protection under the First Amendment than political, religious, and other types of speech.

Kasky lost in the state trial court. The court dismissed the lawsuit, holding that Nike's speech was not commercial and thus deserved full First Amendment protection. The dismissal was upheld by the state Court of Appeal. On further appeal, the California Supreme Court overturned the lower court's decision in a 4 to 3 ruling that characterized Nike's campaign as commercial speech.[3] The state Supreme Court disagreed with Nike that its campaign had full First Amendment protection because it was part of an international debate on issues of strong public concern. According to the court, Nike's campaign included "factual statements about how Nike makes its products."[4] The court said:

> Our holding, based on decisions of the United States Supreme Court, in no way prohibits any business enterprise from speaking out on issues of public importance or from vigorously defending its own labor practices. It means only that when a business enterprise, to promote and defend its sales and profits, makes factual representations about its own products or its own operations, it must speak truthfully.[5]

Some 40 media organizations, including the Reporters Committee for Freedom of the Press, begged to differ with the state Supreme Court, filing a friend-of-the-court brief with the Court when the decision was appealed. They argued that, if upheld, the *Nike* decision would have a "chilling effect" on similar speech.[6]

The U.S. Supreme Court granted *certiorari* and heard oral arguments on April 23, 2003. There were hints of what was to come in the oral arguments that often focused on whether the Court should be hearing the case in the first place since it had never gone to trial.

In June the Court ruled in an unsigned *per curiam* opinion that the writ for certiorari had been "improvidently granted."[7] That decision effectively sent the case back to the trial court. Less than three months later, Nike settled out of court with Kasky by agreeing to pay the Fair

Labor Association (FLA) $1.5 million over three years to fund programs aimed at improving workplace conditions.[8] FLA is a nonprofit coalition of 12 companies including Nike and 185 colleges and universities formed to "promote adherence to international labor standards and improve working conditions worldwide."[9] The case many thought would go a long way toward clarifying the definition of commercial speech ended with a whimper rather than a bang.

The U.S. Supreme Court's nondecision in *Nike* in many ways reflects the struggle of the Court over the years to articulate clear guidelines regarding how much protection commercial speech enjoys. Nevertheless, corporate and commercial speech remains a huge business in the United States just as it is in many other countries, and in any big industry, the possibility of abuse of the public trust is always present. Advertising and other forms of commercial speech are no exception.

Since the days of patent medicines and elixirs that promised cures for ailments from indigestion to baldness in the late 19th and early 20th centuries, there has been concern about false, deceptive, and fraudulent ads. That concern on the part of the government and the public was never translated into regulation until Congress created the Federal Trade Commission in 1914. Many years later, the FTC attempted to regulate advertising. Today, the commission is a prime regulator of commercial speech, although myriad other federal and state agencies are also involved.

This chapter focuses on the regulation of corporate and commercial speech, including advertising, and the development of the "commercial speech doctrine" in the U.S. Supreme Court. The analysis begins with Supreme Court decisions on commercial speech and moves to state and federal restrictions on advertising and other forms of corporate and commercial speech.

The Development of the Commercial Speech Doctrine

As the outcome in the *Nike* case illustrates, the U.S. Supreme Court and other courts struggle with drawing the limits for protection for commercial speech. In fact, the history of involvement of the courts in commercial speech issues is much like a patchwork quilt—myriad confusing and contradictory components that often make it difficult to discern trends and underlying principles. No distinctive evolution of constitutional law on commercial speech occurred. Instead, the U.S. Supreme Court, at least, has at times erratically switched from one principle to another, dependent on the individual circumstances of a particular case. The Court established specific tests for determining whether a particular type of commercial speech has constitutional protection, but these tests have not proved definitive.

In 1942, the first major U.S. Supreme Court case on commercial speech emerged. The public and governmental concern with massive anti-competitive trade practices and fraudulent marketing techniques including false and deceptive advertising at the start of the 20th century was channeled into federal legislation such as the Federal Trade Commission Act of 1914 and the Clayton Act of 1914. Such legislation forbade practices like price fixing and corporate mergers. Later, the Food, Drug and Cosmetic Act of 1938 outlawed the interstate transportation of adulterated or mislabeled foods, drugs, and cosmetics, rather than specifically regulating advertising. The prevailing assumption until the early 1940s was that commercial speech had First Amendment protection and thus could not be severely restricted.

Valentine v. Chrestensen *(1942)*

In 1942, the U.S. Supreme Court tackled head-on the issue of whether commercial speech enjoys First Amendment protection. In *Valentine v. Chrestensen*,[10] the Court held that the First Amendment does *not* apply to "purely commercial advertising." In 1940, F. J. Chrestensen, a Florida resident, moored his submarine formerly owned by the U.S. Navy at a state pier in the East River near New York City. While he was distributing handbills that advertised tours of the sub, the Police Commissioner of New York, Lewis J. Valentine, informed him he was violating a state sanitary code prohibiting distribution of commercial and business advertising on public streets. Valentine told Chrestensen that it was permissible to distribute handbills devoted solely to information or public protest but not commercial handbills. The code effectively banned advertising but not political materials.

Chrestensen was not satisfied and cleverly printed a revision of the original on one side (omitting the admission fee). The other side had no advertising but criticized the City Dock Department for banning the original version of the handbill. The entrepreneur dutifully submitted the new handbill to the Police Commissioner but was rebuffed again. No problem, he was told, with handing out the protest information but no advertising. Chrestensen ignored the warnings, passed out the handbills and was expeditiously restrained by police. He then successfully sought an injunction in District Court for the Southern District of New York to prevent the police from further restraining him. The judge granted only an *interlocutory injunction*, a type of injunction that is effective only until the controversy can be settled on appeal. Thus the police could not prevent Chrestensen from distributing handbills until a higher appellate court made a decision on whether the statute was constitutional. The Second Circuit U.S. Court of Appeals upheld the district court decision.

On further appeal, though, the U.S. Supreme Court, in a decision written by Associate Justice Owen J. Roberts, unanimously reversed the lower court decree. According to the Court:

> This Court has unequivocally held that the streets are proper places for the exercise of the freedom of communicating information and disseminating opinion and that, though the states and municipalities may appropriately regulate the privilege in the public interest, they may not unduly burden or proscribe its employment in these public thoroughfares. We are equally clear that the Constitution imposes no such restraint on government as respects purely commercial advertising.[11]

This decision that enunciates what became known later as the commercial speech doctrine was gradually chipped away over the decades, but it was accepted doctrine until the 1970s. Along the way, the Court attempted to distinguish commercial speech from noncommercial speech but generated more confusion than clarity.

From March through May 1943, the Court decided four cases involving door to door distribution of religious materials by Jehovah's Witnesses. Several First Amendment cases decided by the U.S. Supreme Court including one in 2003 involved this religious sect, always fervent in proselytizing, much to the chagrin of more traditional religious denominations. Anyone who grew up in the rural South or Southwest during the 1950s and 1960s may recall numerous occasions on which Witnesses would canvass the neighborhood door-to-door seeking contributions in return for their religious tracts. The Witnesses persisted in efforts despite having doors slammed in their faces and suffering verbal abuse from people who resented solicitations. They have also generated controversy over decades for their refusal—on religious grounds—to salute the American flag.

Jamison v. Texas *(1943)*

Such persistence often met resistance not only from unsympathetic residents but also by way of local ordinances and state statutes. *Jamison v. Texas* (1943)[12] is a prime example of the selective use of a city ordinance to restrict the activities of religious groups such as the Witnesses. Ella Jamison was convicted in a Texas court of violating a Dallas ordinance banning the distribution of handbills on public streets. She was fined $5 plus court costs for passing out Witness literature.

Under Texas law at that time, Jamison could not appeal the decision to a higher state court. She had to appeal directly to the U.S. Supreme Court, which granted certiorari. In a unanimous opinion written by Justice Hugo L. Black, the Court reversed the conviction on the ground that it violated her First and 14th Amendment rights of freedom of speech and freedom of religion. According to the Court, even though the handbills were on the face commercial, they were protected because of their religious content.

The state argued that *Valentine* should apply because the literature advertised religious books and other works. The Court held that the *Valentine* holding did not affect commercial religious materials of this type. "The mere presence of an advertisement of a religious work on a handbill of the sort distributed here may not subject the handbill to prohibition,"[13] the Court noted. The Court offered as rationale for this exception to the *Valentine* rule that the First Amendment was designed to protect this activity. The state cannot be permitted to ban distribution "merely because the handbills invite the purchase of books for the improved understanding of the religion or because the handbills seek in a lawful fashion to promote the raising of funds for religious purposes."

Murdock v. Pennsylvania *(1943)*

On May 3, 1943, the U.S. Supreme Court issued three separate decisions, all of which dealt with commercial speech and involved Jehovah's Witnesses. Taken together, the majority opinions substantially define the extent to which the state can regulate religious speech within a presumably commercial context. In *Murdock v. Pennsylvania* (1943),[14] the Court reversed the convictions of eight Witnesses for violating a Jeannette, Pennsylvania, ordinance that permitted door-to-door sale of products only with a license that could be obtained only upon payment of a specified fee. No exception was made in the law for religious literature. Although they were not jailed, the eight were ordered to pay fines after they were convicted for violating the ordinance by requesting contributions for religious literature they peddled from door to door.

There was no question that they were guilty, but the defendants unsuccessfully argued before the trial court that the law violated First Amendment rights of freedom of press, speech and religion. On appeal, the Pennsylvania Superior Court and the state supreme court upheld the convictions.

The U.S. Supreme Court ruled in favor of the Witnesses in a 5 to 4 decision written by Associate Justice William O. Douglas. According to the majority, the Witnesses were involved in a religious, not a commercial, venture:

The constitutional rights of those spreading their religious beliefs through the spoken and printed word are not to be gauged by standards governing retailers or wholesalers of books…. The taxes imposed by this ordinance can hardly help but be as severe and telling in their impact on the freedom of press and religion as the 'taxes on knowledge' at which the First Amendment was partly aimed.[15]

Martin v. City of Struthers *(1943)*

The second decision involved a violation of a similar city ordinance by a Jehovah's Witness, but the Supreme Court took a somewhat different tack in striking it down as unconstitutional. In *Martin v. City of Struthers* (1943),[16] the Court in another 5 to 4 split overturned the conviction of Thelma Martin for door-to-door distribution of leaflets advertising a Jehovah's Witness service. She was fined $10 for violating a Struthers, Ohio, ordinance very similar to that in *Murdock*.

Two strange twists to this case contrasted it with *Murdock*. Martin's case was initially rejected on appeal to the U.S. Supreme Court because the justices mistakenly assumed that no constitutional issue had been raised in the lower courts. However, upon a motion for reconsideration, the Court granted a writ of certiorari on the ground that a constitutional question had arisen. The Ohio Supreme Court turned down Martin's appeal because the court concluded no constitutional issue was involved. In striking down the ordinance as a violation of the First and 14th Amendments, the Court also held that it infringed not only on the right of the disseminator of the information but also on the right of area households to receive the information.

The Court acknowledged the aggressiveness of sects such as the Witnesses in door-to-door soliciting. According to the Court, door-to-door solicitations can be regulated under certain conditions, but the law was too broad. The Court noted that an ordinance prohibiting solicitation of homes on which the owners had posted a sign or other notice asking not to be disturbed would be a possible way of overcoming the overreach of this particular law.

Douglas v. City of Jeannette *(1943)*

The third case, interestingly, garnered the unanimous opinion of the Supreme Court but the facts were somewhat different. In *Douglas v. City of Jeannette*,[17] the Court declared that a Jeannette, Pennsylvania, ordinance banning the solicitation of orders for merchandise unless the individual had already obtained a license and paid a fee was unconstitutional. Two distinctions marking this case were that soliciting was not door to door and the solicitation did not involve what is known today as a point of purchase sale (i.e., soliciting for a product that is available on the spot).

Watchtower Bible and Tract Society v. Stratton *(2002)*

In 2002, the U.S. Supreme court handed down another Jehovah's Witness case—this time involving an ordinance approved by an Ohio village of 278 residents that required a door-to-door canvasser to secure a permit from the mayor's office and sign a registration form. In *Watchtower Bible and Tract Society v. Village of Stratton* (2002),[18] the Court ruled 8 to 1 (with only Chief Justice Rehnquist dissenting) that the ordinance violated the First Amendment. The decision capped more than 50 years of cases involving the Witnesses, all of which favored the religious sect. Although the permit required no fee, failure to request a permit was a misdemeanor.

The village argued the ordinance was necessary to protect its residents from fraud, annoyance, and criminal activities. Both a U.S. District Court and the 6th Circuit U.S. Court of Appeals held the ordinance was content-neutral and thus subject to intermediate scrutiny, ruling in favor of Stratton.

The U.S. Supreme Court reversed on grounds that the ordinance was overly broad, covering both commercial and noncommercial speech, including political and religious activities. The Court specifically noted it was not determining whether strict scrutiny was the appropriate level of review because the ordinance was so broad in its impact. The Court did hint that "[h] ad its provisions been construed to apply only to commercial activities and the solicitation of funds, arguably the ordinance would have been tailored to the village's interest in protecting its residents' privacy and preventing fraud." The Court also said, "It is offensive—not only to the values protected by the First Amendment, but to the very notion of a free society—that in the context of everyday public discourse a citizen must first inform the government of her desire to speak to her neighbors and then obtain a permit to do so."[19] The majority opinion did suggest that if the ordinance had been limited to commercial activities and the solicitation of funds, it might not have violated the U.S. Constitution.

Commercial Speech for Professionals and Corporations

This section looks at three major categories of commercial speech—media corporations, non-media corporations, and professionals. Of the three, media corporations have generally made the strongest headway in obtaining protection for commercial speech, but they do not have a perfect win–loss record. Nonmedia corporations have received the most attention from the courts, especially the U.S. Supreme Court. Such corporations have made progress in spite of surprising setbacks, but limits of First Amendment protection for commercial speech have been tested most by professionals, particularly lawyers, who achieved mixed results. The general trend continues to be broader protection for commercial speech but with twists and turns that often defy logic.

First Amendment Rights of Media Corporations

New York Times v. Sullivan *(1964)*

In 1964, the U.S. Supreme Court for the first time issued a major decision involving commercial "political" speech. In the landmark libel decision—the most important libel decision rendered by the Court, *New York Times v. Sullivan*,[20] the Court rejected the argument that First and 14th Amendment freedoms of speech and press did not apply in the case. This is because allegedly libelous information appeared in a paid, commercial advertisement in the newspaper:

The publication here was not a 'commercial' advertisement in the sense in which the word was used in [*Valentine v.*] *Chrestensen*. It communicated information, expressed opinion, recited grievances, protested claimed abuses, and sought financial support on behalf of a movement whose existence and objectives are matters of the highest public interest and concern. That the [*New York*] *Times* was paid for publishing the advertisement is as immaterial in this connection as is the fact that newspapers and books are sold.[21]

The Court went on to rationalize that if the Court had ruled otherwise, the effect would be to discourage newspapers from publishing this type of advertising, which the Court characterized as "editorial advertisements." The Court was particularly concerned that certain groups such as civil rights organizations that do not have ready access to the press would be prevented from disseminating their ideas to a wide audience. As the majority noted, "The effect would be to shackle the First Amendment in its attempt to secure 'the widest possible dissemination of information from diverse and antagonistic sources.... '"[22]

Political communication has been granted greater First Amendment protection than any other form of speech including religious communication, which is a close second. Thus this decision that the *New York Times* did not lose its First Amendment protection because the communication was a paid advertisement easily fits into the Supreme Court's First Amendment mold. The question of whether the commercial speech doctrine would apply in this case was one of the most significant aspects of the *Sullivan* decision, although the new rule enunciated, known as the "actual malice" rule (discussed in Chapter 8), overshadowed the "editorial advertisement" ruling. It could be argued that *Sullivan* was the first step taken by the Supreme Court toward eventually dismembering the commercial speech doctrine by the 1980s, even if *Sullivan* is not perceived as a commercial speech decision.

An important question is whether the Court's reasoning on the commercial speech issue in *Sullivan* is supportable. Would struggling political groups be denied a public forum for their ideas if the press were faced with the possibility of having no First Amendment protection if it published their paid advertisements? Or would the press still be willing to take the risk of no protection in order to obtain the advertising dollars that sustain the commercial media? No one has thoroughly researched this question. But it is likely that if all commercial speech were treated the same for the purposes of the First Amendment, under the expanded protection granted commercial speech in the last two decades, there would be a "chilling" effect. This could work to the disadvantage of political and religious movements that garner little press attention and thus often resort to unconventional communication such as editorial commercials.

Until the early to mid-1970s, the U.S. Supreme Court generally avoided facing constitutional questions involving commercial speech by simply denying certiorari. But the consumer movement beginning in the late 1960s and the polarization of public opinion on the issue of abortion that culminated with *Roe v. Wade*[23] in 1973 had an impact on the type of commercial speech cases reaching the Court. *Roe v. Wade* is the controversial decision granting a woman the constitutional right to an abortion. More specifically, the Court was faced with deciding the constitutionality of governmental restrictions on advertising that did not appear to fall neatly into either a religious or political niche. Was such advertising commercial speech or was it a form of advertising that could be shielded by the First Amendment?

Pittsburgh Press v. Pittsburgh Commission on Human Relations *(1973)*

In 1973, the Court had the opportunity to pull back on the commercial speech doctrine by expanding the context in which commercial speech enjoys full First Amendment protection but chose instead to hold on to *Valentine v. Chrestensen*. The city of Pittsburgh enacted an ordinance in the late 1960s that banned sex discrimination by employers for a broad range of occupations. The *Pittsburgh Press* had long permitted employers placing help-wanted ads in the paper's classified section to list openings under "Jobs—Male Interest," "Jobs—Female Interest," and "Jobs—Male–Female." There was no doubt that these ads effectively promoted sex discrimination by allowing employers to screen out applications from members of the "unwanted" sex. However, the Court was faced with the question of whether such ads were comparable to the ad in *Valentine v. Chrestensen* or the "advertorial" in *New York Times v. Sullivan*. Is it pure commercial speech or a hybrid that can be shielded by the First Amendment?

Pittsburgh Press v. Pittsburgh Commission on Human Relations (1973)[24] began when the Pittsburgh Commission on Human Relations, which had been granted the authority to enforce the city's anti-discrimination ordinance, charged the newspaper with violating the ordinance and, after a hearing, ordered the *Press* to comply with the law. On appeal by the paper, the Court of Common Pleas for Allegheny County affirmed the order. On appeal, the Commonwealth Court of Pennsylvania modified the order to prohibit gender-designated classified ads only for those types of positions for which the ordinance forbade sex discrimination. The newspaper was allowed to carry ads specifying gender for occupations not covered by the law. The Pennsylvania Supreme Court declined to review the case, but the U.S. Supreme Court granted certiorari and heard oral arguments.

In a narrow 5 to 4 decision, the Court held that the ordinance did not violate the First and 14th Amendments by banning illegal gender-specified advertising.

The line-up of the justices was surprising but perhaps a harbinger of other commercial speech cases to come. Associate Justice Lewis F. Powell, Jr. wrote the 5 to 4 decision, and was joined by staunch First Amendment advocates, Justices William J. Brennan, Jr., and Thurgood Marshall. The majority included conservatives, Justices Byron R. White and William H. Rehnquist. Dissenters were Chief Justice Warren Burger, William O. Douglas, Harry A. Blackmun, and Potter Stewart.

How could justices such as Brennan and Marshall justify what is prior restraint on the press? According to the majority, "No suggestion is made in this case that the Ordinance was passed with any purpose of muzzling or curbing the press."[25] Ironically, the Court quoted from *New York Times v. Sullivan* to point to the importance of the First Amendment while finding that the ads resembled those of *Valentine v. Chrestensen* rather than *New York Times v. Sullivan*. The majority opinion went even further, comparing the ad to one for narcotics or prostitution:

> Discrimination in employment is not only commercial activity, it is illegal commercial activity under the Ordinance. We have no doubt that a newspaper constitutionally could be forbidden to publish a want ad proposing a sale of narcotics or soliciting prostitutes. Nor would the result be different if the nature of the transaction were indicated by placement under columns captioned 'Narcotics for Sale' and 'Prostitutes Wanted' rather than stated within the four corners of the advertisement. The illegality in this case may be less overt, but we see no difference in principle here.[26]

The majority simply did not see the state's action in this case as prior restraint even though the effect of the order was to prohibit the newspaper from publishing particular content. As Justice Stewart noted: "So far as I know, this is the first case in this or any other American court that permits a government agency to enter a composing room of a newspaper and dictate to the publisher the layout and the makeup of the newspaper's pages. This is the first such case, but I fear it may not be the last. The camel's nose is in the tent."[27]

Justices Stewart and Douglas acknowledged in the dissent that it was "within the police power of the city of Pittsburgh to prohibit discrimination in private employment on the basis of race, color, religion, ancestry, national origin, place of birth, or sex."[28] But they felt the government had no authority to tell a newspaper in advance what it could and could not publish. Chief Justice Burger dissented on grounds that the decision was an enlargement of the 'commercial speech' doctrine "… and also launches the courts on what I perceive to be a treacherous path of defining what layout and organizational decisions of newspapers are 'sufficiently associated' with the 'commercial' parts of the papers.… "[29]

Bigelow v. Virginia *(1975)*

Was the court headed down a "treacherous path"? Two years later in *Bigelow v. Virginia* (1975)[30] the Court issued another decision in a commercial speech case involving the mass media. Like *Pittsburgh Press*, the case had overtones of prior restraint but with a new twist. This case also illustrates how the opinions in one case can spill over into other decisions on the same topic but on an issue involving much different principles. An apparent spillover in *Pittsburgh Press*, for example, can be surmised by the fact that Justices Brennan and Marshall consistently upheld the constitutionality of anti-discrimination laws and that the newspaper ads effectively promoted sex discrimination. In *Bigelow*, the apparent spillover was evidenced by the fact that Justices White and Rehnquist dissented in *Roe v. Wade* (1973) and in *Bigelow*, which involved newspaper ads for abortions.

In 1971, two years before *Roe v. Wade*, abortion was illegal in Virginia, although it was permitted in some states such as New York. Jeffrey C. Bigelow, a director and managing editor of *The Virginia Weekly* of Charlottesville, ran the following advertisement in his newspaper for a New York City abortion referral service:

UNWANTED PREGNANCY—LET US HELP YOU

Abortions are now legal in New York. There are no residency requirements.

FOR IMMEDIATE PLACEMENT IN ACCREDITED HOSPITALS AND CLINICS AT LOW COST

Contact WOMEN'S PAVILION
515 Madison Avenue
New York, NY 10022
Or call any time: (212) 371-6670 or (212) 371-6650

AVAILABLE 7 DAYS a WEEK
STRICTLY CONFIDENTIAL
We will make all arrangements for you and help you with information and counseling.

Abortion was legal in New York at the time the ad appeared but became illegal later. As you can see, the newspaper ad provided considerable information about abortions in New York including the fact that residency was not required. There was no doubt that the ad was designed to encourage Virginia women to procure abortions in New York. It specifically mentioned that the Women's Pavilion could assist a woman in obtaining "immediate placement in accredited hospitals at low cost" and it would make all arrangements on a "strictly confidential" basis. The newspaper had a high circulation on the University of Virginia campus.

The statute under which Bigelow was prosecuted directly forbade anyone, including by publication, lecture or advertisement, from encouraging or promoting the procurement of an abortion or miscarriage. The editor was convicted of a misdemeanor (the statute made the crime a misdemeanor only) in Albemarle County Court. He appealed to the Albemarle Circuit Court and was granted a *trial de novo* but was convicted again. The Virginia Supreme Court affirmed the new conviction on grounds that the advertisement was purely commercial and therefore not shielded by the umbrella of the First Amendment. The U.S. Supreme Court granted certiorari and sent the case back to the Virginia Supreme Court for further consideration in light of *Roe v. Wade* (1973) and related decisions. Once again, the state supreme court affirmed the conviction, and Bigelow filed another appeal with the U.S. Supreme Court. This time, fate was on his side.

In a resounding 7 to 2 decision, the U.S. Supreme Court reversed Bigelow's conviction. In the majority opinion by Justice Harry A. Blackmun, the Court held the ad did have full First Amendment protection, just as did the ad in *New York Times v. Sullivan*:

> The fact that the particular advertisement in appellant's newspaper had commercial aspects or reflected the advertiser's commercial interests did not negate all First Amendment guarantees.... The advertisement ... did more than simply propose a commercial transaction. It contained factual material of clear 'public interest.'[31]

What material did the Court view as in the public interest? The Court cited the lines, "Abortions are now legal in New York. There are no residency requirements." The Court also said:

> Viewed in its entirety, the advertisement conveyed information of potential interest and value to a diverse audience—not only to readers possibly in need of the services offered, but also those with a general curiosity about, or genuine interest in, the subject matter of the law of another state.... The mere existence of the Women's Pavilion in New York City, with the possibility of its being typical of other organizations there, and the availability of the services offered, were not unnewsworthy.[32]

Notice the Court's reference to *newsworthiness*. In *New York Times v. Sullivan*, the Court did not refer to this factor and merely noted that the ad was not a commercial advertisement in the sense of *Chrestensen* but instead was an "editorial advertisement." How does an ad become newsworthy? Is newsworthiness alone sufficient to warrant full First Amendment protection for an ad or is it to be considered in light of other factors? Would the ad have been protected if it had been nothing more than the name, address, and telephone number of the Women's Pavilion under the heading "Abortion Referral"? In other words, does it enjoy constitutional protection primarily because of the "newsworthy" information it conveyed?

The Court left these questions unanswered, but it was apparent the Court was headed toward expansion of First Amendment rights for a variety of forms of advertising. No matter how hard one tries, it is impossible to reconcile *Chrestensen* with *Bigelow* and even with *New York Times v. Sullivan*. In his dissent, Justice William H. Rehnquist (joined by Justice Byron R. White) characterized the nature of the ad as an exchange of services rather than an exchange of ideas, but the handwriting was on the wall. Both justices also dissented in the *Roe v. Wade* abortion decision.

City of Cincinnati v. Discovery Network, Inc. *(1993)*

Eighteen years after *Bigelow*, the U.S. Supreme Court added icing to the cake when it struck down a city ordinance that barred the distribution of commercial handbills in news racks but imposed no such ban on advertising for traditional newspapers. In *City of Cincinnati v. Discovery Network, Inc.*,[33] the Court affirmed a ruling of the 6th Circuit U.S. Court of Appeals that the ordinance failed the *Hudson* four-prong test, discussed below, including the fourth prong's requirement that the regulation be no more extensive than necessary to advance the government's interest. The 6 to 3 majority opinion written by Justice Stevens said the city had a significant interest in preventing littering, which had become a problem near such news racks. But, the Court contended that the city was not justified in making a distinction between publications that were predominantly advertising and more traditional publications.

The Supreme Court held that the fourth prong of the *Hudson* test imposes a burden of proof on the government in demonstrating a "reasonable fit" between the ends and means chosen to further the substantial government interest. The City of Cincinnati, according to the Court, had not shown "reasonable fit" because the city focused on the content of the handbills rather than the effect of the ordinance in achieving the city's goal of reducing litter. The Court was clearly bothered by the inappropriate distinction the city made between commercial and noncommercial speech. As the majority opinion noted, "In our view, the city's argument attaches more importance to the distinction between commercial speech and noncommercial speech than our cases warrant and seriously underestimates the value of commercial speech." As the Court pointed out, there was no evidence presented by the city that the news racks for handbills contributed more to the litter problem than other news racks.

Dissenters—Chief Justice Rehnquist, joined in his opinion by Justices White and Thomas—strongly disagreed with the majority's reasoning, arguing that the ordinance "burdened less speech than necessary to fully accomplish its [the city's] objective of alleviating the problems caused by the proliferation of news racks on its street corners."

Cincinnati v. Discovery Network seems to be at least a slight broadening of the concept of "reasonable fit" introduced four years earlier in *Board of Trustees of the State University of New York v. Fox*,[34] although the precise boundaries are by no means clear. The handbills or free circulation publications as they are sometimes known do appear to have been considered the press for purposes of the First Amendment, as indicated by the criticism by the Court of the City of Cincinnati for its distinction based on content in enforcing the ordinance. This may at least partially explain why the government lost in a case that, for all practical purposes, involved traditional advertising rather than public interest commercial speech such as that in *Bigelow*. The decision would, without doubt, have been different if the racks had sold baseball collector cards, for example, but are collector cards really different from advertising circulars or even the daily newspaper that must be purchased with coins deposited in the news rack? What if the cards dealt with controversial issues such as drugs, politics, or religion?

First Amendment Rights of Nonmedia Corporations
Virginia State Board of Pharmacy v. Virginia Citizens Consumer Council (1976)

Less than a year after *Bigelow*, *Chrestensen* began its downward spiral. On May 24, 1976, the U.S. Supreme Court for the first time held that truthful commercial speech, even if purely commercial, is protected by the First Amendment. *Virginia State Board of Pharmacy v. Virginia Citizens Consumer Council* (1976)[35] is more of a professional advertising case than either a media or nonmedia corporation case, but it set the pace for future commercial speech decisions. The Court ruled 7 to 1 in the case that a state statute under which licensed pharmacists could be punished for unprofessional conduct for advertising prescription drug prices was unconstitutional. The penalties ranged from small fines to license revocation. The statute was not challenged by pharmacists in the courts but by consumer groups who claimed "the First Amendment entitles the user of prescription drugs to receive information that pharmacists wish to communicate to them through advertising and other promotional means, concerning the prices of such drugs."[36]

The majority opinion by Associate Justice Harry A. Blackmun noted, much to the surprise of many First Amendment scholars, that "in *Bigelow v. Virginia*, the notion of unprotected 'commercial speech' all but passed from the scene." Even a close reading of the Court's opinion in *Bigelow* gives no clear indication that such is the case.

The Court in *Virginia State Board* conceded that a "fragment of hope for the continuing validity of a 'commercial speech' exception arguably may have persisted because of the subject matter of the advertisement in *Bigelow*." The Court then tackled the issue of whether "there is a First Amendment exception for 'commercial speech.'" The Court made clear that *Virginia Pharmacy Board* did not involve cultural, philosophical or political speech, nor was the information newsworthy about commercial matters. Instead, a pharmacist, according to the Court, is attempting to communicate, "I will sell you the X prescription drug at the Y price." Citing *New York Times v. Sullivan*, the Court then noted that it is well established that speech does not lose its First Amendment protection simply because money is spent to purchase it.

According to the justices, "Those whom the suppression of prescription drug price information hits the hardest are the poor, the sick, and particularly the aged." Thus a consumer's interest in such information could be as "keen, if not keener, than his interest in the day's most urgent political debate." The majority opinion strongly criticized Virginia's contention that price advertising would adversely affect the professionalism of pharmacists and harm consumers with low quality service and presumably inferior drugs. Keeping consumers ignorant is not the solution, according to the Court, individuals should be permitted to make their own choices based on information freely available in the marketplace.

Although the justices held that Virginia's statute was unconstitutional, they noted that "some forms of commercial speech regulation are surely permissible." They specifically mentioned untruthful commercial speech such as false and misleading ads and false advertising that causes actual injury. Virginia, in the Court's view, was unconstitutionally suppressing truthful speech that could contribute "to the flow of accurate and reliable information relevant to public and private decision making" for the sake of preventing the dissemination of falsehoods. In other words, the Court was warning the state not to throw the baby out with the bath water. The First Amendment warrants the risk that some false information may sneak into the marketplace so that the truth may prevail.

Justice William H. Rehnquist was the sole dissenter to the Court's decision. His opinion is worthy of note, not so much for its reasoning as for the fact that it represents a strong minority view shared by some professional associations. Rehnquist was particularly concerned that the Court's opinion would open the way "not only for dissemination of price information but for active promotion of prescription drugs, liquor, cigarettes, and other products the use of which it has previously been thought desirable to discourage."[37] To illustrate his point, he satirically penned some "representative" advertisements that a pharmacist might run in the local newspaper:

> Pain getting you down? Insist that your physician prescribe Demoral.
>
> You pay a little more than for aspirin, but you get a lot more relief.
>
> Can't shake the flu? Get a prescription for tetracycline from your doctor today. Don't spend another sleepless night. Ask your doctor to prescribe Seconal without delay.[38]

Eventually, ads for prescription drugs did appear in consumer magazines and newspapers in the mid-1990s when the U.S. Food and Drug Administration began relaxing its rules regarding such advertising. Magazines such as *Parade, Time,* and *Newsweek* regularly carry ads for prescription drugs for allergies, asthma, diabetes, and high cholesterol. In fact, by 2005, the pharmaceutical industry was spending more than $3 billion annually in consumer advertising, often called *direct-to-consumer* or *DTC advertising*. According to a study in the *Journal of the American Medical Association*,[39] such advertising has paid dividends, with physicians writing more prescriptions for advertised drugs in response to requests from their patients. Another study of DTC advertising found that these ads "play a beneficial role in consumer health care decision making," particularly as an educational tool.[40] The study also found that older consumers, to whom much of the advertising is directed, perceived more usefulness in the ads than younger consumers.

The *Bigelow* decision appears to have had little, if any, negative impact on public perceptions of pharmacists. Any concern that the publication of prescription prices would somehow demean pharmacists has long since faded. However, as indicated in the decisions that follow, professional organizations, as a whole—whether they are for lawyers, physicians, or other professionals—continue to harbor fears that advertising will spell the demise of public respect for their particular professions.

One more point in Justice Rehnquist's dissent deserves attention because it represents a vocal, minority view. According to Justice Rehnquist, "The statute ... only forbids pharmacists to publish this price information. There is no prohibition against a consumer group, such as appellees, collecting and publishing comparative price information as to various pharmacies in an area."[38] This view ignores the reality that consumer groups would have to expend considerable time and money to compile such data even though pharmacists are in a much better position because they have direct access to this information. Pharmacists also have a much more effective outlet for communication—newspaper advertising. Most consumer groups could probably not afford to place such advertising. They would have to rely on alternative means such as pamphlets that would likely have limited circulation, particularly among groups—such as the poor and the elderly—who benefit the most from competition among pharmacies. This view has an aura of elitism because it assumes consumers would not be able to effectively and efficiently discern accurate information from deceptive and misleading advertising.

Did *Virginia State Board of Pharmacy* settle the issue once and for all of whether commercial speech had First Amendment protection? Just as *Roe v. Wade* spurred more questions about abortion rights, the Virginia decision left a significant number of unresolved subissues that the Court continues to confront decades later. Three major decisions on the issue were handed down by the next year, and there have been several subsequent rulings. Many of these dealt with advertising of professional services, although other types of commercial speech have been in the spotlight as well.

The first two of the three 1977 decisions are summarized here. The third is deferred to the next section because it deals with advertising by professionals.

Linmark Associates, Inc. v. Willingboro *(1977)*

In *Linmark Associates, Inc. v. Willingboro* (1977),[41] the Court held 8 to 0 (Justice Rehnquist not participating) that a local ordinance banning the posting of "For Sale" and "Sold" signs on lawns violated the First Amendment. The opinion, written by Thurgood Marshall, said that whereas the goal of the ordinance to prevent "white flight" from neighborhoods as they were racially integrated ("block busting") may have been noble, the town had not been able to show such a restriction was necessary or justified under the circumstances. "If dissemination of this information can be restricted, then every locality in the country can suppress any facts that reflect poorly on the locality, so long as a plausible claim can be made that disclosure would cause the recipients of the information to act 'irrationally,'" according to the Court.[42]

Hugh Carey v. Population Services International *(1977)*

In *Hugh Carey v. Population Services International* (1977),[43] a New York education law making it illegal for anyone to sell or distribute nonprescription contraceptives to minors under age 16 and for anyone to advertise or publicly display such contraceptives was declared unconstitutional by a divided court. Population Services International owned Population Planning Associates, a North Carolina corporation that advertised and sold contraceptives to customers of any age via mail order throughout the country, including in New York. (The ads appeared in New York magazines and newspapers.) In applying a *strict scrutiny* test to the statute because of an earlier decision by another divided court that appeared to recognize a limited constitutional right to privacy,[44] Justice William J. Brennan, Jr., writing for the majority, held that the prohibition on distribution of contraceptives violated 14th Amendment due process, but the justices could not agree whether such a ban for minors under the age of 16 was permissible. The Court held the advertising restrictions violated the First Amendment, although the majority could not agree on whether such restrictions are inherently unconstitutional.

First National Bank of Boston v. Bellotti *(1978)*

One year after *Hugh Carey,* the Supreme Court handed down a relatively unnoticed case involving the First Amendment rights of nonmedia corporations. In *First National Bank of Boston v. Bellotti* (1978),[45] the Court struck down as unconstitutional a Massachusetts statute that banned banks and other businesses from attempting to exert direct influence on public opinion unless the issue involved directly and materially affected its business, property, or other assets. The bank had tried to get voters to reject a proposed constitutional amendment granting the legislature authority to enact a progressive (i.e., graduated) personal income tax. In striking it down, the Court for the first time held that nonmedia corporations have First Amendment rights.

Consolidated Edison *and* Central Hudson Gas & Electric *(1980)*

Two years later, the Supreme Court handed down two decisions on the same day dealing with commercial speech rights of public utilities. During the mid- to late 1970s, many public utilities began speaking out on controversial issues such as nuclear energy and environmental regulations and discussing their views in circulars sent with the monthly bills. Both *Consolidated Edison Co. v. Public Service Commission of New York* (1980)[46] and *Central Hudson Gas & Electric Corp. v. Public Service Commission of New York* (1980)[47] involved attempts by the same state regulatory agency to bar a utility from engaging in particular types of commercial speech. The content of the speech differed significantly between the two utilities, but the First Amendment issues were similar.

In 1977, the New York Public Service Commission issued an order barring all public utilities from "using bill inserts to discuss political matters, including the desirability of future development of nuclear power." The order was sparked by a complaint filed by the Natural Resources Defense Council (NRDC), a consumer group opposed to nuclear power, after Consolidated Edison included an item entitled "Independence Is Still a Goal, and Nuclear Power Is Needed to Win the Battle" in its January 1976 monthly insert. The item touted benefits of nuclear energy and noted that they outweighed any risks and that this form of energy was economical, clean, and safe.

The NRDC had asked the electric utility to include a rebuttal written by the NRDC in the next month's insert. When Con Ed refused, the NRDC filed a complaint with the commission and requested that the commission order Con Ed to offer space in the monthly inserts to organizations and individuals holding views opposed to those expressed by the utility on public controversies. Instead of granting the NRDC's request, the commission adopted a policy of prohibiting public utilities from discussing issues of public controversy. The ban was aimed at the topic of nuclear energy, but it imposed prior restraint on all public controversies.

Consolidated Edison challenged the order in court. The New York Supreme Court (an intermediate state appellate court) held that the order was an unconstitutional prior restraint, but the appellate division of the state supreme court reversed and the New York Court of Appeals, the highest appellate court in the state, affirmed. The state court of appeals held that the order was a reasonable time, place, and manner restriction that was designed to protect a legitimate state interest—individual privacy (essentially the right not to be bombarded with utility propaganda).

In a 7 to 2 decision written by Associate Justice Lewis F. Powell, Jr., the U.S. Supreme Court reversed the New York Court of Appeals. According to the Court, the ban was not "(i) a reasonable time, place, and manner restriction, (ii) a permissible subject-matter regulation, or a narrowly tailored means of serving a compelling state interest."[48] The majority opinion specifically noted that "a constitutionally permissible time, place, and manner restriction may not be based upon either the content or subject matter of the speech." This is a reiteration of a well established principle that such prior restraint must be *content-neutral*.

What about the consumer's right of privacy to not be exposed to such controversies when a monthly utility bill is opened? The Court rejected this rationale and a number of other justifications the state offered in its defense for imposing the ban. According to the Court:

> Passengers on public transportation or residents of a neighborhood disturbed by the raucous broadcasts from a passing soundtruck may well be unable to escape an unwanted message. But customers who encounter an objectionable billing insert may "effectively avoid further bombardment of their sensibilities simply by averting their eyes." … The customer of Consolidated Edison may escape exposure to objectionable material simply by transferring the bill insert from envelope to wastebasket.[49]

The Court also rejected the argument that the decision in *Red Lion Broadcasting v. Federal Communications Commission* (1969)[50] (discussed in the next chapter) upholding the Fairness Doctrine justified the ban, noting that the airwaves are limited public resources while billing inserts are not. Even the argument that the ban would prevent consumers from subsidizing the expense of the utility's airing of its controversial views was rejected. There was nothing to indicate that the agency "could not exclude the cost of these bill inserts from the utility's rate base," according to the Court.

In *Central Hudson Gas & Electric v. Public Service Commission of New York* (1980),[51] the U.S. Supreme Court articulated a new four-part analysis for determining whether a particular restriction on commercial speech is constitutional. In 1973, the U.S. suffered an energy crisis brought on by an oil embargo imposed by the Arab cartel known as Organization of Petroleum Exporting Countries (OPEC) in October in retaliation for U.S. support of Israel during the Arab–Israeli War. The ban was lifted on March 18, 1974, after rather severe fuel shortages in this country. The federal government and most states adopted stringent energy conservation measures and launched a public relations effort to encourage Americans to adopt their own conservation methods.

During the energy crisis, the New York Public Service Commission (PSC) ordered the electric utilities in the state including Central Hudson not to advertise or promote the use of electricity. The electric companies complied with the order during the national energy crisis. But after the embargo was lifted in 1974, the effects of the shortage began to wear off, and some public utilities slowly reverted to their traditional promotional advertising. In 1977, the New York PSC adopted a policy statement that continued its ban on promotional advertising even though the energy crisis abated. The statement did not ban all advertising, only "promotional advertising," the commission defined as designed to promote purchase of utility service. Institutional and informational advertising that was not aimed at increasing sales was not prohibited.

Central Hudson Gas & Electric challenged the ban on First and 14th Amendment grounds in court, but the state trial court, intermediate appellate court, and the New York Court of Appeals all held that the order was constitutional. However, in an 8 to 1 opinion written by Justice Lewis F. Powell, Jr., the Supreme Court ruled the ban was unconstitutional. Although there were three separate concurring opinions, only Justice Rehnquist dissented. Justice Powell noted:

> Our decisions have recognized "the 'commonsense' distinction between speech proposing a commercial transaction, which occurs in an area traditionally subject to government regulation, and other varieties of speech." [cites omitted] The Constitution therefore accords a lesser protection to commercial speech than to other constitutionally guaranteed expression.... The protection available for particular commercial expression turns on the nature both of the expression and of the governmental interests served by its regulation. The First Amendment's concern for commercial speech is based on the informational function of advertising. Consequently, there can be no constitutional objection to the suppression of commercial messages that do not accurately inform the public about lawful activity. The government may ban forms of communication more likely to deceive the public than to inform it ... or commercial speech related to illegal activity.[52] [footnotes omitted]

The opinion offered a four-part analysis for courts to apply in commercial speech cases:

> At the outset, we must determine whether the expression is protected by the First Amendment. For commercial speech to come within that provision, it at least must concern lawful activity and not be misleading. Next, we ask whether the asserted governmental interest is substantial. If both inquiries yield positive answers, we must determine whether the regulation directly advances the governmental interest asserted, and whether it is more extensive than necessary to serve that interest.[53]

The Court then applied the analysis to the *Central Hudson* case and determined that the ban did violate the First Amendment. The Court made several interesting points in its analysis. First, the opinion noted that unless there are extraordinary conditions, a monopoly position such as control over the supply of electricity in this case does not change the First Amendment protection accorded the business. Second, although the state's interest in imposing the ban (conserving energy and ensuring fair and efficient rates) was substantial, any negative impact of promotional advertising was "highly speculative." Finally, the Court contended that the state had not demonstrated that its goal of promoting energy conservation could not be accomplished by a less restrictive means than a total ban on promotional advertising.

As with any judicial analysis, the four-step *Central Hudson* test is not as clear and concise as some lower courts would prefer, but it has proven viable in subsequent commercial speech cases. The Court had effectively applied the test, or at least its basic premises, in decisions leading up to *Central Hudson*, but this was the first time the justices had articulated a specific, step-by-step analysis. Not all of the justices agreed with the test. Associate Justice Harry A. Blackmun, joined by William J. Brennan, Jr., indicated in a concurring opinion that the test "is not consistent with our prior cases and does not provide adequate protection for truthful, nonmisleading, noncoercive commercial speech."[54]

According to Justice Blackmun, "If the First Amendment guarantee means anything, it means that, absent clear and present danger, government has no power to restrict expression because of the effect its message is likely to have on the public."[55] Thus Blackmun would extend the commercial speech doctrine to include a much broader range of expression than the *Central Hudson* formula. Justice John Paul Stevens, joined by Justice Brennan, also did not view *Central Hudson* as a commercial speech case. He felt the breadth of the ban exceeded the boundaries of the commercial speech concept: "This ban encompasses a great deal more than mere proposals to engage in certain kinds of commercial transactions." Justice Rehnquist, as would be expected based on his previous dissents in commercial speech cases, believed the state's ban was constitutional as a "permissible state regulation of an economic activity." He once again noted that "the Court unleashed a Pandora's box when it 'elevated' commercial speech to the level of traditional political speech by according it First Amendment protection."[56]

Could it be argued the promotional advertising was a form of political speech under the circumstances in *Central Hudson*? What if the utility had taken a direct stand against the PSC ban in its advertising? What if the company had indirectly promoted electricity by advertising new fuel-efficient appliances? Under Justice Rehnquist's analysis, could the commission have banned all utility company advertising, including "institutional and informational" ads?

First Amendment Protection for Unsolicited Mail Advertising: *Bolger v. Youngs Drug Products Corp.* (1983)

In 1983, the U.S. Supreme Court faced what might initially appear to be a question with a complex answer: is there a First Amendment right to mail *unsolicited* advertising for contraceptives? The answer provided by the Court in *Bolger v. Youngs Drug Products Corp.* (1983)[57] turned out to be rather simple: *yes*. Arriving at the answer was not a simple process. From the long line of cases discussed thus far in this book, it is clear that noncommercial unsolicited mailings have full First Amendment protection. Unsolicited commercial mail also has some First Amendment protection, thanks to *Central Hudson Gas & Electric*.

Youngs Drug Products, one of the largest manufacturers of condoms, planned to regularly send unsolicited advertising matter through the U.S. mail, including a drug store flyer and two pamphlets entitled "Condoms and Human Sexuality" and "Plain Talk about Venereal Disease." Hearing the company's plan, the U.S. Postal Service (USPS) notified the company that such mailings would violate a federal statute that provided "any unsolicited advertisement of matter which is designed, adapted, or intended for preventing conception is nonmailable matter."[58] The USPS rejected Youngs' contention that the law violated the First Amendment. When the manufacturer sought declaratory and injunctive relief from the USPS decision in U.S. District Court for the District of Columbia, the court granted the injunction and declared the statute unconstitutional. The USPS appealed, but the U.S. Supreme Court upheld the lower court ruling.

The threshold question was whether this type of speech was commercial or noncommercial. Surprisingly, the Court opted for the former even though the pamphlets were at least highly informational. One of the pamphlets made numerous references to condoms made by Youngs, whereas the other focused more on generic issues. Thurgood Marshall wrote a majority opinion that agreed with the district court that informational pamphlets constituted commercial speech:

> Most of appellee's mailings fall within the core notion of commercial speech—"speech which does no more than propose a commercial transaction" [citing *Virginia Pharmacy*]. Youngs' informational pamphlets, however, cannot be characterized merely as proposals to engage in commercial transactions. Their proper classification as commercial or noncommercial speech thus presents a closer question. The mere fact that these pamphlets are conceded to be advertisements clearly does not compel the conclusion

that they are commercial speech [citing *New York Times v. Sullivan*]. Similarly, the reference to a specific product does not by itself render the pamphlets commercial speech. Finally, the fact that Youngs has an economic motivation for mailing the pamphlets would clearly be insufficient by itself to turn these materials into commercial speech [citing *Bigelow*]. The combination of all these characteristics, however, provides strong support for the District Court's conclusion that the informational pamphlets are properly characterized as commercial speech.[59]

Finding that the proposed mailings were commercial speech, the Court then applied the *Central Hudson* four-part test for determining whether the specific governmental restrictions on this commercial speech were constitutional. Although the government in this case was federal rather than state, as it had been in earlier cases, the four-part test is still the same. First, the Supreme Court determined that the advertising was not misleading and was not concerned with illegal activities and that it promoted "substantial individual and societal interests," such as family planning and the prevention of venereal disease. The USPS had claimed the substantial government interest was in preventing interference with parents' attempts to discuss birth control matters with their children, but the majority reasoned that the particular statute lent "only the most incremental support for the interest asserted. We can reasonably assume that parents already exercise substantial control over the disposition of mail once it enters their mailbox."[60]

The Court then went on to conclude that the statute was overly broad in achieving its objective. Noting that the unsolicited mailings were "entirely suitable for adults," Justice Marshall's opinion evoked an interesting analogy: the "level of discourse reaching a mailbox cannot be limited to that which would be suitable for a sandbox." This same reasoning has been applied in other contexts, including obscenity, when the argument is made that sexually explicit materials could accidentally fall into the hands of children.

The *Youngs Drug Products* decision is particularly apt today. The number of individuals with the acquired immune deficiency syndrome (AIDS) complex has escalated into a worldwide epidemic. Who would have predicted in 1983 that the U.S. Surgeon General would attempt to mail unsolicited to every household an information booklet on the disease, complete with prevention tips? It seems farfetched that by the end of the decade radio and television public service announcements would appear regularly to warn of the dangers of "unsafe sex" in spreading AIDS, touting condoms as a means of preventing AIDS and that radio and television stations would eventually accept paid advertising for condoms, without even a whimper from the Federal Communications Commission.

First Amendment Rights of Professionals: Lawyer Advertising

In 1977, the U.S. Supreme Court handed down the first of a series of cases involving lawyer advertising. In a split 5 to 4 decision written by Justice Harry A. Blackmun in *Bates v. State Bar of Arizona*,[61] the Court effectively broadened *Virginia Board of Pharmacy* to include the same type of advertising (i.e., prices) for lawyers. Attorney John R. Bates and his partner, Van O'Steen, started a legal service clinic in Phoenix that made extensive use of paralegals, standardized forms and other cost-cutting measures. In 1976, two years after they established the clinic that was designed to handle primarily routine services for lower income clients, the lawyers defied a state bar regulation that forbade advertising by placing an ad in the *Arizona Republican* that simply listed the services their firm offered and typical fees. The ad basically touted the availability of "routine services" for "very reasonable fees." No other claims were made.

At that time, Arizona, like most states, had strict regulations regarding advertising by certain professionals such as physicians and lawyers. These regulations were either in the form of codes enforced by a state licensing arm—such as a medical board or the state bar association—or of state statutes. Such regulations had the rationale that they would prevent deceptive and misleading advertising by these groups and that advertising demeaned the professions. As noted by Justice Rehnquist in his dissent in *Virginia Board of Pharmacy*: "It is undoubtedly arguable that many people in the country regard the choice of shampoo as just as important as who may be elected … but that does not automatically bring information about competing shampoos within the protection of the First Amendment."[62]

Although the Court ruled the Arizona regulation was an unconstitutional infringement on freedom of speech and freedom of the press, the justices had a more difficult time dealing with this case than with the earlier pharmacy decision. As licensed attorneys themselves, the justices no doubt were concerned that a ruling that was too broad in granting lawyers the right to advertise could open a Pandora's box that might ultimately undermine the standards and traditions of the profession. The close 5 to 4 vote certainly reflects that concern, as does the majority opinion itself. As Justice Blackmun indicated in the holding, "The constitutional issue in this case is only whether the State may prevent the publication in a newspaper of appellants' truthful advertisement concerning the availability and terms of routine legal services. We rule simply that the flow of such information may not be restrained."[63]

The Court not only made it clear that this holding was applicable only to the specific type of advertising involved, but it also went to unusual lengths to distinguish permissible versus impermissible forms of advertising. Whereas lawyers may advertise prices for such routine services as simple wills, uncontested bankruptcies, uncontested divorces and adoptions, the Court noted, advertising for more complex services such as contested divorces and estate settlements may be subject to regulation. The Court indicated, as it had in earlier decisions, that false, deceptive and misleading advertising can be restrained. But the majority opinion also mentioned that advertising claims as to the quality of services and in-person solicitations might be justifiably suppressed or limited. The Court noted that a warning or disclaimer could be required for certain kinds of advertising. As might be expected, the justices made no judgment whether such restraints would be upheld. The case did not involve any of this type of advertising. "In sum, we recognize that many of the problems in defining the boundary between the deceptive and nondeceptive advertising remain to be resolved, and we expect that the bar will have a special role to play in assuring that advertising by attorneys flows both freely and smoothly,"[64] the Court said.

Could the Court have broadened the decision to include advertising by other professionals? Over the decades, the Supreme Court has enunciated an overbreadth doctrine on First Amendment issues, which essentially permits individuals challenging a statute on First Amendment grounds to demonstrate that the statute could be applied unconstitutionally in circumstances beyond those at issue in the case. This doctrine flies in the face of the traditional rule in constitutional cases that a statute can be challenged only in relation to the conduct or circumstances at hand. However, in First Amendment cases the Court permits a broader challenge because "an overbroad statute might serve to chill protected speech. First Amendment interests are fragile interests, and a person who contemplates protected activity might be discouraged by the effect of the statute." The justices could clearly have broadened the decision to include advertising by other professionals such as physicians and dentists. But the Court chose not to do so in *Bates* because "the justification for the application of overbreadth analysis applies weakly, if at all, in the ordinary commercial context." According to the majority, advertising is unlikely to be affected by chilling effect because it is "linked to commercial well-being."

What is the importance of this case? Even with the 5 to 4 vote, *Bates* is definitely a broadening of the principles laid down in *Virginia Board of Pharmacy*. But this extension of First Amendment protection to include advertising of routine legal services (*Virginia Board of Pharmacy* dealt only with advertising of prescription drug prices, not the availability of services) was not wide enough to put truthful advertising on par with other forms of speech. The Court chose deliberately from the beginning with *Bigelow* to follow the circuitous route of a case-by-case analysis rather than applying the overbreadth doctrine that would have protected truthful commercial speech to the same extent as political and religious speech. *Bates* raised far more questions than it answered, and many of those questions have yet to be resolved, although the Court wrestled with some of them in subsequent cases.

The dissenters included Chief Justice Warren Burger and Associate Justices Lewis F. Powell, Jr., Potter Stewart, and William H. Rehnquist. Their basic argument was that the ruling was, as Justice Powell stated, "an invitation—by the public-spirited and the selfish lawyers alike—to engage in competitive advertising on an escalating basis." Justice Rehnquist went even further in his dissent. Although Justice Powell indicated in his dissent that some forms of legal advertising might have First Amendment protection, Rehnquist clung to *Valentine v. Chrestensen*: "The *Valentine* distinction was constitutionally sound and practically workable, and I am still unwilling to take even one step down the slippery slope away from it."[65] In subsequent decisions, Rehnquist held that minority view even while serving as the Chief Justice, a role that forced him to seek consensus among the justices in forging more definite rulings.

Lawyer Solicitation: *Ohralik* and *In Re Primus*

Within a year after *Bates*, the Court began a series of decisions that set out the specific parameters of First Amendment protection for commercial speech of attorneys. In *Ohralik v. Ohio State Bar Association* (1978)[66] and *In Re Primus* (1978),[67] the U.S. Supreme Court ruled on the extent to which states may regulate attorneys' solicitation of potential clients. In *Ohralik* the Court upheld the suspension of an attorney by the Ohio Bar Association for his in-person solicitation of two 18-year-old women shortly after they had been in a car accident. The lawyer's efforts resulted in both victims signing contingent fee agreements with him. The state bar association suspended Ohralik even though it was never able to demonstrate any harm to the women from the agreements. In his majority opinion, Justice Lewis F. Powell, Jr. distinguished this type of personal solicitation from the advertising in *Bates*. He said Ohio had a "legitimate and indeed 'compelling'" interest in "preventing those aspects of solicitation that involve fraud, undue influence, intimidation, overreaching, and other forms of 'vexatious conduct.'"

In *In Re Primus*, a South Carolina volunteer American Civil Liberties Union attorney sent a letter to a former patient to solicit her as a potential plaintiff in a suit against a doctor. The lawyer believed the physician had sterilized pregnant women who were allegedly told they would no longer receive Medicaid care unless they agreed to the surgery. Justice Powell, writing for the majority, set aside a public reprimand handed down to the attorney on grounds that the First Amendment right to freedom of speech protected this form of political expression because there was no demonstration of "undue influence, overreaching, misrepresentation, or invasion of privacy."[68] The Court viewed Primus' actions as political, not commercial, expression, while Ohralik was engaging in a commercial transaction. Scholars may characterize such distinction as hair splitting, but the Court saw a difference. Justice Rehnquist dissented in *Primus* because he saw "no principled distinction" between the two cases in which "'ambulance-chasers' suffer one fate and 'civil liberties lawyers' another ... I believe that constitutional inquiry must focus on the character of the conduct which the State seeks to regulate, and not on the motives of the individual lawyers or the nature of the particular litigation involved."[69]

Two years after *Central Hudson*, the Supreme Court ruled that a state may not restrict lawyer advertising to specific types of information. After the *Bates v. State Bar of Arizona* decision in 1977, the Missouri bar adopted some new rules of professional ethics that were believed to be permitted under the principles established in *Bates*. Most state bar associations, which traditionally determine the professional standards for attorneys in the state, have taken a rather conservative approach to advertising. Lawyers, in general, disapprove of most forms of promotion and advertising. When a state or appellate court approves restrictions on advertising imposed by the bar association in one state, the bar associations in other states usually move quickly to adopt those tougher standards if they do not already have them. Lawyers are not the only professionals who abhor advertising. The same sentiment against professional advertising appears to prevail among physicians, pharmacists, nurses, accountants, and so on.

The Missouri restrictions were rather severe, as the U.S. Supreme Court noted in *In Re R. M. J.* (1982),[70] in which the justices unanimously struck down a series of professional ethics rules. "RMJ" was reprimanded for violating several of the rules, including restrictions on information about areas of practice, announcements about office openings, and jurisdictions in which he was admitted to practice. The rules were so strict that only 23 specific terms could be used to describe areas of practice. For example, "RMJ" was reprimanded for using *real estate* instead of *property* in his ad and for listing *contracts* and *securities* as areas of practice. He also ran afoul of the rules by mailing out cards announcing the opening of his office to individuals who were not included in the categories to whom such information could be sent. "RMJ" was also cited for truthfully advertising that he was a member of the Missouri and Illinois bars and that he had been admitted to practice before the U.S. Supreme Court.

The majority opinion, written by Associate Justice Lewis F. Powell, Jr., pointed out that the Missouri bar made no assertions the ads were in any way misleading or inaccurate and thus had demonstrated no substantial state interest in enacting the regulations. Indeed, about all the state had been able to show was that the ads may have approached bad taste. Although the Court held that all of the restrictions challenged were unconstitutional, Justice Powell indicated that the line in the ad in large boldface type proclaiming that "RMJ" was a member of the U.S. Supreme Court bar may have been somewhat misleading and unfortunate. A U.S. Supreme Court rule allows admission to practice before the Court if the attorney has been admitted to practice in the highest court of a state, territory, district, commonwealth, or possession for a minimum of three years and if the person "appears to the Court to be of good moral and professional character." After an application is filed and an admission fee paid, the attorney is sworn in. Thus the vast majority of attorneys are eligible to become members of the Supreme Court bar. Nevertheless, the Court noted there was nothing in the record to indicate that even this information was actually misleading, although "this relatively uninformative fact ... could be misleading to the general public unfamiliar with the requirements of admission to the bar" of the Supreme Court.

The Court found that the other violations, including the mailing of announcement cards to a larger audience than that permitted under the rules[71] and the listing of other jurisdictions to which "RMJ" had been admitted, were not misleading and so were protected by the First Amendment.

The unanimous opinion in this case is not surprising in light of previous Court decisions, including *Bates*. The rules in this case were restrictive. Although the rationale of bar associations for imposing regulations is ostensibly to preserve respect for the dignity of the profession, one effect is to reduce competition among attorneys and prevent legal fees from declining. No mention of such effects was made in the Court's decision, but consumer groups argue that advertising by professionals improves the marketplace for consumers by increasing competition.

Over the decades, lawyers have continued to test the First Amendment limits of advertising. Three cases in the 1980s particularly stand out because lawyers in each case went considerably beyond the guidelines or rules established by their bar associations and yet found constitutional protection in the U.S. Supreme Court. In the first case, *Zauderer v. Office of Disciplinary Counsel* (1985),[72] a Columbus, Ohio, attorney named Philip Q. Zauderer violated the Ohio Disciplinary Rules governing attorneys when he ran a newspaper advertisement that indicated he was willing to handle on a contingent fee basis cases involving women who had been injured by an intra-uterine contraceptive device known as the Dalkon Shield. The ad included an illustration of the device. It claimed a client would owe no fees unless she won damages. Both the illustration and the "no fees" assertion were in clear violation of the Ohio rules. The top part of the ad in bold type with all capital letters asked, "Did you use this IUD?" Along the side was a line drawing of the Dalkon Shield. The ad also noted, "Our law firm is presently representing women on such cases."

The Ohio Office of Disciplinary Counsel disciplined Zauderer for the ad on the grounds that he was soliciting business, had engaged in deceptive advertising, and had included a drawing in the ad. The Ohio Supreme Court upheld the state's disciplinary action, but the U.S. Supreme Court in a 5 to 3 decision held that the Ohio rule regarding solicitation was a violation of the First Amendment. The majority opinion, written by Justice Byron R. White, said the rule was overly broad because it applied to all forms of such advertising—deceptive and nondeceptive. The Court said: "Were we to accept the State's argument in this case [that such solicitations are inherently misleading and therefore subject to the ban], we would have little basis for preventing the Government from suppressing other forms of truthful and nondeceptive advertising simply to spare itself the trouble of distinguishing such advertising from false or deceptive advertising."[73]

All eight of the justices voting found the ban on illustrations was unconstitutional. Six agreed that Zauderer could be disciplined for his claim that "no fees would be owed by the client" because he failed to disclose the client could be held responsible for court costs. While most states permit attorneys to represent clients at no charge and indeed encourage them to act *pro bono* for indigent individuals, courts and state codes of professional conduct generally do not permit attorneys to pay court costs for clients. Although courts usually have the discretion of waiving such costs when warranted, Ohio rules required full disclosure of information regarding contingency fees, and this was constitutionally sound, according to the U.S. Supreme Court.

Zauderer basically stands for the principle that attorneys and other professionals can engage in traditional forms of advertising and promotion so long as such commercial speech is neither misleading nor deceptive. The next case sent shock waves through some legal circles because it appears to have opened the door to a wide variety of advertising. The decision is particularly significant because it answered a major question that remained after *Ohralik, Bates*, and *Zauderer*: *do attorneys have a First Amendment right to solicit clients via direct mail?*

Kentucky attorney Richard D. Shapero requested the Attorneys Advertising Commission, a three-member body created by the Kentucky Supreme Court to regulate attorney advertising,[74] to approve a letter he wished to send to potential clients believed to be facing foreclosure on their home mortgages. The proposed letter urged the recipient to "call my office ... for FREE information on how you can keep your home. Call NOW, don't wait. It may surprise you what I may be able to do for you" [capital letters in the original]. Under the Kentucky Supreme Court rules at that time, attorneys were banned from sending letters or advertisements to potential clients who might need legal assistance because of a change of circumstances such as a divorce, death in the family, or foreclosure. The commission rejected Shapero's letter as a direct solicitation in violation of the State Supreme Court rules. Shapero appealed the decision to the State Supreme Court which ruled against him. But the U.S. Supreme Court ruled 6 to 3 in *Shapero v. Kentucky Bar Association*[75] that the Kentucky rule was a violation of the First and 14th Amendments because it imposed a blanket ban on both deceptive and nondeceptive advertising through the mail. The state had argued the prohibition was necessary to prevent lawyers from exerting undue influence or abusing individuals by taking advantage of potential clients facing serious legal problems.

The majority opinion, written by Justice William H. Brennan, Jr., contended, as the Court did in *Youngs Drug Products*, the potential for undue influence and fraud was significantly less than that of in-person solicitation, which the Court had held in *Ohralik* could be barred. The "File 13" proposition comes into play once again: if you don't like what you receive in the mail, throw it in the trash. Or, as Justice Brennan said, "Unlike the potential client with a badgering advocate breathing down his neck, the recipient of a letter and the reader of an advertisement can effectively avoid further bombardment of his sensibilities simply by averting his eyes."[76]

The attorney, by the way, continued to attract controversy. A year later he became the host of a 6 to 7 p.m. weekly call-in show on an AM radio station which was criticized by the *Louisville Courier-Journal* for allegedly airing inaccurate information. But both the then president-elect of the Kentucky Bar Association and the Chief Justice of the State Supreme Court at the time refused to criticize the program even though the Bar Association and Court were targets for colorful comments.[77]

At the time of that decision, about half of the states permitted solicitation by mail. Now such attorney advertising, so long as it is not deceptive or misleading, is permitted in all states. The State Supreme Court revised its rules to delete this type of advertising as a violation, but still bans false, deceptive, and misleading ads, that are defined as containing "a material misrepresentation of fact or law" regarding (a) the nature of services offered, (b) an attorney's "educational background, employment history, professional experience or other credentials," (c) "a law firm's collective experience in a field of practice," or (d) "the identity of the lawyer(s) who will actually perform the legal services or the location of the office where the services will be performed."[78] The rules also prohibit the use of a nonlawyer in an ad in a way that "suggests or implies that he or she is a lawyer." A similar ban applies to ads in which an actor misrepresents himself as an actual client. The rules also ban props such as a car or truck "that suggests or implies that it was actually involved in a particular legal matter, where such display results in a material misrepresentation." Certain types of ads must carry a disclaimer that "This is an advertisement."[79]

There are specific provisions in those state rules regarding (a) information that must be included in an ad such as the office location and telephone number, (b) advertising that "creates unjustified expectations or makes unsubstantiated comparisons," and (c) "advertising that suggests a likelihood of satisfactory results irrespective of the merits of the particular matter."[80] Those rules are similar, allowing attorneys to voluntarily submit proposed ads to a commission that, for a fee, will review them for compliance.

Another barrier to certain types of lawyer advertising fell in 1990 when the U.S. Supreme Court held in *Peel v. Attorney Registration and Disciplinary Commission of Illinois*[81] that attorneys have a First Amendment right to advertise specialties certified by private or nonbar organizations. The case began when attorney Gary Peel sent a letter to two clients. Peel's letterhead included the statement, "Certified Civil Trial Specialist by the National Board of Trial Advocacy." The information had appeared on his letterhead for three years with no complaints, but the administrative agency of the Illinois Supreme Court, the Attorney Registration and Disciplinary Commission (ARDC), filed a formal complaint against Peel for violating the state Code of Professional Responsibility. According to the code, "A lawyer shall not hold himself out publicly as a specialist, except as follows: patent lawyer, trademark lawyer, admiralty lawyer." After a hearing, the ARDC ruled the attorney had acted improperly and recommended public censure. On appeal, the Illinois Supreme Court upheld the commission's findings, contending that the information on the letterhead was misleading to the public because of the similarity between licensed and certified. The State Supreme Court felt the public could wrongly believe that the attorney "may practice in the field of trial advocacy solely because he is certified by the NBTA." To be certified by the organization, a lawyer must have at least five years of civil trial practice, have acted as lead counsel in at least 15 civil cases, and pass a full-day exam.

In a 5 to 4 decision authored by Justice John Paul Stevens (joined by Justices Brennan, Blackmun, and Kennedy, with Justices Marshall and Brennan concurring separately), the U.S. Supreme Court rejected the state's contention that the letterhead was deceptive. Citing *In Re R. M. J.*, the majority said the claim of certification was information from which "a consumer may or may not draw an inference of the likely quality of an attorney's work in a given area of practice." Thus it was not automatically deceptive or misleading. The Court chided the state for its "paternalistic" rule, noting that this information was essentially no different from the assertion of "practice before the United States Supreme Court" approved in *In Re R. M. J.* The majority compared the certification claim to that of a trademark, noting that "the strength of certification is measured by the quality of the organization for which it stands." The justices said disclosure of *more* information, rather than withholding information, as the state wanted to do, best serves the public interest by educating consumers. Justice Marshall, joined by Brennan, concurred with the Court's judgment that the Illinois regulation was unconstitutional but asserted the letterhead could be misleading. According to these members of the Court, the ban went too far because there were less restrictive ways of accomplishing the same result.

Many attorneys, judges, and bar associations continue to oppose most forms of lawyer advertising, but anyone who regularly watches commercial television has no doubt noticed a proliferation of attorney ads, many of which are as crass and bold as those for new and used cars. Even the conservative American Bar Association (ABA), which for a long time opposed most forms of lawyer advertising, has relented. The rule struck down in *Shapero* was adopted by Kentucky from the ABA's Model Rules of Professional Conduct. (Most state bar associations have adopted these rules, usually with revisions, for their attorneys.) Now the *ABA Journal* carries articles on topics such as successful marketing, including appropriate advertising technique.

The ABA Model Rules of Professional Conduct permit many forms of advertising, including direct mail solicitations of the type challenged in *Shapero*.

The amount attorneys spend on advertising has continued to climb during the years since *Bates*. Some states, such as Texas, cling to stringent rules on ads. In 1988, the year *Shapero* was decided, the State Bar of Texas permitted an attorney to advertise only the law firm's address, the range of legal services offered, and prices.[82] According to a publication of the Yellow Pages Publishers Association, one Texas law firm was cited by the State Bar of Texas for violating its rules when it failed to mention the specific names of lawyers responsible for the areas of specialization cited in a Yellow Pages ad. The same publication noted, on the other hand, that a Florida attorney was apparently not in violation of that state's bar association rules (a version of ABA Rules of Professional Conduct) when his quarter-page spread in the local Yellow Pages proclaimed: "NATIONALLY KNOWN ATTORNEY WITH GUEST APPEARANCES ON 'GOOD MORNING AMERICA,' 'GERALDO,' 'ALAN BURKE' & OTHER SHOWS."[83]

In 1994, the U.S. Supreme issued a ruling in a lawyer advertising case with a new twist. In *Ibanez v. Florida Department of Business and Professional Regulation, Board of Accountancy* (1994),[84] the Court held in the first majority opinion written by Justice Ginsburg that a Florida ban on lawyers advertising that they are also certified public accountants and certified financial planners was a violation of the First Amendment. The new dimension in this case was the placement of the prohibition by the state Board of Accountancy, which licenses and regulates certified public accountants, rather than by the state bar. Silvia Ibanez had placed the initials CPA and CFP in her yellow pages listing and on her business cards and law office stationery. CPA designates a certified public accountant, indicating board licensing. CFP is a designation for a certified financial planner, which is granted after an approved course of study and passing an exam administered by the Certified Financial Planner Board. On appeal, the accountancy board argued that the CPA designation by Ibanez was misleading because, as she had admitted at her hearing, she was practicing law, not accounting. The board contended that the CFP designation was misleading because, in conjunction with CPA, it implied state approval.

The Court unanimously held that the use of CPA was not misleading because Ibanez continued to hold her CPA license and thus the board was punishing her for disseminating truthful commercial speech. No deception and no harm to the public had been demonstrated. Although the accountancy board had reprimanded her for engaging in "false, deceptive, and misleading" advertising, it did not revoke her CPA license nor her CFP authorization. All but Chief Justice Rehnquist and Justice O'Connor believed the CFP designation was neither misleading nor harmful. The latter two justices contended the board could take action against Ibanez for not including a disclaimer to indicate that the CFP board was not affiliated with the state.

Ibanez is a victory for commercial speech. Licensing agencies remain free to impose limits on advertising but restrictions must meet the *Central Hudson* test. Under this standard, the state may ban advertising only if it is false, deceptive, or misleading. It may restrict advertising only if it can show that a restriction directly and materially advances a substantial interest in a manner no more extensive than needed to advance that interest. The Court said, "The State's burden is not slight … '[M]ere speculation or conjecture' will not suffice; rather the State 'must demonstrate that the harms it recites are real and that its restriction will in fact alleviate them to a material degree'" [cite omitted].[85]

In 1995, the U.S. Supreme Court dealt a blow to First Amendment protection for commercial speech. In *Florida Bar v. Went For It, Inc.*,[86] the Court held in a 5 to 4 opinion written by Justice O'Connor (joined by Chief Justice Rehnquist and Associate Justices Scalia, Thomas, and Breyer) that Florida Bar rules prohibiting personal injury attorneys from sending targeted direct mail solicitations to victims or their relatives for 30 days after an accident or disaster do not violate the first and 14th Amendments to the Constitution.

In 1990, the Florida Supreme Court approved with some revisions the state bar association's proposed amendments to the Rules of Professional Conduct that involve advertising.[87] The bar association made the proposals after a two-year study that included hearings, surveys, and public comments about lawyer advertising. An attorney[88] and his wholly owned lawyer referral service, Went For It, Inc., challenged two rules[89] in the U.S. District Court for the Middle District of Florida as unconstitutional. They did this because, taken together, the rules imposed a 30-day blackout after an accident or disaster in which attorneys could not directly or indirectly target victims or relatives for solicitation of business. Prior to the enactment of these rules, the attorney regularly mailed targeted solicitations to victims or their survivors and referred potential clients to other attorneys within 30 days. His suit for declaratory and injunctive relief asked that he be allowed to continue this practice. Both sides asked for summary judgment in their favor, and a magistrate judge to whom the district court referred the case recommended a summary judgment be granted to the bar. The district court rejected his recommendation and issued a summary judgment instead for the plaintiffs.[90] Citing *Bates* and others cited by the trial court, the Eleventh Circuit U.S. Court of Appeals reluctantly affirmed in 1994.[91] The Supreme Court acknowledged in the majority opinion that *Bates* had laid the "foundation" for two decades: "[i]t is well established that lawyer advertising is commercial speech and, as such, is accorded a measure of First Amendment protection." However, that measure of protection is limited, the Court said, noting that *Central Hudson* requires an intermediate level of scrutiny of restrictions on commercial speech.

Applying the *Central Hudson* test, the Court found that (a) the speech being regulated did not concern unlawful activity nor was it misleading, (b) the State Bar had a "substantial interest in protecting the privacy and tranquility of personal injury victims and their loved ones against intrusive, unsolicited contact by lawyers" and a substantial interest in protecting "the flagging reputations of Florida lawyers by preventing them from engaging in conduct that, the Bar Association maintains, 'is universally regarded as deplorable and beneath common decency …'" (c) based on extensive studies and other evidence (including news stories and editorials), that the harms targeted by the rules are "far from illusory," and (d) "[t]he palliative devised by the Bar to address these harms is narrow both in scope and in duration."[92]

Justice Kennedy's dissent in *Florida Bar* is notable because it demonstrates just how thin the majority was, and he minces no words regarding his disdain for the majority opinion. His blistering attack, to which Justices Stevens, Souter, and Ginsburg signed on, criticizes the document ("Summary of Record") the majority relied upon in supporting that the government had a substantial interest:

> This document includes no actual surveys, few indications of sample size or selection procedures, no explanations of methodology, and no discussion of excluded results. There is no description of the statistical universe or scientific framework that permits any productive use of the information the so-called Summary of Record contains. The majority describes this anecdotal matter as "noteworthy for its breadth and detail" ... but when examined, it is noteworthy for its incompetence.[93]

His dissent goes on to say, "Our cases require something more than a few pages of self-serving and unsupported statements by the State to demonstrate that a regulation directly and materially advances the elimination of a real harm when the state seeks to suppress truthful and non-deceptive speech" [cite omitted]. The opinion notes the ban created by the bar association rule is much too broad: "Even assuming that interest [the state's interest] were legitimate, there is a wild disproportion between the harm supposed and the speech ban enforced."[94]

Justice Kennedy's other arguments include (a) mail is not sent to a "captive audience"—it can simply be thrown away, (b) there is no justification for assuming, as the majority does, that information provided in direct mail is "unwelcome or unnecessary" during the 30-day ban, and (c) the ban cuts off information at a time when "prompt legal representation" could be essential. He also notes that "[p]otential clients will not hire lawyers who offend them" and that a "solicitation letter is not a contract." According to Kennedy, "It is most ironic that, for the first time since *Bates v. State Bar of Arizona*, the Court now orders a major retreat from the constitutional guarantees for commercial speech in order to shield its own profession from public criticism." He concludes:

> Today's opinion is a serious departure, not only from our prior decisions involving attorney advertising, but also from the principles that govern the transmission of commercial speech. The Court's opinion reflects a new-found and illegitimate confidence that it, along with the Supreme Court of Florida, knows what is best for the Bar and its clients. Self-assurance has always been the hallmark of a censor. That is why under the First Amendment the public, not the State, has the right and the power to decide what ideas and information are deserving of their adherence....[95]

Advertising by Other Professionals: *Friedman v. Rogers* (1979) and *Thompson v. Western States Medical Center* (2002)

Just as the Court has been reluctant to grant full First Amendment rights to commercial speech of attorneys, it has hesitated to broaden constitutional protection for commercial speech of others. In 1979 in *Friedman v. Rogers*,[96] the justices held 7 to 2 that Texas could prevent optometrists from practicing under a trade name because the state had a "substantial and well-demonstrated" interest in protecting consumers from deceptive and misleading use of optometrical trade names. Three years later, the Court affirmed an opinion by the U.S. Court of Appeals for the Second Circuit[97] that upheld orders by the Federal Trade Commission (FTC) forbidding the American Medical Association and the American Dental Association from imposing total bans on advertising by members of their respective associations. In *American Medical Association v. Federal Trade Commission* (1982),[98] the Supreme Court upheld the appellate court decision without opinion. We do not know why the Court upheld the decision, although the rules did bar truthful advertising by physicians and dentists. The FTC rules are in line with *Bates*—permitting regulation of deceptive and misleading advertising.

In *Thompson v. Western States Medical Center* (2002),[99] the U.S. Supreme Court said in a plurality opinion written by Justice O'Connor that two provisions of the 1997 Food and Drug Administration Modernization Act violated the First Amendment. O'Connor was joined in her opinion by Justices Scalia, Kennedy, and Souter. Justice Thomas concurred in a separate opinion: "I concur because I agree with the Court's application of the test set forth in *Central Hudson Gas & Elec. Corp. v. Public Serv. Comm'n. of N.Y.*, 447 U.S. 557 (1980). I continue, however, to adhere to my view that cases such as this should not be analyzed under the *Central Hudson test*."[100] Chief Justice Rehnquist and Justices Breyer, Stevens and Ginsburg dissented.

The first provision struck down said that pharmacies may generally advertise and promote compounding (combining or mixing ingredients to create medication for a patient's specific needs), but they may not advertise that they compound a particular drug or class of drugs. The second provision said that pharmacists may fill prescriptions for compounded drugs only if the medications are "unsolicited." The Court applied the *Central Hudson* test, rejecting the federal government's arguments that the provisions would protect consumers by stopping pharmacies from doing an end run around the FDA approval process by effectively manufacturing new drugs. According to the plurality opinion, "We have previously rejected the notion that the government has an interest in preventing the dissemination of truthful commercial information in order to prevent members of the public from making bad decisions with the information."[101]

Truthful Commercial Speech: From *Posadas* to *Johanns*

A 5 to 4 decision in 1986, written by Justice William H. Rehnquist, struck what appeared at the time to be a serious blow to the principle that truthful commercial speech concerned with a legal product or service enjoys First Amendment protection. *Posadas de Puerto Rico Associates v. Tourism Company of Puerto Rico* (1986)[102] has never been explicitly overturned. However, it was discredited in subsequent decisions by the Court, including *44 Liquormart v. Rhode Island*,[103] discussed later, in which all but one of the justices either rejected or seriously questioned the *Posadas* rationale. In *Posadas,* the Court applied the four-part *Central Hudson* test for commercial speech to find that a government's restrictions on advertising for legalized gambling were not in violation of the First Amendment. While the Court had indicated since *Bigelow v. Virginia* (1975) and up through *Bolger v. Youngs Drug Products* (1983) that advertising for legal products and services that was not misleading nor deceptive had constitutional protection, *Posadas* appeared, at least then, to have squelched progress made in cases toward putting commercial speech on an equal constitutional footing with noncommercial communication. No matter how much one scrutinizes the reasoning in *Posadas*, it is difficult to square it with the "Three Bs"—*Bigelow, Bates,* and *Bolger.* However, as is seen later in this section, *Posadas* has lost nearly all of its impact today.

In 1948, the Puerto Rican government legalized most types of casino gambling in an effort to beef up its tourism industry. The effort paid off as tourists flocked to the commonwealth.

The 1948 legislation also banned all advertising by casinos to the residents of Puerto Rico. But such advertising was permitted to be directed at tourists within the commonwealth and in the continental United States. Puerto Rican citizens were allowed to use the casinos. A governmental agency, known as the Tourism Company of Puerto Rico, was granted the authority to administer the statute, including the advertising provisions. The Condado Holiday Inn, owned by Posadas de Puerto Rico Associates, defied the ban directed to Puerto Ricans and was fined on several occasions. The hotel consequently filed suit against the government agency, asking for a declaratory judgment that the advertising prohibition was unconstitutional.

After the case traveled through the Puerto Rican judicial system, including a dismissal by the Puerto Rican Supreme Court for lack of a substantive constitutional issue, the U.S. Supreme Court granted a petition for a writ of certiorari. On the threshold question of whether the particular speech in question was commercial or noncommercial, the Court determined that the case involved "the restriction of pure commercial speech which does no more than propose a commercial transaction." The Court applied the *Central Hudson* analysis. It found: (a) the restriction "concerns a lawful activity and is not misleading or fraudulent, at least in the abstract," (b) the "reduction in demand for casino gambling by the residents of Puerto Rico" that the government claimed was the result of the ban constituted the necessary substantial government interest, (c) the statute directly advanced the government's substantial interest because the legislature could reasonably believe that "advertising of casino gambling aimed at the residents … would serve to increase the demand for the product advertised," and (d) the restrictions were "no more extensive than necessary to serve the government's interest."

The casino had argued (a) the statute was too restrictive because it allowed advertising for other types of gambling such as lotteries, horse racing, and cockfighting, (b) the government could more effectively reduce the demand for casino gambling by promulgating speech designed to discourage gambling rather than suppressing speech that promoted this activity, (c) the activity involved here was similar to that in *Bigelow* and, therefore, deserved the protection offered by that case, and (d) once the government legalized gambling, the First Amendment granted protection for advertising related to such activity.

The Court handily rejected all of the appellant's arguments and concluded that the prior restraint had passed the *Central Hudson* test and thus the advertising could make no claim of First Amendment protection. How can the Court justify such severe restrictions on the advertising of a perfectly legitimate activity? Compare gambling with alcohol and tobacco, and you have some indication of the rationale of the Court. The casino had argued that because the government had legalized gambling for tourists and residents, *Bigelow* and its progeny would dictate that the First Amendment would prevent the government from imposing advertising restrictions that were specifically designed to discourage citizens from legal gambling. In other words, once an activity, product or service is legalized, the First Amendment says, "Hands off any advertising, unless it is deceptive or misleading." In strongly rejecting that argument, the Court said the argument should be turned on its head. According to the majority opinion, if a government has the authority to completely prohibit an activity, it could "take the less intrusive step of allowing the conduct, but reducing the demand through restrictions on advertising."[104] The Court went on to mention tobacco, alcohol, and prostitution as examples.

Justice William J. Brennan, Jr. (joined by Thurgood Marshall and Harry A. Blackmun) contended in a dissent that the distinctions between commercial and noncommercial speech did not "justify protecting commercial speech less extensively where, as here, the government seeks to manipulate behavior by depriving citizens of truthful information concerning lawful activities."[105] According to Brennan, even if the government had been able to demonstrate that a substantial interest was involved, there was no evidence that this particular regulation would address that interest. The dissenting opinion argued that the government could have attempted to control harms such as organized crime and prostitution by keeping a tighter rein on the casinos: "It is incumbent upon the government to prove that more limited means are not sufficient to protect its interests, and for a court to decide whether or not the government has sustained this burden."[106]

The lower courts have struggled in interpreting the precise boundaries of "no more extensive than necessary" in the fourth prong of the *Central Hudson Gas & Electric* test, and the U.S. Supreme Court added to the confusion in spite of apparent good intentions. A good illustration of this is the Court's decision in *Board of Trustees of State University of New York v. Fox* (1989).[107] The case involved a First Amendment challenge to a university regulation banning private companies from sponsoring parties in student dormitories when housewares are being promoted. In overturning the rule, the Second Circuit U.S. Court of Appeals held that the standard for determining whether the regulation was no more extensive than necessary was that the state must use the least restrictive measure that could protect the state's interest. At first analysis, this holding may appear to be in line with *Hudson* and even *Posadas*. However, on appeal, the U.S. Supreme Court, in a 6 to 3 decision authored by Antonin Scalia, disagreed with the U.S. Court of Appeals and remanded the case back to the lower court for further findings.

According to the majority, the standard for determining whether a regulation is more extensive than necessary dictates that the restrictions must be "narrowly drawn" and "no more extensive than reasonably necessary" to further government interest. The Court noted that, even for political speech, the "least restrictive measure" test had not been applied in determining the constitutionality of reasonable time, place, and manner restrictions. Instead, the test has been whether regulations are narrowly tailored to promote a significant state interest. The Court noted that a similar test has been applied in determining the validity of restrictions on expressive conduct, including that in a political context. The Court reasoned it would be inappropriate "to apply a more rigid standard" for commercial speech than for other forms of speech that presumably had greater protection. As the Court said, "We think it would be incompatible," given the "subordinate position" of commercial speech, "to apply a more rigid standard in the present context."[108]

How should this test be applied? The state is not required to demonstrate that "the manner of restriction is absolutely the least severe that will achieve the desired end," but a balance, or "fit" as the Court called it, must be found between the asserted governmental interest and the approach taken to accomplish that interest:

> … a fit that is not necessarily perfect, but reasonable; that represents not necessarily the single best disposition but one whose scope is in 'proportion to the interest served …;' that employs not necessarily the least restrictive means but a means narrowly tailored to achieve the desired objective. Within those bounds we leave it to the governmental decision-makers to judge what manner of regulation may be best employed.[109]

The holding represents a significant retreat from the standard that many courts, including the Second Circuit U.S. Court of Appeals, believed applied in commercial speech cases after

Central Hudson Gas & Electric. The new interpretation made it more difficult for governmental restrictions on commercial speech, including advertising, to be struck down as unconstitutional.

Alcohol advertising grabbed the truthful commercial speech spotlight in 1995 when the U.S. Supreme Court struck down a federal statute barring the advertising of the alcohol content of beer. The Federal Alcohol Administration Act (FAAA) of 1935, enacted by Congress after Prohibition died and "strength wars" started among brewers, barred brewers from including the percentage of alcohol on beer labels unless required by state law.[110] In 1987, Coors Brewing Company applied to the federal Bureau of Alcohol, Tobacco and Firearms (BATF) of the Department of Treasury, which administers the Act, for approval of proposed labels and ads that included the percentage of alcohol in its beer. Coors expressed concern about rumors that its beer was weaker than other national brands. The BATF turned down the request on the grounds that it would violate the FAAA and that such advertising and labeling would lead to "strength wars" in which brewers would compete to have the highest alcohol content. The government also argued that such competition would result in more drunkenness and alcoholism and thus more deaths and injuries from drunken driving. Coors then filed suit in U.S. District Court for the District of Colorado, seeking (a) a declaratory judgment that certain provisions of the FAAA violated the First Amendment and (b) an injunction against enforcement of the provisions regarding labeling and advertising of alcohol content. The district court granted Coors' requests. But the 10th Circuit U.S. Court of Appeals reversed the decision and remanded it to the trial court.[111] The appellate court determined that under the *Central Hudson* test the government had shown a substantial interest in suppressing strength wars, but there had been insufficient evidence presented to determine whether the ban would directly advance the interest. Thus the appellate court remanded the case back to the District Court, which upheld the ban on alcohol content ads but struck down the ban on labels. On appeal, the appellate court affirmed,[112] and the case was appealed to the U.S. Supreme Court, which granted certiorari.

In a unanimous decision written by Associate Justice Clarence Thomas with a separate concurring opinion by John Paul Stevens, the Supreme Court held in *Rubin v. Coors Brewing* (1995)[113] that the statutory provision was unconstitutional. Although the Court agreed with the government that its interest in curbing strength wars was sufficiently substantial to meet the *Central Hudson* test, the Court said the ban failed the third and fourth prongs of the test. The Court concluded that the statutory provision "cannot directly and materially advance its [the government's] asserted interest because of the overall irrationality of the Government's regulatory scheme." The Court noted that, although the provision prohibits disclosure of alcohol content on labels unless state law requires it, federal regulations regarding advertising ban statements about alcohol content only in the 18 states specifically prohibiting such advertising content. Thus the laws regarding labels are at odds with those regarding advertising. As the Court saw it, "There is little chance that 205(e)(2) [the labeling ban provision] can directly and materially advance its aim, while other provisions of the same act directly undermine and counteract its effects."

The Supreme Court opinion called the government's evidence *anecdotal* and *educated guesses* regarding the strength wars that would supposedly be fought if the ban were lifted. On the fourth prong of the *Hudson* test, the Court said the regulation was not sufficiently tailored to meet the government's goal. Other options, according to the Court, include directly limiting the alcohol content of beers, banning ads that emphasize high alcohol strength, and limiting the label ban to malt liquors (the market the government believed had the greatest chance of a strength war). The Court suggested that less intrusive forms of the ban might be permitted even though the information being disseminated on the labels and advertisements is truthful information.

In 1996 the U.S. Supreme Court handed down a decision in a case that had the potential to demonstrate just how far the Court was willing to go in protecting truthful commercial speech. Unfortunately, in *44 Liquor Mart v. Racine,*[114] the Court muddied the waters a bit. The case concerned the constitutionality of two Rhode Island statutes.[115] The first law banned the advertising of prices of alcoholic beverages except at the place of sale if sold within the state and so long as the prices were not visible from the street. The second law included a ban on the publication or broadcast of any ads with prices of alcoholic beverages even if for stores in other states. The purpose of the statutes is to discourage consumption of alcohol and maintain control over traffic in alcohol. 44 Liquormart, Inc. and Peoples Super Liquor Stores, Inc., supported by the Rhode Island Liquor Stores Association, successfully challenged the statutory provision in the Rhode Island U.S. District Court, which held it was a violation of the First Amendment.

The case began in 1991 when 44 Liquormart had to pay a $400 fine for a newspaper ad that did not include the prices of alcohol but included the word "WOW" in large letters next to some pictures of vodka and rum. Since the ad featured low prices for peanuts, potato chips, and mixers, the Rhode Island Liquor Control Administrator, charged with enforcing the statutes, ruled there was an implied reference to bargain prices for alcohol, and thus the law had been violated.

The lower court said there was "no empirical evidence that the presence or absence of alcohol price advertising significantly affects levels of alcohol consumption."[116] On appeal, the First Circuit U.S. Court of Appeals reversed, contending the state's action was reasonable and that "[a]dvertising must be generally productive, or so much money would not be spent on it." The court also noted:

> … there would seem to be inherent merit in the State's contention that competitive price advertising would lower prices, and that with lower prices there would be more sales. We would enlarge on this. There are doubtless many buyers whose consumption is sometimes measured by their free money. If a buyer learns that plaintiffs charge less, is he not likely to go there, and then to buy more? Correspondingly, if ignorant of lower prices elsewhere, will he not tend to buy locally, at the higher price, and thus buy less?[117]

The U.S. Supreme Court unanimously reversed, concluding in an opinion written by Justice Stevens that the state had "failed to carry its heavy burden of justifying its complete ban on price advertising." The two statutes and an accompanying state Liquor Control Board Administration regulation violated the First Amendment as applied to the states through the Due Process Clause of the Fourteenth Amendment. Unfortunately, there was no agreement among the justices regarding the appropriate test for making this determination. A plurality of the justices—Stevens, Kennedy, Souter, and Ginsburg—agreed that *Central Hudson* was the correct test.

The plurality agreed that Rhode Island had a substantial government interest in promoting temperance, although noting there was some confusion over what the state meant by *temperance*. The four justices also agreed that even common sense supported the state's argument that a ban on price advertising would elevate prices and that consumption would be lowered as a result. They saw no evidence to support the state's contention that the ban would advance interests in reducing alcohol consumption. The justices said the state could not satisfy the *Central Hudson* requirement that the restriction be no more extensive than necessary.

Chief Justice Rehnquist and Justice Thomas concurred with the Court, but Thomas, in a separate concurring opinion, argued that the *Central Hudson* balancing test should not be applied in commercial speech cases such as this one when "the asserted interest is one that is to be achieved through keeping would-be recipients of the speech in the dark." Later in his opinion he noted that "all attempts to dissuade legal choices by citizens by keeping them ignorant are impermissible." Thomas endorsed the *Virginia Board of Pharmacy* test: "rather than continue to apply a test [*Central Hudson*], a test that makes no sense to me when the asserted state interest is of the type involved here, I would return to the reasoning and holding of *Virginia Pharmacy Bd.*"[118]

The Chief Justice said in his separate opinion that he shared Justice Thomas's "discomfort with the *Central Hudson* test." However, he went on to note, "Since I do not believe we have before us the wherewithal to declare *Central Hudson* wrong—or at least the wherewithal to say what ought to replace it—I must resolve this case in accord with our existing jurisprudence."[119] Thus he was making it clear that he was accepting the application of *Central Hudson* only for now. If the Court were to accept Justice Thomas's analysis in future commercial speech cases—although there is no indication at this point that such is likely to happen—there could be a new era for protection for commercial speech, especially that involving truthful speech. Such a change in direction would be particularly interesting in light of *Florida Bar v. Went for It* (1995).[120] Recall that in *Florida Bar* the Court upheld constitutionality of Florida Bar Association rules prohibiting personal injury attorneys from sending direct mail solicitations to victims and families 30 days after an accident or disaster. The Court applied an intermediate level of scrutiny from the *Central Hudson* test and concluded the bar association had substantial interest in protecting (a) the privacy of victims and their families from intrusion of unsolicited contact by lawyers and (b) public confidence in the legal profession.

44 Liquor Mart and *Rubin v. Coors* and *Florida Bar v. Went for It* illustrate the Court's split personality in commercial speech. When the Court is presented with strong scientific evidence—whether surveys or more rigorous research—to demonstrate substantial state interest and effectiveness of a particular law, it is more likely to side with the government.

A number of recent cases developed within the context of protecting individuals from exposure to material considered inappropriate. In the Fourth Circuit, in the case of *Education Media Company at Virginia Tech, Inc. v. Swecker*, 602 F.3d 583 (4th Cir. 2010) alcohol advertisements in college newspapers were brought under close scrutiny with the knowledge that student publications were read primarily by individuals under the age of 21, a point debated at length in this case. The Virginia Alcoholic Beverage Control Board's restrictions had been challenged on that basis and also the overall influence of such advertisements on consumption were considered, but the Court found that the First Amendment protected such advertisements for alcohol and alcohol prices.

In state court, in the case of *People v. Larsen*, — N.Y.S2nd —, 2010 WL 2991213 (N.Y. Crim. Ct. July 30, 2010), a condom vendor with the company name "Practice Safe Policy" argued that since that corporate entity as well as the name of their prominent products ("Obama Condoms" and "Palin Condoms") should be identified as a form of political speech and provided a First

Amendment exception by virtue of including written matter distinguishing it as "the nation's first brand devoted to showcasing the indecent relations between politics and sex."

The company had been charged with violating a New York statute requiring a license to sell their items on the street in a stated attempt to "turn people's attention from 'minor concerns like the war, the economy or healthcare and instead focus on the truly important issue of the day: Practicing Safe Policy in the bedroom.'" The Court considered whether the condom wrappers could be characterized as "written material" while agreeing that the sale of merchandize could be protected under the First Amendment. The Court concluded that the defendants were primarily occupied with selling goods in spite of what the Court termed "a clunky name," determining that the written material associated with the products were more a part of a sales pitch, as opposed to the expressive quality of information provided as part of political pamphleteering, books, or magazines.

In *City of Tipp City v. Dakin*, 929 N.E.2d 484 (Ohio Ct. App. 2010) business owners were sued for violating a municipal sign ordinance requiring companies to adhere to guidelines or seek a form of exemption. In this case, the Ohio City described a large and colorful "mad scientist" mural depicting a display with a scientist, a beaker, and chemicals had been placed on a company without a permit. The Ohio Court of Appeals judged the mural to invite commercial transaction and thus a form of commercial speech. The Court determined the City's aesthetic and traffic safety considerations of size and color to be overbroad in application and unable to be enforced.

Fruit, Mushrooms and Beef: A Gourmet Meal or a Mystery Recipe?

From 1997 through 2005, the U.S. Supreme Court handed down three decisions involving *compelled funding for advertising*, in which the federal government assessed a fee among certain food producers to promote and advertise their products. *Glickman v. Wileman Brothers & Elliott, Inc., et al.* (1997)[121] arose when California tree fruit growers, handlers, and processors banded together to attempt to overturn a set of federal administrative regulations that required producers to pay for generic advertising of California peaches, plums, and nectarines. Under the Agricultural Marketing Agreement Act of 1937,[122] the producers were exempted from antitrust laws in their marketing but had to pay an assessment for the expenses of administering the program, which included extensive advertising and promotion.

The respondents initially appealed to the U.S. Department of Agriculture, but the agency upheld the regulations. They then appealed to the U.S. District Court, which ruled in favor of the Agriculture Department. On further appeal, the Ninth Circuit U.S. Court of Appeals reversed, applying the *Central Hudson* test and finding the assessment violated the First Amendment because the generic advertising failed both the second and third prongs of the test. The lower appellate court acknowledged that the government had a substantial interest in improving the sales of peaches, plums, and nectarines, but the court said the government had not proven that such advertising and promotion was more effective than individualized ads in increasing consumer demand for the fruits. The court also indicated that the government program was not narrowly tailored because California was the only state with such a program, which provided no credit to companies that did their own advertising. The court noted from the outset that the First Amendment includes the right not to have to financially support others' speech.

In a 5 to 4 decision written by Justice Stevens, the U.S. Supreme Court reversed the Court of Appeals decision, noting that the lower court had dealt with the wrong issue—whether it had raised instead a purely economic policy issue for attention by the President and the Congress.

The Court assumed the latter, pointing out the marketers were gaining considerable economic advantage by being exempt from antitrust laws and the compelled funding was "part of a broader collective enterprise in which their freedom to act independently is already constrained by the regulatory scheme."[123] The opinion went on to note that there are three characteristics of the regulatory scheme that keep the speech in question from falling into a category protected by the First Amendment that would require the Court to review the case under a heightened standard. First, the Court said, the regulations do not prevent the producers from communicating any message with any audience. In other words, no prior restraint is being imposed. Second, they do not force anyone "to engage in any actual or symbolic speech." The lower appellate court felt the regulations compelled speech because the producers had to pay for the advertising. The Supreme Court saw it differently. The Court said the producers are not forced to endorse "any political or ideological views.… Indeed, since all of the respondents are engaged in the business of marketing California nectarines, plums, and peaches, it is fair to presume that they agree with the central message of the speech that is generated by the generic program."[124]

Respondents argued that the assessments violated their First Amendment rights because they had less money to spend for individual advertising, but the Court noted that advertising budgets are often lowered by assessments to cover benefits. "The First Amendment has never been construed to require heightened scrutiny of any financial burden that has the incidental effect of constraining the size of a firm's advertising budget," according to the Court.[125] The justices had no sympathy for the argument that assessments were a form of compelled speech, noting that they did not force respondents to "repeat an objectionable message," to "use their own property to convey an antagonistic ideological message," or "to force them to respond to a hostile message"[126] when they wanted to be silent. The Court clarified that generic advertising "is intended to stimulate consumer demand for an agricultural product in a regulated market. That purpose is legitimate and consistent with the regulatory goals of the overall statutory scheme."[127]

The general message of the Supreme Court in *Glickman* is that you have no basis for a First Amendment complaint when you benefit economically or otherwise from a regulatory scheme that assesses you for the expenses associated with communicating messages with which you have no disagreement. The First Amendment comes into place, the Court seems to be saying, when you are forced to financially support speech, commercial or otherwise, with which you have ideological or similar differences. Even if you disagree with the use being made of the funds that you have had to pay, you still have no basis for a complaint, according to the Court:

> As with other features of the marketing orders, individual producers may not share the views or the interests of others in the same market. But decisions that are made by the majority, if acceptable for other regulatory programs, should be equally so for promotional advertising.[128]

United States v. United Foods *(2001)*

Are peaches, plums, and nectarines different from mushrooms under the First Amendment? In *United States v. United Foods* (2001),[129] the U.S. Supreme Court tackled this question: are the assessments imposed by the Mushroom Promotion, Research and Consumer Information Act of 1990 on members of the mushroom industry for advertising programs in support of the industry a violation of the First Amendment? In a 6 to 3 decision the Court ruled the Mushroom Act was unconstitutional because the compelled speech was not part of a comprehensive regulatory program and thus was not like the tree fruit industry in *Glickman*. The Court said previous restrictions like this, including those in *Glickman*, were not struck down because the objecting members were required to associate for purposes other than the compelled subsidies for speech. The membership in this case was solely for the advertising itself.

One of the major differences between *Glickman* and *United Foods* is that the United Foods Company wanted to advertise that its brand of mushrooms was better than other brands rather than using the generic advertising promoting all mushrooms that its fellow producers favored. United argued that it was effectively being forced to pay for advertising contrary to the advertising it wanted to do. Is the difference really that substantial? *Glickman* and *United Foods* illustrate the thin line the U.S. Supreme Court draws between compelled versus noncompelled speech under the First Amendment.

Johanns v. Livestock Marketing Association *(2005)*

Other agricultural goods, including beef, are affected by federal rules similar to those in *Glickman* and *United Foods*. Under the Beef Promotion and Research Act of 1985 (Beef Act), beef ranchers are assessed $1 per head of cattle to fund generic campaigns such as "Beef, It's What's for Dinner." The Beef Act's primary purpose was to create a national policy for promoting and marketing beef and beef products, including setting up a cattleman's Beef Promotion and Research Board (Beef Board). The amount of money involved was by no means peanuts, with more than $1 billion being collected by the Board from 1988 to 2004. In fiscal year 2000 alone, the Board took in more than $48 million.[130] The Livestock Marketing Association and another group responsible for collecting and paying the checkoff, along with several beef farmers and sellers, sued the U.S. Secretary of Agriculture, the Department of Agriculture, and the Beef Board. They claimed the Beef Act and the assessment or "checkoff" on all sales and importation of beef violated the First Amendment by compelling them to subsidize speech with which they disagreed.

The difference between this case and the previous two cases is in the process by which the product is promoted. The government argued that the advertising and promotion involved government speech, not private speech as in *United Foods* (the mushroom case). The Beef Act directed the Agriculture Secretary to appoint the Board, which then convenes an Operating Committee that submits proposals for funding to the Agriculture Secretary who has the final say on each project.

Is beef more like tree fruit or mushrooms? According to the U.S. Supreme Court in *Johanns v. Livestock Marketing Association* (2005),[131] beef is like neither—at least in how its promotional programs are funded and administered. In a 6 to 3 decision authored by Justice Scalia, the Court held that, because the beef checkoff funds the federal government's own speech—not private speech, the scheme does not violate the First Amendment. The Court noted:

> We have sustained First Amendment challenges to allegedly compelled expression in two categories of cases: true 'compelled speech' cases, in which an individual is

obliged personally to express a message he disagrees with, imposed by the government; and 'compelled subsidy' cases, in which an individual is required by the government to subsidize a message he disagrees with, expressed by a private entity. We have not heretofore considered the First Amendment consequences of government-compelled subsidy of the government's own speech.[132]

In footnote 2, the Court cited several other programs administered by the Department of Agriculture in a way similar to that for beef, including cotton, potatoes, watermelons, popcorn, peanuts, blueberries, avocados, soybeans, pork, honey, eggs, and lamb. The next First Amendment challenge is highly unlikely to come from any of these food industries, but who will be next in line?

The Federal Trade Commission and Other Federal Agencies

The Federal Trade Commission (FTC) has had a colorful history, marred by battles with Congress, the executive branch, consumer advocates, advertisers, and even within the commission itself. However, it has survived, albeit in a different form than when it was created by Congress in 1914. The Federal Trade Commission Act of 1914 stated: "Unfair methods of competition in commerce are hereby declared unlawful. The commission [FTC] is hereby empowered and directed to prevent persons, partnerships, or corporations, except banks and common carriers subject to the Acts to regulate commerce, from using unfair methods of competition in commerce."[133]

Thus the mandate was for the Commission to prevent unfair methods of competition, not to regulate practices that may harm consumers unless such practices affected competition. Most legislation in Congress involves compromises among various interests, and the FTC Act was no exception. Because the U.S. Supreme Court had taken an active role in regulating business with several major decisions on business practices during the early 20th century, advocates on both sides of the regulation coin preferred that a quasi-legislative body or federal agency do the regulating. Both big business, which wanted the trend toward greater monopolization to continue, and antitrust advocates, who pushed for reforms to prevent trade restraint practices, were fearful of the consequences of court intervention, especially from the Supreme Court. Businesses were concerned that certain traditional commercial practices would be restrained or prohibited, whereas antitrust supporters believed the Court would condone or at least refuse to ban anti-competitive trade actions. Both sides lobbied for a federal agency to administer antitrust laws. Unlike today, no consumer activist groups were involved in the lobbying; it was decades before a consumer movement made enough headway to attract the attention of the legislators.

At the same time the FTC Act of 1914 was enacted, Congress also passed the Clayton Antitrust Act,[134] which banned price discrimination, exclusive sales contracts, corporate mergers, inter-corporate stock, and other practices whose effects were to significantly decrease competition or to create a monopoly. The Clayton Act was actually an amendment to the Sherman Antitrust Act of 1890.[135] This prohibited unreasonable interference in interstate and foreign trade, whether by contract and/or conspiracy. The last major revision of the Clayton Act was the 1936 Robinson-Patman Act.[136] This strengthened the Clayton Act by providing severe criminal penalties for businesses that directly or indirectly discriminate in the pricing of similar goods when the impact is to harm competition. It is important to keep this historical background in mind while reviewing FTC regulations on advertising today because the Commission's actions must be evaluated against the backdrop of the 1914 act that created the agency.

The FTC and Deceptive Advertising

The Federal Trade Commission wasted no time after it was created in attacking advertising it deemed deceptive. In 1916 the FTC issued cease-and-desist orders against two companies, both of which advertised clothing made of silk when it was actually made of cotton and other materials.[137] Both companies were charged with engaging in deceptive advertising that resulted in harm either to silk manufacturers or to the silk trade in general. Although the FTC Act makes no mention of deceptive advertising *per se*, the Commission assumed it had authority to ban such advertising. How could the FTC subsume this power? The agency simply characterized deceptive advertising as unfair competition. It was inevitable that, given the blatant abuses of advertising ethics, the Commission would be forced to crack down on deceptive and fraudulent advertising without regard to its effect on the marketplace.

In 1922, the U.S. Supreme Court for the first time found that the FTC had the authority under the 1914 act to directly regulate deceptive ads as an unfair means of competition. In *FTC v. Winstead Hosiery*,[138] the Court upheld a Commission ruling that marketing 10% wool underwear as "Natural Wool" and "Natural Worsted" constituted deceptive advertising. The majority opinion, written by Justice William Brandeis, reasoned that deceptive advertising is unfair competition because it wrongly attracts consumers who would otherwise purchase from manufacturers who do not use unethical advertising. There was an assumption that consumers cannot be expected to distinguish dishonest from honest advertising and thereby may succumb to the deceptive entrepreneurs.

By 1930, regulating false and misleading advertising had become the major portion of the Commission's work as advertising grew by leaps and bounds and the marketplace became more confusing for consumers. This was also a time when advertising agencies burgeoned to handle the marketing demand. In 1931, the FTC suffered what initially appeared to be a major setback in its regulatory efforts when the U.S. Supreme Court ruled unanimously in *FTC v. Raladam Co.*[139] that "unfair trade methods are not *per se* unfair methods of competition." The Court held that false and deceptive advertising must be demonstrated to harm the marketplace (such as injuring a competitor). Raladam had advertised a cure for obesity that it claimed was safe, effective, and convenient. The Commission discounted those claims and sought to ban the advertising but made no assertion on appeal that the advertising had been anticompetitive.

Nearly every week the Commission announces it is either taking action against or has reached a settlement with one or more businesses that have engaged in questionable advertising and marketing. For example, in 2005 the Federal Trade Commission announced that Tropicana Products, owned by Pepsico, had agreed to stop claiming that Healthy Heart brand orange juice can lower the risk of heart disease and stroke. According to news reports, the Commission accused Tropicana of deceiving consumers by claiming that two or three glasses of this particular brand of orange juice could substantially lower blood pressure and cholesterol.[140] The company admitted no guilt but agreed to stop such claims in the future.

Other well-known companies have also been FTC targets. In 1997, the Pizzeria Uno Restaurant chain agreed not to misrepresent the fat content or other nutrients in pizzas with baked crusts. This came after the FTC claimed restaurant ads for "low fat" thin crust pizzas were false and misleading.[141] The same year, Jenny Craig, Inc. settled with the Commission regarding charges that it engaged in deceptive advertising with assertions regarding weight loss maintenance, price, and safety in consumer testimonials and endorsements.[142] Three subsidiaries of Quaker State Corp. agreed in the same year to settle charges that ads for Quaker State's Slick 50 Engine Treatment contained false and unsubstantiated statements.[143]

The Wheeler-Lea Amendments (1938): Regulating Unfair and Deceptive Practices

The setback to the Commission's ability to crack down on deceptive ads in the 1930s was only temporary. The FTC quickly began finding that such advertising was unfair competition. In 1938 Congress gave the agency a boost with passage of the so-called Wheeler-Lea Amendments.[144] These amendments to the 1914 FTC Act granted the Commission broad authority over advertising by permitting it to ban "unfair or deceptive acts or practices in commerce." The 1938 amendments were enacted at a time when there was public concern over marketplace abuses, including the tragic deaths that same year of 100 people who had taken a medication known as elixir sulfanilamide. The Massengill Company, without testing, marketed the drug. In 1938 Congress also enacted the Food, Drug and Cosmetic Act creating the Food and Drug Administration (FDA), which still regulates advertising for drugs, cosmetics, and some consumer products.

In 1975 the FTC Act was revised under the Magnuson–Moss Act to include "unfair or deceptive acts or practices in or affecting commerce."[145] This Act also granted the Commission authority to enact trade regulation rules, which have the force of law and can be targeted at specific industries. *Unfair practices* are defined as those that cause or are "likely to cause substantial injury to consumers which is not reasonably avoidable by consumers themselves and not outweighed by countervailing benefits to consumers or to competition."[146]

FTC Composition and Structure

Like other quasi-legislative, quasi-judicial federal agencies such as the Federal Communications Commission (FCC) and the FDA, the Federal Trade Commission is an independent regulatory agency created by Congress under the authority granted in the Constitution's federal preemption doctrine. There are five commissioners appointed by the President with consent of the Senate for staggered, renewable seven-year terms. The President also designates which member of the five will serve as chair. No more than three commissioners can serve from the same political party. The tradition has been that Presidents appoint the maximum (three) from their political party and then fill any other vacancies from the other political party with individuals whose views are similar to those of their own. However, Presidents can appoint Independents. For example, Mary L. Azcuenaga, an Independent, was appointed to the commission in 1984 and reappointed to a second term in 1991. Pamela Jones Harbour, also an Independent, was appointed as commissioner by President George W. Bush. But such appointments are relatively rare.

The commissioners play a major role in policy and rule making, but the FTC is more than five individuals. There are three bureaus—Competition, Economics, and Consumer Protection—staffed by some 1,200 employees. The Bureau of Competition acts primarily as the agency's antitrust arm, charged with prevention of monopolistic and anticompetitive business practices and anticompetitive mergers. It has the responsibility to investigate alleged violations and make recommendations to the full commission regarding actions. The bureau prepares reports and testimony for Congress and works with the other bureaus and other federal agencies in dealing with anticompetitive practices in areas such as energy for homes and business, prescription drugs and health care, food and high tech industries.[147]

The Bureau of Economics performs three primary functions related to the economic impact of FTC decisions: (a) providing economic advice for enforcement, (b) studying effects of legislative options and regulations, and (c) analyzing market processes.[148] The bureau provided information on telecommunications regulation to Congress when the body was considering the bill now known as the Telecommunications Act of 1996.

The Bureau of Consumer Protection has a mandate "to protect consumers against unfair, deceptive, or fraudulent practices."[149] The Bureau's Advertising Practices Division oversees:

- Claims for foods, drugs, dietary supplements and other products promising health benefits
- Internet health fraud
- Weight-loss ads
- Advertising and marketing directed to children
- Performance claims for computers, Internet service providers and other high tech products and services
- Tobacco and alcohol ads
- Children's online privacy
- Claims about product performance in regional and national mass media, including TV infomercials (program-length commercials), as well as via direct mail to consumers and on the Internet[150]

Infomercials, which frequently appear on late-night cable and satellite television touting everything from cosmetics to miracle car polishes, can easily be mistaken for talk shows because of their format, including a host and a live audience. Since the Federal Communications Commission lifted its limits in 1984 on the percentage of broadcast time that can be devoted to commercials, this form of advertising has flourished.

Other FTC divisions in the Consumer Protection Bureau include *Financial Practices,* which develops policy and enforces laws related to consumer financial and lending practices. The division is also in charge of most of the Commission's consumer privacy programs, including the Fair Credit Reporting Act. The *Division of Marketing Practices* enforces laws against fraudulent marketing practices such as Internet and phone scams, deceptive telemarketing, pyramid sales schemes, and investment scams. The division also enforces the Telemarketing Sales Rule (banning deceptive sales calls and "abusive, unwanted, late-night sales calls") and the Funeral Rule (requiring funeral home directors to disclose prices and other details about their services). The *Division of Enforcement* ensures compliance with FTC orders and enforces various trade regulation rules, guidelines and statutes.[151]

The FTC maintains headquarters at 6th Street and Pennsylvania Avenue N.W. in Washington, DC, with regional offices in Atlanta, Chicago, Cleveland, Dallas, Los Angeles, New York, San Francisco, and Seattle. The staff sizes at regional offices are relatively small compared to the main office, but each regional office usually handles thousands of complaints each year and can initiate investigations that can ultimately lead to a full-scale investigation by the national office.

FTC Modes of Regulation

Investigations

The Federal Trade Commission has a wide range of legal options in its regulation and enforcement activities. The most common are *investigations, consent agreements, trade regulation rules, cease and desist orders*, and *civil and criminal penalties. Investigations* are particularly important tools for FTC enforcement. Contrary to popular opinion, the FTC and other similar federal agencies do not need hundreds or thousands of complaints about a company or practice before they can take action. In fact, the FTC does not need even a single complaint but can instead begin an investigation based solely on information from a news story, a congressional inquiry, or some other credible source. When the agency decides to conduct an investigation, it will first determine whether to publicly announce its intentions or to conduct its work in private. Investigations are usually nonpublic.[152]

Most investigations are initiated by FTC regulatory staff members without formally seeking approval of the full commission, which concentrates its efforts on policy making and major enforcement activities. Because of its rather limited resources, the FTC tends to follow the "squeaky wheel gets the grease" principle—the most flagrant abuses get the most attention. Most investigations die at an early stage but those that survive often take considerable time. If an investigation reveals unfair and deceptive practices by an individual or industry, the staff can then recommend that the full commission take action. The most serious type of initial action is a formal hearing before an administrative law judge or ALJ. The ALJ conducts the hearing under formalized procedures similar to those in a court of law, with each side given an opportunity to present its case following rules of evidence and rules of procedure. The ALJ's decision can be appealed to the full commission, which can exercise its discretion in the matter by rejecting the appeal or ordering a hearing. If the defendant loses and does not appeal to the full commission, the FTC can take appropriate legal action such as issuing cease-and-desist orders, fines, or criminal prosecution. The commission can always overrule the ALJ decision, of course. If a defendant's appeal is rejected by the commission, and after hearing, rules against a defendant, the defendant can appeal the decision to the U.S. Court of Appeals for the circuit in which the defendant resides or does business or in the circuit where the alleged illegal act occurred.

Cease-and-Desist Orders

A *cease-and-desist order* (CDO) issued by the FTC is legally enforceable and prohibits an individual or company from committing a particular act against which an order has been issued. A 1944 FTC case illustrates how this order works. From 1934 to 1939, Charles of the Ritz Distributing Corporation marketed a line of cosmetics, including a Rejuvenescence Cream with sales of about $1 million. In an extensive national advertising campaign, the company claimed the cream contained "a vital organic ingredient" along with "essences and compounds" that "restores natural moisture necessary for a live, healthy skin." The ad also said, "Your face need know no drought years" and that the cream gave the skin "a bloom which is wonderfully rejuvenating" and is "constantly active in keeping your skin clear, radiant, and young looking."[153] In light of some of the hype and puffery that bombards us in advertising, such claims may seem mild. But the FTC ruled, after a hearing, that the advertising was false and deceptive. It issued a CDO prohibiting Charles of the Ritz from using the word *rejuvenescence* or similar terms to describe its cosmetics in any advertising and from representing in any ads that the cream would rejuvenate the skin or restore youth or the appearance of youth to the skin. The company appealed, but the U.S. Circuit Court of Appeals upheld the FTC order.

A cease-and-desist order constitutes prior restraint, but the courts have consistently permitted the FTC and federal agencies to issue such orders so long as a fair hearing is conducted. CDOs are powerful weapons in the FTC arsenal, but they are often time-consuming and expensive. Thus the commission usually attempts other forms of enforcement whenever feasible.

Consent Agreement or Order

A *consent agreement or order* is a relatively painless way of settling disputes over advertising or marketing practices for which the commission believes a company's claims have been deceptive or misleading. If the advertising or practice appears to be fraudulent, it is unlikely the FTC will seek a consent agreement because of the seriousness of the offense. The process is quite simple. The agency staff conducts its usual investigation, which may be brief or protracted. If the evidence points toward deception but it appears little or no harm has occurred to consumers or competitors, the FTC may negotiate a voluntary settlement with the company or business under which it agrees to halt the advertising or practice in dispute. This is in return for the agreement by the FTC not to pursue the case further, assuming no other violations appear. The company or business does not have to admit it violated the law. If it agrees to the terms, the FTC presents an affidavit to its legal representative to sign that assures the ads or practice will be halted. By far, the majority of cases decided by the FTC after an investigation result in a consent agreement or order. Most companies are glad to sign on the dotted line because fighting such accusations can be extremely time-consuming and expensive. It is not unusual for the FTC and the company in their public relations releases and announcements to both emphasize that the consent decree does not imply nor indicate the company has been guilty of any violations. It is merely that the parties have agreed that the advertising or practice in question has ended.

The consent agreement has the same legal effect as an order and thus can be enforced under a threat of contempt. Failure to comply will almost certainly subject the company to a formal hearing and possible fines and other legal sanctions. Thus it is very rare when a company defies a consent decree. The risks of prosecution are simply too high. Under a consent decree, the company agrees to entry of a *final order* and waives all rights to judicial review, i.e., appeals to a court. The commission has to publish the order and allow at least 60 days for public comment before making the order final.

Sometimes the FTC finds it necessary to file suit against a company before a settlement can be reached. In December 2005 the commission announced it had reached a settlement with satellite TV provider DirecTV to pay a $5.335 million fine—the largest civil penalty in the history of the FTC in a consumer protection case—for violating the do-not-call provisions of the

FTC's Telemarketing Sales Rule (TSR) beginning in October 2003.[154] According to the complaint filed by the U.S. Department of Justice for the FTC in U.S. District Court in Los Angeles, the company hired five telemarketing firms to make cold (unsolicited) calls to consumers who were listed on the Do Not Call (DNC) Registry. According to the commission, at least one of the companies also made calls to consumers who had specifically asked not to receive calls from DirecTV and made "abandoned calls" (calls in which the consumer is not connected to a live sales representative within two seconds after the consumer completes his or her greeting), both practices that are illegal under the TSR. As part of the settlement, DirecTV agreed to terminate any marketer of its products and services that the company knows or should know is violating the TSR and to extensively monitor marketers of its products and services. The consent order also included civil penalties of $25,000 and $50,000 against two of the companies and $205,000 and $746,000 against two other companies, but the latter fines were suspended because the companies were unable to pay them.[155]

Around the same time as the DirecTV settlement, the commission also announced it had reached a consent settlement with three companies and their owners for an alleged pyramid or multi-level marketing scheme. The agreement included about $1.5 million in consumer redress, including fines and $600,000 to be paid by the defendants' insurance company.[156]

As an administrative agency, the FTC has the authority to seek preliminary or permanent *injunctions* whenever it appears that a particular practice could cause immediate and irreparable harm to the public or to another business. In the latter case, however, the harmed business is more likely to seek the injunction in court on its own rather than indirectly through the FTC because the indirect route can take considerable time. Usually, the FTC will go the CDO or consent agreement route rather than seek an injunction because the former techniques are quite effective in halting deceptive and misleading advertising and practices.

Trade Regulation Rules

Although much of the enforcement by the FTC is conducted on a case-by-case basis, there are instances in which enforcement is better served by what are often called nonadjudicatory procedures. The most common of these is the *Trade Regulation Rule* (TRR). TRRs provide specific prohibitions on certain practices that are binding on all businesses for whom the rule was designed. Any violation of a TRR can be grounds for an unfair or deceptive act or practice that can subject the offender to civil and even criminal penalties. Although the commission first promulgated TRRs in 1962, its first major and certainly controversial TRR was a requirement in 1964 that all cigarette packaging carry a health warning. That TRR was followed five years later by a requirement that octane ratings be posted on all gasoline pumps. A number of other TRRs have been proposed by the FTC over the years, some of which were eventually promulgated but others died or were substantially weakened by the time the rule-making process was complete.

The following are some of the surviving TRRs that have made direct or indirect impacts on commercial speech:

- **Appliance Labeling** requires disclosure of energy costs or efficiency of home appliances and heating and cooling systems.

- **Games of Chance in the Food Retailing and Gasoline Industries**—requires disclosure of the odds of winning prizes, the random distribution of the winning prize pieces, and publication of the winners' names.
- **The Retail Food Store Advertising and Marketing Practices Rule**, as amended, requires advertised items to be available for sale unless the store notes in the ad that supplies are limited or the store offers a rain check.
- **The Mail or Telephone Order Merchandise Rule** requires businesses to ship mail or telephone purchases when promised or within 30 days if no promise is made.
- **The Used Car Rule** requires dealers to put a buyer's guide on each vehicle with details regarding the warranty and other information.
- **Funeral Rule** requires funeral homes to disclose prices and other information about funerals and services.
- **Telemarketing Sales Rule** requires telemarketers to disclose information that could have an impact on a consumer's decision to buy before he or she agrees to pay for any goods or services.[157]

Some proposed FTC trade regulation rules have brought considerable fire from the industries to be affected and political pressures from Congress. The most notable of these is the commission's recommendation in the late 1970s to prohibit all television advertising directed toward children. This proposal led to an ensuing battle among the commercial TV executives, television critics, and Congress. Congress responded by enacting the Federal Trade Commission Improvement Act in 1980.[158] This Act expanded sanctions available for violation of FTC regulations and broadened the civil remedies available to the courts in cases brought by the commission. It barred the FTC from enacting any TRRs directed at children's TV commercials. The act also limited the FTC's use of funding for consumer groups in FTC cases and required the commission to consider costs versus benefits before issuing rules.

The Act now requires that the FTC enact TRRs only when there is a pattern of deceptiveness evident in the industry, not simply on the basis that the advertising may be unfair. Certainly the most telling provision of the Act was the one creating a legislative veto of any FTC rule if within 90 days of issuance of the rule, both houses of Congress vote against the rule. This legislative veto power was ruled unconstitutional by the U.S. Supreme Court in *Immigration and Naturalization Service v. Chadha* (1980)[159] and thus no longer affects the FTC nor other similar federal agencies.

The Issuance of Trade Regulation Rules

How are TRRs issued? First, the FTC conducts an investigation of trade practices within that particular industry. If the staff uncovers evidence of unfair or deceptive practices such as misleading advertising, the commission can formally initiate the rule-making proceeding. Second, the staff writes a proposed trade regulation rule that is then reviewed by the full commission, which may accept it as is, modify it, or kill it altogether. Third, if a proposed rule is approved for further consideration (not for enactment), a notice is published in the *Federal Register* indicating that a hearing is to be conducted on the proposal and giving the time and location of the hearing. The notice will also indicate the issues to be considered, provide instructions for groups and individual consumers on how to participate, and reprint the text of the proposed rule. Fourth, a hearing or series of hearings is conducted. Not all of the hearings need to be held in Washington; some may take place at any of the FTC regional offices. All formal hearings are open to the public. The press representatives of consumer groups and individual citizens are typically permitted to testify at the hearings. Anyone may file written comments with the commission for consideration with all evidence presented at the hearings, in staff reports, and in the presiding officer's report (the officer is usually a member of the FTC staff versed in procedures). Under rules of the 1975 Federal Trade Commission Act still in effect, if there are disputed issues of material fact, the commission must permit cross-examination of individuals whom the FTC believes to be appropriate and necessary for a full disclosure of the facts.[160]

The full commission then votes on whether to implement the rule as is, to modify it, or to reject it. If it chooses to modify or accept it as is, affected consumers and businesses have the right to appeal the commission's decision in any appropriate U.S. Court of Appeals, including the D.C. Circuit, but the appeal must be filed within 60 days from the time the rule takes effect.

Advisory Opinions

Other nonadjudicatory procedures used by the FTC are *advisory opinions, industry guides,* and *consumer education.* Whereas most state courts and all federal courts are prohibited from issuing advisory opinions, most state and federal agencies, including the FTC, routinely issue such opinions. One of the key limits on FTC advisory opinions is that they can be issued only for contemplated actions, not for actions already taken. For example, if a dog food manufacturer wanted to know whether it could advertise and market a new line of dog food as "Premium Lite" that contains 15% fewer calories than its regular "Premium," it would ask for an advisory opinion so any potential litigation could be avoided. The company would file a written request with the commission describing the advertising under consideration. The FTC legal staff would then review the letter and issue an opinion based on current FTC policy, rules and regulations.

All such advisory opinions become public record and can be used by other advertisers in similar situations. If the advertiser follows the advice in good faith, it cannot be sued by the FTC unless the FTC enacts new rules, which would, of course, require public notice in the *Federal Register,* or the commission decides to rescind its approval, which requires written notification to the party. The FTC will not issue advisory opinions when substantially similar action is part of an official proceeding conducted by the FTC or other agency, when there is ongoing investigation in that area or if issuing an opinion would require lengthy investigation, research or testing.[161]

Industry Guides

While advisory opinions are geared toward businesses and corporations, industry guides are intended to regulate practices of entire industries. For example, the FTC has issued industry guides for the jewelry, precious metals, and pewter industries and for environmental marketing and alternative fueled vehicles. Dozens of these often complex and detailed guides have been issued over the decades for products and services from eyeglasses to health care services. Any business that violates an industry guide faces potential litigation because failure to comply is evidence of unfair or deceptive trade practices.

Consumer Education

Consumer education has been the least controversial of the FTC's nonadministrative functions because these efforts rarely single out a particular business or industry for criticism except when blatant violations are involved. The FTC publishes a wide variety of materials and makes use of press releases, interviews, press conferences, and other public relations techniques to reach consumers. The commission issues dozens of free and inexpensive booklets for business and for consumers on topics such as the Telemarketing Sales Rule, e-commerce and the Internet, franchise and business opportunities, telemarketing, privacy, identity theft, investments, credit, automobiles, energy and environment, and diet, health and fitness.

The FTC is responsible for enforcing its rules and also enforcing specific consumer protection statutes through which Congress has delegated its authority to the commission. These include a broad range of federal laws from the Hobby Protection Act (which requires imitation coins, medals, and similar items be clearly marked "copy" and imitation political items to be marked with the year of manufacture) to the Magnuson–Moss Warranty Act of 1975.[162] This Act requires manufacturers and sellers to disclose warranty information to potential purchasers before they buy consumer products included under the act. The FTC is also responsible for enforcing the Truth-in-Lending Act, the Fair Credit Reporting Act, the Wool Products Labeling Act, the Telemarketing Sales Rule, the Pay-Per-Call Rule, and the Equal Credit Opportunity Act.

Corrective Advertising

Prohibiting misleading and deceptive advertising is a way to protect consumers and ensure fair competition, but outright bans are not always effective or appropriate. Requiring affirmative disclosure can sometimes be an effective remedy. Although the original FTC Act and its revisions make no mention of affirmative disclosure, which usually comes in the form of corrective advertising, the federal courts have generally upheld the right of the FTC to impose requirements on advertisers. As the cases attest, some of the largest corporations have been forced by the commission to modify advertising to include corrective statements.

For example, the Warner-Lambert Company was ordered by the FTC in 1975 to clearly and conspicuously disclose in its next $10 million of advertising for Listerine antiseptic mouthwash: "Contrary to prior advertising, Listerine will not help prevent colds or sore throats or lessen their severity." Listerine had claimed in its advertising that it could prevent, cure, or alleviate the common cold. On appeal, the U.S. Court of Appeals for the DC Circuit held in 1977 in *Warner-Lambert v. FTC*[163] that the commission did "have the power to issue corrective advertising in appropriate cases" but that the preamble, "Contrary to prior advertising," was unwarranted, given the facts in the case. Thus for the next several years, all Listerine print ads and radio and television commercials carried the disclaimer, "Listerine will not help prevent colds or sore throats or lessen their severity."

The FTC complaint against Warner-Lambert was initially filed in 1972 even though Listerine had advertised since 1921 that it would help colds. After four months of hearings at which some 4,000 pages of documents were produced and 46 witnesses testified before an administrative law judge, the ALJ ruled against Warner-Lambert. The company appealed to the full FTC, which basically affirmed the ALJ's decision in 1975. During the next two years, Listerine continued to make the claims until the U.S. Court of Appeals upheld the commission's decision with modification. The U.S. Supreme Court denied certiorari in 1978.[164] Listerine was able to make presumably false assertions for 57 years, including 6 years after the complaint was filed.

The first successful attempt by the FTC to impose an order for corrective advertising came in 1971,[165] the year before the complaint against Listerine was filed. The ITT Continental Baking Company had advertised that Profile Bread could help reduce weight because it contained fewer calories than other similar brands of bread when, in fact, the bread was sliced somewhat thinner than normal and contained only seven fewer calories per slice than "ordinary" bread. ITT was ordered to spend at least 25% of its advertising budget for the following year indicating in its ads that Profile Bread contained only 7 fewer calories than other breads and that this difference would not cause a significant weight reduction.

Other successful FTC efforts to require corrective advertising include Ocean Spray Cranberries, which agreed in 1972 after an FTC complaint to spend 25% of its ad budget for a year informing the public that the term "food energy" used in previous ads referred to calories rather than vitamins and minerals.[166] On rare occasions, the FTC is rebuffed in its push for corrective advertising. In 1978 the U.S. Court of Appeals for the Seventh Circuit held that an egg industry group, the National Commission on Egg Nutrition (NCEN), could not be forced in future advertising or public statements to mention the relationship between egg consumption and heart and circulatory disease. It said, "[M]any medical experts believe increased consumption of dietary cholesterol, including that in eggs, may increase the risk of heart disease."[167] The NCEN, in response to what the FTC described as "anticholesterol attacks on eggs which had resulted in steadily declining per capita egg consumption,"[168] mounted an advertising and public relations counterattack claiming that eggs were harmless and were necessary for human nutrition. For example, some of the advertising asserted that eating eggs does not increase blood cholesterol in a normal person and there is no scientific evidence that egg consumption increases the risk of heart and circulatory disease. The FTC ordered the NCEN to not only stop making such claims but to also issue corrective advertising, as noted.

The U.S. Court of Appeals held that the FTC could prohibit the trade association from disseminating what the commission determined to be false, misleading claims. But the group could be required to issue corrective advertising "only when NCEN chooses to make a representation as to the state of the available evidence or information concerning the controversy [over the connection between egg consumption and increased blood cholesterol and heart disease]."[169] There had been no history of deception, as there had been in *Warner-Lambert v. FTC* (1977) and the original FTC order was broader than necessary to prevent future deception.

Affirmative Disclosure

The Federal Trade Commission has used two other major remedies for deceptive advertising—affirmative disclosure and substantiation. It is not unusual in a consent order or a cease-and-desist order for the commission to require that an advertiser not only refrain from making specific claims but also require that all future advertising make certain disclosures designed to prevent deception, that is, *affirmative disclosures*.

A classic case involving affirmative disclosure is the mid-1960s order by the FTC that the J. B. Williams Co., the distributor of Geritol, state in its commercials that "tiredness and that run-down feeling" were rarely caused by iron-poor blood, which the product claimed to cure.

Geritol advertised heavily on network television, including the *Ted Mack Original Amateur Hour*, that its "iron-rich formula" (primarily vitamins and iron) would cure "iron-poor blood." The ads were particularly aimed at women, who medical experts agree generally need more iron in their diets. As the FTC saw it, the ads failed to mention that Geritol would help only those rare individuals who suffered tiredness as a result of iron deficiency. Geritol was simply a vitamin and iron supplement, not a cure for tiredness. J. B. Williams appealed the FTC order, but the Sixth Circuit U.S. Court of Appeals in 1967 upheld the order.[170] The Geritol story did not end. Six years later the commission fined the company more than $800,000 for allegedly violating a cease-and-desist order, but the Sixth Circuit U.S. Court of Appeals in 1974 ordered a jury trial, at which the company was ordered to pay $280,000 in fines.[171] An example of an affirmative disclosure requirement by Congress rather than the FTC is the set of federal statutes regarding cigarette and smokeless tobacco advertising.

Substantiation

The Federal Trade Commission uses *substantiation* as a mechanism to regulate advertising. The FTC substantiation program began in 1970 when the commission filed a complaint against Pfizer, Inc.,[172] the manufacturer of Un-Burn, an over the counter, nonprescription medication for minor burns and sunburn. The product, which was advertised extensively on radio and television, claimed that it "actually anesthetizes nerves in sensitive sunburned skin" and that it "relieves pain fast." The FTC complaint alleged that the claims and similar ones for Un-Burn had not been substantiated.[173] The commission charged that Pfizer had engaged in unlawful deception and unlawful unfairness in violation of Section 5 of the FTC act.

Unlike other regulatory mechanisms, such as corrective advertising and affirmative disclosure, substantiation essentially places the burden of proof on the advertiser to show that there is scientific evidence to support the particular claim. In other words, the advertiser is forced to prove the truth of the assertions rather than the FTC being forced to prove they are false, as would be the case in a typical complaint for false and deceptive advertising. If a case were to go to trial, the FTC would have the burden of showing that no scientific evidence existed to substantiate the claims. But this could be effectively accomplished with the testimony of expert witnesses and by showing that the advertiser had failed to provide substantiation if requested. Substantiation cases at the FTC have been relatively rare, primarily because a complaint cannot be filed unless the advertiser makes an affirmative product claim without a reasonable basis for that claim, based on adequate and well-controlled scientific tests or studies. This standard, which continues today, does not require that the evidence be overwhelmingly in favor of the product or even that the bulk of the evidence favors the claims. The advertiser simply has to demonstrate that there is a reasonable basis for making the claims. As the FTC noted in the Pfizer decision:

> The question of what constitutes a reasonable basis is essentially a factual issue which will be affected by the interplay of overlapping considerations such as (1) the type and specificity of the claim made, e.g., safety, efficacy, dietary, health, medical; (2) the type of product, e.g., food, drug, potentially hazardous consumer product, other consumer product; (3) the possible consequences of a false claim, e.g., personal injury, property damage; (4) the degree of reliance by consumers on the claims; (5) the type

and accessibility of evidence adequate to form a reasonable basis for making the particular claims.[174]

Suppose you saw the following ad in your local newspaper:

$49.00 OVER FACTORY INVOICE*

EVERY NEW CAR ON OUR LOT

MOORE MOTORS

MAIN STREET

HOMETOWN, HOMESTATE

* Dealer invoice may not reflect dealer cost.

If you visited the dealership, what price would you expect to pay for a new car? Forty-nine dollars more than the dealer paid for the car from the distributor? Forty-nine dollars more than the base vehicle price? Forty-nine dollars above the base vehicle price plus the dealer's cost for accessories? Suppose the disclaimer (indicated by the asterisk) said instead: Invoice price indicates the amount dealer paid distributor for car. Due to various factory rebates, holdbacks and incentives, actual dealer cost is lower than invoice price. Does the latter disclaimer give you a better idea of how to determine how much you would pay for the car in relation to the "actual dealer cost"?

A Fifth Circuit U.S. Court of Appeals tackled these questions in *Joe Conte Toyota Inc. v. Louisiana Motor Vehicle Commission* (1994).[175] The Louisiana Motor Vehicle Commission, which has the authority to regulate automobile dealer advertising in the state, promulgated a set of rules and regulations banning the use of the term "invoice." The regulations were designed to stop misleading ads. In 1985 the Supreme Court of New Jersey upheld a similar ban on the use of "invoice" and "dealer invoice."[176] Joe Conte Toyota sought unsuccessfully in U.S. District Court to have this particular provision (section 20) declared a violation of First Amendment rights. It should be noted that the Toyota dealer did not use any ads that violated the rules but was seeking to have the ban declared unconstitutional so it could, if it so chose, include "invoice" in its ads. Joe Conte submitted a proposed ad, very similar to the first one above, and an alternate proposed ad that had a disclaimer like the second one above.

As you recall from an earlier discussion, under the first prong of the *Central Hudson* test for commercial speech, which we have here, a court must first determine that the expression concerns lawful activity and is not misleading before applying the next three prongs of the test. If the expression is misleading, it simply does not have First Amendment protection. The trial court dismissed the complaint filed by Joe Conte Toyota on the ground that the term "invoice" was inherently misleading in the context of both of the proposed ads. The testimony in the district court did little to bolster the dealer's complaint. One car dealer with 10 years in the business indicated that "invoice" had little meaning because "invoice price" changed over time and from dealer to dealer. Another dealer said "$49.00 over invoice" was basically meaningless for the consumer. Even a sample invoice from Joe Conte Toyota itself revealed four different invoice prices:

[A] base vehicle price at dealer's cost of $14,190.00, a base vehicle price with accessories at dealer's cost of $16,407.30, a total vehicle price with advertising expense, inland freight and handling at dealer's cost of $16,929.30, and a net dealer invoice amount of $16,860.00.[177]

The U.S. Court of Appeals had little trouble deciding, upholding the constitutionality of the commission's regulation and thus affirming the judgment of the lower court. Noting that it agreed with the reasoning of the New Jersey Supreme Court in its 1985 decision, the court said:

... We are satisfied that the proposed advertising copy with the suggested alternative disclaimers is inherently misleading. Because there is ample evidence on the record to support the district court's finding that the use of the word 'invoice' in automobile advertisement [sic] is inherently misleading, its conclusion that the commercial speech in question fell beyond First Amendment protection was not in error. Consequently, there was no need for the court to consider the remaining prongs of the *Central Hudson* test.[178]

Regulation by Other Government Agencies

Although the Federal Trade Commission is the main federal agency responsible for regulating advertising, other federal agencies possess authority to regulate specific types of advertising under certain conditions and state and local government agencies are also involved in the process. The federal agencies include, but are not limited to, the Federal Communications Commission (FCC), the U.S. Postal Service (USPS), the Food and Drug Administration (FDA), the Department of the Treasury, and the Securities and Exchange Commission (SEC). The role of the FCC in regulating broadcast ads, such as its eventual successful attempt to restrict the amount and type of advertising in TV programs to children, is discussed in the next chapter.

The FDA traces its origins to 1927 when the federal Bureau of Chemistry was reorganized into two units—the Food, Drug and Insecticide Administration and the Bureau of Chemistry and Soils. Three years later, the Food, Drug and Insecticide Administration was renamed the Food and Drug Administration. The FDA, an agency of the Department of Health and Human Services (formerly the Department of Health, Education, and Welfare), regulates the advertising of certain foods, prescription and nonprescription drugs, and cosmetics, as provided under the Federal Food, Drug and Cosmetic Act of 1938, as amended. The Food and Drug Administration Act of 1988 placed the FDA under the Department of Health and Human Services with oversight by a Commissioner of Food and Drugs.[179]

The FDA advertising regulations are significantly stronger than those of the FTC. In 1958 Congress approved the Food Additives Amendment requiring manufacturers of new food additives to demonstrate their safety.[180] In the same year the FDA published the first list of almost 200 substances *generally recognized as safe* (GRAS).[181]

Prescription drugs are evaluated by the National Research Council Drug Efficacy Group of the National Academy of Sciences; if a drug is rated less than "effective," the rating must be included in any advertising. All claims in drug advertising regulated by the FDA must be backed by appropriate clinical studies conducted by experts. In 1995 the FDA issued a series of proposed reforms to streamline regulations on the manufacturing of pharmaceuticals, including broadening how manufacturers can promote and advertise approved uses of drugs to health professionals. The FDA was yielding to pressure from prescription drug marketers, consumers (including groups representing AIDS sufferers), and politicians. The FDA also eased the rules regarding the length of time a drug must be tested prior to marketing.

Until 1997 advertising for prescription drugs was restricted primarily to professional publications such as medical and nursing journals. That all changed with the Food and Drug Administration Modernization Act of 1997 under which the FDA eased rules on television and radio advertising of prescription drugs. The new rules allow companies to directly promote a prescription drug's benefits so long as the ads list a toll-free phone number, Internet address, or other means for obtaining information about side effects and risks.[182] Print ads were not affected by the regulations.

By 2005 the amount the pharmaceutical industry was spending on advertising directed at consumers had risen to more than $5 billion.[183] According to a study published that year in the *Journal of the American Medical Association*, when patients ask their physicians for specific prescription drugs they have seen in commercials, the doctors are more likely to prescribe the drugs.[184] Given that earlier research had found that such advertising stimulated consumers to ask for the advertised drugs,[185] this finding is not surprising.

The FDA occasionally gets involved in advertising for other types of products including foods when health claims are touted. In 1997 the agency promulgated a regulation on advertising low-fat, high-fiber foods made from rolled oats, oat bran, and oat flour such as Quaker Oats and General Mills' Cheerios. If foods contain enough soluble fiber, the advertising can claim they are heart-healthy and may reduce the risk of heart disease when they are part of a low-fat diet. This was the first time the FDA allowed a company to assert that a food could help prevent disease.[186]

The other agencies mentioned play a fairly minor role in regulating advertising. The USPS regulates advertising sent via mail but, despite its rather broad authority over such advertising, tends to confine its efforts to blatantly unfair, misleading, and fraudulent cases. Some of this reluctance may be attributed to privacy considerations, but limited resources and deference to the FTC may also explain its conservative approach. The USPS has always been aggressive in prosecuting certain con artist schemes that seem to never die, such as chain letters and "envelope stuffing" job "opportunities" ("make hundreds of thousands of dollars simply by stuffing envelopes in your own home"). The SEC regulates the advertising of stocks, bonds, and other traded securities, whereas the Treasury Department is responsible for enforcing federal statutes regarding the reproduction of paper currency in ads.

Although the great bulk of advertising involves or affects interstate commerce and thus can be regulated by the FTC and other federal agencies, there are exceptions that fall into the regulatory hands of state and local agencies. Because the FTC does not have exclusive control over advertising, ads that cross state lines can under some circumstances be regulated by a state or local agency. A mail order house based in State X advertising in newspapers, on network TV and radio, on local stations, and through the mail could find the FTC overlooking its national ads. The FCC may review broadcast commercials, the state consumer protection agency regulating the ads in the local newspapers and the USPS keeping an eye on mail ads. If the company sells prescription drugs or securities, the picture would be more complicated.

Most states have enacted what have become known as "little FTC acts" or statutes creating state consumer protection agencies modeled after the FTC. Many of these statutes include provisions regarding advertising such as "bait and switch" (deceptive ads in which a low-priced model of a product convinces consumers to visit, then a salesperson persuades them to purchase a high-priced model because the lower-priced one is "sold out" or "not worth it").

Self-Regulation

In an ideal marketplace, consumers would regulate advertising by refusing to buy products that did not live up to their promises and expectations and thus make their distaste known to the manufacturers. Products and services that did not satisfy consumers would thus fade into oblivion. Individual self-regulation does not always work even though most advertisers are honest and make concerted efforts to please. Government regulation is not always effective. To fill the gap as well as to head off government intervention whenever possible, advertisers have established various self-regulatory boards over the years that review and evaluate ads either on a voluntary or, in some cases, nonvoluntary basis. The most powerful of self-regulatory groups was not founded until 1971, but it has become an important broker in advertising.

National Advertising Review Council

In 1971 three major advertising associations—the American Advertising Foundation (AAF), the American Association of Advertising Agencies (AAAA), and the Association of National Advertisers (ANA)—and the Council of Better Business Bureaus (CBBB) created a National Advertising Review Council (NARC) "to foster truth and accuracy in national advertising through voluntary self-regulation." The NARC was given the responsibility of setting up the rules for the National Advertising Division (NAD), the Children's Advertising Review Unit (CARU), and the National Advertising Review Board (NARB). The NAD regularly monitors national ads appearing in all of the major media.

If the NAD determines that an ad may be false, misleading or deceptive, or makes unsubstantiated claims, an investigation is conducted. Investigations can also be initiated on the complaint of another advertiser, consumer group, individual, or local Better Business Bureau. During the investigation, the advertiser is given the opportunity to respond to the allegations. If the NAD concludes that some action is warranted, it will request that the advertiser take the recommended steps, whether they be (a) to cease further advertising that may be misleading, deceptive, or false, (b) to modify future advertising to delete certain claims, or (c) to take some other action.

An NAD decision is not necessarily final. The advertiser can always refuse to comply because the NAD has no governmental authority, or the advertiser can appeal to the NARB. The NARB then selects an ad hoc panel of five individuals to hear the appeal. The NARB also hears appeals from the CARU, which is financed by the children's advertising community. Council membership fees fund NAD and NARB. The NARB upholds the decisions of the NAD, but occasionally will overturn a decision.

Both the NAD and the NARB derive much of their persuasive power from the fact that their parent organization, the CBBB, has considerable clout in the marketplace. Decisions by the NARB cannot be appealed further, but the NARB has no punitive power. The NAD, however, makes very effective use of media publicity to inform consumers about companies that engage in false and misleading advertising. Should an advertiser decide to ignore an NAD/

NARB decision, the NAD can always register a complaint with the FTC or other appropriate federal agency.

The Children's Advertising Review Unit, which focuses on advertising directed toward children, was created in 1974 and operates in a manner similar to the NAD. Each major commercial television network (NBC, CBS, ABC, and Fox) has its own network advertising standards. The networks, for example, refused to carry brand-name commercials for condoms because such advertising violated these codes. In addition, the AAAA requires all members to abide by its Standards of Practice that ban unfair, deceptive, and misleading advertising.

Advertising Ethics and Other Considerations

Although some cynics might argue that advertising ethics is an oxymoron, this is an area of advertising that deserves more attention, especially in the current era of deregulation. Professional associations such as the AAF and AAAA have standards or codes that attempt to articulate ethical standards of their members. Yet some questionable techniques and practices creep through in ads of even some of the largest and most reputable corporations. No doubt some of these can be linked to the rigors of competition, but competition is only part of the equation.

Ads occasionally appear in major newspapers, including Sunday inserts, for indoor TV "dish" antennas. The ads typically include claims that would be difficult to prove false but could confuse or mislead some consumers:

> The [model] looks like an outdoor satellite "dish," but works indoors like ordinary "rabbit ears."

> "Legal in all 50 states. You pay no cable fees because you're NOT getting cable. You pay NO satellite fees because you're NOT using satellite technology or service."

All of these claims are true. Rabbit ear antennas have never been illegal, and purchasers certainly will not get cable or satellite TV with this antenna. They will not have to pay for something they will not get. Other claims are also silly, e.g., "It works entirely with 'RF' technology … to pull in all signals on VHF and UHF from 2 to 82." RF means radio frequency. All receiving antennas use RF technology. Every antenna "pulls" signals out of the air. The ad notes that the antenna "complies with all applicable federal regulations." There are none governing indoor antennas. The "sheer aesthetic superiority of its elegant parabolic design" is presented as "a marketing breakthrough."

In other words, the advertiser thinks the dish looks good and makes a good marketing device. The advertised price for one antenna is 30% higher, thanks to an added $3.00 for shipping and handling. Assertions that there is a limit of "three per address" and that the company reserves "the right to extend above time and quantity guarantees" are equally dubious. Readers who order the antenna probably will not be surprised to get solicitations to order more. The clincher in the ad is the free "Basic Guide to Satellite TV" included with all orders, presumably so buyers can learn about all services "from Disney to XXX movies" that they won't get with the rabbit ears but could receive with a real satellite dish system. By the way, a nice set of rabbit ears (without the parabolic design) can be purchased at Radio Shack and similar stores for $10 and up.

Puffery

Certain examples of a common advertising technique are known as *puffery* or evaluative advertising. The FTC and other federal and state agencies permit puffery so long as such exaggerations do not cross the line and become factual statements that could materially affect an individual's decision to purchase a product. These agencies assume that consumers do not take such claims seriously, and yet some of the most popular brands of products from toiletries to automobiles can trace their dominant market shares to extensive advertising using puffery. Examples include:

> No one has a better chance of winning our contest than you.
> [Translation: Everybody who enters has the same chance of winning or losing.]
> The best time to buy [a computer].
> An unbelievably rich and creamy treat [low-fat ice cream].
> … ends dry skin [skin lotion].
> … bleach makes your wash clean, fresh and wonderful.
> Rich, satisfying taste [cigarettes].
> Exercise takes a lot out of you. Orange juice puts a lot back.
> Introducing the freshest tomato taste [pasta sauce].
> Big discounts every day [discount department store].

These claims can influence consumer decisions, but it is unlikely that any of them would be challenged by the FTC or any other regulatory agency. Puffery, in its traditional form (best, number one, preferred, highest quality, best performer, most economical, lowest-priced, none better, freshest, best tasting, etc.), is an accepted marketing practice that probably causes little harm to consumers, although it conveys little, if any, useful information to a rational consumer.

Testimonials

Another persuasive technique that has become commonplace in advertising in the last few decades, especially in television commercials, is the testimonial or paid endorsement by a well-known personality. Movie stars such as Halle Berry, receives substantial compensation for endorsing products. She would not be hired if her endorsements did not improve sales. Until 1975, the FTC rules were lax regarding testimonials, although the commission has had guidelines for endorsements for many years. The industry guides adopted in 1975[187] focus on endorsers, not company spokespersons. The difference between a spokesperson and an endorser is significant—endorsers are well-known personalities—TV and movie stars, professional athletes, and former politicians—experts or individuals who can claim expertise in a particular area because of experience, education, special training, or a combination thereof.

The guidelines require that a personality or expert be a regular user of the endorsed product and the advertising featuring the endorsement is discontinued if the product is not used by that individual. Guidelines also require that any financial interest by the endorser in the company be disclosed. The guidelines do not require an advertiser to disclose that personalities or experts were paid for testimonials. There is an assumption that consumers know individuals are compensated so there is no need to repeat this fact in every ad. A spokesperson does not have to meet these standards. TV or radio announcers for a headache remedy do not have to actually use the medication. They are simply serving as professional announcers, not endorsers or experts.

Tobacco and Alcohol Advertising: Some Legal and Ethical Issues

Should media outlets refuse to carry questionable advertising and advertising in poor taste? Newspapers and other print media clearly have the right to refuse any and all advertising, thanks to the 1974 U.S. Supreme Court decision in *Miami Herald v. Tornillo*.[188] In this case the Court held that a Florida statute giving political candidates a right of access to editorial space in newspapers that had criticized them or endorsed an opposing candidate was unconstitutional. Now with the death of the Fairness Doctrine, broadcasters presumably can refuse any advertising, except political ads covered by the Equal Opportunities Rule that guarantees candidates for federal office the right to purchase broadcast advertising during certain times.

Washington Post columnist Jane Bryant Quinn criticized the practice of some newspapers that "stubbornly publish work-at-home schemes and offers of loans to bad credit risks, even though they are hardly ever legitimate. Get-rich-quick channels on some cable TV systems are especially bad."[189] Quinn noted that the largest newspaper trade group, the American Newspapers Publishers Association, has no set of voluntary guidelines for advertising and sees no need. She pointed out that the broadcast trade group, the National Association of Broadcasters, once had advertising standards (under a "Code of Good Practice") but they were killed in 1983 when the Justice Department filed an antitrust suit against some of the standards.[190]

Tobacco and tobacco products advertising has been one of the most controversial areas of commercial speech. Tracing its origins all the way back to 1612 when Englishman John Rolfe grew tobacco in Jamestown, Virginia, tobacco has been a commercial enterprise in the United States for almost four centuries.[191] By the 1920s more than a billion cigarettes were sold annually.[192] One of the most important events in the history of tobacco occurred in 1964 when the U.S. Surgeon General issued an official report, directly linking smoking with cancer, heart disease, and other illnesses. Five years later, the U.S. Congress enacted a statute banning advertising for cigarettes and small cigars in all electronic media and designating the Federal Communications Commission as the enforcement agency.[193] The ban took effect in 1971 and was immediately challenged on First Amendment grounds, not by the tobacco industry, but instead by individual broadcasters and their trade association, the National Association of Broadcasters. In *Capital Broadcasting Co. v. Mitchell* (1971),[194] a three-judge district court panel ruled against the broadcasters, holding there was no First Amendment infringement and citing the "unique characteristics of electronic communication that make it subject to regulation in the public interest." Ads for smokeless tobacco in electronic media were banned in 1986.[195]

In 1992 in *Cipollone v. Liggett Group, Inc.*,[196] the U.S. Supreme Court struck another blow against tobacco advertising when it held that the Public Health Cigarette Smoking Act of 1969 did not prohibit suits at common law for fraudulent misrepresentation in tobacco advertising. The next major event in the series arose in 1993 when the staff of the Federal Trade Commission recommended that the agency ban ads for Camel cigarettes that included the cartoon character known as "Old Joe" or "Joe Camel." Studies showed that even young children associated the humped-back character with Camel cigarettes. Within three years after Joe appeared, the illegal sales of Camels to children under 18 reportedly rose from $6 million to a whopping $476 million a year.[197] A 1993 study by the federal Centers for Disease Control and Prevention in

Atlanta found that the three most heavily advertised cigarette brands—Camel, Marlboro, and Newport—controlled 86% of the market for smokers aged 12 to 18, compared to only 35% of the overall market. According to that survey, 3 million adolescents smoked 1 billion packs of cigarettes a year.[198] Another study—this time in the February 23, 1994 *Journal of the American Medical Association*—found that the Virginia Slims "You've Come a Long Way, Baby" campaign persuaded 11- to 17-year-old girls to smoke. Tobacco companies were also criticized for sponsoring auto races as a means of bypassing the TV ban on cigarette commercials.[199]

When R.J. Reynolds spent $42.9 million in major market advertising for Camels in 1993, the FTC voted 3 to 2 to end the investigation, saying there was no evidence to support claims that children were lured to smoke by the campaign, temporarily accepting the arguments of the tobacco industry. U.S. Surgeon General Joycelyn Elders, among other prominent individuals, urged the agency to stop the ads. R.J. Reynolds was by no means off the hook as result of the FTC decision. In 1994 the U.S. Supreme Court denied *certiorari* in an appeal from Reynolds seeking to halt a suit filed against it by San Francisco lawyer Janet Mangini in a California trial court.[200] Mangini sought a permanent injunction against Joe Camel ads and sought to force the company to pay for a national anti-smoking campaign for children. The firm unsuccessfully argued in its appeal that federal law preempted state law in such a case.

The U.S. Food and Drug Administration sent a series of proposals to then-President Bill Clinton in 1995 for regulating nicotine as a drug. One part of the report concluded that the FDA had the authority to regulate nicotine and tobacco under the Food, Drug and Cosmetic Act as "drug delivery devices." The recommendations fell far short of what tobacco critics wanted. But the agency did recommend outlawing cigarette vending machines, banning use of cartoon characters in advertising, and restricting tobacco ads in magazines with substantial youth readerships. Even small steps created controversy. The then-Speaker of the House Newt Gingrich's (R-Ga.) reaction to the report was that the FDA had "lost its mind." The FDA left the implementation of the recommendations to the White House and Congress, where there was resistance.

The first set of regulations aimed at reducing use of cigarettes and smokeless tobacco among adolescents took effect in 1997.[201] The regulations required retail stores to check photo IDs before selling cigarettes or other tobacco products to anyone under the age of 27. They imposed a ban on all outdoor advertising within 1,000 feet of public playgrounds, including those at public parks, elementary and high schools. The FTC had earlier charged that the Joe Camel advertising campaign violated federal law in inducing young people to smoke, resulting in significant harm to their health and safety.[202] The commission minced no words in its allegations against the R.J. Reynolds Tobacco Company, saying the Joe Camel campaign was so successful the percentage of children who smoked Camels eventually outgrew the percentage of adults who smoked the brand. According to the FTC, the company "promoted an addictive and dangerous product through a campaign that was attractive to those too young to purchase cigarettes legally."[203]

In the same month the FDA regulations were promulgated, a group of state attorneys general, health advocates representing 46 states, the District of Columbia, Puerto Rico, the U.S. Virgin Islands, American Samoa, the Northern Mariana Islands, and Guam began negotiations with trial lawyers representing the tobacco companies. On November 23, 1998, the five largest tobacco manufacturers (Brown & Williamson, Lorillard, Philip Morris, R.J. Reynolds, and Liggett & Myers) signed an agreement under which they would pay the states more than

$206 billion over 25 years and accept restrictions on advertising and marketing. When the agreement was reached, four states (Florida, Minnesota, Mississippi, and Texas) had already settled with the manufacturers for $40 billion. Under the agreement, known as the "Attorneys General Master Settlement Agreement":[204] (1) no cartoon characters such as Joe Camel are permitted in tobacco ads; (2) all transit and outdoor tobacco ads, including those on billboards, and tobacco company sponsorships of concerts, team sports and events with a significant youth audience are outlawed; (3) payments promoting tobacco products in movies, TV shows, theater productions, and live performances are banned; and (4) the use of tobacco brand names for stadiums and arenas is prohibited. Mississippi Attorney General Michael Moore (not to be confused with the film-maker of the documentary *Sicko*) led the battle against the industry that resulted in the national settlement, and his state was the first to settle on its own after the proposal was hammered out. And what was the payout? Almost $3.6 billion.[205]

In 1996, after the FDA exercised what it thought was its authority to regulate tobacco products as drugs and devices under the Food, Drug and Cosmetic Act of 1938, the tobacco industry challenged the agency's authority in court. The U.S. District Court sided with the FDA, but the Fourth Circuit U.S. Court of Appeals reversed, holding that Congress had not granted such authority. On further appeal, the U.S. Supreme Court in *Food and Drug Administration v. Brown & Williamson Tobacco Corp. et al.* (2000)[206] upheld in a 5 to 4 decision the lower appellate court ruling. The Supreme Court said that, reading the Act as a whole as well as in the context of later federal tobacco legislation, it was clear that Congress had not delegated the FDA authority to regulate tobacco products as drugs and devices. Soon thereafter, the FDA backed away from its earlier decision, revoking its tobacco regulations. In a more recent case a Massachusetts jury awarded $71 million in compensatory damages from a claim against Lorillard Tobacco Co. in 2010. In this case, an African American woman maintained that she received free samples of Newport cigarettes at the age of 9 as part of a campaign that targeted young blacks in urban neighborhoods. She smoked until her death at the age of 54. She had given her lawyers a videotaped deposition just three weeks before she died. The tobacco company insisted that while it did give free samples to adults to get them to change brands, it never gave free cigarettes to children.

Just as the legal issues associated with tobacco advertising are troublesome and problematic, so are the ethical issues. According to internal memos, the third largest cigarette manufacturer, Brown & Williamson Tobacco Corp., paid more than $950,000 in the early eighties to have its brands featured in more than 20 movies. Sylvester Stallone of *Rocky* fame received at least $300,000 and Sean Connery of the popular James Bond film series also benefited, according to the memos.[207] These movies were seen by millions of teenagers too young to legally smoke.

The ethical question is: *why do many of the mass circulation magazines that have broad readership among young people accept cigarette advertising, knowing the ads are likely to influence young people to smoke and harm their health?* The research on cigarette advertising clearly points in the direction of strong effects of ads on children. For example, a study by Richard Pollay of the University of British Columbia, published in 1996 in the *Journal of Marketing,* found that, on average, when a cigarette brand increased its advertising expenditures by 10%, its market share among adults went up 3% but its market share among teen smokers jumped as much as 9%.[208] According to the Campaign for Tobacco-Free Kids, every day more than 2,000 children in this country become new, regular daily smokers.[209] The campaign particularly criticized the marketing of flavored cigarettes such as "Kauai Kolada," "Twista Lime," Camel "Winter

Warm Toffee" and "Winter MochaMint," and Kool "Caribbean Chill," "Midnight Berry," and "Mocha Taboo." One smokeless tobacco company is marketing flavors such as wintergreen, apple blend, and cherry. The campaign has also criticized Brown & Williamson for promoting its Kool brand with hip-hop music themes, and images.[210] At least one major magazine, *Reader's Digest*, has had a policy for decades that prohibits cigarette and other tobacco product ads, and yet it has continued to be profitable. The *Digest* has few media followers. It is ironic that TV viewers will not see any tobacco ads on television because of the congressional ban, and yet full-page ads for cigarettes pop up as they search their television guides. In 1997 tobacco companies in Japan decided to stop advertising on television, radio, movies, and the Internet, while increasing advertising in magazines and newspapers.[211]

Alcohol advertising has also drawn fire for allegedly catering to youths. A study in the *American Journal of Public Health* by Joel Grude and Patricia Madden showed that beer ads affect children's beliefs about drinking. The research could not demonstrate that the ads affected their later behavior. The survey of fifth and sixth graders found that children are extensively exposed to alcohol advertising and they associate drinking with "romance, sociability and relaxation."[212]

Rules banning all tobacco advertising in newspapers and magazines and on the Internet took effect in the 15 member-countries of the European Union in 2005.[213] The ban also applies to international sporting events. In 2003 Britain, home of three of the largest tobacco companies in the world, effectively banned all tobacco advertising.[214] Bob Iger, CEO of the Walt Disney Company, publicly pledged that all Disney movies, including those produced by Touchstone and Miramax, would no longer portray smoking as of 2007. He also indicated that the company would begin including anti-smoking public service announcements in theaters and on DVDs. About the same time, the Motion Picture Association of America said smoking would be considered in setting movie ratings.

The ethical issues surrounding alcohol and tobacco advertising may or may not clash with First Amendment principles, depending upon which side of the issue the speaker falls. In light of *Central Hudson* and *Coors* and *44 Liquormart*, some of the proposed limitations would probably meet the standards for restricting commercial speech while others would not. Self-regulation is not likely, if the past is any indication, unless the industries feel they have no choice, short of government regulation. So far few major media outlets have dealt with the ethical concerns beyond publicizing them in news stories. Should newspapers and magazines, for example, adopt policies barring alcohol and tobacco ads that are likely to attract the attention of children? Should TV and radio stations consider such restrictions for alcoholic beverages? The study found 685 alcohol commercials in 443 hours of televised sporting events but only 25 public service announcements on the dangers of alcohol during the same time.[215]

In a move heavily criticized by government officials and children's advocacy groups, the Distilled Spirits Council of the United States (DISCUS), a trade association for distillers, announced in 1996 that it was lifting its voluntary ban on the advertising of so-called "hard liquor" (vodka, scotch, rum, whisky, gin, bourbon, etc.) on radio and television.[216] The ban, which many people mistakenly assumed had been imposed either by Congress or the FCC, took effect for radio in 1936 and for television in 1948.[217] It never affected wine and beer commercials, which have been freely broadcast for decades. The ban had actually already been violated earlier in 1996 when the Seagram Co. began carrying ads for its Crown Royal Canadian and Chivas Regal Whisky on a Texas TV station.[218] The ads were responses to years of declining sales.

Many major commercial networks including the traditional sources—ABC, CBS, NBC, and Fox—refused to change their policies prohibiting such advertising, but many local stations including network affiliates and several cable companies were more than happy to accept the ads. One major cable company, Continental Cablevision Inc., accepted the commercials but restricted them to airing from 10:00 p.m. to 2:00 a.m. The then FCC Chair, Reed Hundt, urged in vain for the industry to continue the voluntary ban,[219] and President Bill Clinton had harsh words for the action of the trade association, asking to no avail that the FCC study the effects of liquor advertising.[220] Hundt called the decision to lift the ban "disappointing for parents and dangerous for our kids."[221] More than a year after it broke the voluntary ban, Seagram began inserting six-second disclaimers at the beginning of its ads such as "People of legal drinking age should enjoy alcohol responsibly, but don't drink if you're under 21."[222]

According to a study published in the *Journal of the American Medical Association*, some magazines that attract a sizeable number of teenagers such as *Rolling Stone, Sports Illustrated*, and *People* are likely to contain more advertising than other magazines for liquor and beer.[223] According to the study comparing the advertising content of 35 magazines, for each increase of 1 million readers 12 to 19 years old, a magazine typically had about 60% more beer and liquor ads.[224]

Other Ethical Issues

The *Wall Street Journal* shook the rafters of the publishing industry with a story that detailed how numerous magazine advertisers, including Chrysler, Ford Motor Co. and Colgate-Palmolive Co., insisted that publishers provide them advance notice of potentially controversial articles so they could pull their advertising if they felt it appropriate in the late nineties.[225] Many publishers apparently comply with the requests because they simply cannot afford to lose a major advertiser in the age of emerging online competitors. The problem is that the traditional separation between the advertising and editorial departments breaks down when an advertiser demands prior notice of editorial content.[226] Whether editorial content suffers will vary from magazine to magazine, but there are serious ethical issues involved when a corporation refuses to purchase advertising in a publication unless the publisher gives it advance notice. Advertisers have every right to pick and choose the publications in which they advertise, but should they be permitted to mess with editorial content? If nothing else, readers' perceptions about a magazine and its credibility could be adversely affected if they are led to believe that advertisers can dictate content.

Another controversial issue that has emerged in recent years is the extent to which advertising is sneaking into the mass media, including television, radio, movies and online in the form of product placements. With the advent of devices that permit a consumer to skip TV commercials now in common use in the home, advertisers are having a tough time getting through to viewers. According to *Time* magazine, the percentage of households using electronic devices to skip TV commercials rose from 0 in 2000 to 40% in less than a decade. At the same time, the amount advertisers were spending on product placement on TV rose from about $1 billion in 2000 to an expected $4 billion.[227] Reality shows such as *The Apprentice* and *Survivor* have been particular favorites for product placement. Another new twist on advertising is the so-called "word-of-mouth" radio endorsement in which DJs are paid to plug specific brand products and services in what appear to be spontaneous discussions. One ad agency in Atlanta, for example, specializes in such advertising. Most listeners are unaware they're hearing advertising. For example, two morning show co-hosts might converse for a few minutes between songs about the brand of detergent they used over the weekend to clean their cars or what fast food chain they plan to drop by for lunch later in the day. There are no FCC rules or regulations that ban such advertising nor that prohibit radio hosts from being paid to do such plugs.

Even video games have become a market for advertisers. For example, Jeeps have been placed in Tony Hawk's Underground 2 game, and Pizza Hut appears in the online Everquest II game.[228] Some games—"advergames"—are devoted primarily to promoting a particular product.

Finally, some research indicates that anti-smoking ad campaigns not only do not work but may actually increase smoking, at least among young people. For example, one study found that the more middle school students see such ads, the more likely they are to smoke. [229]

In June, 2009, President Barrack Obama signed the Family Smoking Prevention and Tobacco Control Act giving the Food and Drug Administration the chance to ban advertising geared to children decreasing the amount of nicotine in tobacco products. It also prohibited the use of terms such as "low tar" and "light" as well as sweetened cigarettes often more appealing to young people. Three months later, federal health officials banned the sale of flavored cigarettes such as strawberry, chocolate, and vanilla designed to attract younger smokers while vowing to also address the marketing of small cigars and cigarillos.[230]

Summary and Conclusions

With advertising expenditures continuing to rise, commercial speech has become an important avenue for exercising First Amendment freedoms. Indeed, the media, as we know it today in the United States, could not survive without the continued influx of advertising revenues. Even traditionally noncommercial forms of mass communication, such as public radio and television, have come to rely on advertising, albeit in the form of brief spots and support acknowledgments. The protection granted commercial speech by the courts, particularly the U.S. Supreme Court, has expanded since the unenlightened days of *Valentine v. Chrestensen* (1942). This is thanks to the advances forged in *New York Times v. Sullivan* (1964), *Bigelow v. Virginia* (1975), *Virginia State Board of Pharmacy v. Virginia Citizens Consumer Council* (1976), and progeny as well as cases involving religious speech such as *Watchtower Bible and Tract Society v. Village of Stratton* (2002).

Central Hudson Gas and Electric Corp. v. Public Service Commission (1980) did provide us with a four-part test for determining whether a particular type of commercial speech has First Amendment protection. U.S. Supreme Court decisions such as *Posadas de Puerto Rico Associates v. Tourism Company of Puerto Rico* (1986), *Shapero v. Kentucky Bar Association* (1988), *Board of Trustees of the State University of New York v. Fox* (1989), and *Peel v. Attorney Registration and Disciplinary Commission of Illinois* (1990) have clarified *Central Hudson*'s test and created confusion about its use. Like it or not, the Supreme Court will continue to face commercial speech cases in a variety of contexts until a strong majority on the Court is able to flesh out *Central Hudson* or create a clearer test for determining the scope of constitutional protection for commercial speech. The nondecision in *Nike v. Kasky* (2003) illustrates this struggle of the Court to articulate clear guidelines regarding how much protection commercial speech enjoys. The

Court could always reverse itself and grant commercial speech the same protection as political and religious speech, but that is still unlikely to occur anytime soon.

Coors (1995), *44 Liquormart* (1996), and *Thompson v. Western States Medical Center* (2002) are positive signs that the U.S. Supreme Court is willing under certain circumstances—especially when truthful information is involved that may assist consumers in making marketplace decisions—to broaden First Amendment protection for commercial and corporate speech. But, as *Florida Bar v. Went for It* (1995) and *Glickman* (1997) demonstrate, there are times when the Court will draw the line and find no First Amendment violation when commercial speech is restricted even though the Court would have ruled differently if the speech had involved political or religious content. *Glickman* is troubling because the Court rejected *Central Hudson* as the appropriate test for determining whether a compelled contribution to support a campaign was constitutional. The Court made clear the First Amendment does not bar all compelled contributions to fund advertising, particularly when the advertising does not promote a message with which the contributor disagrees.

Four years later in *United States v. United Foods* (2001), the Court ruled that a statute similar to that in Glickman but regulating mushrooms instead of tree fruit was unconstitutional. The Court said the compelled speech was not part of a comprehensive regulatory program and thus was not like the tree fruit industry in *Glickman*. According to the Court, previous restrictions like those in *Glickman* were not struck down because the objecting members were required to associate for purposes other than the compelled subsidies for speech. In *Johanns v. Livestock Marketing Association* (2005), the Court held that imposing an assessment on all sales and importation of cattle did not violate the First Amendment because the assessment funded the federal government's own speech—not private speech. The difference in this case was that the decisions on expenditures were made by a committee, half of whose members were appointed by the U.S. Secretary of Agriculture and all of whose members could be removed by the Secretary. *Glickman, United Foods*, and *Johanns* illustrate the thin line the U.S. Supreme Court draws between compelled versus noncompelled speech under the First Amendment.

Although the Supreme Court determines the scope of protection granted to various forms of commercial and corporate speech including advertising, federal and state agencies such as the Federal Trade Commission execute day-to-day regulations. The FTC has the most impact on advertising regulation, but state and local agencies share in the process. Congress and the state legislatures also play an important role by enacting specific statutes, usually to restrict or prohibit certain types of advertising. Finally, self-regulation such as that by the National Advertising Division and the National Advertising Review Board work to eliminate false, misleading, and deceptive advertising, even though these entities have no governmental authority and rely on volunteer cooperation from advertisers and pressure from adverse media publicity to halt such advertising.

Self-regulation typically weeds out only the most blatant and egregious abuses, and government enforcement is only a few steps ahead of self-regulation. The media must impose stricter ethical standards for advertising or consumer confidence in advertising will erode. Because the media are never required to accept any particular ads except political ads by broadcasters, there is no rationale for publishing questionable ads even when they may allow media to avoid prosecution. Higher ethical standards for all forms of advertising would lead to more informed and rational consumers, which would, in the long run, benefit rather than harm the mass media.

Tobacco and liquor advertising pose special problems because research indicates that young people are influenced by such messages, even to the point of illegally using the products.

Endnotes

1. Bruce Schreiner and Sarah Skidmore, *Thank you for suing us: Taco Bell Fights Beef Lawsuit with Full Page Ads*, Associated Press, January 28, 2011; and *Taco Bell is Launching an Advertising Campaign to Fight Back*, January 29, 2010, Associated Press, also on The Huffington Post, January 29, 2011, available at http://www.huffingtonpost.com.
2. *See* Shannon McCaffrey, *Supreme Court to Hear Case of Nike's Free Speech*, Lexington (Ky.) Herald-Leader (Knight Ridder Washington Bureau), Jan. 11, 2003, at A9.
3. See *Jeffrey L. Fisher, Nike v. Kasky: Will the Shield of the Commercial Speech Doctrine Become a Sword?* Communication Law. Winter 2003, at 28.
4. *Kasky v. Nike*, 45 P.3d 243 (Cal. 2002).
5. *Id.*
6. *Id.*
7. *Supreme Court Considers Nike Commercial Speech Challenge*, News Media Update (electronic e-mail), vol. 9, no. 9 (May 5, 2003).
8. *Nike v. Kasky*, 539 U.S. 654, 123 S.Ct. 2554, 156 L.Ed.2d 580, 31 Med.L.Rptr. 1865 (2003).
9. *See Nike Settles Controversial First Amendment Case*, Reporters Committee for Freedom of the Press (press release), Sept. 15, 2003.
10. See http://www.fairlabor.org.
11. *Valentine v. Chrestensen*, 316 U.S. 52, 62 S.Ct. 920, 86 L.Ed. 1262, 1 Med.L.Rptr. 1907 (1942).
12. *Id.*
13. *Jamison v. Texas*, 318 U.S. 413, 63 S.Ct. 920, 86 L.Ed. 1262, 1. Med.L.Rptr. 1907 (1943).
14. *Id.*
15. *Murdock v. Pennsylvania*, 319 U.S. 105, 63 S.Ct. 870, 87 L.Ed. 1292 (1943).
16. *Id.*
17. *Martin v. City of Struthers*, 319 U.S. 141, 63 S.Ct. 862, 87 L.Ed. 1313 (1943).
18. *Douglas v. City of Jeannette*, 319 U.S. 157, 63 S.Ct. 877, 87 L.Ed. 1324 (1943).
19. *Watchtower Bible and Tract Society v. Village of Stratton*, 536 U.S. 150, 122 S.Ct. 2080, 153 L.Ed.2d 205 (2003).
20. *Id.*
21. *New York Times v. Sullivan*, 376 U.S. 254, 84 S.Ct. 710, 11 L.Ed.2d 686, 1 Med.L.Rptr. 1527 (1964).
22. *Id.*
23. *Id.*
24. *Roe v. Wade*, 410 U.S. 113, 93 S.Ct. 705, 35 L.Ed.2d 147 (1973).
25. *Pittsburgh Press Co. v. The Pittsburgh Commission on Human Relations*, 413 U.S. 376, 93 S.Ct. 2553, 37 L.Ed.2d 669, 1 Med.L.Rptr. 1908 (1973).
26. *Id.*
27. *Id.*
28. *Id.*
29. *Id.*
30. *Id.*
31. *Bigelow v. Virginia*, 421 U.S. 809, 96 S.Ct. 2222, 44 L.Ed.2d 600, 1 Med.L.Rptr. 1919 (1975).
32. *Id.*
33. *Id.*
34. *City of Cincinnati v. Discovery Network*, 507 U.S. 410, 13 S.Ct. 1505, 123 L.Ed.2d 99, 21 Med.L.Rptr. 1161 (1993).
35. *Board of Trustees of the State University of New York v. Fox*, 492 U.S. 469, 62 S.Ct. 3028, 106 L.Ed.2d 388 (1989).

36. *Virginia State Board of Pharmacy v. Virginia Citizens Consumer Council*, 425 U.S. 748, 96 S.Ct. 1817, 48 L.Ed.2d 346, 1 Med.L.Rptr. 1930 (1976).
37. *Id.*
38. *Id.* (Rehnquist dissent).
39. *Id.*
40. Cited in Betsy Querna, *Pressure from Patients*, U.S. News & World Report, May 9, 2005, at 68.
41. Jisu Huh, Denise E. DeLorme, and Leonard Reid, *The Information Utility of DTC Prescription Drug Advertising*, 81 Journalism Quarterly 788 (2004).
42. *Linmark Associates, Inc. v. Willingboro*, 431 U.S. 85, 97 S.Ct. 1614, 52 L.Ed.2d 155 (1977).
43. *Id.*
44. *Hugh Carey v. Population Services International*, 431 U.S. 678, 97 S.Ct. 2010, 52 L.Ed.2d 675, 2 Med.L.Rptr. 1935
45. *Griswold v. Connecticut*, 381 U.S. 497, 85 S.Ct. 1678, 14 L.Ed.2d 510 (1965).
46. *First National Bank of Boston v. Bellotti*, 435 U.S. 765, 98 S.Ct. 1407, 55 L.Ed.2d 707, 3 Med. L.Rptr. 2105 (1978).
47. *Consolidated Edison Co. v. Public Service Commission of New York*, 444 U.S. 530, 100 S.Ct. 2326, 65 L.Ed.2d 319, 6 Med.L.Rptr. 1518 (1980).
48. *Central Hudson Gas & Electric Corp. v. Public Service Commission of New York*, 447 U.S. 557, 100 S.Ct. 2343, 65 L.Ed.2d 341, 6 Med.L.Rptr. 1497 (1980).
49. *Consolidated Edison Co.*
50. *Id.*
51. *Red Lion Broadcasting v. Federal Communications Commission*, 395 U.S. 367, 89 S.Ct. 1794, 23 L.Ed.2d 371, 1 Med.L.Rptr. 2053 (1969).
52. *Central Hudson Gas & Electric Corp.*
53. *Id.*
54. *Id.*
55. *Id.*
56. *Id.*
57. *Id.*
58. *Bolger v. Youngs Drug Products Corp.*, 463 U.S. 60, 103 S.Ct. 2875, 77 L.Ed. 2d 469 (1983).
59. 39 U.S.C. §3001(e)(2).
60. *Bolger v. Youngs Drug Products Corp.*
61. *Id.*
62. *Bates v. State Bar of Arizona*, 433 U.S. 350, 97 S.Ct. 2691, 53 L.Ed.2d 810, 2 Med.L.Rptr. 2097 (1977).
63. *Virginia State Board of Pharmacy.*
64. *Bates v. State Bar of Arizona.*
65. *Id.*
66. *Id.*
67. *Ohralik v. Ohio State Bar Association*, 436 U.S. 447, 98 S.Ct. 1912, 56 L.Ed.2d 444 (1978).
68. *In Re Primus,* 436 U.S. 412, 98 S.Ct. 1893, 56 L.Ed.2d 417 (1978).
69. *Id.*
70. *Id.*
71. *In re R. M. J.*, 455 U.S. 191, 102 S.Ct. 929, 71 L.Ed.2d 64 (1982).
72. The bar rules permitted attorneys to send such announcements only to "lawyers, clients, former clients, personal friends and relatives."
73. *Zauderer v. Office of Disciplinary Counsel*, 471 U.S. 626, 105 S.Ct. 2265, 85 L.Ed.2d 652 (1985).
74. *Id.*
75. Kentucky Rules of the Supreme Court SCR 7.03.
76. *Shapero v. Kentucky Bar Association*, 486 U.S. 466, 108 S.Ct. 1916, 100 L.Ed.2d 475 (1988).
77. *Id.*
78. Curriden, *Making Airwaves*, American Bar Association Journal 38, 40. (July 1989).
79. Kentucky Rules of the Supreme Court, SCR 3.130–7.01 *et seq.*
80. *Id.*

81. *Id.*
82. *Peel v. Attorney Registration and Disciplinary Commission of Illinois*, 496 U.S. 91, 110 S.Ct. 2281, 110 L.Ed.2d 83 (1990).
83. Attorneys *and Advertising: Yellow Pages and Red Tape?, Yellow Pages Update*, July–August 1988, at 6.
84. *Id.*
85. *Ibanez v. Florida Department of Business and Professional Regulation*, Board of Accountancy, 512 U.S. 136, 114 S.Ct. 2084, 129 L.Ed.2d 118 (1994).
86. *Id.*
87. *Florida Bar v. Went for It, Inc. and John T. Blakely*, 515 U.S. 618, 115 S.Ct. 2371, 132 L.Ed.2d 541, 23 Med.L.Rptr. 1801 (1995).
88. *The Florida Bar: Petition to Amend the Rules Regulating the Bar-Advertising Issues*, 571 So.2d 451 (Fla. 1990).
89. Interestingly, the Court mentions that the attorney in the original suit was disbarred before the case reached the U.S. Supreme Court for reasons unrelated to the case. Another lawyer was then substituted for the appeal.
90. Florida Bar Rules of Professional Conduct 4-7.4(b) and 4-7.8(a).
91. *McHenry v. Florida Bar*, 808 F.Supp. 1543 (M.D. Fla. 1992).
92. *McHenry v. Florida Bar*, 21 F.3d 1038 (11th Cir. 1994). We characterize the appellate court as "reluctantly" affirming because the U.S. Supreme Court said in its decision, "The panel [11th Circuit] noted, in its conclusion, that it was 'disturbed that Bates and its progeny require the decision' that it reached".
93. *Florida Bar.*
94. *Id.* (Kennedy dissent).
95. *Florida Bar.*
96. *Id.*
97. *Friedman v. Rogers*, 440 U.S. 1, 99 S.Ct. 887, 59 L.Ed.2d 100 (1979).
98. *American Medical Association v. Federal Trade Commission*, 638 F.2d 443 (2d Cir. 1980).
99. *American Medical Association v. Federal Trade Commission*, 455 U.S. 676, 102 S.Ct. 1744, 71 L.Ed.2d 546 (1982).
100. *Thompson v. Western States Medical Center*, 535 U.S. 357, 122 S.Ct. 1497, 152 L.Ed.2d 563 (2002).
101. *Id.* (Thomas concurrence).
102. *Id.*
103. *Posadas de Puerto Rico Associates v. Tourism Co. of Puerto Rico*, 478 U.S. 328, 106 S.Ct. 2968, 92 L.Ed.2d 266, 13 Med.L.Rptr. 1033 (1986).
104. *44 Liquor Mart v. Rhode Island*, 517 U.S. 484, 116 S.Ct. 1495, 134 L.Ed.2d 711, 24 Med. L.Rptr. 1673 (1996).
105. *Posadas de Puerto Rico Associates v. Tourism Co. of Puerto Rico.*
106. *Id.* (Brennan dissent).
107. *Id.*
108. *Board of Trustees of the State University of New York v. Fox.*
109. *Id.*
110. *Id.*
111. *See* Federal Alcohol Administration Act, 49 Stat. 977, 27 U.S.C. 201 §5(e)(2).
112. *Adolph Coors Co. v. Brady*, 944 F.2d 1543 (1991).
113. *Adolph Coors Co. v. Bentsen*, 2 F.3d 355 (1993).
114. *Rubin v. Coors Brewing Co.*, 514 U.S. 476, 115 S.Ct. 1585, 131 L.Ed.2d 532, 23 Med.L.Rptr. 1545 (1995).
115. *44 Liquor Mart v. Racine*, 39 F.3d 5, 22 Med.L.Rptr. 2409 (1st Cir. 1994), *rev'g*, 829 F.Supp. 543, 553 (D.R.I. 1993); *44 Liquor Mart v. Rhode Island*, 517 U.S. 484, 116 S.Ct. 1495, 134 L.Ed.2d 711, 24 Med.L.Rptr. 1673 (1996).
116. R.I. Gen. L. §3-8-7 and 2-8-8.1. At dispute also was Regulation 32 of the Rhode Island Liquor Control Administration.
117. *44 Liquormart Inc. v. Rhode Island*, 829 F.Supp. 543, 553 (D.R.I. 1993).

118. *44 Liquor Mart v. Rhode Island,* 39 F.3d 5, 22 Med.L.Rptr. 2409 (1st Cir. 1994).
119. *44 Liquor Mart v. Rhode Island*, 517 U.S. 484 (1996) (Thomas, concurrence).
120. *Id.* (Rehnquist, concurrence).
121. *Florida Bar.*
122. *Glickman, Secretary of Agriculture v. Wileman Brothers & Elliott, Inc., et al.,* 521 U.S. 457, 117 S.Ct. 2130, 138 L.Ed.2d 585 (1997).
123. Agricultural Marketing Agreement Act of 1937 (AMAA), ch. 296, 50 Stat. 246, as amended, 7 U.S.C. §601 *et seq.*
124. *Glickman.*
125. *Id.*
126. *Id.*
127. *Id.*
128. *Id.*
129. *Id.*
130. *United States v. United Foods*, 533 U.S. 405, 121 S.Ct. 2334, 150 L.Ed.2d 438 (2001).
131. *Johanns v. Livestock Marketing Association*, 544 U.S. 550, 125 S.Ct. 2055, 161 L.Ed.2d 896 (2005).
132. *Id.*
133. Id.
134. 38 Stat. 719 (1914).
135. 15 U.S.C. §12-27 (1914).
136. 15 U.S.C. §1-7 (1890).
137. 15 U.S.C. §13 (1936).
138. *Federal Trade Commission v. Yagle,* 1 F.T.C. 13 (1916) and *Federal Trade Commission v. A. Theo. Abbot & Co.,* 1 F.T.C. 16 (1916).
139. *FTC v. Winstead Hosiery*, 258 U.S. 483, 42 S.Ct. 384, 66 L.Ed. 729 (1922).
140. *FTC v. Raladam Co.,* 283 U.S. 643, 51 S.Ct. 587, 75 L.Ed. 1324 (1931).
141. *See Tropicana to Drop Health Claim*, Atlanta Journal-Constitution, June 3, 2005, at F2.
142. FTC File No. 962 3150 (1/22/97).
143. FTC File No. D9260 (5/29/97).
144. FTC File No. D09280 (7/23/97).
145. 52 Stat. 111 (1938).
146. 15 U.S.C. §45(a)(1) (1975).
147. 15 U.S.C. §45(n).
148. *See* http://www.ftc.gov/bcp/conline/pubs/general/guidetoftc.htm.
149. *Id.*
150. *Id.*
151. *Id.*
152. *Id.*
153. *Id.*
154. *Charles of the Ritz Distributing Corp. v. FTC*, 143 F.2d 676 (1944).
155. *See* "DirecTV to Pay $5.3 Million Penalty for Do Not Call Violations" available at http://www.ftc.gov/opa/2005/12/directv.htm. *U.S. and the Federal Trade Commission v. DirecTV* (2005).
156. *Id.*
157. *See* "Alleged Pyramid Scheme Operators Banned from Multi-level Marketing" available at http://www.ftc.gov/opa/2005/12/trekall.htm. *Federal Trade Commission v. Trek Alliance. Inc., et al.* (2005).
158. *See* "Trade Regulations Rules and Industry Guides" available at http://www.ftc.gov/ftc/trr.htm for descriptions of some of these and other TRRs.
159. 94 Stat. 374, 15 U.S.C §45 (1980).
160. *Immigration and Naturalization Service v. Chadha,* 462 U.S. 919, 103 S.Ct. 2764, 77 L.Ed.2d 317 (1983).
161. 15 U.S.C. §45.
162. *See* C.F.R. §1.1–1.4 (1986) for FTC authority to issue such opinions.
163. 15 U.S.C. §2301.

164. 562 F.2d 749 (1977).

165. *Cert. denied*, 435 U.S. 950, 98 S.Ct. 1576, 55 L.Ed.2d 800 (1978).

166. *In Re ITT Continental Baking Co*, 79 F.T.C. 248 (1971).

167. *In Re Ocean Spray Cranberries, Inc.*, 70 F.T.C. 975 (1972).

168. *National Commission on Egg Nutrition v. FTC*, 570 F.2d 187 (7th Cir. 1977), *cert. denied*, 439 U. S. 821, 99 S.Ct. 86, 58 L.Ed.2d 112 (1978).

169. *Id.*

170. *Id.*

171. *J. B. Williams Co., Inc. v. FTC*, 381 F.2d 884 (6th Cir. 1967).

172. *U.S. v. J. B. Williams Co., Inc.*, 498 F.2d 414 (6th Cir. 1974).

173. *In Re Pfizer, Inc.*, 81 F.T.C. 23 (1972).

174. *Id.*

175. *Id.*

176. *Joe Conte Toyota Inc. v. Louisiana Motor Vehicle Commission*, 22 Med.L.Rptr. 1913, 24 F.3d 754 (5th Cir. 1994).

177. *Barry v. Arrow Pontiac, Inc.*, 100 N.J. 57, 494 A.2d 804 (1985).

178. *Joe Conte Toyota Inc. v. Louisiana Motor Vehicle Commission*, citing Brief for Appellee at 11.

179. *Id.*

180. "Milestones in U.S. Food and Drug Law History" available at http://www.fda.gov/opacom/ backgrounders/ miles.html.

181. *Id.*

182. *Id.*

183. *FDA Eases Limits on TV Drug Ads*, Sarasota (Fla.) Herald Tribune (Associated Press), Aug. 9, 1997, at 6D.

184. Virginia Anderson and Bill Hendrick, *Study Finds Dangers in Rosy TV Drug Ads,* Atlantic Journal-Constitution, Jan. 30, 2007, at E1.

185. *Id.*

186. *Id.*

187. *Boxes Can Advertise Oatmeal Heart-Healthy*, Lexington (Ky.) Herald-Leader (Associated Press), Jan. 22, 1997, at A9.

188. 16 C.F.R. §255.1.

189. *Miami Herald v. Tornillo*, 418 U.S. 241, 94 S.Ct. 2831, 41 L.Ed.2d 730, 1 Med.L.Rptr. 1898 (1974).

190. Lexington (Ky.) Herald-Leader, Oct. 6, 1988, at B5 and at B8.

191. *Id.*

192. *Tobacco Timeline*, Lexington (Ky.) Herald-Leader, Sept. 7, 1997, at A12.

193. *Id.*

194. Public Health Cigarette Smoking Act, 15 U.S.C. §1335 (1969).

195. *Capital Broadcasting v. Mitchell*, 333 F.Supp. 582 (D.C. Cir. 1971), *aff'd without opinion,* 405 U.S. 1000, 92 S.Ct. 1289, 31 L.Ed.2d 472 (1972).

196. *See* 15 U.S.C. §4402 (1986).

197. *Cippollone v. Liggett Group, Inc.*, 505 U.S. 504, 112 S.Ct. 2608, 120 L.Ed.2d 407 (1992).

198. *Can First Amendment Save Camel's 'Old Joe'?* Lexington (Ky.) Herald-Leader (Cox News Service), Aug. 14, 1993, at Today-3. For an update see Gardiner Harris, *Targeting Tobacco: cigarette packages will soon come with graphic warning labels meant to shock smokers. Will they prevent teens from getting hooked?* New York Times Upfront, December 13, 2010, and also Gardiner Harris, *Tobacco Rule Proposed in '95 to go Into Effect*, New York Times, March 19, 2010, at A-14.

199. *Cigarette Ads Found To Affect Teen-agers Most*, Lexington (Ky.) Herald-Leader (Associated Press), Aug. 18, 1994, at A3. See Tan Ee Lyn, *China Tobacco Firms Accused of Targeting Children*, Reuters, Shenzhen, China, August 19, 2010.

200. See S. Wollenberg, *Cigarette Makers Bypass TV Ad Ban with Auto Races*, Lexington (Ky.) Herald-Leader (Associated Press), May 28, 1994, at A3.

201. *R.J. Reynolds Tobacco Co. v. Mangini, cert. denied,* 513 U.S. 1016, 115 S.Ct. 577, 130 L.Ed.2d 195 (1994).

202. Regulations Restricting the Sale and Distribution of Cigarettes and Smokeless Tobacco to Protect Children and Adolescents, Final Rule, 61 Fed. Reg. 44395 (August 28, 1996).

203. FTC File No. P884517.

204. *Id.*

205. *See* Joy Johnson Wilson, *Summary of the Attorneys General Master Tobacco Settlement Agreement,* available at http://academic.udayton.edu/health/syllabi/tobacco/summary.htm and http://www.naag.org/settle.htm.

206. Lori Rozsa, *Florida Settles Tobacco Lawsuit for $11.3 Billion,* Lexington (Ky.) Herald-Leader (Knight-Ridder News Service), Aug. 26, 1997, at A1. For an update, see *Lorillard Tobacco Accused of Targeting Black Children,* August 17, 2010, News14.com, available at http://charlotte.news14.com, and *Survey Shows Tobacco Retailers Targeting Children,* at http://www.post-journal.com, downloaded February 7, 2011.

207. *Food and Drug Administration v. Brown & Williamson Tobacco Corp. et al.,* 529 U.S. 120, 120 S.Ct. 1291, 146 L.Ed.2d 121 (2000).

208. *See Firm Spent $950,000 to Plug Tobacco in Movies,* Lexington (Ky.) Herald-Leader (Los Angeles Times), May 19, 1994, at A15.

209. *Cigarette Ads Sway Teens, Study Finds,* Lexington (Ky.) Herald-Leader (wire services), Apr. 4, 1996, at A1.

210. *See* http://www.tobaccofreekids.org.

211. *Id.*

212. *Tobacco Ads,* Lexington (Ky.) Herald-Leader (wire services), October 2, 1997, at A3.

213. L. Neergaard, *TV Ads May Lure Children to Drink Beer, Studies Say,* Lexington (Ky.) Herald-Leader (Associated Press), Feb. 11, 1994, at A1. See also Nicholas D. Kristoff, *Moonshine for Kids?* New York Times, May 23, 2010, at WK-9. And also see, *1 in 4 Young People Binge Drink,* Reuters, New York Times, October 6, 2010, at A-17. This article covers the 2010 report by the Centers for Disease Control and Prevention reporting that one in four U.S. high school students and adults ages 18 to 35 engaged in "binge drinking," defined as having four or more drinks for women and five or more drinks for men within a few hours.

214. Raf Casert, *EU Bans Nearly All Tobacco Ads,* Lexington (Ky.) Herald-Leader (Associated Press), Dec. 3, 2002, at C2.

215. Sue Leeman, *Britain Bans All Ads for Tobacco,* Lexington (Ky.) Herald-Leader (Associated Press), Feb. 15, 2003, at D8.

216. L. Neergaard, *TV Ads May Lure Children To Drink Beer, Studies Say. 1 in 4 Young People Binge Drink,* Reuters, New York Times, October 6, 2010, at A-17.

217. Melanie Wells, *Liquor Group Opts To End TV, Radio Ad Ban,* USA Today, Nov. 8, 1996, at A1. Nicholas D. Kristoff, *Moonshine for Kids?* New York Times, May 23, 2010, at WK-9.

218. Yumiko Ono, *Memo Shows How Seagram Pondered TV Ad*s, Lexington (Ky.) Herald-Leader (Wall Street Journal), June 23, 1996, at Business 5.

219. *FCC: Keep Liquor Ads on Ban Wagon,* Lexington (Ky.) Herald-Leader (wire services and staff reports), November 9, 1997, at A11.

220. Richard A. Serrano, *Clinton Condemns Broadcast Liquor Ads,* Lexington (Ky.) Herald-Leader (Los Angeles Times), Nov. 10, 1996, at A1; Jodi Enda, *Stop Advertising Hard Liquor on TV, Clinton Urges Makers,* Lexington (Ky.) Herald-Leader (Knight-Ridder Washington Bureau), April 2, 1997, at A1.

221. Melanie Wells, *Liquor Group Opts To End TV, Radio Ad Ban* and Nicholas D. Kristoff, *Moonshine for Kids?* New York Times, May 23, 2010, at WK-9.

222. *Seagram Putting Disclaimer at Start of Ads,* Lexington (Ky.) Herald-Leader (wire services), Sept. 16, 1997, at C7.

223. Deanna Bellandi, *Teen Magazines Have More Alcohol Ads, Study Finds,* Lexington (Ky.) Herald-Leader (Associated Press), May 14, 2003, at A6.

224. *Id.*

225. G. Bruce Knecht, *Magazine Advertisers Demand Prior Notice of 'Offensive Articles.'* Wall Street Journal, Apr. 30, 1997, at A1.

226. *See id.*

227. Jeanne McDowell, *Prime-Time Peddling*, Time, May 30, 2005, at 50–51.

228. Gary Gentile, *Ms. Pac-Man Would Wear a Name-Brand Bow Today*, Lexington (Ky.) Herald-Leader (Associated Press), May 24, 2005, at B8.

229. Andrea Jones, *Study: Anti-Smoking Ads Encourage Teen Use*, Atlantic Journal-Constitution, July 20, 2007, at C1. For an update on the complexities of the issue, see also, Perri Klass, M.D., *18 and under: Q. Did You Ever Smoke Pot? A. It's complicated*, New York Times, July 13, 2010, at D-5.

230. Jeff Zeleny, *Occasional Smoker, 47, Signs Tobacco Bill*, New York Times, June 23, 2009, at A-15, and see also Gardiner Harris, *Flavors Banned From Cigarettes to Deter You*, New York Times, September 23, 2009, at A-1.

7

Electronic Mass Media and Telecommunications

It seems as though Family Guy creator, Seth MacFarlane, carefully reviewed the legal definition of broadcast indecency and set out to violate it as literally as he could.

—Tim Winter, President, Parents Television Council.[1]

At the start of Julius Genachowski's tenure as Chair of the Federal Communications Commission (FCC), the Barack Obama appointee indicated that he wanted to keep broadband Internet services deregulated at the same time that watchdog groups questioned his agencies' effectiveness in keeping close scrutiny over key companies providing access to the Web. Meanwhile, supporters on the topic of net neutrality such as Google invited a shift to the FCC authority and stricter rules as a means of keeping the Internet open. At the same time a number of high tech interests settled down after a fairly radical shift in both the media and the nation's economy had taken place.[2]

When the FCC approved so-called net neutrality rules to keep companies providing high speed Internet service from blocking legal content such as the use of Skype visual phone service, the rules were viewed in some quarters as controversial because they required service providers to offer their customers more information on how their networks were going to be being run. And just as controversial was the idea that this government agency would for the first time be taking aggressive steps to keep cable and Internet service companies from "unreasonable discrimination" in offering access to online content. Republicans entering the U.S. House of Representatives almost immediately challenged the FCC Net Neutrality order when they took office. The day the 112th Congress convened and Republicans took over, January 5, 2010, the Internet Freedom Act, backed by 60 representatives, was filed in the House. That act generated a similar response by Republicans in the U.S. Senate.

In terms of broadcast station operations the FCC had been making what were thought to be major in-roads over the course of the previous decade. The Commission altered its philosophy in some important areas such as media cross-ownership and it played a leadership role in the transition to new digital technology just after that with the change in television receivers for the entire nation.

With respect to media ownership, it set new rules restricting how many media outlets a single company or media entity could own in a particular location or market area and both of these changes had a major impact. The digital television (DTV) revolution began with the switch from analog to digital broadcast television when all of the full-power television stations in the nation were required to stop broadcasting in analog and begin telecasting in digital format. As part of a well-orchestrated campaign the FCC urged citizens to purchase digital-to-analog converter boxes since analog television received the over-the-air programming with traditional broadcast antennas ("rabbit ears" or roof antennas) prior to that time. This transition away from analog technology opened up frequencies for additional services including police, fire, and emergency rescue operators, and also provided additional frequencies for advanced wireless services. More important, it permitted TV stations to offer better picture and sound quality. Of course, many subscribers to satellite TV or Direct Broadcast Satellite (DBS) had been receiving local stations' high quality digital television signals through satellite dish for some time.

Regarding FCC's approval of expansion of digital or HD radio to improve audio quality, it:

- Adopted a flexible bandwidth policy permitting a radio station to transmit high quality audio, multiple program streams, and data casting services at its discretion;
- Allowed radio stations to time broker unused digital bandwidth to third parties, subject to certain regulatory requirements; and
- Authorized AM nighttime operations.

Fueling much of the high technology interest from a public policy and regulation point of view are satellite radio systems using high quality audio and expensive talent, primarily XM Satellite Radio Holdings and Sirius Radio—initially separate, which promised to create a new audience, witnessed by the fact that more than 4 million paying subscribers signed up at first for their services in less than three years. Concern over content and control came along with the high jinks these programmers provide such as *Kawabunga Uber Alles*, featuring punk and ska-style surf music over XM and *The Wise Guy Show*, featuring Vinnie Pastore (*The Sopranos*) with "Dr. Pussy's Love Advice." The battle between satellite radio providers and traditional sources began, with established radio names like Eminem, Snoop Dogg, Opie & Anthony, and Howard Stern as initial combatants in the radio space race.[3] When Sirius and XM announced plans to merge into one company with 14 million subscribers in 2007, merged operations seemed bright. Since that time, the company has faced serious financial challenges, another outcome of the economic downturn.

In the context of satellite radio, content issues should not re-merge with regulatory challenges from the FCC, although there was a lot of initial speculation that without regulators to taunt, Stern and company would find their role more challenging. But it is telling to note that Sirius agreed to pay Stern $600 million over five years. And not to be outdone by Sirius, XM later signed a three-year, $55 million contract with Oprah Winfrey for a new channel called "Oprah & Friends" including a variety of programming from self-improvement and fitness to a weekly show with Winfrey herself. By 2006, Sirius had more than 3 million subscribers, and more than 6 million individuals signed with the then rival XM Satellite Radio. Another developing technology permitted Rush Limbaugh listeners to subscribe to "podcasts," homemade digital audio files in MP3 format, a service that began at less than $59 a year. By the middle of

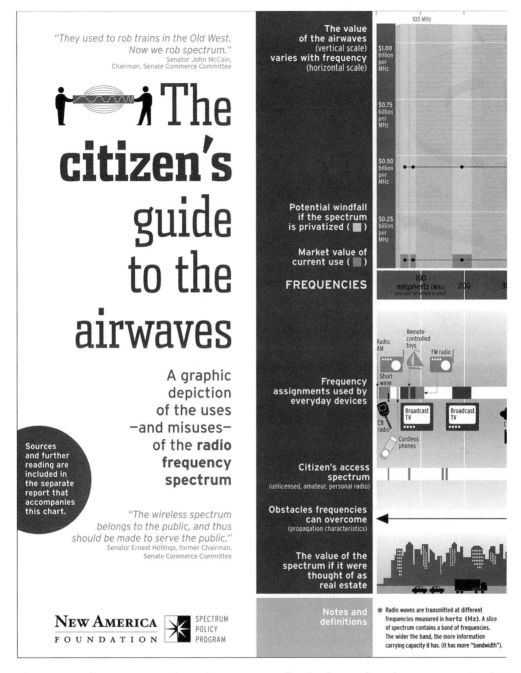

Figure 7.1   "The Citizen's Guide to the Airwaves" offers background on the government's role in regulating the nation's airwaves and the spectrum debate, including the economic, social, and political impact (Reprinted with permission of the New America Foundation, www.Newamerica.net/files/airwaves.pdf).

the decade, the Pew Internet and American Life Project reported that over 20 million Americans owned portable digital players, including iPods. Nearly a third had already downloaded podcasts from the Web, so a revolution in individualized media was well underway.[4]

In addition to satellite broadcasting and podcasting, cell phone companies and their entertainment counterparts were also tapping into television. It would not be too much of a stretch to compare the images from this new technology to over-the-air television's development in the late 1940s as a slide show, the potential is there. Companies taking a serious look at this technology include the established major television networks. Fox News programs and soap opera pilots were delivered to Sprint TV users. One-minute episodes were developed using small digital cameras. Given the integrated nature of delivery systems, the economic potential, and prospects for controversy, the instinct to regulate will no doubt present challenging questions for the FCC.

One of the most interesting questions FCC followers have had to consider, given all of the challenges the Commission has recently faced, is whether the Communications Decency Act has inadvertently fostered indecency. This question was addressed by Dr. William H. Freivogel in an article in *Communication Law and Policy* in Winter 2011. Professor Freivogel, also an attorney, investigated Section 230 of the Communications Decency Act with respect to narrowing the safe harbor of immunity for content liability for material posted by third parties during the development of the Internet. High profile cases involving cyber bullying, pornography, alleged terrorism, racial discrimination particularly in areas such as fair housing have come under scrutiny. Abuse of computer services such as Yahoo and Craigslist have raised issues of subsequent online posting of nude photos, celebrity gossip, solicitations for sex, instances of boyfriends humiliating ex-girlfriends or mere acquaintances, plus those occurring particularly in groups via academic settings, have all led to a rethinking of the basic questions regarding who should be responsible for what on the Internet.

To begin to address the question we may want to consider when regulation of electronic mass media and telecommunications took its last sharp turn back in 1996 when Bill Clinton signed The Telecommunications Act into law. He did so with an electronic pen at the Library of Congress, symbolizing the beginning of an era destined to change the regulatory scheme—from ownership to technology. The Act signaled the end of a decades-long policy of segregating electronic technologies to shield them from competition with each other and the dawn of new policy allowing them to compete and merge in ways that would not have even been considered in the past. Prior to that Act, cable companies were not permitted to intrude into the telephone business, and strict limits were imposed on ownership of broadcast stations for fear a few companies would dominate. Cable and telephone firms now more effectively "duke it out" in the marketplace, and, with few still remaining limits on broadcast ownership, restrictions were liberalized.

To appreciate the significance of the Telecommunications Act, we must first understand how we arrived where we are today. Let's begin with a brief history of over-air or "free" broadcasting.

Origins of Broadcasting

Although many electronic media are *privately* owned, the broadcast spectrum is considered a *public* resource or, more specifically, a *limited public resource.* The technical capacity exists for an almost unlimited number of channels, as spectrum divisions are traditionally known. Yet the courts and the federal government—most notably the Federal Communications Commission—cling to a scarcity rationale in justifying restraints on electronic media that would not pass constitutional muster for the print media. There is no better illustration of this than the U.S. Supreme Court decision in *Turner Broadcasting v. FCC* (1997),[5] in which the Court ruled that Sections 4 and 5 of the Cable Television Consumer Protection and Competition Act of 1992 ("Cable Act") did not violate the First Amendment rights of cable operators. Under the "must carry" provisions of the Act, cable operators were required to carry the signals of local broadcast stations on their systems.

Although the decision concerned the First Amendment rights of cable systems rather than those of broadcasters, the majority opinion written by Justice William Kennedy said the government had a substantial interest in preserving "free, over-the-air local broadcast television" to promote the broad "dissemination of information from a multiplicity of sources" and to promote competition. Such restrictions on print media would never be tolerated by the Court, but the electronic media, including cable television producers remain second-class citizens in the eyes of the Court when it comes to First Amendment rights.

The technical elements for broadcasting—electromagnetic waves, air and space—have always existed, but a means of independently creating radio waves and then receiving them was not created until the late 19th century. If technology had existed a century ago to construct a radio receiver that approached the capabilities of those hand-built by amateur radio experimenters in the 1890s, "transmissions"—including magnetic radiation from "hot spots" on the sun and from lightning and other weather phenomena—could have been picked up. Electromagnetic radiation is the end product of a charged particle (electric field) interacting with a magnetic field.[6] Although radio, television, and similar forms of electromagnetic radiation are characterized as media because they travel over the airwaves or "media," radio waves (which would, of course, include television) can travel without material media—that is, in a vacuum. As early as 1865, a Scottish physicist, James Clerk Maxwell, developed a mathematical theory of electromagnetic radiation that became the first of a series of steps taken by a number of inventors, generally without the knowledge of one another, toward the eventual development of broadcasting as we know it today. Some were scientists, others were visionaries, and a few were opportunists.

The Pioneers

Maxwell's 1873 *A Treatise on Electricity and Magnetism* theorized that electrical and magnetic energy move at the speed of light in transverse waves. Fourteen years later, another physicist— this time a German—conducted experiments involving reflection, refraction, and polarization of magnetic waves. Heinrich Hertz confirmed the existence of radio waves, providing the impetus for other experimenters to study how to harness, transmit, and modify waves so they could transmit information over long distances.

In 1895, an Italian physicist whose name has become synonymous with the wireless telegraph, Guglielmo Marconi, sent what are known today as *long-wave* radio signals over more than a mile. This was an accomplishment on par with the Wright Brothers' first power-driven airplane flight in 1903. For the first time, a scientist had demonstrated that information could be transmitted and received over long distances without benefit of a wire or cable, as had been required for telegraph. Probably no one at the time, including Marconi himself, could have imagined a world a century later whose communication would be virtually controlled by radio waves. But Marconi and others continued their experimentation and made some remarkable achievements within a relatively short time. By 1901, Marconi had picked up the first trans-atlantic wireless transmissions and, although the sounds were neither voice nor music, simply sparks and crackles, the world was on its way to becoming a "global village," as media theorist Marshall McLuhan would later characterize it.

Historians are still divided over when the first voice broadcast occurred. Some claim that a Murray, Kentucky, farmer named Nathan B. Stubblefield broadcast "Hello, Rainey" to his friend, Rainey T. Wells, in a demonstration in 1892, and other scholars attribute the first broadcast to Reginald A. Fessenden, who transmitted a short, impromptu program from Brant Rock, Massachusetts, in 1906 to nearby ships.[7] In 1991 officials of the Smithsonian Institute in Washington, DC, called Stubblefield's work "interesting and even important" to the development of radio but rejected a petition by the farmer's grandson that Stubblefield be recognized as the inventor of radio. In 1904 the first telegraphic transmission of a photograph was accomplished. Although the reproduction was crude by today's standards, it ushered in a new era—news photos could be sent across distances on a timely basis. In 1906 American Lee De Forest announced his invention of the triode, a vacuum tube that permitted the amplification of radio waves. Until the 1960s when the transistor was mass marketed, all radio receivers (and transmitters as well) required vacuum tubes to function. (The transistor was invented as early as 1948. It did not become commonplace in receivers until years later.) In 1910 De Forest made a live broadcast of the great Italian opera singer, Enrico Caruso, and five years later the Bell Telephone Company conducted a series of experiments involving voice transmissions across the Atlantic.[8] One year later on November 17, 1916, De Forest made what is recognized as the first newscast in the United States. Using his experimental station at High Bridge, New York, he recited returns from the Wilson–Hughes presidential election to ham radio operators.[9] No one apparently faulted him for the fact that he ended the broadcast with the wrong result.[10]

Origins of Government Regulation

In 1917 the United States entered World War I and the government subsequently prohibited all private broadcasting until the war ended two years later. By 1919 the groundwork was laid for mass broadcasting with the creation of Radio Corporation of America (RCA) by the three communications giants—General Electric, Westinghouse, and American Telephone and Telegraph. Although there was no indication at the time, the conditions were also set for government regulation. First, newspapers became heavily involved in broadcasting, especially in establishing and owning stations. It would be decades later before strict federal rules were enacted regarding cross-media ownership, but newspaper companies established a foothold in the broadcast marketplace. Papers such as the *Atlanta Journal, Louisville Courier-Journal, St. Louis Post-Dispatch, Chicago Daily News,* and *Milwaukee Journal* had the financial clout to keep stations operating and the news gathering resources, including sports, to fill the airtime.

Radio proliferated and prospered, signaling problems with frequency spectrum allocation. In 1910 Congress passed the Wireless Ship Act, which required all ships leaving any U.S. port to have wireless radios and skilled radio operators on board if they carried 50 passengers. Two years later Congress enacted the Radio Act of 1912, which for the first time required all radio stations to have licenses from the Secretary of Commerce and Labor. The statute also set certain technical requirements and allocated radio bands for exclusive government use.[11] The Act did not limit private broadcast stations to particular frequencies, but the Secretary of Commerce selected 750 kilohertz and 833 kilohertz as the bands on which they were to operate.[12] There was no requirement that the broadcasters operate in "the public interest" nor were there any real restrictions on content. Instead, broadcasters were permitted to operate as they wished without any substantial governmental interference. Unfortunately, the interest of private enterprise in radio grew so quickly that the Commerce Secretary was unable to prevent stations from interfering with one another. Even though many more channels were made available, limits on operating power and hours of operation were imposed and channels were separated by 10 kilohertz, as they still are today in the AM portion of the radio spectrum.[13]

The result was utter chaos as the number of stations escalated from a handful around 1920 to several hundred in 1923 to almost 600 toward the end of 1925, with a backlog of 175 applications for new stations, all wanting to broadcast in essentially the space we call the AM band. As of March 2005 more than 12,700 AM and FM stations were licensed in the United States, with more than 4,700 in the AM band.[14] There is little interference because of strict limits on power, allocated channel space, operating hours, and technical criteria.

With the government giving its *de facto* or tacit approval of private ownership of broadcasting, it was becoming apparent that its role in broadcasting would be as a police officer, not owner. The government did, of course, own and operate certain broadcast facilities for military and security purposes, but these were for private governmental use, not for public dissemination. Because broadcasting did not exist at the time the Constitution was enacted, it contains no provisions specifically dealing with this type of commerce. But it is highly likely that the U.S. Supreme Court would have struck down any constitutional challenges to government ownership of broadcasting, just as it did to government regulation of radio and television. Had the U.S. government or, specifically Congress, chosen not to permit private ownership of the airwaves, our system of broadcasting may have evolved into a system consisting of a mix of private and government ownership—like systems in Great Britain, Japan, and Germany. Other systems exist in which ownership and operations are strictly in the hands of government. The private ownership that we have today was the direct result of a government policy to encourage development of the broadcast system by free enterprise. It was not the product of any *laissez faire* attitude by Congress. The First Amendment clearly prohibits government ownership of the press, which has been interpreted primarily to protect the print media, but no such prohibition applies to the broadcast media. The Supreme Court would probably never allow government takeover of broadcasting today, but the ban would likely be based on public policy and contractual grounds, not on purely constitutional grounds.

Just as debate continues among historians over who made the first voice broadcast, there are conflicting claims as to which station was the first regular broadcasting entity. The first station to be issued a regular (not experimental) broadcasting license, according to official records, was WBZ in Springfield, Massachusetts. The license was granted by the federal government on September 15, 1921.[15] KDKA in Pittsburgh, Pennsylvania, did not receive its license as a regular broadcasting station until several weeks later on November 7, 1921, but mass media historians generally credit KDKA as the first fully licensed commercial broadcast station[16] because it began transmitting news and music on a regular basis beginning in November 1920.

Newspapers and other owners such as the Westinghouse, General Electric, and RCA electronic giants realized rather early the enormous profit potential in broadcasting, although during the early years the income came primarily from the sale of crystal and later vacuum tube radio sets. Newspaper companies generally owned radio stations as a means of promoting the sale of their newspapers. It soon became apparent, however, that the sales of radio sets and newspapers were not the most profitable means of operating radio. Quite simply, the point would be reached at which everyone who could afford a radio receiver would have one, producing revenues only from the sales of second and replacement sets. Instead, broadcasters turned to advertising, which gave the new medium a substantial boost. This gold mine created such an enormous interest in the broadcast business that by the end of 1925, almost 600 radio stations were already on the air, with 175 applications for stations pending.[17] Chaos reigned on the airwaves with at least one station on every available channel and several stations on most channels.

Passive Role of the Courts

The courts were of no assistance in resolving the confusion. A U.S. Court of Appeals ruled that the U.S. Secretary of Commerce could not deny a license to any legally qualified applicant even if the proposed radio station would interfere with the private and governmental stations already on the air.[18] Furthermore, an Illinois District Court held that the Secretary of Commerce could not institute frequency, power, or operation hours restrictions, and a station operating on a different frequency than originally assigned was technically not in violation of the Radio Act of 1912.[19] Even the acting U.S. Attorney General got into the act by declaring that the Secretary of Commerce had no authority under the Radio Act of 1912 to regulate power, frequency, or hours of operation.[20] An exasperated Secretary of Commerce, Herbert C. Hoover (inaugurated 31st U.S. President 3 years later), announced on July 9, 1926, the day after the Attorney General's ruling, that he was giving up attempts to regulate radio, urging stations to self-regulate.[21]

Intervention of Congress: The Radio Act of 1927

Self-regulation never materialized, and on February 23, 1927, Congress stepped into the picture with the Radio Act of 1927 after President Calvin Coolidge had appealed to the legislative body for a solution. As a Supreme Court Justice described the situation 16 years later in *National Broadcasting Co. v. the United States* (1943), "The result [of stations operating without regulations] was confusion and chaos. With everybody on the air, nobody could be heard."[22] One could argue that radio was never given sufficient time to develop an effective system of self-regulation, but the fact remains that even the broadcasters themselves recognized that self-regulation probably would not work in America, at least for the immediate future. With airwaves in such a horrible mess, the potential for profits was substantially reduced because everyone wanted a piece of the spectrum without giving up any privileges.

Federal Radio Commission

The Radio Act of 1927, the first of only three comprehensive broadcast regulatory schemes to be enacted by Congress, was designed to bring order to the chaos and set radio on a path to prosperity. The act created the five-member Federal Radio Commission (FRC) with broad and comprehensive licensing and regulatory authority. The body was granted the authority to issue station licenses and to allocate frequency bands to various services and specific frequencies to individual stations. The commission also had the authority to limit the amount of power a station could use to transmit its signal. Although he was not directly connected with the FRC, the Secretary of Commerce was assigned the responsibility of inspecting radio stations, testing and licensing station operators, and assigning call letters.

The commission took its tasks seriously and immediately began enforcing the rules created under the Act. Some 150 of the 732 stations operating in 1927 eventually left the air. Today, the more than 4,700 commercial AM stations on the air operate in essentially the same frequency space assigned in 1927 but with limits on power and channel separation. This accomplishment can trace its origins to the FRC in 1927, which began the complicated task of reorganizing the broadcast spectrum.

As the FRC progressed in its efforts to administer the Act as "public convenience, interest, or necessity requires," it became apparent that the commission needed expanded regulatory powers and more than simply fine tuning was necessary. Soon after he became President in 1933, Franklin D. Roosevelt asked his recently appointed Commerce Secretary, Daniel C. Roper, to establish an interdepartmental committee to study broadcasting and the FRC. The committee made several recommendations, including creating one federal administrative agency similar to the FRC to regulate all interstate and international communication by wire or broadcasting, not just commercial radio.

Communications Act of 1934

Congress followed the recommendations and enacted the Federal Communications Act of 1934, the second to deal comprehensively with electronic communications. The Act continued to serve as the primary statute under which the FCC functioned until February 1996 when the Telecommunications Act of 1996 became law. Although there had been changes in the form of various amendments to the 1934 Act, the primary provisions of 1934 remained essentially intact until the new 1996 law thoroughly overhauled the regulation of telecommunications and electronic media in this country.

Federal Communications Commission

The 1934 act created a seven-member administrative agency similar to the FRC and renamed it the Federal Communications Commission (FCC). The composition and functions of the FCC were not substantially altered by the 1996 Telecommunications Act, although Congress handed the commission a whole new set of rules and regulations to enforce.

Under Public Law 97-253,[23] enacted in 1982, nearly half a century after the FCC was created, Congress reduced the number of members to five, effective July 1, 1983. Each member is appointed by the President with the advice and consent of the Senate. The President designates one member to serve as chair, who is responsible for organizing and coordinating the FCC's operations and, as would be expected, presides over commission deliberations. Commission members are appointed for five-year terms, with the terms staggered so that one commissioner's term expires each year. If commissioners leave before their terms expire, replacements serve the rest of the unexpired terms (Of course, a replacement may be re-appointed for a five-year term at the end of the original.) No more than three members can serve at the same time from the same political party. When terms expire or openings occur, presidents typically appoint members of their party until a maximum of three has been reached.

An objective of the 1934 Act was to unify the various statutes and rules and regulations affecting interstate communications and place the authority for enforcing them and setting policy under the umbrella of one independent, quasi-judicial, quasi-legislative federal agency. That objective has certainly been accomplished, particularly by the 1996 Act. Nearly every form of electronic communications is now affected by the FCC, including telecommunications, commercial and noncommercial broadcasting, satellite communications, amateur (ham) and citizen's band (CB) radio, cable television, and new technologies such as personal communications services (PCS) and direct broadcast satellite service (DBS). One major exception is governmental services, such as military communications and the Voice of America, the international service operated by the Department of State that broadcasts in more than 100 languages throughout the world.

Section 151 of the Communications Act of 1934 delegated to the FCC the authority to regulate:

> … interstate and foreign commerce in communication by wire and radio so as to make available to all the people of the U.S. a rapid, efficient nationwide and world-wide wire and radio communication service with adequate facilities at reasonable charges for the purpose of national defense [and] for the purpose of promoting safety of life and property.[24]

Section 307 established the standard, which remains today, by which the FCC is to license stations: "public interest, convenience, or necessity."[25] This standard has been affirmed by the courts many times, by the U.S. Supreme Court in the 1943 landmark decision in *National Broadcasting Co. v. United States*.[26] The standard is rather vague, but it essentially grants the FCC very broad regulatory powers.

Limits on FCC Authority

Even with such broad authority, certain limits have been placed on the commission by virtue of the fact that the agency can act only within those parameters enunciated by Congress. The FCC has no jurisdiction over broadcast and related services owned and operated by the U.S. government. A large chunk of the frequency spectrum has been allocated to civilian and military governmental services. Most of the authority for regulating these services has been delegated to the Department of Commerce, although the Department of State through the U.S. Information Agency (USIA) operates international broadcast services such as the Voice of America. At least half of the broadcast space allocated under international treaties is not regulated by the FCC.

One area in which the commission also has very limited authority is advertising. The FCC cannot regulate individual commercials because this power falls under the aegis of the Federal Trade Commission (FTC) and state and local consumer protection agencies. The agency does have the authority to issue guidelines regarding the amount of commercial time allowed in a given hour, but in the early 1980s it began a process of deregulating broadcasting. The commission eliminated its guidelines on commercial limits that had permitted up to 16 minutes of commercials per hour. A station can theoretically carry as much advertising as it wishes. The recourse now to over-commercialization is for the consumer to tune out. It is not unusual for stations and networks to carry as many as a dozen commercials in a row on popular programs whose viewers or listeners are willing to tolerate the clutter. Shorter commercials such as the 10- and 15-second spots add even more to the clutter. The situation has become so bad that many radio stations tout 30- to 60-minute blocks of uninterrupted music in an effort to solve the clutter problem ("10 songs in a row" or "one hour of commercial-free music").

Because the major commercial and noncommercial networks do not broadcast per se, the FCC neither licenses nor directly regulates them. That is not to say, however, that the FCC has no impact on the networks. The parent companies of the major commercial networks and cable network groups—ABC (Walt Disney Company), CBS and UPN (Viacom), Fox Network (News Corp.), NBC and Telemundo (General Electric), CNN and HBO (TimeWarner)—all own and operate radio and television stations licensed by the commission. These owned and operated (O&O) stations must comply with FCC rules and regulations. In addition, the networks are beholden to affiliates (i.e., stations that contract with networks to carry programming for a specified time, usually in exchange for compensation) because affiliates are licensed. Thus a network that provies a program to affiliates violating FCC rules or regulations such as the Equal Opportunities Rule" (sometimes erroneously referred to as the Equal Time rule) would create an uproar among the affiliates who faced the possibilities of FCC citations.

While the network–affiliate relationship has changed dramatically over the years, the networks still attempt to adhere to FCC rules and regulations to avoid causing trouble for affiliates. With network revenues dropping, thanks to the loss of audience shares to competition from cable, satellite television, independent stations (stations with no major network affiliation), video rental stores (such as Blockbuster) and services (such as Netflix) and prerecorded videodiscs (DVDs), the networks scramble to please affiliates. Until Fox began competing in earnest in 1988 by offering its programming to independent television stations, only three major networks were available to split the audience share. The overall influence of the "Big 3" had been a major concern.

Noncommercial networks, such as the Public Broadcasting System (PBS) for television and National Public Radio (NPR), are not licensed by the FCC. PBS and NPR do not own stations and thus are indirectly regulated by the commission. But noncommercial networks must watch their steps, just as the commercial networks do, because survival depends on continued affiliation with local stations. In a speech in 2005, PBS journalist Bill Moyers criticized the complexity of the Corporation for Public Broadcasting (PBS) funding formula and the increased pressure from political quarters. Moyers accused public broadcasters of caving in to partisan political pressures from a Republican White House.

There are also constitutional limits on the FCC, just as there are for other federal agencies. The First Amendment imposes limits on the commission, but a trend throughout the history of broadcast regulation from the 1930s until today has been for the U.S. Supreme Court and other courts to defer to the FCC's perceived expert judgment in determining permissible versus impermissible authority over broadcasting. The U.S. Supreme Court rarely slaps the agency's wrist and even more rarely reverses an FCC decision.

Regulatory Scheme

The concept of *limited public resource* has become synonymous with broadcast regulation and continues to remain the basis on which courts justify considerably stricter government controls over the electronic media than would ever be permitted for the print media under the First Amendment. There is no doubt the airwaves are limited, just as we have limited supplies of water, air, and other resources. However, unlike water and air, the broadcast spectrum is not an exhaustible resource. The airwaves are not *consumed* but merely *occupied*. For example, if a new technology were developed that made it possible for radio stations to occupy only half of the usual frequency space, potentially twice as many stations could broadcast on the same portion of the spectrum. In other words, the real limits on broadcasting are based on technology, *not* consumption.

One new technology that changed the picture was *digital compression* in which video and audio signals are digitally processed to compress them so several times as many signals can be transmitted in the same amount of space required for one signal in the past. All of the newer satellites use this technology. Both Direct Broadcast Satellite systems—DirecTV and Dish Network—offer hundreds of channels and have the capacity to offer thousands of channels of movies, sports, variety, news, music, networks, and pay-per-view programs. The typical cable television system converter now has a capacity for more than 1,000 channels, and fiber optics and integrated circuits capacity is being expanded to thousands of channels.

Why, then, do the courts and often the FCC and Congress cling to the scarcity concept? First, there are still more applicants for the typical broadcast frequency or channel than available frequencies. The demand exceeds the supply, forcing the government to choose among competing applicants. Anyone or any organization can publish a newspaper or magazine without a license (other than the usual business license if the publication is operated as a business). There is no competition for space. Congress chose in 1934 with the Communications Act to adopt a policy of requiring the FCC to grant new and renewal licenses to applicants only "if the public convenience, interest, or necessity will be served thereby."[27] The Telecommunications Act of 1996 did not change that theoretical obligation. The fact remains that in spite of all the new technologies, certain technologies, media, and frequencies are more coveted than others. For example, owning a television station in a major market such as New York or Atlanta can be extremely profitable, especially if the station is a VHF outlet and a major commercial network affiliate. Operating an independent UHF station in a smaller market such as, Lexington, Kentucky, or Columbia, Missouri, even though profitable, would not garner the revenue of New York or Nashville.

Although the courts have never seriously considered alternatives, there are viable options to the current regulatory scheme of awarding licenses on a competing basis, applying the "public interest, convenience, or necessity" standard. In fact, beginning in the early 1980s, the FCC experimented with a lottery program for a relatively new technology[28] known as low-power television (LPTV). In 1982, the commission announced that it would begin accepting applications for a new class of LPTV stations. Those could operate with few program or content restrictions so long as they met technical specifications such as producing no interference with existing full-power television (FPTV) stations and generating a primary signal of no more than approximately 10 miles in any direction. Under the lottery program, the FCC selected among qualified applicants based on a random drawing for allotted frequencies. No attempts made to determine whether an applicant was better qualified than another one or whether one would be more likely to serve the public interest, convenience, or necessity better than another.

Unfortunately, the lottery program moved slowly. The commission was overwhelmed with applications and had a small staff to process them. Despite the slowness, dozens of new LPTV stations did go on the air. LPTV stations can operate on either VHF or UHF channels with an effective radiated power of no more than 3 kilowatts on VHF or 150 watts on UHF. Under the 1982 FCC order, LPTV stations have the discretion of operating as full service channels or simply as translators so long as they have permission from the originating station. As part of its effort to deregulate and promote competition in a free marketplace, the FCC imposed virtually no program restrictions on the LPTV stations, other than the usual rules regarding indecency, obscenity, and so forth. In preparation and build-up to the switch to digital television, the FCC made no provision for LPTV until 2004 when it established a set of rules and policies for digital LPTV, television translator, and television booster stations. In 2006 the agency announced it would begin accepting applications for digital LPTV. Under FCC rules, LPTV stations could choose (a) convert to digital on the existing analog channel or (b) apply for a second digital companion channel that could be operated simultaneously with the analog channel.[29]

LPTV is a perfect illustration of how the commission addressed new technologies. During his administration (1977 to 1981), Jimmy Carter established the National Telecommunications and Information Administration (NTIA) in one of many executive reorganization efforts. One of several functions assigned to the new NTIA was telecommunications applications. The agency was also assigned the role of improving mass communication through the development of new technologies and re-tread of older ones. After a fairly comprehensive study of spectrum allocation, the NTIA concluded that one effective way of increasing the number of television stations on the air, especially for consumers in rural areas, was to lift FCC restrictions permitting low-power TV stations to carry only retransmissions of programming from full-power stations. The FCC somewhat reluctantly accepted the NTIA recommendation in 1982 even though an economic projection from its own staff indicated that LPTV would have an uphill financial battle.

President Carter was replaced by President Ronald Reagan who pushed deregulation in all federal agencies. Thus the FCC (with the "King of Deregulation," Mark Fowler, then at the helm) chose not to impose programming and severe technical restrictions on LPTV. Low-power TV is a hot item, but every new technology from radio to satellites had to take risks before gaining a foothold in the media. Cable television, for example, began in the 1940s but did not become a truly mass medium until the 1970s as the nation became wired.

The FCC discussed LPTV, noting such stations "are operated by diverse groups and organizations—high schools and colleges, churches and religious groups, local governments, large and small businesses and individual citizens."[30] There were no limits on the number of LPTV stations any one entity can own, including cable companies, newspapers, commercial or non-commercial networks.

Low power FM (LPFM) radio is a similar service approved by the FCC "designed to create opportunities for new voices to be heard on the radio."[31] Two types of stations operate under the LPFM service—100-watt stations covering a radius of about 3.5 miles and 10-watt stations with a radius of 1 to 2 miles. Licenses are available only to community-based nonprofit and governmental entities, including educational institutions. Individual or commercial entities as well as existing broadcasters, cable TV companies, newspapers and other media entities do not qualify for LPFM licenses.[32]

The Telecommunications Act of 1996 heaped extensive new responsibilities on the commission, and its budget has grown over the years from $245 million in 2002, to $274 million in 2004, with a $302.5 million budget submitted by President George W. Bush for 2007. The continued growth has raised the ire of some critics.[33]

Federal Communications Commission General Authority

While the FCC, like all federal agencies, has limited authority over the industry it regulates, it clearly plays a major role in both the day-to-day operations and long-term development of telecommunications and broadcasting. The commission regulates a broad range of communications, including broadcast television and radio, cable television, telephone, telegraph, satellites (including direct broadcast satellite services), two-way radio (such as citizens' band and amateur radio), cellular phones, and even certain aspects of the Internet.

Section 326 ("Censorship") of the Communications Act of 1934, still in effect through the Telecommunications Act of 1996, says: "Nothing in this Act shall be understood or construed to give the Commission the power of censorship over the radio communications or signals transmitted by any radio station, and no regulation or condition shall be promulgated or fixed by the Commission which shall interfere with the right of free speech by means of radio communication."[34]

Just as a literal reading of the First Amendment could lead one to conclude that freedom of speech and press are absolute ("Congress shall make no law ..."), someone unfamiliar with regulatory history could assume after reading Section 326 that the FCC played no role in regulating programming. He might assume at the very least that broadcasters enjoy full First Amendment rights ("no regulation ... shall interfere with the right of free speech ..."). Nothing could be further from the truth. The commission is barred from engaging in direct censorship or prior restraint of programs, but a station that persistently flirts with violating FCC rules regarding political broadcasts or indecent and obscene content risks reprimands, fines, and the possibility that its license will be revoked or not renewed.

The Telecommunications Act of 1996 delegated considerable authority to the FCC to carry out the primary objective of the legislation—creating a competitive telecommunications marketplace. The new law directed the commission to conduct 80 different rulemaking proceedings involving hearings and other input from the public and the industry. Some of the new rules were successfully challenged in court, but most survived. Enforcing the Act has taken up much commission time, but the marketplace is becoming more competitive vis-à-vis industry, although media corporations have continued to grow through mergers and buyouts.

FCC Policies Regarding Political Broadcasting

Although indecent programming has been the hot topic into the new millennium and will likely continue to attract attention, the one area of programming that has consistently created the most controversy has been political content. The Fairness Doctrine has also generated considerable heat, but it was dealt a fatal blow by the FCC in August 2011 and appears very unlikely to be resurrected anytime soon.

One of the common misconceptions is that the so-called equal time requirement is a relatively new provision. One reason for this myth may be attributed to the considerable attention the provision received in 1960 when presidential candidates John F. Kennedy and Richard M. Nixon squared off in a live television debate before a national audience. Although it was unclear at the time whether Section 315 applied to presidential debates, Congress nevertheless chose to suspend the provision for the Nixon–Kennedy debates. Two years later, the commission indicated that debates did fall under the rule. Another reason for the myth may be traced to the awareness that Congress amended it several times, although the legislative body chose not to tamper with it in the Telecommunications Act of 1996.

The idea for a provision like Section 315 actually originated with the old Radio Act of 1927. Section 18 of the early act required all broadcasters to provide equal time (or more accurately, equal opportunities) to candidates for public office, once one legally qualified candidate had been granted airtime, whether paid or unpaid. Thus a broadcaster could effectively escape the requirement by simply denying access to all candidates. Section 18 also prohibited a station from censoring any political candidate's broadcast.

Both ideas were adopted in almost the same form when Congress enacted the Communications Act of 1934. Section 315 has been amended three times: in 1952, 1959, and 1972. The provision was significantly strengthened in 1972 with amendments to Section 312.

Section 315: Access for Political Candidates

Part (a) of Section 315 (as currently in force) provides:

Candidates for Public Office

(a) Equal opportunities requirement; censorship prohibition; allowance of station use; news appearances exception; public interest; public issues discussion opportunities. If any licensee shall permit any person who is a legally qualified candidate for any public office to use a broadcasting station, he shall afford equal opportunities to all other such candidates for that office in the use of such broadcasting station: Provided, That such licensee shall have no power of censorship over the material broadcast under the provisions of this section. No obligation is imposed under this subsection upon any licensee to allow the use of its station by any such candidate. Appearance by a legally qualified candidate on any—

(1)   bona fide newscast,
(2)   bona fide news interview,
(3)   bona fide news documentary (if the appearance of the candidate is incidental to the presentation of the subject or subjects covered by the news documentary), or
(4)   on-the-spot coverage of bona fide news events (including but not limited to political conventions and activities incidental thereto),

shall not be deemed to be use of a broadcasting station within the meaning of this subsection. Nothing in the foregoing sentence shall be construed as relieving broadcasters, in connection with the presentation of newscasts, news interviews, news documentaries, and on-the-spot coverage of news events, from the obligation imposed upon them under this Act to operate in the public interest and to afford reasonable opportunity for the discussion of conflicting views on issues of public importance.[35]

Cable Television and the Equal Opportunities Rules

The equal opportunities rules have the greatest impact on over-the-air broadcasts, but cable companies must also comply with them for *origination cablecasting*, which the FCC defines as being subject to the editorial control of the system operator. Cable operators do not have to be concerned with compliance by broadcast stations they carry or by leased access channels or public, educational, and governmental (PEG) channels over which they do not have editorial control. Under the 1992 Cable Consumer Protection and Competition Act, cable companies may restrict indecent or obscene programming on leased access and PEG channels.

Section 315 and Broadcast Stations

Laws are made to be applied as well as interpreted. The Communications Act of 1934, including Section 315, is no exception. The federal courts, especially the U.S. Court of Appeals for the D.C. Circuit, have spent considerable time attempting to determine the legal meanings of terms such as *legally qualified candidate, equal opportunities, no power of censorship,* and *public office.* Sometimes the answers have not been to the FCC's liking, and, as a result, the commission has occasionally altered its rules. For example, in a 1975 case, *Flory v. FCC*,[36] the Seventh Circuit U.S. Court of Appeals ruled, much to the chagrin of the FCC, that a communist party member running as a U.S. Senate candidate in Illinois who had not qualified for inclusion on the ballot was nevertheless a legally qualified candidate because there was the possibility he would be placed on the ballot and, further, he had indicated he planned a write-in candidacy if he did not qualify to be on the ballot.

As it turned out, Ishmael Flory did not gain access to the airwaves because the court held he had not exercised his procedural rights before the commission. The implications of the decision were quite serious. Stations could be forced to grant equal opportunities to candidates based on the probability, or perhaps even only on the possibility that the candidates would run for public office. The commissioners lost little time in responding to the decision by adopting new "Rules Relating to Broadcasts by Legally Qualified Candidates."[37] The rules now define a legally qualified candidate as an individual who has publicly announced his candidacy *and* (not *or*) who "meets the qualifications prescribed by the applicable laws to hold the office for which he is a candidate" *and* either has qualified for a place on the ballot *or* "has publicly committed himself to seeking election by the write-in method *and* is eligible under the applicable law to be voted for by sticker, by writing in his name on the ballot, or other method, *and* makes a substantial showing that he is a bona fide candidate for nomination or office."[38]

In 1999, the FCC acted on a petition from two groups—the Media Access Project and People for the American Way—ruling that candidates for President and Congress should have more flexibility in purchasing ads. The FCC ruled that candidates could not be barred from purchasing ads in lengths of time most useful to them just because broadcasters sell commercial time in shorter increments of 30 and 60 seconds. This reversed an earlier 1994 FCC ruling that broadcasters need not sell legally qualified candidates ads in lengths other than those the station sold to commercial advertisers or programmed during a year period preceding election.

The *ands* and *ors* in the rule can be confusing, but the FCC Political Primer clarifies that a mere announcement by a candidate does not automatically make that person legally qualified. The person must also be eligible to hold the office and either have qualified to be on the ballot or have qualified, as detailed in the rule, as a write-in candidate.[39]

Section 315 has been the subject of substantial litigation over the years, because (a) it is such a sweeping rule and thus affects many political aspirants and all broadcast stations, (b) its language lacks the necessary precision to always make it crystal clear when it applies or does not apply, and (c) it does not stand alone but must instead be interpreted in light of other provisions of the FCC Act, especially Section 312, and sometimes in conjunction with the Fairness Doctrine (when the doctrine was in effect). There have been battles in the courts over who is and is not a candidate, what constitutes a public office, and what is *use* by a station.

FCC Interpretation of Section 315

The FCC has indicated that it takes the publicly announced requirement seriously. During the 1968 presidential campaign, Senator Eugene J. McCarthy, a candidate for the Democratic nomination, requested equal time when President Lyndon Johnson conducted a December 7, 1967, interview with the television networks. At the time, the President had not publicly announced whether he intended to run for re-election. (He later decided not to run.) The commercial networks refused to grant Senator McCarthy equal time. He appealed to the commission which contended that "to attempt to make finding on whether or when the incumbent has become a candidate during the usual, oft-repeated and varying preliminary period would render the statute unworkable," ruling against the senator. The U.S. Court of Appeals affirmed.[40]

The commission has taken a conservative approach in its interpretation of "legally qualified candidate for public office." In 1972, the FCC ruled that the presidential and vice presidential candidates on the Socialist Workers Party ticket were not legally qualified for purposes of Section 315 and Section 312—even though they had filed to be on the ballots in fifteen states, were on the ballots in six, and collected almost a half million signatures on petitions—because neither candidate was at least 35 years old, as required in Article II of the U.S. Constitution.[41] Candidates have the burden of proof in demonstrating they are legally qualified; they must even prove their opponents are legally qualified candidates for the same office. Section 315 technically kicks in only when there are "opposing candidates."[42]

Use of a station has been very broadly construed by the FCC to include broadcasts of old movies and television shows in which a candidate formerly appeared, creating challenges, especially in California with the emergence of Arnold Schwarzenegger as 38th governor of that state. This issue addresses fairness and balance and applies as well to appearances on radio and television that represent part of an individual's regular responsibilities. At the national level, during the 1976 presidential Republican primary campaign, many TV stations were uncertain whether broadcasting old movies in which Ronald Reagan appeared would invite enforcement of Section 315. The FCC moved quickly to relieve any doubt by ruling that when an actor or actress becomes a legally qualified candidate for public office, such appearances constitute use.[43] The equal time to which the opponent would be entitled would be only the amount of time during which the actor appeared, not the entire time the program was broadcast. Similarly, the opponent(s) of a candidate who was a radio or TV personality, host, anchor, or disc jockey would be eligible for time equal only to the amount of time during which the personality was on-air.[44]

Rules regarding broadcasting of debates have changed considerably over the years, beginning with a major overhaul in 1975. Prior to that year, the commission had generally held that debates and press conferences by candidates were not exempt from the equal opportunities rule.

The four major exemptions (bona fide newscasts, news interviews, news documentaries, and on-the-spot coverage of bona fide news events) were not added by Congress until 1959, and the FCC has taken a narrow approach in determining what content was exempt from Section 315.

There were no major regulatory hitches for the three 2004 presidential debates between President George W. Bush and Massachusetts Senator John Kerry at the University of Miami in Coral Gables, Florida, Washington University in St. Louis, Missouri, and Arizona State University in Tempe. The vice presidential debate between Vice President Dick Cheney and North Carolina Senator John Edwards at Case Western Reserve University in Cleveland, Ohio also enjoyed smooth sailing. All four debates were sponsored by the Commission on Presidential Debates (CPD), a nonpartisan, nonprofit, tax-exempt corporation that has sponsored all presidential and vice presidential debates since 1988.

Aspen Institute Rulings on Political Debates

Until 1975 the FCC had held that debates between political candidates and broadcasts of press conferences conducted by candidates did not fall within any of the exemptions under Section 315. In that year, however, the FCC made some surprising rulings that have become known as the *Aspen Institute* decisions. Federal administrative agencies such as the FCC rarely overrule previous decisions, especially relatively recent ones. However, the commission actually did an about-face in *Aspen Institute*[41] when it held that under some conditions, coverage of debates among political candidates and press conferences of candidates would not invoke the equal opportunities provisions of Section 315. Instead, they would be exempt as on-the-spot coverage of bona fide news events. Indeed, the circumstances required for the exemption were essentially the same as those the FCC had ruled in 1962 precluded an exemption.

Why had the earlier decisions been erroneous? According to the FCC, the commissioners had simply misunderstood the legislative history that established Section 315 and Congress had actually intended for broadcasters to cover political news "to the fullest degree" rather than inhibit such coverage. The U.S. Court of Appeals affirmed this reasoning and concluded:

> In creating a broad exemption to the equal time requirements in order to facilitate broadcast coverage of political news, Congress knowingly faced risks of political favoritism by broadcasters, and opted in favor of broader coverage and increased broadcaster discretion. Rather than enumerate specific exempt and nonexempt "uses," Congress opted in favor of legislative generality, preferring to assign that task to the Commission.[46]

Thus a political debate could be considered on-the-spot coverage of a bona fide news event so long as (a) it was arranged by a third party (i.e., someone other than the broadcaster or network), (b) it did not occur in the broadcaster's facilities, (c) it was broadcast live and in its entirety, and (d) the broadcaster's motive in carrying the debate was newsworthiness rather than as a political favor for a particular candidate. In sum, the commissioners gave a blessing for coverage of debates as news events but not as political fodder. Their reasoning was much in line with the contentions in the petitions filed by the Aspen Institute Program on Communications and Society and CBS, Inc., which had triggered the FCC's reexamination of its earlier decisions.

Expansion of Scope of Aspen Decision

The FCC considerably expanded the *Aspen* decision by ruling in 1983 that even debates sponsored by broadcasters themselves would be exempt under Section 315(a)(4) as on-the-spot news coverage.[47] The impact of this decision was felt in many major national and state elections as more and more local and national broadcasters sponsored their own debates. In its ruling, the commission acknowledged that this greater flexibility granted to broadcasters could lead to bias, but opted nevertheless to permit such sponsorship because "Congress intended to permit that risk in order to foster a more informed electorate."[48] According to the FCC, the "common denominator of all exempt programming is bona fide news value."[49] In the same decision, the commissioners killed a previous rule, known as the *one-day rule*, which basically required contemporaneous or near contemporaneous broadcasting to trigger the 315(a)(4) exemption. The *one-day* label came from the fact that the commission generally expected the broadcast coverage of the particular political event to be aired no later than a day after the event.

In lieu of the one-day requirement, the FCC established a "rule of thumb" (the commission's characterization) that a broadcast simply "encompasses news reports of any reasonably recent event intended in good faith by the broadcaster to inform the public and not intended to favor or disfavor any candidate."[50]

The agency has spent considerable time during the last two decades defining *equal opportunities* under Section 315.[51] Some of the examples cited by the FCC of a lack of equal opportunities include (a) unequal audience potential of periods, such as offering candidates the same amount of air time as opponents but at a time when the audience is likely to be smaller, (b) allowing candidates to listen to a recording of an opponent's broadcast before it is aired while denying the opponent the same opportunity, (c) requiring one candidate but not another candidate to submit an advance script, (d) charging unequal rates (a serious *faux pas*), (e) signing an advertising contract with one candidate that effectively excludes opponents from purchasing time, such as selling the candidate most of the available blocks of prime time, and (f) failing to abide by a pre-established interview format.[52] The last example arose in a case in which one candidate had less than 5 minutes of exposure, compared with 16 and 14 minutes for others because a TV station strayed from the format the candidates had agreed to in advance.[53]

FCC's Easing of the Burden of Section 315

Broadcasters generally consider the equal opportunity requirements onerous, at best, and a violation of the First Amendment, at worst, but they have learned to live with them. To its credit, the commission has been lenient with broadcasters who make what it deems good faith efforts to comply with Section 315. The rules themselves have become less burdensome over the decades, because of liberal interpretations of their meaning by the agency and actual rule modifications. Four points illustrate this trend.

First, the FCC has made it clear that stations do not have to notify candidates of an opponent's time and that stations do not have to offer exactly the same time of day on the same day of the week or accept competing political ads on precisely the same program or series.[54] How would candidates know whether a broadcaster has sold time to opponents unless they see or hear ads? Federal regulations require every station to maintain and provide regular public access to a file that contains complete information regarding requests made for time by candidates or others on their behalf, the disposition of each request, and the charges made.[55] In a 1962 decision, the FCC held that candidates effectively have an affirmative duty to check the file if they want the information.[56] The station must promptly put the information in the file in comprehensible form and retain the files for at least two years for public inspection, but it has no obligation to automatically notify opponents when a candidate appears.

Second, the commission has enacted a requirement that is sometimes overlooked by candidates in exercising their equal-opportunity rights—the so-called *seven-day rule*.[57] According to the rule, political candidates must give timely notice to the licensee in order to qualify for air time when an opposing candidate has made use of the station. *Timely notice* is specified as "within one week of the day on which the first prior use, giving rise to the right of equal opportunities, occurred."[58] The rule applies strictly to individuals who are *legally qualified candidates at the time of the broadcasts*.[59] In adopting the rule, the FCC wanted to ensure that stations could make plans prior to the onslaught of a campaign and prevent a candidate from waiting until the election was almost over to get a block of time.[60] The FCC has been strict in enforcement of the rule.

Third, the commission has granted stations considerable leeway with news programs under Section 315(a). For example, if a political candidate appears in a bona fide newscast, opponents are not entitled to equal exposure in that newscast nor any other newscast. Technically, they would not be entitled to news coverage, although public outrage would probably prevent a station from covering one candidate in its news to the exclusion of others. Until August 4, 1987, when the FCC announced its decision to end enforcement of the Fairness Doctrine (reaffirmed in 1988 and officially abolished in 2011),[61] a broadcaster who did not make a good faith effort to provide balanced election news could have faced repercussions from the commission. With the death of the doctrine, communication provisions no longer apply.

Finally, whereas stations have an affirmative duty to provide reasonable access to legally qualified candidates for federal elective office, they always have the option of refusing to sell time in local, county, and state elections. Indeed, Section 315 does not require broadcasters to provide access to candidates in every local, county, and state election, although the FCC, courts, and Congress have indicated that political broadcasting is a significant public service and that stations are expected to devote reasonable time to political races. The decision regarding which elections deserve attention and which can be ignored is left to the discretion of the station.[62]

Section 312: Political Candidates for Federal Offices

In 1972 Congress added Section 312(a)(7):

(a)   The Commission may revoke any station license or construction permit;

(7)   for willful or repeated failure to allow reasonable access to or permit the purchase of reasonable amounts of time for the use of a broadcasting station by a legally qualified candidate for Federal elective office on behalf of his candidacy.[63]

It should be emphasized that Section 315 and other provisions of the Communications Act of 1934 and the Telecommunications Act of 1996 be interpreted in light of Section 312, which codified sanctions available to the FCC. Examples illustrate the flexibility in state and local races. In 1976, the FCC ruled in *Rockefeller for Governor Campaign (WAJR)*[64] that in a state campaign a station is not required to sell air time at all so long as it has offered free reasonable time. In other cases, the commission held that stations cannot be forced to sell a specific time period[65] and a broadcaster does not have to sell time months in advance of an election or sell ad time of a specific length.[66]

An Exception to the Exceptions Under Section 315

Nothing is absolute, including Section 315 exceptions, as illustrated by a rather novel case in 1988.[63] Although most First Amendment challenges to Section 315 have been launched by political candidates rather than journalists, a general assignment reporter for a Sacramento, California, TV station became a candidate for a seat on the council of a nearby town. Because the station believed it would have to offer more than 30 hours of free time to comply with Section 315, William Branch was told to take a leave of absence if he wished to pursue politics. He requested a ruling from the FCC on whether the equal time provisions applied. Citing legislative history of Congress' amendments to the Act, the commissioners ruled against the reporter. On appeal, the U.S. Court of Appeals for the DC Circuit upheld it:

> When a broadcaster's employees are sent out to cover a news story involving other persons, therefore the "bona fide news event" is the activity engaged in by those other persons, not the work done by the employees covering the event. The work done by the broadcaster's employees is not a part of the event, for the event would occur without them and they serve only to communicate it to the public.[68]

Branch also challenged Section 315 as a violation of his constitutional rights, including the First Amendment. The court struck down all three grounds, holding the statute did not extinguish his right to seek political office because no individual has a right of access to broadcast media; Section 315 does not violate the First Amendment because "the first amendment's protections for the press do not apply as powerfully to the broadcast media"; and the provision does not limit "the discretion of broadcast stations to select the particular people who will present news on the air to the public."[69]

Two Hypotheticals

Suppose a station decides to keep a reporter on the air despite political ambitions but limits exposure to no more than 10 minutes per week. The reporter consents to the arrangement and the station dutifully offers free air time to his opponents. However, the station considers this election unworthy of news coverage and thus ignores it. Both reporter and opponents complain that the station has written off the campaign simply because it wants to avoid the awkward situation of having a reporter appear as the subject of a story in the same newscast in which he covers a separate story. How would the FCC rule? In line with the previous discussion, the Commission would probably not second guess the station's news judgment so long as it could demonstrate its decision was based on news judgment, not political or other motives.

What if the station kept the reporter on the air, complied with Section 315 by offering time to all candidates but also covered the campaign, including a press conference by the reporter?

Could you imagine any Section 315 questions? Probably not: given the reasoning of the Court in *Branch v. FCC*. After all, if employees who were legally qualified candidates invoked Section 315 by covering a story, then would it not follow that employees who become subjects of news events do not trigger equal opportunities? Otherwise, they would be receiving discriminatory treatment under the law.

A Big Break for Politicians: Lowest Unit Charge

Public awareness of the equal opportunities rule is weak, but one provision is virtually unknown among voters—the *lowest unit charge* obligation. Section 73.1942 of the FCC Rules and Regulations says:

> (a) *Charges for use of stations.* The charges, if any, made for use of any broadcasting station by any person who is a legally qualified candidate for any public office in connection with his or her campaign for nomination for election, or election, to such office shall not exceed:
>
> (1)   During the 45 days preceding the date of a primary or primary runoff election and during the 60 days preceding the date of a general or special election in which such person is a candidate, the lowest unit charge of the station for the same class and amount of time for the same period.
>
> (i)   A candidate shall be charged no more per unit than the station charges its most favored commercial advertisers for the same classes and amounts of time for the same periods. Any station practices offered to commercial advertisers that enhance the value of advertising spots must be disclosed and made available to candidates on equal terms. Such practices include but are not limited to any discount privileges that affect the value of advertising, such as bonus spots, time-sensitive make goods, preemption priorities, or any other factors that enhance the value of the announcement.[70]

Under these rules stations are not required to offer political candidates lowest unit rates outside the 45- to 60-day time frames, but candidates clearly receive substantial discounts during the effective periods, compared to what they would pay if they were traditional advertisers. In enacting Section 315, Congress left the interpretation of *lowest unit charge* to the FCC, which has traditionally tracked industry sales practices. The computations can be fairly complicated. Suffice it to say that candidates receive rates that compare with high volume advertisers like auto manufacturers.

Cable television systems and direct broadcast satellite providers such as DirecTV and Dish Network are not required to allow political candidates to use their facilities, but, if they do allow such use, they must provide equal opportunities to all other candidates for that office under rules that are quite similar to those for broadcasting stations, including the usual exceptions, such as bona fide newscasts and on-the-spot coverage of bona fide news events.[71] The Commission leaves interpretation of *reasonable access* in the hands of the broadcasters, but it did not grant the industry full latitude.

In a Memorandum Opinion and Order (MO&O) in 1992 the FCC indicated that broadcasting stations can adopt a policy of not selling federal political candidates advertising time during newscasts, but they cannot deny access to candidates during programming adjacent to newscasts unless they do not sell to other advertisers during that time. The time slots before and after news are popular periods for political ads because candidates like having their commercials associated with news and audience ratings traditionally tend to be high, particularly among informed people who vote.

In the MO&O the commission adopted a much more conservative definition of *use* by a political candidate. *Use* now means only those appearances that have the approval of the candidate and does not include spots by organizations and groups such as political action committees (PACs) unless they have the sponsorship or support of the candidate. Prior to this ruling, broadcasters presumably had to offer equal opportunity to opponents when an ad was aired for a candidate even when the person had no direct connection to the commercial. By effectively redefining *use*, the FCC relieved stations of all of the other requirements when such ads appear, including the lowest unit charge and no censorship provisions, as discussed in the next section. Perhaps it is even more significant that the revised definition means that showing a movie, television show, or similar program in which a candidate had previously appeared as an entertainer or corporate head before becoming a candidate will no longer invoke Section 315. No doubt, broadcasters wish this definition had applied when former movie star Ronald Reagan successfully ran for President, an issue revisited in 2007 when U.S. Senator Fred Thompson (R-TN), also then a TV actor on the popular *Law & Order* program formed a presidential exploratory committee.

There is still one potential trap for broadcasters. Because the no-censorship provision no longer applies to ads not approved by a candidate, stations can be held liable for libel and torts stemming from airing PAC and similar ads. Therefore, stations carefully screen these commercials for defamatory statements, obscenities, and other unprotected content, or they can simply refuse to carry them at all.[72]

Censorship of Political Broadcasting

One of the more interesting provisions of Section 315 is its strong prohibition of censorship. Under Section 315 that prohibition is unequivocal ("such licensee shall have no power of censorship over the material broadcast"), but there are no absolutes in government regulation. Two important FCC cases illustrate this point. The first arose in 1956 when A. C. Townley, a provocative candidate for U.S. Senate in North Dakota, in a speech carried on WDAY-TV in Fargo, charged that his opponents and the Farmers' Educational and Cooperative Union had conspired to "establish a Communist Farmers' Union right here in North Dakota."[73] The station told Townley before the program was aired that his statements could be defamatory, but he did not heed the warning. As a consequence, both the candidate and the station were slapped with a $100,000 libel suit in state district court. The trial court judge granted WDAY's motion to dismiss on the ground that Section 315 made the station immune from liability because the statute prohibited censorship so long as a valid use was made by a qualified candidate, as in that case.

In a 4 to 1 decision on appeal by the union, the North Dakota Supreme Court affirmed the lower court ruling. On further appeal, the Supreme Court confronted the question of whether a broadcaster can be held liable for libel when it was expressly forbidden by federal law from censoring the program that carried the potentially libelous statement(s). As discussed in the next chapter, in most states a journalist or media outlet can clearly be held liable for published statements of third parties, depending on the circumstances. But can a plaintiff who has been defamed under these circumstances recover damages from a station?

In a surprisingly close decision in *Farmers' Educational and Cooperative Union of America v. WDAY* (1959),[74] the U.S. Supreme Court affirmed the North Dakota Supreme Court holding. The majority opinion by Justice Hugo L. Black rejected arguments by the union that broadcasters do not need immunity because they can insure themselves or exercise the clause in Section 315 that allows them to deny all political candidates the use of station facilities:

> We have no means of knowing to what extent insurance is available to broadcasting stations, or what it would cost them … While denying all candidates use of stations would protect broadcasters from liability, it would effectively withdraw political discussion from the air … Certainly Congress knew the obvious—that if a licensee could protect himself from liability in no other way but by refusing to broadcast candidates' speeches, the necessary effect would be to hamper the congressional plan to develop broadcasting as a political outlet, rather than to foster it.[75]

The reasoning of the majority in the case was in line with the principle that the marketplace should determine which ideas are accepted and which are rejected. Because radio and television stations have a mandate from Congress to serve the public interest, including the dissemination of political content, under this premise they should not be saddled with unreasonable restrictions. The Court felt it would be unfair to prohibit censorship while holding broadcasters liable for consequences of compliance. In a dissenting opinion, Justice Felix Frankfurter (joined by three other justices) contended that while Section 315 barred censorship, it did not relieve stations of liability under state libel laws. According to Frankfurter, "Section 315 has left to the States the power to determine the nature and extent of the liability, if any, of broadcasters to third persons."[76]

Although this decision answered one major question, a few questions remain. Would this holding apply to all types of content such as national security (especially in light of September 11), invasion of privacy, threats to civil or social order, or obscenity? Does the holding apply in the same way to candidates for federal elective office because there is an affirmative duty to offer reasonable time for these candidates?

Given the usual campaign rhetoric and the visibility of extremists in the political process, it was inevitable that the FCC would confront the issue of whether content that posed a potential threat to society enjoyed immunity from censorship. The WDAY case dealt with an allegedly civil offense against an organization—libel involves personal damages, not social harm. In 1972, the perfect case fell into the commission's lap in the form of self-described "white racist" J. B. Stoner, the same individual who years later was convicted in the bombing of an Alabama church during the 1960s. During his unsuccessful campaign for the Democratic nomination to the U.S. Senate in Georgia, Stoner broadcast the following ad on television and radio:

> I am J. B. Stoner. I am the only candidate for U. S. Senator who is for the white people. I am the only candidate who is against integration. All of the other candidates are race mixers, to one degree or another. I say we must repeal Gambrell's civil rights law.

Gambrell's law takes jobs from us whites and gives those jobs to the niggers. The main reason why niggers want integration is because the niggers want our white women. I am for law and order with the knowledge that you cannot have law and order and niggers too. Vote white. This time vote your convictions by voting white racist J. B. Stoner into the run-off election for U.S. Senator. Thank you.[77]

Various civil rights groups, including the NAACP, petitioned the FCC to issue an order to permit stations to refuse to broadcast political ads that present an "imminent and immediate threat" to public safety and security such as creating racial tension or other social harm. Atlanta TV and radio stations indicated they did not wish to carry the ads but that they were compelled by Section 315. Citing the *Brandenburg v. Ohio* (1969)[78] standard—that even the advocacy of force or of law violation may not be constitutionally prohibited unless "directed to inciting or producing imminent lawless action and is likely to incite or produce such action,"—the Commission refused the request:

> Despite your report of threats of bombing and violence, there does not appear to be that clear and present danger of imminent violence which might warrant interference with speech which does not contain any direct incitement to violence. A contrary conclusion here would permit anyone to prevent a candidate from exercising his rights under Section 315 by threatening a violent reaction. In view of the precise commands of Sections 315 and 326, we are constrained to deny your requests.[79]

The FCC opinion did not make explicit the conditions under which a station could censor political broadcasts invoking the equal opportunities rule because the agency merely cited *Brandenburg* without specifically adopting its precedent. However, "clear and present danger of imminent violence" remains the implicit standard, and the commission has not strayed from it since its invocation in 1972. Some relatively minor forms of censorship have been permitted, but these have had minimal impact on political broadcasting. For instance, although a station may not require candidates to submit copies of their ads or programs in advance, it can review the copy for inaccuracies, potential libel, or other content problems, it can require an advance script or tape if done solely to verify the content is a *use* under the equal opportunities rule, determine length for scheduling purposes, or ascertain that it complies with sponsorship identification rules.[80]

In 1994 the FCC ruled stations could not refuse to carry graphic anti-abortion political advertisements but could confine them to time slots when children were less likely to be in the audience—an action known as "channeling." [81] The ruling came after stations complained to the commission about being forced under the "reasonable access" provisions of the Communications Act of 1934 to carry the explicit ads of candidates such as Michael Bailey, a Republican candidate for Congress from Indiana during the 1992 election.[82] After his television commercials showing graphic images of aborted fetuses appeared, stations were flooded with complaints. Other anti-abortion candidates picked up on the trend, with more than a dozen of them getting permission from Bailey to use his ads. Some viewers even filed lawsuits seeking injunctions to stop the ads.

The stations were in a no-win situation because the FCC's Mass Media Bureau ruled at that time, based on a complaint about similar ads for Republican Congressional candidate that political spots did not meet the FCC criteria for indecency. An earlier informal FCC staff opinion said that programming that stations believe in good faith is indecent could be channeled to *safe harbor* hours of 8:00 p.m. to 6:00 a.m. A few stations used the opinion to justify restricting times when ads were broadcast, but it took the 1994 FCC decision to make it official. The ruling did say that time shifting must be done in good faith based on the nature of the ad and that it could not be done simply because the station disagrees with the message.[83]

Two years after the FCC ruling, the U.S. Court of Appeals for the D.C. Circuit reversed it.[84] The 3 to 0 decision said that nothing in the federal statutes permitted broadcasters "to take the content of a political advertisement into account in determining what constitutes 'reasonable access'" or "to deny a candidate access to adult audiences of his choice simply because significant numbers of children may also be watching television."[85] The court concluded:

> The Commission's Declaratory ruling violates the "reasonable access" requirement section of Section 312(a)(7) by permitting the content-based channeling of non-decent political advertisements, denying qualified candidates the access to the broadcast media envisioned by Congress. The ruling also permits licensees to review the political advertisements and to discriminate against candidates on the basis of their content, in violation of both the 'no censorship' and 'equal opportunities' provisions of Section 315(a).[86]

Section 312(a)(7), as amended by Congress in 2000, specifically exempts "non-commercial educational" broadcast stations, which means public broadcasters do not have to provide airtime to federal candidates. They were required to comply with Section 315 for nonfederal candidates, Section 399 ("support of political candidates prohibited"), "No noncommercial educational broadcasting station may support or oppose any candidate for public office."

Political Editorials and Personal Attack Rules

The FCC had two rules up to 2000: one regarding political editorials and another one on personal attacks affecting how broadcasters treated politicians. Under the rules, if a station or a cable operator (in *cable-casts*) editorially endorsed or opposed a qualified candidate, it had to contact the opponent(s) of the candidate who was endorsed or candidate who was opposed within 24 hours and offer a reasonable time for a response by the candidate or spokesperson. If the editorial was carried within 72 hours before the election, the candidate(s) had to be notified "sufficiently far in advance of the broadcast to enable the candidate or candidates to have a reasonable opportunity to prepare a response and to present it in a timely fashion."[87]

Under the personal attack rule, broadcasting stations were required to grant reasonable access to respond for anyone whose character or integrity had been attacked on the air. The Radio–Television News Directors Association (RTNDA, now RTDNA) and National Association of Broadcasters (NAB) sued the FCC in 1999, to repeal the rules. The NAB had requested that the FCC repeal the rules as early as 1980, but the commission did nothing for several years other than issuing a notice that it was considering such a change. A second petition was essentially ignored. Six years later the U.S. Court of Appeals denied a petition from RTNDA, but told the commission it had six months to make progress toward repealing or modifying the rules. Unfortunately, the commissioners could not agree on what action to take, thanks to a 2 to 2 vote.

The court, upon further appeal in 1998, remanded the case back to the commission, ordering it to take a formal vote and for the two commissioners voting against a change to indicate their reasons. Once again, there was a 2 to 2 split, with FCC Chair William Kennard not participating. The four voting commissioners issued statements explaining their votes. The drama had not ended, however. Almost two months before the next Presidential election in 2000, the agency voted 3 to 2 to suspend the rules for 60 days while conducting a review. By this time, the U.S. Court of Appeals had had enough. One week later—on July 24, 2000—in *Radio–Television News Directors Association v. FCC*,[88] the court recalled its mandate and issued a writ of mandamus "directing the Commission immediately to repeal the personal attack and political editorial rules."

Fairness Doctrine

Of all the issues in which the FCC has been embroiled, probably none has been more controversial than the Fairness Doctrine, because of the long-held desire to have broadcasts as "fair and balanced" as possible. First enunciated by the commission in 1949 in a "Report on Editorializing by Broadcasting Licensees" and clarified *ad infinitum* in numerous rulings since that time, The Fairness Doctrine essentially explained that stations had an affirmative duty to devote a reasonable percentage of time to "consideration and discussion of public issues in the community." In 1959, Congress amended 315(a), which specifies exemptions under the equal opportunities rule, and *presumably* codified (i.e., incorporated into statutory law) the Fairness Doctrine. Section 315 makes no direct mention of the doctrine but Public Law 86-274, which enacted the amendments stated, "Nothing in the foregoing shall be construed as relieving broadcasters from the obligation imposed upon them by this Act to operate in the public interest and to afford reasonable opportunity for the discussion of conflicting views on issues of public importance."[89]

The U.S. Supreme Court for the first time chose to determine the constitutionality of the Fairness Doctrine in 1969. In *Red Lion Broadcasting v. FCC* (1969),[90] the Court held that the doctrine and its allied personal attack rule were not unconstitutional. In a case decided at the same time, *U.S. v. Radio–Television News Directors' Association* (RTNDA), the Court upheld the political editorializing rules. *Red Lion* was used for almost two decades by the commission to justify enforcement of the Fairness Doctrine.

Red Lion arose when WGCB-AM, a small station in Red Lion, Pennsylvania, broadcast a 15-minute program by Reverend Billy James Hargis, as part of a "Christian Crusade" series. On the show, Hargis discussed a book by Fred J. Cook, *Goldwater—Extremist on the Right*, and claimed the author had been fired by a newspaper for making false charges against city officials. Hargis also said Cook had worked for a communist-affiliated publication, had defended Alger Hiss, and had attacked FBI Director J. Edgar Hoover and the Central Intelligence Agency. Cook's book, according to the minister, was intended "to smear and destroy Barry Goldwater."[91] The writer requested free air time to respond to the personal attack under the Fairness Doctrine, but the station refused. The FCC ruled in Cook's favor, and the U.S. Court of Appeals for the D.C. Circuit upheld the decision. In a separate case, the RTNDA had challenged the doctrine and its political editorial rules, which the Seventh Circuit U.S. Court of Appeals declared unconstitutional.

The Supreme Court upheld the D.C. Circuit and overturned the Seventh Circuit ruling, thus upholding the constitutionality of the doctrine and its allied rules. "In light of the fact that the 'public interest' in broadcasting clearly encompasses the presentation of vigorous debate of controversial issues of importance and concern to the public … we think the fairness doctrine and its component personal attack and political editorializing regulations are a legitimate exercise of congressionally delegated authority,"[92] the Court ruled in an 8 to 0 decision written by Justice Byron R. White. The Court emphasized the scarcity of broadcast frequencies and the "legitimate claims of those unable without governmental assistance to gain access to those frequencies for expression of their views" as justification for the doctrine.

In 1984 the commission ruled that WTVH-TV of Syracuse, New York, violated the Fairness Doctrine after the station aired a series of commercials supporting construction of New York State's Nine Mile II nuclear power plant. According to the FCC, the station had "failed to afford a reasonable opportunity for the presentation of viewpoints contrasting to those presented in the advertisements …."[93] In 1985 the FCC issued a long-awaited "Fairness Report," raising doubts about the constitutionality of the doctrine and the public interest.[94] However, the agency said it probably lacked authority to determine the doctrine's constitutionality and announced that it would continue to enforce the doctrine because Congress expected it to do so.

The battle lines began to be drawn with the FCC, the executive branch, broadcasters, and strong First Amendment advocates on one side in 1987, Congress and some public interest groups on the other side, and the courts generally on the sidelines as referees. In *RTNDA v. FCC* and *Meredith Corp. v. FCC* (1987),[95] the U.S. Court of Appeals for the D.C. Circuit remanded *Meredith* to the commission for determination of the constitutionality of the Fairness Doctrine and ordered briefs and oral arguments in *RTNDA* to determine whether the FCC acted improperly when it refused earlier to initiate a rule-making proceeding on the doctrine. The handwriting was on the wall. The FCC announced that "the set of obligations known as the 'fairness doctrine' violated the First Amendment rights of broadcasters."[96] The action came in response to the remand order of the U.S. Court of Appeals in *Meredith.* The FCC went even further in urging the Court to reconsider the scarcity rationale on which it based the 1969 *Red Lion* decision, noting the number of broadcast stations exceeded newspapers. The Commission said the Court should instead apply a traditional First Amendment analysis to broadcasters.

Earlier, Congress had acted swiftly to enact the doctrine into federal law, and such a bill passed both the Senate (59 to 31) and House (302 to 102), but President Reagan vetoed it in 1987. Congress failed to get the necessary two-thirds majority to override. In 1988, the FCC rejected petitions for consideration of its previous decision, but reaffirmed that it would no longer enforce the doctrine. The commission reaffirmed it was not abandoning the equal time and reasonable access provisions of the 1934 Communications Act, as amended, including Sections 312 and 315.[97]

Members of Congress have tried to have a measure codifying the Fairness Doctrine attached to various bills but efforts always fail. The first President Bush made it clear while he was in office that he would veto any bill to which such a measure was attached or separate bills. The FCC gained support on February 10, 1989, when the U.S. Court of Appeals for the D.C. Circuit upheld the FCC's refusal to enforce the Fairness Doctrine against Meredith Corporation and WTVH-TV. The court did not determine whether the doctrine was constitutional, but instead noted: "Although the Commission somewhat entangled its public interest and constitutional findings, we find that the Commission's public interest determination was an independent basis for its decision and was supported by the record. We upheld that determination without reaching the constitutional issue."[98]

After almost a quarter century of not enforcing the Fairness Doctrine, the Federal Communications Commission Chair Julius Genachowski announced in 2011 that the commission had officially abolished the doctrine. Genachowski personally opposed the doctrine, which he characterized as unnecessary and outdated. In a statement accompanying Genachowski's announcement, the FCC Chair said the set of rules held "the potential to chill free speech and the free flow of ideas" and that the doctrine's "elimination would "remove an unnecessary distraction."

The FCC's action did not entirely eliminate all elements of the Fairness Doctrine, but it did effectively kill the most significant rules and policies connected with the doctrine. Much of the opposition to the doctrine have come from politically conservative commentators and conservative religious broadcasters who view it as a serious infringement on their First Amendment rights and as a threat to the programs.[99]

Indecency and Obscenity in Broadcasting and Telecommunications

Government concern with obscene and indecent programming heightened considerably during past decade and has continued well into our new millennium. It appears unlikely to die anytime soon. Much of this focus can be attributed to increased pressures to ban all forms of indecency and obscenity. The pressures historically came from right-wing groups led by conservative stalwarts, television evangelists and organized groups, now advanced by the Parents' Television Council (PTC). PTC regularly tapes and critiques programs and maintains a tracking system, targeting smut and sleaze and challenging the FCC to do something about it. More recently, additional attention has focused on the Internet. The online issues may be magnified, but they are almost as old as broadcasting itself.

In the congressional hearings that eventually led to the enactment of the Radio Act of 1927 and its successor, the Communications Act of 1934, there was discussion about the possibility that radio could be used to carry obscene, indecent, or profane programming. Section 29 of the 1927 Radio Act prohibited the airing of "any obscene, indecent, or profane language, by means of radio communication."[100] The same provision was carried over into Section 326 of the 1934 Communications Act, which also barred the FCC from engaging in censorship of radio communications or from interfering with the right of free speech.[101] While the provision regarding obscene and indecent programs was deleted by Congress in 1948 (the censorship provision was not repealed), but re-codified as part of the Criminal Code:

> *Broadcasting Obscene Language.* Whoever utters any obscene, indecent, or profane language by means of radio communication shall be fined under this title or imprisoned not more than two years, or both.[102]

In comparison with the 21st century's shock radio and R-rated TV, programming in the early decades of radio and TV was prudish. However, that did not stop the Federal Radio Commission and its successor, the FCC, from repressing controversial content. The questions raised by the commission were as effective as legal actions. Even Congress occasionally investigated, at one point holding hearings about certain suggestive Spanish music carried on networks during the 1930s.[103] Actor Edward G. Robinson, Jr., owned a radio station whose license was denied in the 60s because the commission said it had carried programs considered "coarse, vulgar, suggestive and of indecent double meaning" but not indecent or obscene.[104]

Shock or Topless Radio

The term *topless radio* came into vogue in the 1970s in larger markets such as New York and Los Angeles, as a viable format and as target of FCC and congressional inquiries. Topless radio derived its name from the fact that it consisted of talk with a male host discussing explicit sexual matters with listeners, usually females, encouraged to call in. For example, in 1973 WGLD-FM of Oak Park, Illinois, was fined $2,000 for discussions about such practices as oral sex during daytime hours when young children could reasonably be expected in the audience. One excerpt of a WGLD broadcast went:

Female Caller: …I have a craving for peanut butter … so I spread this on my husband's privates and after awhile, I mean I didn't need the peanut butter anymore.
Male host: [laughing] Peanut butter, huh?
Caller: Right. Oh, we can try anything … Any of these women that have called and … have hangups about this … they should try their favorite—you know like—uh
       ….
Host: Whipped cream, marshmallow….[105]

The FCC decided this case and similar sessions violated indecency and obscenity standards of U.S. Criminal Code Section 1464, but indicated the discussion of sex did not automatically risk punishment:

> We are not emphatically saying that sex per se is a forbidden subject on the broadcast medium [*sic*]. We are well aware that sex is a vital human relationship which has concerned humanity over the centuries, and that sex and obscenity are not the same thing. … We are …confronted … [here] with the talk or interview show where clearly the interviewer can readily moderate his handling of the subject matter so as to conform to the basic statutory standards which, as we point out, allow much leeway for provocative material.[106]

The radio station denied wrongdoing but paid the fine. That did not end the matter. Two public interest groups petitioned the commission for reconsideration on the grounds that listeners had a right of access to controversial programs, then appealed to the U.S. Court of Appeals for the D.C. Circuit when the FCC reaffirmed its decision. The appellate court backed the agency: "We conclude that, where a radio call-in show during daytime hours broadcasts explicit discussions of ultimate sexual acts in a titillating context, the Commission does not unconstitutionally infringe upon the public's right to listening alternatives when it determines that the broadcast is obscene."[107]

Two weeks before the FCC notified WGLD-FM of an apparent violation, the board of directors of the National Association of Broadcasters adopted a resolution that "unequivocally deplored and condemned tasteless and vulgar program content, whether explicit or by sexually oriented innuendo."[108]

The debate over indecent programming owes much of its roots to an October 30, 1973, broadcast of comedian George Carlin's recorded monologue, "Filthy Words" on WBAI-FM in New York, owned by the Pacifica Foundation, whose alternative stations have been embroiled in various controversies over content with the FCC. Before the monologue was aired at 2:00 p.m., listeners were warned about offensive language. But weeks later a listener filed a complaint with the FCC, indicating that he had heard the broadcast while driving with his young son. The commission issued a declaratory order granting the complaint but reserved judgment on whether to impose administrative sanctions while noting that its order would become part of the station's file. The FCC held that the language in Carlin's monologue was indecent within the meaning of Section 1464 of the U.S. Criminal Code (Title 18). The commission was concerned especially with the time of the program: "The concept of 'indecent' is intimately connected with the exposure of children to language that describes, in terms patently offensive as measured by contemporary community standards for the broadcast medium, sexual or excretory activities and organs, at times of the day when there is a reasonable risk that children may be in the audience."[109]

The commission's decision, not rendered until February 1975, months after the broadcast, implied the program could have been played at a different time without incurring FCC wrath.

Figure 7.2   American comedian George Carlin performs his stand-up comedy act on stage, 1981 (Ken Howard/Hulton Archive/Getty Images).

"When the number of children is reduced to a minimum, for example during the late evening hours, a different standard might conceivably be used," according to the agency. The FCC did not enunciate a particular standard, nor did it indicate that a lower standard would apply.

Pacifica chose to fight the FCC rather than fold. During the first round of appeals, Pacifica won when the U.S. Court of Appeals for the D.C. Circuit reversed the decision, holding that its actions were tantamount to prior restraint and thus violated the First Amendment. The FCC appealed to the Supreme Court, which reversed the Court of Appeals decision in 1978, siding with the Commission. In a 5 to 4 plurality opinion in *FCC v. Pacifica Foundation* (1978),[110] written by Justice John Paul Stevens, the Court held the FCC could constitutionally prohibit language that was *indecent* even though not *obscene*. (Obscenity involves an appeal to prurient interests or eroticism, whereas indecency does not.) Not surprisingly, the justices split on the decision, leading to the plurality opinion. According to Justice Stevens, whose opinion was supported by four other justices:

> The prohibition against censorship [in §326] unequivocally denies the Commission any power to edit proposed broadcasts in advance and to excise material considered inappropriate for the airwaves. The prohibition, however, has never been construed to deny the Commission the power to review the content of completed broadcasts in the performance of its regulatory duties.[111]

The opinion also noted that "§326 does not limit the Commission's authority to impose sanctions on licensees who engage in obscene, indecent, or profane broadcasting" and that "of all forms of communication, it is broadcasting that has received the most limited First Amendment Protection." The Court's conclusion was troublesome in rationale for individuals who advocate First Amendment rights for broadcast on par with those of other media:

> The Commission's decision rested entirely on a nuisance rationale under which context is all-important. The concept requires consideration of a host of variables. The time of day was emphasized by the Commission. The content of the program in which the language is used will also affect the composition of the audience and differences between radio, television, and perhaps closed-circuit transmissions, may also be relevant. As Mr. Justice Sutherland wrote in citing a much earlier case, a "nuisance may be merely a right thing in the wrong place—like a pig in a parlor instead of the barnyard" We simply hold that when the Commission finds that when a pig has entered the parlor, the exercise of its regulatory power does not depend on proof that the pig is obscene.[112]

Pacifica was only the beginning of growing governmental and public concern with indecent programming, but its holding continues to be invoked by the courts in spite of its plurality status. Indeed, the case became known as the "seven dirty words" decision because Carlin's 12-minute monologue revolved around the seven "words you couldn't say on the public ... airwaves."[113] One misconception surrounding the FCC and Supreme Court's decision is that the seven specific words have been banned from the air. Both the Court and the commission indicated that the monologue, as a whole, broadcast in the specific context (early afternoon when children could be listening) was indecent, not the individual profanities or vulgarities. Note the commission did not take criminal action or pose sanctions; it warned that the offense would be noted in its administrative file.

As much as anyone on the air, Howard Stern has been the subject of FCC scrutiny. As early as 1995, Howard Stern's broadcasts had resulted in total FCC fines of $1.885 million against stations carrying his show. At that time, Stern had been cited more than his nearest competitor. The highest fine up to that date was a paltry $40,000. When Stern's then-employer, Infinity Broadcasting, petitioned the commission for permission to buy Los Angeles station KRTH-FM for $100 million, a record for a radio station in 1994, the FCC balked until Infinity agreed to pay an added fine of $400,000 for Stern's violations. According to the *Washington Post,* Infinity had not paid any of the fines, although the sale was consummated.[114]

New York Post columnist John Podhoretz warned about politics: "Stern's in danger of making the Lenny Bruce mistake. The great dirty comic spent the last few years of his life boring his audience to tears by lecturing them about injustices done to him. Stern's listeners want to hear him talk to strippers and insult his producer's teeth."[115]

The tradition has been to examine the actual words used on the air. The then-FCC Chairman Michael Powell asked commissioners to overturn a decision they had made addressing an expletive ("this is really, really, f-------brilliant") by rock group U-2's lead singer Bono telecast during the NBC broadcast of the 2004 Golden Globe Awards. The initial complaint against the network had been dismissed by the FCC's Enforcement Bureau, which ruled the broadcast of the "F-word" was not obscene because the word was used as an adjective, not to describe a sex act, and constituted a fleeting use that did not warrant liability. However, on appeal, the full commission overturned the bureau's decision, noting "we believe that, given the core meaning of the 'F-Word,' any use of that word or a variation, in any context, inherently has a sexual connotation, and therefore falls within the first prong of our indecency definition."[116] The first prong focuses on the explicitness or graphic nature of the depiction or description of sexual or excretory organs or activities.

When ABC-TV broadcast the movie, *Saving Private Ryan,* which won numerous awards, including a Golden Globes for best motion picture drama, the film was known to focus on the horrors of World War II. The dialogue contains numerous profanities, including the "F-word." ABC affiliates were not given the option of editing out expletives because of the network's contract with the film's owner, and ABC stations chose not to carry the movie. The film was co-introduced by U.S. Senator John McCain (R-Ariz.), a World War II veteran. The broadcast was clearly marked as "TV MA LV" (a rating indicating it was suitable for a mature audience because of explicit language and violence).

Some affiliates decided not to broadcast the film indicating they feared fines. They pointed to the agency's decision in the Bono case and the furor over Janet Jackson and Justin Timberlake's "Nipplegate" appearance during half time at Super Bowl XXXVIII game earlier in the same year. The Super Bowl fiasco, in which Jackson's breast was exposed for 19/32 of a second, resulted in a half million complaints to the FCC. In the aftermath, TV networks and other station owners took a more careful view of on-air performance, including tape delays for "live" performances. The fact that Jackson's breast was shown in view of a national TV audience in prime time created a public outcry, and critics on both sides had a heyday.[117]

The FCC Chair urged an increase in the fine for indecency from $27,500 to $275,000, and the FCC fined Viacom and CBS-owned and-operated stations $550,000 for the indiscretion, even though the network claimed it was blind-sided by the incident. CBS challenged the decision. The incident harkened back to an earlier incident in which 169 FOX stations were hit with complaints for airing what the commission called a "sexually suggestive" bachelor party scene in a reality show, *Married by America*.[118] The agency fined Fox and affiliates $1.183 million or $7,000 for each station carrying the show.

The FCC received complaints about the airing of *Saving Private Ryan*, but ultimately ruled in favor of ABC on grounds that the language in the film, when taken in context, was not indecent.[119] ABC created controversy again when it aired a promo for its series, *Desperate Housewives*, with an actress dropping her towel in front of a Philadelphia Eagles wide receiver in the NFL locker room. The promotion showed only a bare back from the waist up. It was aired during a Monday night football game between the Eagles and the Dallas Cowboys. The commission ruled the promotion may have been sexually suggestive, but was not indecent. [120] Then NBC said it received requests from the FCC for tape of Olympics ceremonies after receiving complaints about scantily clad performers.[121]

The Second Circuit U.S. Court of Appeals held that the FCC's 2003 indecency policy was "arbitrary and capricious" in 2007 and possibly violated the First Amendment. In *Fox Television Stations, Inc. v. FCC* (2007), a three-judge panel ruled that the commission had not provided a "reasoned analysis" in its justification for the new policy. The court did not specifically strike down the policy but instead sent it back to the FCC for reconsideration.

Some Ethical Considerations

It can be argued that *Pacifica* should have let sleeping dogs lie and should not have appealed the FCC decision because taking the case further could lead to an adverse decision and erosion of the First Amendment. No doubt that company felt it could win the case, as it did in federal appellate court, only to be reversed by the Supreme Court. Should the station have appealed the decision?

At the time of the Court's decision, only about 10 million homes subscribed to cable television and Time Inc. had just begun to distribute its Home Box Office Service via satellite to cable systems. One system, DirecTV has nearly 20 million subscribers in the United States.[123]

All of the cable services carry movies and other programs that might easily be characterized as soft-core pornography. Although some services have a policy of showing R-rated and NC-17 movies only at night (usually no earlier than 8:00 p.m.), even PG-13 movies sometimes contain profanity and content that could be considered indecent under traditional over-air broadcast standards. Occasionally, there are consumer complaints about offensive content in movies on these channels, but the FCC has specifically asserted it does not have the authority to fine video and audio subscription services, including cable, satellite television and satellite radio, for indecent content.

For years, many critics of the television industry urged the FCC to mandate that more effective measures—such as requiring a parental lock system on all cable converters—be taken to prevent children from gaining access to inappropriate content. At one time, a special effort had to be made to get access to cable channels outside the normal tuning range of the TV set; but now cable-originated (i.e., those fed from satellites) channels are interspersed with other over-the-air signals.

Talk radio attracted a lot of attention over the years with the great popularity of conservative talk hosts such as Glenn Beck, Rush Limbaugh, Bill O'Reilly, Sean Hannity, and former Watergate convict G. Gordon Liddy. Liddy attracted criticism when he instructed listeners to his show how to effectively shoot federal agents if they invaded a home. "Use head shots," he said, "they've got a vest underneath." Liddy once won the annual First Amendment Award from the National Association of Radio Talk Show Hosts.

Online media postings, including a website belonging to national candidate Sarah Palin, came under fire when the website placed a congressional seat "in the cross-hairs" and was widely criticized in the aftermath of a shooting in Tucson, Arizona, in January, 2011, when six people were shot and U.S. Representative Gabrielle Giffords was critically wounded by a gunman.[124]

Fifteen years earlier, the syndicated *Jenny Jones* television show taped an episode called "Secret Admirers" about men who had secret crushes on other men. The program was never aired because one of the guests, Jonathan Schmitz, shot another guest, Scott Amedure, three days after Amedure disclosed on the show his crush on the other man. Schmitz received a sexually suggestive note from Amedure and shot him in a confrontation. Court TV covered the case in some detail. Schmitz was ultimately convicted for slaying Amedure and sentenced to 25 years in prison. Jones testified at the trial, and was strongly criticized in the press for her confused testimony, which she blamed on the fact that she had been given only one day's notice. Amedure's family subsequently sued Jones and the owner of her show, Warner Brothers, for wrongful death. A Michigan jury found Jones and Warner Brothers liable for more than $29 million in damages, but three years later the state Court of Appeals overturned the verdict, holding that the defendants "had no duty to anticipate and prevent the act of murder committed by Schmitz."

Indecency and Obscenity Continued

The infamous George Carlin "Seven Words You Can't Say" broadcast took place at a time when the FCC was actively involved in regulation. The U.S. Supreme Court decision was handed down just as an era of *deregulation* had begun. That moved from moderation during the late 1970s then accelerated, with an emphasis on market competition beginning in the 1980s. Deregulation never meant complete deregulation. Each commission chose its own areas of emphasis for enforcement, often in line with dictates of Congress in the form of statutes. President Jimmy Carter appointed Charles D. Ferris as chair of the FCC. Ferris coined the term *re-regulation* to characterize the tone of the commission during his tenure. The idea was "to deregulate where markets would work without regulation" while recognizing that "some markets are not competitive enough to be completely deregulated."[125] Robert E. Lee, who served the shortest term as chair of the FCC (four months in 1981) oversaw continuation of the deregulation, which was substantially accelerated in 1981 when Mark Fowler took the helm.

The Fowler Commission became known as the advocate of "unregulation" as it moved to eliminate as many regulations as possible, especially those involving programming. "Let the marketplace decide" were buzz words of the era as rules and regulations fell, often with the rationale that the competitive marketplace was a more efficient and less expensive means of regulation.

What was the impact of deregulation and unregulation on obscenity and indecency? During the decade after Pacifica, the FCC skirted obscenity and indecency issues by announcing that it was limiting application of Pacifica to repeated broadcasts of the "seven dirty words" airing earlier than 10:00 p.m.126 In the entire period from the Pacifica decision until the end of the Fowler administration, not one broadcast station was cited for indecency. For example, after Pacifica, the FCC turned down a petition from a group of citizens, Morality in Media of Massachusetts, to deny renewal of the license of one of the top public television stations, WGBH, Boston. The group complained that the Public Broadcasting Service (PBS) affiliate carried programs with unacceptable language and nudity. Among programs cited was the acclaimed Masterpiece Theatre, produced by WGBH and carried nationally over PBS.

The picture changed in 1987. The commission (a) cited three stations and an amateur ("ham") radio operator for broadcasting obscenities and (b) announced that it would issue a public notice enunciating its position on indecency. Almost two weeks later, the FCC issued its public notice that it was no longer confining enforcement of Section 464 to Carlin obscenities, indicating it would "apply the generic definition of indecency advanced in Pacifica ... *'Language or material that depicts or describes, in terms patently offensive as measured by contemporary community standards for the broadcast medium, sexual or excretory activities or organs.'"*127

Interestingly, even though the commission actually revoked the amateur radio operator's license,128 it took a more lenient approach to the three broadcast licensees, referring one case to the U.S. Department of Justice (which declined to prosecute),129 while taking no specific action against the other two.130 Infinity Broadcasting's station WYSP-FM in Philadelphia simulcast a morning drive-time program from WXRK-FM in New York City, *The Howard Stern Show*, hosted, of course, by its namesake. (Only the Philadelphia station was cited, not the originating station in New York.)

The shock radio citation apparently caught by surprise many stations that were generally comfortable with the deregulatory—or, as some critics characterized it, "unregulatory"—stance of the FCC during Ronald Reagan's presidency under FCC Chairs Mark Fowler (1981 to 1987) and Dennis Patrick (1987 to 1989).131 But the move to stamp out indecency on the air was not abated even with one of industry's own at the helm, Alfred C. Sikes, who indicated on the day before he took over on August 8, 1989, "I hope as chairman of the FCC to help open markets, and I think the competition that results will help people."132 He said that the aggressive moves against obscenity begun by Chair Dennis Patrick would continue: "I see carrying forward that vigorous enforcement." In a citation against Philadelphia's WYSP-FM, which moved in audience ratings for that time slot from near the bottom to third place as a direct result of the "shock" show, 133 the FCC included excerpts it considered indecent:

Howard Stern: Have you ever had sex with an animal?
Caller: No.
Stern: Well, don't knock it. I was sodomized by Lambchop, you know that puppet Shari Lewis holds?
Stern: Baaaaah. That's where I was thinking that Shari Lewis, instead of like sodomizing all the people at the Academy to get that shot on the Emmys she could've had Lambchop do it.134

Shortly after the FCC cited WYSP-FM, Stern encouraged his listeners to voice their disagreement with the commission. "I am the last bastion of the First Amendment," he told them.135 During 1992 and 1993 the FCC issued numerous notices of liability (NALs), including several against stations carrying Stern's show. With an NAL, the FCC cannot force a station to pay a fine unless the station decides not to fight the finding in court or the station loses in court.

Shock radio or its derivations continue on the airwaves, although most of them have toned down since the FCC citations and the aftermath, and some of the most frequently cited individuals such as Howard Stern have moved to satellite radio on grounds that they would have more freedom outside the reach of the FCC. In response to a flood of petitions on both sides of the issue, most from broadcasters and supporters, a request was made in 1987 that the FCC rescind its order and provide clarification of standards of indecency. Among the petitions was one from Morality in Media, asking that specific types of sexually explicit material be banned even if not legally obscene. In its order, the commission called the Morality in Media plan unconstitutional on the ground that the U.S. Supreme Court's holding in *Pacifica* permitted only "reasonable time, place and manner restrictions" on indecent content, not broad restrictions.[135]

In a deft move, the FCC refused to define *patently offensive* from its earlier order and incensed First Amendment advocates by noting that it would not apply *Miller v. California's* (1973)[137] holding that *obscene* material must lack serious literary, artistic, political, or scientific value in evaluating whether broadcast content is *indecent*. According to the FCC, "Merit is simply one of many variables, and it would give this particular variable undue importance if we were to single it out for greater weight or attention than we give other variables.… We must, therefore, reject an approach that would hold that if a work has merit, it is *per se* not indecent."[138]

The FCC emphasized that merit must be included among the variables and that the "ultimate determinative factor … is whether the material, when examined in context, is patently offensive." The order announced, for purposes of evaluating whether material was patently offensive, contemporary community standards (see *Miller*) would be defined as national—an average viewer or listener: "In making the required determination of indecency, Commissioners draw on their knowledge of the views of the average viewer or listener, as well as their general expertise in broadcast matters. The determination reached is thus not one based on a local standard, but one based on a broader standard for broadcasting generally."[139]

Action for Children's Television v. Federal Communications Commission *(ACT I, 1988)*

Further appeals were inevitable, given the potential impact of the original order and the reconsideration order. The culmination of those appeals arrived in the form of a 1988 U.S. Court of Appeals for the D.C. Circuit ruling in *Action for Children's Television v. Federal Communications Commission (ACT I)*.[140] Before the decision arrived, skirmishes occurred. On January 12, 1988, the FCC initiated enforcement action against a TV station for broadcasting purportedly indecent material by announcing that KZKC-TV of Kansas City, Missouri, maybe violated the new indecency standards established earlier.[141] The station had shown at 8:00 p.m. the R-rated movie *Private Lessons*, including scenes of a bare-breasted woman seducing a teenage boy. The owner claimed later the movie had been cut by an inexperienced editor and violated the company's standards. He said the station should not have been fined because the FCC standards were vague and being applied the first time to a TV station.[142] (Earlier citations were against radio.) In June 1988, the FCC voted 2 to 1 (just three commissioners were on board) to levy the maximum fine of $2,000 against the station but delayed assessing it because the U.S. Court of Appeals in *Action for Children's Television v. FCC* ordered the commission to conduct a new hearing regarding the times when indecent material may be aired.

Although there was hope at the time that *Action for Children's Television v. FCC* (1988) would at least provide clearer guidelines regarding indecency, the decision of the court and the congressional action that followed muddied the waters even more. The Court of Appeals ruled the FCC's definition of indecency was not substantially too broad because "merit is properly treated as a factor in determining whether material is patently offensive, but it does not render such material *per se* not indecent."[143] The court reiterated indecent but not obscene material enjoys First Amendment protection, but children's access to indecent material may be regulated through parental oversight to protect unsupervised kids.

The court was less than satisfied with the ratings data the FCC presented to show that large numbers of children were listening and watching during late hours, calling the evidence used in making channeling decisions "insubstantial … and more ritual than real." The midnight or "safe harbor" advice and the FCC's entire position on channeling "was not adequately thought through," the court said. The judges instructed the commission to establish a safe harbor in a rule-making proceeding so the FCC could "afford broadcasters clear notice of reasonably determined times at which indecent material may be safely aired"[144] and ordered re-hearings for two stations.

Within months after the court's decision, Congress, at the urging of conservatives such as the late Senator Jessie Helms (R-N.C.), passed an amendment to an appropriations bill that required the FCC to enforce its indecency policy 24 hours a day, starting January 27, 1989. The commission immediately complied and enacted such a rule. Upon petition, the U.S. Court of Appeals for the D.C. Circuit stayed the FCC rule, pending further review. In the meantime, the Court said, the FCC could gather evidence to support the ban. The Court order did not affect the commission's ability to enforce its safe harbor policy. In 1989 it fined Los Angeles talk radio KFI-AM more than $6,000 for airing indecent remarks during three programs. Topics discussed with callers included penis size and "sexual secrets." The station chose not to appeal and, acting on complaints, the FCC cited and fined others for indecent programming.[145]

In polling regarding reinstatement of a ban, the agency received almost 90,000 complaints. Critic Ron Powers in *GQ* magazine noted that the confrontation between programmers and the government had been building.[146] He pointed out that NBC-TV *Tonight Show* host Jack Paar was forced off the air in the 1950s for a reference to a "water closet," a euphemism for bathroom. Powers felt broadcasters brought suppression on themselves.[147] Ironically, a half century later, rocker Tommy Lee was wished a "Happy (expletive) New Year" on a live broadcast of NBC's *Tonight Show with Jay Leno*.

Action for Children's Television v. Federal Communications Commission *(ACT II, 1991)*

The U.S. Court of Appeals for the D.C. Circuit held in *Action for Children's Television v. Federal Communications Commission (ACT II)* in 1991 that the 24-hour ban was unconstitutional prior restraint because it barred indecent speech, which enjoyed First Amendment protection. The court ordered a stay on the ban, directing the commission to initiate a proceeding to determine when indecent content could be broadcast. The appellate court made it clear the FCC could reinstitute a safe harbor period for indecent speech, but had to do so after addressing the concerns the court had raised in *ACT I*, including "the appropriate definitions of 'children' and 'reasonable risk' for channeling purposes … and the scope of the government's interest in regulating indecent broadcasts."[148] Until the federal appeals court decision, Congress appeared determined to keep a 24-hour ban, as did the FCC. As the FCC General Counsel said before the court's ruling, "Under the Communications Act, the Commission is obliged to enforce an indecency standard; the Commission has consistently articulated a standard for indecency; it has been upheld by the Supreme Court."[149] He also contended indecency "is an area where the Commission has been given, by Congress, a statutory responsibility, and what we're doing is carrying out that congressionally mandated responsibility. It's no more and no less."[150]

In *ACT II*, the D.C. Circuit Court cited both *ACT I* and the 1989 U.S. Supreme Court decision in *Sable Communications v. FCC*[151] to justify its decision. In *Sable Communications* the Supreme Court recognized that Congress could protect children from exposure to dial-a-porn messages (sexually oriented phone services), but it said such restrictions must be strictly limited. Accordingly, the Court held that the federal statute's outright ban on both indecent and obscene interstate commercial telephone messages was unconstitutional. The Court upheld a lower court's decision that the statute could not ban indecent messages but could prohibit obscene messages. The Court specifically rejected the 1978 *FCC v. Pacifica Foundation* decision, discussed earlier, as justification for the ban on indecent phone messages. The Court distinguished *Pacifica* by pointing to the narrowness of the *Pacifica* holding and the "uniquely pervasive" nature of broadcasting that "can intrude on the privacy of the home without prior warning as to program content." According to the Court, "Placing a telephone call is not the same as turning on a radio and being taken by surprise by an indecent message." Thus the justices did not directly confront the 24-hour indecent broadcasting ban because this issue arose independent of the case at hand. On appeal, in 1992 the U.S. Supreme Court denied certiorari in *ACT II*.

Rather than wait for the FCC to come up with a new safe harbor, Congress included a provision in the Public Telecommunications Act of 1992[152] directing the agency to establish regulations banning indecent programming from 6:00 a.m. to midnight. The Act, whose primary purpose was to provide funding for public broadcasting, set the safe harbor hours for public television as 10:00 p.m. to 6:00 a.m. These were for stations that signed off prior to midnight.

Action for Children's Television v. Federal Communications Commission *(ACT III and ACT IV, 1995)*

In *Action for Children's Television v. Federal Communications Commission* (1993),[153] a three-judge panel of the U.S. Court of Appeals for the D.C. Circuit upheld the FCC's new safe harbor regulations. Two years later in *Action for Children's Television v. Federal Communications Commission* (*ACT III*, 1995),[154] an *en banc* court affirmed the panel's decision but expanded the hours for all broadcasters to 10:00 p.m. to 6:00 a.m. so the rules would be uniform for commercial and public television. On appeal, the U.S. Supreme Court denied certiorari. When Action for Children's Television challenged the administrative process the FCC had used in enforcing its indecency rules, including cases the commission had not resolved for years, the U.S. Court of Appeals for the D.C. Circuit ruled in favor of the FCC in what has become known as *ACT IV*. [155] The U.S. Supreme Court denied certiorari in 1996, presumably bringing closure to the issue of what hours could be set for a safe harbor from indecency.

The Telecommunications Act of 1996 contains a provision dealing with sexually explicit adult video programming requiring cable systems and "multi-channel video program distributors" (MVPDs) to scramble programming when carried on channels such as Playboy and Spice that are devoted primarily to sexually oriented content. The scrambling must include both audio and video to prevent nonsubscribers from seeing and hearing the content.[156]

Under the Cable Television Consumer Protection and Competition Act of 1992,[157] cable operators were granted the right to restrict or prohibit indecent programming on leased access channels and public, educational, and governmental (PEG) channels. Leased access channels are leased for commercial use by individuals and organizations not affiliated with the cable company. Most cable systems are required to make such channels available. One section of the Act required cable operators to segregate patently offensive programming to one channel. It also had to block it from viewer access unless a subscriber over the age of 18 asked in writing that access be available. "Patently offensive" programming was defined as obscene under *Miller v. California* (1973) standards and "indecent" was defined as language that describes, in terms patently offensive as measured by contemporary community standards for the broadcast medium, sexual or excretory activities and organs.

Cable companies are not required under federal law to provide PEG channels, but local franchise authorities can require them to offer such channels for use by public, educational, and governmental agencies as a condition for being awarded the local cable franchise.

In *Denver Area Educational Telecommunications Consortium, Inc. v. Federal Communications Commission* (1996),[158] the U.S. Supreme Court had the opportunity to determine whether cable TV followed a print or broadcast model for First Amendment protection or a hybrid. The Court failed to seize the opportunity. It issued a plurality opinion that elicited separate opinions. The case concerned the constitutionality of indecency provisions.

The Court upheld the provision allowing a cable operator to refuse to carry on leased access channels programming reasonably believed to be patently offensive. Unfortunately, the Court could not agree on the rationale. The Court also struck down the provision requiring cable companies to segregate indecent leased access programming to one channel and to scramble the signal except for subscribers who asked in writing that the channel be unscrambled. A majority of justices did agree that this provision was unconstitutional because it was not narrowly tailored to achieve the government objective of protecting children from patently offensive material. The opinion, written by Justice Breyer, noted that other less obtrusive means were available to accomplish the result, namely the V-chip. In a 5 to 4 vote, the Court struck down a provision that allowed cable operators to ban indecent programming from PEG channels but again, could not agree on a rationale.

The Ratings Game: From TV-Y to TV-MA

During the 1990s the major commercial television networks began voluntarily labeling some shows such as the ABC series *NYPD Blue* with an advisory: "Due to some violent content, parental discretion is advised." In the same year, a *Los Angeles Times* poll showed that more than 54% of Americans would support federal guidelines to restrict violence on television.[159] During the next four years, various politicians warned the broadcast industry that legislation might be on the horizon if television violence were not reduced. As a result, major broadcast and cable networks took steps hailed by some in Congress as significant. The steps included hiring an outside group to monitor TV violence and issue annual reports. Cable networks agreed to set up violence ratings systems and install technology that would allow viewers to block certain programs. (Home satellite viewers already had such technology.) In 1994 the industry announced that UCLA's Center on Communications Policy was selected as a monitor as part of a $3.3 million, three-year project. The center studied individual shows rather than making a gross tally, as in previous studies. Prime time programs, including series, movies, and miniseries, on ABC, CBS, Fox, and NBC, as well as Saturday morning children's shows, were monitored, but sports and news were excluded.[160] Studies were conducted on cable. Some examined ratings, warnings, and educational programming.[161]

The television and cable industry initiated a new program ratings system in 1997 modeled after the ratings of the Motion Picture Association of America (MPAA). It had the endorsements of the National Cable Television Association (NCTA) and the National Association of Broadcasters (NAB). The advocacy community, including the American Medical Association (AMA), the American Psychological Association (APA), the National Education Association (NEA), the National PTA, and five other organizations, was also extensively involved in developing the system. Section 551 of the Telecommunications Act of 1996 encouraged, but did not mandate, the industry to "establish voluntary rules for rating video programming that contains sexual, violent or other indecent material about which parents should be informed before it is displayed to children" and display the ratings in the broadcasts.

The Act also required the FCC to consult with public interest groups and members of the public to get their reactions to the voluntary system. Under Section 115, the FCC would have been required to appoint an advisory committee to set up guidelines for a ratings system if the industry had not done so by February 8, 1997—one year after the Telecom Act took effect. Some First Amendment experts questioned whether the system eventually developed could pass constitutional muster because of this provision and political pressures. They reasoned that if a challenger could demonstrate that the pressures and the provision were tantamount to a government mandate, that provision of the Act could be declared to be unconstitutional prior restraint. However, those concerns never arose once the system was developed.

The six age-based categories established by the industry included two for programs aimed solely at children—*TV-Y All Children* (programming appropriate for all children) and *TV-Y7 Directed to Older Children* (programming for children 7 and older). The remaining four categories—*TV-G General Audience* (suitable all ages), *TV-PG Parental Guidance Suggested* (programming may not be suitable for younger children), *TV-14 Parents Strongly Cautioned* (programming may be unsuitable for children younger than 14) and *TV-MA Mature Audiences Only* (programming designed for adults that may be unsuitable for children under 17).

This initial effort was not entirely successful. All of the major broadcast television networks and all major cable television networks eventually adopted the system, but many media researchers as well as parents were less than enthusiastic about the results. For example, one of the studies part of the $3.3 million project mentioned earlier found the system could actually be attracting children to watch violent shows.[162] Research looked at 6,000 programs over two years.

The major criticisms leveled at the system were (a) the ratings gave no indication of the type of content involved—sex, violence, language, etc. and (b) the ratings were confusing, particularly because they were solely age-based. At the urging of the public and members of Congress, the industry eventually revised the system to include violence (V), fantasy violence (FV), coarse language (L), sexual situations (S), and suggestive dialogue (D). The degree of these parameters varied, depending upon the specific rating. For example, a program rated "TV-14 Parents Strongly Cautioned" may contain intense violence, intense sexual situations, strong coarse language or intensely suggestive dialogue, while a "TV-MA Mature Audiences Only" show could have graphic violence, explicit sexual activity or crude, indecent language. The V, FV, L, S, and D symbols indicate the type of content involved. Both the new and the old guidelines apply to all television programming, except news and sports and unedited MPAA-rated movies on premium cable channels such as HBO and Showtime. Premium cable channels carry the MPAA ratings and their own advisories. The rating assigned to a particular program, including the icon and the appropriate content symbols, are shown for at least 15 seconds at the beginnings of all rated programs. Ratings were included in all program guides.

Unlike MPAA ratings assigned by a separate board, the television ratings are chosen by programmers themselves. An advisory board supervises the administration of the ratings system and makes sure the ratings are consistent and accurate, but the board does not assign ratings. All television sets manufactured after February 1998 with 13-inch and larger screens have been required to have technology "designed to enable viewers to block display of all programs with a common rating" (which can be based on the voluntary ratings system or a programmer's own rating system).[163] The V-chip is triggered by a signal transmitted in the TV signal. The Telecommunications Act provision did not require programmers to rate shows, but it did require manufacturers to include technology to block rated shows.

Although programmers do not have to use a ratings system, they are barred under the Telecommunications Act from removing the TV Parental Guidelines signals from the VBI. The ratings icon and information automatically appear on the screen for 15 seconds at the beginning of each program and when activated by remote control action such as changing channels.

The sizzle of competition on the airwaves often drives stations to continue to test the limits of acceptability and encourage government to aggressively defend some parameters. In 1992 Congress included a provision in its bill authorizing funding for public broadcasting that banned "indecent programming" on both radio and TV between 6:00 a.m. and 10:00 p.m. on public stations and 6:00 a.m. and midnight for all other stations. The FCC issued rules implementing the provision. By 2010, the "political correctness" of network decision-making was reflected in the firing of commentator, Juan Williams by NPR because he said he felt uncomfortable when travelling by air when fellow passengers were wearing "Muslim garb."[164]

The NAB had a code of "good practice" from 1929 to 1983, including standards for programming and advertising as well as regulations and procedures. Television and radio had separate but similar codes. Both the family viewing and advertising provisions were challenged as illegal in the late 1970s, and the NAB, facing a long and expensive battle with writers' groups over family viewing and the Justice Department over ad restrictions, killed both the TV and the radio codes in 1983. The family viewing standards adopted by the three commercial networks on April 21, 1975, included a provision that "entertainment programming inappropriate for viewing by a general family audience should not be broadcast during the first hour of network entertainment programming in prime time and in the immediately preceding hour."[165] This essentially restricted TV network programming to family entertainment from 8:00 to 9:00 p.m. during weekdays and 7:00 to 8:00 p.m. on weekends.

It remains to be seen whether the ratings system is actually reducing the amount of objectionable content on television, including violence, but at least the technology is in place and working so viewers, including conscientious parents, can block unsuitable programming from the eyes and ears of children.

Children's Programming

In late 1991 new FCC rules took effect to implement the Children's Television Act (CTA) of 1990, passed by Congress and enacted without the senior President Bush's signature. The statute delegated to the commission the authority to interpret and enforce its provisions, which include a mandate that broadcasters serve the educational needs of children. Under the FCC rules, which have become known as the "Kidvid Rules," the maximum time allocated to commercials during programming directed primarily to children on both commercial and cable television was 10.5 minutes per hour on weekends and 12 minutes per hour on weekdays. The rules at that time did not specify any minimum time that broadcasters had to set aside for children's programming but instead left that decision in the hands of the networks and local stations. Broadcasters, however, had to provide in their files for public inspection summaries of programming that they contended served children. Later, as noted below, the FCC put into place specific programming requirements.

The FCC decided not to clamp down on so-called 30-minute commercials, shows based on characters such as GI Joe, He Man, and Teenage Mutant Ninja Turtles. The commission said this type of program will be considered full commercial time only if the show included paid advertising for the toy of the particular character. However, in March 1993 the FCC announced that these programs and others, *G.I. Joe*, *The Jetsons*, and *The Flintstones*, could no longer count as "educational and informational" programming under the 1990 Act. The commission adopted a notice of inquiry to identify programs that "serve the educational and informational needs of children" and that "further the positive development of children."

Reed Hundt, a telecommunications lawyer, took over as FCC chair in 1993. Hundt opened the commission's first hearing on children's programming in over a decade by telling the broadcast industry "the business of educating kids should be part of the TV business," and he called TV a "battleground" for "the hearts and minds of children."[166] His proposal for improved children's television programming got the nod in 1995 when the commission approved rules that strengthen the Children's Television Act of 1990.

After input from various interest groups and the television industry, the commission gave its final approval in August 1996.[167] Among the changes were a more specific definition of educational or informational programming for children and a requirement that stations specifically identify on-the-air programs they consider educational. The commission members could not agree on whether stations should be required to devote a minimum amount of time to children's programming. Instead, they approved a compromise for stations that broadcast an average of at least three hours a week of educational and informational programming oriented to children 16 and under to receive preferential processing of license renewal.

The 1996 Telecommunications Act had already made it substantially easier for both radio and television stations to renew their licenses by extending licenses to eight years (from five years for TV and seven years for radio). It also severely limits the FCC's authority to deny renewals, to consider license challenges, and to grant conditional approvals.

The FCC significantly enhanced the Kidvid regulations as part of its effort to regulate the transition from analog to digital, high definition television in 2004.[168] Rules applied to both analog and digital television. As with previous rules, they applied solely to broadcasters. They do not affect cable and satellite TV, except for the provisions regarding ads during children's programs. The requirements include three hours of children's programming each week that "further the educational and informational needs of children 16 and under." The shows must be carried between 7:00 a.m. and 10:00 p.m., last at least 30 minutes, and air regularly on a weekly basis. Stations and networks must display a logo throughout such programs with the designation "E/I," indicating educational and informational content. The purpose is to alert parents looking-out for programming for their children. Noncommercial broadcasters are also bound by the new policy, except they do not have to comply with detailed reporting requirements imposed on commercial stations.

Another set of provisions under the digital Kidvid rules establishing requirements on the use of Web site addressed during children's programs created considerable controversy, as did a rule requiring stations multicast (carry both analog and digital signals) to carry an additional 30 minutes of children's programming for each 28-hour block of free digital broadcasts. With the encouragement of West Virginia Senator Jay Rockefeller, the Children's Television Act came under review again in 2010. The Senator raised the issue of commercialization and FCC Chair Genachowski told Rockefeller that he had ordered review of the law. When a cartoon show was proposed wearing a particular brand of kid's sneakers, some external groups proposed reexamination of Children's Television Act policies regarding appearance of commercial characters on cartoon shows.[169]

Regulation of New and Newer Technologies

Cable Television

Although radio and television broadcasting preceded it, cable television is actually a relatively old technology, having been first developed in the 1940s as a means of hauling in signals from distant TV stations to rural areas that had no direct access to over-air broadcast. According to the FCC, in 1950 only 70 communities in the whole country had cable systems.[170] By 1990, it had become a $15 billion industry with access to 80 million homes through more than 8,000 cable systems, of which only 32 had any direct competition. The 14 million subscribers in 1980 had grown to 53.9 million or about 58% of all homes by 1990.[171]

More than 96% of all 110 million American television households now have access to cable, 68% actually receive cable, and 22% receive DBS signals. Satellite is taking its toll on cable generally and in some localities in particular. By May 2005, for example, Springfield, Missouri, the third largest city in that midwestern state, became the first TV market in America to have a greater household penetration for satellite TV (39.6%) than for cable TV (39.2%). Unlike the early cable systems that usually offered no more than three or four VHF signals, to be competitive with emerging television outlets, the typical cable system now offers hundreds of channels. They include local stations, pay-per-view movies and events, public access channels, distant super-stations, and satellite-delivered networks such as USA Network, Lifetime, Black Entertainment Television, the Weather Channel, Home & Garden Television, Spike TV, MTV, Comedy Central, the Syfy Channel, TV Land, and the Cartoon Network. There are now what is commonly known as niche or "within a niche" channels such as Discovery Health Channel and Discovery Home as well as different genres of popular music channels including VH1 Country, VH1 Soul, and VH1 Smooth (jazz). A variety of pay or premium channels is also available from HBO/Cinemax and Showtime/The Movie Channel to adult pay-per-view channels.

Cable has been regulated by the FCC, although not exclusively, since 1965. The 1984 Cable Communications Policy Act, with subsequent amendments, including those of the Telecommunications Act of 1996, is the current regulatory scheme for cable. The FCC has control over some aspects of the industry but local franchising authorities have jurisdiction over other aspects. The basic scheme is that local governments (city, town, or county) grant *franchises* to cable companies to operate local systems, although there are national standards for rate regulation, franchise renewals, and franchise fees.[172] Cable systems are required to register with the commission, but they are not licensed *per se*, as are broadcast stations. The federal rules are primarily in the areas of cross-media ownership and technical specifications. Cable systems must also comply with Sections 312 and 315. One of the most controversial provisions of the Cable Communications Policy Act of 1984 was Section 622, which kept local governments from charging more than 5% of gross revenues for franchising, and Section 623, which prohibited them in most instances from regulating rates for basic and premium services, effective January 1, 1987.[173]

According to a General Accounting Office Report delivered to Congress in 1990, between November 30, 1986 and December 31, 1989, rates for the lowest-priced basic service increased 43% from an average per subscriber of $11.14 to $15.95. By today's standards, those prices are low, but they were considered high by consumer groups at that time. The public and organizations such as the NAB called for cable to be regulated again, and in 1992 Congress passed a new cable regulation bill that was vetoed by the senior President Bush. The Senate and the House, however, overrode the veto, and the legislation took effect. The statute was approved despite a multi-million dollar advertising campaign by the cable television industry to defeat the bill by trying to convince consumers that it would substantially increase cable fees.

Under the statute, the Cable Television Consumer Protection and Competition Act of 1992,[174] (a) the FCC had to establish regulations, administered by local governments, to implement "reasonable" rates for basic cable subscriptions, installation fees, and equipment; (b) the FCC was directed to set standards for reception quality and for customer service, including requests for service and complaints; (c) cable programmers such as Time Warner, which then owned and still owns Home Box Office and Cinemax, were required to license their programming to competitors such as microwave and satellite broadcasters; (d) cable companies had to negotiate compensation agreements with over-the-air stations that had not previously been paid for the retransmission of their signals; and (e) cable companies had to carry signals of local ABC, CBS, NBC, Fox, and PBS affiliates as part of the basic package. The latter is known as the *must-carry* rule.

Nearly all cable operators came under the statute because it exempted only those in a market in which there was a competing company available to at least half of the potential customers and in which a minimum of 15% of the households actually subscribed to the competing firm. Less than 24 hours after Congress overrode the President's veto, the Turner Broadcasting System (TBS) filed suit in U.S. District Court for the District of Columbia to challenge the must-carry provision of the bill as a violation of the First Amendment. The Turner networks included TBS, the Cable News Networks (CNN and CNN Headline News), Turner Network Television, and the Cartoon Network. (Turner Broadcasting System is now owned by Time Warner.) In April 1993 the U.S. District Court for the District of Columbia ruled 2 to 1 in a summary judgment for the government that the must-carry provisions were constitutional. According to the court, "[T]o the extent First Amendment speech is affected at all, it is simply a by-product of the fact that video signals have no other function than to convey information.[175]

In upholding the provisions, the trial court applied the intermediate level of scrutiny established in *United States v. O'Brien* (1968).[176] The majority opinion held that the must-carry provisions were content-neutral and narrowly tailored to protect local broadcasting from cable systems and monopoly power. The cable industry appealed directly to the U.S. Supreme Court, as it was permitted under the Act. The Supreme Court upheld the District Court decision in *Turner Broadcasting System v. Federal Communications Commission* (*Turner I*, 1994),[177] one of the most significant telecommunications legal developments of that decade.

Under Sections 4 and 5 of the Act, cable TV systems are required to devote a portion, generally about one-third, of their channels to local commercial and public broadcast stations. Thanks to these must-carry rules, some cable networks were dropped from certain systems. The C-SPAN public affairs network claimed its signal had been dropped or hours reduced in more than 4.2 million homes.[178] In a 5 to 4 decision written by Justice Kennedy, the Court for the first time said cable TV, at least from the perspective of must-carry rules, enjoys First Amendment protection, but not at the same level as the traditional press. According to the majority:

> There can be no disagreement on an initial premise: Cable programmers and cable operators engage in and transmit speech, and they are entitled to the protection of the speech and press provisions of the First Amendment.
>
> … Although courts and commentators have criticized the scarcity rationale [for broadcast regulation] since its inception, we have declined to question its continuing validity as support for our broadcast jurisprudence.…[179]

The majority opinion went on to note that "the must-carry rules, on their face, impose burdens and confer benefits without reference to the content of speech" and thus are content-neutral. However, the Court said, even a regulation content-neutral on its face may still be content-based if it is designed to regulate speech because of the message it communicates. After further analysis, the Court concluded the provisions were not designed to favor or disfavor any particular content but meant instead "to protect broadcast television from what Congress determined to be unfair competition by cable systems." The opinion rejected the argument of the cable industry that the Court should apply a strict scrutiny test to determine the constitutionality of the provisions. The standard, the Court asserted, should be intermediate level scrutiny of *O'Brien*, as advocated by the district court.

The majority refused to make a final determination on the constitutionality of the provisions because the government had not presented sufficient evidence that the threat to broadcast television—without the rules—was real enough to survive a First Amendment challenge. There had been no evidence showing that stations had gone bankrupt, given up their licenses, or had serious losses of revenues as a result of being dropped from a cable system. The case was remanded to the district court to determine whether, as a four-justice plurality said, "the economic health of local broadcasting is in genuine jeopardy and need of the protections afforded by must-carry" and whether the provisions burdened more speech than necessary to promote the government's interest in preserving over-the-air television.

After a year and a half of fact finding that included consideration of more documents and more expert testimony, the district court, in another split (2 to 1) decision, held that the must-carry provision was narrowly tailored to promote the legitimate government interests. In addition, there was "substantial evidence before Congress" that local broadcasters whose signals were removed from cable systems were likely to "suffer financial harm and possible ruin." The district court found that must-carry had had little effect on the cable companies. The court cited evidence that only slightly more than 1% of all cable channels that had been added since the rules were adopted were broadcast signals that the rules required to be added. Most systems had not been forced to carry additional broadcast signals.

Once again, cable companies appealed the decision directly to the Supreme Court, only to find the highest court in agreement with the district court once again. In *Turner Broadcasting System, Inc. v. Federal Communications Commission (Turner II,* 1997),[180] the Court affirmed the lower court decision in a majority opinion written by Justice Kennedy. The U.S. Supreme Court held, as previously, that "protecting non-cable households from loss of regular television broadcasting service due to competition from cable systems" is a substantial government interest. The court said that regulations promoting such an interest are permissible "even when the individuals or entities subject to particular regulations are engaged in expressive activity protected by the First Amendment."

The Supreme Court cited statistics that were damaging for cable: 94.5% of the cable systems did not have to drop programming as a result of must-carry, 40% of households did not have cable, and 87% of the time cable operators were able to meet the must-carry requirements by adding stations to channels that were not in use.

In 1990 consumers became outraged by another cable regulation but one not initiated by the industry. In 1988, the FCC adopted new syndicated exclusivity ("syndex") rules, similar to those in effect during 1972 to 1980 (when the FCC dropped them). The rules require cable companies to black out syndicated programming available to local viewers from distant television stations such as superstations TBS (Atlanta) and WGN (Chicago) when a local station has signed a contract with a syndicate for exclusive program rights. The syndex rules took effect January 1, 1990, after the D.C. Circuit U.S. Court of Appeals ruled the commission had the authority to enact and enforce them.[181] The rules require that the local station request the blackout, but it is highly unlikely that a station with an exclusive contract with a supplier would not do so because the purpose of the contract is to have exclusive control over the broadcasting of that program in that market, including cable signals. Consumers were initially upset because popular syndicated programs of that era such as *Cheers* and *Teenage Mutant Ninja Turtles* were excised. Network programs are not affected by the rules, but shows that have been on the networks in the past and that may still be running more recent episodes on the networks or have recently finished a network are affected. For example, older reruns of the *Seinfeld* series were syndicated to local stations even though at one time NBC was still showing original episodes and more recent reruns. Complaints abate as viewers adjusted to the changes and cable systems and superstations substituted alternative programming.

There are other FCC rules affecting cable television, but the basic approach of the commission and Congress had been to maintain minimum control, especially in programming. Even the courts handed cable companies victories in rulings by the D.C. Circuit U.S. Court of Appeals in 1985[182] and in 1987[183] that must-carry violated the First Amendment. (The Supreme Court changed that later on).

In 1993, however, a U.S. District Court judge upheld the provision in the 1992 Act known as the *retransmission rule* that required cable companies to negotiate compensation agreements with local affiliates. Under the rule, broadcasters could either require cable companies to carry their signals under the must-carry provisions or to request payment under the 1992 Act. A TV broadcaster had a choice. It could either opt for must-carry and receive no payment and be assured that its signal appeared in the cable lineup or it could opt out of must-carry and negotiate with the cable system to try to get the cable company to pay the station to carry its signal. The TV station, could not have it both ways.

In *Daniels Cablevision, Inc. v. United States* (1993),[184] the U.S. District Court held that even though Congress did not amend the Copyright Act of 1976 to make it an infringement of copyright for cable companies to retransmit signals without permission, it had the right to do essentially the same thing in Cable Television Consumer Protection and Competition Act of 1992. Stations chose must-carry. It produced higher ad revenue, thanks to a larger cable audience, but some stations negotiated. The risk for the station in waiving must-carry was that no agreement could be reached regarding payment. So the cable company then has no obligation to carry.

In the mid-1990s cable television dominated the headlines in industry trade publications when the FCC outlined new rate regulations that established a formula for calculating consumer rates. The commission set rates that were designed to reduce fees, but its follow-up study found a one-third of cable's 58 million subscribers had higher bills. A second round of rate setting was designed to reduce prices for services except for premium and pay-per-view.

The regulation of cable television rates was considerably changed by the Telecommunications Act of 1996. Under Section 303 of the Act, nearly all rate regulations for cable ended by the end of that decade. Prior to that, under certain conditions such as "effective competition" in the market, certain cable companies were not subject to rate regulations. Premium services were not regulated. Only the lowest tier of cable known as basic service, is rate regulated and only by local government franchise authorities approved by the FCC.

The 1996 Telecommunications Act allowed cable firms to provide phone service and phone companies to offer cable. For decades, the U.S. pursued a "two-wire" policy in which video services were to be provided via a cable and phone services were restricted to phone lines, a reflection of the use of old technology.

After originally setting a deadline of January 1, 2007, for TV to switch from analog to solely digital, in February 2006 Congress extended the deadline to February 17, 2009.[185] The greatest impact was on the approximately 15% of Americans who did not subscribe to cable or satellite television and relied on over-the-air stations for programming. Cable and satellite viewers could already receive much digital programming. Legislation set up a $990 million program under which eligible consumers received coupons to purchase digital-to-analog converters that retailed for about $60 each. Under the new statute, the FCC also set to auction the analog television spectrum, which, by some estimates, was worth about $10 billion. Some public interest groups and technology companies pushed the commission to use some of the 700-mHz band for Wi-Fi or wireless broadband networks.[186] Some groups hoped for a "hard date bill" for the transition much sooner. One of them, Senator John McCain (R-Ariz.), the former presidential candidate and something of a bane to the backside of broadcasters on Capitol Hill, introduced legislation that set a final deadline for the transition and called the process by which broadcasters were assigned the digital spectrum a "$70 billion giveaway." McCain was frustrated that so many broadcasters were clearly going to miss the initial FCC deadline.

In spite of delays and uncertainty the move from analog to digital TV went well along with convergence of TV and video with the Internet which produced opportunities for over-air programs and news to be accessible by computer and hand-held device.

Media Ownership

The FCC issued a series of reports that clarified, updated, and revised its media ownership policies after reviews that began under the then FCC Chair Michael Powell. Powell created a Media Ownership Working Group (MOWG) to assess and provide a basis for media ownership policies to address two federal court decisions that struck down related rules and called on the FCC to justify its policies. In *Fox Television Stations v. FCC* (2002),[187] the Third Circuit U.S. Court of Appeals held that the commission's decision in 1998 to retain a cap of 35% (the combined national share of U.S. homes that one owner could reach with commonly owned stations) was arbitrary and capricious. That same year, the U.S. Court of Appeals for the D.C. Circuit ruled in *Sinclair Broadcast Group v. FCC* (2002)[188] that the agency had not provided sufficient justification for national and local ownership rules. The result was a review which included the proviso that the FCC re-examine the issue every two years. The group commissioned 12 studies as part of its process. As a result, the FCC revised: (a) local TV multiple ownership rules, (b) the definition of local radio market, and (c) the national ownership limit, increasing it from 35% to 45%. It kept a dual network rule and revised cross-media for radio/TV and newspaper/broadcast holdings.[189]

The day before those new ownership rules were to go into effect, the Third Circuit U.S. Court of Appeals issued an order preventing the FCC from enacting new rules. This decision followed public opposition to further consolidation. In a setback to regulators and broadcasters, the U.S. Court of Appeals for the D.C. Circuit barred the FCC from relaxing ownership rules. Opposition to new rules was spearheaded by FCC Commissioner Michael J. Copps, a Democrat, who held a number of town hall meetings at universities. Another Democrat on the commission, Jonathan Adelstein, was also outspoken in criticism. Opposition included an unusual alliance of interest groups including the National Rifle Association and National Organization of Women. Groups flooded the FCC with letters.

Congress entered the picture in 2004 by amending the 1996 Telecommunications Act to change the national ownership cap from 35% to 39%. The legislature had planned to keep the cap at 35% but upped it to 39% after it discovered that both News Corp. (Fox's owner) and Viacom (which owned CBS and UPN) were already close to the 39% cap.[190] The result was resolution of the controversial ownership rules, but many critics expected one eventual outcome to be additional reform of FCC rules and policies.

Cross-Ownership

For decades, both FCC rules and federal legislation generally prohibited one entity (corporation, individual, or group) from owning both a radio and a television station or both a commercial broadcast station and a daily newspaper in the same market. The commission began easing the first restriction (both a radio and TV station) through various exceptions, and the 1996 Telecommunications Act directed the FCC to be even more liberal.

As you might expect, media owners tended to challenge traditional decision-making on this subject as not doing nearly enough to deregulate media industries seriously hurt by both the declining economy and the impact of so-called new media, still unable to capitalize by virtue of lagging advertising income and hit hard initially by an economic recession. As you might expect, media consolidation opponents argued that loosening the ban went too far. It was noted how the FCC voted on this very complicated matter only days after hundreds of comments were filed—expressing concern that it could not have possibly considered all of those views.

To demonstrate the agency was listening, in 2007, the FCC completed a comprehensive review of rules governing media market ownership in which the traditional "over air" broadcast stations had been competing with cable TV, satellite radio and TV, and via the Internet. The FCC moved to relax its ban on newspaper/broadcast cross-ownership at that time, one that had been in effect for well over 30 years. The older rules banned cross-ownership by a daily newspaper and broadcast station, for example, operating in the same "market." Under the revised rules, the FCC said that it would evaluate proposed cross-ownership combinations on a "case-by-case basis" to determine whether they would promote additional competition, localism, and diversity. In changing its philosophy and policies, the FCC at that time established a complex framework with assumptions distinguishing between the make-up of various media markets and how they might be best structured. In the top 20 markets—the FCC said that it would presume a combination with a major newspaper and a TV station could be a good thing, or in its terminology "in the public interest" if: (1) the TV station was not ranked among the top four stations in that market, and (2) at least eight independently owned major media voices (newspapers and/or full-power TV stations) remain after a proposed transaction concluded. The Commission announced that it would also consider:

- the extent to which the combination will increase the amount of local news in the market;
- whether each media outlet in the combination will exercise independent news judgment;
- the level of already existing media concentration in the market;
- financial condition of newspaper and TV station, and whether a new owner plans to invest in newsroom operations if either media outlet is in financial distress.

These rules do not limit the number of TV stations a single entity may own nationwide, as long as the station's group collectively reaches no more than 39% of the nation with TV households, with UHF channels (14 and above) count less than TV stations on VHF channels (13 and below). The rules prohibit a merger among any two of the more traditional, existing TV networks: ABC, CBS, Fox, and NBC. It allows an entity to own two TV stations in the same market if either (a) the station's service areas do not overlap; or (b) at least one of the stations is not ranked in the top four stations in that market (based on market share), and at least eight independently owned TV stations would remain in the market after the proposed combination.

In terms of local broadcast cross-ownership the rule allows common ownership of up to two TV stations and several radio stations in a market, as long as the combination complies with the local radio and local TV ownership limits. In the largest markets, an entity may own up to two TV stations and six radio stations (or one TV station and seven radio stations). Rules imposes restrictions based on a sliding scale varying by market size: (a) in a radio market with 45 or more stations, an entity may own up to eight radio stations, no more than five may be in the same service (AM or FM); (b) in a radio market with between 30 and 44 radio stations, an entity may own up to seven radio stations, no more than four of which are in the same service; (c) in a radio market with between 15 and 29 radio stations, an entity may own up to six radio stations, no more than four of which are in the same service; and (d) in a radio market with 14 or fewer radio stations, an entity may own up to five radio stations, no more than three of which are in the same service, as long as the entity does not own more than 50% of all stations in that market.

National Ownership Rules

There are more than 1,500 television and 12,000 radio stations in the country. The rules originally restricted ownership to 1 TV, 1 AM, and 1 FM station in the whole country, but they were later eased to include an ownership limit of 12 television stations, 20 FM, and 20 AM radio stations. The 1996 Telecommunications Act substituted the 12-station limit on TV stations for an "audience reach" limit of no more than 35% of national television households. As noted earlier, thanks to the 1994 amendment to the Telecommunications Act, the limit is now 39%. The Act killed the limit on the number of radio stations that can be owned nationally and now allows one entity to own five to eight radio stations in the same market, depending upon the size of the local market. Now in the top markets, up to eight radio stations can have the same owner so long as no more than five are either AM or FM stations. The large radio chain, Clear Channel, former home of shock jock Howard Stern, went from 43 stations to 1,376.[191] Radio ads accounted for almost half of the company's revenue out of a total of $8.6 billion including income from billboards and entertainment.[192]

In the year following the enactment of the Telecommunications Act, a multitude of media mergers and buyouts included: (a) the $6.8 billion Time Warner merger with Turner Broadcasting, resulting in the world's largest media corporation,[193] (b) the purchase of Bell Atlantic by Nynex for $22.1 billion, forming the largest regional telephone company in the country, and (c) the $3.9 billion merger of Westinghouse Electric Corp. and Infinity Broadcasting Corp.[194] Prior to the Act, Walt Disney Co. had bought Capital Cities/ABC for $18.5 billion and Westinghouse had acquired CBS Inc. for $5.4 billion.[195] Capital Cities/ABC owned the ABC television and radio networks and TV and radio stations, magazines, and newspapers. Disney owned part of the ESPN and the A&E cable networks, and produced popular programs on ABC-TV. The merger created one of the largest media and entertainment conglomerates in the world.

Local and Long Distance Telephone Services

After the 1984 breakup of the old American Telephone and Telegraph Co. monopoly by a consent decree (known as the Modified Final Judgment), seven regional companies ("Baby Bells" or Bell Operating Companies—BOCs) emerged. These Baby Bells were restricted to providing local and intrastate phone service. Under the 1996 Telecommunications Act, they were permitted to offer long distance service and video with local telephone companies.[196]

In a $67 billion buyout in 2006, AT&T acquired BellSouth with few regulatory hurdles, illustrating that the once strong concern one company could monopolize an entire industry—which led to the forced breakup of AT&T in 1984—has given way to the idea that bigger may actually be better or at least create more competition. Two years prior to AT&T's purchase of BellSouth, Cingular Wireless had purchased AT&T Wireless for $41 billion, and a year later SBC bought AT&T (not AT&T Wireless) for $16 billion, with the merged company adopting

AT&T rather than SBC as its new name.[197] The new AT&T had 70 million land-line subscribers and 10 million broadband customers with plans to compete with cable and satellite companies in providing video programming.[198]

Satellite Television Rules

Under the Satellite Home Viewer Extension and Reauthorization Act of 2004 (SHVERA),[199] DBS companies (Dish and DirecTV) were allowed to retransmit local broadcast stations in local markets, just as cable companies were able to do for decades. This is known as *local-into-local service*. The Act also required DBS providers to make it possible for subscribers to receive local stations on the same antenna dish as other signals and thus no longer have to erect two antennas, as some subscribers formerly had to do. This Act and other changes in FCC rules leveled the playing field for cable and DBS, although cable subscribers still outnumber DBS subscribers.

Technological Developments

The broadcast regulation picture is in a state of flux in many areas as new technologies are developed and new forms of content are introduced. For several years, Europe and Japan experimented with high-definition television (HDTV), including over-the-air broadcasts. This revolutionary technology, which is also known as advanced television (ATV), is available and still growing in popularity in the United States, thanks to the 1996 Telecommunications Act and the switch from analog to digital, as discussed earlier.

Digital television and high-definition are not the same, although they are intertwined in the U.S. system. Digital television is a means of sending television signals and has actually been available for some time in the United States through satellite TV services such as DirecTV and Dish Network. The traditional means of transmission was analog, what you used to see when you watched over-air and cable.[200]

The United States had been behind other countries in offering digital television because the FCC decided in 1990 that HDTV broadcasts would be "simulcast" so that sets that used analog transmission would not become obsolete, or at least not immediately. Under this initial arrangement, stations broadcast two signals—one analog and the other digital—for consumers with HDTV receivers. Analog color TV sets had only 525 lines per inch rather than the 700-plus lines of systems in other countries. This is because the Commission chose to restrict the color system to a technology that was compatible with existing black-and-white sets rather than choose a system with superior color and picture quality that would render black-and-white sets obsolete. This two-channel format would prevent the newer HDTV technology from being held back by the older format. Only in 1997 did the FCC finally, after delay, finalize the digital standard.[201]

In terms of radio, cognitive radios may eventually enable parties to negotiate for spectrum use on an ad hoc or real-time basis, without the need for prior agreements between all parties."[202] If such an approach were adopted, it could revolutionize the delivery of audio and eventually video services, making traditional broadcast content regulations obsolete and transforming broadcasting as we knew it into a system like the Internet. As the scarcity rationale faded into the sunset, broadcasters requested full First Amendment protection.

The first step in this direction may have begun in the early nineties when United States Satellite Broadcasting (USSB) and Hughes Electronics agreed to build and operate the first direct broadcast satellite (DBS) system, using an 18-inch dish offering more than 100 channels. Thomson Consumer Electronics agreed to manufacture and sell the satellite receivers. Two years later, DirecTV signed agreements with major cable TV services to offer a line-up similar to cable. DirecTV offered complementary rather than competing services using the same satellites. By the middle of that decade new high-power direct satellite services began offering 150 channels of digital TV to consumers who purchased the system.[203] The system is typically offered for free, including installation, with an agreement to purchase a programming package.

DirecTV provides digital television for both residential and commercial customers in the Unied States and Latin America. It has grown exponentially and consistently argued that it should not be subject to FCC regulations in technological areas.[204] DBS became the fastest growing consumer electronics product in history, selling more than 3 million receivers by 1997.[205] DBS services have continued to broaden, including the availability of Internet access. With DSL providers such as AT&T offering discount bundles that include DBS, local and long distance telephone, and broadband access—all in one package for a price less than the total of all services purchased separately—DBS. Cable companies offer similar packages.

One FCC decision that particularly boosted DBS prospects was implementation of a provision in the 1996 Telecommunications Act prohibiting unreasonable restrictions by state and local laws including zoning, building regulations, homeowner association rules, and restrictions when an individual has a direct or indirect property ownership. Government agencies and homeowner associations were allowed to impose guidelines on the placement of antennas. But the guidelines allow the owner to be able to receive direct broadcast satellite service and video programming services such as wireless cable with a dish of up to 1 meter (39 inches) in diameter. In other words, even private homeowner associations can no longer prohibit placement of smaller satellite antennas. Such bans, which were once common, are now generally preempted by the Act and the FCC rules.

Two broadcast television networks also went on the air in the 1990s—Warner Brothers Television Network (WB) and the United Paramount Network (UPN). UPN was owned by CBS Corporation (which is owned by parent Viacom), and WB was owned by Warner Brothers Entertainment (which is owned by parent Time Warner). CBS and Warner Brothers announced that the UPN and WB networks would operate under a joint venture known as the CW.

As with the airline industry when it was deregulated, some telecommunications and media companies did go under in the scramble to compete, but large conglomerates continued to gain a more substantial piece of the pie. No one could have seriously predicted the specific impact of the reform wrought by the 1996 Telecommunications Act. Changes were enormous, with a new age of telecommunications underway. Except for academic critics such as Robert McChesney who offered explanations regarding the impact of changes on democracy, the broader picture was seldom reported, except in business news and growing concerns on partisan reporting.

The issue of vertical integration did attract national press attention following Janet Jackson's Super Bowl "moment," with questions raised about how much control Viacom (CBS) had over content of its subsidiaries. Similar objections are sometimes raised about product placement and lewd themes presented on programs.

Indecent, edgy content is one regulatory challenge facing the FCC as new technologies pro-liferate. Each new technology brings issues. When the agency approved satellite radio, it never envisioned the service would become the home for Howard Stern. When the shock jock—then one of the most visible over-air radio talents—announced he was abandoning his home in favor of satellite, he talked about the move in First Amendment terms—pitching it as a means to avoid government intrusion. The economic "hit" for pay services took later-on considerably altered their financial prospects.

And such a move was not cheap. Listeners paid a monthly fee to receive a package of chan-nels. Decoders were built for use in autos. Major auto manufacturers offer an audio service as factory-installed options in vehicle lines. The day may come when vehicles will include dual band with over-air and satellite as standard equipment.

Internet Neutrality Rules

Initiating new rules in the area of what it termed Internet Neutrality, the FCC adopted on Dec. 21, 2010, "In the matter of preserving the Open Internet Broadband Industry Practices." The almost 200-page order from the FCC on this topic contained several specific provisions. The order noted especially the need for Internet protections and a new level of transparency requir-ing all broadband providers to disclose information about their network management practices, their performance of service and the commercial terms the employed, providing information for consumers to make informed choices regarding the use of their services. [206]

This FCC report and order also established a prohibition by wire-based broadband provid-ers from blocking any legal Web-based content and services requiring broadband providers to allow harmless devices to be connected to their networks. Exemptions on no-blocking rules for mobile broadband carriers included not being able to prohibit providers from blocking some of the Web content and services. It would not limit blocking services that compete with a carriers' voice or video telephony and the new rules barred wired but not mobile broadband providers from unreasonable discrimination against legal network traffic. Specialized services were ini-tially exempt from these rules.

Any commercial agreements between broadband providers and other companies allowing types of Web traffic was said to likely violate the prohibition on unreasonable discrimination. Those types of agreements would raise cause for concern and possibly harm innovation and overall investment in the Internet. The report said broadband customers and providers of Web applications and services would be able to file informal complaints through the FCC's website without paying a fee and that others can also file formal complaints after notifying the provider.

The FCC added that it would permit requests for expedited action on any complaints that were issued. In making all of this clear to the public, the FCC also announced it would monitor the mobile broadband industry for signs of any anti-consumer behavior or instances in which some providers might hurt the prospects for the Internet by acting in an anti-competitive way.

Summary and Conclusions

For nearly 10 decades, broadcasting has been regulated as a limited public resource. Space on the broadcast spectrum has been occupied by those required to serve "the public interest, convenience and necessity." The governing body in this regulatory scheme has been the Federal Communications Commission since the Communications Act of 1934. The commission has taken different approaches at different times toward regulating broadcasting and telecommunications from extensive regulation to deregulation. Much of the movement, however, has been in the direction of providing marketplace incentives for competition. The Telecommunications Act of 1996 provided incentives by allowing forms of broadcasting and telecommunications to begin to compete on a level playing field.

Broadcast programming is another area where deregulation took hold, as reflected in the FCC's abandonment of the Fairness Doctrine, which Congress sometimes threatens to revive through codification, so far to no avail. It appears that for the future, the agency will continue to enforce the equal opportunity rules and political programming regulations unless the U.S. Supreme Court declares the scarcity rationale invalid for imposing greater First Amendment restrictions. That scenario appears unlikely although breaches of good taste in over-air network programming and resultant public fall-out have encouraged a recasting of the FCC's position.

The one area of programming for both cable and broadcasting where the FCC has tightened the reins is indecency, whose regulation has support from Congress, the executive branch, and especially the public. Although the *ACLU v. Reno* (1997)[207] decision, as discussed later in Chapter 9, struck down the indecency provisions of the Communications Decency Act of 1996 as they applied to the Internet, the U.S. Supreme Court decision by no means affected the regulation of indecency in broadcasting and other forms of telecommunications.

Newer technologies are changing not only the technology of broadcast and telecommunications, but also forcing a rethinking of the entire regulatory scheme. Individualized media including "Cognitive" or "smart" radio may also force a rethinking of approaches to assigning the radio frequency spectrum. For the short term, the FCC may continue to be challenged by the public's unhappiness with what it sees and hears as the agency expands its efforts to target developing areas for evaluation. Viewers have often tended to be more offended by bad language on TV than by depictions of bad behavior including nudity, and violence A new strain of criticism has focused on the political extremes represented by cable news networks such as FOX and MSNBC which provide a continuing coverage from partisan perspectives.[208] Concerns may continue to be addressed so long as some of the vestiges of a scarcity rationale receive the blessing of the FCC, the courts, and the executive branch, but new regulatory models reflective of the growth of the Internet are also likely to further emerge in the long term.

Endnotes

1. Quoted in *Is "Family Guy" Creator Seth Macfarlane Taunting the FCC? Joe Flint, Company Town: The Business behind the Show*, Washington Post, May 4, 2010.
2. Cecilia Kang, *FCC Chairman Genachowski Expected to Leave Broadband Services Deregulated*, Washington Post, May 3, 2010, and Jim Puzzanghera, *'Net Neutrality' Wins Approval from FCC*, St. Louis Post-Dispatch, December 22, 2010.
3. See Anna Marie Cox, *Howard Stern and the Satellite Wars*, Wired, Mar. 2005, at 133; Betsy Streisand, *Radio Shock Waves: Satellite Versions Hope to Attract Listeners with High-Voltage, Distinctive Line-up*, U.S. News & World Report, Feb. 14, 2005 at 50.
4. *See More TV Coming to Your Cell Phone*, Las Vegas (Nev.) Review-Journal (Orange County Register), May 14, 2005, at B10; *Space Race*, Fortune, May 16, 2005, at 42; and David Sheets, *Limbaugh Joins the Ranks of the Podcasters*, St. Louis (Mo.) Post-Dispatch, May 18, 2005, at A28.

5. *Turner Broadcasting System, Inc. v. Federal Communications Commission*, 520 U.S. 180, 117 S.Ct. 1174, 137 L.Ed. 369, 25 Med.L.Rptr. 1449 (1997).

6. *See* Jerry Kang, *Communications Law and Policy: Cases and Materials*, 8–10 (2nd ed., 2005) for an explanation of electro-magnetic waves.

7. *See* W. D. Sloan and J .D. Startt, *The Media in America: A History*, 417–418 (6th ed., 2005).

8. *Id.*

9. J. E. Kraft, Frederic R. Leigh, and D. Godfrey, *Electronic Media*, 21 (2001).

10. *Id.*

11. *National Broadcasting Co. (NBC) v. United States*, 319 U.S. 190, 63 S.Ct. 997, 87 L.Ed. 1344, 1 Med.L.Rptr. 1965 (1943).

12. *Id.*

13. Broadcast frequencies are now measured in hertz (kilo-, mega-, giga-, etc.), the international unit for cycles per second, in honor of Heinrich Hertz, discussed earlier. Until the early 1990s, the designation was simply cycles per second (kilocycles, megacycles).

14. *See World Radio and TV Handbook 2006*, 406 (60th ed., 2005).

15. *See* D. Copeland and D. Hatcher, *Mass Communication in the Global Age*, 188 (2004).

16. J.E. Kraft, Frederic R. Leigh, and D. Godfrey, *Electronic Media*, 21 (2001).

17. *NBC v. U.S.*

18. *Hoover v. Intercity Radio Co.*, 52 App.D.C. 339, 286 F. 1003 (1925), cited in *NBC v. U.S.*

19. *United States v. Zenith Radio Corp.*, 12 F.2d 614 (1926), cited in *NBC v. U.S.*

20 35 Ops. Atty. Gen. 126 (1926), cited in *NBC v. U.S.*

21. *NBC v. U.S.*

22. *Id.*

23. 47 U.S.C. §154(a).

24. 47 U.S.C. §151(a).

25. 47 U.S.C. §307.

26. *NBC v. U.S.*

27. 47 U.S.C. §307(a). *See also NBC v. U.S.*

28. Low-power television has actually been available since 1956 but under the guise of satellite or translator stations that simply retransmitted the signal of an existing full-power station to increase or improve the coverage area of the originating station.

29. FCC Public Notice DA 06-123 (Jan. 26, 2006), Announcement of Filing Window for LPTV and TV Translator Digital Companion Channel Applications from May 1, 2006 through May 12, 2006 (Report AUC-06-85-A, Auction 85).

30. *See Low Power Television (LPTV) Service* on the FCC website at http://www.fcc.gov/cgb/ consumerfacts/lptv.html.

31. *See Low Power FM Radio (LPFM)* on the FCC website at http://www.fcc.gov/cgb/consumerfacts/lpfm.html.

32. *Id.*

33. Mathew Rodriquez, *Moyers Articulates His Growing Concern with Less Access to Government Records*, Quill, Oct./Nov. 2004, at 10.

34. 47 U.S.C. §326.

35. 47 U.S.C. §315(9).

36. *Flory v. FCC*, 528 F.2d 124 (7th Cir. 1975).

37. 60 F.C.C.2d 615 (1976).

38. FCC, *The Law of Political Broadcasting and Cablecasting: A Political Primer* (1984 FCC *Primer*) at 5. See also FCC Acts on Petition, Report. MM 99-12, (Sept. 8, 1999), unofficial announcement of commission action and *MCI v. FCC*, 515 F 2d 385 (D.C. Cir. 1974).

39. *Id.* at 7.

40. *Sen. Eugene J. McCarthy*, 11 F.C.C. 2d 511, 1 Med.L.Rptr. 2205 (1968); *aff'd*, 390 F.2d 471(D.C. Cir. 1968).

41. *Socialist Workers Party*, 39 F.C.C.2d 89 (1972).

42. *Red Lion Broadcasting v. FCC* and *U.S. v. Radio Television News Directors' Association*, 395 U.S. 367, 89 S.Ct.1794, 23 L.Ed.2d 371, 1 Med.L.Rptr. 2053 (1969).

43. *Adrian Weiss* (Ronald Reagan Films), 58 F.C.C.2d 342 (1976); *review denied,* 58 F.C.C.2d 1389 (1976).

44. *Mutual Film Corp. v. Industrial Commission of Ohio*, 236 U.S. 230, 35 S.Ct. 387, 59 L.Ed. 552 (1915); *Joseph Burstyn, Inc. v. Wilson*, 343 U.S. 495 (1952).

45. *Petition of Aspen Institute and CBS, Inc.,* 55 F.C.C. 2d 697 (1975); *aff'd sub nom., Chisholm et al. v. FCC,* 538 F.2d 349 (D.C. Cir., 1976), 1 Med.L.Rptr. 2207; *cert. denied,* 429 U.S. 890, 97 S.Ct. 247, 50 L.Ed.2d 173 (1976).

46. *Chisholm et al. v. FCC,* 1 Med.L.Rptr. 2220.

47. *Henry Geller,* 95 F.C.C.2d 1236 (1983); *aff'd sub nom., League of Women Voters v. FCC,* 731 F.2d 995 (1984).

48. *Id.*

49. *Id.*

50. *Id.*

51. *Telecommunications Research and Action Center v. FCC*, 801 F.2d 501 (D.C Cir. 1986), cert. denied, 482 U.S. 919 (1987).

52. *Meredith Corp. v. FCC*, 809 F.2d 63 (D.C. Cir. 1987).

53. Socialist Workers Party, 26 F.C.C.2d 485 (1970).

54. FCC, 1984 Primer, at 36.

55. 47 C.F.R. §73.1940(d).

56. *Norman William Seemann*, Esq., 40 F.C.C. 341 (1962).

57. 47 C.F.R. §73.1940(e).

58. *Id.*

59. *Syracuse Peace Council v. FCC*, 867 F. 2d 654 (D.C. Cir., 1989); *cert. denied*, 493 U.S. 1019 (1990). *See also Kansas AFL-CIO v. FCC*, 11 F.3d 1430 (8th Cir. 1993).

60. *Id.*

61. FCC Report MM-319, *Mass Media Action,* Mar. 24, 1988.

62. *Pacifica Foundation, Inc.*, 2 F.C.C.R. 2698 (1987); *Regents of the University of California*, 2 F.C.C.R. 2703 (1987).

63. 47 U.S.C. §312(a)(7).

64. *Rockefeller for Governor Campaign (WAJR),* 59 F.C.C.2d 646 (1976).

65. *W. Roy Smith,* 18 F.C.C.2d 747 (1969).

66. *Dan Walker (WMAQ),* 57 F.C.C.2d 799 (1975).

67. *Branch v. FCC,* 824 F.2d 37 (D.C. Cir. 1987), 14 Med.L.Rptr. 1465; *cert. denied,* 485 U.S. 959, 108 S.Ct. 1220, 99 L.Ed.2d 421 (1988).

68. *Id.*

69. *Id.*

70. 47 C.F.R. §73.1942 (2006) (candidate rates).

71. 47 C.F.R. §76.205–206 (cable television) and 47 C.F.R. §25.701 (direct broadcast satellite) (2006).

72. Codification of the Commission's Political Programming Policies, 7 F.C.C.R. 678 (1991); Gross, *New Political Programming Policies of the FCC,* 10 Com. Law 3 (Fall 1992).

73. *Farmers' Educational and Cooperative Union v. WDAY,* 360 U.S. 525, 79 S.Ct. 1302, 3 L.Ed. 1407 (1959).

74. *Id.*

75. *Id.*

76. *Id.*

77. *Atlanta NAACP,* 36 F.C.C.2d 635 (1972); M. Murray, *J.B. Stoner and Free Speech: How Free Is Free?* Western Communication Journal, Winter 1974, at 18.

78. *Brandenburg v. Ohio,* 395 U.S. 444, 89 S.Ct. 1827, 23 L.Ed.2d. 430 (1969).

79. *Atlanta NAACP.*

80. FCC, *1984 Primer,* at 44.

81. *In the Matter of Petition for Declaratory Ruling Concerning Section 312(a)(7) of the Communications Act.*

82. FCC Memorandum and Opinion Order 94-249 (1994).

83. *Television Stations Must Run, But May Reschedule, Graphic Anti-Abortion Political Advertisements,* News Media & Law (Winter 1995), at 35.

84. *Becker et al. v. FCC,* 95 F.3d 75 (D.C. Cir. 1996).

85. *Id.*

86. *Id.*

87. 47 C.F.R. §73.123(c).

88. *Radio–Television News Directors Association v. FCC,* 299 F.3d 269, 28 Med.L.Rptr. 2465. *(D.C. Cir. 2000).*

88. Pub. L. 86-274, 73 Stat. 557 (1959).

90. Red Lion Broadcasting v. FCC and U.S. v. Radio Television News Directors' Association, 395. U.S. 367, 89 S.Ct. 1794, 23 L.Ed.2d 371, 1 Med.L.Rptr. 2053 (1969).

91. *Id.*

92. *Id.*

93. Syracuse Peace Council, 99 F.C.C.2d 1389 (1984); recon. denied, 59 R.R.2d (P&F) 179 (1985); remanded sub nom., *Meredith Corp. v. FCC,* 809 F.2d 863 (D.C. Cir. 1987); *Syracuse Peace Council et. al v. FCC,* 867 F.2d 654, 16 Med.L.Rptr. 1225 (1989).

94. *Report Concerning General Fairness Doctrine Obligations of Broadcast Licensees,* 102 F.C.C.2d 143 (1985).

95. *Radio Television News Directors' Association v. FCC,* 809 F.2d 860 and Meredith Corp. v. FCC, 809 F.2d 863 (D.C. Cir. 1987).

96. *FCC Ends Enforcement of Fairness Doctrine, Report MM-265,* Aug. 4, 1987. Memorandum Opinion and Order (FCC 87-266).

97. *FCC Reaffirms Decision to End Enforcement of Fairness Doctrine; Denies Various Requests for Reconsideration, Report MM-319,* Mar. 24, 1988; Memorandum Opinion and Order (FCC 88-131).

98. Syracuse Peace Council v. FCC (consolidated with *Geller v. FCC*), 867 F.2d 654 (D.C. Cir. 1989).

99. *See* Celia King, *FCC removes Fairness Doctrine from the books,* Washington Post, online at http://www. washingtonpost.com/blogs/post-tech/post/fcc-removes-fairness-doctrine-from-the-books/2011/08/22/ gIQAwHwsWJ_blog.html; Shannon Bream, *Opponents Praise End of FCC's Fairness Doctrine, but Some Worry About Similar Tactics,* June 9, 2011, FoxNews.com online at: http://www.foxnews.com/ politics/2011/06/09/death-sentence-for-fairness-doctrine/; and Zara Golden, FCC *Kills Off Outdated 'Fairness Doctrine' Once And For All,* Mediaite, August 22, 2011, at http://www.mediaite.com/online/ fcc-kills-off-outdated-fairness-doctrine- once-and-for-all/.

100. Radio Act of 1927, §29.

101. Communications Act of 1934, §326.

102. U.S. Criminal Code, 18 U.S.C. §1464.

103. National Association of Broadcasters, *Broadcast Regulation 89: A Mid-Year Report,* 102 (1989).

104. *Id.*

105. *Sonderling Broadcasting Corp. (WGLD-FM),* 27 R.R.2d 285 (F.C.C. 1973); *reaff'd,* 41 F.C.C. 777, 27 R.R.2d 1508 (1973).

106. *Id.*

107. *Illinois Citizens Committee for Broadcasting v. FCC,* 515 F.2d 397, 31 R.R.2d 1523 (D.C. Cir. 1974).

108. National Association of Broadcasters, at 103.

109. *Pacifica Foundation,* 56 F.C.C.2d 94 (1975).

110. *Pacifica Foundation v. FCC,* 556 F.2d 9 (D.C. Cir. 1979).

111. *FCC v. Pacifica Foundation,* 438 U.S. 726, 98 S.Ct. 3026, 57 L.Ed.2d 1073, 3 Med.L.Rptr. 2553 (1978).

112. *Id.*

113. For the curious, the words that will "curve your spine, grow hair on your hands and maybe even bring us ... peace without honor ... and a bourbon," according to Carlin, are *shit, piss, fuck, cunt, cocksucker, motherfucker,* and *tits.* References to *shit* and *fuck* comprise a major portion of the 12-minute skit.

114. Paul Farhi, *War of the Worlds,* The Washington Post Magazine, May 21, 1995, at 12.

115. John Podhoretz, *More Than a Jerk,* New York Post, July 2, 2004, at 31.

116. *Complaints against Various Broadcast Licensees Regarding Their Airing of the "Golden Globe Awards" Program,* 19 F.C.C.R. 4975 (2004).

117. Amy Schatz, *FCC Loses another Indecency Case*, Wall Street Journal, January 5, 2011, at A-1.

118. *Complaints against Various Television Licensees Regarding Their Broadcast of the Fox Television Network Program "Married By America" on April 7, 2003,* 19 F.C.C.R. 20191 (2004).

119. *Complaints Against Various Television Licensees Regarding Their Broadcast November 11, 2004 of the ABC Television Network's Presentation of the Film "Saving Private Ryan,"* 20 F.C.C.R. 4516 (2005).

120. *Complaints Against Various Television Licensees Regarding the ABC Television Network's November 15, 2004 Broadcast of "Monday Night Football,"* 20 F.C.C.R. 5481 (2005).

121. Interview with Sirius XM Radio CEO Mel Karmazin, *Charlie Rose Show*, Public Broadcasting Service, December 31, 2009.

122. *Fox Television Stations, Inc. v. FCC*, 2007 U.S. App. LEXIS 12868 (2nd Cir. 2007). *In the Matter of Various Complaints Regarding CNN's Airing of the 2004 Democratic National Convention,* 20 F.C.C.R. 6070 (2005); *In the Matter of Various Complaints against the Cable/Satellite Television Program "Nip/Tuck,"* 20 F.C.C.R. 4255 (2005). . *Graves v. Warner Brothers,* 253 Mich. App. 486, 656 N.W.2d 195 (2002).

123. *Hearst, Direct TV Reach Deal on Programming Fees,* Associated press, December 30, 2010; 5:42 pm. Fifty Years in Communications (1984), at 30.

124. Pauline Arrillaga and Amanda Lee Myers, *Suspect Charged in Mass Shooting, Painted Himself into a Dark Social Corner, ,* New York Times, January 10, 2011, at A-1. WGBH Foundation, 69 F.C.C.2d 1250, 43 R.R.2d 1436 (1978). New Indecency Enforcement Standards to be Applied to All Broadcast and Amateur Licenses, 2 F.C.C.R.2726, 62 R.R.2d 1218 (1987).

125. *Hearst, Direct TV Reach Deal on Programming Fees, Associated Press,* December 30, 2010; 5:42 pm.

126. Matter of David Hildebrand, 2 F.C.C.R. 2708, 2712 n. 9, 62 R.R.2d 1208, 1209–1210, n. 12 (1987). The FCC revoked the license even though the record showed there were only 66 hams under 17 in the whole Los Angeles area. See Feldman, The FCC and Regulation of Broadcast Indecency: Is there a National Broadcast Standard in the Audience? 41 Fed. Com. L. J. 369, at n. 69.

127. *Pacifica Foundation,* 2 F.C.C.R. 2698, 62 R.R.2d 1191 (1987). The U.S. Department of Justice has primary responsibility for enforcing Section 464 for specific violations, while the FCC can use violations in revoking or refusing to renew a broadcast license.

128. *Regents of the University of California,* 2 F.C.C.R. 2703, 62 R.R.2d 1199 (1987). *Infinity Broadcasting Corp. of Pennsylvania,* 2 F.C.C.R. 2705, 62 R.R.2d 1202 (1987).

129. *Raunch Radio Stirs Debate,* Gannetteer, July–Aug. 1987, at 14.

130. *More Competition Is Goal of Sikes as Head of FCC,* St. Louis Post Dispatch, Aug. 8, 1989.

131. *See Indecency, "Marketplace" Issues Dominate FCC Confirmation Scene,* Television/Radio Age, Aug. 7, 1989, at 12.

132. *Infinity Broadcasting,* 2 F.C.C.R. 2705 (1987).

133. Quoted in *Perspectives* (Overheard), Newsweek, May 4, 1987, at 17.

134. *Infinity Broadcasting Corp. of Pennsylvania* (Reconsideration Order), 3 F.C.C.R. 930, 64 R.R.2d 211 (1987).

135. *Miller v. California* (1973), 413 U.S. 15, 93 S.Ct. 2607, 37 L.Ed.2d 419, 1 Med.L.Rptr. 1409 (1973).

136. *Infinity Broadcasting* at 933.

137. *Id.*

138. *Action for Children's Television v. FCC (ACT I).* 852 F.2d 1332, 65 R.R.2d 45, 15 Med. L.Rptr. 1907 (D.C. Cir. 1988).

139. Lexington (Ky.) Herald-Leader (Associated Press), Jan. 13, 1988, at A1.

140. Cincinnati Post (Associated Press), June 23, 1988, at A12.

141. *ACT I.*

142. *Id.*

143. *FCC Fines Two South Florida Stations for Indecency,* The Brechner Report, Nov. 1989, at 1.

144. Interview on National Public Radio's All Things Considered newscast, July 15, 1990.

145. *Id.*

146. *Action for Children's Television v. FCC (ACT II),* 932 F.2d 1504, 18 Med.L.Rptr. 2153 (D.C. Cir. 1991), cert. denied, 503 U.S. 913, 112 S.Ct. 1281, 117 L.Ed.2d 507 (1992).

147. *Interview,* 8 Com. Law 21, No. 1 (1990).

148. *Id.*

149. *Sable Communications of California Inc. v. FCC,* 492 U.S. 115, 109 S.Ct. 2829, 106 L.Ed.2d 93, 16 Med.L.Rptr. 1961 (1989).

150. Public Telecommunications Act of 1992, 106 Stat. 949, 954.

151. *Action for Children's Television v. FCC,* 11 F.3d 170 (D.C. Cir. 1993).

152. *Action for Children's Television v. FCC (ACT III),* 58 F.3d 654 (D.C. Cir. *en banc* 1995).

153. *Action for Children's Television v. FCC (ACT IV),* 59 F.3d 1249 (D.C. Cir. *en banc* 1995).

154. 47 U.S.C. §641(a).

155. Pub. L. 102-385 (1992).

156. *Denver Area Educational Telecommunications Consortium, Inc. et al. v. Federal Communications Commission et al.,* 518 U.S. 737, 116 S.Ct. 2374, 135 L.Ed.2d 888 (1996).

157. *Americans' Concern Rising over TV Violence, Poll Says,* Lexington (Ky.) Herald-Leader (Wire Services), Dec. 18, 1993, at A6.

158. *4 Networks Hire UCLA Group to Monitor Violence on TV,* Lexington (Ky.) Herald-Leader (Knight-Ridder News Service), June 30, 1994, at A5.

159. J. Tranquada, *Violence Debate Simmers While Studies Conducted,* Lexington (Ky.) Herald-Leader (Los Angeles Daily News), Aug. 2, 1994, at Today-11.

160. Larry Williams, *Biff! Pow! TV Rating System Not Working as Planned,* Lexington (Ky.) Herald-Leader (Knight-Ridder Washington Bureau), Mar. 27, 1997, at A3.

161. 47 U.S.C. §§303(w) and 303(x). Public Telecommunications Act of 1993 §16(a), Pub. L. 102-356, 106 Stat. 949.

162. Elizabeth Jensen, *NPR Executive who fired Juan Williams Resigns,* New York Times, January 6, 2011, at A-1.

163. Program Standards (Family Viewing Considerations), NAB Television Code (1978).

164. Jake Stump, *Changes Ahead for Children's TV: FCC to Review 1990 Programming Law,* Charleston (W.V.) Daily Mail, July 24, 2009.

165. Policies and Rules Concerning Children's Television, MM Docket 93-48. *Also* Children's Television Obligations of Digital Television Broadcasters, 19 FCC Rcd 22943 (2004).

166. *In the Matter of Children's Television Obligations of Digital Television Broadcasters,* 19 F.C.C.R. 22997 (2004).

167. Jake Stump, *Changes Ahead for Children's TV: FCC to review 1990 programming law,* Charleston (WV) Daily Mail, July 24, 2009, at 5-A, and also *The Cartoons Are Coming!* Editorial, Las Vegas Review-Journal, September 16, 2010, at 6-B.

168. FCC: Broadcasting and Cable Television 11 (1988).

169. Tom Shales, *The Great American Cable Tangle* (Outlook), The Washington Post, June 10, 1990, at C1.

170. Hobson, *Does the 1984 Cable Act Franchise 'Video Programming'?* 8 Com. L. 3, (1990).

171. Cable Communications Policy Act of 1984, Pub.L. 98-549, 98 Stat. 2779, 47 U.S.C. §521–559.

172. Cable Television Consumer Protection and Competition Act of 1992, Pub. L. 102-385, 106 Stat. 1460, 47 U.S.C. §§325, 521, 534, 535, 543, and 548.

173. *Turner Broadcasting System, Inc. v. FCC,* 819 F.Supp. 32 (D.C. Cir. 1993).

174. *United States v. O'Brien,* 391 U.S. 367, 88 S.Ct. 1673, 20 L.Ed.2d 672 (1968).

175. *Turner Broadcasting System, Inc. v. FCC (Turner I),* 512 U.S. 622, 114 S.Ct. 2445, 129 L.Ed.2d 497 (1994).

176. Wall Street Journal, June 14, 1994, at A15.

177. *Turner I* (1994).

178. *Turner Broadcasting System, Inc. v. FCC (Turner II),* 520 U.S. 180, 117 S.Ct. 1174, 137 L.Ed.2d 369, 25 Med.L.Rptr. 1449 (1997).

179. *United Video Inc. v. FCC,* 800 F.2d 1173, 66 R.R.2d 1865 (D.C. Cir. 1989).

180. *Quincy Cable TV, Inc. v. FCC,* 768 F.2d 1434 (D.C. Cir. 1985); *cert. denied,* 476 U.S. 1169, 106 S.Ct. 2889, 90 L.Ed.2d 977 (1986).

181. *Century Communications Corp. v. FCC,* 835 F.2d 292 (D.C. Cir. 1987); *clarified,* 837 F.2d 517 (D.C. Cir. 1988); *cert. denied,* 486 U.S. 1032, 108 S.Ct. 2014, 100 L.Ed.2d 602 (1988).

182. *Daniels Cablevision, Inc. v. United States,* 835 F.Supp. 1 (D.C. Cir. 1993).

183. Anne Broache, *Early 2009 Set for End of Analog TV,* cnet news.com, retrieved March 1, 2006, from http://news.com.
184. *Id.*
185. *Fox Television Stations v. FCC,* 280 F.3d 1027 (D.C. Cir. 2002).
186. *Sinclair Broadcast Group v. FCC,* 284 F.3d 148 (D.C. Cir. 2002).
187. *2003 Biennial Review,* 18 F.C.C.R. 13620 (2003), *rev'd and remanded, Prometheus Radio Project v. FCC,* 373 F.3d 372 (3rd Cir. 2004).
188. Consolidated Appropriations Act of 2004, Pub. L. 108-199, §325, 118 Stat. 3, §99.
189. John Eggerton, *Broadcasters Weigh In on FCC's 2007 Media Ownership Rule Revision: Deadline for Briefs in Third Circuit Bourt's Hearing Arrives,* Broadcasting & Cable, May 17, 2010.
190. *Id.*
191. Skip Wollenberg, *Turner-Time Warner Deal Backed,* Lexington (Ky.) Herald-Leader (Associated Press), Sept. 13, 1996, at C9.
192. *FCC OKs Westinghouse, Infinity Radio Deal,* Lexington (Ky.) Herald-Leader (Wire Services), Dec. 27, 1996, at C8.
193. Neil Hickey, *So Big: The Telecommunications Act at Year One,* Columbia Journalism Review, Jan-Feb. 1997, at 23.
194. Richard E. Wiley, *Developments in Communication Law,* in 2 Communications Law 114 (1997).
195. Satellite Home Viewer Extension and Reauthorization Act of 2004 *(SHVERA),* Title IX, Consolidated Appropriations Act of 2005 (H.R. 4818).
196. *Id.*
197. Jim Motavalli, *HD Radio: Is it the Auto Industry's Next Big Thing?* Mother Nature Network, January, 4, 2011.
198. Todd Spangler, DirecTV: Leave our Set-Top Out of It, Newsline, December 21, 2009, at 32-A.
199. Georg Szalai, *Top TV Execs Debate Retransmission Consent Changes in D.C.,* HollywoodReporter.com, November 17, 2010.
200. *In the Matter of Facilitating Opportunities for Flexible, Efficient, and Reliable Spectrum Use Employing Cognitive Radio Technologies,* 20 F.C.C.R. 5486 (2005).
201. Jay Hylsky, *DSS: Past, Present and Future,* Satellite Direct, Dec. 1997, at 30.
202. See Georg Szalai, *Malone: DirecTV Flying High,* HollywoodReporter.com, June 4, 2008.
203. Todd Spangler, *DirecTV: Leave our Set-Top Out of It,* Newsline, December 21, 2009, at 32-A.
204. *Id.*
205. Joe Flint, *Internet Issues Bog down Comcast-NBS Merger,* Los Angeles Times, December 10, 2010, at 1-B.
206. *Reno et al. v. American Civil Liberties Union et al.,* 521 U.S. 844, 117 S.Ct. 2329, 138 L.Ed.2d 874.
207. Vincent Carroll, *Bully in the Free Speech Debate,* Denver Post, November 20, 2010, at B-11;
208. *What can we Say?* Editorial, Investor's Daily, November 19, 2010, at A-12.; and John Eggerton, *Rassmussen Poll Finds Little Support for Net Regs,* Broadcasting & Cable, December 28, 2010 at 10.

8

Libel

The chilling effect is gone. The SPEECH Act says, "Go ahead and publish whatever you find is important."

—Rachel Ehrenfeld, quoted in "SPEECH act Protects Against Libel Tourism," *The News Media & the Law* (Fall, 2010, p. 21)

The most basic tenets of newsgathering come under fire and sometimes appear to be "up for grabs" in defamation cases, especially when key elements of reporting—as in who said what to whom—come under critical scrutiny. In addition, frequently it is the most prominent members of society—public officials and public figures—who sue media defendants for libel. Complicating things is the new technology that has expanded the context—the platform, the scope, and the prospects for such charges.

One breath of fresh air in this area arrived in August, 2010 when President Barrack Obama signed legislation, known as the SPEECH ACT (Securing the Protection of our Enduring and Established Constitutional Heritage) protecting writers from Britain's libel laws. This was regarded as a response to a suit involving American academic Dr. Rachel Ehrenfeld sued by a businessman on grounds that her book, *Funding Evil*, libeled him.

While the frequency of defamation and privacy lawsuits has reached an all time low in the United States, as new media and social networking opportunities continue to emerge and evolve, many experts anticipate additional related, legal challenges via online venues. This is because of the growing attention such cases received. The first instance in which a well-known person was accused of slandering someone over the popular micro-blog network Twitter arrived in 2009. Courtney Michelle Love, the widow of the rock group Nirvana's leader Kurt Cobain, was sued by her former fashion designer for allegedly defaming her. Love had written about Dawn Simorangkir, on both Twitter and MySpace and in a libel suit filed in Los Angeles Superior Court, the Austin, Texas, based fashion designer claimed that Love had used Twitter to disseminate "an obsessive and delusional crusade" of malicious libel against her in multiple public forums. These included online marketplaces where Simorangkir conducted business. In court documents Simorangkir of the "Boudoir Queen" clothing line, claimed that Courtney

Michelle Love had also libeled her on her MySpace page. The designer alleged that Love had commissioned her initially to create clothing but then balked when invoiced to pay for the work created on her behalf. The case alleged that Love had subsequently sought retribution against the fashion designer.

Earlier in that same decade, Courtney Love had been involved in other legal disputes. These revolved around her alleged failure to meet contractual obligations to Geffen/Universal on the number of albums she was contracted to produce, but litigation also involved, to some extent, her own group's public image—and later, specifically, the ownership and control of Nirvana L.L.C. assets and the highly anticipated release of the group's last song "You Know Your Right." After the death of lead singer Kurt Cobain, Love and the group's former band members, Dave Grohl and Krist Novoselic, fought over ownership of that work. Love's own band Hole, had been involved in a lawsuit with Geffen/Universal, taking the position that Universal Music Group obtained Geffen after Love signed her contract with them. When Nirvana's last song was recorded in January of 1994, just a few months before Cobain died, Love maintained that her creative partner was the singular vision of the rock group Nirvana. When an agreement was reached in 2002 the song spent four weeks at number one and the album containing it, once it was released, also did well, starting out in the top ten.

As part of a settlement in the first case, musician and actress Courtney Love agreed to start paying what her attorney described as a "modest settlement" amounting to $430,000 to Dawn Simorangkir in March 2011. If the case had gone to trial it would have been the first involving a high-profile celebrity regarding statements posted on social media, but Love's attorney concluded "I think everybody decided enough is enough." The representative for the fashion designer noted that this was not a groundbreaking case, but one that sent a message to be careful what you say online because you are not exempt from legal exposure just because you use social media.[1]

In another case, involving another west coast celebrity, a BBC-TV presenter (a role roughly equivalent to TV anchor in the United States), Anna Richardson, sued former California Governor Arnold Schwarzenegger and two of his political aides in 2005 for comments they made regarding her charge that the former movie actor groped her years before. Richardson claimed the three tried to ruin her reputation by dismissing her assertions that Schwarzenegger had touched her inappropriately at a press event and alleging that she had encouraged this behavior. Making the claim even more compelling as a libel case was the fact that the story was reported on the Internet, placing it in an international context. Jurisdictional questions arose over whether Schwarzenegger could be a defendant in a British court case, because Richardson also made the claim that she was libeled in an online article in the *Los Angeles Times*. A British appeal court ruled the governor's spokesperson could be served with libel proceedings abroad, so the case raised the specter of well-known figures embroiled in an international dispute involving their good names, brought about in part through online venues.[2]

The next month MSNBC's Joe Scarborough lambasted Schwarzenegger on his program, saying: "You know, this guy has been in so much trouble. He's got sagging poll numbers. He's got political groups criticizing his every move. And now the governator is making all his enemies' job easier. According to the *London Evening Standard*, Arnold recently went on Howard Stern's radio show and offered his theory on how to end premenstrual syndrome, saying: 'If we get rid of the moon, womens [sic], whose menstrual cycles are governed by the moon, will not get PMS. They will stop bitching and whining.'" The problem from a reporting and ethical point of view was that Schwarzenegger made no such statements. *Washington Post* columnist Anne Schroeder followed up by noting an impersonator on the Stern radio program apparently said those things. She encouraged Scarborough to clarify the mistake. The governor's spokesperson called on news outlets to perform due diligence in the sourcing of information.[3]

A month later, former New York Governor Mario Cuomo settled a $15 million libel suit he initiated against the author and publisher of a book, *The Best Democracy Money Can Buy*. The book's author, Greg Palast, and the publisher, Plume, a unit of Penguin Putnam Inc., were named in the suit. The book alleged that Cuomo had improperly influenced a federal judge, convincing the judge to toss out a verdict against a utility company that allegedly lied about the cost of a nuclear power plant it wanted to build. In the end, the author wrote a letter to Cuomo clarifying his meaning.[4]

In another instance involving celebrity status that began as a California state law defamation action, famed O. J. Simpson attorney Johnnie L. Cochran, Jr. sued a former client and others who, according to the state trial court, falsely claimed that Cochran owed the client money. The defendants also picketed Cochran's office with signs that Cochran claimed included insulting and defamatory statements. Before he died, Cochran also alleged that picketers chased him while chanting threats and insults, all aimed at forcing him to pay the former client money to stop the activities. Without a court order, every indication was that this behavior would continue.

The trial court granted Cochran's request for a permanent injunction against former clients Ulysses Tory and Ruth Craft, banning such picketing as well as ordering the defendants to stop making oral statements about the lawyer and his law firm in any public setting. The California Court of Appeal affirmed the trial court decision. The U.S. Supreme Court granted certiorari and heard oral arguments in March 2005. One week later, Cochran died. At Cochran's attorney's request, Cochran's widow was then substituted as the respondent in the case. In *Tory v. Cochran* (2005),[5] the U.S. Supreme Court ruled 7 to 2 that Cochran's death did not make the case moot because the injunction remained in effect under state law until a court overturned it. The Court went on to note that Cochran's death negated any need to rule on any basic First Amendment issues in the case. The Court said:

> Rather, we need only point out that the injunction, as written, has now lost its underlying rationale. Since picketing Cochran and his law offices while engaging in injunction-forbidden speech could no longer achieve the objectives that the trial court had in mind (*i.e.*, coercing Cochran to pay a "tribute" for desisting in this activity), the grounds for the injunction are much diminished, if they have not disappeared altogether. Consequently the injunction, as written, now amounts to an overly broad prior restraint upon speech, lacking plausible justification.[6]

Some First Amendment supporters hoped that the Supreme Court would rule against Cochran on the ground that prior restraint could not be imposed on potentially defamatory statements and that such statements can be punished only after the fact. However, the Court found a way around such a ruling due to Cochran's death.[7]

Another area in which professional journalists provide the most unique and potentially important service to readers, viewers, and listeners is in conducting investigations. However, the results of their investigative work have come under increased scrutiny in cases in which their sources have sought to remain anonymous. In 2005, Ohio's largest daily newspaper, the

Cleveland Plain Dealer, withheld publication of two major investigative articles because they were based on illegally leaked documents. The paper's lawyers advised against publication for fear of culpability in the event that reporters were forced to divulge their sources. This legal advisory occurred against the backdrop of the jailing of *New York Times* reporter Judith Miller for refusing to divulge the identity of a confidential source. The source, Vice President Cheney's Chief of Staff, Lewis "Scooter" Libby, later gave permission to be identified and Miller was released from jail. Previous to that, a *Times* magazine reporter, Mathew Cooper, was released by a source from the promise of confidentiality in another case in which this reporter was spared from doing time in jail.[8]

These kinds of complex issues are no longer unique. The modern media age with its new information technology has led to concerns about around-the-clock reporting. These concerns include the selection and placement of stories and photos for online news sources and the difficulty of handling personal tragedies that are televised and then endlessly repeated. An example of how such deadline pressures can come into play involved Detroit journalist Mitch Albom, who authored popular books including *Tuesdays with Morrie*. Albom was accused of fabricating the attendance of two athletes at an event that they had promised to attend, but were unable to do so. One of the oddest aspects was that so many people came to Albom's defense even though he admitted making up the story to meet his deadline.[9] In other instances, the issue of what constitutes news is also open to interpretation.

In recent years there has been an increased effort to force bloggers to identify themselves and their sources. Some experts argue that independent online news providers, while maintaining status as journalists, do not gather information in the traditional news gathering sense. Media law experts have insisted that bloggers, while unorthodox and inventive in their methodology, should be held accountable for libelous content they create. Experts also argue that fictional material must be clearly labeled as fiction.

In the initial phases of cyber-bullying cases involving the suicides of teenage girls over Internet messages, a great deal of effort was made to initially try to keep the details out of the media. The media is often sympathetic to such concerns for fear of having "copy cat" activity on the part of some impressionable youngsters. But in some cases, the nature of the case and the nature of the story involving impersonators resulted instead in a great deal of coverage. The first of these cases involved 13-year-old Megan Meier of Dardenne Prairie, Missouri, who hanged herself from a support beam in her bedroom closet after receiving cruel and insulting messages over the Internet. It turned out that those messages did not emanate from the source that had been identified to her on the Internet—a teenage boy, but instead, they came from the mother of one of her neighbors. This case eventually resulted in the introduction of a House Bill, April 2, 2009, H.R. 1966: Megan Meier Cyberbullying Prevention Act, designed to prevent people from using the Internet to "coerce, intimidate, harass, or cause substantial emotional distress to a person." But the bill was also criticized on grounds that it might be used as a form of censorship or simply as a means of getting-back at people you do not like.

The second case revolved around the death of Chelsea Abram of St. Peters, Missouri, who shot herself in the stomach with her father's .22 caliber pistol on January 2, 2006, after she said that she was raped months earlier by a man she had met online as it turned-out, another impersonator, a 22-year-old adult male who identified himself online as being 16 years old. Once charges were made and the story appeared in the press, the young woman started to be taunted by students at her school. She transferred to an alternative school but suffered quite a lot because of what had happened to her.[10]

Actors and film celebrities are often involved in the most prominent libel cases in the news. A now historic case involving television comedian Carol Burnett revolved around a story published in the tabloid *National Enquirer* alleging that she had gotten into an argument in a Washington, D.C., restaurant with former U.S. Secretary of State Henry Kissinger. The allegations were found to be false and a Los Angeles jury awarded Burnett $1.6 million. An appellate court later reduced the award to $200,000, which Burnett used to create a scholarship for journalism students.[11]

Controversial film director Roman Polanski won a libel case in a British court against the magazine *Vanity Fair* in 2005. The magazine published an article in 2002 that said that Polanski had propositioned a woman in a New York City restaurant. The article claimed this event happened soon after his wife, actress Sharon Tate, was murdered by Charles Manson's cult followers in the highly sensational case, later the subject of the popular book *Helter Skelter*. Polanski testified from Paris that he had been libeled "for the sake of a lurid anecdote." After the trial, *Vanity Fair* editor Graydon Carter reflected on some international aspects of the case, saying that he found it amazing that someone who lived in France could sue a magazine published in America in a British courtroom. There was also speculation by Carter that Polanski testified from Paris because of fear that if he entered Britain he could be extradited to the United States to face child sex charges made years earlier. *Vanity Fair* was ordered to pay Polanski 175,000 pounds sterling.[12]

Polanski continued to receive strong press scrutiny when under house arrest in Switzerland while awaiting possible extradition to the United States, and his situation was complicated further when his lawyers filed an appeals petition in March 2010 revealing sealed testimony about some secret dealings between high-ranking prosecutors and the judge in the director's original sex crimes case, by then 33 years old. A documentary about that case, *Roman Polanski: Wanted and Desired*, alleged improper contact between the original judge—Laurence J. Rittenband—now deceased, and former prosecutor two years earlier. The incidents repeated in the 2010 filing involved contact between that Judge and one or two other prosecutors. A 68-page petition asked the California Court of Appeals for the Second District, in Los Angeles, to act on an emergency basis so that the court should free Polanski by imposing a sentence for time he served, or make sealed testimony alleging wrongdoing available to Swiss authorities holding him.

According to that petition, the inappropriate contact was described in sealed testimony by the deputy district attorney who prosecuted Polanski after his 1977 arrest on a series of charges, including rape and sodomy, resulting from a sexual encounter with a 13-year-old-girl. According to that petition, prosecutors met in the summer of 1977 with the judge, after he was told that they intended to file an application to disqualify the judge because of misconduct. The judge was said to have admitted misconduct, according to the petition, but they were denied permission to file a disqualification motion. Polanski fled the United States in 1978 after serving 42 days in prison while undergoing psychiatric tests, but before final sentencing under a plea agreement.

Years later, Polanski was arrested on his way to a film festival in Zurich and spent months in a Swiss prison and under house arrest. Polanski's lawyers argued that as a result he should not be extradited, because the judge had promised—affirmed in sealed testimony—to sentence him to no more than 90 days in jail, and an extradition treaty between the United States and Switzerland applies only to longer sentences. California prosecutors said at the time that questions about Polanski's sentence and any official misconduct should not be considered until he ended fugitive status, in spite of an appeals court ruling that urged, but did not order, sentencing him while abroad, to finally put a definitive end to the case. The Swiss freed Polanski in July 2010 saying the United States had failed to turn over documents they had requested. To most observers, the continuing saga of his case pointed to the complexities of such cases involving people in the entertainment industry, especially those in Hollywood.

Athletes are also involved in many lawsuits and claims about their bad behavior off the field or basketball court. They often dominate news coverage. Pick up a sports review list of top performers in any area of competition and note the large number of lawsuits that some of these individuals attract. Interestingly, that aspect of their celebrity status is often brought up in their defense. Baseball's Bo Jackson, a stellar Chicago athlete—and former player for the White Sox, filed suit in 2005 over a story challenging statements by a "dietary expert" that he had lost his hip due to anabolic steroid use. Jackson called the statement appearing in two California newspapers "hitting below the belt," but the follow-to such situations regarding comments regarding star athletes shows that there is often very little long term effects in terms of their popularity."[13]

In the same year, the Seventh Circuit U.S. Court of Appeals in Chicago dismissed a libel lawsuit revolving around a *Chicago Sun-Times* columnist's statements concerning basketball star Michael Jordan's former mistress. The column said that his mistress was working in an "old profession." The court said that could be construed to have innocent meaning, not prostitution, but simply demeaning oneself for money. Los Angeles Lakers basketball player Kobe Bryant was also the subject of a protracted public and widely reported legal battle in which he was charged with rape. Since that time, professional football quarterbacks such as Michael Vick and Bret Favre have been built-up but also tainted by press attention. The result is much second guessing about the nature and extent of the coverage. The scope of public scrutiny also sometimes creates impetus for prominent people to react outside the bounds of their own legal counsel. When Louisville basketball coach, Rick Pitino, admitted to having engaged in sexual activity with a woman in 2003, he subsequently said that he felt compelled to speak out to the news media in response to further allegations, which he described as a "total fabrication of the truth," and "pure hell" for his wife and his family. It was noted that those follow-up statements went against the advice of his attorney. There is a long history of defining, addressing and documenting legal issues involved in such cases.[14]

In 1971 William L. Prosser, who until his death was considered the country's foremost authority on the law of torts, published the last edition of his hornbook. A *hornbook* explains fundamental principles in a given field of law, and is useful for anyone who wants an overview of an area such as torts. Both appellate and trial courts occasionally refer to "hornbook law" to show that a legal principle has been generally accepted. In *Law of Torts*, Prosser noted:

> It must be confessed ... there is a great deal of the law of defamation that makes no sense. It contains anomalies and absurdities for which no legal writer ever has a kind word, and it is a curious compound of a strict liability imposed upon innocent defendants, as rigid and extreme as anything found in the law....[15]

Little has changed in the decades since Prosser published these statements even though the U.S. Supreme Court alone has issued dozens of opinions on defamation and thousands of libel trials and lower appellate court decisions have been published. The law of defamation continues to defy logic even with the libel treatment that arrived with the *New York Times v. Sullivan* decision by the Supreme Court in 1964.[16] Some rules have been established—enough for hornbooks. However, defamation law is complicated, confusing, cumbersome, and often unsettling for journalists.

Research has found a potential "chilling effect" of libel suits on the media. Studies consistently show that even the best newspapers, broadcast stations, and networks have lost major libel suits, some to the tune of millions of dollars. They also show that threatened and actual libel suits can "chill" large and small media outlets into being less aggressive and overly cautious in their reporting and editing and also that public perception of libel is inaccurate, in terms of understanding concepts including actual malice and pleading truth as a defense.[17]

Libel seminars are common at meetings of trade associations such as the Newspaper Association of America, American Society of Newspaper Editors, Investigative Reporters and Editors, Inc., National Association of Broadcasters, Society of Professional Journalists and Women in Communications, Inc. These seminars are widely attended because journalists and publishers see the writing on the wall since the stakes are very high for corporate owners.

According to figures compiled by the Media Law Resource Center (MLRC), news organizations are sued less frequently for libel than in the past. In addition, they often win cases. The success rate of media defendants in libel cases reached record highs a decade ago. At one point, 82.3% of libel cases were dismissed with summary judgments, and 83.6% of those that did go to trial were decided in favor of the defendants. Current studies show declines in the number of libel trials and the chance of a defendant having a libel verdict in favor of the plaintiff overturned on appeal or having a verdict in the defendant's favor (about 81.6%, a drop from recent years).[18]

According to MLRC's report on trials and damages, at mid-decade the percentage of "wins" by media defendants continues to rise while the total number of such trials per year is on the decline. There were a dozen trials against media defendants as recently as 2004 and the defendants won seven trials. In trials won by plaintiffs, the average award was $3.4 million. In the two decades since the MLRC started to keep statistics, the number of trials has declined. Media defendants have fared best against plaintiffs classified as public figures, winning more than 40% of those cases.[19]

The MLRC has concentrated recent attention on the emergence of online bloggers, tweets, and cyber-bully cases often involving or targeting underage teens. In the complete postings, MLRC includes the status of cases, updates on cases, and links to all court documents. The most widely discussed case involving was *U.S. v. Drew*, Crim. No. 08-00582 (C.D. Cal. indictment filed May 15, 2008). The case as presented by MLRC, Legal Actions Against Bloggers, reviewed its status as a conviction on three misdemeanor charges, acquittal on three of the felony charges, hung jury on one felony charge (C.D. Cal. Nov. 30, 2008); felony charge dismissed (Dec. 31, 2008); convictions reversed on post-trial motions (preliminary ruling July 2, 2009).[20]

Other online examples of MLRC cases pending or dismissed with related documents also include a criminal case, also in Missouri, in which a middle-aged woman allegedly posted a teen-aged girl's picture and contact information to the "Casual Encounters" section of Craigslist after having a fight with the 17-year-old. The person was charged in the wake of the Lori Drew case. The attorney in this third case asserted that the constitutionality of the statute would be challenged while the accused in that case was released on bond but barred from using a computer or the Internet.

In a case in Illinois Circuit Court a mother sued on behalf of a minor son, alleging defendants, minors who knew the plaintiff created a fake Facebook profile using a real photo and cell number, on which was posted racist and sexual comments that appeared to have been written by the plaintiff. That lawsuit claimed defamation, false light, and intentional infliction of emotional distress.

In another case involving social media and Facebook, *Finkel v. Facebook*, No. 102578-2009 (N.Y. Sup. Ct. filed Feb. 16, 2009), claims against Facebook were dismissed (Sept. 15, 2009) when a high school graduate sued classmates and their parents over postings to a private Facebook group, "90 Cents Short of a Dollar." The suit against Facebook in this case claimed it asserted ownership of material posted to its site. It argued the site's terms of use made it publisher of the material, not immune from liability under section 230 of the Communications Decency Act. On September 15, 2009, a New York Supreme Court Justice dismissed the claims against Facebook, rejecting the plaintiff's argument that section 230 did not apply.

Celebrity charges in some cases emanating from otherwise anonymous sources are just a few of the other kinds of cases such as these, regularly outlined by the MLRC and showing the broad scope of the issues involved. They also included, for example, *Siegal v. Kardashian*, No. 09-93439 CA 15 (Fla. Cir. Ct. Dec. 29, 2009). In this instance, a website called Dr. Siegal's Cookie Diet contained a page linking to news articles and press mentions of a particular diet. Several of these links suggested that Kim Kardashian of the popular reality cable series *Keeping up with the Kardashians* had been a fan of this diet. At one point Kardashian allegedly tweeted that she thought the diet was "unhealthy" and that the company was lying. Her lawyers followed up and sent the site a cease and desist letter asking that all references to her be taken down. A suit was brought alleging that both the doctor and the company were defamed by the Tweets. In the aftermath, there were subsequently no links on The Cookie Diet site to Kardashian.

In another celebrity-related case, *Salisbury v. Gawker Media LLC*, No. 2009-60340-393 (Tex. Dist. Ct. file Oct. 16, 2009), a former NFL quarterback, ESPN analyst, and sports radio host Sean Salisbury sued Gawker Media over posts on the company's blog which he alleged led to his being fired from media positions, thus limiting employment. That suit revolved around several postings to a blog over a two-year period alleging Salisbury acted inappropriately towards female co-workers. While posts attributed such allegations and linked to other sources, Salisbury's attorney told the McKinney (Tex.) *Courier-Gazette* his client targeted this particular blog because of its "concerted" efforts.

In *Save-A-Life Foundation v. Baratz*, No. 2007-CH-12022 (Ill. Cir. Ct. filed May 3, 2007) and *Save-A-Life Foundation, Inc. v. Heimlich et al.*, No. 1:08-cv-06022 (N.D. Ill), a Chicago-based foundation which teaches and promotes use of the Heimlich maneuver sued critics of the first aid procedure and its creator, Dr. Henry Heimlich. Among critics named in that suit was Jason Harp, who maintained the Cincinnati Beacon blog (www.cincinnatibeacon.com), and Peter Heimlich, Henry Heimlich's son, who had his own website (http://medfraud.info/). The foundation sought an injunction against the critics' comments. And in its amended complaint, the foundation added American Broadcasting Company, WLS-TV in Chicago, and reporter Chuck Goudie as defendants concerning two stories on the controversy. In January of 2009, the case was moved to federal court. And later, in July of that year, the plaintiff voluntarily withdrew it.

With legal challenges to the media still likely, why aren't some attorneys uncorking bottles of champagne? One major reason is that megabuck awards can still hit a major mainstream media company hard and awards by juries against the media can extend over many years, thus tying up company resources. In one of the all-time leading awards in media libel, a jury awarded $58 million in damages to Vic Feazell, the former district attorney for McLennan County, Texas, against Dallas station WFAA and reporter Charles Duncan in 1991. Feazell claimed he had been libeled in an investigative series that accused him of taking bribes to settle drunk driving charges. Feazell was later indicted on bribery and racketeering but was subsequently acquitted on all counts.[21]

That award broke a previous record of $34 million awarded by a jury against The Philadelphia Inquirer to Richard A. Sprague, a former first assistant district attorney in Philadelphia.[22] The $34 million award included $2.5 million in compensatory damages and $31.5 million in punitive damages based upon a series of editorials and articles written by a reporter who had been successfully prosecuted by the attorney for illegal wiretapping a year earlier and had promised to "get" the prosecutor.[23] Twenty-three years after the articles and editorials appeared, the Inquirer settled out of court. Two months after a $58 million jury award against the WFAA-TV station owner, the A. H. Belo Corporation announced it had reached an out-of-court settlement.

A seven-person federal jury also sent shock waves throughout the media in 1997 when it awarded a defunct bond brokerage firm, Money Management Analytical Research (MMAR) of Houston, Texas, a record $222.7 in a libel suit against the Wall Street Journal.[24] The award included $22.7 million in actual damages and $200 million in punitive damages. The jury also awarded $20,000 in punitive damages against the reporter, Laura Jereski. The story, "Regulators Study Texas Securities Firm and Its Louisiana Pension Fund Trades," implied that MMAR may have defrauded the Louisiana State Employees Pension Fund and that the company's founders had earned tens of millions of dollars in profits. The jury determined that five of eight statements at issue were false, including that the firm spent $2 million in one year for limousines, that it kept losses secret and used deceptive or fraudulent information to get the state pension fund to buy securities. The company went bankrupt less than a month after the story appeared. Jereski had interviewed more than 30 sources for the story, on which she had worked for four months. The judge threw out the $200 million award for punitive damages. He said the plaintiffs had not demonstrated the article was printed with malice. He allowed $22.7 million in compensatory damages, along with interest and court costs, to stand.[25]

The other fear is that million dollar awards are not limited to "big" media. In 2003, juries in two different states awarded six figure sums—$1.5 million combined in libel cases against small newspapers in Massachusetts and Minnesota.[26] The Boston Phoenix published allegations of child abuse against a county prosecutor and lost the case to the tune of $950,000. A small Minnesota newspaper, the Chanhassen Villager, implied a plot against a former administrator existed due to a grudge, the result of editorials that ended up costing $625,000 in damages in state court. An attorney for the Minnesota Newspaper Association maintained the size of the award could bankrupt two-thirds of the newspapers in that state.[27]

A jury awarded a former county judge executive $1 million against a small weekly paper in Kentucky. He lost re-election by one vote. Damages were $160,000 for lost wages, $340,000 for personal hardship, and $500,000 in punitive damages. The plaintiff had to demonstrate actual malice on the part of the newspaper since he was a public figure. It focused on his contention that the editorials were part of a plan to remove him. The decision was appealed and overturned. On further appeal the Kentucky Supreme Court upheld. The plaintiff filed a second libel suit against the paper, its editor, and publisher which was held by the judge.[28]

The history of defamation is replete with examples of complex stories involving people who have served in more than one capacity, often in complicated public roles. In *Robert R. Thomas v.*

Bill Page, et al., a sitting justice of the Illinois Supreme Court (also a former Chicago Bears football player) sued the Kane County Chronicle. Kane County is outside Chicago in the western suburb of Geneva. Thomas sued a columnist, an editor, and the paper's parent division because of two columns he alleged had defamed and placed him in a false light. The columns questioned the judge's ethics in decisions he had made, implying that he acted more like a politician than a judge. This was of special concern because Illinois Supreme Court justices are elected to office.[29] As a result, six Illinois Supreme Court justices later requested to quash subpoenas for documents related to this libel suit. The justices also asserted their belief that they were exempt from a standard procedure of listing documents they believed to be privileged.[30]

In a case involving investigative reporting about office holders in Seattle, Washington, the plaintiffs alleged that KING-TV aired two broadcasts that were defamatory, invaded their privacy, and placed one plaintiff in a false light. The first story repeated allegations about one plaintiff making personal use of city equipment and rental cars as well as unnecessarily scheduling overtime. The story concluded with an attempt to interview her on a public street, asking her whether she owed the city money. The news broadcasts centered on the charges specified and a trip to Las Vegas by one plaintiff. The station's report claimed that the plaintiff attended very little of a professional meeting that was the supposed purpose of the trip, but instead spent time gambling and shopping.[31]

The defendants were subject to a variety of claims in this case including alleged violations of the federal Racketeer Influenced and Corrupt Organizations (RICO) Act, as well as civil rights violations. The plaintiff's defamation claims were dismissed by the trial court judge citing lack of specificity. The RICO claims were dismissed as were false light and emotional distress claims against one plaintiff. The court denied KING's motion to dismiss other claims. The defendant's motion to dismiss a request for damages was granted.[32]

The Boston Globe appealed a $2.1 million verdict that the paper and one of its reporters were ordered to pay to a medical doctor who maintained she was libeled by a story about a Globe columnist who was killed by an accidental chemotherapy overdose. The doctor sued the Globe, arguing that she was erroneously identified in the article. In *Ayash v. Dana-Farber Cancer Institute and Others*, a trial judge found the Globe and its reporter liable in 2001, entering a judgment to punish them for refusing to comply with a court order to disclose sources. The jury decided only on the amount of damages, holding the newspaper liable for $1.6 million and the reporter for $420,000. The doctor wanted the identities of the confidential sources to demonstrate that privacy had been invaded.[33]

In cases involving health matters, the financial stakes can be especially high. Philip Morris Companies, Inc. once filed a $10 billion libel suit against the American Broadcasting Company for a story on ABC-TV claiming the tobacco industry spiked cigarettes with extra nicotine so smokers would get addicted, thus increasing tobacco sales. Afterward, R.J. Reynolds Tobacco Co. filed a similar suit for the same segment. Philip Morris filed its suit in state circuit court in Virginia, and subpoenaed material from telephone companies, a rental car firm, and credit card issuers, trying to track the identity of ABC's source, code-named "Deep Cough."[34]

ABC, in turn, filed a motion for a protective order to quash the subpoenas, but the trial court judge in the case turned down the network's request. He ruled that the subpoenas were not protected by qualified privilege, as ABC argued, and thus the subpoenas were valid. Both suits were settled out of court. The network made an apology and agreed to settle to avoid further litigation. ABC paid the plaintiffs' legal fees and expenses, believed to be more than

$2.5 million. Then three TV stations quit carrying anti-tobacco commercials placed by a state health services department after being told by R.J. Reynolds Tobacco Co. they might be sued for libel.[35]

Other defamation suits of note have included an early $100 million suit filed by Michael Jackson against a syndicated TV show, *Hard Copy*, and Los Angeles radio station KABC-AM for broadcasting a story about a 27-minute videotape allegedly showing Jackson engaging in sexual romps with a 13-year-old boy. This occurred before Jackson was accused and acquitted of similar allegations. Another was a $100 million libel suit filed by the Boston Celtics against the *Wall Street Journal* for a front page story in which several physicians averred that star Reggie Lewis could have died from cocaine abuse rather than a heart condition. In the wake of the O. J. Simpson trial and charges against Michael Jackson much later that resulted in acquittals, professional athletes and entertainers became regular targets for special press coverage.

Documentary filmmaker Michael Moore was hit with a libel suit filed by the brother of Oklahoma City bombing conspirator Terry Nichols (serving two life sentences without parole in the bombing that killed 168 people). Nichols' brother James maintained that Michael Moore's 2002 film, *Bowling for Columbine*, accused him of being an accomplice in the bombing through statements that were "half-truths or total untruths." Among items in question was one phrase in the film alleging federal agents couldn't "get the goods" on James Nichols.[36] The implication was that the terrorist's brother was involved, but able to evade prosecution. Moore and his attorneys took the position that filmgoers understood statements in his films are opinions—not facts, with First Amendment protection.

Many libel cases involve the First Amendment defense. One case involved a media figure operating behind the scenes. Lou DiBella, a former executive with Home Box Office (HBO) sued Bernard Hopkins, who became middleweight boxing champion of the world. DiBella had left HBO but retained several dates for fights that he had arranged. Before leaving, DiBella had discussions with Hopkins about representing and marketing him in the future. They agreed by way of a handshake and Hopkins agreed to pay DiBella $50,000 as an advance fee for future services, which he later paid. Once DiBella left HBO, he began to advise Hopkins. The previously agreed-upon fight dates were filled by Hopkins. These were all fights he later won.[37] In the aftermath, Hopkins stopped communicating with DiBella and was interviewed for the online boxing publication, MaxBoxing.com, in which Hopkins said:

> Understand, every time I fought (the past couple of years), Lou DiBella got paid, even when he was with HBO, which is f**king wrong. What I'm saying is that the bottom line is, the Syd Vanderpool fight, should an HBO employee accept $50,000 while he's still working for HBO? ... So if they want the cat out [of] the bag, then let's let the f**king cat out of the bag....[38]

Hopkins made allegations of a relationship between fight dates and business dealings. He repeated them in an article in the *Boston Globe* ("Hopkins Hops Around") on December 24, 2001, in an article published January 10, 2002 in the *Philadelphia Daily News,* and on ESPN Radio. DiBella sued Hopkins for libel. A jury returned a verdict in DiBella's favor based on Hopkins' original interview. On appeal, DiBella challenged the trial court judges' jury instructions with respect to burden of proof necessary to show libel.

In his cross appeal, Hopkins claimed the libel judgment violated his freedom of speech, that DiBella failed to prove falsity and actual malice, and that there was inconsistency based on the fact that the assertions appeared three times in the media but only one was shown to be libelous. Libel claims in this case arose under New York law. The jury did not find other dissemination of allegations from other sources libelous, though Hopkins undoubtedly made them. The judgment in *Lou DiBella and DiBella Entertainment v. Bernard Hopkins* was upheld by the second Circuit U.S. Court of Appeals. This dispute arose between individuals—with the mass media caught in the middle.[39]

When it comes to the status of individuals in libel and defamation cases, the attention has by no means been limited to professional sports. An Alabama judge once threw out claims in a defamation suit based on the public figure status of two University of Alabama assistant football coaches. A $60 million lawsuit had been filed initially against the NCAA in December 2002, claiming the association had defamed the coaches when it implicated them in a recruitment scandal that led to the loss of 21 student scholarships and probation for the program. The state trial court judge held both men were public figures.[40] The message was clear—coaches who attract media attention and are then associated with scandals at former institutions will be considered public figures for purposes of libel and required to demonstrate actual malice. A libel suit filed by one of the coaches against *Time, Inc.* was later settled out of court.[41]

High-profile cases sometimes involve individuals who initially welcome publicity, but attention results in disclosure of unsavory personal matters for public consumption. In one case in Louisville, Kentucky, a former TV morning show host sought $2.7 million in damages, claiming she had been defamed by her former boyfriend, a former radio host, by malicious on-air comments he made after they stopped dating. The radio host called the former TV morning show host "the devil" and made other comments regarding breast implants, personal hygiene, and undergarments. His attorney called her "a spurned suitor." The radio host was subsequently fired and relocated to another city and. the plaintiff relocated as well. The verdict in the case, which took the jury two hours to decide, cleared the radio host on all claims. Although members of the jury expressed concern about the nature of on the air statements, they were reluctant to find the defendant acted with actual malice.[42]

The fact remains that libel suits make up a disproportionate share of litigation against the media and invasion of privacy and other torts also continue to appear. Until recent years, the number of megabuck verdicts appeared to be increasing, with juries determined to punish the press for perceived transgressions. Every media professional must be familiar with the basic principles of libel, and know how to avoid libel suits and successfully defend those that still occur despite the best intentions.

Origins of Defamation

Defamation, which includes both libel and slander, is very old. It is difficult to determine exactly how old, as evidenced by the different origins ascribed by experts to each of these two causes of action. Prosser traces modern day defamation to 16th and 17th century England when the ecclesiastical and common law courts battled over jurisdiction in slander cases.[43] Later, political libel or sedition developed in the notorious Star Chamber cases as printing became prevalent. Michael Gartner traced *libel* to the Latin *libellus,* meaning "little book" to signify pamphlets that were published to broadcast rumors about the famous or the not-so-famous during the Elizabethan era.[44] Prominent First Amendment attorney Bruce Sanford notes that

Anglo-American libel can be traced to remedies provided to defamed individuals as early as pre-Norman times, with the church becoming the first major arbiter.[45]

Four types of libel developed in England—sedition, defamation, blasphemy, and obscene libel.[46] *Sedition* or *seditious libel*, as discussed *infra*, was and still is criticism of the government and/or government officials. From the mid-15th century until its abolition by Parliament in 1641, the English Star Chamber secretly tried without a jury and imposed torture on individuals who spoke ill of the monarchy. The fate for committing an offense may have been worse than death. In 1636, William Prynn was pilloried in stocks in the public square, had his ears cut off, was fined 10,000 pounds, and then was imprisoned for life for denouncing plays and other activities in a book that was deemed to criticize the queen by inference.[47] John Twyn suffered an even more horrible demise in 1663 for advocating that a ruler should be accountable to the people. He was sentenced by the judge to first be hanged by the neck then, while alive, cut down and castrated, after which his intestines were taken out and burned while he remained alive. Finally, he was to be beheaded and quartered.[48] No mention was apparently made about what was to be done if he died before he had a chance to see his body parts removed!

Defamation, also known as *private libel* and handled at first by the ecclesiastical courts, gradually became a common law offense with requirements somewhat similar to those of libel and slander today. *Blasphemy* or *blasphemous libel* was principally criticism of God, Christ, the church, or church leaders. It is nonexistent today in the United States but is still alive and well in some countries and caught many individuals in its vise until the mid-19th century in England. Finally, *obscenity* or *obscene libel* was not a concern until about the early 19th century with the spread of Methodism. However, as *Regina v. Hicklin* (1868) illustrates,[49] obscenity was suppressed by the mid-19th century in both England and the United States, which adopted the *Hicklin* rule until 1957.[50]

Libel versus Slander

With the proliferation of printing, *defamation,* or information that tends to subject an individual or entity such as a corporation to public hatred, contempt, or ridicule, involved a new factor—the multiplying of harm to one's reputation through widespread dissemination via publication. *Slander* (oral defamation) and libel (printed defamation) became separate torts with somewhat different rules. The reasons for this distinction were mired in historic inconsistencies, but the distinction continues. Some states, for example, treat broadcast defamation as slander, although others follow the recommendation of the Restatement (Second) of Torts that print and electronic media be treated the same—that is, that both be considered libel.[51]

The distinction between libel and slander is very important because in most jurisdictions *special damages* must be demonstrated by plaintiffs before they can recover any damages unless the slander falls into one of four categories: (a) imputation of crime; (b) imputation of a loathsome disease such as leprosy or a venereal disease; (c) imputations affecting one's trade, business, profession or calling; and (d) imputation of unchastity. Special damages are specific pecuniary losses or what are commonly called "out-of-pocket" expenses. They are difficult to prove in slander cases, but they do not have to occur if slander fits into one of the four traditional pegs.

Except for broadcasting in a few jurisdictions, slander is not a major problem. Broadcasters generally do not object to falling into the slander category because they have much greater protection against slander than libel. A few jurisdictions differentiate slander and libel in other ways. Georgia, for example, characterizes broadcast defamation as "defamacast."[52] Kentucky[53] and some other states treat both print and broadcast defamation as slander but have somewhat different rules for defamation in the two types of media.[54] Most distinctions have no real practical effect unless it is a matter of categorizing one as slander and the other as libel.

Libel Per Se versus Libel Per Quod

Some courts have traditionally made a distinction between *libel per se* (statements defamatory on their face) and *libel per quod* (statements not defamatory on their face but defamatory with reference to extrinsic facts or circumstances). These distinctions are less than clear at common law and in state statutes. However, according to the general rule, special harm must be shown for a plaintiff to recover for libel per se but this does not have to be demonstrated for libel per quod. Even this distinction has become blurred over the decades and centuries. Attorney Robert Sack points out, "In New York, the state of case law [on libel per se versus libel per quod] is so confusing and contradictory that it is impossible to be certain what the rule is."[55] New York is not alone. According to Sack, at least nine states[56] appear to have rules that all libelous statements are treated as libel per se, thus not requiring proof of special harm.[57]

There have been thousands of libel per se cases. Some resulted in awards for plaintiffs; others did not. ESPN sports TV network once broadcast a retraction after one of its announcers said that a particular professional baseball pitcher transferred from a private university to a community college because he "failed his grades."[58]

In *Bryson v. News America Publications Inc.* (1996),[59] the Supreme Court of Illinois held that a story entitled "Bryson" in *Seventeen* magazine was libelous per se because it characterized a woman as a "slut." Under Illinois law, one of the categories in which a written or spoken statement is defamatory per se is the false claim that a person has engaged in "fornication or adultery."[60] The article was labeled "fiction" and used only the plaintiff's last name (Bryson), but the Illinois Supreme Court noted that the name "is not so common that we must find, as a matter of law, that no reasonable person would believe that the article was about the plaintiff."[61] The plaintiff's name was Kimberly Bryson, and she and the defendant, Lucy Logsdon, had attended high school together. The article's namesake was a native of southern Illinois, the same area as the plaintiff, who claimed there were 23 other similarities between her and the fictional character.

These examples show how libel on its face can potentially get a publication or an individual into trouble. First Amendment attorney Bruce Sanford compiled a list of what he termed "red flag" words that can lead to a suit if improperly handled: *fascist, booze-hound, fawning sycophant,* and *stool pigeon.*[62] Many of these are prime illustrations of libel per se.

Libel per quod can be troublesome for journalists because words do not automatically throw up a red flag. Publishing the statement that a woman is pregnant is not defamatory on its face. What if she is elderly? Ninety-six-year-old Nellie Mitchell won $650,000 in compensatory damages and $850,000 in punitive damages from the *Sun* after a jury trial in Arkansas U.S. District Court.[63] The supermarket tabloid published her picture with an article in which it said a 101-year-old Australian news carrier quit her route because a millionaire customer got her pregnant. A *Sun* editor admitted during the trial the story was fabricated but Mitchell's photo was used because he assumed she was dead. The *Sun's* attorney argued that Mitchell was not libeled because "most reasonable people recognize that the stories [in the *Sun*] are essentially fiction."[64]

What about the discrepancy in age or false assertion that she lived in Australia? The last two facts, while false, are probably not defamatory because they would probably not harm one's reputation unless special circumstances existed—such as falsely indicating that a married man lived in Australia when his friends, acquaintances, and family knew his spouse was living elsewhere. At trial, these extrinsic facts and circumstances are relevant in showing information was false and defamatory even though they were not widely known nor even known by the defendant. If the jurisdiction requires a showing of special damages, as some states do, before recovery by the plaintiff or if the libel per quod does not fall within one of the special categories under slander, a suit would be unsuccessful. In general, such damages need not be demonstrated.

Trade Libel

Most libel suits involve people, companies, or organizations, but a growing number involve product disparagement or *trade libel,* which requires proof of four elements: (1) publication of a false statement that disparages the quality of a product; (2) actual malice (reckless disregard for truth or knowledge of falsity); (3) intent to harm, awareness of the likelihood of harm or a reasonable basis for awareness; and (4) special damages.[65]

A prominent, now historic, case of trade libel is *Engler et al. v. Lyman et al.* (1998).[66] Top-rated talk show host Oprah Winfrey, her production company, and a guest on her April 16, 1996, syndicated program were sued for $6.7 million by Amarillo, Texas, cattle rancher Paul Engler and Cactus Feeders, a Texas cattle producer. The suit was filed after Howard Lyman, a vegetarian and director of the Humane Society's Eating with a Conscience campaign, and Winfrey made negative comments about beef. Lyman claimed on *The Oprah Winfrey Show* that 100,000 cows die for no apparent reason and are ground up and fed to other cows. If even one of the dead cows had "mad cow disease," thousands of other cows might be infected as a result, according to Lyman. Other guests on the show, appearing before Lyman made his comments, played down the risks of transmittal of the disease to humans through beef.

Mad cow disease, or bovine spongiform encephalopathy, became a major health issue in Great Britain beginning in the 1980s and is still a concern there as well as in the United States. There were reports that the disease, which destroys the brain, might be linked to illness in humans. The disease is thought to be picked up by cows through feed containing ground-up sheep parts.

After Lyman commented, Winfrey exclaimed, "It has just stopped me from eating another burger." After the show, cattle prices fell from 62 cents a pound to 55 cents, and Engler claimed he lost $6.7 million.[67] Engler sued under a Texas statute. At the time, Texas was one of 13 states with what became known as "veggie libel" statutes because they allow a company, individual, or industry harmed as a result of disparaging comments made about a perishable food product to recover damages. Winfrey moved her program to Amarillo, Texas, where the case was tried by a jury in federal court. After 5½ hours of deliberation, the jury vindicated Winfrey, finding that no harm occurred because she did not defame cattle producers by providing false information. The Third Circuit U.S. Court of Appeals upheld the decision in 2000 and Winfrey's reputation for fairness was intact although one of the appeals judges wrote that she believed cattle to be covered by the law.[68]

Winfrey settled another lawsuit in March 2010. That suit was brought by the headmistress she accused of not properly running her girls' school in Johannesburg, South Africa. A trial had been due to start in Philadelphia, but the settlement occurred two weeks prior. The details of the settlement were confidential but a joint statement announced parties met "woman to woman" without lawyers; happy that they could resolve the dispute peacefully. The head of the school had claimed earlier that Winfrey had defamed her after some students claimed they had been sexually abused at the school. She denied charges of abuse when Winfrey said that she had failed to deal with the scandal. The head of that school also initially claimed that she was never told about the abuse but afterwards had trouble finding a job after Winfrey said she "lost confidence" in her.

States began considering veggie libel laws after CBS, the National Defense Resource Council, Fenton Communications, Inc., and three CBS network affiliates successfully defended a suit filed by 11 Washington State apple growers who sued after a report by *60 Minutes* that claimed Alar, a chemical growth regulator sprayed on apples, could cause cancer. The report entitled "A is for Apple" called Alar the "most potent cancer-causing agent in our food supply." It did not mention apple growers nor refer to Washington or Washington apples per se. According to growers, it (a) implied "red apples were poisonous, dangerous or harmful for human consumption," (b) did not "distinguish … between red apples that were Alar-treated and those red apples that were untreated," and (c) failed to include "advocates for the healthy, safe nature of all red apples." The apple growers contended they lost more than $130 million as a result of the broadcast.

The U.S. District Court judge denied the defendants' motion to dismiss. The defendants argued that the report was not "of and concerning" the plaintiffs—i.e., it did not identify the plaintiffs, but the judge held that the "of and concerning" rule did not apply because the suit was a product disparagement suit, not traditional defamation. The district court held the broadcast "was 'of and concerning' all apples" since it "clearly targeted every apple in the U.S." Thus every apple grower would have standing to sue. After a year of discovery including depositions from experts on both sides, CBS successfully sought a summary judgment. The court ruled that the claims in the program could not be proven false and that the defendants should be able to reasonably rely on government data.

In *Auvil v. CBS "60 Minutes"* (1995),[69] the Ninth Circuit U.S. Court of Appeals affirmed, saying plaintiffs "failed to raise an issue of material fact as to the falsity of the broadcast." CBS said: "For all the cosmic questions posed, the ultimate issue in the Alar case really was whether optimists can recover for product disparagement against those who publicize the views of pessimists."[70]

First Amendment experts generally view such laws as unconstitutional. Washington State had no such statute at the time of the broadcast so the plaintiffs had to rely on common law. Professor Robert D. Richards noted, "If lawmakers are concerned about the reputation of locally grown produce, they should concentrate their efforts on regulating the types of pesticides used rather than the reports about how such chemicals potentially harm consumers."[71]

Another case—this one in Britain—attracted a lot of media attention because McDonald's Corp. spent an estimated $16 million to win a trade libel suit against two vegetarian activists.

They handed out pamphlets outside a McDonald's in Britain, claiming the company abused animals, exploited kids in ads, promoted poor diet, and paid low wages. After the longest trial in British history—314 days including 130 witnesses and 40,000 pages of documents—the fast-food chain was awarded $98,000 in damages.[72]

Other examples of alleged trade libel include two suits filed against Consumers Union (CU), publisher of *Consumer Reports*, for damaging the sales of the Suzuki Samurai after reporting that the sports utility vehicle (SUV) rolled over easily in road tests. In one year sales fell from 77,000 to less than 1,500.[73] Suzuki sued after the magazine republished the report in a 60th anniversary edition. The product disparagement case was later settled.[74]

In a case of David versus Goliath, New York attorney Aaron Lichtman successfully defended a libel suit filed against him by a restaurant after he put a sign in his office window that simply said "Bad Food." His office was directly above the restaurant. The case was dismissed by a trial court judge who ruled the sign had First Amendment protection.[75]

The Typical Libel Case

There is probably no typical libel suit because every case has its own unique aspects, as even big-name suits have demonstrated. However, it may be useful to focus on a fairly typical case before a discussion of libel elements.

E. W. Scripps Co., The Kentucky Post and Al Salvato v. Louis A. Ball

E. W. Scripps Co., The Kentucky Post and Al Salvato v. Louis A. Ball[76] began when a newspaper owned by Scripps Howard and the third largest daily in the state, *The Kentucky Post,* published the first of a two-part series by reporter Al Salvato on the allegedly poor performance of a county attorney.[77] The second part appeared two days later) The articles primarily dealt with the prosecutor's allegedly lenient handling of repeat offenders and strained police relationships. Both stories were lead articles each day and were headed "Portrait of a Prosecutor." The major subhead in the first article was: "Lou Ball's Record Lags Behind Others." The second's was "Serious Gap with the Police." Both were accompanied by large graphs, photos, and other visual elements. An editorial entitled "Our Challenge to Lou Ball" appeared later and called on Ball to improve his record. The paper had also earlier published a critical editorial. Although the series did not claim Ball was corrupt, it implied he was not doing a good job. A team of lawyers checked and rechecked the stories before publication.[78]

Later, the prosecutor filed a libel suit against the *Post*, claiming the series and editorials were false and published with actual malice. The U.S. Supreme Court defined *actual malice* as reckless disregard for the truth or knowledge of falsity in *New York Times v. Sullivan* (1964) and held that public officials must show actual malice before they can recover for libel. Less than a year after the series appeared and after months of discovery and legal maneuvers, including the *Post* filing a motion to dismiss that was rejected by the judge, the trial began in Campbell Circuit Court. It lasted seven days and included testimony that Salvato, the reporter, bore a grudge against Ball because of an incident at a high school football game in which a police officer made the reporter leave. The officer had been called to investigate a report that Salvato was "trying to get some girls to take some dope with him," but he decided not to arrest Salvato after Salvato said he was working on a story on drug use among young people. The grudge against Ball supposedly arose when the prosecutor failed to pursue Salvato's complaint against police. During the trial, Salvato was questioned about how he conducted research for the series. He testified that he spent three months reviewing records of nearly 3,000 cases and interviewed more than 40 people, including Ball and three assistants.[79]

The plaintiff's attorney argued there was evidence of actual malice, including the notation "good case" scribbled by the reporter on cases—such as a felony charge reduced to a misdemeanor—and that Salvato had used a statement by a former narcotics officer that criminals "couldn't have a better friend" than Ball even though a judge who knew the officer had told the reporter he was "a very poor police officer, totally unreliable." Ball's attorney claimed this and other allegations— such as that the prosecutor had lost about half the cases taken to trial in the last six years and he failed to assist a county attorney investigating misdemeanor obscenity charges involving an adult theater—were false and defamatory.[80]

The *Post's* attorneys countered that all allegations had been checked and rechecked, the reporter had no grudge against Ball, and most statements were protected by the First Amendment. The stories contained inaccuracies, which the newspaper's attorneys contended were minor and had no impact on the readers' perception of Ball. For example, figures in one graph had been accidentally transposed so that Ball's record appeared worse than was the actual case. The defense noted Ball did not point out the mistake when he was shown the graph before publication and asked to comment on the story.[81]

After deliberating a few hours, the jury returned a verdict in favor of Ball awarding $175,000 in actual damages but no punitive damages. The *Post* appealed and nearly two years after the jury decision and almost three years after the series appeared the state Court of Appeals reversed the trial court. It held "there is no clear and convincing evidence that these articles were published with the requisite knowledge of falsity or reckless disregard for the truth necessary to remove from constitutional protection." Ball appealed and the state Supreme Court heard oral arguments. That court delayed its decision until a case it considered to be similar, *Harte-Hanks Communications, Inc. v. Connaughton* (1989),[82] was handed down by the U.S. Supreme Court. *Harte-Hanks* upheld a jury finding of actual malice by the Hamilton (Ohio) *Journal News* in publishing a story and editorial about a candidate. Connaughton won $5,000 in compensatory damages and $195,000 in punitive.

One year later, the state Supreme Court heard re-arguments in the case. The state Supreme Court reversed the state court of appeals decision and reinstated the trial court award (with interest) to Ball. In a unanimous opinion (6 to 0), the Kentucky Supreme Court ruled:

> ... as constrained by the decisions of the United States Supreme Court regarding the First Amendment protection of freedom of the press, including the mandate that appellate judges in such cases "exercise independent judgment and determine whether the record establishes actual malice with convincing clarity" [citing *Bose v. Consumers Union of the United States* (1984)[83]], we reverse the Court of Appeals and reinstate the judgment of the trial court.[84]

The state supreme court felt that the jury could reasonably infer that the *Post* reporter held a grudge against the prosecutor because of the incident at the high school game and from a statement made by Salvato to Ball in a phone conversation, presumably implying a threat that Ball would be "hearing from" him. The court ruled there was evidence presented at trial that statements were false and defamatory, including the "they couldn't have a better friend" comment from the former narcotics officer and claim he lost half the cases he took to trial. The court rejected the idea that some statements were opinions enjoying First Amendment protection. It noted the refusal to publish a retraction as evidence of actual malice.

The newspaper petitioned the U.S. Supreme Court to grant a writ of certiorari, but the Court turned it down, 6½ years after the series appeared. The newspaper's insurance reportedly covered most legal fees, but the *Post* probably paid $50,000 to $100,000 as a deductible in the award to Ball plus a percentage (typically 20%) of the amount above the deductible.[85] Reporter Al Salvato died in 2006 after a long and distinguished career in journalism.

E. W. Scripps et al. v. Ball is typical of libel suits the media face in four ways, although circumstances differ. First, the plaintiff was a public official and had to demonstrate with clear and convincing evidence or "convincing clarity" that the defendant published the story with actual malice, as required under *New York Times v. Sullivan* (1964). Public figures and public officials have a heavier evidentiary burden to meet in successfully suing for libel than private individuals, but they are more likely to sue. Three factors explain this. First, public officials and public figures get more media attention than private people. They are supposedly more newsworthy. Second, public officials and public figures usually have greater finances and can persevere more than private citizens who may not be able to afford court costs and attorney fees. Because they are in the limelight, public figures depend on positive reputations for a livelihood. When an image is hurt, damages mount.

A second way in which *E. W. Scripps v. Ball* typifies libel lies in how it meandered through the courts. While the trend appears to have reversed by now, plaintiffs in the past were more likely than defendants to win libel suits. More libel suits are settled out of court than ever reach trial or they are dismissed before trial. Many are settled with payment to plaintiffs. Media defendants cannot count juries among friends, as witnessed by major megabuck awards.

Third, the treatment accorded the *Post* in the courts reflects the trends in other courts. Whereas a lower appellate court may occasionally reverse a libel award, higher appellate courts, especially state supreme courts, are just as likely to uphold. State and federal appellate courts are following the lead of the U.S. Supreme Court. That is why state Supreme Court delayed its decision on the appeal until *Harte-Hanks Communications v. Connaughton* could be decided. Contrary to that Supreme Court's conclusions, the facts in *Harte-Hanks* were different from those in *E. W. Scripps*. The evidence of actual malice was substantially stronger in *Harte-Hanks*. The only pieces of evidence of actual malice they could point to in *E. W. Scripps* were the "grudge" theory, the "good case" marks on reporter's notes, the contention he "selectively interviewed only a few persons hostile to Ball as background" while "choosing not to interview those who could contradict their claims," and the "[criminals] couldn't have a better friend" statement by the ex-police officer.

The case points out how attorneys on the opposing side can highlight seemingly innocent mistakes even veteran journalists might commit and sway a jury toward the plaintiff's side. No story, no matter how much time is spent researching, writing, editing, and fact checking, is perfect. There will always be one more source who should have been interviewed, a misspelled name, wrong age, or transposed graph. Juries hold reporters and editors to high standards—so high, in fact, that they are sometimes impossible to meet. Juries are not journalists' peers. They focus on a story in dispute and fail to put the journalistic process into perspective by realizing that a reporter or editor usually cannot concentrate on only one story. To the jury, mistakes are unforgivable, no matter how minor. In the eyes of the jurors, mistakes reflect sloppy reporting.

In addition to the financial toll of libel suits, there is the time of individual reporters or editors spent under fire, as they face hours of depositions by opposing attorneys, briefings, and pretrial preparations conducted by their lawyers. Time spent in preparing a case and appearing in court is time away from the news. The toll can be enormous even when a media defendant wins.[86]

Elements of Libel

As with any tort, libel requires elements be established before a plaintiff can win a suit and recover damages. This section examines these with examples in case law, especially from the U.S. Supreme Court. While there is agreement on the general nature of each requirement, there are differences among courts and statutes in the role each element plays in the whole libel picture. Inconsistencies and confusion abound.

The Restatement (Second) of Torts[87] enumerates elements for a *prima facie* case of libel. These include: (a) a false and defamatory statement of and concerning another *(identification)*, (b) communication that is not privileged to a third party *(publication)*, (c) negligence or greater *fault* on the part of the plaintiff, and (d) actual injury arising from publication of the statement *(harm)*. The first element can actually be broken down into three requirements—*defamation, falsity, and identification*.

Defamation

To be libelous, a statement must be defamatory. The words in and of themselves may be defamatory *(libel per se)* or they may be defamatory only when extrinsic facts and circumstances are known *(libel per quod)*. Nevertheless, they must be such that they would or could injure the reputation of a person or other entity such as a business. A common definition of *libel* is information that tends to subject a person to public hatred, contempt, or ridicule or tends to demean individuals in their profession or business. Statements that tend to enhance a person's reputation, although they may be false, generally are not actionable. However, there may be instances in which it could trigger an invasion of privacy. Characterizing a person as well educated, intelligent, or kind would not be libelous, even if false, simply because such information does not harm the person's *reputation*, which is usually defined as standing in the community (i.e., what others think about that person).

The question of whether a statement is defamatory is crucial in many libel cases because it is often easy to establish most of the other elements, such as falsity, publication, and identification. Examples of information that the U.S. Supreme Court has upheld as defamatory or sent back to a trial court or a lower appellate court with the presumption that it was defamatory include:

1. A magazine's false accusation that a college football coach had conspired with another coach to "fix" a game [*Curtis Publishing Co. v. Butts* (1967)][88]
2. A magazine's false claim that an attorney for a family in its suit against a police officer for killing their son had been an official of a "Marxist League" advocating "violent seizure

Steps in a Libel or Slander Case

Prepared by Mark Sableman

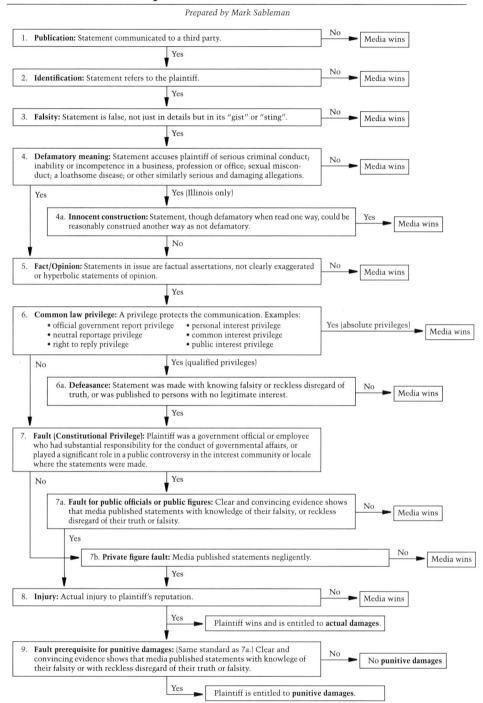

T H O M P S O N C O B U R N LLP

Figure 8.1 Steps in a Libel or Slander Case. (Prepared by Mark Sableman, Thompson Coburn LLP. Reprinted with permission.)

of our government" and that the attorney was a "Leninist" and a "communist" [*Gertz v. Welch* (1974)][89]

3. A magazine's statement that a multimillionaire's divorce was granted due to adultery when it had been for "a gross lack of domestication" on both sides [*Time v. Firestone* (1976)][90]

4. A credit reporting agency's circulation of a false statement that a contractor had filed for bankruptcy [*Dun & Bradstreet, Inc. v. Green-moss Builders, Inc.* (1985)][91]

The following have been held as not defamatory under the particular circumstances:

1. A statement during a pay-per-view World Championship Wrestling (WCW) event by a WCW creative director that the professional wrestler known as "Hulk Hogan" was a "god damn politician ... who doesn't give a shit about this company." The director, Vince Russo, was playing his scripted role as a member of WCW at the time. The professional wrestler was performing in his Hulk Hogan character. However, Russo strayed from his script and went on to note that the viewers would "never see that piece of shit again," called Hogan a "big bald son of a bitch," and told Hogan to "kiss my ass." A Georgia trial court granted a summary judgment in favor of the defendant on the ground the comments did not constitute factual statements but were merely rhetorical hyperbole made primarily to advance the storyline and role he had assumed [*Bollea v. World Championship Wrestling, Inc.* (2005)].[92]

2. A parody ad in *Hustler* magazine, in which the Rev. Jerry Falwell was depicted as having had sex with his mother in an outhouse [*Hustler Magazine and Larry C. Flynt v. Jerry Falwell* (1988)].[93] The U.S. Supreme Court reversed a jury decision awarding Falwell damages for intentional infliction of emotional distress. (The jurors had found that no libel had occurred.) There was no basis for a libel suit or for an emotional distress suit, according to the Supreme Court, because the parody had not been touted as factual or understood as such by readers.

Falsity

By virtue of its definition, libelous information must be false. Thus *truth* is an absolute defense. Most state statutes make it clear that truth, if demonstrated, is a complete defense to libel. Truth is typically not an issue in libel trials, especially those involving the mass media, because defamation suits that survive a motion to dismiss usually involve false information. Inaccuracies, even those that may initially appear to be minor, traditionally trip up reporters and editors.

An important issue that sometimes does arise about the element of falsity is whether the plaintiff has the burden of proving information is false or a defendant has the burden of showing the published statements are true. The assumption has been that public officials and public figures in libel suits have the burden of proving falsity. The Supreme Court's decision in *New York Times v. Sullivan* (1964)[94] requires public officials (and public figures, as enunciated later by the Court) to *show actual malice,* but, who has the burden in cases involving private figures?

In *Philadelphia Newspapers v. Hepps* (1986),[95] the Supreme Court answered one-half of the question when it held that a private individual suing a media defendant for libel over a matter of public concern must demonstrate that the information published was false. In other words,

Figure 8.2   November 1982 Hustler magazine parody. (Reprinted with permission from Larry Flynt.)

the media defendant does not have the burden of proving truth. In its 5 to 4 decision written by Justice Sandra Day O'Connor, the Court ruled unconstitutional the interpretation by some state courts that *Gertz v. Welch* permitted a court to assume the information was false unless proven otherwise by the defendant. Instead, the Court said a plaintiff must prove with clear and convincing evidence that the allegedly defamatory statements are false when they involve a matter of public concern. The Court appeared to leave the door open for state and lower courts to adopt a common law position that the burden is on the defendant to prove truth and apply the rule to situations involving non-media defendants in controversies. Two justices, Brennan and Blackmun, said the Court's rules were applicable to non-media defendants.

Identification

Before a person or corporation can be libeled, readers must link the defamatory information to that individual or entity. A reputation obviously cannot be harmed if no one understands to whom the defamatory information refers. However, identification does not have to be by name. Instead, the identification can be established with extrinsic facts. This latter process is known as *colloquium*.

Ordinarily, identification is not an issue in a libel case because the plaintiff is actually named or enough information is provided about the person in the story so there is little or no doubt about the individual's identity. There are three typical situations in which colloquium may be an issue: (a) stories in which no specific individual is named but allegations are inferred to a particular person, (b) fictionalized stories and stories employing pseudonyms, and (c) group libel.

A Florida case is a good illustration of the first situation. A Florida automobile mechanic sued ABC-TV for libel after his back was shown in a report on auto repair scams. The segment was an excerpt from a video secretly recorded by police. In the tape, mechanic Steven Berry is shown with his back to the camera while he works under a car's hood. The network filed a motion to dismiss Berry's suit on several grounds, including that Berry was not identifiable, and the U.S. District Court judge granted the motion.[96]

In *Bryson v. News America Publications*, only the last name was included in the article. Given the fact that Bryson is not a common name, a reasonable person could assume that the term "slut" referred to the plaintiff, according to the court. What if a different last name had been used but the other 24 alleged similarities remained? Would these similarities be enough to satisfy identification? It depends.

The second category, *fictionalization*, is illustrated in two cases: one involving a fictional Miss Wyoming and the other a fictional psychiatrist. In the first, *Pring v. Penthouse International, Ltd.* (1982),[97] Kimberli Jayne Pring, one-time Miss Wyoming in the Miss America contest, won $25 million in punitive damages and $1.5 million in actual damages from *Penthouse* magazine in a jury trial. The trial court judge reduced the punitive award to $12.5 million. The jury awarded Pring $10,000 actual and $25,000 punitive damages against author, Philip Cioffari. The adult magazine published a fictitious story about "Charlene," a fictional Miss Wyoming and champion baton twirler, as Pring had been, with another talent, or at least imagined she had another talent in the article—she could make men levitate by performing fellatio on them.

The article described three incidents during which Charlene (a) levitates a football player from her school by performing oral sex; (b) performs the same act on the football coach, while the audience applauds; and (c) performs a fellatio-like act on her baton, which stops the orchestra. The trial court jury and judge had no problem associating the alleged libel with the real former Miss Wyoming, and, on appeal, the 10th Circuit U.S. Court of Appeals accepted that determination (i.e., the article identified the plaintiff). However, the appeals court reversed the award, ruling the story was "complete fantasy," saying, "It is impossible to believe that anyone could understand that levitation could be accomplished by oral sex before a national audience or anywhere else. The incidents charged were impossible. The setting was impossible." Thus, the descriptions were "obviously a complete fantasy."[98] The appellate court reversed the verdict on grounds the story was too unbelievable to be libelous, rather than for lack of identification. The judges said labeling a story as fiction is not enough, the test being whether the charged portions in context could be reasonably understood as describing facts about the plaintiff or real events in which she participated. If it could not be understood as such, portions could not be taken literally.[99]

The Court of Appeals characterized the story as "gross, unpleasant, crude, distorted" and an attempt to ridicule the contest and contestants, without redeeming features. The court felt the story had First Amendment protection because the Constitution was intended to cover a "vast divergence in views and ideas." Would the appellate court have decided differently if the story had concerned acts that were not impossible? What if the nonsexual talent for both beauty contestants had been unusual: playing the piano while seated backward or speaking simultaneously in five languages?

The second example of fictionalization, *Bindrim v. Mitchell* (1979),[100] sheds light on these questions. Best-seller author Gwen Davis Mitchell decided to write a novel about leisure-class women. In an effort to gather background information for the book, she attended a nude therapy session offered by Paul Bindrim, a licensed clinical psychologist and author. Bindrim used a technique known as nude marathon in group therapy to get clients to shed inhibitions. Mitchell was allowed to attend only if she would agree in writing not to take photos, write articles, or in any way to disclose what happened. Mitchell told the psychologist she had no intentions of writing about the marathon. She was attending solely for therapy.

Two months later, Mitchell contracted with Doubleday to write her novel and received a $150,000 advance. The completed novel, *Touching,* included an account of a nude encounter session in southern California led by a fictional "Dr. Simon Herford." Bindrim sued for libel and breach of contract. He cited passages in the book as libelous, including the false implication that he used obscenities in therapy sessions and other inaccurate portrayals of what occurred at the nude marathon sessions. A jury awarded the plaintiff $38,000 against the author for libel, $25,000 in punitive damages against the publisher for libel, and $12,000 against the author on the contract claim. The total award was later reduced to $50,000. The Second Appellate District California Court of Appeal modified the amount of damages but affirmed the decision. The California Supreme Court and the U.S. Supreme Court rejected further appeals.

The California Court of Appeals had no problem with the question of whether Bindrim was identified: "There is overwhelming evidence that plaintiff and 'Herford' [the fictional doctor] were one." The trial court and the appellate court reached this conclusion in spite of major differences in characteristics. The book character is described as a "fat Santa Claus type with long white hair, white sideburns, a cherubic rosy face and rosy forearms," but Bindrim had short hair and shaved. The book character was an M.D. and Bindrim held a Ph.D. Their names were different. Common links convincing the court were nude marathon techniques and the similarity between a transcript of the encounter the author attended and one in the book. The court relied on the identification by several witnesses of the fictional Dr. Herford as Bindrim, the real psychologist.

Although *Bindrim v. Mitchell* is binding only in California's Second Appellate District, it has been influential in other cases. It invoked a common rule of identification employed in other jurisdictions—whether a reasonable person exposed to the work would understand the fictional character as referring to the real person. That is the key difference between *Bindrim* and *Pring*. Although the appellate court ruling in *Pring* was handed down in a different jurisdiction three years after *Bindrim,* the basic rule of identification was essentially the same. The *Penthouse* story was hype and fantasy. *Touching* hit close to home with descriptions of therapy sessions fairly close to what could have happened but did not.

What role did the contract Mitchell signed about nondisclosure play? Initially, the jury awarded Bindrim $12,000 in damages on the contract claim, but the trial court judge struck down the award. The appellate court upheld the judge's decision, noting that because Mitchell was a bona fide patient, she could write whatever she wished about what occurred in spite of the contract. Thus, the contract clause was unenforceable. It is clear from the case that even when fictional names are employed, authors must be cautious about how close their descriptions of fictional events are to the factual situations on which they are based. Changing names does not always protect the innocent.

Group Libel

One situation in which identification is nearly always an issue is *group libel*—defamatory comments directed at a specific group. The general rule is the larger the group, the less likely a member of the group has been defamed. Group libel suits are fairly common but are usually dismissed, unless they involve a small group. The late NBC-TV *Tonight Show* host, Johnny Carson, was once sued for $5 million by a dentist for jokes Carson told about dentists.[101] The jokes were directed at dentists in general, not the one whose letter Carson read on the air before a monologue. The suit was dismissed. Dentists compose too large a group for group libel.

Similar suits have been filed against film companies for depictions of ethnic groups in popular films. A U.S. District Court judge dismissed a class action suit he characterized as bordering "on the frivolous" filed against the Public Broadcasting System for airing the controversial documentary, *Death of a Princess*.[102] Plaintiffs sought $20 million in damages on behalf of all Muslims, who the plaintiffs asserted were defamed by the film's depiction of the execution of a Saudi Arabian princess for adultery. The total number of individuals alleged to have been defamed was 600 million. The court indicated that defamation of such a group "would render meaningless the rights guaranteed by the First Amendment to explore issues of public import."[103]

Similarly, a specific chain of businesses would not be permitted to recover for group libel unless its size was small. The founder of Kentucky Fried Chicken, the late Colonel Sanders, was known for commenting on the franchise products after he sold the company but for which he still served as a spokesperson. In a published story he said the gravy on mashed potatoes was "horrible" and the potatoes had "no nutrition," adding "[T]hat new 'crispy' recipe is nothing in the world but a damn fried dough-ball stuck on some chicken." A franchise owner sued on behalf of 5,000 franchised restaurants. The suit was dismissed by the Kentucky Supreme Court because the owner could not demonstrate that the comments referred to him or any of the other franchisees.[104]

A group of 637 net fishermen sued three Orlando, Florida, TV stations for libel after they broadcast paid political ads criticizing opposition to a state constitutional amendment to ban net fishing in coastal waters.[105] (The amendment was approved by voters.) A trial court judge dismissed the suit because the group was considered too large. A state court of appeals upheld the decision.[106] In its *per curiam* opinion, the appellate court aligned with jurisdictions recognizing that for a group defamation to be actionable by a member of the group when there is no specific reference to an individual, the group must be small enough for the defamation to be reasonably understood to refer to that member.[107]

The court cited cases from other jurisdictions to support its decision, including one in which a Nigerian businessman unsuccessfully sued for libel on behalf of 500 other Nigerian businesspeople after a *60 Minutes* segment about Nigerians engaged in allegedly fraudulent international business.[108] Another summary judgment was granted in a suit brought on behalf of almost 1 million Michigan hunters over a *60 Minutes* broadcast that criticized hunters.[109]

In a case similar to the Orlando suit, a group of 436 fishermen sued four Jacksonville, Florida, TV stations for airing the same ads.[110] The state appeals court was critical of the ads, calling them "false and fraudulent and clearly intended to mislead voters in the State of Florida."[111] Even after the stations were told by an outside source the ads were fraudulent, they continued to air them, "[k]nowing the words and images selected were false and fraudulent," according to the court. It said the stations were "actors and participants in the use of false and defamatory material in a negligent manner without reasonable care as to whether the defamatory advertisements were true or false."[112] The opinion suggested legislation.[113] The court concluded the plaintiffs had been unable to demonstrate the defamatory ads were *of and concerning* them because of the group's size.

William Prosser noted in his *Law of Torts* that 25 persons had become a general rule in determining whether a group is small enough for individual members to have been defamed by libelous statements about the group as a whole.[114] Some jurisdictions appear to apply such a rule of thumb, but it is not universal. The U.S. Supreme Court has never dealt directly with the issue of whether group libel is possible. It may someday have the opportunity with concern over "politically correct" speech. Universities have enacted codes of conduct that bar students and faculty from uttering racial, sexual, ethnic, and religious slurs in public on campus, including classes and school functions. Recent examples have emerged involving references to September 11 and the treatment of minority groups. Penalties for violations range from reprimands to expulsion or faculty firing. The purpose of such codes is to prevent libel of certain groups. They could be challenged as unconstitutional prior restraint or as unenforceable because the size of the group makes it impossible to establish *colloquium*—that is, that the libelous statements individually harm the group's members.

One case attracted considerable media attention more than a decade ago. A white male undergraduate student at the time, Eden Jacobowitz, was charged for violating the University of Pennsylvania's racial harassment policy. He faced charges after yelling "Shut up, you water buffalo" from his dormitory to five African American women, who he said were noisy. He contended the term *water buffalo* was not racist. The women filed a complaint but later dropped it. Jacobowitz sued the university for intentional infliction of emotional distress. The two sides settled out of court about five years after the incident, with the university admitting no harm or fault.[115]

There are at least two major points of view on group libel. On the one side are those individuals who believe the press should be held accountable for group libel under certain circumstances—such as racial, ethnic, and religious slurs when they cause substantial harm. The Rutgers women's basketball team in 2007 demanded and received an apology from CBS radio talk show host Don Imus after he referred to the players as "nappy-headed hos" on his program. Imus was initially dropped from several stations and then fired several days later by CBS. Racial and ethnic jokes are rife with stereotypes but publications employing them still have First Amendment protection. Presumably no mainstream publisher would present defamatory information but defamatory on line sources are sometimes brought to public attention. On the other hand, scholars argue that there should be no control over the press in uttering whatever group slurs and defamations it wishes to publish unless the comments would lead directly to violence. One writer characterized the two perspectives as "communitarian" and "liberal," respectively.[117] More recently special concerns have been expressed regarding the use of the term "person of interest" or "persons of interest." Use of those terms by authorities in controversial, unsolved criminal cases has raised some red flags with civil libertarians. The terms emerge almost in the same sense that the old "usual suspects" phrase was used to describe those who fit a certain profile. There is concern for persons unjustly accused of committing a crime by implication, as was the case in the press coverage of Richard Jewell and the Atlanta Olympics bombing.

Publication

The second element that must be demonstrated in a libel case, *publication*, is typically the easiest for a plaintiff to prove because the allegedly libelous information has appeared in a news story, documentary, book, or similar outlet. All that is required is simply that the information was communicated to a third party. There is usually no dispute about whether publication has occurred. On rare occasions, publication may be in question. For example, suppose a TV news director sends a confidential memo to one of the reporters falsely accusing him of doctoring his expense vouchers (i.e., inflating mileage or meal costs). The director types the memo and sends it in a sealed envelope to the reporter. Has publication occurred? The answer is *absolutely not*. The information has not been transmitted to the necessary third party. What if the reporter then shares the memo with others? Publication failed. An individual cannot communicate a defamatory message and then claim she has been libeled. In other words, self-publication will not work. If the alleged libeler publishes the defamatory remarks and then the person who is the object of the comments passes the information on to others, the libeler is certainly not off the hook. The key is that self-publication does not affect the outcome one way or another.

What if the director has a secretary type the memo, but the director still marks the envelope *confidential* and does not share the information with anyone else? Publication has been committed even if these three individuals are the only ones who actually see the memo. An equivalent situation happened when two reporters at the *Alton* (Illinois) *Telegraph* sent a confidential memorandum to an attorney in the U.S. Department of Justice summarizing information they gathered in an investigation they had conducted about possible organized crime ties with a major local contractor and a local bank. The reporters sent information, much of which was unsubstantiated, to fulfill a promise to share results of their investigations with the Justice Department in exchange for cooperation. Each page of the memo was marked *confidential* and the reporters noted some charges were unsubstantiated.[117]

The attorney to whom the memo was directed left the Justice Department soon after the memo was delivered. The memo eventually fell into the hands of Federal Home Loan Bank Board (FHLBB) officials after Justice Department employees passed it on with a suggestion that the bank board review the files of a savings and loan (S&L) association to determine whether loans to the developer had been proper. The memo from the reporters, which was never acted on by the Justice Department, had intimated possible ties to organized crime, although these links were not substantiated. The review indicated that improper loans had been made. The company lost several construction projects. The lawyer for the S&L vice president who had facilitated the loans discovered the existence of the confidential memo through a federal Freedom of Information Act request. By this time, the S&L was under control of the FHLBB and the construction enterprise had fallen apart. The reporters and the paper were sued for libel even though the allegedly libelous information was never published. The reporters merely sent the memo in an effort to get help in verifying unsubstantiated allegations to which the Justice Department had never responded.

Eleven years after the memo was sent, an Illinois Circuit Court jury awarded $6.7 million in compensatory damages and $2.5 million in punitive damages for a total of $9.2 million, more than the paper was worth.[118] At the time it was the largest U.S. libel award. An Illinois appellate court denied the newspaper's appeal on grounds it lacked jurisdiction because the newspaper failed to post a $13.8 million bond.[119] The newspaper did not have the funds to post bond and filed for bankruptcy. After the dust settled in bankruptcy proceedings, the *Telegraph* and insurers agreed to pay $1.4 million. The defense legal expenses alone were reportedly more than $600,000, which the paper itself had to pay.[120]

Privilege: Absolute, Qualified, and Constitutional

The element of *publication* also involves the concept of privilege. If defamatory information is privileged, the defamed person cannot recover damages even though the statements may have been false and caused harm. Thus, privilege can act as a defense to a libel suit. There are two basic types of privilege—**absolute** (sometimes called "unconditional") and **qualified** (known as "conditional" and "limited"). There is a third type known as **constitutional privilege** arising from the U.S. Constitution but, unlike absolute privilege, it originates indirectly from the First Amendment rather than from a specific provision in the Constitution. This third type of privilege did not exist until *New York Times v. Sullivan* in 1964 when the U.S. Supreme Court announced that press or media defendants could not be held liable for defaming public officials unless plaintiffs could demonstrate actual malice.

Except in one rare situation involving the broadcast media, as elaborated shortly, the press does not enjoy *absolute privilege.* Instead, this is a defense to libel that can generally be claimed only by participants, including officials in official proceedings. The best example of absolute privilege, one typically not connected with the media, lies in the Speech or Debate clause of the U.S. Constitution. Article I, Section 6 states: "They [Senators and Representatives] shall in all Cases, except Treason, Felony and Breach of the Peace, be privileged from Arrest during their attendance at the Session of their respective Houses, and in going to and returning from the same; and for any Speech or Debate in either House, they shall not be questioned in any other Place."

This clause ensures that any member of Congress cannot be held legally liable for any remarks made as part of an official proceeding in the Senate or the House, regardless of the harm they may cause, unless tantamount to a criminal act. A senator would not be immune from prosecution for plotting a murder or committing criminal fraud even though it occurred during a Senate hearing. A senator could make defamatory remarks about private citizens with impunity as U.S. Senator Joseph McCarthy did during the early 1950s when he launched attacks on alleged communists in a series of Senate hearings. The 2005 George Clooney film, *Good Night and Good Luck*, dramatizes McCarthy's attacks, including his infamous battle with famed CBS journalist Edward R. Murrow, who played a key role in McCarthy's downfall, especially with his famous March 9, 1954, *See It Now* broadcast. The senator's claims—that communists occupied government positions, aided by communist sympathizers—were never substantiated. However, McCarthy remained immune in spite of eventual censure by his fellow senators on December 2, 1954. The junior senator from Wisconsin died three years later.

During the McCarthy era, there was widespread abuse of the absolute privilege, but this defense remains alive, thanks to the U.S. Constitution. Since the 1930s, members of the U.S. House of Representatives have invoked a ritual known as "one-minute speeches." A member can speak for 60 seconds on any issue. The speeches require prior approval of the Speaker of the House, but this is always granted.[121] Sometimes these presentations become heated and controversial, but the tradition continues.

Hutchinson v. Proxmire *(1979)*

Another Wisconsin senator, William Proxmire, discovered that absolute privilege has limits. In 1975, the senator initiated a satirical "Golden Fleece of the Month Award" to publicize examples of what he considered wasteful government spending. He cited federal agencies, including the National Science Foundation, Office of Naval Research, and National Aeronautics and Space Administration, which funded research by Ronald R. Hutchinson, director of research at the Kalamazoo, Michigan, State Mental Hospital. Hutchinson received more than $500,000 over a seven-year period to conduct a study of emotional behavior in animals to devise an objective measure of aggression. The tests included exposing animals to aggravating stimuli to see how they reacted to stress. Proxmire's legislative assistant, Morton Schwartz, who had alerted the senator to Hutchinson's research, prepared a speech announcing the award to the Senate, along with an advance press release almost identical to the speech that was sent to 275 members of the media. Later, the senator mentioned the research and award in a newsletter sent to about 100,000 constituents and others, and he talked about it on TV. The next year Proxmire listed "Golden Fleece" awards for the previous year, including Hutchinson's. Proxmire mentioned Hutchinson by name in his speech and press release, but not in other publicity.

Among the comments by the senator in the release and in the Senate speech was: "Dr. Hutchinson's studies should make the taxpayers as well as the monkeys grind their teeth. In fact, the good doctor has made a fortune from his monkeys and in the process made a monkey out of the American taxpayer."[122] Hutchinson filed suit against Proxmire and Schwartz, claiming that as a result of publicity, he "suffered a loss of respect in his profession ... suffered injury to his feelings ... [had] been humiliated, held up to public scorn, suffered extreme mental anguish and physical illness and pain." He contended that he lost income and the ability to earn future income.

The defendants in the libel suit made a two-prong attack on the plaintiff's claims. First, they moved for change of venue from Wisconsin to the District of Columbia and for summary judgment on grounds that such criticism enjoyed absolute privilege under the Speech or Debate clause as well as protection under the First Amendment. Second, Proxmire and Schwartz argued that the researcher was both a public figure and a public official and thus had to demonstrate *actual malice* under *New York Times v. Sullivan*. No actual malice existed, according to the defendants.

The federal district court judge did not rule on the change of venue motion but did grant summary judgment in favor of the defendants. The judge said the Speech or Debate clause included investigative activities related to research and afforded Schwartz and Proxmire absolute immunity. The trial court also held that the press release "was no different [from a Constitutional perspective] from a radio or television broadcast of his speech from the Senate floor."[123]

The District Court further held that Hutchinson was a public figure because of his "long involvement with publicly-funded research, his active solicitation of federal and state grants, the local press coverage of his research, and the public interest in the expenditure of public funds on the precise activities in which he voluntarily participated."[124] The Seventh Circuit U.S. Court of Appeals affirmed the District Court ruling.[125] When Hutchinson appealed the decision to the U.S. Supreme Court, Proxmire and Schwartz said that newsletters, press releases, and appearances were protected by the Speech or Debate clause because they were necessary to communicate with Congress. They also argued this was essential for members of Congress to inform constituents.

On appeal, the U.S. Supreme Court, in an 8 to 1 decision written by Chief Justice Burger, reversed and remanded to the U.S. Court of Appeals. The Court noted that a literal reading of the clause would confine its application strictly to speech or debate within the walls of either house, but the Court previously ruled that committee hearings had absolute protection even if held outside chambers and committee reports enjoyed the same status. The majority opinion held that the objective of the clause was to protect legislative activities: "A speech by Proxmire in the Senate would be wholly immune and would be available to other members of Congress and the public in the Congressional record. But neither the newsletters nor the press release was 'essential to the deliberations of the Senate' and neither was part of the deliberative process."[126]

The second issue the Court had to deal with was the status of Hutchinson. Although both the trial court and the lower appellate court ruled the researcher was a "limited public figure" (see *Gertz v. Welch* later in this chapter) for purpose of comment on his receipt of federal funds, the Supreme Court held he was not a public figure, and thus he did not have to demonstrate actual malice. According to the Court, his activities and public profile "are much like those of countless members of his profession. His published writings reach a relatively small category of professionals concerned with research in human behavior. To the extent his published writings became a matter of controversy it was a consequence of the Golden Fleece Award."[127] The Court emphasized that "Hutchinson did not thrust himself or his views into public controversy to influence others" and that he did not have the requisite regular and continuing access to the news media to be classified as a public figure.

The lessons in *Hutchinson* are (a) absolute privilege has limits even when public officials utter the defamatory statements as part of their perceived official duties, and (b) individuals do not become public figures or officials simply by virtue of their attraction of government funding nor can they be made public figures by the creation of a controversy by someone else. In other words, don't thrust individuals into the limelight and then claim that they are public figures.

State and Local Recognition of Privilege

There are other examples of absolute privilege, but litigation involving them is rare. Most state constitutions contain a provision that parallels the federal Speech or Debate clause so that state lawmakers can debate without fear of libel or another tort as long as they are participating in an official proceeding. Sometimes local governments enact ordinances granting protection for officials. In federal and state courts, judges and trial participants can claim absolute privilege for remarks made during official proceedings. This does not mean witnesses can lie. They may be immune from libel or torts such as invasion of privacy, but can still be charged with perjury or false swearing.

There has been only one modern day instance in which the Supreme Court has recognized absolute privilege for the media. In a split (5 to 4) decision in *Farmers' Educational and Cooperative Union of America v. WDAY* (1959),[128] the justices held that because the Federal Communications Act of 1934 bars censorship of political speech by radio and TV stations, they can carry required broadcasts, including commercials under the Equal Opportunities Rule under Section 315, and claim absolute immunity from libel suits that may arise from defamatory statements. The ruling itself was not a great surprise because fairness would dictate that the government cannot require a station to carry a broadcast without any censorship and then subject it to potential liability for having complied with the law, but the narrow vote was somewhat surprising. The Court did indicate that the political opponent or whoever uttered the defamatory statements in the broadcast did not have absolute immunity and thus could face a libel suit.

Qualified Privilege

Qualified, conditional or limited privilege (a rose by any other name …) is the most common type of privilege available to the mass media. In proceedings such as legislative hearings and debates, the judicial process (grand jury deliberations, preliminary hearings, trials, etc.) and meetings of government agencies as well as for public records, the press has a qualified right to report information even though it may be defamatory. There is an important condition: *the report must be fair and honest.* Different states employ somewhat different language in specifying the condition, but the gist of it is still the same—the report must be an accurate account of what transpired or what is in the record and it must not be biased so as to unfairly defame an individual or other entity.

The requirement is not that the information be truthful; instead the report must be an accurate rendition. In most jurisdictions, if a plaintiff can prove that the publication was for an improper motive such as revenge or malice, the qualified privilege is defeated. The best tactic for journalists to demonstrate fairness is to show that they were acting to keep readers or viewers informed about a matter of public interest, emphasizing that citizens have a right to know what occurs in government proceedings. Minor errors such as a misspelled name (unless someone can claim the misspelled version) or slightly altering a quote for brevity (which is still an error and thus should not be done even though it may not prove fatal) are usually not enough to lose the privilege defense, but a minor oversight can lead to serious consequences. *Time* magazine learned this in *Time, Inc. v. Mary Alice Firestone.*[129]

Time, Inc. v. Mary Alice Firestone *(1976)*

In 1961 Mary Alice Firestone separated from her husband, Russell Firestone, heir to the Firestone fortune. She later filed a complaint for separate maintenance in a state trial court in Palm Beach, Florida. Russell Firestone counterclaimed with a request for divorce on grounds of extreme cruelty and adultery. After a trial with testimony from both sides about the other party's extramarital affairs, the Florida judge granted a divorce in a confusing judgment. He said, in part:

According to certain testimony in behalf of [Russell Firestone], extramarital escapades of [Mary Alice Firestone] were bizarre and of an amatory nature which would have made Dr. Freud's hair curl. Other testimony, in [her] behalf, would indicate that the defendant was guilty of bounding from one bed partner to another with the erotic zest of a satyr. The court is inclined to discount much of this testimony as unreliable. Nevertheless, it is the conclusion and finding of the court that neither party is domesticated, within the meaning of that term as used by the Supreme Court of Florida.... In the present case, it is abundantly clear from the evidence of marital discord that neither of the parties has shown the least susceptibility to domestication, and that the marriage should be dissolved.[130]

Thus the judge was granting the divorce on the ground of lack of domesticity, not on the grounds of extreme cruelty and adultery, although his decision was not entirely clear. The divorce proceedings received extensive local and national publicity, and Mary Alice Firestone held press conferences during the proceedings. *Time* was operating under a tight deadline to get the story published. The divorce decree was announced Saturday. The next deadline for the magazine was Sunday. *Time's* New York bureau heard the decision from an Associated Press wire story indicating "Russell A. Firestone had been granted a divorce from his third wife, whom 'he had accused of adultery and extreme cruelty.'" In its evening edition, the *New York Daily News* published a similar report. *Time's* New York staff got similar information from a bureau and a stringer in Palm Beach, place of the trial. With four sources, *Time* staff wrote this item appearing in the "Milestones" section the following week:

Divorced. By Russell A. Firestone Jr., 41, heir to the tire fortune: Mary Alice Sullivan Firestone, 32, his third wife; a one-time Palm Beach schoolteacher; on grounds of extreme cruelty and adultery; after six years of marriage, one son; in West Palm Beach, Fla. The 17-month intermittent trial produced enough testimony of extramarital adventures on both sides, said the judge, "to make Dr. Freud's hair curl."[131]

A few weeks later, Mary Alice Firestone requested a retraction of the article, claiming that a portion of it was "false, malicious and defamatory." (Florida law, similar to laws of many states, requires that a demand for retraction be made before a libel suit can be filed and allows the defendant to mitigate damages, if published.) *Time* refused and a suit ensued. In a jury trial in which the plaintiff called witnesses to testify that she suffered anxiety and concern over the inaccurate report, Firestone testified that she feared her young son would be adversely affected by the report. Prior to trial, she withdrew her claim for damages to reputation, asking for compensatory damages for harm other than to reputation, as permitted under Florida law. A sympathetic jury awarded her $100,000 in compensatory damages.

On appeal, Florida's Fourth Circuit Court of Appeals overturned the decision on the grounds that the article was fair and no damages had been demonstrated. The Florida Supreme Court reinstated damages on the basis that false information in the report was clear and convincing evidence of negligence. In a 5 to 3 decision, the U.S. Supreme Court vacated the state Supreme Court decision and sent it back to state court to determine fault, as required under the Court's decision in *Gertz v. Welch* (1994). The Court said under *Gertz* Mary Alice Firestone was a private figure and thus had to demonstrate only that the magazine was negligent, not that it had acted with actual malice. According to the Court, "Respondent did not assume any role of especial prominence in the affairs of society, other than perhaps Palm Beach society, and she did not thrust herself to the forefront of any particular public controversy in order to influence the resolution of the issues involved in it."[132]

The decision, written by William H. Rehnquist, noted, "Dissolution of a marriage through judicial proceedings is not the sort of 'public controversy' referred to in *Gertz*, even though the marital difficulties of extremely wealthy individuals may be of interest to some of the public."[133] The Court rejected *Time's* argument that the report was protected from libel because it was "factually correct" and "faithfully reproduced the precise meaning of the divorce judgment." Accordingly, for the report to have been accurate, "the divorce … must have been based on a finding … that [Russell Firestone's] wife had committed extreme cruelty towards him *and* that she had been guilty of adultery," not the case, the court said, in light of the trial court's findings.[134] Two years after the U.S. Supreme Court decision, Mary Alice Firestone's attorneys announced that she was dropping the suit because the original jury's verdict had vindicated her.

One difficult problem faced by the media is determining precisely when qualified privilege can be invoked. State laws vary with some granting protection in a range of circumstances from pretrial proceedings and government subcommittee meetings to public records whereas others are more narrowly drawn. The key is to be accurate and fair regardless of deadline or other pressures. In footnote 5 of its *Time* decision, the Supreme Court indicated that it appeared none of the magazine's employees had seen the Firestone divorce decree before the article appeared. *Time's* attorneys indicated in their appeal that the weekly would have published an identical statement even if the staff had seen the actual judgment before the story was written. The fact remains that a journalist versed in legal matters, as all journalists need to be, might have spotted the error. The third type of privilege, *constitutional privilege,* arose in *New York Times v. Sullivan* (1964).[135]

Negligence or Greater Fault: *New York Times v. Sullivan* (1964)

In 1964, the U.S. Supreme Court recognized a new defense to libel known as *constitutional privilege* in a decision that the Court continues to affirm while simultaneously narrowing its application. In *New York Times v. Sullivan,* the Court established the so-called *actual malice* rule that requires public officials to show defamatory material disseminated by a media defendant was published with knowledge it was false or with reckless disregard for whether it was false or true.

Although only the essentials of the case's history will be laid out here, there are some sources that everyone should read to gain a fuller understanding of this important decision. These include Anthony Lewis' *Make No Law: The Sullivan Case and the First Amendment* (1991), Peter E. Kane's *Errors, Lies, and Libel* (1992), and Rodney A. Smolla's *Suing the Press: Libel, The Media, and Power* (1986). Each offers its unique version of the case in a way that the reader will truly appreciate the importance of the decision that has affected media law for decades.[136]

On Tuesday, March 29, 1960, the *New York Times* published a full page advertisement entitled "Heed Their Rising Voices." Although the ad's descriptions of civil rights violations were faithful to real events in the South, the details of what had occurred in Montgomery, Alabama, were inaccurate. As Smolla pointed out, the black students who demonstrated on the capitol steps in Montgomery sang the *The Star Spangled Banner* instead of *My Country 'Tis of Thee*; the nine black students were expelled from college for demanding service at a lunch counter in the county courthouse rather than for leading the demonstration; and police had never "ringed" the Alabama State College campus, although they had been called to campus three times in connection with civil rights protests.[137] Other errors included the claim that Dr. Martin Luther King, Jr. had been arrested seven times (he was arrested four times) and that police ("Southern violators") had twice bombed his home (they were never implicated and reportedly attempted to determine who committed the violence).[138]

Soon after the ad appeared, the *New York Times* was sued by several Alabama politicians, including Governor John Patterson and L. B. Sullivan, a Montgomery city commissioner. The *Times* printed a retraction, as requested by the governor, but rejected the request for a retraction from Sullivan, who, as Commissioner of Public Affairs, was in charge of the police department. Nowhere in the ad is any mention made of Sullivan or his position. Sullivan successfully contended at trial that use of the term *police* implicated him because his duties entailed supervising the police department. He also claimed that he was implicated by reference to "Southern violators," which he asserted meant Montgomery County police because arrests would have been handled by police.

Sullivan's attorneys called witnesses to indicate whether the ad was "of and concerning" the plaintiff, as required under Alabama libel law. All of them said they associated the allegedly defamatory statements with Sullivan or the police department.[139] Although lawyers for the newspaper argued Sullivan was not identified, the jury and the trial court judge were convinced otherwise. The paper's attorneys raised defenses of privilege, truth, and lack of malice. In reversing the Alabama Supreme Court, the U.S. Supreme Court did not buy Sullivan's contention that he was identified in the ad. According to Justice Brennan's majority opinion:

> [The evidence] was incapable of supporting the jury's finding that the allegedly libelous statements were made "of and concerning" respondent [Sullivan]. Respondent relies upon the words of the advertisement and the testimony of six witnesses to establish a connection between it and himself.... There was no reference to respondent in the advertisement, either by name or official position.[140]

The Court noted that several of the allegedly libelous statements did not concern police and reference to "they" "could not reasonably be read as accusing [Sullivan] of personal involvement in the acts in question."[141] The Court went on to say, "Although the statements may be taken as referring to the police, they did not on their face make even an oblique reference to [Sullivan] as an individual."[142] The justices reasoned that identification must be established through testimony of witnesses for the plaintiff, but "none of them suggested any basis for the belief that [Sullivan] himself was attacked in the advertisement beyond the bare fact that he was in overall charge of the police department and thus bore official responsibility for police conduct."[143] If identification or colloquium could be established on this basis, as the Alabama Supreme Court indicated in upholding the verdict, then criticism of government (seditious libel) would rear its ugly head because any criticism of government could easily become criticism of government officials and therefore be punished. According to the U.S. Supreme Court:

> Raising as it does the possibility that a good-faith critic of government will be penalized for his criticism, the proposition relied on by the Alabama courts strikes at the very center of the constitutionally protected area of free expression. [footnote omitted]

> We hold that such a proposition may not be constitutionally utilized to establish that an otherwise impersonal attack on government operations was libel of an official responsible for those operations. Since it was relied on exclusively here, and there was no other evidence to connect the statements with [Sullivan], the evidence was constitutionally insufficient to support a finding that the statements referred to [Sullivan].[144]

The Court did not rule out public officials being able to sue for libel for criticism in connection with their official duties, but the Court was not willing to permit plaintiffs such as Sullivan to infer libel simply because government actions connected with them were criticized. This aspect of *Sullivan* is often overlooked in discussions of the case, although lack of identification was a clearly a major reason the U.S. Supreme Court reversed the Alabama Supreme Court's upholding of the trial court verdict against the *Times*.

At the time the *New York Times* decision originated, the climate for civil rights, especially in the South, was hostile. The trial judge announced before the trial began in earnest that the 14th Amendment "has no standing whatever in this Court, it is a pariah and an outcast."[145]

The 14th Amendment was ratified after the Civil War. It was aimed at ensuring individuals would be protected against state actions that attempted to override rights guaranteed under the U.S. Constitution. ("No State shall make or enforce any law which shall abridge the privileges or immunities of citizens of the United States.") This amendment, interpreted by the Supreme Court, assures all persons have the same rights as state citizens as they do as U.S. citizens. That meant a state or local government can impose no greater restriction on free speech or press freedom than what the federal government may impose, as the Court made clear in 1925 in *Gitlow v. New York*.[146]

The judge in *Sullivan* permitted several of the jurors in the trial to be seated in the jury box with Confederate uniforms. They had just participated in a re-enactment of the swearing in of Confederate President Jefferson Davis.[147] Seating at the trial was segregated by race. During the trial, one of Sullivan's attorneys, Calvin Whitesell, appeared to be saying *nigger* instead of *Negro* when he read the ad to the jury.[148] One defense raised by the *Times* was lack of *in personam* jurisdiction by the state court because only 394 copies out of a circulation of 650,000 had been distributed in the state. The trial court judge rejected the motion.

The local lawyer for the newspaper, T. Eric Embry, made what is known as a *special appearance*—a procedure by which an attorney is allowed to make a onetime appearance before a court to challenge its jurisdiction. With a special appearance, unlike a general appearance, the attorney is not agreeing for the client to come under the authority of the court, but simply to come before the judge to argue that the court does not have the authority to hear the case. He followed steps enunciated by Judge Jones in a book the judge had written, entitled *Alabama Pleading and Practice*, only to have the judge overrule his own book. The judge declared Embry's presence was a *general appearance*, subjecting Embry's client to the court's jurisdiction.[149]

At the time of the *New York Times* trial, Alabama, like a few other states, had a strict liability libel statute. Under this, a judge instructs a jury that once the statements are determined to be libelous per se (as he ruled) and are not privileged, to find the defendants liable, the jury needs only to find that they had published the ad and the statements were "made of and concerning" the plaintiff. The jury was told because the statements were libelous per se, "the law … implies legal injury from the bare fact of publication itself," "falsity and malice are presumed." "General damages need not be alleged or proved but are presumed," and "punitive damages may be awarded by the jury even though the amount of actual damages is neither found nor shown."[150]

After a three day trial, the jury deliberated for two hours and awarded the plaintiff the full amount he sought—$500,000—against the *Times* and four ministers, also defendants. It was at that time the largest libel judgment in the state's history. The jury gave no indication of how much of the award was for actual damages and how much for punitive damages. The Alabama Supreme Court sprung no surprises in its decision on appeal, sustaining the trial court verdict in its entirety. The U.S. Supreme Court granted certiorari and heard oral arguments on January 6, 1964. Two months later, the Court handed down its historic unanimous opinion written by Justice William Brennan.

Actual Malice Requirement

Federal courts, including the U.S. Supreme Court, are barred from hearing cases that do not involve a *federal question* (or diversity if the case originates in U.S. District Court). *Federal question* means the case must concern the U.S. Constitution, Acts of Congress, treaties or another area in which jurisdiction has been granted to the federal courts. Thus the Supreme Court had to find jurisdictional authority before it could hear the appeal from the *New York Times*. The Court readily disposed of both major arguments against its jurisdictional power over the case. First, the Court rejected the contention of the Alabama Supreme Court that the case involved private action, not state action, and that the 14th Amendment could not be invoked. The Court said the fact that the case involved a civil suit in common law was irrelevant because the "test is not the form in which state power has been applied but, whatever the form, whether such power has in fact been exercised."[151] The Court had no problem finding state action in Alabama's attempt to impose restrictions on the constitutional rights of the defendants.

Second, the justices disagreed with the Alabama courts that First Amendment rights were inapplicable in the case because the libel involved a paid commercial advertisement. Noting that this argument relied on *Valentine v. Chrestensen*, the Supreme Court said the *Times* ad was not a commercial ad in the sense of *Chrestensen*. The Court instead characterized it as an *editorial advertisement* that "communicated information, expressed opinion, recited grievances, protested claimed abuses, and sought financial support on behalf of a movement whose existence and objectives are matters of the highest public interest and concern."[152] The Court felt public officials should take the heat of criticism, even when false information is involved:

> Thus we consider this case against the background of a profound national commitment to the principle that debate on public issues should be uninhibited, robust, and wide-open, and that it may well include vehement, caustic, and sometimes unpleasantly sharp attacks on government and public officials. [citations omitted] The present advertisement, as an expression of grievance and protest on one of the major public issues of our time, would seem clearly to qualify for the constitutional protection. The question is whether it forfeits that protection by the falsity of some of its factual statements and by its alleged defamation of respondent.[153]

In another significant part of the decision, the Court rejected the ruling of the Alabama court that the First Amendment's limit on repression of freedom of speech and freedom of the press under criminal statutes such as the federal Sedition Act did not apply to state civil libel statutes. "[W]hat a State may not constitutionally bring about by means of a criminal statute is likewise beyond the reach of prosecution under a civil statute," according to the Court. The justices enunciated a new actual malice rule: "The constitutional guarantees require, we think, a federal rule that prohibits a public official from recovering damages for a defamatory false-hood relating to his official conduct unless he proves that the statement was made with actual malice—that is, with the knowledge that it was false or with reckless disregard of whether it was false or not."[154]

With this statement, the U.S. Supreme Court set a new standard for determining when media defendants can be held liable for publication of defamatory information about public officials. For the first time, the Court was granting First Amendment protection for false, defamatory statements under certain conditions. As subsequent cases have demonstrated, proving actual malice with convincing clarity (as the Court said was necessary) is a tough but by no means impossible burden for a libel plaintiff. When it applied this standard to the *Sullivan* case, the Court ruled in favor of the *New York Times* and the other four defendants.

More than four decades after *New York Times v. Sullivan* was handed down, much of the general public is unaware of the case and the principle it established. One statewide survey found that almost seven out of ten respondents felt that if a newspaper accidentally used false information in an editorial criticizing a well-known person, that individual would be justified in suing for libel.[155] Similar surveys in other states would likely find the same results, although the Supreme Court made it clear that public officials (later extended to public figures) would not be able to recover for accidental disclosure of false information that would constitute neg-ligence, not the requisite actual malice.

Garrison v. Louisiana (1964): The Death of Criminal Libel?

The U.S. Supreme Court later expanded the actual malice rule to apply to criminal libel. In *Jim Garrison v. Louisiana* (1964),[156] the Court unanimously reversed the conviction of Orleans Parish (Louisiana) District Attorney Jim Garrison[157] for criminal libel for attacking the conduct of eight judges of his parish's criminal district court at a press conference. Garrison attributed a large backlog of cases to "the inefficiency, laziness, and excessive vacations of the judges" and accused them of hampering his efforts to enforce state vice laws by refusing to approve dis-bursements for the expenses of undercover investigations of vice in New Orleans. He was tried without a jury by a judge in another parish and convicted of criminal libel under a Louisiana statute providing criminal penalties for the utterance of truthful statements with actual malice ("hatred, ill will or enmity or a wanton desire to injure") and for false statements about public officials unless made "in reasonable belief of truth." The Louisiana Supreme Court upheld the conviction. The U.S. Supreme Court reversed.

The Louisiana statute was unconstitutional, according to majority opinion. Neither civil nor criminal liability can be imposed for false statements about official conduct unless statements are made with knowledge of falsity or reckless disregard for truth. The actual malice rule of *Sullivan* now applied to both civil and criminal libel for criticism of officials. The Court took an opportunity to clarify the meaning of *actual malice* by defining the term to include having "serious doubts" about the truth of the publication and uttering "false statements made with … [a] high degree of awareness of their probable falsity." The justices indicated that the use of a "calculated falsehood" would not be immune from liability and that the *New York Times* rule "absolutely prohibits punishment of truthful criticism" of the official conduct of public officials.

The Court did not toll the death of criminal defamation in *Garrison v. Louisiana*. Twelve years before *Garrison,* the Court upheld the constitutionality of an Illinois criminal libel statute. In *Beauharnais v. Illinois* (1952),[158] the Court upheld a statute that made it a crime to "… sell, or offer for sale, advertise or publish, present or exhibit in any public place in this state any lithograph, moving picture, play drama or sketch, which … portrays depravity, criminality, unchastity, or lack of virtue of a class of citizens, of any race, color, creed or religion to contempt, derision, or obloquy, or which is productive of breach of the peace or riots.…"[159]

Beauharnais, president of the White Circle League, was convicted by a jury of violating the statute and fined $200. He distributed racist leaflets on streets in Chicago urging the mayor and city council "to halt the further encroachment, harassment and invasion of white people, their property, neighborhoods and persons, by the Negro" and called upon "[o]ne million self-respecting white people in Chicago to unite … If persuasion and the need to prevent the white race from becoming mongrelized by the negro will not unite us, then the aggressions … rapes, robberies, knives, guns and marijuana of the negro, surely will."[160]

The Court rejected Beauharnais' argument that the statute violated his free speech and press rights guaranteed against states under the 14th Amendment Due Process clause. According to the 5 to 4 majority decision, libelous statements, including criminal libel, are not protected by the Constitution. *Beauharnais* has never been directly overturned by the Court although dissenting opinions of Justices Black, Reed, Douglas, and Jackson have found more favor over the decades. *Beauharnais*, in fact, continues to be cited by the Court to support the principle that libelous speech does not have First Amendment protection, including its citation in 1992 in *R.A.V. v. City of St. Paul*,[161] which struck down a city ordinance used to punish teenagers for allegedly burning a cross on the lawn of an African American family.

Two years after *Garrison*, the U.S. Supreme Court handed down another decision involving criminal libel—this time, common law rather than statutory law—without specifically referring to *Sullivan's* actual malice rule. In *Steve Ashton v. Kentucky* (1966),[162] a unanimous court reversed the conviction of a man who had committed the common law offense of criminal defamation by circulating a pamphlet in Hazard, Kentucky, during a bitter labor battle. It criticized the city police chief, sheriff, and owner of a local newspaper for not supporting striking miners. Steve Ashton accused the sheriff of "probably" buying off the jury "for a few thousand dollars" and state police of escorting "scabs into the mines and hold[ing] the pickets at gunpoint." The trial judge, who fined Ashton $3,000 and sentenced him to 6 months in prison, defined criminal libel as "any writing calculated to create disturbances of the peace, corrupt the public morals, or lead to any act, which, when done, is indictable." In the majority opinion, the Court held such a law was too vague because punishing someone for publishing that tends to breach the peace makes that person "a criminal simply because his neighbors have no self-control and cannot refrain from violence." Three months before *Ashton,* the U.S. Supreme Court elaborated on circumstances under which a public official can be defamed under *Sullivan,* including how to separate criticism of officials from criticism of government. In *Alfred D. Rosenblatt v. Frank P. Baer* (1966),[163] six justices, in an opinion written by Justice Brennan, reversed a jury award of damages to a former supervisor of county recreation against a local unpaid newspaper columnist. The columnist alleged mismanagement by a ski resort after the plaintiff was discharged and claimed, "On any sort of comparative basis, the Area this year is doing literally hundreds of percent BETTER than last year." The column made no mention of the plaintiff, but the jury and trial court judge felt the criticism referred to the former supervisor. The Court said, "in the absence of sufficient evidence that the attack focused on the plaintiff, an otherwise impersonal attack on governmental operations cannot be utilized to establish a libel of those administering the operations."[164]

The decision clearly defined *public official*, which the Court said "applies at the very least to those among the hierarchy of government employees who have, or appear to the public to have, substantial responsibility for or control over the conduct of governmental affairs."[165]

New York Times' Progeny: Extending the Actual Malice Rule

Three years after *Sullivan*, the U.S. Supreme Court extended application of the *actual malice rule* to *public figures*, which the Court defined as persons who thrust themselves "into the 'vortex' of an important public controversy." In *Curtis Publishing Co. v. Butts* and *Associated Press v. Walker* (1967),[166] the Court combined two cases whose trial court decisions had been made prior to *New York Times v. Sullivan*. University of Georgia Athletic Director Wallace Butts was awarded $60,000 in general damages and $3 million in punitive damages by a jury for an article in the *Saturday Evening Post* magazine that accused him and legendary Alabama football coach, Paul "Bear" Bryant, of fixing a game between the schools. The magazine relied on information from an Atlanta insurance salesman who said he accidentally overheard a phone conversation between the men. The judge reduced the award to $460,000, and upon appeal by the publisher, the Fifth Circuit U.S. Court of Appeals affirmed. The U.S. Supreme Court also upheld the verdict.

The second case involved an Associated Press story about retired Army General Edwin Walker, which erroneously said he had led a violent crowd of protesters at the University of Mississippi to block federal marshals attempting to carry out a court order permitting James Meredith, an African American, to enroll at the segregated public university. Walker won $500,000 in compensatory damages and $300,000 in punitive damages in a jury trial, but the judge struck the award of punitive damages. The U.S. Supreme Court reversed the verdict.

In a plurality opinion written by Justice Harlan, the Court distinguished the two cases. Both individuals were public figures, according to the Court, but the evidence indicated "the Butts story was in no sense 'hot news' and the editors of the magazine recognized the need for a thorough investigation of the serious charges. Elementary precautions were, nevertheless, ignored." The Court found the second case much different:

> There the trial court found the evidence insufficient to support more than a finding of even ordinary negligence and the Court of Civil Appeals supported the trial court's view of the evidence … In contrast to the *Butts* article, the dispatch which concerns us in *Walker* was news which required immediate dissemination. The Associated Press received the information from a correspondent who was present at the scene of the events and gave every indication of being trustworthy and competent.[167]

The plurality opinion also advocated a different test for actual malice in the case of public figures versus public officials: "We consider and would hold that a 'public figure' who is not a public official may also recover damages for a defamatory falsehood whose substance makes substantial danger to reputation apparent, on a showing of highly unreasonable conduct constituting an extreme departure from the standards of investigation and reporting ordinarily adhered to by responsible publishers."[168] This test attracted support of only three justices besides Harlan. Since then, some state courts and an occasional federal court have cited the test as appropriate, but the U.S. Supreme Court has never explicitly adopted this standard.

The same year as *Curtis Publishing,* the Court ruled in a *per curiam* opinion that a county clerk up for reelection in West Virginia had failed to demonstrate actual malice with the convincing clarity required under the *New York Times* standard when he was attacked in three local newspaper editorials. In *Beckley Newspapers Corp. v. C. Harold Hanks* (1967),[169] the Court reversed a $5,000 jury verdict because the evidence showed no "high degree of awareness of … probable falsity."

Serious doubts became the buzzwords for actual malice in 1968 when the Court ruled 8 to 1 in *Phil A. St. Amant v. Herman A. Thompson*[170] that a public official failed to show defamatory statements about him in a televised political speech were made with actual malice. According to the opinion written by Justice White: "There must be sufficient evidence to permit the conclusion that the defendant in fact entertained serious doubts as to the truth of his publication. Publishing with such doubts shows reckless disregard for truth or falsity and demonstrates actual malice."[171]

Two years after *St. Amant,* the U.S. Supreme Court held in *Greenbelt Cooperative Publishing Assoc. v. Charles Bresler* (1970)[172] that use of the term *blackmail* in referring to a real estate developer's negotiating stance could not be reasonably understood as a criminal accusation because it was merely rhetorical hyperbole. The Court overturned a $17,500 jury verdict for the defendant.

In a similar vein, the Court reversed the $20,000 jury verdict evenly split against a newspaper and the distributor of a syndicated column for referring to the criminal records of one of several candidates for the U.S. Senate primary in New Hampshire and for calling him a "former small-time bootlegger." According to the Court, the judge in *Monitor Patriot Co. v. Roselle A. Roy* (1971)[173] erroneously instructed the jury that actual malice had to be shown only if the libel concerned the plaintiff's fitness for office. The judge allowed the jury to determine whether the alleged conduct was relevant, but the U.S. Supreme Court said "a charge of criminal conduct, no matter how remote in time or place, can never be irrelevant to an official's or candidate's fitness for office for purposes of application" of the actual malice rule.[174]

In *Time, Inc. v. Pape* (1971)[175] the justices attempted to clarify the actual malice rule in a complex case. The Court's analysis focused on whether omission of the qualifier "alleged" in a *Time* magazine story about an incident reported in a commission's report could be considered by a jury as evidence of actual malice. Characterizing the report as "extravagantly ambiguous," the Court's majority felt failure on the magazine's part was "at most an error of judgment rather than reckless disregard of the truth" and could not be construed as actual malice, which the defendant would have needed to demonstrate because he was considered a public figure.

In *Ocala Star-Banner Co. v. Leonard Damron* (1971),[176] the Supreme Court wrestled with an issue similar to that in *Monitor Patriot Company*—whether a false report of the alleged criminal misconduct of a public official is relevant to the person's qualifications. The case arose when a small daily newspaper accidentally used the name of the plaintiff instead of his brother who had been charged with perjury. The mistake was committed by an editor who had been at the paper for about a month. Citing *Monitor Patriot,* the Court reversed a $22,000 verdict awarding compensatory damages.

The Court issued another libel decision in 1971, *George A. Rosenbloom v. Metro-media*,[177] a plurality opinion that the justices subsequently rejected. The essence of the ruling was that both public figures and private individuals involved in events of public concern must demonstrate actual malice. That view was never adopted by a majority of justices, although some state courts applied versions of it. The Court was obviously struggling to give meaning to the actual malice rule. On the tenth anniversary of *New York Times v. Sullivan,* the U.S. Supreme Court had the opportunity to deal with questions that continued to surround its 1964 landmark decision.

Gertz v. Welch (1974):
Handing the Standard of Care for Private Individuals Back to the States

In *Elmer Gertz v. Robert Welch, Inc.* (1974),[178] the Court for the first time dealt with the standard of care to be applied in the case of a private figure. In a 5 to 4 opinion, second only to *New York Times v. Sullivan* in its stature among libel rulings, the justices held that each state may set its own standard so long as the standard is not one of strict liability. A defendant cannot be held liable simply because defamatory information was published, but instead the plaintiff must show, at the very least, that the defendant violated the prevailing standard of care. In other words, the defendant must, at a minimum, have acted unreasonably. In some states, this means the defendant did not do what a reasonable journalist would have done. In other states the standard is *reasonable person.*

The case began when Elmer Gertz, a well-known Chicago attorney, was severely criticized in *American Opinion*, a magazine published by the right-wing John Birch Society. Gertz had represented the Nelson family in a civil suit against a Chicago police officer, Richard Nuccio, who had been convicted of second degree murder in the death of their son. Although Gertz had played no role in the criminal proceeding against Nuccio, the magazine article, entitled "Frame-Up: Richard Nuccio and the War on Police," accused the attorney of being an architect in a frame-up against police. The story said the police file on Gertz took "a big Irish cop to lift," that he had been an official of the "Marxist League for Industrial Democracy," and that he was a "Leninist," a "Communist fronter," and a former officer of the National Lawyers Guild. The article described the guild as a communist organization that "probably did more than any other outfit to plan the communist attack on the Chicago police during the 1968 Democratic Convention."

The statements were false. Gertz had no criminal record. There was no evidence that he was a "Leninist" or "Communist fronter," and he had never been a member of the Marxist League. He had been a member of the National Lawyers Guild 15 years earlier, but there was no evidence that he or the organization had taken any part in demonstrations. Robert Welch, the magazine's managing editor, "made no effort to verify or substantiate the charges" against Gertz, according to the Court. "The principal issue in this case is whether a newspaper or broadcaster that publishes defamatory falsehoods about an individual who is neither a public official nor a public figure may claim a constitutional privilege against the liability for the injury inflicted by those statements,"[179] the Court said.

Gertz won $50,000 in damages in a jury trial against the magazine, but the judge instructed the jury that the plaintiff was a private individual, not a public figure, concluding after the verdict that the actual malice standard of *New York Times v. Sullivan* should have been applied instead of the state's negligence standard. He issued a *jnov* overturning the jury's decision. The U.S. Supreme Court reversed the trial court decision and ordered a new trial.

Many states now have a *negligence* standard. Alaska, Colorado, Indiana, and New Jersey adopted an actual malice standard for private figures. New York imposes a gross irresponsibility standard, and it is unclear from four states—Connecticut, Louisiana, Montana, and New Hampshire—exactly what rule applies.[180]

The Court made two more significant points in *Gertz*. First, it determined that Gertz was not a public figure:

> He played a minimal role at the coroner's inquest, and his participation related solely to his representation of a private client. He took no part in the criminal prosecution of Officer Nuccio. Moreover, he never discussed either the civil or criminal litigation with the press and was never quoted as having done so. He plainly did not thrust himself into the vortex of this public issue, nor did he engage the public's attention in an attempt to influence its outcome.[181]

The Court further indicated there are two types of public figures. One type is a person who has achieved such "pervasive fame or notoriety that he [she] becomes a public figure for all purposes and in all contexts." This type of public figure is now generally called an *all-purpose public figure.* The second and more common type of public figure is "an individual [who] voluntarily injects [her] himself or is drawn into a public controversy, becoming a public figure for a limited range of issues." This category is known as a *limited-purpose public figure.*

Under the *Gertz* rationale, both the all-purpose public figure and the public official must show actual malice before they can recover any damages for libel unless the libelous statements do not relate to their public performance. However, limited-purpose public figures need to demonstrate actual malice only if the libelous matter concerns the public issue or issues on which they have voluntarily thrust themselves into the vortex. The private individual need demonstrate only that the particular standard of care was violated, which is typically negligence, a much lower standard than actual malice. The Court said that "hypothetically, it may be possible for someone to become a public figure through no purposeful action of his [her] own, but the instances of truly involuntary public figures must be exceedingly rare."[182] The instances are so rare that since *Gertz* was handed down, the U.S. Supreme Court has yet to uphold a libel decision in which a plaintiff was classified as an involuntary public figure. It is safe to assume when reporting about people who have somehow been involuntarily thrust into the public spotlight that they are private figures, not public figures for libel purposes. Elmer Gertz, Mary Alice Firestone, and Ronald R. Hutchinson were all private figures, not public figures.

What about Richard Jewell? When a bomb exploded in summer 1996 at Centennial Olympic Park in Atlanta, killing one person and injuring 111 others, Jewell became a hero because he had discovered a suspicious knapsack, alerted police, and helped clear people away. Three days later, the 33-year-old security guard was questioned by the FBI under circumstances for which Attorney General Janet Reno made an apology months later.[183] The *Atlanta Journal-Constitution* was the first media outlet to identify Jewell as a "prime suspect," citing anonymous sources. Others followed suit including CNN, *Time* magazine, and NBC-TV. For the next 88 days, the FBI kept Jewell and his apartment where he lived with his mother under surveillance, and followed him with an entourage. His apartment was searched and his mother interviewed, as were acquaintances and former employers, but he was never arrested or charged with any crimes. Throughout the ordeal, he was the subject of intense media coverage. On October 26, 1996, the U.S. Department of Justice sent his attorney a letter, saying, "Based on evidence developed to date, your client Richard Jewell is not considered a target of the federal criminal investigation into the bombing."[184]

Jewell sued or threatened to sue several media outlets for libel and invasion of privacy, including WABC-AM in New York (owned by Walt Disney Co.), the *New York Post,* NBC-TV, CNN, and the *Atlanta Journal-Constitution.* Most media law experts quoted in news accounts and in an article in the *American Bar Association Journal* generally agreed that Jewell had little chance of winning his lawsuits, primarily because they believed he would likely be considered a public figure for purposes of libel and thus would have to prove actual malice.[185] They pointed to the fact that Jewell had voluntarily granted interviews, especially after the bombing. An attorney for Jewell criticized the media for crossing the ethical line and prematurely judging his client.[186]

NBC became the first media outlet to settle with Jewell, paying him an estimated $500,000 for comments made by the then-dominant news anchor Tom Brokaw.[187] CNN also settled for an undisclosed amount. *Time* made no payment, but indicated in a "clarification" that it regretted what "may have been some inaccurate or incomplete" statements.[188] In the final analysis, Richard Jewell was cleared of all charges and all allegations made in the media against him. The media did not fare as well. Other prominent news organizations including Cox Enterprises (parent to the *Atlanta Journal-Constitution*) and the *New York Post* were targeted for their inaccurate coverage and misreporting of aspects of Richard Jewell's story. Some news outlets, including CNN, continue to maintain their coverage was fair and accurate. The Georgia Court of Appeals ruled that reporters did not have to reveal confidential sources unless Jewell could show a need for this sensitive information. In *Jewell v. Atlanta Journal-Constitution* (2001), the state appellate court also ruled that Jewell had become a voluntary public figure, pointing to his "ten interviews and one photo shoot in three days," most of them to the national press.[189]

In the current environment, particularly in the aftermath of the World Trade Center Attack of September 11, 2001, and subsequent bombings in Madrid, Spain and London, England, among others, similar concerns have been expressed regarding use of the terms, "person of interest" or "persons of interest." Army scientist Steven J. Hatfill, for example, requested in 2005 that a federal court of appeals reinstate a lawsuit claiming the *New York Times* had ruined his reputation by publishing false accusations implying that he was responsible for the deadly anthrax mailings of 2001. Then U.S. Attorney General John Ashcroft had labeled Hatfill a "person of interest."[190]

In *Gertz* the U.S. Supreme Court indicated that *self-help* is an important factor for courts to consider in distinguishing categories of libel plaintiffs. Is there an opportunity to address an unfounded allegation, contradict a lie, or correct an error, thereby minimizing adverse impact on a person's reputation? The Court in *Gertz* noted that private individuals usually lack "effective opportunities for rebuttal," whereas those who seek public office "must accept certain necessary consequences of that involvement in public affairs." This point was clearly a warning of what was to come. The Court held that no libel plaintiffs—public or private—could recover punitive damages unless the person demonstrated actual malice. The Court noted, "It is necessary to restrict defamation plaintiffs who do not prove knowledge of falsity or reckless disregard for the truth to compensation for actual injury."[191] The justices declined to define *actual injury*, deferring instead to the trial courts. They did indicate that the term was not to be limited to "out-of-pocket loss" but could include "personal humiliation, and mental anguish and suffering."

Dun & Bradstreet, Inc. v. Greenmoss Builders, Inc. (1985): *Gertz* Clarified or Modified?

In 1985, the U.S. Supreme Court upheld in a split 5 to 4 vote a jury award of punitive damages. In this case, the trial court judge had not instructed the jury that a showing of actual malice was required. On appeal of the trial court decision, the Vermont Supreme Court upheld the award on the ground that *Gertz* was not applicable to non-media defendants. In *Dun & Bradstreet, Inc. v. Greenmoss Builders, Inc.*,[192] Justice Powell, joined by Justices Rehnquist and O'Connor, disagreed with the state supreme court. Powell said that for matters of private concern, states could determine whether punitive and presumed damages require a showing of actual malice.

The case began when Dun & Bradstreet, a credit reporting agency, sent a confidential report to five clients that falsely reported that Greenmoss Builders, a construction contractor, had gone bankrupt. Greenmoss won $50,000 in compensatory damages and $300,000 in punitive damages. Justice Powell noted that the report did not concern a matter of public interest but instead was "speech solely in the individual interest of the speaker" and its confidential subscribers. Some First Amendment experts viewed the decision as nothing more than a reaffirmation of *Gertz* because, as Justice Brennan indicated in his dissent, at least six justices appeared to agree that the press ("institutional media") has no greater or lesser protection against defamation than other defendants. Other experts disagreed, asserting that the Court was granting states the opportunity to lower the Gertz standard for punitive damages below actual malice.

Harte-Hanks Communications, Inc. v. Connaughton (1989): A Public Official Recovers for Actual Malice

Only rarely has the Supreme Court permitted a public official to recover damages. The Court took the opportunity to do so in *Harte-Hanks Communications, Inc. v. Connaughton*.[193] This case involved a front-page story in the Hamilton, Ohio, *Journal-News*, which quoted Alice Thompson, a grand jury witness, as saying that municipal judge candidate Daniel Connaughton, had used "dirty tricks" in his campaign and had offered her and her sister jobs and a vacation in Florida "in appreciation" for help in an ongoing investigation of bribery charges against incumbent James Dolan's director of court services. The gist of the story was that Connaughton had engaged in a smear campaign against Dolan. The story was published a month before the election in which the newspaper supported Dolan.

After he lost the election, Connaughton sued the *Journal-News* for libel. A jury awarded $5,000 in compensatory damages and $195,000 in punitive damages. A court of appeals upheld the decision and the U.S. Supreme Court unanimously affirmed. In an opinion written by Justice Stevens, the Court pointed to strong evidence of actual malice, as determined by the trial court. The paper did not bother to interview the one witness that both the plaintiff and Thompson said could verify conflicting accounts of events surrounding alleged charges—

Thompson's sister, Patty Stephens: "It is utterly bewildering in light of the fact that the *Journal-News* committed substantial resources to investigating Thompson's claims, yet chose not to interview Stephens—while denials coming from Connaughton's supporters might be explained as motivated by a desire to assist Connaughton, a denial from Stephens would quickly put an end to the story."[194]

The reporter and editors deliberately chose not to listen to tape recordings of the original interview in which Thompson made her allegations of dirty tricks. There was evidence that Thompson may not have been a credible witness. She had a criminal record, had been treated for mental instability, and her version of events was disputed by six witnesses. Finally, the newspaper printed an editorial before its investigative story appeared, indicating that damaging information would appear later about the candidates during the final days of the campaign. To the Court, this showed a lack of concern for unearthing the truth or bias against Connaughton. There was conflicting testimony at trial from the newspaper's own staff about how the story was investigated.

Bose Corporation v. Consumers Union of the United States (1984): De Novo Review

The Supreme Court dealt with one other important, related issue in the *Harte-Hanks* case—whether the appellate court had conducted the required de novo review established in *Bose Corporation v. Consumers Union of the United States*[195] on the 20th anniversary of *New York Times v. Sullivan* and the 10th anniversary of *Gertz v. Welch*.

Bose began with an article in the May 1970 *Consumer Reports* rating stereo speakers, which claimed that the Bose 901 speaker system reproduced the sound of individual musical instruments in such a way that they "tended to wander about the room." According to testimony at the trial, the sounds tended to wander "along the wall" between the speakers, not "about the room." The judge ruled the company was a public figure but that there was clear and convincing evidence of actual malice. A U.S. District Court judge at a second trial ordered Consumers Union to pay $115,296 in damages to compensate Dr. Amar G. Bose, who had invented the innovative speaker system, for $9,000 he had said he spent to counter the bad publicity and $106,296 in lost sales.

On appeal, the First Circuit U.S. Court of Appeals agreed that the article was "disparaging" but reversed the district court decision after conducting a de novo review or independent review of both the facts and the law in the case and finding there was no evidence of actual malice. Bose appealed the appellate court's decision on the ground that Rule 52(a) of the Federal Rules of Civil Procedure (which bars federal appeals courts from determining facts in a case unless the trial court's decision was "clearly erroneous") should have been the standard of review, not a de novo review. The U.S. Supreme Court affirmed the court of appeals decision, holding that federal appellate courts must conduct a de novo review "in order to preserve the precious liberties established and ordained by the Constitution" in cases related to First Amendment issues. Note that such a review is mandatory if an appeal involving the First Amendment is considered in the federal courts; it is not optional.

In *Harte-Hanks,* the Supreme Court found that the court of appeals conducted the independent review mandated in *Bose* and thus did not give undue weight to the jury's findings.

Michael Milkovich v. Lorain Journal Company (1990): Protection for Opinion

In *dicta* in the *Gertz* case, the Court said, "Under the First Amendment there is no such thing as a false idea." To some courts and media defendants, this implied that ideas or opinions were libel-proof. However, *dicta* (officially known as *obiter dicta* or "remarks by the way")[196] are comments or opinions of a judge not directly related to the issue or question in the case and thus not meant to represent the law.

In *Michael Milkovich v. Lorain Journal Company* (1990),[197] in a 7 to 2 decision written by Chief Justice Rehnquist, the Court ruled that the First Amendment does not require a separate privilege for statements of opinion. The justices held that the protection offered by *New York Times v. Sullivan, Curtis Publishing Co. v. Butts,* and *Gertz v. Welch* is sufficient for both opinions and statements of fact:

> Thus, where a statement of "opinion" on a matter of public concern reasonably implies false and defamatory facts regarding public figures or officials, those individuals must show that such statements were made with knowledge of their false implications or with reckless disregard of their truth. Similarly, where such a statement involves a private figure on a matter of public concern, a plaintiff must show that the false connotations were made with some level of fault as required by *Gertz.* Finally, the enhanced appellate review required by *Bose Corp.* provides assurance that the foregoing determinations will be made in a manner so as not to "constitute a forbidden intrusion of the field of free expression."[198]

Milkovich concerned a sports column that said a high school wrestling coach "had beat the system with the big lie" and that "anyone who attended the meet … knows in his heart that [Milkovich, the plaintiff] lied at the hearing after giving his solemn oath to tell the truth." The Supreme Court said that a "reasonable fact finder could conclude that the statements in the … column imply an assertion that Milkovich [the plaintiff] perjured himself in a judicial proceeding." According to the majority, "The article did not use the sort of loose, figurative, or hyperbolic language that would negate the impression that [the columnist] was seriously maintaining Milkovich committed perjury."199 The Court reversed the trial court's summary judgment in favor of the newspaper.

Many journalists found the decision unsettling, but one First Amendment attorney has characterized the decision in "purely legal terms" as "little more than judicial tinkering, unlikely to have more than a marginal impact, especially on mass media with the sophistication, resources and guts to do their jobs aggressively."[200] Charles N. Davis found in his research that libel suits since *Milkovich* involving opinion often result in summary judgment in favor of the defense. The study "suggests the many gloomy predictions made in the wake of *Milkovich* were overstated and concludes that most statements of opinion are still protected by the libel doctrines created in earlier Supreme Court decisions."[201]

A good illustration to support this premise is *NBC Subsidiary (KCNC-TV), Inc. v. The Living Will Center* (1994),[202] in which the Colorado Supreme Court ruled 4 to 3 that characterizing a company's marketing of living will kits a "scam" was constitutionally privileged as opinion. The case arose when the station aired two segments in its afternoon newscasts about the Living

Will Center, which sold a $29.95 kit enabling a person to draft and execute a living will. A medical ethicist commented in one of the reports that when people get the kits they will realize they have been "totally taken," adding that he thought the marketing was a "scam." Newscasts pointed out that the living will forms could be obtained free from the University of Colorado Health Sciences Center and that the company's president was neither a lawyer nor a doctor. Reversing a lower appellate court, the state supreme court said, "The terms 'scam' and 'taken' as well as the substance and gist of the broadcasts neither contain or imply a verifiable fact nor can they be reasonably understood as an assertion of actual fact about [the center's] product."[203]

It is rare for any appellate court to reconsider a case and reverse itself upon a request for a rehearing, but that is what happened in 1994. Much to the amazement of observers on both sides, the U.S. Court of Appeals for the D.C. Circuit concluded it had made a mistake in a previous decision. In *Moldea v. New York Times Co. (Moldea I,* 1994),[204] the Court of appeals in a 2 to 1 decision reinstated writer Dan E. Moldea's suit against the *New York Times*, which had won a summary judgment in the U.S. District Court for the District of Columbia. The suit involved a review of Moldea's book, *Interference: How Organized Crime Influences Professional Football*, in the *New York Times Book Review*. The reviewer, sportswriter Gerald Eskenazi, said, "… there is too much sloppy journalism to trust the bulk of this book's 512 pages—including its whopping 64 pages of footnotes." Moldea claimed five other passages in the negative review were defamatory, including the reviewer's statement that the author had characterized a meeting involving Joe Namath as "sinister" and that Moldea was reviving "the discredited notion" that the owner of a West Coast football team had "met foul play when he drowned in Florida 10 years ago."

Moldea I held that "the term [sloppy] has obvious, measurable effects when applied to the field of investigative journalism" and thus criticized his abilities as a journalist. The court rejected the plaintiff's contention that three of the statements in question were actionable but ruled that the statements regarding the "sinister" meeting and "discredited notion" could be verified and thus should be sent to a jury for determination of their truth or falsity. Upon reconsideration, the three-member panel did an about-turn. In *Moldea II,* the court unanimously held "the challenged statements in the *Times* review are supportable interpretations of *Interference,* that as a matter of law the review is substantially true. Accordingly, we affirm the District Court's grant of summary judgment in favor of the *Times*."[205]

In admitting the appellate court's mistake in the first ruling, a circuit court judge said the majority's first opinion was "misguided" and "applied an inappropriate standard." The court said it was "highly debatable" whether the "sloppy journalism" characterization was verifiable. The book examples were "supportable interpretations." The judges were troubled by the "sinister meeting" reference but said it "does not come within the compass of 'incremental harm.'"

Under the *incremental harm doctrine,* the harm created by the allegedly false information is compared to the harm created by any true information. In other words, if a story accurately describes someone in a negative way but at the same time uses false information, the plaintiff would lose because the published truth was more damaging than the falsehoods. As the court noted, "Because the review relies principally on statements that are true, supportable opinions or supportable interpretations to justify the 'sloppy [footnote omitted] journalism' assessment, we are constrained to find that it is substantially true and therefore not actionable."[206] As media defense attorney Lee Levine said, "*Moldea II* may not warrant … [dancing in the streets] … but journalists do have reason to permit themselves a little jig in the privacy of their newsrooms."[207]

Different states have different approaches to protect opinions in light of *Milkovich*. Some states continue to offer more protection for opinions than factual statements while others adhere to the idea that opinions have no special protection. The most common approach, as illustrated in a Florida case, is to grant protection to statements of opinion when facts supporting the opinions are either contained in the report or the statements are based upon facts that are publicly known. In *Miami Child's World v. Sunbeam Television Corp.* (1996),[208] a Florida appellate court held that a TV station and its reporter could not be found liable for libel for broadcasting a news report about a company's business with the Miami Beach City Commission that the report called a "rip-off," "inside deal," and "land giveaway." The court said the descriptions were reasonable in light of the factual statements that were used to support the characterizations.

Masson v. New Yorker Magazine (1991): Altered Quotes

In *Masson v. New Yorker Magazine* (1991),[209] the U.S. Supreme Court reversed a Ninth Circuit U.S. Court of Appeals decision upholding a summary judgment by a California U.S. District Court judge in favor of a magazine, author, and book publisher. The Supreme Court held that although a libel defendant's intentional alteration of direct quotes did not automatically equate with actual malice, such changes could constitute an issue of fact to be presented to a jury. The Court was particularly bothered by a passage in which the plaintiff, psychoanalyst Jeffrey Masson, was quoted as saying Sigmund Freud Archive officials had characterized him as an "intellectual gigolo" when a tape recording contained a much different statement. The opinion also suggested the term *actual malice* not be used in jury instructions because of the confusion surrounding the term. According to the Court, "[I]t is better practice that the jury instructions refer to publication of a statement with knowledge of falsity or reckless disregard as to truth or falsity." In 1993 a U.S. District Court jury in San Francisco in a retrial determined that the author, Janet Malcolm, had libeled Masson, but the case ended in a mistrial when the jury could not agree on damages.

Injury

There is one final element for proof of libel: The plaintiff must be injured. Damages fall into five major categories: (a) nominal, (b) special, (c) general, (d) actual, and (e) punitive. The U.S. Supreme Court has never dealt directly with nominal damages, but there is some question whether such damages are still available after *Gertz*,[210] in which the Court said that compensation can be made only for actual injury, which the Court broadly defined. Nominal damages are symbolic, such as the award of $1, a way of recognizing that a plaintiff has been defamed but no real harm occurred.

Special damages are awarded to libel plaintiffs to compensate for out-of-pocket, pecuniary (economic) harm. The judge in the *Bose* trial awarded the plaintiff special damages representing his actual loss of sales because of the critical review. Ordinarily, plaintiffs do not seek special damages in libel cases because they are fairly difficult to demonstrate.

General damages are awarded to libel plaintiffs to compensate them for losses that cannot necessarily be measured. In 1986 a federal district court jury awarded Brown & Williamson

Tobacco Corp. $3 million in general or compensatory damages and $2 million in punitive damages against CBS for a commentary on a network-owned television station, WBBM-TV in Chicago, which accused the company of advertising its Viceroy cigarettes so children would associate smoking with sex, alcohol, and marijuana. The judge reduced the compensatory damages to $1 because he said the company had failed to show loss of sales. In 1987 the Seventh Circuit U.S. Court of Appeals upheld the punitive damages but restored the $1 million compensatory damages. The U.S. Supreme Court denied certiorari.[211]

With *Gertz* and its requirement of actual injury for all plaintiffs, *actual damages* have become the norm. As the Court indicated in *Gertz,* these can be awarded for such injuries as harm to reputation, humiliation, and mental anguish. In *Hustler Magazine and Larry C. Flynt v. Jerry Falwell,*[212] the U.S. District Court jury verdict awarded the TV evangelist $200,000 in damages, including $100,000 in compensatory damages and $50,000 each against the magazine and its publisher in punitive damages for intentional infliction of emotional distress. *Hustler* had published a parody of a Campari Liqueur ad in which Falwell talked about his "first time" (see Figure 8.2). The Campari ads referred to the "first time" celebrities tasted the liqueur, but the magazine parody included a picture of Falwell with the text of a fictional interview in which he describes his "first time" as incest with his mother in an outhouse.

The Supreme Court ruled that because the jury had determined Falwell had not been libeled, the minister was not entitled to damages for intentional infliction of emotional distress. The majority opinion written by Chief Justice Rehnquist said, "There is no doubt that the caricature of respondent and his mother published in *Hustler* is at best a distant cousin of the political cartoons ... [of Thomas Nast] ... and a rather poor cousin at that."[213] To recover such damages, the plaintiff would have to show that the publication contained a false statement of fact which was made with actual malice, which Falwell had failed to do, according to the Court. The moral of this story: intentional infliction of emotional distress will be virtually impossible to demonstrate for libelous statements unless plaintiffs can show that they were also defamed and, for a public figure, that the statements were published or broadcast with actual malice.

Finally, *punitive damages* are designed to send a message to defendants and to punish them for the libel. There is no real cap on such damages, although judges will often reduce huge awards. Entertainer Wayne Newton initially won $19 million in compensatory and punitive damages from NBC for a TV news report that he claimed falsely implied that the Mafia and mob sources helped him purchase the Aladdin in exchange for a hidden share of the hotel and casino and that he had lied under oath to Nevada gaming authorities about his relationship with the Mafia. The trial court judge reduced the amount to $225,000 for physical and mental injury, $50,000 as presumed damages to reputation, and $5 million in punitive damages. The Ninth Circuit U.S. Court of Appeals overturned the verdict, and the U. S. Supreme Court denied certiorari.[214]

Punitive damages, in general, have received a lot of attention, both from the media and from politicians. Everyone from the Internal Revenue Service (which, with the support of the Supreme Court, considers punitive damages taxable)[215] to the courts have addressed punitive damages. With each new president, the U.S. Congress usually makes noise about imposing caps on punitive damages for torts such as medical malpractice. The U.S. Supreme Court's decision in *Honda Motor Co. v. Oberg* (1994)[216] was beneficial to some libel defendants, especially those in states where judges tend to lack discretion to review jury awards of punitive damages. Although this case concerned a provision of a state constitution, state and federal statutes that attempt to accomplish the same result—the preservation of jury punitive damage awards—could not survive scrutiny of the Due Process clause. This assures judges the right to review, reduce, or overturn punitive damages. The impact of that Court's decision was minimal since the majority of jurisdictions already have a review mechanism.

In *BMW of North America v. Gore* (1997),[217] the U.S. Supreme Court established guidelines for punitive damages. The case began when Ira Gore Jr., a physician, bought a new BMW sports sedan for $40,750.88 from a Birmingham, Alabama, dealer. He later took the car to a detailer to make the car look "snazzier." A detailer told Gore that the car appeared to have been repainted—apparently due to acid rain damage. Gore sued BMW, asking for $500,000 in compensatory and punitive damages. At trial, BMW admitted it had had a policy of selling cars as new if they had been repaired after being damaged during manufacture or transportation, if the damage did not exceed 3% of the suggested retail price.

Gore requested $4 million in punitive damages. He presented evidence at the trial that BMW had sold about 1,000 damaged cars in the country since 1983 and that his car was worth about $4,000 less than it would have been if it had not been repainted ($4,000 × 1,000 cars = $4 million). The jury obliged and awarded $4 million in punitive damages and $4,000 in compensatory damages. The Alabama Supreme Court upheld the award but halved punitive damages.

In a 5 to 4 decision, the U.S. Supreme Court held that the $2 million award was grossly excessive and thus violated the Due Process clause of the 14th Amendment. The Court made it clear that a state has a legitimate interest in punishing unlawful conduct and preventing repetition but cannot set policies for the whole country by punishing parties for conduct that occurred in other states. The award should have been made based upon what happened in Alabama. BMW sold only 14 such cars in Alabama since 1983.

Next, the Court pointed to three guideposts to be used in determining whether the award was excessive because the defendant did not have fair notice of the conduct for which it could be punished as well as the severity of the penalties, as required under the Constitution. Under each guidepost, BMW was not given fair notice, thereby rendering the $2 million punitive award "grossly excessive." The Court said a court must first look at "the *degree of reprehensibility* (emphasis added) of the defendant's conduct." It noted that Gore's damages were "purely economic" because repainting had no effect on his auto's performance, safety features, or appearance, and there was no evidence that the company had acted in bad faith, made deliberate false statements or engaged in affirmative misconduct.

The second guidepost is "*the ratio between the plaintiff's compensatory damages and the amount of punitive damages*" (emphasis added). The Court said, "Although it is not possible to draw a mathematical bright line between the constitutionally acceptable and the constitutionally unacceptable that would fit every case … the ratio here (the punitive award is 500 times the compensatory award) is clearly outside the acceptable range."[218] The last guidepost is the *difference between the punitive damages award and "the criminal or civil sanctions that could be imposed for comparable misconduct*" (emphasis added). Again, the award against BMW failed the test. The Court pointed out that the maximum fine in Alabama at the time was only $2,000, similar to maximums in other states. The Court concluded: "… we are fully convinced that the grossly excessive award imposed in this case transcends the constitutional limit."[219]

The U.S. Supreme Court remanded the case back to the Alabama Supreme Court, which reduced the punitive damages to $50,000.[220] According to legal affairs journalist Mark

Thompson, federal and state courts have frequently used the *BMW* ruling to substantially cut multimillion-dollar punitive awards, with federal courts doing so more often than state courts.[221] One often cited case involved a woman who convinced a jury to award her $2.7 million in damages against McDonald's Corporation for severe burns sustained when hot coffee she ordered at a drive-thru spilled in her lap. A judge reduced the award to $480,000. The case was eventually settled out of court.

In a 5–4 decision written by Justice Stephen G. Breyer, the U.S. Supreme Court vacated a $79.5 million judgment against tobacco giant Philip Morris USA in 2007. In *Philip Morris USA v. Williams*,[222] the Court held that it is a violation of the due process clause when a jury is permitted to base a punitive damage award "upon its desire to punish the defendant for harming persons who are not before the court" such as victims not represented by the parties. The case arose after a jury awarded $821,000 in compensatory damages and $79.5 million in punitive damages for deceit in marketing that led to the death of a smoker. In practical terms this means that juries must base punitive damages on the harm to the plaintiff(s) not to other individuals who may be been victims as well.

Defenses to Libel

There are five major defenses to libel and three ways for a defendant to attack libel and either have the case dismissed or mitigate damages. The five hard-line defenses are truth, privilege (absolute and qualified), fair comment and criticism, consent, and the statute of limitations. The other three methods of attack are retraction or correction, libel-proof plaintiff, and neutral reportage.

Truth

Since the John Peter Zenger trial in 1735, truth has been a defense to libel, or at least to criminal libel, in America. Every state permits truth as a defense in some form. Truth must be published with "justification" or "good motives" in many states, but this is theoretical and probably would not survive a constitutional challenge in light of *New York Times v. Sullivan*. In its decision in the case, the Court prominently mentioned the value of truth and, in some circumstances even falsehoods, in the uninhibited and robust debate that we cherish on controversial issues of public importance. Thus, it can be safely assumed that truth is an absolute bar to a successful libel suit. There are two problems that interfere with this defense. First, most libel suits do not involve truthful information. Plaintiffs generally do not sue unless the information is false. Whether there are damages or the degree of falsity is sufficient to warrant a suit may be questionable, but nearly always a suit that survives a motion to dismiss involves false information.

In *Philadelphia Newspapers, Inc. v. Maurice S. Hepps* (1986),[223] the U.S. Supreme Court ruled in a 5 to 4 opinion written by Justice O'Connor that when a private individual sues the media for libel and the information published is a matter of public concern, the plaintiff has the burden of demonstrating the allegedly defamatory statements were false. Thus a suit fails if the plaintiff does not provide clear and convincing evidence that the information was false. The defendant does not have the burden of showing the information was true. Although the

Court did not indicate in its ruling that this requirement would prevail for public figures and public officials, there is little doubt that this would be the standard. It is highly unlikely that the Court would impose a tougher standard of proof on private individuals than on public figures and public officials.

The Court did not indicate what the rule would be in cases involving private individuals and nonpublic issues. It would be safe to assume from the split vote and the fact that the Court chose to specifically tie the rule to matters of public concern that states would make their own determinations of the burden of proof in non-public matters whether they involve private individuals or public figures, especially limited-purpose public figures, as defined in *Gertz*. The public issue in *Philadelphia Newspapers* was alleged ties of a franchised business to organized crime and the use of these supposed ties to allegedly influence the state's government.

Privilege

As discussed earlier in this chapter, there are three major types of privilege—absolute, conditional, and constitutional. The latter two are most useful as defenses. Each type has limited applicability, but all have proven useful in specific situations. Public figures and public officials occasionally win libel suits from sympathetic juries, but the vast majority of those verdicts have damages reduced or are tossed out altogether by an appellate court conducting a de novo review. The key is having an individual declared a public official or public figure. One libel case[224] involving the *Lexington* (Kentucky) *Herald-Leader*, in which the first author of this text served the defense as an expert witness before trial, illustrates the point. A former University of Pittsburgh assistant basketball coach sued the newspaper for information about him in a 1986 reprint of an earlier article that alleged he made an improper recruiting offer to a high school player. Before the trial began, Fayette Circuit Court Judge James E. Keller ruled that the plaintiff coach was not a public figure. As the suit neared trial, he reversed himself and ruled the plaintiff was a public figure and would have to show actual malice.

After the plaintiff's attorney had presented his side at the trial itself, the judge granted the defense's motion for a directed verdict on the ground that the plaintiff had not met his burden of proof. The plaintiff appealed the decision to the Kentucky Court of Appeals, which reversed the trial court decision, and ruled the individual was not a public figure and the directed verdict was not warranted. The defendants then appealed the decision to the state's supreme court, which affirmed the lower appellate court's holding and ordered a new trial. The U.S. Supreme Court denied certiorari. The case was settled out of court for an undisclosed sum.

This case illustrates the extreme importance of the constitutional privilege mandated by *New York Times v. Sullivan*. It is far easier to prove negligence, which was the standard of care for private individuals in the Kentucky case, than actual malice. Conditional privilege can also be excellent protection, but it is conditional—journalists must take steps, sometimes unusual ones, to ensure reporting is fair and honest. Otherwise, they can expect no protection from the statutes.

The New Jersey Supreme Court made an exception to its long standing principle that most businesses are private figures rather than public figures for purposes of libel. In *Turf Lawnmower Repair, Inc. v. Bergen Record Corporation* (1995),[225] the court ruled that a "regular" business—in this case, a lawnmower repair company—had to demonstrate that a newspaper published a story with actual malice when the business was involved in matters of public health and safety and was subject to substantial government regulation or involved in practices that could violate consumer protection laws. About the same time, the Supreme Court of Louisiana unanimously ruled in *Romero v. Thomson Newspapers* (1995)[226] that a private figure, a physician, involved in a matter of great public concern was required to show actual malice to recover for libel. Dr. Alton Romero, an obstetrician, sued the Lafayette, Louisiana, *Daily Advertiser* after it published a story based on a report by the Public Citizens Health Research Group about the performance of unnecessary Caesarean sections. The story quoted the organization's director as saying, "Louisiana's women are being butchered by their obstetricians in the way they do so many C-sections." The story concluded with a quote from the administrator of the local hospital asserting that the high rate there can be attributed to the only obstetrician, Dr. Romero, who "is nearing retirement and only attends long-time patients who have had previous children—the category of women most likely to have a Caesarean."

Dr. Romero argued that the article contained several false statements including that he was nearing retirement (which the administrator denied saying but said he had instead indicated that Romero was "semi-retired") and that the hospital had the highest C-section rate in the country. The trial court dismissed the newspaper's motion for a summary judgment, and the state Court of Appeals refused to hear the case. However, the state Supreme Court accepted the appeal and reversed the ruling. The court said the "butchering" quote was protected hyperbole that "was not of and concerning" the plaintiff and that the other statements were substantially true and published without actual malice, which Dr. Romero had to demonstrate because of the issue involved.

One First Amendment expert advocates a new test for determining whether an individual is a public figure for purposes of libel. John R. Bender of the University of Nebraska at Lincoln proposes having only one category of public figure—not the two types from *Gertz* (general-purpose and limited-purpose). His test would consist of three questions:

1. Does the plaintiff occupy a position in the community's social, political, or economic life that would allow him or her to exercise appreciably more influence over matters of general or public interest than could ordinary citizens?
2. Does the plaintiff have a reputation within the community as one who possesses a degree of influence over matters of general or public interest appreciably greater than that of the ordinary citizen?
3. Has the plaintiff participated in or tried to influence, to a degree greater than that of the ordinary citizen, the decision-making process on any matter of general or public interest?[227]

Bender's test focuses on influence and involvement in matters of public concern rather than celebrity, prominence, and notoriety—traditional indicators of status as a public figure.

Fair Comment and Criticism

Fair comment and criticism is opinion in slightly different clothing. Both the common law and statutes have generally permitted criticism of matters of public concern and of public individuals in their public performance, whether political, artistic, literary, or whatever. Contrary to what some doomsayers contend, *Milkovich* did not kill fair comment and criticism, nor did it kill opinion. Facts that are cloaked (in the eyes of the Court, at least) in the guise of opinions have no greater protection than other factual statements. There have been a few isolated instances, and *Milkovich* is one, in which commentary was considered libelous. The fact remains that comment and criticism of public persons and public events—so long as they are (a) based on facts the source believes to be true but not factual statements per se, and (b) not published with malice—are protected. Scathing reviews of movies and books and slams at public officials are alive and well but must be opinions, not statements of fact. A movie review that says a lead actor was "extremely convincing in his role as a hardened drug addict" is protected, but an assertion that he was such a "convincing actor that one would think he may have had experience with such drugs before taking on the role as addict" may step over the line. It could result in a successful lawsuit.

During Bill Clinton's presidency two videotapes produced by a California organization called Citizens for Honest Government were offered for sale on the Rev. Jerry Falwell's TV program, *The Old Time Gospel Hour*.[228] The tapes, *Bill Clinton's Circle of Power* and *The Clinton Chronicles,* made allegations characterizing Clinton as a drug addict and murderer. Should such tapes qualify as fair comment, especially when the target was then still serving in office?

Consent

Consent, if it can be demonstrated, is a good defense, but rarely available because individuals and corporations rarely grant permission to a journalist to disseminate defamatory information about themselves. Permission must be granted voluntarily, intelligently, and knowingly. As with torts such as invasion of privacy, minors generally cannot grant consent.

Ethical Concerns with Consent

Consent involves an ethical concern. When individuals, whether they are public figures or private ones, grant permission to communicate potentially damaging information about themselves, a red flag should go up. The person may be mentally unstable or even setting up the journalist for a potential lawsuit. Obviously, there may be occasions in which information that is potentially harmful to someone may be disclosed by that person and be newsworthy. A political candidate responding to an attack by an opponent could, in a weak moment, say something like, "I admit that I have had extramarital affairs in the past, but I haven't had one in the past two years. I've reformed." Such disclosures could be relevant and deadline pressures would dictate that only limited verification could be achieved. Consent would be a strong defense in the case if the politician knew he was revealing information for public consumption. If he named past liaisons, their names should probably not be publicized for ethical reasons. No purpose is served by disseminating such information.

Statute of Limitations

A U.S. Supreme Court decision, *Kathy Keeton v. Hustler Magazine* (1984),[229] involved an interesting aspect of the statute of limitations defense. If a defendant can show that a defamation suit was filed even one day past deadline under the statute, the suit must be dismissed, no matter how much harm has occurred. This defense, if successful, is complete.

Kathy Keeton, associate publisher of *Penthouse* magazine and the common law wife of publisher Robert C. Guccione, filed a defamation suit against *Hustler* magazine for a series of items published between September 1975 and May 1976, including a cartoon in the May issue alleging Guccione had infected Keeton with a venereal disease. Keeton first filed suit in Ohio against Larry Flynt, *Hustler's* publisher, but the case was dismissed because the statute of limitations had tolled. Keeton then sued the defendant in New Hampshire because it was the only state of the 50 whose statute of limitations could be met. At that time New Hampshire's limit was six years. The legislature later reduced it to three years (still longer than the one-year limits in most states). Keeton was a resident of New York and had no contact with New Hampshire. *Hustler* had only a limited contact with the state through the 10,000 to 15,000 copies of the magazine distributed each month.

A U.S. District Court judge ruled that the state's *long-arm statute* (a statute under which a state under certain circumstances, known as *minimum* contacts, can establish jurisdiction over an out-of-state resident) was too short to reach Flynt in Ohio. The U.S. Court of Appeals for the First Circuit affirmed the decision, but a unanimous U.S. Supreme Court held that the limited circulation of the magazine was sufficient to constitute the minimum contacts.

Keeton could take advantage of what is known as the *single publication rule*, the Court said, which exists in some states to permit a libel plaintiff to file one action in one jurisdiction for damages suffered in other jurisdictions. The Court rejected the defendant's argument that application of the single publication rule and the longer statute of limitations was unfair. Justice Rehnquist noted in the Court's opinion: "New Hampshire ... has a substantial interest in cooperating with other States, through the 'single publication rule' to provide a forum for efficiently litigating all issues and damages arising out of a libel in a unitary proceeding."[230]

In *Iain Calder and John South v. Shirley Jones* (1984),[231] the Court held that actress Shirley Jones, who lived in California, could file suit in her home state and county against the *National Enquirer*—a tabloid with a circulation of 4 million, of which 60,000 copies were sold weekly in California. As with *Keeton,* the Court said the test of "minimum contacts" was met even though neither reporter nor editor had visited the state during story preparation.

An unusual twist to the statute of limitations defense arose in a billion-dollar libel suit filed by stockbroker Julian H. Robertson, Jr. against *Business Week* publisher McGraw-Hill Companies, Inc.[232] The print version of an article entitled "The Fall of the Wizard of Wall Street" was published on March 22, 1996, and Robertson filed suit on March 24, 1997, right on time for New York's one-year statute of limitations because March 22 fell on a weekend. However, the electronic version of the magazine was placed online on March 21. If March 21 counted as the publication date, the plaintiff would have missed the statute of limitations.

A media defendant should assume that the statute of limitations for the state in which it does most business or has its home office may not necessarily be the statute that prevails in a suit. As both *Keeton* and *Calder* demonstrate, establishing the necessary contacts asserting long-arm jurisdiction over a defendant is not difficult.

Other Defensive Maneuvers

There are several alternatives that defendants are sometimes forced to use or otherwise choose to assert in lieu of or in addition to the traditional defenses. Technically, these are not defenses, although they can sometimes serve to mitigate or eliminate damages. The most common of these is correction or retraction. This incomplete defense is available in most states under a statute that permits a potential defendant to publish a bona fide correction of a previously published false statement. This may work so long as it appears within a specified time after it is requested by the subject of the statement published in a position as prominent as the original item.

These statutes are usually strict and operate only if a time limitation is met and a correction admits an error and provides correct information. Publishing or broadcasting a correction has a primary benefit. It typically prevents a plaintiff from recovering punitive damages. The party is usually still allowed to seek actual, special, and compensatory damages. The correction/retraction has the disadvantage that it is, in effect, an admission of negligence. It also brings attention to the media error. However, if a journalist has "goofed," this may be the best strategy for avoiding punitive damages and may, in fact, satisfy the aggrieved party. Studies on libel indicate that plaintiffs are often not seeking monetary awards when they believe they have been defamed, but simply want an apology so their reputations remain intact.[233] The decision on whether to issue a correction or retraction is difficult because of a risk of having to pay damages other than punitive, and it may be made tough with little time—days or hours—to decide.

Apologies can sometimes prevent a libel suit, but they have no real legal standing unless they are in the form of a retraction/correction or part of an out-of-court settlement. For example, Internet service provider Prodigy Services Co. apologized to an investment firm in 1995 for messages posted on Prodigy's computer bulletin board. The messages posted by an anonymous consumer were highly critical of the investment company.[234]

A lawyer and former companion to Anna Nicole Smith, Howard K. Stern—not to be confused with the radio host of the same name brought a defamation suit against the author and publisher of a book *Blonde Ambition: The Untold Story behind Anna Nicole Smith's Death* based on statements repeated about him. In *Stern v. Cosby*, 654 F. Supp. 2nd 258 (S.D.N.Y. 2009) the court rejected the argument that he was "libel proof" just because allegations were different than other statements made about him elsewhere.[235] The wording of an insult or in cases of what might best be termed "on-air name calling" will often determine whether an apology is necessary. Two radio talk show hosts at San Francisco radio station KLLC called a local woman a "skank," "chicken butt," and "local loser" because of participation in TV's Who Wants to Marry a Millionaire? The woman sued, but a judge determined that the terms were "too vague" to be found true or false.[236]

In some cases, the issue of libel has become a consequence of press coverage. In one instance, the *Boston Herald* published 17 articles and columns in the aftermath of a case in 2002, in which a judge was alleged to have told a prosecutor "tell her to get over it," in a rape trial. The judge denied ever having made that comment. What complicated the case further was an exchange between *Herald* reporter Dave Wedge and the host of Fox TV's *O'Reilly Factor*, in which the reporter was pressed by Bill O'Reilly to verify that the judge actually made that statement. The judge sued for libel on grounds that the attribution related to his official role as judge, alleging actual malice, well beyond basic errors in reporting. In a discussion of the case on the PBS *News Hour*, authors Alex Jones and Alicia Mundy noted the difficulty of reviewing details when the orientation of some talk television programs is "action." Jones maintained that in that environment sources are "being pushed to say as much as they can be pushed to say and sometimes you can get caught in the heat of a situation and misspeak." [237]

Libel-proof plaintiffs are very rare but there are individuals whose reputations are so damaged by their own actions, they have no reputation to defend. Two possible examples are convicted mass murderers and former political leaders convicted of multiple felonies. In *Lamb v. Rizzo* (2004), [238] the Tenth Circuit U.S. Court of Appeals upheld a trial court ruling that, if given the opportunity, the Kansas Supreme Court would likely recognize the libel-proof plaintiff defense. The state trial court had ruled against a felon serving three consecutive life sentences for murder and kidnapping who sued a newspaper reporter for libel. The journalist published an article containing false and inaccurate statements about the criminal. The story correctly reported that the plaintiff had made a violent escape from prison and had taken hostages. However, it incorrectly said he raped two of the victims and abducted one victim while prowling shopping centers "dressed as a woman."

According to the federal appellate court, the plaintiff's reputation had been damaged so extensively by his life sentences that no further harm could occur: "[T]here comes a time when the individual's reputation for specific conduct, or his general reputation for honesty and fair dealing is sufficiently low in the public's estimation" that he becomes libel-proof. [239]

The idea of this defensive maneuver is to claim that the person's reputation has been so lowered in the eyes of the public that the individual cannot be harmed with false, defamatory statements. Even when dealing with notorious criminals, a journalist should follow the same precautions to prevent a potential libel suit. Almost everyone has some redeeming quality that could be infringed upon.

The most controversial of alternative defense strategies is *neutral reportage*. In *Edwards v. National Audubon Society* (1977),[240] the Second Circuit U.S. Court of Appeals held that neutral reportage was a viable defense. However, this ruling is limited to the Second Circuit only, although a few state courts have recognized the defense and several have specifically rejected it or narrowed its application to very limited circumstances. The requirements for this defense are the charges (a) must be serious and newsworthy and create or concern an important public controversy, (b) must be uttered by a responsible person or organization, (c) must relate to a public figure or public official, and (d) must be accurately and disinterestingly reported.

Neutral reportage grants the media an opportunity to act responsibly when allegations about prominent individuals emerge that are hard to confirm, are made by a supposedly trustworthy source, and are newsworthy. Important ethical concerns have to be considered before this kind of information is disseminated. Occasionally, such allegations turn out to be false and before the truth becomes known, harm is done. Prominent people and organizations sometimes make charges about opponents during the heat of political campaigns, in the midst of pronounced controversies. Even where neutral reportage is available, it should be invoked only when strongly justified and thus not used as a shield to report sensational information or information that is not newsworthy.

The Uniform Correction or Clarification of Defamation Act

After more than three years of work, the National Conference of Commissioners on Uniform State Laws formally approved a document known as the "Uniform Correction or Clarification of Defamation Act" (UCCA) in 1993. The House of Delegates of the American Bar Association, as expected, approved the proposed legislation in a 176 to 130 vote. It was submitted to the legislatures of each of the 50 states. As with the Uniform Commercial Code, which was adopted in every state except Louisiana to govern commercial transactions, the UCCA attempted to establish libel law uniformity throughout the entire country. Unlike "model laws" that give uniformity to the law in a particular area and allow for state differences, "uniform laws" are designed for more strict uniformity so there is greater predictability. Some major provisions of the UCCA include:

1. The Act applies to any defamation action against any defendant brought by any plaintiff. This includes libel as well as slander, private individuals as well as public figures. It also includes defamation, false light, intentional infliction of emotional distress—in fact, any cause of action if it is based upon injury to reputation or emotional distress if related to the dissemination of allegedly false information.
2. All plaintiffs must formally request of any defendant a "correction or clarification" within 90 days after learning that allegedly defamatory statements have been communicated about them.
3. If such a request us not made within the 90 days, the plaintiff can recover in any suit only for economic loss such as lost income—no punitive damages and no damages for general injury to reputation or for emotional distress.
4. The allegedly defamed individual or entity can be required by the defendant to provide all "reasonably available" relevant information about the allegedly false statements.
5. The correction or clarification must be "timely," as defined under the Act.
6. Even if a defendant has up to that point refused to publish a correction or clarification, an offer to correct or clarify can be made prior to the beginning of the trial. If the offer is dismissed, but the defendant must pay reasonable attorney fees owed by the plaintiff. If the offer is turned down, the plaintiff is entitled only to provable economic losses and reasonable attorney fees. [241]

The UCCA received a warm welcome, especially among the media. As communications lawyers Lee J. Levine and Daniel Waggoner (both involved in drafting the Act), conclude:

> … if the Conference is successful in securing the Act's passage throughout the United States, the national news media will be governed by one 'uniform' set of rules affecting corrections and clarifications. Such uniformity should serve to minimize uncertainty, reduce risk, and lead to a more predictable and rational system for resolving such disputes.[242]

The reception among journalists was not uniformly warm. Jane Kirtley, attorney and executive director of the Reporters Committee for Freedom of the Press at that time, now professor at the University of Minnesota, believed the Act should operate as a model rather than a uniform law so individual states can decide whether to adopt it: "Only they can determine whether, taken as a whole, the statute will be an improvement over their existing state law. It should not be foisted upon them, untested and untried."[243]

Libel and the Internet

The new frontier for libel suits is the information superhighway. A reporter for a trade publication *Communications Daily* once settled a lawsuit filed against him for an item he sent on an electronic news service on the Internet. The item was critical of a direct marketing firm. As part of the settlement, the reporter agreed to pay a $64 court fee and submit questions to the company two days in advance before making any comments about it.[244] That was easy to handle.

In a more complex and costly case, Stratton Oakmont Inc. sued the Prodigy online service, which was jointly owned by Sears and IBM, for $200 million for allegedly defamatory statements made by a subscriber about the securities investment banking firm on a discussion forum. The subscriber was initially sued, but he was later dropped from the suit. His statements included that the firm's offering was "a major criminal fraud," that the company's president was "soon to be proven criminal," and that the firm was a "cult of brokers who either lie for a living or get fired."

The crucial question in this case was whether such services are to be treated like a book or like a bookstore. Prodigy argued that its service was like a bookstore or a telephone system, and that it should not be held responsible for subscriber conversations. The bank contended the service was akin to a book and therefore the owners should be held responsible for the content. In *Stratton Oakmont Inc. v. Prodigy Services Co.*,[245] a New York Supreme Court judge held that Prodigy exercised sufficient editorial control over contents of the bulletin board, particularly in reviewing messages posted by subscribers, that it served an editorial function.

In reaction to the ruling, Congress included a "Good Samaritan" provision in the Communications Decency Act (CDA), effectively overruling the decision. The CDA was signed into law and took effect on February 8, 1996. Under it, "No provider or user of an interactive computer service shall be treated as the publisher or speaker of any information provided by another information content provider" and no provider or user can be held liable for "any action voluntarily taken in good faith to restrict access to or availability of" objectionable content.[246]

Two other important early Internet libel cases were *Zeran v. America Online* (1997)[247] and *Blumenthal v. America Online* (1997).[248] In *Zeran,* the Fourth U.S. Circuit Court of Appeals upheld a U.S. District Court decision that an Internet service provider (ISP), America Online, could not be held liable for not quickly removing allegedly libelous messages about a person. The messages had been posted anonymously as part of a promotion for "Naughty Oklahoma T-shirts" six days after the Oklahoma City bombing. The messages referred interested purchasers to "Ken" and listed the plaintiff's Seattle phone number, the number of his home-based business. The plaintiff, Kenneth Zeran, received angry phone calls, and even death threats. He unsuccessfully argued in his lawsuit that even after he notified AOL, the ISP unreasonably delayed removing messages. A U.S. District Court dismissed Zeran's lawsuit, citing the Good Samaritan provision of the Communications Decency Act, and the appellate court affirmed the decision.

In the *Blumenthal* case, a columnist and his wife, Sidney and Jacqueline Blumenthal, sued AOL for a story written by gossip columnist Matt Drudge in "The Drudge Report," a column for AOL subscribers. The column alleged that Sidney Blumenthal had a history of spouse abuse. The case differed from earlier Internet libel cases because AOL paid Drudge to write his column and quickly removed the column, once given notice. Because the Blumenthals were well known as public figures (as aides in President Bill Clinton's White House), they needed to demonstrate the report was published with actual malice, including on the part of AOL. According to the Court, "While it appears to this Court that AOL in this case has taken advantage of all the benefits conferred by Congress in the Communications Decency Act, and then some, without accepting any of the burdens that Congress intended, the statutory language is clear: AOL is immune from suit, and the Court therefore must grant its motion for summary judgment."[249]

Blumenthal became even better known as he later testified on President Clinton's behalf at the President's impeachment hearing and was quoted as having allegedly told free-lance journalist Christopher Hitchens that Monica Lewinsky was a "stalker" of Clinton. [250] This raised news coverage issues that anticipated events in the political arena because of Blumenthal status as a journalist.

National political campaigns have been rife with charges and countercharges concerning use of the Internet and other forms of media. In 2004, that included news documentaries, traditionally objective, focusing on candidates, their reputations, and decisions. These included Michael Moore's *Farenheit 9/11* and *Going Upriver: The Long War of John Kerry*. In one instance, a fake photo of Kerry with Jane Fonda was circulated on the Internet.[251]

In the wake of many challenges faced by bloggers, one major news organization, CBS News, created its own blog for analysis of its coverage. After errors occurred in a CBS News *60 Minutes* report on then-President George Bush's National Guard service, that network launched CBS Public Eye in September 2005 as a means of letting the public ask questions of the news staff and follow up important stories. For the first week of coverage CBS provided video of an editorial meeting. The blog was organized to report to the president of CBS Digital Media rather than CBS News' president under whom the mistakes had been initially broadcast. In more recent years, coverage of political figures such as Sarah Palin included special attention to their use of blogs and the Internet.[252]

Summary and Conclusions

Libel is false and defamatory information that harms a person's reputation and subjects a person to public hatred, contempt, or ridicule. Libel continues to be a serious threat to the news media, especially because the U.S. Supreme Court has made it easier, although still difficult, for public figures, public officials, and private individuals to successfully sue for libel. This trend has occurred despite the precedent established in *New York Times v. Sullivan* and later in *Curtis Publishing Company v. Butts* and *Associated Press v. Walker* requiring public officials and public figures suing media defendants to demonstrate *actual malice* (reckless disregard for the truth or knowledge of falsity).

Of all the defenses, *truth* and *constitutional privilege* are the most effective. Truth is an absolute defense. Constitutional privilege under *New York Times v. Sullivan* and its progeny requires a public official or public figure to demonstrate clear and convincing evidence of actual malice. Private individuals in most states need to show only negligence to win a libel suit, but must also prove actual malice to obtain punitive damages, at least when the alleged defamatory statements concern an issue of public importance. Other viable defenses include *qualified privilege*, *statute of limitations*, and *consent*. However, the latter two are not typically applicable. Hurdles to recover punitive damages can be high. They are designed to punish offenders rather than to compensate the offended.

The trend in the past in both state and federal courts has been toward permitting more plaintiffs to succeed, especially when media defendants have acted irresponsibly, but the most recent trends indicate a swing in favor of media defendants. To mitigate damages, the media should consider publishing a *correction/retraction*. However, such action must be taken with care because it effectively means an admission of negligence or guilt. Finally, *neutral reportage* is a limited defense that must be used responsibly in the few jurisdictions where it is recognized.

The shape of libel has changed significantly with the advent of new technology. These changes will hopefully translate to good news for the media with greater recognition of individual and press rights under the First Amendment. The battle ground for future libel and other torts, such as invasion of privacy, is the Internet. As more users come on board, it is inevitable that more and more libelous information will appear, as subscribers become, in effect, gatekeepers and publishers. The Good Samaritan provision of the Communications Decency Act of 1996 provided protection for Internet service providers, but protection is limited and does not shield journalists and consumers who post messages from potential libel suits, particularly given the international nature of those messages.

Endnotes

1. The resolution of the first case involving Courtney Love appears in *Courtney Love Settles Twitter Defamation Case*, New York Times, March 17, 2011, at C-2   For details on this and related cases, see *No More 'Libel Tourists,'* Washington Post, August 13, 2010, at A-18, and Roy Greenslade, *Obama Seals off US Journalists and Authors from Britain's Libel Laws*, The Guardian, August 11, 2010 at A-15. Regarding other Love court cases: Sheila Marikar, *Courtney Love's 'Malicious' Twitter Rants Revealed: Rocker Courtney Love Sued After Allegedly Defaming Designer on Twitter, MySpace,* ABC News, April 2009; Gene Stout, *Cobain Band, Widow Fight over Son,* Seattle Post-Intelligencer, June 29, at 2-1; and Holly Millea, *Love is a Battlefield*, Entertainment Weekly, 29 March 2002: 34-41.

2. BBC News World Edition, *UK Judge Allows Arnie Libel Case*, Mar. 23, 2005. Katharine Q. Seelye, Jacques Steinberg, and David F. Gallagher, *Bloggers as News Media Trophy Hunters*, New York Times, Feb. 14, 2005, at C1.

3. Ironically, the then-Governor Schwarzenegger generally had been getting favorable press in America, on a par with his former movie star status. *See* Margaret Talev and Gary Delsohn, *Travels with Arnold*, American Journalism Review, Feb./Mar. 2005, at 43. See also editorials, *Silly Libel Law Punishes Truth*, Kansas City Star, August 13, 2010, at A-19, and *No More 'Libel Tourists': Congress Steps in to Protect Writers*. Washington Post, August 13, 2010, at A-18. For further background, see Anne Schroeder, *Names and Faces: Scarborough Unfair?* Washington Post, May 6, 2005, at C3; Greg Mitchell, *The Gannon Case*: *Blogs Roll Again*, Editor & Publisher, Mar. 2005, Vol. 138, No. 3, at 26; and *Supremes Let Stand Ruling That 'Dallas Observer' Piece Was Satire, Not Libel*, Editor & Publisher (A.P.) on line, June 6, 2005 at http://www.editorandpublisher.com/Article/Supremes-Let-Stand-Ruling-That-Dallas-Observer-Piece-Was-Satire-Not-Libel. And http://abcnews.go.com/US/mother-arnold-schwarzeneggers-love-child-revealed/story?id=13626896

4. Samuel Maul, *New York's Former Governor Cuomo Settles Libel Suit with Publisher, Author*, Associated Press Worldstream, May 10, 2005, 10:35 PM GMT edition.

5. *Tory v. Cochran*, 544 U.S. 734, 125 S.Ct. 2108, 161 L.Ed.2d 1042, 33 Med.L.Rptr. 1737 (2005).

6. *Id.*

7. Bill Mears, *Free Speech Rights and Defamation Clash in High Court Case: Justices Weigh Case Involving Johnnie Cochran, Dissatisfied Client*, CNN online, Mar. 29, 2005.

8. Robert D. McFadden, *Newspaper Withheld Stories for Fear of Retribution,* St Louis Post-Dispatch (New York Times News Service), July 9, 2005, at A23.

9. David Lyman, *Style and Culture; Stained by Permanent Ink; Bestselling Writer and Beloved Detroit Sports*

Columnist Mitch Albom Finds Himself in Odd Position: Under Fire, Los Angeles Times, Apr. 22, 2005, at E1

10 Joel Currier, *Teen's Turmoil Stated On-Line*, St. Louis Post-Dispatch, November 23, 2007, at C-1; and Shane Anthony and Joel Currier, *Woman Accused of Cyber-bullying*, St. Louis Post-Dispatch, August, 18, 2009, at A-1.

11. *Burnett v. National Enquirer*, 144 Cal.App.3d 991, 193 Cal.Rptr. 206 (1983).

12. BBC News (online UK edition), *Director Polanski Wins Libel Case,* July 22, 2005; Robert Siegel, *Michael Horsnell Discusses Roman Polanski's Libel Suit,* interview on National Public Radio's *All Things Considered*, July 22, 2005. For update, see: Michael Cieply, "Polanski Breaks His Silence on Sex-Crime Case," St. Louis Post-Dispatch, May 3, 2010, at A-18, and Henry Chu, *Swiss Free Filmmaker Polanski*, St. Louis Post-Dispatch, July 13, 2010, at A-16.

13. *See*, for example, http://espn.go.com/blog/chicago/white-sox/post/_/id/1654/ramirez-to-sox-far-from-done

14. Regarding Michael Jordan and his mistress' claims, *Knafel v. Chicago Sun-Times*, see Geoffrey Norman, *Ain't Nobody Like Mike*, National Review on line, Feb. 7, 2003; David Dukevich, *Faces of the Week*, Forbes.com, June 13, 2003; *Mistress' Libel Suit Over Prostitution Dismissed*, Reporter's Committee for Freedom of the Press, July 5, 2005. See also, Michael McCarthy, *Woods 'Failing' in Media Blitz, Experts Say*, USA Today, November 19, 2010, at C-1.

15. William Prosser, Law of Torts 737 (1971).

16. *New York Times Co. v. L. B. Sullivan* and *Ralph D. Abernathy et al. v. L. B. Sullivan*, 376 U.S. 454, 84 S.Ct. 10, 11 L.Ed.2d 686, 1 Med.L.Rptr. 1527 (1964).

17. *Media Won Seven of 12 Trials in 2004*, Media Law Resource Center, Feb. 25, 2005. Beyond numbers, regarding effects of libel and changing attitudes over time, see Hansen and Moore, *Chilling the Messenger: The Impact of Libel on Community Newspapers*, 11(2) Newspaper Research Journal 86 (1990); Hansen and Moore, *Public Attitudes Toward Libel: Do Newspaper Readers and Editors See Eye to Eye?*, 13 (3) Newspaper Research J. 2 (1992).

18. Mark Fitzgerald, *Number of Newspaper Libel Trials is Declining, Group Says*, Editor & Publisher online edition, Mar. 8, 2005;

19 *Media Won Seven of 12 Trials in 2004*, Media Law Resource Center (press release), Feb. 25, 2005.

20 For a discussion of related issues involving young people and false identity on the web, see Tamar Lewin, *Teenage Insults, Scrawled on Web, Not on Walls*, New York Times, May 6, 2010, at A-1; or Monica Davey, *Online Talk, Suicides and a Thorny Court Case,* New York Times, May 14, 2010, at A-1. For blogging cases from the Media Law Research Center: http://mlrcblogsuits.blogspot.com/.

21. *$58 Million Awarded in Biggest Libel Verdict*, New York Times (Associated Press), Apr. 21, 1991, at 1.

22. *Id.*

23. The award came in the second trial. The newspaper had successfully appealed a 1983 verdict in favor of the plaintiff but lost on retrial. See also Joan Thompson, *$222 Million Is Most Ever By Libel Jury*, Lexington (Ky.) Herald-Leader (Associated Press), Mar. 21, 1997, at A17.

24. *Judge Erases Bulk of Record Libel Award*, Dallas Morning News (Bloomberg News), May 24, 1997, at F3. See also,*Wall Street Journal Told To Pay Out for Libel; $222.7 Million Award Breaks Record*, Roanoke (Va.) Times & World News (Associated Press), Mar. 22, 1997, at A8, and News Media & Law., March 28, 1997, for an account of how the case developed.

25. *Id.*

26. *Id.*

27. *Id.*

28. *Id.*

28. *The Land of Libelin'?* Editor & Publisher, Nov. 2004, Vol. 137, No. 11, at 21.

30. *Justices to Judge: Quash Subpoenas for Papers*, Chicago Daily Law Bulletin, Sept. 2, 2004.

31. *Gloria Marks and Mamie D. Hill v. City of Seattle,* 32 Media L. Rep. 1949 (U.S.D.C. W.D. Wash. 2003).

32. *Id.*

33. *Two Publications Fare Well in Libel Appeals, But Boston Globe Hit with $2.1 Million Verdict*, the News Media & the Law, Spring, 2002, at 32.

34. *Tobacco Companies Launch a Barrage of Subpoenas Seeking Reporters' Records,* News Media & Law

(Winter 1995), at 3; *Philip Morris Companies v. American Broadcasting Companies*, 36 Va. Civ. 1 (Va. Cir. Ct. 1995); *TV Stations Yank Anti-Smoking Ads*, Lexington (Ky.) Herald-Leader (Wire Services), Oct. 14, 1994, at C9.

35. Jill Rosen, *Et Tu, 'Nightline'?* American Journalism Review, Feb./Mar. 2004, at 18.
36. JoAnne Viviano, *Lawyer Urges Judge to Dismiss Libel Lawsuit Against Filmmaker Michael Moore*, Associated Press, July 1, 2005, BC cycle.
37. *Lou DiBella and Dibella Entertainment, Inc. v. Bernard Hopkins*, 403 F.3d 102 (2nd Cir. 2005).
38. *Id.*
39. *Id.*
40. Brad Wolverton, *NCAA Splits Rulings in Alabama Lawsuits*, Chronicle of Higher Education, July 22, 2005, at A25; Jamie Schuman, *Judge Dismisses Charges by Coaches Against NCAA*, Chronicle of Higher Education, Aug. 5, 2005, at A34. See Libby Sander, *NCAA Rules are 'a Lawyer's Paradise,'* Chronicle of Higher Education, June 22, 2010, at A33.
41. Mike Bolton, *Libel Suit Settled; Price Feels Relieved Sports Illustrated Still Stands Behind Article,* Birmingham (Ala.) News, Oct. 11, 2005, at A1.
42. *Media Victories in Louisville and Chicago*. Media Law Resource Center; *Divita-Ziegler: Verdict is In*, WLKY 32 (The Louisville Channel), May 24, 2005.
43. Prosser, *supra,* note 12.
44. Michael Gartner, *Spreading the Word on Libellus*, Hartford Courant, Aug. 9, 1991 at C3.
45. Bruce W. Sanford, *Libel and Privacy* (2005) contains a review by a foremost First Amendment scholar/attorney of libel development—a superb reference source for journalists.
46. Tedford, Herbeck, and Haiman, *Freedom of Speech in the United States* 14 (2005)—an informative discussion of the history of each of these types of libel.
47. *Id., Howell's State Trials* 513 (1663).
48. *Id.*, at 32, excerpted from *Howell's State Trials* 513 (1663).
49. *Regina v. Hicklin, L.R.,* 3 Q.B. 360 (1868).
50. *See* Tedford, at 16–21 for a discussion of the history of each of these four types of libel.
51. Restatement (Second) of Torts §568A (1977).
52. Ga. Code Ann. (2005).
53. Ky. Rev. Stat. §§ 411.051, 411.061, and 411.062 (2005).
54. Kentucky Revised Statutes distinguish between "newspaper libel" and "actions against a radio or television broadcasting station" for "a defamatory statement" in the process of making a qualifying correction (retraction).
55. Robert D. Sack, *Common Law Libel and the Press: A Primer,* in 1 Communication Law 45 (2003).
56. Delaware, Iowa, Minnesota, Mississippi, New Jersey, Pennsylvania, Texas, Vermont, and Washington.
57. Sack, at 41.
58. *Pitcher Says ESPN Remarks Were Off Base,* Lexington (Ky.) Herald-Leader (wire service), Oct. 1, 1990, at B2. See also, Michael McCarthy, *Woods 'Failing" in Media Blitz, Experts Say*, USA Today, November 19, 2010, at C-1.
59. *Bryson v. News America Publications*, 174 Ill.2d 77, 672 N.E.2d 1207, 25 Med.L.Rptr. 1321 (1996).
60. Robert D. Sack, supra note 56; Article Describing Plaintiff as "Slut" Defamatory Per Se, Says Illinois Supreme Court, First Amendment Legal Watch, Vol. 1, No. 49, Oct. 21, 1996.
61. *Bryson v. News America Publications.*
62. Sanford, *Libel and Privacy.*
63. *Mitchell v. Globe International Publishing, Inc.,* 773 F.Supp. 1235 (W.D. Ark. 1991); Woman, 96, is Awarded $1.5 Million in Sun Libel Suit, Lexington (Ky.) Herald-Leader (Associated Press), Dec. 6, 1991, at A6.
64. *The Truth Is Lies Are No Defense*, 14 Presstime 60, Jan. 1992 (No. 1).
65. Restatement (Second) of Torts §§ 623A, 626, and 633 (1977); Chad E. Milton et al., *Emerging Publication Torts,* in Libel Litigation 665 (1994).
66. Mark Babineck, *Cattlemen Sue Oprah, Using 'Veggie Libel' Law*, Lexington (Ky.) Herald-Leader (Associated Press), June 17, 1997, at B4; Aaron Epstein, *Food 'Libel' Laws Get First Test in Oprah Winfrey Case,* Lexington (Ky.) Herald-Leader (Knight-Ridder), Dec. 29, 1997, at A1.

67. Babineck, *supra,* note 67.
68. *Engler v. Winfrey*, 201 F.3d 680 (2000); *Federal Appeals Court: Oprah Guilty of Melodrama But Not Libel*, Associated Press, online edition, Feb. 9, 2000; *LDRC Issues Bulletin On Agricultural Disparagement Laws, Provides Lawyers with Tools to Fight These Laws Around Country*, Media Law Resources Center (press release), May 18, 1998; BBC News World Edition, *Oprah Food Libel Claim Rejected*, Feb. 18, 1998; David Hudson, *Oprah's Battle with Beef Ranchers Became First Amendment Cause Celebre, Defamation and the First Amendment,* Freedom Forum First Amendment Center, retrieved Oct. 14, 2005, vrom http://www.freedomforum.org; Marvin Hyenga, Texas Cattle Feeders Take on Oprah Winfrey—Testing the Veggie Libel Law, Aug, 1998, http://www.extensioniastate.edu.
69. *Auvil v. CBS "60 Minutes,"* 836 F.Supp. 740, 21 Med.L.Rptr. 2059 (E.D. Wash. 1993); 800 F.Supp. 928, 20 Med.L.Rptr. 1361 (E.D. Wash. 1992); 67 F.3d 816, 23 Med.L.Rptr. 2454 (9th Cir. 1995); *cert. denied,* 517 U.S. 1167, 116 S.Ct. 1567, 134 L.Ed.2d 666 (1996).
70. Bruce E. H. Johnson and Susanna M. Lowy, *Does Life Exist on Mars? Litigating Falsity in a Non-'Of and Concerning' World*, 12 Comunication Law, Summer 1994, at 1.
71. Robert D. Richards, *Food Defamation Laws Might Damage Free Speech*, Lexington (Ky.) Herald-Leader (Washington Post), Apr. 18, 1996, at A15.
72. Dirk Beveridge, *McDonald's Wins Libel Suit Against 2 Britons,* Lexington (Ky.) Herald-Leader (Associated Press), June 20, 1997, at B7; Dirk Beveridge, *Charges Sting McDonald's Despite Libel Suit Victory,* Lexington (Ky.) Herald-Leader (Associated Press), June 21, 1997, at A11; *McDonald's Won't Attempt To Stop Vegetarians' Fliers*, Lexington (Ky.) Herald-Leader (Associated Press), July 19, 1997, at A11.
73. James R. Healey, *Isuzu Sues Consumers Union Over Trooper Tests,* USA Today, Aug. 1, 1997, at B3.
74. *Suzuki and Consumers Union Agree on Dismissal of Law Suit,* ConsumerReports.org, News Update, July 2004.
75. *Restaurant Critic: Lawyer's Sign Starts Food Fight* ("Obiter Dicta"), 82 A.B.A. J. 14 (July 1996).
76. E. W. Scripps Co., *The Kentucky Post and Al Salvato v. Louis A. Ball*, 801 S.W.2d 684, 18 Med.L.Rptr. 1545 (Ky. 1990), cert. denied, 499 U.S. 976, 111 S.Ct. 162, 113 L.Ed.2d 719 (1991).
77. *A. America, Anatomy of a Libel Suit*, Presstime, Vol. 13, No. 5, May 1991, at 6.
78. *Id.*
79. *Id.*
80. *Id.*
81. *Id.*
82. *Harte-Hanks Communications, Inc. v Daniel Connaughton*, 491 U.S. 657, 109 S.Ct. 2678, 105 L.Ed.2d 562, 16 Med.L.Rptr. 1881 (1989).
83. *Bose Corp. v. Consumers Union of the U.S., Inc.,* 466 U.S. 485, 104 S.Ct. 1949, 80 L.Ed.2d 502, 10 Med.L.Rptr. 1625 (1984).
84. *E. W. Scripps Co. v. Louis A. Ball.*
85. *See A. America, Anatomy of a Libel Suit*, supra, note 78.
86. *Id.*
87. Restatement (Second) of Torts §558 (1977).
88. *Curtis Publishing Co. v. Wallace Butts* and *Associated Press v. Edwin A. Walker*, 388 U.S. 130, 87S.Ct. 1975, 18 L.Ed.2d 1094, 1 Med.L.Rptr. 1568 (1967).
89. *Elmer Gertz v. Robert Welch, Inc.,* 418 U.S. 323, 94 S.Ct. 2997, 41 L.Ed.2d 789, 1 Med. L.Rptr. 1633 (1974).
90. *Time, Inc. v. Mary Alice Firestone*, 424 U.S. 448, 96 S.Ct. 958, 47 L.Ed.2d 154, 1 Med.L.Rptr. 1665 (1976).
91. *Dun & Bradstreet, Inc. v. Greenmoss Builders, Inc.,* 472 U.S. 749, 105 S.Ct. 2939, 86 L.E 2d 593, 11 Med.L.Rptr. 2417 (1985).
92. *Bollea v. World Championship Wrestling, Inc.,* 610 S.E.2d 92 (Ga. Ct. App. 2005).
93. *Hustler Magazine and Larry C. Flynt v. Jerry Falwell,* 485 U.S. 46, 108 S.Ct. 876, 99 L.Ed.2d 41, 14 Med.L.Rptr. 2281 (1988).
94. *New York Times v. Sullivan.*
95. *Philadelphia Newspapers, Inc. et al. v. Maurice S. Hepps et al.,* 475 U.S. 767, 106 S.Ct. 1558, 89 L.Ed.2d 783, 12 Med.L.Rptr. 1977 (1986).

96. *Berry v. Capital Cities/ABC Inc.*, No. 93-208-Civ-OC-10 (Dec. 8, 1994); *Federal District Court Awards "PrimeTime Live" Summary Judgment in Defamation Suit,* Brechner Center Rep. (University of Florida Brechner Center for Freedom of Information, Gainesville, Fla.), Feb. 1995, at 2.

97. *Pring v. Penthouse International, Ltd.,* 7 Med.L.Rptr. 1101 (D. Wyo. 1981), *rev'd,* 695 F.2d 438, 8 Med.L.Rptr. 2409 (10th Cir. 1982), *cert. denied,* 462 U.S. 1132, 103 S.Ct. 3112, 77 L.Ed.2d 1367 (1983). The author, Philip Cioffari, Ph.D., was a professor at a New Jersey school.

98. *Pring v. Penthouse International, Ltd.,* 695 F.2d 438, 8 Med.L.Rptr. 2409 (10th Cir. 1982).

99. *Id.*

100. *Paul Bindrim v. Gwen Davis Mitchell et al.,* 155 Cal.Rptr. 29, 5 Med.L.Rptr. 1113 (Cal. App. 1979), *cert. denied,* 444 U.S. 984, 100 S.Ct. 490, 62 L.Ed.2d 412, *rehearing denied,* 444 U.S. 1040, 100 S.Ct. 713, 62 L.Ed.2d 675 (1980).

101. *Carson's Dentist Jokes Bring $5 Million Lawsuit,* Lexington (Ky.) Herald-Leader (wire services), Sept. 4, 1987, at A2.

102. *Mansour v. Fanning,* 506 F.Supp. 186, 6 Med.L.Rptr. 2055 (D.C. N.Cal. 1980).

103. *Id.*

104. *Kentucky Fried Chicken, Inc. v. Sanders,* 563 S.W.2d 8 (Ky. 1978).

105. *Adams v. WFTV,* 691 So.2d 557, 25 Med.L.Rptr. 2242 (Fla. App. 1997); *Group Libel Suit Dismissal Upheld,* Brechner Center Rep. (University of Florida Brechner Center for Freedom of Information, Gainesville, Fla.), June 1997, at 1.

106. *Adams v. WFTV.*

107. *Id.*

108. *Anyanwu v. Columbia Broadcasting System Inc.,* 887 F.Supp. 690 (S.D. N.Y. 1995).

109. *Michigan United Conservation Clubs v. Columbia Broadcasting System Inc.,* 665 F.2d 110 (6th Cir. 1981).

110. *Thomas v. WJKS,* 699 So.2d 800 (Fla. App. 1997); *Another Group Libel Suit Thrown Out of Court,* Brechner Center Rep. (University of Florida Brechner Center for Freedom of Information, Gainesville, Fla.), March 1996, at 1.

111. *Id.*

112. *Id.*

113. *Id.*

114. Prosser, *supra,* note 12, at 750.

115. Julianne Basinger, *Penn Settles Lawsuit Filed by Student Involved in 'Water Buffalo' Incident,* Academe Today (online service of the Chronicle of Higher Education), Sept. 9, 1997.

116. Note, *A Communitarian Defense of Group Libel Laws,* 101 Harvard Law Review 682 (1988).

117. *See* Kane, *Errors, Lies and Libel,* 113–120 (1992) for an informative account of how the case developed.

118. Kane, *supra.*

119. *Alton Telegraph Printing Co. v. Green,* 438 N.E.2d 203, 8 Med.L.Rptr. 1345 (1982).

120. Kane, *supra,* at 118.

121. Christopher Maloney, *Presidential Politics Interrupt House Floor Proceedings,* C-SPAN Update, Oct. 10, 1988.

122. *Ronald R. Hutchinson v. William Proxmire and Morton Schwartz,* 443 U.S. 111, 99 S.Ct. 2675, 61 L.Ed.2d 411, 5 Med.L.Rptr. 1279 (1979).

123. *Hutchinson v. Proxmire,* 431 F. Supp. 1311, 2 Med.L.Rptr. 1769 (W.D Wis. 1977).

124. *Id.*

125. *Hutchinson v. Proxmire,* 579 F.2d 1027, 4 Med.L.Rptr. 1016 (7th Cir. 1978).

126. *Hutchinson v. Proxmire* (1979).

127. *Id.*

128. *Farmers' Educational and Cooperative Union of America v. WDAY,* 360 U.S. 525, 79 S.Ct.1302, 3 L.Ed.2d 1407 (1959).

129. *Time, Inc. v. Mary Alice Firestone.*

130. *Id.,* quoting the trial court judge's decision.

131. *Id.*

132. *Id.*

133. *Id.*

134. *Id.*
135. *New York Times v. Sullivan.*
136. *Id.* Also Rodney Smolla, *Suing the Press: Libel, the Media and Power* (1986), 26–52; Anthony Lewis, *Make No Law: The Sullivan Case and the First Amendment* (1991) for accounts of Sullivan. Lewis includes the first draft of Associate Justice Brennan's unanimous opinion. It is interesting to compare it with the final version.
137. *Id.*
138. *New York Times v. Sullivan.*
139. *Id.*
140. *Id.*
141. *Id.*
142. *Id.*
143. *Id.*
144. Smolla, supra, at 33.
145. *Benjamin Gitlow v. New York*, 268 U.S. 652, 45 S.Ct. 625, 69 L.Ed.1138 (1925).
146. Lewis, supra, at 25–26.
147. *Id.* at 27.
148. *Id.* at 25–26.
149. *New York Times v. Sullivan,* quoting the trial court judge.
150. *Id.*
151. *Id.*
152. *Id.*
153. *Id.*
154. Hansen and Moore, *Public Attitudes Toward Libel: Do Newspaper Readers and Editors See Eye to Eye?*
155. *Jim Garrison v. Louisiana,* 379 U.S. 64, 85 S.Ct. 209, 13 L.Ed.2d 125, 1 Med.L.Rptr. 1548 (1964).
156. Garrison portrayed himself in Oliver Stone's film about the JFK Assassination, *JFK.*
157. *Beauharnais v. Illinois,* 343 U.S. 250, 72 S.Ct. 725, 96 L.Ed. 919 (1952).
158. Cited in *id.*
159. Cited in *id.*
160. *R.A.V. v. City of St. Paul,* 505 U.S. 377, 112 S.Ct. 2538, 120 L.Ed.2d 305 (1992).
161. *Steve Ashton v. Kentucky,* 384 U.S. 195, 86 S.Ct. 1407, 16 L.Ed.2d 469 (1966).
162. *Alfred D. Rosenblatt v. Frank P. Baer,* 383 U.S. 75, 86 S.Ct. 669, 15 L.Ed.2d 597, 1 Med. L.Rptr. 1558 (1966).
163. *Id.*
164. *Id.*
165. *Curtis Publishing Co. v. Wallace Butts* and *Associated Press v. Edwin A. Walker* (1967).
166. *Id.*
167. *Id.*
168. *Beckley Newspapers Corp. v. C. Harold Hanks,* 389 U.S. 81, 88 S.Ct. 197, 19 L.Ed.2d 248, 1 Med.L.Rptr. 1585 (1967).
169. *Phil A. St. Amant v. Herman A. Thompson,* 390 U.S. 727, 88 S.Ct. 1323, 20 L.Ed.2d 262, 1 Med.L.Rptr. 1586 (1968).
170. *Id.*
171. *Greenbelt Cooperative Publishing Assoc. v. Charles S. Bresler* (1970).
172. *Monitor Patriot Co. v. Roselle A. Roy,* 401 U.S. 265, 91 S.Ct. 621, 28 L.Ed.2d 35, 1 Med. L.Rptr. 1619 (1971).
173. *Id.*
174. *Time, Inc. v. Frank Pape,* 401 U.S. 265, 91 S.Ct. 633, 28 L.Ed.2d 45, 1 Med.L.Rptr. 1627 (1971).
175. *Ocala Star-Banner Co. v. Leonard Damron,* 401 U.S. 295, 91 S.Ct. 628, 1 Med.L.Rptr. 1624 (1971).
176. *George A. Rosenbloom v. Metromedia,* 403 U.S. 29, 91 S.Ct. 1811, 29 L.Ed.2d 296, 1 Med. L.Rptr. 1597 (1971).
177. *Elmer Gertz v. Robert Welch, Inc.* (1974).
178. *Id.*

179. John B. McCroy et al., *Constitutional Privilege in Libel Law,* in 1 Comunication Law, 418–430 (2003).

180. *Elmer Gertz v. Robert Welch, Inc.* (1974).

181. *Id.*

182. *Kevin Johnson, Attorney General, Too, Apologizes to Jewell,* USA Today, Aug. 1, 1997, at A4.

183. Kevin Johnson and Gary Fields, *Jewell Investigation Unmasks FBI 'Tricks',* USA Today, Nov. 8, 1996, at A13; Roberto Suro, *FBI Accused of Ruse to Have Jewell Waive Rights in Bomb Investigation,* Lexington (Ky.) Herald-Leader (Washington Post), Nov. 10, 1996, at A16; *U.S. Drops Ex-Guard as Suspect in Bombing,* Lexington (Ky.) Herald-Leader (wire services), Oct. 27, 1996, at A1.

184. Tony Mauro, *Experts Doubt Jewell Has Case for Lawsuits,* USA Today, Aug. 13, 1996, at A3.

185. *Eager Media Judged Jewell Prematurely, Lawyer Contends,* 3 Freedom Forum News 1 (Nov. 11, 1996).

186. *Olympic Bombing Suspect Cleared, Threatens to Sue,* CNN online version, Oct. 26, 1996; Kevin Johnson, *Jewell, CNN Settle; Paper Sued,* USA Today, Jan. 29, 1997, at A1; Kevin Johnson, *Media Shy from Lawsuits,* USA Today, Jan. 29, 1997, at A5; *Georgia Policy Protects Source Even if Shield Law Does Not,* Atlanta Journal-Constitution, Oct. 10, 2001, http://www.gannett. com/go/newswatch/2001/december/nw1228-4.htm; *Richard Jewell Still Seeking Newspaper's Sources,* Associated Press, Aug. 5, 2003, http://www.firstamendmentcenter.org/news.aspx?id=11789; *60 Minutes II: Falsely Accused,* CBS News, June 26, 2002, http://www.cbsnews.com/stories/2002/ 01/02/60II/main322892.shtml.

187. For more on the Jewell case, see Mark Curriden, *Rebuilding a Reputation,* 83 A.B.A. J. 20 (Jan.1997); Angie Cannon, *Jewell Says He's Haunted by FBI Inquiry Memories,* Lexington (Ky.) Herald-Leader (Knight-Ridder), July 31, 1997, at A5.

188. *Jewell v. Atlanta Journal-Constitution,* 251 Ga.App. 808, 817, 555 S.E.2d 175, 183, 29 Med. L.Rptr. 2537 (2001), *petition for cert. denied,* 537 U.S. 814 (2002).

189. Larry O'Dell, *'Persons of Interest' in Anthrax Case Seek to Revive Libel Claim,* Associated Press, May 24, 2005.

190. *Elmer Gertz v. Robert Welch, Inc.* (1974).

191. *Dun & Bradstreet, Inc. v. Greenmoss Builders, Inc.*

192. *Harte-Hanks Communications, Inc. v. Connaughton.*

193. *Id.*

194. *Bose Corp. v. Consumers Union of the U.S., Inc.* (1984).

195. *Black's Law Dictionary* 409 (5th ed. 1979).

196. *Milkovich v. Lorain Journal Co.,* 497 U.S. 1, 110 S. Ct. 2695, 111 L.Ed.2d 1, 17 Med.L.Rptr. 2009 (1990). Milkovich later settled out of court with the newspaper.

197. *Id.*

198. *Id.*

199. Harold W. Fuson, *A Yawn for Milkovich,* 79 Quill 23, (July–Aug. 1991).

200. Charles N. Davis, *Libel and Statements of Opinion Before and After Milkovich,* 15 Newspaper Research J. 104 (Summer 1994).

201. *NBC Subsidiary (KCNC-TV), Inc. v. The Living Will Center,* 879 P.2d 6 (Colo. 1994).

202. *Claim That Living Will Kit is "Scam" Privileged,* News Media & Law, Fall 1994, at 7.

203. *Moldea v. New York Times Co. (Moldea I),* 15 F.3d 1137, 22 Med.L.Rptr. 1321 (D.C. Cir. 1994); *Moldea v. New York Times Co. (Moldea II),* 22 F.3d 310, 22 Med.L.Rptr. 1673 (D.C. Cir. 1994).

204. *Moldea II.*

205. *Id.*

206. Lee Levine, *Diving Catch,* A. Journalism Rev., July–Aug. 1994, at 37.

207. *Miami Child's World v. Sunbeam Television Corp.,* 669 So.2d 336 (Fla. 3d DCA 1996); Dana J. McElroy and Gary M. Held, *Decision Revives Protection for Opinion in Florida,* Brechner Center Rep. (University of Florida Brechner Center for Freedom of Information, Gainesville, Fla.), June 1996, at 4.

208. *Masson v. New Yorker Magazine, Inc.,* 501 U.S. 496, 111 S.Ct. 2419, 115 L.Ed.2d 447, 18 Med.L.Rptr. 2241 (1991).

209. Sack, *supra,* at 84–85.

210. *Brown & Williamson Tobacco Corp. v. Jacobson,* 827 F.2d 1119, 14 Med.L.Rptr. 1497 (7th Cir. 1987), *cert. denied,* 485 U.S. 993,108 S.Ct. 1302, 99 L.Ed.2d 512 (1988).

211. *Hustler Magazine and Larry C. Flynt v. Jerry Falwell* (1988).

212. *Id.*

213. *Newton v. NBC.*

214. Kevin *M. O'Gilvie and Stephanie L. O'Gilvie, Minors v. United States*, 519 U.S. 79, 117 S.Ct.452, 136 L.Ed.2d 454 (1996).

215. *Honda Motor Co. Ltd. et al. V. Oberg*, 512 U.S. 415, 114 S.Ct.2331, 129 L.Ed.2d 336 (1994).

216. *BMW of North America Inc. v. Ira Gore Jr.,* 517 U.S. 559, 116 S.Ct.1589, 134 L.Ed.2d 809 (1996).

217. *Id.*

218. *Id.*

219. Terry Carter, *State Court Slashes BMW Paint Award*, 83 A.B.A. J. 34 (Aug.1997).

220. Mark Thompson, *Applying the Brakes to Punitives,* 83 A.B.A. J. 68 (Sept. 1997).

221. *Philip Morris USA v. Mayola Williams*, 127 S.Ct. 1057, 166 L.Ed.2d 940 (2007).

222. *Philadelphia Newspapers, Inc. v. Hepps* (1986).

223. *Reggie Warford v. Lexington Herald-Leader et al.*, 789 S.W. 2d 758, 17 Med.L.Rptr. 1785 (Ky. 1990), *cert. denied*, 498 U.S. 1047, 111 S.Ct 754, 112 L.Ed.2d 774 (1991).

224. *Turf Lawnmower Repair, Inc. v. Bergen Record Corporation,* 139 N.J. 392, 65 A.2d 417, 23 Med. L.Rptr. 1609 (N.J. 1995); *cert. denied*, 516 U.S. 1066, 116 S.Ct. 752, 133 L.Ed.2d 700 (1996).

225. *Romero v. Thomson Newspapers*, 648 So.2d 866 (La. Sup. Ct. 1995), *cert. denied,* 515 U.S. 1131, 115 S.Ct. 2556, 132 L.Ed.2d 810 (1995).

226. John R. Bender, *Of Jellyfish and Community Leaders: Redefining the Public Figure in Libel Litigation,* paper presented to Convention of the Association for Education in Journalism and Mass Communication, Chicago, July 1997.

227. George J. Church, *The Clinton Hater's Video Library,* Time, Aug. 1, 1994, at 21.

228. *Kathy Keeton v. Hustler Magazine, Inc.,* 465 U.S. 770, 104 S.Ct. 1473, 79 L.Ed.2d 790, 10 Med.L.Rptr. 1405 (1984).

229. *Id.*

230. *Iain Calder and John South v. Shirley Jones*, 465 U.S. 783, 104 S.Ct. 1482, 79 L.Ed.2d 804, 10 Med.L.Rptr. 1401 (1984).

231. *Publication-Date Debate: Online or On Paper,* First Amendment Legal Watch, Vol. 2, No. 45, Nov. 10, 1997.

232. Libel Reform Project of the Annenberg Washington Program Proposal for the Reform of Libel Law 9-10 (1988) and Gannett Center for Media Studies, the Cost of Libel: Economic and Policy Implications (Conference Report) 1 (1986).

233. Patricia G. Barnes, *Who's Sorry Now?* 83 A.B.A. J. 20 (Jan. 1997).

234. See example, Caryn James, *Ever Changing Fame, as Fluid as it is Fleeting,* New York Times, April 11, 2007, at B-8. And *Communications Law in the Digital Age 2010*, PLI, Vol. 3, at 19.

235. *Roger L. Sandler, The Chicken Butt Case*, Electronic Media Law, 2005, at 159.

236. *Using the Reporter's Remarks on TV as Evidence,* News Hour, Dec. 16, 2004, pbs.org/newshour/ bb/media/july-dec04/libel_12-16.html; Alice Mundy, *Libel Suit Takes Aim at Reporter's Words on TV*, Washington Post, retrieved from http://www.washingtonpost.com/wp-dyn/articles/A62088-2004Dec13.html, Dec. 14, 2004, at A1; and also Kristen Rasmussen, *Can I Quote You on That? Even If you Didn't Say it This Time, But You've Said it Before?* News Media and the Law, Fall 2010, 18-19.

237. *Lamb v. Rizzo*, 391 F.3d 1133 (10th Cir. 2004).

238. *Id.*

239. *Edwards v. National Audubon Society* 556 F.2d 113 (2d Cir. 1977), *cert. denied, sub. nom.; Edwards v. New York Times,* 434 U.S. 1002, 98 S.Ct. 647, 54 L.Ed.2d 498, 3 Med.L.Rptr. 1560 (1977); *McCroy et al., supra, note 180,* at 591–592.

240. Lee J. Levine and Daniel M. Waggoner, *The Uniform Correction or Clarification of Defamation Act: Overview of the Act,* 11 Comunication Law, Winter 1994, at 8.

241. *Id.,* at 11.

242. Jane E. Kirtley, *The Uniform Correction or Clarification of Defamation Act: Puncturing a Trial Balloon,* 11 Communication Law Winter, 1994, at 12.

243. Jamie Prime, *Shallow Pockets,* 82 Quill 30 (Oct. 1994).

244. *Stratton Oakmont Inc. v. Prodigy Services Co.*, 23 Med.L.Rptr. 1794 (N.Y. Sup. 1995); Jeffrey P. Cunard and Jennifer B. Coplan, *Cyberliability 2005: Select Developments*, 2 Communication Law 41 (2005).

245. Communications Decency Act of 1996, 47 U.S.C. §223.

246. *Kenneth Zeran v. America Online Inc.*, 958 F.Supp. 1124, 25 Med.L.Rptr. 1609 (E.D. Virginia 1997); 129 F.3d 327 (4th Cir. 1997); *AOL Not Liable for Third-Party Defamatory Me*ssages, First Amendment Legal Watch, Vol. 2, No. 47, Nov. 26, 1997.

247. *Blumenthal v. Drudge*, 992 F.Supp. 44 (D.D.C. 1998); Jeffrey P. Cunard and Jennifer B. Coplan, *supra,* note 242.

248. *Blumenthal v. Drudge.*

249. *House Prosecutors Urge Senate to Call Witnesses Who Challenge Blumenthals' Testimony*, Court-TV online, Feb. 8, 1999.

250. Geneva Overholser and Kathleen Hall Jamieson, *The Press* (2005), at 437. For examples involving journalists such as Chris Mathews*, see* Bob Baker, *Mr. Motor Mouth*, Los Angeles Times, July 25, 2004, E1; David Bauder, *Mathews Fights His Way Back into the Spotlight*, Las Vegas Sun, Sept. 13, 2004, at E2, and *Palin Responds to Critics, Expresses Sorrow*, St. Louis Post-Dispatch, January 13, 2011.

251. Jennifer Dorroh, *Eye on CBS, The Network Launches a Blog to Scrutinize Its News Operation*, American Journalism Review, Oct./Nov. 2005, at 14; Jacques Steinberg and Bill Carter, *CBS Dismisses 4 Over Broadcast on Bush Service, Moves After An Inquiry, Investigators Say Program Should Not Have Been Allowed to Air*, New York Times, Jan. 11, 2005, at C6; Lisa Kennedy, *For Filmmakers, It's Open Season on Politics*, Denver Post, Sept. 10, 2004, at E22, at A-8, and Kristen Rasmussen, *Can I Quote You on That? Even If you didn't Say it this Time, But you've said it before?* News Media and the Law, Fall 2010, 18–19.

9

Indecency, Obscenity, and Pornography

For generations there has been a societal consensus about sexual material getting limited First Amendment coverage. You're asking us to go into an entirely new area where there is no consensus.

—Justice Anthony Kennedy, quoted in "Justices Take up Ban on Violent Games," USA TODAY, November 3, 2010, p. 3-A

As in other evolving areas of media law, much attention has been paid recently to the so-called new media, particularly Internet related activity and especially those areas involving children's use of online content including violent video games and pornographic content depicting children. Two relatively recent cases symbolic of these areas, *Entertainment Software Association v. Swanson*, 519F.3d 768 (8th Cir. 2008) and *Video Software Dealers Association v. Schwarzenegger*, 556 F 3d 950 (9th Cir. 2009), reaffirmed rulings that content-based regulation of free speech is subject to scrutiny so that violent speech is considered protected, while specifying violent content that may appeal to "morbid interests" is open for review and *U.S. v. Williams*, 128 S. Ct. 1830 (2008), in which the U.S. Supreme Court upheld a federal law prohibiting child pornography in cases in which material is thought to depict real children.

Supreme Court justices have questioned the validity of a ban on violent video games in the state of California by prohibiting the sale or rental of video games depicting "killing, maiming, dismemberment or sexually assaulting an image of a human being," as states have done over time for sexually explicit material. Video game manufacturers said the ban is too broad and Justice Anton Scalia questioned whether a state could actually define "deviant" violence, adding "Some of the Grimm's fairy tales are quite grim."

Outside of the strict purview of children, while courts have continued to go back and forth on related content matters, some major fines by the FCC have focused attention on government efforts to address indecency on traditional over-the air media, due, in large measure, to consumer response. One installment of an animated FOX-TV sit-com *Family Guy* reportedly generated almost 200,000 complaints to the FCC. The plot of the episode involved horse semen, and the first complaint registered against it came from Dan Isett of the Parents Television Council, a media watchdog group. FOX-TV also reportedly received 150,000 complaints when a camera panned the stands at a professional football game showing one fan wearing a t-shirt with lettering suggesting that the opposing team do something physically impossible to themselves.

The Fox Broadcasting Company, facing an FCC fine of $1.2 million, took issue with federal regulators who said that an episode of *Married by America* that aired April 7, 2003, featuring male and female Las Vegas strippers in sexual motif was indecent and patently offensive. The FCC clarified: "Although the nudity was pixilated, even a child would have known that the strippers were topless and that sexual activity was being shown."[1] On that occasion, in the wake of the exposure of Janet Jackson's breast (aka "Nipplegate") during the 2004 Super Bowl half-time show on CBS, the FCC voted unanimously to fine each of 169 Fox affiliates airing the *Married by America* program $7,000, totaling $1.183 million.

The Supreme Court's initial decision against the FCC in the Super Bowl halftime program and Fox programs occurred against the backdrop of a large number of cases accumulated on the topic of indecency. During his nomination hearing, FCC Commissioner Robert McDowell said that it was time for the Commission to begin to address and "clear-out" the backlog of what was estimated to be over a million indecency complaints. In the wake of that statement Communication attorneys noted a larger number of complaints not about nudity or profanity but episodes of widely distributed series such as *Dr. Phil* on the subject of masturbation. The FCC attorneys made a point of saying such a complaint—while not within the purview of previously addressed areas, still required action on the broadcaster's part including a compilation of evidence—tapes, scripts, or explanation of why it was not indecent.

After court decisions concerning the continuingly controversial Super Bowl halftime peep-show revelations including *CBS Corp. v FCC*, 2008 WL 2789307 (3d Cir. July 21, 2008), CBS has fought on, consistently taking the position that it in no way intended to air "potentially indecent material." Six years after initially telecast, in 2010, the U.S. Supreme Court directed the Third Circuit Court of Appeals in a supplemental brief to take yet another look at this case. The first time the broadcast was considered, the Court ruled the FCC's fine over the incident was "arbitrary and capricious."

The Supreme Court also overturned a similar finding by the Second Circuit Appeals Court against the FCC's fleeting profanity decision in the Fox Billboard Awards case, anticipating review by the Third Circuit Court of Appeals. But following-up on new oral arguments of February 23, 2010, the Third Circuit took the unusual step of asking for more information from both sides on what is often termed "mens rea" or in popular terminology "guilty mind," asking in effect, what level of intent on CBS' part could justify such a fine?

CBS argued that any way you evaluated the situation the company should not be held liable since it did not even intend to broadcast any potentially indecent material. It said further that the FCC must show CBS' intent to violate the law. The FCC countered in the supplemental brief that even if CBS did not intend to broadcast that particular content, it did intend to broadcast a "live" half-time show, and doing that, it failed to take any steps to prevent the action that took place. The FCC renewed its request that the court remand the case for further explanation of the specific part of the laws the FCC relied on in imposing the initial fine and to resolve the issue of whether a "video delay" was available at the time of the broadcast, ostensibly rendering CBS's conduct "reckless."

Beyond these efforts to address transgressions by the so-called traditional media, as indicated at the start of this chapter most emerging cases address issues raised by the growth of obscenity and indecency on the Internet, including protecting children from online sexually explicit materials. A concerted effort by the federal government along these lines was best represented by Congress' creation of the Commission on Online Child Protection (COPA). The commission released a report at the start of the last decade, evaluating child protection policies and technologies including accessibility, costs, and methods of protection such as monitoring and family contracts. It identified the need for a public education campaign to alert the nation to the growth of online materials harmful to minors and methods available to protect children online.

The commission noted the growth of this material and encouraged government support for legislation to address it. It also attempted to offer industry and the private sector the incentive to engage in a national debate to address the next generation of systems for identifying, evaluating, and labeling content to protect young people. While the results have been uneven, the government, working especially with public libraries, made the first meaningful effort to identify a serious, growing problem and has taken the first few small steps to address it. Within this context, it is important to note much of the potentially harmful material originates abroad.

Other new technologies geared toward adults have created new venues for sexually explicit materials or porn. The demise of American Exxxtasy, an X-rated satellite subscription service, is an interesting illustration of the ongoing clash between purveyors of pornography doing legal battle with local, state, and federal government officials. It is also an unusual example of the type of gap that occasionally emerges between new media and law enforcement. The public and customers of obscene materials play a minor role in the inevitable battle. Public opinion polls consistently find that most citizens consider proliferation of sexually explicit materials to be a problem. But they do not favor actions by police because they feel adults should be able to judge for themselves and consume even works explicitly depicting sexual conduct unless depictions include minors, violence, or deviant sex. Meanwhile, statutes imposing strict bans on child pornography enjoy widespread public support.

It is instructive to consider the complex history of technology in such matters since the old-style over-the-air broadcast of sketchy material is now provided primarily via satellite and cable. Officials of Home Dish Only (HDO) Satellite Network, the parent corporation of American Exxxtasy, pleaded guilty in 1990 to two misdemeanor charges of distributing obscene materials. Less than a year later, the company pled guilty to federal charges of broadcasting obscenity via satellite to New York and Utah. HDO transmitted its signal around the country from New York for four years via satellite space leased from GTE, a major satellite owner. X-rated movies were carried after 8:00 p.m. and scrambled so only the 30,000 paying subscribers could legally view them. The service was not available to cable subscribers, only to satellite dish owners.

How was HDO indicted and ultimately forced to plead guilty to obscenity charges or face likely conviction by juries in the state and federal courts? Amexxx is an example of how the law eventually caught up with technology. HDO was able to carry its XXX-rated channel nationwide and bypass cable systems via the same technology that transformed a small UHF television station owned by Ted Turner into Superstation TBS—geostationary satellites that spin with the earth's orbit. Section 639 of the Cable Communications Policy Act of 1984 provides: "Whoever transmits over any cable system any matter which is obscene or otherwise unprotected by the Constitution of the United States shall be fined not more than $10,000 or imprisoned not more than two years, or both."[2] Notice that the provision made no mention of satellite transmission or subscription TV. That omission was remedied with Public Law 100-690 in 1988:

§1468. Distributing Obscene Material by Cable or Subscription Television.

(a)   Whoever knowingly utters any obscene language or distributes any obscene matter by means of cable television or subscription services on television, shall be punished by imprisonment for not more than 2 years or by a fine in accordance with this title or both.

(b)   As used in this section, the term "distribute" means to send, transmit, retransmit, telecast, broadcast, or cablecast, including by wire, microwave, or satellite, or to produce or provide material for such distribution.

(c)   Nothing in this chapter, or the Cable Communications Policy Act of 1984, or any other provision of Federal law, is intended to interfere with or preempt the power of the States, including political subdivisions thereof, to regulate the uttering of language that is otherwise obscene or otherwise unprotected by the Constitution or the distribution of matter that is obscene or otherwise unprotected by the Constitution, of any sort, by means of cable television or subscription services on television.[3]

By including "satellite" in the definition of "distribute," Congress granted the FBI the authority to prosecute Amexxx. Note that the section included a clause (item c) that makes it clear the states still retained the authority to conduct their own prosecutions. In fact, Montgomery County, Alabama's District Attorney Jimmy Evans, who was a candidate for state attorney general at the time, was the first official to prosecute HDO. He convinced an Alabama grand jury to indict four executives of the network for allegedly violating state obscenity statutes. Eventually, HDO pled guilty to two misdemeanor charges of distributing obscene material and was fined $5,000 and forced to pay $75,000 each to two children's homes.

According to rumors in the satellite industry trade press at the time of the prosecutions, Alabama authorities were alerted to Amexxx after school officials discovered that high school students were distributing among their peers tapes of the network's programming, some of which may have been recorded with pirated or illegal descramblers. FBI agents filed their charges after an agent purchased a decoder and paid a subscription fee to watch the programming. The agency began its 13-month investigation after dish owners complained about Amexxx's unscrambled commercials. HDO pled guilty before it could be indicted by a federal grand jury. HDO was fined $150,000 on a single count of broadcasting obscenity via satellite and agreed to a consent decree under which it erased all of its X-rated movie inventory.[4]

In addition to American Exxxtasy, HDO offered a premium movie service known as Stardust and an R-rated adult service called Tuxxedo, both of which folded shortly after Alabama indictments, apparently because revenues of Amexxx were subsidizing the other services. All three services were available only to dish owners.

Although American Exxxtasy is gone, current satellite dish services offer X-rated programming. DirecTV offers adult channels. Dish offers adults-only channels, one described on its website as an "uncensored channel delivering the wildest situations the adult world has to offer." Some of the adult channels, including Playboy, feature sexually oriented viewer call-in shows. And the satellite services are not the only media outlets offering explicit adult programming. Most cable systems offer a similar array of pay channels. The Internet was still relatively new in the mid-1990s when federal and state authorities began a crackdown on X-rated material. For example, one couple was convicted in U.S. District Court in Memphis, Tennessee, in

1994 for transmitting obscenity via interstate phone lines on a member-only electronic bulletin board. The service operated from California but was prosecuted in Tennessee after one complaint. Owners were convicted on 11 counts of obscenity, but acquitted of charges of child pornography. Some of the pictures transmitted via e-mail included scenes of bestiality and sexual fetishes.[5] Sophisticated tracking software is used to identify children who have been used in making pornography.[6]

About the same time, the FBI arrested a 20-year-old University of Michigan student for posting a story on the Internet that included discussions about his fantasy of raping, killing, and torturing a classmate whom he named. The events discussed with a fellow Internet user never occurred, and the student never made any threats against his classmate. The student was charged with five counts of transmitting by e-mail a threat to kidnap or injure. However, a U.S. District Court Judge ruled that the discussions had First Amendment protection and dismissed the charges. The student was jailed for 29 days after he was charged. The suicide of a Rutgers University student exposed on the Internet by fellow students as having engaged in homosexual activity and the earlier mass murders at Virginia Tech have forced another reevaluation of the influence of new technology on criminal behavior and also how academic institutions can best share information when attacks become public.

At the level of mass media, pushing the so-called decency envelope further has also become more commonplace with the emergence of satellite radio. In what some critics called "lewd" and a set-back to feminism, one bawdy female radio host heard on Sirius Satellite Radio calling herself the "Radiochick" invited female guests to strip in the studio while advising male callers on such issues as how to cheat on their girlfriends. Of course, what is considered "lewd" and what is regarded as "smut" are often left to the audience, and then as we know from studies of psychology, selective perception comes into play.[7]

From *Hicklin* to *Roth*: An Emerging Definition of Obscenity

In the case outlined earlier, it took a federal statute for the national government and the state of Alabama to successfully prosecute HDO for transmitting obscenity via satellite, but a U.S. Supreme Court decision 17 years earlier provided foundation for its demise.

Obscenity has been suppressed and prosecuted throughout history, always somehow managing to survive even when it was forced to go underground, and it has actually thrived during some eras. Until 1957 the U.S. Supreme Court avoided getting embroiled in defining obscenity, relying instead on lower courts to enunciate the boundaries of acceptable sexually oriented speech.

The two major influences on obscenity prosecutions from approximately the mid-19th century to the mid-20th century were an American named Anthony Comstock and an 1868 British court decision known as *Regina v. Hicklin*.[8] Comstock lived from 1844 to 1915. He founded and directed the New York Society for the Suppression of Vice, which was instrumental in lobbying state and federal legislators to enact statutes strictly regulating obscenity. The statutes whose passage he spearheaded were popularly known as "Comstock laws." The federal law was enforced primarily by the U.S. Post Office, which had the authority to bar the mailing of obscene materials and to prosecute violators. During much of the time he was involved in suppression Comstock was a special agent of the Post Office reportedly receiving shares of proceeds from the fines imposed on offenders. The current federal statute and many state statutes still reflect the cries of the anti-obscenity crusades.

Regina v. Hicklin

Regina v. Hicklin began when British Trial Court Judge Hicklin enforced an anti-obscenity law by ordering the confiscation and destruction of copies of a pamphlet entitled *The Confessional Unmasked*, which included depictions of sexual acts. The trial court's decision was upheld on appeal to the Queen's Bench in an opinion by Lord Chief Justice Cockburn, who formulated what become known as the Hicklin test for determining obscenity: "whither the tendency of the matter charged as obscene is to deprave and corrupt those whose minds are open to such immoral influences and into whose hands a publication of this sort might fall."[9]

The test essentially barred all sexually oriented materials because (a) an entire publication could be considered obscene if *any* portion, no matter how small, could "deprave and corrupt"; and (b) the work was obscene if it would deprave and corrupt the minds of even the most sensitive and easily influenced individuals, including children. In fact, successful prosecution did not require that the Crown demonstrate the materials actually fell into the hands of susceptible people but merely that they *could* end up there. By taking isolated passages out of context and convincing judges and juries that these passages could stimulate immoral thoughts within children and other sensitive individuals, the state could successfully censor almost any publication referring to sexual conduct.

Until the Civil War (1861 to 1865), public concern in the United States over obscenity was not high. But when stories appeared about soldiers reading and viewing allegedly pornographic materials, the stage was set for severe suppression of such works after the war. With Anthony Comstock at the helm, legislators and judges responded by enforcing statutes already on the books and enacting new laws where needed. Because the U.S. Supreme Court had never dealt with the issue head-on, the lower courts, both state and federal, generally adopted the handy *Hicklin* definition complete with the isolated passage and sensitive individual provisions.

U.S. v. Ulysses

The tide against this oppressive rule began to turn in 1934 when U.S. District Court Judge John M. Woolsey in New York held that James Joyce's *Ulysses* was not obscene and, therefore, could be imported into the United States.[10] (Customs officers had prohibited the book's entry into this country.) Judge Woolsey rejected the *Hicklin* rule and instead offered a new test that nevertheless kept some elements of the old rule. According to Judge Woolsey, a work is obscene if it "tends to stir the sex impulses or to lead to sexually impure and lustful thoughts. Whether a particular book would tend to excite such impulses must be the test by the court's opinion as to its effect [judged as a whole] on a person with average sex instincts."[11]

Thus the isolated passages provision of *Hicklin* was replaced by the requirement that the work must be judged in its entirety and that the court must look at the effect of the material on the average person ("a person with average sex instincts"), not on sensitive individuals. Another significant change was the substitution of "lead to sexually impure and lustful thoughts" for "deprave and corrupt." This essentially meant that the work must be sexually exciting, not merely corrupting or, as later court decisions said, including those of the U.S. Supreme Court, the material must appeal to prurient interests. There is still debate among scholars over how much influence the *Ulysses* holding had on modern obscenity tests, but it is clear that *Hicklin* was crumbling away by the time of *Ulysses* and the U.S. Supreme Court would eventually have to intervene to bring some consistency to obscenity prosecutions.

One year later, the Second Circuit U.S. Court of Appeals affirmed the lower court decision, and the federal government chose not to appeal the ruling, thus denying the U.S. Supreme Court the opportunity to consider the case. *Ulysses* miraculously survived the *Hicklin* sword, primarily because of an enlightened jurist who realized the book deserved First Amendment protection, but other literary works were not so fortunate and were at least temporarily banned thanks to *Hicklin*. These have included Henry Miller's *Tropic of Cancer*, Ernest Hemingway's *For Whom the Bell Tolls*, Erskine Caldwell's *Tobacco Road*, William Faulkner's *Mosquitoes,* and Dr. Alan Guttmacher's *Complete Book of Birth Control*.[12]

Butler v. Michigan: *Rejecting the* Hicklin *Standard*

Except for a few isolated decisions involving matters that were more procedural than substantive, the U.S. Supreme Court waited until 1957 to assume the task of defining obscenity. In *Butler v. Michigan* (1957)[13] the Court struck down as unconstitutional a provision in the Michigan Penal Code that banned any material "tending to incite minors to violent or depraved or immoral acts manifestly tending to the corruption of the morals of youth." According to the unanimous opinion by Justice Felix Frankfurter:

> The State insists that, by thus quarantining the general reading public against books not too rugged for grown men and women in order to shield juvenile innocence, it is exercising its power to promote the general welfare. Surely this is to burn the house to roast the pig…. We have before us legislation not reasonably restricted to the evil with which it is said to deal. The incidence of this enactment is to reduce the adult population of Michigan to reading only what is fit for children.[14]

Roth v. U.S. *and* Alberts v. California *(1957):* *A New Obscenity Standard*

The *Butler* decision was especially significant because it specifically rejected the *Hicklin* standard on which the Michigan statute had been patterned and thus paved the way for the Court's landmark ruling exactly four months later in *Roth v. U.S.* and *Alberts v. California* (1957).[15] Samuel Roth was convicted by a jury in the U.S. District Court of the Southern District of New York for violating *federal* obscenity statutes—more specifically, the Comstock Act—barring the mailing of obscene materials. He had allegedly mailed obscene circulars, ads, and a book, *American Aphrodite*. His conviction was affirmed by a federal appeals court.

Mail order entrepreneur David S. Alberts was sentenced by a California municipal court for violating obscenity provisions of the California Penal Code. His conviction in a bench trial was upheld by a federal appeals court. The U.S. Supreme Court struggled with the case, as evidenced by the 5 to 4 majority opinion, which included a 7 to 2 vote upholding the conviction of Alberts and a 6 to 3 vote affirming Roth's conviction. The majority decision, written by Justice William Brennan who had been nominated only a few months earlier by President Eisenhower, offered broader protection for sexual expression than had been previously granted. But the Court made it clear that obscene speech did not fall under the First Amendment. The Court began by settling the issue:

> The dispositive question is whether obscenity is utterance within the area of protected speech and press. Although this is the first time the question has been squarely presented to this Court, either under the First Amendment or the Fourteenth Amendment, expressions found in numerous opinions indicate that this Court has always assumed that obscenity is not protected by the freedoms of speech and press.[16]

The significance of this point is that once material has been properly deemed obscene by a court, prior restraint can be imposed within the limitations of *Near v. Minnesota* (1931).[17] Justice Brennan went on to note:

> All ideas having even the slightest redeeming social importance—unorthodox ideas, controversial ideas, even ideas hateful to the prevailing climate of opinion—have the full protection of the guaranties [of the First and Fourteenth Amendments], unless excludable because they encroach upon the limited area of more important interests. But implicit in the history of the First Amendment is the rejection of obscenity as utterly without redeeming social importance.... We hold that obscenity is not within the area of constitutionally protected speech or press.[18]

The last statement led to this test being characterized as the "utter" standard for judging obscenity. There are four prongs to the test: (a) whether to the average person, (b) applying contemporary community standards, (c) the dominant theme of the material taken as a whole (d) appeals to prurient interest. The Supreme Court has spent the decades since this decision attempting to define terms such as: *average person, contemporary community standards,* and *prurient interest.* The Court made a good faith but unsuccessful effort to distinguish sex from obscenity:

> Sex and obscenity are not synonymous. Obscene material is material which deals with sex in a manner appealing to prurient interest. The portrayal of sex, e.g., in art, literature and scientific works, is not itself sufficient reason to deny material the constitutional protection of freedom of speech and press. Sex, a great and mysterious motive force in human life, has indisputably been a subject of absorbing interest to mankind through the ages; it is one of the vital problems of human interest and public concern.[19]

Smith v. California *(1959): The Requirement of Scienter*

The next piece in the perplexing obscenity puzzle emerged two years later in *Smith v. California* (1959)[20] in which the U.S. Supreme Court unanimously reversed the conviction of a Los Angeles bookstore owner for violating a municipal ordinance barring the possession of any obscene or indecent writings, including books, in any place of business. Justice Brennan was able to garner the agreement of four other justices (although they were not the same four who had joined him in *Roth*) in holding that the ordinance was unconstitutional because the city law made booksellers liable even if they were unaware of the contents of the book. The other four justices concurred in the result but with different reasoning. According to the majority, in order to pass constitutional muster, such an ordinance must require the government to prove *scienter*—that is, the individual had knowledge of the contents of the allegedly obscene materials. Otherwise, the Court reasoned, a chilling effect would prevail:

> If the bookseller is criminally liable without knowledge of the contents and the [ordinance] fulfills its purpose, he will tend to restrict the books he sells to those he has inspected; and thus the State will have imposed a restriction upon the distribution of constitutionally protected as well as obscene literature.... And the bookseller's burden would become the public's burden, for by restricting him the public's access to reading matter would be restricted. If the contents of bookshops and periodical stands were restricted to material of which their proprietors had made an inspection, they might be depleted indeed.[21]

State statutes now typically include this element of *scienter* as essential for an obscenity conviction. Kentucky's penal code dealing with the distribution of obscene matter, for example, reads: "A person is guilty of distribution of obscene matter when, *having knowledge of its content and character ...*" (emphasis added).[22] Georgia's parallel statute stipulates that the offense of distributing materials occurs when a person disseminates obscene material "knowing the obscene nature thereof" and defines "knowing" as "either actual or constructive knowledge of the obscene contents of the subject matter, and a person has constructive knowledge ... if he has knowledge of the facts which would put a reasonable and prudent person on notice as to the suspect nature of the material."[23]

The U.S. Supreme Court handed down a major opinion dealing with *scienter* in obscenity prosecutions in 1994. In *United States v. X-Citement Video*,[24] the Court ruled 7 to 2 in a decision that the language of the Protection of Children Against Sexual Exploitation Act of 1977 could be properly read to include a *scienter* requirement. Justices Thomas and Scalia dissented. A video owner and operator challenged his conviction under the Act for selling 49 tapes featuring porn queen Traci Lords in sexually explicit films made while she was under age. The defendant sold the tapes to undercover police and shipped eight more Traci Lords' tapes to the same policeman in Hawaii. The majority opinion engaged in an interesting grammar exercise that ultimately reversed a Ninth Circuit U.S. Court of Appeals ruling. The lower appellate court held the Act as unconstitutional because it did not require defendants to know one of the performers was a minor.

The Supreme Court decision is a good illustration of how the Court will make every effort to construe an obscenity statute to meet the *scienter* requirement. Two sections of the Act were in dispute, "knowingly" appearing in both. The adverb is placed next to "transports or ships" and "receives, or distributes" rather than appearing with "involves the use of a minor engaging in sexually explicit conduct." The appellate court had opted for "the most natural grammatical reading"—that "knowingly" did not modify "involves the use ..." According to the Court, there is a "standard presumption in favor of a *scienter* requirement." That presumption would favor a finding that "knowingly" included use of a minor.

Manual Enterprises v. Day *(1962): Patent Offensiveness*

In 1962 the U. S. Supreme Court considered a new aspect of the definition of obscenity: sexual explicitness or what has become known as *patent offensiveness*. In *Manual Enterprises v. Day*,[25] a majority of justices led by Justice John M. Harlan overturned a U.S. Post Office Department ban against the mailing of several gay oriented magazines with titles such as *MANual, Grecian Pictorial,* and *Trim* that the court characterized as "dismally unpleasant, uncouth and tawdry."

Why were the magazines protected? They featured male nudity but were not patently offensive. Justice Harlan noted the Post Office had not been able to ban materials featuring female nudity, and male nudes were no more objectionable than female nudity even if directed to homosexuals. *Patently offensive* was added as a new requirement to the definition of obscene. What is *patently offensive?* The Court says material that "affronts community standards."

But what *community* is used to determine community standards? This question has been one of the most troublesome faced by the Court. Two years after *Manual Enterprises,* the U.S. Supreme Court attempted to define this important concept when it reversed the conviction of the manager of a movie theater in Cleveland Heights, Ohio. He had been convicted in a bench trial of two counts of possessing and showing *Les Amants* ("The Lovers"), which included a fairly explicit but brief love scene. His punishment was a $2,500 fine; his convictions were upheld by an intermediate state appellate court and by the Ohio Supreme Court.

The effort of the Court to define the concept added to the confusion and signaled further trouble ahead. Six justices in *Jacobellis v. Ohio* (1964)[26] agreed that Nico Jacobellis had been wrongly convicted. They splintered in reasoning, resulting in a plurality. Pieced together, opinions supporting a reversal appeared to point to a national standard in line with what the Court enunciated earlier in *Roth and Alberts.* The case illustrates how complex and difficult it is to define *community* for purposes of obscenity.

Most memorable from *Jacobellis* was a now-famous statement in Justice Potter Stewart's concurring opinion attempting to define *obscenity*: "I know it when I see it, and the motion picture involved in this case is not that." Stewart's statement has been ridiculed and satirized for obtuseness, but he was making the point that obscenity convictions should be limited to what is typically characterized as hard core pornography, not works merely dealing with sex.

On the same day as *Jacobellis,* the justices handed down another obscenity decision, but this one dealt with a different controversy—whether an adversary hearing must be held to determine that materials are obscene before a search warrant is approved. Once again, the justices splintered. Seven justices agreed in *A Quantity of Copies of Books v. Kansas* (1964)[27] that a state statute permitting prosecutors to obtain warrants for the seizure of allegedly obscene materials without an adversarial hearing was unconstitutional. They disagreed on the reasoning.

According to the Court, under the Constitution, materials that had been determined to be obscene by a judge could be seized and then legally destroyed. However, the Kansas statute allowed a seizure order to be executed before any adversarial hearing was held. In effect, prosecutors were serving as judges in determining what was and what was not obscene. According to a plurality opinion authored by Brennan, the statute posed a danger that the public would be denied access to non-obscene, constitutionally protected works to punish the obscene.

Freedman v. Maryland *(1965):*
The Constitutionality of Censorship Boards

A similar sticky issue arose in 1965 in *Freedman v. Maryland,*[28] although by then the justices had begun to agree some on procedural points even though other important matters continued to elude them. In *Freedman,* the Court unanimously struck down a Maryland statute that mandated that movie exhibitors submit their films in advance to a state board of censors.

Justice Brennan wrote the majority opinion that declared the law a clear violation of the First Amendment. The Court said the statute placed the burden of proof on the exhibitor and failed to provide a means for prompt judicial scrutiny of an adverse decision by the board, which granted licenses only for those films that it approved as not being obscene.

Ronald Freedman was convicted for showing a film, *Revenge at Daybreak*, prior to submitting it to the censorship body. Interestingly, the board indicated in its arguments against Freedman's appeal of his conviction that the film was not obscene. It would have been approved if reviewed. The Court saw the board's action as unconstitutional prior restraint because the law "fails to provide adequate safeguards against undue inhibition of protected expression."[29]

The Court held that, to escape the First Amendment axe, "a non-criminal process which requires the prior submission of a film to a censor" must have three procedural safeguards:

> First, the burden of proving that the film is unprotected expression must rest on the censor.... Second, while the State may require advance submission of all films ... the requirement cannot be administered in a manner which would lend an effect of finality to the censor's determination whether a film constitutes protected expression.... [Third] the procedure must also assure a prompt final judicial decision, to minimize the deterrent effect of an interim and possibly erroneous denial of a license.[30]

The Fanny Hill Case: Applying the "Utter" Test

On March 21, 1966, the U.S. Supreme Court announced three decisions focusing on obscenity, each of which touched on a different aspect of the controversy that refused to go away. In *A Book Named "John Cleland's Memoirs of a Woman of Pleasure" v. Attorney General of Massachusetts*,[31] the Court reversed a ruling that the famous 1750 British novel popularly known as *Fanny Hill* was obscene. The book had been widely available in this country since the early 19th century, but Massachusetts was determined to ban it. The book had been reissued in 1963 by G. P. Putnam's Sons Publishers. The commonwealth banned the novel in spite of the fact that the publisher had orders from many universities and libraries, including the Library of Congress.

Fanny Hill is not a book for the faint of heart although its language is rather reserved by modern standards. As the prosecuting attorney noted at the hearing that led to the ban, the work describes several acts of heterosexual intercourse, male and female homosexuality, flagellation and female masturbation. Nevertheless, expert witnesses at the proceeding testified that the book had literary, cultural, and educational value.

Once again, the U.S. Supreme Court struggled with the nature of obscenity. Six members of the Court voted to reverse the equity court ruling and declare *Fanny Hill* was not obscene, but no majority opinion surfaced. Instead, Justice Brennan forged a plurality opinion with Chief Justice Warren and Associate Justice Abe Fortas that strongly reaffirmed the three-pronged *Roth* test. The opinion said the Massachusetts Supreme Court erred in ruling a jury could declare the book obscene without finding that the work was "utterly without redeeming social value." According to Justice Brennan, *any* redeeming social value is sufficient to save a work:

> We defined obscenity in *Roth* in the following terms: "whether to the average person, applying contemporary community standards, the dominant theme of the material taken as a whole appeals to prurient interest." [citation omitted] Under this definition,

… three elements must coalesce: it must be established that (a) the dominant theme of the material taken as a whole appeals to a prurient interest in sex; (b) the material is patently offensive because it affronts contemporary community standards relating to the description or representation of sexual matters; and (c) the material is utterly without redeeming social value.[32]

Ginzburg v. U.S. *(1966): Pandering*

The central issue of the second case handed down on March 21, 1966, was the role of *pandering*, or the way in which a work is promoted and advertised, in determining whether material is obscene. In *Ginzburg v. U.S.* (1966),[33] Justice Brennan was able to attract four other justices, including the Chief Justice, for a majority opinion affirming the 28-count conviction of Ralph Ginzburg for engaging in "the business of purveying textual or graphic matter openly advertised to appeal to the erotic interest of customers." The dissenting voices of the remaining four justices were unusually strong in condemning the majority holding.

Ginzburg was convicted, fined $28,000, and sentenced to five years in prison for violating federal obscenity statutes by mailing *Eros*, a magazine dealing with sex; *Liaison*, a biweekly sex-oriented newsletter; and a book entitled *The Housewife's Handbook on Selective Promiscuity*. Where did Ginzburg go wrong? The materials he distributed were probably not obscene, a point conceded by the prosecution. As Justice Brennan noted in his opinion, the prosecutor "charged the offense in the context of the circumstances of production, sale, and publicity and assumed that, standing alone, the publications themselves might not be obscene." Yet Justice Brennan and four of his colleagues upheld the conviction because, as Justice Brennan said, Ginzburg had shown the "leer of the sensualist." The Court extended the message that if distributors promote works in a manner that emphasizes non-redeeming social value or sexual provocativeness, the materials can be assumed to be obscene. This assumption applies, putting aside the promotion or pandering, to materials otherwise not obscene. According to the majority opinion:

> We agree that the question of obscenity may include consideration of the setting in which the publications were presented…. Each of the accused publications was originated or sold as stock in trade of the sordid business of pandering…. Where the purveyor's sole emphasis is on the sexually provocative aspects of his publications, that fact may be decisive in the determination of obscenity…. In close cases evidence of pandering may be probative with respect to the nature of the material in question and thus satisfy the *Roth* test.[34]

The dissenters were as fractured in their reasoning as the majority, but they shared a conviction that the majority had made a serious error in its decision to uphold Ginzburg's sentence. Justice Hugo L. Black took his usual stand that the federal government had no authority under the Constitution to censor any speech or expression of ideas. He said, "As bad and obnoxious as I believe governmental censorship is in a Nation that has accepted the First Amendment as its basic ideal for freedom, I am compelled to say that censorship that would stamp certain books and literature as illegal in advance of publication or conviction would in some ways be preferable to the unpredictable book-by-book censorship into which we have now drifted."[35]

Justice Douglas continued with his consistent theme contending "the First Amendment does not permit the censorship of expression not brigaded with illegal action," a relatively absolutist view that he clung to until he retired from the Court in 1975. Justice Harlan concurred with the dissenters on grounds that government could ban only hard-core pornography, a category into which he felt these materials did not fall. Finally, Justice Stewart dissented because he believed that censorship "is the hallmark of an authoritarian regime. In upholding and enforcing the Bill of Rights, this Court has no power to pick or to choose."

Mishkin v. New York *(1966): Obscenity Directed to Deviants*

The third and final decision handed down on that same day involved an intriguing argument by an obscenity defendant. Edward Mishkin was sentenced to three years in prison and fined $12,500 for selling obscene books that Justice Brennan said in his majority opinion "depict such deviations as sado-masochism, fetishism and homosexuality." Typical titles were *Dance with the Dominant Whip* and *Mrs. Tyrant's Finishing School*, hard-core porn featuring explicit sexual depictions. But Mishkin argued on appeal that they did not meet the *Roth* test for prurient interest because the average person would find them unappealing rather than sexually stimulating. The Court called his bluff and upheld his conviction in *Mishkin v. New York* (1966). According to the Court, "Where the material is designed for and primarily disseminated to a clearly defined sexual group, rather than the public at large, the prurient-appeal requirement of the *Roth* test is satisfied if the dominant theme of the material taken as a whole appeals to the prurient interest in sex of the members of that group."[36]

Although *Roth* is no longer the test for determining obscenity, *Mishkin* has never been overturned and presumably still dictates the rule of determining the reference group for prurient appeal—go to the group to which the work is directed. As Mishkin soon learned, there is no loophole for evading the prurient appeal requirement.

In *Mishkin*, the Court said the materials were aimed at those individuals interested in the particular "deviant sexual practices." Does this mean magazines depicting gay men and lesbian women will pass the prurient appeal test if they sexually excite or stimulate members of these groups? The Court in *Mishkin* apparently assumed that the specific type of sex shown determined the prurient-appeal reference group, i.e., books focusing on sadomasochism would be judged by prurient appeal to the average sadomasochist and so on.

Yet, studies have shown the vast majority of pornography is geared to heterosexual males, although there is also now a flourishing market for gay material. Judging by legal cases, little material has been historically geared to lesbians and female heterosexuals, even though the vast majority of books, magazines, videos, and so on, available from above-ground sources such as adult bookstores and the adult sections of local video rental outlets portray heterosexual and purported "lesbian" couplings. In other words, the reference group cannot always be determined by simply reviewing the types of sex depicted, as illustrated by the fact that the primary audience for sexually explicit works portraying lesbians is considered to be male heterosexuals, not lesbians. The predominant consumers of gay materials are homosexual men. Which reference group is used to determine the *average person* for the *Roth* prurient interest test? The Court has avoided the issue, allowing lower courts to make the determination, resulting in inconsistency.

Ginsberg v. New York *(1968): Variable Obscenity Laws*

After its 1966 triple holdings, the U.S. Supreme Court apparently became so frustrated that it effectively abandoned its efforts to define obscenity until the "seven year itch" hit in *Miller v. California* (1973).[37] By 1967 the Court was ready to admit it had reached a deadlock. There was no agreement among its members as to the meaning of obscenity, even for those who had stuck together in reversing and affirming lower court obscenity convictions.

In a *per curiam* decision in *Redrup v. New York* (1967),[38] a majority of the justices outlined their individual tests and reversed the conviction of a clerk at a New York City newsstand for selling the paperbacks titled *Lust Pool* and *Shame Agent* to plain-clothed police. As part of the same decision, the Court also reversed the conviction of a Kentucky bookstore owner for allowing a female clerk to sell two magazines, *High Heels* and *Spree*. The majority overturned a civil decision by a prosecuting attorney in Arkansas who declared some magazines obscene, including *Gent, Swank, Bachelor, Modern Man, Cavalcade, Gentleman, Ace,* and *Sir*.

In its brief, unsigned opinion, the Court acknowledged the reversals were in order regardless of the test. For the next two years, the Court handled obscenity cases, which climbed in number, by denying certiorari or by reversing convictions whenever at least five justices, applying individual tests, could agree the particular materials in question were not obscene. Dozens of cases were handled this way, without benefit of oral arguments or written opinions. The iron was not hot enough to strike. That would change.

The next year the Court upheld the constitutionality of a New York statute known as a *variable obscenity law*. In *Ginsberg v. New York* (1968)[39] (not to be confused with *Ginzburg v. United States* two years earlier), a 6 to 3 majority ruled that the statute, which prohibited the knowing sale to individuals under 17 years old of "materials harmful to minors" regardless of whether the works would be obscene to adults, was constitutional. The decision was not a major surprise. The most liberal courts have approved good-faith efforts to protect children from products readily available to adults such as alcohol and cigarettes. That trend has continued with the Court consistently upholding child pornography or "kiddie porn" laws that apply much stronger standards for children than for adults.

The case arose when Sam's Stationery and Luncheonette, operated on Long Island by Sam Ginsberg and his wife, sold two "girlie" magazines to a 16-year-old boy. The magazines had already been declared not obscene by the U.S. Supreme Court. This happened the year before in *Redrup v. New York*. But the judge convicted Ginsberg for violating a state statute. The statute established minors as the group used to determine whether the materials were harmful, appealed to prurient interest and so on, when such materials were knowingly distributed to minors. The general purpose of the law was to keep works that were perfectly permissible for sale to adults out of the hands of minors. The judge suspended Ginsberg's conviction. The defendant appealed anyway. Ginsberg also attacked the statute as void for vagueness because of its use of the concept "harmful to minors" and other terminology, but the Court refused to accept this argument as well.

On the same day as *Ginsberg*, the Court struck down a Dallas, Texas, ordinance in *Interstate Circuit v. Dallas* (1968),[40] which banned the showing of a film to persons under age 16 if it portrayed "sexual promiscuity" that would "create the impression on young persons that such conduct is profitable, desirable, acceptable, respectable, praiseworthy or commonly accepted … [or] … its calculated or dominant effect on young person's is substantially to arouse sexual desire." The fatal flaw in the ordinance, according to Justice Thurgood Marshall and five other justices was that it was unconstitutionally vague in failing to enunciate appropriately narrow standards and definitions. Two other members of the Court concurred with the result on the ground that obscene materials enjoyed First Amendment protection. In his dissent, Justice Harlan maintained, "The current approach has required us to spend an inordinate amount of time in the absurd business of perusing and viewing the miserable stuff that pours into the Court, all to no better end than second-guessing judges."[41] Justice Harlan consistently noted in his opinions—both concurring and dissenting—that no significant First Amendment concerns were involved in obscenity cases but instead individual states should be permitted to determine what sexually oriented materials should be censored and what should flourish.

Stanley v. Georgia *(1969): Privacy and Obscenity*

The road from *Roth* to *Miller* took a surprising turn in 1969 when the U.S. Supreme Court unanimously held that individuals could not be punished for the mere possession of obscene materials in their own home. In *Stanley v. Georgia* (1969),[42] the justices reversed the conviction of a suspected bookmaker for violating a state statute that barred the knowing possession of obscene works, even in one's personal residence.

In an opinion, joined by five of his colleagues, Justice Marshall reversed Stanley's conviction on First and Fourth Amendment grounds, although the focus in the decision was on privacy concerns, as the Court emphasized in later cases. The police had discovered three sexually explicit 8-mm films in a desk drawer in the defendant's bedroom during the execution of a search warrant for evidence of illegal gambling. The police used a projector found nearby to view the movies and then promptly charged Stanley with possession of obscene materials. No bookmaking evidence was found.

For purposes of the case, the defendant stipulated that the films were obscene, and thus the issue became primarily one of right of privacy. All nine justices agreed that Stanley's conviction should be overturned but for different reasons (as the Court usually did in obscenity cases). According to Justice Marshall's majority opinion:

> Fundamental is the right to be free, except in very limited circumstances, from unwanted government intrusion into one's privacy.... Mere categorization of these films as "obscene" is insufficient justification for such a drastic invasion of personal liberties guaranteed by the First and Fourteenth Amendments. Whatever may be the justifications for other statutes regulating obscenity, we do not think they reach into the privacy of one's own home. If the First Amendment means anything, it means that a State has no business telling a man, sitting alone in his own house, what books he may read or what films he may watch.[43]

The Court particularly rejected Georgia's argument that a state has a right to punish individuals for possession of such materials even in their own home because exposure to obscenity leads to deviant sexual conduct and violent sexual crimes. Instead, the Court said that just as the state cannot prohibit the possession of chemistry books on the ground that it may lead to the manufacture of home-made spirits, it cannot prohibit the mere possession of obscenity on the basis that it may cause antisocial conduct.

1970 Presidential Commission on Obscenity and Pornography

There were two major developments in 1970, neither of which had major impact on the regulation of obscenity but both signaling beginning of a new era in obscenity law, albeit not necessarily in line with what was expected. First, the 1970 Presidential Commission on Obscenity and Pornography issued a report.

William B. Lockhart, former dean of the University of Minnesota Law School, chaired the commission. He was appointed by President Lyndon Johnson. The 18-member group was charged with the mission of studying the obscenity and pornography trade to determine its nature and scope, including its impact on adults and minors, and to make recommendations for restricting obscenity within constitutional parameters. After spending thousands of hours and more than $2 million studying the problem, the body filed a report whose content reflects the same ambiguity so evident on the U.S. Supreme Court. Only 12 of the 18 members joined the majority report that made the following surprising recommendations:

1. An end to all censorship of materials directed to consenting adults, but a continuation of strong obscenity laws governing minors, including their depiction in sexually explicit works. The commission noted that after an extensive review of studies on effects, it found scant evidence that reading or viewing sexually explicit materials lead to antisocial conduct, criminal activity or sexual deviance.
2. Enactment of strong statutes to protect children from exposure to obscene materials, primarily photos, films, and other visual representations.
3. Enactment of legislation to restrict pandering and techniques directed at unwilling individuals including unsolicited mail and public displays.
4. A comprehensive sex education curriculum in public schools, for both elementary and secondary school students.

By the time the commission finished its work in 1970, Richard M. Nixon was President and the country headed in a conservative direction. Nixon rejected the commission's report, characterizing it as "morally bankrupt." The U.S. Senate moved in with a resolution supported by 60 members and opposed by only 5. Public criticism was also intense, leading Nixon to vow to appoint U.S. Supreme Court justices who opposed relaxed regulations on obscenity.

President Nixon had already successfully nominated conservative Associate Justice Warren Burger to replace liberal Chief Justice Earl Warren, who stepped down in 1969. Harry A. Blackmun was then appointed in 1970 to fill the slot opened by the resignation of Abe Fortas after he withdrew his name for nomination as Chief Justice.

Miller v. California (1973): Conjunctive Test of Obscenity

For the next three years, the U.S. Supreme Court issued no major decisions dealing directly with obscenity. It began a relatively short wait for a new majority coalition to emerge. Nixon saw his wish come true as the liberal majority was replaced by a new conservative majority, including two more Nixon nominees, Lewis F. Powell and William H. Rehnquist, both of whom joined the Court in 1972.

Fourteen years later Justice Rehnquist became Chief Justice.. The earlier conservative majority consisted of Chief Justice Burger and Associate Justice Byron R. White (a conservative, at least on obscenity issues, nominated by President John F. Kennedy in 1962).

Justice Burger deftly used the authority granted him as chief justice to avoid scheduling any oral arguments in cases involving obscenity, except for two fairly minor decisions in 1971: *United States v. Reidel*[44] and *United States v. Thirty-Seven Photographs*.[45] In *Reidel*, the usual majority rejected the reasoning of a U.S. District Court judge that, because *Stanley* permitted the possession of obscene materials in a private home, the federal statute banning the mailing of obscene works to private residences, including those of consenting adults, was unconstitutional. Led by Justice White, the majority found the trial court's decision much broader than that intended in *Roth* and *Stanley*: "*Roth* has squarely placed obscenity and its distribution outside the reach of the First Amendment. *Stanley* did not overrule *Roth* and we decline to do so now."

The second decision concerned whether *Stanley* extended to the luggage of a tourist arriving from overseas. The same majority refused to broaden *Stanley*, ruling that no zone of privacy existed for purposes of obscenity carried in one's luggage and the federal statute permitting prosecution for possession was constitutional.

By 1973 the necessary five-person majority had coalesced and the Court was in a position to utter the final word on obscenity by once and for all defining this elusive concept. On June 21, 1973, just before its 1972–1973 term ended, the Court issued *five* separate opinions that established the current test for obscenity. In fact, since that time the justices have steered clear of obscenity cases except to fine tune the *Miller* test, as it has become known. However, the justices have not avoided indecency cases.

In each of the five cases, the 5 to 4 vote line-up was the same, with the thin but nevertheless effective majority of Chief Justice Burger and Associate Justices Powell, Rehnquist, White, and Blackmun and the outnumbered but adamant minority of Associate Justices Douglas, Stewart, Marshall, and Brennan. Justice Brennan was the architect of several of the majority opinions (including *Roth*) that rejected First Amendment protection for obscenity, but in the second of five cases, *Paris Adult Theatre I v. Slaton*,[46] Justice Brennan explained his conversion in a strongly worded dissent:

> Our experience with the *Roth* [case] has certainly taught us that the outright suppression of obscenity cannot be reconciled with the fundamental principles of the First and Fourteenth Amendments. For we have failed to formulate a standard that sharply distinguishes protected from unprotected speech, and out of necessity, we have resorted to the *Redrup* approach, which resolves cases as between the parties, but offers only the most obscure guidance to legislation, adjudication by other courts, and primary conduct. By disposing of cases through summary reversal or denial of *certiorari* we have deliberately and effectively obscured the rationale underlying the decisions. It comes as no surprise that judicial attempts to follow our lead conscientiously have often ended in hopeless confusion.[47]

This section focuses only on the first two cases—*Miller v. California*[48] and *Paris Adult Theatre I*—because they are the most important and established the modern test for obscenity. The decisions were written by Justice Burger, who formulated a new three-prong obscenity test.

In *Miller* the Court remanded the conviction of Marvin Miller back to the state appellate court to determine the outcome of his appeal in light of the new test enunciated by the Court. Miller had been convicted of a misdemeanor for violating the California Penal Code by conducting a mass mailing campaign advertising the sale of illustrated, sexually explicit books. Five copies of the brochures were sent unsolicited to a restaurant and were opened by the owner and his mother. Inside were ads for four books (*Intercourse, Man-Woman, Sex Orgies Illustrated,* and *An Illustrated History of Pornography*) and a film titled *Marital Intercourse.* As the Court noted, "While the brochures contain some descriptive printed material, primarily they consist of pictures and drawings very explicitly depicting men and women in groups of two or more engaging in a variety of sexual activities, with genitals often prominently displayed."[49] After summarizing the background of the case, Chief Justice Burger's opinion quickly framed the issue:

> This case involves the application of a State's criminal obscenity statute to a situation in which sexually explicit materials have been thrust by aggressive sales action upon unwilling recipients who had in no way indicated any desire to receive such materials. This Court has recognized that the States have a legitimate interest in prohibiting dissemination or exhibition of obscene material when the mode of dissemination carries with it a significant danger of offending the sensibilities of unwilling recipients or of exposure to juveniles.... It is in this context that we are called on to define the standards which must be used to identify obscene material that a State may regulate without infringing on the First Amendment as applicable to the States through the Fourteenth Amendment.[50] (footnote and citations omitted)

The Court used the "unwilling recipient" principle (which even the 1970 President's Commission on obscenity endorsed) as a diving board to plunge into a new definition of obscenity. The justices could easily have upheld Miller's conviction using almost any of its previous decisions, but the majority was obviously determined to establish a new test. *Paris Adult Theatre I* presented the perfect opportunity to apply the new test in a broader context—a public setting in which only consenting adults were involved and minors and unwilling recipients were excluded. In *Miller*, the Court:

1. *Reaffirmed the holding in Roth and subsequent cases that "obscene material is unprotected by the First Amendment."*
2. *Strongly criticized the plurality opinion in Memoirs, especially the "utterly without redeeming social importance" prong*: "Thus, even as they repeated the words of Roth, the *Memoirs* plurality produced a drastically altered test that called on the prosecution to prove a negative, i.e., that the material was 'utterly without redeeming social value'—a burden virtually impossible to discharge under our criminal standards of proof."
3. *Formulated a new three-prong conjunctive test for obscenity:* "The basic guidelines for the trier of fact must be: (a) whether 'the average person, applying contemporary community standards' would find that the work taken as a whole appeals to the prurient interest ...; (b) whether the work depicts or describes, in a patently offensive way, sexual conduct specifically defined by the applicable state law; and (c) whether the work, taken as a whole, lacks serious literary, artistic, political, or scientific value."

4. *Cited examples of what a state could define under the second prong.* These included "(a) [P]atently offensive representations or descriptions of ultimate sex acts, normal or perverted, actual or simulated. (b) Patently offensive representations or descriptions of masturbation, excretory functions, and lewd exhibition of the genitals."

5. *Indicated that only hard-core sexual conduct was to be punished under the new test:* "Under the holdings announced today, no one will be subject to prosecution for the sale or exposure of obscene materials unless these materials depict or describe patently offensive 'hard core' sexual conduct specifically defined by the regulating state law, as written or construed."

6. *Held that "obscenity is to be determined by applying 'contemporary community standards,'... not 'national standards.'"* In fact, the Court held that the requirement under California's statute that the jury evaluate the materials with reference to the "contemporary community standards of the State of California" was constitutional. As the Court had indicated earlier, "It is neither realistic nor constitutionally sound to read the First Amendment as requiring that the people of Maine or Mississippi accept public depiction of conduct found tolerable in Las Vegas, or New York City."

In a bitter dissent, Justice Douglas lambasted the majority for, in effect, making a criminal law *ex post facto* (which is impermissible under the U.S. Constitution) by devising a new test that "would put a publisher behind bars under a new law improvised by the courts after the publication." He also repeated his contention from previous obscenity cases that judges were never given the constitutional authority to define obscenity. Justice Brennan, joined by Justices Stewart and Marshall, referred in a one-paragraph dissent to his dissenting opinion in *Paris Adult Theatre I*, noting that his view in the latter substantially departed from his prior opinions.

In *Paris Adult Theatre I*, two Atlanta "adult" theaters and their owners and managers were sued in civil procedure by the local district attorney to enjoin them from showing two movies, *Magic Mirror* and *It All Comes Out in the End.*

The Georgia Supreme Court characterized the latter in its decision on appeal as "hard core pornography" leaving "little to the imagination," although by today's standards the movies would probably fall into either the R or NC-17 ratings of the Motion Picture Association of America (MPAA).

The films did feature, as the Court noted, scenes of simulated fellatio, cunnilingus, and group sex. But according to photographs presented to the trial court, which dismissed the prosecutor's complaint, the theaters' entrance (two theaters sharing a common entrance) was conventional and inoffensive and displayed no pictures. Two signs proclaimed: "Atlanta's Finest Mature Feature Films" and "Adult Theatre—You must be 21 and be able to prove it. If viewing the nude body offends you, please Do Not Enter." The Georgia Supreme Court reversed the trial court decision and the U.S. Supreme Court, in a 5 to 4 vote, vacated and remanded the case back to the state supreme court for reconsideration in light of *Miller.*

The majority opinion by the Chief Justice agreed with the Georgia Supreme Court that the movie houses did not enjoy constitutional protection even though the state appellate court assumed they showed the films only to consenting, paying adults and minors were never permitted to enter. The justices made it clear that whereas it had consistently recognized a state's legitimate interest in regulating the exposure of obscenity to juveniles and non-consenting adults, these were by no means the only legitimate state interests permitting regulation of obscene works:

In particular, we hold that there are legitimate state interests at stake in stemming the tide of commercialized obscenity, even assuming it is feasible to enforce effective safeguards against exposure to juveniles and passersby. Rights and interests "other than those of the advocates are involved." … These include the interest of the public in the quality of life and the total community environment, the tone of commerce in the great city centers, and, possibly, the public safety itself.[51] (footnotes and citations omitted)

The opinion then cited the Hill-Link Minority Report of the Commission on Obscenity and Pornography (the 1970 Presidential Commission). Both the majority and the dissenting opinions in *Paris Adult Theatre I* and *Miller* made little reference to the commission's report, although it was the most comprehensive study ever made of the obscenity problem.

In *Paris Adult Theatre I*, the majority cited a passage from the main presidential commission report acknowledging a split among medical experts over a link between exposure to pornography and antisocial conduct. The opinion also cited the commission's minority report's claim that female and male juveniles are among the "heavy users and most highly exposed people to pornography." In a dissenting opinion, joined by Justices Stewart and Marshall, Brennan included one footnoted reference to the commission's report. It claimed no empirical research had found evidence "that exposure to explicit sexual materials plays a significant role in the causation of delinquent or criminal behavior [in] youth or adults."

Thus, the Presidential Commission report received little attention from the Court in its deliberations. Public attention was minimal except for rejection of the report by President Nixon and the Senate.

In a dissenting opinion, Justice Douglas commended Brennan in his effort to "forsake the low road" and join the side of the dissenters. According to Douglas, there is "no constitutional basis for fashioning a rule that makes a publisher, producer, bookseller, librarian, or movie house operator criminally responsible, when he fails to take affirmative steps to protect the consumer against literature, books, or movies offensive to those who temporarily occupy the seats of the mighty" (footnote omitted).[52]

Justice Brennan's dissent is well worth reading in its entirety even by those who vehemently disagree with him. Substantially longer than the majority opinion, it traces the 16-year history of the Supreme Court's attempts to define obscenity and eloquently describes what many jurists consider to be the four main options in dealing with obscenity:

1. *Draw a new line between protected and unprotected speech while still allowing states to suppress all unprotected materials.* This would take the issue of obscenity out of federal hands and put it exclusively in regulatory hands.
2. *Accept the new test enunciated by the Court.*
3. *Leave enforcement primarily in the hands of juries with the Supreme Court and other appellate courts intervening only "in cases of extreme departure from prevailing standards."*
4. *Adopt the view that the First Amendment bars the suppression of any sexually oriented expression, as advocated by Justices Black and Douglas.*

Justice Brennan then went on to advocate a fifth option:

Allow sexually oriented materials to be controlled under the 1st and 14th Amendments only in the manner of their distribution and only when there are strong and legitimate state interests such as the protection of juveniles and non-consenting adults. In other words, consenting adults would make their own choices about what to see and read without interference from government.

Brennan opted for the last approach; he felt it had flaws but that they were less serious and obtrusive than those of the other options.

Aftermath of *Miller* and *Paris Adult Theatre I*

Relatively few obscenity cases have been granted certiorari since *Miller et al.*, and the limited number of decisions that have been handed down contained no major surprises. In the year following *Miller*, the Court issued two obscenity decisions on the same day.

Hamling v. U.S. (1974)[53] tied a couple of the many loose ends left in *Miller*. The Court affirmed the federal obscenity convictions of four individuals and two corporations for mailing approximately 55,000 copies of a brochure throughout the country advertising *The Illustrated Presidential Report of the Commission on Obscenity and Pornography*. The jury was unable to reach a verdict on charges that the illustrated report itself was obscene. The single-sheet brochure (printed on both sides) included:

> a full page splash of pictures portraying heterosexual and homosexual intercourse, sodomy and a variety of deviate sexual acts. Specifically, a group picture of nine persons, one male engaged in masturbation, a female masturbating two males, two couples engaged in intercourse in reverse fashion while one female participant engages in fellatio of a male; a second group picture of six persons, two males masturbating, two fellatrices practicing the act, each bearing a clear depiction of ejaculated seminal fluid on their faces; two persons with the female engaged in the act of fellatio and the male in female masturbation by hand; two separate pictures of males engaged in cunnilinction; a film strip of six frames depicting lesbian love scenes including a cunnilinguist in action and female masturbation with another's hand and a vibrator, and two frames, one depicting a woman mouthing the penis of a horse, and a second poising the same for entrance into her vagina.[54]

The reverse side of the brochure contained an order form and paragraphs touting the "research" value of the book and chiding "Mr. President" for suppressing the report. The Ninth Circuit U.S. Court of Appeals had no difficulty affirming the convictions nor did the U.S. Supreme Court. The primary issue was what rules of law would govern obscenity convictions, like this one, decided in trial and lower appellate courts before *Miller* was handed down.

The 5 to 4 opinion authored by Justice Rehnquist held (a) that jurors in federal obscenity cases can draw on the knowledge of the local community in determining standards; (b) that jurors can, if they wish, ignore the testimony of experts because they are experts ("average persons"); and (c) that the prosecution is required to show only a defendant had knowledge of the contents in order to prove *scienter*, not that the defendant knew materials were obscene.

Billy Jenkins v. Georgia *(1974): Mere Nudity Is Not Enough*

In the second case, *Billy Jenkins v. Georgia* (1974),[55] the Court reversed the conviction of a theater operator accused of distributing obscene materials by showing the film *Carnal Knowledge* at an Albany, Georgia, drive-in. In 1972 (before *Miller* was decided), law enforcement officers seized the film while Jenkins was showing it and charged him with violation of state obscenity statutes. Two months later, a jury convicted him. He was fined $750 and given 12 months' probation.

In a split decision, the state court affirmed the conviction while acknowledging the definition of obscenity in the state statute was "considerably more restrictive" than the test in *Miller*, which had recently been handed down. In an opinion written by Justice Rehnquist, the Court unanimously overturned the trial court. The Court considered it relevant that the film had received favorable reviews from critics and was on many "Ten Best" lists for 1971. According to the majority opinion:

> Our own viewing of the film satisfies us that 'Carnal Knowledge' could not be found under the *Miller* standards to depict sexual conduct in a patently offensive way.... While the subject matter of the picture is, in a broader sense, sex, and there are scenes in which sexual conduct including 'ultimate sex acts' is to be understood to be taking place, the camera does not focus on the bodies of the actors at such times. There is no exhibition of the actors' genitals, lewd or otherwise, during these scenes. There are occasional scenes of nudity, but nudity alone is not enough to make material legally obscene under the *Miller* standards.[56]

These two cases provide examples of what the Court had in mind for protected versus unprotected works when it fashioned the *Miller* test. The *Hamling* brochure was clearly hard core sexual content, but *Carnal Knowledge* was far from patently offensive.

The *Jenkins* case is a frightening illustration of how suppressive prosecutors and juries can be in judging works they deem offensive. No doubt, there are many more examples of censorship of constitutionally protected materials that never sought redemption from what some critics deemed "the High Court of Obscenity."

Child Pornography

The courts have recognized children as a protected class for a long time and thus worthy in some situations of stronger protection by the government than that warranted for adults. Only within the last few decades have both Congress and the courts made a significant effort to protect children from exploitation such as child labor and sexual abuse. As late as 1918 the U.S. Supreme Court held that Congress lacked the authority under the Constitution's Commerce clause to ban the interstate transportation of goods made by children under 14 years of age.[57] Two decades later, the Court reversed the decision, noting that the 1918 decision "has not been followed" and "should be and is now overruled."[58]

Eventually, the concern for protecting children broadened to include preventing them from having access to pornography and stopping the creation and dissemination of child pornography or "kiddie porn," as it is popularly known. During the mid-1970s several states and the

U.S. Congress responded to public outrage over the perceived proliferation of child pornography as detailed in various media reports.

New York enacted one of the toughest statutes[59] in the country in 1977, the same year a new federal statute took effect, the "Protection of Children against Sexual Exploitation Act of 1977."[60] Both statutes provided stiff fines and prison sentences for individuals convicted of using minors to engage in sexually explicit acts for still and moving image cameras of any type.

Paul Ira Ferber, owner of a Manhattan store, was convicted in a New York trial court on two counts of violating child pornography laws for selling to an undercover police officer two films showing young boys under the age of 16 masturbating. The state's highest court, the New York Court of Appeals, reversed the conviction on the ground the state statute was under-inclusive and over-broad.

In *New York v. Ferber* (1982),[61] the U.S. Supreme Court reversed and remanded the case to the state Court of Appeals. In the 6 to 3 decision written by Justice White, the Court said the constitutional standards for child pornography are not the same as those for adult materials. According to the justices, states could impose stricter bans on materials involving the sexual depiction and conduct of minors and ban such materials even if they did not meet the legal definition of obscenity in *Miller*. The Court noted that 47 states already had such laws and that the regulations could go beyond *Miller* because "the prevention of sexual exploitation and abuse of children constitutes a government objective of surpassing importance." However, the Court did say that criminal liability may not be imposed unless *scienter* is shown on the part of the defendant.

The U.S. Supreme Court answered a question left in the air after the *Ferber* decision: *Does the Stanley bar against prosecution for possession of obscene materials in the privacy of one's home cover child pornography?* In *Ferber* the Court held that the same standards did not apply for child pornography as for adult materials because children are a protected class and "the use of children as subjects of pornographic materials is harmful to the physiological, emotional and mental health of the child."[62]

In *Osborne v. Ohio* (1990),[63] the Court upheld 6 to 3 a state kiddie porn statute that included penalties for the private possession of child pornography. In the decision written by Justice White, who was joined by Chief Justice Rehnquist and Associate Justices Blackmun, O'Connor, Scalia, and Kennedy, the Court said:

> The threshold question in this case is whether Ohio may constitutionally proscribe the possession and viewing of child pornography, or whether as Osborne argues, our decision in *Stanley v. Georgia* ... compels the contrary result.... We find this case distinct from *Stanley* because the interests underlying child pornography prohibitions far exceed the interests justifying the Georgia law at issue in *Stanley*. (citation omitted)[64]

The majority opinion went on to note, "Given the importance of the State's interest in protecting the victims of child pornography, we cannot fault Ohio for attempting to stamp out this vice at all levels of the distribution chain."[65]

The case began when 61-year-old Clyde Osborne was prosecuted after police searched his home on a tip and found an album containing four sexually explicit photos of a boy believed to be 13 or 14 years old. The state statute, which the Court upheld, specifically banned the possession of lewd material or material that focused on the genitals of a minor. The law also forbade the possession or viewing of "any material or performance that shows a minor" nude. There were exceptions in the statute for photos taken by parents and for photos with an artistic, medical or scientific purpose. Osborne was sentenced to six months in prison and fined $100. He was granted a new trial by the U.S. Supreme Court on the ground that the jury that had convicted him had not been properly instructed. However, Ohio's statute stood intact because it met constitutional muster.

A concern related to child pornography has been how to keep sexually oriented materials out of the hands of minors. State and local governments have enacted statutes or ordinances requiring all businesses that sell such magazines, books, videos, and other works to place them where children cannot see or peruse them. Virginia had such a statute, challenged as unconstitutional by the American Booksellers Association. In *Virginia v. American Booksellers Association* (1988),[66] the U.S. Supreme Court remanded a ruling by the Fourth U.S. Circuit Court of Appeals that the state statute was unconstitutionally over-broad back to the court on the ground that the lower appellate court's decision was not supported by the record.[67] On remand,[68] the circuit court ruled the statute did not violate the First and Fourteenth Amendments because, as construed by the state supreme court, it penalized only businesses that knowingly permitted or failed to act reasonably to prevent minors from gaining access to such materials and only when the works lacked serious literary, artistic, political or scientific value "for a legitimate minority of normal, older adolescents." Thus, according to the federal appellate court, the statute gave establishments adequate notice of what was prohibited. The U.S. Supreme Court denied certiorari on the American Booksellers Association's appeal of the Fourth Circuit decision.[69]

In 1996 Congress passed the Child Pornography Prevention Act,[70] which broadened the definition of child pornography to include computer-simulated images created by a process known as "morphing." The Act was challenged as unconstitutional in federal court by various civil liberties organizations and the adult-trade industry, but in *Ashcroft v. Free Speech Coalition* (2002)[71] the U.S. Supreme Court held in a 6 to 3 opinion that two provisions of the Act, §2256(8)(B) and §2256(8)(D), violated the First Amendment because they were over-broad. The first section banned a wide range of sexually explicit images, including virtual child pornography ("morphing") and images that appeared to depict minors, including the use of youthful looking adults or computer images. It did not matter whether the images actually portrayed minors. What mattered was whether the images appeared to be of minors. The second section was a pandering provision that focused on how the work was promoted, more specifically, whether the promotion "conveys the impression" that it contained sexually explicit scenes of minors even if there were no such scenes. According to the majority opinion written by Justice Kennedy:

> Our society, like other cultures, has empathy and enduring fascination with the lives and destinies of the young. Art and literature express the vital interest we all have in the formative years we ourselves once knew, when wounds can be so grievous, disappointment so profound, and mistaken choices so tragic, but when moral acts and self-fulfillment are still in reach. Whether or not the films we mention [the Court specifically mentioned "Traffic" and "American Beauty"] violate the CPPA, they explore themes within the wide sweep of the statute's prohibitions. If these films, or hundreds of others of lesser note that explore those subjects, contain a single graphic depiction

of sexual activity within the statutory definition, the possessor of the film would be subject to severe punishment without inquiry into the work's redeeming value. This is inconsistent with an essential First Amendment rule: the artistic merit of a work does not depend on the presence of a single explicit scene.[72]

The Court cited both *Ferber* and *Miller*, noting the CPPA was inconsistent with *Miller* because under the Act, the government did not have to demonstrate the materials appealed to prurient interests nor that they were patently offensive. The Court said, unlike *Ferber*, no direct link could be demonstrated between the materials and the sexual abuse of children in this case. The CPPA banned speech that recorded no crime and created no victims in its production, according to the Court.[73] The Court also rejected the government's other arguments, including the point that the Act was needed to prevent pedophiles from using virtual pornography to trap children online, noting this argument "runs afoul of the principle that speech within the rights of adults to hear may not be silenced completely in an attempt to shield children from it."

In response to the case, the government established a national database to help trace missing children and assist in prosecutions. In an effort to protect privacy, the database does not include the names of victims but instead lists law enforcement personnel who can testify that victims are real children. The database is maintained by the Customs Cybersmuggling Center with the cooperation of the National Center for Missing and Exploited Children.[74] In 1997 an Oklahoma district judge found that the 1979 Oscar-winning film, *The Tin Drum*, based on the classic novel by Gunter Gräss, was obscene under Oklahoma law because it depicts a young boy having oral sex with a teen-age girl. The movie and novel focus on the trauma suffered by a young boy in Nazi Germany during World War II. The case arose after Oklahomans for Children and Families, an anti-pornography organization, notified police that the R-rated film was in the local public library and in six local video rental stores. Police confiscated the one library copy as well as copies from the video outlets.[75] They also served warrants on three individuals who had copies in their homes.

Syndicated columnist Leonard Pitts, Jr. criticized the decision, particularly for its perceived chilling effect on the First Amendment. "I find myself reminded that the biggest problem with freedom of speech is its operating assumption: that we should risk being capsized in swill in order that we might occasionally be blinded by light."[76] Unusual cases crop up from time to time such as the conviction of an inmate in a Minnesota prison for selling child pornography over the Internet. He had accessed the Internet through a computer at the prison.[77] In both *Los Angeles v. Alameda Books* and *Ashcroft v. Free Speech Coalition,* the U.S. Supreme Court held 7 to 2 that certain provisions of the Child Pornography Prevention Act (CPPA) were too broad and therefore unconstitutional. Specific issues regarded the virtual depiction of children far reaching without the actual use of real children.[78] In addition, in *Ashcroft v. American Civil Liberties Union* (2002), the U.S. Supreme Court determined that the nature of the material as provided in the Child Online Protection Act (COPA) did not mean the statute was too broad. In *Connection Distributing Co. v. Keisler*, 505 F.3d 545 (6th Cir.2007), a federal statute requiring detailed record-keeping by anyone producing photographs of sexually explicit conduct was designed to eliminate child pornography by requiring record-keeping spurred controversy and so the debate over the availability, extent, and nature of child pornography over the Internet continues.[79]

Zoning and Other Restrictions

Zoning is one of the most effective ways local governments have discovered for regulating obscenity. The courts, including the U.S. Supreme Court, have generally backed authorities in their efforts to use zoning laws as a means of restricting adult stores and theaters to certain areas and barring them from other areas, so long as they do not impose an absolute ban. For example, in *City of Renton v. Playtime Theatres* (1986),[80] the Supreme Court held that a Renton, Washington, zoning ordinance restricting so-called adult theaters from operating within 1,000 feet of any residential zone, single or multiple family housing, school, park, or church was constitutional. According to the 7 to 2 opinion, the law represented a legitimate state response to problems generated by such establishments and did not infringe on First Amendment and Fourteenth Amendment freedoms even though it restricted showing non-obscene plays, films, and printed works. Ten years earlier, the Court upheld a similar zoning ordinance in Detroit, noting that the ordinance did not totally ban such businesses but merely restricted to certain areas of the city. Both ordinances, the Court said, were reasonable time, place, and manner restrictions permissible under the Constitution.

In a second case, *Arcara v. Cloud Books* (1986),[81] the U.S. Supreme Court gave the constitutional nod of approval to a New York state statute under which an adult bookstore was prosecuted and then shut down. An undercover investigation by the local county sheriff's department allegedly revealed illegal sexual activities, including prostitution, taking place in the store. One deputy testified that he witnessed customers masturbating, fondling one another, and performing fellatio as well as prostitutes soliciting.

A 6 to 3 opinion by Chief Justice Burger compared the situation to the draft card burning in *U.S. v. O'Brien* (1968),[82] which the Court asserted is a form of expressive conduct. Furthermore, the majority contended, sexual activities such as these have even less protection than draft card burning: "Unlike ... symbolic draft card burning ... the sexual conduct carried on in this case manifests absolutely no element of protected expression."[83] Dissenters pointed out that the store itself was closed to prevent the activities by imposing liability on owners rather than simply punishing conduct.

In 1996 a New York City trial court judge ruled that the city's zoning law, which restricted businesses selling sexually-oriented materials to specific parts of the city, did not violate the First Amendment.[84] One of the visible results of the ruling was most of the formerly prominent adult businesses in the district moved.

Attorney General Commission on Pornography Report

An event calling attention to the pornography issue was the release, amid fanfare, of a $500,000 study in the 1980s entitled *The Attorney General Commission on Pornography Report.*[85] The 11-person commission, appointed by President Ronald Reagan's Attorney General, Edwin Meese, a year earlier, made 92 recommendations, many of which were opposite of those of the presidential commission from the previous decade. With two members dissenting, the commission recommended or endorsed:

1. Stronger state and federal obscenity statutes;
2. A ban on all obscene shows on cable television;
3. A ban on "dial-a-porn" telephone services;
4. Increased involvement of citizen groups against businesses that sell, distribute, or produce sexually explicit materials, including picketing and boycotting;
5. Creation of a high-level U.S. Department of Justice task force on obscenity;
6. New laws permitting the federal government to confiscate the assets of businesses that violate obscenity laws;
7. Prosecution of producers, actors, and actresses involved in pornographic films under prostitution laws;
8. Enactment of legislation making a second-offense arrest under obscenity laws a felony rather than a misdemeanor.[86]

Many criticisms were leveled at the group from organizations such as the American Civil Liberties Union, First Amendment societies, and professional journalism associations. These groups maintained most of the recommendations would be unconstitutional if carried out and the commission produced little scientific evidence to support conclusions that exposure to sexually violent materials can cause antisocial acts of violence and possibly unlawful acts.[87]

The Commission acknowledged when the report was released that it relied heavily on common sense and testimony of expert witnesses rather than scientific studies. The two dissenting members accused the commission of bias and distortion, noting that most of the more than 200 witnesses were opposed to pornography.[88]

Some of the recommendations of the commission have been implemented such as tougher obscenity statutes. Others have not. The commission recommended that federal and state government step up obscenity prosecutions through the use of RICO (Racketeering Influenced and Corrupt Organizations) statutes. In 1970 Congress passed the RICO provision as part of the Organized Crime Control Act.[89] It was amended in 1984 to include obscenity convictions, which gave the federal government the chance to seek stiffer fines and prison sentences against distributors and sellers of pornography as well as a forfeiture of assets when a pattern of racketeering could be demonstrated in court.[90]

The statute was successful in cracking down on interstate trafficking in porn. In *Fort Wayne Books v. Indiana* (1989),[91] the Court ruled that a state RICO-type statute was not unconstitutionally vague in its language permitting the prosecution of obscenity as a form of racketeering, but held pretrial seizure of allegedly obscene materials violated the First Amendment, so in effect, prior restraint.

The case arose when two adult bookstore owners were separately charged with violating Indiana's RICO statute. One of the defendants challenged the statute as unconstitutional on grounds it permitted seizure of his entire inventory. The Court agreed that his assets could not be seized unless rigorous safeguards laid out in *Freedman v. Maryland* and other cases were employed, but it did not strike down the statute. According to the Court, "While a single copy of a book or film may be seized and retained for evidentiary purposes based on a finding of probable cause, books or films may not be taken out of circulation completely until there has been a determination of obscenity after an adversary hearing."[92]

The message of the Court is clear: books, films, magazines, and other forms of expression must be treated as if they have First Amendment protection until a determination has been made by a court that they are obscene. Thus prosecutors cannot seize materials in the same way they confiscate illegal drugs and weapons.

The Court upheld the constitutionality of the federal RICO statute in obscenity prosecutions. In *Alexander v. United States*,[93] the owner of adult-oriented businesses had been convicted of selling obscene items at his stores in violation of both the federal RICO act and federal obscenity statutes. The U.S. District Court had not only given the defendant a prison term and fined him but also ordered him to forfeit his businesses and approximately $9 million he earned in profit. The Supreme Court noted that in this case the forfeiture had occurred after required procedures had been followed. Interestingly, the Court remanded the case back to the lower appellate court to determine whether the forfeiture, fine, and prison term combined had violated the Eighth Amendment prohibition against excessive fines and cruel and unusual punishments.

One other important recommendation of the commission saw the light of day, the establishment of a federal obscenity task force. Attorney General Edwin Meese set up a National Obscenity Enforcement Unit within the Justice Department. It was involved in prosecutions against alleged pornographers.

Occasionally, an obscenity decision by the U.S. Supreme Court provides a surprise. An example is *Pope v. Illinois* (1987).[94] That case involved the prosecution of two adult bookstore clerks who sold magazines to Rockford, Illinois, detectives which the prosecution claimed were in violation of the state obscenity statute. When the judge instructed the jury, he faithfully reviewed the *Miller* three-prong test. But he told jurors that in applying the "LAPS" prong (Does the material in question lack serious literary, artistic, political, or scientific value?), they should do so "by determining how it would be viewed by ordinary adults in the whole state of Illinois." In other words, they were to apply a state standard in determining the "LAPS" value. After separate trials, defendants challenged their convictions on grounds that the Illinois statute was a violation of First Amendment because it invoked state standards.

In a 5 to 4 decision, the Supreme Court agreed with the challengers and remanded the cases back to the state appellate court. The Court held that the "LAPS" determination should be made based on a "reasonable person" thus invoking a national standard:

> Just as the ideas a work represents need not obtain majority approval to merit protection, neither, insofar as the First Amendment is concerned, does the value of the work vary from community to community based on the degree of local acceptance it has won. [95]

The justices emphasized that *Miller* was never intended to protect only works in which the majority would find value but instead to provide a First Amendment shield for materials for which a minority would ascribe value. With application of the reasonable person standard, the Court felt minority views would be better protected than with the use of local community standards.

The defendants in *Pope* were not entirely off the hook. The Court indicated that the state appellate court was to review the case and determine beyond a reasonable doubt whether the erroneous instruction by the judge affected the outcomes in trials. If the mistake were simply a "harmless error," the convictions should stand upon remand, according to the majority opinion.[96]

Examples of Obscenity Prosecutions

The long-term impact of the *Miller* decision has been exactly what the U. S. Supreme Court intended with its three-prong test. Different jurisdictions have shown different degrees of tolerance of sexually explicit materials. Some cities and towns use selective prosecution to rid themselves of adult bookstores and theaters. Communities tolerate the availability of such works, permitting local video stores, for example, to rent and sell Walt Disney's *Cinderella* in the Family section and XXX-rated *Nancy Nurse* and *Turn up the Heat* in another section accessible only to adults. The latter two films were being shown at an adult theater in Sarasota, Florida, in 1991, when actor Paul Reubens, also known as "Pee-wee Herman," was arrested and later pleaded no contest to a charge of indecent exposure.[97]

Two other examples illustrate the complexity and inconsistencies of obscenity prosecutions. In the first case, U.S. District Court Judge Jose Gonzalez of the Southern District of Florida ruled in a 62-page decision that an album entitled *As Nasty as They Wanna Be* by the once highly controversial rap group 2 Live Crew was obscene under Florida law. This was a case of applying the standards established in *Miller*.[98]

The civil suit was prompted by a county circuit court judge's ruling that there was probable cause to believe the album was obscene. The county judge was acting on a request from Broward County Sheriff Nick Navarro be granted authority to arrest shopkeepers who continued to sell the album. More than 1.7 million copies had been purchased nationwide before the court's decision. The sheriff was acting, he said, based on complaints from local citizens. After the county judge's probable cause ruling, the sheriff and his deputies distributed copies of the ruling to record stores throughout the county and threatened to arrest anyone who sold the album. Attorneys for 2 Live Crew filed suit against the sheriff after sales of the record in the area were effectively stopped. The rap group sought a declaratory judgment that the album was not obscene and a restraining order to prevent the sheriff from stopping sales.

U.S. District Court Judge Gonzalez ruled the music was obscene after a trial in *Skyywalker Records, Inc. v. Navarro*.[99] According to the judge, both the *ex parte* application from the sheriff and the county judge's order itself violated the due process standards for prior restraint established in *Freedman v. Maryland*. He went on to declare the album obscene because it appealed to prurient interests, was patently offensive as defined by state law, and lacked serious literary, artistic, political, or scientific value. Judge Gonzalez did not prohibit sale of the album nor did he find there was any criminal liability because the decision was based on a civil suit. According to the district court judge:

> It [the album] is an appeal to 'dirty' thoughts and the loins, not to the intellect and the mind.… The recording depicts sexual conduct in graphic detail. The specificity of the descriptions makes the audio message analogous to a camera with a zoom lens, focusing on the sights and sounds of various … sex acts. It cannot be reasonably argued that the violence, perversion, abuse of women, graphic descriptions of all forms of sexual conduct, and microscopic descriptions of human genitalia contained in this recording are comedic art.[100]

The decision was the first time a federal judge declared a record album or CD obscene. Although the main impact of the decision, as expected, was a substantial increase in sales of the album around the country, at least one record shop owner was arrested the next day after the judge's decision. E-C Records proprietor Charles Freeman was arrested by six deputies of the Broward County Sheriff's Department after he sold the album to an undercover officer. He was hand-cuffed, taken to jail, and charged with a misdemeanor of distributing obscene material.[101]

Four days after the ruling, Broward County Sheriff's deputies arrested, as they had promised after the judge's ruling, two members of 2 Live Crew after the band performed an adults-only show at a Hollywood, Florida, nightclub.[102] Like Charles Freeman, the band members faced a maximum penalty of $1,000 and/or a year in jail. A third member of the four-person band was arrested and charged later. The band members went on trial in October 1990, and a jury acquitted all three members after a two-week trial in which much of the evidence consisted of a poor videotape recording of the performance. The jury deliberated only about two hours before reaching its verdict.[103]

The controversy eventually died down, but, ironically, a band known as Too Much Joy was arrested in August of the same year by Broward County deputies. It played songs from the 2 Live Crew Album to 350 people in a Hollywood, Florida, nightclub to protest the federal district court decision declaring the album obscene.[104] In May 1992 the Eleventh Circuit U.S. Court of Appeals overturned the district court ruling. A three-judge panel of the appellate court ruled that Sheriff Navarro had not proven *As Nasty as They Wanna Be* met a legal defini-tion of obscenity established in *Miller*.[105]

Interestingly, the 2 Live Crew album carried a warning label as part of a voluntary uniform label system unveiled by the Recording Industry Association of America (RIAA). RIAA mem-bers produce more than 90% of the records, tapes, and CDs sold in the country.[106] The system is strictly voluntary, although most recording companies have complied. The warning labels are placed on music products that contain material believed objectionable to children such as lyrics dealing with sex, violence, drugs, and bigotry.

Neither RIAA nor the National Association of Recording Merchandisers (NARM) publicly supported 2 Live Crew in its civil suit.[107] Two weeks before the 2 Live Crew acquittals, the Contemporary Arts Center of Cincinnati, Ohio, and its director, Dennis Barrie, were found not guilty of charges that they pandered obscenity when the gallery featured a controversial exhibit of photographs by the late Robert Mapplethorpe. The jury also cleared the defendants of two charges of exhibiting nude photos of children. The center and its director were indicted by a Hamilton County grand jury the same day the exhibit opened.

The 20-year retrospective of the acclaimed photographer's work, entitled "The Perfect Moment," consisted of 175 photographs, including five homosexual pictures and two of chil-dren. One of the five homosexual pictures includes a male urinating into the mouth of another male, and the others are of various sex acts. One of the photos is of a very young girl sitting on a porch with her skirt up to reveal her genitals, and the other is of a young boy standing nude on a couch. Most of the other photos in the display were of flowers and nude male and female figures.

According to press reports, the gallery spent $350,000 in legal expenses to defend itself at the two-week jury trial, and the city spent $14,550 in the prosecution.[108] More than 40,000 individuals paid to see the show during its first three weeks and another 40,000 reportedly saw it before it ended its run. In contrast to the 2 Live Crew case, First Amendment groups from around the country supported the defendants in the Cincinnati trial. The exhibit was able to continue because the center successfully sought an injunction from a U.S. District Court judge to bar city and county law enforcement officers from confiscating or otherwise interfering with the exhibit until a judicial determination had been made that the photographs were obscene.[109]

In 1997, 22-year-old Andrew Love was arrested in an Ocala, Florida, mall parking lot and charged with violating the state's obscenity statute for wearing a T-shirt promoting the British band, Cradle of Filth. The T-shirt pictured a topless nun masturbating. At trial, Love's attorney argued the shirt was not obscene because it was protected political commentary. The prosecutor claimed that, as required under Florida law to be obscene, the average person would find that the T-shirt: (1) appealed to a prurient, morbid, or shameful interest in sex, applying contemporary community standards, (2) depicted sexual material in a patently offensive way, and (3) when taken as a whole, was devoid of any serious literary, artistic, political or scientific value. The six-person jury acquitted Love.[110]

There is probably no modern figure more closely associated with obscenity than *Hustler* magazine publisher Larry Flynt, who was the subject of director Milos Forman's 1997 movie, *The People v. Larry Flynt.* The publisher frequently reminds anyone who will listen that if the First Amendment protects a "scumbag" like him, it protects everyone.[111] In *An Unseemly Man: My Life as Pornographer, Pundit, and Social Outcast,* Flynt, who presides over a multimillion dollar, sexually-oriented publishing empire, admits to having sex with a chicken when he was nine. While conceding Flynt's First Amendment right to protest, feminist Gloria Steinem, founding editor of *Ms. Magazine* and a Flynt critic, argued in the *New York Times* that if he had published "the same cruel images even of animals [that he published of women], the movie [*The People v. Larry Flynt*] would never have been made."[112]

Flynt was convicted in Hamilton County, Ohio, of 15 counts of obscenity, including pandering, in 1977. His conviction was later reversed by an appeals court. He was never retried, but in April 1998 he was indicted on 15 felony counts in the same county for selling 16 sexually explicit videos at his Hustler store in Cincinnati. The charges included nine counts of pandering obscenity, three counts of disseminating materials harmful to minors, two counts of conspiracy to engage in a pattern of corrupt activity, and one count of engaging in such activity.[113]

Informed critics are quick to point out that the company selling more X-rated films every year than Larry Flynt and *Playboy*, more than $200 million annually out of an estimated $10 billion, is DirecTV which General Motors sold to Rupert Murdoch's News Corp. in 2003. Republican presidential candidate Mitt Romney, who has spoken out strongly against pornography in this country, was harshly criticized in 2007 for not attempting to get the Marriott Hotel chain out of the pay-per-view hotel movie distribution business. Romney served on the Marriott board for nine years, including as chair of the audit committee. Like most major hotels, Marriott makes sexually explicit movies available via patron TV sets.

Obscenity versus Indecency

The U.S. Supreme Court and other appellate and trial courts have not confined their deliberations to obscene speech when it comes to sexually oriented or other offensive materials. They have also tackled *indecency.* From a legal perspective, there is one major difference between *indecency* and *obscenity.* The latter must appeal to prurient interests, but the former need not. Both usually involve nudity and sex in some form, although their impact on the average person is different, according to the courts. There is one other major difference: indecent speech enjoys constitutional protection in some contexts, but obscenity can never count on the First Amendment.

Some examples of speech that could be considered indecent but are very likely not obscene appear in Madonna's documentary film, *Truth or Dare*. The film shows Madonna exposing her breasts, Madonna simulating oral sex with a bottle, two male dancers kissing one another, a friend of the singer discussing a lesbian relationship, Madonna simulating orgasm from masturbation during a concert, and profanity. A media critic might argue that the "material girl" has changed her tune, but her R-rated movie would never pass the *Miller* conjunctive test because it might be judged to hold some literary value and does not appeal to prurient interests.[114]

Indecency on Cable Television

Cable television outlets face severe criminal penalties under both federal and state statutes if they carry obscene programming. The Cable Television and Consumer Protection and Competition Act of 1992 contained several provisions regarding obscene and indecent programs.[115] These include a provision allowing cable operators to deny access to anyone seeking to lease a channel to carry programming that the operator "reasonably believes describes or depicts sexual or excretory activities or organs in a patently offensive manner as measured by contemporary community standards." This phrasing is very much in line with the FCC's definition of indecency in broadcasting.

The Act provides for civil and criminal liability for cable operators who carry obscene programs on public, educational and governmental (PEG) and leased access channels. The FCC was directed under the Act to establish rules. The rules (1) require cable operators who carry indecent programming on leased access channels to block the channels unless the consumer requests in writing that the channel not be blocked, and (b) allow cable operators to ban "obscene material, sexually explicit conduct, or material soliciting or promoting unlawful conduct."

The Commission began the appropriate rule making proceedings shortly after the Act took effect, and in June 1995 the U.S. Court of Appeals for the D.C. Circuit in a 6 to 4 decision upheld the indecency and obscenity provisions of the Act and the FCC's implementation of them.[116] The circuit court reasoned that there was no violation of the First Amendment because there was no absolute ban on indecent programs and cable operators had a choice on whether to block such programming. On appeal, the U.S. Supreme Court granted certiorari in 1996.

In *Denver Area Educational Telecommunications Consortium v. Federal Communications Commission* (1997),[117] the Supreme Court affirmed in part and reversed in part the D.C. Circuit decision. There were enough concurring and dissenting opinions in the case to make one's head swim, pointing to the extreme difficulty justices have in determining the standards that should apply to indecent content on cable television. Justice Breyer, joined by Justices Stevens, O'Connor, Kennedy, Souter, and Ginsburg, held that Section 10(b) violated the First Amendment. That section applies only to leased access channels and requires cable operators to confine any "patently offensive" programming to a single channel and to automatically block the programming unless a subscriber makes a written request that the channel not be blocked.

The Court said this provision was not narrowly tailored enough to achieve the government's legitimate objective of protecting children from such content. According to the Court, there were other less restrictive means of protecting minors such as V-chips and lockboxes that allow parents to selectively block access.

In a 7 to 2 vote, the Court upheld the constitutionality of Section 10(a), which permits cable operators to refuse to carry programming on commercially leased access channels if the cable company "reasonably believes" the programming "depicts ... sexual activities or organs in a patently offensive manner." Unfortunately, a majority of the justices could not agree on the rationale for upholding the provision.

In a closer vote (5 to 4), the Court ruled that Section 10(c), which allows cable operators to refuse to carry what they believe is indecent programming on local PEG channels, is unconstitutional. Once again, there was no agreement among the majority regarding why the provision violated the First Amendment.

The case did little to resolve the issue of how far the government can go in regulating indecency on cable television. About all the justices could agree on are that the need to protect children from such programming is a compelling government interest and that requiring cable companies to block indecent programming on local access channels is impermissible when the consumer has to take the initiative to unblock the programming. In *U.S. v. Playboy Entertainment Group, Inc.*, the U.S. Supreme Court ruled that Section 505 of the Telecommunications Act of 1996 was unconstitutional because it was not the least restrictive means of addressing children's exposure to sexually explicit programming on cable. The Court applied the strict scrutiny test, as the court had done in *Sable Communications v. FCC* (1989) regarding indecent phone sex.

Indecency on the Internet

Even when Bill Clinton was President and he signed into law the Telecommunications Act of 1996, one of the provisions of the statute, the Communications Decency Act (CDA),[118] was immediately challenged in the courts. Under the Act, anyone who uses a computer to transmit indecent material faces possible imprisonment of up to two years and fines up to $500,000. At a Freedom Forum seminar a month after the law took effect, U.S. Senator Patrick Leahy (D-Vt.), who had voted against the measure, characterized the CDA as "unconstitutional."[119]

Because Congress knew the provision was likely to be challenged, it included a provision in the CDA that the federal courts would grant expedited review. The U.S. District Court for the Eastern District of Pennsylvania quickly granted a temporary restraining order that barred enforcement of the CDA, pending appellate court review.[120] After hearing oral arguments and reviewing reams of documents filed in the case, a special three-judge panel headed by Chief Judge Sloviter of the Third Circuit U.S. Court of Appeals unanimously agreed to granting a preliminary injunction requested by the American Civil Liberties Union, the American Library Association, several online services, the Society of Professional Journalists, and 50,000 Internet users.[121] Defendants in the case included U.S. Attorney General Janet Reno and the Department of Justice. In its decision, the court viewed the Internet as more analogous to the telephone or to the print media than the broadcast media and pointed to the fact that one person can literally speak instantaneously to millions of people around the world.

According to the separate opinion of one member of the panel, District Judge Stewart Dalzell, "Any content-based regulation of the Internet, no matter how benign the purpose, could burn the global village to roast the pig." Two provisions of the Act were challenged—one dealing with "indecent" communication (which the Act did not define)[122] and the other dealing with "patently offensive" communication, which was defined in traditional terms similar to that in broadcasting as "measured by contemporary community standards ... [the depiction or description of] ..., sexual or excretory activities or organs."[123]

To obtain a preliminary injunction, which would be effective only until overturned or upheld on appeal, a plaintiff must show "a reasonable probability of eventual success in the litigation" and that the person or entity would suffer irreparable harm if the law was enforced. According to the panel, the plaintiffs had demonstrated this. The U.S. Supreme Court heard oral arguments in the appeal on March 19, 1997. On June 26, its next-to-last day for business for the session, the Court issued its decision in *Reno v. ACLU* (1997).[124] In a 7 to 2 opinion authored by Justice John Paul Stevens, the Court struck down as unconstitutional both the "indecent transmission" and "patently offensive display" provisions of the Communications Decency Act.

In affirming the district court decision, the Supreme Court distinguished regulation of the Internet from broadcast and cable regulation. It said: "Neither before nor after the enactment of the CDA have the vast democratic fora [sik] of the Internet been subject to the type of government supervision and regulation that has attended the broadcast industry [citing *Pacifica*]. Moreover, the Internet is not as 'invasive' as radio and television."[125]

The Court acknowledged that sexually explicit material from "the modestly titillating to the hardest core" could be found on the Internet and that, once it was available in any community, it was accessible everywhere. However, the Court noted that "users seldom encounter such content accidentally" and that software had been developed to allow parents to control access by their children. The Court conceded that current software could not screen sexually explicit images but the technology was developing to block such content.

The Court applied a "strict scrutiny" analysis, almost guaranteeing that the provisions would be struck down. (Prior restraint rarely survives "strict scrutiny" review by the Court.) There were serious flaws in the CDA provisions, according to the majority opinion. They included: (a) parents are not allowed to consent to their children's access to restricted materials, (b) the provisions are not limited to commercial transactions, (c) "indecent" is not defined in the Act, and (d) there is no requirement that "patently offensive" material lack socially redeeming value. The Court said that the CDA lacked precision that the *First Amendment* requires when a statute regulates the content of speech. In order to deny minors, it suppressed speech that adults had a right to receive and address to one another. The burden on adult speech is unacceptable if less restrictive alternatives would be as effective in achieving a legitimate purpose.[126]

The government clearly has an interest in protecting children, but "that interest does not justify an unnecessarily broad suppression of speech addressed to adults." The majority opinion went on to characterize the breadth of the CDA's coverage as "wholly unprecedented." The government had argued before the Supreme Court, although not before the district court, that it had an interest in promoting growth of the Internet. But that court was not convinced, saying:

> The Government apparently assumes that the unregulated availability of 'indecent' and 'patently offensive' material on the Internet is driving countless citizens away from the medium because of the risk of exposing themselves or their children to harmful material.
>
> We find this argument singularly unpersuasive. The dramatic expansion of this new marketplace of ideas contradicts the factual basis of this contention. The record dem-

onstrates that the growth of the Internet has been and continues to be phenomenal. As a matter of constitutional tradition, in the absence of evidence to the contrary, we presume that governmental regulation of the content of speech is more likely to interfere with the free exchange of ideas than to encourage it. The interest in encouraging freedom of expression in a democratic society outweighs any theoretical but unproven benefit of censorship.[127]

As expected, advocates for strong First Amendment rights for the Internet reacted with great joy to the ruling, which attracted more media attention than almost any other Supreme Court decision at that time. Their glee was certainly warranted because the Court clearly saw cyberspace as an uncharted medium worthy of strong First Amendment protection—at least at that time. But there were hints in the majority opinion, even then, that the Court might be willing to entertain some restrictions on the Internet.

First, the Court agreed to allow the portion of the CDA dealing with obscene content to stand. The CDA included a severability clause that allowed the Court to leave intact those provisions and terms that were determined to be constitutional, while severing those portions of the legislation that were unacceptable. In other words, the Court could simply strike those provisions and terms that presented constitutional problems, while allowing the rest of the Act to remain in effect. The Court rejected this opportunity, except for the term *obscene* in Section 223(a), which it allowed to remain. The net effect of this move by the Court was to keep alive the ban on obscene content on the Internet.

Second, throughout the majority opinion, the Court emphasized that the major problem with the two provisions of the Act was the breadth with which it swept in protected speech because of its vagueness. The Court noted, for example, that it agreed "with the District Court's conclusion that the CDA places an unacceptably heavy burden on protected speech, and that the defenses [advanced by the Government] do not constitute the sort of 'narrow tailoring' that will save an otherwise patently invalid unconstitutional provision."[128] Thus the Court appears to be hinting that it might be willing to entertain a better-drafted statute.

Phone Indecency

Another area of obscenity and indecency in which the FCC has become involved is the so-called dial-a-porn telephone services that use various call prefixes to offer sexually explicit recordings. In some cases, this involves two-way conversations about sex with callers, who are charged fees for a minute or more. Dial-a-porn had become big business by the time Congress acted in 1988 to amend Section 223(b) of the 1934 Federal Communications Act to ban both indecent and obscene interstate telephone messages. The purpose of the amendment was clearly to crack down on the dial-a-porn services.

Sable Communications, one of the services, which had been operating for five years, filed suit against the FCC, seeking a declaratory judgment that the indecency and obscenity portions of the amendment violated the First and Fourteenth Amendments to the Constitution. In *Sable Communications of California v. FCC* (1988),[129] the U.S. Supreme Court upheld a U.S. District Court decision that the amendment's indecency provision but not the obscenity provision violated the Constitution. The Court ruled 6 to 3 in an opinion written by Justice

White that, in its present form, the law "has the invalid effect of limiting the content of adult conversations to that which is suitable for children to hear. It is another case of 'burning up the house to roast the pig.'" The justices felt that the legislation had not been narrowly drawn enough to promote the government's legitimate interest in protecting children from exposure to indecent telephone messages.

In response to the *Sable* decision, Congress passed a new amendment sponsored by Senator Jessie Helms (R-N.C.) that revised Section 223 of the Federal Communications Act of 1934 to ban the use of a telephone for "any indecent communication for commercial purposes which is available to any person under 18 years of age or to any other person without that person's consent, regardless of whether the maker of such communication placed the call." The law requires phone companies to block access to dial-a-porn services unless the customer requests access in writing. In 1990 the FCC issued rules that defined telephone indecency as descriptions of "sexual or excretory activities or organs in a patently offensive manner as measured by contemporary community standards for the telephone medium." This was essentially the same as its definition for indecency for broadcasting. The FCC also promulgated new rules that established a defense for such telephone services if they gave written notice to the telephone company that they provided such communications or if they required an identification code before transmitting the messages or scrambled messages only decipherable by someone with a descrambler.

One of the providers of dial-a-porn, Dial Information Services of New York, and three similar companies sought an injunction in U.S. District Court in Manhattan to prevent the commission from implementing the Helms amendment.[130] Two days before the law was to take effect, U.S. District Judge Robert P. Paterson granted the request on the grounds that the law was likely unconstitutional because it required common carriers (telephone companies) to make a prior determination of whether particular speech was or was not indecent and the term *indecency* was too vague. Paterson also said the law did not, as required, use the least restrictive means of imposing prior restraint to keep minors from obtaining access to the messages. The FCC appealed. In a 3 to 0 ruling in *Dial Information Services of New York Corp. v. Thornburgh*,[131] the Second Circuit U.S. Court of Appeals reversed the trial court decision. It held that the statute's definition of indecency was adequately defined and the regulations were not unconstitutional prior restraint because the services merely had to classify their messages, not halt them, and any adults attempting access to the services could still do so by simply stating their intent in advance. According to the Court of Appeals, "It always is more effective to lock the barn before the horse is stolen."[132] The U.S. Supreme Court denied certiorari.[133]

Live Nudity and the First Amendment

Finally, the U. S. Supreme Court has become the final arbiter in deciding whether nude dancing has constitutional protection. Obviously, live performances that are deemed obscene can be banned, but what about non-obscene nude performances? The Court has traditionally kept its views on the issue undercover, but it was inevitable that the justices had to give either a green or a red light to state statutes around the country that bar or restrict nude public performances.

The Court first became involved in the constitutional aspects of nude dancing in 1956. It upheld an obscenity conviction of a stripper on grounds that the statute was a valid exercise of a state's police authority.[134] For the next 16 years, the justices denied certiorari when such cases were appealed, but in 1972 the Supreme Court upheld a California statute that prohibited acts of "gross sexuality," which included sexually explicit live entertainment where alcohol was served.[135] Several similar decisions followed in which the Court essentially held that both nude and topless dancing in businesses where alcohol was served could be prohibited.[136] Only one Supreme Court decision gave any reprieve to nude dancing and that occurred in 1975 when the Court unanimously overturned a preliminary injunction issued by a New York trial court judge against three North Hempstead bars that featured topless dancing.[137] The U.S. Supreme Court said the state statute involved was too broad and therefore unconstitutional because it applied to all live entertainment, including artistic works. This decision was cited for many years as granting First Amendment protection to nude dancing. But that was a serious misinterpretation because it was clear that the Court was not trying to protect traditional nude dancing in bars but to protect plays and socially redeeming works that might include some nudity.

The Court has wrestled with the issue of whether nude dancing enjoyed First Amendment protection as speech or expression or whether it was really conduct. In *Barnes v. Glen Theatre* (1991),[138] the justices lined up 5 to 4 against the dancers by upholding an Indiana public indecency statute that required female strip-tease dancers to wear at least G-strings and pasties in their performances. The Supreme Court overturned a Seventh Circuit U.S. Court of Appeals ruling involving dancers at the Kitty Kat Lounge in South Bend, Indiana, that "non-obscene nude dancing performed as entertainment is expression and as such is entitled to limited" First Amendment protection. The plurality opinion written by Chief Justice Rehnquist who was joined by O'Connor and Kennedy said: "Nude dancing of the kind sought to be performed here is expressive conduct within the outer perimeters of the First Amendment, though we view it as only marginally so." That protection, however, is overridden by the state's interest in protecting morals and public order. "The requirement that the dancers don pasties and G-strings," Rehnquist said, "does not deprive the dance of whatever erotic message it conveys; it simply makes the message slightly less erotic."

Associate Justice David Souter concurred only with the result of the case, asserting that the statute was a valid exercise of the state's interest in preventing prostitution, sexual assault, and other crimes. Justice Scalia also concurred with the Court's judgment but on the ground that the statute involved no First Amendment issues. Justices Marshall (who resigned at the end of the Court's term and was replaced by Clarence Thomas), Blackmun, Stevens, and White dissented on the ground that the dancing was protected expression.

In a follow-up to *Barnes v. Glen Theatre*, the Supreme Court ruled 5 to 4 in two different opinions that a Pennsylvania ordinance requiring exotic dancers to wear G-strings and pasties while performing was constitutional. [139] In this case, *City of Erie v. Pap's A.M.*, the court in 2000 said cities may bar nude dancing to deter the secondary effects of criminal activity associated with adult only businesses. This is consistent with government interest in regulating public safety, health, and morals.[140]

Indecency and the Arts

Although the third prong of the *Miller* test for obscenity makes it clear that materials having serious artistic value by definition cannot be obscene, the arts have continued to suffer at the hands of some government officials. One of the most publicized cases involving censorship of the arts is *National Endowment for the Arts v. Karen Finley*.[141] The case focused on the constitutionality of a statute enacted by Congress requiring the head of the National Endowment for the Arts (NEA) to take into account "general standards of decency and respect for the diverse beliefs and views of the American public"[142] when making decisions regarding grants.

The same year the Act was passed, Karen Finley and three other artists sued the NEA. They claimed that the "decency" provision of the law violated their First Amendment rights.[143] Finley received NEA support before the statute was enacted for a performance in which she appears on stage nude, covered with chocolate, and says "God is death."[144] Her grant and those of some other artists and performers spurred Congress into taking steps to stop such funding, including the 1990 Act. The U.S. Supreme Court in an 8 to 1 ruling in June 1998 upheld the law for NEA to consider decency when deciding whether artists would receive government support.

At the start, the United States District Court for the Central District of California ruled in 1992 in favor of Finley and the other plaintiffs, holding that the law was unconstitutionally vague and "gives rise to the danger of arbitrary and discriminatory application."[145] Four years later, the Ninth Circuit U.S. Court of Appeals in a 2 to 1 vote affirmed the lower court decision.[146] According to the majority opinion, "Even when the Government is funding speech, it may not distinguish between speakers on the basis of the speaker's viewpoint or otherwise aim at the suppression of dangerous ideas." The Court held at that time, "Government funding of the arts, in the circumstances of this case, must be viewpoint neutral."[147] But in the final analysis the Supreme Court decided in 1998 that the NEA could consider decency standards in awarding grants. The opinion in the case was written by Justice Sandra Day O'Connor, and the only dissenting opinion was filed by Justice David Souter. One of the central figures in the case, Karen Finley, continued to present performance art and, in 2000, her book *A Different Kind of Intimacy: The Collected Writings of Karen Finley* was published.[148]

Ethical Dilemmas Facing the Media in Obscenity and Indecency Cases

Obscenity cases such as police raids on adult bookstores and indecency cases like *Barnes* generally attract considerable media attention, although their impact to the First Amendment may arguably not be as strong as other less "sexy" restraints on free expression. Public officials inevitably damn the evils of pornography and indecency, often confusing the two and thereby add to misunderstanding. Taken out of context, even the mildest forms of depiction of sex and nudity can appear offensive, as Georgia prosecutors demonstrated in a dispute over the movie *Carnal Knowledge* in *Jenkins v. Georgia*. But, as the Court said in the decision, *Miller* requires that hard core depictions be involved. Nudity alone is not enough.

A close reading of the plurality opinion in *Barnes* and the concurring opinions, though, reveals a rather different attitude of the Court—one that sees virtually no protection in nude expression. There may be a difference between live nude performances and nude photographs or film, but the fact remains that each form involves expression. The only real difference is that one is live and therefore ephemeral, and the other is recorded and thus more permanent. Yet the less permanent form enjoys virtually no protection, and the more permanent one can count on substantially greater protection. Thus a dancer at the Kitty Kat must wear pasties and G-strings, but if she becomes a *Playboy* centerfold, she can bare all. The venue does make a difference as the *City of Erie v. Pap's A.M.* case showed, with the U.S. Supreme Court saying that cities may bar nude dancing to hamper deleterious secondary effects, especially an increase in crime.

This situation touches on the first of five major ethical dilemmas facing the news media in covering obscenity and indecency stories: How far should journalists go in defending individuals and organizations that test the First Amendment to its limits? Neither the Kitty Kat dancers nor 2 Live Crew attracted much support from the news media and even the Cincinnati Contemporary Center for the Arts gained only limited editorial favor from the news media in fighting prosecution over the Mapplethorpe photo exhibit. The Larry Flynts of the world can count on even less support even when movies about them portray them as heroes.

As the late U.S. Supreme Court Justices William O. Douglas, William Brennan, and Thurgood Marshall eloquently argued, the First Amendment must be strong in order for it to have meaning. Protecting thoughts is not enough; we must protect the expression of thoughts. Most of the major news media such as the *New York Times* and major chains such as Gannett, Knight-Ridder, and Scripps Howard continue to fight in editorials and in other ways against restrictions on freedom of speech and freedom of the press. They do this even when situations and individuals involved have no popular support, especially from politicians, although the exposure of national government secrets in the United States and elsewhere, through Wikileaks in 2010 provided a number of series concerns.

The protection of states secrets commands serious attention but perhaps erotic dancers do not deserve First Amendment protection? But where is the line drawn beyond nude dancing? What about plays with nudity? Why should the latter be considered First Amendment expression when the former, as noted in *Barnes*, is "within the outer perimeters … only marginally so"? Is it because the audience for one is a group of blue-collar, middle-age males, whereas the other attracts people with an interest in art and culture?

A second dilemma facing journalists in dealing with obscenity and indecency is deciding how graphic or detailed descriptions of cases should be. During the final Senate Judiciary Committee hearing on the nomination of Clarence Thomas as associate justice of the Supreme Court, some of the testimony from his former associate, Anita Hill, and others about Thomas' alleged sexual harassment of her was graphic. There were references to a pubic hair on a Coke can and a porn star named "Long Dong Silver."

The Cable News Network (CNN) and other networks carried testimony "live" to one of the largest television audiences ever of a Senate hearing. Some people were angered that this content was aired without editing. Most were surprised that the sexually explicit references were not deleted but the importance of the process appeared in this case to trump all of the "off-color" content.

During the Palm Beach, Florida, trial in which a Kennedy family cousin, William Kennedy Smith was acquitted of an alleged rape, explicit testimony about semen, ejaculation, and lack of a condom was carried live by Court TV with portions on CNN. The person's identity was blocked by some media outlets until an interview on ABC TV's *PrimeTime Live* and once the defendant was acquitted.

Both the Smith trial and Judge Thomas' confirmation hearings significantly boosted CNN's ratings.[149] Criticism from the public bolstered ratings, and the senior White House officials indicated that those events should not have been televised because of offensive language. Later, broadcast reports during the impeachment hearings of Bill Clinton raised eyebrows, particularly details of sex with White House intern Monica Lewinsky.

Figure 9.1   *Time* magazine cover dated February 2, 1998 (DSK/AFP/Getty Images).

Independent Counsel Kenneth Starr provided Congress with a detailed 445-page report including explicit descriptions of sex acts. Starr's report mentioned oral sex 92 times, genitalia 39, phone sex 29, and sexual activity between Clinton and Lewinsky in the White House 10 times. In his book *Sex Sells! The Media's Journey from Repression to Obsession*, Rodger Streitmatter maintained that sex was lurking as a background issue until the semen stain was reported on Lewinsky's dress as part of the story. That would seem to make it difficult for journalists to ignore, but liberal columnists and even members of the public cried foul because the reports were considered so salacious—and too detailed. But despite the protests, ratings remained high. [150]

Conservative talk show host Bill O'Reilly was sued for sexual harassment by a Fox News Channel producer in 2004. Fox filed a countersuit against the producer and her attorney. Included in the producer's charges were allegations that O'Reilly, her boss, had in phone conversations suggested that she "buy a vibrator and was clearly excited."[151] O'Reilly disclosed that the producer's attorney demanded $60 million in what he termed "hush money" not to file the lawsuit. O'Reilly countered that the charges represented a "politically motivated extortion attempt." At the end of the day, the public was exposed to statements quoted as part of phone sex conversations raising questions of bad manners and bad taste.

Media critics generally split on whether the intense attention by the press in some of these cases is really warranted. Some question whether the language should have been included. But certainly a strong argument can be made that the public must be exposed to the grit in such situations in order to understand and evaluate the situation. Anita Hill's explicit references in the case of Supreme Court nominee Clarence Thomas clearly were relevant in explaining her charges. The Smith rape trial was handled in the courtroom the way almost any other rape trial would be, including explicit testimony that the jury had to hear as evidence.

A third and related dilemma is whether the print and electronic media should include the specific words and pictures in indecency and obscenity cases. Obviously, it would be highly irresponsible for a TV or radio newscast, especially in prime time, to broadcast words such as those in *Pacifica Foundation* even though they may be integral to understanding a story. When a local campus radio station that had drawn the ire of some members of the community for its music lyrics is challenged, the words may be unnecessary for understanding's sake. But, is there a context in which those words can be repeated so the reader does not have to rely on rumors to know the language involved? What about the use of a sidebar inside a newspaper or a cautionary preliminary note in a late night newscast? Is it better to use euphemisms such as "explicit sexual references," "bodily functions," and "offensive language"? How about omitting letters as in f--k, s--t, and p--s or simply f--, s--?

Different news organizations handle these situations in different ways, but every station, newspaper, and magazine should have a written, clear policy about how these kinds of stories are to be covered. Regardless of how it is done, readers will complain, and so news organizations need to be able to easily explain why specific language did or did not appear.

A similar sensitive problem sometimes arises when police conduct raids of adult theaters and bookstores. How do you convey to a reader or viewer the kinds of materials confiscated or the specific act that the actor known as Pee Wee Herman allegedly committed at an adult theater in Sarasota, Florida? Some of the news stories about the incident simply said that Paul Reubens had been charged with indecent exposure; others stated that he was arrested for masturbating. There seemed to be much greater concern about how parents should explain to children what had happened to Pee Wee Herman than the legal fate of Paul Reubens. In fact, there was more space devoted in the news media to the reactions of parents and children than to resolution of the case. When Reubens pleaded "no contest" and paid a $50 fine, the decision warranted little more than a 15-second blip on a TV monitor.

Typically, newspapers and television newscasts will show police loading marked boxes and cartons when they conduct a search of an adult bookstore, and the public is invariably left with no idea of the exact materials seized. Were the books and videos the same as those available in more proper establishments, such as chain drug stores, convenient marts (behind the counter, of course), and the local video rental store (in that special adult section)? Or are the works truly hard core? It is certainly not necessary for reporters to hold up copies of the pages or to show excerpts from the X-rated movies, but should they not at least be more specific about the kinds of sex featured? The press is also placed in the odd position of being faced with the dilemma of giving attention to performers, especially so-called shock jocks on radio, who often appear to have contrived outrageous events to simply attract attention for the purpose of gaining publicity and notoriety.

The consumer is usually quite interested in knowing whether deviant conduct such as bestiality and child pornography is depicted or if the works are typical heterosexual and homosexual depictions familiar to most adults. Why should members of the public know less about the nature of such materials than the jury and judge who will be deciding the defendant's fate? In murder and other criminal trials, the public usually has more information available to it than the jury, which is restricted from seeing and hearing certain kinds of information. Why should the reverse be true in obscenity and indecency cases?

With stories about nudity and sex, some newspapers and magazines as well as television shows carry edited versions of recordings, pictures, and so on. In these cases, the nudity is blurred out or the profanities replaced, as in re-runs of *The Sopranos* or *Dexter,* just enough to offer the public a good idea of the subject matter but not enough to incur outrage from government officials. Are these techniques more ethical than exposing the consumer to the actual nudity or words, or are they simply a means of avoiding the wrath of the FCC and angry viewers or readers? On the other hand, it certainly could be argued that providing even the edited versions is really only a convenient cover for attracting a larger audience with titillations and tasteless promos. Where should the line be drawn?

A fourth dilemma involves whether the media should accept (a) advertising for adult bookstores, theaters, and movies (with or without provocative titles and visuals) and/or (b) advertising for ordinary products that contain offensive language or full or partial nudity. The broadcast industry has been far more conservative than newspapers on this issue. This is undoubtedly because of concerns about FCC actions, but all of the mass media, except some magazines, have traditionally rejected both types of advertising even though there is virtually no fear they would ever be prosecuted, even in the most conservative communities. They probably fear public pressure.

Some media outlets compromise by permitting adult establishments to advertise but not to mention specific titles (whether or not highly offensive) or to use terms such as *X-rated, explicit material,* and so forth. Some even carry ads from adult escort firms and dial-a-porn services, usually under the rationale that the media cannot make judgments about acceptability of businesses so long as they are offering a legitimate product or service.

Media outlets can never be required to carry any particular ad or form of advertising, but at least one newspaper has been caught in a bind over legal notices. The *Boston Globe* once rather reluctantly published a 2½″ × 15½″ legal notice listing titles of 355 allegedly pornographic books and magazines seized by police.[152] Under a 1945 Massachusetts statute, publications could not be officially prosecuted as obscene until a legal notice was published in a Boston newspaper and one in a newspaper in the county where the materials are seized. Many of the titles were quite graphic and included profanities. Examples included such titles as *Mother's into Bondage* and *Sextraverts.*[153]

Another Boston daily, the *Boston Herald,* refused to publish the ad, as it had the right to do. Both the *Globe* and the *Times-Union* in Springfield, Massachusetts, where the publications were confiscated, published the ad twice, as stipulated in the statute. The *Globe* included a notice with the ad indicating that it was published to comply with state law, whereas the *Times-Union* ran no disclaimer but did run an editorial saying that the legal notice was not an endorsement of the prosecutor's actions.

The final dilemma is one that the news media rarely face. But it is one that, nevertheless, can be rather difficult to resolve: *How specific should a story be about an incident involving indecency or pornography when there is no major concern about offending language or nudity but instead a concern about the possibility of copycats?* A prime example of this problem is illustrated in a Fifth Circuit U.S. Court of Appeals decision in 1987, *Herceg v. Hustler*.[154] The appellate court held that *Hustler* magazine could not be held liable for the death of a 17-year-old boy occurring after he attempted a technique described in the magazine. The article offered detailed information about *autoerotic asphyxia*, in which a person affixes a rope to stop breathing at the peak of sexual stimulation.

The case originally received little press attention, probably because editors feared attracting more individuals to read the article and possibly attempt the same act. The article, according to the court decision, did stress the "often-fatal dangers" of the practice, recommended "readers seeking unique forms of sexual release DO NOT ATTEMPT this method," and indicated that the information was "presented here solely for an educational purpose." Even when the decision was handed down by the appellate court, most newspapers and broadcast news either overlooked or ignored it, even though it had considerable public interest.

Similar safety issues arose when MTV's *Jackass* series featured outrageous stunts. A number of suits resulted from imitations of death-defying stunts gone bad, inflicted on themselves by watchers of this program. Even with a disclaimer telling viewers that they should not attempt to recreate or perform anything that they saw on the series, MTV was left trying to defend the airing of these stunts and the injuries to some viewers. With claims that the programming had in some manner instigated personal injury, MTV repeatedly added that the program was rated not suitable for those under 18.

Generally, there is no liability even for media outlets that originally carry such a story of extremely violent acts and certainly no fear of liability for news coverage about such cases, no matter how detailed they may be. But reporting themes of behavior can be problematic and cause concern. For example, the press is aware of the copycat implications of reporting clusters of suicides by young people, including high school and even college students. But, is it ethical to carry a number of these stories, particularly at times when individuals and communities may be under stress? And if they demand attention, how far do you go in covering these kinds of stories? Should the technique be outlined with a warning and the hope that it will educate individuals who might be tempted and even possibly save some lives? On the other hand, should the specific issue be mentioned when it would provide ready access to someone who might model the incident? What are the ethical responsibilities in these situations that invoke concerns as in "copycat suicides"?

Summary and Conclusions

Obscenity, pornography, and *indecency* are terms often used interchangeably by the public and sometimes even by journalists, but they are not synonymous. Pornography is simply a layperson's term for obscenity, a term used by the courts, but there are major differences between obscenity and indecency in the eye of the law. **Obscenity**, as defined by the U.S. Supreme Court in *Miller v. California* in 1973 requires (a) that the average person, applying contemporary community standards, find the work as a whole appeals to prurient interests, (b) that the work depict or describe in a patently offensive way sexual conduct specifically defined by state law, and (c) that the work, taken as a whole, lacks serious literary, artistic, political, or scientific value. This standard is conjunctive, which means that all three prongs of the test must be met before a work can be declared legally obscene.

Contrary to popular opinion, featuring explicit sex alone or nudity alone is not enough. As the Supreme Court said in *Jenkins v. Georgia*, the conduct depicted must be hard core sexual activity, not simply nudity or offensive conduct. However, even explicit sex is not enough, as illustrated by an advisory jury's decision in 1981 in a case involving the movie *Caligula*.[155] Penthouse International, the owner of the film, filed a request in equity court for a declaration that the film was not obscene and an injunction to enjoin the Solicitor General of Fulton County (Atlanta), Georgia, from arresting or prosecuting anyone connected with the film's distribution—as he had threatened to do if the film were shown in his jurisdiction.

An advisory jury determined that the film was patently offensive and its sexual depictions an affront to community standards, but, viewed as a whole, the film did not appeal to the average person's prurient interest in sex (applying contemporary community standards). The judge in the case also found that, based on expert testimony, the movie had both serious and artistic value. Thus the film was not obscene even though it contained "a prolonged and explicit lesbian love scene" and "is a dizzying display of bodies, genitals, orgies, heterosexual and homosexual activity, masturbation, bodily functions, and sexual conduct and excesses of all varieties."[156] To be obscene, a work must pass all *three* prongs of the *Miller* test, not just one or two.

It is still relatively rare for a newspaper or radio or television station to be prosecuted for obscenity, although magazines, books, and films occasionally face such charges. Indecency is generally not a major problem for the print media, but broadcasters and cable operators still have to worry about offending the FCC and Congress. Indecency, unlike obscenity, need not appeal to prurient interest, and thus is easier to demonstrate, especially when explicit sexual expressions and terms are used.

In *Barnes v. Glen Theatre* (1991), the U.S. Supreme Court held that a state could bar nude dancing. But the majority could not agree on a rationale, indicating that the Court could at some point rule that some forms of nude dancing may have First Amendment protection, just not the kind displayed at the Kitty Kat Lounge, although the decision in *City of Erie v. Paps* acknowledges a relationship between community standards for decency and consequences occurring beyond the local strip club door.[157]

Both obscenity and indecency continue to draw inordinate attention from politicians and police, but the U.S. Supreme Court generally appears to be steering away from becoming the high court of obscenity again. Any future decisions in this area are likely to be little more than fine tuning, as the Court did in *Pope v. Illinois* (1987), the last step determining the level of authority involved in each of the three prongs of the *Miller* standard. We now know that prong one relates to *local community standards*, prong two to *state standards*, and the third prong (the LAPS test) must look to *national standards*.

The Motion Picture Association of America—the industry association that rates movies voluntarily submitted from G to X based on their level of violence, sex, and offensive language—

abolished the X-rating in 1990 and replaced it with NC-17 (no children under 17 admitted) in response to public criticism of its rating system, complaints of unwarranted censorship from filmmakers and critics, and the extensive use of the X-rating by the pornographic film business which the MPAA had not trademarked. The first movie to get the NC-17 rating was *Henry and June.* Very few MPAA films ever received a final X-rating anyway, although some acclaimed productions such as *Midnight Cowboy, Last Tango in Paris,* and *Clockwork Orange* were released with the tag. Now, however, X is left for the adult movies that primarily serve as video industry products.

As illustrated by *Reno v. ACLU* (1997), the technology now facing the most serious assault from authorities over alleged indecency and pornography is the home computer. Many of the software catalogs, including those selling public domain programs and shareware, sell sexually explicit disks containing adult sex games or actual computer images of explicit sex.[158] Will computer-simulated sex be possible with the next wave of video technology known as *virtual reality*, which makes three-dimensional images possible with a personal computer. How will libraries remain accessible while protecting children from online predators? These issues are widely debated.[159] In the first instance, the U.S. Supreme Court has already ruled that child pornography created through digitalization or morphing cannot be prosecuted when no children were involved. Every meeting of librarians includes sessions regarding online access.

Over-the-air broadcasters have become very frustrated by shrinking audiences and increased competition from sources offering content on the fringe of good taste or bad manners. They are annoyed that federal regulators have stepped up to challenge the content of their programs while their satellite and direct TV cable competitors have become much less inhibited. Some of the most popular television shows focused by key demographic groups of the past decade such as *The Sopranos* and *Sex in the City* were programmed over cable outlets, in this case HBO, with scant scrutiny by the FCC. Meanwhile, the over-the-air broadcasters are left to defend what would appear by comparison to be relatively minor annoyances. Because of the spectrum of cases, particularly *Reno v. ACLU, U.S. v. American Library Association, Ashcroft v. Free Speech Coalition*, and also *Ashcroft v. ACLU,* the Internet has become a battleground medium for an information war over access to indecent content. This occurs while the states and Congress attempt to work around the court decisions to protect children. Requirements for schools and libraries to employ filtering software and demanding that Internet service providers create special domain codes for sites deemed offensive or harmful to children continue to create minefields in this war.

Satellite, cable television and radio continue to push the boundaries of indecency and obscenity, but occasionally even these media have to pull back. XM Satellite radio's *Opie and Anthony* once apologized for airing a homeless man's comment on their show that he would like to have sex with the then Secretary of State Condoleezza Rice, Laura Bush, and Queen Elizabeth. The program hosts were given a 30-day suspension from their show by XM.[160]

Endnotes

1. *Fox Takes Issue with FCC Finding*, Las Vegas (Nev.) Review-Journal (Associated Press), Oct. 14, 2004, at A11 and also, *See*: John Eggerton, "CBS: No Statute by Which We Can Be Fined for Super Bowl Reveal: Company says it did not intend to air "potentially indecent material," *Broadcasting & Cable,* May 21, 2010.

2. 47 U.S.C. §559 (2005).

3. Pub. L. 100-690, 102 Stat. 4181, Nov. 18, 1988.

4. *Cuomo Refuses Extradition of Programming Execs*, Onsat, July 22, 1990, at 8; *HDO Pleads Guilty*, Onsat, Dec. 9, 1990, at 105; *HDO Pleads Guilty to Federal Charges*, Onsat, Jan. 6, 1991, at 6.

5. *Couple Guilty in Computer Porn Case*, Lexington (Ky.) Herald-Leader, July 29, 1994, at A5; Leslie Miller, *Panel Agrees: Rethink Net Porn Laws*, USA Today, Oct. 17, 2000, at D3; Robert S. Greenberger, *High Court Strikes Down Ban on 'Virtual' Child Pornography*, Wall Street Journal, Apr. 17, 2002, at A4; David G. Savage, *Not Real? Not Porn*, A.B.A. J. 88, June 2002, at 34.

6. *See* Jennifer Lee, *New U.S. Database Will Track Abusers, Children in Porn*, Lexington (Ky.) Herald-Leader (New York Times News Service), Feb. 9, 2003, at A18.

7. Rebecca Miller, *Lewd 'Radiochick' Gains Following*, Atlanta Journal-Constitution (Associated Press), July 24, 2005, at MS-2; Jamie Gumbrecht, *Nipplegate One Year Later: American Media Still Reeling, but 'Desperate' to Provide Smut*, Lexington (Ky.) Herald Leader, Feb. 6, 2005, at C14. Note the quote in response to the question: "Do you think *Desperate Housewives* can be restricted?" Answer: "No. People favor keeping airwaves from being filled with smut, but if it's a show they like, they don't see smut. They say, 'Well that's not what I'm talking about. I'm talking about that hard core stuff.'"

9. *Regina v. Hicklin*, L.R., 3 Q.B. 360 (1868).

10. *Regina v. Hicklin*.

11. *United States v. One Book Called "Ulysses,"* 5 F.Supp. 182 (S.D. N.Y. 1933).

12. *United States v. One Book Called "Ulysses,"* 72 F.2d 705 (1934).

13. R. J. Wagman, *The First Amendment Book* 203 (1991).

14. *Alfred E. Butler v. State of Michigan*, 352 U.S. 380, 77 S.Ct. 524, 1 L.Ed.2d 412 (1957).

15. *Id.*

16. *Samuel Roth v. United States* and *David S. Alberts v. California*, 354 U.S. 476, 77 S.Ct. 1304, 1 L.Ed.2d 1498, 1 Med.L.Rptr. 1375 (1957).

17. *Id.*

18. *Near v. Minnesota*, 283 U.S. 697, 51 S.Ct. 625, 75 L.Ed. 1357, 1 Med.L.Rptr. 1001 (1931).

19. *Roth v. United States* and *Alberts v. California*.

20. *Id.*

21. *Eleazor Smith v. California*, 361 U.S. 147, 80 S.Ct. 215, 4 L.Ed.2d 205 (1959).

22. *Id.*

23. Ky. Rev. Stat. §531.020 (1996).

24. Ga. Code Ann. §16-12-80 (1997).

25. *United States v. X-Citement Video*, 513 U.S. 64, 115 S.Ct. 464, 130 L.Ed.2d 372 (1994).

26. *Manual Enterprises, Inc. v. Day, Postmaster General of the United States*, 370 U.S. 478, 82 S.Ct. 1432, 8 L.Ed.2d 639 (1962).

27. *Nico Jacobellis v. Ohio*, 378 U.S. 184, 84 S.Ct. 1676, 12 L.Ed.2d 793 (1964).

28. *A Quantity of Books et al. v. Kansas*, 378 U.S. 205, 84 S.Ct. 1723, 12 L.Ed.2d 809 (1964).

29. *Ronald L. Freedman v. Maryland*, 380 U.S. 51, 85 S.Ct. 734, 13 L.Ed.2d 649 (1965).

30. *Id.*

31. *Id.*

32. *A Book Named John Cleland's Memoirs of a Woman of Pleasure et al. v. Attorney General of Massachusetts*, 383 U.S. 413, 86 S.Ct. 975, 16 L.Ed.2d 1, 1 Med.L.Rptr. 1390 (1966).

33. *Id.*

34. *Ralph Ginzburg et al. v. U.S.*, 383 U.S. 463, 86 S.Ct. 942, 16 L.Ed.2d 31, 1 Med.L.Rptr. 1409 (1966).

35. *Id.*

36. *Id.*

37. *Edward Mishkin v. New York*, 383 U.S. 502, 86 S.Ct. 958, 16 L.Ed.2d 56 (1966).

38. *Marvin Miller v. California*, 413 U.S. 15, 93 S.Ct. 2607, 37 L.Ed.2d 419, 1 Med.L.Rptr. 1441 (1973).

39. *Robert Redrup v. New York, William L. Austin v. Kentucky*, and *Gent et al. v. Arkansas*, 386 U.S. 767, 87 S.Ct. 1414, 18 L.Ed.2d 515 (1967).

40. *Ginsberg v. New York*, 390 U.S. 629, 88 S.Ct. 1274, 20 L.Ed.2d 195, 1 Med.L.Rptr. 1424 (1968).

41. *Interstate Circuit, Inc. v. Dallas and United Artists Corp. v. Dallas,* 390 U.S. 676, 88 S.Ct. 1298, 20 L.Ed.2d 225 (1968).

42. *Id.*

43. *Robert Eli Stanley v. Georgia,* 394 U.S. 557, 89 S.Ct. 1243, 22 L.Ed.2d 542 (1969).

44. *Id.*

45. *United States v. Reidel,* 402 U.S. 351, 91 S.Ct. 1410, 28 L.Ed.2d 813 (1971).

46. *United States v. Thirty-Seven Photographs,* 402 U.S. 363, 91 S.Ct. 1400, 28 L.Ed.2d 822, 1 Med.L.Rptr. 1130 (1971).

47. *Paris Adult Theatre I et al. v. Lewis R. Slaton, District Attorney, Atlanta Judicial Circuit, et al.,* 413 U.S. 49, 93 S.Ct. 2628, 37 L.Ed.2d 445, 1 Med.L.Rptr. 1454 (1973).

48. *Id.*

49. *Marvin Miller v. California,* 413 U.S. 15, 93 S.Ct. 2607, 37 L.Ed.2d 419, 1 Med.L.Rptr. 1441 (1973).

50. *Id.*

51. *Id.*

52. *Paris Adult Theatre I.*

53. *Id.*

54. *William L. Hamling et al. v. U.S.,* 418 U.S. 87, 94 S.Ct. 2887, 41 L.Ed.2d 590, 1 Med.L.Rptr. 1479 (1974).

55. *Id.*

56. *Billy Jenkins v. Georgia,* 418 U.S. 153, 94 S.Ct. 2750, 41 L.Ed.2d 642,1 Med.L.Rptr. 1504 (1974).

57. *Id.*

58. *Hammer v. Dagenhart,* 247 U.S. 251, 38 S.Ct. 529, 62 L.Ed.2d 1101 (1918).

59. *United States v. Darby,* 312 U.S. 100, 61 S.Ct. 451, 85 L.Ed.2d 609 (1941).

60. Penal Law, Art. 263, §263.05ff (1977).

61. Protection of Children Against Sexual Exploitation Act of 1977, Pub. L. 95-225, 18 U.S.C. §2251–2253 (1996).

62. *New York v. Paul Ira Ferber,* 458 U.S. 747, 102 S.Ct. 3348, 73 L.Ed.2d 1113, 8 Med.L.Rptr. 1809 (1982).

63. *Id.*

64. *Osborne v. Ohio,* 495 U.S. 103, 110 S.Ct. 1691, 109 L.Ed.2d 98 (1990).

65. *Id.*

66. *Id.*

67. *Virginia v. American Booksellers Association,* 484 U.S. 383, 108 S.Ct. 636, 98 L.Ed.2d 782, 14 Med.L.Rptr. 2145 (1988).

68. Before remanding the case, the U.S. Supreme Court had the Virginia Supreme Court respond to the certified questions regarding statutory construction.

69. *American Booksellers Association v. Virginia,* 882 F.2d 125 (4th Cir.1989).

70. *American Booksellers Association v. Virginia, cert. denied,* 494 U.S. 1056, 110 S.Ct. 1525, 108 L.Ed.2d 764 (1990).

71. Child Pornography Prevention Act of 1996, Pub. L. 104-208, 18 U.S.C. §2251 (1996).

72. *Ashcroft v. Free Speech Coalition,* 535 U.S. 234, 122 S.Ct. 1389, 152 L.Ed.2d 403 (2002).

73. *Id.*

74. *Bookseller Charged with Selling Child Porn,* Lexington (Ky.) Herald-Leader (staff and wire reports), Feb. 20, 1998, at A5.

75. John Stamper, *Hotline Targets Internet Child Porn,* Lexington (Ky.) Herald-Leader (Knight-Ridder), Mar. 10, 1990, at E2. For an update on new technology applications, see Jennifer Lee, *New U.S. Database Will Track Abusers, Children in Porn*, Lexington Herald-Leader (New York Times News Service), Feb. 9, 2003, at A18.

76. *Award-Winning Film Ruled Obscene by Oklahoma Judge,* First Amendment Legal Watch, First Amendment Center at Vanderbilt University, July 10, 1997, Vol. 2, No. 27.

77. Leonard Pitts Jr., *Law Is Clumsy in Choosing Between Art and Obscenity,* Lexington (Ky.) Herald-Leader (Knight-Ridder), July 5, 1997, at A13.

78. *City of L.A. v. Alameda Books, Inc., et al.,* 535 U.S. 426, 466 (U.S. 2002).
79. Conclusions in the case of *City of Los Angeles v. Alameda Books, Inc., et al,* 535 U.S. 426, 466 (U.S. 2002) were based on a 1977 study of Hollywood, California, concluding that concentrations of adult entertainment establishments were often associated with high crime density.
80. *What to Do About the Children's Internet Protection Act,* National Coalition against Censorship Newsletter: Censorship News, 91, Fall 2003, at 4; Debbie Holt, *Filters on Net Access at Libraries Upheld,* Atlanta Journal-Constitution, June 24, 2003, at A5.
81. *City of Renton et al. v. Playtime Theatres, Inc., et al.,* 475 U.S. 41, 106 S.Ct. 925, 89 L.Ed.2d 29 (1986).
82. *Richard Arcara, District Attorney of Erie County v. Cloud Books, Inc.,* 478 U.S. 697, 106 S.Ct. 3172, 92 L.Ed.2d 568 (1986).
83. *United States v. O'Brien,* 391 U.S. 367, 88 S.Ct. 1673, 20 L.Ed.2d 672 (1968).
84. *Richard Arcara, District Attorney of Erie County v. Cloud Books, Inc.*
85. *New York Judge Upholds City's Sex Shop Zoning Law,* First Amendment Legal Watch, First Amendment Center at Vanderbilt University, Oct. 21, 1996, Vol. 1, No. 49.
86. Attorney General Commission on Pornography Final Report (July 1986).
87. McDonald, *Sex Crimes, Porno Linked, Report Says,* Atlanta Constitution, July 10, 1986, at A2.
88. *Id.*
89. *Id.*
90. Racketeering Influenced and Corrupt Organizations (RICO) Act of 1970, 18 U.S.C. §1961-68 (1996); Timothy Egan, *Mainstream Corporations Sell Lots of Sex,* Lexington (Ky.) Herald-Leader (New York Times News Service), Oct. 25, 2000, at A3.
91. Blodgett, *RICO v. First Amendment,* 73 A.B.A. J. 17 (Nov. 1987).
92. *Fort Wayne Books, Inc. v. Indiana,* 489 U.S. 46, 109 S.Ct. 916, 103 L.Ed.2d 34, 16 Med. L.Rptr. 1337 (1989).
93. *Id.*
94. *Alexander v. United States,* 509 U.S. 544, 113 S.Ct. 2766, 125 L.Ed.2d 441, 21 Med.L.Rptr. 1609 (1993).
95. *Richard Pope and Charles G. Morrison v. Illinois,* 481 U.S. 497, 107 S.Ct. 1918, 95 L.Ed.2d 439, 14 Med.L.Rptr. 1001 (1987).
96. *Id.*
97. *Id.*
98. *State Offers Pee-Wee Deal for Plea of No Contest,* Lexington (Ky.) Herald-Leader (Associated Press), Oct. 30, 1991, at A8.
99. McFadden, *Experts Shocked by Obscenity Decision,* Lexington (Ky.) Herald-Leader (New York Times News Service), June 9, 1990, at A2; Parker, *Federal Judge Finds Rap LP Obscene,* Washington Post, June 7, 1990, at A1.
100. *Skyywalker Records, Inc. v. Navarro,* 739 F.Supp. 578, 17 Med.L.Rptr. 2073 (S.D. Fla. 1990).
101. *Id.*
102. *Man Arrested for Selling Controversial Rap Record,* Lexington (Ky.) Herald-Leader (Associated Press), June 9, 1990, at A2.
103. Parker, *Rap Singers Charged with Obscenity,* Washington Post, June 11, 1990, at A1.
104. *2 Live Crew Beats Obscenity Rap,* Lexington (Ky.), Herald-Leader (Associated Press), Oct. 21, 1990, at A10.
105. *Performers Arrested Over "Nasty" Songs* Lexington (Ky.), Herald-Leader (Associated Press), Aug. 12, 1990, at A10.
106. *Luke Records, Inc. v. Navarro,* 960 F.2d 134, 20 Med.L.Rptr. 1114 (11th Cir. 1992).
107. Andrews, *Recording Industry Unveils Warning Sticker,* Lexington (Ky.) Herald-Leader (Associated Press), May 10, 1990, at Al.
108. Harrington, *In the Wake of 2 Live Crew,* Washington Post, June 8, 1990, at Bl.
109. *Obscenity Verdict Hasn't Changed Cincinnati Chief's Outlook,* Lexington (Ky.) Herald-Leader (Associated Press), Nov. 12, 1990, at A5.
110. *Contemporary Arts Center v. Ney,* 735 F.Supp. 743 (S.D. Ohio 1990).

111. M. L. Lyke, *From Contempt to Respect*, Lexington (Ky.), Herald-Leader (Seattle Post-Intelligencer), Jan. 10, 1997, at W-18.
112. Gloria Steinem, *Flynt Is a Hustler, Not a Hero*, Lexington (Ky.) Herald-Leader (New York Times News Service), Jan. 12, 1997, at E2.
113. *Flynt To Be Arraigned May 1 in Cincinnati*, Lexington (Ky.) Herald-Leader (Associated Press), Apr. 17, 1998, at B7.
114. On a somewhat related topic on the role that women are playing in this area, see Mireya Navarro, *Rising Entrepreneurs in Sex-Related Businesses? Women*, Lexington (Ky.) Herald-Leader (New York Times News Service), Feb. 21, 2004, at A3.
115. Cable Television and Consumer Protection Act of 1992, Pub. L. 102-385, 106 Stat. 1484, 47 U.S.C. §532 (1998).
116. *Alliance for Community Media v. FCC*, 56 F.3d 105 (D.C. Cir. 1995, en banc).
117. *Denver Area Educational Telecommunications Consortium v. FCC* and *Alliance for Community Media v. FCC*, 518 U.S. 727, 116 S.Ct. 2374, 135 L.Ed.2d 888 (1997).
118. Communications Decency Act of 1996, Pub. L. 104-104, Title V, 110 Stat. 56, 47 U.S.C. §609 (1998).
119. *Saving Children or Sacrificing Rights?* Freedom Forum News, Apr 8, 1996, at 1.
120. *American Civil Liberties Union et al. v. Janet Reno, Attorney General of the United States, et al.*, 929 F.Supp. 824 (U.S.D.C. E.D. Pa. 1996). The subsequent Attorney General, John Ashcroft, fought for CIPA. He faced an early defeat but then prevailed. See 2002 U.S. Dist. Lexis 9537 and 539 U.S. 194 (2003). See also Jason Krause, *Can Anyone Stop Internet Porn?* A.B.A. J., Sept. 2002, at 56.
121. *American Civil Liberties Union et al. v. Janet Reno, Attorney General of the United States, et al.*
122. Communications Decency Act of 1996 §223(a).
123. Communications Decency Act of 1996 §223(d).
124. *Janet Reno, Attorney General of the United States, et al. v. American Civil Liberties Union et al.*, 521 U.S. 844, 117 S.Ct. 2329, 138 L.Ed.2d 874, 25 Med.L.Rptr. 1833. (1997).
125. *Id.*
126. *Id.*
127. *Id.*
128. *Id.*
129. *Sable Communications of California v. FCC*, 492 U.S. 115, 109 S.Ct. 2829, 106 L.Ed.2d. 93 (1989).
130. *Courts Approve Restrictions on "Dial-A-Porn,"* News Media & Law, Fall 1991, at 40.
131. *Dial Information Services Corp. of New York v. Thornburgh*, 938 F.2d 1535 (2nd Cir. 1991).
132. Richard Carelli, *Clampdown on Dial-A-Porn Calls Upheld*, Lexington (Ky.) Herald-Leader (Associated Press), January 28, 1992, at Al.
133. *Phone Porn Restraints Are Upheld for Children*, Lexington (Ky.) Herald-Leader (Associated Press), July 17, 1991, at   B5.
134. *Adams Newark Theatre Co. v. City of Newark*, 354 U.S. 931, 77 S.Ct. 1395, 1 L.Ed.2d 1533 (1957).
135. *California v. LaRue*, 409 U.S. 109, 93 S.Ct. 390, 34 L.Ed.2d 342 (1972).
136. *New York State Liquor Authority v. Bellanca*, 452 U.S. 714, 101 S.Ct. 2599, 69 L.Ed.2d 357, 7 Med.L.Rptr. 1500 (1981); *City of Newport, Kentucky v. Iacobucci*, 479 U.S. 92, 107 S.Ct. 383, 93 L.Ed.2d 334 (1986).
137. *Doran v. Salem Inn, Inc.*, 422 U.S. 922, 95 S.Ct. 2561, 45 L.Ed.2d 648 (1975).
138. *Barnes v. Glen Theatre, Inc.*, 501 U.S. 560,111 S.Ct. 2456, 115 L.Ed.2d 504 (1991).
139. *City of Erie v. Pops, A.M.* 529 U.S. 277 (2000) 282.
140. Joan Bertin, *Indecency Again*, National Coalition against Censorship Newsletter: Censorship News, Spring 2004, at 3.
141. *National Endowment for the Arts et al. v. Karen Finley et al., cert. granted*, 118 S.Ct. 554, 139 L.Ed.2d 396 (1997).
142. 20 U.S.C. §954(d)(1) (1998).
143. Paulette Walker Campbell, *In Supreme Court Hearing, Justices Seem to Have Mixed Views of Law on NEA Grants*, Academe Today (online version of Chronicle of Higher Education), Apr. 1, 1998.
144. *Id.*
145. *Karen Finley et al. v. National Endowment for the Arts et al.*, 795 F.Supp. 1457 (U.S.D.C. C.D. Calif., 1992).

146. *Karen Finley et al. v. National Endowment for the Arts et al.,* 100 F.3d 671 (9th Cir. 1994).

147. *Id.*

148. *National Endowment for the Arts et al. v. Karen Finley et al.,* cert. granted, 1998; Mel Gussow, *The Supreme Court: The Artist,* New York Times, June 26, 1998, at A17; Kyle MacMillan, *Artist Finley Still Ruffling Some Feathers: Icon of the Culture Wars Brings Show to Boulder,* Denver Post, Sept. 9, 2003, at F1.

149. *William Kennedy Smith Trial Boosts CNN Ratings,* Lexington (Ky.) Herald-Leader (Knight Ridder News Service), Dec. 14, 1991, at B3. Diane Sawyer's interview with Bowman helped one ABC-TV magazine program get its highest ratings ever: *Bowman Nets Top TV Rating,* Lexington (Ky.) Herald-Leader (wire services), Dec. 21, 1991, at A3.

150. Carl Sessions Stepp, *The American Media's Sex Addiction,* American Journalism Review, August/Sept. 2005, at 75, reviewing Rodger Streitmatter, *Sex Sells! The Media's Journey from Repression to Obsession,* (2005).

151. *Producer Sues Bill O'Reilly,* Las Vegas (Nev.) Review Journal, Oct. 14, 2004, at 11-A.

152. *Papers Run Obscenity Ads to Comply with Law,* Presstime, May 1991, at 46.

153. *Id.*

154. *Herceg v. Hustler,* 814 F.2d 1017 (5th Cir. 1987); Diamond and Primm, *Rediscovering Traditional Tort Typologies to Determine Media Liability for Physical Injuries: From the Mickey Mouse Club to Hustler Magazine,* 10 Hastings Comment L.J. 969–997 (1988) contains an insightful analysis of this decision and other claims of liability for physical injuries caused by media publication.

155. *Penthouse International v. Hinson McAuliffe,* 702 F.2d 925, 7 Med.L.Rptr. 1798 (N.D. Ga. 1981); *aff'd by evenly divided court,* 717 F.2d 517 (11th Cir. 1983).

156. *Id.*

157. *City of Erie v. Pops,* A.M. 529 U.S. 277 (2000).

158. O'Connell, *Future Computers Will Turn Sexual Fantasy into "Reality,"* Lexington Herald-Leader (Orlando Sentinel), May 6, 1991, at B3.

159. Regarding the Children's Internet Protection Act, see Debbie Holt, *Filters on Net Access at Libraries Upheld,* Atlanta Journal-Constitution, June 24, 2003, at A5 and *What to Do About the Children's Internet Protection Act,* National Coalition against Censorship Newsletter: Censorship News 91, Fall 2003, at 4.

160. This same duo was fired by CBS Radio in 2002 for airing a promotional contest in which a couple claimed to have had sex in New York's St. Patrick's Cathedral. XM hired them two years later. *See* Jacques Steinberg, *XM Radio Takes Two Hosts Off the Air for 30 Days,* New York Times, May 16, 2007, at E2.

10

Right of Privacy

Big Brother in the form of an increasingly powerful government and in an increasingly powerful private sector will pile the records high with reasons why privacy should give way to national security, to law and order, to efficiency of operation, to scientific advancement and the like.

— Justice William O. Douglas

At the beginning of 2011 legislative sessions, U.S. lawmakers were examining recommendations for "do not track" mechanisms used as a means of monitoring Internet users. There was general agreement that consumers needed to better understand how information was being collected and used as a consequence of their Internet use. On the one hand, they sought support for a system to try to prevent the tracking of children's use of the Internet for commercial purposes, for example, but also questioned how such a system might work, in light of potentially undermining the development of more free, advertising-supported content, especially at a time when the nation was still facing a very demanding economic recovery.[1]

At another level in the national government, much of the discussion was couched in terms of national security. The September 11, 2001, attacks on America created an era of heightened security throughout the entire nation. Nevertheless, the collecting of data on private citizens by way of phone record scrutiny then became a major issue, when *USA Today* disclosed that the U.S. spy agency, the National Security Agency (NSA), was secretly collecting phone call records of tens of millions of Americans. The fact that the NSA did not get prior approval from a court to pursue electronic surveillance on domestic phone calls in this particular instance gave the White House the unenviable task of attempting to explain how, why, and by whom such decisions were made. The explanation of policy at that time was that the USA Patriot Act of 2001 (Uniting and Strengthening America by Providing Appropriate Tools to Intercept and Obstruct Terrorism Act) had given the government the authority to take unusual security measures to protect its citizens.

On the other hand, this challenge came as a follow-up to earlier disclosures that customer records had received scrutiny in other contexts. Most notably, this included passenger records

481

from major airlines including American and Delta and an earlier incident, when the government, anticipating a possible New Year's Eve attack on Las Vegas, put together the records of over a quarter of a million hotel guests and airplane passengers, even though no credible threat of an attack was ever uncovered. The *Las Vegas Review-Journal* reported that air passengers and hotel guests in Nevada had their records scrutinized.[2] In a similar vein, requests for customer records from search engines AOL, Yahoo, Microsoft, and Google by the U.S. Department of Justice resulted in all but Google handing over material. Subsequent attention has been paid to body scanning technology at the nation's airports and invasion of personal privacy.

Using pattern recognition, key words, and other sophisticated techniques, computers sift through massive amounts of data and produce profiles of consumer interests and tastes, areas that customers have consistently argued to be off limits for purposes of sharing or selling to outsiders.

The *New York Times* reported that President George W. Bush once authorized eavesdropping without warrants by the NSA. The companies involved in the requests including AT&T Inc., BellSouth Corp., and Verizon Communications Inc. all issued statements clarifying that they protected customer privacy and followed the law but refused to provide additional details. Verizon Wireless and T-Mobile USA Inc. denied having given material to NSA and another telecommunications company, Qwest Communications International Inc., said it had refused to turn over records. The Electronic Frontier Foundation alleged in a class action federal lawsuit that AT&T gave NSA direct access to records of millions of voice messages and Internet data.

After the public disclosure of the collection of records President Bush indicated that the government was "not mining or trolling" through lives of millions of innocent Americans and then reinforced that all efforts were focused on links to terrorists—"Al Qaeda and known affiliates." President Bush also clarified that the information sought was only related to phone numbers, time and frequency of calls, not the nature of what was said, data similar to those on typical cell phone bills each month but for both land-based and cell phone calls. While experts debated the legality, the nominee for head of the CIA at that time, General Michael Hayden, who was in charge of NSA when the surveillance program began, provided the Senate Judiciary Committee with information on NSA activities. Senator Jon Kyl, Chair of the Senate's anti-terrorism subcommittee, added: "This is nuts. We're in a war and we got to collect intelligence on the enemy, and you can't tell the enemy in advance how you're going to do it, and discussing all this stuff in public leads to that."[3]

In the aftermath of disclosures media outlets editorialized about the activity and often tied improvements in technology to growing concerns. Marc Rotenberg, executive director of the Electronic Privacy Information Center in Washington, D.C., noted, "Ten years ago, they wouldn't have compiled such a database because they didn't have the technological tools to use it once they did compile it."[4] Hayden was quickly confirmed by the U.S. Senate as the CIA head.

Several months prior to the *USA Today* story, media reports revealed that NSA had another program that did involve monitoring and recording phone conversations and e-mail messages without a court warrant—in this case, calls and e-mails within the United States involving suspected terrorists in other countries. Prior to September 11, 2001, revelation of such projects would have likely led to public outrage. Hayden received mostly praise for NSA accomplishments.

A federal judge ruled in March 2010 that the National Security Agency's surveillance without warrants was illegal. This rejected attempts by President Barack Obama's administration to keep secret the counterterrorism policies of his predecessor. Judge Vaughn R. Walker of the U.S. District Court in San Francisco ruled that the government had violated a federal statute requiring court approval for domestic surveillance intercepting phone calls in the aftermath of September 11th, 2001. The judge characterized expansive use of a so-called state secrets privilege tantamount to "unfettered executive branch discretion," with potential for abuse.[5]

Ironically, the U. S. Senate Committee on Commerce, Science, and Transportation, had earlier commended an FCC Chairman, Kevin Martin for having undertaken statutory authority to protect consumer telephone records. He appeared before the House of Representatives and testified that noncompliance by telecommunications carriers could face strong enforcement action if they violated Section 222 of the Communications Act consistent with the customer proprietary network, protecting confidentiality of customer calling activity and billing records.[6] At the same time, former *New York Times* reporter Judith Miller was in federal appeals court fighting over the government's right to access her phone records to discover which sources she called in an effort to assess information about the government's plan to search offices of two Islamic organizations after the September 11 attacks.[7]

An even better indicator of how the concept of privacy has changed in a post-September 11 world is the fact that, according to a Washington Post–ABC News poll taken by the Gallup Organization shortly after that *USA Today* story appeared, almost two-thirds of Americans, including 44% who strongly approved the project, said such efforts were acceptable in the war on terror[8] concluding "The battle of fighting terrorism, in a lot of our research, seems to be more important to the public than what they perceive as violations of their privacy—so far."[9]

By comparison, other countries used a variety of other methods to address security issues. China utilized a variety of censorship tools known more generally as "The Great Firewall" and up until March of 2010 most major media companies like Google accepted self-censorship as one price of doing business in an ever growing market. But that approach stopped when Google, who claimed it was increasingly becoming a target for hacking attacks from inside China, redirected its online traffic to a Hong Kong-based site, which it did not censor. Even though the U.S. Congress appropriated $35 million for grants to develop technology to circumvent Internet censorship and the U.S. Secretary of State Hilary Clinton championed Internet freedom on that subject, the State Department said it played no role in Google's decision to move out of China.

In theory at least, Americans continue to place a high value on privacy at a time when privacy rights are viewed as being eaten away by court decisions and statutes such as the USA Patriot Act of 2001[10] which significantly expanded the authority of the government to obtain information and tangible items via warrants as part of an investigation "to protect against international terrorism or clandestine intelligence activities." That authority included library records of individuals even if not suspected terrorists, business records, and financial information. In addition, under FCC order, all cell phones have global positioning system (GPS) chips so 911 calls can be tracked to the locations of phones.[11] Modern technologies such as these sometimes make a mockery of the concept of privacy. Coupled with the high value corporations and other business entities attach to personal information, it is not surprising that consumers are more tolerant of the use of techniques once considered obtrusive and unwarranted, yet still maintained personal privacy is worth preserving. We particularly abhor media intrusions and yet have an appetite that is difficult to satisfy sometimes when it comes to certain types of news.

An early example of how this appetite morphed into a bit of an addiction occurred when a former Miami model Donna Rice suddenly acquired unwanted celebrity status when the mass media around the country revealed that she had spent a night with presidential candidate Gary Hart in his Washington, D.C. townhouse. The *Miami Herald*, which broke the story, secretly stationed reporters outside Hart's residence (but not on his property) to watch him around the clock. Stories followed with details about the relationship between Rice and Hart, who dropped his campaign for the Democratic nomination as a result. Although the stories created considerable controversy over whether Hart, who was married at the time, and Rice had been victims of an invasion of privacy, no lawsuits were ever filed. Both individuals heavily criticized the media. In an article for the Overseas Press Club of America, *Dateline*, Rice wrote:

> I felt like a piece of chum tossed as bait into shark-infested waters. It was impossible for me to resume my normal life, and I retreated into seclusion. Silence seemed to be my only alternative since I chose not to exploit the situation.... My silence was the result of shock, a natural discretion that led me to salvage whatever shreds of privacy I could and a sense of responsibility that I should not impede the political process.[12]

Several months later she again became an object of controversy when she literally fled the Cincinnati Convention Center, where she had been scheduled to speak on the subject of media exploitation to the annual convention of the Society of Professional Journalists (SPJ). Rice was a "no show" for the panel after she saw that cameras and microphones were poised for the occasion. She issued a written statement that "it was my original understanding that this panel discussion was private and essentially off the record. But when I arrived a few minutes ago and saw the cameras, lights and tape recorders, I realized this wasn't the forum I had anticipated."[13] SPJ officials claimed that Rice had been told the press would be covering the session.

More recent cases involving Presidential Candidate John Edwards and international golf sensation, Tiger Woods, have resulted in a dearth of unwanted press attention focusing primarily on their personal lives. The caveat about the media building up a public person as a means to tearing them down seems to set the standard. In other recent instances, particularly outside the United States, celebrities have sought protection from an overly aggressive press arguing that the public's right to know must be balanced with privacy rights. In Great Britain, actors Michael Douglas and Catherine Zeta-Jones once sued a publication over unauthorized use of their wedding photos when the star couple had arranged an exclusive deal for publication of pictures with a rival publication. Zeta-Jones and Douglas won their court challenge on grounds that one publisher had an exclusive confidentiality agreement that the stars negotiated in advance.[14] That same year, model Naomi Campbell won a direct appeal to the British House of Lords concerning a story and photo related to her attendance at Narcotics Anonymous meetings. A high court ruled in her favor and the publication was required to pay court costs and more than $6,000.[15]

A great deal of attention is currently being paid to the methods used to extract information. High technology direct mail companies, called "data cowboys" by professor Bryan Pfaffenberger of the University of Virginia, acquire information about Internet users through "cookies," or software transferring code from websites to a user's hard drive.[16] The cookies allow a company to compile data about consumers, including the websites visited, computer configurations, and more—without consumer knowledge. The information is usually sold to advertisers for marketing, just as magazines and organizations sell lists to others for marketing and advertising. Some computer users know how to detect and delete cookies; others are unaware of the process.

Every time a user visits a website on the Internet, uses a credit card, telephones an 800 or 900 number, writes a check, rents a car, registers at a hotel, joins a club, orders merchandise from a catalog or through a TV shopping network, visits a physician, an emergency room, or hospital, or even notifies the post office of a change of address, personal privacy has been potentially invaded. Usually no law has been violated. Today's sophisticated computers make it possible for a wide range of government agencies, businesses, and even private individuals to access large amounts of personal information, legally and without your consent.

Credit reporting bureaus have drawn considerable flak because they are legally permitted to gather highly sensitive credit information about individuals and businesses and sell that information under certain conditions for a profit to various enterprises. Optical scanners, combined with credit card and check transactions, can compile very detailed information about individual shopping patterns. Some of the largest corporations sponsor point-of-sale data collection systems.

The largest collector of private information is the U.S. government, with the Internal Revenue Service at the top of the collector group. The Census Bureau has records on nearly everyone in the country but is prohibited by federal law from sharing any of this information, except for statistics that do not identify individuals. The FBI alone has more than 20 million criminal files and, under J. Edgar Hoover, violated civil liberties it was established to protect.

In one of many out-of-court settlements with individuals over the years, the FBI paid the widow of American Communist Party leader William Albertson $170,000 in 1989 for planting a report on Albertson during the 1960s that falsely accused him of being an FBI informer.[17] Court documents in the case revealed that the agency had tracked Albertson for five years, wiretapped thousands of phone conversations, intercepted mail, and monitored his bank account, all apparently without legal authority.[18]

With identity theft emerging as the nation's top financial crime, special attention is being paid to online access to financial information. However, the heightened awareness to the potential for this type of crime stands in stark contrast to an Annenberg Public Policy Center poll in which nearly half of the 1,500 Internet users surveyed did not know that websites can share information about them without their knowledge.[19] Consumer purchasing behavior and personal spending habits are among the most sought-after bits of information online, while privacy policies regarding the use of such information are still under study.

In a National Public Radio interview, Marc Rotenberg, executive director of the Electronic Privacy Information Center at Georgetown University, pointed to the importance of e-mail privacy. In response to challenges to the service provider Yahoo!, he suggested that in the future, individuals might want to specify in their wills what should be done with their e-mail. He encouraged the courts to get involved in this area with the likelihood that in lieu of a formal individual decision, an Internet service provider has discretion to make decisions on an individual's behalf.[20]

Probably the most serious threat to personal and even corporate privacy is the proliferation of data banks whose information can be readily accessed with a few keystrokes on a computer. Much of the information available about individuals and businesses can be obtained quickly online and locally at no or low cost. Courthouses contain a wealth of public information about personal transactions and ownership—listings of all real estate and personal property, including vehicles and large equipment registered to individuals and companies. You can even ascertain how much a property sold for and its assessed value and license plate numbers of all vehicles. Of course, any lawsuits or other civil or criminal actions taken against or on behalf of persons and organizations are also usually matters of public record. Many state, local, and federal courthouses today have converted records to computer data that can be readily accessed.

Walt Disney World announced that it would be asking for fingerprint scans from all persons 10 years old and above for theme park admittance in 2005. Theme park guests were asked to make peace signs for the scanning of the index and middle fingers in an effort to limit access to persons who purchased tickets or obtained special passes. Almost immediately, privacy organizations including the Electronic Privacy Information Center objected on grounds that guests were not informed as to how long the fingerprints would be retained nor for what other purposes the information might be used. Tied closely to the issue were added concerns regarding surveillance in public places, which included plans for research facilities in which so called living laboratories would offer opportunities to study individual consumer behavior. Citing privacy violations, the theme park fingerprint policy was challenged on grounds that the amount and type of data far exceeded traditional security demands for entrance to government facilities or even nuclear power plants.[21]

The federal government is the largest repository of personal data files. Over the years, various statutes have been enacted to prevent most agencies from sharing information with other agencies, but there have been a number of largely unsuccessful attempts to permit a linking of computer files. Privacy became a flash point in the aftermath of the September 11 attack on America. There was a heightened sense of awareness to the potential use of new technology to protect nation security interests. However, this was followed by increasing concerns about intrusion and overlapping privacy regulations in the United States and abroad, as noted earlier. The need to acquire intelligence data linked to terrorists was being weighted in this era in which new technology has been advanced along with unprecedented opportunities to acquire personal information in such areas as banking and medical records.

The general public has become better informed about sacrifices individuals were beginning to make in the interest of national security, further complicating the philosophical issues associated with a patchwork of privacy laws and regulations developing across jurisdictions and applying to such broad areas as medical records, banking, protection from spam, and protection of children from online predators or cyber-bullies.

The suicide of a 15-year-old South Hadley, Massachusetts, high school freshman student, Phoebe Prince, after being the continuing target of a rash of bullying—including cyber-bullying; both inside and outside of her high school, led some people to believe that the Massachusetts state legislature would address bullying, and they quickly set about the task with both houses of the state legislature quickly approving such a bill. The thinking was that a stronger legal position against such bullies might give schools more tools to address the growing issue as computers and cell phones allowed traditional playground bullies to morph into an electronic menace, including female "bad girls" who taunted some fellow students and previously functioned "under the radar." This type of activity was also investigated with the knowledge that such bullies often functioned with an anonymous chorus of online cheerleaders from their schools urging on the bad behavior.

Accounts of the death also described the circumstances for the newly arrived student from

County Clare, Ireland, and that she had yet to master American culture. In the aftermath of the death, it was said that she had been hounded to her grave by bullies from her new school which included using text messages and social networking websites to target her. The thinking was that if the laws in this area became stricter, schools would be able to address bullies' online tactics before another vulnerable student felt there was no escape from harassment. But the free speech protections and legal constraints, central to the U.S. Constitution, make it difficult to address cyber-bullying. And schools are not permitted to discipline a student for off-campus speech unless it causes what the courts have called a "substantial disruption" to the climate of the school. And the U.S. Supreme Court has left that term, *substantial disruption*, deliberately vague. And since no one has a definitive picture for the term, every school is left to try to figure it out.

Dr. Elizabeth Englander, head of the Massachusetts Aggression Reduction Center (MARC), often pointed out that legislative attention typically focuses on what schools can do to address and then try to reduce bullying, adding that the parents are the key element in reducing the problem while stressing that almost all cyber-bullying by teenagers takes place on computers at home. Parents don't know what their children are up to online, and they generally don't talk about it. And Englander conducted extensive research showing cyber-bullies could not be legislated into better behavior.

About a quarter of the students surveyed said they had been the target of traditional "in-your-face" bullying; but almost 60% experienced cyber-bullying. Between 5% and 7% of students admitted to being traditional bullies themselves; and a little over a quarter admitted to being cyber-bullies. Nearly 70% of high school teenagers said their parents either didn't worry or very rarely worried about cyber-bullying, while a little over half said their parents put no restrictions whatsoever on how long or what they did online. Englander said that bullying had become a public health issue and educational programs on other tough teen issues such as teen smoking and drunk-driving had led to a sizeable reduction in those problem areas. She also noted the need to give schools more guidance on when they might legally intervene in a situation, as a means of teaching them what they can do to address a teen at risk.

In spite of the legal restrictions Englander encouraged schools to have regular informational meetings with those identified as bullies as a means of supporting victims to ensure there is less likely to be bullying at school. But all of her advisories concluded with a finger pointed squarely at the bully's parents as the ultimate disciplinarians and overseers of computer use, in their role in the home.

The immediate follow-up to this case was that Massachusetts legal authorities spelled out a litany of charges against the nine teenagers accused of subjecting the 15-year-old to almost three months of tortuous harassment before she hanged herself. This suicide had sparked statewide horror and also prompted intense public debate on the nature of bullying. The Northwestern District Attorney in this case, Elizabeth Scheibel, outlined the charges and faulted officials at South Hadley High School, saying her investigation determined the girl's harassment had been "common knowledge" at the school, contradicting previous assertions by administrators' that they had been unaware of the problems faced by the student until after her death. In presenting the charges, Scheibel also described the student's last day at school, saying her investigation found the Irish immigrant was being taunted in the hallways and bombarded by a series of vulgar insults, subjected to verbal harassment and the threat of physical abuse, her death being the result of a nearly-three month campaign of verbally assaultive behavior and threats of physical harm.

As she studied in the library during lunch that day, for example, the accused students alleg-edly hounded her openly while other students and a teacher observed. Witnesses alerted school administrators only after her death. She said online harassment played only a secondary role, although a prominent columnist for the *Boston Globe*, Kevin Cullen, reported that some of the student bullies allegedly involved in this case even posted mocking statements on their Face-book page, after the death had taken place.[22]

The nature of charges from criminal harassment and civil rights violations to stalking and statutory rape cast a very wide net in the case. This hinted at a very forceful strategy of using many legal avenues in the pursuit of convictions. School officials became the target of an incredible amount of criticism in the press, and the prosecutors' assertions regarding the lack of parental and school oversight prompted some parents to also pressure School Committee mem-bers to take action against administrators at the school. Administrators said they were unaware of the bullying until after the student's death. But Prosecutor Scheibel said that students, some teachers and administrators were well aware of the harassment of Prince and that her mother had actually spoken with two school staff members about her daughter's troubles. Scheibel said the school's inaction was "troublesome" but did not constitute criminal behavior but lack of understanding of harassment associated with teen dating was prevalent at the school.

Because of a volatile economy, another key interest in privacy cases relates to personal finances. Financial experts urge consumers to scrutinize their credit card bills regularly and check their credit reports at least once a year to ensure they are accurate. Mistakes are common. When reports are legitimately shared with creditors and others, some errors can have serious consequences for consumers. Under federal law, credit bureaus are required, upon request, to send free copies to individuals who have been denied credit as results of reports and to allow anyone affected by negative information in a report to insert an explanation of up to 100 words. Consumers can order free copies of their reports once a year from the big three bureaus— Experian, Equifax, and TransUnion. The reports can even be ordered via the Internet.

Caller identification (CID) service has become extremely popular for both land-based and cell phones, but it faced strong criticism in some circles when telephone companies first mar-keted the service decades ago. To the phone companies who sell the service as a deterrent against obscene and other harassing calls, CID is another customer convenience for increasing revenues. To civil libertarians, the service is an unwarranted invasion of privacy that promises the demise of the anonymous phone call.[23] The phone companies won, civil libertarians lost, and CID is now part of American culture, along with call forwarding, call waiting, and voice mail. Not all consumers are concerned about the privacy issue and see CID as a convenient means of privately screening numbers and preventing harassment calls.

The technology gets more sophisticated each day as the opportunities increase for invad-ing privacy. In a *Time* cover story, published at the end of the last decade, the magazine listed 15 everyday events that provide for lessened privacy, including bank machines, prescription drug purchases, phone calls, cellular phones, voter registration, credit cards, sweepstake entries, electronic tolls, mail order purchases, and e-mail.[24] That same year, a story in the *ABA Jour-nal* cited three technologies that represent even greater threats—magnetic gradient measuring, back-scattered x-ray imaging, and passive millimeter wave imaging. The first technology uses fluctuations in the earth's magnetic field to locate any metals, including weapons, inside a building. The second bounces minimal doses of x-rays off a person's skin to create an image of a body, such as that of a passenger in an airport. The third can detect a body's electromagnetic waves as well as any objects on a person.[25]

With the improvement of thermal imaging and similar body scans technology for the purpose of detecting hidden weapons in a less intrusive way, personal privacy has become a bigger and even more complicated issue at the nation's airports. The concept of privacy is a broad issue that actually encompasses a bundle of individual rights that derive from myriad sources—from common law to statutes to the Constitution. Most Western societies have imposed various restrictions to ensure at least some semblance of individual privacy. The First, Fourth, and Fifth Amendments to the Constitution specify certain conditions under which privacy must be reserved. The First Amendment provides for freedom of press, speech, and religion as a means of ensuring that one's political beliefs and expressions may not be suppressed or adversely used by the government. The Fourth Amendment recognizes a right to be protected "against unreasonable searches and seizures," a right that has been broadened over the years, and the Fifth Amendment guarantees against self-incrimination, prohibiting the government from forcing persons to testify against themselves in criminal actions. Many Western constitutions make similar guarantees, but in some cultures, the concept of privacy has a much different meaning.

A fight over the Supreme Court nomination of Judge Robert Bork arose over privacy in 1987 when the candidate, who was nominated by President Ronald Reagan, responded to questions at his Senate hearing about the issue of privacy by saying that he could not find such a right in the Constitution.[26] Bork was a vocal proponent of the strict constructionist judicial philosophy that holds that judges should interpret the U.S. Constitution in light of the original intent of the framers. The U.S. Senate rejected his nomination in a 58 to 42 vote, but one of the ironic outcomes of the hearing was the eventual enactment of the Video Privacy Protection Act of 1988.[27] During Bork's nomination, a list of videos he had rented was leaked to the press. There was nothing particularly provocative, but Congress felt compelled to pass legislation banning the "wrongful disclosure of video tape rental or sale records."[28]

Almost two decades later, privacy issues arose in the complex process to fill positions of U.S. Supreme Court Justices by the George W. Bush administration to replace the late U.S. Chief Justice William Rehnquist and Associate Justice Sandra Day O'Connor. The dilemma arose again when Congressional lawmakers questioned whether privacy issues should take on a special status in the post-September 11 era. After a 78 to 22 vote of approval from the Senate in 2005, U.S. Court of Appeals Judge John Roberts was sworn in as the 17th Chief Justice of the United States. The following year another U.S. Court of Appeals Judge, Samuel Alito, replaced Justice O'Connor, after a 58 to 42 vote of approval from the Senate. Both justices were queried about rights to privacy. Both dodged the question of whether such rights could be found in the U.S. Constitution, noting instead the importance of respecting U.S. Supreme Court precedents on the issue.

Some scholars argue we have entered a new age in which information technology now offers instantaneous access to information in formerly protected areas— protected somewhat by previously slow, cumbersome technology. Eugene Volokh, a UCLA law professor and former clerk to Justice Sandra Day O'Connor, has pointed to the need to rethink privacy law in an era in which government documents can be easily and instantaneously retrieved. He points out how a lot of personal information has been considered part of the public record, though seldom accessed.[29] Now, at a time when personal information such as birth dates, addresses, and property ownerships can be downloaded and placed in aggregate form, new questions arise about acquisition, storage, and judicious use of such material.

Professor Irvin Altman once examined privacy as a generic process concluding it is present in all cultures regulating privacy.[30] Those differences can be dramatic. Among Indians of central Brazil, houses tend to be placed so people can be seen as they move around. Housing is communal, people enter dwellings without announcing themselves; but secret paths and clearings in surrounding woods allow them to get away. In Balinese culture, families live in homes surrounded by walls. Entrances to doors are narrow. Only family and friends enter without permission. Members of a Moslem sect in Northern Africa wear sleeveless outer garments. Men wear veils and headdresses that permit only their eyes to be uncovered; veils are always worn.[31]

Judicial Origins of a Right of Privacy

Virtually every treatise or text on the origins of the tort of invasion of privacy in the United States traces its development to an 1890 *Harvard Law Review* article by Boston lawyers Samuel D. Warren and Louis D. Brandeis.[32] Brandeis was appointed 26 years later as an Associate Justice of the Supreme Court of the United States, where he served until 1939. The article—one of the most influential law reviews on invasion of privacy—appeared at the height of the era of "yellow journalism." This was the heyday of editors and publishers such as Joseph Pulitzer and William Randolph Hearst, whose newspapers appealed to the masses by reflecting the times.

From the end of the Civil War (1865) to the end of the 19th century, "industrialization, mechanization, and urbanization brought extensive social, cultural, and political changes: the rise of the city, improved transportation and communication, educational advances, political unrest, and the rise of the labor movement."[33] It was inevitable that a sense of loss of privacy would develop, especially among the well-heeled and prominent lawyers like Brandeis and Warren. They no doubt scorned the focus on sensationalism in news, just as they probably mourned the extent to which a growing population meant a decrease in physical privacy or "personal space." Some critics would argue those descriptions of news still ring true: "When personal gossip attains the dignity of print, and crowds the space available for matters of real interest to the community, what wonder that the ignorant and thoughtless mistake its relative importance."[34]

In their article, Brandeis and Warren proposed a new tort of invasion of privacy that would today fall into the category of *unreasonable publication of embarrassing private matters*. They did not deal directly with the other three categories of invasion of privacy—*intrusion, appropriation,* and *false light*. Libel was already a tort in most jurisdictions at that time, and they drew on principles of libel for their tort of invasion of privacy concept, in which words as well as pictures would be subject to liability and damages would be available for mental anguish and other harm. However, the two authors asserted that, unlike libel, truth should not be a valid defense to invasion of privacy. The focus was the concern that private affairs of prominent and well-heeled not become the subjects of intense scrutiny. To some extent, this remains a concern, although invasion of privacy has been broadened to include private individuals (i.e., nonpublic figures), but much of the litigation links to public figures who felt privacy was violated.

The ideas enunciated by Brandeis and Warren attracted attention among legal scholars, but no court was prepared to recognize a common law right of privacy and no legislature was willing to take the initiative to enact a statute granting such a right. The New York courts had the first opportunity to acknowledge a common law right of privacy, but chose to defer to the legislature. After a lithographed image of her appeared without her consent in an extensive advertising campaign for "The Flour of the Family," an attractive young girl named Abigail Roberson sued the flour company for invasion of privacy. The trial court and lower appellate court ruled Roberson was entitled to damages for the humiliation, embarrassment, and emotional distress she had suffered because of the ads. However, in a 4–3 decision in *Roberson v. Rochester Folding Box Company* (1902),[35] the New York Court of Appeals (the highest appellate court in the state) rejected her claim on grounds that (a) no previous precedent had established a right of privacy; (b) if the trial court decision were permitted to prevail, a flood of litigation would inevitably follow; (c) it would be difficult to limit application of such a right, if recognized, to appropriate circumstances; and (d) such a right might unduly restrict freedom of speech and press. The court also implied that creation of such a right was more the province of the legislature than the courts. The court did cite Brandeis and Warren but rejected arguments. In their strong dissent, the three dissenting judges attacked the majority for its failure to recognize privacy as an inherent right.

Both the public and politicians assailed the decision. The New York Court of Appeals decision sufficiently outraged the state legislature to enact a statute the next year (1903) that provided both civil and criminal liability for "a person, firm or corporation that uses for advertising purposes, or the purposes of trade, the name, portrait or picture of any living person without having first obtained the written consent of such person."[36] The law included minors such as Roberson in its protection, requiring that consent be obtained from a parent or guardian. The statute did not protect the use of a dead person's name or image, and consent was an absolute defense. A few states still do not recognize a right of privacy for the deceased, but the trend is toward granting a right of publicity even after death. The statute made the offense a misdemeanor, but permitted compensatory and punitive damages in a civil suit. That statutory provision in altered form still survives today, although New York statutes now include other privacy torts such as intrusion.

In 1905 Georgia became the first state to recognize a common law right of privacy. Once again, however, it was not a broad right of privacy but, similar to the right granted in New York, it was limited to commercial use or appropriation. Paolo Pavesich, an Atlanta artist, awoke one morning to find his photograph and a testimonial in a newspaper advertisement for the New England Life Insurance Company. The ad was quite complimentary of Pavesich; it portrayed him as handsome and successful, touting virtues of good life insurance. Unfortunately, he had not consented for his picture to appear in the ad and testimonial had been made up by a copywriter.

In *Pavesich v. New England Life Insurance Company* (1905),[37] the Georgia Supreme Court reversed the trial court decision, which dismissed Pavesich's claim for damages. The court rejected *Roberson* holding (which was binding only in New York) and bought arguments advanced by Warren and Brandeis. It was some time before other courts jumped on the bandwagon, but when they hopped aboard, they limited right to commercial use. Many courts refused to recognize it until the 1930s and 1940s when value of endorsements became apparent.

Why did it take so long for courts and legislatures to act? The courts were probably reluctant because they tend to avoid establishing sweeping precedents. Instead, they defer to legislatures because precedents are difficult to overturn but statutes can be changed by simply enacting new legislation. Legislatures likely did not get involved because there was no strong public pressure until incidents such as the *Roberson* case pointed to the need for privacy protection. Pulitzer, Hearst, Scripps and their colleagues gave readers heavy doses of sensationalism, including facts about the private lives of public figures, but they wrote about ordinary people in a positive light except when they were involved in alleged criminal activities. The huge success of the "new journalism" newspapers demonstrated an insatiable public appetite for private information. The U.S. Constitution and most state constitutions do not enumerate privacy rights other than prohibiting unreasonable search and seizure and self-incrimination. There was simply no overriding concern with privacy at the time they were written.

Why was this right restricted principally to appropriation for so long? Why not include other privacy rights? Physical intrusion was fairly difficult to accomplish because people had no phones to tap, no recording devices, no microphones to hide, and so on, and the tort of trespass was already available to prevent someone from intruding on another's land or physical solitude.

The torts of false light, publicizing private matters, and appropriation all involve publication. The New York Court of Appeals in *Roberson* pointed to a possible explanation for excluding these torts. It noted that any injury Roberson may have suffered was mental, not physical, and that targets of publicity might actually be pleased to get such attention. In other words, Roberson should have been flattered that a company would want to use her image.

What Is the Right of Privacy?

Black's Law Dictionary defines right of privacy as "the right to be let alone; the right of a person to be free from unwarranted publicity."[38] William L. Prosser, foremost authority on the law of torts until his death, delineated invasion of privacy in four torts:

1. *Appropriation* of one person's name or likeness for the benefit or advantage of another
2. *Intrusion* upon an individual's physical solitude or seclusion
3. *Public disclosure* of highly objectionable private facts
4. Publicity that places and individual in a *false light* in the public eye[39]

This chapter examines each of these four torts of invasion of privacy. Although each is distinct from the others, they also overlap. It is common for two or more of the torts to arise from the same facts, but each tort is reviewed separately and overlapping characteristics are noted.

Appropriation

Appropriation is by far the oldest form of invasion of privacy recognized at common law, as *Pavesich* demonstrates, but it is the one tort of the four that poses minimal problems for the mass media. The courts have generally held that even though newspapers, magazines, and broadcasters make substantial profits from the dissemination of stories about people from the ordinary person to the millionaire movie star, they cannot be held liable for appropriation so long as the profit-making is incidental to the use. CBS does not have to get consent or pay a rock group when *60 Minutes* does a feature on them. NBC need not seek permission of the

President when the *Nightly News* covers a presidential press conference. However, the media are not relieved of liability for strictly commercial use of a person's name, image, or likeness.

There have been some interesting examples of alleged appropriation. The late host of *Mr. Rogers' Neighborhood* of the Public Broadcasting System, once convinced Burger King Corporation to pull a 30-second commercial aired around the country. The commercial that cost $150,000 to produce featured a "Mr. Rodney" teaching viewers to say "McFrying" (taking a whack at Burger King's competitor). According to news reports, the ad had appeared about two dozen times on the major commercial TV networks and 30 to 40 times in typical major markets.[40] Mr. Rogers never sued, but the commercials were cut after he complained. About the same time, Eddie Murphy was doing his ghetto-ized version of *Mr. Rogers' Neighborhood* on *Saturday Night Live*. Murphy's skits were some of the most popular segments on the comedy show at that time and no challenge occurred then.

Film director Woody Allen once received $425,000 in an out-of-court settlement with National Video, Inc., after the video rental franchise firm used look-alike Phil Boroff in an advertisement in 1984. As part of the settlement, Allen dropped suits against Boroff and his agency, Ron Smith Celebrity Look-Alikes. There was no disclaimer and Allen was not mentioned by name in the ad, although two of his movies, *Bananas* and *Annie Hall,* appear alongside two films, *The Maltese Falcon* and *Casablanca*, featured prominently.[41]

Vanna White of TV's *Wheel of Fortune* game show sued Samsung Electronics of California for $1 million for using what she claimed was her likeness to sell its brand of consumer electronics without her consent. In 1992 the Ninth Circuit U.S. Court of Appeals unanimously dismissed White's claim of appropriation, ruling that her name and likeness had not been used, but a majority of the court upheld her common law claim for misappropriation of her identity.[42] The United States Supreme Court denied certiorari.

In *Rosa Parks v. LaFace Records* (2003),[43] the Sixth Circuit U.S. Court of Appeals ruled that civil rights icon Rosa Parks had a cause of action against the rap group OutKast for unauthorized use of her name as title of a song. Parks, who died in 2005, became a well-known civil rights figure after she refused to give up her seat on a city bus in Montgomery, Alabama, to a white passenger, leading to her arrest. Her defiance eventually resulted in a boycott of the bus company spearheaded by Dr. Martin Luther King, Jr. Historians trace the start of the civil rights movement to her action.[44]

Parks claimed the use of her name in the song constituted false advertising under the Lanham (federal trademark) Act and her right of publicity had been infringed. The federal appellate court reversed a U.S. District Court summary judgment in favor of OutKast. The appellate court said the test was whether the title had "artistic relevance" to the original work or whether it "explicitly misleads as to the source or the content of the work" (citing earlier precedent).[45]

The court rejected the Outkast's defense that the use was metaphorical and symbolic, noting the group said in an interview they had not intended for the song to refer to Parks or the civil rights movement but to send a message that other rap artists could not compete with them and thus should "move to the back of the bus," a phrase repeated in the song. The court characterized the chorus as "pure egomania," probably a disguised ad intended only to attract attention.

Interestingly, after Rosa Parks died, a dispute developed over her estate, including appropriation rights for her name and image. Parks, who was 92 when she passed away, left the bulk of her estate to a nonprofit organization, the Rosa and Raymond Parks Institute for Self Development. Her will was challenged by relatives, who then reached an out-of-court settlement.

Before his famous name was tarnished by his off the course behavior, the same appellate court ruled against golfer Tiger Woods in *ETW Corp. v. Jireh Publishing* (2003)[46] when he sued a publisher for marketing limited edition prints by "America's sports artist" Rick Rush. The prints commemorated Woods' early win in the Masters' Tournament, featuring him in three different poses with other famous golfers and the famed Augusta, Georgia, clubhouse in the background. The court said the prints were not violations of Woods' right of publicity nor the Lanham Act but were protected by the First Amendment because they focused on an "historic sporting event" and the artist had added a significant creative component.[47]

Why do sports and entertainment celebrities and other public figures go to great lengths, including litigation, to protect their images from unauthorized commercial exploitation? The simple answer is economics. The amounts of the out-of-court settlements and even jury awards are typically not high, but the long-term potential for earnings from authorized endorsements for some public figures can be very lucrative.

The number of television and film stars and famous athletes who have made commercial endorsements over the years is large, with some figures becoming more famous for their commercials than their career feats. Few celebrities reject the opportunity to sell major brand products and services because the compensation can be quite attractive and the work involved in doing such ads is typically not demanding or time consuming. A few stars refuse to sell rights in the United States out of concern that their images could be become tainted here, but nevertheless appear in ads in other countries where less stigma may be attached to endorsements. Much of the stigma or perceived loss of professional credibility connected with endorsements has actually disappeared even in the United States as more celebrities hop on the endorsement bandwagon. A recent trend is for celebrities to lend voices but not their names or images for commercial use.

Digital imaging now makes it possible to have the images of deceased celebrities endorse products in digitized commercials in which they never appeared when alive. For years, deceased stars have been featured in still photos endorsing products and services, but beginning in the 1990s they began popping up in videos. The deceased celebrities included John Wayne, Humphrey Bogart, and Ed Sullivan.[48] Forty-five states and the District of Columbia now recognize appropriation or misappropriation as a privacy tort. Only Iowa, Montana, North Dakota, South Dakota, and Wyoming have not directly recognized this cause of action. In Oregon, the state supreme court has not adopted the tort, but it has been recognized by the intermediate appellate court. In Alaska, there have been no reported cases since 1926.[49]

Appropriation is not limited to public figures. Private individuals can also recover for appropriation. It is quite rare for such persons to sue and even rarer for them to win awards, but some have prevailed. There are two major reasons for the lack of cases. First, private individuals appear in the media less frequently than public officials and public figures. Second, private individuals have a tough task in demonstrating substantial damages, especially in establishing lost potential earnings. Although the plaintiff in an appropriation case theoretically need only demonstrate (a) commercial use and (b) identification (i.e., that a reasonable person could recognize the image or name used as that of the plaintiff), in reality, some commercial gain must usually be shown to allow recovery of significant damages. Because the market value of commercial use of a private figure's image, name, or likeness is usually severely limited, damages are usually low.

Although only living persons may secure damages for the other types of privacy invasion, appropriation is different. Courts in three states—Georgia, New Jersey, and Utah—have said the appropriation right is descendible (may be passed to heirs). Ten states—California (50 years), Florida (40 years), Illinois (50 years), Kentucky (50 years), Nebraska, Nevada, Oklahoma, Tennessee, Texas, and Virginia (20 years)—have enacted statutes that permit the heirs of a deceased figure to assume and control publicity rights for a time after the person's death. The statutes in five states —Arizona, Massachusetts, New York, Rhode Island, and Wisconsin—either bar the survival of such rights after death or a court in the state has interpreted the statute to impose a ban.[50]

U.S. News & World Report readers were once surprised when they opened their magazine to find theoretical physicist Albert Einstein gracing an ad for an Olympic Wood Preservative. Although Einstein died in 1955, his image and name were licensed by his heirs to a Beverly Hills agency that also licensed Marilyn Monroe (who died in 1962) and even Sigmund Freud (1856–1939).[51] The Little Tramp Character of Charlie Chaplin (who died in 1977) has appeared in IBM commercials, and other deceased notables appear in ads. The length of time during which the right of publicity is protected after death varies from state to state, with some extending protection as long as 50 years after death. No advertiser should ever assume that protection no longer exists for appropriation after an individual dies because the result of using such an image without consent could serve as an unnecessary and expensive lesson.

Hugo Zacchini v. Scripps-Howard Broadcasting Company *(1977)*

Only one appropriation case has been decided by the U.S. Supreme Court, although a growing number of cases are meandering through the lower federal and state courts. In *Hugo Zacchini v. Scripps-Howard Broadcasting Company* (1977),[52] a case whose impact on appropriation is not entirely clear, the Supreme Court ruled that a TV station could be held liable for invasion of privacy for broadcasting the entire act of a performer. What was the "entire act"? About 15 seconds of Hugo Zacchini shot from a cannon to a net 200 feet away. Interestingly, the filmed performance was shown during a regular 11:00 p.m. newscast, not as part of an entertainment program. Newsworthiness is a limited defense to three of the four types of invasion of privacy—but not intrusion. Thus, if newsworthiness could have been demonstrated in this case, the result would have been different.

A freelance reporter for WEWS-TV in Cleveland recorded the human cannonball at a county fair despite the fact that on the previous day Zacchini had specifically denied the reporter's request. Reporters had free access to the fair, and the general public was charged an admission fee that included Zacchini's act. Moreover, the commentary by the anchors that accompanied the film clip on the TV station was quite favorable, encouraging viewers to attend the fair and to see the human cannonball's performance.

Zacchini claimed, however, that broadcast of his act without his consent violated his right of publicity and he was entitled to $25,000 in damages for harm to his *professional* privacy. In his suit, the performer took an unusual tack—he contended that by showing the entire act, the station deprived him of potential revenue. As the Supreme Court of the United States noted in its narrow 5 to 4 decision:

> If … respondent [the TV station] had merely reported that petitioner was performing at the fair and described or commented on his act, with or without showing his picture

on television, we would have a very different case.… His complaint is that respondent filmed his entire act and displayed that film on television for the public to see and enjoy.[53]

The state trial court had granted the station summary judgment in the $25,000 suit, but an intermediate state appeals court reversed the decision. The Ohio Supreme Court reversed again, holding that the station had a First and a Fourteenth Amendment right to broadcast the act as a matter of public interest in the absence of intent to injure the plaintiff or to appropriate his work. The U.S. Supreme Court disagreed strongly with the state supreme court. The Ohio Supreme Court had relied heavily on *Time Inc. v. Hill* (1967),[54] discussed *in the section on false light*, but Justice Byron White, writing for the Supreme Court majority, noted major differences in the two torts involved—false light and appropriation. The majority argued that (a) the state's interest in providing a cause of action was different for the two, and (b) the two torts differ considerably in the extent to which they restrict the flow of information to the public.

On the first point, the Court noted that false light involves reputation, parallel to libel, but the right of publicity is linked to "the proprietary interest of the individual in his act in part to encourage such entertainment." The appropriate parallel for right of publicity is patent and copyright law, according to the Court. For the second point, the majority asserted that false light victims want to minimize publicity, but the typical plaintiff in a right of publicity case usually wants extensive publicity as "long as he gets the commercial benefit of such publication."[55] In other words, false light plaintiffs want to stay out of the limelight whereas right of publicity plaintiffs want media attention on their terms—that is, with financial compensation.

No other appropriation case has ever been decided by the U.S. Supreme Court, and even *Zacchini* was not a full-blown or pure appropriation case because it dealt specifically with the *right of publicity*, a tort that some states including Ohio treat somewhat differently from appropriation. States that make a distinction generally do so by confining a right of publicity to celebrities who can demonstrate commercial value of their names, images, or likenesses and require that the public figures have either sold or could have sold such rights. This illustrates, again, why it is much easier for a public figure to recover for appropriation or right of publicity than a private individual. Obviously, a right-of-publicity plaintiff does not have to be a nationally prominent or even a regional celebrity. Zacchini was no media star. In fact, although very few people then knew or now know of him and his act, the Supreme Court permitted him to pursue his appropriation claim.

Zacchini left many questions. Is a right of publicity triggered only by the unauthorized dissemination of an entire work or could this right apply for *substantial portions* of a work, similar to copyright infringement? Does this right survive the death of a person and thus become transferable to heirs? (Although some states, as noted earlier, recognize a right of publicity that survives the individual, this right has not been recognized by the Supreme Court.) Does the right extend to private individuals or is it restricted to public performers or public figures? Would the Court have ruled differently if Zacchini had been shot out of the cannon during a small company reception or if he had simply been an audience volunteer? What if his act had been filmed as part of a public celebration for which the human cannonball had been paid by the local government or a corporate sponsor, but for which the audience was not charged admission?

Although appropriation is virtually unheard of in the U.S. Supreme Court, many cases have been decided in lower federal courts and state courts. Certain names that crop up frequently are most valuable from a publicity perspective. Elvis Presley's name has appeared in several cases. His name has become even more valuable after his death because his popularity has soared and royalties and income from rights have poured into his estate.

The executors of Presley's estate have been aggressive in protecting these rights. As a result, they have been involved in almost a dozen suits against nonprofit and commercial enterprises that have attempted to cash in on the Elvis name. Three of those cases are reviewed here because they illustrate the complexity and range of application of the right of publicity.

The Elvis Cases—All Shook Up?

Three days after Elvis Presley died on August 16, 1977, a company known as Pro Arts marketed a poster entitled "In Memory." Above the photograph of Presley was the epithet "1935–1977." The copyright to the photograph had been purchased by Pro Arts from a staff photographer for the *Atlanta Journal*. Five days after it began distributing the poster, the company notified Boxcar Enterprises, the Tennessee Corporation established by Presley and his manager, Col. Tom Parker, for the sublicensing to other companies for the manufacture, distribution, and sale of merchandise bearing the Elvis name and likeness. Two days after Presley's death, Boxcar Enterprises had granted another company, Factors etc., the exclusive license to commercially use the image. Factors told Pro Arts to immediately halt sale of the poster or risk a suit. Pro Arts ignored the warning and filed suit in a U.S. District Court in *Ohio* seeking a declaratory judgment that it had not infringed on Factors' rights. Factors, in turn, successfully sought a preliminary injunction in U.S. District Court in New York to halt any further distribution or sale of the posters and any other Elvis merchandise. On appeal to the U.S. Court of Appeals for the Second Circuit, the lower court injunction was upheld:

> In conclusion, we hold that the district court did not abuse its discretion in granting the injunction since Factors has demonstrated a strong likelihood of success on the merits at trial. Factors possesses the exclusive right to print and distribute Elvis Presley memorabilia.… Pro Arts infringed that right by printing and distributing the Elvis Presley poster, a poster whose publication was not privileged as a newsworthy event.[56]

The defendant, Pro Arts, had claimed in district court and in the appellate court that (a) the right of publicity did not survive the death of a celebrity and (b) it was privileged, as a matter of law, in printing and distributing the poster because it commemorated a newsworthy event. The U.S. Court of Appeals handily rejected both arguments. The court noted that the duration of any right of publicity was governed by state law—in this case, New York law—because this was a case involving diversity jurisdiction. (In federal court, *state* law prevails.) Even though the appellate court could find no New York state court cases directly addressing the issue, it cited *Memphis Development Foundation v. Factors, Etc., Inc.* (1977)[57] and *Price v. Hal Roach Studios, Inc.* (1975)[58]—to support its position that the right of publicity did survive a celebrity's death.

In *Memphis Development Foundation*, a U.S. District Court in Tennessee held that Factors etc. (the same company in the case at hand) had been legally granted exclusive rights to capitalize on and publicize Presley's name and likeness, that the right of publicity survives a celebrity's death, and that Factors was entitled to a preliminary injunction to prevent the non-profit Memphis Development Foundation from giving away eight-inch pewter replicas to anyone who contributed $25.00 or more toward a $200,000 fund to cast and erect a bronze statue of Presley.

Factors did not contest the right of the organization to commission and erect the statue, only the specific right to distribute replicas. It is unlikely that erecting a statue under these conditions for public display with no admission charge would be considered a violation of the right of publicity. Why then would distribution of the replicas at no profit but solely for the purpose of financing the statue be a violation? Non-profit status does *not* automatically grant a corporation a license to essentially deprive an owner or authorized user of profits from a work. The non-profit organization stands in essentially the same stead as a "for profit" enterprise. Deprivation is deprivation, regardless of the worthiness of the cause.

What is the underlying rationale for permitting states to extend a right of publicity beyond a person's death? Harm to the individual's reputation is not at stake because courts have consistently ruled that other rights of privacy—where they are recognized, such as publication of private matters, intrusion and false light—do *not* survive a person's death. Nearly all state and federal courts that have been presented the question have held that an individual cannot be defamed once he or she has died. The answer lies in a judicial doctrine known as *unjust enrichment*. This doctrine, grounded in principles of equity and justice, holds that "one person should not be permitted unjustly to enrich himself at expense of another, but should be required to make restitution of or for property or benefits received, retained or appropriated."[59]

The intent of this judicially created doctrine is that an individual or company should not receive a windfall at the expense of another because of an event in which it played no role. Thus the issue is pure and simple economics. Why should Factors etc. be forced to give up its legitimately purchased rights and, undoubtedly, highly lucrative profits for the undeserved and unjust benefit of anyone who chose to cash in on Presley's fame after his death? It could be argued that the death of a celebrity is only another market factor that a company should keep in mind when negotiating the terms of a licensing pact. Why should only one or a limited number of individuals profit from the use of a celebrity's status after his or her death? Why not provide everyone the opportunity to compete equally? There has never been any constitutionally recognized right of publicity either before or after a person's death, whether a celebrity or not, but the decision of whether to grant a right of publicity that survives death is strictly a policy matter in the hands of legislators.

In *Price v. Hal Roach Studios, Inc.*, a U.S. District Court, applying New York law, held that the deaths of comic actors Stanley Laurel and Oliver Hardy did not extinguish any assigned rights of publicity. The court concluded that whereas death is a "logical conclusion" to a right of privacy, there "appears to be no logical reason to terminate" an assignable right of publicity.[60]

On appeal, the U.S. Court of Appeals for the Sixth Circuit in 1980 in a rather brief opinion reversed the U.S. District Court decision. In *Memphis Development v. Factors Etc.* (1980),[61] the federal appeals court held that Presley's right to publicity, even if exercised and exploited while he was alive, did not survive his death and thus was *not* inheritable. The U.S. Supreme Court refused to hear a further appeal, and four years later Tennessee enacted a statute that granted a right of publicity beyond a person's death.[62] In 1987 in *Elvis Presley Enterprises v. Elvisly Yours*,[63] the Sixth Circuit Court finally recognized a descendible right of publicity but under Tennessee *common law* in line with an earlier Tennessee Court of Appeals decision.[64]

One other case involving the proverbial King of Rock n' Roll deserves mention. In 1981 in

Estate of Presley v. Russen,[65] a U.S. District Court in New Jersey ruled that impersonator Rob Russen violated Presley's right of publicity with his "Big EL Show." Russen argued that he had a First Amendment right to impersonate the celebrity, but the court held that no such right existed because the show was designed to be entertaining rather than informative. Impersonators are rarely sued for infringement because they generally do not fare well, given public fickleness, but the courts are quick to side against impersonators who can be mistaken for the "real thing" or when blatant commercial use is involved in advertising contexts, even if the individual has died.

What about a prominent figure who did not commercially exploit an image during his lifetime? A Georgia court tackled this question in 1982 in *Martin Luther King, Jr., Center for Social Change, Inc. v. American Heritage Products, Inc.*[66] The Georgia Supreme Court held that the King Center could be granted an injunction against American Heritage to prevent it from marketing busts of the famed civil rights leader who was assassinated in 1968, even though King had clearly *not* commercially exploited his name or image during his life. Other questions arose regarding the use of King's "I Have a Dream" speech placed in commercial contexts.

In a controversial move in 2006, the King estate put an extensive collection of Dr. King's personal writings and other documents up for auction. However, before the auction could take place, the estate reached an agreement for the sale of the materials, which included drafts of the famous "I Have a Dream" speech, to a group of prominent companies and individuals in Atlanta for more than $32 million. Under the agreement, the collection was eventually transferred to King's undergraduate alma mater, Morehouse College. The $32 million price covered only the right to physically possess the collection including displaying the materials and making them available to researchers, but it did not include intellectual property rights, including copyright, trademark, and appropriation rights. The estate retained control of rights, which are undoubtedly worth many times the price paid for the collection itself.

In a legal battle that lasted more than eight years, a three-judge panel of the Missouri Court of Appeals in St. Louis in 2006 upheld a $15 million jury award to former hockey player Tony Twist against Todd McFarlane and his company for the use of the player's name in the comic series "Spawn." The strip features a violent mob boss with the same name as the player. Twist originally sued in 1997 but a $24.5 million award was thrown out by a judge, with the Missouri Supreme Court eventually ordering a new trial, ruling McFarlane had no First Amendment protection in using Twist's name. The second jury handed down the $15 million judgment.[67]

Thus far the cases we have considered involved the use of a person's name or act, but appropriation can occur with other attributes. In 1962, Johnny Carson became the host of *The Tonight Show* on NBC-TV. As the show's popularity grew over the years, the host became synonymous in the public's eye with "Here's Johnny," the introduction used on every show until he retired in 1992. (Various substitute co-hosts bellowed or blurted out the slogan, but permanent co-host Ed McMahon had the edge.) Like other celebrities, Carson licensed ventures over the years from Here's Johnny Restaurants to Johnny Carson clothing. In 1976, Earl Braxton of Michigan founded a company known as: Here's Johnny Portable Toilets Inc. The toilets were marketed under the slogan, "The World's Foremost Commodian."

Carson was not amused and filed suit against the company for unfair competition, federal and state trademark infringement, and invasion of privacy and publicity rights. His requests for damages and an injunction to prohibit further use of the "Here's Johnny" slogan were denied by the trial court on grounds that Carson had failed to demonstrate a likelihood of confusion between toilets and products licensed by the TV host and that the right of privacy and right of publicity extended to a name or likeness, not to a slogan.

Carson appealed the trial court decision and eventually in *Carson v. Here's Johnny Portable Toilets, Inc.*,[68] the U.S. Court of Appeals for the Sixth Circuit disagreed with the lower court, holding "that a celebrity's identity may be appropriated in various ways. It is our view that, under the existing authorities, a celebrity's legal right of publicity is invaded whenever his identity is intentionally appropriated for commercial purposes." The court then noted that if the company had actually used Carson's name ("J. William Carson Portable Toilet" or the "John William Carson Portable Toilet") there would have been no violation of Carson's right of publicity because his identity as a celebrity would not have been appropriated.

Would "Johnny Carson Portable Toilets" have been an infringement? What about simply "Carson Portable Toilets"? What harm did Carson suffer? Was he deprived of potential revenues from licensed products under his name? Would the general public be so naive as to believe that Carson had endorsed the toilets? Evaluate *Estate of Elvis Presley v. Russen*, discussed earlier, in light of this case. How likely that someone would mistake impersonator Russen with the established King of Rock 'n Roll? And don't impersonators and toilet distributors increase interest in a celebrity and potentially stimulate sales of their licensed products? That may be debatable but the doctrine of unjust enrichment dictates that one person should not be unduly enriched at the expense of another.

Defenses to Appropriation

There are only two viable defenses to either appropriation or violation of the right of publicity: *consent* and *newsworthiness*. Consent is clearly the strongest defense, but newsworthiness is sometimes helpful, depending on the context. Consent, if knowingly offered in good faith, is usually an airtight defense, especially if it has been granted in writing. Oral agreements and even implied consent can be valid but their applicability varies from state to state and with the surrounding circumstances. It is not necessary that a person be compensated for commercial use of his or her name or persona, but very few celebrities or even private individuals are willing to grant consent *gratis*—money usually talks. Most media outlets have standardized release forms that assure informed consent, but there are traps for the unwary. For example, a person must have legal capacity to sign an agreement or otherwise grant consent. Thus a parent or guardian must usually sign for minors. Another pitfall is to assume that the consent is broad enough to cover all circumstances and all time.

In 1982 singer/actress Cher was awarded more than $663,000 in damages by a U.S. District Court judge in California in a suit against *Forum* and *Penthouse* magazines, the weekly tabloid *Star*, and freelance author Fred Robbins for violation of Cher's right of publicity.[69] Cher had consented to an interview with Robbins under the assumption that it was to be published in *US* magazine. *US* was not interested in the proposed article and paid Robbins a "kill fee" for his work. A "kill fee" is generally paid to a writer for a commissioned work that the publication decides not to use. The writer usually retains the right to submit the work elsewhere. Robbins sold the interview to the *Star*, a tabloid that competes with the *National Enquirer* at the supermarket checkout, and to *Forum*, a sexually oriented discussion magazine owned primarily by Penthouse International, which also owns *Penthouse* magazine.

Both publications carried the interview, but took different approaches in marketing and displaying the story. *Forum* placed ads in more than two dozen newspapers, aired radio commercials, and printed subscription tear-outs that touted, "There are certain things that Cher won't tell *People* and would never tell *US*. So join Cher and *Forum's* hundreds of thousands of other adventurous readers today." The promotions included Cher's name and likeness. The front cover of the *Forum* issue that carried the interview included "Exclusive: Cher Talks Straight" in large type. The *Forum* story briefly mentioned Robbins at the beginning, but the format implied that *Forum* had conducted the interview. The *Star* published the interview as a two-part series beginning in March 1981, with the banner headline "Exclusive Series: Cher, My Life, My Husband, and My Many, Many Men."

On appeal, in *Cher v. Forum International, Ltd.* (1982),[70] the Ninth Circuit U.S. Court of Appeals overturned the trial court award of $369,000 against the *Star* on grounds that Cher had not been able to demonstrate that the magazine acted with *actual malice*, as required for false light under *Time v. Hill*.[61] The appellate court, however, upheld a $269,000 judgment against *Forum*. In 1983 the Supreme Court of the United States denied certiorari.

Clearly, written consent can work to the advantage of the creator of an intellectual property ultimately involved in commercial use. When she was 10 years old, actress-model Brooke Shields posed nude for photographer Gary Gross, who had paid $450 for the written consent of Shields' mother for virtually unlimited publication rights. The photographs were published but attracted little attention until several years later at which time Shields garnered attention as a fashion model and actress, including appearing nude in a movie *Pretty Baby* about a New Orleans brothel. Shields sought an injunction to halt further publication of the photos, and the New York Supreme Court ruled in her favor on grounds that the signed agreement could later be revoked because she was a minor at the time.[72] The New York Court of Appeals, the state's highest court, reversed, holding that the privacy statute allowed a parent to grant consent on behalf of a minor.[73]

What if an individual signs a broad consent agreement, but major changes are made in the use of the person's name, their image, or likeness? What if a professional model is paid to pose for a series of photographs but then the context is severely altered? Two cases illustrate how the courts treat such situations. In a historic case in 1959, the New York Supreme Court ruled that even though Mary Jane Russell had signed a broad release form that ostensibly granted Avedon Bookstore rights to use her picture for advertising purposes, the model could recover damages for subsequent use of her image by others.[74] Avedon sold a photo of Russell to a bed sheet company that, in turn, considerably altered it and used the new version in a provocative series of ads. The state supreme court held that the extensive alteration negated the agreement because the photo was not the same to which Russell had originally granted consent.

A later case involving men's magazines illustrates a similar point. In the early 1980s, aspiring actress Robyn Douglass posed nude with another woman in suggestive poses for a photographer. Douglass signed a standard release form granting *Playboy* the right to publish photos of her but only without the other woman. Later *Hustler* publisher Larry Flynt purchased the photos and, according to court testimony, was verbally assured that the actress had consented to the use of the pictures. When the nude pictures appeared in *Hustler*, Douglass sued the magazine on grounds that her right of publicity had been violated, had suffered intentional infliction of emotional distress, and placed in a false light because of the nature of the magazine. The Seventh Circuit U.S. Court of Appeals[75] reduced trial court damages to the extent to which they were based on emotional distress from appearing in *Hustler* because she already voluntarily appeared in the buff in *Playboy*. The court ruled against her on the false light claim, but upheld right of publicity noting that being depicted as voluntarily associated with a magazine like *Hustler* "is unquestionably degrading."[76]

The only other defense to appropriation and right of publicity is *newsworthiness,* but this defense is rather difficult to evoke in a commercial context and rarely works for a media defendant. *Zacchini v. Scripps-Howard*[77] illustrates the dilemma of claiming newsworthiness even when the use is clearly in a traditional news context. Recall that Zacchini's act appeared in a regular newscast on the television station. It was apparently not shown in a promotional segment or used in a direct way to commercially exploit his performance. The only pecuniary gain the station may have gained would have been potentially higher advertising revenues from increased ratings. Such a gain is unlikely, because ratings used to determine ad rates are generally measured over a period of a month, not one show for one night. The Court was concerned that the "broadcast of a film of petitioner's (Zacchini's) entire act poses a substantial threat to the economic value of the performance."[78] The Court noted that the Ohio statute had "recognized what may be the strongest case for a 'right of publicity'—involving not the appropriation of an entertainer's reputation—but the appropriation of the very activity by which the entertainer acquired his reputation in the first place."[79]

Sports Illustrated (*SI*) once used a photograph of a major sports figure, New York Jets' quarterback and Super Bowl hero Joe Namath in its subscription promotion. The photo, which had been taken during the Super Bowl in which the Jets had captured the title in spite of being underdogs, was used in ads in the magazine as well as in other periodicals. Namath sued the magazine for appropriation but a New York County Supreme Court held that because the state statute allowed incidental but not direct use of newsworthy photographs even in a commercial context, Namath had no cause of action.[80] The court said that as "long as the reproduction was used to illustrate the quality and content of the periodical in which it originally appeared, the law accords an exempt status to incidental advertising of the news medium itself."[81] Note that the court clearly considered *Sports Illustrated* a news medium, not an entertainment medium, and the photo had been used in earlier stories in the magazine. The idea was that it was unlikely that someone would see Namath's appearance as his endorsement of the periodical.

What if *SI* had used a photo that one of its photographers had taken but had *not* been published in the magazine? What if *SI* had tried to entice subscribers with a photo it had purchased from a newspaper that had previously published the picture, although the photo had never been in *SI*? The results may have been different because there could be an impression left on potential subscribers that Namath may have endorsed the magazine rather than offering a look at the types of stories that readers would find in its issues.

An even earlier case illustrates this idea. In the late 1950s, *Holiday* magazine published a photo of a popular actress Shirley Booth while she was vacationing at a Jamaica resort. Booth had granted consent for the photo but was outraged months later when the same picture appeared in promotional ads for *Holiday* in other periodicals. Booth sued the magazine for appropriation under the New York statute and won $17,500 in damages from the trial court. On appeal, a New York Supreme Court reversed, holding that such use was incidental and permissible under the statute.[82] *Holiday* was not a "news magazine" in the traditional sense, but the principle established here and reinforced in the later *Namath* case would appear to protect both "non-news" and news media in typical promotional campaigns that tout the kinds of stories the reader can expect to see in that media outlet.

Throughout this discussion of appropriation and right of publicity, we have dealt only with commercialization of *human* names, images, and likenesses. Today, there are animals whose names and images clearly have commercial value and thus potential rights of publicity. Some of them have been prominent for a long time, and others are just gaining fame. The older cases include Lassie (actually several dogs) and Trigger, Roy Rogers' horse. Although animal names can usually be trademarked to protect use of the name, what prevents someone from marketing a painting or selling a photograph of a famous animal? Probably not much, but the picture has been changing. According to one law journal article,[83] the owners of two famous horses, Secretariat and Easy Goer, contributed publicity rights for their horses to a non-profit foundation for equine medical research. To make commercial use of the horses' names, one had to acquire a license and pay a 10% to 15% royalty.[84] Some legal scholars argue that a horse is a horse, others contend that certain equine names are so valuable they deserve the protection. The U.S. Supreme Court has not handed down any appropriation decisions since *Zacchini*.

Intrusion

The tort of intrusion bears many similarities to the tort of *trespass*, which at common law is basically unlawful interference with an individual's personal possessions (personality) or real property (realty). Even accidental or unintentional interference can be the basis for a trespass claim because injury is generally considered to have occurred simply because the person has intruded on the property, even if there is no actual physical harm. In a similar vein, intrusion is the only one of the four torts of invasion of privacy that does *not* require publication. The fact that the intrusion occurred, regardless of any dissemination of information obtained as a result, is sufficient to constitute harm. Publication can increase damages, but the tort then most likely becomes the publication of private matters coupled with intrusion. If a reporter eavesdrops on the private conversations of the local mayor by illegally bugging her phone and publishes a story about the conversations he overheard in which the official conducted drug deals, the reporter could clearly be held liable for wiretapping (intrusion) but may be able to avoid liability for the stories because they are newsworthy. In most circumstances, the reporter can even be held liable for invasion of privacy for disclosing illegally obtained information.

How does intrusion occur? Is there a difference in liability between wiretapping a phone and using a telephoto lens from a public street to catch two people making love on a couch in their own home or between a surreptitious recording by a reporter of interviews with her sources versus videotapes shot while standing on private property without consent? Each situation is different, depending on factors, including the particular jurisdiction in which the alleged intrusion occurred.

The rules regarding intrusion are intricate, complex, and inconsistent. Some basic rules are universal, but beyond these axioms, the road can be treacherous. It is clearly illegal to wiretap a phone, except one's own, without consent of the owner and usually of any and all parties to the conversation or without a court order (if you are a law enforcement official). Even court orders can be granted only on a showing of *probable* cause, which requires reasonable grounds to suspect that an individual is committing or is likely to commit a crime. The basic test under the

Fourth Amendment, according to the courts, is whether the apparent facts and circumstances in the situation would lead a reasonably prudent person to believe that a crime had occurred or was about to occur. Mere suspicion, without some supporting evidence, is not sufficient to justify search and seizure or the issuance of a warrant. The courts have permitted warrantless searches and seizures under special circumstances such as when a police officer witnesses a crime or when obtaining a warrant is impractical (e.g., when an officer is pursuing a fleeing felon). Traditional intrusion by the government such as surreptitious recording, wiretapping and eavesdropping always requires a court order or warrant, but there is no requirement that the government notify the individual until formally charged.

Dietemann v. Time, Inc. (1971)

Journalists on their own never have court authority to commit intrusion, no matter how justified the ends may be. If they are working with authorities, they may or may not be legally permitted to intrude on an individual's privacy. The most cited case on journalistic intrusion is *Dietemann v. Time, Inc.* (1971).[85] The Ninth Circuit U.S. Court of Appeals reached its decision in the case on a narrow set of facts involving primarily California common law and the First Amendment. (The federal courts had jurisdiction. This was a diversity case.) In its November 1, 1963, edition, *Life* magazine carried an article entitled "Crackdown on Quackery," which characterized Dietemann as a quack doctor, and included two photographs taken secretly at his home about five weeks earlier. The magazine editors had reached an agreement with the Los Angeles County District Attorney's office to send two reporters posing as husband and wife to the home armed with a hidden camera and microphone that transmitted conversations to a tape recorder in a parked car occupied by another magazine staff member, an assistant district attorney, and a state Department of Public Health Investigator.

The purpose of the reporters' visit was to obtain information for use as evidence to prosecute Dietemann for practicing medicine without a license, but the investigators had agreed that the magazine could use the information for a story. The district court described the plaintiff (Dietemann) as "a disabled veteran with little education … engaged in the practice of clay, minerals, and herbs—as practiced, simple quackery."[86] The two *Life* journalists did not identify themselves as reporters, but instead pretended to be potential clients. The female reporter asked the quack doctor to diagnose a lump in her breast. After examining her, Dietemann concluded that she had eaten some rancid butter 11 years, 9 months, and 7 days earlier. One of the secret photos published by the magazine was of the plaintiff with his hand on the upper portion of the reporter's breast. The trial court and the appeals court emphasized that Dietemann was a journeyman plumber who claimed to be a scientist, not a doctor, and that he "practiced" out of his home. He did not advertise, had no telephone, and did not charge a fee for his services, although he accepted "contributions." He was ultimately convicted for practicing medicine without a license after pleading *nolo contendere* to the charges. (The story was published in *Life* before his conviction.)

The U.S. District Court awarded the plaintiff $1,000 in general damages for invasion of privacy, and the U.S. Court of Appeals upheld that judgment. The appellate court rejected the magazine's argument that the First Amendment immunized it from liability for its secret recordings on grounds that tape recorders are "indispensable tools of investigative reporting."

According to the majority opinion, "The First Amendment has never been construed to accord newsmen immunity from torts or crimes committed during the course of newsgathering."[87]

But weren't the journalists acting, in effect, as agents of the police because they had consent of the district attorney's office, cooperating with the D.A. and the health department? The court cleverly skirted this issue by holding that because the plaintiff had proven a cause of action for invasion of privacy under California law and because the defendants could not shield their actions with the First Amendment, the latter issue was moot.

Legal scholars and courts have split among themselves on the importance of *Dietemann*. Some courts have basically rejected the holding or diluted its impact by distinguishing the case as involving a narrow set of circumstances; other courts, probably the majority, cling to the principle that "the First Amendment is not a license to trespass, to steal, or to intrude by electronic means into the precincts of another's home or office. [footnote omitted] It does not become a license simply because the person subjected to the intrusion is reasonably suspected of committing a crime."[88] Although all courts and legal scholars would agree that the First Amendment is not a license to intrude, there are major differences over the definition of intrusion. This court was very careful to separate the physical act of intrusion from publication, which is definitely in line with the traditional meaning of intrusion. In other words, no publication is required for intrusion. However, publication can substantially enhance damages, as the appellate court held in permitting the plaintiff to seek damages for additional emotional distress as a result of the publication. This presents a win–win situation for the plaintiff and a lose–lose one for the defendant because the defendant is not allowed to claim a publication privilege for intrusion and the plaintiff can ask for additional damages from publication.

Pearson v. Dodd (1969)

Most courts would likely still rule as the Ninth Circuit Court did in 1971—that *Dietemann's* holding has become more limited to the circumstances in the case, which included the private home setting, misrepresentation of identification by the journalists, and the direct use of eavesdropping devices by reporters. In fact, even this court circumscribed the case by footnoting that its facts were different from those of *Pearson v. Dodd*[89] decided two years earlier by the U.S. Court of Appeals.

In *Pearson*, the U.S. District Court for the District of Columbia granted a partial summary judgment for Senator Thomas Dodd of Connecticut for conversion against syndicated newspaper columnists Drew Pearson and Jack Anderson but denied a judgment for intrusion. The appeals court reversed the judgment for intrusion and affirmed the denial of the judgment for *conversion*. Conversion is an old tort that lies in the unauthorized control over another's property so rightful owners are deprived of rights of possession. Unlike theft, normally a criminal action, conversion is a civil action. The owner can be granted damages in addition to return of property. The higher court ruled there was no basis for Dodd's claims.

The facts of the case are similar to those that can occur in some investigative stories, especially those involving the misdeeds of politicians. Two former employees of the U.S. senator secretly entered his office, removed confidential documents from his files, made photocopies, and returned the originals without consulting with their ex-boss. The documents, which contained details of alleged misdeeds of the politician, were then turned over to Pearson and

Anderson, who used the information to write six syndicated newspaper columns that offered their "version of … [Dodd's] relationship with certain lobbyists for foreign interests, and gave an interpretative biographical sketch of … [his] public career."[90]

The columnists admitted that they knew the documents were purloined, but claimed, in defense, that they had not actually participated in securing them. Two members of Dodd's current staff had gone with the ex-employees during some of the visits, but Anderson and Pearson had apparently played no role other than publishing the information. The journalists also argued that Dodd had no cause of action for invasion of privacy even for publication of the private information because it was in the public interest. The appellate court agreed, holding that the columnists could not be held liable for damages for invasion of privacy from the publication or for intrusion. In a majority opinion written by Circuit Judge J. Skelly Wright, the court said:

> If we were to hold appellants liable for invasion of privacy on these facts, we would establish the proposition that one who receives information from an intruder, knowing it has been obtained by improper intrusion, is guilty of a tort. In an untried and developing area of tort law, we are not prepared to go so far.[91]

Of course, Pearson and Anderson did more than listen. They spread the information throughout the country, with resulting considerable harm to the senator's career and reputation. The information, however, "was of obvious public interest," according to the decision. The court also rejected Dodd's claim of conversion because the "documents were removed from the files at night, photocopied, and returned to the files undamaged before office operations resumed in the morning … [Dodd] was clearly not substantially deprived of his use of them."[92]

The key defense in this case was the lack of participation by defendants in intruding on the plaintiff's privacy. Neither Pearson nor Anderson nor anyone directly associated with them was involved in obtaining the documents from Dodd's office. There was, however, a difference in *Dietemann*: reporters carried eavesdropping devices into the plaintiff's home.

Bartnicki v. Vopper (2001)

In a case bearing some similarities to *Pearson*, the U.S. Supreme Court held in *Bartnicki v. Vopper* (2001)[93] that the First Amendment protected the broadcast of a recording of an illegally intercepted cell phone conversation that had been sent anonymously to a radio commentator who had played it on his show. Applying intermediate scrutiny, the Supreme Court noted the case involved "the repeated intentional disclosure of an illegally intercepted cellular telephone conversation about a public issue. The persons who made the disclosures did not participate in the interception, but they did know—or at least had reason to know—that the interception was unlawful."[94] The case involved a call made to a local teachers' union president by a union negotiator to discuss the status of collective bargaining talks. In the recording the union president said, "If they're not going to move for three percent, we're going to have to go to their, their homes [of school board members] … to blow off their front porches, we'll have to do some work on some of those guys."

The recording was initially carried on the commentator's program. He had received it from the head of a local taxpayers' group opposed to the union's demands. He testified that he had found the tape in his mailbox. Other media outlets including a local newspaper publicized the contents of the tape. The parties to the cell phone conversation sued the commentator and the head of the taxpayers' group in a civil suit for damages based on invasion of their privacy. They claimed the disclosure violated Title III of the Omnibus Crime Control and Safe Streets Act of 1968,[95] generally banning the willful interception of wire, electronic, and oral communications as well as the disclosure of such communication by anyone who knows or has reason to know of the illegal interception.

According to the majority opinion, privacy interests must be "balanced against the interest in publishing matters of public importance." In this case, the Court said "a stranger's illegal conduct does not suffice to remove the First Amendment shield from speech about a matter of public concern."[96] The Court specifically cited both *New York Times v. Sullivan* and *Florida Star v. B.J.F.* in its reasoning.

In *Boehner v. McDermott*,[97] a panel of the U.S. Court of Appeals for the D.C. Circuit ruled 2-1 in 2006 that Representative James McDermott (D-Wash) did not enjoy First Amendment protection when he violated the same statute at issue in *Bartnicki* by disclosing a tape recording of a cell phone conversation that had been sent to him by a Florida couple who intercepted the call via a police radio scanner. In the recording, U.S. House Majority Leader John H. Boehmer (R-Ohio) and other Republican Party leaders discuss how then House Speaker Newt Gingrich (R-Ga.) might be willing to accept a reprimand and fine if the House Ethics Committee would forgo a hearing on ethics violations.[98] The majority opinion in the appeal reasoned that Rep. Boehner, the defendant in the case, clearly knew the couple had illegally intercepted and recorded the call and thus the tape had not been lawfully obtained, even though Boehner had played no role in the interception.

The court cited *Bartnicki*, noting that the tape in that case had been legally obtained. McDermott argued that *Bartnicki* meant that anyone who received such a copy had First Amendment protection. However, according to the appellate court:

> The eavesdropping statute may not itself make receiving a tape of an illegally-intercepted conversation illegal.... But it does not follow that anyone who receives a copy of such a conversation has obtained it legally and has a First Amendment right to disclose it. If that were the case, then the holding in *Bartnicki* is not "narrow" as the Court stressed, but very broad indeed. On the other hand, to hold that a person who knowingly receives a tape from an illegal interceptor either aids and abets the interceptor's second violation (the disclosure), or participates in an illegal transaction would be to take the Court at its word. It also helps explain why the Court thought it so significant that the illegal interceptor in *Bartnicki* was unknown ... and why the Court distinguished this case on that ground.... [cites and footnotes omitted][99]

Florida Publishing Company v. Fletcher (1976): Implied Consent

In an often-cited Florida Supreme Court decision in 1976, *Florida Publishing Company v. Fletcher*,[100] the state supreme court ruled that an "implied consent" based on the "doctrine of common custom and usage" prevented Mrs. Klenna Ann Fletcher from recovering damages for trespass, invasion of privacy, and wrongful infliction of emotional distress. Fletcher's 17-year-old daughter died alone in her home when a fire of unknown origin gutted the house. In

Florida, as in many states, fire marshals and police permit reporters and news photographers to follow them as they conduct their investigations. A photographer for the *Florida Times-Union* took a picture of a "silhouette" that remained on the floor of the house after Fletcher's body had been taken away. The photo was taken at the request of a fire marshal who had run out of his own film and needed another picture. A copy of the photo was turned over to the investigators for their files, but the picture was also published with others from the fire in the newspaper.

Unfortunately, Cindy Fletcher's mother, who was out of town at the time of the death, first learned of the tragedy and its suspicious circumstances (possible arson) when photos and story appeared in the paper. Her suit for invasion of privacy (intrusion) was dismissed by the trial court, which granted summary judgments for the defendants on two counts, one for a combined trespass and invasion of privacy and another for wrongful infliction of emotional distress. An intermediate state appellate court held that Fletcher should have been able to pursue the trespass claim at trial.

The Florida Supreme Court ruled against Fletcher on all three counts, and the U.S. Supreme Court denied certiorari.[101] The state supreme court reasoned, as did the trial court judge, that "it is common usage, custom and practice for the news media to enter private premises and homes to report on matters of public interest or a public event."[102] The court emphasized that the photographer's entry was at the invitation of investigators, but that "implied consent would, of course, vanish if one were informed not to enter at that time by the owner or possessor or by their direction."[103]

The court was imposing three requisite conditions before the media can be relieved of liability. First, there must be a standing agreement or at least general public acceptance that journalists are permitted to enter private premises in such situations. Second, the matter must be of public interest or a public event. Finally, the owner or other person(s) entitled to possession of the property (such as a renter or lessee) must either not be present at the time to object or be present but not object. This decision was by a state supreme court. It establishes no precedent in other jurisdictions; the holding has been favorably cited by other courts, but never upheld by the U.S. Supreme Court.

Some aspects of this decision are unclear. The Florida Supreme Court did not indicate whether all three of the conditions must always be present. What if the owner objected but there was a strong public interest to be served and authorities had granted consent? What if the owner granted consent but the investigators objected? Could an event be so public or could the public interest be so strong as to override the objections?

Ethical Considerations

Beyond legal questions, however, are a number of ethical concerns in such situations. Assuming the newspaper knew that Fletcher had not been notified of her daughter's death (which was unclear from the court's decision), should it have published the pictures and the story? What if the pictures had included the body, not just a silhouette?

Newspaper and magazine reporters often draw the ire of the public and occasionally the courts when they are perceived to intrude on privacy. But the most intense criticism has been directed at photographers and electronic journalists, thanks to the images the public has seen of obtrusive microphones thrust into the faces of the families of victims of tragedies or the prying eye of the still photographer focused on the victim's body. Sensationalized news constitutes a relatively small proportion of news coverage, but courts and the public pay greater attention to the unusual. Some of these potential intrusions lead to litigation, whereas others merely lead to irate phone calls and letters to the editor.

The Associated Press distributed a photo obtained from a member newspaper in California that showed the parents and two brothers of a young boy's family in intense mourning in 1985 just as the boy's body is pulled from an area where he had drowned. The picture was particularly shocking because the body appeared prominently in the foreground of the uncropped version. Public criticism was vehement, including a bomb threat and more than 500 irate phone calls.[104]

When a Pan American jet exploded in mid-air over Lockerbie, Scotland, in 1988, killing all 270 people aboard, the media immediately converged on Syracuse, New York, because 35 of the passengers were students from Syracuse University. Press coverage was intrusive. At a campus memorial service, "Photographers jammed the aisles and balconies with bulky TV equipment, and they triggered blinding strobe lights and noisy motor drives on still cameras. The service was more like a press conference than a prayer vigil."[105] Several reporters called friends and family of the dead within hours; they resorted to interviewing students as they walked on campus, snapping their photos as they succumbed to grief. These scenes of supposedly private mourning appeared nationwide, countless times in the newspapers and on television.

Among the most complex recent stories involving coverage of death are protests at military funerals. A Kansas Church took the position that God is punishing the United States for "the sin of homosexuality." The family of one dead Marine won an initial $5 million judgment from the protesters which was later overturned and the U.S. Supreme Court later agreed to hear the case.

Was there an invasion of privacy by the media in all of these situations? From a legal perspective, the answer is *absolutely not*. Public events invite scrutiny. The drowning occurred in a public area, in plain view of anyone. The accident was newsworthy, of course, and there was no reasonable expectation of privacy. The plane explosion was of legitimate public concern, but didn't individuals attending the memorial service expect some privacy? Perhaps, but by permitting the media to cover the service, the university waived a right to assert a claim of intrusion, including presence of cameras. Interestingly, university public relations personnel reportedly provided journalists with detailed information about when and where the memorial service would be held. By the second service, reporters and photographers were confined to the balconies.[106]

The case involving protests at military services will likely focus on limits on where protests may be held as a means of protecting the dignity of memorials and funeral services. Two of the traditional codes of media ethics connected with decision-making deal specifically with privacy: (a) the *Society of Professional Journalists Code of Ethics* and (b) the *Radio–Television News Directors Association Code (now RTDNA)*. The *National Press Photographers Association Code of Ethics* and the NPPA *Digital Manipulation Policy* does not include direct references to privacy. The SPJ Code has dealt with privacy in two sections. Under "Seek Truth and Report It," the code declares that *journalists should*:

> Avoid undercover or other surreptitious methods of gathering information except when traditional open methods will not yield information vital to the public. Use of such methods should be explained as part of the story.[107]

Under "Minimize Harm," the SPJ Code says that *journalists should:*

> Recognize that private people have a greater right to control information about themselves than do public officials and others who seek power, influence or attention. Only an overriding public need can justify intrusion into anyone's privacy.[108]

The previous SPJ Code said simply: "The news media must guard against invading a person's right to privacy." There are other statements in the new code that touch on privacy: "Show good taste. Avoid pandering to lurid curiosity." Journalists are also told in that section ("Minimize Harm"): "Be cautious about identifying juvenile suspects or victims of sex crimes."

When and how does a journalist know that "traditional open methods" will not work? What is an "overriding public need"? How much stronger are privacy rights of private people than public figures? Are rights confined to limits specified under law, or are there limits defined by ethical standards broader than legal standards dictating certain kinds of intrusion (beyond privacy concerns) may be legal but *unethical?* The RTDNA code was more general, noting members "respect the dignity, privacy and well-being of people with whom they deal."[109]

Public Places

One principle regarding expectation of privacy rings loud and clear from the courts—individuals who appear in public places, whether they are public or private figures, expect less privacy than in private settings. The difficulty for the media is distinguishing between public versus private. Suppose a television reporter is assigned by a news director to cover alleged health code violations by local restaurants. The reporter is handed a list of establishments cited by the city health services administration. She selects one from the list and enters unannounced with cameras rolling. The result is chaos: waiting customers leave in anger, patrons dash off without paying, and others hide behind napkins or under tables. Can she be held liable for intrusion?

An incident similar to this led to a jury verdict in favor of a restaurant for $1,200 in compensatory damages and $250,000 in punitive damages. On appeal, the compensatory damages stood, but the case went back for retrial on the punitive award, which the judge ultimately dismissed.[110] In 1972, a reporter for Channel 2 TV (owned by CBS) in New York not only paid a surprise visit with cameras rolling and lights bright, but continued to record the ensuing confusion after the manager asked the crew to stop. Although the diner received only $2,500, probably less than court costs and attorneys' fees, the New York Supreme Court (Appellate Division) rejected CBS' claim of First Amendment protection. Citing *Dietemann v. Time,*[111] the court reiterated that the First Amendment has never been interpreted to grant journalistic immunity from crimes and torts committed during news gathering.

It is interesting to note that the action was for trespass, not intrusion, because, in line with the Restatement (Second) of Torts,[112] most courts have held that corporations and businesses do not have a right of privacy. But the consequences of trespass can be just as severe as those for intrusion, as this case illustrates and the famous Food Lion case demonstrated in the 1990s.

When ABC-TV's *Primetime Live* sent producers to work undercover at three Food Lion supermarkets in North and South Carolina, the producers recorded more than 40 hours of videotape with cameras hidden in their wigs and battery packs and other equipment strapped to their bodies over three days.[113] ABC aired a 25-minute story in 1992 based on its investigative work that included accusations that the grocery chain engaged in unsanitary practices such as selling repackaged, out-of-date meat washed in bleach, cheese gnawed by rats, decaying produce, and contaminated fish. The producers had been able to get behind the scenes at Food Lion stores by getting hired with doctored résumés. They did not reveal to Food Lion they were journalists.

Food Lion got wind of the program before it was broadcast and convinced a North Carolina trial court judge to issue an order banning the network from showing any excerpts from the videotapes taken with the secret cameras. However, ABC was able to continue with the segment after convincing a federal court judge to overturn the state court restraining order. Food Lion, headquartered in Salisbury, North Carolina, had about 1,100 stores in 14 states at the time.

The next year the company sued (a) the network, (b) its parent company (Capital Cities/ABC at that time), (c) senior investigative producer Ira Rosen, (d) executive producer Rick Kaplan, and (e) the two producers (Dale and Barnett) for civil fraud, trespass, and breach of loyalty. The civil fraud claim was based on the fact that the two producers lied on their résumés and failed to give their true identities. The trespass claim was related to the fact that the two gained access to nonpublic work areas under false pretenses. The breach of loyalty claim related to the presumed commitment an employee makes to act in good faith on behalf of an employer.

After the report aired, Food Lion's sales dropped and it's publicly traded stock fell sharply, and the company said it was forced to close 84 stores and fire 3,500 employees. At the trial in U.S. District Court in Greensboro, North Carolina, the grocery store chain asked for $2,432.35 in actual damages, including wages it had paid to the two producers during their employment at Food Lion. It sought up to $2.5 billion in punitive damages. The food chain chose not to challenge the accuracy of the report in court. They did not sue for libel, but outside the courtroom it claimed there were program inaccuracies. The jurors never saw the *PrimeTime* segment. Food Lion's attorneys showed several hours of out-takes from the hidden cameras.[114]

Three years later, in December, 1996 the jury returned a verdict in favor of Food Lion, awarding the company $1,402 in actual damages, representing the amount the food chain paid to train the two producers.[115] On January 22, 1997 the jury determined that Capital Cities/ABC Inc. should pay $4 million and ABC Inc. $1.5 million in punitive damages. The jury assessed the program's executive producer $35,000 and senior producer $10,750 in punitive damages.

In light of the U.S. Supreme Court decision in *BMW v. Gore*[116] a year earlier, it was inevitable that the award would be reduced or overturned. The punitive damages were almost 4,000 times the actual damages—far out of line with the 500-to-1 ratio that the Supreme Court had found unacceptable in *Gore*. In August 1997, U.S. District Court Judge Carlton Tilley lowered the punitive damages to $315,000 on the ground that the ratio of actual to punitive damages was excessive. Two months later, Food Lion agreed to accept the reduced award, but ABC filed an appeal with the U.S. Court of Appeals for the Fourth Circuit. Two years later, the Fourth Circuit reversed "the judgment to the extent it provides that the ABC defendants committed fraud and awards compensatory damages of $1,400 and punitive damages of $315,000 on that claim." The court affirmed "the judgment to the extent it provides that Dale and Barnett breached their duty of loyalty to Food Lion and committed a trespass" and awarded total damages of $2.00 on the latter claims.[117]

Even when they appear in public places, individuals certainly do not give up all rights of privacy. The classic illustration of this is *Galella v. Onassis* (1973),[118] in which Jacqueline Kennedy

Onassis successfully sought an injunction restricting Ron Galella's attempts to photograph her and her children. The celebrity photographer routinely staked out Onassis by keeping a constant watch on her movements and those of her children. Galella was usually careful to take his pictures only in public places such as sidewalks and schools. However, according to the court, he once came uncomfortably close to Onassis in a power boat while she was swimming, often jumped and postured while taking pictures of her at a theater opening, customarily bribed doorkeepers, and even romanced a family servant so he would know family movements. Galella was detained and arrested on a criminal complaint by Secret Service agents in an incident involving John Kennedy, Jr. while he was bicycling in Central Park. After his acquittal on the charges, Galella sued the agents and Onassis for false arrest and malicious prosecution. Onassis denied any role in the arrest and countersued Galella for invasion of privacy, assault and battery, harassment, and intentional infliction of emotional distress.

A U.S. District Court granted a temporary restraining order that forbade Galella from "harassing, alarming, startling, tormenting, touching [Onassis] … or her children … and from blocking their movements in the public places and thoroughfares, invading their immediate zone of privacy by means of physical movements, gestures or with photographic equipment and from performing any act reasonably calculated to place the lives and safety of the defendant [Onassis] … and her children in jeopardy."[119]

Within two months, the "paparazzo" (as Galella called himself, which literally meant "annoying insect," according to the Court of Appeals) was back in the District Court for violating the order. The U.S. District Court granted a new order, as a result, that required the photographer to keep 100 yards from the Onassis apartment in New York and 50 yards from Onassis and her children.[120] The order also prohibited surveillance. After a six-week trial consolidating Galella's claims and Onassis' counterclaims, the U.S. District Court dismissed the celebrity photographer's claim and granted a broad injunction that included a provision keeping Galella from approaching within 100 yards of the Onassis home, within 100 yards of either child's school, and within 75 yards of either child or within 50 yards of Onassis.

The U.S. Court of Appeals for the Second Circuit modified the trial court's order by cutting the zone of protection to 25 feet, banning the photographer from touching Onassis, forbidding him from blocking her movement in public places and thoroughfares, and engaging in "any conduct which would reasonably be foreseen to harass, alarm or frighten" Onassis. The appeals court also enjoined Galella from "(a) entering the children's schools or play areas; (b) engaging in action calculated or reasonably foreseen to place the children's safety or well-being in jeopardy, or which could threaten or create physical injury; (c) taking any action which could reasonably be foreseen to harass, alarm, or frighten the children; and (d) from approaching within thirty (30) feet of the children."[121] The Appeals Court applied a balancing test:

> Of course legitimate countervailing social needs may warrant some intrusion despite an individual's reasonable expectation of privacy and freedom from harassment. However the interference allowed may be no greater than that necessary to protect the overriding public interest. Mrs. Onassis was found to be a public figure and thus subject to news coverage.[122]

It is important to realize that Galella's actions were extreme. It was difficult for the family to go anywhere in public without facing the photographer's flashing lights and clicking cameras.

The freelancer made considerable sums from his sales of the photos and continued to do so even after the unfavorable decision. The Court of Appeals noted that, as modified, the order still fully allowed Galella the opportunity to photograph and report on Onassis' public activities and that "any prior restraint on news gathering is minuscule and fully supported by the findings."[123] Unfortunately, the court order did not halt Galella's surveillance. Nine years later he was found in contempt of court for repeated violations of the order and had to pay a $10,000 fine.[124] According to press reports, he finally relented and focused his efforts on other celebrities.

The Onassis case is the exception. According to the general rule, at least as recognized by most courts, individuals have little claim to invasion of privacy on grounds of intrusion when they appear in public. But a claim may exist on grounds such as false light or appropriation.

Photojournalists around the world appear to have become more sensitive to how they cover celebrities after Princess Diana's death. A great deal of public scorn was heaped upon them after it became apparent that the photographers pursuing the Mercedes in which she rode may have played a role in the accident or that they displayed more concern with getting a photo of the crash than trying to assist the individuals in the car. Whether this reaction to the criticism will translate into permanent changes in the way such photographers do business remains to be seen, but the incident pointed out extremes of the profession.

A good illustration of how the general rule regarding public places is in *Cefalu v. Globe Newspaper*,[125] in which a Massachusetts Court of Appeals upheld a trial court's summary judgment in favor of the *Boston Globe*. Angelo Cefalu claimed the newspaper had libeled him and invaded privacy by publishing a photograph of individuals, including him, lined up to collect unemployment benefits in a state office building. The photographer obtained consent of the public information officer who announced to people standing in line that the photographer was taking a picture from the rear and anyone who did not wish to be in the picture could face the front or step out of line.

Unfortunately, Cefalu did not hear the announcement, and his face was one of the few in the picture that is recognizable. He was in the line, not to pick up a check but rather to serve as translator for a non-English-speaking friend. The photo was published in April 1973 without complaint from Cefalu, who, according to the court, even displayed the photo in his home. But the next year, the paper selected the photo from its file for a feature story on unemployment. The captions for each photo were similar; no one's name or other identification was mentioned. In upholding the trial court's summary judgment in favor of the newspaper, the appellate court noted that publication of the photo was not actionable:

> The notion of right of privacy is founded on the idea that individuals may hold close certain manuscripts, family photographs, or private conduct which is no business of the public and the publicizing of which is, therefore, offensive. *The appearance of a person in a public place necessarily involves doffing the cloak of privacy which the law protects.*[126]

Private Places

Under the Fourth Amendment to the U.S. Constitution, "The rights of the people to be secure in their persons, houses, papers, and effects, against unreasonable searches and seizures, shall not be violated, and no Warrants shall issue, but upon probable cause, supported by Oath or affirmation, and particularly describing the place to be searched, and the persons or things to be seized."[127] In the past decade, especially in the past few years, the U.S. Supreme Court has broadened the authority of the government to conduct searches without warrants within the limits of the Fourth Amendment. In 1991, the Court ruled 6–3 that police who suspect contraband is hidden in a car may legally search the vehicle and any closed container inside.[128]

The decision effectively overturned a series of earlier rulings by the Court that held that police, under most circumstances, had to obtain a search warrant to open a closed container such as luggage. A week earlier, the Court held that once a driver had given authorities consent to search a car, they could also open containers in the vehicle. In both cases, the majority favorably cited the 1925 case of *Carroll v. United States*,[129] in which the Court had upheld a search without a warrant of an automobile being driven on a highway so long as there was probable cause. The rationale was that any contraband (in this case, liquor) could be quickly moved during the interim in which a search warrant was sought. Under the leadership of Chief Justice John Roberts, the U.S. Supreme Court has narrowed individual rights under the Fourth Amendment, as illustrated in *Hudson v. Michigan* (2006).[130] The case involved the execution of a search warrant by Detroit police at a private residence for suspected illegal narcotics and weapons. When officers executed the warrant, they did not follow the knock-and-announce rule, which requires police under the Fourth Amendment to knock on the door of a home first, identify themselves and then indicate their purpose for entering before executing a warrant or making an arrest without a warrant. The state admitted that it had not followed the rule in the case but claimed that the evidence police seized and that was ultimately used to convict the defendant did not have to be suppressed because of the violation. The U.S. Supreme Court agreed, holding that the social costs had to be weighed against deterrence and that the social costs considerably outweighed deterrence. The social costs, according to the Court, included the risks that dangerous criminals would be set free, that police officers could be harmed and that evidence could be destroyed. The justices acknowledged privacy issues were involved but said they were considerably outweighed by social costs. According to the Court, "[T]he rule has never protected one's interest in preventing the government from seeing or taking evidence described in a warrant. Since the interests violated here have nothing to do with the seizure of the evidence, the exclusionary rule is inapplicable."[131]

The Fourth Amendment protects individuals only against governmental intrusion, *not* against intrusion by nongovernmental entities such as private corporations and news media. The trend is toward granting government greater latitude in gaining access to what were formerly considered to be private places, but federal and state statutes have continued to bolster the rights of citizens to be free of intrusion from nongovernmental entities. It is ironic that the only U.S. Supreme Court decision recognizing a general constitutional right of privacy involved governmental intrusion, yet intrusion has been granted greater legitimacy by courts at the same time that nongovernmental intrusion is more restricted.

Griswold v. Connecticut (1965)

In *Griswold v. Connecticut* (1965),[132] the Court ruled that a state statute forbidding the use of contraceptives and the dissemination of birth control information even to married couples was unconstitutional because it infringed on a right to marital privacy. The Connecticut law provided a fine of up to $50 and/or up to 60 days in prison for a violation. The test case arose after a member of the state Planned Parenthood League and a physician were arrested and fined $100 each for giving information about contraceptives to married couples. In striking down the statute, the majority opinion written by Justice Douglas found that "specific guarantees in the Bill of Rights … create zones of privacy."[133] The sources for these emanations, according to the Court, include the First Amendment right of association, the Third Amendment ban against the quartering of soldiers in a private home without consent during peacetime, the Fourth Amendment guarantee against unreasonable search and seizure, the Fifth Amendment self-incrimination clause, and, finally, the Ninth Amendment, which provides that "the enumeration in the Constitution, of certain rights, shall not be construed to deny or disparage others retained by the people."[134]

This constitutional right of privacy against governmental intrusion is by no means absolute, of course, as demonstrated in decisions by the U.S. Supreme Court such as (1) *Bowers v. Hardwick* (1986)[135] upholding a state statute forbidding consensual homosexual activity even in a private home, (2) *Webster v. Reproductive Health Services* (1989),[136] a 5 to 4 decision upholding a Missouri statute placing restrictions on abortion that appeared to circumvent the Court's 1973 holding in *Roe v. Wade*[137] recognizing a woman's right to have an abortion under guidelines established by the Court, and (3) *Planned Parenthood of Southeastern Pennsylvania v. Casey* (1992),[138] a 5 to 4 decision in which a bitterly divided Court reaffirmed *Roe v. Wade* but with a new test and with new limitations.

In *Planned Parenthood*, the plurality opinion said that although a woman still has the constitutional right to decide whether or not to have an abortion, states could impose restrictions such as requiring a woman to wait 24 hours before undergoing an abortion and to be informed about abortion risks and alternatives. The Supreme Court did strike down the portion of the Pennsylvania statute being tested that required a woman to tell her husband of her intent to seek an abortion. Instead of the traditional strict scrutiny test, the test for determining the constitutionality of abortion restrictions, according to the Court, should be whether they impose an "undue burden" on a woman's right of choice. Only two justices—Blackmun, who wrote the majority opinion in *Roe*, and Stevens—voted to apply the original "strict scrutiny" test of *Roe*. The four remaining justices said *Roe* should be overturned. As privacy rights against governmental intrusion erode, privacy parameters against intrusion by others are expanding.

Changing times or new societal attitudes can lead to changing opinions from the U.S. Supreme Court. In 2003 the Court overturned its decision in *Bowers*, holding in *Lawrence v. Texas* (2003)[139] that a state statute criminalizing "deviate sexual intercourse" between individuals of the same sex was unconstitutional. In a majority decision written by Justice Kennedy, the Court held that the statute violated the liberty and privacy protections of the due process clause of the Fourteenth Amendment. Justice O'Connor concurred in the judgment but on the ground that the law violated the equal protection clause of the same amendment. If this case had been heard by the current Supreme Court, the decision would most likely still have gone the same way, although by a 5 to 4 instead of a 6 to 3 vote. Justice Kennedy was joined in his opinion by Justices Stevens, Souter, Ginsburg, and Breyer. Two of the dissenters, Justices Scalia and Thomas, are still on the Court. Chief Justice John Roberts replaced Chief Justice Rehnquist and Justice O'Connor has been succeeded by Justice Samuel Alito. Roberts and Alito would likely have joined Scalia and Thomas, had they been on the Court at the time.

In *Lawrence*, the Court made it clear that the statute was clearly unconstitutional because it attempted to illegally control an intimate relationship that consenting adults possessed the liberty in which to engage and that the statute served no legitimate governmental interest that could justify intrusion into the personal and private lives of citizens. The two men involved in the case were convicted and fined $200 each for criminal conduct after they were observed engaging in anal sexual intercourse when police officers entered an apartment in response to a reported weapons complaint. Many of the intrusion concerns revolve around surveillance.

In 1986 Congress passed the Electronic Communications Privacy Act, which provides:

> An offense can be punished by a fine of up to $10,000 and/or imprisonment of up to five years.[141] Anyone found guilty of manufacturing, distributing, possessing, or advertising such devices can be fined up to $10,000 and/or imprisoned for up to five years.[142] Most states have similar statutes because the federal statutes, under the Constitution, can regulate the transmission of interstate or foreign communications or communications affecting foreign commerce. Federal laws cannot regulate communication that is purely intrastate. There are numerous exceptions under the law, including law enforcement officials with a court order and monitoring by the Federal Communications Commission to enforce the Communications Act of 1934.

Participant Monitoring

One important exception is consensual or participant monitoring, as specified in Section 2511:

> It shall not be unlawful under this chapter for a person not acting under color of law to intercept a wire, oral, or electronic communication where such person is a party to the communication or where one of the parties to the communication has given prior consent to such interception unless such communication is intercepted for the purpose of committing any criminal or tortious act in violation of the Constitution or laws of the United States or of any state.[143]

Prior to the 1986 Electronic Communications Privacy Act, this provision included "injurious purpose" with criminal and tortious acts. The Act passed in 1968 as the Omnibus Crime Control and Safe Streets Act. The two key words were deleted, however, in the 1986 act, primarily in response to a 1984 Sixth Circuit U.S. Court of Appeals decision in *Boddie v. the American Broadcasting Companies*.[144] That case arose when ABC's *20/20* carried "Injustice for All" a story by Geraldo Rivera, investigating allegations that an Ohio judge granted leniency to female criminal defendants who had sex with him. Rivera interviewed an unwed mother of four, who had received a lenient sentence from the judge, although she claimed she had not had sex with him. The interview was recorded with a hidden video camera and microphone.

When excerpts of the interview were broadcast, Rivera alleged that a friend of individual had sex with the judge on her behalf. She sued the network and Rivera 19 months later for libel, false light, and civil violation of the federal statute. The trial court judge dismissed the eavesdropping claim, and a jury ruled there had been no libel or invasion of privacy. The Sixth Circuit U.S. Court of Appeals sent the case back to trial court, ruling the wiretapping claim had been improperly dismissed. Before the case was retried, Congress passed the 1986 act with revisions designed to permit surreptitious recording for news gathering under participant monitoring.

When retried, the district court judge dismissed the suit on the grounds that the 1986 revision simply clarified, rather than changed, previous law and that Congress had not meant for "injurious purpose" to include news gathering. It was appealed, and the U.S. Court of Appeals for the Sixth Circuit affirmed the dismissal on grounds that the "injurious purpose" language was vague, holding that the trial court judge had erred when he dismissed claims on the basis that the 1986 revisions had clarified the old law.[145]

Although the Court of Appeals decision is binding only in the Sixth Circuit, it recognizes the right of news organizations as well as the public to secretly record conversations in person, via phone, or by other means when they are parties to the conversation or when they have consent of *one* of the parties. The appellate court made it clear "even though the statute is not explicitly aimed at speech, uncertainty about its scope is likely to inhibit news gathering and reporting."[146]

Although the trial court and the appellate court agreed that the case should have been dismissed on different grounds, both decisions reveal an undercurrent that should concern journalists. By erroneously ascribing the basis for the dismissal to clarification in the 1986 revision, the district court was indicating that, had Congress chosen to broaden the statute to include claims, Congress would have been permitted to do so. In other words, Congress would not have violated the First Amendment.

This situation is particularly troubling in light of the legislative history of the Act, which shows that Senate sponsors and supporters of the revision expressed on the record that permitting civil damages under the wiretap statute would violate the First Amendment. Even the appellate court decision strikes a discordant note because the court also refused to dismiss the claim on grounds that the "injurious act" language specifically violated the First Amendment but instead clung to the notion of *constitutional vagueness*. The higher court gave no indication that an authorization of civil suits would violate the Constitution.

Only 12 states—California, Connecticut, Florida, Illinois, Maryland, Massachusetts, Michigan, Montana, Nevada, New Hampshire, Pennsylvania, and Washington—now prohibit recording a conversation unless all participants have consented.[147] Twenty-four states ban use of hidden cameras in private places; some are specifically applied to instances involving nudity.[148]

Journalists and others who secretly record conversations by phone or other means risk criminal and civil penalties in those jurisdictions. *The rule in these states is that you must have consent of all parties before recording.* Even in the other states and for interstate calls under the federal rules, there are other risks. Although the Communications Act of 1934, in its current form, makes no mention of secret recordings by broadcasters, the Federal Communications Commission, regulating broadcast as well as common carriers such as telephone companies, still has rules that require telephone companies to cancel a customer's service when the person records phone conversations without notifying all parties with an audio tone or "beep." In addition, all radio and television stations must inform any participant if a *telephone* conversation is being recorded for broadcast. The later rule does not require that an audible tone be transmitted, but instead that the participants must be given reasonable verbal notice at the time.

One of the false assumptions of most computer users is that by pressing or clicking the delete button, they are actually deleting a file. All that is accomplished with this step is simply freeing up the space on the hard drive or disk so that it can be written over, if needed. In other words, hitting "delete" tells the computer that it can put something else in that space if the need arises later, not that the file is erased. Most computer users are also not aware that computer servers routinely back up files, making deleted files available. A cottage industry has as emerged in which computer experts retrieve deleted files as part of the discovery process. As Attorney Chad A. McGowan concluded in a *Georgia Bar Journal* article, "Counsel should not overlook deleted files on an opponent's computer systems because it is possible those files can be recovered. The files marked as deleted might just contain the telltale memo, e-mail or piece of correspondence necessary to prove your client's case."[149] The threat of e-mail discovery is driving corporations to negotiate settlements in lawsuits rather than face the time and expense of discovery.

Most states now use digitalized photos for driver licenses, raising privacy concerns about police misuse and even commercial exploitation because the photos are stored the same way as other electronic records. Anyone can gain access to an individual's picture as easily as getting an address, unless records were not made part of the public record. The National Press Photographers Association has a *Digital Manipulation Policy* including specific guidelines for dealing with digital images.

Cell phones continue to be a major privacy concern even though it is illegal to intercept conversations without a court order. Many people who use these devices do not realize they function like radio transmitters. A federal statute bans anyone from selling or manufacturing a radio receiver capable of intercepting cellular phone conversations, but many broadband receivers had already been sold before the law took effect. It is also simple to modify a cell phone to pick up other phone conversations. In the famous O. J. Simpson Bronco chase in Los Angeles in 1994, police were monitoring Simpson's cellular conversations as the chase was being broadcast.

The radio conversations of police, firefighters, ambulance drivers, etc., can be overheard by anyone who owns a scanner or similar device, but Section 605(a) of the Federal Communications Act prohibits interception and divulgence of such transmissions.

One famous intercepted cellular phone call was that of former U.S. House Speaker Newt Gingrich in 1996. A Florida couple taped the call between Gingrich and Republican leaders and then shared it with the ranking Democrat on the House Ethics Committee. A transcript of the call, which had been picked on a radio scanner, was published in the *New York Times*, the *Atlanta Journal-Constitution*, and *Roll Call*, a Capitol Hill newspaper.[150] The couple entered into a plea bargain with federal officials, agreeing to pay a $1,000 fine in exchange for being charged only with illegally intercepting a cellular phone call.[151]

In *Vernonia School District 47J v. Acton* (1995),[152] the U.S. Supreme Court upheld the constitutionality of an Oregon public school district's Student Athlete Drug Policy (SADP) that authorized random urinalysis drug testing of students in athletic programs. The case began when a student refused to take the test and was not allowed to play football. He and his parents sued on grounds that the policy violated his Fourth and Fourteenth Amendment rights and the state constitution. The U.S. District Court denied the claims, but the Ninth Circuit U.S. Court of Appeals reversed, holding the policy violated federal and state constitutions.

In a 6–3 decision, the Court held that the policy was constitutional. The Court said such testing does constitute a "search" under the Fourth Amendment, but that its "reasonableness is judged by balancing the intrusion on the individual's Fourth Amendment interests against the promotion of legitimate government interests." The justices reasoned that children in the temporary custody of the state have less of a legitimate expectation of privacy and that the deterrence of drug use is sufficiently important to override privacy interests in the situation: "Taking into account all the factors we have considered above—the decreased expectation of privacy, the relative unobtrusiveness of the search, and the severity of the need met by the search—we conclude Vernonia's Policy is reasonable and hence constitutional."[153]

The U.S. Supreme Court struck down as unconstitutional a Georgia statute in 1997 requiring candidates for certain public offices to certify that they had taken a urinalysis drug test at least 30 days before they qualified for nomination or election and that the result was negative. In *Chandler v. Miller* (1997),[154] the Court held in an 8–1 opinion that such a required test did not fall within the limited category of constitutionally permissible suspicion less searches such as what was permitted in *Vernonia School District 47J*. The Court noted, "Our precedents establish that the proffered special need for drug testing must be substantial—important enough to override the individual's acknowledged privacy interest, sufficiently vital to suppress the Fourth Amendment's normal requirement of individualized suspicion."[155] Georgia failed to show special need.

The Court was not as concerned with how the test was administered as it was with the fact that no special need was demonstrated. Noting that the state allowed the candidate to take the test in the office of his or her own physician and that the results are provided to the candidate first, the Court did not find the testing process particularly invasive. The justices were not convinced that the requirement would deter unlawful drug users from seeking office, pointing out that the candidate could schedule the test date and thus abstain for a pretest period to get a negative result. The state also presented no evidence that there was a drug problem among elected state officials, the Court said: "The need revealed, in short, is symbolic, not 'special,' as that term draws meaning from our case law."[156] The Court concluded:

> We reiterate, too, that where the risk to public safety is substantial and real, blanket suspicion less searches calibrated to the risk may rank as 'reasonable'—for example, searches now routine at airports and at entrances to courts and other official buildings. [cite omitted] But where, as in this case, public safety is not genuinely in jeopardy, the *Fourth Amendment* precludes the suspicion less search, no matter how conveniently arranged.[157]

The majority opinion noted that it was expressing no opinion on whether a state could impose a requirement that candidates certify they were in good health based upon a medical examination, a point Chief Justice Rehnquist, in dissent, did not find convincing: "It is all but inconceivable that a case involving that sort of requirement (medical examination) could be decided differently than the present case; the same sort of urinalysis would be involved."[158]

The formal need for and understanding of privacy was reinforced by the U.S. Congress in 2002. An ombudsman-like position was created to uphold the Privacy Act. Initially, some watch dog groups expressed concern that a Homeland Security chief privacy officer would be nothing more than a rubber stamp for the government's anti-terror initiatives. But the person placed in charge, O'Connor Kelly, was subsequently credited for implementing training programs for government managers and negotiating an information sharing agreement with the European Union, which already had privacy protections. O'Connor had been employed as legal counsel for an Internet company, Double Click, Inc. As Homeland Security's chief privacy officer, she was credited for delaying use of a program called Secure Flight, which attempted to gain information on airline travelers using commercial databases.[159]

Impact of Codes of Ethics

None of the major codes of ethics directly mentions surreptitious monitoring or recording, and the journalistic community appears divided on the propriety of common investigative reporting techniques that the public, by and large, considers improper, such as misrepresentation, sifting through an individual's trash, and accepting or using documents stolen by someone else without the cooperation of the media organization. The Society of Professional Journalists Code of Ethics does say under "Seek Truth and Report It" that journalists should "avoid undercover or other surreptitious methods of gathering information except when traditional open methods will not reveal information vital to the public."

Is it ethical for journalists to hound controversial figures wherever they go and to write about and photograph personal tragedies with cameras, notepads, and microphones at hand? There were many tragic and telling moments captured on film and in print during the Vietnam War, some of which are said to have altered public support of the war such as the picture of the naked Vietnamese girl screaming as she flees a napalm attack and the photo of the south Vietnamese soldier shooting the captured Viet Cong soldier through the head. In spite of severe restraints imposed by the military on the press during the Persian Gulf War, some of the stories and photos published were graphic and poignant. *Detroit Free Press* photographer David Turnley won accolades for one of the war's "most memorable" pictures—an American soldier sobbing after he discovers that the body in a bag in the helicopter ferrying him to a hospital is his friend.[160] CNN videos and photos of the desecration of an American soldier's body by Somali citizens immortalized in the film *Black Hawk Down* intensified public pressure to remove U.S. troops from Somalia. *USA Today* carried a front-page photo of that scene.

The wars in Iraq and Afghanistan have seen their share of privacy controversies, including an initial Pentagon clamp-down on photos of coffins in official custody carrying the bodies of soldiers killed in the war. The restriction was enacted after the publication of photos of flag-draped coffins being transported in Iraq for transport to the United States. The U.S. military itself made photos available of the lifeless face of Abu Musab al-Zarqawi, the leader of the terrorist organization Al-Qaeda in Iraq, when he was killed by bombs dropped by U.S. warplanes. However, in general, the war in Iraq did not generate nearly as much graphic coverage in the mass media as previous wars, although videos of beheadings of Americans and others, including the murder of *Wall Street Journal* reporter Daniel Pearl in Pakistan, were available on the Internet.

Defenses to Intrusion

There is only one sure-fire defense to intrusion: consent. In those 37 states that permit participant monitoring, the consent needs to come from only one participant, which can include the individual actually making the recording. What if a call to one of the other 13 states comes from one of the 37 states? Would the law of the participant monitoring state prevail or the law of the other state apply? In *Kearney v. Salomon Smith Barney* (2006),[161] the Supreme Court of California answered that question for that state. Applying California's choice-of-law rules, the California high court said the state had a "strong and continuing interest in protecting the privacy of its residents" and thus could ban secretly recorded phone conversations between its citizens and out-of-state callers. The case arose when a national brokerage corporation was sued for secretly recording its telephone calls to California customers. The company made the calls from Georgia, which permits such taping so long as one party consents. The California Supreme Court indicated that Georgia did "have a legitimate interest in protecting its companies from unexpected liability based on past actions that were lawful in Georgia," and thus upheld the dismissal of claims for damages and restitution by the lower court.

Even in those 13 states that require consent of all parties, a form of implied consent can sometimes be invoked, as illustrated in *Florida Publishing Co. v. Fletcher* and *Cassidy v. ABC*. Because publication is not required for intrusion to occur, *newsworthiness* and *privilege* are not available as defenses for the intrusion itself, although they may provide protection for a defendant for publication of the information. A reporter who illegally obtained documents indicating that the local police chief has been involved in drug trafficking would probably not face a suit for disclosing information but might be charged with criminal offenses and possibly have to pay civil damages for the intrusion. Ethically, journalists should avoid secret recording and monitoring unless (a) the information is being obtained via a strictly legal means, (b) there is no other effective way of obtaining the information, and (c) publishing the information would definitely serve the public interest.

Publication of Private Matters

This third tort of invasion of privacy goes by several names. The basic elements are the same. They include publication of private matters and public disclosure of private facts. No one's life, even a U.S. President's, is entirely an open book. In general, the more prominent the individual, the less protection that person enjoys from unwanted publication of private affairs. This tort has three basic elements as indicated in the Restatement (Second) of Torts: "One who gives publicity to a matter concerning the private life of another is subject to liability to the other for invasion of his privacy, if the matter published is of a kind that (a) would be highly offensive to a reasonable person, and (b) is not of legitimate public interest."[162]

Publication

The first element, *publication*, is generally easy for a plaintiff to demonstrate and is usually not in dispute. Unlike libel, which requires that the defamatory information be communicated merely to a third party, public disclosure of private facts must be fairly widespread because this is a tort of publicity, not simply communication. Thus embarrassing facts jotted in a reporter's notebook would not be sufficient to meet the publication requirement nor would an internal memo about a worker that is circulated among supervisors. An in-house newsletter for employees and a gossip column in a small weekly newspaper would satisfy the criterion.

Offensiveness

The second element, *offensiveness*, has been defined differently in different jurisdictions and is often litigated. A critical aspect is that the published facts must be highly offensive, not simply embarrassing, to the reasonable person. This determination is always a jury question (i.e., fact) in a jury trial because jurors in a community are presumed to judge as reasonable people, just as in obscenity cases, whether contemporary community standards are violated. The courts have been strict in applying the standard, much to the chagrin of the public, which tends to view more of a person's private life as worthy of protection.

When U.S. Court of Appeals Judge Robert Bork was unsuccessfully nominated as a U.S. Supreme Court justice in the late eighties, a small weekly newspaper in Washington, D.C., *City Paper*, obtained a list of movies that he had rented from a local video store. The newspaper published the list along with a story that attempted to explore the "inner workings of Robert Bork's mind" as revealed by video rentals. The Senate Judiciary Committee, which reviews Supreme Court nominees, was outraged, as was the majority of Congress, and enacted the Video Privacy Protection Act of 1988,[163] popularly known as the "Bork law." This statute provides civil damages but *no criminal penalties* against "video tape service providers" (presumably stores, although the wording is vague) that disclose "personally identifiable information concerning any consumer." Anyone "aggrieved" by the "wrongful disclosure of video tape rental or sale records" may recover actual damages of at least $2,500 and punitive damages for intentional disclosure. The law has had no adverse impact on the press thus far, and it is unclear whether any entity other than rental stores is covered. In fact, there have apparently been no suits yet against anyone for violating the statute. The law may very well be unconstitutional prior restraint, but it epitomizes the gap between zones of privacy versus those dictated by legislation. It is highly unlikely that a court would consider public disclosure of one's video preferences offensive, but Congress was ready to carve out this area of privacy.

In 1989 a deranged and disgruntled former employee at Standard Gravure Corporation wounded 13 and killed 8 workers at the plant with a Chinese-made AK-47 assault rifle in a shooting spree before taking his own life with a pistol. The next day the *Louisville Courier-Journal* published a front-page photograph of one of the murder victims sprawled on the floor. The photo did not identify the victim, but part of his face was visible. The newspaper was besieged with public criticism for publishing the controversial picture, which it sold to *Newsweek* and other publications. Editor David Hawpe defended his paper's use of the picture, noting that the decision came after extensive discussion with other editors. "We did think about the impact such a picture might have on the family and friends of the victim," according to Hawpe. "The photo did what I wanted it to do by showing the reality of what assault weapons are capable of. A less graphic photograph would not have been as effective."[164]

The family of the victim sued the paper for invasion of privacy and intentional infliction of emotional distress, but a Kentucky Circuit Court judge dismissed the suit on grounds that the photo was newsworthy, that the family had no basis for a claim because dead individuals have no right of privacy under state law (other than appropriation) and that publication of the photo did not constitute extreme and outrageous conduct necessary for proving intentional infliction of emotional distress. A Kentucky Court of Appeals upheld the dismissal, the Kentucky Supreme Court declined to review, and the Supreme Court of the United States denied certiorari.[165]

The public was similarly upset a month earlier when a video and still photos taken from it appeared in the media, showing a man alleged to be U.S. hostage Lt. Col. William Richard Higgins dangling from a gallows. The tape was released by pro-Iranian extremists who said they had tried and executed the U.S. officer, who was captured while serving in a U.N. observer group. During the recent Iraq War, the release of videos of the decapitations of civilians has caused even greater alarm.

Cox Broadcasting Corp. v. Martin Cohn (1975)

Most states have statutes prohibiting the publication of rape victims' names, but a decision by the U.S. Supreme Court in 1975 in *Cox Broadcasting Corp. v. Martin Cohn*[166] declared a Georgia statute unconstitutional that made it a misdemeanor to publish or broadcast the name or identity of any female who may have been raped or against whom a rape may have been attempted. The law violated the First and Fourteenth Amendments because it permitted civil liability against a television station that accurately reported the name of a rape victim it had obtained from a public record. In August 1971, 17-year-old Cynthia Cohn was gang raped and murdered. Five of the six youths who had been indicted in the case pled guilty to rape or attempted rape after murder charges were dropped. The sixth defendant pled not guilty and was bound over for trial later. While he was covering the proceedings, a reporter for WSB-TV in Atlanta, where the crime occurred, obtained the victim's name from the indictments, which were available as public records. In the evening newscast, the reporter used Cynthia Cohn's name in a report about the proceedings, and the report was rebroadcast the next morning. Cohn's father filed suit against the station, claiming that his right to privacy had been invaded by disclosure of his deceased daughter's name. A state trial court granted summary judgment in favor of Martin Cohn and ordered a jury trial to determine damages. The Georgia Supreme Court ruled that the trial court had erred in construing a civil cause of action based on the criminal statute but that Cohn could sue under a common law right of privacy. On appeal, the U.S. Supreme Court reversed:

> In placing the information in the public domain on official court records, the State must be presumed to have concluded that the public interest was thereby being served. Public records by their very nature are of interest to those concerned with the administration of government, and a public benefit is performed by the reporting of the true contents of the records by the media. The freedom of the press to publish that information appears to us to be one of critical importance to our type of government in which the citizenry is the final judge of the proper conduct of public business.[167]

Although the Georgia Supreme Court escaped the issue of the constitutionality of the state statute by holding that it did not provide a civil cause of action, the U.S. Supreme Court held, in effect, that the statute did create such a cause of action and was a violation of the First and Fourth Amendments. To prevent the press from being punished either in a civil or criminal suit, the Court had to go further, by holding that a constitutional privilege existed to give the media the right to publish truthful information obtained from public records. Thus this decision covers a broad range of information, not simply rape victim names. The Court did *not* say that rape victims' names could not be protected, but that such information could be published with impunity once it had become public record.

Florida Star v. B.J.F. (1989)

Fourteen years after *Cox Broadcasting v. Cohn*, the Supreme Court of the United States decided another case involving the publication of a rape victim's name. There are several parallels between the two cases but there were two major and interesting differences. The name in the 1989 case was accidentally published and was not in a court record. B.J.F. (the Court used only her initials to respect privacy) reported to the Duval County, Florida, sheriff's department that she had been robbed and sexually assaulted by an unknown man. The department issued a report based on her information and placed the report, as it routinely did for reported crimes, in the press room, accessible to anyone. The report included the victim's full name. A reporter-trainee for the *Florida Star*, a weekly newspaper that serves Jacksonville with a circulation of about 18,000, used the information to write a story for the "Police Reports" section of the paper:

> [B.J.F.'s full name] reported on Thursday, October 20, she was crossing Brentwood Park, which is in the 500 block of Golfair Boulevard, enroute to her bus stop, when an unknown black man ran up behind the lady and placed a knife to her neck and told her not to yell. The suspect then undressed the lady and had sexual intercourse with her before fleeing the scene with her 60 cents, Timex watch and gold necklace. Patrol efforts have been suspended concerning this incident because of a lack of evidence.[168]

Like most newspapers, the *Florida Star* had a written internal policy against publishing the names of sexual offense victims. B.J.F.'s name had been accidentally published. The report was one of 54 police reports that appeared that day in the paper. The victim sued both the *Star* and the sheriff's department for negligence. Prior to trial, the department settled out of court by agreeing to pay B.J.F. $2,500 in damages. After a day-long trial at which the woman testified that she had suffered emotional distress from threatening phone calls and other incidents as a result of the story, a jury awarded her $75,000 in compensatory damages and $25,000 in punitive damages. A state appeals court upheld the decision, and the U.S. Supreme granted certiorari. In *Florida Star v. B.J.F.* (1989), the Supreme Court ruled 5–4 in favor of the newspaper but disappointed most journalists by refusing to extend First Amendment protection:

> Our holding today is limited. We do not hold that truthful publication is automatically constitutionally protected, or that there is no zone of personal privacy within which the State may protect the individual from intrusion by the press, or even that a State may never punish publication of the name of a victim of a sexual offense. We hold only that where a newspaper publishes truthful information which it has lawfully obtained, punishment may be imposed, if at all, only when narrowly tailored to a state interest of the highest order, and that no such interest is satisfactorily served by imposing liability under 794.03 [the Florida statute] to appellant [the *Star*] under the facts of the case.[169]

The Court based its decision on *Cox v. Cohn* (1975) and two other cases, *Oklahoma Publishing Co. v. Oklahoma County District Court* (1977)[171] and *Smith v. Daily Mail Publishing Co.* (1979).[171] In Oklahoma Publishing Co. the Court held in a per curiam opinion that a trial court judge's order prohibiting the press from publishing the name and photo of an 11-year-old boy charged with murder was unconstitutional prior restraint because the hearing at which his name was revealed was open to the public. In Smith, a West Virginia statute was unanimously declared unconstitutional because it imposed criminal penalties for publishing, without permission from a juvenile court judge, the identity of a juvenile offender even when the information was lawfully obtained. Smith was a narrow decision. There was no question of unlawful access to court proceedings, privacy or of prejudicial publicity. In such a situation, the Court said "state officials may not constitutionally punish publication of the information absent a need to further a state interest of the highest order."[172] In neither Smith nor Florida Star had the state demonstrated such an interest. In the latter decision the Court said it could "not rule out the possibility that, in a proper case, imposing civil sanctions for publication of a rape victim might be so overwhelmingly necessary to advance these interests [privacy of victims of sex offenses, physical safety of such victims and encouraging victims to report offenses without fear of exposure] as to satisfy the [Smith v.] Daily Mail standard."[173]

Two situations, both of which occurred in 1991, illustrate the complexity of the issue of whether rape victims' names should be made public. In the first, Palm Beach (Florida) County Circuit Court Judge Mary Lupo issued a gag order in the trial of 30-year-old William Kennedy Smith, a nephew of Massachusetts Senator Edward Kennedy. Smith was charged with second-degree sexual battery and misdemeanor battery in connection with the alleged rape of a young woman at his family's Palm Beach estate. The gag order itself was not highly unusual in such a case even though it barred all participants in the case, including all potential witnesses, from discussing the case outside the courtroom. What were unusual were the events that eventually led to the restrictive order. Before Smith was ever charged, several newspapers and NBC News identified the 29-year-old woman who had filed charges against him. The alleged victim was named first in a London tabloid newspaper and then in the U.S. tabloid the *National Enquirer*. The newspapers also published her photograph, broadcast shortly thereafter by NBC.

Although most news organizations have either written or unwritten policies against publishing the names of victims of sexual assault, several newspapers including the *New York Times* identified the woman. The Associated Press and newspapers such as the *Miami Herald* did not use the woman's name.[174] However many of the news organizations that have such a policy do permit disclosure of the identity when individuals choose to make their names public.

The *Des Moines* (Iowa) *Register*, which did identify the Palm Beach alleged rape victim, won a Pulitzer Prize a week earlier for a five-part series on the rape of a young woman, who gave consent for her name to be published so people would understand how rape brutalizes victims and should not be treated as just another crime. She decided to tell her story after the editor wrote a column arguing that withholding names of rape victims added to the stigma.[175]

In another case, the one involving a relative of the Kennedy clan of Massachusetts, after acquittal in a rape charge, the up to that time anonymous accuser went public to criticize the jury's verdict and gave interviews on several national talk shows. At that point, nearly all of the news media in the country then revealed her name. Interestingly, the *Globe*, the Florida-based tabloid that was among the first media outlets to publish the name of Smith's accuser, was charged with violating Florida's statute barring the publication of rape victims' names. The Palm Beach County Judge ultimately ruled that the law was unconstitutional on its face and as applied by prosecutors and dismissed the charge.[176]

The second occurrence attracted little media attention but may have been a significant development. In an unusual move, the U.S. Supreme Court identified a rape victim in a court decision. In a 7 to 2 opinion written by Justice Sandra Day O'Connor, the Court held that a defendant in a rape case may be barred under some circumstances from introducing evidence at trial of a previous sexual relationship with the victim. That decision of May, 1991, which had no direct bearing on First Amendment law, was nevertheless overshadowed by the identification. Justice O'Connor refused to indicate whether her action was intentional or an oversight, but no efforts were made to convince the media to omit the name. In a publicized rape case, charges against NBA star Kobe Bryant were dropped after allegations of sexual activity were made against his accuser.

If victims of sexual assaults should have their names kept confidential, what about the victims of other crimes? Should the name and address of a man who fell into an investment scam be revealed? What about the name and address of a woman who was robbed in front of a restaurant? Crime stories have been a staple of news since the penny press of the 1830s. However, except in sex offenses, victims of crimes have routinely been named in reports. In fact, many newspapers, such as the *Florida Star*, routinely carry a police blotter or summary log that is often one of the widest read sections, according to readership surveys.

In a very unfortunate twist on privacy rights and potential press abuse in November 2006, a crew from the award-winning *Dateline NBC* television series "To Catch a Predator" was situated outside of the North Texas home of an individual identified as part of its "sting operation," along with local police seeking his arrest, when the accused committed suicide. Louis "Bill" Conradt, Jr. had been a Texas prosecutor caught in the pedophile sting operation in Murphy, Texas and was identified as having solicited sex from someone he thought was a 13-year-old boy, but turned out to be police authorities. Conradt's sister announced in 2007 she had retained legal counsel, Baron Associates of Brooklyn, NY. Her attorney, Bruce Baron, indicated that his client could, due to *Dateline's* involvement in the situation, pursue several legal courses of action against NBC–Universal, including, among other things, wrongful death, violation of the decedent's civil and constitutional rights, extreme emotional distress, and the loss to his estate in "compensatory and punitive damages exceeding $100 million."

NBC noted that up to that time, there had not been a lawsuit filed on behalf of Conradt's estate and the company would vigorously defend itself against such a suit, if one were forthcoming. But at the same time, some media-related sources pointed out that Conradt had never actually met with any young boys and that the NBC program's relationship with police and, to some extent, another external organization—Perverted Justice—amounted to a form of entrapment, via the Internet. The partnership of the police with such outside entities and, particularly, members of the press can often raise red flags, although the performance of the *Dateline NBC* series was complicated by its relatively high rate of success in helping to catch sexual predators using the Internet, individuals operating previously "under the police radar" who might otherwise go undetected.[177]

Briscoe v. Reader's Digest (1971)

Sometimes the individuals *who commit crimes* cry foul. One case, *Briscoe v. Reader's Digest*, is typical of the dilemma news media face in identifying people who have been convicted of past crimes. Marvin Briscoe, who with an accomplice had hijacked a truck in 1956, was convicted and then rehabilitated. Eleven years later *Reader's Digest* published a story entitled "The Big Business of Hijacking," which included this sentence in its report on how truckers were fighting back against thieves: "Typical of many beginners, Marvin Briscoe and Garland Russell [his accomplice] stole a 'valuable-looking' truck in Danville, Ky., and then fought a gun battle with the local police, only to learn that they had hijacked four bowling pin spotters."[178]

No mention was made of when the incident took place. Briscoe sued for willful and malicious invasion of privacy as a result of this publication of what he contended were "embarrassing private facts about plaintiffs past life." A California Superior Court dismissed the case in favor of *Reader's Digest*, but on appeal, the Supreme Court of California reversed, holding that Briscoe could recover damages if he could demonstrate the magazine invaded his privacy with reckless disregard for facts a reasonable person would find highly offensive:

> First … a jury could reasonably find that plaintiff's identity in connection with incidents of his past life was in this case of minimal social value.… Second, a jury might find that revealing one's past for all to see is grossly offensive to most people in America.… Third, in no way can plaintiff be said to have voluntarily consented to the publicity accorded him here. He committed a crime. He was punished. He was rehabilitated. And he became for 11 years, an obscure and law abiding citizen. His every effort was to forget and have others forget that he had once hijacked a truck.[179]

Notice the court's intense concern with promoting rehabilitation by protecting the privacy of those who have become good citizens. The discordant note in this decision and those that followed in the U.S. Supreme Court is that a news medium could be punished for publishing truthful information contained in a public record. *Florida Star v. B.J.F.* points in this direction, as does *Cox v. Cohn*.

Would the decision have been different if the magazine mentioned the year? Briscoe would still have suffered, as he pointed out in his complaint, because his 11-year-old daughter and friends and acquaintances were not aware of his criminal history. Is it ethical to publish the name of someone who is rehabilitated? At what point should a media outlet no longer identify a convicted criminal? One year? How about five years or perhaps immediately after release from jail? Should the period of time vary with the crime or the sentence? It is not unusual for newspapers, magazines, and the electronic media to cover the releases of notorious criminals after they have served their terms. Does this serve the "compelling interest" of society, at least as perceived by this court, "in rehabilitating criminals and returning them as productive and law-abiding citizens"?[180] Does the public's need to know override this interest and the interest of individuals in protecting the privacy of their past?

When the *Briscoe* case went back to the trial court, it was removed to the U.S. District Court for the Central District of California. The federal trial court issued a summary judgment in 1972 in favor of the magazine, holding that the information was newsworthy, that it was published without malice or recklessness, that it was not an invasion of privacy, and that it was thus protected by the First Amendment. Judge Lawrence T. Lydick pointed out in his opinion that Briscoe had actually been imprisoned in Kentucky until December 1961, that on his release he was placed on federal probation until December 1964 and on state parole until February 1969, almost a year after the article appeared. The judge also indicated that his name and exploits were clearly remembered by the people in his hometown even at the time of the new trial.

Virgil v. Time (1975)

A few years later the Ninth U.S. Circuit of Appeals dealt with another unusual invasion of privacy case arising in California. In *Virgil v. Time* (1975)[181] the court held that a 1971 story in *Sports Illustrated* containing embarrassing facts about a body surfer's private life could claim First Amendment protection only if the information was shown to be newsworthy and of legitimate public interest. The story focused on surfing at the Wedge, a beach near Newport Beach, California, considered the most dangerous place in the world for body surfing. Mike Virgil, who had a reputation for being the biggest daredevil of surfers at the beach, was among the individuals described and was quoted in the 11-page article. Among the quotes attributed to Virgil are:

> I quit my job, left home and moved to Mammoth Mountain. At the ski lodge there one night I dove headfirst down a flight of stairs—just because. Because why? Well, there were these chicks all around. I thought it would be groovy. Was I drunk? I think I might have been. Every summer I'd work construction and dive off billboards to hurt myself or drop loads of lumber on myself to collect unemployment compensation so I could surf at the Wedge. Would I fake injuries? No, I wouldn't fake them. I'd be damn injured. But I would recover. I guess I used to live a pretty reckless life. I think I might have been drunk most of the time…. [in discussing his aggressiveness as a child] I bit off the cheek of a Negro in a 6-against-30 gang fight. They had tire irons with them.[182]

The article quoted Virgil's wife as saying, "Mike also eats spiders and other insects and things." According to the story, "Perhaps because much of his time was spent engaged in such activity, Virgil never learned how to read." A photo caption read, "Mike Virgil, the wild man of the Wedge, thinks it possible his brain is being slowly destroyed."[183]

While Virgil admitted in his complaint alleging invasion of privacy by the magazine that he had willingly talked with the reporter, he claimed that he "revoked all consent" when he learned the article contained negative statements about him. He had learned about the references to "bizarre incidents in his life that were not directly related to surfing" from a staff member who had telephoned him and his wife to verify information. At that time, Virgil told the checker that he did not want to be mentioned in the story and that he wanted the article stopped. Despite Virgil's opposition, *SI* published the story. The surfer filed suit. At trial the U.S. District Court denied Time, Inc.'s motion for summary judgment, and the trial court's decision was upheld on appeal to the Ninth Circuit, which then remanded the case back to the trial court. The U.S. Supreme Court denied certiorari on further appeal.[184] The district court ruled in favor of *Sports Illustrated* on grounds that the information in the story was newsworthy. The court did question whether the specific details about Virgil, such as diving down stairs and eating insects, were of legitimate public interest but concluded that this information helped the reader understand the frame of mind of people who are involved in high risk sports.[185]

Defenses to Publishing Private Matters

There are three basic defenses to publicizing private matters, none of which offers absolute protection: consent, privilege, and newsworthiness. As *Virgil v. Time* illustrates, *consent* can be revoked if done so reasonably. Virgil had willingly talked with the *Sports Illustrated* reporter and had disclosed embarrassing facts, but the court had no problem with his claim that he revoked his consent prior to publication by telling the checker that he wanted the story halted because he had discovered that the portrait would not be so flattering. As with the other torts of invasion of privacy, the consent must be voluntary—explicit or implicit. The individual who is granting the consent must possess the legal and mental capacity to do so.

Journalists should clearly identify themselves when interviewing potential sources and make it clear, whether by phone or in person, that the information may be used in a story. They should **never** promise a source that nothing negative will be used or that the story will take a particular approach. A practice in some news organizations is to have a copy editor check quotes and facts with sources to make sure information is accurate. Unfortunately, this can lead to situations such as the one in *Virgil v. Time* in which an important source may have second thoughts and then attempt to revoke consent. On the other hand, this approach is an effective way of documenting consent. If it appears controversy may arise and lead to a possible suit, the reporter or editor should get consent in writing or, at the very least, have an independent witness or tape recorder at hand.

Privilege, whether constitutional or under common law, is usually the strongest defense, as demonstrated in the *Florida Star* decision. *Constitutional privilege* simply means *First Amendment protection*. *Florida Star v. B.J.F.* made it clear that truthful information from public records does not enjoy absolute privilege because a state could conceivably demonstrate that prohibiting disclosure would further a state interest. The Florida statute has the fatal flaw that it applied only to an "instrument of mass communication," thus singling out the press for punishment. The statute also failed constitutional muster because it imposed a negligence per se standard, which did not permit findings on a case-by-case basis to determine whether a reasonable person would find the information highly offensive. Because the government has the burden of demonstrating state interest, a defendant remains relatively free to publish information from a public record made in good faith.

A common law privilege exists in some jurisdictions for publishing public records, but *Cox Broadcasting* and *Florida Star* make privilege unnecessary because the Court recognized a constitutional privilege in both cases that provided as much protection. Although some journalists and legal scholars are concerned that the Court did not broaden the sweep of the First Amendment to include all information in public records, the protection provided under *Florida Star* should be sufficient to permit anyone to publish truthful information lawfully obtained from a public record under almost any circumstances, including negligence, with impunity.

Newsworthiness is similar to common law privilege and is recognized as common law. It extends beyond public records and public proceedings to include matters that are of public interest. The U.S. Supreme Court has avoided directly confronting the question of whether newsworthiness itself is a viable defense to the publication of private matters, but state and lower federal courts have tackled this issue and recognized this defense. One of the earliest cases involved a child prodigy who became famous in 1910. He lectured to distinguished mathematicians on "four-dimensional bodies" at age 11 and graduated from Harvard when he was 16. William James Sidis subsequently avoided publicity, but was the unwilling subject of a brief biographical sketch and cartoon in 1937 in *The New Yorker*. Information was also published about him in a story in the magazine four months later, and an advertisement appeared in the publication to announce the first story.

According to the Second Circuit U.S. Court of Appeals in *Sidis v. F-R Publishing Corp.* (1940),[186] the initial article, which said Sidis had a "certain childlike charm," was "a ruthless exposure of a once public character, who has since sought and has now been deprived of the seclusion of private life."[187] The sketch was part of a regular feature in the magazine that described current and past personalities, with the latter appearing under the title, "Where Are They Now?" The Sidis piece was subtitled "April Fool" (Sidis was born on April 1) and described how the math genius was now "an insignificant clerk" who collected streetcar transfers and lived in an untidy room.

The Court of Appeals affirmed the District Court's dismissal of the invasion of privacy and malicious libel suit Sidis filed against the magazine, holding that even though the plaintiff had "cloaked himself in obscurity," his private life since he sought seclusion was nevertheless "a matter of public concern. The article in *The New Yorker* sketched the life of an unusual personality, and it possessed considerable popular news interest."[188] However, the court noted that it was not deciding whether newsworthiness was always a complete defense.

The approach taken by this court, although now more than 50 years old, is still being taken by other courts. Newsworthiness is not a high and mighty concept that requires a demonstrated *need* for the public to know but instead can be framed in the context of what people want to know. The Sidis story served no noble cause—people were just curious about the status of someone who once enjoyed the limelight.

Many newspapers and magazines carry sidebars or vignettes recalling events from the past under such titles as "25 Years Ago Today" highlighting old news. Often, the individuals whose names appear in these stories are shocked and some have sued for invasion of privacy. These items are different from the *Reader's Digest* story about Briscoe because they make clear the date of the event, and they are different from the Sidis article because they do not focus on one person and they do not indicate current status. Yet they can expose an individual to unwanted publicity. Nearly all cases involving this type story have been decided in favor of the mass media.

In 1976, the *Des Moines* (Iowa) *Sunday Register* published a long investigative feature about alleged illegal activities at a county home, including deaths from scalding baths, sterilization of young women residents who were mentally disabled, and improper shipments of prescription drugs. The article mentioned that an 18-year-old woman named Robin Woody had been sterilized in 1970 with consent of her mother. It included quotes from an interview with the psychiatrist for the Jasper County Home, who characterized Woody as an "impulsive, hair-triggered, young girl."[189] The feature gave other details of the sterilization and noted that Woody had been discharged from the home at the end of 1971 and her mother did not know where she was living. Although the newspaper did not know at the time the article was published, Robin Woody had become Robin Howard and, according to her petition to the court, had "led a quiet and respectable life and made friends and acquaintances who were not aware of her surgery."[190]

Robin Howard sued the newspaper and its reporter for disclosure of the information, but the Iowa District Court issued a summary judgment in favor of the defendants on the grounds that the article was "newsworthy and was not shockingly offensive or distasteful and was not a sensational prying into Plaintiff's private life for its own sake."[191] The trial court noted that newsworthiness was the most compelling reason for its decision.

On appeal, the Iowa Supreme Court upheld the district court's summary judgment. The appellate court concluded that the plaintiff's name and the details of her sterilization had been obtained from public records (working files in the governor's office provided by an administrative assistant at the request of the reporter) and that the fact of the sterilization was a public rather than a private fact and a matter of legitimate public concern. According to the court:

> In the sense of serving an appropriate news function, the disclosure contributed constructively to the impact of the article. It offered a personalized frame of reference to which the reader could relate, fostering perception and understanding. Moreover, it lent specificity and credibility to the report. In this way the disclosure served as an effective means of accomplishing the intended news function. It had positive communicative value in attracting the reader's attention to the article's subject matter and in supporting expression of the underlying theme.[192]

The court was not willing to say it was necessary for the newspaper to name names, but said the *Register* had the right to treat identity as a matter of legitimate concern.

In 1975 ex-marine Oliver Sipple knocked a gun out of the hand of Sara Jane Moore just as she was attempting to fire a second shot at President Gerald Ford in San Francisco. His heroic act attracted extensive national media attention. The *San Francisco Chronicle* and other publications revealed that Sipple was a homosexual, a fact he had not disclosed to family members in the Midwest, although he was well-known and active in San Francisco's gay community, having marched in several gay parades. When Sipple sued for invasion of privacy, a California trial court judge granted summary judgment for the *Chronicle*. The California Court of Appeals upheld the lower court decision on grounds that Sipple's sexual orientation was public, not private, in this case and that this information was newsworthy.[193]

According to the court, even though Sipple probably did not realize the consequences of his act at the time, his effort nevertheless attracted legitimate media attention that was "not limited to the event that itself arouses the public interest."[194] The court also contended that the coverage of his homosexuality arose from "legitimate political considerations, i.e., to dispel the false public opinions that gays were timid, weak and unheroic figures and to raise the equally important political question whether the President of the United States entertained a discriminatory attitude or bias against a minority group such as homosexuals."[195]

State and federal courts are sometimes uneven in their application of the newsworthiness defense, as illustrated by two cases in 2005. In the first case, a U.S. District Court judge issued a summary judgment for the defendants in an Oklahoma civil case in which *Harper's Magazine* and one of its photographers was sued for publishing pictures of an open casket at the funeral of a National Guard member killed in Iraq.[196]

The judge said the First Amendment protected the magazine's right to publish photos of the funeral because it was public and newsworthy. The judge acknowledged a right of privacy enjoyed by the family, but held that the public right to know should prevail. Almost 1,200 people attended: the governor and members of the press, including the photographer, who had been invited as well. The family had claimed in its lawsuit that three privacy torts had occurred: appropriation, publication of private facts, and intrusion. The court dismissed all three as well as other claims, including intentional infliction of emotional distress and false representation.[197]

In the second case, the U.S. Court of Appeals for the D.C. Circuit ruled that the D.C. Freedom of Information Act and the Drivers Privacy Protection Act of 1994 (discussed in the next chapter) protected the disclosure of the addresses of drivers who had been ticketed after cameras captured them running red lights in Washington, D.C. According to a three-judge panel, the plaintiff failed to demonstrate public interest would be served by release of information.[198]

Student Privacy Rights

Under the Family Educational Rights and Privacy Act of 1974 (FERPA), also known as the Buckley Amendment, elementary and secondary schools as well as colleges and universities that receive federal funding face the potential loss of such funding if they release students' educational records. The original purpose of the Act was to grant students and parents the right to restrict access to students' educational records without written consent. The Act has been amended over the decades to allow public and/or government access to specific types of information, including decisions involving students disciplined for sex offenses and violent acts. The Campus Sex Crimes Prevention Act, which took effect in 2002, requires convicted sex offenders already registered in states to notify colleges and universities to which they apply and attend of their convictions. The statute also requires higher education institutions to make public how students, staff, and faculty can access information about sex offenders on campus.[199] Some records, including law enforcement, employee, and alumni records, are not covered.[200]

The U.S. Supreme Court handed down two cases, just months apart in 2002, dealing with FERPA. In the first case, *Owasso Independent School District No. I-011 v. Falvo*,[201] the Court held in a unanimous decision (with Justice Scalia concurring) that peer grading and students calling out peers' grades in the classroom do not violate FERPA. The Court ruled such information did not constitute education records defined by the Act as "records, files documents, and other materials" with information directly related to a student that "are maintained by an educational agency or institution or by a person acting for such agency or institution."[202] The Court reasoned even if one assumes a teacher's grade book is an education record, there is no score until the grade is recorded, including calling out scores, not "maintained" per se.

In *Owasso* the U.S. Supreme Court noted that it assumed but was not deciding whether FERPA provided private parties with the right to sue for violations, but exactly four months later the Court ruled that a university student whose records were improperly disclosed by the institution had no right under FERPA to sue to enforce the statute and thus could not recover damages for any violations. In *Gonzaga University v. Doe* (2002),[203] the Court reversed a jury award of compensatory and punitive damages against Gonzaga, a private institution in Washington state. The university was sued by an individual whose affidavit certifying good moral character to teach in a public elementary school was denied when he was a student after a teacher certification specialist began an investigation of it. The teacher had overheard two students discussing allegations that the plaintiff had engaged in sexual misconduct. At the time of the suit, the state required every new teacher to have a certificate of good moral character from the institution from which he or she graduated. According to the Court, the remedy for such FERPA violations was a cutoff of federal funds, as provided in the statute, not civil damages.

In the aftermath of multi-murders on its campus in 2007, Virginia Tech officials said they were reviewing the impact of state and federal privacy laws on communication within the university, including between counseling services and academic affairs, maintaining privacy laws had prevented campus police from knowing whether the assailant Seung-Hui Cho had been hospitalized for mental illness, as he had been ordered to by a local judge. U.S. Department of Education later issued a determination in May, 2010 saying University officials failed "to issue adequate warnings in a timely manner in response to the tragic events of April 16, 2007." [204]

The Internet has created some interesting privacy dilemmas in recent years for high school and college students, especially in the use of MySpace.com, a commercial social networking service. The service began in 2004 and only two years later was purchased by News Corp., the media conglomerate that also owns Fox television and radio, for $580 million in cash. At the time of the purchase the website already had more than 80 million members, primarily teens and college students, although some parents and other adults are also members. There is no charge for creating an account on the site, which is supported by advertising. The basic idea of MySpace and similar services such as Facebook.com, Friendster, and 360 (owned by Yahoo) is to provide individual sites on the server so members can share information with each other, including photos, videos, personal preferences, and other details.[205] Among the problems with such services is that the sites are available for viewing not only by friends but by school authorities, law enforcement, and even sexual predators.[206] Other websites such as Blip TV, Google Video, Vimeo, and YouTube are popular with college students because they allow users to post video clips. Some of these postings, as well as those on student blogs, have attracted the attention of college officials concerned about the depiction of illegal behavior such as underage drinking and public indecency. Two 17-year-olds were charged with setting 17 fires in Maryland in 2006 after they bragged about their crimes on their sites on MySpace.com.[207]

Identity theft has become a serious problem in this country, and college campuses have not been immune from the problem. Lexis-Nexis and IBM announced a joint effort with universities and law enforcement agencies around the country in 2006 to establish a new center to focus on identity theft.[208] According to media reports, more than 20 million individuals had suffered identity theft in just a three year period.[209] Even Lexis-Nexis experienced a security breach in which data on more than 300,000 citizens were stolen.[210] About the same time, the University of Kentucky revealed that data on some 1,300 current and former employees, including social security numbers, had been accidentally made public on the Internet for almost three weeks before the error was discovered. [211] The previous year ChoicePoint said it may have accidentally sold personal information on 140,000 citizens to criminals who had pretended to be legitimate businesses. One of the publicized and largest thefts of data involved a stolen laptop computer, eventually recovered containing the Department of Veteran Affairs personnel records of more than 26.5 million individuals.[212] Apparently no records were used to commit identity theft, but the department came under heavy fire from members of Congress and the public.

Health Insurance Portability and Accountability Act of 2003 (HIPAA)

On April 14, 2003, a new federal medical privacy law known as the Health Insurance Portability and Accountability Act (HIPAA)[213] took effect. The statute does not directly apply to journalists or the news media. It regulates only entities that bill or are paid for medical services or that transmit electronic payments including health insurance plans, medical facilities, and health care professionals. HIPAA bans entities affected from disclosing, unless a patient consents, "personally identifying information such as names, addresses or specific medical condition."[214] The statute says that hospitals and other medical facilities must specifically ask patients whether they want information about them made public. If a patient does not agree that the information can be publicly disclosed, the facility cannot even disclose the person's condition or even indicate whether the person is dead or being transferred.[215] This means, for example, that a hospital generally cannot give the media a patient's name, although it presumably can confirm whether a particular individual is hospitalized as well as the person's general medical condition, age range, and home state or region.[216] As attorneys Andrew Mar and Alison Page Howard point out on the website for the First Amendment Center at Vanderbilt University, the Act "does not apply to every entity that has a health-care function." [217] In addition, as they note, "Health-care information the media obtains independently is not subject to HIPAA and may be published or broadcast freely, subject to limitations and internal policies on printing information about minors or the deceased."[218]

On paper, at least, HIPAA does have teeth. Under the statute, the U.S. Department of Health and Human Services (HHS) has the authority to levy fines of up to $100 for civil violations with a maximum fine of $25,000. Criminal violations carry a fine of up to $250,000 and 10 years in prison.[219] According to a *Washington Post* story three years after the Act took effect, in spite of more than 19,000 complaints filed, the federal government had prosecuted only two criminal violations and imposed no civil fines.[220]

False Light

In this age of docudramas and fictionalized accounts of public and private events, from the sad stories of Marilyn Monroe to the tragic shooting of James Brady (presidential press secretary, wounded along with President Ronald Reagan), it may be surprising to some that the tort of false light is alive and well. The Restatement (Second) of Torts defines false light as:

> One who gives publicity to a matter concerning another that places the other before the public in a false light is subject to liability to the other for invasion of privacy, if (a) the false light in which the other was placed would be highly offensive to a reasonable person, and (b) the actor had knowledge of or acted in reckless disregard as to the falsity of the publicized matter and the false light in which the other would be placed.[221]

Thus false light shares elements of both publicizing private matters and libel but is still different from both. Whereas the information must be false and must be published with reckless disregard for the truth or knowing the information was false (what the Supreme Court of the United States characterized as "actual malice" from *New York Times v. Sullivan* until it retreated from this term in 1991), it need not be defamatory. Only two false light cases have been decided by the U.S. Supreme Court, and although both were hailed as significant decisions, they only began to draw the boundaries of this amorphous, hybrid tort.

False light law suits typically originate with individuals involuntarily attracting media attention that distorts or fictionalizes their lives or the events in which they were involved. Generally, they are private people who want no media attention, even if sympathetic or positive. Each of the two Supreme Court decisions illustrates the false light trap.

Time Inc. v. Hill (1967): Extending Actual Malice Rule to False Light

The first, *Time Inc. v. Hill* (1967),[222] arose when *Life* published an article in February 1955 entitled "True Crime Inspires Tense Play," with the subtitle, "The ordeal of a family trapped by convicts gives Broadway a new thriller, 'The Desperate Hours.'" The feature described how three years earlier the James Hill family had been held prisoners in their home outside Philadelphia by three escaped convicts. It went on to note that Joseph Hayes' novel, *The Desperate Hours*, had been inspired by the family's ordeal and the story had been reenacted in a Broadway play.

The *Life* piece characterized the play as an "expertly acted ... heart stopping account of how a family rose to heroism in a crisis." The magazine staff photographed the play while it was running in Philadelphia and took some of the actors and actresses to the house where the Hills lived at the time of the incident for pictures. (The Hills no longer lived in the house.) The two pages following the text included an enactment of the beating of the son by one of the convicts, called a "brutish convict," and the "daring daughter" biting the hand of one of the thugs to force him to drop his gun. Another photo showed an actor portraying the father throwing a gun through the door after a "brave try" to save his family fails. While it was true that James Hill and his wife and five children were held hostage in their Whitemarsh, Pennsylvania, home by three convicts for 19 hours, the family was released unharmed and members told reporters afterward that the convicts had treated them courteously, had not molested them, and had not been violent. Two of the convicts were killed later in an encounter with police, and the Hills moved to Connecticut where they tried to avoid press attention.

Several months later, a novel appeared with a fictionalized account of the event in which a family of four is held hostage by three escaped convicts. The convicts in the novel beat the father and son and verbally assaulted the daughter. The play was based on the book. James Hill sued for invasion of privacy in New York, claiming that the magazine had used the family's name for trade purposes (i.e., appropriation), the article was a "fictionalization" as prohibited under New York's privacy statute, and the article portrayed the family in false light. A jury awarded him $50,000 in compensatory and $25,000 in punitive damages. On appeal, the Appellate Division of the New York Supreme Court ordered a new trial but upheld the jury's verdict of liability. At the new trial on damages, the Appellate Division (a trial court despite the name) awarded Hill $30,000 in compensatory damages and no punitive damages. (In effect, the judge—a jury trial was waived—reduced the damages to $30,000.) The New York Court of Appeals, New York's highest court, affirmed.

The United States Supreme Court reversed the decision of the New York Court of Appeals in an opinion written by Justice Brennan: "We hold that the constitutional protections for speech and press preclude the application of the New York statute to redress false reports of matters of public interest in the absence of proof that the defendant published the report with knowledge of its falsity or in reckless disregard of the truth."[223]

The Court extended the actual malice rule of *New York Times v. Sullivan* (1964)[224] to include false light when the matter was one of public interest. In its 5 to 4 decision, the Court ruled that the content of the *Life* article was a matter of public interest and remanded the case back to the state appellate court. The Court also dismissed the claim that the article was published for trade purposes, noting that the publication of books, newspapers, and magazines for profit does not constitute trade purposes. After 11 years of litigation, James Hill dropped his suit.

Cantrell v. Forest City Publishing Co. (1974)

Seven years after *Time v. Hill*, the U.S. Supreme Court decided the second and, thus far, last of the false light cases. *Cantrell v. Forest City Publishing Co.*[225] was the ideal case to clarify *Time v. Hill*. Ten days before Christmas in 1967, 44 people, including Melvin Cantrell, were killed when the Silver Bridge spanning the Ohio River at Point Pleasant, West Virginia, collapsed. Joseph Eszterhas, a reporter for the *Cleveland* (Ohio) *Plain Dealer*, wrote a prize-winning feature about the funeral of Cantrell and the impact of his death on his wife and children. Five months later, the reporter and a photographer visited Point Pleasant for a follow-up. The two stopped by the Cantrell home and talked with the children for about an hour while Margaret Mae Cantrell, Melvin Cantrell's widow, was away. The photographer, Richard Conway, took 50 pictures.

The result was the lead feature, "Legacy of the Silver Bridge," in the August 4, 1968, Sunday *Plain Dealer Magazine*. The story focused on "the family's abject poverty; the children's old, ill-fitting clothes and the deteriorating condition of their home."[226] The photos and text were used, as with the original piece, to demonstrate the effects of the disaster on the community. Unfortunately, the article contained several inaccuracies and false statements, including the following paragraph:

> Margaret Cantrell will talk neither about what happened nor about how they are doing. She wears the same mask of nonexpression she wore at the funeral. She is a proud woman. Her world has changed. She says that after it happened, the people in the town offered to help them out with money and they refused to take it.[227]

The reporter had never talked with Ms. Cantrell because she was not home at the time. Thus these statements were apparent fabrications. According to the Court, there were other misrepresentations in the descriptions of the family's poverty and "the dirty and dilapidated conditions of the Cantrell home."[228] Ms. Cantrell filed a diversity action against the reporter, photographer, and newspaper in the U.S. District Court for the Northern District of Ohio, alleging that the story made the family the object of pity and ridicule and caused "outrage, mental distress, shame and humiliation."[229] The federal trial court jury awarded Cantrell $60,000 in compensatory damages for false light. The district court judge dismissed Cantrell's claim for punitive damages, supposedly on the ground that no common law malice had been demonstrated. The judge did rule that Cantrell could recover actual or compensatory damages if she could convince the jury that the misrepresentations and false information had been published with "actual malice," as enunciated by the Supreme Court in *Time v. Hill*.

Since the landmark *New York Times v. Sullivan* decision in 1964, there has been considerable confusion over the difference between *common law malice* (evil intent arising from hatred, revenge, or ill will) and *actual malice* (reckless disregard for truth or knowledge of falsity). In its 1991 decision in *Masson v. The New Yorker Magazine, Inc.*, the U.S. Supreme Court suggested abandoning the term *actual malice* and said that the courts should instead refer to *knowing* or *reckless falsehood*. *Cantrell v. Forest City Publishing Co.* illustrates this wisdom.

On appeal, the Sixth Circuit U.S. Court of Appeals reversed the trial court decision because it interpreted the judge's finding that Cantrell had not presented sufficient evidence that the publication "was done maliciously within the legal definition of that term" to mean that there was no actual malice. The intermediate appellate court held that the defendants' motion for a directed verdict in their favor should have been granted under the *Time v. Hill* standard for false light actions. But the U.S. Supreme Court noted: "Although the verbal record of the District Court proceedings is not entirely unambiguous, the conclusion is inescapable that the District Judge was referring to the common law standard of malice rather than to the *New York Times* 'actual malice' standard when he dismissed the punitive damages claims."[230] Therefore, the Supreme Court reversed the Court of Appeals, holding that:

> The District Judge was clearly correct in believing that the evidence introduced at trial was sufficient to support a jury finding that the respondents, Joseph Eszterhas and Forest City Publishing Co. had published knowing or reckless falsehoods about the Cantrells. [The Court indicated in a footnote here that "there was insufficient evidence to support the jury's verdict against the photographer Conway" because his testimony that his photos were fair and accurate depictions was not challenged and there was no evidence that he was responsible for the inaccuracies and misstatements in the article.] There was no dispute during the trial that Eszterhas who did not testify must have known that a number of the statements in the feature story were untrue.[231]

The Court characterized the reporter's implication that Cantrell had been at home during the visit and his description of her "mask of nonexpression" as "calculated falsehoods," justifying the jury decision that he had portrayed the family "in a false light through knowing or reckless untruth."[232] A major question that remained unanswered at the time of the *Cantrell* decision was the impact of *Gertz v. Welch* (1974) on the false light tort: "whether a State may constitutionally apply a more relaxed standard of liability for a publisher or broadcaster of false statements injurious to a private individual under a false light theory of invasion of privacy, or whether the constitutional standard announced in *Time v. Hill* applies to all false light cases."[233]

The question is still unanswered because all of the parties accepted the *Time v. Hill* standard and thus the Supreme Court did not have to deal with this issue. One fact is clear, however: a solid 8 to 1 majority reaffirmed the position in *Time v. Hill*, which had been decided by a thin 5 to 4 margin. Only Justice William O. Douglas dissented: "It seems clear that in matters of public importance such as the present news reporting, there must be freedom from damages lest the press be frightened into playing a more ignoble role than the Framers visualized."[234] The message of *Cantrell* is clear: actual malice can be demonstrated in false light cases.

It is instructive to compare the editorial decision making in the two false light cases. In *Time v. Hill*, the *Life* article was prepared under the direction of its entertainment editor. The director of the play, which was based on the fictionalized account in the book, suggested that the editor generate a story, and about the same time, the editor met a friend of the book's author, Joseph Hayes, who told the editor in a casual discussion that the book had been based on a real incident. The entertainment editor contacted Hayes, who confirmed the connection and arranged for the editor to see the former Hill home.

As the Court pointed out, "Neither then nor thereafter did Prideaux [the editor] question Hayes about the extent to which the play was based on the incident."[235] Prideaux's file for the story included news clippings with details about the incident, including the lack of violence, as well as a *New York Times* article by Hayes indicating that the book was a composite of stories about incidents in various locales. The first draft of the *Life* feature did not mention the Hills by name except in the caption for one photo. The draft mentioned that the play was a "somewhat fictionalized" account of the Hill incident, and a research assistant assigned to check the accuracy of the story inserted a question mark over the words, "somewhat fictionalized." When the draft was reviewed by a copy editor, he changed the first sentence to focus on the Hill incident, using the family's name, deleted "somewhat fictionalized," and added the statements that the novel was "inspired" by the incident and that the play was a "re-enactment."

In the *Cantrell* case, the Supreme Court offered little detail on the editorial review process other than that the story was the reporter's idea but was approved by the editor. But the justices obviously were convinced that the reporter had fabricated key points in the story and that falsehoods and misrepresentations had escaped scrutiny of the editorial process. The Court agreed with the lower appellate court that the photographs did not cast the family in a false light.

The circumstances under which the photographer and reporter entered the home to talk with the children while the mother was gone are unclear, but apparently no suit was filed for intrusion or publication of private matters. Could a case have also been built for these torts?

Defenses to False Light

As with the other torts of invasion of privacy, consent is a defense, but individuals rarely agree to have false information published about them. But if it can be demonstrated by preponderance of the evidence that the person had the legal capacity to grant consent and did so voluntarily and in good faith and did not revoke such consent, a suit for false light would theoretically fail. Jurors and judges, like anyone else, tend not to believe, however, that plaintiffs would consent to publication of falsehoods about themselves. Because journalists have an ethical and sometimes legal obligation to be accurate and truthful, jurors and judges are usually not sympathetic when a reporter or editor touts consent as a defense to publishing falsehoods. Consent can be a two-edged sword as a defense. By claiming consent, the journalist is admitting an ethical abrogation.

Newsworthiness is also a weak, if not impossible, defense. Alone, it simply does not work. However, newsworthiness can be a viable defense in conjunction with constitutional privilege. As the Court indicated in *Time v. Hill* and reiterated in *Cantrell v. Forest City Publishing Co.*, plaintiffs suing the media for publishing false information on matters of public interest must demonstrate actual malice (reckless or knowing falsehoods) before recovering for false light. If the subject matter is newsworthy, even if the information is false, actual malice must be shown. Unfortunately, the scope of this constitutional privilege remains unclear to this day because the Court has never determined whether a state could institute a lower standard such as negligence in a matter involving a private individual.

The majority opinion raised this question without answering it, indicating that the Court may someday respond. With a solid coalition of conservative justices on First Amendment issues now on the Supreme Court, it is highly likely that the Court would apply the *Gertz* holding for libel to false light cases, thus permitting states to lower the standard to negligence for private individuals. In fact, when such a case arrives at the Court, the vote could be 9 to 0.

One question has never been tackled by the U.S. Supreme Court, but the Court's response could have a major impact on false light and even libel: is there a constitutional privilege (even limited) to publish false information from the public record when such falsehoods are published without actual malice? *Florida Star v. B.J.F.* and *Cox v. Cohn* dealt only with truthful information in public records, and *Cantrell v. Forest City Publishing Co.* and *Time v. Hill* dealt with false information not in public records. It is very difficult to predict how the Court would deal with this issue or even if the Court will consider such a case. Journalists must be diligent and avoid publishing false information even if the information is published in good faith. Negligence is easy to demonstrate and this may eventually become the point at which liability occurs in false light cases.

False light has not been recognized as a tort in every state—i.e., although the majority do; by statute or at common law. The list recognizing such claims continues to grow, including the Ohio Supreme Court in 2007. States that still do not recognize this tort include Minnesota, Virginia, and North Carolina.

Summary and Conclusions

As the concern of citizens over governmental and corporate snooping intensifies and as communication technologies advance faster than legislation can respond to limit their potential to invade privacy, journalists can expect more suits for invasion of privacy. Because of the September 11, 2001, attacks and the resulting heightened concern with preventing global terrorism, Americans have become, according to University of Minnesota Professor Jane Kirtley, "schizophrenic" about the role of the press. Kirtley was responding at the time to a national poll for the Pew Research Center for the People and the Press.[236] Of the over 2,000 participants, half believed that the news media harm national security interests when they publish stories such as those about the secret program in which the federal government checked the bank records of U.S. citizens it suspected had ties to foreign terrorists. In the same poll, almost two-thirds of Americans felt the stories "told citizens something they should know about." [237] An earlier poll had found similar results when the public was asked about the secret program that allowed the National Security Agency to conduct warrantless eavesdropping on phone calls and e-mail messages of Americans suspected of having ties to foreign terrorists.[238]

When privacy issues pop up related to new technologies, it is not unusual for cell phones to be targets. This pervasive technology seems particularly vulnerable to intrusions on privacy, as demonstrated in a legal experiment by a phone security company. After the company purchased 10 used cell phones on eBay, its software experts had little difficulty reviving a wide variety of sensitive data on each of the phones. The data included bank account numbers, passwords, and e-mails that the former owners undoubtedly assumed had been deleted. In fact, the company found enough information on those 10 phones to equal 27,000 pages of printouts.[239] Flash memory, an inexpensive technology, makes cell phones convenient to use but also susceptible to intrusion.

Where do the mass media fit into this picture? Of the four torts of invasion of privacy—intrusion, appropriation, publicizing private matters, and false light—the latter two pose the greatest potential liability for the mass media. Statutory and constitutional laws regarding intrusion have been well delineated by legislatures and the courts, although some of the newer technologies such as cell phones present interesting challenges.

Federal law prohibits the manufacture, import, and sale of radio receivers that can pick up cell phone conversations, and yet there are still older receivers that were sold before the Act took effect that can intercept calls. It is also relatively easy, although illegal, for someone to modify a general coverage radio receiver so it can pick up cellular phone calls. Calls on cordless phones are even easier to intercept. Most news rooms have scanners that legally receive police, fire, and other public services, but listening to cell phone conversations is verboten.

How much bite federal and state laws have on eavesdropping with the use of newer technologies remains to be seen, but reporters and editors fortunately are rarely involved in intrusion suits. Journalists sometimes do lawfully acquire from third parties cell and land phone recordings that may have been illegally made but may contain especially newsworthy information. Journalists in such cases generally cannot be prosecuted nor held liable for possessing and disseminating such recordings if they played no role in acquiring them in the first place, as the U.S. Supreme Court held in *Bartnicki v. Vopper*. However, as the federal appeals court indicated in *Boehner v. McDermott*, this principle does not grant a blanket First Amendment license to disclose such information.

One area where intrusion has already created problems is computer technology, particularly the Internet. It is quite easy for an individual or a corporation to compile information based upon a consumer's visits to websites, without the person having any knowledge of snooping, which is often perfectly legal. The compilation of electronic databases that contain highly personal information and that can be quickly accessed also poses some serious threats to individual privacy. Journalists are already seeing a backlash as abuses of such information appear, even though they may not have been directly involved in such abuses.

New technology and the Internet have created anxiety about identity theft as well as having personal details shared with strangers. As part of an investigation into the crash that killed famed NASCAR driver Dale Earnhardt the *Orlando Sentinel* requested copies of the autopsy photos—not to publish the photos but rather just to look at them to gauge the effect of the crash. This led to a great deal of public outrage against the newspaper and a Florida bill removing autopsy photos from the domain of public records. A trend to limit access to public information including recordings of 911 calls have resulted in the banning of the release of such information in four states, with many others exploring similar measures with respect the release of birth and marriage records, pending court cases and requests for the names of those who oppose a law giving gays more rights in Washington state.

As with the Katrina disaster in New Orleans, when the Federal Emergency Management Agency (FEMA) paid out billions to residents who claimed damages, many media outlets suspecting possible waste and fraud requested names and addresses of those receiving money. FEMA said "no" in Florida until the judge of the federal appeals court, Judge Stanley Marcus, told FEMA to release the addresses noting the court could not find any privacy interests that even began to outweigh the public interest in this case. One other technology that has more recently attracted attention is radio frequency identification (RFID). According to an *ABA Journal* article:

> RFID is one of dozens of new technologies unleashed in the past half decade. Although few companies go so far as to implant RFID devices in employees, many institutions and individuals are using biometrics such as facial or iris recognition, fingerprint scans and satellite navigation technology to keep track of employees, children and even the elderly.[240]

The article said, "many Americans embrace new technologies for their convenience and the promise of greater security. Some legal experts worry that the law is not keeping pace with the introduction of ever-more invasive and pervasive technologies with potential for abuse, fraud or identity theft."[241] The Supreme Court may have anticipated in *Kyllo v. United States* (2001)[242] that the nation's privacy concerns would move over to its airports but in their decision in that case, the Court held that police use of thermal imaging devices from a public street to track down an indoor marijuana manufacturing operation without a search warrant violated the Fourth Amendment ban on unreasonable searches and seizures. However, as one writer notes:

> Experts now say the decision may be less protective of privacy rights in the home than it first seemed. In *Kyllo*, the majority also held that a reliance on technology that is in 'general public use,' or that only replicates what a naked-eye observer could see from a public vantage point, is not a search—even when the location being viewed is the interior of a home. [243]

What implications does this have for the media? If history is any indication, the media may expect broader protection under the First Amendment for disclosing information that has been obtained through the use of technologies in general use, so long as there are no specific legal restrictions. Cell phone cameras represent one illustration. Because of the proliferation of this technology, it is rare that any major public event, even unexpected, is not photographed or video recorded by witnesses. Our expectation of privacy at newsworthy events has lessened, as a result.

Appropriation has generally not been a major problem for journalists because the celebrities of the world are well rewarded by corporations for commercial use of their names, images, and likenesses. Unless the situation approaches that of *Zacchini v. Scripps-Howard Publishing Co.*, it is unlikely a plaintiff will be successful in a suit for appropriation in a news context. Consent is always the best insurance when a potential commercial context appears because newsworthiness is not a defense to appropriation.

Publication of private matters and false light will continue to be troublesome for the media. The Supreme Court could further broaden constitutional privilege for these two torts and further restrict other defenses such as newsworthiness and consent, a weak shield anyway. When dealing with private matters, journalists should make sure a strong public interest is to be served and, whenever possible, that they are dealing with public figures or public officials. Obviously, all news stories and features cannot focus on public people, but reporters and editors must be wary of traps when private individuals are involved because legislatures, courts, and the public (from which jurors—are drawn) firmly believe that privacy for ordinary citizens is being eroded and the media are responsible for some of the erosion. The events of September 11, 2001, made the public more tolerant of governmental intrusion on private lives of citizens, but journalists should not count on this tolerance translating to broader First Amendment protection for the press.

Finally, the boundaries of false light are obscure but likely to become clearer in the future, especially if the relatively new area of privacy becomes a hotbed of litigation. False light requires no defamation but harm to an individual as a result of false information, including fictionalization. Thus a suit that might be unsuccessful as libel may strike false light gold.

Endnotes

1. Edward Wyatt, *Legislators Support Internet Privacy, but Question How to do It,* New York Times, December 3, 2010, at B-3.
2. *Climate Has Changed for Data Privacy; Other Companies Have Shared Customer Info with Government,* USA Today, May 12, 2006, at B1; Arshad Mohammed and Terence O'Hara, *NSA Program Further Blurs Line on Privacy; Consumers Grow Accustomed to Surrendering Personal Data,* Washington Post, May 13, 2006, and Josh Gerstein, *'This is Nuts,' Kyl Says of Leak,* New York Sun, May 12, 2006, at A1. Laurie Kellman and Donna Cassata, Associated Press Online, May 11, 2006; Eric Lichtblau and Scott Shane, *Bush Is Pressed over New Report on Surveillance,* New York Times, May 12, 2006, at A1.
3. Mark Clayton, *Mining Data to Nab Terrorists: Fair?* Christian Science Monitor, May 15, 2006, at 1; Douglas Birch, *Does Anyone Have Any Privacy Left?* Baltimore Sun, May 12, 2006.
4. Charlie Savage and James Risen, *Wiretaps are Ruled Illegal,* St. Louis Post-Dispatch, April 1, 2010, at A-6.
5. Charlie Savage, Justice Dept. to Limit Use of State Secrets Privilege, New York Times, September 22, 2009, located at http://www.nytimes.com/2009/09/23/us/politics/23secrets.html?hp).
6. Testimony by Conrad Burns, "Protecting Telephone Call Records," Capital Hill Hearing Testimony, Committee on Senate Commerce, Science and Transportation Subcommittee on Consumer Affairs, Product Safety and Insurance, Feb. 8, 2006.
7. Kati Cornell Smith, *Miller Fights Subpoena,* New York Post, Feb. 14, 2006, at 21.
8. Arshad Mohammed and Terence O'Hara, *Feds Can Tap River of Data: Consumer Privacy Spotty,* Atlanta Journal-Constitution (Washington Post), May 14, 2006, at A1.
9. *Id.*
10. Uniting and Strengthening America by Providing Appropriate Tools to Intercept and Obstruct Terrorism Act (USA Patriot Act) of 2001.
11. Katherine Shrader and Donna Cassata, *Call Tracking Stirs Uproar: Bush Assures Civil Liberties Are Protected,* Atlanta Journal-Constitution (Associated Press), May 12, 2006, at A1.
12. Donna Rice, *Back from the Eye of the Media Hurricane, 'The Woman in Question' Writes about the Perils of the Press,* Dateline, Apr. 19, 1988, at 20.
13. *Journalistic Soul-Searching Follows Snub by Donna Rice,* Cincinnati Post, Nov. 19, 1988, at Al.
14. Beth Gardiner, *"Naomi Campbell Wins Britain Peers Case,"* Associated Press Online, May 6, 2004; Mark Pearson, *Press Freedom Suffers for Celebrity Security,* The Australian, Feb. 3, 2005.
15. *Id.*
16. *Protect Your Privacy on the Internet,* 3 Ga. B. J. 32 (Dec. 1997).
17. *FBI Pays Widow of U.S. Communist for 1984 Frame-Up,* Lexington (Ky.) Herald-Leader, Oct. 27, 1987, at A3.
18. *Id.*
19. Joseph Turow, Lauren Feldman and Kim Meltzer, *Open to Exploitation: American Shoppers Online and Off, Report from the Annenberg Public Policy Center,* University of Pennsylvania, 2005, at 12; Federal Trade Commission. (May 2000), *Privacy Online: Fair Information Practices in the Electronic Marketplace* available at http://www.ftc.gov/reports/privacy/2000/privacy2000.pdf.
20. Liane Hansen, NPR Weekend Edition, National Public Radio, Apr. 24, 2005.
21. *Theme Parks and Your Privacy,* Electronic Privacy Information Center, Oct. 12, 2005.
22. Peter Schworm and Brian Ballou, *9 Teens Charged in Girl's Bullying,* Boston Globe, March 30, 2010, at A-1. *See* also, Kevin Cullen, *The Untouchable Mean Girls,* Boston Globe, January 24, 2010; and also, Kevin Cullen's *No Safe Haven for Bullies,* Boston Globe, February 2, 2010, 1-A.
23. Endejan, 8 Com. L. 6, No. 2 (1990) for a thorough discussion of the impact of CID.
24. Joshua Quittner, *Invasion of Privacy,* Time, Aug. 25, 1997, at 28.
25. Mark Hansen, *No Place To Hide,* 83 A.B.A. J. 44 (Aug. 1997).
26. Mary Deibel, *Court Established Right to Privacy 40 Years Ago This Week,* Scripps-Howard News, June 6, 2005.
27. Video Privacy Protection Act of 1988, 100 P.L. 618, 102 Stat. 3195, 18 U.S.C. §2710.
28. *Id.*

29. Scott Canon, *Debate Over Right to Privacy Roils a Nation and Its Courts,* Kansas City Star (Knight Ridder), Oct. 17, 2005; *Will Roberts Leave You Alone?* USA Today, Aug. 16, 2005, A12.

30. I. Altman, *Privacy Regulation: Culturally Universal or Culturally Specific?* 33 Journal of Social Issues Vol. 66, No. 3 (1977).

31. *Id.*, at 72–77.

32. S. D. Warren and L. D. Brandeis, *The Right to Privacy,* 4 Harvard Law Review 193 (1890).

33. W. Agee, P. Ault, and E. Emery, *Introduction to Mass Communications,* 83–89 (9th ed. 1988).

34. Warren and Brandeis, supra.

35. *Roberson v. Rochester Folding Box Co.,* 171 N.Y. 538, 64 N.E. 442 (1902).

36. New York Civil Rights Law §50–51 (current law).

37. *Pavesich v. New England Life Insurance Co.,* 122 Ga. 190, 50 S.E. 68 (1905).

38. *Black's Law Dictionary* 1075 (5th ed. 1979).

39. W. Prosser and W. Keeton, *Handbook of the Law of Torts* 851–866 (5th ed. 1984).

40. *Burger King Learns Fast Lesson from Mr. Rogers,* Lexington (Ky.) Herald-Leader (Associated Press), May 9, 1984, at B15.

41. *Allen v. National Video,* 610 F. Supp. 612 (S.D. N.Y. 1985).

42. *Vanna White v. Samsung Electronics America Inc.,* 971 F.2d 1395, 20 Med.L.Rptr. 1457 (9th Cir. 1992), *cert. denied,* 508 U.S. 951, 113 S.Ct. 2443, 124 L.Ed.2d 660 (1993).

43. *Rosa Parks v. LaFace Records,* 76 F. Supp.2d 775 (E.D. Mich. 1999), *rev'd,* 329 F.3d 437 (6th Cir. 2003).

44. *Id.*

45. *Id.*

46. *ETW Corp. v. Jireh Publishing, Inc.,* 99 F. Supp.2d 829 (N.D. Ohio 2000), *aff'd,* 332 F.3d 915 (6th Cir. 2003).

47. *Id.*

48. Henry Sheehan, *High-Tech TV Ads Bring Celebrities To Life,* Lexington (Ky.) Herald-Leader (Orange County Register), Nov. 4, 1996, at Your Money-11.

49. Media Law Resource Center, Media Privacy and Related Law 1589–1597 (2004).

50. Victor A. Kovner, Elizabeth A. McNamara, Suzanne L. Telsey and Robert Walther, *Newsgathering, Invasion of Privacy and Related Torts,* 1 Communications Law, 967 (2005).

51. Lexington (Ky.) Herald-Leader, June 10, 1989, at A12.

52. *Hugo Zacchini v. Scripps-Howard Broadcasting Co.,* 433 U.S. 562, 97 S.Ct. 2849, 53 L.Ed.2d 965, 2 Med.L.Rptr. 1199 (1977).

53. *Id.*

54. *Time, Inc. v. James J. Hill,* 385 U.S. 374, 87 S.Ct. 534, 17 L.Ed.2d 456, 1 Med.L.Rptr. 1791 (1967).

55. *Hugo Zacchini v. Scripps-Howard Broadcasting Co.*

56. *Factors Etc., Inc. v. Pro Arts, Inc.,* 579 F.2d 215, 4 Med.L.Rptr. 1144 (2d Cir. 1978), *cert. denied,* 440 U.S. 908, 99 S.Ct. 1215, 59 L.Ed.2d 455 (1979).

57. *Memphis Development Corp. v. Factors Etc.,* 441 F.Supp. 1323, 3 Med.L.Rptr. 2012 (W.D. Tenn. 1977).

58. *Price v. Hal Roach Studios Inc.,* 400 F.Supp. 836 (S.D. N.Y. 1975).

59. *Black's Law Dictionary,* 1377.

60. *Price v. Hal Roach Studios Inc.,* at 844.

61. *Memphis Development Corp. v. Factors Etc.,* 616 F.2d 956, 5 Med.L.Rptr. 2521 (6th Cir. 1980), *cert. denied,* 449 U.S. 953, 101 S.Ct. 358, 66 L.Ed.2d 217 (1980).

62. Tenn. Code Ann. §47-25-1101 et seq. (Personal Rights Protection Act of 1984).

63. *Elvis Presley Enterprises v. Elvisly Yours,* 817 F.2d 104, 14 Med.L.Rptr. 1053 (6th Cir. 1987).

64. *State ex rel. Presley v. Crowell,* 733 S.W.2d 89, 14 Med.L.Rptr. 1043 (Tenn. App. 1987). Had the court *not* recognized a *common law right* that existed prior to the statute in 1984, there would be a question of whether Presley's name and image had protection from date of his death in 1977 to the effective date of the statute—a period of about seven years.

65. *Estate of Elvis Presley v. Russen,* 513 F.Supp. 1339 (D. N.J. 1981).

66. *Martin Luther King, Jr. Center for Social Change Inc., v. American Heritage Products, Inc.,* 250 Ga. 135, 296 S.E.2d 697, 8 Med.L.Rptr. 2377 (1982).

67. Robert Patrick, *State Appeals Court Upholds Jury Award to Tony Twist*, St. Louis Post-Dispatch, June 21, 2006, at B2.

68. *Carson v. Here's Johnny Portable Toilets Inc.*, 698 F.2d 831, 9 Med.L.Rptr. 1153 (6th Cir. 1983).

69. *Cher v. Forum International Ltd.*, 7 Med.L.Rptr. 2593 (C.D. Cal. 1982).

70. *Cher v. Forum International Ltd.*, 692 F.2d. 634, 8 Med.L.Rptr. 2484 (9th Cir. 1982), *cert. denied*, 462 U.S. 1120, 103 S.Ct. 3089, 77 L.Ed.2d 1350 (1983).

71. *Time, Inc. v. Hill.*

72. The photographs were non-obscene poses of Shields nude in a bathtub. Shields made no claim that they were pornographic.

73. *Shields v. Gross*, 451 N.Y.S.2d 419 (App. Div. 1982), 58 N.Y.2d 338, 448 N.E.2d 108 (N.Y. 1983).

74. *Mary Jane Russell v. Marlboro Books*, 183 N.Y.S.2d 8 (1959).

75. *Douglass v. Hustler Magazine*, 759 F.2d. 1128 (7th Cir. 1985), cert. denied, 475 U.S. 1094, 109 S.Ct. 377, 109 L.Ed.2d 892 (1986).

76. *Id.*

77. *Hugo Zacchini v. Scripps-Howard Broadcasting.*

78. *Id.*

79. *Id.*

80. *Namath v. Sports Illustrated*, 371 N.Y.S.2d 10 (N.Y. Sup. Ct. App. Div. 1962).

81. *Id.*

82. *Booth v. Curtis Publishing Co.*, 15 A.D.2d 343, 223 N.Y.S.2d 737 (N.Y. Sup. Ct. App. Div. 1962).

83. M. Ament and R. J. Emmett, *The Right of Publicity in Thoroughbreds: An Issue of Dollars and Horse Sense*, 10 Louisville Law, 14, No. 2 (1990).

84. *Id.*

85. *Dietemann v. Time Inc.*, 449 F.2d 245, 1 Med.L.Rptr. 2417 (9th Cir. 1971).

86. *Dietemann v. Time Inc.*, 284 F.Supp. 925 (C.D. Calif. 1968).

87. *Dietemann v. Time Inc.* (1971).

88. *Id.*

89. *Pearson v. Dodd*, 410 F.2d 701, 1 Med.L.Rptr. 1809, *cert. denied*, 395 U.S. 947, 89 S.Ct. 2021, 23 L.Ed.2d 465 (1969).

90. *Pearson v. Dodd*, 410 F.2d 701 (D.C. Cir.).

91. *Id.*

92. *Id.*

93. *Bartnicki v. Vopper*, 532 U.S. 514, 121 S.Ct. 1753, 149 L.Ed.2d 787 (2001).

94. *Id.*

95. Omnibus Crime Control and Safe Streets Act of 1968, 18 U.S.C. §2511.

96. *Bartnicki v. Vopper.*

97. *Boehner v. McDermott*, 441 F.3d 1010, 34 Med.L.Rptr. 1481 (D.C. Cir. 2006).

98. *Federal Appeals Court Finds McDermott in Violation of Wiretap Law*, Silha Center Bulletin 17–18 (Winter 2006).

99. *Boehner v. McDermott.*

100. *Florida Publishing Co. v. Fletcher*, 340 So.2d 914, 2 Med.L.Rptr. 1088 (Fla. 1976), *cert. denied*, 431 U.S. 930 (1977).

101. *Id.*

102. *Id.*

103. *Id.*

104. Reporters Committee for Freedom of the Press, *Photographers' Guide to Privacy*, News Media & Law (Summer 1986), at 2.

105. Wisnia, *Private Grief, Public Exposure*, Quill 28 (July 1989).

106. *Id.*, at 29.

107. *Society of Professional Journalists Code* (Appendix A).

108. *Id.*

109. *Radio–Television News Directors Association Code* §3; Candace Cummins Gauthier, *Privacy Invasion by the News Media: Three Ethical Models*, Journal of Mass Media Ethics, 17(1), 20–34 (2002).

110. *Le Mistral v. Columbia Broadcasting System*, 61 A.D.2d 491, 402 N.Y.S.2d 815, 3 Med. L.Rptr. 1913 (1978).
111. *Dietemann v. Time, Inc.* (1971).
112. Restatement (Second) of Torts §6521, comment c (1977).
113. Scott Andron, *Food Lion versus ABC*, Quill 15 (Mar. 1997); John Siegenthaler and David L. Hudson Jr., *Going Undercover*, Quill 17 (Mar. 1997); Paul McMasters, *It Didn't Have To Come To This*, Quill 18 (Mar. 1997).
114. Scott Andron, *Food Lion versus ABC.*
115. *Food Lion, Inc. v. Capital Cities/ABC, Inc.*, 887 F.Supp. 811, 23 Med.L.Rptr. 1673 (M.D. N.C. 1995); *judgment aff'd in part, rev'd in part*, 194 F.3d505 (4th Cir. 1999).
116. *BMW of North America, Inc. v. Ira Gore Jr.*, 517 U.S. 559,
117. S.Ct. 1589, 134 L.Ed.2d 809 (1996).
118. *Id.*
119. *Galella v. Onassis*, 353 F.Supp. 196 (S.D. N.Y. 1972), *aff'd*, 487 F.2d 986, 1 Med.L.Rptr. 2425 (2d Cir. 1973).
120. *Id.*
121. *Id.*
122. *Id.*
123. *Id.*
124. *Galella v. Onassis*, 533 F.Supp. 1076 (S.D. N.Y. 1982).
125. *Cefalu v. Globe Newspaper Co.*, 391 N.E.2d 935, 5 Med.L.Rptr. 1940, (Mass. App. Ct. 1979).
126. *Id.*
127. U.S. Constitution, Amendment IV.
128. *California v. Acevedo*, 500 U.S. 565, 111 S.Ct. 1982, 114 L.Ed.2d 619 (1991).
129. *Carroll v. United States*, 267 U.S. 132, 45 S.Ct. 280, 69 L.Ed. 543 (1925).
130. *Hudson v. Michigan,* 126 S.Ct. 2159, 165 L.Ed.2d 56 (2006).
131. *Id.*
132. *Griswold v. Connecticut*, 381 U.S. 479, 85 S.Ct. 1678, 14 L.Ed.2d 510 (1965).
133. *Id.*
134. U.S. Constitution, Amendment IX.
135. *Bowers v. Hardwick*, 478 U.S. 186, 106 S.Ct. 2841, 92 L.Ed.2d 140 (1986).
136. *Webster v. Reproductive Health Services*, 492 U.S. 490, 109 S.Ct. 3040, 106 L.Ed.2d 410 (1989).
137. *Roe v. Wade*, 410 U.S. 113, 93 S.Ct. 705, 35 L.Ed.2d 147 (1973).
138. *Planned Parenthood of Southeastern Pennsylvania v. Casey*, 505 U.S. 833, 112 S.Ct. 2791, 120 L.Ed.2d 674 (1992).
139. *Lawrence v. Texas*, 539 U.S. 558, 123 S.Ct. 2472, 156 L.Ed.2d 508 (2003).
140. 18 U.S.C. §2510–2521.
141. *Id.* at §2511(4).
142. *Id.* at §2512(1).
143. *Id.,* at §2511(2) (d).
144. *Boddie v. American Broadcasting Cos.*, 731 F.2d 333, 10 Med.L.Rptr. 1923 (6th Cir. 1984).
145. *Boddie v. American Broadcasting Cos.*, 694 F.Supp. 1304, 16 Med.L.Rptr. 1100 (N.D. Ohio 1988), *aff'd* 881 F.2d 267 (6th Cir. 1989).
146. *Id.*
147. Victor A. Kovner, Elizabeth A. McNamara, Suzanne L. Telsey, and Robert Walther, at 574.
148. *Id.,* at 578.
149. Chad A. McGowan, *Discovering Deleted Computer Files*, 2 Ga. B. J. 20 (Apr. 1996).
150. *Attorney Subpoenaed Over Intercepted Call,* Lexington (Ky.) Herald-Leader (Associated Press), June 8, 1997, at A7.
151. *Couple Who Taped Gingrich Charged,* Lexington (Ky.) Herald-Leader (Associated Press), Apr. 24, 1997, at A3.
152. *Vernonia School District 47J v. Acton*, 515 U.S. 646, 115 S.Ct. 2386, 132 L.Ed.2d 564 (1995).
153. *Id.*

154. *Walker L. Chandler, et al. v. Zell Miller, et al.*, 520 U.S. 305, 117 S.Ct. 1295, 137 L.Ed.2d 513 (1997).
155. *Id.*
156. *Id.*
157. *Id.*
158. *Id.* (Rehnquist dissent).
159. Sara Kehaulani Goo and Spencer S. Hsu, *First Privacy Officer Calls 'Experiment' a Success: Official is lauded for Protecting Citizen Rights,* Washington Post, Sept. 29, 2005, at A21.
160. *What Really Happens in War,* Parade, June 9, 1991, at 4.
161. *Kearney v. Salomon Smith Barney,* 2006 Cal. Lexis 8362 (2006).
162. Restatement (Second) of Torts § 652D.
163. Video Privacy Protection Act of 1988, 100 P.L. 618, 18 U.S.C. §2710, 102 Stat. 3195.
164. Hughes, *A Photo that Had to Be Used*, 1 Fineline 3, No. 7 (1989).
165. *Barger v. Louisville Courier-Journal,* 20 Med.L.Rptr. 1189 (1992).
166. *Cox Broadcasting v. Cohn,* 420 U.S. 469, 95 S.Ct. 1029, 43 L.Ed.2d 328, 1 Med.L.Rptr. 1819 (1975).
167. *Id.*
168. *Florida Star v. B.J.F.,* 491 U.S. 524, 109 S.Ct. 2603, 105 L.Ed.2d 443, 16 Med.L.Rptr. 1801 (1989).
169. *Id.*
170. *Oklahoma Publishing Co. V. Oklahoma County District Court,* 430 U.S. 308, 97 S.Ct. 1045, 51 L.Ed.2d 355, 2 Med.L.Rptr. 1456 (1977).
171. *Smith v. Daily Mail Publishing Co.,* 443 U.S. 97, 99 S.Ct. 2667, 61 L.Ed.2d 399, 5 Med.L.Rptr. 1305 (1979).
172. *Id.*
173. *Florida Star v. B.J.F.*
174. Donnelly, *To Name or Not To Name Alleged Victim,* Lexington (Ky.) Herald Leader (Knight-Ridder News Service), Apr. 18, 1991, at A3.
175. Janis, *Behind Every Pulitzer, There's Another Story: The Winner's,* Gannetteer, June 1991, at 2.
176. *Florida v. Globe Communications., Inc.,* No. 91-11008, slip op. (Palm Beach County Ct., Oct. 24, 1991); Linda Deutsch, *Secrecy in Celebrity Cases Raises Concern About Justice System,* Las Vegas Review Journal, July 24, 2004, at A7.
177. *See* "Murphy Releases Names in 'Dateline NBC' Sting: North Texas 'Dateline' Sting Nets More Than 20 Arrests: NBC5i.com, Channel 5, Dallas/Fort Worth. Posted: 12:52 p.m., CST, November 6, 2006; "NBC 'Catch a Predator' Sting Shakes up Texas Town," Associated Press, June 28, 2007; and also Marisa Guthrie, "Sister of Man Featured on Dateline's To Catch a Predator Retains Legal Representation," Broadcasting & Cable, July 17, 2007.
178. *Briscoe v. Reader's Digest,* 4 Cal.3d 529, 483 P.2d 34, 1 Med.L.Rptr. 1845 (Cal. Sup. Ct. 1971).
179. *Id.*
180. *Briscoe v. Reader's Digest,* 1 Med.L.Rptr. 1852 (U.S.D.C. C.D. Cal., 1972).
181. *Virgil v. Time,* 527 F.2d 1122, 1 Med.L.Rptr. 1835 (9th Cir. 1975).
182. *Id.*
183. *Id.*
184. *Time v. Virgil, cert. denied,* 425 U.S. 998, 96 S.Ct. 2215, 48 L.Ed.2d 823 (1976).
185. *Virgil v. Sports Illustrated,* 424 F.Supp. 1286 (S.D. Cal. 1976).
186. *Sidis v. F-R Publishing Corp.,* 113 F.2d 806, 1 Med.L.Rptr. 1775 (2d Cir. 1940).
187. *Id.*
188. *Id.*
189. *Howard v. Des Moines Register and Tribune Co.,* 3 Med.L.Rptr. 2304 (Iowa D.C. 1978).
190. *Howard v. Des Moines Register and Tribune Co.,* 283 N.W.2d 289, 5 Med.L.Rptr. 1667 (Iowa 1979), *cert. denied,* 445 U.S. 904, 100 S.Ct. 1081, 63 L.Ed.2d 320 (1980).
191. *Howard v. Des Moines Register and Tribune Co.* (1979).
192. *Id.*
193. *Sipple v. Chronicle Publishing Co.,* 154 Cal.App.3d 1040, 201 Cal. Rptr. 665, 10 Med.L.Rptr. 1690 (1984).
194. *Id.*

195. *Id.*
196. Casey Murray, *Open-Casket Picture Not Invasion of Privacy*, News Media Update (Reporters Committee for Freedom of the Press), Vol. 12, No. 1 (Jan. 9, 2006).
197. *Id.*
198. Corinna Zarek, *D.C. Red-Light Camera Records Ruled Private*, News Media Update (Reporters Committee for Freedom of the Press), Vol. 12, No. 1 (Jan. 9, 2006).
199. Dave Roland, *FOI on Campus*, First Amendment Center, available at Elia Powers, *Balancing Safety and Student Privacy*, June 21, 2006.
200. Elia Powers, *Balancing Safety and Student Privacy.*
201. *Owasso Independent School District No. I-011 v. Falvo*, 534 U.S. 426, 122 S.Ct. 934, 151 L.Ed.2d 896 (2002).
202. Family Educational Rights and Privacy Act of 1974 (FERPA), 20 U.S.C. §1232g, 88 Stat. 571.
203. *Gonzaga University v. Doe*, 536 U.S. 273, 122 S.Ct. 2268, 153 L.Ed.2d 309 (2002).
204. Tonia Moxley, *Department of Education: Va Tech Broke Clery Act Rules During April 16 Shootings: May Affect Two Lawsuits,* Roanoke Times, May 19, 2010, at A1.
205. Anick Jesdanum, *Where's the Party These Days? At MySpace.com*, Lexington (Ky.) Herald-Leader, Feb.13, 2006, at A3.
206. Ken Leebow, *Adults Need to Take a Look at MySpace*, Atlanta Journal-Constitution, June 23, 2006, at A11.
207. *Bragging on MySpace.com Busts Teens*, Atlanta Journal-Constitution (wire services), May 14, 2006, at A13.
208. Tim Mullin, *Companies, Colleges, Launch ID Theft Study*, Atlanta Journal-Constitution, June 29, 2006, at C3.
209. *Id.*
210. *Id.*
211. Art Jester, *UK Employees at Risk for Identity Theft*, Lexington (Ky.) Herald-Leader, June 2, 2006, at A1.
212. Hope Yen, *VA Hasn't Fixed Data Controls, Panel Told*, Lexington (Ky.) Herald-Leader Associated Press), June 15, 2006, at A3.
213. Health Insurance Portability and Accountability Act (HIPAA), 42 U.S.C. §13d-6 (2003).
214. Andrew M. Mar and Alison Page Howard, *HIPAA & Newsgathering.*
215. *Id.*
216. *Id.*
217. *Id.*
218. Rob Stein, *Medical Privacy Law Nets No Fine*, Washington Post, June 7, 2006, at A1.
219. *Id.*
220. *Privacy Law Frustrates a Daughter—and Journalists*, Associated Press, March 16, 2006.
221. Restatement (Second) of Torts §652E (1981).
222. *Time, Inc. v. Hill*, 385 U.S. 374, 87 S.Ct. 534, 17 L.Ed.2d 456, 1 Med.L.Rptr. 1791 (1967).
223. *Id.*
224. *New York Times v. Sullivan*, 376 U.S. 254, 11 L.Ed.2d 686, 84 S.Ct. 710, 1 Med.L.Rptr. 1527 (1964).
225. *Cantrell v. Forest City Publishing Co.*, 419 U.S. 245, 95 S.Ct. 465, 42 L.Ed.2d 419, 1 Med. L.Rptr. 1815 (1974).
226. *Id.*
227. *Id.*
228. *Id.*
229. *Id.*
230. *Id.*
231. *Id.*
232. *Id.*
233. *Id.*
234. *Time v. Hill.*
235. *Id.*

236. Rebecca Carr, *Nation Torn Over News vs. Security*, Atlanta Journal-Constitution, Aug. 23, 2006, at A12.
237. *Id.*
238. *Id.*
239. Ted Bridis, *Indiscreet Cellphones*, Atlanta Journal-Constitution (Associated Press), Aug. 31, 2006, at C3.
240. Margaret Graham Tebo, *Who's Watching the Watchers*, 92 A.B.A. J. 36 (June 2006).
241. *Id.*
242. *Kyllo v. United States*, 533 U.S. 27, 121 S.Ct. 2038, 150 L.Ed.2d 94 (2001).
243. Mark Hansen, *Who Could Be Watching*, 92 A.B.A. J. 39 (June 2006).

11

Press and Public Access to the Judicial Processes, Records, Places, and Meetings

Talk of transparency is fine, but there's little value in having a window on government if the blinds are closed.[1]

—Ken Paulson

New technology is expanding the parameters of what information is shared—and needs to shared, with the public—and also recorded or archived for posterity. In February, 2010, White House attorneys said for example, that any "tweet" by President Barrack Obama's press spokesperson, Robert Gibbs, would need to be archived along with e-mails and anything else that he produced in his job at the White House as part of the Presidential Records Act of 1978. Gibbs had asked for the clarification when he started using Twitter early in 2010. The attorneys further clarified that unless someone responded directly to Gibbs, and only Gibbs—such online interaction should be regarded as analogous to sending e-mail to the White House.[2]

The First Amendment protects the press in two important areas. First, the government cannot interfere with the publication of material except under unusual circumstances such as when national security is at stake. Second, publishers generally do not have to fear criminal sanctions. However, the U.S. Supreme Court has never explicitly recognized a First Amendment right to gather information.

In those rare instances in which the Court has enunciated the rights of the media to have access to information, places, or events such as criminal trials, the Court has done so on the ground that the press acts as a surrogate for the public. The Court clings to the principle that the press can claim no greater rights of access than those afforded the public under the U.S. Constitution. Thus the press faces the unfortunate dilemma of having broad freedom to publish but considerably less freedom to ferret out the truth. The situation may be due largely to the fact that the press at the time the Constitution was written consisted primarily of "party organs" financed by political and other special interest groups that had little concern with objectivity, fairness, and truth. They were simply seeking to inform and influence their constituents and to criticize their opponents, not necessarily to serve as a watchdog over the government.

In the 1970s, the doors to records, places, and especially the judicial process began to open, thanks to a series of U.S. Supreme Court rulings and a flurry of state and federal freedom of information statutes. This chapter reviews the progress as well as the limits journalists face in seeking information. It also explores the parallel ethical problems that sometimes call for self-restraint even when the law permits access and disclosure.

Access to Judicial Processes and Judicial Records

As we explore access to the judicial process and judicial records, you will see that the U.S. Supreme Court—as do most other courts—generally looks to what media law attorneys Dan Paul, Richard Ovelmen, and Enrique D. Arana call two "complementary" considerations. First, has the particular judicial process "been historically open to the public"? Second, would access "contribute to the self-governing function and further the democratic process"?[3] Let's begin with criminal trials.

Richmond Newspapers v. Virginia *(1980): Criminal Trials*

Since the adoption of the Bill of Rights in 1791, the Sixth Amendment has guaranteed, among other rights, the right of a criminal defendant "to a speedy and public trial, by an impartial jury of the State and district wherein the crime shall have been committed." The U.S. Supreme Court has wrestled for more than two centuries with issues such as the criteria for an impartial jury and the meaning of *speedy*, but the Court never directly acknowledged a constitutional right of public access to judicial proceedings until 1980 when the justices held 7 to 1 in *Richmond Newspapers v. Virginia*[4] that the First and Fourteenth Amendments guarantee the press and the public the right to attend criminal trials. According to the Court, the right is not absolute, but "absent an overriding interest articulated in findings, the trial of a criminal case must be open to the public."

The case involved a defendant who was being tried for the fourth time on a murder charge. The first trial had been reversed on appeal and the two subsequent trials were declared mistrials. When the defense attorney moved that the trial be closed, the state trial court judge granted the request. Neither the prosecutor nor the two newspaper reporters who were present in the courtroom at the time objected to the closure. However, the reporters did file a motion later that day, asking that the order be vacated, but the judge denied the request. The following day, the judge granted a motion by the defense to strike the prosecution's evidence. He then dismissed the jury and ruled the defendant was not guilty. All during this time, of course, the proceedings were closed to the press and to the public. The Virginia Supreme Court dismissed the appeal by the newspaper that the judge's closure order be overturned.

One aspect of the Supreme Court's decision that was puzzling to some journalists was that, with six different opinions among the seven justices in the majority, there was no clear indication whether the issue was a First or a Sixth Amendment right. Chief Justice Warren Burger was joined by Justices Byron White and John Paul Stevens in the Court's holding that "the right to attend criminal trials is implicit in the guarantees of the First Amendment; without the freedom to attend such trials, which people have exercised for centuries, important aspects of speech and 'of the press could be eviscerated'" (citing *Branzburg v. Hayes*, 1972).[5]

In separate opinions, Justices White, Stevens, Potter Stewart, and Harry Blackmun each explained why they voted to reverse the decision of the state appellate court that upheld the trial court judge's decision to close the trial. In his three-sentence concurring opinion, Justice White criticized the Court for not having recognized the right to attend criminal trials under the Sixth Amendment one year earlier in *Gannett Co. v. DePasquale* (1979).[6] In his separate concurring opinion, Justice Stevens characterized the case as a "watershed" but chided the Court for not recognizing a right of access in *Houchins v. KQED*[7] two years earlier. In *Houchins*, the Court had ruled in a plurality opinion written by Chief Justice Burger that the First and Fourteenth Amendments do not grant the press the right of access to a jail that is "different from or greater than" the right enjoyed by the public. Thus the Court held that a sheriff could deny a TV station access to the portion of a jail where a suicide had occurred because he had also excluded the public from such access.

In his separate concurring opinion, Justice Blackmun stuck to his view earlier in *Gannett Co. v. DePasquale* that the right to a public trial could be found explicitly in the Sixth Amendment but that "the First Amendment must provide some measure of protection for public access to the trial."[8] Justice Stewart argued in his concurring opinion that the First and Fourteenth Amendments clearly grant the public and the press the right of access to both civil and criminal trials. Justice William J. Brennan, Jr., joined by Justice Thurgood Marshall, said in his lengthy concurring opinion that the First Amendment barred judges and the parties from having sole discretion in closing criminal trials.

The lone dissenter, Justice William Rehnquist, said he could find no prohibition against closing a trial to the public and the press anywhere in the Constitution, including the First, Sixth, Ninth, or any other amendments. Justice Rehnquist would instead defer to the states and to the people to make the judgment of whether trials should be open. He made no reference to the meaning of "public trial" under the Sixth Amendment, although he had joined the majority in *Gannett Co. v. DePasquale,* which held that "members of the public have no constitutional right under the Sixth and Fourteenth Amendments to attend criminal trials."[9]

The Court tackled three more major cases dealing with right of access to the judicial process after *Richmond Newspapers v. Virginia,* and in each case found a constitutional right, but continued to quibble over the origins of the right. The result was confusion over whether the right arises from the Sixth Amendment or the First Amendment.

The Court is not the only body ambivalent about opening the judicial process to press and public scrutiny. Lawyers, judges and the public are split on the issue as well. Some judges have little hesitation in closing criminal trials and pretrial proceedings to the public and the press, whereas others take extraordinary measures to ensure public access while protecting the rights of the defendant. First Amendment attorneys generally favor open trials and open proceedings, and criminal defense lawyers are sometimes more comfortable with closed proceedings, especially in highly visible cases that are likely to attract media attention.

Why are courts so concerned with open proceedings? The most common fears are (a) a public trial can bias jurors and thus prevent a defendant from receiving a fair trial; (b) the presence of the news media will seriously affect the courtroom decorum and ultimately the judicial process; and (c) extensive publicity may adversely affect the defendant and other witnesses, including the victim. Justice Rehnquist raised none of these issues in his lone dissent. Instead, he based his decision on the idea that the Court had no constitutional authority to review lower court decisions in such cases.

There are some major societal benefits to open trials. First, an open trial can go a long way toward ensuring that a defendant does get a fair trial by subjecting the whole process to public scrutiny. Secret justice may not be justice served. In his concurring opinion, Justice Brennan (joined by Justice Marshall) emphasized this point:

> Secrecy is profoundly inimical to this demonstrative purpose of the trial process. Open trials assure the public that procedural rights are respected, and that justice is afforded equally. Closed trials breed suspicion of prejudice and arbitrariness, which in turn spawns disrespect for law. Public access is essential, therefore, if trial adjudication is to achieve the objective of maintaining public confidence in the administration of justice.[10]

Without question, a judge is far less likely to violate a defendant's constitutional rights under the light of public and press scrutiny than in a closed courtroom in which no one other than the lawyers can take the judge to task. Of course, journalists have no right to directly intervene in the proceedings, but they can certainly inform the public when the rules of evidence or procedure are not properly followed, for example, or when an attorney appears to be incompetent. Simply providing a blow-by-blow account of the trial is, in and of itself, an important service for the public. Only journalists can effectively do that.

Second, we have a tradition in the United States of openness in the judicial process as a means of demonstrating that the public has a stake in the trial. After all, public funds are involved in almost every aspect of a trial from the judge's salary to the operation of the courtroom itself, and, in the case of a criminal trial, the state or the public is the entity against which the alleged crime has been committed. Justice Brennan invoked history several times in his concurring opinion, pointing out that public trials are rooted in our English common law heritage. "As a matter of law and virtually immemorial custom, public trials have been the essentially unwavering rule in ancestral England and in our own Nation," according to Justice Brennan. This ties in with the idea that there is "an historical presumption of access," as Paul et al. note.[11]

Do public trials prevent jurors from rendering impartial verdicts, and, if so, would closing trials ensure unbiased decisions? Some criminal trials attract so much pretrial media attention that the courts automatically assume that extraordinary measures must be taken even during *voir dire*. One example is the O. J. Simpson criminal trial in 1995 in which the ex-professional football player was acquitted of the murders of his ex-wife, Nicole Simpson Brown, and her friend, Ronald Goldman. Another example is the 1997 trial of Timothy McVeigh, who was sentenced to death by a jury and executed four years later for his role in the Oklahoma City bombing of the Alfred P. Murrah Federal Building that resulted in the deaths of 168 children and adults. The Simpson murder trial was televised, while McVeigh's trial was not. In both cases, thousands of news stories appeared about each defendant, and hundreds of potential jurors were questioned during *voir dire* before final panels were selected. Most individuals were dismissed as potential jurors because they indicated they had seen and heard some of the massive publicity and thus were presumably biased.

Nebraska Press Association v. Judge Stuart *(1976)*

The principles laid down by the Court in *Near v. Minnesota* (1931)[12] and *Nebraska Press Association v. Judge Stuart* (1976)[13] effectively restrict judges from exercising control over pretrial and during-trial publicity, although they can certainly control what takes place in the courtroom. In *Near,* the Court said that the government could impose prior restraint against the press only in exceptional circumstances, such as obscene publications or a potential violation of national security. In *Nebraska Press Association,* the Court unanimously held that a state trial court judge's restrictive order on the news media was unconstitutional because the judge had failed to exhaust other measures for ensuring a fair trial short of prior restraint: "We reaffirm that the guarantees of freedom of expression are not an absolute prohibition under all circumstances, but the barriers to prior restraint remain high and the presumption against its use continues intact."[14]

In a law review article entitled "Who Is an Impartial Juror in an Age of Mass Media?" Newton Minow and Fred Cate concluded:

> To think that jurors wholly unacquainted with the facts of a notorious case can be impaneled today is to dream. Anyone meeting that standard of ignorance should be suspect. The search for a jury is a chimera. It is also unnecessary. Knowledgeable jurors today, like 800 years ago, can form an impartial jury. In fact, the very diversity of views and experiences that they possess is the best guarantee of an impartial jury.[15]

The authors note that in 12th century England where the jury system was invented, an individual had to be familiar with the parties as well as the circumstances in the case before he was eligible. Strangers could not serve.

In an indirect way, the U.S. Supreme Court has agreed with the premise that knowledgeable jurors can be impartial. In *Murphy v. Florida* (1975),[16] the Court held that Jack Roland Murphy, known as "Murph the Surf," was not denied a fair trial even though members of the jury that convicted him of the 1968 robbery of a Miami home had learned of the defendant's prior felony conviction and other facts from news stories. Murphy unsuccessfully argued that the extensive media coverage he received primarily because of his flamboyant life style and his earlier conviction for stealing the Star of India sapphire prejudiced the jury. Murphy cited *Irvin v. Dowd,*[17] *Rideau v. Louisiana,*[18] *Estes v. Texas,*[19] and *Sheppard v. Maxwell*[20] to support his contention that "persons who have learned from news sources of a defendant's prior criminal record are presumed to be prejudiced."[21] In each of these cases, the Supreme Court reversed a criminal conviction in state court "obtained in a trial atmosphere that had been utterly corrupted by press coverage."[22]

According to the majority opinion written by Justice Thurgood Marshall, the "constitutional standard of fairness requires that a defendant have 'a panel of impartial, indifferent jurors,'" but "[q]ualified jurors need not, however, be totally ignorant of the facts and issues involved."

The Court had no difficulty distinguishing this case from *Dowd, Rideau, Estes,* and *Sheppard.* It noted that, at the trial, Murphy did not object to the jurors selected and that he did not cross-examine any of the prosecution witnesses. His objections came after he had already been convicted. Furthermore, the Court noted, when it reviewed the *voir dire* transcript, it could find only one bit of dialogue that showed any possibility of partiality by a juror. That involved a juror who had said, in response to a hypothetical question, that his prior impressions of the defendant could dispose him to convict. The Court found the incident insignificant, however, given that the man was asked leading questions by the defense and that his other testimony indicated that "he had no deep impressions" of the accused.

Dowd was different, the Court said, because "the rural community in which the trial was held had been subjected to a barrage of inflammatory publicity immediately prior to trial, including information on the defendant's prior convictions, his confession to 24 burglaries and six murders including the one for which he was tried, and his unaccepted offer to plead guilty in order to avoid the death sentence."[23]

In *Rideau,* the Court pointed out, a confession by the defendant had been broadcast three times by a local television station. "*Sheppard* arose from a trial infected not only by a background of extremely inflammatory publicity but also by a courthouse given over to accommodate the public appetite for carnival," according to the Court. Finally, the trial in *Estes* took place in "a circus atmosphere" with journalists allowed to sit within the bar of the court, which was overrun with television cameras.[24]

Irvin v. Dowd *(1961)*

In *Irvin v. Dowd* (1961), the Court held unanimously that "Mad Dog Irvin" (as he was known in the press) had been denied Fourteenth Amendment due process and thus was entitled to a new trial. Under the Fourteenth Amendment all citizens are guaranteed fair procedures when state action is involved, and they are protected against unfair taking of their property by the state. Irvin's complaint was that proper procedures were not followed during his trial.

The U.S. Supreme Court vacated the decision by the Seventh Circuit U.S. Court of Appeals, which had turned down Irvin's request for a writ of habeas corpus. The Supreme Court pointed to the fact that 8 of the 12 jurors in the case had indicated during *voir dire* that they thought he was guilty of the murder for which he was being tried. Although he was tried and convicted of one murder, Irvin was supposedly linked to six murders. All eight of the jurors said they were familiar with the facts and circumstances, including Irvin's confession to six murders. They had acquired this information from the massive press coverage the story received, but all 12 told the judge they could still be impartial and fair. As the Court noted:

> No doubt each juror was sincere when he said that he would be fair and impartial to petitioner [Irvin], but the psychological impact requiring such a declaration before one's fellows is often its father. Where so many, so many times, admitted prejudice, such a statement of impartiality can be given little weight. As one of the jurors put it, "You can't forget what you hear and see." With his life at stake, it is not requiring too much that petitioner be tried in an atmosphere undisturbed by so huge a wave of public passion and by a jury other than one in which two-thirds of the members admit, before hearing any testimony, to possessing a belief in his guilt.[25] [citations omitted]

The barrage of publicity in the immediate vicinity where Irvin was tried included stories about crimes he had committed as a juvenile, about convictions 20 years earlier for arson and burglary, and about a court-martial on AWOL charges during the war. There were also head-lines about his police lineup identification, a planned lie detector test and, of course, his confession. Many of the news stories characterized the defendant as the "confessed slayer of six." One story described him as remorseless and having no conscience but noted that he had been declared sane by his court-appointed physicians.

Rideau v. Louisiana *(1963)*

In *Rideau v. Louisiana* (1963), the Court reversed the death penalty of Wilbert Rideau, convicted of armed robbery, kidnapping, and murder. Rideau was accused of robbing a bank in Lake Charles, Louisiana, in 1961, kidnapping three bank employees and killing one of them. The Court held that his right to due process had been violated because the state trial court refused to grant a change of venue.

Most people in Calcasieu Parish, including the jurors, had seen a film broadcast three times on television in which the defendant confessed to the sheriff in a 20-minute interview, without benefit of an attorney, that he had committed the alleged crimes. The Court was concerned because three members of the jury said during *voir dire* that they had seen the televised confession at least once. Further, two members of the jury were deputy sheriffs of the parish in which the trial occurred. The Court harshly criticized the trial proceedings:

> The case before us does not involve police brutality. The kangaroo court proceedings in this case involved a more subtle but no less real deprivation of due process of law. Under our Constitution's guarantee of due process, a person accused of committing a crime is vouchsafed basic minimal rights. Among these are the right to counsel, the right to plead not guilty, and the right to be tried in a courtroom presided over by a judge. Yet in this case the people of Calcasieu Parish saw and heard, not once but three times, a "trial" of Rideau in a jail, presided over by a sheriff, where there was no lawyer to advise Rideau of his right to stand mute."[26]

The story of Wilbert Rideau did not end with the U.S. Supreme Court decision. Rideau was tried, convicted and sentenced to death again a year later by another all-white, all-male jury. However, a U.S. Court of Appeals overturned that decision on the basis that the prosecution had struck several potential jurors because of their perceived opposition to the death penalty. A third trial in 1970 by another all-white, all-male jury also resulted in the death penalty. The Louisiana Supreme Court overturned the death penalty but allowed the conviction to stand. Several years later Rideau become editor of the Louisiana State Penitentiary magazine, *The Angolite,* which won several journalistic awards under his editorship.

Rideau went on to become what many considered a model prisoner, including producing or co-producing several award-winning documentaries and co-authoring a book on criminal justice. Despite being recommended four times over the years by the state pardon board for release, he remained in prison. In 2000 he won the right to another trial—thanks to a decision by the Fifth Circuit U.S. Court of Appeals in New Orleans. He was re-indicted 18 months later and then tried again in January 2005 by a racially diverse jury that convicted him of manslaughter. After the court sentenced him to the 44 years he had already served, he left the courtroom a free man.[27]

Estes v. Texas *(1965)*

The circumstances compelling the Supreme Court to overturn the swindling conviction of the petitioner in *Estes v. Texas* (1965) involved more than simply jury prejudice. The Court held that the Fourteenth Amendment due process rights of financier Billy Sol Estes had been violated primarily because of the publicity associated with a pretrial hearing that had been carried live on both television and radio. Some portions of the trial were also broadcast,[28] and news photography was permitted throughout the trial.

The Court was clearly unhappy with the massive pretrial and during-trial publicity, but its greatest concern was the presence of cameras at the two-day pretrial hearing, which included at least 12 camera persons continually snapping still pictures or recording motion pictures, cables and wires "snaked across the courtroom floor," three microphones on the judge's bench, and others aimed at the jury box and the attorney's table. By the time of the trial, the judge had imposed rather severe restriction on press coverage, and the trial was moved about 500 miles away. The Supreme Court did hint that cameras would return someday to the courtrooms:

> It is said that the ever-advancing techniques of public communication and the adjustment of the public to its presence may bring about a change in the effect of telecasting upon the fairness of criminal trials. But we are not dealing here with future developments in the field of electronics. Our judgment cannot be rested on the hypothesis of tomorrow but must take the facts as they are presented today.[29]

Chandler v. Florida *(1981): Cameras in the Courtroom*

The facts indeed did change as the technology changed, leading the court to rule in *Chandler v. Florida*[30] 16 years later that a state could permit broadcast and still photography coverage of criminal proceedings because cameras and microphones in courtrooms were no longer inherent violations of a defendant's Fourteenth Amendment rights, contrary to the holding in *Estes v. Texas*. The majority opinion in *Estes* cited four major reasons for banning cameras from the courtroom: (a) the negative impact on jurors, especially in biasing the jury and in distracting its members; (b) impairment of the quality of the testimony of witnesses (the idea that witnesses may alter their testimony when cameras and mikes are present); (c) interference with judges in doing their job; and (d) potential negative impact on the defendant, including harassment. As the Court noted:

> Trial by television is … foreign to our systems…. Telecasting may also deprive an accused of effective counsel. The distractions, intrusions into confidential attorney–client relationships and the temptation offered by television to play to the public office might often have a direct effect not only upon the lawyers, but the judge, the jury and the witnesses.[30] [citation omitted]

Both the First Amendment Center at Vanderbilt University and the Radio–Television Digital News Association (RTDNA) maintain online state-by-state summaries of restrictions on courtroom news coverage.[31] According to the First Amendment Center compilation, among the 50 states and the District of Columbia, only the latter expressly bans both appellate and trial court electronic news. The summary also notes that 16 states allow only appellate court coverage, 15 states have restrictions barring coverage of certain types of cases or coverage of witnesses who object to being recorded, and 19 states permit news coverage in most states.[32] In its state-by-state guide to cameras in the courtroom, RTDNA divides coverage into three tiers. The first tier ("states that allow the most coverage") includes 19 states. Some 15 states fall into the second tier ("states with restrictions prohibiting coverage of important types of cases, or prohibiting coverage of all or large categories of witnesses who object to coverage of their testimony"). The remaining 16 states are in the third tier ("states that allow appellate coverage only, or that have such restricting trial coverage rules essentially preventing coverage").[33]

Thus, in spite of enormous advances in communication technology and with public attitudes now more favorable toward such coverage, general bans still remain in several states and in the federal system. The most restrictive states include two of the most populous—Illinois and New York. In *Courtroom Television Network v. State of New York* (2005),[34] the New York Court of Appeals, the state's highest appellate court, ruled 7 to 0 that there is no state constitutional right to televise court proceedings. The court upheld the constitutionality of Civil Rights Law Section 52 that bans audiovisual coverage of most courtroom proceedings in New York. According to the court:

> Civil Rights Law Section 52 does not prevent the press, including television journalists, from attending trials and reporting on the proceedings. What they cannot do under the statute is bring cameras into the courtroom. This is not a restriction on the openness of court proceedings but rather on what means can be used in order to gather news. The media's access is thus guaranteed. But it does not extend to a right to televise those proceedings.[35] [citation omitted]

Ironically, audiovisual coverage was allowed in New York for almost a decade, ending in 1997 when the state statute expired. In 2005 the Illinois Supreme Court dismissed without comment a petition from various news organizations to allow electronic coverage of trials.[36]

When the Court TV cable network debuted in mid-1991, there were no outcries of sensationalism or complaints about lack of due process. Indeed, the network had an enormous variety of civil and criminal trials from which to choose to fill its 24-hour programming. The network got a particularly significant boost in its ratings with the O. J. Simpson criminal trial in 1994–1995, as did CNN and other cable networks that also broadcast the murder trial.

Through improved television access to the courts and growing viewer appetites for courtroom drama, Court TV has done well, both financially and in the number of viewers. When he appeared before the U.S. Senate Judiciary Committee in November 2005, Henry Schleiff, chair and CEO of the network, pointed to a variety of cases the network had carried that he said demonstrated the value of televised court proceedings. He said the network had already covered more than 900 cases including the 2000 broadcast of the trial of four New York police officers accused of firing 41 bullets in the slaying of unarmed West African immigrant Amadou Diallo. The officers claimed they thought the victim was reaching for a weapon at the time of the shooting. They were acquitted by the jury.

In his testimony before the Judiciary Committee, Schleiff noted that "the public's acceptance of the verdict was widely attributed to the fact that the public had been able to watch and listen to the proceedings unfold with their own eyes and ears."[37] Other cases he cited included a live telecast from Las Vegas of the trial of a former topless dancer and her beau who were accused of forcing heroin down the throat of a former casino owner and then digging up millions of dollars worth of silver their victim had stored in an underground vault. Both defendants were convicted.

Court TV coverage also included cases involving children such as 15-year-old Christopher Pittman who claimed his use of the Zoloft antidepressant led him to murder his grandparents when he was 12. Prosecutors argued at the 2005 trial that it was the grandparents' discipline of the boy after an incident in which he had choked another child on a school bus that led to the murders. Pittman was convicted and given 30 years in prison. In the same year, the network broadcast the trial of 80-year-old Edgar Ray Killen for the 1967 murders of three civil rights workers. The defendant claimed he was at a wake at the time of the killings, but the prosecution successfully argued that he coordinated the crimes. He was found guilty of manslaughter.

Schleiff concluded his comments by arguing for televised coverage of U.S. Supreme Court oral arguments. Over the years, including during the dispute over the 2000 presidential election, the Supreme Court has permitted the delayed but same-day broadcasts of audio recordings of a few historic cases. However, the Court still bans video cameras and live coverage. "The American people deserve to see their judicial system in action, at all levels," according to Schleiff. "The American people deserve to see this window on a system of justice now opened and for the sun to shine in upon it. Indeed, the American people deserve to have cameras permitted in our nation's federal courtrooms."[38] So far, that has not occurred.

Thanks to high-speed technology, with the beginning of its new term on October 2, 2006, the U.S. Supreme Court began making transcripts of oral arguments available free online to anyone on the same day they are heard in court. The website is www.supremecourtus.gov. Prior to that, the transcripts were usually available online within two weeks after the oral arguments. In 2007 the Court provided digital access for the first time to videotaped evidence cited in an opinion. The link for the clip was included, with access made available via the Court's website. The clip featured a video recording of a high-speed police chase in Atlanta taken with a camera mounted on the dashboard of the cruiser.

In *Chandler,* two men were convicted of conspiracy to commit burglary, grand larceny, and possession of burglary tools after they were charged with breaking and entering a popular Miami Beach restaurant. (Both were Miami Beach police officers at the time of their arrests.) The trial attracted considerable media attention, and cameras were in the courtroom, as permitted under experimental Florida Supreme Court rules. The cameras were in place only during *voir dire,* during the testimony of the prosecution's chief witness, and during closing arguments. The witness was an amateur radio operator who had overheard and recorded conversations between the defendants on their police walkie-talkies while they were committing the burglary. Less than three minutes of the trial were actually broadcast.

Before the trial, the defendants had been unsuccessful in persuading the Florida Supreme Court to declare the experimental rules unconstitutional. They also could not convince the trial court judge to sequester the jury because of the television coverage, although he did instruct the jury not to watch or read anything in the media about the case. The defendants were convicted on all counts and moved for a new trial on the ground that they had been denied a fair and impartial trial because of the television coverage. The Florida District Court affirmed the convictions, and the Florida Supreme Court declined to review.

Noting that it had no supervisory jurisdiction over state courts, the U.S. Supreme Court made it clear that it was limited to whether the mere presence of media cameras in the courtroom was sufficient to deny the defendants their constitutional right to a fair trial. According to the Court, there is no prohibition in the U.S. Constitution against a state's experimental use of cameras in the courtroom.

Ironically, *Chandler v. Florida*, which recognized no constitutional right of access but merely held that the Constitution does not bar states from allowing radio, television, and photographic coverage of criminal proceedings, has probably had a greater impact on opening the judicial process than *Richmond Newspapers v. Virginia*, which did recognize a constitutional right of access to criminal trials by the press and the public. The public still generally distrusts broadcast coverage of trials, as the fallout from the O. J. Simpson murder trial demonstrated in 1995, but such coverage is becoming more accepted and routine.

The federal court system has been among the least progressive in opening the courts to electronic news coverage. From 1990 to 1993 as part of a pilot program, the Judicial Conference (a 27-member federal body that determines rules and policies for the federal courts) allowed video and still camera coverage of civil proceedings in eight federal district and appellate courts, including the Second Circuit U.S. Court of Appeals in New York and the Ninth Circuit in San Francisco. By all accounts, the program was highly successful, with judges overwhelmingly saying their attitudes toward cameras in the courtroom continued to be favorable, as they had been before the experiment.[39] The committee charged with analyzing the results of the pilot recommended giving judges the authority to permit access to cameras in civil proceedings, but the Judicial Conference voted not to follow the recommendation. In 1996 the conference voted down the idea again. The Conference has allowed further experimentation by appellate courts in specific cases.[40]

Closing Criminal Trials

Are there situations in which criminal proceedings, including trials, can be closed without violating the First Amendment? *Richmond Newspapers v. Virginia* provides at least a partial answer. According to the Court, the trial of a criminal case must be open to the public, "absent an overriding interest articulated in findings."[41] The Court, however, took no pains to explain "overriding interest," but did distinguish the case from *Gannett v. DePasquale* by noting that "both the majority [which upheld the closure of a criminal pretrial hearing as constitutional] and dissenting opinions ... agreed that open trials were part of the common law tradition."[42]

Unfortunately, the justices did not overrule *Gannett v. DePasquale*, which led Justice Byron White to argue in his concurring opinion in *Richmond Newspapers v. Virginia* that the latter case "would have been unnecessary had *Gannett* ... construed the Sixth Amendment to forbid excluding the public from criminal proceedings except in narrowly defined circumstances."[43]

Richmond Newspapers was a particularly appropriate case for testing this implicit right of access in the Constitution because it involved a defendant who had already been tried three times and specifically requested closure with no objection from the prosecution. The defendant's first conviction of second degree murder was reversed because improper evidence was introduced at trial, and the second and third trials ended in mistrials. Because the defendant asked that the trial be closed, he effectively waived his right to a public trial. Thus a First Amendment rationale was necessary if the trial were to remain open.

One of the more puzzling aspects of the decision is that the majority opinion (written by then Chief Justice Warren Burger) said it was "not crucial" to characterize the decision as "right of access" or a "right to gather information." The Court did note that the "explicit, guaranteed rights to speak and to publish concerning what takes place at a trial would lose much meaning if access to observe the trial could, as it was here, be foreclosed arbitrarily."[44]

The vast majority of states forbid coverage of juvenile cases, testimony by victims of sex crimes, domestic relations (divorces, adoption proceedings, child custody disputes, etc.), trade secrets, and *voir dire*.

Sheppard v. Maxwell *(1966): Prejudicial Publicity*

Although it was technically not an access case, *Sheppard v. Maxwell* (1966)[45] was a watershed decision involving the Fourteenth Amendment rights of defendants, especially in highly publicized cases. It also played a major role in a movement by lower courts away from openness that began in the early 1990s. Indeed, the Court's decision served as a lightning rod for many state courts to close trials even though the justices clearly did not intend to send a message that press and public access should be restricted beyond the suggestions made for preventing a crowded courtroom.

The circumstances in the case are particularly important in understanding the Court's decision. Samuel H. Sheppard, a prominent Ohio osteopath, was tried and convicted by a jury of second degree murder after his wife, Marilyn, was bludgeoned to death in their Bay Village home in suburban Cleveland. The Supreme Court's opinion describes the case in considerable detail, but some highlights bear mentioning. Sheppard was a suspect in the murder from the beginning. He claimed that he had fallen asleep on a couch the night his wife was murdered in her bedroom, and that he had heard her cry out in the early morning. When he ran upstairs to her bedroom, he saw a "form" standing over her bed and was then knocked unconscious when he struggled with the "form." When he regained consciousness, he checked his wife and believed she was dead after he could not get a pulse. He then checked on his son, found him unharmed and chased the "form" out the door onto the lake shore, where he again lost consciousness.[46]

The publicity surrounding the case and the trial was unbelievable and on par with that in the 1934 trial of Bruno Hauptmann in the kidnap–murder of the 19-month-old son of famed aviator Charles Lindbergh. The indiscretions of the press in that case led the American Bar Association three years later to adopt Canon 35, which effectively forbade broadcast coverage and still photos in courtrooms for more than four decades.

A few examples from the *Sheppard* case will give a sense of why the Court denounced the "carnival atmosphere at trial." The headlines, stories, and editorials in the Cleveland newspapers were relentless and merciless in their accusations against the defendant. Some typical examples among the dozens cited by the Court:

1. At the coroner's request before the trial, Sheppard re-enacted the tragedy at his home, but he had to wait outside for the coroner to arrive because the house was placed in protective custody until after the trial. Because news reporters had apparently been invited on the tour by the coroner, they reported his performance in detail, complete with photographs.

2. When the defendant refused a lie detector test, front-page newspaper headlines screamed "Doctor Balks at Lie Test; Retells Story" and "'Loved My Wife, She Loved Me,' Sheppard Tells News Reporter."

3. Later, front-page editorials claimed someone was "getting away with murder" and called on the coroner to conduct an inquest: "Why No Inquest? Do It Now, Dr. Gerber." When the hearing was conducted, it took place in a local school gymnasium, complete with live broadcast microphones, a swarm of photographers and reporters and several hundred spectators. Sheppard was questioned for five and one-half hours about his actions on the night of the murder, an illicit affair, and his married life. His attorneys were present but were not allowed to participate.

4. Later stories and editorials focused on evidence that was never introduced at trial and on reports of numerous extramarital affairs, even though the evidence at trial included an affair with only one woman, Susan Hayes, the subject of dozens of news stories.

5. Sheppard was not formally charged until more than a month after the murder, and during that time the editorials and headlines ranged from "Why Isn't Sam Sheppard in Jail?" to "New Murder Evidence Is Found, Police Say" and "Dr. Sam Faces Quiz at Jail on Marilyn's Fear of Him."

6. The trial occurred two weeks before the November general election in which the chief prosecutor was a candidate for common pleas judge and the trial judge was a candidate to succeed himself. All three Cleveland newspapers published the names and addresses of prospective jurors and during the trial the jurors became media celebrities. During the trial, which was held in a small courtroom (26 by 48 feet), 20 newspaper and wire service reporters were seated within 3 feet of the jury box. A local radio station was even allowed to broadcast from a room next door to where the jurors recessed and later deliberated in the case. Each day, witnesses, the attorneys, and the jurors were photographed as they entered and left the courtroom, and although photos were not permitted during the trial itself, they were permitted during the recesses. In fact, pictures of the jury appeared more than 40 times in the newspapers.

7. The jurors were never sequestered during the trial and were allowed to watch, hear, and read all the massive publicity during the trial, which even included a national broadcast by the famous Walter Winchell in which he asserted that a woman under arrest for robbery in New York City said she was Sam Sheppard's mistress and had borne his child. The judge merely politely "admonished" the jurors not to allow such stories to affect their judgment.

As the Court summarized in its 8–1 decision ordering a new trial for Sheppard, "[B]edlam reigned at the courthouse during the trial and newsmen took over practically the entire courtroom, hounding most of the participants in the trial, especially Sheppard."[47] As a result, Sheppard was denied a fair trial in violation of his Fourteenth Amendment due process rights, according to the Court. At the second trial, 12 years after the first, the physician was acquitted.

In spite of the fact that Dr. Sheppard had been the subject of highly prejudicial, intense publicity, the Court recommended remedies short of prior restraint:

> Bearing in mind the massive pretrial publicity, the judge should have adopted stricter rules governing the use of the courtroom by newsmen.... The number of reporters in the courtroom itself could have been limited at the first sign that their presence would disrupt the trial. They should not have been placed inside the bar. Furthermore, the judge should have more closely regulated the conduct of newsmen in the courtroom....

Secondly, the court should have insulated the witnesses. All of the newspapers and radio stations apparently interviewed prospective witnesses at will, and in many instances disclosed their testimony....

Thirdly, the judge should have made some effort to control the release of leads, information, and gossip to the press by police officers, witnesses, and the counsel for both sides. Much of the information was inaccurate, leading to groundless rumors and confusion.[48]

The Court also suggested other remedies, including (a) continuance or postponing the case until prejudicial publicity subsided, (b) transferring to another county not permeated by the publicity, (c) sequestration of the jury to keep its members from being exposed to prejudicial publicity, and (d) ordering a new trial if publicity threatened a defendant's due process rights after a trial has begun. It is significant that the Court did not cite restrictive (gag) orders on the press as a judicial remedy but instead favored restricting the parties, witnesses, and attorneys.

Unfortunately, many courts interpreted the *Sheppard* holding as a license to impose restrictive orders on the press anyway, prodding the Court to eventually rule out such censorship under most circumstances in a series of rulings that culminated in the decision in 1976 in *Nebraska Press Association v. Stuart,* in which the Court held that restrictive orders against the press are "presumptively unconstitutional" and cannot be issued except in rare circumstances and then only after other measures less restrictive of the First Amendment are exhausted.

Until *Richmond Newspapers,* the Supreme Court appeared to be moving toward restricting press access to the judicial process, as witnessed by the 5–4 decision in *Gannett v. DePasquale,* upholding the closure of pretrial hearings. In *Pell v. Procunier* (1974)[49] and *William B. Saxbe v. the Washington Post Co.* (1974),[50] the Court decided 5–4 that journalists have no constitutional rights of access to prisons or their inmates beyond those enjoyed by the public. *Pell* upheld a California Department of Corrections regulation barring the news media from interviewing "specific individual inmates." Four prisoners and three journalists had challenged the rule as a violation of their First and Fourteenth Amendment rights of free speech.

According to the Court, "It is one thing to say that a journalist is free to seek out sources of information not available to members of the general public. It is quite another thing to suggest that the Constitution imposes upon government the affirmative duty to make available to journalists sources of information not available to members of the public generally."[51] The Court accepted the state's rationale that media interviews can turn certain inmates into celebrities and thus create disciplinary problems for these and other prisoners.

In *Saxbe,* issued on the same day as *Pell,* the Court upheld a federal rule similar to that of California that prohibited personal interviews by journalists with individually designated federal inmates in medium- and maximum-security prisons. The justices saw no major differences between the two regulations and noted that the federal rule "does not place the press in any less advantageous position than the public generally."[52] The *Washington Post* had filed suit after it was denied access to prisoners who had allegedly been punished for their involvement in strike negotiations at two federal facilities. In its reasoning, the Court relied heavily on *Branzburg v. Hayes* (1972),[53] which held 5 to 4 that the First Amendment grants no special privileges to journalists against revealing confidential sources or confidential information to grand juries.

Pell and *Saxbe* were basically reaffirmed four years later in a plurality opinion in *Houchins v. KQED* (1978),[54] in which the Court held that a broadcaster's First and Fourteenth Amendment rights were not violated when the station was denied access to the portion of a county jail where a suicide had occurred. According to the Court, "Neither the First Amendment nor Fourteenth Amendment mandates a right of access to government information or sources of information within the government's control. Under our holdings in [*Pell* and *Saxbe*], until the political branches decree otherwise, as they are free to do, the media has [sic] no special right of access to the Alameda County Jail [the facility in question] different from or greater than that accorded the public generally."[55] The station could use other sources, the Court noted, such as inmate letters, former inmates, public officials, and prisoners' attorneys to gain the information it sought about conditions at the facility.

A number of trials since Sheppard have attracted intense, unrelenting media attention such as the Charles Manson murders, but the O. J. Simpson murder trial probably set the record for media coverage. Simpson was charged in June 1994 with the murders of his former wife, Nicole Brown Simpson, and her friend, Ronald Goldman. All of the major proceedings were broadcast live, and nearly every major newspaper in the country carried front page stories and photos during dramatic points in the trial. An estimated 95 million viewers watched at least a portion of the bizarre June 17 Los Angeles freeway chase carried live by CNN and many TV stations, thanks to cameras mounted on helicopters.[56] The trial attracted even more viewers and set new records several times for CNN, Court TV, and the big four commercial networks— ABC, CBS, Fox, and NBC. The coverage made trial participants such as Brian "Kato" Kaelin, Deputy District Attorney Marcia Clark, Defense Attorneys Johnny Cochran and Robert J. Shapiro, and, of course, L.A. Detective Mark Fuhrman household names. In fact, the reading of the jury's verdict of acquittal had one of the largest live TV audiences in history.

Both sides in the Simpson case argued to prevent the release of some of the evidence such as crime scene photographs and medical records. The trial and the events surrounding it severely tested the ethical and legal limits on the mass media, and the trial went down as one of the major media events of the century. The principles laid down by *Sheppard* and its progeny assured that Simpson got a fair trial even with the intense pretrial and during-trial publicity. There were surprisingly few clashes between the judiciary and the press over access. During the early part of the trial, Judge Lance Ito temporarily barred *The Daily News* of Los Angeles, the city's second largest newspaper, from the courtroom for publishing the details of a jury questionnaire the day before it was officially released. However, the paper was quickly allowed to return to the courtroom.

When Simpson was tried for the wrongful deaths of Brown and Goldman in the civil case in 1996 through 1997, Judge Hiroshi Fujisaki issued a blanket gag order on all participants and banned all television and radio recording from the courtroom. The trial concluded in February 1997 with a $33.5 million judgment against the defendant.

The aftermath of the Simpson trials, especially the criminal trial, was a strong backlash against the media as well as against lawyers. In California, the site of both Simpson trials, a rash of "O. J. laws" were proposed, and some of them were enacted. These included a new rule by the state Judicial Council granting trial court judges more authority to ban cameras in the courtroom as well as a new state bar association rule that severely restricts the ability of attorneys to make out-of-court comments that could influence in-court proceedings.[57] In several high-profile trials held after the Simpson murder trial, trial court judges specifically cited the Simpson case as justification for banning cameras in states where cameras had become relatively routine. These included the trials of John Salvi, who was convicted for murdering two women and injuring five others at two Massachusetts abortion clinics, and of Richard Allen Davis, convicted of kidnapping 12-year-old Polly Klaas from her bedroom in her California home and then killing her.[58]

The backlash prompted American Bar Association President N. Lee Cooper to caution his fellow bar members not to "base our approach to court coverage on fears generated by isolated media trials."[59] "We must always separate problems of court coverage from problems with the courts themselves," he noted.

There may even have been some spillover from the Simpson trials into the public views about the media coverage of Independent Counsel Kenneth W. Starr's 1998 investigation of President Clinton's reported affair with 21-year-old White House intern Monica Lewinsky. Many members of the public apparently saw the news coverage as just another example of media excess, chastising the press for its intrusive reporting while, at the same time, devouring the stories focusing on the investigation. A *Washington Post* poll, for example, found that 56% of those surveyed thought Clinton had been treated unfairly and 75% said the Lewinsky story was getting too much coverage, but broadcast and cable news ratings continued to surge, as did the circulation of news magazines and newspapers such as *USA Today.*[60]

Richard Nixon v. Warner Communications (1978): Right of Access to Public Recordings

In a 1978 decision that has had limited impact on the press because of its rather unusual circumstances, the Court ruled 5–4 that no First Amendment rights were violated when the press was denied permission to copy, broadcast, and sell to the public recordings of White House conversations played during one of the Watergate trials. *Richard Nixon v. Warner Communications*[61] was unusual in that Warner was requesting copies of tapes that had already been played at trial but were in the custody of the Administrator of General Services under authority granted by the Presidential Recordings Act approved by Congress.

Robert K. Smith v. Daily Mail Publishing Co. (1979): *Publishing Juvenile Offender Names*

Exactly one year later the Court unanimously struck down as unconstitutional a West Virginia statute that provided criminal penalties for publication, without the written permission of the juvenile court, of truthful information that had been lawfully acquired concerning the identity of a juvenile offender. In *Robert K. Smith v. Daily Mail Publishing Co.* (1979),[62] the justices said the asserted state interest of insuring the anonymity of juveniles involved in juvenile court proceedings was not sufficient to override the First Amendment's restrictions against prior restraint. The Charleston (West Virginia) *Daily Mail* and the Charleston *Gazette* published the name of a 14-year-old junior high student who had been charged with shooting a 15-year-old classmate to death at school. Reporters and photographers first heard about the shooting on a police radio and then were given the alleged assailant's name by several eyewitnesses, the police, and an assistant prosecutor. After the name and photo of the teenage defendant appeared in the papers, a grand jury indicted both publications for violating the state statute, although no indictments were issued against three local radio stations who broadcast the name. (The statute applied only to newspapers, not to the electronic or other media, a deficiency duly noted by the Court in its decision.)

The holding in the case was narrow, as then Chief Justice Warren Burger indicated, because "there is no issue before us of unlawful press access to confidential judicial proceedings [citations omitted]; there is no issue here of privacy or prejudicial pre-trial publicity."[63] Indeed, Justice Rehnquist, while concurring in the judgment of the Court, noted, "I think that a generally effective ban on publication that applied to all forms of mass communication, electronic and print media alike, would be constitutional."[64] The Court's opinion, representing the other seven justices voting in the case—Justice Powell took no part in the consideration or decision of the case—held that a state statute punishing the publication of the name of a juvenile defendant could never serve a "state interest of the highest order," as required to justify prior restraint. The majority opinion cited, among other decisions, *Landmark Communications Inc. v. Virginia* (1978),[65] *Cox Broadcasting Corp. v. Cohn* (1975),[66] and *Oklahoma Publishing Co. v. District Court* (1977).[67]

In *Landmark*, the Supreme Court ruled 7 to 0 that a Virginia statute subjecting individuals, including newspapers, to criminal sanctions for disclosing information regarding proceedings before a state judicial review commission was a violation of the First Amendment. The case arose when the *Virginian Pilot* published an article accurately reporting details of an investigation of a state judge by the Virginia Judicial Inquiry and Review Commission. One month later, a state grand jury indicted the company that owned the newspaper for violating the statute by "unlawfully divulg[ing] the identification of a judge of a court not of record, and stating that the judge was the subject of an investigation and hearing" by the commission. In a bench trial, Landmark was fined $500 and ordered to pay court costs. The company appealed and the Supreme Court held that the First Amendment does not allow "the criminal punishment of third persons who are strangers to the inquiry, including news media, for divulging or publishing truthful information regarding confidential proceedings" of the Judicial Inquiry and Review Commission.[68]

The Court noted that the issue was narrow because the case was neither concerned with application of the statute to someone who obtained the information illegally and then divulged it nor with the authority to keep such a commission's proceedings confidential. But it was, nevertheless, an important victory for news gathering because it reinforced the principle that truthful information legally obtained enjoys First Amendment protection even when such information includes details of closed judicial proceedings. This protection is not absolute, of course, as the Court noted in both *Landmark* and *Smith,* but the state has a heavy burden in demonstrating that its interests outweigh those of the First Amendment. While admitting in *Landmark* that premature disclosure of the commission's proceedings could pose some risk of injury to the judge, judicial system, or operation of the commission itself, the Court said "much of the risk can be eliminated through careful internal procedures to protect the confidentiality of Commission proceedings."[69]

In *Cox Broadcasting,* the U.S. Supreme Court declared unconstitutional a Georgia statute that made the press criminally and civilly liable for publishing the name of a rape victim even when such information was obtained from public records.[70] In *Oklahoma Publishing Co.,* the Court held that a state court injunction barring the press from publishing the identity or photograph of an 11-year-old boy on trial in juvenile court was unconstitutional prior restraint.[71] The Court struck down the judge's order because he had already allowed reporters and other members of the public to attend a hearing in the case in which the information was disclosed. Once truthful information is "publicly revealed" or "in the public domain," it cannot be banned, according to the Court.

Globe Newspaper Co. v. Norfolk County Superior Court *(1982)*: *Unconstitutionality of Mandatory Closures*

In 1982 the U.S. Supreme Court issued the first of three rulings that appeared to significantly broaden the holding in *Richmond Newspapers* (1980) that criminal trials were under the Constitution presumptively open to the press and the public. While the first decision, *Globe Newspaper Co. v. Norfolk County Superior Court* (1982),[72] did not deal directly with the scope of *Richmond Newspapers,* it still paved the way for the two subsequent cases that confronted this issue. In *Globe Newspaper,* the Court in a 6–3 opinion struck down as unconstitutional a Massachusetts statute that the state Supreme Judicial Court construed to require judges to exclude the press and the public in trials for certain sexual offenses involving a victim under the age of 18 during the time the victim is testifying. The key factor in the case was *mandatory closure*—the judge had no discretion. Liberally quoting its decision in *Richmond Newspapers,* the Court rejected the state's contentions that the statute was necessary to protect "minor victims of sex crimes from further trauma and embarrassment" and to encourage "such victims to come forward and testify in a truthful and credible manner." According to the majority opinion:

> Although the right of access to criminal trials is of a constitutional stature, it is not absolute. But the circumstances under which the press and the public can be barred from a criminal trial are limited; the State's justification in denying access must be a weighty one. Where, as in the present case, the State attempts to deny the right of access in order to inhibit the disclosure of sensitive information, it must be shown that the denial is necessitated by a compelling governmental interest, and is narrowly tailored to serve that interest.[73]

The justices agreed that the first asserted state interest was compelling but that mandatory closure was not justified because "the circumstances of a particular case may affect the significance of the interest. A trial court can determine on a case-by-case basis whether closure is necessary to protect the welfare of a minor victim."[74] The Supreme Court was not convinced at all on the second asserted interest because the press and the public are allowed to see the transcript and to talk with court personnel and other individuals and thus ascertain the substance of victims' testimony and even their identities. Thus the Court left the door open for closure on a case-by-case basis, while clearly prohibiting mandatory closure as unconstitutional prior restraint.

Press Enterprise I *(1984) and* Press Enterprise II *(1986)*: *Right of Access to Voir Dire and Preliminary Hearings*

Press Enterprise I (1984)[75] and *Press Enterprise II* (1986),[76] as they have become known, opened up *voir dire* and preliminary hearings, at least as they are conducted in California, to the press and the public. *Press Enterprise I* is particularly significant because the Court for the first time held that the jury selection process is part of a criminal trial and thus presumptively open under the First and Fourteenth Amendments. The unanimous decision reiterated that the "presumption of openness may be overcome only by an overriding interest based on findings that closure is essential to preserve higher values and is narrowly tailored to serve that interest."[77]

In *Press Enterprise I,* the newspaper was denied access to most of the *voir dire* in a trial for the rape and murder of a teenage girl. The judge allowed the press to attend the "general *voir dire*" but closed the courtroom when the attorneys questioned individual jurors. In all, only three days of the six weeks of *voir dire* were open, and the judge refused to allow a transcript of the process to be released to the public. The jury selection process could under some circumstances invoke a compelling government interest, but no such interest had been demonstrated in this case, according to the Court. An example cited by the justices of such a justified closure might be to protect an individual's privacy when a prospective juror had privately told the judge that she or a member of her family had been raped but had not prosecuted the offender because of the trauma and embarrassment from disclosure.

Two years later in *Press Enterprise II,* the Supreme Court held 7 to 2 that the press and the public enjoyed a limited First Amendment right of access in criminal cases to preliminary hearings. The holding was quite narrow because the Court emphasized that it applied only to such hearings "as they are conducted in California" where "because of its extensive scope, the preliminary hearing is often the most important in the criminal proceeding."[78] The case began when the newspaper was denied access to a 41-day preliminary hearing for a nurse charged with the murders of 12 patients. The defendant requested closure, and the magistrate in the case not only granted the motion but also sealed the record. The prosecution moved to have the transcript released and the trial court agreed to do so when the defendant waived the right to a jury trial, but the California Supreme Court reversed the trial court decision. The U.S. Supreme Court reversed, holding that "California preliminary hearings are sufficiently like a trial" to warrant a First Amendment right of access unless the state can demonstrate an overriding interest sufficient to overcome the presumption of openness.

Summary and Conclusions

Since *Press Enterprise II* the U.S. Supreme Court has not considered whether other portions of the criminal judicial process, including preliminary hearings in states that do not follow the California model, fall under the holding in *Richmond Newspapers*. The composition of the Court has changed completely since 1986, except for Justice Stevens who voted with the majority in *Press Enterprise II.* Given the current composition of the Court with Justice John Roberts at the helm it does not appear likely that the Court will, even if given the opportunity, broaden the scope of the limited First Amendment right of access to the criminal judicial process.

The chances are even slimmer that the Court will recognize anytime soon a constitutional right of the press and the public to attend civil trials and related proceedings. Such a move would be a bold and unprecedented step toward truly opening the judicial system to the public, which it was designed to serve in the first place. Civil trials are now routinely open, with closures relatively unusual, in state and federal courts, but most federal and many state civil trials continue to be closed to electronic media coverage. The U.S. Supreme Court has always opened its formal proceedings, although not its deliberations, including oral arguments and the reading of decisions to the public, but the justices continue to ban cameras in the courtroom except for ceremonial occasions.

As the Court has indicated in each of its decisions dealing with access to the judicial process, the right of public and press access is not absolute, but the burden on the state to justify closure must necessarily be heavy. The trials of Bruno Hauptmann, Dr. Sam Sheppard, and even the O. J. Simpson murder trial were aberrations and should be viewed as such by the courts. Openness clearly promotes fairness and justice because it subjects the judicial system to press and public scrutiny, which is essential in an age in which the public appears to have lost some of its faith in the process.

Access to Places

No Special Right of Access to Public and Private Places by the Press

Although access to the judicial process has significantly expanded over the decades, press and public access to places, especially government institutions, has actually become more restricted, especially since the attacks of September 11, 2001. However, not all of the restrictions can be attributed to the aftermath of the attacks. As early as 1972 in *Branzburg v. Hayes*, the U.S. Supreme Court hinted at what might be in store for the future:

> Despite the fact that newsgathering may be hampered, the press is regularly excluded from grand jury proceedings, our own conferences, the meetings of other official bodies gathered in executive session, and the meetings of private organizations. Newsmen have no constitutional right of access to the scenes of crime or disaster when the general public is excluded, and they may be prohibited from attending or publishing information about trials if such restrictions are necessary to assure a defendant a fair trial before an impartial jury.[79]

Two years later the Court began drawing the boundaries with its decisions regarding access to prisons in *Pell v. Procunier* and *Saxbe v. the Washington Post*. The task of defining the specific limitations, though, was left to other courts and legislators but the Supreme Court certainly set the tone: so long as the media are granted the same privileges as the general public in gaining access to places, no First Amendment rights are violated.

Access to public property is generally much easier than private property, especially where a public forum exists, but there are times and circumstances when it is reasonable, according to the courts, to limit access even to public places and public events. Disasters and wars are prime examples in which authorities can severely restrict press and public access even though an event of great public interest may be involved.

During both the 1991 Persian Gulf War and the more recent wars in Afghanistan and Iraq, the U.S. military imposed restrictions on news media access. During the war in Iraq, journalists were embedded with United States troops and thus permitted to actually travel in fatigues or uniforms with soldiers on patrol and on maneuvers. Most press associations were pleased to have such access even when the military imposed embargoes on when and what they could report. However, as journalist Irwin Gratz, then President of the Society of Professional Journalists, told a group of colleagues in 2005, the federal government made less information about the Iraq War available to the public than it did about other battles before the September

11, 2001, attacks. According to Gratz, "The Bush administration has been working overtime to keep as much information secret as it can."[80]

During 2001 after the September 11 terrorist attacks, the United States military initiated combat operations in Afghanistan in its global war on terrorism. *Hustler* magazine publisher Larry Flynt asked the Department of Defense (DOD) to allow correspondents to accompany ground troops during combat. When Flynt was denied such access, he sued the DOD, claiming that his First Amendment rights had been violated. Flynt argued that the Constitution guaranteed journalists the right to travel with the military in combat. A U.S. District Court judge denied his claim and refused to grant an injunction against the DOD in enforcing such restrictions. On appeal, the U.S. Court of Appeals for the D.C. Circuit affirmed the district court decision in *Flynt v. Rumsfeld* (2004).[81] The appellate court held there was no such First Amendment right. This decision makes it clear that the military can determine if and when journalists can be embedded with troops in combat.

Execution is another area in which journalists have sometimes had difficulty gaining access in spite of the tradition at most executions that at least one member of the press be present during the proceeding. California, for example, unsuccessfully attempted to allow access to executions only after prisoners were taken to the chamber to be executed, tied down and had the intravenous lines started. However, that restriction was struck down as a violation of the First Amendment by the Ninth Circuit U.S. Court of Appeals in *California First Amendment Coalition v. Woodford* (2002).[82]

Typically, unless journalists can demonstrate either that (a) the government authorities acted unreasonably or in an arbitrary and capricious manner in blocking access or (b) the government discriminated against the press by blocking media access while allowing the public to enter the area, they will lose. Even when the public is given access, the media do not automatically have a right to full access by bringing cameras and other video and audio recording equipment. Journalists simply have the right to treatment equal to that granted to the public. Most police departments, especially in larger metropolitan areas, have written guidelines for dealing with the press at accidents and disasters. Although these are usually not legally binding because they are merely guidelines rather than administrative regulations, journalists, including news photographers, should be familiar with them. Often such guidelines are drawn up after consultation with the press. When they prove unworkable or unreasonable, the media should pressure police department administrators to change them. The changes are more likely to occur when the press makes a concerted and organized effort through professional associations such as area press clubs and the local chapters of the Society of Professional Journalists.

Restrictions on press intrusion on private property are usually rather severe, as was illustrated in 1979 when several reporters and photographers were arrested and later convicted of criminal trespassing after they entered a nuclear power plant construction site known as Black Fox Station in Rogers County, Oklahoma. The plant was owned by the Public Service Co. of Oklahoma (PSO), which had a record of denying access to the plant to the news media and the public. The arrests occurred after the reporters followed a group of antinuclear protestors as they crossed a border fence to enter the privately owned nuclear power plant site.

The Oklahoma District Court judge ruled that whereas "there is a First Amendment right of the news media to reasonable access to the news such as is available to the public generally," this right must be weighed against several opposing state interests.[83] (Although the power company was technically privately owned, the judge treated it as a governmental entity for purposes of the case because its operation was heavily regulated by the state and federal governments.) He then ruled that the reporters' First Amendment rights were not violated because the state had the duty to maintain public order and enforce criminal statutes and to protect property. The state Criminal Court of Appeals, in upholding the $25 fines imposed on each of the journalists by the trial court, held that the First Amendment does not guarantee the press access to property "simply because it is owned or controlled by the government."[84]

During the Vietnam War the press played a major role in reversing public opinion from strong support to doubts and opposition; the Persian Gulf War saw a return to "a patriotic press," the norm in wartime.[85] Media critic and columnist Richard Reeves, for example, suggested that the Cable News Network, which was the primary source for news about the war for most Americans according to opinion polls, should have been called PNN (Pentagon News Network).[86]

Wars inevitably invoke different rules for access for both the press and the public, but access can be restricted even when it means that significant news events will not be covered, both in peacetime and during war. The Iraq War revealed one of the major ethical dilemmas facing journalists: *should the press agree to "voluntary" restrictions by the government in covering an important event when the restraint would otherwise likely be unconstitutional?*

It is imperative that the news media aggressively fight at all times for access to places and information on behalf of the public and the press when such access is essential to effectively gathering accurate data about events of public interest. However, voluntary restraint is justified under some circumstances, such as when national security would clearly be endangered. Nevertheless, the press must always be wary of agreeing to withhold information simply because the government has threatened to revoke a journalist's credentials or because the government has indicated it will deny access unless the news media exercise self-restraint. Sometimes the press may need to challenge the government even when public sentiment is strongly against journalists, as occurred during both the Gulf War and the war in Iraq.

One of the more controversial steps that some news organizations have taken is to work with governmental authorities, such as police and fire departments, to develop a system for issuing press passes. Such arrangements are becoming more common, but some journalists fear the result may be less rather than greater access. Presumably, under this argument, the guidelines established for the use of the passes offer authorities the chance to prevent the media from going where they want to go at crime and disaster scenes under the guise of a formal agreement that the press has promised to respect.

Access to Records

When it comes to gathering news, reporters and editors still rely most heavily on personal sources—experts, officials, politicians, eyewitnesses, ordinary individuals, lawyers, and so on—for information, but written as well as computerized records usually provide much of the material that goes into a typical news story.

These records can include birth, marriage, and death certificates; divorce decrees; court documents; government agency materials; property deeds; and even telephone books and city directories. Although the focus of this section is on obtaining public documents, private individuals should not be overlooked as sources of records, especially of non-public materials. In fact, when you are writing a story, it sometimes may be more expeditious to consult a nongovernmental source for a copy of a legal document than to wait for days or months for a government agency to release the information. However, you should make sure in such a case that your source is absolutely trustworthy and reliable (and thus will not give you an altered document) and that the person did not illegally acquire the document (such as by stealing it from an office).

This chapter can provide only a summary of the process for legally obtaining public documents, but several useful guides may be consulted for further information.[87] Each of the 50 states has its own statutes regarding access to public government records, but two federal statutes deal specifically with U.S. government documents: the 1966 Freedom of Information Act (FOIA)[88] and the 1974 Privacy Act.[89]

1966 Freedom of Information Act

The FOIA celebrated its 40th anniversary in 2006. The Act, which President Lyndon Johnson reluctantly signed into law on July 4, 1966, generally mandates that all federal executive and independent regulatory agencies (a) publish in the *Federal Register* descriptions of their central and field organizations and the employees from whom and the process by which the public can obtain records from them; (b) make available for public inspection all final opinions and orders made in the adjudication of cases as well as statements of policy and interpretation adopted by the agencies, administrative manuals as well as current indexes providing identifying information to the public about any policy, decision, rule or regulation issued, adopted or promulgated by the agencies after July 4, 1967 (the effective date of the act).

Each agency is also required to publish at least quarterly and distribute copies of each index and to promulgate regulations regarding the schedule of fees for the processing of FOIA requests and the conditions under which fees will be reduced or waived. The upshot is that every agency must, on request, indicate the procedures and fees involved in obtaining records and make documents readily available.

There are some limitations to the Act. First, it applies only to federal agencies, not to state and local agencies, although all 50 states have similar statutes that make such records available at the state and local levels. Second, nine exemptions and three exclusions prevent many documents from being accessible. Third, the statute does not apply to the courts nor to Congress, which conveniently exempted itself from the law. Finally, the information is not free, although agencies cannot charge for the first two hours of search time nor for the first 100 pages of photocopies if the request is for noncommercial use. Even if fees are charged, a waiver or reduction can be granted when disclosure of the information would serve the public interest because it will likely contribute significantly to public understanding of the operations or activities of the government and the information requested would not primarily serve the requester's commercial interests.

Journalists routinely ask for this waiver because news stories based on such documents generally do increase public awareness about the activities of government and news gathering is one of the purposes Congress had in mind when the statute was written. Indeed, this is reflected by the fact that an agency can impose reasonable standard charges for document search, duplication, and review when the information is for commercial use, but it can charge educational or noncommercial scientific institutions and representatives of the news media only for duplication, not for search and review. The nine exemptions that permit an agency to withhold a record from the public are:

1. Matters specifically authorized under criteria established by an executive order to be kept secret in the interest of national defense or foreign policy and properly classified
2. Matters related solely to the internal personnel rules and practices of an agency
3. Matters exempted under another federal statute
4. Trade secrets and commercial or financial information obtained from a person and privileged or confidential
5. Inter-agency or intra-agency memoranda or letters
6. Personnel and medical files and similar files, the disclosure of which would constitute a clearly unwarranted invasion of privacy
7. Records or information compiled for law enforcement whose disclosure (a) could reasonably be expected to interfere with enforcement proceedings, (b) would deprive a person of the right to a fair trial, (c) could reasonably be expected to be an unwarranted invasion of privacy, (d) could reasonably be expected to identify a confidential source, (e) would include law enforcement techniques, procedures or guidelines for investigations or prosecutions, or (f) could reasonably be expected to endanger the life or physical safety of someone
8. Matters concerning the examination, operation, or condition of a financial institution
9. Geological and geophysical information and data, including maps, concerning wells[90]

An agency cannot refuse to provide a record simply because some of the information in it would fall under one or more of the exemptions. Instead the FOIA provides that any "reasonably segregable portion of a record shall be provided to any person requesting such record" after deletion of the portions which are exempt.[91] The exemptions also do not prevent an agency from releasing information even if it falls within one of the exemptions, depending upon the particular exemption and the circumstances.[92]

In 1996 Congress approved an amendment to the Freedom of Information Act known as the Electronic Freedom of Information Act.[93] The amendment requires agencies to "provide records in any ... format requested ... if the record is readily reproducible by that agency in that form or format" and requires them to "make reasonable efforts to search" for electronic records. Both records and indexes must be made available in electronic form for all records created after November 1, 1966. The traditional time limits for providing records can be extended under "exceptional circumstances" such as the need to review and process voluminous records requested by one person or organization. The period for the agency to determine whether to comply with a request was extended from 10 to 20 days by the amendment, but there is a provision that permits anyone with a "compelling need" to have expedited access to records. Examples of compelling needs are an "imminent threat to the life or physical safety" of a person and when a person primarily is involved in disseminating urgent information to the public about "actual or alleged Federal Government activity."[94] Some examples of stories that emerged from documents released under the FOIA include:

- Surveillance reports by the Department of Defense disclosing that the federal agency had monitored e-mail messages of students at four universities who were planning protests against the war in Iraq and against the military's don't-ask-don't-tell policy for gay and lesbian members.[95]

- A series in the *St. Louis Post-Dispatch* entitled "Broken Promises, Broken Lives" about 21 deaths and 665 injuries among mentally ill and mentally disabled individuals in government-supervised institutions in Missouri over six years.[96]
- An investigative series in the *Los Angeles Times* about serious problems with the country's organ transplant system.[97]

State open records laws have also led to disclosure of information about major national events, including the 2006 release of recordings of hundreds of phone calls, most involving firefighters and dispatchers, from the September 11, 2001, New York World Trade Center attacks. The recordings were made public after the *New York Times* and relatives of victims of the attacks sued the city for their release.[98] A year earlier thousands of pages of emergency workers' oral histories and radio transmissions had been released. Five months earlier the city also released transcripts of 130 calls made by individuals trapped in the twin towers. Out of concern for potential invasion of privacy, some recordings were not made public, including those of 10 civilians calling from inside the towers.[99]

Several of the exemptions have been tested in court and thus deserve some discussion. A loophole in Exemption 1 became apparent in 1973 when the U.S. Supreme Court held that the exemption (as then worded, without a reference to "properly classified") did not permit a U.S. district court to conduct even an *in camera* inspection of records concerning an underground nuclear test, thus effectively granting the executive branch the sole discretion in determining what could be classified.[100] Congress rather quickly remedied that problem with a 1974 amendment that granted the courts the authority to conduct *in camera* inspections of documents whose disclosure is sought to determine whether they have been properly classified.[101] Unfortunately, much of the impact of the new law was buffered by the fact that Congress instructed the courts to grant considerable deference to agencies in making the determination on matters of national security, and the federal courts have followed the directions well. The provision also has few teeth because the President determines by executive order the particular classification system.

That system was followed by then President Ronald Reagan until 1995 and then continued by President George Bush. Under Executive Order 12356,[102] the test for classification was simply whether disclosure could reasonably be expected to endanger national security, and the classification could continue for as long as its disclosure could harm national security—theoretically forever (although the executive order did permit agencies to establish predetermined declassification dates at their discretion). The executive order even permitted documents that had been declassified to be reclassified, *after* an FOIA request had been filed. In other words, an agency could classify a document that was not already classified *after* it was requested under the FOIA.[103]

On April 17, 1995, the picture changed fairly dramatically when President Bill Clinton issued Executive Order 12958.[104] The order reflected President Clinton's "presumption of disclosure" philosophy that information should be classified when strongly justified. One of the most important parts of the order was that if "there is significant doubt about the need to classify the information, it shall not be classified."

Other significant developments in the history of the FOIA include (1) a new exemption added under the Homeland Security Act in November 2002 that permits federal, state, and local agencies to withhold information from the public about "critical infrastructure,"[105] (2) Executive Order 13392 ("Improving Agency Disclosure") signed by President George W. Bush on December 14, 2005, requiring federal agencies to improve their processing of FOIA requests and become more "citizen-centered and results-oriented," including designating a chief FOIA officer.[106] President Barack Obama followed suit with an Executive Order 13526, setting goals for the declassification and promoting the use of declassification by use of new technology.

Department of Air Force v. Rose *(1976): Exemption 2*

Only one major U.S. Supreme Court decision has dealt directly with Exemption 2. In 1976 the Court ruled 5–3 in *Department of Air Force v. Rose*[107] that this exemption did not exempt from disclosure Air Force Academy case summaries, with identifying information excised, of honors and ethics code hearings because the purpose of the provision was to relieve federal agencies of the task of assembling and maintaining records that have no reasonable public interest value and thus are not applicable to matters of "genuine and significant public interest." The case arose when the *New York Law Review* was denied access to summaries of honors and ethics hearings even though the academy routinely posted this information and distributed it to faculty and administrators. The Air Force Academy also contended the records could be withheld under Exemption 6, but the Court rejected that argument as well, holding that "Exemption 6 does not protect against disclosure every incidental invasion of privacy—only such disclosures as constitute 'clearly unwarranted' invasions of personal privacy."[108] The majority opinion, written by Justice Brennan, noted that the case summaries revealed no names, and listed cadets "determined to be guilty." The summaries were widely disseminated within the academy.

Exemption 3

The purpose of Exemption 3 is to allow government agencies to withhold information even though it would otherwise have to be disclosed under the FOIA if a statute already permitted such withholding. The first big test of this exemption arrived in 1975 in *FAA v. Robertson*[109] in which the U.S. Supreme Court was asked to determine whether Congress intended for the disclosure requirements of the FOIA to apply to statutes that had allowed confidential information to be withheld before the Act took effect in 1966. The FOIA itself was not clear about this, and the Court accordingly ruled that such information fell under Exemption 3 and thus could be kept secret. The case concerned a provision of the Federal Aviation Act that gave agency officials extremely broad authority to keep certain documents secret in the "interest of the public."

Congress immediately jumped into the fray and in 1976 passed an amendment to the FOIA that essentially overruled the Court's decision, although the amendment does allow the withholding of information under either one of two circumstances: (1) if the statute "requires that the matters be withheld from the public in such a manner as to leave no discretion on the issue," or (2) the statute "establishes particular criteria for withholding or refers to particular types of matters to be withheld."[110] The courts have generally interpreted these provisions to mean that a statute must either explicitly refer to the FOIA regarding the information to be exempted or the information exempted must be of the type that the FOIA allows to be exempt.

In *Consumer Product Safety Commission v. GTE Sylvania* (1980),[111] the Court held that the Consumer Product Safety Commission (CPSC) was bound under the 1972 Consumer Product Safety Act rather than the FOIA in disclosing television-related accident reports. The commission released reports from television manufacturers to two consumer organizations, Consumers Union and the Public Citizen's Health Research Group, including reports provided by the companies to the commission at the commission's request. The companies claimed the reports were confidential. Under the 1972 Act, the agency was required to notify the manufacturers at least 30 days before the information was released so they would have an opportunity to respond in advance. In a unanimous opinion written by Justice Rehnquist, the Court ruled that the CPSC Act took priority over the FOIA and thus the commission should not have released the report without the 30 days' notice.

In another case, *CIA v. Sims* (1985),[112] the Court unanimously held that the names of 185 researchers at more than 80 universities who had received funding from the Central Intelligence Agency to study the effects on humans of mind-altering drugs did not have to be disclosed under the FOIA. Even though two people had reportedly died and others suffered mental problems as a result of the MKULTRA experiments—including use of the powerful LSD hallucinogen, which in some cases had been administered without the knowledge of the individuals—the Court ruled the National Security Act of 1947 took priority.

Under the Act, Congress granted the CIA director the authority to prevent unauthorized disclosure of intelligence sources. CIA files on the project were declassified in 1970, four years after the project ended.[113] The CIA made public all but 21 names of participating universities when a request was filed by the Public Citizen Health Research Group. The CIA claimed these 21 schools had been promised confidentiality. The Court, in line with the intent of Congress, gave considerable deference to the agency, noting that Congress had granted the CIA director "very broad authority to protect from disclosure all sources of intelligence information."[114]

It is clear from this decision that the U.S. Supreme Court strongly defers to agency heads in determining the kinds of information that can be withheld under Exemption 3. Often that authority lies in the enabling statute that created the agency. This was illustrated two years after *CIA v. Sims* when the Court held in *Church of Scientology v. IRS* (1987)[115] that tax returns filed with the Internal Revenue Service met the criteria for the second category established by Congress in its 1976 FOIA amendment (the statute "establishes particular criteria for withholding or refers to particular types of matters to be withheld").

One year later, the Court dealt with the sticky issue of whether federal presentence reports had to be disclosed. In *U.S. Department of Justice v. Julian* (1988),[116] the Court held that the U.S. Parole Commission and Reorganization Act and Rule 32 of the Federal Rules of Criminal Procedure prevent only specific types of information to be withheld. These include the probation officer's sentencing recommendations, information from confidential sources, diagnostic opinions, and information that could cause personal harm. Anything else in a report has to be disclosed unless another exemption applies.

Exemption 4

The first test of Exemption 4 came in 1979 in *Chrysler Corp. v. Brown*,[117] in which the U.S. Supreme Court ruled in what is known as a "reverse FOIA suit" that the FOIA gave federal agencies the authority to release certain kinds of information that private corporations and individuals had submitted to the agency, including trade secrets and other types of confidential information. The case arose when the Defense Logistics Agency (DLA) received a FOIA request for information about Chrysler's affirmative action policies. Chrysler had been required under federal statutes to provide the information to the Department of Labor because the company had several contracts with the federal government. (The DLA is the equal opportunity employment compliance agency for the Department of Defense.) Before the DLA could release the information, which it had decided should be publicly disclosed, Chrysler successfully sought an injunction in U.S. District Court for the District of Delaware to bar release of the data. The Third Circuit U.S. Court of Appeals overturned the trial court order, and the U.S. Supreme Court upheld the lower appellate court ruling and remanded the case back to the district court. The Court unanimously held that the FOIA did not grant the company any private right of action to stop such disclosures even when they involve possible trade secrets. The Court gave the message that the FOIA is a disclosure statute and thus the exemptions *permit but do not require* federal agencies to withhold the release of documents that fall within one or more of the exemptions.

The impact of the *Chrysler* decision was buffered somewhat by a 1986 executive order issued by President Reagan,[118] which required agencies to notify companies when an FOIA request has been filed for information they have submitted. The order also allowed the corporation to comment on whether the data should be released and provides a 10-day period for the company to seek an injunction or other relief in court to stop the release if the agency decides to grant the FOIA request.

Exemption 5

Exemption 5 was designed to protect pre-decisional information, such as working drafts of documents, preliminary reports, tentative recommendations, and similar materials that are parts of the decision-making process. The idea is that agency personnel should be able to discuss matters under consideration without fear of disclosure before a final decision is made. Once a decision is final, of course, an agency is required to release the specific details, but administrators can engage in freewheeling, confidential exchanges while matters are under consideration. This exemption also includes agency–attorney communications as well as information obtained by the government in civil suits during the discovery phase when agencies are involved in the litigation.

The U.S. Supreme Court made it clear in *National Labor Relations Board v. Sears, Roebuck & Co.* (1975)[119] that Exemption 5 does not apply to "final opinions" that explain actions already taken by an agency and agency decisions that have already been made and thus are really "final dispositions." In other words, once a decision reaches the level of having some finality, it is no longer a privileged document under civil discovery, and an attorney on the other side or anyone else is entitled to see it. On the other hand, the Court also made it clear that attorney work products do fall under the exemption, and, therefore, memoranda prepared by a government attorney in anticipation of litigation do not have to be disclosed. Such memoranda would include litigation strategies indicating an attorney's approach to a case.

Four years later in *Federal Open Market Committee v. David R. Merrill* (1979),[120] the Court ruled that the Federal Reserve Board could, as permitted by law, delay the release of certain monetary policy directives during the time they are in effect, usually a month, after which they appear in the *Federal Register*. According to the Court, this information met the definition of intra-agency memoranda "not available by law to a party other than another agency in litigation with the agency."

Later, in *Federal Trade Commission v. Grolier, Inc.* (1983),[121] the U.S. Supreme Court ruled that the work products of government attorneys met the criteria of Exemption 5, regardless of the status of the litigation involved. The effect of the decision was to make the working documents of federal agency attorneys privileged until the government chose to make them public so long as such documents would traditionally be privileged under the Federal Rules of Civil Procedure.

The case involved an FOIA request filed by Grolier, an encyclopedia publisher, with the Federal Trade Commission (FTC) for documents compiled by FTC attorneys in a lawsuit against the company for deceptive sales practices. The suit was dismissed with prejudice (meaning the commission could not bring the same suit again against the publisher). According to its own testimony at trial, Grolier had sought the documents to determine how much the FTC had learned about its sales techniques through secret monitoring of door-to-door salespersons. The Court sided with the commission, however, contending that because it was silent about the status of litigation, Exemption 5 included work product materials even when the litigation had presumably ended.

In *United States v. Weber Aircraft Corp.* (1984),[122] the U.S. Supreme Court ruled that confidential but unsworn information given during an investigation of the crash of an Air Force plane was protected from disclosure under Exemption 5. According to the Court, the statements "unquestionably" met the criteria for "intra-agency memorandums or letters" and were furthermore protected from civil discovery under a long-established principle known as the *Machin* privilege, under which confidential statements made to air crash safety investigators do not have to be revealed during pretrial discovery. The case involved a pilot who was injured in an Air Force plane crash and sought information provided to investigators in order to help him in his suit against the company that manufactured the plane.

Exemption 6: **U.S. Department of State v. Washington Post Co.** *(1982)*

Exemption 6 has spurred considerable controversy and litigation. The first U.S. Supreme Court case involving the exemption was handed down in a unanimous decision in 1982. It held that "similar files" included information about the citizenship status of foreign nationals. *U.S. Department of State v. Washington Post Co.*[123] concerned an FOIA request filed by the *Washington Post* with the U.S. Department of State to determine whether two Iranian nationals living in Iran had valid U.S. passports. The Supreme Court ruled in favor of the State Department denial, agreeing that disclosure could constitute "a clearly unwarranted invasion of the personal privacy" of the two men because disclosure could threaten their safety in Iran where intense anti-American feelings prevailed. The justices remanded the case back to the District of Columbia U.S. Court of Appeals for a final determination.

The Supreme Court rejected the newspaper's claim that the "similar files" term was not intended to include all files with personal information but instead those with intimate details and highly personal information. According to the Court, Congress intended for the exemption to include detailed government documents on a person that "can be identified as applying to that individual," thus granting a broad definition to "similar files."

A rather unusual case involving Exemption 6 developed in 1986 when the *New York Times* sought the tape recording of the astronauts' voice communications just prior to the tragic explosion of the space shuttle *Challenger* on January 28 of that year. All seven crew members died as the space shuttle self-destructed 73 seconds after lift-off. In *New York Times v. NASA*,[124] the District of Columbia U.S. Circuit Court of Appeals affirmed a U.S. District Court decision ordering NASA to release the tape. The appellate court applied a two-prong test in determining whether the recording fell under the exemption: "The threshold question is whether the material at issue is contained in a personnel, medical, or similar file. If it is, the court must then balance the individual and governmental interests involved in order to determine whether disclosure would constitute a clearly unwarranted invasion of privacy" (citations omitted).[125]

The District Court ruled that the tape did not meet the threshold requirement and the Court of Appeals affirmed, concluding "that the information recorded on the tape is 'unrelated to any particular person' and therefore is not a similar file."[126] In 1990 the D.C. Circuit met *en banc* (with the full court participating rather than a panel of three) and reversed the earlier decision, holding that the tape was sufficiently similar to personnel and medical files so as to fall under Exemption 6. Upon remand, the District Court then ruled that releasing the tape would constitute a "clearly unwarranted" invasion of privacy and thus the tape was not made available.[127]

In 1991 the U.S. Supreme Court held that disclosure of unredacted reports of confidential interviews with Haitian nationals who had tried to illegally enter the United States would meet Exemption 6's requirement that they "would constitute a clearly unwarranted invasion of personal privacy." According to the Court in *United States Department of State v. Ray* (1991),[128] the individual's right of privacy had to be balanced against the public right to know under the FOIA. The Court recognized the legitimate public interest in knowing whether the government was doing an adequate job in monitoring Haiti's compliance with an agreement it had made with the United States to not prosecute illegal aliens when they were sent back to Haiti. The Court said, however, that the redacted interview summaries the Department of State had made available were sufficient to satisfy the public interest, noting that the unredacted summaries would make it easy to identify the people interviewed and possibly make them and their families vulnerable to embarrassment and retaliation.

The records had been requested by a Florida attorney representing Haitians seeking political asylum in this country and three of his clients. The summaries turned over to him by the government ran about 96 pages.

In *United States Department of Defense v. Federal Labor Relations Authority* (1994),[129] a unanimous court ruled that the Privacy Act of 1974 forbids the disclosure of employee addresses to collective bargaining representatives who request access under the Federal Service Labor–Management Relations Statute. The opinion was written by Justice Thomas, with Justice Souter filing a concurring opinion and Justice Ginsburg filing an opinion concurring in the judgment. Two labor unions had filed unfair labor practice charges with the FLRA after the federal government gave them names and work stations but refused to turn over home addresses of agency employees represented by the unions. The labor statute requires federal agencies "to the extent not prohibited by law" to provide unions with information necessary for collective bargaining. The agencies contended revealing home addresses was a violation of the Privacy Act. The FLRA ruled in favor of the unions, rejecting the government agencies' argument.

On appeal, the Fifth Circuit U.S. Court of Appeals ruled in favor of the FLRA and the unions. The divided panel said the Privacy Act does not forbid disclosure of personal information if such disclosure was required under the FOIA. The court said that only Exemption 6 of the FOIA potentially applied in the situation but that since the FOIA applies only secondarily to the labor statute, "it is proper for the federal court to consider the public interest embroiled in the statute which generates the disclosure request."[130]

Applying this standard, the appeals court held that the public interest purpose of the labor statute would mean there was no "clearly unwarranted invasion of privacy" under Exemption 6. In other words, the court was ruling that because Exemption 6 did not apply, the FOIA's broad mandate for disclosure would require disclosure of the addresses and, in turn, the Privacy Act would give FLRA the authority to order disclosure.

The U.S. Supreme Court disagreed, holding that the FOIA no longer required disclosure, as the Supreme Court had indicated in another case discussed in this chapter, *U.S. Department of Justice v. Reporters Committee for Freedom of the Press* (1989), which focuses on Exemption 7. The test, as discussed below, in determining whether this case was an unwarranted invasion of privacy involved balancing the public interest in disclosure against the public interest Congress intended to serve in passing the legislation:

> … the only relevant 'public interest in disclosure' to be weighed in this balance is the extent to which the disclosure would serve the 'core purpose of the FOIA,' which is 'contribut(ing) significantly to public understanding of the operations or activities of the government' [citing *DOJ v. Reporters Committee*].[131]

Under this test, the Court said, the purpose for which the information is sought does not determine whether there is an unwarranted invasion of privacy. The Court went on to note, "The relevant public interest supporting disclosure is negligible, at best," whereas "it is clear that the individual privacy interest that would be protected by nondisclosure is far from insignificant." Thus the Court held:

> Because the privacy interest of bargaining unit employees in nondisclosure of their home addresses substantially outweighs the negligible FOIA-related public interest in disclosure, we conclude that the disclosure would constitute a 'clearly unwarranted invasion of personal privacy.'[132]

This ruling clearly broadens the sweep of *Department of Justice v. Reporters Committee for Freedom of the Press,* but, as Justice Souter said in his brief concurring opinion, "[I]t does not ultimately resolve the relationship between the Labor Statute and all of the Privacy Act exemptions potentially available to respondents.…"

In *Dobronski v. the Federal Communications Commission* (1994),[133] the Ninth Circuit U.S. Court of Appeals ruled the sick leave records of a Federal Communications Commission official must be disclosed under the FOIA. The Court said anyone, including a private citizen, has the right to find out whether public officials have abused their offices. The records involved allegations that an employee had taken unauthorized paid vacation time. The three-judge panel said the public interest in revealing corruption outweighs any minimal privacy interest the official may have in keeping the records closed.

In the aftermath of four hurricanes in Florida in 2004, the South Florida *Sun-Sentinel* newspaper asked the Federal Emergency Management Agency (FEMA) for the names and addresses of disaster claimants, the names and identification numbers of FEMA inspectors, and various e-mail messages. FEMA denied the request, citing Exemption 4 and Exemption 6 under the FOIA as well as the Privacy Act. On appeal of the FEMA denial, the U.S. District Court for the Southern District of Florida ruled in *Sun-Sentinel v. U.S. Department of Homeland Security* (2006)[134] that Exemption 6 did apply to release of the names. However, the court held that the exemption did not apply to release of the home addresses and neither exemption applied to the names and identification numbers of the FEMA inspectors. Thus this information was required to be released, according to the court, which also ordered the release of all but two e-mail messages of FEMA officials. The two exempt messages included legal advice from FEMA's general counsel, which the court said fell within the scope of attorney–client privilege.

Exemption 7: Department of Justice v. Reporters Committee for Freedom of the Press *(1989)*

A great deal of litigation has focused on Exemption 7. It is clear in Exemption 7 that the FOIA generally does not apply to records or information compiled for law enforcement purposes. However, such information is unavailable only to the extent that release of the information would meet one or more of the six standards listed in the exemption, for example, a disclosure that would interfere with judicial proceedings, disclose a confidential source, or endanger the life or physical safety of a person. One of the most important U.S. Supreme Court decisions involving the exemption occurred in 1989 in *Department of Justice v. Reporters Committee for Freedom of the Press*[135] in which the Court unanimously ruled that reporters have no right under the FOIA to obtain computerized FBI criminal identification records, commonly known as rap sheets.

The Reporters Committee and CBS reporter Robert Schakne sought the FBI rap sheet on Charles Medico, whose company had allegedly won defense contracts with the U.S. government with the assistance of a member of the House of Representatives to whom the company had made substantial campaign contributions. The Justice Department refused to release the information on the ground that the disclosure "could reasonably be expected to be an unwarranted invasion of personal privacy," although it did release the records of Medico's three brothers who were also allegedly involved in the scheme after they died. The committee argued that much of the information in the rap sheets had already been made public anyway in state and local police and court records, but the Court disagreed: "Plainly there is a vast difference between the public records that might be found after a diligent search of courthouse files, county archives, and local police stations throughout the country and a computerized summary located in a single clearinghouse of information."[136]

The Court also noted that the FBI maintains rap sheets on more than 24 million individuals and keeps the information on file until a person dies or attains age 80. The central purpose, according to the opinion written by Justice Stevens, "is to ensure that the government's activities be open to the sharp eye of public scrutiny, not that the information about private citizens that happens to be in the warehouse of government be so disclosed."[137]

In an earlier decision, the Court upheld the National Labor Relations Board's refusal to disclose potential witnesses' statements collected during a federal investigation of the labor practices of a tire company.[138] The majority opinion said that the information met the criteria of "investigatory records compiled for law enforcement purposes" that could reasonably be expected to interfere with enforcement proceedings.

In 1982 the Court ruled 5–4 in *FBI v. Abramson*[139] that Exemption 7 was broad enough to include information originally compiled in the form of law enforcement records that had been summarized as a new document not created for law enforcement. Howard Abramson, a freelance writer, was denied his FOIA request for a memo written by former FBI Director J. Edgar Hoover to Watergate conspirator John Erlichmann. Abramson was also denied access to some 63 pages of "name check" summaries on various political targets of President Nixon's administration. According to the Court, once an agency has determined the information was compiled for a legitimate law enforcement purpose and that disclosure would cause one of the six types of harm, the information continued to be exempt even if recreated in a new form.

Following the reported suicide of President Bill Clinton's Deputy Counsel Vincent Foster, Jr. in 1993, five government investigations were conducted, including one by Independent Counsel Kenneth Starr. Because Foster's body was found in Fort Marcy Park on federal property, the United States Park Police conducted the initial investigation into his death, including taking 10 color photos of his body at the death scene. The investigation concluded that Foster had shot himself with a revolver. Other investigations reached similar conclusions.

Alan Favish, an associate counsel for an organization known as Accuracy in Media (AIM), sued on behalf of AIM for release of the death scene photos by the U.S. Office of Independent Counsel (OIC). After the U.S. District Court for the District of Columbia ruled against the release, Favish then requested as a private citizen the release of the 10 body photos and another photo showing Foster's eyeglasses. After the OIC denied the request and the district court affirmed, the Ninth Circuit U.S. Court of Appeals remanded the case back to District Court, which then ordered the release of five of the photos. The government appealed this decision to the Ninth Circuit again, which affirmed the release of four of the photos.

In *National Archives and Records Administration v. Favish* (2004),[140] the U.S. Supreme Court held for the first time that the surviving family members of a deceased individual whose records were sought through an FOIA request had privacy interests under the Act. The decision authored by Justice Kennedy unanimously reversed the lower appellate court decision. The Court ruled that the "FOIA recognizes surviving family members' rights to personal privacy with respect to their close relative's death-scene images" and that in this case the "family's privacy interest outweigh[ed] the public interest in disclosure." The Court went on to note:

> As a general rule, citizens seeking documents subject to FOIA disclosure are not required to explain why they seek the information. However, when Exemption 7(C)'s privacy concerns are present, the requestor must show that public interest sought to be advanced is a significant one, an interest more specific than having the information for its own sake, and that the information is likely to advance that interest.[141]

The U.S. Supreme Court seemed particularly persuaded in its decision by a sworn declaration of Foster's sister filed in the District Court, stating that the family had been inundated with requests from what she called "political and commercial opportunists" who planned to profit from her brother's suicide. Shelia Foster Anthony described how she had been "horrified and devastated" by one photo that had already been leaked to the press. She said, "Every time

I see it I have nightmares and heart-pounding insomnia as I visualize how he must have spent his last few minutes and seconds of his life." [142]

Exemptions 8 and 9

The last two exemptions have stimulated little litigation, primarily because the courts have given agencies broad leeway in withholding information under them. The U.S. Supreme Court has not dealt directly with either exemption.

There are also three exclusions under the FOIA. As the Federal Citizen Information Center (FCIC) of the U.S. General Services Administration (GSA) notes in its online guide to accessing federal records, "The three exclusions, which are rarely used, pertain to especially sensitive law enforcement and national security matters."[143] Exclusions work differently from exemptions. They permit federal law enforcement agencies to "treat the records as not subject to the requirements" of the FOIA. In other words, when these records are involved, the agency holding the record can simply respond that no record responsive to the FOIA request exists.[144] Thus the agency does not even have to indicate that a record exists.

Federal Freedom of Information Act Today

The Federal Freedom of Information Act, which was strengthened by the Freedom of Information Reform Act of 1986 and broadened by the Electronic Freedom of Information Act in 1996 to include electronic records, has generally granted much greater access of the press and the public to federal records. Unfortunately, the courts and the executive branch continue to place barriers to such access. Occasionally, Congress knocks down the obstacles with mending legislation, but progress has been relatively slow.

According to the 2006 annual report by OpenTheGovernment.org, there has been "a continued expansion of government secrecy across a broad array of agencies and actions."[145] Some of the statistics cited in the report include:

- There was a slight decline in the number of documents classified in 2005 (14.2 million) than in the previous year (15.6 million), but the rate was still almost double the number in 2001, the year of the September 11 terrorist attacks.
- For each dollar spent declassifying old documents, the federal government spent $134 to create and store new secret documents in 2005.
- State legislatures in 2005 enacted twice as many new laws restricting access as they passed to increase access to public records.
- More than 2,000 secret surveillance orders were approved by the Foreign Intelligence Surveillance Court in 2005, more than double the number five years earlier. The court has turned down only four federal government requests for surveillance orders since it was established in 1980.[146]

The report concluded that some protections are necessary for unclassified information, such as personal privacy information or trade secrets. The federal government, however, has greatly expanded its ability to control unclassified public information through vague restrictions that give government officials wide latitude to declare information beyond the public's reach. Such unchecked secrecy threatens accountability in government and promotes conflicts of interest by allowing those with an interest in disclosure or concealment to decide between openness or secrecy.[147]

Improper classification has apparently become a serious problem. According to an official audit by the National Archives, 36% of more than 25,000 records removed were improperly reclassified under classification standards set up under a 1995 executive order.[148] To combat this problem, the Archive's Information Security Oversight Office issued new reclassification guidelines in 2006, by which all of the agencies agreed to abide. *Parade* magazine cited examples of information that had been classified that most people would agree did not warrant classification including:

- Names of illegal aliens convicted in this country of violent crimes such as murder and rape
- Notes of inspectors from the Mine Safety and Health Administration that are no longer classified
- Daily CIA intelligence briefings prepared for President Lyndon Johnson in the 1960s
- Except for 1963, 1997 and 1998 (which have been declassified), the annual budget for American intelligence, including the CIA[149]

Americans apparently share the same skepticism as journalists when it comes to government secrecy, according to a 2006 Scripps Howard News Service poll. Of the more than 1,000 U.S. citizens surveyed, nearly one in six believed the federal government has "too much secrecy." When asked whether "public access to government records is critical to the functioning of good government," 62% said such access was critical. About half of the respondents said FOI laws offered the public about the right amount of access, and more than a quarter said the laws did not provide enough access.[150]

Although the FOIA requires federal agencies to respond to requests within 20 working days of receipt (not counting Saturdays, Sundays, and federal holidays), in practice the wait is often much longer—sometimes years. According to a National Security Archive (NSA) audit, the oldest unfilled FOIA request belongs to William Aceves, a professor at California Western School of Law who filed four requests in 1989 while he was a graduate student at the University of Southern California.[151] Aceves was seeking information about the federal government's Freedom of Navigation Program. The government has provided some of the information, including blank, redacted pages but not everything he requested. The 2006 NSA audit included a list of the top 10 oldest unfilled requests, including two requests for information about the Berlin Crisis in 1958 in which the Soviet Union (as it was known at that time) gave the United States, Britain, and France six months to withdraw from West Berlin.[152]

Some changes have been instituted to attempt to speed up the process, including an executive order issued by President George W. Bush in 2005 that requires each federal agency affected by the FOIA to have at least one "FOIA Requester Service Center" that can be contacted to find out the status of a pending request. Each agency also has a "FOIA Public Liaison" who can be contacted when there is a complaint about service by one of the centers. Under some circumstances, an agency, if requested, can conduct "expedited processing" of a request. A study of 13 Cabinet departments and 9 agencies by the Coalition of Journalists for Open Government found that the number of unprocessed requests increased from 104,225 in 2004 to 148,603 in 2005, with unprocessed requests rising from 20% to 31% of the total. The report also found a decline in the number of federal employees handling FOIA requests over the years.[153]

Even with the FOIA policy changes enacted by President George W. Bush, many journalists and First Amendment scholars were highly critical of the administrations' overall record in enforcing the statute. According to First Amendment scholar Jane Kirtley, the "administration's contempt for the public right to know amounts to an organized assault on freedom of information that is unprecedented since the enactment of the Freedom of Information Act forty years ago."[154]

The strongest damage to the FOIA's attempt to broaden public access to government records may have been inflicted by the three U.S. Supreme Court privacy-related decisions. As First Amendment scholars Martin Halstuk and Bill Chamberlin note in their analysis of the FOIA and privacy protection, "In the aggregate, the *Washington Post, Reporters Committee* and *Favish* opinions have resulted in an FOIA framework that has significantly diminished the FOIA-related public interest while expanding the statute's privacy protections. The framework has no basis in either the plain text or legislative history of the statute...."[155]

Halstuk and Chamberlin ultimately conclude that the "Court's current FOIA policy privacy framework is the product of judicial overreaching grounded in historical revisionism that is clearly at odds with the bedrock democratic principles of accountability and transparent governance in an open society, as envisioned by FOIA's framers 40 years ago."[156]

Although not part of the FOIA, a provision in the Department of Homeland Security Appropriations Act of 2007 that funded the department requires federal agencies that handle unclassified information that is kept out of the public eye for security reasons (called "sensitive security information" or SSI) must review the information after three years to determine whether withholding the information is justified. The government agency must follow specific procedures in conducting the review.

Privacy Act of 1974

During the final week of its 94th Session, the U.S. Congress hastily passed the Privacy Act of 1974,[157] whose primary purposes were to set limits on personal information gathered about citizens by the federal government and to guarantee individuals, except under certain conditions, the right to see records collected about them and to have corrections made in those records that are inaccurate or incomplete.

The Act, as with the FOIA, applies only to documents held by agencies in the executive branch of the U.S. government. It does not apply to state and local governments. Only the individual who is the subject of the records or that person's authorized agent has the right of access. The Act includes 10 exemptions: (1) information compiled in reasonable anticipation of a civil action or proceeding, (2) Central Intelligence Agency records, (3) law enforcement records, (4) national security information covered under the FOIA, (5) materials compiled for law enforcement purposes and criminal investigations, (6) Secret Service records, (7) statistical records, (8) confidential information provided in connection with civilian employment, military service, federal contracts, etc., (9) testing and examination materials used to determine individual qualifications for federal employment, and (10) confidential information given in connection with the potential promotion of an individual in the armed services.[158] The Act applies only to records that are kept as part of a "system" of records and does *not* apply to Congress or the courts. As with the FOIA, there is no central government office where one can ask for records. Instead, a person has to go to each agency to make a request. As with the FOIA, requests have to be filed with the specific agency holding the record. There is no central federal office for processing requests or time limit for agencies to fulfill requests, although most agencies have adopted the same time limits as those under the FOIA. If an individual finds inaccurate information in a file, that person has the right, with proper documentation, to have the record corrected. Denials can be appealed, and even if the denial stands, a person has a right to submit a statement of explanation that the agency is required to attach to any nonexempt records.[159]

The Act provides both criminal and civil penalties. A government employee who knowingly discloses information without authority to do so under the Act can be found guilty of a misdemeanor and fined not more than $5,000.[160] Similar penalties are provided for a person who requests information under false pretenses.[161]

Driver's Privacy Protection Act of 1994

In 1994 Congress passed the Driver's Privacy Protection Act,[162] after 21-year-old actress Rebecca Schaeffer was murdered by a deranged fan in July 1989. Robert John Bardo was convicted of murder for shooting the star of the *My Sister Sam* television show in the doorway of her Los Angeles apartment.[163] He had obtained her address by requesting her driver's records.

Under the Act, which took effect in 1997, severe restrictions were imposed on the release by the states of personal information from motor vehicle records, driver's licenses, and auto registrations. The information included a person's photograph, social security number, driver identification number, name, address, medical conditions or disabilities, and phone number. Excluded from the Act was information about auto accidents, driving violations, and the driver's status. Civil penalties of up to $5,000 per day can be levied against any department of motor vehicles that fails to comply with the Act. States were allowed to enact "opt-out" laws or adopt policies that give motorists the opportunity to decide whether to keep the information confidential, and 29 states chose to do so before the law took effect.[164]

Journalists generally oppose such statutes, citing instances in which such information had served the public good, including stories exposing pilots and school bus drivers who had been convicted of drunken driving and other serious violations and yet remained on the job.[165] Various press associations lobbied to overturn the statute, and in 1997 South Carolina Attorney General Charlie Condon, joined by the Newspaper Association of America, the American Society of Newspaper Editors, and five state press associations, succeeded in getting the law declared unconstitutional, at least in South Carolina.

U.S. District Court Judge Dennis Shepp ruled in *Condon v. Reno* (1977)[166] that the Act violated the Tenth Amendment's Commerce Clause (which provides that the powers not delegated to the federal government "are reserved to the States"). Judge Shepp relied heavily upon the U.S. Supreme Court decision in *Printz v. United States* (1997),[167] which declared unconstitutional a provision of the so-called Brady bill that required local law enforcement officials to perform background checks on anyone applying for a handgun license. The district court decision prevents enforcement of the law only in South Carolina. The strategy of journalism associations has been to challenge the statute on Tenth Amendment, rather than First Amendment, grounds because the courts are unlikely to recognize any First Amendment right of access to such records.

Access to Meetings

Access to meetings of federal, state, and local governmental agencies is no longer a major problem for the mass media. Since Congress passed the Government in the Sunshine Act,[168] which took effect on March 12, 1977, the meetings of all major federal agencies (such as the Federal Trade Commission and the Federal Communications Commission) have been open to the press and to the public. The exceptions are parallel to those of the FOIA, with two additions: (a) agencies responsible for regulating financial institutions, currencies, securities, and commodities can close meetings that could lead to "significant financial speculation" or "significantly endanger the stability of a financial institution" and (b) meetings involving certain litigation matters such as issuing a subpoena or initiating a civil action. There have been few legal challenges to those meetings that have been closed, although some agencies are much more likely than others to broadly apply the exemptions. All 50 states and the District of Columbia have similar open meetings statutes, with some states offering greater access by having fewer exemptions and opening up more agencies.

Summary and Conclusions

The Freedom of Information Act of 1966 and the Government in the Sunshine Act of 1977 have provided the news media and the public with much broader access to federal government agency records and meetings. Both Acts, but particularly the FOIA, have had to be amended over the years to cope with adverse court rulings and changing technologies. One of the most significant changes to the FOIA was the Electronic Freedom of Information Act of 1996, which granted greater access to electronic records and required agencies to make records readily available in electronic form. The Privacy Act of 1974 provides access for individuals to federal records collected and maintained about them and sets limits on the types of information the federal government can seek and keep about private citizens. Each of the statutes, of course, has exceptions, and much of the litigation surrounding them has involved these "exemptions."

All states have statutes similar to the FOIA and the Government in the Sunshine Act, although the extent of access varies from state to state. In general, state and local governments have been more restrictive than the federal government in providing access, although the situation may be changing toward more openness. When the U.S. Congress passed the Driver's Privacy Protection Act of 1994, a state government—South Carolina—led the way, accompanied by press associations, in challenging the Act, which severely restricted public and media access to state motor vehicle records.

A 2005 executive order known as Improving Agency Disclosure of Information reaffirmed that the FOIA "has provided an important means through which the public can obtain information regarding the activities of federal agencies" and required federal agencies to make their FOIA efforts "citizen-centered and results-oriented."[169] In spite of these good intentions, the fact remains that the trends are toward greater restrictions by federal, state, and local government agencies on access to information and to meetings. The OpenTheGovernment. org report discussed above clearly pointed to such trends. The September 11, 2001, attacks on America and the resulting legislative and judicial reaction, including the USA Patriot Act, have particularly made it easier to classify documents even when there is little justification.

A good illustration of this trend is the experience of the Sunshine Project, a group that opposes the proliferation of biological weapons. The organization filed an FOIA request with East Carolina University in 2006, seeking documents the institution held on how it oversaw research on biological weapons.[170] The University denied access to many of the records on national security grounds. By accident, the university included both the redacted documents as well as a series of e-mail messages it had apparently intended to withhold. In comparing the original documents with the redacted ones, Sunshine Project discovered what had been deleted. The redacted information included (a) a discussion among officials on whether they should withhold information about herpes research, (b) minutes of a university committee focusing on a defective waste incinerator, and (c) the phrase, "no gas in lab."[171]

To some extent, there exists somewhat of a contrast between the approach of the federal government and those of state governments. For example, the trend in state courts is to allow cameras in courtrooms, but the general ban on cameras in the federal courts continues. This is in spite of the fact that an experimental project in the federal courts demonstrated clearly that there were no substantial adverse effects from the use of still and video cameras in the courtroom.

How does the public fit into the picture? According to most opinion polls, Americans remain ambivalent about access, especially to records. This ambivalence undoubtedly reflects intensifying public concern over what it sees as a serious erosion of individual privacy. On the other hand, we continue to expect the news media to serve the watchdog role, especially with the declining confidence in the government, including elected and appointed officials.

The general trend has been for more federal agencies to release records. President Bill Clinton's executive order in 1995 began automatic declassification of records more than 25 years old, unless an agency specifically requests an exemption. The order was to take effect in 2000, but was later extended to 2003 and then given another three-year reprieve by President George W. Bush, who refused, however, to grant further extensions. As a result, hundreds of millions of pages have been released (with much of it now available online) by the CIA, FBI, National Security Agency and other agencies.[172]

As a further overhaul of the executive branch's system for protecting classified national security information, President Barack Obama issued another executive order, Number 13526, on January 29, 2009. This order allowed the government to classify certain types of information related to national security after they have been requested. And in doing so, President Obama indicated that no information should stay classified indefinitely. In this order and an accompanying presidential memorandum to agency heads, he signaled that government should try harder to make information public whenever possible, including requiring agencies to regularly review information they classify to eliminate obsolete secrecy requirements. This move eliminated a rule put in place by former President George W. Bush that allowed the leader of the intelligence community to veto decisions by an interagency panel to declassify information. Given this change, spy agencies who object to decisions would have to appeal directly to the president. This Executive Order also established a National Declassification Center at the National Archives to speed declassification of documents by centralizing the review, rather than sending them to different agencies. It also set a four-year deadline for processing 400-million-pages of records, including archives related to historical military operations during World War II, the Korean War, and the war in Vietnam.[173] Even more recently, in the wake of massive disclosures of classified documents via Wikileaks, many foreign governments and NATO have had to revisit their policy of information gathering as previously unreported information has been shared across international boundaries. [174]

Endnotes

1. *Privacy vs. Public Right to Know*, USA Today, March 18, 2010, at 11-A.
2. Mimi Hall, *Press Secretary's Tweets on Record*, USA TODAY, February 18, 2010, at 7-A.
3. Dan Paul, Richard J. Ovelmen, and Enrique D. Arana, *Access*, in 1 Communications Law 91 (2005). *See Reynolds v. United States*, 98 U.S. 145, 25 L.Ed. 244 (1878). The Court, in affirming the constitutionality of a federal law making bigamy a crime in the territories, rejected a motion for a new trial on the ground that the trial judge had allowed an individual to serve on the jury who, it was asserted, "'believed' he had formed an opinion which he had never expressed, and which he did not think would influence his verdict on hearing the testimony."
4. *Richmond Newspapers, Inc. v. Virginia*, 448 U.S. 555, 100 S.Ct. 2814, 65 L.Ed.2d 973, 6 Med. L.Rptr. 1833 (1980).
5. *Paul M. Branzburg v. John P. Hayes, In the Matter of Paul Pappas*, and *U.S. v. Earl Caldwell*, 408 U.S. 665, 92 S.Ct. 2646, 33 L.Ed.2d 626, 1 Med.L.Rptr. 2617 (1972).
6. *Gannett Co., Inc. v. Daniel A. DePasquale*, 443 U.S. 368, 99 S.Ct. 2898, 61 L.Ed.2d 608, 5 Med.L.Rptr. 1337 (1979).
7. *Thomas L. Houchins, Sheriff of the County of Alameda, Calif., v. KQED, Inc.*, 438 U.S. 1, 98 S.Ct. 2588, 57 L.Ed.2d 553, 3 Med.L.Rptr. 2521 (1978).
8. *Gannett v. DePasquale.*
9. *Id.*
10. *Richmond Newspapers, Inc. v. Virginia* (Brennan concurrence).
11. Dan Paul, Richard J. Ovelmen, and Enrique D. Arana.
12. *J. M. Near v. Minnesota*, 283 U.S. 697, 51 S.Ct. 625, 75 L.Ed. 1357, 1 Med.L.Rptr. 1001 (1931).
13. *Nebraska Press Association v. Judge Hugh Stuart*, 427 U.S. 539, 96 S.Ct. 2791, 49 L.Ed.2d 683, 1 Med.L.Rptr. 1059 (1976).
14. *Id.*
15. Minow and Cates, *Who Is an Impartial Juror in an Age of Mass Media?*, 40 American University Law Review 631 (1991).
16. *Murphy v. Florida*, 421 U.S. 794, 95 S.Ct. 2031, 44 L.Ed.2d 589, 1 Med.L.Rptr. 1232 (1975).
17. *Irvin v. Dowd*, 366 U.S. 717, 81 S.Ct. 1639, 6 L.Ed.2d 751, 1 Med.L.Rptr. 1178 (1961).
18. *Rideau v. Louisiana*, 373 U.S. 723, 83 S.Ct. 1417, 10 L.Ed.2d 663, 1 Med.L.Rptr. (1963).
19. *Estes v. Texas*, 381 U.S. 532, 85 S.Ct. 1628, 14 L.Ed.2d, 1 Med.L.Rptr. 1187 (1965).
20. *Sheppard v. Maxwell*, 384 U.S. 333, 86 S.Ct. 1507, 16 L.Ed.2d 600, 1 Med.L.Rptr. 1220 (1966).
21. *Murphy v. Florida.*
22. *Id.*
23. *Id.*
24. *Id.*
25. *Irvin v. Dowd.*
26. *Rideau v. Louisiana.*
27. *See* Dwight Garner, *One Man's Hard Road*, reviewed in New York Times, May 4, 2010 at C-1. For additional background on Wilbert Rideau and his trials, see the "Wilbert Rideau" entry for Wikipedia at http://en.wikipedia.org/wiki/Wilbert_Rideau.
28. While the judge banned live broadcasting during most of the trial, the opening statements and closing arguments of the prosecutor, the return of the jury's verdict, and the receipt of the verdict by the judge

were broadcast live. Other portions of the trial were recorded by a camera behind a camouflaged booth and broadcast later as clips during the local newscasts. News photographers were also restricted to the booth area.

29. *Estes v. Texas.*
30. *Noel Chandler and Robert Granger v. Florida,* 449 U.S. 560, 101 S.Ct. 802, 66 L.Ed.2d 740, 7 Med.L.Rptr. 1041 (1981).
31. Beth Chesterman, *Restrictions on Courtroom News Coverage,* First Amendment Center at Vanderbilt University (Aug. 16, 2006), available at http://www.firstamendmentcenter.org; Radio–Television News Directors Association and Foundation, Freedom of Information, *Cameras in the Court: A State-by-State Guide,* available at http://www.rtndf.org/foi/scc.shtml.
32. Chesterman, *Restrictions on Courtroom News Coverage, supra,* note 31.
33. Radio–Television News Directors Association and Foundation, Freedom of Information, *Cameras in the Court: A State-by-State Guide, supra,* note 31.
34. *Courtroom Television Network v. State of New York,* 5 N.Y.3d 222, 833 N.E.2d 1197, 33 Med.L.Rptr. 1887 (2005).
35. *Id.*
36. *Illinois High Court Rejects Bid to Allow Cameras in Courtrooms* (Associated Press), First Amendment Center at Vanderbilt University (Sept. 15, 2005), available at http://www.firstamendmentcenter.org.
37. *Cameras in the Courtroom,* Cong. Q, Testimony by Henry Schleiff to U.S. Senate Judiciary Committee, Nov. 9, 2005.
38. *Id.*
39. *Would Cameras Change the Court?,* News Media & Law, Spring 2006, at 22.
40. *Id.*
41. *Richmond Newspapers, Inc. v. Virginia.*
42. *Id.*
43. *Id.*
44. *Id.*
45. *Sheppard v. Maxwell.*
46. The old network TV series, *The Fugitive* was loosely based on the Sheppard story, as was the 1993 movie by the same name in which Dr. Richard Kimble is hunted down by ruthless U.S. Marshall Sam Gerard.
47. *Sheppard v. Maxwell.*
48. *Id.*
49. *Pell v. Procunier,* 417 U.S. 817, 94 S.Ct. 2800, 41 L.Ed.2d 495 (1974).
50. *William B. Saxbe v. the Washington Post Co.,* 417 U.S. 843, 94 S.Ct. 2811, 41 L.Ed.2d 514 (1974).
51. *Pell v. Procunier.*
52. *William B. Saxbe v. the Washington Post Co.*
53. *Branzburg v. Hayes.*
54. *Thomas L. Houchins v. KQED,* 438 U.S. 1, 98 S.Ct. 2588, 57 L.Ed.2d 553, 3 Med.L.Rptr. 2521 (1977).
55. *Id.*
56. J. Lafayette, *Chasing the Juice: O.J. Saga Throws Media Into Overdrive,* Electronic Media, June 27, 1994, at 1.
57. B. J. Palermo, *A Rush to Reform: Critics Fear Some Simpson-Inspired Changes Are Misguided,* 83 American Bar Association Journal 20 (Apr. 1997).
58. Tony Mauro, *Simpson Trial Aftermath: Courts Closing Doors,* First Amendment News, Mar. 1996, at 1. 59 N. Lee Cooper, *Don't Get Trampled by Media Circus,* 83 A.B.A. J. 8 (Feb. 1997).
59. *N. Lee Cooper, Don't Get Trampled by Media Circus, 83, A.B.A. J. 8 (Feb. 1997).*
60. *Public Fed Up with Coverage But Can't Resist,* Lexington (Ky.) Herald-Leader (Washington Post), Feb. 13, 1998, at A11.
61. *Richard Nixon v. Warner Communications,* 435 U.S. 589, 98 S.Ct. 1306, 55 L.Ed.2d 570, 3 Med.L.Rptr. 2074 (1978).
62. *Robert K. Smith v. Daily Mail Publishing Co.,* 443 U.S. 97, 99 S.Ct. 2667, 61 L.Ed.2d 399, 5 Med.L.Rptr. 1305 (1979).
63. *Id.*

64. *Id.*
65. *Landmark Communications, Inc. v. Commonwealth of Virginia*, 435 U.S. 829, 98 S.Ct. 1535, 56 L.Ed.2d 1, 3 Med.L.Rptr. 2153 (1978).
66. *Cox Broadcasting Corp. et al. v. Martin Cohn*, 420 U.S. 469, 95 S.Ct. 1029, 43 L.Ed.2d 328, 1 Med.L.Rptr. 1819 (1975).
67. *Oklahoma Publishing Co. v. District Court in and for Oklahoma County*, 430 U.S. 308, 97 S.Ct. 1045, 51 L.Ed.2d 355, 2 Med.L.Rptr. 1456 (1977).
68. *Landmark Communications v. Virginia.*
69. *Id.*
70. *Cox Broadcasting v. Cohn.*
71. *Oklahoma Publishing v. District Court.*
72. *Globe Newspaper Co. v. Norfolk County Superior Court*, 457 U.S. 596, 102 S.Ct. 2613, 73 L.Ed.2d 248, 8 Med.L.Rptr. 1689 (1982).
73. *Id.*
74. *Id.*
75. *Press Enterprise Co. v. Riverside County Superior Court* (*Press Enterprise I*), 464 U.S. 501, 104 S.Ct. 819, 78 L.Ed.2d 629, 10 Med.L.Rptr. 1161 (1984).
76. *Press Enterprise Co. v. Riverside County Superior Court* (*Press Enterprise II*), 478 U.S. 1, 106 S.Ct. 2735, 92 L.Ed.2d 1, 13 Med.L.Rptr. 1001 (1986).
77. *Press Enterprise I.*
78. *Press Enterprise II.*
79. *Branzburg v. Hayes.*
80. John Huotari, *SPJ Chief: Media Must Probe; Journalists Should Challenge Restrictions on Information*, Knoxville News-Sentinel, May 21, 2005, at B2.
81. *Flynt v. Rumsfeld*, 355 F.3d 697, 32 Med.L.Rptr. 1289 (D.C. Cir. 2004).
82. *California First Amendment Center Coalition et al. v. Woodford et al.*, 299 F.3d 868, 30 Med.L.Rptr. 2345 (9th Cir. 2002).
83. *State of Oklahoma v. Benjamin Bernstein et al.*, 5 Med.L.Rptr. 2313, *aff'd*, *Stahl v. Oklahoma*, 665 P.2d 839, 9 Med.L.Rptr. 1945 (Okl. Crim. 1983), *cert. denied*, 464 U.S. 1069, 104 S.Ct. 973, 79 L.Ed.2d 212 (1984).
84. *Stahl v. Oklahoma.*
85. K. Seelye and D. Polman, *Military Reined in Media, Held Tight*, Lexington (Ky.) Herald-Leader (Knight Ridder News Service), Mar. 28, 1991, at D14.
86. *Id.*
87. Three good official sources for more information are: (1) *Your Right to Federal Records*, U.S. General Services Administration and U.S. Department of Justice (joint publication usually updated annually and available at http://www.pueblo.gsa.gov/cic), (2) *DOJ FOIA Guide*, U.S. Department of Justice (updated every two years and available at http://www.usdoj.gov/oip), and (3) *A Citizen's Guide to the FOIA* (2005, 85-page guide prepared by the House Committee on Government Reform). These federal publications include the text of the FOIA and an overview of the Privacy Act of 1974. You can download them free through links on the U.S. Department of Justice FOIA website: http://www.usdoj.gov/04foia. You can also consult the Society of Professional Journalist's Annual FOI Report.
88. Freedom of Information Act of 1966, 5 U.S.C. §552, as amended (2002).
89. Privacy Act of 1974, 5 U.S.C. §552a, as amended (2000).
90. 5 U.S.C. §552a(6)(C)(b)(1–9).
91. 5 U.S.C. §552a(6)(C).
92. Federal Communications Commission FOIA website: http://www.fcc.gov/foia.
93. 5 U.S.C. §552 (Electronic Freedom of Information Act Amendments of 1996), 104 Pub. L. 231, 110 Stat. 3048 (1996).
94. *Id.*
95. Samantha Henig, *Pentagon Surveillance of Student Groups as Security Threats Extended to Monitoring E-Mail, Reports Show*, Chronicle of Higher Education (electronic edition), July 6, 2006.
96. Brea Jones, *FOIA After Forty*, Quill, Sept. 2006, at 28.97 *Id.*

97. *Id.*
98. *Terrorism Developments*, Atlanta Journal-Constitution (news services), Aug. 17, 2006, at A4.
99. *Id.*
100. *Environmental Protection Agency v. Mink*, 410 U.S. 73, 93 S.Ct. 827, 35 L.Ed.2nd 119, 1 Med. L.Rptr. 2448 (1973).
101. Pub. L. 93-502, 88 Stat. 1561 (1974).
102. Executive Order 12,356, 3 C.F.R. (1983).
103. During his term, President Jimmy Carter, in contrast, issued an executive order that mandated a review of all classified material every 20 to 30 years, whereas the Reagan order required that a classified document be reviewed once, at the   time the initial classification occurred.
104. Executive Order 12,958 (1995).
105. *Id.*
106. Brea Jones, *FOIA After Forty, supra,* note 96; Federal Communications Commission FOIA website: http://www.fcc.gov/foia.
107. *Department of the Air Force et al. v. Michael T. Rose et al.*, 425 U.S. 352, 96 S.Ct. 1592, 48 L.Ed.2d 11, 1 Med.L.Rptr. 2509 (1976).
108. *Id.*
109. *Federal Aviation Administration v. Robertson,* 422 U.S. 255, 95 S.Ct. 2140, 45 L.Ed.2d 164 (1975).
110. Pub. L. 94-409, §5(b)(3), 5 U.S.C. §552(b)(3), 90 Stat, 1241 (1976).
111. *Consumer Product Safety Commission v. GTE Sylvania, Inc.*, 447 U.S. 102, 100 S.Ct. 2051, 64 L.Ed.2d 766 (1980).
112. *CIA v. Sims*, 471 U.S. 159, 105 S.Ct. 1881, 85 L.Ed.2d 173 (1985).
113. The MKULTRA project lasted from 1953 to 1966.
114. *CIA v. Sims.*
115. *Church of Scientology v. Internal Revenue Service*, 484 U.S. 9, 99 S.Ct. 1705, 60 L.Ed.2d 208, 4 Med.L.Rptr. 218 (1987).
116. *U.S. Department of Justice v. Julian*, 486 U.S. 1, 99 S.Ct. 1705, 60 L.Ed.2d 208, 4 Med.L.Rptr. 218 (1988).
117. *Chrysler Corp. v. Harold Brown, Secretary of Defense*, 441 U.S. 281, 99 S.Ct. 1705, 60 L.Ed.2d 208, 4 Med.L.Rptr. 218 (1979).
118. Executive Order 12,600 (1986).
119. *National Labor Relations Board v. Sears, Roebuck & Co.*, 421 U.S. 132, 95 S.Ct. 1504, 44 L.Ed.2d 29, 1 Med.L.Rptr. 2471 (1975).
120. *Federal Open Market Committee v. David R. Merrill*, 443 U.S. 340, 99 S.Ct. 2800, 61 L.Ed.2d 587 (1979).
121. *Federal Trade Commission v. Grolier, Inc.*, 462 U.S. 19, 103 S.Ct. 2209, 76 L.Ed.2d 387, 9 Med.L.Rptr. 1737 (1983).
122. *United States v. Weber Aircraft Corp.*, 465 U.S. 792, 104 S.Ct. 1488, 79 L.Ed.2d 814, 10 Med. L.Rptr. 1477 (1984).
123. *U.S. Department of State v. Washington Post Co.*, 456 U.S. 595, 102 S.Ct. 1957, 72 L.Ed.2d 358, 8 Med.L.Rptr. 1521 (1982).
124. *New York Times Co. v. National Aeronautics and Space Administration*, 852 F.2d 602, 15 Med.L.Rptr. 2012 (D.C. Cir. 1988).
125. *Id.*
126. *Id.*
127. *New York Times Co. v. National Aeronautics and Space Administration*, 920 F.2d 1002, 18 Med.L.Rptr. 1465 (D.C. Cir. 1990) (*en banc*); 782 F.Supp. 628, 19 Med.L.Rptr. 1688 (D.D.C. 1991).
128. *United States Department of State v. Michael D. Ray*, 502 U.S. 164, 112 S.Ct. 541, 116 L.Ed.2d 526, 19 Med.L.Rptr. 1641 (1991).
129. *United States Department of Defense v. Federal Labor Relations Authority*, 510 U.S. 487, 114 S.Ct. 1006, 127 L.Ed.2d 325, 22 Med.L.Rptr. 1417 (1994).
130. *United States Department of Defense v. Federal Labor Relations Authority*, 975 F.2d 1105 (1992).
131. United States Department of Defense (1994).

132. *Id.*
133. *Mark Dobronski v. the Federal Communications Commission*, 17 F.3d 275 (9th Cir. 1994).
134. *Sun-Sentinel Company v. United States Department of Homeland Security*, 431 F.Supp.2d 1258, 34 Med.L.Rptr. 1741 (2006).
135. *Department of Justice v. Reporters Committee for Freedom of the Press*, 489 U.S. 749, 109 S.Ct. 1468, 103 L.Ed.2d 774, 16 Med.L.Rptr. 1545 (1989).
136. *Id.*
137. *Id.*
138. *National Labor Relations Board v. Robbins Tire and Rubber Co.*, 437 U.S. 214, 98 S.Ct. 2311, 57 L.Ed.2d 159 (1978).
139. *Federal Bureau of Investigation v. Howard S. Abramson*, 456 U.S. 615, 102 S.Ct. 2054, 72 L.Ed.2d 376 (1982).
140. *National Archives and Records Administration v. Favish*, 541 U.S. 1057, 124 S.Ct. 2198, 158 L.Ed.2d 768 (2004).
141. *Id.*
142. *Id.*
143. Your Right to Federal Records, *supra,* note 87.
144. DOJ FOIA Guide, *supra,* note 87.
145. OpenTheGovernment.org, Secrecy Report Card (Sept. 2, 2006).
146. *Id.*
147. *Id.*
148. *Freedom of Information: Archive Audit Shows 1 in 3 Records Improperly Reclassified,* Quill, June/July 2006, at 6.
149. *What Should Be Classified,* Parade, Feb. 28, 2006, at 5.
150. Thomas Hargrove and Guido Stempel, III, *Poll Finds Americans Concerned About Government Secrecy,* Scripps Howard News Service, Mar. 9, 2006.
151. *FOIA Facts: Requests Can Linger in Limbo for Years*, Atlanta Journal-Constitution, Mar. 12, 2006, at C4.
152. *Id.*
153. *Feds Leaving More FOIA Requests Unanswered,* Quill, Sept. 2006, at 12.
154. Jane E. Kirtley, *Transparency and Accountability in a Time of Terror: The Bush Administration's Assault on Freedom of Information,* 11 Communication Law & Policy 479 (2006).
155. Martin E. Halstuk and Bill F. Chamberlin, *The Freedom of Information Act 1966–2006: A Retrospective on the Rise of Privacy Protection Over the Public Interest in Knowing What the Government's Up To*, 11 Communication Law & Policy 511 (2006).
156. *Id.*
157. Privacy Act of 1974, Pub. L. 93-579, 5 U.S.C. §55 2a (1974).
158. 5 U.S.C. §552a(d)(5), §552a(j), and §552a(k)(1)–(7).
159. Your Right to Federal Records, *supra,* note 87.
160. 5 U.S.C. §552a(i)(1).
161. 5 U.S.C. §552a(i)(3).
162. Driver's Privacy Protection Act of 1994, Pub. L. 103-322, 18 U.S.C. §§2721–2725 (1994).
163. Bardo was prosecuted by none other than Marcia Clark, the lead prosecutor in the 1994 O. J. Simpson murder trial.
164. Lauri Schumacher, *Driver Records Still in Jeopardy,* Quill, Sept. 1997, at 23.
165. Kyle E. Niederpruem, *Driver Act Now State Fight,* Quill, Oct. 1996, at 45.
166. *Charlie Condon et al. v. Janet Reno et al.*, 972 F.Supp. 977, 25 Med.L.Rptr. 2313 (D. S.C. 1997).
167. *Jay Printz v. United States*, 521 U.S. 88, 117 S.Ct. 2365, 138 L.Ed.2d 914 (1997).
168. Government in the Sunshine Act, 5 U.S.C. §552b (1976).
169. Federal Communications Commission FOIA website: http://www.fcc.gov/foia.
170. Scott Jaschik, *Unintended Sunshine,* at http://www.insidehighereducation.com (Aug. 23, 2006).
171. *Id.*

172. *See* Scott Shane, *Secret Files Declassified at Year's End*, Atlanta Journal-Constitution, Dec. 26, 2006, at A7.

173. Charlie Savage, *Obama Curbs Secrecy of Classified Documents*, New York Times, December 29, 2009, at A-1.

174. *See* Eric Schmitt, *In Disclosing Documents, WikiLeaks Seeks 'Transparency,'* New York Times, July 25, 2010, at A-1; Andrew Malcolm, *WikiLeaks Classified Documents Leak Out on Twitter*, Los Angeles Times, November 28, 2010, C-2; and Robert Winnett and Andy Bloxham, *Afghanistan War Logs: 90,000 Documents Revealed by WikiLeaks,* The (London) Telelgraph, July 26, 2010, at A-1.

12

Intellectual Property

It's a strange world of language in which skating on thin ice can get you into hot water.

—Frank P. Jones[1]

Copyrights, trademarks, and patents are typically grouped into an area of the law that has become known as *intellectual property*. Trade secrets are sometimes included in this area as well. The constitutional origins of intellectual property, at least for copyrights and patents, can be traced to Article I, Section 8, of the U.S. Constitution, which provides, among other powers, that Congress shall have the authority "[t]o promote the Progress of Science and useful Arts, by securing for limited Times to Authors and Inventors the exclusive Right to their respective Writings and Discoveries." Patents and copyrights are regulated almost exclusively by federal statutes (Title 35 and Title 17 of the U.S. Code, respectively) since Congress has chosen to invoke the preemption doctrine granted under Article VI of the U.S. Constitution (known as the supremacy clause), which provides in part:

> … This Constitution, and the Laws of the United States which shall be made in Pursuance thereof; and all Treaties made, or which shall be made, under the Authority of the United States, shall be the supreme law of the Land; and the Judges in every State shall be bound thereby, any Thing in the Constitution or Laws of any State to the Contrary notwithstanding.

Exclusive federal regulation of copyrights and patents is also justified under the commerce clause in Article I, Section 8 of the U.S. Constitution which provides that Congress shall have the power "[t]o regulate Commerce with foreign Nations, and among the several States, and with the Indian Tribes."

Trademarks and trade secrets, on the other hand, involve both state and federal law as well as common law, although state laws are not permitted to conflict with federal law. Trademark law can be found primarily in Title 15 of the United States Code (known as the Lanham Act or the Trademark Act of 1946). Trademarks, which identify goods, and service marks, which identify services, may be registered and have protection under either state or federal statutes. Trade secrets usually are not registered under federal law, except as they relate to a patent application, because registration is ordinarily a public record, which would defeat the purpose of a trade secret.

Patents, Including Creation and Duration

While the U.S. Copyright Office is an arm of the Library of Congress, the United States Patent and Trademark Office (which, as the name indicates, handles both patents and trademarks) is an agency of the Department of Commerce headed by the Commissioner of Patents and Trademarks who is also an Assistant Secretary of Commerce. The office, which celebrated its 200th anniversary, was created by President Thomas Jefferson, an inventor (see Figure 12.1). The office has processed more than 7 million applications, with about 3,500 approved each week and increasing.[2] Because of this growth and the fact that the number of patent examiners has not kept pace, the average time between the filing of an application and the initial approval decision grew from about seven and one-half months in 1993 to more than 20

Figure 12.1 Who is the only U.S. President to be awarded a patent? If you answered Thomas Jefferson, that's a good guess. Unfortunately, it's wrong (although Jefferson was an inventor). The correct response is Abraham Lincoln, who patented a device to lift boats over shoals without losing their cargoes (Courtesy of the Library of Congress, LC-USZ62-16377).

months in 2005, according to a study by the National Academy of Public Administration.[3] By 2011 the Patent and Trademark Office had a backlog of almost 700,000 patent applications, but that number was expected to decline considerably thanks to the new America Invents Act. The Act created up to 2,000 new examiners and switched the U.S. to a "first-to-file" from a "first to invent" system.

Patents, trademarks, and copyrights are all forms of *exclusive* (i.e., monopolistic) *control* that owners, who can be individuals or companies, can exercise to ensure that others generally cannot market, use, or sell the work, invention, or mark without consent of the owner. Until June 8, 1995, patents generally had protection for 17 years from the date the patent was issued, after which they passed to the public domain and could be used, marketed, or sold to anyone without consent.

However, in 1989 Congress revised the patent law, including establishing a new 20-year term for protection, measured strictly from the filing date, for any patent filed after June 8, 1995.[5] In some cases, the 20-year period can be extended for a maximum of 5 years when marketing time was lost because of regulatory delay.[6] The 20-year period was chosen because it has been the standard of the rest of the industrialized world for some time. The new law also grants greater authority to the U.S. government to seize imports entering the United States when they infringe on patents owned by a U.S. company or citizen, and it creates a means by which a provisional application can be filed while the inventor prepares a regular application, that must be filed within one year.

When a patent for a popular drug or invention expires, the impact on the marketplace can be strong, as witnessed by the proliferation of marketers of the aspartame artificial sweetener. When the Monsanto Company's patent expired, the Nutra Sweet name continued to be protected as a trademark, but other companies could and did market aspartame under their own names or simply as a generic product with approval of the U.S. Food and Drug Administration, which regulates artificial sweeteners.

The three basic types of patents are *utility, plant*, and *design*. Patents on mechanical devices, electrical and electronic circuits, chemicals, and similar items are known as utility patents.[7] Plant patents apply to the invention or asexual reproduction of a distinct new variety of a natural plant,[8] and design patents are issued for new, original, and ornamental designs.[9] In 1994 the U.S. Court of Appeals for the Federal Circuit, which hears all appeals from all decisions in patent infringement suits,[10] ruled that computer software could be patented, even though mathematical formulas and algorithms cannot be patented. In *In Re Alappat*, the court reasoned that software "creates a new machine, because a general purpose computer in effect becomes a special purpose computer once it is programmed."[11]

Securing a patent is typically only the first step in the process. Before an invention can be marketed, approval from other federal and state agencies may be needed. A new food product or drug would typically require a green light from the FDA. Protecting a name under which an invention is to be sold requires compliance with provisions of trademark laws and probably trademark registration at some point. Unlike the trademark and copyright laws, patent law is incredibly complex, and the process of obtaining a patent is expensive, time-consuming, and complicated. Most attorneys have a limited knowledge of patent law. The filing fees for a basic application for a small entity (defined as an independent inventor, small business, or nonprofit organization), except for design, plant, and provisional applications, are $75.00 if filed electronically and $155.00 if not filed electronically. All other entities must pay $310.00. The filing fees for design, plant, and provisional applications are $105.00 for small entities and $210.00

for others. (Small entities always pay half the fee of other entities.) To determine whether a potential patent is novel, as required, inventors can conduct their own searches online at the U.S. Patent and Trademark Office website (www.uspto.gov). However, because of the complexity of the process and the considerable time involved, many inventors hire either the Patent and Trademark Office at an hourly rate or an attorney to perform the search. That can add up to thousands of dollars to filing costs.

In 1995 new patent rules took effect that allow inventors to file provisional patent applications allowing protection from infringement for a year without having to demonstrate that the invention has already been built and used (a requirement for protection under traditional patent law). During the one-year interim, the person is given the opportunity to market the invention without fear of the idea being stolen.

Under federal statute, an invention cannot be patented if "the subject matter as a whole would have been obvious at the time the invention was made to a person having ordinary skill in the art...."[12] Many patent applications have failed because the inventions were too obvious.

Patent infringement is a serious matter and can result in extensive damages, as illustrated in the infringement suit filed by Polaroid against Eastman Kodak over instant photography.[13] When the dust had settled in 1986, Eastman Kodak was ordered to pay Polaroid more than $1 billion in damages and prohibited from further sales of instant photo cameras, film, and related products. The suit was based on patents granted to Polaroid in the 1970s. In 2007 Microsoft lost a patent case filed against it by Alcatel-Lucent in a jury trial in U.S. District Court in San Diego. The jury verdict against Microsoft was to the tune of $1.52 billion—the largest patent judgment on record. The dispute centered on the use of MP3 technology.[14]

In 2006 a U.S. District Court jury awarded TiVo, Inc. almost $74 million in damages for patent infringement against the parent company of Dish satellite network, EchoStar Communications.[15] TiVo filed the lawsuit after the satellite company used its own version of a digital video recorder (DVR), a device first marketed by TiVo that allow television viewers to pause and rewind live television and to skip through commercials. TiVo already had an agreement for the use of its DVR with Dish's competitor, DirecTV, and was negotiating with some cable operators. Since the stakes can be quite high, patent holders for popular inventions rigorously defend their rights even against small-time entrepreneurs and companies. Patents are generally granted on a first-come-first-served basis, and the race to the finish line can be intense when competitors battle. When two or more claimants apply separately for patents on essentially similar inventions, the PTO will hold an interference proceeding, complete with motions and testimony, to ascertain the rightful inventor.[16]

One of the remedies available for patent infringement is a permanent injunction against the infringer. The traditional test for determining whether such a remedy is warranted in other areas of the law has involved four factors. First, the plaintiff must have suffered irreparable injury. Second, remedies at law (an injunction is an equitable remedy, as discussed in Chapter 1) are inadequate to compensate for the injury. (Remedies at law are primarily damages.) Third, in balancing the hardships between the plaintiff and the defendant, a remedy in equity is justified. Finally, public interest would not be disserved by a permanent injunction.

In *eBay, Inc. v. MERCEXCHANGE, L.L.C.* (2006),[17] the U.S. Supreme Court unanimously held that this four-factor test was the appropriate one for permanent injunctions under the U.S. Patent Act. The Court saw no reason to make a "major departure from the long tradition of equity practice. The case arose after eBay and MERCEXCHANGE could not agree on the terms for MERCEXCHANGE's purchase of a license for eBay's business method.

When America's top economist and the former Chair of the Federal Reserve, Alan Greenspan, clarified how a major shift had taken place in the economic products of the United States, he noted how those products had become "predominantly conceptual." It sounded more than a little revolutionary at the time, but Greenspan was emphasizing ideas and innovations in the field of intellectual property in the first part of the 21st century had replaced more traditional and tangible assets of personal property in the form of land and raw materials. He added that as a consequence of the shift, the management of those intellectual property assets was becoming a much more critical concern for the American corporate culture.[18]

A shift to a more aggressive identification of corporate property in the form of new and innovative ideas had taken place and forced corporate America to revise its business model and to take special stock of software development, technology, and all of the special things in the field of mass media and communication that distinguish one creative company from another. With this recognition in mind, it became more commonplace for companies to attempt to expand the scope of their corporate intellectual property claims by identifying, patenting, and licensing new ideas and innovations much more quickly and then aggressively litigating to protect them by maintaining control and exclusivity.

The last decade, the number of patent applications nearly doubled, with almost half of that growth in the U.S. coming in telecommunications and technical information.[19] This exponential growth was spurred by a mindset that encourages more and more intellectual property claims as well as an ensuing debate as to whether this growth might actually have a positive effect once those innovations are more widely known and better understood and appreciated. As experts point out, patents only allow temporary rights, and the full disclosure of new ideas often has the effect of spurring others to test those innovations. More businesses can become known for innovations in a particular area of expertise. This reinforces the likelihood they will share ideas with competitors in their fields of specialization by virtue of wanting to rush ahead with new ideas and the subsequent marketing of property to others.

The U.S. Supreme Court handed down two major decisions involving patents in 2007. Both effectively reduce the breadth of patent protection. In *KSR International Co. v. Tele-flex, Inc.,*[20] the Court unanimously ruled that a more flexible standard applied determining whether a patent was obvious (and thus not worthy of protection). The ruling clearly makes it more difficult to secure a patent. In the second, *Microsoft v. AT&T Corp.,*[21] the Court held 7–1 that Section 271(f) of the 1984 Patent Act does not cover defendants who make and sell infringing copies of software in other countries.

Trade Secrets

Trade secrets can take many forms, including formulas, plans, processes, devices, and compounds. The distinguishing characteristics are (a) that a trade secret has commercial value by virtue of the fact that it gives the owner a business advantage over competitors because they are not familiar with it, and (b) it is known only to those individuals who have a need to know it. Under the both state and federal laws governing trade secrets, they must be kept secret, particularly from competitors or potential competitors, to warrant protection. For example, North

Carolina defines misappropriation of a trade secret as the "acquisition, disclosure, or use of a trade secret of another without express or implied authority or consent" unless the trade secret was derived independently, by reverse engineering or from someone who had authority to disclose the secret.[22] The Illinois Trade Secrets Act defines a trade secret as "information, including but not limited to, technical or nontechnical data, a formula, pattern, compilation, program, device, method, technique, drawing, process, financial data...."[23]

Remedies for appropriation of trade secrets include damages as well as injunctions, whenever appropriate, especially where it is likely that a trade secret will be further disclosed if an injunction is not issued and that such disclosure would likely result in irreparable harm to a business. For example, Pepsico successfully sought an injunction in a U.S. District Court in Illinois in 1994 to prevent one of its former officers from assuming a position with Quaker Oats for six months and preventing him from forever disclosing trade secrets regarding Pepsico's annual operating plan. The Seventh Circuit U.S. Court of Appeals upheld the injunction.[24] The annual strategic plan included marketing strategies for Pepsico to position its AllSport drink to compete with Quaker's Gatorade.

In 1996 the U.S. Congress passed the Economic Espionage Act of 1996,[25] which makes the theft of trade secrets a criminal offense. The statute, which amends Title 18 of the U.S. Code, imposes stiff penalties for the theft of trade secrets in general. It also provides penalties of up to $500,000 or imprisonment of up to 15 years for individuals who steal trade secrets that benefit a foreign government or other entity, and up to $10 million for organizations that commit such offenses.

Federal statutes, including the Freedom of Information Act,[26] which otherwise require disclosure of information held by federal agencies, contain exemptions for trade secrets. The federal Trade Secrets Act,[27] in fact, imposes criminal sanctions on federal employees who disclose certain kinds of confidential information disclosed to the government, including trade secrets and confidential statistical data.[28]

The U.S. Supreme Court has decided few cases over the years directly involving trade secrets, probably because the lower federal courts generally are not involved in such cases unless they involve parties from two or more different states ("diversity jurisdiction") or concern federal employees or federal law. Since 1974, in fact, the Supreme Court has decided only six cases focusing on trade secrets. In a 1974 case, *Kewanee Oil Co. v. Bicron Corp.,*[29] the Court held that Ohio's trade secret law was not preempted by federal patent law, noting among other points that the federal patent policy of encouraging invention is not harmed by the existence of other incentives to invention such as state trade secret statutes.

In 1986 in *Dow Chemical v. United States,*[30] the Court held that the U.S. Environmental Protection Agency was acting within its authority when it employed a commercial aerial photographer to take photographs from public airspace of a chemical plant after the agency had been denied access by the company for an on-site inspection. The Court said such observations were legitimate even though the company's competitors might be barred from such action under state trade secrets law. The opinion noted that governments generally do not try to appropriate trade secrets from private enterprises and that state unfair competition laws do not define the Fourth Amendment's provision regarding unreasonable search and seizure.

In 1984 in *Ruckelshaus v. Monsanto Co.,*[31] the Court held that under certain conditions, disclosure of a trade secret by a government agency could constitute a "taking" under the Fifth Amendment, particularly when such disclosure interferes with what the Court called "reasonable investment-backed expectations." Without deciding whether there actually was a Fifth Amendment violation in the case, the Court said that trade secrets that enjoyed protection under state law could constitute "property" for purposes of the Fifth Amendment despite their intangible nature. The Court pointed out the fact that the EPA had promised confidentiality in exchange for disclosure of the information to the agency that the company had designated as trade secrets at the time of submission.

Trademarks, Including Federal and State Protection and Renewal

Trademarks are extremely important in communication law, as witnessed by the fact that trademark battles can be intense and drawn out, with millions and sometimes even billions of dollars at stake. The basic purpose of a trademark is to enable a consumer who can be a private individual or a business conglomerate to identify the origin of a product or service. Identifying the origin does not necessarily mean knowing the specific manufacturer, distributor, or franchise. The idea is that a consumer should be able to have confidence that all goods with a specific trademark are associated with a common source.

For example, when a viewer sees a television commercial for Hershey's Kisses, the person can assume that all Kisses come from Hershey's. However, that does not mean the consumer can assume that all candy bearing the Hershey's trademark is necessarily actually made by the same company but simply that Hershey's has given its consent for and presumably imposed its standards on the distribution of the products under its name.

Through the effective marketing and communication of its trademark, an owner can build up invaluable market goodwill. Think about the value of trademarks such as Coca-Cola, McDonald's, IBM, Kodak, Xerox, Sony, Dell, iPod, Apple, and Walt Disney. Coca-Cola is such a valuable trademark that the corporation has licensed its own line of clothing. Walt Disney licenses or produces thousands of products, including toys, movies, clothes, games and, of course, its own entertainment complexes throughout the world. It even owns its own broadcasting network—ABC. Neither Disney nor Coca-Cola actually manufactures the goods bearing their names, but they instead have contracts with other firms that grant permission for the use of their marks.

The success of Starbucks worldwide has resulted in numerous cases in which the Seattle-based company forced a potential, but much smaller competitor, to stop using its trademark name, or one very similar. In Galveston, Texas, a beer called Star Bock was challenged on grounds that people would associate that name with Starbucks products, and in Astoria, Oregon, a judge told coffee shop proprietor Samantha Buck, also known as Sam Buck, that use of her name infringed on Starbucks' trademark. In the eastern United States, a federal judge ruled that a New Hampshire micro-roaster selling "Charbucks," a dark coffee blend, the naming of which the owner described as an attempt to warn customers of its dark quality, did not harm Starbucks.[32]

U.S. District Court Judge Laura Taylor Swain of New York said the coffee roasting company known as the Black Bear Micro Roastery had obviously intended to take advantage of the similarity in names but did not mislead customers about any relationship between the two companies. The judge noted major differences in company logos and signage with respect to the image, the color, or the format used, and she added that Charbucks was not used as a stand-alone word in any company advertising or promotional campaign.[33] Starbucks has also fought to protect its trademarks in emerging coffee markets such as Russia and China.[34]

Trademark Dilution: Moseley and Moseley v. V Secret Catalogue, Inc. *(2003)*

The purpose of the Federal Trademark Dilution Act (FTDA) of 1995[35] is to protect "famous" trademarks against uses that blur the distinctiveness of a mark or tend to tarnish or disparage it. The term "dilution" is used to address the lessening of a mark used to identify and distinguish particular goods and services. There is considerable confusion about how much impact a new mark might have on a more established one, and this has led to some court cases focusing on the similarity of names used by companies or individuals.

Victoria's Secret is distinctive trademark of a well-established company known primarily for its stores and catalogues specializing in women's lingerie. In 1998 Victor and Cathy Moseley opened their Victor's Secret shop in Elizabethtown, Kentucky. The Moseleys' small shop near Fort Knox carried adult videos and novelties as well as lingerie. After an army colonel sent a copy of an ad for Victor's Secret to V Secret Catalogue, Inc., the owner of the Victoria's Secret trademark and parent company of the lingerie stores, the company asked the Moseleys to halt use of Victor's Secret. They claimed the use of their store's name was not an attempt to associate their single retail store with the bigger company, and that they had adopted the business name simply to avoid disclosing the existence of the shop to Victor Moseley's employer. The couple responded by changing the shop's name to Victor's Little Secret.

V Secret Catalog subsequently sued the Moseleys, claiming the use of Victor's Little Secret constituted (a) trademark infringement under federal law, (b) unfair competition, (c) trademark dilution, and (d) trademark infringement under common law. When the Moseleys refused to stop using the name, a lawsuit ensued, with a U.S. District Court ruling in favor of the plaintiffs on the trademark dilution claim. The Sixth Circuit U.S. Court of Appeals affirmed. The courts were convinced that although there was no likelihood of confusion regarding the names, the names were still sufficiently similar to dilute the more famous trademark and potentially tarnish the better known Victoria's Secret.[36]

In *Moseley and Moseley v. V Secret Catalogue, Inc.* (2003),[37] the U.S. Supreme Court unanimously held that the FTDA requires proof of actual dilution, not the mere "likelihood" of harm, as typically required under state statutes. The Court said there was insufficient evidence to support the dilution claim: "There is a complete absence of evidence of any lessening of the Victoria's Secret" mark's capacity to identify and distinguish goods or services sold in Victoria's Secret stores or advertised in catalogs."

The Court did say that a mark must be both famous and distinctive to qualify for legal protection under the Act. However, the issue of what actually constitutes the "blurring" of a distinctive mark was not resolved in the decision written by Justice Stevens, with a concurring opinion by Justice Kennedy. The Court affirmed that objective proof of actual injury to a famous mark is a prerequisite for relief, but the loss of sales or distinct profits was not required. Although the Court did not specify precisely how to prove actual dilution, it did indicate that the standard is actual dilution, not just the likelihood of dilution.

In another case involving Victoria's Secret, a *Sports Illustrated* swimsuit model was prohibited from even launching a brand of women's panties with the words "sexy little things" on them because a U.S. District Judge ruled that could result in trademark infringement. The case arose because Victoria's Secret had used the exact same label, "Sexy Little Things," since 2004 on products sold in retail stores, via catalogues, and online. Even though the developers of the product maintained that a trademark using that name had not been registered by Victoria's Secret, the judge's assessment of evidence, including product marketing, and the fact that the descriptive phrase was suggestive, not just descriptive, entitled "Sexy Little Things" greater legal protection.[38]

Apple Computer Inc. and Apple Corps Ltd., the commercial licensing agency for The Beatles, have fought in the courts for decades over the use of the apple logo. Apple Computer's logo is a cartoon-like apple with a bite missing while Apple Corps' logo is a shiny green apple. The two companies reached an agreement in 1991 that they would not compete with each other's business, but 15 years later, they were back in court. Apple Corps sued Apple Computer in a British court for using the apple logo for its iTunes Music Store. The judge in the case ruled in favor of Apple Computer.[39]

Service marks are essentially the same as trademarks, except that they identify services rather than goods. Famous service marks include Enterprise, Hertz, Avis, Home Box Office, The Movie Channel, Showtime, Citicorp, WalMart, and True Value. To avoid repetition, we will use the term "trademark" to refer to both trademarks and service marks throughout this chapter.

Trademark and Service Mark Registration

The Patent and Trademark Office handles both trademarks and patents, but trademark registration is much different and far less expensive than registration for patents. In fact, copyright registration and trademark registration involve quite similar processes, even though they are administered by different federal agencies. However, the similarities between trademarks and copyrights end there. Unlike copyrights and patents, trademarks do not derive their origin from the U.S. Constitution, although the authority of Congress to regulate trademarks and service marks comes from the Constitution, more specifically, the commerce clause.

Trademarks and service marks are statutory creations of the states and the federal government. Since trademark laws vary considerably from state to state, state laws will not be discussed here. However, some trademarks and service marks—those that are not used nor intended to be used in interstate and/or international commerce between the United States and another country—can be registered and protected only under state law. Before a trademark or service mark can be registered under federal law (i.e., the Lanham Act), the owner must either (a) use the mark on goods that are shipped or sold in interstate or international commerce, or (b) have a bona fide intention to use the mark in such commerce.[40]

Until the Trademark Law Revision Act of 1988,[41] which became effective November 16, 1989, a trademark essentially had to actually have been used in some form of interstate commerce, but the 1988 law permits registration so long as there is a bona fide intent to use it in interstate commerce. Nevertheless, trademarks that are strictly for intrastate use are registered with the Secretary of State in the state where they will be used.

Colors can be trademarked, under the right circumstances, as demonstrated in *Qualitex Company v. Jacobson Products, Inc.* (1995).[42] A unanimous U.S. Supreme Court held that the Lanham Trademark Act of 1946 does allow trademark registration of a color. However, the opinion, written by Justice Breyer, said that the special shade of green-gold used to identify dry cleaning press pads made by Qualitex had acquired the requisite secondary meaning under the Lanham Act. Jacobson Products, a competitor to Qualitex, had challenged the trademark registration and unsuccessfully argued that such registration would create uncertainty about what shades of color a competitor could use and that it was unworkable because of the limited supply of colors. Qualitex had won in U.S. District Court but lost in the Ninth Circuit Court of Appeals. The Supreme Court reversed the appellate court decision.

Sounds can be registered. In 1978 the Trademark Trial and Appeal Board recognized the combination of the musical notes G, E, and C used by the National Broadcasting Company as a valid trademark, while denying the registration of the sound of a ship's bell.[43] The roar of the MGM lion has been registered as a trademark for some time. Harley-Davidson, Inc., which already owns the rights to the word "Hog," applied for a trademark on its engine sound, but several competitors, including Suzuki, Honda, and Kawasaki, opposed the registration. Before he was acquitted on two murder counts, O. J. Simpson applied for registration of the O. J. mark for use on a series of goods, including clothing and footballs, video games, playing cards, newsletters, and jigsaw puzzles. Simpson's lawyers later sued several dozen clothing manufacturers and retail stores for selling goods with Simpson's name or likeness.

The registration process and protection under federal law for trademarks and service marks are the same. Under the Lanham Act, a trademark is defined as "… any word, name, symbol, or device, or any combination thereof adopted and used by a manufacturer or merchant to identify his or her goods or services."[44] Thus a trademark can be a slogan, design, or even a distinctive sound so long as it identifies and distinguishes goods or services. The key characteristics are identification and distinction.

Among the other changes wrought by the Trademark Revision Act of 1988 is that use prior to registration of a trademark is no longer necessary. Now, a trademark owner needs only to have a bona fide intention to use the mark. The 1988 law also cut the term of registration in half from 20 years to 10 years. Unlike copyrights and patents, that have limited durations, trademarks can last indefinitely if an owner takes appropriate steps to ensure that infringers are prosecuted and that the mark does not revert to the public domain. Protection can also be lost by abandonment. Contrary to popular myth, registration is not necessary for a trademark to have protection. As with copyrights, there are some important advantages to registration, but it is not required. Among the advantages are that registration:

1. Provides *prima facie* evidence of first use of the mark in interstate commerce and of the validity of the registration.
2. Permits an owner to sue in federal court (U.S. District Court) for infringement.
3. Allows lost profits, court costs, attorneys' fees, criminal penalties, and treble damages, in some cases, to be sought.
4. Serves as constructive notice of an ownership claim, preventing someone from claiming that a trademark was used because of a good faith belief that no one else had claim to it. In other words, once a mark is registered, any potential user has an obligation to check the registry to ascertain that no one else owns the mark.
5. Establishes a basis for foreign registration.

Registration is a fairly simple process, although it is more complicated than copyright registration and much easier than securing a patent. First, the owner or his or her attorney files an application form available on the Patent and Trademark Office website that includes (a) the name and mailing address of the applicant, (b) a clear drawing of the mark, (c) a listing of the goods or services, and (d) a $375.00 (paper) or $325.00 (electronic) filing fee for each class of goods or services for which the owner is applying. If the mark has been used in commerce, the application must also include a sworn statement that the mark is in use in commerce. Once the PTO has received the application materials, a trademark examining attorney must decide whether the mark can actually be registered.

This decision is then sent to the applicant about three months after the application is filed. A refusal can be appealed to the Trademark Trial and Appeal Board, an administrative tribunal in the PTO. Further refusal can then be appealed to a U.S. District Court and to the U.S. Court of Appeals for the Federal Circuit. The U.S. Supreme Court has jurisdiction to hear further appeals, but rarely does so. Once approval is granted, the mark is published in the *Trademark Official Gazette*, a weekly bulletin from the PTO. Anyone opposing the registration has 30 days after the publication to file a protest with the Trademark Trial and Appeal Board, which acts very much like a trial court. If there is no opposition, about 12 weeks after the mark is published, the registration then becomes official if the application was based upon actual use. If the application is, instead, based upon an intention to use the mark, the trademark owner then has six months to either use the mark in commerce or request a six-month extension. Once the mark is used, a statement-of-use form must be filed.

There is now a rebuttable presumption that if a trademark is not used for three years, it has been abandoned. Under a rebuttable presumption, the owner has the burden of demonstrating that the trademark was in use in any infringement suit.

Journalists should become acquainted with the registration process in case they deal with stories about trademarks because it can play a major role in determining the outcome of an infringement suit or a suit over ownership of the mark. A good start is the online PTO booklet, *Basic Facts About Trademarks*. The U.S. Trademark Association, a private organization in New York City, also distributes informative materials, and the American Bar Association's Section on Intellectual Property Law has published a booklet, *What Is a Trademark?*

Grounds on which marks can be excluded from registration include that the mark:

1. Disparages or falsely suggests a connection with people, organizations, beliefs, or national symbols or brings them into contempt or disrepute.
2. Consists of or simulates the flag, coat of arms, or other insignia of the United States, a state, a city, or any foreign country.
3. Is immoral, deceptive, or scandalous.
4. Is the name, portrait, or signature of a living person unless he or she has given permission.
5. Is the name, portrait, or signature of a deceased U.S. President while his or her surviving spouse is alive unless the spouse has given consent.
6. Is so similar to a mark previously registered that it would be likely to confuse or deceive a reasonable person.
7. Is simply descriptive or deceptively misdescriptive of the goods or services.

If an applicant can demonstrate that a mark already being used in commerce has become distinctive enough that the public now identifies the goods or services with the mark, it can be registered even if it is merely descriptive.

Trademark registration is not restricted to commercial enterprises, of course. Nonprofit organizations, trade associations, and other groups as well as individuals can register trademarks. For example, the Society of Professional Journalists (SPJ) registered its name and logo along with the name Sigma Delta Chi. Trade names such as International Business Machines Corporation and Pepsi-Cola Bottling Company cannot be registered as trademarks under the federal statute, but the name associated with the product or service (i.e., IBM, Pepsi-Cola, etc.) can be registered and the corporation name can be filed and registered with the appropriate official (usually the Secretary of State) in each state.

Some of the owners of popular trademarks such as Xerox, IBM, Kleenex, and Kodak sometimes purchase ads in media trade publications such as *Editor & Publisher, Broadcasting & Cable,* and the *Quill* (published by SPJ) informing journalists that their names are registered trademarks and should be identified as such. Many famous former trademarks such as cornflakes, linoleum, mimeograph, escalator, and raisin bran went into public domain and thus lost their protection as trademarks because they were abandoned or the owners did not aggressively fight infringers. Some companies often send out press releases and buy ads requesting that their trademarks be used as proper adjectives in connection with their products and services and not as verbs. Advertisers are particularly irked when news stories mention trademarks without identifying them as such.

Some companies have reputations for notifying media outlets when they believe their trademarks have been used inappropriately, probably because they feel this is one way of demonstrating a strong effort to protect their marks in case an infringement occurs and they have to counter the claim from a defendant that a mark has become generic and no longer worthy of protection. While a company would have no real basis for claiming infringement simply because a news or feature story made generic use of a trademark, savvy advertisers and public relations practitioners remind reporters, editors, and other journalists from time to time that good journalistic practice dictates appropriate acknowledgment of trademarks.

Thousands of court battles have been fought over trademarks over the years about products from beer to cars. Even universities have entered the fray. Toyota and Mead Data General once fought in U.S. District Court over Toyota's use of Lexus as the trademark for its luxury cars. Mead Data argued that the car line name was so similar to Lexis, the trademark for Mead's computerized information retrieval service, that consumers would be confused. Toyota argued that consumers did not confuse Pulsar cars by Nissan with Pulsar watches or Lotus computer software with Lotus autos. Ultimately, a U.S. District Court Judge agreed with Toyota and permitted the registration, and the Second Circuit U.S. Court of Appeals upheld the decision.[45] Toyota later changed the logo for the cars under its own name to one with three ellipses.

The PTO Trademark Trial and Appeal Board affirmed the decision of the trademark examining attorney that Churchill Downs, Inc., in Louisville, Kentucky, be allowed to register The Kentucky Derby as a trademark for use on various consumer goods. The registration had been challenged by a gift shop operator who argued that the slogan was merely descriptive or generic. Products licensed include Derby-Pie, a delicious chocolate and pecan pie that spawned numerous copycats, none of which can bear the Derby-Pie trademark without consent. Derby-Pie is licensed to Kern's Kitchen Inc., a Louisville baking company. The company has been aggressive, as trademark owners must be, in protecting its trademark. In 1994 Kern's successfully sought a court order to ban Nestlé USA from using the term "derby pie" after Nestlé printed a "derby pie" recipe on the back of some of its chocolate chip packages. Twelve years later when a "Kentucky Derby Pie" recipe showed up on a Nestlé-owned website, meals.com, Kern's filed a motion in court, claiming Nestlé had violated the earlier order.[46]

Harvard University was the last Ivy League school to register its name as a trademark. More than 100 colleges and universities have registered their names as trademarks. Usually the schools then license their products through one of the major licensing firms for a set fee and a percentage of the profits from the sales of products. The battles over university names can sometimes get interesting, as witnessed by the fight between Ohio State University and Ohio University in 1997 over the use of the word "Ohio." Ohio University registered the name as a trademark in 1993, but Ohio State University did not find out about it until three years later.[47]

Pizza Hut and Donatos Pizza reached an out-of-court settlement in 1997 when Pizza Hut agreed to pay its smaller rival an undisclosed sum to be able to call its new pizza "The Edge," not to be confused with the U2 musician. Donatos had sued Pizza Hut for trademark infringement after Pizza Hut launched a $55 million advertising campaign for The Edge. Donatos said the name was substantially similar to its "Edge to Edge," which it had been using for years.[48] The Maine Lobster Promotion Council and the National Pork Producers Council, both trade organizations for promoting their respective products, clashed in federal court after negotiations broke down over the lobster group's use of the term "Ultimate White Meat," which the pork folks argued was too similar to its use of "The Other White Meat," registered as a trademark four years earlier.[49]

Some registration attempts have been unsuccessful such as Anheuser-Busch Inc.'s failed effort to use the LA mark for its low alcohol beer. The Seventh Circuit U.S. Court of Appeals upheld the decision of a U.S. District Court that LA was merely descriptive and thus had not acquired the requisite secondary meaning, or distinctiveness. According to the court, the common sense view is:

> ...that, as a practical matter, initials do not usually differ significantly in their trademark role from the description words that they represent ... [and thus] ... there is a heavy burden on a trademark claimant seeking to show an independent meaning of initials apart from the descriptive words which are their source.[50]

Once a federal registration is issued by the PTO (usually about six months after an application is filed if there is no opposition from another party and if the trademark examining attorney gives approval), the owner gives notice of registration by using the ® symbol or the phrase "Registered in U.S. Patent and Trademark Office," or the abbreviation "Reg. U.S. Pat. & Tm. Off." These registration indications cannot be used before registration, but the owner is free to use TM or SM as symbols for trademark and service mark, respectively, although he or she is not required to do so. Recall that under the federal statute, registration is not required for trademark protection, although there are many advantages to registration, as enumerated above.

The Trademark Law Revision Act of 1988 made another important change that may have an impact on some nontraditional forms of communication, especially parodies. The Act includes a provision that permits a trademark owner to recover damages and, under other provisions of the Act, obtain an injunction for product or service misrepresentation. The provision applies only to commercial use, not to political communication or editorial content, but it appears aimed at specific product disparagement, although some forms may continue to be protected such as that in *L.L. Bean, Inc. v. Drake Publishers, Inc.* (1987).[51]

When Drake published a sex catalog parodying L.L. Bean's clothing catalog, L.L. Bean filed suit, claiming that *L.L. Beam's Back To School-Sex-Catalog* violated Maine's anti-dilution statute. (Such statutes are aimed at protecting trademarks and similar names from suffering disparagement and thus having their commercial value chipped away through unauthorized use.) The First Circuit U.S. Court of Appeals ruled that since the sex catalog was a noncommercial use, the anti-dilution statute could not be used under the First Amendment to prohibit its publication. (L.L. Bean sought an injunction.) If the sex catalog had been an attempt to actually market products instead of simply an artistic endeavor and had it been published after the new Act took effect in 1989, the Court would probably have ruled in favor of L.L. Bean.

Two common mistakes most people make with trademarks are (a) confusing trademarks with other forms of intellectual property, especially copyrights, and (b) failing to recognize trademarks. An example of the first type of error occurred in news stories about the NC-17 rating system instituted by the Motion Picture Association of America (MPAA). Several major newspapers and at least one wire service reported pornographic movie makers started using the noncopyrighted X rating in the early 1970s, but the NC-17 rating is copyrighted. The truth is that none of the ratings are copyrighted. They are instead registered trademarks. Names and titles cannot be copyrighted, but they can become trademarks. Open the entertainment section of your favorite newspaper and you will clearly see the registered trademark symbol after the rating of each movie, along with the MPAA symbol, also a trademark. The MPAA deliberately chose not to protect the X rating, but it did so by not registering it as a trademark rather than not copyrighting it (which it could not do anyway). The distinction between a trademark and a copyright is very important, and journalists should learn the difference before using the terms, just as they would make sure to use the correct spelling of a spokesperson's name in a news story.

The second type of mistake is the most common. Most national advertisers know the importance of identifying trademarks, especially their own, but it is not unusual for local and regional advertisers to omit the trademark symbol, particularly when referring to the products of competitors, such as in comparative ads.

Trademarks may be big business, but trademark protection is by no means restricted to profit making enterprises. The word *Olympic* and the Olympic symbol (three intertwined circles and five intertwined circles) are registered trademarks of the International Olympic Committee. Indeed, many businesses, including the U.S. Postal Service, Delta Airlines, and United Parcel Service have paid fees for the use of the Olympic trademarks, and yet *Olympic* is often used in news stories as a generic term. In 1987 the U.S. Supreme Court in a 5–4 decision held that the United States Olympic Committee had the exclusive right to use the term and symbol and could therefore bar a homosexual group from using the trademark in its gay olympics events.[52] On the profit making side, *Star Wars* is a trademark, having been registered by Lucasfilm, Ltd., owned by George Lucas and others, during the height of *Star Wars* mania.

The BBB symbol of the Better Business Bureau is a registered trademark, but the walking fingers logo of yellow page fame is not a trademark. The L'eggs package for women's hosiery is now history because the Sara Lee Corp. phased out the containers in favor of cardboard packaging that is less harmful to the environment, but both the old and the new containers are registered trademarks. (Distinctive packaging can be trademarked.) Sometimes trademarks are changed or even taken off the market at the behest of the government or sometimes because of consumer perceptions. The Kellogg Co. changed the name of its Heartwise cereal to Fiberwise under pressure from the U.S. Food and Drug Administration, which has a policy of discouraging the use of "heart" in brand names.

The U.S. Federal Trade Commission also rescinded its initial approval of Powermaster as a brand name for a beer with a higher than usual percentage of alcohol because it has a policy of banning brand names of alcohol that promote the alcohol content. The Procter & Gamble Co. redesigned its decades-old moon-and-stars trademark, including eliminating the curly hairs in the man's beard that looked like sixes. The company filed lawsuits and repeatedly issued statements that attempted to dispel rumors that P&G supported Satan because of the sixes that appeared in the symbol's beard. (The number 666 is mentioned in the Book of Revelation in the Bible in connection with the devil.) The company continued using the trademark in revised form, but it also uses two newer symbols, Procter & Gamble and P&G in a script-like format. In 1985 P&G began omitting the moon-and-stars emblem from most of its products. The company continues to use the symbol (in revised form) in some places.

Even radio and television call letters and sounds can be trademarked, and many stations have registered their calls and distinctive sound identifications to differentiate them in a highly competitive market in which call letters readily alert listeners and viewers to their favorite channels and frequencies such as K-FNS, Fox 100, Cozy'95, Double-Q, and Rock 105.

Trademark names are often linked to current trends. For example, prior to the start of the new millennium, the U.S. Patent and Trademark Office recorded registrations for 117 trademarks that included the word "millennium" and more than 1,500 with the number "2000." The registrations included *Playboy* magazine's slogan, Official Magazine of the Millennium and one company's use of Class of 2000 for its line of clothing.

Most the cases involving loss of property are deadly serious or they usually would not be taken to court. Occasionally, the nature of a case will bring a smile even to litigants and the judge involved in it. In February, 2010, the celebrated North Face apparel company faced court-ordered mediation to resolve litigation it had initiated with South Butt LLC, over the use of its brand, claiming it infringed on its trademark name and logo. South Butt LLC was started by a University of Missouri student with products sold over the counter in a Ladue, Missouri, pharmacy. The core of the dispute was the infringement lawsuit in which North Face made the claim against the small, upstart apparel company. Missouri Eastern District Judge Rodney W. Sippel ruled against South Butt's request that the lawsuit be dismissed noting that he did not find it implausible that the logo being used by South Butt could cause confusion or dilute the North Face brand. The Judge began his order by quoting humorist Franklin P. Jones: "It's a strange world of language in which skating on thin ice can get you into hot water." In reflecting on the claims in this case—and the humor injected into consideration of it—University of Missouri Journalism Law Professor, Sandy Davidson, recalled the similar use of humor in a trademark case involving Hormel, maker of Spam. In suing over the use of the name "Spa'am" in a motion picture starring Muppets cartoon character, Miss Piggy, an appeals court wrote: "In one little can, Spam contains the five major food groups: Snouts. Ears. Feet. Tails. Brains.' (One) might think Hormel would welcome the association with a genuine source of pork." Professor Davidson suggested that the case was also inherently funny and certainly invited this kind of response from the judge.[53]

Two final notes about trademarks. First, they can last indefinitely so long as they are aggressively protected to avoid dilution and infringement. As noted earlier, registration lasts ten years, but it can be renewed every ten years by filing a renewal application during the six months before the registration ends. (A renewal request can be made only during the six months before the last registration expires—not before and not later.) Second, trademarks, like patents and copyrights, can be sold and transferred by a written agreement or contract just like other types of property. When corporations merge and large companies acquire smaller ones, the trademarks are often among the most valuable assets. Consumers rely very heavily on brand names and trademarks in their decisions, which is why a company will pay hundreds of millions of dollars to acquire an already well-established trademark for a brand of candy bar, for instance, rather than market a similar candy bar under a new trademark. An existing brand is a sure winner; a new name could be a huge risk.

Summary

Trademarks have considerable protection under both state and federal law, but trademark holders must take aggressive steps to ensure that their marks do not become diluted and risk going into the public domain. Most advertisers and other commercial and noncommercial enterprises also constantly monitor the use of their trademarks for possible infringement, while making sure they treat the trademarks of others with appropriate respect.

Copyright

On January 1, 1978, the law of copyright changed dramatically when the Copyright Act of 1976 took effect, and the pieces of what was once a colossal mess acquired some long-needed order. Prior to January 1, 1978, copyrights were governed principally by a federal statute known as the Copyright Act of 1909 that had been revised on numerous occasions over a period of almost 70 years to try to accommodate new technologies and unresolved problems. In 1909 we had no computers, compact disks, photocopy machines, satellites, or television broadcasts, and even radio had reached only an experimental stage. Copyright infringement was certainly possible, and authors definitely needed protection, but it was much more difficult during that time than it is today to make unauthorized use of a person's creative work.

The idea of copyright, though, was not new even in 1909. Copyright laws arose as early as the 15th century in Europe with the development of movable type and mass printing, but they were employed largely as a mechanism for prior restraint in the form of licensing and not as a means for protecting authors. The first federal copyright statute was enacted by Congress in 1790, one year after the U.S. Constitution was ratified and a year before the Bill of Rights took effect. A two-tiered system emerged with the federal statute principally protecting published works and state common law governing unpublished works. That system essentially continued with the 1909 law but was eviscerated by the 1976 statute in favor of a system that made common law copyright unnecessary and theoretically nonexistent.

Congress is often criticized for its laborious, cumbersome, and time-consuming decision making, and some of that criticism may be in order for the deliberations involved in formulating a new copyright statute in the 1970s. But the end result was a well-crafted, albeit imperfect, federal law that differs substantially from the old 1909 scheme. Even the premises of the two are at odds. As Kitch and Perlman note, "Under the old law the starting principle was: the owner shall have the exclusive right to copy his copies. Under the new the principle is: the owner shall have the exclusive right to exploit his work."[54] The new law is clearly an author-oriented statute that offers tremendous protection to the creators of original works of authorship.

Closely aligned with Internet copyright concerns in the intellectual property arena are emerging issues involving Internet link law. In a groundbreaking article in *Berkeley Technology Law Journal* outlining the status of the law related to linkages and content on the Internet, St. Louis attorney Mark Sableman outlined cases that engendered considerable interest in linking content from one source to another. In many instances similar names emerge in such cases to potentially confuse those who go to one site expecting one company's content but finding instead another with perhaps a similar name, or else merely by way of establishing linkages between a personal website and Dilbert cartoons or content linked to *Playboy* magazine or newspaper front pages. While linking has often been regarded as fair use by the courts, particularly when we can assume that use of content including trademarks or icons hyperlinking to other sites would be understood to be separate property that would not blur or tarnish an owner's mark or offer the impression that some form of sponsorship or endorsement exists, there have been occasions in which linking offered "frames" from what might otherwise be considered rather innocuous sources, but then added commercial content or advertising.

Some individuals have intentionally used corporate logos and links in an effort to disparage a company's services or products. Sableman discusses one such case, *Bally Total Fitness Holding Corp. v. Faber*[55] in which a health club owner sued an unhappy customer for his "Bally's Sucks" web page, in which he used the plaintiff's trademark. Bally's also objected to a link from the defendant's site to another link that it considered pornographic in nature. The court had to determine whether a reasonable consumer would consider the site to have been sponsored by Bally. It ruled a reasonable consumer would not. Sableman also raised the related issue of whether, once someone has entered such a site and then been given the opportunity to exit, a link established to an avowedly family-friendly or family-oriented site somehow tarnishes or diminishes the mark.[56] He also revisited the issue of whether association to a business or organization via a link could be deemed to potentially hurt one's reputation through association with an organization or one known to be of lesser or even formally labeled to represent lower quality, such as fan sites existing exclusively to critique a particular broadcast series or a national sports franchise.[57] Cases involving database rights and protection of copyright will obviously invite additional scrutiny and litigation as time goes by. So we can likely expect a continuing interest in this area.

The Old versus New Law

Some of the major differences between the old and the new copyright statutes are:

1. Under the new law, the duration of copyright protection was considerably increased, even for works that began their protection under the old law. The general term of protection for most works is now the author's lifetime plus 70 years, compared to two 28-year terms under the old law. The initial term was lifetime plus 50 years, but in 1998 President Bill Clinton signed into law the Sonny Bono Copyright Extension Act that increased the U.S. term to the international standard of lifetime plus 50 years.
2. Under the old law, works could generally claim federal copyright protection only if they were published; publication is not required under the new law.
3. The scope of both "exclusive rights" (rights initially conferred solely on the creator of the work) and the types of works included were considerably expanded under the new law.
4. Registration is no longer necessary for copyright protection.

Nature of Copyright under the New Law

Because the Copyright Act of 1976 effectively killed common law copyright, under which states offered perpetual protection for unpublished works, copyright is now strictly a federal statutory matter. More precisely, it arises from Title 17 of the U.S. Code Sections 101–810 and subsequent revisions. Under Section 102, copyright protection extends to "original works of authorship fixed in any tangible medium of expression, now known or later developed, from which they can be perceived, reproduced, or otherwise communicated, either directly or with the aid of a machine or device." This section enumerates seven categories under works of authorship: (a) literary works; (b) musical works, including any accompanying words; (c) dramatic works, including any accompanying music; (d) pantomimes and choreographic works; (e) pictorial, graphic, and sculptural works; (f) motion pictures and other audiovisual works; and (g) sound recordings.

Section 102(b) notes that copyright protection does not extend to "any idea, procedure, process, system, method of operation, concept, principle, or discovery, regardless of the form in which it is described, explained, illustrated, or embodied in such work." Some of these entities may enjoy protection as trademarks, trade secrets, or patents, but they cannot be copyrighted even though works in which they appear can be copyrighted. Section 103 specifies that compilations and derivative works have copyright protection, but this protection extends only to the material contributed by the author of a compilation or derivative work. Thus any preexisting material used in a derivative work or compilation does not gain additional protection but maintains the same protection it had originally. In other words, you cannot expand the protection a work originally enjoyed by using it, whether in whole or in part, in another work such as a derivative work or compilation. Section 101, which contains definitions of terms in the statute, defines a compilation as "… a work formed by the collection and assembling of preexisting materials or of data that are selected, coordinated, or arranged in such a way that the resulting work as a whole constitutes an original work of authorship." Compilations also include collective works. A compilation can be further defined as "… a work, such as a periodical issue, anthology, or encyclopedia, in which a number of contributions, constituting separate and independent works in themselves, are assembled into a collective whole." A derivative work is:

> … a work based upon one or more preexisting works, such as a translation, musical arrangement, dramatization, fictionalization, motion picture version, sound recording, art reproduction, abridgment, condensation, or any other form in which a work may be recast, transformed, or adapted. A work consisting of editorial revisions, annotations, elaborations, or other modifications, which, as a whole, represent an original work of authorship, is a 'derivative work.'[58]

The key differences between a compilation and a derivative work are that (a) a compilation consists of a pulling together of separate works or pieces of works already created whereas a derivative work can trace its origins to one previous work, and (b) the key creative element in a compilation is the way in which the preexisting works are compiled to create the whole, i.e., the new work, but the creative dimensions of a derivative work are basically independent of the previous work.

The film *Gone With the Wind*, which was based on Margaret Mitchell's book by the same name, is an example of a derivative work. An anthology of poems by Robert Frost, which consisted of poems previously published on their own or in even in other anthologies is an illustration of a compilation that is also a collective work. With certain exemptions such as "fair use" and compulsory licensing for nondramatic musical works, the owner, who is usually the creator, of an original work of authorship acquires exclusive rights that only that person can exercise or authorize others to exercise.

Exclusivity is a very important concept under the current copyright law because copyright owners are essentially granted a monopoly over the use of their works. No matter how valuable a work may be in terms of its scholarship, commercial value, artistic quality, or contribution to society, its copyright owner has the exclusive right to control its use and dissemination during the duration of the copyright. For example, Margaret Mitchell's heirs, who inherited the rights to her novel when she was killed when hit by an auto in 1949, nixed any sequels to the enormously popular book and movie until 1988 when Warner Books paid $4.5 million at an estate auction for the right to publish a sequel, although the estate retained the right to choose the author. A series of sequels, including books and movies, would probably have brought in millions of dollars in royalties, but *Gone With the Wind* devotees dying to learn the fate of Rhett and Scarlett had to wait until 1991 for Alexandra Ripley's *Scarlett: Tomorrow Is Another Day*. The 768-page sequel was published simultaneously in 40 countries, with excerpts in *Life* magazine. The television movie followed three years later—all six hours plus commercials. The second sequel to *Gone with the Wind* was published in 2007. The publisher, St. Martin's Press, paid the Margaret Mitchell estate $4.5 million for the right to publish the book *Rhett Butler's People* authored by Donald McCaig.

Under Section 106 these exclusive rights are:

1. To reproduce the copyrighted work in copies or phonorecords;
2. To prepare derivative works based upon the copyrighted work;
3. To distribute copies or phonorecords of the copyrighted work to the public by sale or other transfer of ownership, or by rental, lease, or lending;
4. In the case of literary, musical, dramatic, and choreographic works, pantomimes, and motion pictures and other audiovisual works, to perform the copyrighted work publicly;
5. In the case of literary, musical, dramatic, and choreographic works, pantomimes, and pictorial, graphic, or sculptural works, including the individual images of a motion picture or other audiovisual work, to display the copyrighted work publicly.

Actual ownership of a work, as opposed to ownership of the copyrights to a work, does not convey any copyrights. For example, if Jan Smurf purchases a videocassette of Walt Disney's (a registered trademark) *Cinderella* (a copyrighted work) at her local Wal-Mart (another registered trademark), she can play the tape to her heart's content in her own home and even invite her friends for an evening of viewing on a big-screen television. However, she does not have the right to make a copy of the tape nor even to play it at a neighborhood fund-raiser for the homeless, no matter how worthy the cause. She does not even have the right to make her own edited version of the film. In other words, purchasing the cassette merely gave her the right to use it in the form in which it was intended to be used—nothing more. She could, of course, lend the movie to a neighbor or even sell her copy to a stranger as long as it was a bona fide copy, and not a pirated version, just as she could with a book or other physical object. Thus her rights are strictly tangible; she has no intangible rights.

The Rev. Martin Luther King Jr.'s estate reached an agreement for the sale of many of the civil rights leader's personal materials, including drafts of the famous "I Have a Dream" speech, to a group of prominent companies and individuals in Atlanta for more than $32 million. Under the agreement, the collection was eventually transferred to King's undergraduate alma mater, Morehouse College. The $32 million sale price covered only the right to physically possess the collection, including displaying the materials and making them available to researchers, but it did not include intellectual property rights, including copyright, trademark, and appropriation rights. The estate retained control of those rights, which are probably worth many times the price of the collection alone.

Exclusive rights do not necessarily translate into absolute control over a work, once the work is sold. Under what is known as the first sale doctrine, for example, when a copyright owner sells or gives away a copy of a particular work, the owner essentially gives up the exclusive right to vend that specific copy, including the right to prevent it from being transferred to someone else. Under Section 109(a) of the new Copyright Act, "Notwithstanding the provisions of Section 106(3), the owner of a particular copy or phonorecord lawfully made under this title, or any person authorized by such owner, is entitled, without the authority of the copyright owner, to sell or otherwise dispose of the possession of that copy or phonorecord." That is why video rental stores do not have to get permission of the copyright owner to rent videocassettes, so long as the copies rented were legally purchased.

However, Section 109(b) provides an exception for computer programs, based on the Computer Software Rental Agreements Act of 1990,[59] which bars the rental, lease, and lending of computer programs, except for nonprofit libraries and nonprofit educational institutions for nonprofit purposes if a proper copyright warning is posted on the copies. The section also does not apply to video games designed strictly for playing, such as video game modules and computer programs embodied in machines such that the programs ordinarily cannot be copied. The record industry had a similar amendment passed in 1984 for the commercial rentals of phonorecords, except those acquired before October 4, 1984.[60]

In 1998 in *Quality King Distributors, Inc. v. L'anza Research International, Inc.,*[61] the U.S. Supreme Court handed down a decision focusing on the first sale doctrine. Although the case involved the resale of hair care products, the Court's ruling had implications for the sale of other products including videos and CDs by discounters such as Wal-Mart. The dispute involved the multibillion dollar "gray market" in which certain American-made products are initially sold abroad and then resold back in the United States.[62]

L'anza Research International sold its line of hair care products in the United States only to distributors who contracted to resell them within specific geographic areas and solely to authorized retailers such as barber shops and hair salons. The company advertised and promoted its shampoos and other products in this country but limited its advertising in other countries. As a result, the prices were substantially lower abroad. Both the domestic and the imported versions of the products carried copyrighted labels.

One of the company's distributors in Great Britain sold several tons of the products to another distributor in Malta, which, in turn, sold the products to Quality King Distributors. Without permission of L'anza, Quality King resold them at deeply discounted prices to unauthorized retailers in the United States. L'anza then sued Quality King, claiming its exclusive rights under the Copyright Act of 1976 had been violated. A U.S. District Court issued a summary judgment in favor of L'anza after rejecting Quality King's first sale defense. The Ninth

Circuit Court of Appeals affirmed the trial court decision, but the Supreme Court held that the doctrine was applicable to imported copies. According to the Court, "The whole point of the first sale doctrine is that once the copyright owner places a copyrighted item in the stream of commerce by selling it, he has exhausted his exclusive statutory right to control its distribution."[63] The Clinton administration, represented by the Solicitor General of the United States, had argued on the side of L'anza, contending that five international trade agreements had already been reached to allow domestic copyright owners to stop unauthorized importation of validly copyrighted copies of works. The Supreme Court, however, called these actions "irrelevant" to interpretation of the Copyright Act.

This decision does not in any way grant the purchaser of a copyrighted work the right to alter the work and then resell it nor to make copies of the work and sell them. It does, however, grant major discounters and other retailers the right to resell copyrighted products or products with copyrighted labels that have been brought back into the United States after being sold abroad.

Creation of Copyright

Probably the most important difference between the old and the new copyright statutes is the point at which copyright protection begins. Under the 1909 statute, federal copyright protection generally could not be invoked until a work had been published with notice of copyright. There were a few exceptions to this general rule, but unpublished works were basically protected only under state law or what was known as common law copyright, as mentioned earlier. Common law copyright certainly had some advantages, including perpetual protection for unpublished works, but, with each state having its own common law, there was no uniformity. The 1976 Copyright Law solved this problem very easily. Copyright exists automatically:

> ... in original works of authorship fixed in any tangible medium of expression, now known or later developed, from which they can be perceived, reproduced, or otherwise communicated, either directly or with the aid of a machine or device.[64]

No registration is necessary. No publication is required. Not even a copyright notice has to be placed on the work for it to be copyrighted. This is one of the most difficult aspects of copyright for laypersons, including mass media practitioners, to understand. In the copyright workshops for laypersons taught by the author of this text, the most frequently asked question is, "What do I do to copyright my book (or other creative work)?" The answer is simply "nothing" because the work was copyrighted the very second it was created in a tangible medium. Nothing could be simpler. No hocus-pocus, smoking mirrors, or other magic. Not even a government form to complete.

The question the person actually wants answered is, "How do I register the copyright for my work?" There are definitely some major advantages to registration, but this step is absolutely not essential to secure copyright protection. The only requirements are creation and fixation in a tangible medium. A work is created under the statute "when it is fixed in a copy or phonorecord for the first time."[65] Thus a work cannot be copyrighted if it exists only in the mind of its creator, but once it is fixed in a tangible medium, the protection begins.

When a work is developed over time, the portion that is fixed at a particular time is considered the work at that time. For instance, the copyrighted portion of this textbook at the time these words are being written on the computer processor consists of everything written thus far to the end of this sentence. If a work is prepared in different versions, each version is a separate work for purposes of copyright. Thus the first edition of this book is considered a separate work from the second edition and so on. When is a work actually fixed in a medium? According to Section 101:

> A work is 'fixed' in a tangible medium of expression when its embodiment in a copy or phonorecord, by or under authority of the author, is sufficiently permanent or stable to permit it to be perceived, reproduced, or otherwise communicated for a period of more than transitory duration. A work consisting of sounds, images, or both, that are being transmitted, is 'fixed' for purposes of this title if a fixation of the work is being made simultaneously with its transmission.[66]

Suppose an enterprising skywriter composes a love poem in the sky to her fiancé during halftime in the final game of the World Series. A few miles away another romantic scribbles in the ocean sand the opening of a modernized version of the great film epic, *Beach Blanket Bingo*. How can these two original works of authorship be copyrighted? Both face a major obstacle— they are not yet fixed in a tangible medium of expression. Almost as soon as the love poem is written in the sky, it evaporates into thin air. Thus its transitory nature prevents it from being "fixed" for purposes of copyright. The same holds true for the film's opening sequence since it ends up blowing in the wind. How do we "fix" them? An easy way would be to write them on a piece of paper or perhaps photograph or videotape them before they fade. But won't paper eventually deteriorate? (The yellowed and tattered newspaper clippings from our glory days in high school are testament to this.) Fixation does not require permanency—only, as indicated above, that the medium be sufficiently permanent or stable to allow it to be perceived, copied, or otherwise communicated for more than a transitory duration.

Copyright law must be flexible enough to accommodate new technologies, but this idea is not new. In *Burrow-Giles Lithographic Company v. Sarony* (1884),[67] the U.S. Supreme Court ruled for the first time that photographs enjoyed copyright protection even though the Copyright Act of 1790 written nearly 50 years before the invention of photography made no mention of this medium, of course. In the decision, the Court pointed to the fact that Congress had included maps and charts in the first Copyright Act. The case arose after renowned New York studio photographer Napoleon Sarony sued a printer for copyright infringement after it made at least 85,000 copies of a photo Sarony had taken of the notorious British playwright, novelist and poet Oscar Wilde. The Court said the photo was "an original work of art ... and of a class of inventions for which the Constitution intended that Congress should secure to him [Sarony] the exclusive right to use, publish and sell...."[68] Six years later, the U.S. Supreme Court justices visited New York and sat for a photo taken by Sarony to commemorate the 100th birthday of the U.S. federal judiciary.[69]

Copyright Owners

There is a world of difference between the treatment of copyright ownership under the 1909 statute and co-existing common law and the treatment under the Copyright Act of 1976. Prior to January 1, 1978 (the effective date of the new statute), when an author, artist, or other creator sold his or her copyright, the presumption was that all rights had been transferred unless rights were specifically reserved, usually in writing. An artist who sold her original painting to someone effectively transferred copyright ownership as well because the common law recognized that the sales of certain types of creative works invoked transfer of the copyright to the purchaser. Now the presumption works in the opposite direction. None of the exclusive rights enumerated above nor any subdivision of those rights can be legally transferred by the copyright owner unless the transfer is in writing and signed by the copyright owner or the owner's legal representative.

Under the new statute, unless a work is a "work made for hire," the copyright is immediately vested in the creator. If a work has more than one creator (i.e., joint authorship), the copyright belongs to all of them. The creator or creators can, of course, transfer their rights but the transfer of any exclusive rights must be in writing. Oral agreements are sufficient for the transfer of nonexclusive rights. For example, a freelance artist could have a valid oral agreement with an advertising agency to create a series of drawings to be used in commercials for a life insurance company. At the same time, she could have an agreement with a magazine to prepare similar illustrations for a feature story.

On the other hand, if the artist chose to transfer an exclusive right such as the sole right to reproduce the drawings or even a subdivided right such as the right to reproduce the drawings in commercials or the right to produce a derivative work such as a training film based on the drawings, she would need to make the transfer in writing for it to be binding. The sole exception to this rule is a work made for hire, which exists in two situations, as defined in Section 101:

> (1) a work prepared by an employee within the scope of his or her employment; or
> (2) a work specially ordered or commissioned for use as a contribution to a collective work, as part of a motion picture or other audiovisual work, as a translation, as a supplementary work, as a compilation, as an instructional text, as a test, as answer material for a test, or as an atlas, if the parties expressly agree in a written instrument signed by them that the work shall be considered a work made for hire.

In the case of a work made for hire, the employer is considered the author for purposes of copyright and automatically acquires all rights, exclusive and nonexclusive, unless the parties have signed an agreement to the contrary. Thus the employer effectively attains the status of creator of the work. A regular, full-time reporter for a newspaper, for instance, would have no rights to the copy she created for the paper. The newspaper would own the copyright.

On the other hand, a photo sold by a freelance photographer for use in a news story normally would not be a work made for hire unless the photographer, who is contractually an independent contractor, and the newspaper firm had signed a contract specifically stating that the photo would be a work made for hire.

NBC-TV *Tonight* host Jay Leno once caught the wrath of shock jock Howard Stern over the rights to show a tape of his show on which Stern was a guest. The shock jock had appeared three months earlier on the show with two women in bikinis who kissed on the lips while the show was taped. When the show was broadcast later, that scene was edited, and NBC refused to grant Stern the rights to re-broadcast the unedited version on his E! cable program. Even though Stern appeared on the show, NBC, not the shock jock, owned the copyright.[70]

Work Made for Hire: Community for Creative Non-Violence v. Reid *(1989)*

Freelancers create much of the copyrighted material today, and work made for hire principles play a major role in the copyright status of their creative output. Unfortunately, the 1976 law left a gaping hole on this issue because even though the statute defines dozens of terms from an "anonymous work" to a "work made for hire," there is no definition of "employer," "employee," or "scope of … employment." In 1989, however, the U.S. Supreme Court settled some perplexing questions regarding work made for hire by enunciating a clear principle for determining whether an individual is an employee. In *Community for Creative Non-Violence v. Reid* (1989),[71] in an opinion written by Justice Thurgood Marshall, the Court unanimously held:

> To determine whether a work is for hire under the Act [Copyright Act of 1976], a court must first ascertain, using principles of general common law of agency, whether the work was prepared by an employer or an independent contractor. After making this determination, the court can apply the appropriate subsection of Section 101.

The Court then indicated those factors under the general common law of agency to be applied in determining whether the hired party is an employee or an independent contractor, including:

> … the hiring party's right to control the manner and means by which the product is accomplished. Among the other factors relevant to this inquiry are the skill required; the source of the instrumentalities and tools; the location of the work; the duration of the relationship between the parties; whether the hiring party has the right to assign additional projects to the hired party; the extent of the hired party's discretion over when and how long to work; the method of payment; the hired party's role in hiring and paying assistants; whether the work is part of the regular business of the hiring party; whether the hiring party is in business; the provision of employee benefits; and the tax treatment of the hired party.… No one of these factors is determinative. [footnotes omitted][72]

Agency law deals with the relationship between two individuals or between an individual and a corporation or other entity in which the person performs a task for the other within the context of employer–employee, employer–independent contractor, or other similar relationships. The factors mentioned by the Court are among those cited by other courts in determining the relationship. Note the Court's holding that no one of these is determinative; instead all of the factors are considered as a whole in the analysis. The facts of *CCNV v. Reid* are rather interesting and provide insight into the Court's reasoning and its conclusion that sculptor James Earl Reid was an independent contractor. They also reinforce the need for written agreements in such situations.

In 1985 CCNV, a Washington, D.C. nonprofit organization for eliminating homelessness in America, reached an oral agreement with a sculptor to produce a statue with life-sized figures for display in the annual Christmas season Pageant of Peace in Washington. The original idea for the display came from association members. After negotiations over price and the materials used to make the statue, Reid and CCNV agreed to limit the cost to no more than $15,000, excluding Reid's donated services. The sculpture was made from a synthetic material to keep costs down. Reid was given a $3,000 advance. At the suggestion of a trustee of the organization,

Reid observed homeless people both at CCNV's Washington shelter and on the streets for ideas on how to portray the figures in the statue to be titled "Third World America."

Throughout November and the first half of December, Reid worked exclusively on the statue in his Baltimore studio, where he was visited by several members of the agency who checked on his progress and coordinated construction of the statue's base, which CCNV built on its own. CCNV paid Reid in installments, and he used the funds to pay a dozen or so people over time who served as assistants during the process. During their visits, CCNV representatives made suggestions about the design and construction of the sculpture, and the artist accepted most of them such as depicting the family (a man, woman, and infant) with their personal belongings in a shopping cart rather than in a suitcase, as Reid had wanted.

When Reid delivered the completed work on December 24, 1985, he received the final installment of the agreed price of $15,000. CCNV then placed the statue on its base (a steam grate) and displayed it for a month near the pageant, after which it was returned to Reid for minor repairs. Several weeks later a trustee devised plans to take the work on a fund-raising tour of several cities and the creator objected because he felt the statue would not withstand the tour. When asked that the sculpture be returned, Reid refused, registered the work in his name with the U.S. Copyright Office and announced his intentions to take the sculpture on a less ambitious tour than CCNV had planned. The trustee immediately filed copyright registration in the agency's name and CCNV then sued Reid and his photographer (who never appeared in court and claimed no interest in the work) for return of the sculpture and a decision on copyright ownership.

A U.S. District Court judge granted a preliminary injunction, ordering that the piece be returned to CCNV. (Injunctions are among the remedies available to copyright owners against infringers.) At the end of a two-day bench trial, the court decided that CCNV exclusively owned the copyright to the sculpture since it was a work made for hire under Section 101 of the Copyright Act.

According to the district court, the agency was "the motivating force" in the creation of the piece and Reid was an employee for purposes of copyright. The U.S. Court of Appeals for the District of Columbia held that Reid owned the copyright because the sculpture was not a work made for hire and thus reversed the trial court ruling and remanded the case.

According to the appellate court, "Third World America" was not a work made for hire under any of the provisions of the Copyright Act, including Section 101. Applying agency law principles, the court thus held that Reid was an independent contractor, not an employee, although the court did remand the case back to the trial court to determine whether Reid and CCNV may have been joint authors. The U.S. Supreme Court affirmed the decision of the U.S. Court of Appeals and remanded the case back to the trial court to determine whether CCNV and Reid were joint authors of the work.

Although *CCNV v. Reid* did not settle all of the questions surrounding the concept of work made for hire, it gave clearer guidance for the lower federal courts and remains one of the most important copyright cases decided by the Court since the new law took effect. At the time the case was decided, there were several conflicting lower appellate court holdings on the issue. Now it is clear that the presumption will be that a work is not a work made for hire unless a written agreement indicates the existence of the traditional employer–employee relationship. The legislative history of the 1976 Act provides strong evidence that Congress meant to establish two mutually exclusive ways for a work to acquire work made for hire status, as indicated in Section 101.

The Court also pointed out that "only enumerated categories of commissioned works may be accorded work for hire status … [and that the] … hiring party's right to control the product simply is not determinative." The Court specifically rejected an "actual control test" that CCNV argued should be determinative. Under such a test, the hiring party could claim the copyright if it closely monitored the production of the work, but the Supreme Court said this approach "would impede Congress' paramount goal in revising the 1976 Act of enhancing predictability and certainty of copyright ownership." The Court went on to note:

> … Because that test hinges on whether the hiring party has closely monitored the production process, the parties would not know until late in the process, if not until the work is completed, whether a work will ultimately fall within Section 101(1).[73]

The idea, as the Court believed Congress intended in 1976, is that it must be clear at the time a work is created who owns the copyright.

Works Not Protected by Copyright

People unfamiliar with the law wrongly assume that any creative work can be protected by copyright. While the 1976 statute is broad, certain types of works do not fall under its wings. The most obvious example is a work that has not been fixed in a tangible medium, but the Copyright Act excludes "any idea, procedure, process, system, method of operation, concept, principle, or discovery."[74] While such works have no protection in and of themselves, expressions of them can be copyrighted.

A university professor who writes a textbook based on his ideas about mass communication law and ethics, for example, cannot protect his ideas *per se*, but the expression of those ideas—a book—is copyrighted the moment it is created and put in a tangible medium. Titles, names, short phrases, slogans, familiar symbols and designs, and mere listings of ingredients and contents have no copyright protection, although these may enjoy other forms of legal protection such as trademarks. Any attorney practicing copyright law can verify one of the most common questions clients ask: "What do I need to do to copyright this great idea I have?" The shocking answer is "Sorry. You can't copyright an idea; you can only copyright the expression of that idea." After a discussion about original works of authorship, tangible media, and automatic copyright, the client usually recovers from the shock.

A 1980 Second Circuit U.S. Court of Appeals decision demonstrates how the courts divide the line between an idea and the expression of an idea. In *Hoehling v. Universal City Studios, Inc.* (1980),[75] the federal appellate court ruled that Universal had not infringed on the copyright of A. A. Hoehling's book, *Who Destroyed the Hindenburg?* in a movie about the explosion of the German dirigible at Lakehurst, New Jersey, in 1937. The film was based on a book by Michael Mooney published in 1972, 10 years after Hoehling's work.

Both books theorized that Eric Spehl, a disgruntled crew member who was among the 36 people killed in the disaster, had planted a bomb. While the 1975 movie, which was a fictionalized account of the event, used a pseudonym for Spehl, its thesis about the cause of the tragedy was similar to the theory in Hoehling's book. (Investigators concluded that the airship blew up after static electricity ignited hydrogen fuel, but speculation still abounds.)

A U.S. District Court judge issued a summary judgment in favor of Universal City Studios, and the U.S. Circuit Court of Appeals upheld the lower court's decision. According to the court:

> A grant of copyright in a published work secures for its author a limited monopoly over the expression it contains. The copyright provides a financial incentive to those who would add to the corpus of existing knowledge by creating original works. Nevertheless, the protection afforded the copyright holder has never extended to history, be it documentary fact or explanatory hypothesis. The rationale for this doctrine is that the cause of knowledge is best served when history is the common property of all, and each generation remains free to draw upon the discoveries and insights of the past. Accordingly, the scope of copyright in historical accounts in narrow indeed, embracing no more than the author's original expression of particular facts and theories already in the public domain.[76]

Hoehling claimed there were other similarities, including random duplication of phrases and the chronology of the story, but the court saw no problem with such overlap:

> … For example, all three works [Hoehling had sued the author of a second work with a similar thesis as well] contain a scene in a German beer hall, in which the airship's crew engages in revelry prior to the voyage. Other claimed similarities concern common German greetings of the period such as 'Heil Hitler,' or songs such as the German National anthem. These elements, however, are merely *scenes a faire*, that is, 'incidents, characters or settings which are as a practical matter indispensable, or at least standard, in the treatment of a given topic.' [footnote omitted][77]

Four more categories of work also lack copyright protection:

1. Any work of the United States Government, although the Government can have copyrights transferred to it by assignment, bequest or other means. State and local governments are not precluded from copyrighting works; only the federal government comes under this rule.
2. Works consisting wholly of common information having no original authorship such as standard calendars, weight and measure charts, rulers, etc. Works that contain such information can be copyrighted even though the information itself cannot be. For instance, a calendar with illustrations of herbs for each month could be copyrighted but the copyright would extend only to the illustrations and original work, not the calendar itself.
3. Public domain works, i.e., works that were never copyrighted or whose copyright duration has expired.
4. Facts.

The Copyright Act of 1976 prohibits the federal government from copyrighting works it creates, but the government can acquire copyright for works it did not create. U.S. postage stamp designs are copyrighted, as witnessed by the copyright notices in the margins of sheets and booklets, in spite of the fact that the U.S. Postal Service is a semiautonomous federal agency. Typically, the Postal Service contracts with freelance artists who design the stamps and then transfer the copyrights to the agency. Classic stamps featuring media greats Joseph Pulitzer and Edward R. Murrow, for example, require permission for their commercial use.

Most government works such as Federal Trade Commission pamphlets on fraudulent telephone schemes and U.S. Public Health Service studies on AIDS are not copyrighted. Beginning March 1, 1989 (when the United States joined the Berne Convention), publications incorporating noncopyrighted U.S. government works or portions of such works were required to carry notices indicating that such use had been made. These publications were also required to specify either (a) the portion or portions of the work that are federal government material, or (b) the portion or portions of the work for which the author is asserting copyright. Such a notice is no longer mandatory, but the U.S. Copyright Office still recommends that such a notice be posted to prevent innocent infringement.[78]

Remember that under the 1909 law, copyright protection lasted for a maximum of two terms of 28 years each for a total of 56 years. Even works copyrighted before the new law took effect had the period of protection extended, but any work that was copyrighted prior to 1903 or any work whose copyright was not timely renewed no longer has protection. Thus some works copyrighted as late as 1949 went into the public domain because no copyright renewal application was filed. For that reason you can find great prices on some old movies and television shows, including classics, at your local Wal-Mart or Target. Copyright owners simply did not bother at the time to renew the copyrights.

Once a work becomes public domain property, no royalties have to be paid and no permission needs to be sought from any owner. Usually, the copyright owners felt some works had no viable market. No videocassette recorders and no iPods were around, and it was thought that television viewers had lost interest in old films and vintage TV shows. However, copyright owners who had foresight filed applications for renewal and were amply rewarded when the VCR and cable television created a market for nostalgia.

During World War II, "Rosie the Riveter" became a famous icon for women who provided logistical support for the war by working in factories, government offices, and other settings. Two of the posters bearing the image of "Rosie" (who was actually a collection of various women—not just one woman) became particularly well known. One was created by J. Howard Miller and the other by Norman Rockwell. Rockwell copyrighted his poster but Miller did not. Guess which one has been more widely used? Miller's image, of course, because there is no charge to reproduce it.

The consequences of failing to renew a copyright were evident in a 2003 decision handed down by the U.S. Supreme Court that involved the intersection of copyright and trademark law. *Dastar Corp. v. Twentieth Century Fox Film Corp.*[79] addressed the question of whether the owner of a work whose copyright has expired has the right to sue others who copy the work once it goes into the public domain and then palm it off as their own ("reverse passing off") and whether those who do can be held liable for violating the Lanham (trademark) Act. The case arose after Dastar issued a set of videos entitled *World War II Campaigns in Europe* made from copies of a television series based on General Dwight D. Eisenhower's World War II book, *Crusade in Europe*. (Eisenhower later became U.S. President.) An affiliate of Twentieth Century Fox Film acquired exclusive television rights for the book from Doubleday, the book's publisher. In

1975 Doubleday renewed the book's copyright, but Twentieth Century Fox did not renew the copyright to the television series when it expired in 1977. The broadcast originally aired in 1949.

Later SFM Entertainment and New Line Home Video bought exclusive rights from Fox to manufacture and distribute the series on video. Dastar released its video set with no attribution or acknowledgment to Fox, SFM Entertainment, or New Line Home Video and priced it much lower than the SFM–New Line videos. The U.S. Supreme Court held that Section 43(a) of the Lanham Act, which deals with false or misleading designation of origin, did not bar "the unaccredited copying of an uncopyrighted work." According to the Court in its 8-0 decision, Dastar had simply "taken a creative work in the public domain, copied it, made modifications (arguably minor) and produced its very own series of videotapes." The Court said "origin" under the Lanham Act referred to the origin of the physical products (the tapes), not the creator of the underlying work that had been copied.[80]

Even under the 1909 statute, facts alone could not be copyrighted. The expression of facts does enjoy protection, of course. Thus while news cannot be copyrighted, newscasts can be. In *Miller v. Universal City Studios* (1981),[81] the Second U.S. Circuit Court of Appeals overturned a U.S. District Court decision that Universal had infringed the copyright of Gene Miller, a Pulitzer Prize-winning reporter for the *Miami Herald*, in a book entitled *83 Hours Till Dawn*, about Barbara Mackle. Mackle was rescued after being kidnapped and buried underground for five days in a box in which she could have survived for only a week. The trial court was impressed by the approximately 2,500 hours Miller said he had spent researching and writing the book: "To this court it doesn't square with reason or common sense to believe that Gene Miller would have undertaken the research required … if the author thought that upon completion of the book a movie producer or television network could simply come along and take the profits of the books and his research from him."[82]

Although there were several similarities between Miller's book and the script for Universal's docudrama, *The Longest Night*, including some factual errors, the appellate court ordered a new trial on the ground that "the case was presented and argued to the jury on a false premise: that the labor of research by an author is protected by copyright."[83] The court indicated that Miller had presented sufficient evidence that an infringement may have occurred but on other theories of copyright law, not on the basis of research alone.

"The valuable distinction in copyright law between facts and expression of facts cannot be maintained if research is held to be copyrightable. There is no rational basis for distinguishing between facts and the research involved in obtaining the facts,"[84] according to the Appeals Court.

In 1991 the U.S. Supreme Court attempted to clarify the concept of *originality*, which is closely linked to the facts versus compilation of facts distinction. In *Feist Publications, Inc. v. Rural Telephone Service Co.,*[85] the Court unanimously held, in an opinion by Justice O'Connor, that the white pages of a telephone directory could not be copyrighted. The case involved a telephone book publisher that used the names and telephone numbers from a telephone company's directory to compile its own area-wide telephone directories. The Court noted that while the telephone company could claim copyright ownership to the directory as a whole, it could not prevent a competitor from using its compilation of names, towns, and phone numbers to create its own directory. Facts are not copyrightable, the justices said, but compilations of facts can generally be copyrighted.

The decision stressed that hard work or "sweat of the brow" is not enough; there must be originality, which the Court characterized as the *sine qua non* of copyright. "To be sure, the requisite level of creativity is extremely low; even a slight amount will suffice," Justice O'Connor wrote. She went on to note that originality and novelty are not the same for purposes of copyright and cited the example of two poets who independently create the same poem: "Neither work is novel, yet both are original and, hence, copyrightable."

Next, a moment of silence, please. In 2002 a British composer settled out of court for £100,000 (about $180,000) with the estate of American composer John Cage, whose 1952 composition entitled *4'33"* consisted of 4 minutes and 33 seconds of silence. British composer Mike Batt had included a song entitled "A One Minute Silence" on an album for his rock band, The Planets, that was—you guessed it! —60 seconds of silence, and Batt credited the "song" to "Batt/Cage."[86] However, before a British court could rule in the case, Batt settled with the John Cage Trust, and both sides were apparently happy.

Misappropriation and Unfair Competition

Misappropriation is a broad tort that covers a variety of situations, including the commercial use of a person's name, image, or likeness. This common law creature, also known as unfair competition, has been incorporated into most state statutes and in the federal Lanham Act, the same statute that in 1947 revised trademark law. It is occasionally invoked in addition to or in lieu of a copyright infringement suit. The idea of the tort, as illustrated in the classic U.S. Supreme Court decision in *International News Service v. Associated Press* (1918)[87] is that one should not be permitted to compete unfairly through the misappropriation of the toils of another, especially by palming off another's work as one's own. Like copyright infringement, misappropriation is a form of intellectual theft but it usually does not quite approach the standards for copyright infringement.

In *INS v. AP*, the International News Service (INS) owned by the infamous "yellow journalism" publisher William Randolph Hearst, admitted pirating AP stories from early editions of AP member newspapers and from AP bulletin boards. AP claimed that INS also bribed AP employees to get stories before they were actually sent to AP newspapers. INS editors rewrote some of the stories and sent others verbatim to its own subscribers. In its defense, INS claimed that since the AP did not copyright its stories, the information was therefore in the public domain. INS also claimed that it could not get information about World War I because INS reporters had been denied access to the Allied countries as a result of Hearst's pro-German stance.

In a 7–1 decision, the U.S. Supreme Court upheld a Second Circuit Court of Appeals decision granting AP an injunction against INS's use of AP stories. The Court reasoned that while the Constitution does not grant a monopoly, even for a limited period, to the first person to communicate a news event, INS's methods were "an unauthorized interference with the normal operation [of AP's business] … precisely at the point where the profit is to be reaped."[88] The justices concluded that INS's misappropriation of AP's stories created unfair competition that could therefore be prohibited.

Copyright Duration

The term of copyright was fairly simple prior to enactment of the Copyright Act of 1976. Under the 1909 statute, copyright protection began on the day the work was published or on the date

Table 12.1 Copyright Duration in Years[89]

	Identifying Status			
	Author Named	**Pseudonym**	**Anonymous**	**Work for Hire**
Created before 1/1/78	95*	95*	95*	95*
Created after 1/1/78	Life of author + 70**	95/120***	95/120****	95/120****

*   If renewal is filed during last (28th) year of first term.
**   If more than one author, life of last surviving author plus 70 years.
***   Extends 95 years from publication or 120 years from creation, whichever comes first unless the author's real name is indicated on the copyright registration form in which case the term is the same as an "author named" work.
****   Extends 95 years from publication or 120 years from creation, whichever comes first.

it was registered if unpublished and continued for 28 years. If the copyright were renewed by filing the appropriate form and fee with the Copyright Office during the 28th year, the protection continued for another 28-year term and then the work went into the public domain. The new statute is much more generous, but the precise term of protection depends upon a number of factors including whether the work was created before, on, or after January 1, 1978, whether the work is made for hire, and the identifying status of the work. Table 12.1 is an attempt to simplify duration.

For works that had already secured federal copyright protection before January 1, 1978, an additional 19 years of protection was tacked on to the previous maximum of 56 years, assuming the copyright owner filed or files a renewal application during the last year of the first term of 28 years. In effect, this provision created a relatively easy way of equalizing duration of copyright under the 1909 law with duration under the 1976 statute. Congress could have chosen to make the periods precisely the same, but this would have made the calculations extremely difficult since the old law was not tied to an author's life and copyright protection did not begin until registration or publication.

Beginning in 1962, while Congress was debating the provisions of a long-overdue new statute to replace the 1909 one, a series of Congressional enactments extended the second term of all renewed copyrights that would have expired between September 19, 1962, and December 31, 1976.[90] Then a provision of the 1976 Act extended the period further by granting an automatic maximum of 75 years protection for copyrighted works that had already been renewed and began their second term anytime from December 31, 1976 to December 31, 1977. The extension was automatic because no additional forms had to be filed for the extension (only the renewal form for the second term).

In October 1998, in one of its last acts before adjournment, the 105th Congress passed the Sonny Bono Copyright Term Extension Act, which President Bill Clinton signed into law. The result of extensive lobbying by the Walt Disney Company, the Act granted corporations exclusive copyright of their works for 95 years, 20 years longer than the Copyright Act of 1976 had granted. It also extended the copyright of authors to lifetime plus 70 years, compared to the previous provision of lifetime plus 50 years. The European Union had already granted similar protection for its members in 1995. Congress also approved the Fairness in Music Licensing Act, supported by the National Restaurant Association, which contained a controversial provision exempting restaurants and bars smaller than 3,750 gross square feet and retail businesses of 2,000 square feet or less from paying licensing fees for background music. Larger businesses are also exempt if they use no more than four TV sets or six speakers.

Taken as a whole, the prior extensions and the Sonny Bono Copyright Term Extension Act effectively grant a maximum of 95 years of protection for all copyrighted works that had not lost copyright protection before September 19, 1962. Protection was lost, of course, if the copyrighted work had fallen into the public domain prior to that date either because of a lack of renewal or expiration of both copyright terms. Thus the only way one can safely assume that a work is not copyrighted is to check the copyright notice on the work or the date on the registration form in the copyright office and determine that it was copyrighted more than 95 years ago.

Works Created but Neither Published nor Copyrighted before January 1, 1978

Under the present law, neither publication nor registration is required for copyright but, as already noted, one of these conditions must have been met under the old statute. But what about those works that were never copyrighted but instead were filed away in a drawer or framed on Aunt Sally's wall? Because there was no effective way of establishing a date of creation for these works, Congress had to devise a different scheme for determining how long they were to be protected or even whether they could be copyrighted at all. The solution was simple, although the calculations are a bit complicated. The legislators opted to automatically protect these works, which had enjoyed common law protection in individual states but were no longer shielded by the common law since the new law explicitly nixed common law copyright.

The duration of protection for such works is computed the same way as works created on or after January 1, 1978—life of the author (or last surviving author if more than one) plus 70 years for works whose author is identified or if pseudonymous and the author's actual name is indicated on the registration form. For anonymous works and works made for hire, the protection is 95 years from publication or 120 years from creation, whichever is shorter.

Anyone or any entity, including advertisers and public relations firms, attempting to use works created prior to January 1, 1978, and not previously copyrighted through registration or publication must be very cautious because even very old works may still have copyright protection. This provision in the law is not widely known, even among media professionals. The same defenses, such as fair use, apply to these works as to newer works, but communication practitioners are sometimes lulled into making extensive use of old, unpublished, and unregistered materials on the assumption that they are in the public domain when, in fact, they may still be copyrighted.

Copyright Renewal

For works created on or after January 1, 1978, there is no renewal. When an author has been dead 70 years or for some pseudonymous and all anonymous works and works made for hire, the copyright death bell tolls after 95 or 120 years and anyone can make use of the work in any way he or she sees fit. From January 1, 1978 to June 25, 1992, the copyright also expired if the owner of a work copyrighted prior to January 1, 1978, failed to file a renewal application during the last year of the first 28-year copyright term.

However, all of this changed on June 26, 1992, when Public Law 102-307 took effect. This law, which amended Section 304(a) of the U.S. Copyright Act of 1976, automatically extended copyrights secured between January 1, 1964 and December 31, 1977, an additional 47 years, thus eliminating the need for filing a renewal application. The previous law specifically required that all renewals be filed between December 31 of the 27th year and December 31 of the 28th year of the first term. If renewal was not achieved during the one-year time frame, the work permanently lost protection. With this automatic extension granted by the 1992 law, renewal has become a moot issue. One final note: all copyright terms run to the end of the calendar year in which the copyright would otherwise expire, thus granting as much as a year of additional protection for some works. For example, a painting by an artist who died on January 1, 2007, would be copyrighted automatically until December 31, 2077.

Copyright Notice

One of the most persistent myths about copyright, perhaps due to the fact that the 1909 statutory requirements were so rigid, is that a copyright notice cannot be placed on a work unless it has been registered. Nothing could be further from the truth. The new law not only permits posting of the copyright notice on all works— registered and unregistered—but actually encourages this practice. Under the 1909 law, published works that did not bear a copyright notice were lost forever in the twilight zone of public domain. Unless they were registered, unpublished works had no federal protection anyway and thus a copyright notice was irrelevant. Until March 1, 1989, when the United States joined the Berne Convention for the Protection of Literary and Artistic Works,[91] published works were required to post correct copyright notices or risk losing protection. Even an incorrect notice subjected a work to possible loss of protection.

Copyright notice is now optional for all works published on or after March 1, 1989, although it is still highly recommended that the notice be posted anyway, as discussed shortly. Copyright notice is still mandatory for works published before March 1, 1989, although failure to include the notice or giving an incorrect notice does not automatically negate the copyright, as it did under the 1909 law. Instead, the copyright owner is permitted to take certain steps, as provided in Sections 405 and 406 of the statute, to preserve the copyright. These steps include (1) registering the work before it is published or before the omission took place or within five years after the error occurs, and (2) making a reasonable effort to post a correct notice on all subsequent copies.[92] If these steps are not followed, the work will automatically go into the public domain in the United States five years after publication. The work may continue to have protection in some other countries, depending upon their copyright provisions. Some omissions are not considered serious enough to require correction such as failing to place the notice on only a few copies, dating a notice more than a year later after the first publication, and omitting the © symbol or the word "Copyright" or the "Copr" abbreviation.

Although not mandatory for works first published on or after March 1, 1989, a copyright notice is highly recommended since it gives the world notice that the work is protected and provides useful information, including the copyright owner and year of publication, to anyone who may wish to seek permission to use the work. Providing the notice also prevents an individual or organization from claiming innocent infringement as a defense to unauthorized use. Under Section 405(b) of the Copyright Act, a person who infringes on a copyrighted work by relying innocently upon the omission of a copyright notice on a work published before March 1, 1989, cannot be held liable for actual or statutory damages before being notified by the owner of the infringement.[93] The "innocent infringer" must demonstrate that he or she was misled by the omission of notice and can still be sued for any profits from the infringement, if the court allows.

Similar provisions in the statute provide an innocent infringement defense for works first published without notice on or after March 1, 1989. Under Section 401(d) (dealing with "visually perceptible copies") and Section 402(d) ("phonorecords of sound recordings"), if the correct copyright notice appears on the copies of the work to which an infringer had access, the defendant cannot claim innocent infringement in mitigation of actual or statutory damages (except for employees of nonprofit educational institutions, libraries and archives and employees of public broadcasting entities under certain conditions). Thus it is very important that all published works carry a proper copyright notice, even though it is no longer required.

Under the 1976 statute, copyright notice has never been required for unpublished works, but unpublished works have always been permitted to carry the notice. An individual or organization cannot use the defense of innocent infringement for unauthorized use of an unpublished work. This defense is available for published works that omit the notice. Freelancers, in particular, are often hesitant about posting a notice on unpublished materials, especially those submitted for review, because they believe publishers will be offended. This is, unfortunately, a misconception. The 1976 Copyright Act was designed to offer strong protection to original works of authorship, and the creators of those works should not be reluctant to exercise their rights and to notify others of their intentions. They have nothing to lose by posting a copyright notice on all works—published and unpublished.

Proper Notice

For purposes of notice, the copyright law divides works into two categories:

1. Visually perceptible copies ("copies from which the work can be visually perceived, either directly or with the aid of a machine or device"[94])
2. Phonorecords of sound recordings[95]

The first category includes all copyrighted works except phonorecords of sound recordings. The distinction is important because the notices are different for the two. For visually perceptible the key three elements of notice are:

1. The symbol © (C encircled) or the word "Copyright" or the abbreviation "Copr"
2. The year of first publication
3. The name of the copyright owner

Examples of proper notices are:

1. © 2012 Roy L. Moore and Michael D. Murray
2. Copyright 2012 Roy L. Moore and Michael D. Murray
3. Copr. 2012 Roy L. Moore and Michael D. Murray

The first example is the one most recommended since it is the only form acceptable under the Universal Copyright Convention (UCC) of which the United States is a member. The UCC was founded in Geneva, Switzerland, in 1952 to attempt to bring international uniformity to copyright and revised its rules at a meeting in Paris in 1971 (which the United States implemented on July 10, 1974). For phonorecords of sound recordings, the notice is the same except the symbol ℗ (P encircled) is used instead of the © symbol "Copyright," or "Copr." An example is: ℗ 2012 Roy L. Moore.

If a work is unpublished, there is no mandatory form for notice since notice is not required anyway, but a recommended form is: Unpublished work © 2007 Roy L. Moore.

For works that incorporate U.S. government materials, the notice must include a statement distinguishing the author's work from the U.S. government work, if published before March 1, 1989.

Two examples are:

1. © 2012 Roy L. Moore. Copyright claimed for all information except information from U.S. government documents on pages 100–110.
2. © 2012 Roy L. Moore. Chapter 10 and photo on page 11 are U.S. government works.

Similar notices should be placed on works published after March 1, 1989, although no longer required. They are particularly useful for informing potential users which portions you are copyrighting.

Placement of Notice

The copyright statute is fairly vague about where a copyright notice should be placed, but the Copyright Office has issued regulations that are quite specific, although flexible.[96] The statute says simply that for visually perceptible copies, "The notice shall be affixed to copies in such manner and location as to give reasonable notice of the claim of copyright."[97] Congress delegated authority to prescribe regulations regarding notice to the Copyright Office in the same provision.[98] A similar provision governs phonorecords: "The notice shall be placed on the surface of the phonorecord, or on the phonorecord label or container, in such a manner and location as to give reasonable notice of the claim of copyright."[99]

Examples of conforming positions of notice in the Copyright Office regulations for books are (1) title page, (2) page immediately following the title page, (3) either side of front or back cover, and (4) first or last page of the main body of the work.[100] For collective works, only one copyright notice needs to be given, i.e., it is not necessary (although it is permissible) for each separate work to carry its own notice. Collective works include magazines, journals, encyclopedias, newspapers, and anthologies. The exception to this rule is advertising. If an advertiser wishes to comply with notice requirements, it must include a separate notice either to defeat a defense for innocent infringement or to comply with international regulations.

Copyright Infringement

The Copyright Act of 1976 has considerable teeth for punishing infringers. Chapter 5 of the Act provides a wide variety of remedies, including civil and criminal penalties and injunctions. The 1989 revision implementing the Berne Convention treaty increased the penalties even more. The statute sends a clear message that copyright infringement does not pay. An infringer is defined as "[a]nyone who violates any of the exclusive rights of the copyright owner … or who imports copies or phonorecords into the United States in violation of section 602" ("Infringing importation of copies or phonorecords").[101] The list of individuals and organizations who have been sued (many successfully) for copyright infringement reads like a *Who's Who*. Star-ware Publishing Corp. and its president were ordered by a U.S. District Court judge to pay Playboy Enterprises $1.1 million in damages for downloading photographs from a computer bulletin board and then putting them on a CD-ROM for sale. Playboy was also awarded $50,000 for trademark infringement.[102] Walt Disney Productions ordered the Very Important Babies Daycare Center in Hallandale, Florida, to remove paintings of Mickey and Minnie Mouse, Donald Duck and Goofy from its walls because of copyright infringement.[103] The characters themselves are trademarks, but their depictions, such as drawings, are copyrighted.

In 2006 a U.S. District Court judge in Philadelphia ordered Multistate Legal Studies, Inc. (MLS) to pay $12 million in damages to the National Conference of Bar Examiners (NCBE) for copying 113 questions from the Multistate Bar Exam (MBE) for use in bar exam preparation courses.[104] NCBE administers the MBE, which includes multiple-choice questions and an essay and is required for attorney licensing in most states. Most states also require their own state-oriented exams as well.

MLS admitted it had hired individuals to take the MBE and then used that information to write its own simulated exam for individuals who take its Preliminary Multistate Bar Review (PMBR) courses. The company claimed the questions in dispute constituted only 113 out of its bank of more than 3,000 questions.[105] The MBE includes 200 multiple-choice questions, of which 60 are usually from previous exams. Retired MBE questions are available for a licensing fee. The District Court judge calculated the damages based on the $16 million that PMBR earned in annual gross revenues.[106]

Among other things, the enactment of the Family Entertainment and Copyright Act of 2005 in concert with the Artists' Rights and Theft Prevention Act of 2005 prohibits the use of audiovisual recording devices to transmit or copy motion pictures or other works prior to their commercial release. This makes it clear that the bootlegging of intellectual property in the form of tapes and DVDs violates federal law.[107] But it is important to note that music and motion picture companies have used the common law tort of copyright infringement rather than relying solely on federal regulation to address the problems they faced in illegal copying and downloading and are continuing to crack down on free downloads of their intellectual property.

The music industry has aggressively challenged and won suits against illegal computer file sharing on P2P networks and also gotten injunctions to effectively close down distribution sites such as Napster. The music trade association RIAA also brought hundreds of suits against individuals downloading free music and began a massive over-the-air education campaign to let the young American public know that theft is theft, regardless of the mode of transmission, and would be aggressively prosecuted. What was once considered so obscure and primitive as to be almost a laughing matter—such as the scene in a classic episode of the TV comedy program *Seinfeld* in which Kramer videotapes a movie in a theatre so he can sell bootleg copies—is now the target of lawyers and prosecutors. These suits are increasing in frequency and complexity.[108]

In a lawsuit brought by motion picture companies against individuals who were alleged to have offered bootlegged movies online, two Virginia residents were the subjects of a suit brought by the Motion Picture Association of America. This copyright infringement lawsuit was filed along with five others in 2006 in U.S. District Court for the Central District of California. The suit named Warner Brothers Entertainment and Twentieth Century Fox Film Corp. as plaintiffs alleging that copyrighted titles of popular films such as *Napoleon Dynamite* and *Batman Returns* had been sold on the eBay Internet marketplace auction. The complaint stated that the copies were obviously counterfeit because the disks did not contain legitimate file structures and the packaging was different. At the time, a MPAA representative indicated that a total of 37 similar suits had been filed since November of 2006. Other lawsuits had been filed on behalf of MPAA members including Paramount Pictures, Sony Pictures, and Universal City Studios.[109]

Legal research firms have entered the fray. After three years of litigation, West Publishing Co. and Mead Data Central, two computerized legal research companies, agreed to a settlement in 1988 under which Mead would pay license fees to use West's case reporting scheme known as Star Pagination from West's copyrighted National Reporter System.[110] Mead, which, as indicated earlier, owned the Lexis computer research service, claimed that West's system could not be copyrighted because it lacked originality and was therefore tantamount to public property.

Even when West Publishing Co. merged with Thomson Corp. in 1996, West continued its battle to establish copyright protection for the Star Pagination system. The next year a U.S. District Court judge in New York issued a summary judgment in favor of one of West's competitors, Matthew Bender,[111] but another U.S. District Court judge—this one in West's home state of Minnesota—reaffirmed an earlier Eighth Circuit Court of Appeals decision, granting West protection for its copyright claims.[112] The Minnesota case was eventually settled with an agreement under which the other publisher, Oasis Publishing Co., was granted a license for a reasonable fee to include West's pagination system in a CD-ROM of Florida case law.[113]

Garrison Keillor, the star of National Public Radio's (NPR) *A Prairie Home Companion* and the Robert Altman film of the same name, sued the noncommercial radio network in 1988 for copyright infringement after NPR included a Keillor speech in its catalog of cassettes offered for sale. The tape contained Keillor's presentation to the National Press Club which was carried live on NPR. Keillor claimed he owned the rights to the recording and that he had never granted NPR permission to tape and distribute it. The two parties reached an out-of-court settlement in which the radio network agreed to make available 400 cassettes of the speech free to anyone who requested one.[114]

Although infringement suits usually attract little, if any, attention in the mass media except in cases involving major figures, the stakes can be quite high, especially with videotaped movies and computer software. Two motion picture industry executives, John D. Maatta of N.I.W.S. Productions (a subsidiary of Lorimar Telepictures) and Lorin Brennan of Carolco Pictures, indicate that video piracy takes two basic forms: (1) unauthorized duplication and sale in which a pirate acquires a master, makes duplicates, and then sells them, and (2) "second generation" video piracy in which a pirate forges copyright documents so it appears he or she is the legitimate owner and then goes to another country and forces the rightful owner to prove its claim of title.[115]

International Protection Against Copyright Infringement

U.S. companies are able to take criminal and civil action against infringers in other countries because of various international agreements the United States has signed and conventions treaties we have joined. However, it should be noted that there is no universal international copyright, but instead the treatment afforded works copyrighted in the United States differs considerably from country to country. One of the earliest international copyright agreements was the 1910 Buenos Aires Convention, which the United States joined in 1911 with several Latin American states, including Argentina, Bolivia, and Panama, but there are even earlier bilateral agreements such as the one made with Cuba in 1903 that is still in effect.

The two most important international copyright conventions are the Universal Copyright Convention (UCC) and the Berne Union for the Protection of Literary and Artistic Property (Berne Convention). Both have substantially simplified international copyright by bringing some consistency in international protection. The United States joined the UCC in 1955 and revisions made at a subsequent UCC in 1971 became effective here in 1974. The most sweeping changes in international copyright were wrought by the Berne Convention, which met first in Berlin in 1908 and most recently in Paris in 1971. The United States, however, did not join the convention until March 1, 1989, after 78 other nations were already members. Some of the changes caused by the federal Act implementing Berne membership were fairly substantial.

The most important impact was that the United States must treat the copyrighted works of nationals of other Berne Convention countries the same as it treats works of its own citizens, and member countries must offer at least the same protection for U.S. works as they do for those of their own citizens.[116] The result has been more U.S. firms hauling more international pirates into courts in their own countries so they can be punished. This enables them to really hit the infringers where it hurts— the pocketbook. Finally, all works created on or after March 1, 1989, by citizens of Berne Convention countries and all works first published in a Berne Convention country enjoy automatic protection in the United States. No registration or other formality is necessary.

On January 1, 1996, the International Agreement on Trade-Related Aspects on Intellectual Property Rights (TRIPS), which was part of the General Agreement on Tariffs and Trade (GATT), took effect. The agreement, which affects all members of the World Trade Organization including the United States, allows copyright protection to be automatically restored under certain conditions to works from other countries that had gone into the public domain in the United States. This restoration of copyright, for example, applies to works from countries that had no copyright agreements with the United States at the time the work was published or works that did not have the requisite copyright notice before the Berne implementation act removed that formality.

American authors have also been hauled into the courts of other countries for alleged copyright infringement. Dan Brown, author of one of the most popular novels of all time, *The Da Vinci Code*, and his publisher, Random House, were sued in a British court by two of the three authors of a 1982 nonfiction, historical book, *Holy Blood, Holy Grail*. They claimed Brown had appropriated the central theme of their book. In *Baigent v. Random House Group* (2006),[117] a London High Court of Justice judge dismissed the copyright infringement claim, ordering the plaintiffs to pay 85% of the defendants' several million dollars in legal fees. He also denied them the opportunity to appeal the decision.

Defenses to Infringement

There are seven major defenses to copyright infringement, although the first one is technically not a defense but a mitigation of damages: (a) innocent infringement, (b) consent, (c) compulsory license (for certain types of works), (d) public property, (e) statute of limitations, (f) expiration of copyright or public domain and (g) fair use. Each of the first six will be briefly explained, and then fair use will be treated in detail.

Innocent Infringement

Innocent infringement, as indicated earlier, occurs when a person uses a copyrighted work without consent upon the good faith assumption that the work is not copyrighted because the work has been publicly distributed without a copyright notice. The innocent infringer must prove that he or she was misled by the omission of such notice and can still be liable, at the court's discretion, for profits made from the infringement, although the person would not have to pay actual or statutory damages. Thus this claim, if proven, merely mitigates damages; the innocent infringer can still have to fork over any profits.

There are two major limitations to this defense. First, an individual cannot claim innocent infringement in the case of works published after March 1, 1989, the effective date of the Berne Convention Implementation Act of 1988. (The Berne Convention does not require a copyright notice on any works—published or unpublished—and thus effectively prohibits a claim of innocent infringement.) Second, innocent infringement can be claimed only for published works, not for unpublished works since a copyright notice was not required for unpublished works even before March 1, 1989.

Consent

As noted earlier, the transfer of any of the exclusive rights and any subdivision of those rights must be in writing to be effective. This means, quite simply, that consent in most cases must be written. The typical way in which a right is transferred is through a contract. The Copyright Office does not publish a model contract, but there are dozens of copyright and intellectual property handbooks—some geared to attorneys and others aimed at laypersons—that provide sample agreements. Section 205 of the 1976 Copyright Act allows, but does not require, parties to record transfer agreements in the Copyright Office.[118]

With such a recording, the individual to whom a right or rights have been transferred gains some important legal advantages. Recording serves as constructive notice[119] of the terms of the agreement to other parties if certain conditions have been met.[120] Recordation also provides a public record of the terms of the agreement and, if certain conditions are met, establishes priorities between conflicting transfers.[121] It is extremely important that recordations of transfers comply completely with the provisions in Section 205 and rules of the Copyright Office. A fee must also be paid for each document containing one title. Additional titles are extra. All transfer documents are first checked by the Copyright Office to make sure they comply with the requirements and are then catalogued and microfilmed for the public record.[122] Anyone can gain access to copies of the documents through the Copyright Office's online computer file known as COHD or by using the microfilm readers and printers in the Copyright Card Catalog in the Library of Congress in Washington, D.C.[123]

Another provision in the statute deals with terminations of transfers. Under Section 203, a copyright owner can terminate a grant of any exclusive or nonexclusive right after 35 years by notifying the individual or organization to whom the right was transferred.[124] This is an often overlooked provision that can certainly work to the advantage of a copyright owner. It applies to both works that were created on and after January 1, 1978, as well as those created before that date so long as the transfer of rights was executed on or after the date. (Of course, the work must not have already lost copyright protection.) The owner can make the termination effective any time during a 5-year period beginning at the end of 35 years from the date of execution of the transfer or from date of publication, if the transfer involves publication, to the end of 40 years from the day the transfer was effective, whichever term ends first.[125]

This special termination of transfers provision does not apply to works made for hire nor to a grant to prepare a specific derivative work.[126] Termination of transfers is another fringe benefit of the new copyright law that can be very useful, especially when a work is slow in gaining popularity. The exception regarding derivative works simply provides that where an author has granted someone the right to a particular derivative work, that right cannot be terminated if the specific derivative work has been completed before the five-year termination window. The author can, however, terminate the right of the person to any other derivative works. Thanks to this provision, in 2011 thousands of artists and songwriters began filing notices with the copyright office that they plan to request that copyrights be returned to them in 2013. The provision requires an advance notice of two years.

Compulsory License

One of the most controversial and complicated provisions of the Copyright Act of 1976 was Section 111, which provides a mechanism by which the "secondary transmission of a primary transmission embodying a performance or display of a work is not an infringement of copyright …"[127] if certain conditions are met. For example, the management of a hotel, apartment complex, or similar type of housing can retransmit the signals of local television and radio stations to the private lodgings of guests or residents if no direct charge is made so long as the secondary transmission is not done by a cable system.[128]

This is a rather complex area of copyright law that deals with cable and satellite transmissions of television programs, phonorecords, jukeboxes, and noncommercial broadcasting. The idea is that by paying a specified fee to the government, the record company or other entity such as a cable company can make use of certain copyrighted works such as songs or television signals without obtaining consent from the copyright holder. Until December 1993, the rates were set by a three-person Copyright Royalty Tribunal, which also distributed the fees (royalties) to the appropriate owners after deducting an amount for overhead. The tribunal was eliminated in 1993 and its powers transferred to ad hoc arbitration panels set up by the Librarian of Congress. The Licensing Division in the U.S. Copyright Office administers the statutory license provisions of the federal copyright statute, including collecting and distributing fees.[129]

The primary beneficiaries of the royalties generated by compulsory licensing have been program syndicators, represented principally by the Motion Picture Association of America (MPAA). This group has typically received more than two-thirds of the licensing revenue each year, but there are several other recipients, including the music industry, represented by the American Society of Composers, Authors and Publishers (ASCAP), Broadcast Music Inc. (BMI), professional and college sports associations, and National Public Radio (NPR).

Other Types of Licensing

There is one other mechanism for licensing that enables a potential user of a copyrighted work to avoid having to negotiate with individual copyright owners: the blanket license. Blanket licenses, purchased for a fee based on a percentage of a radio or television station's revenue, allow a broadcaster to publicly perform any of the music for which the licensing agency has acquired a nonexclusive right. The two primary licensing agencies in the United States are ASCAP and BMI.[130] Both organizations serve similar functions. ASCAP, a membership association of approximately 30,000 composers, authors, and publishers founded in 1914, has nonexclusive rights to more than 3 million musical compositions. BMI, a nonprofit corporation formed in 1939, has about 50,000 writer and publisher affiliates and holds nonexclusive rights to the public performance of more than one million musical compositions. Both agencies grant blanket licenses to broadcast stations so they can use any of the music licensed to the agencies without having to obtain the permission of individual copyright owners. Unlike the old law, the 1976 statute makes it clear that playing a recorded copyrighted song without consent or a license is infringement.

Thus while radio stations for many years paid no royalties when they played recorded music (which they usually obtained free from recording industry promoters anyway), they must now pay royalties even if they actually purchased the records. At one time record companies and performers were happy to have air time and therefore did not object to the scheme under which they provided free copies in return for air play.

However, many copyright owners realized they were losing considerable sums in royalties with the arrangement and successfully pushed Congress to include broadcast use under public performances protected by the new statute. Blanket licensing is an efficient mechanism for collecting the millions of dollars in royalties since individual copyright owners are not faced with the onerous task of monitoring broadcast stations around the country to catch copyright violators and then prosecute them. Instead the licensing agency can handle this. The income from the fees garnered by each agency is distributed, after a deduction for administrative expenses, to the copyright owners with whom the agency has an agreement.

Typically, the composer of a licensed song gets the same share of royalties as the publisher. A blanket license normally grants a TV station two types of rights: synchronization rights and performance rights. A "sync" right allows the licensee to copy a musical recording onto the soundtrack of a film or videotape in synchronization with action so a single work is produced. A performance right allows the station to transmit the work to the public, either live or recorded. Both ASCAP and BMI also offer a program license that grants a broadcaster the right to as many of the compositions licensed by the agency that the stations wishes on a specific program. The fee for this license is a set percent of the advertising revenue from the program.

Over the years, blanket licensing has survived a number of legal challenges, including *Buffalo Broadcasting Co. v. American Society of Composers, Authors and Publishers* (1984),[131] in which the Second Circuit U.S. Court of Appeals overturned a U.S. District Court decision that blanket licensing constituted an unlawful restraint of trade. The District Court's injunction against ASCAP and BMI to prevent them from licensing nondramatic music performance rights to local stations for syndicated programming was also lifted by the Court of Appeals. On further appeal, the U.S. Supreme Court denied certiorari.[132]

Broadcasters are not the only ones affected by licensing. In 1982, the Second Circuit U.S. Court of Appeals held that Gap clothing stores could be enjoined for copyright infringement for playing copyrighted music without a license.[133] The company retransmitted a radio station's signal over speaker systems to customers in its stores. There are dozens of music services such as Muzak, Super Radio, and the Instore Satellite Network that offer stores and other public facilities audio services. Most are delivered via satellite and are unscrambled, but they cannot be broadcast without consent, which involves paying a monthly fee with the proceeds shared with owners of the copyrighted music, including composers and publishers. An office, store, or other business (whether for-profit or nonprofit) does not have the right to rebroadcast radio signals even if they are from a local commercial or noncommercial station because the station's blanket license covers only the original broadcast, not any other "public performance." A secretary who listens to a favorite country and western station at the office each day is not engaging in copyright infringement, but a metropolitan newspaper that retransmits the local top 40 station to its 50 individual offices in the building without consent is likely in violation.

Finally, it is no secret that ASCAP, BMI, and other licensing agencies routinely monitor radio and television stations and visit restaurants, bars, department stores, and other public facilities to spot potential copyright infringers who are usually warned and threatened with a lawsuit if they do not halt infringement or obtain a blanket or other appropriate license. Millions of dollars are at stake, and the copyright law provides writers, artists, performers, composers, and publishers with powerful tools of enforcement, as indicated below. Licensing agencies are merely acting on behalf of their members or affiliates in aggressively pursuing infringers.

Public Property

Certain kinds of works are considered public property because they have no original authorship and, as such, cannot be copyrighted. These include "standard calendars, height and weight charts, tape measures and rulers, and lists or tables taken from public documents or other common sources."[134] Public property also includes works created by the federal government, as noted earlier, but bear in mind that the U.S. government can have copyrights transferred to it by individuals who are not regular government employees.

Although not required because of the Berne Convention, a copyright notice will usually be posted on those works for which the government is claiming copyright under a transfer, but the government usually does not include a notice on noncopyrighted works to inform the reader that the work is in the public domain. Instead, the idea of the government appears to be that it is not necessary to inform the public that a particular government work can be used without consent. U.S. government bookstores such as the main store in Washington, D.C. carry thousands of noncopyrighted government works for sale ranging from Congressional reports to wildlife posters that can be reproduced without consent. Most of the materials are printed by the U.S. Government Printing Office.

Statute of Limitations

The statute of limitations for both criminal and civil violations of copyright is three years. According to Section 507, "No criminal proceeding shall be maintained … unless it is commenced within three years after the cause of action arose"[138] and "No civil action shall be maintained … unless it is commenced within three years after the claim accrued."[139] Thus a plaintiff has a fairly lengthy period in which to file an infringement suit against an alleged offender, and the federal government (usually the Federal Bureau of Investigation) must file any criminal charges against an alleged infringer within the three years.

If such actions are not initiated within that time, the statute of limitations imposes a complete bar, no matter how serious or extensive the infringement. For example, an unscrupulous writer who uses another writer's chapter without consent in his book published in January 2002 could be sued anytime until January 2005 for the initial publication. However, if he continues to publish the book with the pirated chapter, he can still be held liable in February 2011 for a book he permitted to be sold in March 2000 even though the initial infringement occurred more than three years earlier. Thus each publication, sale, etc., constitutes a separate and new infringement. Because the statute of limitations is relatively long, it is rarely used as a defense to either criminal or civil infringement.

Expiration of Copyright

In 1893 Patty Smith Hill and her sister, Mildred J. Hill, two kindergarten and Sunday school teachers from Louisville, Kentucky, composed a melody whose lyrics later become the famous song, "Happy Birthday to You."[140] The song was not published and copyrighted, however, until 1935. In 1988 the Sengstack family of Princeton, New Jersey, which for 50 years had owned Birchtree Ltd., the company that owned the copyright to the song,[141] sold the company along with the rights to "Happy Birthday to You" to Warner Chappell (a division of Warner Communications, Inc. and the largest music publisher in the world) for a reported $25 million.[142] Why did Warner want the copyright to the song? According to the *Guinness Book of World Records*, it is one of the three most popular songs in the English language, along with "Auld Lang Syne" and "For He's a Jolly Good Fellow."[143]

The good news is that the song garners royalties of about $1 million a year, but the bad news is that it became a public domain work in 2010 when its 75-year-old copyright expired. The other two popular songs are already in the public domain because their copyrights have long expired. "Happy Birthday to You" lives on. Interestingly, the Sengstack family sold the copyright reportedly because Birchtree did not have the resources to aggressively protect the copyright and market the song.[144]

Until the song attracted attention with its sale, most people assumed that it was not copyrighted. Every day the song is sung at thousands of birthday parties and no royalty is paid since it would be difficult to enforce the copyright in those situations, but when the song is sung on television or radio or its lyrics appear in an advertisement, a royalty is due and chances are very good that it is paid since Warner rightfully protects the songs for which it owns the copyright. It is essential that anyone, including journalists, make absolutely sure that a work's copyright has expired before assuming that it is in the public domain and making use of the work without consent. Once a copyright expires, a work remains in the public domain forever, but copyright duration under the new law is extensive, both for works that were copyrighted before the statute took effect and those created on or after January 1, 1978.

Fair Use

Fair use is the one defense to copyright infringement with which most people are familiar. Unfortunately, it is also the most misunderstood concept about copyright, as the various myths about fair use can attest. **Myth one**: If less than 10% of a work is used, that's fair use. **The**

truth: There is no specified amount, either in the statute or in case law. **Myth two**: If you acknowledge (i.e., give credit) when you include excerpts from another's work, that's fair use and no consent need to be obtained. **The truth**: Fair use has nothing to do with whether you give credit. In fact, as noted above, when you acknowledge using the other person's work, you are, in a sense, admitting possible infringement if you do not have a legitimate defense.

Myth three: If the use would seem fair to a reasonable person, then it's fair use. **The truth**: If you have a "gut feeling" that what you are doing is unfair or wrong, you are probably treading on dangerous ground and committing infringement. But, on the other hand, if you feel comfortable, your actions still may not be fair use. For example, many people see nothing wrong with burning a compact disc if they already own it. Under the statute, this is not permissible as fair use, and even though one's chances of being sued in such a case are virtually nil during home use, the act is, nevertheless, infringement.

A final myth: Fair use is a First Amendment right. **The truth**: Nothing could be further from the truth. Fair use has always been a common law creature that was given federal statutory life only in 1978 when the new law took effect. Interestingly, the courts, including the U.S. Supreme Court, in recent years have either ignored or dismissed claims of First Amendment or other Constitutional protection by defendants in fair use cases. **The moral**: Use the statute as a "fair use" shield, but do not expect the First Amendment to save you when you have used copyrighted material without consent.

What Is Fair Use?

Congress included dozens of definitions in the Copyright Act of 1976 from "anonymous work" to "widow" and "widower," but fair use is deliberately not among them because the legislators had difficulty defining the concept, as indicated in a 1976 report of the House of Representatives Judiciary Committee:

> The judicial doctrine of fair use, one of the most important and well-established limitations on the exclusive right of copyright owners, would be given express statutory recognition for the first time in section 107. The claim that a defendant's acts constituted a fair use rather than an infringement has been raised as a defense in innumerable copyright actions over the years, and there is ample case law recognizing the existence of the doctrine and applying it … Although the courts have considered and ruled upon the fair use doctrine over and over again, no real definition of the concept has ever emerged. Indeed, since the doctrine is an equitable rule of reason, no generally applicable definition is possible, and each case raising the question must be decided on its own facts.[145]

Thus Congress chose instead to incorporate into Section 107 four criteria that had evolved from the courts in determining fair use:

> … In determining whether the use made of a work in a particular case is fair use the factors to be considered shall include (1) the purpose and character of the use, including whether such use is of a commercial nature or is for nonprofit educational purposes; (2) the nature of the copyrighted work; (3) the amount and substantiality of the portion used in relation to the copyrighted work as a whole; and (4) the effect of the use upon the potential market for or value of the copyrighted work.[146]

Section 107 mentions specific examples of purposes that can involve fair use, including "criticism, comment, news reporting, teaching (including multiple copies for classroom use), scholarship, or research."[147]

While it is not part of the statute and it cannot be used to definitively determine the intent of Congress in enacting the Copyright Act, the House Report gives an indication of the law's purpose. The statement of the fair use doctrine in Section 107 offers some guidance to users in determining when the principles of the doctrine apply. However, the endless variety of situations and combinations of circumstances that can arise in particular cases precludes the formulation of exact rules in the statute. The bill endorses the purpose and general scope of the judicial doctrine of fair use, but there is no disposition to freeze the doctrine in the statute, especially during a period of rapid technological change. Beyond a very broad statutory explanation of what fair use is and some of the criteria applicable to it, the courts must be free to adapt the doctrine to particular situations on a case-by-case basis. Section 107 is intended to restate the present judicial doctrine of fair use, not to change, narrow, or enlarge it in any way.[148]

Thus Congress chose to establish broad guidelines and trust the courts to determine on a case-by-case basis what is and is not fair use, and that is exactly what the courts have done, occasionally even revealing gaps in the statute. There have been hundreds of court decisions dealing with fair use, both under the 1909 statute and the 1976 one, but this section will focus on those that have had a major impact and/or illustrate important aspects of the concept. Each of the four factors is important, but none is, by itself, determinative. Instead, the courts evaluate each situation in light of all four and attempt to strike a balance among them, as illustrated in a 1968 decision by a U.S. District Court in New York. In *Time, Inc. v. Bernard Geis Associates*,[149] the federal trial court ruled that the author and publisher of a book containing charcoal sketches of frames from the famous copyrighted Zapruder film of President John F. Kennedy's assassination constituted fair use. When Kennedy was killed on November 22, 1963, amateur photographer Abraham Zapruder took color 8mm moving pictures of the shooting. Zapruder had three copies made, of which two were given to the U.S. Secret Service with the understanding that they would not be made public but used only for the government's investigation. He then signed a contract with *Life* under which the magazine acquired ownership of all three copies for $150,000. *Life* subsequently published individual frames of the film in various issues but did not register its copyright until 1967, although the magazine issues in which the frames appeared had already been registered.

Bernard Geis Associates negotiated unsuccessfully with Time, Inc. (the publisher of *Life*) for the right to publish several frames from the Zapruder film in a book, *Six Seconds in Dallas*, by Josiah Thomas.[150] After being denied the right, Thomas and the publisher hired a professional artist to draw charcoal sketches of the frames, 22 of which appeared in the book when it was published in late 1967. Time, Inc. sued for copyright infringement, and Bernard Geis claimed fair use as a defense and that *Life* had no valid copyright in the film. A U.S. District Court judge balanced each of the four factors (listed above) and issued a summary judgment in favor of Bernard Geis Associates. Judge Wyatt determined that Time, Inc. had a valid copyright but the book had made fair use of the film and therefore had not infringed:

> There is a public interest in having the fullest information available on the murder of President Kennedy. Thomas conducted serious work on the subject and has a theory entitled to public consideration. While doubtless the theory could be explained with sketches of the type used at page 87 of the Book and in The *Saturday Evening Post*, the

explanation actually made in the Book with copies is easier to understand. The Book is not bought because it contained the Zapruder pictures; the Book is bought because of the theory of Thomas and its explanation, supported by Zapruder pictures. There seems little, if any, injury to plaintiff, the copyright owner. There is no competition between plaintiff and defendants. Plaintiff does not sell the Zapruder pictures as such and no market for the copyrighted work appears to be affected. Defendants do not publish a magazine. There are projects for use by plaintiff of the film in the future as a motion picture or in books, but the effect of the use of certain frames in the Book on such projects is speculative. It seems more reasonable to speculate that the Book would, if anything, enhance the value of the copyrighted work; it is difficult to see any decrease in its value.[151]

While this case was decided prior to the 1976 statute, it illustrates well how courts balance the factors. Notice that the court was particularly concerned about factor four—the effect of the use upon the potential market for or value of the copyrighted work. The judge made it clear that the two parties were not in competition; indeed the book could even increase the value of the film. He also weighed the public interest served in line with factor one. In another part of the decision, the Court noted that while Thomas had made "deliberate appropriation in the book, in defiance of the copyright owner, it was not the night-time activities of Thomas that enabled defendants to reproduce Zapruder frames in the book. They could have secured such frames from the National Archives, or they could have used the reproductions in the Warren Report or in the issues of *Life* itself."[152]

In 1997 the Assassination Records Review Board, a federal board, officially ruled 5 to 0 that the Zapruder film permanently belonged to the American people. This action meant that the Zapruder family would have to turn over the film to the federal government by August 1, 1998. The action is similar to a government agency declaring eminent domain over a piece of land to build a highway. The Zapruders had to be compensated for the film, just as the government would compensate a property owner for taking the person's land. According to press reports, the family had earned almost $1 million over the years from selling reproduction rights.[153] Copies are now available from the government.

In 1985 the U.S. Supreme Court issued an important fair use decision. In *Harper & Row v. Nation Enterprises*[154] the Court held in a 6–3 decision written by Justice Sandra Day O'Connor that *Nation* magazine had infringed the copyright jointly owned by Harper & Row and Reader's Digest Association to the unpublished memoirs of former President Gerald Ford.

Shortly after he left office, Gerald Ford signed a contract with Harper & Row and *Reader's Digest* to publish his then-unwritten autobiography. Ford granted the two publishers the right to publish the manuscript in book form and as a serial ("first serial rights"). They later sold *Time* magazine the exclusive right to excerpt 7,500 words from Ford's account of his pardon of former President Richard M. Nixon for any crimes connected with the 1972 attempted burglary by Nixon operatives of the Democratic campaign headquarters at the Watergate office building in Washington, D.C. (Nixon was forced to resign from the presidency as a result of his involvement in the cover-up of the burglary.) The contract with *Time* included provisions that the magazine would be allowed to publish the excerpt approximately one week before the book would be shipped to bookstores and that *Time* retained the right to renegotiate part of its payment if the material in the book were published before the excerpt. However, in March 1979 an unidentified source furnished the editor of the *Nation*, a monthly political magazine, with a copy of the unpublished manuscript, *A Time to Heal: The Autobiography of Gerald R. Ford*.

Before *Time* could publish its excerpt the next month, the *Nation* carried a 2,250 word feature that included verbatim quotes of 300 to 400 words from the original manuscript. These quotes, according to the Court, comprised about 13% of the *Nation* article, and the editor made no independent commentary nor did any independent research because, as he admitted at trial, he wanted to scoop *Time*. *Time* thus decided not to publish its excerpt and refused to pay Harper & Row and Reader's Digest Association the remaining $12,500 of the $25,000 it had agreed to pay for the prepublication rights. Harper & Row and Reader's Digest then filed suit against the *Nation* for copyright infringement. The U.S. District Court for the Southern District of New York ruled against the *Nation* in its defense of fair use and awarded the plaintiffs $12,500 in actual damages for copyright infringement. However, the Second Circuit U.S. Court of Appeals reversed, holding that while the memoirs were copyrighted, the *Nation*'s disclosure of the information was "politically significant" and newsworthy and thus fair use. The U.S. Supreme Court disagreed with the lower appellate court. The Court analyzed the case in light of each of the four factors but paid particular attention to the fourth factor:

> In evaluating character and purpose [factor one] we cannot ignore the *Nation's* stated purpose of scooping the forthcoming hardcover and *Time* abstracts. The *Nation*'s use had not merely the incidental effect but the intended purpose of supplanting the copyright holder's commercially valuable right of first publication.... The fact that a work is unpublished is a critical element of its "nature." [citations omitted] Our prior discussion establishes that the scope of fair use is narrower with respect to unpublished works. While even substantial quotations might qualify as fair use in a review of a published work or a news account of a speech that had been delivered to the public or disseminated to the press.... the author's right to control the first public appearance of his expression weighs against such use of the work before its release. The right of first publication encompasses not only the choice whether to publish at all, but also the choices when, where and in what form first to publish a work.[155]

On the third factor (amount and substantiality), the Court noted that while "the words actually quoted were an insubstantial portion" of the book, the *Nation*, as the District Court said, "took what was essentially the heart of the book."[156] The Court cited the *Nation* editor's own testimony at trial as evidence that he selected the passages he ultimately published "precisely because they qualitatively embodied Ford's distinctive expression."[157]

On the last factor (effect of the use on the potential market), the Court was particularly critical of the *Nation's* action and its impact. Noting that this factor "is undoubtedly the single most important element of fair use," the majority pointed to the trial court's finding of an actual effect on the market, not simply a potential effect:

> ... *Time's* cancellation of its projected serialization and its refusal to pay the $12,500 were the direct result of the infringement... Rarely will a case of copyright infringement present such clear cut evidence of actual damage. Petitioners [Harper & Row and Reader's Digest] assured *Time* that there would be no other authorized publication of any portion of the unpublished manuscript prior to April 23, 1979.[158]

The justices went on to contend, "Placed in a broader perspective, a fair use doctrine that permits extensive prepublication quotations from an unreleased manuscript without the copyright owner's consent poses substantial potential for damage to the marketability of first serialization rights in general."[159] Thus *Harper & Row v. Nation Enterprises* has typically been classified as an "unpublished works" case, but at least one copyright expert viewed the holding "is more properly understood as an attempt by the Court to protect the right of authors to choose the timing of the first publication of their soon-to-be-published works."[160]

Three major points emerge from this decision. First, a defense of fair use is less likely to succeed in the case of an unpublished work than with a published work. Would the *Nation* have won if all the circumstances had been the same except that the extensive excerpt from Ford's memoirs had already appeared in *Time*? What if both the book and the *Time* excerpt had already been published? The Court apparently assumed that the manuscript had been purloined, even though the *Nation* editor himself had apparently not been directly involved. This allegation hurt the magazine's claim that the information was in the public interest.

As the Court iterated, the book took two years to produce, including hundreds of taped interviews that had to be distilled into a single work. If one were allowed to profit from taking another's work under these circumstances, the Court felt authors would be discouraged from creating original works, thereby depriving the public of important historical information. In other words, if a writer faces the risk that his or her work will garner no rewards such as royalties, that person is unlikely to be interested in conducting the research and making the effort to produce work that might ultimately add to public knowledge.

The Court was also concerned that offering protection for *Nation* in this case would establish a precedent in which the defense of fair use would be broadened so much that it would "effectively destroy any expectation in the work of a public figure."[161]

The principles established in *Harper & Row v. Nation Enterprises* played a major role two years later in an important copyright decision by the Second Circuit U.S. Court of Appeals. In *Salinger v. Random House* (1987),[162] the federal appellate court granted an injunction sought by reclusive writer J.D. Salinger (author of the classic novel, *The Catcher in the Rye*) against publication of Ian Hamilton's unauthorized biography, *J.D. Salinger: A Writing Life*. Hamilton made extensive use of information, including direct quotes, he had obtained from some 70 copyrighted letters Salinger had sent to various individuals who had, in turn, donated them to several university libraries. Although the biographer had substantially altered the book before it went to press after complaints from Salinger, the writer was not satisfied and filed suit for copyright infringement. The U.S. District Court sided with Hamilton and refused to issue the injunction (one of the remedies available for infringement) because it felt most of the material used from the letters was protected by fair use since it consisted primarily of Salinger's ideas expressed in Hamilton's words rather than from quotes of Salinger.

The U.S. Court of Appeals reversed, holding that Hamilton was not protected by fair use and that, under *Harper & Row v. Nation*, unpublished works "normally enjoy complete protection against copying any protected expression."[163] According to the appellate court, "Public awareness of the expressive content of the letters will have to await either Salinger's decision to publish or the expiration of his copyright."[164] Interestingly, Salinger indicated that he had no intentions of publishing the letters, but since he wrote them, the copyright belonged to him, not the recipients. Thus he had every right to halt publication of their content, in the eyes of the court. The U.S. Supreme Court denied certiorari in the case.

Two years later, the Second Circuit tackled the fair use issue once again in a case that has particularly troubled many First Amendment experts, not because of its outcome but because of the court's opinion. In *New Era Publications International v. Henry Holt & Co.*,[165] the Court of Appeals affirmed a U.S. District Court decision not to grant an injunction against publication of a highly critical and unauthorized biography of the controversial L. Ron Hubbard, founder of the Church of Scientology. Applying the principles established in *Salinger v. Random House*, District Court Judge Pierre N. Leval had ruled that Russell Miller's *Bare-Faced Messiah: The True Story of L. Ron Hubbard* had infringed on the copyrights held by New Era Publications to Hubbard's writings because "there is a body of material of small, but more than negligible size, which, given the strong presumption against fair use of unpublished material, cannot be held to pass the fair use test."[166] However, Judge Leval ruled an injunction was not appropriate. First Amendment concerns about prior restraint outweighed the copyright owner's interests in the case and New Era could still seek damages (another infringement remedy).

The Second Circuit Court upheld the trial court decision but on the ground of *laches*, not fair use. Laches is the equitable doctrine that when a party unreasonably delays asserting a right or a claim to the detriment of the other party, its request will be dismissed. New Era had failed to make any effort to protect its copyrights until the biography was published even though it had clearly been aware for several years that Miller's work was underway. "The prejudice suffered by Holt as a result of New Era's unreasonable and inexcusable delay in bringing action invokes the bar of laches."[167] Miller had gathered most of his information about Hubbard from court documents, interviews with Hubbard acquaintances, news stories, and Hubbard's own writings, including letters and diaries.

The appellate court particularly noted its displeasure with the U.S. District Court Judge's analysis, especially his First Amendment concerns. "We are not persuaded … that any First Amendment concerns not accommodated by the Copyright Act are implicated in this action."[168] The U.S. Court of Appeals felt that the biography was a more serious infringement than the trial court had claimed. Henry Holt filed a request for rehearing on the issue of fair use in the case even though it had won on the laches ground, but the appellate court rejected the request in a sharply divided 7 to 5 opinion.[169]

One year later, the same appellate court in another fair use case involving another unauthorized biography of L. Ron Hubbard overturned a U.S. District Court injunction against publication of Jonathan Caven-Atack's *A Piece of Blue Sky: Scientology, Dianetics and L. Ron Hubbard Exposed*. In *New Era Publications International v. Carol Publishing Group*,[170] the Second Circuit U.S. Court of Appeals ruled in favor of Carol Publishing (which had published the biography) on all four of the fair use factors. The appellate court felt the materials used in the work were particularly protected because they had been taken from dozens of published works rather than Hubbard's unpublished writings.

The court noted that the works were factual and that the scope of fair use is greater for factual than nonfactual writing and that the materials used in the biography were neither qualitatively nor quantitatively substantial. Finally, the court said that while the book was intended to make profits and that it might "discourage potential purchasers of the authorized biography [which New Era planned to publish], this is not necessarily actionable under the copyright laws … Harm to the market for a copyrighted work or its derivatives caused by a 'devastating critique' that 'diminished sales by convincing the public that the original work was of poor quality' is not 'within the scope of copyright protection.'" [citations omitted][171] While the last decision provided comfort for biographers and others who use primarily published materials, the earlier decisions continue to haunt those who want to use unpublished documents.

The aftermath of the *Salinger v. Random House* and *New Era Publications v. Holt* decisions, according to one news account, was self-censorship by book publishers with "the authors themselves try[ing] to figure out history in a straitjacket."[172] While Second Circuit opinions are binding only on federal courts in Vermont, Connecticut, and New York, the opinions have traditionally been very influential on courts in other circuits. The U.S. Supreme Court denied certiorari in both cases. In the meantime, researchers can be expected to exercise care in using unpublished materials, including those of public figures, even when the information is readily accessible to the public in libraries and other places. *Harper & Row v. Nation* may have opened a can of worms that will haunt or at least chill the dissemination of information based on unpublished materials used without the consent of the author or other copyright owner. In 1992 President George H. W. Bush signed legislation that amended Section 107 of the Copyright Act to include: "The fact that such a work is unpublished shall not itself bar a finding of fair use if such finding is made upon consideration of the above factors."[173] Had this provision been in effect at the time the Copyright Act of 1976 took effect, *Salinger* and similar cases may well have been decided differently.

There have been many occasions in which literary works have been at the basis of contentious legal battles when the estate of a major artist has maintained control over a particular work. For example, Stanford Professor Carol Loeb Shloss with the support of the Center for the Internet and Society—also situated at Stanford Law School—fought a protracted legal battle over James Joyce's literary masterpiece *Ulysses*. The Stanford professor wanted to write a book about Joyce's family and sought the use of quotes from letters exchanged between family members, particularly Lucia Joyce—the subject of Shloss' book, and daughter of James Joyce. The remaining heir of the Joyce estate, Stephen Joyce, nixed that idea. Since he controls his grandfather's work until 2012, Professor Schloss filed suit, taking the position that under fair use, as a form of commentary and criticism, she did not need Stephen Joyce's permission to use the quotes.[174] But when her book, *Lucia Joyce: To Dance in the Wake,* was published in 2003, her publisher, Farrar, Straus & Giroux, deleted material to avoid a conflict with the copyright owner. Schloss argued that the evidence to support some of her book's claims was deleted. The case raises many questions about protracted ownership and access that have yet to be resolved.

In another test case of fair use in 1992, *American Geophysical Union v. Texaco,*[175] U.S. District Court Judge Pierre N. Leval ruled that it was not fair under Section 107 when a Texaco scientist made single copies of articles from the *Journal of Catalysis.* The parties in the case, Texaco (as defendant) and American Geophysical Union and 82 other publishers of scientific and technical journals (as plaintiffs), agreed in advance to a limited-issue bench (nonjury) trial. Both sides stipulated that the scope of the trial would be limited to the photocopying of eight articles by the one scientist from the one journal.

According to the testimony at trial, Texaco scientists, including one whose name was drawn at random for the case, routinely had the company library make single copies of articles from journals to which the company subscribes. The advantages of this approach include permitting the workers to keep easily referenced files in their desks or on office shelves, eliminating the risks of errors when data are transcribed from articles and taken back to lab, making it possible for them to take articles home to read. The judge held this was not fair use and was thus an infringement because (a) Texaco's use was for commercial gain, (b) substantial portions of the works were copied, and (c) Texaco's use deprived the copyright holder of potential royalties. One solution suggested by the judge was for the company to obtain clearance from the non-profit Copyright Clearance Center, which grants blanket advanced permission to photocopy for a specified fee.

In 1994 the Second Circuit U.S. Court of Appeals in an interlocutory appeal[176] from the district court upheld the trial court's decision but with somewhat different reasoning.[177] The appellate court held that three of the four fair use factors, including the purpose and character of use (first factor) and the fourth factor (effect upon potential market and value), favored the publisher. The majority opinion disagreed with a dissenting opinion filed by a Circuit Judge, who contended that the majority's ruling would require that an intellectual property lawyer be posted at each photocopy machine. As the majority saw it, all Texaco had to do in the circumstances of the case was to take advantage of existing licensing schemes or work out one on its own. A year later, the Second Circuit amended its ruling to note that its decision was limited to the specific question of whether photocopying by the company's 400 or 500 scientists was fair use.

According to the court, "We do not deal with the question of copying by an individual, for personal use in research or otherwise, recognizing that under fair use doctrine or the *de minimis* doctrine, such a practice by an individual might well not constitute an infringement."[178] The message the appellate court seemed to be sending is that photocopying on an individual basis for research would not ordinarily constitute copyright infringement. The problem in this case was that Texaco had a policy of encouraging photocopying—at least single copies—by scientists as a group, which meant there was the potential for hundreds of copies of the articles, presumably depriving the publishers of potential royalties. Keep in mind that Texaco had legal journal subscriptions, but that it is a commercial enterprise.

Because of the nature of the work conducted at the nation's colleges and universities, intellectual property concerns are always very high on the list of issues under regular scrutiny. There are extensive lists of breaches of security involving intellectual property by privacy and cyber-security organizations involving educational institutions due to their aggressive collection of student data involving such obvious areas as grades and other academic records but also covering issues such as online purchases by students and alumni. By the same token, academic institutions tend to be more willing than businesses to report online theft.[179]

Two major court decisions have had particularly important impacts on the use of copyrighted materials in higher education. On March 28, 1991, U.S. District Court Judge Constance Baker Motley of the Southern District of New York issued a decision that has had a major effect on how colleges and universities use copyrighted materials in the classroom. In *Basic Books, Inc. v. Kinko's Graphics Corp.*,[180] the federal trial court judge soundly rejected Kinko's claim that the fair use doctrine permitted it to photocopy, without consent, anthologies of copyrighted materials as part of its Professor Publishing program under which the firm photocopied journal articles, book chapters, and other copyrighted materials selected by university instructors as readings for classes. These anthologies were then sold for profit to students. The suit was filed in April 1989 by eight publishers who said two of the stores owned by the graphics company had engaged in copyright infringement by photocopying substantial portions of 12 books for use at New York University, Columbia University, and the New School for Social Research. Neither the schools nor the professors involved were named as defendants.[181]

In her 57-page opinion, Judge Motley held that Kinko's had intentionally violated the copyright statute and ordered the chain to pay $510,000 in actual damages as well as the plaintiffs' court costs and attorneys' fees. She also issued an injunction barring the company from photocopying and selling copies of copyrighted materials without obtaining the consent of copyright owners and paying requested royalties. As a result, Kinko's changed its Professor Publishing program policies to comply with the court order, including obtaining permission for photocopying any copyrighted material from the copyright owner or requiring a professor to obtain permission even when he or she believes the photocopying to be protected under fair use.[182] Kinko's eventually got out of the business of producing course packets.

Copyright claims have been further complicated by the digital role developed in the new millennium by libraries scanning their collections against the backdrop of two lawsuits by groups of publishers and authors. A book digitization project initiated by the massive search engine Google was subject to negotiations in August 2006 with the University of California system that would provide access to its collection of over 30 million books. That agreement provided for the scanning along with what would join those library holdings of the University of Michigan, as well as Harvard, Stanford, and Oxford Universities. At about that same time, the University of California system and thirty other universities were also involved in another mass digitization project involving Yahoo and Microsoft. This last agreement was publicly negotiated on behalf of the Open Content Alliance (OCA) using an open-source model in which all copyright holders would have an individual say as to whether their works could be scanned.[183]

In other litigation involving higher education and new technology, Blackboard, Inc. sued a rival, Desire2Learn Inc., over alleged patent infringement. A debate ensued about whether Blackboard's patent was overly broad in covering course management and course content via e-learning and thus allegedly stifling competition among commercial providers, a claim that Blackboard, Inc. firmly rejected. Blackboard also indicated at that time that its objective was not to target colleges and universities, some of which had online education services and content management software running for some time.[184]

In 1986, a U.S. District Court judge in California granted summary judgment for the University of California, Los Angeles, in a copyright infringement suit filed against the university by BV Engineering, a computer software company based in California. The company asked for $70,000 in damages from UCLA for allegedly making unauthorized copies of seven computer programs and user manuals for which BV Engineering owned the copyright. The federal trial court judge ruled that the 11th Amendment to the U.S. Constitution barred state-supported institutions from being successfully sued under federal laws, including the Copyright Act of 1976, unless Congress specifically allowed such litigation or the state has explicitly waived its immunity.[185]

In *BV Engineering v. University of California at Los Angeles* (1988),[186] the Ninth Circuit U.S. Court of Appeals upheld the lower court decision, and in 1989, the U.S. Supreme Court denied certiorari. Because the case simply pointed to a gap in the 1976 statute, Congress quickly revised the federal copyright statute with little opposition. Even universities supported the bill because they too own copyrights that they protect from infringement by state agencies.

The impact of the case was rather minimal even before the new law because the court's holding did not exempt individual professors from being held liable nor did it prevent a copyright owner from seeking an injunction against a state agency for infringement. The decision merely barred BV Engineering from obtaining damages, thanks to an oversight by Congress.

Under the revision, effective November 15, 1990,[187] the definition of "anyone" for purposes of infringement now includes "any State, any instrumentality of a State, and any officer or employee of a State or instrumentality of a State acting in his or her official capacity."[188]

The Act makes it clear that any state, instrumentality, officer, or employee of a state acting in official capacity shall not be immune under the Eleventh Amendment of the Constitution of the United States or under any other doctrine of sovereign immunity from suit in federal court for copyright infringement.[189] The revised statute also preserved the same remedies, including actual and statutory damages for infringement available to nongovernmental entities.[190] The net effect of that law was to put state governments in the same position as everyone else (except the federal government) for purposes of copyright infringement.

Section 107 of the 1976 statute specifically mentions criticism, comment, and news reporting as purposes that can be considered fair use, but, as the courts have made clear, these uses do not always enjoy protection in an infringement suit. A U.S. District Court Judge in Atlanta awarded WSB-TV· $108,000 plus attorneys' fees and court costs against TV News Clips for videotaping portions of the station's local newscasts and selling them to the public in 1991.[191] The court also issued a permanent injunction barring the company from making any further copies of newscasts or offering them for sale. The news clips service charged clients $65 for the first program and $30 each for additional programs. The same company was earlier ordered to pay $35 in damages to another Atlanta station, WXIA-TV,[192] which eventually obtained an injunction prohibiting the service from making copies of the station's newscasts.[193]

In 1991 several Los Angeles police were indicted for assault and other charges for allegedly beating or failing to stop the beating of an area motorist pulled over for speeding. George Holliday, an amateur photographer, videotaped the beating from his apartment window. The videotape was shown hundreds of times on stations across the country and the networks after it was allegedly distributed by a Los Angeles TV station without consent of Holliday, who owned the copyright to the tape, registered with the Copyright Office. Holliday's attorney reportedly mailed letters to more than 900 television stations around the country demanding payment for use of the film. Whether stations are protected under the fair use doctrine has not been determined, but it is likely that stations would be held liable when a tape is copyrighted and not considered a public document nor in the public domain.

In 1992 Gordon Lish won a $2,000 judgment for copyright infringement against *Harper's,* which had published more than half of the fiction writer–editor–teacher's unpublished letter to his students. In *Lish v. Harper's Magazine Foundation,*[194] U.S. District Court Judge Morris E. Lasker's ruling rejected the magazine's claim of fair use because the evidence supported Lish on the first three factors associated with fair use, although the publication had little or no impact on the market for the letter (fourth factor).

On March 7, 1994, the U.S. Supreme Court handed down its decision in the long-awaited case of *Luther R. Campbell a.k.a. Luke Skyywalker v. Acuff-Rose Music, Inc.*[195] The original song, "Oh, Pretty Woman," was written by Roy Orbison and William Dees in 1964. Twenty-five years later, Luther R. Campbell wrote a song, "Pretty Woman," which was intended to satirize the original work. Orbison and Dees' song is a rock ballad about a man's fantasies concerning a woman he sees walking down the street. Campbell's tune, on the other hand, is a rap song that includes lines such as "Big hairy woman you need to shave that stuff," and "Two timin' woman girl you know you ain't right."

Campbell asked Acuff-Rose Music, Inc., the copyright owner of the original song, for a license to use the song in a rap version by 2 Live Crew, but Acuff-Rose refused. 2 Live Crew recorded its version anyway on the album *As Clean as They Wanna Be*, which sold almost 250,000 copies in less than a year. Acuff-Rose filed a copyright infringement suit in U.S. District Court. The trial court granted a summary judgment for the defendants on the ground that the 2 Live Crew song was a parody of the original and fair use under the Copyright Act of 1976.

On appeal, the Sixth Circuit U.S. Court of Appeals reversed the trial court in a 2–1 decision, holding that the 2 Live Crew song's "blatantly commercial purpose … prevents this parody from being fair use." The appellate court analyzed the song on the four factors of fair use under Section 107 of the Copyright Act and found (1) every commercial use, as was the case here, is presumptively unfair (factor one, purpose and character of use), (2) this work fell within the categories of work the copyright intended to protect (factor two, nature of the copyrighted work), (3) by "taking the heart of the original and making it the heart of a new work," 2 Live Crew had taken too much (factor three, amount and substantiality) and (4) since "the use of the work is wholly commercial, … we presume a likelihood of future harm to Acuff-Rose exists" (factor four, effect on the potential market).

The U.S. Supreme Court also invoked the four factors but came to a different conclusion, noting that on the first factor, parodies by definition must draw to some extent upon the original work they are criticizing.

> … For the purposes of Copyright law, the nub of the definitions, and the heart of any parodist's claim to quote from existing material, is the use of some elements of a prior author's composition to create a new one that, at least in part, comments on the author's works.[196]

The Court went on, "The threshold question when fair use is raised in defense of parody is whether a parodic character may reasonably be perceived." The justices said the 2 Live Crew song "reasonably could be perceived as commenting on the original or criticizing it, to some degree. 2 Live Crew juxtaposes the romantic musings of a man whose fantasy comes true, with degrading taunts, a bawdy demand for sex, and a sigh of relief from paternal responsibility."

The first factor is only one factor in the fair use determination, according to the Court, and commercial use should not be presumptively considered unfair. The Supreme Court spent little time with the second factor, noting that this criterion had never been much help "in separating the fair use sheep from the infringing goats in a parody case."

The Court differed substantially with the Court of Appeals on the third factor. The opinion noted that while parodists cannot "skim the cream and get away scot free," the lower court "was insufficiently appreciative of parody's need for the recognizable sight or sound when it ruled 2 Live Crew's use unreasonable as a matter of law. The Supreme Court could not make a final determination from the record on the fourth factor. The opinion noted that the defendants put themselves at a disadvantage in moving for summary judgment "when they failed to address the effect on the market for rap derivatives, and confined themselves to uncontroverted submissions that there was likely no effect on the market for the original." Nevertheless, the Court did not see this as a fatal flaw and criticized the appellate court for applying the presumption that commercial use was unfair use on this factor, as it had done on the first factor. Parodies and the originals usually serve different markets, according to the justices. "We do not, of course, suggest that a parody may not harm the market at all, but when a lethal parody, like a scathing theater review, kills demand for the original, it does not produce a harm cognizable under the Copyright Act," the Court said. The key is whether the parody is acting as a substitute or as criticism. In reversing the judgment and remanding it back to the trial court, the Supreme Court held:

> It was error for the Court of Appeals to conclude that the commercial nature of 2 Live Crew's parody of 'Oh Pretty Woman' rendered it presumptively unfair. No such evidentiary presumption is available to address either the first factor, the character and purpose of the use, or the fourth, market harm, in determining whether a transformative use, such as parody, is a fair one. The court also erred in holding that 2 Live Crew had necessarily copied excessively from the Orbison original, considering the parodic purpose of the use.[197]

Soon after the Copyright Act of 1976 was passed, a group of authors, educators and publishers met and drafted fair use guidelines for educators who wanted to make use of copyrighted works. The guidelines were eventually made part of the *Congressional Record*, and are widely used by the courts in interpreting "educational use" under fair use doctrine. Unfortunately, the guidelines did not include multimedia use because new technologies such as electronic digitalization were not in popular use at that time.

In September 1994 the Consortium of College and University Media Centers set up a committee of educators and representatives of various copyright owners, including major publishers, recording firms, and motion picture producers, to draft guidelines for fair use of multimedia by educators. In a satellite broadcast three years later, the committee released the final version of its "Fair Use Guidelines for Educational Multimedia."[198] The guidelines were the result of extensive discussion and negotiations among the committee's members. Although they do not constitute a legal document *per se,* the guidelines are useful in court decisions regarding educators' use of copyrighted materials in multimedia projects because they are now also in the *Congressional Record*. They also represent an agreement among the diverse copyright owners represented that they will not pursue claims for copyright infringement when the guidelines are followed.

The list of endorsers includes such heavy hitters as the Association of American Publishers, the Business Software Alliance, the Magazine Publishers of America, the McGraw-Hill Companies, Microsoft Corporation, the Motion Picture Association of America, the National Cable Television Association, the Newspaper Association of America, the Software Publishers Association, Time Warner Inc., West Publishing Company, and Viacom, Inc. The guidelines were supported, but not endorsed by the U.S. National Endowment for the Arts, the U.S. Copyright Office and the U.S. Patent and Trademark Office.

The guidelines are aimed specifically at educators and students who want to use multimedia in classroom projects. They do not include the display or broadcast of whole works such as digital images or dramatic works. Separate subcommittees were established to deal with the latter uses.

Under the new guidelines, a professor or student may, for example, use 30 seconds or 10%, whichever is less, of a single musical work, and the individual may make only a limited number of copies of videos, CD-ROMs, etc. that incorporate the copyrighted materials. There are restrictions as well on the use of such works for distance education programs, including the requirement that access be controlled through passwords and other security measures.[199]

As of 2002, the Technology, Education and Copyright Harmonization (TEACH) Act was signed into law by President George W. Bush as part of justice reauthorization legislation (H.R. 2215). That initiative, while requiring institutions to vigorously enforce copyright protections, became integrated into sections of that law (Title 17, U.S. Code) in an effort to bring opportunities to so-called distance learning students in line with those who study in the traditional classroom format.

A group of freelance writers later sued the *New York Times* and four other companies for reproducing their work in electronic form without authorization. The suit involved 21 articles published between 1990 and 1993. The publishers, including the *Times, Newsday,* Time Inc., and the *Atlantic Monthly,* had sold to the other defendants—University Microfilms Inc. and the Mead Corporation (now Lexis/Nexis)—the right to include the stories in databases and CD-ROMs. The writers had been compensated for the use of their works in print but argued they were entitled to additional royalties on the ground that electronic reproduction was a separate or new publication, not a revision of the original.

The companies argued that the electronic format was part of the original collective work for which the writers had sold the rights. Under the Copyright Act of 1976, the creator of a "collective work," which all of the parties agreed was involved in this case, transfers only the right to reproduce and distribute the creator's particular contribution to the work, including any revisions, unless there is a different agreement in writing. Thus the key question in the case was whether publishing the articles in the electronic databases constituted a new work or simply a revision of the original. In 1997 U.S. District Court Judge Sonia Sotomayor in New York sided with the defendants. In *Jonathan Tasini et al. v. The New York Times Co. et al.* (1997),[200] the trial court judge granted the defendants' motion for summary judgment, holding that they had not exceeded their authority under Sections 101 and 201 (c) of the Copyright Act. The Second Circuit U.S. Court of Appeals reversed the trial court decision, and the publishers appealed. On further appeal, the U.S. Supreme Court upheld the Court of Appeals decision. In *The New York Times Co. et al. v. Jonathan Tasini* (2001), the Supreme Court ruled:

> For copyright purposes, although the transfer of a work between media does not alter the character of that work, the transfer of newspaper and magazine articles to computer databases—unlike the conversion of newsprint to microfilm—does not represent a mere conversion of intact periodicals (or revisions of periodicals) from one medium to another, for (1) the databases offer users individual articles, not intact periodicals, and (2) media neutrality should protect freelance authors' rights in their individual articles to the extent those articles are now presented individually, outside the collective work context, within the databases' new media.[201]

This was a clear victory for freelancers because the Court made it clear that their rights under the Copyright Act had been infringed by the reproduction and distribution of their articles by the electronic publishers in a manner in which they had not been authorized. The Court also ruled that the print publishers had also engaged in copyright infringement by contracting with the electronic publishers to reproduce the articles in the databases. The result has been that print publishers now obtain permission to reproduce the articles electronically either sometime before they are included in databases or as part of the original contract. The latter appears to be more common.

The generic term "Web2.0" has been adopted to describe the new high tech wave of changes now underway, fulfilling the early promise of innovation and wide participation of the early digital era. But right along with that some new issues have emerged in the quest to protect copyright while providing access and generating new creative material. One of the most interesting examples involves YouTube, a website where people post and watch home-grown videos. It started when two dot.com survivors of Santa Monica, California, Chris DeWolfe and Tom Anderson, planned a site consisting exclusively of material that young people would bring to it. Within a year, 35,000 videos were added to the site each day and issues started to arise regarding the sources of some of the material. Since much of it originated with network television, copyright issues emerged along with the recognition that such a massive number of viewer–participants might represent more of a marketing opportunity than a source of copyright infringement.[202]

Beyond the obvious attention it attracted and the immense opportunities it created, the YouTube site, along with MySpace.com and Flickr.com, a photo sharing page, were also credited with launching the careers of some previously unknown writers, performers, and photographers, including Brooke Bradack who received a contract with talk show host Carson Daly shortly after posting her own Internet videos on YouTube. A comedian, Dane Cook, used MySpace to launch his career, which included an appearance on NBC's *Saturday Night Live*. In June 2006, one source suggested that as many as 13 million people had visited the YouTube site that year, generating additional incredible interest in the mainstream media. Flickr.com, purchased by Yahoo for an estimated $35 million, was obviously interested in the large base of users and free contributors. MySpace.com was quickly purchased by Rupert Murdoch. In the case of YouTube, the ownership of much of the source material remained at issue. Proponents of such sites trumpeted the self-service, collaborative nature of such endeavors along with the harnessing of so-called collective intelligence as a means of coming up with new ideas. Detractors continue to point to the frequency of the use of copyright material uploaded without permission.[203]

In 2006 Google purchased YouTube for $1.65 billion, and five months later Viacom, the parent company of CBS, MTV, Nickelodeon, Comedy Central, and other cable networks sued YouTube for $1 billion for what it characterized as "massive copyright infringement." The complaint also sought an injunction against further infringement. Viacom claimed YouTube made available on its website thousands of clips of Viacom programs without permission.[204]

Digital Millennium Copyright Act of 1998

Twenty years after the Copyright Act of 1976 took effect, the Act was substantially expanded with the Digital Millennium Copyright Act of 1998 (DMCA),[205] signed into law by President Bill Clinton. The statute implemented two 1996 World Intellectual Property Organization (WIPO) treaties and dealt with some of the copyright issues the 1976 Act did not address. These included (a) adding limitations on the liability of online service providers for copyright infringement involving specific types of activities, (b) creating an exemption for making copies of computer programs by activating a computer for maintenance or repair, and (c) amending the Digital Performance Right in Sound Recordings Act of 1995 (DPRA), which created, for the first time in U.S. copyright history, a limited performance right in the digital transmission of sound recordings by FCC-licensed terrestrial broadcast stations. The latter change expanded the rights of broadcasters to make digital transmissions of sound recordings on the Internet using streaming audio technologies.

This right is by no means free, even for public (noncommercial) broadcasters, as demonstrated by the settlement reached between college radio stations and the recording industry in 2003 to reduce the fees they were required to pay under a fee structure announced the year before by the Librarian of Congress. The librarian was authorized to set the fees under the DMCA, but neither commercial nor noncommercial stations were happy with the fees that were set following recommendations to the librarian from an arbitration panel. The commercial stations had negotiated a lower rate before the noncommercial stations began their negotiations. The commercial station rate is lower than that set by the librarian but still higher than the rate ultimately agreed upon for noncommercial stations.[206] The new rates were retroactive, meaning the stations had to pay royalties that had not been previously collected, going back to 2000. A noncommercial station at a college with under 10,000 students generally pays a $500 annual fee for Webcasting. At colleges with more than 10,000 students, the standard fee is $500 for Webcasting rights only. The stations have to pay separate fees for broadcasting sound recordings over the air.

The limitations on the liability of online service providers for copyright infringement came into play in 2006 when YouTube was sued for copyright infringement for the first time. Independent photographer Robert Tur, well known for filming the 1992 Los Angeles riots, including the beating of Reginald Denny, sought $150,000 for each time the video was uploaded to the service. He also sought an injunction against any additional use of his work. The video was removed from the server, although YouTube took the position at the time that under the 1998 Digital Millennium Copyright Act, the company was protected from being sued based on the actions of customers.[207] YouTube was later the source of 5 million streams in less than a month for one skit from *Saturday Night Live* featuring a rap version of *Chronicles of Narnia*. NBC Universal demanded that YouTube remove the skit.[208]

Remedies for Infringement

Under Section 501(a) of the current copyright statute, anyone (including state agencies and officials) who violates any of the exclusive rights of the copyright owner is an infringer. The statute provides a wide range of remedies from injunctions to criminal penalties, although it does not codify common law infringement. To prove infringement, a plaintiff must demonstrate that (a) he or she owns the copyright to the infringed work, and (b) the defendant(s) copied the work.

The latter involves proving the defendant(s) had access to the work and that the two works are substantially similar. Proving ownership is usually not difficult since the owner simply has to produce sufficient evidence that he or she created the work or that the rights to the work were transferred to him or her. Registration is one way of establishing this since it constitutes prima facie evidence in court of the validity of the copyright if it is made prior to or within five years after publication. Sometimes ownership may be in dispute, however, as illustrated in a 1990 decision by the U.S. Supreme Court involving the 1954 Alfred Hitchcock movie *Rear Window*. In *Stewart v. Abend*,[209] the U.S. Supreme Court ruled 6–3 that actor James Stewart and the late film director Alfred Hitchcock had violated the copyright of Sheldon Abend to

Rear Window when they released the film in 1981 for television and in 1983 put it on videocassette and videodisc.

The complicated story began in 1942 when a short story entitled "It Had to Be Murder" by Cornell Woolrich appeared in *Dime Detective* magazine. In 1945 Woolrich sold the movie rights only, not the copyright itself, to the story to B.G. De Sylva Productions for $9,250 with an agreement that De Sylva would have the same rights for the renewal period (which under the statute at that time was an additional 28 years). De Sylva then sold the movie rights in 1953 to a production company owned by Stewart and Hitchcock, which made the story into the still highly popular classic film, *Rear Window*.[210]

When Woolrich died in 1968, he left his estate, including copyrights to his works, to Columbia University. Chase Manhattan Bank, the executor for Woolrich's estate, renewed the copyright and in 1971 sold the renewed movie rights to "It Had to Be Murder" to Sheldon Abend, a literary agent, for $650.[210] In that same year, the movie was made available for television, and Abend informed Stewart, Hitchcock's estate, and MCA, Inc. (which released the film) that he would sue for copyright infringement if the movie were distributed further. When MCA ignored the warning and allowed ABC Television to broadcast *Rear Window*, Abend made good on his threat and sued. The parties eventually settled out of court, with Abend getting $25,000. The saga continued, however.

In 1977, the Second Circuit U.S. Court of Appeals held that a company which had acquired derivative rights to a work still retained those rights even if the transfer of rights from the original work expired. MCA relied on that holding since *Rear Window* was a derivative work and re-released the film in 1983 on videocassette and for cable television. Abend filed suit once again. It was dismissed by a U.S. District Court judge.

On appeal, the Ninth Circuit U.S. Court of Appeals reversed, and the U.S. Supreme Court upheld the decision, 6–3. Abend stood to make millions of dollars in profits because the re-release had generated more than $12 million worldwide by the time of the Supreme Court decision plus another $5 million in profits from release on home video.[212] Writing for the majority, Justice Sandra Day O'Connor said the 1977 Second Circuit decision was wrong. The 1909 statute in effect at the time of the ruling provided that the original copyright to a work continued, if renewed, even if derivative rights have been granted. Thus derivative rights expire when the original copyright expires, and the owner of the original rights can prevent the owner of the derivative rights from continuing to use the work. The Court was not sympathetic to the complaint by MCA, Stewart, and Hitchcock's heirs that "they will have to pay more for the use of works that they have employed in creating their own works.… [S]uch a result was contemplated by Congress and is consistent with the goals of the Copyright Act."[213] The decision affected hundreds of films and was estimated to cost the movie industry millions of dollars.[214]

In the area of trademark infringement, the use of names within an entertainment context often presents litigants with an increasingly challenging and complex burden of proof. On June 27, 2006, a Southern California rock band filed a complaint in U.S. District Court against the CBS television reality program *Rock Star: Supernova*, with a claim under unfair competition and trademark infringement that it used the "Supernova" mark first.[215]

According to the lawsuit, that group had performed under the Supernova name previously and even released three albums and also some singles under that name. The lawsuit noted that representatives of Mark Burnett Productions had filed seven U.S. trademark applications for the name "Supernova" and two for "Rock Star: Supernova." The CBS program hosted by rocker Dave Navarro followed the plights of 15 contestants hoping to appear as the lead singer with the newly formed group consisting of former members from well-known rock groups: Metallica, Guns N' Roses, and Motley Crue. Defendants Mark Burnett, CBS, and the members of the new rock group (Tommy Lee, Gilby Clarke, and Jason Newstead) were not obligated to answer the lawsuit when it was first reported in the press because it had not yet been served. But at that time, some astute television observers commented on the difficulty of coming up with creative, original names in an ever-expanding universe of intellectual property. At the time of this particular suit, the *Television Business Report* (*TVBR*), while emphasizing the seriousness of such legal challenges, reviewed the names of some continuingly popular rock groups such as Paul Revere and the Raiders, noting with tongue in check that one member of that particular rock group was actually named Paul Revere, indicating that care must be taken with historical names, especially those that still hold currency. To avoid messy legal actions, *TVBR* suggested that rock groups might want to look back to American history and consider less contentious names such as "Rock Star: Mugwump or Rock Star: Millard Fillmore."[216]

Demonstrating access is usually a relatively simple matter, especially when a work has been widely distributed, but occasionally a defendant is able to prove lack of access. A typical example occurred when rocker Mick Jagger successfully fought a copyright infringement suit in 1988 for his hit song "Just Another Night."[217] Reggae musician Patrick Alley claimed the chorus from Jagger's song had been lifted from the 1979 recording "Just Another Night." Alley claimed that Jagger had access to his song through a drummer who had played on both records and that Jagger probably heard Alley's song when it was played on several smaller New York radio stations. Jagger denied he had heard the song, and a U.S. District Court jury in New York ruled in his favor after hearing testimony from the defendant that included him singing some of his lyrics.[218]

Substantial similarity is typically the key in deciding an infringement case. Although it was rendered prior to enactment of the current copyright statute, a 1977 ruling by the Ninth Circuit U.S. Court of Appeals has become a leading case related to criteria for evaluating substantial similarity. In cases of direct copying such as a chapter, extensive excerpts, and appropriation of exact wording, proof of copying is usually cut and dried, but indirect proof is typically all that can be shown and this can be done with evidence of substantial similarity.

In *Sid and Marty Krofft Television Productions, Inc. v. McDonald's Corp.* (1977),[219] the creators of the show *H.R. Pufnstuf* successfully claimed that McDonald's television commercials infringed on their copyright because the McDonaldland setting in the hamburger chain's ads and the characters portrayed in them were substantially similar to those in *H.R. Pufnstuf*. The U.S. Court of Appeals applied a two-prong test in reaching its conclusion. First, is there substantial similarity between the underlying general ideas of the two works? If the answer is "no," there is no infringement. If "yes," the second question is, is there substantial similarity in the manner of expression of the two works? If "yes," there is infringement. If no, the lawsuit fails. Both of these are questions of fact for a jury to determine or for the judge in a bench trial. Substantial similarity is often difficult for a plaintiff to prove on the two questions, but as the *Krofft* case illustrates, it can be done. The court found that McDonaldland and H.R. Pufnstuf's Living Island had substantially similar characters, scenery, dialogue, and other features. Some of the most damning evidence presented at trial was that former Krofft employees had helped design and build McDonaldland.[220]

A classic case of substantial similarity involved the highly popular movie *Jaws*. In 1982 a U.S. District Court in California found that the movie *Great White* was substantially similar to *Jaws* and, therefore, an infringement.[221] The similarities were striking, as the court noted, including similar characters (an English sea captain and a shark hunter who together track a vicious shark), a similar plot, and virtually identical opening and closing sequences. The judge in the case felt that it was obvious that "the creators of *Great White* wished to be as closely connected with the plaintiff's motion picture *Jaws* as possible."[222] The producers of the infringing movie were ordered to pay damages, and an injunction was issued to ban further distribution of the film. *Great White* was dead in the water with no sequels in sight.

The similarities were also striking in a 1989 Seventh Circuit U.S. Court of Appeals decision involving greeting cards.[223] For two years, Ruolo designed distinctive greeting cards for Russ Berrie & Co. under a contract granting the latter the exclusive right to produce and sell them as its "Feeling Sensitive" line.

When the contract expired and Ruolo notified the company that it would not be renewed, Berrie marketed a similar line of cards known as "Touching You." The appeals court upheld a jury decision that Berrie had infringed because the cards were substantially similar. They were designed for similar occasions and were identical in size and layout. Both cards featured two colored stripes on the left side on which a foil butterfly was superimposed and one colored stripe on the right side. Both series of cards were printed on cream-colored paper with handwritten messages in brown ink. The Court of Appeals characterized the action as trade dress infringement in which the substantial similarities lie in the overall image or "look and feel" of the works, as evidenced in size, shape, color, graphics, packaging, and other visual aspects. The appellate court upheld the jury award of $4.3 million.

This same "look and feel test" is often applied in determining infringement in computer software cases. According to one author, though, "[W]hile broad protection may be given by some courts to the structure, sequence and organization of a program, copyright law provides no general protection for the overall 'look and feel' of a computer program."[224] The authors predict that patent law will emerge to grant the necessary protection that copyright law does not provide for computer software.[225]

By passing the Sonny Bono Copyright Term Extension Act (CTEA) in 1998, as discussed earlier, the U. S. Congress included 20 years of additional copyright protection. This Act amended earlier 1976 legislation. The new Act, named after the late Congressman who had once been an entertainer and also spouse of Mary Bono, his widow and Congressional successor. As noted earlier, this Act was heavily supported by the Walt Disney Company and thus acquired the pejorative nickname of "The Mickey Mouse Protection Act," a back-handed reference to aggressive corporate legal activity and efforts to further extend copyright ownership for creative works. Critics of such efforts point to the large number of Disney works based on earlier published literary material existing in the public domain as a counterpoint to successful efforts by Disney to protect its characters, brands, and logos.[226]

A challenge to CTEA also came in the form of *Eldred v. Ashcroft* (2003),[227] in which Stanford Law Professor Lawrence Lessig represented noncommercial website operator Eric Eldred in asking the Court to strike down the Act on First Amendment and other constitutional grounds. Eldred argued that the extension exceeded Congress' authority under the copyright clause portion of Article I, Section 8, clause 8 of the U.S. Constitution ("by securing for limited times"). He also argued the extension violated the free speech provision of the First Amendment. U.S.

District Court Judge June Green rejected the arguments, and the decision was appealed. The U.S. Court of Appeals upheld the decision. On further appeal, the U.S. Supreme Court ruled 7–2 that the Act was constitutional. The majority opinion written by Judge Ruth Bader Ginsberg pointed to earlier copyright acts, holding that Congress had not exceeded its authority and that the Act did not violate the First Amendment. The Court applied the intermediate scrutiny test, ruling that strict scrutiny did not apply.

Professor Lessig, founder of the Center for the Internet and Society, has written extensively on copyright duration, arguing for openness and availability, as quickly as possible.[228] He has proposed the idea of a creative commons license under which artists would make their works available for free under certain conditions prior to publication, specifying the restrictions, if any, in a link next to the work or by embedding it in an MP3, PDF, or other file.[229] For example, an artist could require that any reuse credit the author or that such use be only noncommercial. The creator could also put the work immediately in the public domain.

Injunctions, Impoundment, and Disposition

Under Section 502 of the Copyright Act, federal courts can grant both temporary and permanent ("final") injunctions to prevent infringement once infringement has been proven. The permanent injunction against *Great White* is an example of how this form of equitable relief can be effective. With the injunction, the movie could no longer be distributed, shown, or sold anywhere in the United States. While injunctions are clearly forms of prior restraint, the courts have indicated they are constitutionally permissible to prevent further infringement of intellectual property rights. A mere threatened infringement is usually not sufficient to warrant an injunction, but once infringement is proven, an injunction becomes a potent weapon available for the copyright owner. As with all injunctions, violations can subject a defendant to citation for contempt and fines as determined by the court.

Section 503 provides two other effective remedies: impoundment and disposition. Impoundment involves the government seizing potentially infringing materials or forcing a defendant to turn them over to the custody of the court until a case is decided. In its final decision, the court can also "order the destruction or other reasonable disposition of all copies or phonorecords" determined to violate copyright.[230] The federal courts rarely have to resort to these remedies, but they clearly have the authority to use them.

Damages and Profits

The most common remedy for infringement is an award of damages. A copyright owner who files suit against an alleged infringer can opt at any time before the court issues its decision (before "final judgment") for either actual damages along with any additional profits or statutory damages, but the owner cannot recover both. Under Section 504 an infringer can be liable for actual damages caused by the infringement plus any profits attributable to the infringement. All the copyright owner needs to show at trial to establish the amount of profit is the infringer's gross revenue.[231] A defendant can offset the profits awarded the plaintiff by proving deductible expenses and any portion of the profits that did not come from the infringement. Otherwise, the defendant may have to surrender all profits. There is no limit on the amount of actual damages a copyright owner can recover so long as sufficient evidence demonstrates the extent of the harm suffered. As with all civil suits in federal courts, judges have a responsibility to ensure that awards are not excessive in light of the evidence presented at trial. However, the judge and jury have considerable discretion in determining what is reasonable.

The 1988 revision of the Copyright Act[232] substantially increased the amount of statutory damages available. If the copyright owner of an infringed work chooses statutory damages instead of actual damages and profits, he or she may obtain an award from $750 (minimum) to $30,000 (maximum) for each work infringed, depending upon what the court considers an appropriate amount. If the copyright owner can prove that the infringement was willful, she or he can recover, at the court's discretion, up to $150,000 for each work.[233] On the other hand, if the infringer can convince the court that she or he was not aware or had no reason to believe infringement occurred (i.e., innocent infringement), the court can reduce the statutory damages.[234]

A fair use provision is tucked away in Section 504 under which "an employer or agent of a nonprofit educational institution, library, or archives acting within the scope of his or her employment … cannot be held liable for statutory damages for infringement in reproducing a work if the person believed and had reasonable grounds for believing that the use was a fair use." A similar exception is made for public broadcasting employees who infringe by performing or reproducing a published nondramatic literary work.

President Clinton signed the No Electronic Theft Act into law on January 6, 1998.[235] Under this law, federal prosecutors can charge individuals who illegally copy or distribute copyrighted materials on the Internet even when they made no money from doing so. The Act, which amends provisions of Titles 17 and 18 of the U.S. Code, was in response to a 1994 decision by a U.S. District Court in Massachusetts to dismiss the charges against a Massachusetts Institute of Technology student accused of using the MIT computer system to illegally distribute millions of dollars in software. The judge threw out the charges on the ground that he had made no commercial or private financial gain.

The No Electronic Theft Act made it a felony to copy or to distribute 10 or more copies of a copyrighted work with a cumulative retail value of more than $2,500, with penalties of up to five years in prison and fines of up to $250,000. A second or subsequent offense can lead to imprisonment of up to six years. It is a misdemeanor under the law to make or distribute during any 180-day period one or more copies of a work with a total retail value of more than $1,000. A misdemeanor violation can be punished with a maximum of one year in prison and a fine of up to $100,000. For both felonies and misdemeanors, prosecutors have to demonstrate that the acts were willful and not protected under the fair use doctrine.

Even though the bulk of the anti-theft attention was directed at major corporations, experts in the field were quick to point out that small business owners, especially in particular smaller pockets of creativity in the country where intellectual property innovations are plentiful, also need to be aware of their rights. Some areas, evidenced by the filing of many patents, also demonstrate the need to take the threat very seriously. For example, in 2005, close to 3,000 patents alone were issued to small businesses and individuals in Ohio.

While signs of such innovation ranked Ohio eighth overall in patents issued, it also demonstrates the extent and the need for small companies in such locales to be willing to fight in court to maintain their intellectual property rights. While larger companies in bigger communities known for such innovation often have in-house capability to fight intellectual property right challenges and claims, the smaller, family-owned companies were also targeted by the federal and Ohio local governments to increase their overall awareness of the extent of the crime and seek to enforce their rights beyond both local and national levels. As the problem becomes more pronounced, more pervasive, and more troublesome, smaller companies can find themselves spending half or more of a marketing budget on lawsuits just fighting patent infringement to protect intellectual resources.[236]

The result of the government's efforts in this area has been impressive although a lot more obviously needs to be done. But in the short time since the federal government began to target the need for recognition of the problem and litigation in the area as a means of protection, defendants prosecuted for intellectual property theft increased 97% from October 2004 to the end of 2005. A large number of computer hacking and intellectual property units were established nationwide and comprehensive training programs were conducted for federal cyber prosecutors to address computer crime. In 2005, searches of 22 major online piracy groups were executed and prosecutors obtained indictments against 44 defendants, with 10 convictions the following year.[237]

It also took action to stop counterfeiting operations and obtained felony conspiracy and copyright convictions against nearly two dozen software, music, and movie pirates. The federal government also continued efforts to intervene in court actions to defend copyright owners' use of civil subpoenas to identify anonymous Internet users alleged to be involved in copyright infringement.

Other Remedies for Infringement

Under Section 505, the court can award court costs (i.e., the full cost of litigation for that side) and reasonable attorney's fees to whichever side wins.[238] These remedies are at the discretion of the judge. Finally, under certain circumstances, anyone who willfully infringes for commercial or private financial gain can be fined up to $250,000 and/or imprisoned for a maximum of five years. These offenses include such actions as reproducing or distributing during any 180-day period at least 1,000 phonorecords or copies of one or more sound recordings[239] or at least 65 copies of one or more motion pictures or other audiovisual works.[240]

Most videotape recordings now carry the standard Federal Bureau of Investigation warning, complete with seal, at the beginning of the tapes. The FBI is the primary police authority for enforcing the criminal provisions of the copyright statutes. The statutes also include a provision making it a federal crime to traffic in counterfeit labels for phonorecords and copies of motion pictures and other audiovisual works.[241]

In spite of its best efforts, Congress left some gaps in the copyright law, many of which have been closed with various amendments enacted since the legislation originally passed in 1976. The most prominent gap, at least from the consumer perspective, was revealed in the one U.S. Supreme Court copyright decision with which the public is familiar: *Sony Corporation of America v. Universal City Studios, Inc.* (1984).[242] The *Sony* decision or "Betamax case," as it is popularly known, is one of the most misinterpreted and misunderstood cases involving copyright since the statute took effect. Some of the misunderstanding can be traced to inaccuracies in news stories about the decision and to the apparent general attitude among the public that home videotaping is a fair use and should not be regulated.

The case developed when Universal Studios, Walt Disney Productions, and other television production companies sued the Sony Corporation[243] for contributory copyright infringement.

The production companies claimed the Japanese firm marketed to the public the technology to infringe on copyrighted works. This infringement occurred, according to the plaintiffs, when consumers used Sony's Betamax VCRs[244] to record copyrighted programs broadcast on local stations, including "time shifting," or recording for later use programs not viewed at the time they were broadcast. (The Court characterized this practice as the principal use of a VCR by the average owner.)

A U.S. District Court judge for the Central District of California ruled that recording broadcasts carried on the public airwaves was fair use of copyrighted works and thus Sony could not be held liable as a contributory infringer even if such home recording were infringement. The Ninth Circuit U.S. Court of Appeals reversed the trial court's decision, but the U.S. Supreme Court reversed the appellate court ruling. In a very narrow decision that dealt only with Sony's liability for manufacturing and marketing the recorders, the Court agreed with the district court that the company was not guilty of contributory infringement. In a 5–4 opinion written by Justice John Paul Stevens, the Court concluded that home time-shifting was fair use:

> In summary, the record and findings of the District Court lead us to two conclusions. First, Sony demonstrated a significant likelihood that substantial numbers of copyright holders who license their works for broadcast on free television would not object to having their broadcasts time shifted by private viewers. And second, respondents failed to demonstrate that time shifting would cause any likelihood of nonminimal harm to the potential market for, or the value of, their copyrighted works. The Betamax is, therefore, capable of substantial noninfringing uses. Sony's sale of such equipment to the general public does not constitute contributory infringement of respondents' rights.[245]

The Court went on to note that there is no indication in the Copyright Act that Congress intended to make it unlawful for consumers to record programs for later viewing in homes or to prohibit the sale of recorders. "It may well be that Congress will take a fresh look at this new technology, just as it so often has examined other innovations in the past. But it is not our job to apply laws that have not yet been written."[246] After the decision, several bills were proposed in Congress to respond to the Court's holding such as taxing recorders and blank tape, but most legislators apparently felt the political fallout from such legislation would be too great.

The Sony decision, which barely attracted a majority of the justices, left many unanswered questions. Is videotaping at home an infringement? The Court said that the record supported the trial court's decision that home time shifting was fair use, but the fair use doctrine does not mention such use as permissible. In fact, a literal application of the four criteria for fair use would appear not to protect this practice. For example, home taping typically involves recording an entire program (under the third factor, more than a substantial portion), its purpose is entertainment rather than nonprofit educational use (factor one) and, contrary to the Court's musings, such taping likely negatively affects the potential market for the work (factor four). Is it fair use to record cable television programs, including pay channels? Is it fair use to edit programs while they are being recorded by deleting commercials, for example? Do recorded programs have to be erased as soon as they are viewed, or is it fair use to archive them for future multiple viewings?

Registration

Even though registration is no longer required for copyright protection,[247] there are some major advantages, and the process is relatively simple. The advantages include:

1. Public record of the copyright;
2. Standing in court to file suit for infringement;
3. If made within five years of publication, *prima facie* evidence in court of the copyright's validity;
4. If made within three months after publication or prior to infringement, the availability of statutory damages and attorney's fees.

Registration may be made any time for the duration of the copyright by sending the following in a single envelope or package to the copyright office:

1. A completed application form (different types of works have different forms);
2. A $65 filing fee for registration via paper or $35 for online registration (for most works);
3. One copy or phonorecord if the work is unpublished or was first published outside the United States, or two copies or phonorecords if the work was first published in the United States.

There are seven standard forms for original registration, and three of them have short versions. In addition, Form CA is used to correct or amplify information given on an earlier form and Form RE is for renewals. Of the standard forms, TX and its short form are for registration of published and unpublished nondramatic literary works. Form TX is also used for reference works, directories, catalogs, and compilations of information. Form VA is used for works of the visual arts such as sculptures and architecture and works used in the sale or advertising of goods and services if the copyrightable material is primarily pictorial or graphic. Motion pictures and other audiovisual works require Form PA. Form SR is for sound recordings, and Form G/DN is a special form for registering a month's issues of a daily newspaper and GR/CP is a supplementary form for the registration of group contributions to periodicals. Form SE is for serials such as periodicals, newspapers, annuals, journals, proceedings, and transactions of societies.

Registration is effective the day the copyright office receives the properly completed application, fee, and materials. Certificates can take as long as four months, but most are mailed within one to two months. The certificates are simply copies of the form signed and dated by the copyright office.

Another option is preregistration, which is available for works that have a history of prerelease infringement. The work must also be unpublished but be in the process of preparation for commercial distribution. The application is only online and requires a $100 filing fee.[248]

Copyright Protection for Newer Technologies

Copyright protection exists for a wide range of technologies, including computer programs, automated databases, and semiconductor chips (also known as mask works). Computer programs have been the subject of considerable litigation even with the new statute, but the courts have made it clear that computer software enjoys copyright protection. In June 1988 the copyright office announced, after public hearings and a review of public comments, that it would "require that all copyrightable expression embodied in a computer program owned by the same claimant, including computer screen displays, be registered on a single application form" (Form TX or PA).[249] Until that time, conflicting court opinions had created confusion over whether a single form could be used. Now the question appears resolved, although other new technologies will undoubtedly raise other questions. The courts have also made it clear that copyright protection covers object codes, source codes, and microcodes in software as well as the overall structure of a program or its "look and feel."

The copyright statute does not specifically mention automated data bases, but the copyright office and the courts interpret the legislative history of the Act to include automated data bases as compilations of facts and thus literary works.[250] Such data bases, as with all copyrightable works, must involve originality and not simply be mere mechanical collections of information.[251] Finally, semiconductor chips (sometimes called integrated circuits) were added to the list of copyrightable works with the Semiconductor Chip Protection Act of 1984.[252] The provisions regarding these mask works differ some from those of other works.

Moral Rights

The most controversial issue in the debate over whether the United States should join the Berne Convention was Article 6, which requires convention members to protect the moral rights or *droit moral* of authors. These rights are entirely independent of copyright, but by agreeing to adhere to the convention the United States is obligated to abide by all of the provisions, including those involving moral rights.

Moral rights fall into two categories under the convention: *paternity rights* and *integrity rights*, both of which have been formally recognized in many other countries for some time. Paternity rights involve the right to be credited as the author of a work and to prevent others from attributing a work to you that is essentially not your work. For example, a publisher who, without consent, omitted the name of the primary author from a book or a magazine editor who, without consent, falsely attributed an article to a well-known author to sell more copies or lend credibility to the magazine would be violating paternity rights. (Even if the famous author contributed a small amount to the work, his name cannot be used without his consent.) Integrity rights basically involve "the right to object to distortion, other alteration of a work, or derogatory action prejudicial to the author's honor or reputation in relation to the work."[253]

A classic example of the latter was the 1976 Second Circuit U.S. Court of Appeals decision that the ABC Television Network violated the copyright of the British comedy troupe known as Monty Python of *Monty Python's Flying Circus* fame when the network edited the programs to make room for commercials.[254] The court held that the changes significantly impaired the integrity of the works and that Monty Python had the right to prevent "distortion or truncation" of its creations. The court cited common law, copyright law, and Section 43(a) of the Lanham Act dealing with unfair competition for its authority. Even though the comedy team had granted the British Broadcasting Corp. the right to license the programs overseas, that right did not include allowing licensees to significantly distort them.

In 2001, a U.S. Court of Appeals for the Ninth Circuit issued an injunction that effectively shut down Napster, the source of free music that was downloaded, played, and shared via MP3 files over the Internet. While the court injunction was appealed, it signaled Napster's eventual decline although it subsequently started a legal ad-supported service in 2006 to try to compete with Apple Computer's iTunes.[255] But the broader context of the earlier blatant copyright infringement— music files downloaded and shared without any charge—was viewed within the backdrop of a precipitous drop in CD sales. As with some other online distribution systems, corporate America was caught in an interesting and somewhat controversial dilemma. While seeing a rise in illegal use of products through advancement of the new technology, corporations were faced with a precipitous decline in overall interest by legal means. They had to become more creative and investigate new strategies.

These are the same kinds of challenges faced by the mainstream television industry when other sources such as YouTube developed an interest in online or so-called viral video programming built on user-generated or user-selected content, described by supporters as the democratization of the mass media, with opportunities to retrieve content more at the consumer's disposal. And thus a new debate emerged about whether such efforts at sharing streaming video should be encouraged rather than aggressively litigated as fiercely as in the past. Interestingly, NBC allowed some material lifted from *Saturday Night Live* to remain on YouTube for a while, although it eventually called for its removal, leading some to believe that the major players were taking a closer look at the impact and potential of this development. Most of the subsequent corporate legal activity involving the democratization of the so-called new media has focused on the means of recouping costs from the lawful sharing of content by including some form of encryption device, whether the source is audio or video.[256]

Plagiarism

Plagiarism, or the misappropriation of another's intellectual or creative works, is a recurrent problem. It is often difficult to demonstrate plagiarism, but accusations crop up from time to time. In 2000 WSPD-AM in Toledo, Ohio, signed a consent order with *The Blade*, a Toledo newspaper, under which the station agreed to give proper attribution to the paper when it used information from *The Blade* on the air.[257] The owner of the newspaper had sued the station, claiming the broadcaster was stealing published stories and passing them off as its own. The newspaper was particularly concerned about a morning radio host whose slogan was "I read *The Blade* so you don't have to," which both sides agreed was a satirical statement. Nevertheless, under the agreement the host had to clearly indicate that the stories on which he commented were written by *The Blade*. In 2003 *Syllabus* magazine apologized after it published an article entitled "Probing for Plagiarism in the Virtual Classroom" that had apparently plagiarized passages from an article published a year earlier by another author in a different publication.[258]

In 2003 BYU NewsNet, a student-managed news organization at Brigham Young University, voluntarily forfeited two national awards for innovative Web design when the student editors determined that a substantial portion of their website was rather similar to a basic site discussed in a software design guide published by another organization.[259] The perception, which research indicates is probably accurate, that plagiarism by students has become a serious problem on college campuses has led many universities to subscribe to anti-plagiarism software such as TurnItIn and MyDropBox. These programs allow student papers to be checked and a report issued indicating any plagiarism detected.[260]

In 2006 19-year-old Harvard sophomore Kaavya Viswananathan, who had signed a half-million dollar contract with Little, Brown & Co., a major publisher, admitted that she had used substantial portions of the work of writer Megan McCafferty in her first novel, *How Opal Mehta Got Kissed, Got Wild, and Got a Life*.[261] The book was ultimately withdrawn from sale.

Romance writer Janet Dailey, who has sold more books than any other female in the country,[262] publicly admitted in 1997 that she borrowed ideas and passages for her novel *Notorious* from Nora Roberts' book *Sweet Revenge*. Roberts is also a best-selling romance author. Dailey attributed her plagiarism to a psychological disorder for which she was being treated.[263]

Award-winning writer, poet, and sculptor Barbara Chase-Riboud settled out of court in 1998 with film producer Steven Spielberg and Dreamworks SKG after Chase-Riboud had sued Spielberg and the studio for plagiarism. Chase-Riboud claimed the movie *Amistad* used characters, events, and dialogue from her book *Echo of Lions*. Both the book and the film revolved around the revolt by Africans on a Spanish slave ship bound for the United States, which led two years later to an historic decision by the U.S. Supreme Court. John Quincy Adams, a former President of the United States, served before the Supreme Court as the attorney for the Africans, who were granted their freedom by the Court.

Chase-Riboud asked for $10 million in damages and for a preliminary injunction to stop the movie's premiere in 1997. The U.S. District Court for the Central District of California denied Chase-Riboud's motion for the injunction, and the movie made its scheduled debut in theaters around the country. The plagiarism suit was allowed to move forward until a settlement was reached, under which Chase-Riboud dropped her suit and complimented the studio and Spielberg on their film.

Most actions of this type do not result in lawsuits for copyright infringement, but the resultant negative publicity is often punishing. Smart journalists and smart journalism students know that when there is any doubt about whether a reader, listener, or viewer (including a professor) might be misled into thinking that a work is entirely original when it is not, clear attribution is essential for both expressions and ideas. Attribution will not prevent a successful lawsuit for copyright infringement, but it can at least alleviate perceptions of plagiarism.

The tendency of Internet users to copy, share, and swap their music files came to a head in 2001 when the record industry sued the highly popular file sharing Napster network in the Ninth Circuit Court of Appeals. The court sided with the industry and agreed that the exchange of recorded music via Napster's file sharing created and also encouraged copyright infringement. Subsequent related cases focused more on individual file sharers with special attention given to college students, as opposed to the corporate software providers, as a means of establishing where most of the activity was taking place.[264]

But some degree of uncertainty still exists regarding who is at fault in such cases because the courts have often had to reconsider whether companies are actually encouraging copyright infringement or merely providing the means to do so. In the aftermath of cases focusing on peer-to-peer file sharing, for example, tens of thousands of sites, particularly those situated at the nation's colleges and universities, were shut down in a major crackdown on music theft and as a means of underscoring the pervasiveness of the crime.

As awareness of the value of intellectual policy has grown along with the growth of the Internet and increased opportunities for theft via computer, the U.S. government has increasingly targeted that area for attention. In March 2004 former Attorney General John Ashcroft set up a government task force specifically targeted to address the field of intellectual property and designed to review developments and make recommendations on how enforcement efforts might improve. The Justice Department had already announced strategies to aggressively prosecute Internet crime such as computer intrusion, copyright and trademark violation, theft of trade secrets, and economic espionage, as well as theft of high tech components for computers. Beyond that, the Justice Department had announced its commitment to work with local law enforcement agencies to see that crimes were reported and information shared across jurisdictional boundaries. The department increased relationships with high tech communities and local governments by way of offering subject area experts in intellectual property law and additional legal advice for collection of digital evidence to pursue criminals in this area. In less than eight months the task force returned with a number of added recommendations including suggestions regarding prevention and international cooperation. With the awareness that intellectual property thefts were costing American companies over $250 billion each year, Ashcroft's successor in the U.S. Attorney General's office, Alberto Gonzalez, followed up on those recommendations—appointing new members for this extended government task force and directing them to implement the recommendations of the previous government report. Then working with the U.S. Patent and Trademark Office, close to a million dollars was earmarked for piracy prevention under the Justice Department.[265]

In conjunction with the release of the 2006 progress report on intellectual property and as a follow-up to government initiatives to crack down on piracy, the U.S. Attorney General's office announced that in addition to 25 cities such as Baltimore and Philadelphia previously targeted for attention, 7 new cities would create new computer hacking and intellectual property (CHIP) units. In targeting additional cities such as San Diego, the new CHIP units would provide special prosecutors trained in detecting intellectual property theft in their districts with an eye to preventing cyber crime. These stepped-up government efforts, also including seminars and websites devoted to the problem, were part of an informational initiative called the Strategy Targeting Organized Piracy (STOP!) to target e-commerce by informing small business owners of the potential for cyber theft and criminally prosecuting hackers and others using technology to maliciously steal or propagate code that would disrupt the flow of normal business operations. These increased education efforts and government-inspired litigation were considered very logical in light of the fact that California alone by 2004 had more than one million small business operators exporting over $1 billion in products. Intellectually property-based companies, particularly in that area known internationally for creativity and innovation, were especially keen on eliminating the potential for piracy and counterfeiting.[266]

Hollywood movie studios and major record labels won another legal war when Grokster, once regarded as a major safe haven for digital pirates, decided to stop operating in November 2005. Five months earlier, the Supreme Court issued its unanimous opinion in the peer-to-peer file swapping case in *Metro-Goldwyn-Mayer Studios v. Grokster* (2005).[267] The case revolved around whether distributors of file sharing software such as Grokster would be liable for copyright infringement by program users. The case was complicated by the fact that thousands of Americans swapped files online. The Supreme Court's decision in this case was that file swapping companies could be sued by the recording industry and others that were hurt by the practice. The Court also said such companies could be held liable in cases in which the software was found to be part of the business model and intended for an illegal purpose.

Justice Souter, writing for a unanimous Court, emphasized the need for balance between the values of creative pursuits through copyright protection and promoting innovation through new technology.

Grokster addressed growing concerns of balance between copyright interests and technology providers in the age of growing consumer use of sophisticated digital technology. It tightened the previous Supreme Court decision regarding the use of technology, specifically Betamax, in *Sony Corp. v. Universal Studios Inc.*,[268] which held that sellers of VCRs were not liable for user copyright infringement when there was also substantial noninfringing use of their product. In that case the Court said that the Sony Corporation could not be sued if the owners of their copying machines used them to record illegally. The case extended consideration of whether the actual intent of the business was to violate copyright, especially in instances in which over 90% of the use was illegal.

The case appeared against the backdrop of a U.S. Department of Justice study finding a 26% increase in suspects charged with intellectual property theft from 1994 to 2002. The number of people convicted for that crime rose more than 50% in the same time frame, while the federal government increased efforts to provide greater public awareness of the nature and extent of the crime. Using *Star Wars* as an example, the United States Under Secretary of Commerce for Intellectual Property, Jon Dudas, pointed out how copying and downloading computer games, video games, DVDs, and music from such a popular Hollywood film was stealing someone else's property, emphasizing how respect for the work of others was an important part of the American educational process.[269]

Grokster, a software developer, was utilized as a peer-to-peer operation. The U.S. Supreme Court decision came in the wake of Napster, a company serving as a middleman that was forced by the Ninth Circuit U.S. Court of Appeals to fold its operations in 2001. After abuses became known, Napster and the other national file sharing companies had started to change their formats to charge users for downloading files, with a percentage of profits going to the artists and creators of the works. Some legal scholars, such as Rod Smolla, have revisited the issue as presenting a generational challenge to the extent that a large number of young people do not view the downloading of an artist's work in the same category as stealing a CD off the shelves of the local Wal-Mart, Walgreens, or Target.[270]

In *Grokster* the Court sent the case back to district court for trial, noting that the entertainment industry could file privacy lawsuits against companies that encouraged the theft of movies and music over the Internet.[271] Grokster had been accused of being responsible, by way of encouraging or "inducing" the illegal downloading of copyrighted files by running file sharing software to enable the download of music and movies online to a large number of users. After the decision, Grokster agreed to settle the suit, pay the plaintiffs $50 million in damages, and immediately shut down its website. At that time, Grokster's website posted in part: "There are legal services for downloading music and movies. This service is not one of them."[272] In the aftermath of the *Grokster* verdict, many entertainment sources claimed that the Supreme Court's decision in this case almost immediately enhanced the growth of legal music services and improved the prospects for legitimate peer-to-peer markets.[273]

Television programs are often bootlegged and flow freely on the Web, but some online services such as Google now offer legal downloads of popular programs such as *CSI, Star Trek: Voyager* and even TV classics such as *I Love Lucy*.[274] AOL's online network, In2TV, offered almost 5,000 episodes of 100 classic television series such as *Welcome Back, Kotter*, while Yahoo had contemporary hits such as *Apprentice* with Donald Trump and *Two and a Half Men* as well as news reports and more than 10,000 music videos.[275]

Hollywood feature-length motion pictures continue to be pirated, typically on DVD, sometimes even before they appear on the silver screen, in China, Russia, and other countries. Intellectual property experts agree that this type of theft will continue until the creative and artistic communities in those countries begin to suffer financially as well because their works are pirated. Only then is it likely that governments in such countries will crack down on piracy. In the meantime, some innovative techniques are emerging to counter this problem. For example, in 2006 Hollywood director Steven Soderbergh introduced a $1.7 million crime drama entitled *Bubble*, which simultaneously opened in theatres, on high definition cable, and on DVD. This experiment was conducted by Mark Cuban and Todd Wagner, who owned the Landmark Theatre chain, which they had purchased with the proceeds from the sale of their company, Broadcast.com, to Yahoo for almost $6 billion.[276] The experiment was not universally praised because it broke the conventional approach of showing a movie in theatres for at least a month, followed by the release of the DVD and then showings on pay cable, followed by free television. This business model assumes that viewers will pay at least twice to see the same movie but in different formats. The simultaneous release business model is aimed at making a film available to 90% of the consumers who would be unlikely to see the initial theatrical release, including youths, a traditionally strong market for films.[277] Whether this approach will slow illegal copying and the pirating of motion pictures remains to be seen. But the integration of some of the most creative technology and their interface with companies on which they rely is also resulting in interesting court challenges. The founders of Skype, for example, filed suit on September 16, 2009 against eBay, the owner of their Internet telephone technology, alleging that the auction site violated a copyright agreement that it would not share the proprietary code powering the service. The suit was officially brought by another company which was also owned by Skype founders: Niklas Zennstrom and Janus Friis. Trouble for that company, Joltid, which also founded a video-sharing site, began when eBay moved to sell most of Skype to three private equity firms. The Skype founders argued that such a sale would violate eBay's license to Skype's peer-to-peer technology, which they still technically owned. Making the case even more interesting, in March, 2009, Joltid filed the same suit in British court. eBay was optimistic about the chances of winning the case at the time of the filing, but at the same time started working on contingency plans just in case it had to turn over its technology.

Summary and Conclusions

Copyrights, trademarks, and patents fall under an area of the law known as *intellectual property*, which also usually includes trade secrets. The constitutional origins of intellectual property, at least for copyrights and patents, can be traced to Article I, Section 8 of the U.S. Constitution. There are three basic types of patents: *utility, plant,* and *design*. Patents generally have protection for 20 years. Trade secrets, on the other hand, can theoretically be protected in perpetuity, if certain conditions are met.

Trademarks have considerable protection under both state and federal law, but trademark holders must take aggressive steps to ensure that their marks do not become diluted and risk going into the public domain. Most advertisers and other commercial and noncommercial enterprises also constantly monitor the use of their trademarks for possible infringement, while making sure they treat the trademarks of others with appropriate respect.

Copyright, on the other hand, is strictly a federal matter, since enactment of the Copyright Act of 1976, which eliminated state copyright laws and common law copyright. The Act made other substantial changes in copyright law, not the least of which was significantly increasing the amount and duration of copyright protection for original works of authorship. Public perceptions and even those of communication professionals still consist of myths and distortions that bear little relationship to the real world of copyright. Many writers and artists still find it difficult to believe that copyright protection exists automatically upon creation of a work in a tangible medium without benefit of registration and that attribution alone does not protect one from a successful infringement suit. The concept of fair use is even more difficult to comprehend, and the courts as well as Congress have added to the confusion.

Nevertheless, the federal copyright statute is a powerful arsenal for the creators of original works of authorship. The fact that copyrighted works, other than works made for hire and anonymous works, are protected under the Sonny Bono Copyright Extension Act for 70 years beyond the last surviving author's death reflects the tone of the law. It is an authors' law—plain and simple—and journalists must be cautious in using the expressions of others. The law is not very forgiving, as attested by its provisions granting remedies from injunctions and damages to criminal penalties.

Congress continues to fill gaps that are occasionally detected by courts, especially as new technologies from electronic digitalization to distance education via the Internet become more prevalent. The fair use doctrine continues to add to the confusion, but guidelines such as those drafted for educational multimedia by the Consortium of College and University Media Centers are positive steps. Cutting-edge technologies will also continue to be developed to thwart would-be pirates, such as encryption techniques to curb the illegal copying of movies and music, including those delivered via modems, cable, and satellite.[278]

The most serious problem, at least from the perspective of industry, continues to be pirating, including illegal downloading on the Internet. One year after the U.S. Supreme Court handed down the *Grokster* ruling, illegal file sharing was apparently still alive and well. In the year following *Grokster*, the Recording Industry Association of America (RIAA) sued some 6,000 individuals for what it considered illegal downloading. With 10 million or more people around the world clicking into peer-to-peer technology each month, according to one report,[279] and with most file sharing likely illegal, it is obvious why the recording industry continues its fight to catch pirates, even when they are individual consumers rather than organized offenders.

In July 2009, the U.S. Justice Department confirmed that it was conducting an antitrust investigation into the settlement of a lawsuit that groups representing various authors and publishers had filed against Google. A $125 million settlement in October 2009 was designed to resolve a class action lawsuit filed earlier by the Authors Guild and the Association of American Publishers against Google. In that suit, the authors and publishers said Google's move to digitize books and make them available via its Book Search service was a violation of copyright law. The U.S. Justice Department said it was reviewing concerns that the agreement violated the Sherman Antitrust Act. The settlement gave Google the right to display books online, and to profit by selling access of titles by selling subscriptions to libraries and institutions. Revenue would be shared by Google, the authors, and publishers, so the Justice Department investigation was viewed as an indication to some observers that it was reviewing the complaints so that the agreement granted Google exclusive rights to also profit from so-called orphan works—those out of print books and authors or rights holders who were not known or at least could be found.[280]

Endnotes

1. Quoted in the Atlanta Journal-Constitution, June 22, 2006, at E9, indicating his approval of methods used by copyright owners to frustrate computer users when they attempt to illegally exchange audio and video files on the Internet.
2. Michael S. Malone, *The Smother of Invention*, Forbes, June 24, 2002, at 32.
3. Jeff Nesmith, *Tech Innovations Swamp U.S. Patent Office*, Atlanta Journal-Constitution, Aug. 27, 2006, at B1.
4. *Id.*
5. Pub. L. 100-418 (1989).
6. Pub. L. 98-417 (1984) and Pub. L. 100-670 (1988) had granted such an extension for drugs, but the 1989 Act broadened the extension to include patents for other inventions and discoveries.
7. 35 U.S.C. §101.
8. 35 U.S.C. §161.
9. 35 U.S.C. §171.
10. All patent infringement suits must be brought in the U.S. District Court. Other federal courts and state courts have no jurisdiction. Appeals from the U.S. District Court are then heard exclusively by the U.S. Court of Appeals for the Federal Circuit. Upon a writ of certiorari, a discretionary writ, the U.S. Supreme Court can, if it so chooses, hear any appeals from the Federal Circuit.
11. *In Re Alappat*, 33 F.3d 1526, 13 U.S.P.Q. 2d 1545 (Fed. Cir. 1994).
12. 35 U.S.C. §103.
13. *Polaroid v. Eastman Kodak*, 789 F.2d 1556, 229 U.S.P.Q. 561 (Fed. Cir. 1986), *cert. denied*, 479 U.S. 850, 107 S.Ct. 178, 93 L.Ed.2d 114 (1986).
14. *See* Saul Hansell, *Microsoft Loses Case over Patents*, New York Times, Feb. 23, 2007, at C9.
15. David Koenig, *TiVo Jury Doesn't Pause: It's a $74 Million Settlement*, Madison.com (Associated Press), Apr. 14, 2006.
16. For a succinct overview of patent law basics, *see* Larry Roberts, *Patent Law for the General Practitioner*, 9 Ga. B.J. 10 (Aug. 2003).
17. *eBay, Inc. v. MERCEXCHANGE, L.L.C.*, 126 S.Ct. 1837, 164 L.Ed.2d 641 (2006).
18. *A Market for Ideas*, Economist, U.S. Edition (Oct. 22, 2005).
19. *Id.*
20. *KSR International Co. v. Teleflex, Inc.*, 127 S.Ct. 1727, 1671. Ed.2d 705 (2007).
21. *Microsoft v. AT&T Corp.*, 127 S.Ct. 1746, 167 L. Ed.2d 737 (2007).
22. N.C. Gen. Stat. §66-152(1).
23. 764 ILCS 1065/3(a).
24. *Pepsico, Inc. v. Redmond and the Quaker Oats Co.*, 54 F.3d 1262, 35 U.S.P.Q. 2d (BNA) 1010 (7th Cir. 1995).
25. Economic Espionage Act of 1996, Pub. L. 104-294, 110 Stat. 3488 (1996).
26. 5 U.S.C. §552.
27. 18 U.S.C. §1905.
28. *Chrysler Corp. v. Brown*, 441 U.S. 281, 99 S.Ct. 1705, 60 L.Ed.2d 208 (1979).
29. *Kewanee Oil Co. v. Bicron Corp.*, 416 U.S. 470, 94 S.Ct. 1879, 40 L.Ed.2d 315 (1974).
30. *Dow Chemical Co. v. United States*, 476 U.S. 227, 106 S.Ct. 1819, 90 L.Ed.2d 226 (1986).
31. *Ruckelshaus v. Monsanto Co.*, 467 U.S. 986, 104 S.Ct. 2862, 81 L.Ed.2d 815 (1984).
32. Kevin Moran, *'Star Bock' Beer Has Coffee Giant Starbucks Steamed*, Houston Chronicle, June 7, 2005; *Judge Nixes Sambuck's Coffee Shop Name*, Associated Press Online, December 7, 2005; John Stossel, *Give Me a Break: Sambucks and Trademarks*, ABC News, 20/20, Dec. 9, 2005.

33. Starbucks vs. 'Charbucks': Judge Says No Trademark Infringement, Associated Press, Dec. 28, 2005.

34. Maria Levitov, Starbucks Reclaims Trademark, Moscow Times, July 15, 2005; Starbucks Wins Legal Brew in Shanghai Against Chinese Copycat," Agence France Press, Jan. 2, 2006.

35. Federal Trademark Dilution Act (FTDA), 15 U.S.C. §1125(c) (1995).

36. Dickerson M. Dowling, Dilution in the Post-Victoria's Secret World, Computer & Internet Law, Dec. 2004, at 6.

37. Moseley and Moseley v. V Secret Catalogue, Inc., 537 U.S. 418, 123 S.Ct. 1115, 155 L.Ed.2d 1 (2003).

38. Larry Neumeister, Judge Rules Against Sports Illustrated Model in Sexy Panties Flap, Associated Press, Jan. 11, 2006.

39. *See* Apple Corps Loses ITunes Suit, 9 May, 2006 at http://www.washingtonpost.com/wp-dyn/content/article/2006/05/08/AR2006050800235.html

40. U.S. Department of Commerce, Patent and Trademark Office, Basic Facts about Trademarks at http://www.uspto.gov.

41. Pub. L. 100-667 (1988).

42. *Qualitex Company v. Jacobson Products, Inc,* 514 U.S. 159, 115 S.Ct. 1300, 131 L.Ed.2d 248 (1995).

43. *In Re General Electric Co.,* 199 U.S. P.Q. 560 (T.T.A.B. 1978).

44. 15 U.S.C. § 1051.

45. *Mead Data Central, Inc. v. Toyota Motor Sales, U.S.A., Inc.,* 875 F.2d 1026, 10 U.S. P.Q.2d 1961 (2nd Cir. 1989); Prather, *How Toyota Got 'Lexus' for Name of New Car,* Lexington (Ky.) Herald-Leader, Jan. 11, 1989, at A1.

46. Bruce Schreiner, *Kerns Is Vigilant About Derby-Pie,* Lexington (Ky.) Herald-Leader, May 6, 2006, at C2.

47. David Adams, *Universities Fighting for Right to Use 'Ohio,'* Lexington (Ky.) Herald-Leader, Nov. 27, 1997, at A25.

48. James Prichard, *Donatos Gets a Piece of the Pie, But Pizza Hut Keeps Its 'Edge,'* Lexington (Ky.) Herald-Leader (Associated Press), Oct. 30, 1997, at D2.

49. *Litigating Against Lobsters Described as 'Absurd,'* First Amendment Legal Watch, First Amendment Center at Vanderbilt University, July 29, 1997, Vol. 2, No. 30.

50. *G. Heileman Brewing Co., Inc. v. Anheuser-Busch, Inc.,* 873 F.2d 985 (1989); *LA Law,* A.B.A. J., Aug. 1989, at 92.

51. *L.L. Bean, Inc. v. Drake Publishers, Inc.,* 811 F.2d 26, 13 Med.L.Rptr. 2009 (1st Cir. 1987).

52. *San Francisco Arts and Athletics, Inc. v. United States Olympic Committee,* 483 U.S. 522, 107 S.Ct. 925, 97 L.Ed.2d 427 (1987).

53. *See* Todd C. Frankel, *A Smile from 'South Butt' Judge,* St. Louis Post- Dispatch, February 11, 2-010, at A-8.

54. Kitch and Perlman, *Legal Regulation of the Competitive Process* 622 (1979).

55. *Bally Total Fitness Holding Corp. v. Faber,* 29 F.Supp. 2d 1161 (C.D. Cal. 1998).

56. Mark Sableman, Link Law Revisited: Internet Linking Law at Five Years, 16 BERKELEY L. 1314 (fall 2001).

57. Ericka S. Koster and Jim Shatz-Akin, *Set Phasers on Stun: Handling Internet Fan Sites* Computer Law Journal, Jan. 1998, at 18.

58. 17 U.S.C. §101.

59. Computer Software Rental Amendments Act of 1990, Title VIII of Pub. L. 101-650, 104 Stat. 5089 (1990).

60. Record Rental Amendment, Pub. L. 98-450, 98 Stat. 1727 (1984).

61. *Quality King Distributors, Inc. v. L'Anza Research International, Inc.,* 66 U.S. L.W. 4188 (1998).

62. Joan Biskupic, *Discounters Get a Break from High Court,* Lexington (Ky.) Herald-Leader (Washington Post), Mar. 10, 1998, at E2.

63. *Quality King Distributors, Inc. v. L'Anza Research International, Inc.* (1998).

64. 17 U.S.C. §102(a).

65. 17 U.S.C. §101.

66. *Id.*

67. *Burrow-Giles Lithographic Company v. Sarony,* 111 U.S. 53, 4 S.Ct. 279, 28 L.Ed. 349 (1984).

68. *Id.*

69. Mitch Tuchman, *Supremely Wilde*, Smithsonian, May 2004, at 17, an interesting discussion of the history of this case.

70. Huff, *Leno Says Stern Should Blame NBC, Not Him,* Lexington (Ky.) Herald-Leader, Feb. 16, 1996, at Weekender-8.

71. *Community for Creative Non-Violence v. Reid*, 490 U.S. 730, 109 S.Ct. 2166, 104 L.Ed.2d 811, 16 Med.L.Rptr. 1769 (1989).

72. *Id.*

73. *Id.*

74. 17 U.S.C. §102.

75. *Hoehling v. Universal City Studios, Inc.*, 618 F.2d 972, 6 Med.L.Rptr. 1053 (2d Cir. 1980), *cert. denied,* 449 U.S. 841 (1980).

76. *Id.*

77. *Id.*

78. U.S. Copyright Office, *Copyright Basics*, available at http://www.copyright.gov.

79. *Dastar Corp. v. Twentieth Century Fox*, 539 U.S. 23, 123 S.Ct. 2041, 156 L.Ed.2d 18 (2003).

80. Linda Greenhouse, *Justices Reject Using Trademark Law in Case About Old War Footage*, New York Times online (http://www.nytimes.com), June 3, 2003.

81. *Miller v. Universal City Studios, Inc.*, 650 F.2d 1365, 7 Med.L.Rptr. 1735 (5th Cir. 1981).

82. *Miller v. Universal City Studios, Inc.*, 460 F.Supp. 984 (S.D. Fla. 1978).

83. *Id.*

84. *Id.*

85. *Feist Publications, Inc. v. Rural Telephone Service Co.*, 499 U.S. 340, 111 S.Ct. 1282, 113 L.Ed.2d 358, 18 Med.L.Rptr. 1889 (1991).

86. *Composer Pays for Piece of Silence,* CNN.com, Sept. 23, 2002.

87. *International News Service v. Associated Press*, 248 U.S. 215, 39 S.Ct. 68, 63 L.Ed. 211 (1918).

88. *Id.*

89. For a much more detailed listing of copyright terms, see *Copyright Term and the Public Domain in the United States* at http://www.copyright.cornell.edu/resources/publicdomain.cfm.

90. Pub. L. 87-668, 89-142, 90-141, 90-416, 91-147, 91-555, 92-170, 92-566, and 93-573.

91. Berne Convention Implementation Act of 1988, Pub. L. 100-568, 102 Stat. 2853.

92. 17 U.S.C. §§405 and 406.

93. 17 U.S.C. §405(b).

94. 17 U.S.C. §401(a).

95. 17 U.S.C. §402(a).

96. 37 C.F.R. §201.20 for complete regulations. They are summarized in U.S. Copyright Office, *Copyright Notice*, available at http://www.copyright.gov.

97. 17 U.S.C. §401(c) (1996).

98. *Id.*

99. 17 U.S.C. §402(c) (1996).

100. 37 C.F.R. §201.20(d) and Copyright Notice.

101. 17 U.S.C. §501(a) (1996).

102. *Playboy Enterprises, Inc. v. Starware Publishing Corp.*, 900 F.Supp. 438 (S.D. Fla. 1995).

103. *Before You Wish Upon A Star, Better Check the Copyright*, Lexington (Ky.) Herald-Leader (wire services), May 1, 1989, at A12.

104. *National Conference of Bar Examiners v. Multistate Legal Studies, Inc.,* Civil Action 0403282-JF (E.D. Pa. 2006).

105. Geri L. Dreiling, *A Costly Case of Cribbing,* American Bar Association Journal e-Report, Sept. 2, 2006, available at http://www.abanet.org.

106. *National Conference of Bar Examiners v. Multistate Legal Studies, Inc.*

107. Family Entertainment and Copyright Act of 2005, 109 P. Law. 9, 119 Stat. 218 (2005).

108. Martin E. Segal, *Don't Take Your Camcorder to the Movies,* Miami Herald, Aug. 7, 2006.

109. Lindsey Nair, *Radford Pair Named in Movie Lawsuit,* Roanoke (Virginia) Times, Aug. 2, 2006.

110. Blodgett, *West, Mead Data Central Settle,* A.B.A. J., Sept. 1, 1988, at 36.

111. *Matthew Bender and HyperLaw, Inc. v. West Publishing Co.*, 42 U.S. P.Q.2d 1930, 25 Med. L.Rptr. 1856 (S.D. N.Y. 1997).

112. *Oasis Publishing Co. v. West Publishing Co.*, 924 F.Supp. 918 (1996).

113 Laura Gatland, *West Settles Copyright Suit*, American Bar Association Journal, Oct. 1997, at 37.

114. *Garrison Keillor Settles Suit with National Public Radio*, Cincinnati Post, June 24, 1988, at A2.

115. John Maatta and Lorin Brennan, 10 Hastings Comment L.J. 1081 (1988).

116. U.S. Copyright Office, *International Copyright Relations of the United States;* for a complete list of countries having copyright agreements with the United States see http://copyright.gov.

117. *Baigent v. Random House Group*, EWHC 719 (2006).

118. 17 U.S.C. §205.

119. Constructive notice is a legal term implying or imputing that the public has been notified in the eyes of the law by being provided a means for learning such information. In other words, by recording the agreement in the copyright office, the transferor and transferee have met any public notice requirements since anyone who examined the copies of the documents in the copyright office would know the terms of the agreement. This is in contrast to actual notice in which the parties have formally provided other parties with actual copies of the documents.

120. 17 U.S.C. §205(c)(1) and (2).

121. 17 U.S.C. §205(d) and (e).

122. U.S. Copyright Office, Recordation of Transfers and Other Documents, http://www.copyright.gov.

123. *Id.*

124. 17 U.S.C. §205.

125. 17 U.S.C. §203(a)(3).

126. 17 U.S.C. §203(b)(1).

127. 17 U.S.C. §111.

128. 17 U.S.C. §111(a)(1).

129. U.S. Copyright Office, Licensing Division at http://www.copyright.gov.

130. Another licensing agency is SESAC, Inc. (once known as the Society of European State Authors and Composers), but ASCAP and BMI dominate the field.

131. *Buffalo Broadcasting Co., Inc. v. American Society of Composers, Authors and Publishers*, 744 F.2d 917 (2d Cir. 1984), *cert. denied*, 469 U.S. 1211, 105 S.Ct. 1181, 84 L.Ed.2d 329 (1985).

132. *Id.*

133. *Id.*

134. *Id.*

135. *Id.*

136. *Sailor Music et al. v. The Gap Stores, Inc.*, 668 F.2d 84 (2nd Cir. 1981), *cert. denied*, 456 U.S. 945, 102 S.Ct. 2012, 72 L.Ed.2d 468 (1982).

137. Copyright Basics.

138. 17 U.S.C. §507(a).

139. 17 U.S.C. §507(b).

140. *$25 Million Deal Includes Ownership of Birthday Song*, Lexington (Ky.) Herald-Leader (New York Times News Service), Dec. 20, 1988, at A4.

141. *For A Song: 'Happy Birthday to You' May Sell for $12 Million*, Lexington (Ky.) Herald-Leader (New York Times News Service), Oct. 20, 1988, at A2.

142. *$25 Million Deal Includes Ownership of Birthday Song, supra.*

143. *Id.*

144. *Id.*

145. H.R. 94-1476, 94th Cong., 2nd Sess. 65 (1976). Excerpts reproduced in U.S. Copyright Office, Reproduction of Copyrighted Works by Educators and Librarians, http://www.copyright.gov.

146. 17 U.S.C. § 107.

147. *Id.*

148. H.R. 94-1476, *supra.*

149. *Time, Inc. v. Bernard Geis Associates*, 293 F.Supp. 130 (S.D. N.Y. 1968).

150. Bernard Geis Associates had offered all profits from the book to Time, Inc. in return for a license to use the copyrighted frames in the book, but the magazine publisher rejected the offer.

151. *Time, Inc. v. Bernard Geis Associates.*

152. *Id.*

153. *U.S. Begins Legal Seizure of Film of Kennedy Slaying,* Lexington (Ky.) Herald-Leader (Associated Press), Apr. 25, 1997, at A16.

154. *Harper & Row Publishers, Inc. and The Reader's Digest Association, Inc. v. Nation Enterprises,* 471 U.S. 539, 105 S.Ct. 2218, 88 L.Ed.2d 588, 11 Med.L.Rptr. 1969 (1985).

155. *Id.*

156. *Id.*

157. *Id.*

158. *Id.*

159. *Id.*

160. Vittor, *'Fair Use' of Unpublished Materials: 'Widow Censors,' Copyright and the First Amendment,* Comunications Law, Fall 1989, at 1.

161. *Harper & Row v. Nation Enterprises.*

162. *Salinger v. Random House,* 811 F.2d 90, 13 Med.L.Rptr. 1954 (2d Cir. 1987), *cert. denied,* 484 U.S. 890, 108 S.Ct. 213, 98 L.Ed.2d 177 (1987).

163. *Id.*

164. *Id.*

165. *New Era Publications International v. Henry Holt & Co.,* 873 F.2d 576, 16 Med.L.Rptr. 1559 (2d Cir. 1989).

166. *Id.*

167. *Id.*

168. *Id.*

169. *New Era Publications International v. Henry Holt & Co., reh'g denied,* 884 F.2d 659, 16 Med. L.Rptr. 2224 (2d Cir. 1989).

170. *New Era Publications International v. Carol Publishing Group,* 904 F.2d 152, 17 Med.L.Rptr. 1913 (2d Cir. 1990).

171. *Id.*

172. Kaplan, *The End of History? A Copyright Controversy Leads to Self-Censorship,* Newsweek, Dec. 25, 1989, at 80.

173. Pub. L. 102-492 (Oct. 24, 1992).

174. Lisa M. Krieger, *Copyright Suit Challenges What's Public vs. Private,* San Jose Mercury News, Aug. 4, 2006.

175. *American Geophysical Union v. Texaco,* 85 Civ. 3446, 802 F.Supp. 1 (S.D. N.Y. 1992).

176. Under the Federal Interlocutory Appeals Act, 28 U.S.C. §1292(b), a U.S. Court of Appeals can review any interlocutory order (an interim order pending final disposition of a controversy) in a civil case if the district court judge states in the decision that there is a controlling question of law on which there is apparent disagreement in the courts. The judge in this case had issued such an order so the appellate court could make the final determination.

177. *American Geophysical Union v. Texaco,* 37 F.3d 881, 32 U.S. P.Q. 2d 1545 (2nd Cir. 1994).

178. *American Geophysical Union v. Texaco,* 60 F.3d 913 (2d Cir. 1995).

179. Mary Beth Markein, *Colleges Are Textbook Cases of Cybersecurity Breaches,* USA Today, Aug. 2, 2006.

180. *Basic Books, Inc. v. Kinko's Graphics Corp.,* 758 F.Supp. 1522 (S.D. N.Y. 1991).

181. Watkins, *Photocopying Chain Found in Violation of Copyright Law,* Chronic;e of Higher Education, Apr. 3, 1991, at A1.

182. March 29, 1991, letter from Paul J. Orfalea, chairperson of Kinko's, distributed to university and college professors.

183. Scott Carlson, *U. of California Is in Talks to Join Google's Library-Scanning Project,* Chronicle of Higher Education, Aug. 11, 2006, at A29.

184. Dan Carnevale, *Blackboard Sues Rival Over Alleged Patent Infringement,* Chronicle of Higher Education, Aug. 11, 2006, at A30.

185. The 11th Amendment (adopted in 1798) says: "The Judicial power of the United States shall not be construed to extend to any suit in law or equity, commenced or prosecuted against one of the United States by Citizens of another State, or by Citizens or Subjects of any Foreign State."

186. *BV Engineering v. University of California at Los Angeles*, 858 F.2d 1394 (9th Cir. 1988).

187. Copyright Remedy Clarification Act of 1990, Pub. L. 101-553, 17 U.S.C. §§501(a) and 511.

188. 17 U.S.C. §501(a).

189. 17 U.S.C. §511(a).

190. 17 U.S.C. §511(b).

191. *Court Clips Wings of Atlanta Video Clipping Service*, Broadcasting, June 10, 1991, at 63.

192. Thompson, *Ruling on Right to Copy TV News Clips   Decides Little*, Atlanta Journal, Oct. 14, 1983, at A16.

193. *Court Clips Wings of Atlanta Video Clipping Service, supra.*

194. *Lish v. Harper's Magazine Foundation*, 807 F.Supp. 1090, 20 Med.L.Rptr. 2073 (S.D. N.Y. 1992); Reske, *Gordon Lish's $2,000 Letter*, AmericanBar.Association Journal, Feb. 1993, at 28.

195. *Luther R. Campbell a.k.a. Luke Skyywalker v. Acuff-Rose Music, Inc.*, 510 U.S. 569, 114 S.Ct. 1164, 127 L.Ed.2d 500, 22 Med.L.Rptr. 1353 (1994).

196. *Id.*

197. *Id.*

198. Consortium of College and University Media Centers, *Fair Use Guidelines for Educational Multimedia* (1996).

199. *Id.* More information about the guidelines can be found at http://www.libraries.psu.edu/avs/.

200. *Jonathan Tasini et al. v. the New York Times Co. et al.*, 981 F.Supp. 841 (1997).

201. *The New York Times Co. et al. v. Jonathan Tasini*, 533 U.S. 483, 121 S.Ct. 2381, 150 L.Ed.2d 500 (2001).

202. Heather Green, *Whose Video Is It, Anyway?* Business Week On-Line, July 28, 2006, at 38; *YouTube Launches Its Own Web Stars*, USA Today, July 18, 2006, at D1.

203. Stephen Levy and Brad Stone, *The New Wisdom of the Web*, Newsweek, Apr. 2006; John Jurgensen, *Moguls of the New Media*, Wall Street Journal, July 29, 2006, at 1.

204. *See* Daisy Whitney, *Viacom Escalates YouTube Copyright Fight*, Television Week, March 13, 2007, available at http://www.TVweek.com; Miguel Helft and Geraldine Fabrikant, *Whose Tube?*, New York Times, March 14, 2007, at C1.

205. The Digital Millennium Copyright Act of 1998, Pub. L. 105-304, 112 Stat. 2860 (Oct. 28, 1998). For a detailed explanation of the Act, *see* U.S. Copyright Office, *Digital Millennium Copyright Act of 1998* (U.S. Copyright Office Summary), available at http://www.copyright.gov.

206. Dan Carnevale, *College Radio Stations Reach Deal with Record Companies for Lower Web-casting Fees*, Chronicle of Higher Education (online edition) June 3, 2003.

207. Antony Bruner, et al., *The Latest news from .biz: YouTube Sued*, Hollywood Reporter, July 29, 2006.

208. Thomas K. Arnold, *Stream Turns to Deluge,* USA Today, July 5, 2006, at D5.

209. *Stewart v. Abend*, 495 U.S. 207, 110 S.Ct. 1750, 109 L.Ed.2d 184 (1990).

210. Epstein, *Court Ruling Could Pull Classic Videos from Shelves*, Lexington (Ky.) Herald-Leader (Knight Ridder News Service), Apr. 25, 1990, at A1. By 1990, the re-release had generated more than $12 million worldwide.

211. *Rohauer v. Killiam Shows*, 551 F.2d 484 (2d Cir. 1977), *cert. denied*, 431 U.S. 949, 97 S.Ct. 2666, 53 L.Ed.2d 266 (1977).

212. Epstein, *supra.*

213. *Steward v. Abend.*

214. Epstein, *supra.*

215. *Band Sues 'Rock Star' Over Supernova Name: Attorney for Mark Burnett Says Show Has Legal Right to Use Name*, Associated Press, MSNBC, July 11, 2006.

216. *TVBR Observation: Will CBS Supernova Flame Out?* Television Business Report, Aug. 14, 2006.

217. *Jagger Gets Satisfaction in Lawsuit Over Song*, Lexington (Ky.) Herald-Leader (Associated Press), Apr. 27, 1988, at A2.

218. *Id.*

219. *Sid and Marty Krofft Television Productions, Inc. v. McDonald's Corp.*, 562 F.2d 1157 (9th Cir. 1977).

220. *Id.*

221. *Universal City Studios, Inc. v. Film Ventures International, Inc.*, 543 F.Supp. 1134 (C.D. Calif1982).

222. *Id.*

223. *Ruolo v. Russ Berrie & Co.*, 886 F.2d 931 (7th Cir. 1989).

224. Abramson, *'Look and Feel' of Computer Software*, Case and Comment, Jan–Feb. 1990, at 3.

225. *Id.*

226. M. Sableman, *Link Law: The Emerging Law of Internet Hyperlinks*, 4 Communication Law and Policy 585 (1999).

227. *Eldred v. Ashcroft*, 537 U.S. 186, 123 S.Ct. 769, 154 L.Ed.2d 683 (2003).

228. Lawrence Lessig, *Free Culture: The Future of Ideas and Code and Other Laws of Cyberspace* (2004) and *The Future of Ideas: The Fate of the Commons in a Connected World* (2001); http://www. lessig.org.

229. Andy Raskin, *Giving It Away (For Fun and Profit)*, Business 2.0, May 2004, at 112.

230. 17 U.S.C. §503(b).

231. 17 U.S.C. §504(b).

232. Pub. L. 100-568, 102 Stat. 2853, 2860 (1988).

233. The amounts prior to the October 31, 1988, enactment of the new law were $250 and $10,000, respectively.

234. 17 U.S.C. §504(c)(2).

235. No Electronic Theft (NET) Act, Pub. L. 105-147, 111 Stat. 2678 (1997).

236. Jeffery Sheban, *Firms in Ohio Hurt by Illegal Copying; Intellectual Propety Theft 'Getting Worse*, The Columbus (Ohio) Dispatch, May 17, 2006, at D1.

237. *Fact Sheet: Department of Justice Increases Enforcement and Protection of Intellectual Property*, U.S. Newswire, Mar. 30, 2006.

238. 17 U.S.C. §505.

239. 17 U.S.C. §506 (1994) and 18 U.S.C. §2319(b)(1)(A).

240. 18 U.S.C. §2319(b)(1)(B).

241. 18 U.S.C. §2318.

242. *Sony Corp. of America v. Universal City Studios, Inc.*, 465 U.S.1112, 104 S.Ct. 1619, 80 L.Ed.2d 1480 (1984).

243. At the time of the Court's decision these devices were called video tape recorders or VTRs, but the terminology later became videocassette recorders (VCRs), a forerunner of today's DVD technology.

244. Betamax VCRs used the Beta format, which lost out to the VHS format, but at the time of the suit, Beta was the dominant format. Even Sony eventually abandoned Beta for VHS in its VCRs for home use. Although some technical experts still argue that the Beta format was superior to VHS, VHS won the battle, primarily because manufacturers of VHS recorders outmaneuvered Beta in the marketplace.

245. *Sony Corp. of America v. Universal City Studios, Inc.*

246. *Id.*

247. Public Law 102-307, enacted on June 26, 1992, made even renewal registration optional by automatically extending the duration of copyright obtained between January 1, 1964 and December 31, 1977 to an additional 47-year period. No registration renewal needs to be filed for this extension. There are some advantages to renewal registration, however. *See* U.S. Copyright Office, Renewal of Copyright, http://www.copyright.gov. One of the advantages is that such registration serves as *prima facie* evidence of the validity of the copyright, just as it does with an original registration.

248. *Copyright Basics.*

249. U.S. Copyright Office, *Copyright Registration for Computer Programs*, http://www.copyright.gov.

250. U.S. Copyright Office, *Copyright Registration for Automated Data Databases*, http://www.copyright.gov.

251. The Copyright Act defines a "compilation" as "a work formed by the collection and assembling of pre-existing materials or of data that are selected, coordinated, or arranged in such a way that the resulting work as a whole constitutes an original work of authorship." *See* 17 U.S.C. §101.

252. Pub. L. 98-62 (1984).

253. *Id.*

254. *Gilliam v. American Broadcasting Cos., Inc.*, 538 F.2d 14 (2d Cir. 1976).

255. Rob Lever, *Blast from the Past: Napster Tries Free Music*, with a Twist, Agence France Presse, May 4, 2006.

256. Neal Conan, "Viral Video and the Rise of YouTube," *Talk of the Nation*, National Public Radio, June 6, 2006; Andrew Wallenstein, *Catch YouTube if You Can,* Hollywood Reporter, Mar. 21, 2006.

257. *See* Stefan Walther, Bloopers, Canadian Association of Journalists Media Magazine, Winter 2001, at http://caj.ca/wp-content/uploads/2010/mediamag/winter2001/bloopers.html

258. Dan Carnevale, *Magazine's Essay on Plagiarism Seems to Have Been Partly Plagiarized*, Chronicle of Higher Education (online edition), May 28, 2003.

259. Brock Read, *News Organization at Brigham Young U. Returns Awards for Copied Web-Site Design*, Chronicle of Higher Educucation (online edition), June 3, 2003.

260. Mary Pilon, *Anti-Plagiarism Programs Look Over Students' Work*, USA Today, May 23, 2006, at D10.

261. David Mehegan, *Author's Apology Not Accepted,* Lexington (Ky.) Herald-Leader (Boston Globe), Apr. 26, 2006, at B8.

262. David Streitfeld, *Romance World Is Dark, Stormy over Plagiarism,* Lexington (Ky.) Herald-Leader (Washington Post), July 31, 1997, at A3; Nanci Hellmich, *For Janet Dailey, A Romance Gone Sour,* USA Today, July 31, 1997, at D1.

263. David Streitfeld, *Romance World Is Dark, Stormy over Plagiarism.*

264. L. Eko, *Many Spiders, One World Wide Web:Towards a Typology of Internet Regulation*, Communication Law and Policy, 6, 445, 2001.

265. *Justice Department Highlights Progress in Intellectual Property Protectio*n, Techweb, June 19, 2006.

266. U.S. Government Brings Anti-Counterfeiting, Piracy Program to Southern California, U.S. Fed News, Feb. 27, 2006.

267. *Metro-Goldwyn-Mayer Studios v. Grokster*, 543 U.S. 913, 125 S.Ct. 2764, 162 L.Ed.2d 781 (2005).

268. *Sony Corp. v. Universal Studios Inc.,* 464 U.S. 417 (1984).

269. Michelle Witte, *The Daily via U-Wire*, University Wire, June 29, 2005; and "Supreme Court Decision on Peer-to-Peer File Sharing," *Talk of the Nation*, National Public Radio (NPR), June 27, 2005.

270. Rod Smolla, *You Say Napster, I Say Grokster*, Slate Magazine, Dec. 13, 2004.

271. Mary Beth Peters, *Copyright Infringement and File Sharing*, Capital Hill Testimony, Committee on the Senate Judiciary, Congressional Quarterly, Sept. 28, 2005.

272. Ted Bridis, *Grokster Downloading Service Shuts Down in Piracy Settlement*, Associated Press, Nov. 7, 2005; William Triplett, *Grokster Sings Swan Song,* Variety, Nov. 8, 2005, at 4.

273. Brooks Boliek, *It's Over for Grokster*, Hollywood Reporter, Nov. 8, 2005. Susan Butler, *Legal Matters: Grokster Shackled*, Billboard.Com, Nov. 26, 2005.

274. *5,000 Channels: TV on the Internet*, Time, Jan. 23, 2006, at 69.

275. *Id.*

276. Sean Smith, *When the 'Bubble' Bursts*, Newsweek, Jan. 23, 2006, at 65.

277. *Id.*

278. *Agreement Will Curb Illegal Copying of Music, Movies,* Lexington (Ky.) Herald-Leader, Feb. 20, 1998, at B6.

279. John Boudreau, *Illegal File Sharing Showing No Letup*, Seattle Times (seattletimes.com), July 3, 2006.

280. See Miguel Helft, "U.S. Inquiry Is Confirmed Into Google Books Deal" *New York Times*, July 2, 2009, at B-1.

13

International and Foreign Law

*Kyu Ho Youm**

I make difficult decisions such as assessing the risk that the Ayatollah Khomeini might sue the magazine for libel.

—C. Thomas Dienes, former general counsel for *U.S. News & World Report, 23* Journal of Legal Reform 1 (1989).

Which country will most likely fit the status report on freedom of speech and the press below?

- Access to government records is not a constitutional right;
- Journalists have not much constitutional privilege to protect sources;
- Defamation remains a crime;
- Advertising is less protected than non-commercial speech, although it's true and not illegal.

One more revelatory hint: This country is ranked 20th in a global press freedom survey of 175 nations.[1] Believe it or not, the answer to the question is the United States, which is often touted as an "exception" in its commitment to freedom of expression.[2] America does not necessarily lead the rest of the world in its freedom of speech and the press. Indeed, it is trailing in some areas. One media law commentator stated, "[T]he sweeping free-speech assumption about the U.S. exceptionalism is more debatable than ever, with First Amendment precepts continuing to unfold, as Americans endeavor to balance free speech with other competing sociopolitical interests amid unprecedented challenges at home and abroad."[3]

Meanwhile, the Parliament of Iceland was scheduled to vote in 2010 on its Icelandic Modern Media Initiative (IMMI) to offer more press freedom in Iceland than in any other place by,

---

* The author is the Jonathan Marshall First Amendment Chair Professor in the School of Journalism and Communication at the University of Oregon. Portions of this Chapter are drawn from the author's published research in several law journals, including the *Journal of International Media & Entertainment Law, Communication Law & Policy, George Washington Law Review, Hastings Communications & Entertainment Law Journal,* and *Stanford Journal of International Law* or from his presented papers at AEJMC (Association for Education in Journalism and Mass Communication) and other scholarly conventions. For this Chapter the author has substantially revised and updated them, where warranted.

among other things, strengthening news source and whistleblower protections, adopting anti-SLAPP (Strategic Lawsuits Against Public Participation) law, immunizing internet service providers (ISPs) from liability, limiting prior restraint, expanding freedom of information (FOI), and banning "libel tourism."[4]

"To a considerable extent," a journalism and media law scholar commented, "the Initiative is borrowing from the 100-plus years of the US experience with freedom of speech and the press. Not surprising."[5] He stressed, however, that the Initiative went beyond the First Amendment. He considered it an example of the international and foreign laws that "are sometimes more proactive in press freedom than US law."[6]

The international and comparative understanding of media law is increasingly relevant. It is not only for journalism and communication scholars and students but also for practicing lawyers and journalists. The accelerated globalization of the media thanks to the Internet[7] entails more than instantaneous and interactive communication among individuals and institutions in the United States and abroad. It raises a host of legal challenges for the news media, especially those transnational U.S. media. They often force journalists and media lawyers to engage in risk assessment. The quote at the beginning of this chapter by Thomas Dienes is further evidence of these wide-ranging and diverse concerns. [8]

Another case in point: The *New York Times* blocked access for U.K. readers to its August 28, 2006, edition online and did not deliver any of its offline editions for that day to the United Kingdom. The August 28, 2006, edition of the *New York Times* contained an article detailing suspects in England who were allegedly plotting to blow up transatlantic airlines. In explaining its unprecedented decision to forgo its distribution to England, whether in hard or soft copies, this American newspaper stated: "On advice of legal counsel, this article is unavailable to readers of nytimes.com in Britain. This arises from the requirement in British law that prohibits publication of prejudicial information about the defendants prior to trial."[9]

Regardless, now nearly every area of American media law is closely intertwined with international and foreign law. In recent years, freedom of speech and the press has become "a subject of practical importance."[10] Some international media law issues are more familiar than others. Libel, privacy, and other media liability-related issues have attracted more in-depth attention for a longer period of time,[11] while access to information, hate speech, journalistic privilege, and commercial speech have emerged as an area of interest to media and non-media students and practitioners.[12] Enforcement of foreign court judgments has also concerned American journalists, lawyers, and judges.[13]

Given the growing need for American students to develop global and comparative perspectives on media law,[14] this chapter offers an international and comparative approach to some of the media law topics discussed in this book. At the outset, meanwhile, it should be acknowledged that the discussion of international and foreign media law ought to be deliberately selective. This is largely because a single book chapter is not capacious enough to address the fast expanding international and foreign law,[15] and also some media law topics are more significant than others.

Among the more significant and thus more widely discussed international and foreign media law topics are hate speech, defamation, privacy, right of reply as access to the press, journalistic privilege, freedom of information, commercial speech, and foreign court judgments against U.S. media. This chapter examines these discrete topics. Some topics are discussed in more detail than others.

I. Freedom of Expression: Hate Speech as a Crime

Hate speech is protected in the United States. The First Amendment attorney Floyd Abrams explains:

> We protect it under the broad legal umbrella provided by the First Amendment. There is an inevitable trade-off in doing so. By broadly protecting such speech, we avoid the risks of suppressing valuable speech that could be argued to be unacceptably offensive to others.... Perhaps most important, we avoid legitimizing direct governmental censorship of speech based upon content."[16]

But the First Amendment protection of hate speech makes American law diverge from the law of many other liberal democracies.[17] University of London professor Eric Heinze noted that the U.S. approach to hate speech "looks increasingly like an anomaly."[18]

All the major international human rights treaties recognize hate speech bans. Article 20(2) of the International Covenant on Civil and Political Rights (ICCPR) provides: "Any advocacy of national, racial or religious hatred that constitutes incitement to discrimination, hostility or violence shall be prohibited by law."[19] The International Convention on the Elimination of All Forms of Racial Discrimination (CERD) is stronger in requiring all state parties to the treaty to declare as a criminal offence "all dissemination of ideas based on racial superiority or hatred, incitement to racial discrimination,... the provision of any assistance to racial activities," and participation in "organizations, and also organized and all other propaganda activities, which promote and incite racial discrimination."[20]

The regional human rights conventions for Europe, Americas, and Africa prohibit hate speech.[21] But they have been occasionally interpreted in such a way as to protect hate speech. Although it is distinguishable from the U.S. Supreme Court in *Brandenburg v. Ohio*,[22] for example, the majority of the European Court of Human Rights in *Jersild v. Denmark*[23] held that a journalist's conviction under a Danish hate speech law violated Article 10 the European Convention of Human Rights (ECHR).

As noted earlier, the U.S. prohibition of hate speech is exceptional. Sandra Coliver of Article 19 called American hate speech law in the early 1990s "the United States' dramatically different approach from that of Europe and the rest of the world."[24]

The oft-discussed *Yahoo!* case[25] capsulized how far a sovereign nation is willing to go in regulating hate speech online by punishing the originating source of the content. It began in April 2000, when two French anti-hate groups, La Ligue Contre le Racisme et l'Antisemitisme (League Against Racism and Anti-Semitism; LICRA) and L'Union des Etudiants Juifs de France (French Union of Jewish Students; UEJF), demanded that Yahoo! "cease presenting Nazi objects for sale" on its U.S. auction site and stop "hosting" on its Webpage service Nazi-related writing such as an English-language translation of *Mein Kampf.*

The French censorship advocacy groups sued Yahoo! Inc. and Yahoo! France in Paris, claiming that Yahoo! violated a French criminal statute, the Nazi Symbols Act, which prohibits the public display in France of Nazi-related "uniforms, insignia or emblems."[26] The French groups asked the trial court in Paris to order Yahoo! Inc. and Yahoo! France to "institute the necessary measures to prevent the display and sale on its site Yahoo.com of Nazi objects" in France.[27]

Characterizing the exhibition of Nazi objects on its site for sale is a violation of the French criminal code on hate speech, French Judge Jean-Jacques Gomez held that it constituted "more an affront to the collective memory of a country profoundly traumatized by the atrocities committed by Nazis against its citizens." He found that through its actions, Yahoo! committed "a wrong in the territory of France, a wrong whose unintentional character is averred but which has caused damage … to LICRA and UEJF."[28]

In May 2000, the French court issued an interim order directing Yahoo! to "take all necessary measures" to "dissuade and render impossible" any access to the Yahoo! Internet auction service displaying Nazi artifacts and to any other site or service "that may be construed as constituting an apology for Nazism or a contesting of Nazi crimes."[29] The court also gave Yahoo! two months to come up with technical proposals to implement its order.

In July 2000, Yahoo! told Judge Gomez that it would be "technically impossible" for the company to comply with his May 22 order. To determine the validity of Yahoo!'s alleged impossibility of implementing technical measures under his order, Judge Gomez convened a panel of three technology experts. The experts reported in November 2000 that some 70% of the Internet Protocol addresses of French users or users residing in French territory could be correctly identified by specialized providers using specialized databases.[30] Further, the panel added that if Yahoo! asked its users whose IP address is ambiguous to "provide a *declaration of nationality*," it could achieve "a filtering success rate approaching 90%." [31]

In "reaffirm[ing]" its order of May 22, 2000, the French court directed Yahoo!, among others, to (1) re-engineer its content servers in the United States and elsewhere to enable them to recognize French IP addresses and block access to Nazi material by end-users assigned such IP addresses; (2) require end-users with "ambiguous" IP addresses to declare their nationalities when they arrive at Yahoo!'s home page or when they initiate any search using the word "Nazi"; and (3) comply with the court order within three months or face penalty of 100,000 Francs (approximately U.S.$13,300) for each day of non-compliance.[32] The court denied the anti-hate groups' request to enforce its order or impose any penalties directed at Yahoo! Inc. against Yahoo! France.[33]

The French court judgment was hailed as a moral and cultural victory for those who supported the advocacy groups who stated that "French have a right to be shielded from the commercialization of Nazi objects."[34] And the Movement Against Racism and for Friendship Among Peoples in France considers the ruling a warning against the Internet's becoming "an extra-legal zone" governed by the "permissive" nature of the First Amendment to the U.S. Constitution.[35]

To those who see the unlimited value of the Internet as a "unique new medium of communication" in expanding freedom of expression, Judge Gomez's order against Yahoo! is "a predictable consequence of the global character of the Internet and the conflicts that will inevitably arise concerning speech protected by the U.S. Constitution but forbidden by repressive laws elsewhere."[36] Nonetheless, it has set a major legal precedent establishing that Internet companies, no matter where they're located, must pay extra attention to local laws in any countries from which their Websites are accessible.[37] While disavowing its intent to fully comply with the French ruling, Yahoo! has removed Nazi merchandise from its French-based site and inserted warnings on links to its auction site in the United States. On the other hand, Yahoo! has filed suit in U.S. federal district seeking a declaratory judgment that the French court decision cannot be enforced in the United States.

II. Defamation: Reputation Still a Priority

Legal protection against injury of a person's reputation is a "reasonable transcultural goal of the law."[38] The critical question is how to accommodate freedom of the press against the law of defamation, whether civil or criminal.[39] In the United States, reputation is not a fundamental right under the U.S. Constitution.[40] By contrast, it is recognized as a human right by the Universal Declaration of Human Rights[41] and the ICCPR. In the past few decades, however, freedom of speech and the press has been expanded at the expense of the right to reputation in a growing number of free-press countries. U.S. libel law is characterized by the First Amendment principle requiring that "speech be overprotected in order to assure that it is not under-protected."[42] Its "actual malice" rule represents America's unique libel law standard.[43]

A. *European Court of Human Rights on Defamation*

According to a 2006 study of 52 European Court of Human Rights (ECtHR) libel cases under Article 10(2),[44] the European Court found free-speech violations in 39 cases, i.e., 75%.[45] From a comparative perspective, the score card of the ECHR on free speech vs. reputation is profoundly significant in that it is not much different from that of American media libel jurisprudence.

The European court's frequent findings of Article 10 violations in defamation cases involving politicians over the years were presaged by *Lingens v. Austria*,[46] the ECtHR's landmark ruling on freedom of the press and libel law. For the first time the European court interpreted the "for the protection of the reputation or rights of others" clause of Article 10(2) in the context of criminal libel involving politicians.

The ECtHR enunciated First Amendment-like principles regarding the freedom of political speech and the need for politicians to accept criticism. The Court reasoned why politicians are different from nonpoliticians in libel law:

> The limits of acceptable criticism are .... wider as regards a politician as such than as regards a private individual. Unlike the latter, the former inevitably and knowingly lays himself open to close scrutiny of his every word and deed by both journalists and the public at large, and he must consequently display a greater degree of tolerance. No doubt Article 10(2) enables the reputation of others—that is to say, of all individuals—to be protected, and this protection extends to politicians too, even when they are not acting in their private capacity; but in such cases the requirements of such protection have to be weighted in relation to the interests of open discussion of political issues.[47]

The *Lingens* Court took issue with the Austrian Criminal Code, which limited Lingens' defense of his defamatory statements to proving that they were true. Because Lingens' comments were not provable facts but "value judgments," the court found that he was exercising not his right to distribute information but his freedom of opinion.[48]

The ECtHR's distinction between statements of fact and value judgments is important in that it is identical to American libel law on fact vs. opinion. Although its contours are still evolving, the European Court's protection of value judgments is in line with the libertarian reading of freedom of ideas and the right to hold opinions under Article 10. In every case, the

European court has applied the value judgment standard in favor of freedom of expression over reputational interest, especially when political expression was at issue.

Under Article 10 on freedom of expression vs. reputation, civil servants are more protected than politicians, but they are less protected than private persons. In *Thoma v. Luxembourg*,[49] the ECtHR stated:

> Civil servants acting in an official capacity are, like politicians, subject to wider limits of acceptable criticisms than private individuals. However, it cannot be said that civil servants knowingly lay themselves open to close scrutiny of their every word and deed to the extent politicians do and should therefore be treated on an equal footing with the latter when it comes to criticism of their conduct.[50]

Protection of civil servants from defamation is noticeably vigorous when it comes to judges and similar officials working for the judicial bodies. The ECtHR tends to be more deferential to the states' "margin of appreciation"[51] in punishing criticism of the judiciary. *Prager & Oberschlick v. Austria*[52] was one of the significant civil servant libel cases in which the European court gave more latitude to the states in Article 10's margin of appreciation. The ECtHR recognized the press's right and duty to question the functioning of the system of justice, which it termed "essential for any democratic society."[53] However, the Court added thus:

> Regard must ... be had to the special role of the judiciary in society. As the guarantor of justice, a fundamental value in a law-governed State, it must enjoy public confidence if it is to be successful in carrying out its duties. It may therefore prove necessary to protect such confidence against destructive attacks that are essentially unfounded, especially in view of the fact that judges who have been criticized are subject to a duty of discretion that precludes them from replying.[54]

Private citizens deserve more protection of their reputations than politicians or civil servants, the European Court stated. In reality, however, private persons should not be overly sanguine. When they are defamed by the news media in relation to issues of public interest, they are less likely to be protected. Thus, private libel plaintiffs under Article 10 face a similar situation that private figures do in American libel law. *Bergens Tidende & Others v. Norway*,[55] a 2000 private libel case, shows how conscious the ECtHR is of the public watchdog role of the news media in balancing freedom of expression with the reputation of a private individual. The European Court warned the state authorities against overreaching their margin of appreciation when the press plays its "vital role of 'public watchdog'" in imparting information on matters of public concern.[56] The Court expressed its qualms about interjecting itself into the role of dictating news reporting methods:

> [N]ews reporting based on interviews constitutes on [sic] of the most important means whereby the press is able to play its vital role of "public watchdog." The methods of objective and balanced reporting may vary considerably, depending among other things on the medium in question; it is not for the Court, any more than it is for the national courts, to substitute its own views for those of the press as to what techniques of reporting should be adopted by journalists.[57]

B. United Kingdom: The Evolving "Public Interest" Defense

In May 2010, before introducing his libel reform bill[58] to Parliament, Lord Anthony Lester lamented the media-unfriendly British libel law: "The job of the legislature and judiciary is to balance those conflicting freedoms [i.e., freedom of speech v. reputation]. In England, that balance has become skewed: libel law gives robust protection to reputation, but it increasingly does so at the expense of freedom of speech."[59]

English libel law is still similar to the pre-*Sullivan* American law, although it has been supplemented and clarified by statutes. It is based on the rule of "strict liability." The libel rule was derived from the ancient doctrine: "Whatever a man publishes, he publishes at his peril."[60]

The 1938 *Restatement of Torts* of the United States summarizes the U.K. libel law: "To create liability for defamation there must be an unprivileged publication of false and defamatory matter of another, which (a) is actionable irrespective of special harm, or (b) if not so actionable, is the legal cause of special harm to the other."[61] Thus, the plaintiff is entitled to damages for a false and defamatory statement as long as it was published on an unprivileged occasion, regardless of the defendant's innocence in the publication.

In making a prima facie libel case, the plaintiff has to prove that the defendant communicated a defamatory statement about the plaintiff.[62] No actual injury to reputation is required in establishing a cause of action. Further, the plaintiff has to plead falsity but not prove it. The English libel law recognizes three primary defenses for libel—truth (justification), fair comment and criticism, and fair report privilege.[63]

Whether justified or not, London is often called the "libel capital of the world."[64] It is the favored forum particularly for those American public plaintiffs who wish to avoid the *Sullivan* requirements in their home country.[65] But this moniker is not entirely accurate. While freedom of the press in England does not enjoy the kind of "preferred position" that it does in American law, it has certainly had notable achievements.

Although "actual malice" in the *Sullivan* sense has yet to be accepted, *Sullivan* has been approvingly cited in English libel cases. A case in point is *Derbyshire County Council v. Times Newspapers, Ltd.*,[66] the landmark case of the House of Lords in 1993. A local government body cannot sue for defamation under the common law of England, the Lords held in repudiation of seditious libel and in favor of political speech. Citing *Sullivan* and a 1923 Illinois case, *City of Chicago v. Tribune Co.*,[67] Lord Keith reasoned, "While these decisions were related most directly to the provisions of the American Constitution concerned with securing freedom of speech, the public interest considerations which underlaid [sic] them are no less valid in this country."[68]

In *Reynolds v. Times Newspapers Ltd.*,[69] the House of Lords rejected the media defendant's argument that "political information" should be privileged in English law in a fashion similar to the "actual malice" rule of American libel law. *Reynolds* arose when the *Sunday Times* published a story about former Prime Minister Albert Reynolds of Ireland. The story accused Reynolds of misleading the Dáil (parliament) and his cabinet colleagues. When sued for libel, the newspaper sought unsuccessfully to defend itself on the ground that it had a qualified privilege to publish the story because the public had a legitimate interest in knowing about Reynolds as an Irish *Taoiseach* (prime minister).

In the leading judgment in the House of Lords, Lord Nicholls stated that the privileged category of political speech would provide inadequate protection for reputation. "Moreover," he added, "it would be unsound in principle to distinguish political discussion from discussion of other matters of serious public concern."[70]

Nonetheless, Lord Nicholls enthusiastically endorsed freedom of the press to conduct investigative journalism:

> [T]he court should have particular regard to the importance of freedom of expression. The press discharges vital functions as a bloodhound as well as a watchdog. The court should be slow to conclude that a publication was not in the public interest and, therefore, the public had no right to know, especially when the information is in the field of political discussion. Any lingering doubts should be resolved in favour of publication.[71]

Lord Nicholls formulated a 10-factor qualified privilege test for "responsible journalism" on matters of public interest:

1. The seriousness of the allegation. The more serious the charge, the more the public is misinformed and the individual harmed, if the allegation is not true.
2. The nature of the information, and the extent to which the subject matter is a matter of public concern.
3. The source of the information. Some informants have no direct knowledge of the events. Some have their own axes to grind, or are being paid for their stories.
4. The status of the information. The allegation may have already been the subject of an investigation.
5. The steps taken to verify the information.
6. The urgency of the matter. News is often a perishable commodity.
7. Whether comment was sought from the claimant. He may have information others do not possess or have not disclosed. An approach to the claimant will not always be necessary.
8. Whether the article contained the gist of the claimant's side of the story.
9. The tone of the article. A newspaper can raise queries or call for an investigation. It need not adopt allegations as statements of fact.
10. The circumstances of the publication including the timing.[72]

The *Reynolds* criteria were expected to provide the British news media with greater protection. But the post-*Reynolds* case law has left the news media dismayed about the judicial application of the *Reynolds* multifactor analysis. The media have found their scorecard in the *Reynolds* defense lopsidedly disappointing.[73] It led journalists and their employers to wonder about the chilling effect of *Reynolds* on news reporting.[74]

These and related concerns persuaded the House of Lords to revisit the public interest defense in 2006. In *Jameel v. Wall Street Journal Europe,* appeal to Britain's highest court centered on "the scope and application of ... *Reynolds* privilege" as the threshold issue.[75]

Jameel started in February of 2002, when the *Journal Europe* reported that Saudi businessman Mohammed Jameel's bank accounts were among several Saudi accounts monitored by Saudi authorities at the request of the U.S. government. The monitoring of the bank accounts was designed "to prevent them from being used, wittingly or unwittingly, for the funneling of funds to terrorist organizations."[76] This information was attributed to "U.S. officials and Saudis familiar with the issue."[77]

The High Court of Justice ruled in 2003 that publication of the story was not in the public interest because it flouted an agreement between the U.S. and Saudi authorities to keep their monitoring program secret.[78] Moreover, the article could be defended only if the newspaper had a "social or moral duty" to publish it.[79] The trial court also found that Jameel should have been given time to comment on the article's allegations before its publication.[80] The Court of Appeal upheld the trial court's ruling, regarding the *Journal Europe*'s refusal to withhold its publication as "fatal" to its *Reynolds* defense.[81]

In reviewing the lower court decisions in *Jameel*, the House of Lords wondered whether the *Reynolds* privilege had been applied the way they originally intended, i.e., to expand freedom of the press to publish stories of public interest. Writing the leading opinion in *Jameel*, Lord Hoffmann bemoaned the "little impact" of *Reynolds* on the libel trials. He added, "It is therefore necessary to restate the [*Reynolds*] principles."[82]

Reminding that the privilege conditions in *Reynolds* were addressed "only in very general terms," Lord Hoffmann described the circumstances in *Jameel* as epitomizing the privilege's applicability as a libel defense.[83] In determining whether the *Reynolds* privilege should protect a news story from liability, he set forth a three-prong test:

- Was the subject matter of the article a matter of public interest?[84]
- Was there justification for including the defamatory statements in the article?[85]
- Were the methods used in gathering and publishing the news information "responsible and fair"?[86]

According to Lord Hoffmann, the public interest test for evaluating the substance of the article is a question of law for the judge, not one of fact for the jury. The *Journal Europe* story "easily passes that test," he stated. "The thrust of the article as a whole was to inform the public that the Saudis were cooperating with the U.S. Treasury in monitoring accounts. It was a serious contribution in measured tone to a subject of very considerable importance."[87]

To answer whether the *Journal Europe* was justifiable in including the defamatory statement in the precipitating article about Jameel, Lord Hoffmann observed that the allegation made "a real contribution to the public interest element" of the story. At the same time, he showed keen sensitivity to journalistic presentation of news stories while cautioning against judicial overstepping:

> Allowance must be made for editorial judgment. If the article as a whole is in the public interest, opinions may reasonably differ over which details are needed to convey the general message. The fact that the judge, with the advantage of leisure and hindsight, might have made a different editorial decision should not destroy the defence. That would make the publication of articles which are, *ex hypothesi,* in the public interest, too risky and would discourage investigative reporting.[88]

Lord Hoffmann disagreed with the lower courts that Jameel should not have been named in the article. He found the inclusion of the name "important" and "necessary" to the story because it established that the Saudis' cooperation with the U.S. government in fighting terrorism reached the "heartland of the Saudi business world." He dismissed resorting to "a prominent Saudi businessman" in the story, instead of naming Jameel, as ineffectual in serving the *Journal Europe*'s intended purpose of publishing the article.[89]

Lord Hoffmann clarified the kind of "responsible journalism" that Lord Nicholls considered in enumerating his 10-factor *Reynolds* privilege. He emphasized that the *Reynolds* factors were not intended as "tests which the publication has to pass," but they "should in suitable cases be taken into account." A judge who is hostile to the public interest defense in *Reynolds,* Lord Hoffmann said, can turn the 10 factors into ten hurdles for the media to scale "at any of which the defense may fail."[90] This contradicts the intent of *Reynolds* because judges must apply the standards of journalistic conduct it requires "in a practical and flexible manner" while taking into account the realities of news reporting.

On whether the responsible journalism standards were met by the *Journal Europe* in publishing the Jameel story, Lord Hoffmann focused on three aspects of the *Journal* news reporting: verification of the story, opportunity for Jameel to comment on the story, and propriety of the story's publication.

Lord Hoffmann criticized the trial judge for his misdirection to the jury that the story should be assumed to be false unless the *Journal Europe* sought to prove the truth. Given that *Reynolds* concerns the public interest of the material and the conduct of the journalists at the time of news reporting, Lord Hoffmann stated, it was irrelevant to the *Reynolds* defense that a defamatory statement was not proved to be true.[91] Significantly, Lord Hoffmann noted application of the *Reynolds* defense in "reportage" cases, which do not hinge on the truth or falsity determination as a relevant factor.[92] Here, the news media's inability to prove the truth of the defamatory statement is a nonissue in applying *Reynolds*.

After dissecting at length the *Journal Europe* reporters' verification of the story, Lord Hoffmann found convincing the evidence provided by the Washington, D.C., reporter in relation to his "ritual or code" between reporter and source in Washington.[93] Regarding the *Journal Europe*'s failure to give Jameel time to comment on the story, he said, "Failure to report the plaintiff's explanation is a factor to be taken into account. Depending upon the circumstances, it may be a weighty factor. But it should not be elevated into a rigid rule of law."[94] Lord Hoffmann was skeptical about the realistic value of asking Jameel for comment under the circumstances involved. According to Lord Hoffmann, Jameel could only have said that he knew of no reason for his bank account to be monitored simply because he was not aware of the secret monitoring program. So, no matter what Jameel had to explain, it would have added little to what the *Journal Europe*'s reporters already knew.[95]

III. Privacy as an Evolving Culture-bound Right

Media law professor Doreen Weisenhaus at the University of Hong Kong noted that the news media's "excessive privacy intrusion" has led the public, governments, and others to protect an individual's right to privacy.[96] Now privacy is more widely recognized as a right, although it is still evolving. Recently a British media lawyer said that privacy in England "has come a long a way." She added that British courts are aware of their obligation to protect privacy for individuals.[97] Especially noteworthy is a growing interest in privacy law for an international and comparative study.[98] American law usually serves as a frame of reference for international and foreign courts when balancing privacy with freedom of the press. For the United States has more experience with privacy vs. press freedom than any other culture as it does in other areas of free speech jurisprudence.

Privacy, as guaranteed in a number of international human rights agreements, tends to be more culture-bound and less definable cross-nationally. Its conceptual ambiguity is pointed out by communication law scholar Franklyn Haiman:

> What will be considered presumptuous, intrusive, or embarrassing by an individual depends in large measure on the value which the person's culture places on privacy, and that is a highly variable phenomenon. Not only do primitive cultures tend to have far less concern than modern industrialized societies about individual privacy in general but the specific kinds of behavior that are thought to require seclusion differ from culture to culture.[99]

The striking difference between U.S. and non-U.S. law on privacy is "a right to be let alone," which was highlighted by the ECtHR in *Von Hannover v. Germany.*[100] Applying Article 8 of the ECHR on privacy,[101] the European court rejected the German Constitutional Court's decision that Princess Caroline of Monaco, a public figure "par excellence," had no right to prevent the tabloid media from publishing photographs of her without her consent or knowledge.

In the landmark case of 2004, the ECtHR has developed a "fair balance" test for assessing an individual's right to respect for his private life vis-à-vis the public's and the media's competing interests. The Court, characterizing the ECHR's guarantee of privacy not as "theoretical or illusory" but as "practical and effective,"[102] held:

> [A] fundamental distinction needs to be made between reporting facts—even controversial ones—capable of contributing to a debate in a democratic society relating to politicians in the exercise of their functions ... and reporting details of the private life of an individual who ... does not exercise official functions. While in the former case the press exercises its vital role of "watchdog" in a democracy by contributing to "impart[ing] information and ideas on matters of public interest,["] it does not do so in the latter case.[103]

While acknowledging the public's right to be informed as "an essential right in a democratic society that can extend to the private life of public figures in some special circumstances," the Court concluded that the violation of Princess Caroline's privacy at issue did not concern a matter of public or political interest.[104] Rather, the Court said the publication of the photos and articles about her was solely aimed to "satisfy the curiosity of a particular readership" regarding her private life, hence no contribution to any debate of public interest to society.[105]

In Anglo-American law, prior restraint in libel and privacy law is a non-issue, although in Japan, France, Germany, and other countries, it is not necessarily proscribed. Japanese courts "have not shied away from exercising prior restraint."[106] Professor Eric Barendt, author of the leading comparative study, *Freedom of Speech*, wrote that "in many jurisdictions courts may grant injunctions to stop the issue of publications which, it is argued, would amount to a breach of confidence, [or] infringe personal privacy...."[107]

Nonetheless, the prior restraint-averse English law on privacy is now being challenged by Max Mosley, president of the *Fédération Internationale de l'Automobile* (FI), as a violation of Article 8 of ECHR. No doubt it is a case to watch because it may (re)define privacy as a human right beyond what it did in the *Von Hannover* case.[108]

In July 2008, Mosley won a ruling from the High Court of London that the *News of the World* breached his privacy by publishing an article claiming that he had engaged with prostitutes in a sadomasochistic "orgy" with a Nazi theme. The court in *Max Mosley v. News Group Newspapers Ltd.*[109] agreed with Mosley that there was no Nazi theme in his sexual activities with five prostitutes in a private apartment that the tabloid newspaper secretly filmed and that the article and pictures published in the newspaper did not deal with a matter of public interest.

The High Court Judge Sir David Eady reasoned that Mosley had a "reasonable expectation" of privacy for his sexual activities that took place on private premises and that did not involve violations of the criminal law.[110] He stated: "There was no public interest or other justification for the clandestine recording, for the publication of the resulting information and still photographs, or for the placing of the video extracts on The News of the World Web site—all of this on a massive scale."[111]

Meanwhile, Mosley unsuccessfully sought interim injunction against further publication of the challenged story and an order that the footage be prevented from being further shown on the *News of the World*'s website.[112] Judge Eady rejected his request for the injunction. He explained that "the material was so widely accessible that an [injunctive] order ... would have made very little practical difference."[113] He added: "The dam has effectively burst."[114]

In submitting an application for a ruling by the ECtHR in September 2008, Mosley claimed that the United Kingdom violates ECHR by failing to require news media to notify a person before publication of an article that might infringe his intimate privacy by publishing personal information into the public domain so that he may seek an injunction to restrain such publication.[115]

In response to Mosley's argument, one of the three media organizations as interveners in the ECtHR case countered in March 2010, finding no "necessity" for a pre-publication notification as a legal duty for the media: *"Such a duty would be wrong in principle; it would be unworkable in practice; it would constitute an unwarranted and disproportionate interference with freedom of expression."*[116]

IV. Access to the Press: Right of Reply Recognized

In Anglo-American law, the right of reply as "a statutory right for a defamed person to respond to the precipitating libelous publication"[117] is rarely accepted as a right to access the press. But the right of reply is increasingly recognized in foreign and international law.

The American Convention on Human Rights provides for a right to reply for those "injured by inaccurate or offensive statements or ideas."[118] The ECtHR reads a right of reply into the European Convention on Human Rights.[119] In 2004, the Council of Europe revised its 1974 right of reply resolution to reflect many major technological developments in the media.[120] The U.N. Convention on the International Right of Correction is not necessarily as "academic and largely ineffective" as it was dismissively described in 1980.[121] The number of the Convention's signatories is growing, albeit slowly.

Further, the right of reply has been thriving in U.S.-influenced countries,[122] although it is passé in American broadcasting law and has been a non-issue for American print media. Some countries recognize it as a constitutional right, while others treat it as a statutory regulation. France and Germany epitomize the right of reply as a way to balance reputational interest with a free press. In South Korea, the right of reply has facilitated more access for ordinary citizens to their news media since it was introduced into Korean law in 1980.[123]

A. France

The French Press Freedom Act of 1881, which is still in force, delineates the right of reply in two ways: *droit de reponse* (right of reply) for ordinary individuals and *droit de rectification* (right of rectification) for government officials:

> Article 12. The director [of the publication] must insert free of charge, at the head of the very next number of the newspaper or written periodical, all corrections which have been sent to it by a trustee of the public authority, on the subject of his pubic functions which have been incorrectly reported by the said newspaper or periodical. However, these corrections shall not exceed double the article to which they will respond. In case of violation, the director will be punished by a fine of from 360 to 3,600 francs.

> Article 13. The director [of the publication] must insert, within 3 days of their receipt, the responses of all persons named or designated in the newspaper or daily written periodical, under penalty of a fine of 180 to1,800 francs; without prejudice to other penalties or damages to which the article might give rise. In that which concerns non-daily newspapers or written periodicals, the director, under the same sanctions, shall insert the response in the number which follows two days after receipt. This insertion must be made in the same place and in the same print as the article which provoked it and without any alteration.[124]

The right of reply under Article 13 is available to anyone insofar the person was mentioned and regardless of whether the original statement was defamatory or not.[125] The French reply law makes no distinction between expression of opinion and statements of fact. Consequently, its primary aim was not to assert the public interest in truth but to protect the interests of individuals.[126] The right of reply in France can be denied if the request exceeds the statutory length and has nothing to do with the initial article.[127]

The French right of rectification under Article 12 is narrower than the right of reply because rectification is only applicable to statements of fact and not to opinion. Also, it is limited to news stories concerning a government official whose conduct relating to his official duties was incorrectly reported by the press.[128]

No right of reply for publication of photographs exists in French law.[129] But there is a separate right of reply for the broadcasting media. The 1982 law, as amended in 2004, allows the right of reply for television and radio broadcasting. It is different from the Press Freedom Act. The broadcasting law permits replies only "if the initial communication on the air is considered as defamatory," which is not requisite under the print and Internet statutes.[130] Further, the right of reply in French law is available to all those who have been charged with criminal violations and then acquitted.[131]

In March 2007, the French government submitted to the European Commission a draft decree for enforcement of the digital economy law on the right of reply that implemented the EU e-commerce directive.[132] The draft decree stipulates that the right of reply is granted if the challenged Internet site refused a direct reply opportunity through forums or chat rooms. But it does not cover the right of reply for the general public or for third-party claimants.[133] The decree's "debatable" provisions relate to the claimant's option to forgo the right of reply in exchange for the webmaster's agreement to modify or eliminate the original article complained of and the maximum length of the reply in connection with the article in discussion.[134]

B. Germany

Germany is not absolute in its constitutional guarantees of freedom of the press.[135] Under the Basic Law of Germany, press powers "shall find their limits in the provisions of general laws ... in the right to violability of personal honour."[136] The right of reply under German law is derived from the rights of personality and identity guaranteed by the Basic Law.[137] It is further based on Article 5, which reads: "These [speech and press] rights are limited by the provisions of the general laws" including the press law. Nonetheless, the Basic Law still prohibits the "essential content" of the basic rights from being restricted by application of the general laws.[138]

Under the Hamburg Press Act (*Hamburgischen Pressegesetz*), the right of reply is restricted to a statement of fact. The Hamburg press law states: "The responsible editor and publisher of a periodical printed work are obliged to publish the reply of a person or body concerned in a *factual* statement made in the work. This obligation extends to all subsidiary editions of the work in which the statement has appeared."[139] Thus, opinion and subjective expression of value judgments are excluded from the right of reply.

Every person or authority affected by a statement in the press can request a reply. Included in the wide scope of the law are private individuals, associations, companies, and public authorities, both German and foreign. Among the periodical printed works, which are subject to the right of reply provisions are newspapers, magazines, and other mass media such as radio, television, and films, appearing "at permanent if irregular intervals of not more than six months."[140]

The content of the reply cannot include matters punishable by law such as defamatory charges.[141] Also, the length of the reply must not exceed that of the original statement complained of.[142] If the reply is disproportionately long, the editor and publisher can reject it. The reply must be asserted "immediately and at latest within three months" of the publications.[143]

The Hamburg statute requires that the reply be published in the next issue if the issue is not yet typeset for printing.[144] The news periodical must publish the reply in the same section of the periodical and in the same type as the challenged statement.[145] In the case of broadcasting media, the reply must be broadcast immediately to the same receiving area and at an equivalent time to the precipitating broadcast.[146] No interpolations or omissions of the reply are allowed under the law.[147] The reply is printed free of charge "unless the text complained of appeared as an advertisement."[148] A letter to the editor cannot be a substitute for the reply. The news medium can publish its own editorial comment on the reply in the same issue if it focuses on factual statements.[149]

The Hamburg press law exempts fair and accurate reports of the open proceedings of the three branches of federal government and local and state governments.[150] The rationale of this provision consists in "preventing political opponents from continuing in the press the debate which took place in Parliament."[151] The right of reply is not recognized for purely commercial expression.[152]

If the news media refuse to comply with the reply request, the reply claim can be enforced through an ordinary judicial process.[153] On application of the legitimate complainant, the civil court of the place of the periodical in question may issue a provisional injunction to have the reply published.[154]

In January 1998, the Constitutional Court of Germany unanimously rejected a challenge to the Hamburg Press Act on the right of reply and correction.[155] In upholding the Hamburg law, the Court weighed freedom of the press against an individual's reputation and his right of personality. The Court stated that freedom of the press includes "freedom of formulating press publications" as its central element. The news media's editorial decisions include determining what topics to report and which articles to publish. They also extend to the news media decisions regarding how to present the articles and where to place them within the particular issue.[156]

Nonetheless, the Hamburg right of reply law is a "general law" under the Constitution because it does not restrict the freedom of opinion or a particular type of opinions. Rather, the law protects the general right of personality, which is guaranteed by the Basic Law.[157] Further, the Court did not consider the Hamburg right of reply statute disproportionate in limiting freedom of the press while protecting the individual against the dangers to the person's right of personality from the press. The Court took note of the inherent challenge facing individuals when their personal matters are incorrectly reported by the news media.

Given the scope and influence of news reporting, the individual cannot as a rule counter the news media with the prospect of the same publicity. In an effort to equalize the playing field for the press vs. individuals, the Court wrote, lawmakers have a duty under the right of personality principle to safeguard the individuals against the media's impact on their personal sphere.[158] Included in the legislative options is the legal guarantee that those affected by news reporting can respond through their own words. This legal opportunity of reply for individuals contributes to the "free, individual and public formation of opinion under Article 5(1) of the Basic Law, according to the Court, because "besides the information from the press, the reader is informed from the point of view of the person affected as well."[159]

To the question of whether the right of reply is superfluous in protecting an individual's personality as a right, the Constitutional Court answered No. While the reply can, under certain prerequisites, supplement an injunction, a correction, or a retraction, or compensation, in addition to the punishment of the persons responsible for the precipitating statement, none of the civil or criminal remedies permits the person affected to reply to the media story about them. Besides, retraction and correction are not as prompt as the claim to a right of reply because they require a time-consuming finding of the untruth of the original stories.[160]

To the Constitutional Court, protection of an individual's personality through the right of reply is not a terrible handicap to press freedom. The Court cited three reasons. First, given that the right of reply must always be tied to the original news story, only the person who was the object of the press discussion can demand a reply. Second, the reply is limited to factual communication, and statements of opinion are excluded. Finally, the reply claim will be qualified by the subject matter and scope of the original article within a reasonable framework.[161]

The Constitutional Court found no merit in the objection to the right of reply that the right of reply requires no injury to one's honor or no proof of falsity of the original news article or the truth of the statement in reply. The Court distinguished reputation from the right of personality as a basis for the right of reply. Personal honor as a justification for restricting press freedom constitutes an "important component" of the right of personality. The Court said, however, that a person's personality can still be impaired by media representations while his honor remains intact.[162]

The Constitutional Court characterized as inconsequential in constitutional law the news media's assertion that a reply should be denied when the media believe in their challenged articles. The Court reasoned:

> The fact that a statement in reply is independent of the truth is a consequence of the
> requirement that follows from the State duty of protection for the right of personality

to guarantee the same publicity. The speech realization of the claim to give an answer would fail if the proceedings were burdened with the elucidation of the question of truth.[163]

V. Journalistic Privilege: Right to Protect Sources Recognized

The journalist's privilege to keep confidential sources is not entirely a legal matter. It is also an ethical issue. In his comparative survey of international journalists, mass communication scholar David H. Weaver concluded: "[T]here was a high level of agreement among all journalists, suggesting a near-universal professional norm of protecting confidential sources."[164]

A. Foreign Law

Although the journalist's privilege is not recognized as a right under the First Amendment to the U.S. Constitution, it is more widely accepted around the world, especially in democratic polities.

1. Argentina

The Constitution of Argentina, amended in 1994, protects the confidential information of registered journalists unconditionally. Article 43 of the Constitution stipulates: "The secret nature of the sources of journalistic information shall not be impaired."[165] The journalist's privilege for the Argentine press is intertwined with freedom to receive information, along with the freedom to impart information, as part of the right to freedom of thought and expression, under Article 13(1) of the American Convention on Human Rights,[166] an international instrument with the same rank as the Argentine Constitution.

2. Australia

The Evidence Act protects confidential information a journalist obtains in his "professional" capacity.[167] Nonetheless, the journalistic source protection is balanced with other competing interests. In granting and rejecting the journalist's privilege, Australian courts weigh "such factors as the probative value of the evidence, its importance, the nature of the claim or defense and the subject matter of the proceeding, the availability of the evidence from other sources, the extent of harm to the confider, whether the evidence is necessary to establish innocence in a criminal case."[168]

Thus far, Australian courts have refused to place press freedom in a preferred position over society's interest in a fair trial. "[T]here is a paramount interest in the administration of justice which requires that cases be tried by courts on the relevant and admissible evidence," the High Court of Australia held in 1988.[169] "The role of the media in collecting and disseminating information to the public does not give rise to a public interest which can be allowed to prevail over the public interest of a litigant in securing a trial of his action on the basis of the relevant and admissible evidence."[170]

The Australian High Court also looked at factors beyond the balancing of press freedom and the right to evidentiary proof. The Court pointed out the additional benefit of compelling the media to disclose their sources:

The liability of the media and of journalists to disclose their sources of information in the interests of justice is itself a valuable sanction which will encourage the media to exercise with due responsibility its great powers which are capable of being abused to the detriment of the individual. The recognition of an immunity from disclosure of sources of information would enable irresponsible persons to shelter behind anonymous, or even fictitious, sources.[171]

3. Canada

In May 2010, the Supreme Court of Canada refused to recognize a blanket privilege for journalists under the Constitution or common law. Instead, the Court held that the journalistic privilege can be claimed on a case-by-case basis. In *Regina v. National Post*,[172] the landmark case on press freedom in Canada, the Canadian high court ruled on whether journalists may avoid being compelled by a court to reveal their confidential sources to government authorities.

Justice Ian Binnie stated that partial or total "journalist-confidential source" privilege may be asserted if the journalist can satisfy four criteria adapted from the *Wigmore* test[173] for establishing confidentiality at common law. The burden of proof is on the journalist, he said. Thus, a journalist's promise of confidentiality will be recognized if the journalist proves that:

> First, the communication must originate in a confidence that the identity of the informant will not be disclosed. Second, the confidence must be essential to the relationship in which the communication arises. Third, the relationship must be one which should be "sedulously fostered" in the public good…. Finally, if all of these requirements are met, the court must consider whether in the instant case the public interest served by protecting the identity of the informant from disclosure outweighs the public interest in getting at the truth.[174]

Justice Binnie also ruled that journalists are not entitled to a common law "class privilege" similar to lawyer-client privilege that "presumably cloaks in confidentiality" information resulting from the relationship.[175] Noting that class privileges are rare, he said, only legislatures can create them in Canada.[176]

4. Germany

The right to refuse testimony is provided by federal law in Germany.[177] The Criminal Procedure Code allows "individuals who are or were professionally involved in the preparation, production or dissemination of periodically printed matter or radio broadcasts" to refuse to testify "concerning information received by them in their professional capacity insofar as this concerns contributions, documentation and information for the editorial element of their activity," unless "they have been released from their obligation of secrecy."[178] Likewise, the Civil Procedure Code provides that individuals, including journalists, who have had facts confided to them because of their profession may refuse to testify concerning those facts unless the source consents to the disclosure.[179]

Most Länder (state) laws recognize journalists' right to keep their sources confidential. A good example is the North Rhine Westphalia Press Law, which states:

> Editors, journalists, publishers, printers and others involved in the production or publication of periodical literature in a professional capacity can refuse to give evidence as

to the person of the author, sender or confidant of an item published in the editorial section of the paper or communication intended wholly or partly for such publication or about its contents.[180]

The constitutional protection of journalistic sources is much weaker than statutory protections at the federal and state level. But the Constitutional Court of Germany has recognized the journalist's privilege. The Court held protection of confidential sources essential to journalists in doing their professional duties.[181] Journalists are not required to reveal their sources unless their value in uncovering malfeasance outweighs the interest in the administration of justice.[182]

5. Japan

Japan appears to have been among the earliest of Western democracies to grapple with the journalist's privilege as a legal issue. As early as 1952, the Supreme Court of Japan considered a news reporter's refusal to divulge confidential sources under the privileged communication clause of the Code of Criminal Procedure.[183] The Supreme Court refused to accord privileged status to journalists, noting that establishing such a journalistic privilege was up to lawmakers.[184]

Japanese journalists are protected by the Code of Civil Procedure, which provides for the right of witnesses to refuse to disclose their "professional secrets."[185] Article 281 stipulates that "[a] witness may refuse to testify … [i]n a case where he is questioned with respect to matters relating to a technical or professional secret."[186] News reporters as witnesses may withhold their confidential information on sources "unless it one-sidedly closes off the pursuit of evidence so as to result in an unfair trial."[187]

In addition, the Supreme Court of Japan has recognized protection of journalistic sources, even when they are not confidential, as a matter of press freedom under the Constitution of Japan. Indeed, three years before the U.S. Supreme Court in *Branzburg* rejected the journalist's privilege as a right, the Supreme Court of Japan in the *Hakata Railway Station* case noted the need to balance source disclosure in a criminal trial with the news media's freedom to gather information:

> It should be said that we cannot but restrict the freedom of news-gathering activity to a certain degree when the data collected by news media is considered to be necessary as evidence in order to secure such a fair criminal trial. Even in such a case, however, the character, mode and gravity of the crime which is the object of the trial, evidential value of the data and the existence of the necessity for the realization of a fair criminal trial should be considered at first, and then they should be balanced with the degree of the hindrance to the freedom of news-gathering activity which would occur when news media are obliged to submit the collected data as evidence with the extent of its consequential influence upon the freedom of news report and with all other necessary considerations. Even when the use of the data as evidence in a criminal trial is considered to be inevitable, the regard should be paid lest the disadvantage to be suffered by news media should exceed the indispensable degree.[188]

6. Norway

Norway's Civil Procedure Code protects journalists and editors of newspapers, periodicals, and broadcasts against compelled disclosure of their sources. But the journalist's privilege is overridden if the confidential information sought is particularly important. To resolve a case, courts balance the conflicting interests of the parties in weighing whether the information is necessary. If the information is available through non-news media sources, courts do not require media disclosure.

7. Sweden

Sweden is one of the most media-friendly nations in protecting the journalist's privilege.[189] The privilege is a constitutional right under the Freedom of the Press Act, which is one of the three parts of the Swedish Constitution. The Freedom of the Press Act, first adopted in 1766, established the right of anonymity of "authors" in 1812. When it was strengthened in 1949, it protected news sources especially for the print media.[190] Singularly significant is that the Swedish shield law, one of the strongest in Europe, empowers sources to take criminal prosecution against journalists if their confidential identity is revealed without their authorization.[191] It further forbids public officials to inquire about the journalistic sources. If public officials violate the law, they face fines or one year in jail.[192]

Not surprisingly, however, the journalist's privilege is not absolute in Swedish law. Courts may order source disclosure when national security is at stake, or when high treason, espionage or other similar crimes are involved.[193] Exceptions to the source protection are also allowed when a court finds it "of exceptional importance" that a source is a witness in a crime and when information specifically made secret by statute is revealed.[194]

8. United Kingdom

No English court had upheld a common law right of the news media to withhold their confidential sources.[195] In the 1981 case, *British Steel Corp. v. Granada Television Ltd.*, the House of Lords stated flatly that "[n]o public interest in the press not being forced to disclose their sources of information at the trial has yet been recognised; and there are insufficient grounds for holding that such an interest ought to exist."[196]

The common law rejection of the reporter's privilege, except in the limited "newspaper rule" context,[197] was changed by the Contempt of Court Act in 1981. Section 10 provides:

> No court may require a person to disclose, nor is any person guilty of contempt for refusing to disclose, the source of information contained in a publication for which he is responsible, unless it be established to the satisfaction of the court that disclosure is necessary in the interests of justice or national security or for the prevention of disorder or crime.[198]

The Contempt of Court Act was a radical departure from the judicial rejection of the journalist's privilege in that it was a statutory effort to strike a balance between journalists' right to gather and publish information and competing pubic interests. Protection of confidential sources was supposed to be the norm, not the exception, insofar as its statutory exceptions were concerned.

But the practical value of the Contempt of Court Act has been limited. In their initial application of the Act, English courts have broadly interpreted the exceptions.[199] Even more disconcerting from a media perspective, the courts have yet to formulate a standard for determining public interest in the free flow of information. Rather, they find that the level of public interest in freedom of expression varies from case to case, as is the societal interest in informational disclosure by the press.[200] Nonetheless, the English law on the journalist's privilege has led courts to recognize the right to nondisclosure of news sources as an aspect of press freedom which can be protected.

B. International Law

International law on the journalist's privilege has emerged as an issue of increasing significance since the mid-1990s. Two human rights courts have considered claims that the confidentiality of journalistic sources is part of a right to freedom of expression. The ECtHR declared in 1996 that journalists have a right not to disclose their sources unless an overriding countervailing interest outweighs the confidentiality of news sources.[201] The International Criminal Tribunal for the former Yugoslavia (ICTY) held in 2002 that war correspondents cannot be compelled to testify about their sources, except under extraordinary circumstances.[202]

1. European Court of Human Rights in Goodwin v. United Kingdom

William Goodwin, a journalist for the *Engineer* magazine in England, obtained information from his source that Tetra Ltd. was raising a £5 million loan while experiencing financial difficulties. The unpaid and unsolicited information was provided on an "unattributable" basis.[203] When learning that Goodwin was writing a story on the basis of the confidential information, Tetra obtained an ex parte interim injunction against the *Engineer* publishing any information from the corporate plan.[204]

Meanwhile, Tetra asked the High Court of Justice in London to order Goodwin to identify his confidential source. Judge Hoffmann of the High Court of Justice ordered Goodwin to identify his confidential source.[205] Goodwin's appeal to the Court of Appeal to stay the High Court's order was rejected.[206] Following the House of Lords' dismissal of the appeal, Goodwin complained to the European Commission on Human Rights.[207]

The Commission held that the English courts' disclosure order failed to meet the "necessary in a democratic society" test.[208] The Commission expansively considered the journalist's privilege as an important element of press freedom in a democracy. The Commission did not find the kind of justifiable circumstances that required a departure from the "fundamental" human rights principle that news sources should be protected from disclosure.

The ECtHR adopted the conclusions of the European Commission. The Court concentrated on the overarching issue: Was the disclosure order the kind of interference with Goodwin's freedom of expression that could be justified as "necessary in a democratic society"? In assessing what kind of measures are acceptable in restricting freedom of expression, the European Court said, the national authorities may exercise "a certain margin of appreciation." Nonetheless, the margin of appreciation is considerably narrow when freedom of the press is at stake. The Court held that disclosure of journalistic sources interferes with "the interest of democratic society in ensuring and maintaining a free press" and thus calls for the "most careful scrutiny" by the court.[209]

The European Court expounded on freedom of expression as an "essential foundation of a democratic society" and more specifically noted the "safeguards that a free press needs in serving its crucial role as a watchdog." The court was especially emphatic about the journalistic privilege as part of freedom of the press:

Protection of journalistic sources is one of the basis conditions for press freedom, as is reflected in the laws and the professional codes of conduct in a number of Contracting States and is affirmed in several international instruments on journalistic freedoms. Without such protection, sources may be deterred from assisting the press in informing the public on matters of public interest. As a result the vital public watchdog role of the press may be undermined and the ability of the press to provide accurate and reliable information may be adversely affected. Having regard to the importance of the protection of journalistic sources for press freedom in a democratic society and the potentially chilling effect an order of source disclosure has on the exercise of that freedom, such a measure cannot be compatible with Article 10 of the Convention unless it is justified by an overriding requirement in the public interest.[210]

In applying this "most careful" scrutiny of the interference with press freedom, the court found little value in the compelled disclosure of Goodwin's source because it aimed to a very large extent to achieve the same purpose already being achieved by the injunction, i.e., to prevent further distribution of the confidential material contained in Tetra's corporate plan.[211]

2. International Criminal Tribunal for the Former Yugoslavia in the Randal Case

In February 1993, *Washington Post* reporter Jonathan Randal published a story in the *Washington Post*, which was partly based on his interview with Radoslav Brdjanin, then the Bosnian Serb housing administrator. Randal quoted Brdjanin as saying that he "believes the 'exodus' of non-Serbs should be carried out peacefully, so as to 'create an ethnically clean space through voluntary movement.'"[212]

When the prosecution wanted to have Randal's article admitted as evidence to prove Brdjanin's intention to "cleanse" northwestern Bosnia of non-Serb people, Brdjanin sought Randal's appearance for cross examination. When Randal declined the prosecution's request to testify voluntarily, the Trial Chamber of the ICTY issued a subpoena to him, and he challenged the subpoena.

Randal argued that the ICTY's power to subpoena witnesses could be constrained by various public policy concerns. The public interest privilege of journalists to avoid compulsory process brings about the "outstanding benefits" for international criminal justice. According to Randal, media coverage in combat zones provides the public with important information about international conflicts, and it also offers evidentiary material for investigation of war crimes.[213] Compelling journalists to give testimony before international criminal courts against what they have observed or interviewed would likely curtail the benefits of war reporting.

Randal called attention to the Geneva Conventions (rule 97) and the ECHR (Article 10) as legal safeguards adopted to protect journalists. He noted the watchdog role of the news media, as recognized by the ECtHR and the IACHR. [214] He also posited that the journalist's privilege has been recognized by the United States and other countries.

In June 2002, the Trial Chamber dismissed Randal's motion to set aside the subpoena. The Trial Chamber acknowledged the vital role of news reporting on conflict areas in apprizing the world of the horrors of the conflict and journalists' contribution in establishing the ICTY. Nonetheless, it did not want a journalist's privilege to be framed in such a way as to allow the journalist to determine the usefulness of his news reporting to the criminal tribunal as possible evidence.[215]

The Trial Chamber did accept the journalistic privilege as articulated in *Goodwin*. It considered the *Goodwin* test of the ECtHR as a benchmark in that to uphold a standard lower than *Goodwin* would constitute "a step in the wrong direction, a step backward, and a severe blow" to journalistic freedom of expression and freedom of the media.[216] Yet the Trial Chamber found the *Goodwin* standard inapposite in the *Randal* case, since it involved no confidential information.[217]

On appeal, Randal argued that the Trial Chamber had erred in not recognizing a testimonial privilege for journalists and in finding, on the facts of the case, that he should be compelled to testify. In December 2002, the Appeals Chamber of the ICTY unanimously reversed the Trial Chamber's ruling and set aside the subpoena to Randal.[218]

The Appeals Chamber embraced a widely accepted proposition that a vigorous press is indispensable to open societies, and compelling journalists frequently and casually to produce evidence will hinder their newsgathering abilities. The EtCHR's recognition of the watchdog role of the news media and shield laws in several countries showcased the proposition.[219]

The Appeals Chamber viewed the public interest in protecting the integrity of war correspondents in newsgathering as "particularly clear and weighty." This was all the more so, given that news reporting in war zones is replete with difficulties in its information gathering and distribution, and plays a vital role in publicizing the horrors of international and regional conflicts and in helping international courts investigate war crimes.[220]

The Appeals Chamber also broadened the concept of the public's interest in the work of war correspondents. It drew an important but often overlooked conceptual linkage of war reporting to people's access to information as a positive right under the Universal Declaration of Human Rights. The Appeals Chamber stated: "[T]he right to freedom of expression includes not merely the right of journalists and media organizations freely to communicate information. It also incorporates a right of members of the public to receive information."[221]

The Appeals Chamber was convinced that forcing war correspondents to give testimony could exert a "great" harmful impact upon their newsgathering activity and their personal safety.[222] It countered the Trial Chamber by stating that the impact is no different regardless of whether the testimony of war correspondents involved confidential sources.[223]

As to what test would balance appropriately the public interest in war correspondents' work with the public interest in the administration of justice through access to all relevant evidence, the Appeals Chamber enunciated its own test for determining when a war correspondent can be subpoenaed:

> First, the petitioning party must demonstrate that the evidence sought is of direct and important value in determining a core issue in the case.

> Second, it must demonstrate that the evidence sought cannot reasonably be obtained elsewhere.[224]

The Appeals Chamber did not apply its two-prong test to the facts. Instead, it left the Trial Chamber to apply the test if the prosecution or Brdjanin still wanted Randal to testify.[225] In obiter dictum, however, the Appeals Chamber stated that it "finds it difficult to imagine [Randal's] testimony could be of direct and important value to determining a core issue in the case,"[226] for Randal spoke no Serbo-Croatian and relied on another journalist for interpretation for his interview with Brdjanin.

VI. Freedom of Information: A "Veritable Revolution" in Free Speech

Whether or not it is a human right, access to government-held information, often known as "freedom of information," is more widely recognized than ever.[227] In his 2008 international and comparative law analysis of access to information, the leading FOI expert Toby Mendel noted "a veritable revolution" in the right to information:

> Whereas in 1990 only 13 countries had adopted national right to information laws, upwards of 70 such laws have now been adopted globally, and they are under active consideration in another 20–30 countries.... In 1990, the right to information was seen predominantly as an administrative governances reform whereas today it is increasingly being seen as a fundamental human right. [228]

The impact of the FOI revolution on various countries is increasingly evident. In late June of 2010, the *New York Times* reported that the 5-year-old Right to Information Act[229] of India has empowered the Asian country's 1.2 billion citizens to demand access to almost any information from their government.[230] In April 2010, Jamie P. Horsley, a research scholar at Yale Law School, stated in her informative study of the FOI law[231] in China, officially known as the People's Republic of China (PRC): "Thus far, the widespread and assertive citizen utilization of the fledgling OGI [Open Government Information] system bodes well for the continued, if uneven, development of a more open and responsive Chinese government and realization of the Chinese people's right to know."[232]

A. Access to Information as a Human Right in International Law

Freedom of information was referred to as part of freedom of expression in general, not as a specific right to access to government records, by the Universal Declaration of Human Rights and the International Covenant on Civil and Political Rights (ICCPR). But it has been read into various international human rights treaties like ICCPR as their interpretations adapt to the changing times. The UN Special Rapporteur on Freedom of Opinion and Expression, for example, has stated that the universal right to free expression includes the right to access information by the State.

The regional human rights organizations—the Organization of American States, the Council of Europe, and the African Union—recognize access to government information through their own foundational documents such as the IACHR (Article 13), the ECHR (Article 10), and the African Charter on Human and Peoples' Rights (Article 9).

The European Court of Human Rights[233] and the Inter-American Court of Human Rights have recognized that the "freedom to receive and impart information and ideas," as guaranteed by the Universal Declaration of Human Rights as well as by regional human rights treaties, extends to a right to receive information of public interest held by State authorities.

In April 2009, the ECtHR in *Társaság a Szabadságjogokért v. Hungary*[234] held for the first time in the ECHR history that the freedom of expression clause of ECHR applies to access to information as a right: "[T]he law cannot allow arbitrary restrictions which may become a form of indirect censorship should the authorities create obstacles to the gathering of information."[235]

This ECtHR case on FOI arose from the Hungarian Constitutional Court's denial of the applicant Hungarian Civil Liberties Union's request for access to a parliamentarian's complaint that asked the Court to review some recent amendments to the Criminal Code. While noting that Article 10 of ECHR does not create "a general right of access to administrative data and documents,"[236] the ECtHR pointed out its consistent recognition that "the public has a right to receive information of general interest."[237] The European court found that the Hungarian Constitutional Court's "monopoly of information thus amounted to a form of censorship" in violation of the Hungarian Civil Liberties Union's right to freedom of expression under ECHR.[238] The ECtHR concluded that the Hungarian government's interference with the applicant's freedom of expression in the case was not "necessary in a democratic society" and constituted a violation of Article 10 of ECHR.[239]

Similar to the ECtHR ruling on access to information was the IACHR's decision of September 2006 in *Claude Reyes v Chile*.[240] The IACHR held that the American Convention on Human Rights on freedom of expression included an implied right of general access to government held information. The Court held:

> By expressly stipulating the right to "seek" and "receive" "information," Article 13 of the Convention protects the right of all individuals to request access to State-held information, with the exceptions permitted by the restrictions established in the Convention. Consequently, this article protects the right of the individual to receive such information and the positive obligation of the State to provide it, so that the individual may have access to such information or receive an answer that includes a justification when, for any reason permitted by the Convention, the State is allowed to restrict access to the information in a specific case. [241]

The IACHR continued that the government should provide the requested information with no need for the requester to prove his "direct interest or personal involvement" unless there is a legitimate restriction on the release of the information. [242] The delivery of government records to an individual can allow its distribution to society so that the public can assess it. Consequently, the IACHR stated, "the right to freedom of thought and expression includes the protection of the right of access to State-held information, which also clearly includes the two dimensions, individual and social, of the right to freedom of thought and expression that must be guaranteed simultaneously by the State." [243]

This seminal IACHR case on FOI started when the Chilean government rejected Marcel Claude Reyes and others' request for a copy of the government's report on its assessment of the risks of a U.S. company's logging project in Chile. Claude Reyes and others challenged their government's denial of their FOI request judicially. Their claim was rejected by the Chilean courts, including the Supreme Court of Chile.[244]

B. China, India, and South Korea's Experience with FOI

A U.S.-born British information campaigner, Heather Brooke, wrote in her recent book about the access to information issues in England:

> It is one thing for a politician to say he or she is committed to transparency and direct accountability; it is another entirely to act on those commitments. In the absence of meaningful journalism and direct accountability there is freedom of information. FOI offers a legal approach to get official information out of the hand of those in power.[245]

In varying degrees, the FOI stories of three Asian nations—China, India, and South Korea—illuminate the right to information as a transformative agent in society.

China's Law on "Disclosure of Government Information": Not Entirely a Rhetorical Gimmick

The PRC Constitution does not guarantee access to information as a right for Chinese citizens, and various statutes emphasize government secrecy. But the State Council, the cabinet of the PRC government, promulgated China's first information statute in 2007, which took effect on May 1, 2008.[246] The FOI law was to a certain extent in response to external pressure toward more openness, but the domestic agenda of the Chinese government was more responsible for its enactment: to share more information for economic development, to improve the quality of life for the people, to enhance the trust between the government and the public, to control government corruption, and to ensure better governance.[247]

An American expert on Chinese law was cautiously optimistic in her 2010 assessment of the PRC's freedom of information. Although there is much work for the government to do in clarifying, strengthening, and revising the open access regulations, she noted, "[t]hus far, the widespread and assertive citizen utilization of the fledgling OGI [Open Government Information] system bodes well for the continued, if uneven, development of a more open and responsive Chinese government and realization of the Chinese people's right to know."[248]

The FOI law of China aims to ensure citizens, legal persons, and other organizations access to "government information" as a right.[249] It is designed to promote the transparency of the governing process and to advance the rule-of-law administration for the people's life and socio-economic activities.[250] "Government information" is "information produced or acquired and recorded or kept in certain forms by administrative organs in the process of performing their duties." Thus, the law does not cover the People's congresses, political consultative conferences, courts, and procuracies.[251] Meanwhile, Article 37 stipulates that the public enterprises and institutions in education, health, family planning, public utilities, environmental protection, transportation, "or any other field closely related to the people's interests" are subject to the FOI provisions.[252]

Access to information in China is through the government's voluntary actions[253] or through the government's response to information requests.[254] Government agencies have 20 business days to release information after its creation or revisions if it is for voluntary release.[255] When replying to an application for government information disclosure, an administrative organ shall handle the request "on the spot" if possible. If not, the government agency has to reply to the informational request within 15 workdays. If the time frame is extended for reply, the extension should be no more than 15 business days.[256]

Although the disclosure request does not hinge on the content of the government information involved,[257] Article 13 states that citizens, legal persons, and other organizations may request information "in light of their special needs for production, living, or scientific research." This may lead to a needs test, which diverges from prior local Chinese or international FOI practice, and thus limits the freedom of information in China.[258]

Disclosure is not necessarily a priority over non-disclosure in China. Disclosure of government records is qualified by an array of conditions, such as that information should concern the "vital interests" of citizens and others.[259] The Chinese information law is distinguished from the U.S. Freedom of Information Act; the former, unlike the latter, provides for no specific categories of information that is exempt from disclosure. The Chinese law tends to be overly general when it prohibits disclosure of information from affecting "national security, public security, economic security, or social stability."[260] These nondisclosure principles are supplemented by Article 14: Privacy and state and commercial secrets may justify nondisclosure of information, while the government may release it if it believes that withholding such information would exert a "great influence" on public interests.[261]

The General Office of the State Council is in charge of "promoting, guiding, coordinating, and supervising the government information disclosure work of the whole nation."[262] This is significant because the institutional mechanism to implement the law is fundamental to the law's eventual success. But it is not clear how the General Office maintains impartiality and independence in carrying out its statutory functions.

If a government agency's FOI action violates the "legal rights and interests" of any citizen, legal person, or any other organization, administrative appeals or lawsuits are a further mechanism for the supervision and safeguarding of the access to records in China.[263] In addition, the Chinese law, like the OPEN Government Act of the United States, holds government officials personally responsible for their "serious" violations of the statutory requirements. Among the enumerated circumstances that constitute the violations of the law are:

1. Failing to fulfill the obligation of disclosing government information according to law;
    Failing to update the contents of disclosed government information, directory for government information disclosure and   catalogue of government information disclosure in a timely manner;
    Charging fees by violating the relevant provisions;
    Providing government information in the form of paid services through any other organization or individual;
    Disclosing the government information that should not be disclosed;
    Other behaviors going against these provisions.[264]

The "right to know" law has been quite a "culture change" for government agencies and their personnel in China. This should be no surprise to those familiar with freedom of information as a right around the world. But the challenge facing the Chinese government might have been deep-rooted institutionally and societally. Government secrecy and bureaucratic inertia have been entrenched in Chinese society for many years. Uplifting about China's FOI record study, however, is the law's positive impact on the Chinese people and their government. As the 2010 Chinese FOI law has concluded, while the Chinese news media are not yet actively using the law, a wide range of citizens and groups are exercising their access right and willing to challenge when their informational requests are rejected. Second, many Chinese citizens obtain government information because government agencies are disseminating more information voluntarily or in response to the FOI requests from the public—or as a result of administrative appeals or lawsuits. Finally, the public demand for greater informational disclosure in China is beginning to affect the government policies.[265]

India's Right to Information Act: The World's "Most Exciting Experiment" with FOI[266]
As FOI researcher Toby Mendel reported in 2008, the Right to Information Act (RTIA) of India is "more significantly progressive" than its earlier one and that its implementation has

been "positive."[267] More recently, the *New York Times* noted that the RTIA "has clearly begun to tilt the balance of power, long skewed toward bureaucrats and politicians" in India.[268]

The Constitution of India contains no explicit recognition of the right to know. In 1975, however, the Supreme Court of India read access to government information into the right to freedom of expression under the Constitution.[269] In 1982, the Supreme Court ruled again that informational access was implicitly part of the constitutional guarantee of freedom of speech and expression and that secrecy was "an exception justified only where the strictest requirement of public interest so demands."[270]

The RTIA, which superseded the Freedom of Information Act of 2002,[271] went into force in its entirety in October 2005. The law lays out the right to information for citizens to "secure access to information" controlled by the government and to "promote transparency and accountability" of public authorities.[272] Its preamble recognizes a possibility that access to information conflicts with other public interests and the need to "harmonise these conflicting interests while preserving the paramountcy of the democratic ideal."

"Information" subject to disclosure under the RTIA is defined as:

> [A]ny material in any form, including records, documents, memos, e-mails, opinions, advices, press releases, circulars, orders, logbooks, contracts, reports, papers, samples, models, data materials held in any electronic form and information relating to any private body which can be accessed by a public authority under any other law for the time being in force.[273]

The Indian law is broad in its institutional application. That is, a public body is "any authority or body or institution of self government" established by or under the Constitution, any law passed by the Parliament or a state legislature, or any notification or order issued by government. The law extends to any body owned, controlled, or substantially financed by government, including a non-governmental organization.[274]

The RTIA is considerably proactive in releasing government information to the public. Every administrative authority must, within 120 days of the law's enactment, publish a wide range of information, including: particulars of their organization, functions, and duties, the procedure followed in the decision-making process, the directory of their officers and employees, the budget allocated to each of its agency, the details in respect to the information, available to or held by it, reduced in an electronic form, the particulars of facilities available to citizens for obtaining information, and the names, designations, and other particulars of the Public Information Officer (PIO).[275] Besides, government agencies are required to make a "constant endeavour" to provide as much information as possible to the public at regular intervals and widely and in such form and manner easily accessible to the public. Further, the informational dissemination should be cost-effective, language-friendly, and communication-accessible.[276]

The RTIA states that, subject to its provisions, "all citizens shall have the right to information."[277] Access requests must be submitted to a PIO in writing or electronically.[278] No reason is required to be given for a request for information. Also, the law does not require "any ... personal details" from the information applicant except those necessary for contacting him or her.[279]

The PIO is required to respond in writing within 30 days or if the information concerns the life or liberty of a person, within 48 hours.[280] If there is no response within these timelines, the government agency is deemed to have denied the request.[281]

Access may be conditional upon the payment of a fee if the fee shall be "reasonable." The fee may be waived for those below the poverty level.[282] From a pro-access perspective, it is noteworthy that no fee may be charged when a public agency fails the time limits required for responses.[283]

As with other FOI laws around the world, access to information in India is not absolute. It should be weighed against other competing interests. So, the RTIA lists 11 specific exceptions:

- Information, [the] disclosure of which would prejudicially affect the sovereignty and integrity of India, the security, strategic, scientific, or economic interests of the State, relation with foreign state or lead to incitement of an offence;
- Information which has been expressly forbidden to be published by any court of law or tribunal or the disclosure of which may constitute contempt of court;
- Information, the disclosure of which would cause a breach of privilege of Parliament or the State Legislature;
- Information including commercial confidence, trade secrets, or intellectual property, the disclosure of which would harm the competitive position of a third party, unless the competent authority is satisfied that larger public interest warrants the disclosure of such information;
- Information available to a person in his fiduciary relationship, unless the competent authority is satisfied that the larger public interest warrants the disclosure of such information;
- Information received in confidence from foreign government;
- Information, the disclosure of which would endanger the life or physical safety of any person or identify the source information or assistance given in confidence for law enforcement or security purposes;
- Information which would impede the process of investigation or apprehension or prosecution of offenders;
- Cabinet papers including records of deliberations of the Council of Ministers, Secretaries and other officers.
- Information which relates to personal information, the disclosure of which has no relationship to any public activity or interest or which would cause unwarranted invasion of the privacy of the individual unless the Central Public Information Officer or the State Public Information Officer or the appellate authority, as the case may be, is satisfied that the larger public interest justifies the disclosure of such information.[284]

Most important, however, the RTIA includes an override clause relating to the exemptions. Section 22 explicitly overrides inconsistent provisions in other laws "for the time being in force," including the Official Secrets Act of 1923.[285] Further, the law makes the exemptions discretionary. That is, if public interest in disclosure of information outweighs the harm to the protected interests, the public authority may release the information regardless of the exemptions.[286] Also, the exemptions do not apply to historical disclosures when the requested information relates to any matter that took place 20 years before the request was made.[287] Still this historical disclosure provision does not kick in the exceptions for sovereignty, security, strategic interests, relations with other States, the privileges of Parliament and cabinet papers.[288] The law also provides for partial disclosure of a record that can be reasonably severed from any exempted part.[289]

Any person who did not receive the reply to his or her information request within the specified time frame or who is aggrieved by an FOI decision under the law[290] may, within 30 days, to appeal the denial of information to an officer who is senior in rank to the responsible PIO.[291] The second appeal should be made to the central or state information commission within 90 days. The appeal must be processed within 30 days or an extended period of up to 45 days.[292] The burden of justifying the refusal of the requested information is on the PIO involved.[293] The information commission's decision is binding.

The RTIA includes sanctions against PIOs. If an information commission determines that a POI has, with no reasonable cause, refused to accept an informational request, failed to provide information within the requisite time limit, denied the request in bad faith, knowingly given incorrect, incomplete, or misleading information, or destroyed information, which was the subject of the request, or obstructed in any manner access to the information, the POI is subject to a penalty of 250 rupees each day until the information at issue is released. The maximum penalty should not exceed 25,000 rupees.[294] The onus of proving that he or she has acted "reasonably and diligently" is on the PIO.

The law bars courts from adjudicating FOI complaints as a remedial option for the information applicant.[295] According to David Banisar, who has extensively researched freedom of information as a human right, "[A]s the right to information is a constitutional right, it would appear that citizens still have the right to go to the High Court or Supreme Court if they feel their right has been infringed."[296]

To make the law closer to reality than in the past, the RTIA requires the government authorities to actively monitor and promote the law.[297] In addition, the government may develop and organize educational programs to help the public to better understand how to exercise the FOI rights.[298]

In his 2010 analysis of the RTIA, law professor Alasdair Roberts at Suffolk University has noted: "Although the law has clearly done good already, substantial challenges remain to be overcome."[299] He pointed out the barriers for India's rural poor in using the law and the threat to enforcement capabilities stemming from the appeals to information commissions. He further called attention to the Indian government's "repeated attempts" to amend the law in order to restrict the right to information.[300]

Nonetheless, Roberts cautioned against viewing the RTIA pessimistically. "Most importantly, problems of implementation have not induced a sense of fatalism among the RTIA's advocates, either within and outside government," he stated. "On the contrary, there is still broadly shared optimism that problems can be worked out and the potential of the law fully realized."[301]

South Korea: An Earlier Adopter of FOI in Transitioning to Democracy

South Korea is a fascinating FOI case study. The FOI law in Korea has been one of the most liberalizing statutes that "make the government increasingly transparent."[302] The Constitution of Korea has no specific provision on the right to information. Freedom of information has been inferred from freedom of expression: "All citizens shall enjoy freedom of speech and the press, and freedom of assembly and association."[303]

The special law governing the access to information in Korea is the Official Information Disclosure Act enacted in 1996.[304] It covers "any State agency, local government, government-invested institution."[305] "Any State agency" encompasses the three branches of the government—that is, the National Assembly, the judicial branch, and the executive branch—and the Constitutional Court, and the National Election Commission. So, it is wider in its scope than the Freedom of Information Act of the United States, which does not apply to Congress and the federal courts.

The Korean law defines "information" as "matters recorded" in documents (including electronic documents), drawings, pictures, films, tapes, slides, and other media that public institutions create and manage as part of their official duties.[306]

Significantly, the broadcasting media, *both* public and private, are subject to disclosure of information under the Broadcasting Act.[307] The access to information requirement of the Broadcasting Act applies to all the broadcasting stations, except KBS (Korean Broadcasting System), a government-invested corporation, and EBS (Educational Broadcasting System). KBS and EBS as public institutions are subject to the Official Information Disclosure Act.

While no specific government agency or public institutions are exempted from the access to information obligations under the Official Information Disclosure Act, the Act is sweeping in exempting "any information" collected or created by national security agencies in order to analyze national security interests.[308]

In recognition of the conflicting interests involved, the Act stipulates several grounds of exemptions to information disclosures, which include:

1. Information specifically exempted by the Act and other laws;
2. Information relating to national security, national defence, unification, diplomatic relations, etc.;
3. Information harmful to the protection of individuals' lives, physical safety, and properties;
4. Information relating to ongoing trials, to crime investigation and prevention, institution and maintenance of indictments, or the execution of sentence and security disposition;
5. Information relating to audit, supervision, inspection, tests, regulations, tendering contract, the development of technology, the management of personal affairs, decision-making processes and internal review processes, etc.;
6. Information relating to management and trade secrets of corporations, organizations, or individuals;
7. Information relating to real estate and the acts of cornering and hoarding real estate.[309]

The Korean law does not discriminate non-citizens against citizens in accessing government records. Not only Korean citizens but also foreigners can file FOI requests to the government bodies and public institutions that are subject to the law. But the foreigners' requests have to comply with a relevant presidential decree.[310]

There is no limitation on the format of access requests. Requests may be filed electronically as well as in writing or in person. The public institutions under the FOI law can charge for the actual cost of disclosing information.[311] Fees are waived or reduced when the purpose of using the requested information is recognized to be for maintaining and promoting public welfare.[312] The deadlines for handling FOI-related matters are 10 days for answering the request from the date when the request was received[313] and 20 days for refusing the request for information.[314]

When a public institution decides not to disclose information, it must "promptly" notify in writing the requester of its nondisclosure decision.[315] In the case of a refusal of access, the Act requires that the reasons for the decision be explained to the requester.[316]

Even if the third party refuses to authorize access to information it has supplied to the government, the public body can make its own decision on whether to allow the access to the information. Third parties cannot exercise a veto over the FOI decisions by government authorities. There is no such thing as the reverse FOI application of the exemptions to denial of access requests.[317]

Individuals whose information requests have been denied may seek redress by filing for an administrative hearing under the Administrative Litigation Act.[318] More Koreans and public interest groups resort to the Administrative Litigation Act to challenge the denials of their access requests.

In the first FOI case,[319] the Constitutional Court extended Article 21 of the Constitution on freedom of expression to access to government records. The Court held:

> Freedom of speech and press guaranteed by Article 21 of the Constitution envisages free expression and communication of ideas and opinions that require free formation of ideas as a precondition. Free formation of ideas is in turn made possible by guaranteeing access to sufficient information. Right to access, collection and processing of information, namely the right to know, is therefore covered by the freedom of expression. The core of right to know is people's right to know with respect to the information held by the government, that is, general right to request disclosure of information from the government (claim-right).[320]

The Court stated, however, that the right to know is not absolute and it can be reasonably restricted by balancing the interest secured by the restriction and the infringement on the right to know: "Generally, the right to know must be broadly protected to a person making the request with interest as long as it poses no threat to public interest. Disclosure, at least to a person with direct interest, is mandatory."[321]

In another important FOI case, the Constitutional Court affirmed that a sufficient guarantee of access to information makes freedom of speech and the press a reality.[322] Interestingly, the Court drew upon the U.N. Declaration of Human Rights as well as the Constitution of Korea for its conclusion that the right to know is naturally included in the freedom of expression.[323]

In an FOI case of 2004, the Supreme Court set forth a balancing test in ruling on when access requests are denied by the government. *Chung Dong-yon v. Chief Public Prosecutor, the Seoul District Prosecutor's Office*,[324] stemmed from an FOI request by Chung, who participated in the Kwangjoo Democratization Movement of 1980, to Seoul District Prosecutor's Office. Chung asked the records of his and others' unsuccessful damage lawsuit against the prosecutors who refused to prosecute former Presidents Chun Doo Hwan and Roh Tae Woo in connection with their illegal military revolt of 1979, and the bloody Kwangjoo movement of 1980.

The Prosecutor's Office rejected Chung's request on the ground that he had no legitimate interest in accessing the information because the lawsuit he initiated against the prosecutors had already been completed. Chung disagreed, contending that the rejection of his FOI request violated the Official Information Disclosure Act.

In upholding a lower court's ruling in favor of Chung, the Supreme Court drew the line on when information requests can be denied. The requests are rejected, the Court stated, when they collide with the State and societal interests in national security, maintaining law and order, and ensuring public welfare or when they violate the basic rights of criminal suspects and witnesses to safeguard their reputation, private secrets, life and physical safety and tranquility.[325]

Lawyers for a Democratic Society requested the copies of the released U.S. government documents about the political situation in South Korea in 1979 and 1980. The Ministry of Foreign Affairs denied the information request, arguing that the contents of the U.S. documents have been already reported by Korean news media. Thus the plaintiffs could use them to form their own opinions, and their right to know was not violated. It also maintained that when the U.S. government provided the documents to the Ministry of Foreign Affairs, the U.S. government expressed its wish that Korean citizens would ask the U.S. government for access under the U.S. law.[326]

In September 1999, the Supreme Court in *Lawyers for a Democratic Society v. Ministry of Foreign Affairs*[327] disagreed with the Ministry of Foreign Affairs. In affirming its balancing test in FOI, the Court held: "There are certain limits on the citizens' right to access to information based on the people's right to know. But the benefits from the limitations should be weighed against those from their restrictions."[328] The Court concluded that there was no evidence that the damage to the State interest would arise from the release of the U.S. government records, and the lawyer group's request for the records had overstepped the citizens' right of access to information through the right to know.[329]

VII. Commercial Expression: Still Second Class in Free Speech Jurisprudence

Commercial speech is a significant area of comparative law on freedom of expression in the United States and Europe in that it illustrates "how courts protecting citizens' constitutional or fundamental rights apply similar methods of scrutiny when dealing with comparable issues."[330] The ECtHR has increasingly expanded freedom of expression to commercial speech over the years. In the United States and Europe, however, the legal status of commercial speech is still evolving, although there is no denying that commercial speech is more protected now than ever.

Article 10(2) of the European Convention on Human Rights sets the criteria for evaluation of all restrictions on expression, whether commercial or not. To a certain extent, it is true that "[d]ifferent tests are not used for different types of expression"[331] in Article 10, at least not to the same degree as they are in the First Amendment jurisprudence of the U.S. Supreme Court. Indeed, there is not a distinctive "commercial speech" doctrine in ECtHR case law like the one of the U.S. Supreme Court. However, commercial speech is ranked low in the case law of the ECtHR.

The European court is usually more willing to accept the regulation of advertising than it is to accept the regulation of noncommercial speech. Therefore, its doctrinal approach to advertising law is no different from that of the U.S. Supreme Court. Furthermore, the different degree of the margin of appreciation under Article 10(2) illustrates a judicial discrimination against commercial speech.

X and Church of Scientology v. Sweden,[332] the first commercial speech case under the ECHR, is a good example. This 1979 case involved an injunction against the Swedish Scientology Church's certain misleading statements in advertising a device called the E-meter.[333] In adjudicating the statements at issue in the E-meter advertisement, the European Commission of Human Rights made a distinction between informational or descriptive advertisements about a religious faith and commercial advertisements that offer products for sale. Thus, when religious advertisements promote the sale of goods for commercial purposes, they are not for dissemination of religious beliefs. According to the Commission, because the advertisements challenged aimed to persuade people to buy the E-meter, it was commercial.[334]

On whether the Swedish government had authority to restrict the Scientology Church's freedom of expression, the Commission held that the necessity requirement of Article 10(2) must be interpreted less strictly when commercial speech is restricted. It observed that most of the ECHR state parties have statutes for commercial speech to protect consumers from deceptive advertising.[335] Although commercial speech is not necessarily unprotected under the ECHR, the Commission held, "the level of protection must be less than that accorded to the expression of 'political' ideas, in the broadest sense, with which the values underpinning the concept of freedom of expression in the Convention are chiefly concerned."[336]

In 1994, the ECtHR addressed whether advertising is protected or unprotected expression. In *Casado Coca v. Spain*,[337] the Court stated unequivocally that Article 10, in guaranteeing freedom of expression to everyone, does not concern whether expression is profit-motivated or not.[338] It found that "Article 10 does not apply solely to certain types of information or ideas or forms of expression, in particular those of a political nature; it also encompasses artistic expression, information of a commercial nature … and even light music and commercials transmitted by cable."[339] However, the ECtHR granted the national authorities a wide margin of appreciation in unfair competition and advertising.[340]

Meanwhile, the Court indicated its willingness to review the margin of appreciation more strictly when truthful advertising is subject to regulation. Advertising may be restricted to prevent unfair competition and misleading advertising. But the Court continued: "In some contexts, the publication of even objective, truthful advertisements might be restricted …. *Any such restrictions must, however, be closely scrutinized by the Court, which must weigh the requirements of those particular features against the advertising in question.*"[341]

In connection with lawyer advertising at issue, the Court in *Casado Coca* emphasized that "the rules governing the profession, particularly in the sphere of advertising, vary from one country to another according to cultural tradition"[342] and that they change in most ECHR member states with varying degrees.[343] Hence, the complex nature of the lawyer advertising regulations place the national authorities in a better position than the ECtHR to balance the conflicting interests involved.[344] Significantly, however, the Court implied that restrictions on lawyer advertising would be more strictly reviewed in the post-*Casado Coca* years if the advertisement rules in the ECHR nations are liberalized and lawyers are given greater freedom in advertising.[345]

In an earlier *professional* commercial speech case, *Barthold v. Germany*,[346] the ECtHR found an Article 10 violation in a German court's injunction against a veterinary surgeon in discussing what he said in a newspaper interview about after-hours services. The veterinarian was charged by a veterinarians' association with violation of the Rules of Professional Conduct and the Unfair Competition Act because, in the association's view, he sought publicity for his own veterinary clinic.[347]

The German restrictions on professional publicity and advertising, the ECtHR said, violated the free speech rights of the members of professional veterinarians and the watchdog role of the news media. Noting the crucial role of the press in a democratic society, the Court stated that "[t]he injunction … does not achieve a fair balance between the … interests at stake." [348] The Court further held:

> A criterion as strict as this in approaching the matter of advertising and publicity in the liberal profession is not consonant with freedom of expression. Its application risks discouraging members of the liberal professions from contributing to public debate on topics affecting the life of the community if ever there is the slightest likelihood of their utterances being treated as entailing, to some degree, an advertising effect. By the same token, application of a criterion such as this is liable to hamper the press in the performance of its task of purveyor of information and public watchdog.[349]

In its leading but controversial commercial speech case, *Markt Intern & Beermann v. Gemany*,[350] the ECtHR was less than analytical in applying the balancing test in commercial speech. This 1990 case led the Court to rule on an injunction imposed on a publishing firm, Markt Intern, and its editor-in-chief, Klaus Beermann. Markt Intern and Beermann tried to promote the interests of small- and medium-sized retail businesses against competition of large-scale distribution companies. They were sanctioned for publishing in their weekly newsletters an article critical of the business practices of an English mail-order firm, Cosmetic Club International. They were ordered not to repeat the statements published in their newsletter.[351] Although Markt Intern was not a competitor against the Club, the German courts held that the publishing firm had violated the 1909 Unfair Competition Act, because its publication disadvantaged the Club while advancing the interests of its competitors.[352] In embracing the interests of the Club's competitors while attacking the Club's commercial interests, Markt Intern did not act as an organ of the press.[353]

The European Commission of Human Rights ruled 12 to 1 that Germany had violated Markt Intern's right to free speech under the ECHR.[354] Nonetheless, the ECtHR disagreed with the Commission. In its 10–9 opinion, the Court adopted the German courts' reasoning in toto: Markt Intern's newsletter at issue was not directly aimed at the general public but focused on a limited circle of traders conveying information of a commercial nature.[355] Recognizing a wide margin of appreciation for the national authorities in advertising regulation, the Court said:

> Such a margin of appreciation is essential in commercial matters and, in particular, in an area as complex and fluctuating as that of unfair competition. Otherwise, the European Court of Human Rights would have to undertake a re-examination of the facts and all the circumstances of each case. The Court must confine its review to the question whether the measures taken on the national level are justifiable in principle and proportionate.[356]

The ECtHR is wary of the chilling effect of the wider margin of appreciation on commercial speech and freedom of expression relating to debates of public concern. In *Hertel v. Switzerland*,[357] the injunction against a Swiss scientist in connection with a magazine article about his research was held to violate Article 10 of the ECHR. The article concerned Hans U. Hertel's findings that food prepared in microwave ovens was harmful to health. The Swiss courts proscribed Hertel from speaking about the danger of microwave ovens to health and from using the image of death in publications and speeches on microwave ovens. The Federal Court of Switzerland ruled that any scientist is "wholly free" to present his expertise in the academic community. Where competition is involved and a research discovery is still in dispute, however, a scientist must not misuse his unconfirmed opinion "as a disguised form of positive or negative advertising" of his own work or the work of others.[358]

In deciding whether they had a "pressing social need" to impose an injunction on Hertel, the ECtHR accorded the Swiss authorities some margin of appreciation. This was especially the case with commercial matters in unfair competition, according to the Court.[359] Nonetheless, the margin of appreciation must be reduced "when what is at stake is not a given individual's purely 'commercial' statements, but his participation in a debate affecting the general interest … over public health."[360] To the Court, Hertel's publication in a general-interest magazine was not a commercial advertisement but for a debate, which stood in sharp contrast with *Markt Intern* and *Jacubowski*. Thus, the Court more carefully examined whether the Swiss authorities' enforcement of the 1986 Unfair Competition Act accorded with its intended aim.

In balancing Hertel's right to free speech with the interests of microwave ovens makers, the ECtHR paid close attention to Hertel's role—lack thereof—in publishing the journal's article about his research findings and to the tone of his research paper quoted in the article. Hertel had nothing to do with the editing, illustrating, and headlining of the journal's article and his comments on microwave ovens were qualified. His only role in the journal's article was that he sent a copy of his research paper to the journal editor.[361] Meanwhile, the Court could not detect any substantial adverse impact of the journal article on the sale of microwave ovens in Switzerland.[362] So, it questioned the proportionality of the Swiss authorities' measure to its intended objective. The Court held:

> The effect of the injunction was thus partly to censor the applicant's work and sub-stantially to reduce his ability to put forward in public views which have their place in a public debate whose existence cannot be denied. It matters little that his opinion is a minority one and may appear to be devoid of merit since, in a sphere in which it is unlikely that any certainty exists, it would be particularly unreasonable to restrict freedom of expression only to generally accepted ideas.[363]

"Cause advertising" is given more protection than purely commercial advertising under Article 10. In *Vgt Verein Gegen Tierfabriken v. Switzerland,*[364] an animal rights association wanted to run an advertisement on television to encourage people to eat less meat. The European Court reiterated a wider margin of appreciation for commercial speech.[365] The Court held, however, that the animal rights film at issue was not commercial because it did not persuade the public to purchase a particular product, but it reflected controversial views relating to modern society.[366] Because the advertisement was political, the Swiss government's discretion in restricting it was reduced.

The Court acknowledged a possibility that freedom of the broadcasting media will be cur-tailed at the expense of the public's right to information if powerful financial groups dominate commercial advertising on radio and television. It considered pluralism in information and ideas essential to freedom of information in a democratic society. In this context, the Court said the audio-visual media should be guided by the principle of pluralism.[367]

The European Court concluded that the statutory prohibition of political advertising in Switzerland was supported by no "relevant and sufficient" reasons. It rejected the Swiss govern-ment's assertion that political advertising was prohibited from broadcasting media, but not in print media since "television had a stronger effect on the public on account of its dissemination and immediacy."[368] The Court said the differential treatment of the broadcast and print media for political advertising was not particularly pressing.

Further, the Court stated that the animal rights organization was not a financially power-ful group that was committed to undermining the independence of the television broadcaster, unduly influencing public opinion, or endangering the equality of opportunity among the different forces of society. Instead of abusing a competitive advantage, the organization merely wanted to participate in an ongoing debate on animal protection.[369]

The ECtHR in *Demuth v. Switzerland*[370] also took into account the broadcast media's pro-found impact on society in upholding the Swiss government's denial of a license to Car Tv AG. Noting that Car Tv AG's primary purpose was to promote car sales, the Court observed that "in view of their [audio-visual media] strong impact on the public, domestic authorities may aim at preventing a one-sided range of commercial television programmes on offer."[371] When issuing broadcasting licenses, the national authorities may weigh pluralism in broadcasting to ensure the quality and balance of broadcasting programs. The Court concluded that the licensing require-ments of the Swiss Radio and Television Act did not exceed the margin of appreciation given to the Swiss government. The particular political circumstances in Switzerland compelled the authorities to consider sensitive political criteria such as cultural and linguistic pluralism.[372]

Comparative advertising cannot be subject to an injunction unless it is overbroad. The 2003 case of *Krone Verlag GmbH & Co. KG v. Austria (No. 3)*[373] is illustrative. The Salzburg edi-tion of *Neue Kronenzeitung*, one of the daily newspapers owned by KG in Vienna, published an advertisement for subscriptions for the newspaper in which its monthly subscription rates were compared with those of another regional newspaper. The advertisement called the *Neue Kronenzeitung* the "best" local newspaper.[374] The Austrian courts issued an injunction against the *Neue Kronenzeitung* under Austria's Unfair Competition Act. The Linz Court of Appeal banned the newspaper from comparing its subscription prices with those of its competitor unless its comparison included the differences in their news reporting styles.[375]

The ECtHR rejected the Austrian government's measure against the *Neue Kronenzeitung* because its consequences would impact future advertising profoundly. Mandating inclusion of information about the differences between the compared newspaper in their news reporting styles, according to the Court, is "far too broad, impairing the very essence of price comparison."[376]

VIII. U.S. Media Sued Abroad: Enforcement of Foreign Court Judgments

The real world is taking over cyberspace slowly but inexorably. A growing number of govern-ments, for example, have taken legal actions against Internet access-providers and publishers, "using old-fashioned laws, in old-fashioned courts."[377] The notion of the borderless or "a-geo-graphical" Internet, to the dismay of many cyber-libertarians, is more often tested these days.[378] And application of local laws to the Internet world within several countries substantiates the unmistakable resiliency of old-style geographical boundaries in the era of the Internet.[379]

In 2005, for example, the Ontario Court of Appeal agreed with the *Washington Post* that a former U.N. official's libel lawsuit against the American newspaper be dismissed because it had nothing to do with Canada. The Canadian court held: "[T]here is simply no real and substan-tial connection between this action and Ontario and that it is not appropriate for the courts of Ontario to assume jurisdiction."[380] Most significantly, the High Court of Australia stated in 2002 that when a defamatory statement is accessible to and read by ISP subscribers in an Aus-tralian state, a court of that state has jurisdiction to hear an action for defamation relating to the statement.[381]

The growing need for an understanding of foreign law has become more acute in recent years because "broadcasts and publications transcend the boundaries of one state, or even one country, causing complicated problems for potential libel plaintiffs."[382]

Judging from the expanding case law of the United States on enforcement of foreign judgments, the principles of comity are likely to be of little help to those wishing to bring their foreign judgments to America for enforcement. Two earlier (i.e., pre-SPEECH Act) cases are illustrative.

A. New York Court in Bachchan Rejects an English Judgment

In *Bachchan v. India Abroad Publications, Inc.,*[383] a 1992 libel case, the plaintiff, an Indian national living in London, asked a New York State trial court to enforce an English libel verdict. *Bachchan* resulted from a British High Court of Justice libel judgment against India Abroad Publications, Inc. The case against the New York-based publications company concerned a defamatory story about the plaintiff. The defendant transmitted the story to an Indian news agency, pursuant to an agreement between them, for distribution to Indian newspapers. The wire service story appeared in the *India Abroad*, the defendant's English-language weekly, which was reprinted and distributed in England by the defendant's English subsidiary, India Abroad UK.[384]

Bachchan sued India Abroad Publications in February 1990 as a result of the wire service story. He amended his libel claim to include an action against India Abroad UK for its distribution of the *India Abroad* article. At the English jury trial, the High Court of Justice in London applied the "strict liability" standard of the English common law of libel. The jury awarded Bachchan damages and attorney's fees of £40,000 (U.S.$70,000).[385]

Since the judgment could not be enforced in England because there were no assets available in England,[386] the plaintiff asked a New York court to enforce the British libel ruling against the defendant. India Abroad argued against enforcement of the British judgment on the ground that the ruling was "fundamentally at odds with the core constitutional protections" of the First Amendment.[387] Characterizing the judgment as "plainly repugnant" to the public policy of New York, the defendant maintained that the English judgment would fall within an exception to the recognition of foreign judgments.[388]

Justice Shirley Fingerhood of the New York court held that if the foreign judgment is repugnant to the policy embodied in both the federal and state constitutions, "the refusal to recognize the judgment should be, and it is deemed to be, 'constitutionally mandatory.'"[389] Comparing English with American libel law, Justice Fingerhood mentioned the strict liability rule still adhered to by British courts but rejected by American courts.[390] She also noted that the burden of proof standards employed by the English and U.S. courts were significantly different.[391]

Applying the U.S. Supreme Court's rejection in *Gertz v. Robert Welch, Inc.*[392] of the strict liability standard and *Philadelphia Newspapers, Inc. v. Hepps*[393] on the burden of proof, the New York court expressed strong reservations about the British law, which places the burden of proving truth upon media defendants in libel litigation.[394] The court observed: "The 'chilling' effect is no different where liability results from enforcement in the United States of a foreign judgment obtained where the burden of proving truth is upon media defendants."[395] Thus, the court found Bachchan's judgment unenforceable in New York.

The New York court's refusal to recognize the British judgment also was based on the difference between the liability standards of English and New York law. Under English law, plaintiff

Bachchan was not required to prove any degree of fault on the part of India Abroad. Noting that, under New York libel law, a private plaintiff must meet a "gross irresponsibility" standard in media libel actions for publications of public concern,[396] the court doubted whether Bachchan could have proved that the defendant's actions in disseminating the news story constituted gross negligence.

The *Bachchan* decision has established a legal precedent that foreign libel judgments will not be recognized and enforced by American courts if they contravene First Amendment guarantees. It has sent a clear signal to actual and potential plaintiffs in extraterritorial litigation against American media: "If you want to use the American judicial process, be prepared to meet the requirements of the First Amendment." Five years after, *Bachchan* was explicitly invoked by the Maryland Court of Appeals in another libel case pitting an English plaintiff against an American defendant.

B. Maryland's Highest Court Applies Bachchan in Matusevitch

In November 1997, Maryland's highest court rejected the recognition of an English court's libel ruling. The Maryland Court of Appeals in *Telnikoff v. Matusevitch*[397] reasoned that the English libel standards which were applied to the English libel judgment were so "repugnant" to the public policy of Maryland that the judgment should not be recognized for enforcement.[398] *Telnikoff*, the first *appellate* court ruling in the United States on foreign libel judgments, resulted from an English libel decision of 1992 against Vladimir Matusevitch, a U.S. citizen then living in England, for libel.[399] The English libel ruling related to Matusevitch's letter to the editor that had appeared in the London *Daily Telegraph*. The letter was Matusevitch's response to Vladimir Telnikoff's op-ed article in the *Daily Telegraph*.

In his letter to the editor, Matusevitch, a Soviet Jewish emigre to the United States, argued that as a "racialist (anti-Semitic)," Telnikoff demanded a change in the recruitment policy of the BBC Russian Service "from *professional testing* to a *blood* test."[400] Telnikoff sued Matusevitch for libel, alleging that he had been "gravely injured" in his reputation as a result of Matusevitch's letter.

In granting Matusevitch's motion for summary judgment, the High Court of Justice in London ruled that no jury would find that the letter was "unfair comment" or that Matusevitch was malicious in writing the letter.[401] The trial court, pointing out that Telnikoff, in writing an article of public interest, invited comment from the public, stated that Matusevitch "is entitled in this country to express extreme views on a matter of public interest, provided he does not overstep the boundary of what is permitted, and expresses the views honestly and without ulterior motives."[402]

The U.K. Court of Appeal agreed with the High Court that Matusevitch's letter, read together with Telnikoff's opinion article, was comment, not a statement of fact, and that no reasonable jury could have held that Matusevitch's primary motive had been to injure Telnikoff, and that there was no evidence of malice on the part of Matusevitch in publishing his letter.[403]

Telnikoff appealed again and the House of Lords, the highest court in England, affirmed in part, reversed in part, and remanded. The Law Lords agreed unanimously that Telnikoff had failed to establish malice on Matusevitch's part and thus could not defeat the fair comment defense if the letter was comment as distinguished from fact.[404] The majority, however, rejected the contextual reading of defamatory comment like Matusevitch's letter, which was accepted by the Court of Appeal and the High Court of Justice. According to the House of Lords, "the letter must be considered on its own. The readers of the letter must have included a substantial number of persons who had not read the article or who, if they had read it, did not have its terms fully in mind."[405]

Following a jury trial on remand, the jury returned a verdict for Telnikoff in the amount of £240,000, or U.S.$416,000.[406] He was strictly liable for his letter regardless of his state of mind. Judgment was entered on March 16, 1992.

When the English libel judgment could not be enforced in England, Telnikoff in December 1993 asked the Circuit Court for Montgomery County, Maryland, to enforce the libel ruling against Matusevitch.[407] Matusevitch, a U.S. citizen, moved as a journalist for Radio Free Europe/Radio Liberty from London to the corporation's headquarters in Washington. He was living in Maryland.[408]

Matusevitch countersued by filing a civil rights action against Telnikoff in the U.S. District Court for the District of Maryland. He argued that the recognition and enforcement of the British judgment would deprive him of his free speech rights under the U.S. Constitution and the state Constitution of Maryland because the judgment was repugnant to the Constitutions. The case was moved to the U.S. District Court for the District of Columbia in May 1994.

U.S. District Judge Ricardo M. Urbina ruled that a foreign libel judgment cannot be enforced in the United States if it is based on the libel standards that are contrary to U.S. law.[409] He found that Telnikoff's English judgment was "repugnant" and not enforceable. He concluded that enforcement of the judgment would deprive Matusevitch of his constitutional right to free speech and free press as a U.S. citizen.[410]

Telnikoff appealed Judge Urbina's decision to the District of Columbia Circuit. After hearing oral argument, the U.S. Court of Appeals for the District of Columbia Circuit certified to the Maryland Court of Appeals a question whether recognition of Telnikoff's foreign judgment would be repugnant to the public policy of Maryland.[411]

The Maryland Court of Appeals answered the certified question in the affirmative. In refusing to recognize Telnikoff's libel judgment, Maryland's highest court relied extensively on the American and Maryland constitutional history relative to the public policy, which favored "a much broader and more protective freedom of the press than ever provided for under English law."[412]

First, in Maryland the *Gertz* principle on fault in libel actions applies "regardless of whether the allegedly defamatory statement involved a statement of public concern and regardless of whether the action was against a media defendant or a non-media defendant."[413] Second, in all defamation actions in Maryland, neither presumed nor punitive damages may be recovered unless the plaintiff establishes liability under the "actual malice" standard of *Sullivan*.[414] And finally, Maryland law does not allow recovery unless "actual malice" is established in defamation cases where the defamatory statement enjoys a conditional privilege.[415]

In its comparison of English libel standards with those of Maryland, the Maryland Court of Appeals took special note of the "unchanged" principles governing English defamation actions from the earlier common law era.[416] The court called attention to the English courts' adherence to the strict liability standard, the presumptive falsity of defamatory statements, the defeat of qualified privilege with no proof of "actual malice," and no distinction between private and public figures and between statements of public and private concern.[417] The court concluded: "[P]resent Maryland defamation law is totally different from English defamation law in virtually every significant respect."[418]

As an illustration of the sharp contrast between English and Maryland law, the Maryland Court of Appeals took issue with the English court's reasoning underlying its judgment in favor of Telnikoff. Telnikoff would have been considered a public figure and thus required to prove "actual malice" for recovery under Maryland law. But the English courts allowed him to recover damages notwithstanding the absence of "actual malice."[419] Telnikoff was not required to prove the falsity of Matusevitch's letter. Rather, falsity was presumed under English law, which was contrary to Maryland law.[420] The Maryland court also questioned the way Matusevitch's letter was examined. The court pointed out that the letter was examined not in context but in isolation, which was incompatible with the present libel law of the United States.[421]

The Court characterized the libel law principles which applied to Telnikoff's suit in England as "so contrary to Maryland defamation law, and to the policy of freedom of the press underlying Maryland, that Telnikoff's judgment should be denied recognition under principles of comity."[422] The Maryland court's rejection of the *Telnikoff* judgment was also based on the court's concern that "recognition of English defamation judgments could well lead to wholesale circumvention of fundamental public policy in Maryland and the rest of the country."[423]

The impact of *Telnikoff*, of course, will not be limited to the traditional mass media. The case would provide a judicial road map on cyberspace defamation in that "[c]omputer networks simply offer unparalleled opportunities for injuring individual reputations anywhere in the world. In light of this potential for international defamation and forum shopping, more U.S. residents may soon select from a number of favorable forums, such as England, and choose to file defamation suits abroad."[424]

IV. Summary and Conclusions

Now media law has become more global, although a nation-state remains relevant in setting the boundaries on freedom of speech and the press. This is all the more manifest, given that media law is increasingly affected by Internet communication that, more often than not, defies the borders.

But it should be noted that some areas of media law are more culture-dictated than others. Hence, they ought to reflect their differing value priorities entrenched in their societies, whether political or nonpolitical. For example, hate speech is prohibited as a crime around the world, but not in the United States, where it is protected by the First Amendment.

Likewise, reputation is more a human right globally and thus is as highly regarded as freedom of expression, if not more. Yet the balancing of reputation with free speech reveals a fascinating process for a nation's commitment to political democracy. Defamation of government officials and politicians in various rule-of-law nations, as illustrated by U.K. and ECHR law, is given more leeway than that of private individuals. In this connection, the theoretical and doctrinal impact of the U.S. "actual malice" rule on the global media law is significant.

Privacy is still evolving as a right, and judges and lawmakers are drawing its contours. The ECtHR rulings on privacy are expected to influence how it is weighed against other competing interests. From a press freedom perspective, what should constitute a matter of legitimate interest to the public will be more searchingly examined in the years to come.

The right of reply in Germany, France, and other nations showcases how freedom of the press is expanded as an affirmative concept instead of as a traditionally passive notion. Most important, it contributes to the marketplace of ideas as an equalizer for those outside the institutional press in countering the otherwise media-dominant distribution of information. At the same time, it enriches the quality as well as the quantity of the informational exchange.

The international and foreign law on the journalistic privilege to protect confidential sources and on the access to information stand out from U.S. law in that the former tends to be more liberal than the latter in varying degrees. This may be surprising because American law has inspired the development of the international and foreign law over the years.

As a rule, advertising as commercial speech is less protected than political or public speech, regardless of whether it is supposed not to be discriminated against in free speech jurisprudence, albeit as a matter of principle.

Meanwhile, the interaction between American and foreign media law is most dramatically illustrated when U.S. courts refuse to enforce foreign court judgments on First Amendment grounds. Because the newly enacted SPEECH Act prohibits U.S. courts from recognizing foreign judgments against American media, there will be less "libel tourism" to England and other countries. Yet it is not clear what the law's practical impact will be on the transnational American media that maintain substantial assets abroad.

In any case, international and foreign law affords a valuable opportunity for us to critically learn how our American media law protects freedom of speech and the press as a right. So, it helps us to better appreciate our First Amendment right to speak freely and with a sense of discernment.

Endnotes

1. Reporters Without Border for Press Freedom, *Press Freedom Index 2009*, at http://bit.ly/9oOlMx (last visited May 29, 2010).
2. Frederick Schauer, *The Exceptional First Amendment*, in American Exceptionalism and Human Rights 29 (Michael Ignatieff ed., 2005).
3. Kyu Ho Youm, *Comparative Essay: America's Evolving Freedoms*, 86 Journalism & Mass Communication Quarterly 636 (spring 2009).
4. *Icelandic Modern Media Initiative,* http://immi.is/?l=en&p=vision (last visited May 31, 2010). "Libel tourism" refers to "the use of libel judgments procured in jurisdictions with claimant-friendly libel laws [and little or no connection to the author or purported libelous material] to chill free speech in the United States." *Ehrenfeld v. Bin Mahfouz,* 881 N.E.2d 830, 834 (N.Y. 2007). At least eight states have adopted or consider adopting anti-libel tourism law. Congress has passed an anti-libel tourism statute, titled the SPEECH [Securing the Protection of our Enduring and Established Constitutional Heritage] Act, which President Barack Obama signed on August 10, 2010. For the text of the SPEECH Act, see http://bit.ly/cFEbHO (last visited Aug. 29, 2010). For a discussion of the SPEECH Act, see *Victory for Writing,* New York Times, July 22, 2010, at http://nyti.ms/acJpOw (last visited Aug. 29, 2010).
5. Kyu Ho Youm, *Iceland's Free Speech Initiative Improves upon US First Amendment Exceptionalism,* Jurist, March 8, 2010, at http://bit.ly/aP7YmR (last visited May 31, 2010).
6. *Id.*
7. From a media law perspective, American media law attorney Richard N. Winfield observed:
   This trend [of media law's increasing internationalization] is explained by the Internet, with its nearly infinite and instantaneous capacity to distribute problematic copy and liability exposure everywhere; and by the global reach of powerful media conglomerates by satellite television and by the efforts of states to assert sovereignty over their information space and protect it.
   Richard N. Winfield, *Globalization Comes to Media Law*, 1 Journal of International Media & Entertainment Law 109, 109 (2006). *See also* Ashley Packard, Digital Media Law, at vi (2009).

8. C. Thomas Dienes, *Libel Reform: An Appraisal,* 23 Journal of Legal Reform 1 (1989).

9. Catherine Spratt, *British Blockade*, News Media & Law, Fall 2006, at 26–27.

10. Eric Barendt, *Freedom of Speech*, at v (2d ed. 2005).

11. *See,* e.g., Peter F. Carter-Ruck, Libel and Slander (1972). This "bible" on international and foreign defamation law has been revised. The revised and expanded edition of the book is *Carter-Ruck on Libel & Privacy* (6th ed., Cameron Doley and Alastair Mullins eds. 2010). *See also International Libel and Privacy Handbook* (Charles J. Glasser Jr. ed., 2d ed. 2009); *The International Libel Handbook* (Nick Braithwaite ed., 1995). Especially noteworthy is Dean Rodney Smolla's expanded discussion of foreign law in his oft-cited U.S. libel law treatise, *Law of Defamation*. In 2010, Dean Smolla added Australia, New Zealand, and South Africa to Canada and the United Kingdom in his foreign law discussion. *See* Rodney A. Smolla, *Law of Defamation* § 1:9.80 (Australia), § 1:9.85 (New Zealand), and § 1:9.90 (South Africa) (2010).

12. See, e.g., Toby Mendel, *Freedom of Information: A Comparative Legal Survey* (2d ed. 2008); *Extreme Speech and Democracy* (Ivan Hare & James Weinstein eds., 2009); Kyu Ho Youm, *International and Comparative Law on the Journalist's Privilege: The Randal Case as a Lesson for the American Press*, 1 Journal of International Media & Entertainment Law 10 (2006).

13. See, e.g., Ashley Packard, *The Borders of Free Expression* (2009).

14. Although not in the context of media law, the value of examining global issues to law courses in the United States is compellingly argued:

    [S]ome threshold level of exposure to comparative and international law is essential for today's students to understand the meaning, interpretation and practical impact of the individual rights guarantees contained within the U.S. Constitution. In addition, of course, international law is a direct source of constitutional law. Moreover, exposure to foreign law helps prepare students for practice in a globalized society. Limited exposure will not, of course, lead to a deep understanding of other constitutions or legal systems. It is, however, an important start, which will alert students to the potential applicability of global issues to legal questions as they enter practice.

    Alan Brownstein & Leslie Gielow Jacobs, *Global Issues in Freedom of Speech and Religion*, at iii (2009).

15. For a look at the sheer volume of foreign and international media and related law in the world, see *Media, Advertising & Entertainment Law Throughout the World* (Andrew B. Ulmer ed., 2010). This loose-leaf service, annually supplemented, covers 39 countries.

16. Floyd Abrams, *Speaking Freely: Trials of the First Amendment* 278 (2005). For a recent insightful discussion of the First Amendment and its relevance to the world in the 21st century, see Lee C. Bollinger, *Uninhibited, Robust, and Wide-open: A free Press for a New Century* (2010), at 78.

17. *See* Schauer, *supra* note 2, at 32.

18. Eric Heinze, *Wild-West Cowboys versus Cheese-Eating Surrender Monkeys: Some Problems in Comparative Approaches to Hate Speech*, in Extreme Speech and Democracy, *supra* note 12, at 186.

19. International Covenant on Civil and Political Rights (ICCPR), art. 20(2).

20. International Convention on the Elimination of All Forms of Racial Discrimination (CERD), art. 4.

21. *See generally* Ivan Hare, *Extreme Speech Under International and Regional Human Rights Standards*, in Extreme Speech and Democracy, *supra* note 12, at 62-80.

22. *Brandenburg v. Ohio*, 395 U.S. 444 (1969).

23. *Jersild v. Denmark*, 19 E.H.R. R. 1 (1995). *See also Lehideux and Isorni v. France,* 30 E.H.R.R. 665 (1998).

24. Sandra Coliver, *Hate Speech Laws: Do They Work?, in* Striking a Balance: Hate Speech, Freedom of Expression and Non-Discrimination 372 (1992), quoted *in* Peter Molnar, *Towards Improved Law and Policy on "Hate Speech"—The "Clear and Present Danger" Test in Hungary*, in Extreme Speech and Democracy, *supra* note 12, at 237. For a comparative discussion of hate speech, see Michael Rosenfeld, *Hate Speech in Constitutional Jurisprudence: A Comparative Analysis,* 24 Cardozo Law Review 1523 (2003).

25. *Yahoo! Inc. v. La Ligue Contre le Racisme et l'Antisemitisme*, 145 F. Supp. 2d 1168 (N.D. Cal. 2001).

26. *Id.* at 1172.

27. French Union of Jewish Students v. Yahoo! Inc., No. N° RG: 00/05308, 00/05309, Interim Court

Order of the County Court of Paris (May 22, 2000) (Gomez, J.) (translated copy of May 22, 2000, order).

28. *Id.*

29. *Id.*

30. *Id.*

31. *Id.*

32. *Id.*

33. *Id.*

34. Pierre-Antoine Souchard, *French Judge Sets New Cyberspace Parameter Rules Against Yahoo in Auction Case*, Record, Nov. 21, 2000, at A1.

35. Carl Honori, *Should Nazi Items Be Off-Limits on Net?*, Chicago Sun-Times, Aug. 10, 2000, at 55.

36. Brief Amici Curiae in Support of Plaintiff's Motion for Summary Judgment at 1, Yahoo! Inc. v. La Ligue Contre le Racisme et l'Antisemitisme, No. C00-21275 JF (N.D. Cal. filed April 6, 2001), at 1-2.

37. David Pringle, *Some Worry French Ruling on Yahoo! Will Work to Deter Investments in Europe*, Wall Street Journal, Jan. 20, 2000, at B2.

38. Lawrence W. Beer, *Freedom of Expression in Japan: A Study in Comparative Law, Politics, and Society* 314 (1984).

39. Although criminal libel is dubious as a matter of free speech law in the United States, it remains on the books in more than a dozen jurisdictions, and it is still enforced. *See* David Pritchard, *Rethinking Criminal Libel: An Empirical Study,* 14 Communication Law & Policy 1, 3 (2009). This makes it all the more noteworthy that criminal libel has been abolished in England, Ireland, Mexico, and other countries. *See Mexico Decriminalises Defamation, Libel and Slander,* April 19, 2007, at http://bit.ly/cpcRV3 (last visited May 31, 2010). *See also* James Cohen, *OSCE Media Freedom Representative Welcomes Ireland's Decriminalization of Defamation, Calls for Crime of "Blasphemy" to be Abolished,* International Free Press Society, Jan. 12, 2010, at http://bit.ly/bAksaA (last visited May 31, 2010); *Criminal Libel and Sedition Offences Abolished,* Press Gazette, Jan. 13, 2010, at http://bit.ly/asXJia (last visited May 31, 2010). For a measured argument in favor of supplanting criminal libel law with civil libel law, see the concurring opinion of IACHR President Sergio Garcia Ramirez in *Herrera-Ulloa v. Costa Rica*, July 2, 2004, at 5–6, at http://bit.ly/bWNfZh (pdf).

40. *See Paul v. Davis*, 424 U.S. 693 (1976).

41. Universal Declaration of Human Rights, art. 12 ("No one shall be subjected to … attacks upon his honor and reputation. Everyone has the right to the protection of the law against such interference or attacks.").

42. Harry Kalven, *The* New York Times *Case: A Note on "The Central Meaning of the First Amendment,"* Sup. Ct. Rev. 213 (1964).

43. The U.S. "actual malice" defense has influenced international and foreign law as a source of doctrinal inspiration. Although not as widely as some press freedom advocates wish, "actual malice" has been accepted by several countries, including Argentina, Bosnia, Hungary, India, and the Philippines. *See* Kyu Ho Youm, New York Times v. Sullivan: *Impact on Freedom of the Press Abroad*, Communications Law, Fall 2004, at 12.

44. Article 10 of the European Convention on Human Rights states:
1. Everyone has the right to freedom of expression. This right shall include freedom to hold opinions and to receive and impart information and ideas without interference by public authority and regardless of frontiers. This article shall not prevent States from requiring the licensing of broadcasting, television or cinema enterprises.
2. The exercise of these freedoms, since it carries with it duties and responsibilities, may be subject to such formalities, conditions, restrictions, or penalties as are prescribed by law and are necessary in a democratic society, in the interests of national security, territorial integrity, or public safety, for the prevention of disorder or crime, for the protection of health or morals, for the protection of the reputation or rights of others, for preventing the disclosure of information received in confidence, or for maintaining the authority and impartiality of the judiciary. European Convention on Human Rights, art. 10

45. Dan Kozlowski, *"For the Protection of the Reputation or Rights of Others": The European Court of Human*

Rights' Interpretation of the Defamation Exception in Article 10(2), 11 Communication Law & Policy 140 (2006) (citation omitted).

46. *Lingens v. Austria*, 8 E.H.R.R. 407 (1986).
47. *Id.* ¶ 42.
48. *Id.* ¶ 45.
49. *Thoma v. Luxembourg*, 36 E.H.R.R. 21 (2003).
50. *Id.* ¶ 47.
51. The doctrine of "margin of appreciation" allows the governments of the ECHR member states some discretion, subject to the ECtHR supervisioin, in balancing freedom under the ECHR with conflicting interests such as reputation, privacy, and the right to a fair trial. This doctrine was first articulated by the ECtHR in *Handyside v. United Kingdom*:

    In particular, it is not possible to find in the domestic law of the various Contracting States a uniform European conception of morals. The view taken by their respective laws of the requirements of morals varies from time to time and from place to place, especially in our era which is characterised by a rapid and far-reaching evolution of opinions on the subject. By reason of their direct and continuous contact with the vital forces of their countries, State authorities are in principle in a better position than the international judge to give an opinion on the exact content of these requirements as well as on the "necessity" of a "restriction" or "penalty" intended to meet them.... Nevertheless, it is for the national authorities to make the initial assessment of the reality of the pressing social need implied by the notion of "necessity" in this context.

    Consequently, Article 10 para. 2 (art. 10-2) leaves to the Contracting States a margin of appreciation. This margin is given both to the domestic legislator ("prescribed by law") and to the bodies, judicial amongst others, that are called upon to interpret and apply the laws in force ....

    Nevertheless, Article 10 para. 2 (art. 10-2) does not give the Contracting States an unlimited power of appreciation. The Court, which, with the Commission, is responsible for ensuring the observance of those States' engagements (Article 19) (art. 19), is empowered to give the final ruling on whether a "restriction" or "penalty" is reconcilable with freedom of expression as protected by Article 10 (art. 10). The domestic margin of appreciation thus goes hand in hand with a European supervision. Such supervision concerns both the aim of the measure challenged and its "necessity"; it covers not only the basic legislation but also the decision applying it, even one given by an independent court....

    *Handyside v. United Kingdom,*1 E.C.H.R. 737, 753-54 (1979).
52. *Prager & Oberschlick v. Austria*, 21 E.H.R.R. 1 (1996).
53. *Id.* ¶ 35.
54. *Id.*
55. *Bergens Tidende & Others v. Norway*, 31 E.H.R.R. 420 (2001).
56. *Id.* ¶ 49.
57. *Id.* ¶ 57 (citation omitted).
58. For the text of Lord Lester's "Defamation Bill," see http://bit.ly/ctUOvv (pdf) (last visited May 29, 2010). For a discussion of the Defamation Bill, see *Lord Lester's Defamation Bill—An Overview*, Inforrm's Blog, May 27, 2010, at http://bit.ly/9Qft1Q (last visited June 1, 2010).
59. Lord Lester, *Redressing the Balance*, Times (London), May 25, 2010, at http://bit.ly/9qHYhP (last visited May 29, 2009). A most recent example of the abusive application of U.K. libel law is vividly portrayed by Simon Singh, who was sued for defamation in connection with his comment on the medical claims by chiropractors. Simon Singh, *Reform of Our Libel Law Is Long Overdue*, Telegraph, May 25, 2010, at http://bit.ly/aBvkWs (last visited May 29, 2010).
60. *Peck v. Tribune Co.*, 214 U.S. 185, 189 (1909) (quoting Lord Mansfield in *Rex v. Woofdall* [1774] Lofft 776, 781, 98 Eng. Rep. 914, 916).
61. *Restatement of Torts* § 559 (1938). One archaic libel rule that constrains U.K. media is the "multiple publication" rule, which makes a publisher liable for each republication of a libelous statement, "no matter how long after first publication." Anthony Lester, *Free Speech—the Gloves Are Off*, Sunday Times (London), May 30, 2010, http://bit.ly/blsdEX (last visited June 1, 2010). U.S. libel law follows the "single-publication" rule in which "a plaintiff in a libel suit against a publisher has only one claim for

each mass publication, not a claim for every book or issue in that run." Black's Law Dictionary 677 (9th ed. 2009).

62. *Id.* § 558.

63. For a concise discussion of English defamation law, see Anna Frankum et al., *United Kingdom*, in Media, Advertising & Entertainment Law Throughout the World, *supra* note 15, §§ 36:11-36:16.

64. Geoffrey Robertson & Andrew Nicol, *Media Law* 93 (5th ed. 2008).

65. Winfield, *supra* note 7, at 110. *See generally* David Hooper, *Reputations Under Fire* 428–48 (2000).

66. *Derbyshire County Council v. Times Newspapers, Ltd.* [1993] A.C. 534 (H.L.).

67. *City of Chicago v. Tribune Co.*, 307 Ill. 595 (1923).

68. *Derbyshire,* at 548 (opinion of Lord Keith).

69. *Reynolds v. Times Newspapers Ltd.* [1999] 4 All E.R. 609 (H.L.).

70. *Id.* at 625 (opinion of Lord Nicholls).

71. *Id.* at 626.

72. *Id.* "Responsible journalism" as a libel defense in English law has inspired the Canadian Supreme Court to adopt "responsible communication" in a 2009 landmark decision for freedom of the traditional *and* non-traditional (i.e., Internet) media. In enunciating "public interest responsible communication" as a new libel defense, the Supreme Court of Canada held in December 2009:

A. The publication is on a matter of public interest
and:
B. The publisher was diligent in trying to verify the allegation, having regard to:
   (a) the seriousness of the allegation;
   (b) the public importance of the matter;
   (c) the urgency of the matter;
   (d) the status and reliability of the source;
   (e) whether the plaintiff's side of the story was sought and accurately reported;
   (f) whether the inclusion of the defamatory statement was justifiable;
   (g) whether the defamatory statement's public interest lay in the fact that it was made rather than its truth ("reportage"); and
   (h) any other relevant circumstances.

Grant v. Torstar, 2009 SCC 61, ¶ 126

73. Richard Rampton, *Lowering the Hurdles—for Serious Journalism*, Times (London), Oct. 24, 2006, at 1 (noting that the success rate of the defense between 1999 and 2006 was no more than 20%).

74. *See* Catherine Spratt, *A New Day in the U.K.,* News Media & Law, Winter 2007, at 24 (noting that "[r]ather than using the criteria as flexible guidelines, the lower courts were applying them as a checklist that must be met in order to use the defense").

75. *Jameel v. Wall Street Journal Europe* [2006] U.K.H.L. 44.

76. *Id.* ¶ 4 (opinion of Lord Bingham).

77. *Id.*

78. Stuart D. Karle, *Jameel on Appeal: Reynolds Revisited,* Communication Law Review, Fall 2006, at 8.

79. *Jameel,* ¶ 57 (opinion of Lord Hoffmann).

80. *Id.* ¶ 82.

81. *Id.*

82. *Id.* ¶ 38

83. *Id.* ¶ 47.

84. *Id.* ¶ 48.

85. *Id.* ¶ 51.

86. *Id.* ¶ 53.

87. *Id.* ¶ 49.

88. *Id.* ¶ 51.

89. *Id.* ¶ 52.

90. *Id.* ¶ 56.

91. *Id.* ¶ 62.

92. *Id. See also id.* ¶ 35 (stating that the *Journal Europe*'s news reporting was "the sort of neutral, investigative journalism which *Reynolds* privilege exists to protect") (opinion of Lord Bingham). Although the House of Lords in *Jameel* did not refer to the American "neutral reportage" doctrine, "reportage" in U.K. law has its genesis in the 2nd U.S. Circuit Court of Appeals' decision of 1977, *Edwards v. National Audubon Society*, 556 F.2d 113 (2d Cir. 1977). *See generally* Kyu Ho Youm, *The "Neutral Reportage" Doctrine in English Law: U.K. Courts Embrace the Floundering U.S. Libel Defense* (presented at the convention of the Association for Education in Journalism and Mass Communication in Chicago, Aug. 6–9, 2008).

93. *Id.* ¶ 78.

94. *Id.* ¶ 80.

95. *Id.* ¶ 84.

96. Doreen Weisenhaus, Hong Kong Media Law 104 (2007).

97. Amber Melville-Brown, *Shooting Stars: Privacy Claims in the UK*, in International Libel & Privacy Handbook, *supra* note 11, at 426.

98. *See generally* Michael Tugendhat & Iain Christie, *The Law of Privacy and the Media* (2d ed. 2011). For an excellent, up-to-date overview of privacy as a right in European law, see Amber Melville-Bown, *Opinion: "Private Lives—Part 2"*, Inforrm's Blog, at http://bit.ly/aCy1G3 (last visited June 1, 2010).

99. Franklyn S. Haiman, Speech and Law in a Free Society 61 (1981).

100. http://bit.ly/aertBU (pdf) (last visited May 31, 2010). Unlike in the U.S. and U.K., invasion of privacy can be a criminal matter in Italy, Germany, and the Netherlands. In February 2010, for example, three Google executives were sentenced to suspended three years in jail for violation of the privacy of a disabled boy, who a video posted on YouTube showed was being bullied. Amber Melville-Brown, *Opinion: "Private Lives—Part 1,"* Inforrm's Blog, May 29, 2010, at http://bit.ly/dmakU1 (last visited June 10, 2010).

101. Article 8 of the ECHR states: "Everyone has the right to respect for his private and family life, his home and his correspondence." European Convention on Human Rights, art. 8.

102. *Von Hannover v. Germany,* [2004] ECHR 294, ¶ 71.

103. *Id.* ¶ 63 (internal citation omitted).

104. *Id.* ¶ 64.

105. *Id.* ¶ 65.

106. Mark D. West, *Secrets, Sex, and Spectacle: The Rules of Scandal in Japan and the United States* 64 (2006).

107. Barendt, *supra* note 10, at 117.

108. For a forceful argument in favor of prior restraint in privacy law under ECHR, see Gavin Phillipson, *Max Mosley Goes to Strasbourg: Article 8, Claimant Notification and Interim Injunctions*, 1 Journal of Media Law 73 (2009).

109. *Mosely v. News Group Newspapers Ltd.* [2008] EWHC 1777(QB).

110. *Id.* ¶ 232.

111. *Id.* ¶ 233.

112. *Mosley v. News Group Newspapers Ltd.* [2008] EWHC 687 (QB).

113. *Id.* ¶ 36.

114. *Id.*

115. *Supplemental Statement About the Facts and Violations,* Mosley v. United Kingdom, Jan. 14, 2009, ¶1. For a discussion of Mosley's brief and the U.K. government's argument, see *Mosley ECHR—Submissions of the Applicant and the UK Government*, May 3, 2010, http://bit.ly/afik6j (last visited May 31, 2010).

116. Mosley v. United Kingdom, *Submissions on Behalf of the Media Lawyers Association* (third party intervener), March 10, 2010, ¶ 51. For a discussion of the media amici curiae briefs filed in the ECtHR, see *Mosley ECHR Case—the Media Submissions*, April 9, 2010, http://bit.ly/cs19u9 (last visited May 31, 2010).

117. Jae-Jin Lee, *Right of Reply*, in International Encyclopedia of Communication (Wolfgang Donsbach ed., 2008), http://bit.ly/awYD5Y (last visited May 29, 2010).

118. American Convention on Human Rights, art. 14.

119. Melnychuk v. Ukraine, European Court of Human Rights, Application No. 28743/03, July 5, 2005.

120. Recommendation on the Right of Reply in the New Environment, Nov. 17, 2004, CM(2004)206.

121. Sean MacBride, *Many Voices, One World* 249 (1980).

122. *See* Amit M. Schejter, *The Fairness Doctrine is Dead and Living in Israel*, 51 Federal Communications Law Journal. 281 (1999).

123. Jae-Jin Lee & Sung-Hoon Lee, *The Right of Reply System for the Last Two Decades in South Korea*, Korean Journal of Journalism & Communication Studies 409 (special English ed. 2001) (citation omitted).

124. Franklyn S. Haiman, *Citizen Access to the Media: A Cross-Cultural Analysis of Four Democracies* 12 (1987).

125. Dominique Mondoloni, "France," in *International Libel & Privacy Handbook*, *supra* note 11, at 289.

126. Zechariah Chafee Jr., *Government and Mass Communications* 149 (1947).

127. Mondoloni, *supra* note 125, at 290.

128. Chafee, *supra* note 126, at 152.

129. Mondoloni*, supra* note 125, at 296 n.5.

130. *Id.*

131. Emmanuel E. Paraschos, *Media Law and Regulation in the European Union: National, Transnational and U.S. Perspectives* 79–80 (1998).

132. EDRI, "French Draft Decree Regarding the Right to Reply on the Internet," March 28, 2007, at http://www.edri.org/edrigram/number5.6/right-to-reply-france (last visited June 6, 2010).

133. *Id.*

134. *Id.*

135. *See* Article 5 of the Basic Law of Germany ("Freedom of the press and freedom of reporting by means of broadcasts and films shall be guaranteed. There shall be no censorship"). Basic Law of Germany, promulgated in 1939 and amended in 2006, art. 5(1)

136. Basic Law of Germany, art. 5(2).

137. Article 1 of the Basic Law on human dignity states in pertinent part:
Human dignity shall be inviolable. To respect and protect it shall be the duty of all state authority:
The German people therefore acknowledge inviolable and inalienable human rights as the basis of every community, of peace and of justice in the world.
Article 2 on personal freedoms provides as follows:
Every person shall have the right to the free development of his personality insofar as he does not violate the rights of others or offend against the constitutional order or the moral law;
Every person shall have the right to life and physical integrity. Freedom of the person shall be inviolable. These rights may be interfered with only pursuant to a law.
Basic Law of Germany, arts. 1, 2 (last amended 2006).

138. Basic Law of Germany, art. 5(2).

139. Hamburg Press Act, ¶11(1) (emphasis added).

140. *Id.* ¶7(4).

141. *Id.* ¶11(2).

142. *Id.*

143. *Id.*

144. *Id.* ¶11(3).

145. *Id.*

146. *Id.* ¶11(6).

147. *Id.*

148. *Id.*

149. *Id.*

150. *Id.* ¶11(5).

151. Urs Schwartz, *Press Law for Our Times* 83 (1966).

152. Martin Löffler, *The 'Gendarstellungsrecht' in the Federal Republic of Germany*, in Martin Löffler et al., Das Gegendarstellungrecht in Europa: Möglichkeite der Harmonisierung (The Right of Reply in Europe: Possibilities of Harmonization) 191 (1974).

153. Hamburg Press Act, ¶11(4).

154. *Id.*

155. BverG, 1 BvR 1861/93 (Jan. 14, 1998). The author's analysis of the German Constitutional Court's

1998 ruling on the Hamburg Press Act is based on the English translation of the court's opinion, as provided by Raymond Youngs, senior research fellow at the Institute of Global Law, University College London and senior lecturer at Kingston University in England.

156. *Id.* ¶71.
157. *Id.* ¶78.
158. *Id.* ¶79 (citation omitted).
159. *Id.* (citation omitted).
160. *Id.* ¶80.
161. *Id.* ¶81.
162. *Id.* ¶82.
163. *Id.* ¶83.
164. Beate Josephi, *Journalistis: International Profiles,* in Global Journalism: Topical Issues and Media Systems 148 (Arnold S. de Beer ed., 5th ed. 2009) (citing D. H. Weaver, *Journalists: International Profiles,* in Global Journalism: Topical Issues and Media Systems (Arnold S. de Beer & John C. Merrill eds., 4th ed. 2004).
165. Constitution of Argentina, art. 43.
166. Article 13 of the American Convention on Human Rights states:
Everyone has the right to freedom of thought and expression. This right includes freedom to seek, receive, and impart information and ideas of all kinds, regard less of frontiers, either orally, in writing, in print, in the form of art, or through any other medium of one's choices.
167. Peter *Protection of Journalists' Sources Under Foreign and International Law,* Media Law Resource Center White Paper on the Reporter's Privilege 188 (2004).
168. *Id.*
169. *John Fairfax & Sons Ltd. v. Cojuangco,* 165 C.L.R. 346, 354 (1988).
170. *Id*
171. *Id.* at 355
172. *R. v. National Post,* 2010 SCC 16.
173. John Henry Wigmore's criteria for confidentiality at common law:
The communications must originate in a *confidence* that they will not be disclosed.
    This element of *confidentiality must be essential* to the full and satisfactory maintenance of the relation between the parties.
The *relation* must be one which in the opinion of the community ought to be sedulously *fostered.*
The *injury* that would inure to the relation by the disclosure of the communications must be *greater than the benefit* thereby gained for the correct disposal of litigation.
8 John Henry Wigmore, *Evidence in Trials at Common Law* § 2285 (John T. McNaughton rev. 1961).
174. *National Post,* ¶ 53 (citations omitted).
175. *Id.* ¶ 42.
176. *Id.*
177. Abrams & Hawkes, *supra* note 167, at 192.
178. *Id.*
179. *Id.*
180. *Id.* (quoting North Rhine Westphalia Press Law, ¶ 24(1)).
181. *Id.*
182. *Id.* (citation omitted).
183. Beer, *supra* note 38, at 290.
184. *Id*
185. Code of Civil Procedure, art. 281(1)(3) (quoted in Beer, *supra* note 38, at 308 n.49).
186. *Id*
187. Beer, *supra* note 38, at 290.
188. *Id.* (quoting Hakata Railway Station, 1969 (Shi) No. 68, Supreme Court, 26 November 1969).
189. It should come as no surprise that Wikileaks, which publishes anonymous documents from governments and other organizations, is benefiting from the Swedish whistleblower act. *Swedish Law Gives*

Shelter to Controversial Wikileaks Site, April 9, 2010, EurActive Netowrk, at http://bit.ly/a73Tcc (last visited May 29, 2010).

190. John E. Nichols, *Swedish Shield Law and Its Impact on Criminal Justice in Sweden,* 60 Journalism Quarterly 253, 253-54 (1983).
191. *Id.* at 254.
192. *Id.*
193. *Id.*
194. *Id.*
195. David Feldman, *Civil Liberties and Human Rights in England and Wales* 849 (2d ed. 2002).
196. [1981] A.C. 1096, 1120.
197. Lord Denning explains the "newspaper rule" in *British Steel Corp. v. Granada Television Ltd.* as follows: [W]hen a plaintiff sues a newspaper for damages for libel, the newspaper will not be compelled to disclose its source of information: at any rate in answer to interrogatories administered in interlocutory proceedings before trial…. Sometimes this is put as a rule of practice—on the ground that it is not necessary at the interlocutory stage to discover the name of the informant. At other times it is put as a rule of law—on the ground that the plaintiff has an adequate remedy in damages against the newspaper and that it is not in the public interest that the name of the informant should be disclosed - else the sources of information would dry up.
    British Steel Corp. v. Granada Television Ltd. [1981] AC 1096 1128 (H.L.).
198. Contempt of Court Act, 1981, c.10.
199. Feldman, *supra* note 195, at 852 (citation omitted).
200. Kelly Buchanan, *Freedom of Expression and International Criminal Law: An Analysis of the Decision to Create a Testimonial Privilege for Journalists,* 35 Victoria University Wellington Law Review 609, 630-31 (2004) (citation omitted).
201. *See Goodwin v. United Kingdom,* 22 E.H.R.R. 123 (1996).
202. *See Prosecutor v. Brdjanin and Talic,* Case No. IT-99-36-AR73.9 (2002) [hereinafter "Appeals Chamber Decision"]
203. *Goodwin,* 22 E.H.R.R. at 126.
204. *Id.*
205. *Id.* at127 (quoting Judge Hoffmann).
206. *Id.* at 129 (quoting Lord Donaldson of the Court of Appeal).
207. *Id.* at 132.
208. *Id.* at 137.
209. *Id.*
210. *Id.* at 143 (citation omitted).
211. *Id.* at 144.
212. Jonathan C. Randal, *Preserving the Fruits of Ethnic Cleansing; Bosnian Serbs, Expulsion Victims See Campaign as Beyond Reversal,"* Washington Post, Feb. 11, 1993, at A34.
213. Appeals Chamber Decision, *supra* note 202, ¶ 11.
214. *Id.* ¶ 13 .
215. *Id.* ¶ 25.
216. *Id.* ¶ 31.
217. *Id.*
218. *Id.* ¶ 56.
219. *Id.* ¶ 35 (citations omitted).
220. *Id.* ¶ 36 (citations omitted).
221. *Id.* ¶ 37.
222. *Id.*
223. *Id.* ¶ 42.
224. *Id.* ¶ 50.
225. *Id.* ¶ 55.
226. *Id.* ¶ 54.

227. For the comprehensive resources on freedom of information in international and foreign law, see free-dominfo.org: The Global Network of Freedom of Information Advocates, at http://www.freedominfo.org/resources/ (last visited July 11, 2010); Right2Info: Good Law and Practice, at http://right2info.org/ (last visited July 11, 2010).

228. *See* Mendel, *supra* note 12, at 3.

229. Right to Information Act, 2005, No. 22 of 2005 (June 15, 2005). For the text of the Right to Information Act, see http://bit.ly/b0QYS8 (last visited July 11, 2010) [hereinafter RTIA].

230. Lydia Polgreen, *Right-to-Know Law Gives India's Poor a Lever,* New York Times, June 28, 2010, http://nyti.ms/9MtpcR (last visited July 11, 2010).

231. For the text of the "Provisions of the People's Republic of China on the Disclosure of Government Information," see *Freedom of Information in China,* at http://chinesefoi.org/regulation.aspx (last visited July 11, 2010) [hereinafter "Chinese DGI Provisions"].

232. Jamie P. Horsley, *Update on China's Open Government Information Regulations: Surprising Public Demand Yielding Some Positive Results,* at http://bit.ly/cY1DbP (last visited July 11, 2010) [hereinafter Horsley, *Update on China's OGI Regulations*].

233. For a concise discussion of the ECtHR on freedom of information, Hugh Tomlinson, *Freedom of Expression and Freedom of Information: Part1 The European Convention,* at http://bit.ly/b0cx3d (last visited May 30, 2010).

234. *Társaság a Szabadságjogokért v. Hungary,* European Court of Human Rights, April 14, 2009.

235. *Id.* ¶ 27.

236. *Id.* ¶ 35.

237. *Id.* ¶ 26.

238. *Id.* ¶ 28.

239. *Id.* ¶ 39.

240. *Claude Reyes et al. v. Chile, Inter-American Court of Human Rights*, Sept. 19, 2006.

241. *Id.* ¶ 77 (citation omitted).

242. *Id.*

243. *Id.*

244. *Id.* ¶ 57(31).

245. Heather Brooke, *The Silent State: Secrets, Surveillance and the Myth of British Democracy* 251 (2010).

246. The national FOI law of China is based on various local open government information legislation in more than 30 provinces and municipalities throughout China since 2002. Jamie P. Horsley, *China Adopts First Nationwide Open Government Information Regulations*, at 1 (n.d.) [hereinafter Horsley, *China's Adoption of Open Government Information Regulations*].

247. *Id.* at 1.

248. Horsley, *Update on China's OGI Regulations, supra* note 232.

249. "Chinese DGI Provisions," *supra* note 231, art. 1.

250. *Id.*

251. Horsley, *China's Adoption of Open Government Information Regulations, supra* note 246, at 2.

252. "Chinese DGI Provisions," *supra* note 231, art. 37.

253. *See e.g., id.* art. 9 (stating that "[a]n administrative organ shall voluntarily disclose the government information satisfying" any of the statutory requirements).

254. *See id.* art. 13 (stating that "citizens, legal persons, or other organizations may, in light of their special needs for production, living, or scientific research, apply to the departments under the State Council, the local people's governments at various levels and the departments of the local people's government at or above the county level for accessing the relevant government information").

255. *Id.* art. 18.

256. *Id.* art. 24.

257. *Id.* art. 20.

258. Horsley, *China's Adoption of Open Government Information Regulations, supra* note 246, at 5.

259. Chinese DGI Provisions, *supra* note 231, art. 9.

260. *Id.* art. 8.

261. *Id.* art. 13.

262. *Id.* art. 3.

263. *Id.* art. 33.

264. *Id.* art. 35.

265. Horsley, *Update on China's OGI Regulations, supra* note 232.

266. Alasdair Roberts, *A Great and Revolutionary Law?: The First Four Years of India's Right to Informa-tion Act*, Pub. Admin. L. 27 (forthcoming), at http://ssrn.com/abstracts=1527858 (last visited Aug. 29, 2010). This law review article is a must read for those interested in India's freedom of information because it offers analytical insights and valuable up-to-date information on RTIA.

267. Mendel, *supra* note 12, at 55, 56.

268. Polgreen, *supra* note 230.

269. David Banisar, Freedom of Information Around the World: A Global Survey of Access to Government Information Laws 84 (2006) (citing State of Uttar Pradesh v. Raj Narain and Others [1975] 4 SCC 428).

270. Toby, *supra* note 12, at 55 (citing S.P. Gupta v. President of India [1982] AIR (SC) 149, p. 234).

271. The FOIA of 2002 was adopted in January 2003 but never came into force. Banisar, *supra* note 269, at 85.

272. RTIA preamble.

273. *Id.* § 2(f).

274. *Id.* § 2(h).

275. *Id.* § 4(1)b.

276. *Id.* § 4(2)-(4).

277. *Id.* § 3.

278. *Id.* § 6(1).

279. *Id.* § 6(2).

280. *Id.* § 7(1).

281. *Id.* § 7(2).

282. *Id.* § 7(5).

283. *Id.* § 7(6).

284. *Id.* § 8(1).

285. *Id.* § 22.

286. *Id.* § 8(2).

287. *Id.* § 8(3).

288. *Id.*

289. *Id.* § 10(1).

290. *Id.* § 18(1).

291. *Id.* § 19(1).

292. *Id.* § 19(6).

293. *Id.* § 19(5).

294. *Id.* § 20(1).

295. *Id.* § 23.

296. Banisar, *supra* note 269, at 84.

297. RTIA § 25(1).

298. *Id.* § 26 (1).

299. Roberts, *supra* note 266, at 25.

300. *Id.*

301. *Id.* at 26-27

302. *Speaking Out for Free Expression: 1987–2007 and Beyond* 165–66 (2008).

303. Constitution of South Korea, art. 21(1).

304. Law No. 5242, Dec. 31, 1996, wholly amended by Law No. 7127, Jan. 29, 2004, last amended by Law No. 8871, Feb. 29, 2008.

305. Official Information Disclosure Act, art. 2-3.

306. *Id.* art. 2-1.

307. Broadcasting Act, art. 90(5), Law No. 6139, Jan. 12, 2000, last amended by Law No. 8867 (2008).

308. Official Information Disclosure Act, art. 4(3).

309 *Id.* art. 10(1).

310. *Id.* art. 5.

311. *Id.* art. 17(1).

312. *Id.* art. 17(2).

313. *Id.* art. 11(1).

314. *Id.* art. 11(5).

315. *Id.* art. 13(4).

316. *Id.*

317. Although not identical to American law on third parties' invocation of various FOIA exemptions, Korean law is similar to the reasoning of the U.S. Supreme Court in *Chrysler Corp. v. Brown*, 441 U.S. 281 (1979).

318. Official Information Disclosure Act, art. 20.

319. The "Forests Survey Inspection Request" case, Constitutional Court, 88 Honma 22, Sept. 4, 1989.

320. *Id.*

321. *Id.*

322. Constitutional Court, 90 Honma 133, May 13, 1991.

323. *Id.*

324. *Chung Dong-yon v. Chief Public Prosecutor, Seoul District Prosecutor's Office*, Supreme Court, 2003 Du 1370, Sept. 23, 2004. The appellant's first name was not included in the Supreme Court opinion, but the *Law Times* of Oct. 25, 2005, identifies Chung by his full name.

325. *Chung Dong-yon*, 2003 Du 1370.

326. *Lawyers for a Democratic Society v. Ministry of Foreign Affairs*, Supreme Court, 97 Nu 5114, Sept. 21, 1999.

327. *Id.*

328. *Id.*

329. *Id.*

330. Walter van Gerven, *The European Union: A Polity of States and Peoples* 250 (2005).

331. Karie Hollerbach, *Expression Here and Abroad: A Comparative Analysis of the United States Supreme Court's and the European Court of Human Rights' Commercial Speech Doctrine* (May 23–27, 2003) (paper presented at the ICA convention, San Diego, CA), 1.

332. *X and Church of Scientology v. Sweden*, 16 D&R 68 (1979).

333. The E-meter was "an electronic instrument for measuring the mental state of an individual" especially after confession to determine "whether or not the confessing person has been relieved of the spiritual impediment of his sins."

334. *X and Church of Scientology*, 16 D&R 68.

335. *Id.*

336. *Id.*

337. Cosado Coca v. Spain, 18 E.H.R.R. 1 (1994).

338. *Id.* ¶ 35.

339. *Id.*

340. *Id.* ¶ 50.

341. *Id.* ¶ 51 (emphasis added).

342. *Id.* ¶ 54.

343. *Id.*

344. *Id.* ¶ 55.

345. *Id.* ¶ 56. Noting the "material time" relevant to its judgment, the ECtHR held that the authorities in Spain did not overstep their boundaries in regulating the lawyer advertising. *Id.*

346. *Barthold v. Germany*, 7 E.H.R.R. 383 (1985).

347. *Id.* ¶ 16.

348. *Id.* ¶ 58.

349. *Id.*

350. *Beermann v. Gemany*, 12 E.H.R.R. 161 (1990).

351. *Id.* ¶ 13.
352. *Id.* ¶ 18.
353. *Id.*
354. *Id.* ¶ 22.
355. *Id.* ¶ 26.
356. *Id.* ¶ 33.
357. *Hertel v. Switzerland*, 28 E.H.R.R. 534 (1998).
358. *Id.* ¶ 23.
359. *Id.* ¶ 47.
360. *Id.* ¶ 47.
361. *Id.* ¶ 50.
362. *Id.*
363. *Id.*
364. *Vgt Verein Gegen Tierfabriken v. Switzerland*, 34 E.H.R.R. 4 (2002).
365. *Id.* ¶ 69.
366. *Id.* ¶ 70.
367. *Id.* ¶ 73.
368. *Id.* ¶ 74.
369. *Id.* ¶ 75.
370. *Demuth v. Switzerland,* 38 E.H.R.R. 20 (2004).
371. *Id.* ¶ 43.
372. *Id.* ¶ 44.
373. *Krone Verlag GmbH & Co. KG v. Austria* (No. 3), 42 E.H.R.R. 28 (2006).
374. *Id.* ¶ 10.
375. *Id.* ¶ 14.
376. *Id.* ¶ 33.
377. *The Internet's New Borders*, Economist, Aug. 11, 2001, at 9.
378. *See generally* Jack Goldsmith & Tim Wu, *Who Controls the Internet: Illusions of a Borderless World* (2006).
379. Lisa Guernsey, *Welcome to the Web. Passport, Please?* New York Times, March 15, 2001, at D1.
380. *Bangoura v. Washington Post*, 258 D.L.R. (4th) 341 ¶ 46 (2005).
381. *Dow Jones & Co. v. Gutnick,* 194 A.L.R. 433 (2002).
382. Kyu Ho Youm, *Defamation*, in Communication and the Law 121 (W. Wat Hopkins ed., 2010 ed. 2010).
383. *Bachchan v. India Abroad Publications, Inc.,* 585 N.Y.S.2d 661 (N.Y. Sup. Ct.1992).
384. *Id.*
385. *Id.* at 662.
386. Robin Pogrebin, *A N.Y. Court Refuses to Enforce Decision in U.K. Libel Case*, New York Observer, May 4, 1992, at 1.
387. Memorandum of Law in Opposition to Plaintiff's Motion to Enforce a Foreign Judgment at 11, *Bachchan*, 585 N.Y.S.2d 661.
388. *Id.* at 17–18. "A foreign country judgment need not be recognized if ... the cause of action on which the judgment is based is repugnant to the public policy of this state." N.Y. Civ. Prac. L. & R. § 5304 (McKinney 2000).
389. *Bachchan*, 585 N.Y.S.2d at 662.
390. *Id.* at 663.
391. *Id.*
392. *Gertz v. Robert Welch, Inc.*, 418 U.S. 323 (1974).
393. *Philadelphia Newspapers, Inc. v. Hepps*, 475 U.S. 767 (1986).
394. *Bachchan*, 585 N.Y.S.2d at 664.
395. *Id.*
396. *Id.*
397. *Telnikoff v. Matusevitch*, 702 A.2d 230, 249 (Md. 1997).
398. *Id.*

399. Brief for Appellee at 3, 6, 11, Matusevitch v. Telnikoff, 877 F. Supp. 1 (D.D.C. 1995) (No. 95-7138).

400. *Id.* at Pocket B: Defendant's Letter to the Daily Telegraph.

401. *Telnikoff v. Matusevitch*, Judgment of May 25, 1989 (No. MR/0365), High Court of Justice, slip op., at 65.

402. *Id.* at 66.

403. *Telnikoff v. Matusevitch*, 3 All E.R. 865 (C.A. 1990).

404. *Telnikoff v. Matusevitch*, 4 All E.R. 817, 825 (1991) (per Lord Keith).

405. *Id.* at 822.

406. Joint Appendix to Appellate Brief at 517, *Matusevitch v. Telnikoff*, 877 F. Supp. 1 (D.D.C. 1995) (No. 95-7138).

407. *Id.* at 77-79.

408. Brief for Appellee, *supra* note 399, at 3-4.

409. *Matusevitch v. Telnikoff*, 877 F. Supp. 1, 4 (D.D.C. 1995).

410. *Id.*

411. *Telnikoff*, 702 A.2d 230, 236 (Md. 1997).

412. *Id.* at 240.

413. *Id.* at 246 (citing Jacron Sales Co. Sindorf, 276 Md. 580, 592, 350 A.2d 688, 695 (1976)).

414. *Id.* (citing *Jacron*, 276 Md. at 601, 350 A.2d at 700).

415. *Id.* at 246-47 (citing *Jacron*, 276 Md. at 599-601, 350 A.2d at 699-700).

416. *Id.* at 247 (citations omitted).

417. *Id.* at 247-48

418. *Id.* at 248.

419. *Id.* at 249.

420. *Id.*

421. *Id.*

422. *Id.*

423. *Id.* at 250.

424. Eric J. McCarthy, *Networking in Cyberspace: Electronic Defamation and the Potential for International Forum Shopping*, 16 University Pennsylvania Journal of International Business 527, 551 (1995).

Case Index

Subject Index